Aging in the 1980s

Psychological Issues

Leonard W. Poon, Editor

Associate Editors

Marilyn Albert
James Birren
David Chiriboga
Margaret Gatz
Steven Harkins
Gail Marsh
John Nesselroade
Joyce Parr
Anderson Smith
Lillian Troll
M. Virtrue Williams

American Psychological Association
Washington, D.C.

Library of Congress Cataloging in Publication Data

Main entry under title:
Aging in the 1980s.

   Bibliography: p.
   Includes indexes.
   1. Aging—Psychological aspects. I. Poon, Leonard W. [DNLM: 1. Aging. 2. Aged—
Psychology. WT150 A2673]

BF724.55.A35A36   155.67   80-18515
ISBN 0-912704-15-2

Published by the American Psychological Association, Inc.
1200 Seventeenth Street, N.W., Washington, D.C. 20036
Copyright © 1980 by the American Psychological Association.
All rights reserved.

Printed in the United States of America.

Contents

v

Preface

This is the third volume on aging issued by the American Psychological Association. *Psychological Aspects of Aging*, published in 1956 and edited by J. E. Anderson, summarized the literature existing at that time. *The Psychology of Adult Development and Aging*, edited by Carl Eisdorfer and M. Powell Lawton and published in 1973, was prepared by a task force organized to represent APA at the White House Conference on Aging in November 1971. This second volume published the recommendations of the task force, together with in-depth reviews of the major areas of research on the psychology of aging.

Once again a substantial amount of information has accumulated that can help to direct our thinking about psychological aging in the next decade. The present volume has multiple purposes: to summarize and put into perspective selected issues on the psychology of aging and to establish research directions for the 1980s; to identify what we now know and what we need to know about nine selected areas in the field of aging; and to provide a framework to guide the deliberations of the participants at two projected conferences on aging—the 1981 White House Conference on Aging, and the tentatively scheduled 1982 World Assembly on Aging.

In attempting to fulfill these purposes I have aimed to present complementary and competing views from researchers and clinicians of different backgrounds. The success of this book will eventually be determined by the amount of controversy it creates and the new thinking it stimulates. Accordingly, *Aging in the 1980s* has been designed for a wide audience. It is intended to serve as a sourcebook to supplement and complement existing literature for researchers, practitioners, clinicians, graduate and postgraduate students, as well

as the professionals and the policymakers in the field of aging and allied sciences. Abstracts have been provided to make each chapter accessible to lay readers.

Nine major areas of research in aging are explored in this volume: clinical issues, neuropsychological issues, psychophysiological issues, psychopharmacological issues, cognitive issues, stress and coping, environmental issues, interpersonal relations, and methodological issues. For each of these areas, one or more associate editors were directed to identify and review the outstanding issues, to integrate new and old theories and data, and to provide directions for the next steps to be taken by researchers in the 1980s. Most sections of the book were presented in a series of symposia held at the 87th annual meeting of the American Psychological Association in New York City, in September 1979.

From its inception to publication, *Aging in the 1980s* has taken about two years. I would like first to acknowledge the organizational effort, the creativity and responsiveness, and the tenacious insistence on high quality, of the 11 associate editors, all of whom put aside heavy schedules to meet our strict deadlines. I also thank the 83 other contributors whose work appears in the 43 chapters of this book. In order to guarantee the widest circulation at the lowest possible publication cost, and consistent with APA policy, neither these contributors nor the editors have received personal financial return for the preparation of this book.

I am grateful to many other people whose participation ultimately shaped this book. Congressman Robert Drinan and his associate Elizabeth Bankowski, Robert Butler and Leonard Jakubczak of the National Institue on Aging, Barry Lebowitz of the National Institute of Mental Health, and Marguerite T. Hays and Earl Freed of the Veterans Administration all provided valuable information on national fiscal policies and priorities. Harold Brody, Bernice Neugarten, Martha Storandt, and many other acknowledged and anonymous reviewers and advisors contributed to the improvement of specific chapters and sections. Finally, Bernard Stotsky shared his broad gerontological experience in reviewing the final manuscript.

I would like to give special acknowledgment to Anita DeVivo, Executive Editor of APA publications, and her staff, especially Brenda Bryant and Shelley Hammond, who were involved in all stages of the publication process, and to Geraldine Stevens, whose experience, patience, and knowledge contributed to the technical integrity of the book. And finally, I thank the staff of the Mental Performance and Aging Laboratory, especially Diane Williams and Susan Carroll, for their unfailing efficiency and good humor in providing administrative assistance.

Leonard W. Poon

Contributors

Marilyn S. Albert, PhD Research Psychologist, Department of Neurology, Beth Israel Hospital, Boston; Lecturer, Departments of Neurology and Psychiatry, Harvard Medical School; Research Associate, Department of Neurology, Boston University School of Medicine; Department of Psychology, Veterans Administration Medical Center, Boston, Massachusetts

Judith L. Alpert, PhD Associate Professor, Department of Educational Psychology, New York University

David Arenberg, PhD Chief, Learning and Problem Solving Section, Gerontology Research Center, National Institute on Aging, National Institutes of Health, Baltimore, Maryland

Paul B. Baltes, PhD Professor of Human Development, College of Human Development, Division of Individual and Family Studies, Pennsylvania State University

Raymond T. Bartus, PhD Senior Scientist, CNS Biology Department, Medical Research Division, American Cyanamid Company, Pearl River, New York

James E. Birren, PhD Executive Director, Ethel Percy Andrus Gerontology Center, University of Southern California

Lenore S. Blum, PhD Assistant Professor of Education, Graduate Program in Counseling Psychology, Northwestern University

James A. Blumenthal, PhD Clinical Assistant Professor of Medical Psychology, Department of Psychiatry, Duke University Medical Center; Senior Fellow, Duke University Center for the Study of Aging and Human Development

John Cerella, PhD Research Psychologist, Geriatric Research, Educational and Clinical Center, Veterans Administration Outpatient Clinic, Boston, Massachusetts

Thomas J. Chippendale, PhD, MD Resident, Department of Neurology, University of California, San Diego

David A. Chiriboga, PhD Associate Professor of Psychology in Residence, Human Development and Aging Program, University of California, San Francisco

Victor G. Cicirelli, PhD Professor of Developmental and Aging Psychology, Department of Psychological Sciences, Purdue University

Frances Cohen, PhD Assistant Professor of Medical Psychology, Graduate Group in Psychology, Department of Psychiatry, School of Medicine, University of California, San Francisco

Ralph L. Cooper, PhD Assistant Medical Research Professor, Division of Medical Psychology, Department of Psychiatry, Duke University Medical Center; Senior Fellow, Duke University Center for the Study of Aging and Human Development

Walter R. Cunningham, PhD Associate Professor, Department of Psychology, University of Florida

Loraine Cutler, PhD Postdoctoral Fellow, Texas Research Institute of Mental Sciences, Texas Medical Center, Houston, Texas

Solomon Cytrynbaum, PhD Associate Professor of Education and Clinical Psychology; Director, Graduate Program in Counseling Psychology; Coordinator, Adult Development and Intervention Area, Counseling Psychology, Northwestern University

Warren L. Danziger, PhD Research Assistant, Department of Neurology, Washington University School of Medicine

Claire Darley, BA Psychology Technician, Veterans Administration Medical Center, Palo Alto, California

Kenneth L. Davis, MD Chief of Psychiatry, Veterans Administration Medical Center, Bronx, New York

Leonard R. Derogatis, PhD Associate Professor and Director of Medical Psychology, Department of Psychiatry; Assistant Professor of Oncology; Director of Research, Sexual Behavior Consultation Unit, Johns Hopkins University School of Medicine

George Fein, PhD Research Psychologist, Veterans Administration Medical Center, San Francisco; Assistant Professor of Medical Psychology, University of California, San Francisco

Irwin Feinberg, MD Director, Sleep Research Laboratory, Veterans Administration Medical Center, New York, New York; Professor of Psychiatry, New York University College of Medicine

Steven Ferris, PhD Director, Geriatric Study and Treatment Program; Assistant Professor, Department of Psychiatry, New York University Medical Center

Thomas C. Floyd, MA Research Psychologist, Veterans Administration Medical Center, San Francisco, California

Judith M. Ford, PhD   Research Psychologist, Veterans Administration Medical Center, Palo Alto, California; Research Scholar, Department of Psychiatry and Behavioral Sciences, Stanford University Medical School

James L. Fozard, PhD   Director, Patient Treatment Service, Office of Extended Care, Veterans Administration Central Office, Washington, D.C.

Dolores E. Gallagher, PhD   Assistant Director, Adult Counseling Center, Ethel Percy Andrus Gerontology Center, University of Southern California

Margaret Gatz, PhD   Associate Professor and Director of Clinical Aging, Department of Psychology; Senior Staff Associate, Ethel Percy Andrus Gerontology Center, University of Southern California

Samuel Gershon, MD   Professor of Psychiatry, Department of Psychiatry, New York University Medical Center

Leonard M. Giambra, PhD   Research Psychologist, Gerontology Research Center, National Institute on Aging, National Institutes of Health, Baltimore, Maryland

Douglas S. Goodin, MD   Resident, Department of Neurology, University of California, San Francisco

Judith O. Harker, PhD   Postdoctoral Research Fellow, Ethel Percy Andrus Gerontology Center, University of Southern California

Stephen W. Harkins, PhD   Associate Professor, Departments of Gerontology and Psychiatry, Medical College of Virginia, Virginia Commonwealth University

Joellen T. Hartley, PhD   Postdoctoral Research Fellow, Ethel Percy Andrus Gerontology Center, University of Southern California

Christopher K. Hertzog, PhD   Postdoctoral Research Fellow, Department of Psychology, University of Washington

John L. Horn, PhD   Professor, Department of Psychology, University of Denver

Mardi J. Horowitz, MD   Professor of Psychiatry; Director, Center for the Study of Neuroses, Langley Porter Institute, University of California, San Francisco

Sandra C. Howell, MPH, PhD   Associate Professor of Behavioral Science, Department of Architecture, Massachusetts Institute of Technology

William J. Hoyer, PhD   Associate Professor, Department of Psychology, Syracuse University

Robert A. Jensen, PhD   Assistant Research Psychobiologist, Department of Psychobiology, University of California, Irvine

Terry L. Jernigan, PhD   Research Psychologist, Veterans Administration Medical Center, Palo Alto, California

Iseli K. Krauss, EDD   Assistant Professor, Department of Psychology; Research Associate, Ethel Percy Andrus Gerontology Center, University of Southern California

Erich W. Labouvie, PhD   Associate Professor of Psychology, Center for Alcohol Studies and Department of Psychology, Rutgers—The State University, New Brunswick

M. Powell Lawton, PhD   Director, Behavioral Research, Philadelphia Geriatric Center, Philadelphia, Pennsylvania

Martin Lenhardt, PhD   Associate Professor of Otolaryngology, Medical College of Virginia, Virginia Commonwealth University

Sandra M. Levy, PhD   Health Scientist Administrator, National Cancer Institute, National Institutes of Health, Washington, D.C.; Assistant Professor of Medical Psychology, Department of Psychiatry, Johns Hopkins University School of Medicine; Visiting Associate Professor of Psychology, University of Maryland Baltimore County

Lawrence E. Marks, PhD   Associate Fellow, John B. Pierce Foundation Laboratory, New Haven, Connecticut; Associate Professor, Departments of Epidemiology and Psychology, Yale University School of Medicine

Gail R. Marsh, PhD   Associate Professor of Medical Psychology, Department of Psychiatry, Duke University Medical Center; Senior Fellow, Duke University Center for the Study of Aging and Human Development

Joe L. Martinez, Jr., PhD   Associate Research Psychobiologist, Department of Psychobiology, University of California, Irvine

J. Jack McArdle, PhD   Research Associate, Department of Psychology, University of Denver

James L. McGaugh, PhD   Executive Vice Chancellor and Professor, Department of Psychobiology, University of California, Irvine

M. Colleen McNamara, PhD   Postdoctoral Fellow, Center for the Study of Aging and Human Development, Duke University Medical Center

Rita B. Messing, PhD   Associate Research Psychobiologist, Department of Psychobiology, University of California, Irvine

Henry J. Michalewski, PhD   Research Associate, Ethel Percy Andrus Gerontology Center, University of Southern California

Francis T. Miller, PhD   Associate Professor, Department of Psychiatry, University of North Carolina, Chapel Hill

Richard C. Mohs, PhD   Psychologist, Veterans Administration Medical Center, Bronx, New York; Assistant Professor, Department of Psychiatry, Mount Sinai School of Medicine of the City University of New York

John R. Nesselroade, PhD   Professor of Human Development, College of Human Development, Division of Individual and Family Studies, Pennsylvania State University

Kathy Newport, BA   Research Assistant, Department of Psychology, Washington University

John B. Nowlin, MD   Associate Professor of Community and Family Medicine, Duke University Medical Center; Senior Fellow, Duke University Center for the Study of Aging and Human Development

Phyllis J. Oster, PhD   Research Associate, Department of Psychology, Washington University

Joyce Parr, PhD   Executive Director, Foundation for Aging Research, Clearwater, Florida; Adjunct Associate Research Scholar/Scientist, University of South Florida

Robert Patrick, MA   Doctoral Candidate, Graduate Program in Counseling Psychology, Northwestern University

Adolf Pfefferbaum, MD   Assistant Professor, Department of Psychiatry and Behavioral Sciences, Stanford University School of Medicine

Dana J. Plude, MA   Doctoral Candidate, Department of Psychology, Syracuse University

Leonard W. Poon, PhD Research Psychologist and Director, Mental Performance and Aging Laboratory, Geriatric Research, Educational and Clinical Center, Veterans Administration Outpatient Clinic, Boston, Massachusetts; Instructor in Psychology, Department of Psychiatry, Massachusetts General Hospital and Harvard Medical School

Leonard J. Price, PhD Postdoctoral Fellow, Department of Psychiatry, University of California, San Francisco

Barry Reisberg, MD Assistant Professor of Psychiatry, Department of Psychiatry, New York University Medical Center

Mary Sue Richardson, PhD Associate Professor, Department of Counselor Education, New York University

Rick J. Scheidt, PhD Assistant Professor, Department of Family and Child Development, Kansas State University

Ilene C. Siegler, PhD Associate Professor of Medical Psychology, Department of Psychiatry, Duke University Medical Center; Senior Fellow, Duke University Center for the Study of Aging and Human Development

Anderson D. Smith, PhD Associate Professor of Psychology, School of Psychology, Georgia Institute of Technology

David B. D. Smith, PhD Associate Professor, Human Factors Department, University of Southern California

Michael A. Smyer, PhD Assistant Professor, College of Human Development, Pennsylvania State University

Kenneth C. Squires, PhD Assistant Adjunct Professor, Department of Neurology, University of California, Irvine

Arnold Starr, MD Professor and Chair, Department of Neurology, University of California, Irvine

Jan Stein, MA Doctoral Candidate, Graduate Program in Counseling Psychology, Northwestern University

John A. Stern, PhD Professor of Psychology, Washington University; Director of Research, Malcolm Bliss Mental Health Center, St. Louis, Missouri

Joseph C. Stevens, PhD Fellow, John B. Pierce Foundation Laboratory, New Haven, Connecticut; Senior Research Psychologist and Lecturer in Psychology, Yale University

Larry W. Thompson, PhD Director, Adult Counseling Center, Ethel Percy Andrus Gerontology Center, University of Southern California

W. Gary Thompson, PhD Postdoctoral Fellow, Duke University Center for the Study of Aging and Human Development

Lillian E. Troll, PhD Professor of Psychology, University College, Rutgers—The State University, New Brunswick

Beatriz J. Vasguez, PhD Assistant Research Psychobiologist, Department of Psychobiology, University of California, Irvine

David Wadner, MA Doctoral Candidate, Graduate Program in Counseling Psychology, Northwestern University

David A. Walsh, PhD Assistant Professor, Department of Psychology; Research Associate, Ethel Percy Andrus Gerontology Center, University of Southern California

Alan T. Welford, ScD Professor Emeritus of Psychology, University of Adelaide, Adelaide, South Australia

Carole Wilk, MA Doctoral Candidate, Graduate Program in Counseling Psychology, Northwestern University

Diane M. Williams, BA Research Assistant, Geriatric Research, Educational and Clinical Center, Veterans Administration Outpatient Clinic, Boston, Massachusetts

M. Virtrue Williams, PhD Research Coordinator, Ethel Percy Andrus Gerontology Center, University of Southern California; Research Psychologist, Human Memory Research Laboratory, Veterans Administration Medical Center, Sepulveda, California

Sherry L. Willis, PhD Associate Professor of Human Development, College of Human Development, Division of Individual and Family Studies, Pennsylvania State University

Nancy Wilner, BA Research Specialist in Psychiatry, Center for the Study of Neuroses; Lecturer, Langley Porter Institute, University of California, San Francisco

Paul G. Windley, ArchD Associate Professor, Department of Architecture, Kansas State University

Kathy S. Wrege, BA Graduate Student, Department of Psychobiology, University of California, Irvine

Anita M. Woods, MA Research Assistant, Ethel Percy Andrus Gerontology Center, University of Southern California

Leslie M. Zatz, MD Chief, Radiology Service, Veterans Administration Medical Center, Palo Alto, California; Professor of Radiology, Stanford University School of Medicine

Leonard W. Poon and Alan T. Welford

Prologue
A Historical Perspective

The psychology of aging has matured as a scientific discipline in the last 50 years. The history of its development has been carefully chronicled by the late Klaus Riegel in two major reviews of the discipline (Birren & Schaie, 1977; Eisdorfer & Lawton, 1973). The purpose of this prologue is to extend and to bring up to date the historical perspective by describing the recent growth of both the research literature and national and international developments.

Literature

The literature in the psychology of aging began to become substantial only after World War II. Earlier publication on the psychology of aging had begun with G. Stanley Hall's 1922 book *Senescence: The Last Half of Life* and the work of Walter Miles and his associates in the 1930s. One journal on aging existed in 1940, the *Zeitschrift für Altersforschung*; now there are more than 30 such journals around the world. The field of aging has itself come of age, thanks to the persistent efforts of Nathan W. Shock, who single-handedly produced *A Classified Bibliography of Gerontology and Geriatrics* in 1951, 1957, and 1963, which has appeared in quarterly supplements in the *Journal of Gerontology* since 1956 and in bimonthly supplements since 1974. The proliferation of the literature in the last 50 years can be seen in the graph on the next page, which summarizes the number of publications on psychological aging from 1880 to 1979. The graph updates similar efforts by Riegel (1973, 1977) on the number of publications from 1920 to 1968. The

year 1968 saw 235 publications, and in 1979 there were 635 publications, a 270% increase in the last 11 years.

The most common areas of investigation in the literature on psychological aging were categorized by Riegel (1973) into nine clusters. In descending order of frequency in the literature, they are (1) intellectual deterioration, (2) general intellectual changes, (3) vocabulary achievements, (4) verbal skills, (5) psychomotor skills, (6) short-term retention, (7) dichotic listening, (8) studies of adjustment, and (9) social variables.

Several publications both summarized and integrated available data and theories on psychological aging. Even before publication of the present volume, the American Psychological Association exerted leadership by publishing two volumes that summarized the available psychological literature on aging. The first was based on an APA conference held in 1955 and was edited by Anderson (1956). The second brought together the existing body of psychological information on aging for the White House Conference on Aging and was edited by Eisdorfer and Lawton (1973). In the same year a major introductory textbook on the psychology of aging was written by Botwinick (1973), who reviewed the existing literature and its implications. In addition, James E. Birren has edited two handbooks on the psychology of aging. The first (Birren, 1959) climaxed 10 years of thinking on the need for a comprehensive handbook, and the impetus for its accomplishment came from a recommendation made at a conference held in Palm Beach in 1956 and funded by the Training Branch of the National Institute of Mental Health. The second handbook, edited with K. Warner Schaie (Birren & Schaie,

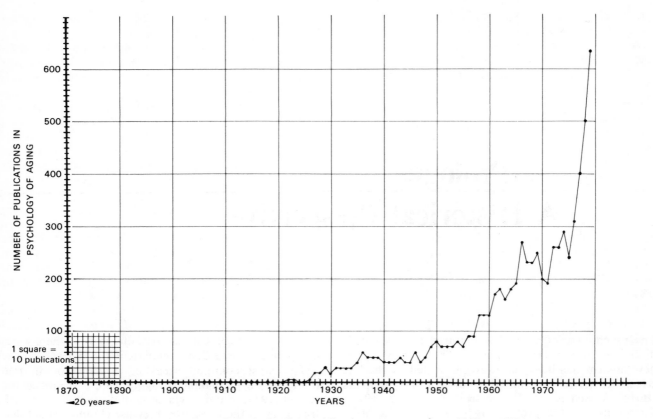

Number of psychological aging publications per year from 1880 to 1979.

1977), took five years to compile and is one of a series of three handbooks in the discipline of gerontology. It represents the work of 42 contributors who concentrated on historical and theoretical perspectives of biological, environmental, health, and behavioral issues.

Other integrative efforts on psychological aging theories and data can be found in the periodic updates devoted to aging in the *Annual Review of Psychology*—by Birren (1960), Botwinick (1970), Chown and Heron (1965), and Schaie and Gribbin (1975)—and in edited review volumes such as those by Baltes and Schaie (1973), Goulet and Baltes (1970), Neugarten (1968), and Talland (1968).

Efforts to advance and promote research in the psychology of aging through integrated reviews continued in the late 1970s and early 1980s. Some examples are (1) a review of the clinical psychology of aging—an area that had received little attention until recently—initiated and edited by Storandt, Siegler, and Elias in 1979; (2) the *Annual Review of Gerontology and Geriatrics*, edited by Eisdorfer in 1980; and (3) a review of memory and aging from experimental and clinical perspectives by contributors from both fields (Poon, Fozard, Cermak, Arenberg, & Thompson, 1980). It is too early to assess the impact of these publications. However, it seems fair to state that in the last 30 years, periodic reviews of the trends and developments in the psychology of aging have become essential not only to consolidate the ever-increasing amount of information available but also to assure meaningful directions for the years ahead.

International Development and Cooperation

The aging phenomenon truly transcends race, color, religion, and language barriers. It is understandable, therefore, that the study of aging has quickly acquired the sign of maturity in a scientific discipline implied by the coming together of scientists from the far corners of the world to cooperate on a common set of objectives.

In the 1940s and 1950s two significant developments formed a foundation for gerontology as a science: first, the development of gerontological institutes in a number of different countries, and second, the establishment in 1950 of the International Association of Gerontology (IAG). Biomedical aspects of aging have traditionally received major emphasis, but in recent years the study of psychosocial or behavioral aspects of aging has gained significant ground, especially in the United States, England, and Germany.

In the United States private resources created the opportunity for the early development of gerontology. In 1940 the Macy Foundation gave a one-year grant to the National Institutes of Health for the establishment of a research unit on aging; this research unit subsequently became the Gerontological Research Center in Baltimore under the auspices of the National Institute on Aging. Other private foundations, such as the Xerox Corporation and the Forest Park Foundation of Peoria, Illinois, supported important early efforts in gerontological research.

The establishment of that first research unit on aging was followed by the founding in 1942 of the American Geriatric Society and in 1945 of the American Gerontological Society and the American Psychological Association's Division of Maturity and Old Age. These organizations implemented the exchange of ideas among gerontologists and contributed to the directions of the discipline's growth.

In the United States, the federal government, through the National Institutes of Health, began to support gerontological activities in 1952. In the decade of the 1970s, gerontological activities have been funded by, among others, the National Institute of General Medical Sciences, the National Institute of Mental Health, the National Heart and Lung Institute, the National Institute of Child Health and Human Development, the National Institute on Aging, the Veterans Administration, the Administration on Aging, and the National Science Foundation.

In Britain, the beginnings of modern gerontology were initiated by the Nuffield Foundation, which in the mid-1940s sponsored three research projects on (1) the accommodation of old people, which led to the Rowntree (1947) report *Old People*, (2) medical needs of old people, which led to the book *The Social Medicine of Old Age* by J. H. Sheldon (1948), and (3) work capacities and psychological performances in relation to age, which led to the publication of *Skill and Age* and *Ageing and Human Skill* by A. T. Welford in 1951 and 1958, respectively.

In 1954 the Nuffield Foundation sponsored a research group under K. F. H. Murrell at Bristol University to continue the work begun by A. T. Welford, and at the same time the British Medical Research Council funded a unit to study aging in industry under A. Heron at Liverpool University. It is worth noting that the Nuffield Foundation had the vision to support the first large-scale study of psychological aging under Sir Frederic Bartlett and A. T. Welford at Cambridge, and that their pioneering work ulti-

mately set the stage for subsequent research in the United States and abroad.

While biological aging has received the bulk of attention from institutes of gerontology in Europe, the Middle East, and Asia, psychological aging research is beginning to flourish in Germany. There have been significant advances in gerontological studies on cognitive theories of personality, psychological and social responses to life stress, intergenerational relations, attitudes on health, psychological aspects of leisure behavior, sex differences, and longitudinal changes in cognitive functions.

With increased attention focused on aging processes, international cooperation and communication are inevitable. The first international conference on senility was conducted in Kiev, Russia, in 1938. The International Association of Gerontology, founded in 1950, has held meetings every three years since that time. Of these, three have taken place in the United States, and one each in England, Italy, Denmark, Austria, Russia, Israel, and Japan. In the last four international meetings, the psychological and social sciences have been well represented, along with clinical medicine and biological sciences. At these meetings the importance of interdisciplinary cooperation has been recognized in the scheduling of symposia combining psychological sciences and other disciplines.

In the last 30 years the psychology of aging has grown, together with its allied biological sciences, into a vital discipline with a developing network for shared information and communication. There can be little doubt that the leaders in securing international communication have been, in gerontology as a whole, Nathan W. Shock, and in psychological gerontology, James E. Birren. Their unwavering dedication should be applauded.

National Development for Basic Psychological Aging Research

In 1952 the National Heart Institute supported five gerontological research projects with a total funding of $67,000 (Murphy, 1976); today more than 30 federal departments and agencies support gerontology-related activities. Among these agencies, the Administration on Aging gives major support to policy and applications research, while the National Institute on Aging (NIA), the National Institute of Mental Health (NIMH), and the Veterans Administration (VA) supply the major support for basic psychological aging research. A brief synopsis follows of the three agencies that sponsor basic research in aging.

The first national program on aging was organized at the Adult Development and Aging Branch (ADAB) of the National Institute of Child Health and Human Development (NICHD) in 1963. The ADAB staff was subsequently transferred to NIA at its establishment in July 1975. NIA supported intramural (within-agency) research at the Gerontology Research Center at the Baltimore City Hospitals, with a budget that has totaled $5.5, $6.1, and $7.9 million for the fiscal years 1976, 1977, and 1978, respectively. Extramural research and training at universities, medical schools, and hospitals, and other nonprofit research contracts totaled $12.6, $21.7, and $26.5 million, respectively, for fiscal years 1976, 1977, and 1978.

The table compares the NIA commitment to behavioral and social science research with its commitment to biological science research in the last three years (L. Jakubczak, personal communication, 1979). As the table shows, biological research support increased 119% for fiscal year 1979, while the behavioral and social science support increased 45%. The proportion of behavioral to biological science support varied between 21% and 23% during the three years. Clearly, even though there has been a significant increase in allocations for research, the behavioral sciences have not kept pace with the biological sciences.

Research on the mental health of the aged has been supported by NIMH since 1960. In 1976 the Center for Studies of the Mental Health of the Aging was granted funds specifically for studies of the aged person. NIMH expenditures on aging totaled $15.04, $16.45, and $22.32 million for fiscal years 1977, 1978, and 1979, respectively. Approximately 57% of the NIMH expenditure is budgeted for mental health services, 30% for research, and 13% for training, with approximately 25% of the total budget assigned to the behavioral and psychological domain (B. Lebowitz, personal communication, 1979).

The VA has a long-standing commitment to the care of aging veterans and to the advancement of knowledge on the aging processes (see Coppinger, 1967). There are about 3 million veterans over 65 years of age today, and about 7 million are projected to be over 65 in 1990 ("The Aging Veteran," 1977). Since the VA is required by law (Public Law 95-581, Section a) to care for aging veterans, the need is critical for aging research, training of geriatric and gerontological personnel, and clinical demonstration of innovative health and mental health delivery techniques for the care of the aged. While NIA and NIMH support both intra- and extramural research, the VA supports only intramural aging research in its various VA medical centers, domiciliaries, nursing homes, and outpatient facilities. The VA appropriated $1.4, $1.7, and $3.0 million, respectively, in fiscal years 1977, 1978, and 1979, for aging research. Of these funds, approximately 16% was earmarked for behavioral aging research (R. Hays, personal communication, 1980). The VA commitment to aging was further strengthened by the establishment in 1975 of eight Geriatric Research, Educational, and Clinical Centers (GRECC) around the nation, of which five are actively involved in psychological aging research.

Aging in the 1980s: An Introduction

Selection of topics in this volume is predicated on a model in which psychological aging is considered from a systems perspective, with the person, the environment, health, and behavior interacting over time. Changes in one influence the status of the others. The

Research Support for Biological Sciences and Behavioral and Social Sciences in Fiscal Years 1977, 1978, and 1979 at the National Institute on Aging

Research area	FY 77		FY 78		FY 79	
	$(millions)	No. projects	$(millions)	No. projects	$(millions)	No. projects
Biological sciences						
Cellular	4.45	58	6.22	72	11.71	151
Molecular/biochemistry	4.99	74	6.15	78	8.75	110
Biophysiological/biopathology	5.66	75	7.69	95	12.59	163
Total	15.10	207	20.06	245	33.05	424
Behavioral and social sciences						
Behavioral processes[a]	1.14	12	1.24	14	1.39	16
Cognition[b]	1.44	22	1.41	22	1.77	31
Social psychology	1.67	13	1.53	15	1.48	17
Demography, family, sociology	1.63	17	1.90	27	3.87	53
Total	5.88	64	6.08	78	8.51	117
Proportion of behavioral compared to biological support	28%		23%		20.5%	

[a] Sensory perceptions, motivation, animal behavior, etc.
[b] Learning, memory, problem solving, etc.

chapters that follow examine the discrete effects of environment, health, and behavior, as well as the combined effects of all three, on the aging person.

Section 1 examines the mental health delivery system for older adults, as well as relevant issues in the clinical diagnosis and treatment of maladaptive behaviors. In Sections 2, 3, and 4 the recent breakthroughs in neuropsychological, psychophysiological, and psychopharmacological techniques are discussed in relation to the understanding, assessment, and treatment of senile dementia and decline in cognitive functions. Normative age changes in cognitive, attentional, and perceptual processes and behavioral slowing are examined in Section 5, Parts 1 and 2.

Section 6 discusses the contribution of the environment to the well-being of the aged and proposes environmental changes that may facilitate successful adaptation of the elderly. The influence of interpersonal and family environment is examined in Section 7.

Both the environment and the health and personality of the aged person have the capacity either to provide support or induce stress, and these conditions may promote normal or maladaptive behavior. Section 8 examines the relations between the stresses encountered and the coping mechanisms adopted over the life span.

Section 9 examines such methodological issues as between- and within-subject research design, mathematical models of the aging processes, and the application of signal detection theory in aging research.

An epilogue concludes the volume with some thoughts on how to proceed from here and a last word that attempts to establish continuity between what has been done and what lies ahead.

REFERENCES

The aging veteran: Present and future medical needs (VA Technical Report). Washington, D.C.: Veterans Administration Report, October, 1977.

Anderson, J. E. (Ed.). *Psychological aspects of aging.* Washington, D.C.: American Psychological Association, 1956.

Baltes, P. B., & Schaie, K. W. (Eds.). *Life-span developmental psychology: Personality and socialization.* New York: Academic Press, 1973.

Birren, J. E. (Ed.). *Handbook of aging and the individual: Psychological and biological aspects.* Chicago: University of Chicago Press, 1959.

Birren, J. E. Psychological aspects of aging. *Annual Review of Psychology,* 1960, *11*, 131–160.

Birren, J. E., & Schaie, K. W. (Eds.). *Handbook of the psychology of aging.* New York: Van Nostrand Reinhold, 1977.

Botwinick, J. Geropsychology. *Annual Review of Psychology,* 1970, *21*, 239–272.

Botwinick, J. *Aging and behavior.* New York: Springer, 1973.

Chown, S. M., & Heron, A. Psychological aspects of aging in man. *Annual Review of Psychology,* 1965, *16*, 417–450.

Coppinger, N. W. The psychological aspects of aging: A prospectus for research in the Veterans Administration. *Gerontologist,* 1967, *7*, 1–80.

Eisdorfer, C. (Ed.). *Annual review of gerontology and geriatrics.* New York: Springer, 1980.

Eisdorfer, C., & Lawton, M. P. (Eds.). *The psychology of adult development and aging.* Washington, D.C.: American Psychological Association, 1973.

Goulet, L. R., & Baltes, P. B. (Eds.). *Life-span developmental psychology: Research and theory.* New York: Academic Press, 1970.

Hall, G. S. *Senescence: The last half of life.* New York: Appleton, 1922.

Murphy, D. G. Report from the National Institute on Aging: The research grant support mechanism. *Journal of Gerontology,* 1976, *31*, 696–704.

Neugarten, B. L. (Ed.). *Middle age and aging.* Chicago: University of Chicago Press, 1968.

Poon, L. W., Fozard, J. L., Cermak, L. S., Arenberg, D., & Thompson, L. W. (Eds.). *New directions in memory and aging: Proceedings of the G. A. Talland Memorial Conference.* Hillsdale, N.J.: Lawrence Erlbaum, 1980.

Riegel, K. F. On the history of psychological gerontology. In C. Eisdorfer & M. P. Lawton (Eds.), *The psychology of adult development and aging.* Washington, D.C.: American Psychological Association, 1973.

Riegel, K. F. History of psychological gerontology. In J. E. Birren & K. W. Schaie (Eds.), *Handbook of the psychology of aging.* New York: Van Nostrand Reinhold, 1977.

Rowntree, B. S. (Chair). *Old people: Report of a survey committee on the problems of ageing in the care of old people.* London: Oxford University Press for the Nuffield Foundation, 1947.

Schaie, K. W., & Gribbin, K. Adult development and aging. *Annual Review of Psychology,* 1975, *26*, 65–96.

Sheldon, H. *The social medicine of old age.* London: Oxford University Press, 1948.

Shock, N. W. *A classified bibliography of gerontology and geriatrics.* Stanford, Calif.: Stanford University Press, 1951.

Shock, N. W. *A classified bibliography of gerontology and geriatrics.* Stanford, Calif.: Stanford University Press, 1957.

Shock, N. W. *A classified bibliography of gerontology and geriatrics.* Stanford, Calif.: Stanford University Press, 1963.

Storandt, M., Siegler, I. C., & Elias, M. F. (Eds.). *The clinical psychology of aging.* New York: Plenum Press, 1979.

Talland, G. A. (Ed.), *Human aging and behavior.* New York: Academic Press, 1968.

Welford, A. T. *Skill and age.* London: Oxford University Press, 1951.

Welford, A. T. *Aging and human skill.* London: Oxford University Press, 1958.

Clinical Issues

Margaret Gatz, *Section Editor*

Introduction

This section presents some major issues confronting the clinical psychology of aging in the 1980s. To consider these issues requires a look at the history of clinical psychology. Witmer founded the first psychological clinic in 1896, with an emphasis on diagnosis. The first major professional role of the psychologist was to serve as a tester. This role included personnel selection during World War I and later the assessment of psychopathology. The second professional role was that of therapist. This role, initially a response to the psychiatric toll of World War II, evolved by the 1950s into the Boulder model of a scientist-professional. The third role, that of the community psychologist, began to be defined in the 1960s as concern grew about the broader social context of mental illness and of positive mental health. Like developmental stages, each new role entailed a redefinition and reorganization of previous roles. Thus, a community-oriented psychologist may do assessment and program evaluation, counseling and consultation, crisis intervention, and community organization. The three roles are considered in the three chapters of this section. In the first chapter, the aged are viewed within the larger system of the delivery of mental health services. The second chapter focuses on assessment. The third chapter discusses psychopathology and treatment, both in the community and in the institution.

Both the number of older adults in the United States and the percentage of the population that they constitute have increased. In 1970, 9.9% of the population were age 65 or older. Between the 1960 and 1970 censuses, the number of aged increased by 21.1%, while the number of those under 65 increased by only 12.5% (Brotman, 1973). By 1978 there were over 24 million citizens aged 65 or older, or 11% of the population (U.S. Department of Commerce, 1979a). By 1985 that percentage is expected to be 11.4, and it will reach a maximum population percentage of 11.7 by 1990 (USDC, 1977).

What are the mental health needs of older adults? Social indicators and epidemiological data provide a basis for making such estimates.

The social-indicators approach uses data derived from public reports to identify subgroups of the population at risk for mental illness. For instance, older adults are overrepresented among the poor and the near-poor, comprising nearly 30% of those in the United States with an annual income below $3200 (USDC, 1979b). Women tend to live longer than men, so that many aged women are widows. In addition, generally decreasing mortality rates have meant that within the older population more than one third are age 75 or above (USDC, 1979c). Another relevant social indicator is household composition. The number of persons 65 and older who were living either alone or with unrelated others increased from 2.3 million in 1960 to 7 million by 1978. Vulnerability is additive, as seen in the fact that 38% of people 75 and older live alone. Another social indicator is race: In recent years the number of minority aged have increased. In 1978,

8% of blacks were aged 65 or older (USDC, 1979c). At the same time, mortality rates for minority aged have been increasing over the period 1962–1976. Jackson (1979) explained the implications:

> To put it more simply . . . only the fittest of blacks now reach old age. If this assumption is valid . . . it portends an increasing need for mental health services to functionally impaired aged black males and their families in the future. (p. 79)

These social-indicator data provide one estimate of the need for both preventive and ameliorative mental health services within a community. Other estimates of need for services are derived from epidemiological data.

In 1973 Kramer, Taube, and Redick summarized seven studies of prevalence rates for mental illness among noninstitutionalized older age groups. Based on this literature, they estimated that from 10% to 20% of persons age 65 and over were in need of mental health services. Blenkner's survey of the noninstitutionalized population of New York City 60 years of age and over indicated that from 14% to 16% were mentally impaired (Blenkner, Bloom, Wasser, & Nielsen, 1971). Some other specific epidemiological data elaborate these figures. Older adults account for roughly 25% of reported suicides each year (Butler & Lewis, 1977). Alcohol and drug abuse are also problems. In a recent national survey of agencies serving individuals with drinking problems, 18% of the clientele were 55 years or older (Wood, 1978). A collation of data from a number of community-level surveys (Gunner-Swenson & Jensen, 1976) suggests that the prevalence of senile dementia among the elderly in the community is from around 3% to 5%. Within the institutional setting, it has been estimated that 58% of all nursing-home residents are considered confused some or most of the time (National Center for Health Statistics, 1977), the majority of them presumably suffering from senile dementia and related conditions. Another important aspect of these rates is that among older adults who appear to suffer from senile dementia, as many as one-third may in fact have reversible (acute) brain syndromes stemming from errors in medication, malnutrition, metabolic imbalance, or other causes (Libow, 1977).

In summary, while differing methods and criteria for psychiatric diagnoses among the community studies make it difficult to come to firm population estimates, taken together, these statistics provide ample reason for psychologists to be concerned with the mental health of the aged. The three chapters in this section discuss how well older adults have been served, review what assessment and therapeutic practices have been shown to be effective, and suggest what the 1980s will offer.

REFERENCES

Blenkner, M., Bloom, M., Wasser, E., & Nielsen, M. A research and demonstration project of protective services. *Social Casework*, 1971, *52*, 483–499.

Brotman, H. B. Who are the aging? In E. W. Busse & E. Pfeiffer (Eds.), *Mental illness in later life*. Washington, D.C.: American Psychiatric Association, 1973.

Butler, R. N., & Lewis, M. *Aging and mental health*. St. Louis, Mo.: Mosby, 1977.

Gunner-Swenson, F., & Jensen, K. Frequency of mental disorders in old age. *Acta Psychiatrica Scandinavica*, 1976, *53*, 283–297.

Jackson, J. J. Epidemiological aspects of mental illness among aged black women and men. *Journal of Minority Aging*, 1979, *4*, 76–87.

Kramer, M., Taube, C. A., & Redick, R. W. Patterns of use of psychiatric facilities by the aged: Past, present, and future. In C. Eisdorfer & M. P. Lawton (Eds.), *The psychology of adult development and aging*. Washington, D.C.: American Psychological Association, 1973.

Libow, L. S. Senile dementia and "pseudo-senility": Clinical diagnosis. In C. Eisdorfer & R. O. Friedel (Eds.), *Cognitive and emotional disturbance in the elderly*. Chicago: Year Book Medical Publishers, 1977.

National Center for Health Statistics. Profile of chronic illness in nursing homes. In *Vital and health statistics* (Series 13, No. 29). Hyattsville, Md.: U.S. Department of Health, Education and Welfare, 1977.

U.S. Department of Commerce, Bureau of the Census. *Projections of the population of the United States 1977–2050* (Current Population Reports, Series P-25, No. 704). Washington, D.C.: U.S. Government Printing Office, 1977.

U.S. Department of Commerce, Bureau of the Census. *Estimates of the population of the United States by age, sex, and race, 1976 to 1978* (Current Population Reports, Series P-25, No. 805). Washington, D.C.: U.S. Government Printing Office, 1979. (a)

U.S. Department of Commerce, Bureau of the Census. *Money income in 1977 of families and persons in the United States* (Current Population Reports, Series P-60, No. 118). Washington, D.C.: U.S. Government Printing Office, 1979. (b)

U.S. Department of Commerce, Bureau of the Census. *Social and economic characteristics of the older population 1978* (Current Population Reports, Series P-23, No. 85). Washington, D.C.: U.S. Government Printing Office, 1979. (c)

Wood, W. G. The elderly alcoholic: Some diagnostic problems and considerations. In M. Storandt, I. C. Siegler, & M. F. Elias (Eds.), *The clinical psychology of aging*. New York: Plenum Press, 1978.

Margaret Gatz, Michael A. Smyer, and M. Powell Lawton

CHAPTER

1

The Mental Health System and the Older Adult

Neither the mental health system nor the aging network has adequate services to meet the mental health needs of older adults. Past efforts may have been limited by several factors: an individually focused service model, overemphasis on socialization activities, and professional self-interest. The lack of programs to serve older adults with senile dementia and their families highlights these issues. Psychologists of the 1980s must consult in the many settings where older people are found. In doing so, they should provide both direct and preventive services, with a goal of optimizing development.

The 1960s were the time of the Great Society and large-scale social action, while the 1970s marked the beginning of recognition of limited resources and the reemergence of individualism. These changing themes have been reflected both in policies toward aging and in the organization of mental health services. In this chapter, we begin by reviewing mental health programs and policies of the 1960s and 1970s. Next, we focus on developments in public policy and services to the aged during this period. We then consider the impact of these systems on the older individual, using senile dementia and depression to illustrate the issues we have raised. Finally, we discuss the prospects for mental health and aging in the 1980s and beyond.

Mental Health Programs and Policies

In the mental health arena, the 1960s heralded community mental health legislation. Fifteen years later,

there was a recognition that implementation had not matched the ideology of this movement. Community mental health centers were meeting neither the original broad social goals nor the more limited goals of getting community-based mental health services to those most in need.

Prior to the 1960s, publicly funded mental hospitals were the primary location for treatment of the mentally ill. The number of patients in these facilities peaked around 1955. Thereafter, the inpatient population declined because of two major factors: (a) an increased use of drugs that could control socially unacceptable behavior on an outpatient basis, and (b) the acceptance of geographic decentralization within the state hospital setting, which brought about an emphasis on community placement and follow-up (Bloom, 1975).

Several pieces of legislation in the 1960s shaped the growth of federally funded community-based treatment programs for the mentally ill. The most significant piece of legislation was the Community Mental Health Centers Act of 1963, which declared that access to mental health services was a civil right of all citizens. In addition, three substantive elements of the act shaped mental health efforts for the next 15 years: (a) the creation of geographically based catchment areas; (b) the designation of five essential services to

We wish to thank the following people for their assistance and comments: Adrienne Cole, Steven Danish, Ray Horn, Gert Langerud, Pat Piper.

be provided by each center (inpatient, outpatient, emergency services, partial hospitalization, and consultation and education); and (c) the establishment of a funding scheme that required shared responsibility on the federal, state, and local levels (Bloom, 1975).

Two additional developments that shaped patterns of use of mental health services were the Social Security Amendments of 1965 and the expansion of private insurance coverage to include mental health care reimbursement (Kramer, Taube, & Redick, 1973). The Social Security Amendments, which funded Medicare and Medicaid, provided coverage for use of general hospitals and extended-care facilities. In the private sector, insurance coverage further contributed to increased use of psychiatric facilities within general hospitals as well as to the growth of private fee-for-service practice.

By 1968 the pattern of mental health services for older adults had increased in complexity. By this time fewer patients of all ages were living in state mental hospitals when compared to the patient census of the mid-1950s. In 1968, for example, 13% of discharges were 65 or older. At this point, however, the trend toward deinstitutionalization was less marked for the older population than for middle-aged adults. There were still 140,000 patients 65 and over in mental hospitals, representing 30% of all patients (National Institute of Mental Health, 1978a; Redick, Kramer, & Taube, 1973). The state mental hospital thus remained the site of treatment for demented elderly—new admissions with organic brain syndromes—and for chronically mentally impaired—aged schizophrenics who had been admitted when they were young (Kahn, 1975).

While admission rates to state mental hospitals were declining, admissions to psychiatric facilities within general hospitals and to extended-care facilities were on the increase for the older population. There was a dramatic growth on the part of the nursing home industry in the late 1960s. Between 1963 and 1969, for example, the resident nursing-home population increased slightly more than 75%. At the same time, the public share of nursing-home expenditures increased significantly (from 38% in 1965 to 64% in 1967) with the passage of Medicare and Medicaid (Butler, 1975). Although these extended-care facilities were designed within a medical framework, their residents had significant mental health problems as well as physical disabilities (Kane & Kane, 1978; Wack & Rodin, 1978). Some unknown but substantial proportion of the increase in nursing-home residents was due to the deinstitutionalization movement in the mental hospitals. The 1972 amendments to the Social Security Act marked the beginning of the Supplemen-

tal Security Income Program. Its funds were prohibited to residents of institutions. Therefore, to an even greater degree, unregulated boarding homes and hotels for single-room occupancy became depositories for older mental hospital patients in the name of "normalization" (Levine, 1979). There is some evidence that this pattern of irresponsible discharge is on the decline. Nonetheless, a variety of non-mental-health facilities remain badly in need of mental health services and consultation.

Between 1963 and 1978, the Community Mental Health Centers Act remained the centerpiece of legislative activities in mental health. The act was amended in 1967, 1968, 1970, 1973, and 1975. It was only in 1975 that specialized services for the mentally ill elderly were mandated. This requirement was in response to the underutilization of community mental health centers by older adults. For example, Redick et al. (1973) noted that in 1969, 4% of the patient-care episodes in community mental health centers were with adults 65 years of age or older. This 4% figure is lower than one would expect, since older adults comprise over 10% of the general population, and epidemiological studies indicate that the prevalence of mental disorders increases with age. This proportion has remained stable through 1977, the last year for which figures are available (National Institute of Mental Health, 1978b).

Even within the community mental health centers, the older adult was likely to receive a biased sample of the range of services available. Sue (1976) reported that after ethnicity, age was the best predictor of the type of service a patient was assigned to within the community mental health center (e.g., group rather than individual therapy, paraprofessional rather than professional therapist). This pattern is consistent with Kahn's (1975) report of the distribution of community mental health services in 1971 for the caseload of patients over age 65. The elderly accounted for 7% of the inpatient population, 3% of the outpatient population, and 2% of the partial hospitalization services rendered.

The individualism of the 1970s was accompanied by freedom-of-choice legislation and a consequent increase in the number of fee-for-service mental health practitioners. Thus, along with federally funded community mental health centers, psychologists in private practice became another important source of mental health services. A number of professional psychology programs were begun, some in freestanding schools. As a result, the practicing psychologist has become an increasingly important force in health care delivery by the private sector. For example, it recently has been estimated that 23,000 psychologists are working as health care providers and that over half of the time spent by psychologists providing health services is on a private-practice fee-for-service, rather than a salaried, basis (Gottfredson & Dyer, 1978).

To what extent are these psychological practitioners meeting the mental health needs of older adults? These practitioners' involvement is of necessity limited by their numbers. Storandt (1977) estimated that fewer than 100 professionals had received formal training in clinical psychology and aging. In a national survey of clinical psychologists, Dye (1978) identified fewer than 400 who were seeing older adult clients. Similarly, Mills, Wellner, and VandenBos (1979) found that 28 of the 25,510 psychologists listed in the *National Register of Health Service Providers* reported that over 75% of their clientele were age 65 or older and that these 28 practitioners were significantly older than other groups of psychologists. Perhaps the most optimistic estimate comes from Dörken and Webb (1979), who reported that nearly 7% of the clients of fee-for-service psychologists were age 65 or older. Again, older psychologists tended to see more of the older clientele.

In summary, as Kramer et al. (1973) and Kahn (1975) have noted, the net result of the mental health movement that began in the 1960s was a perhaps paradoxical increase in custodianship in the care of the aged. Inpatient care still accounted for 85% of psychiatric treatment for older adults. At the same time, many older adults dropped out of or never entered into the mental health system. Instead, other settings (such as nursing homes) became the service destinations for the mentally impaired elderly.

In 1977 the President convened a Commission on Mental Health. (In contrast to the 1959 Joint Commission on Mental Illness and Health, however, the commission reported to the Secretary of Health, Education and Welfare, rather than directly to the President.) The need for a commission arose, in part, from the recognition that community mental health centers were not meeting the goal of providing equal access to mental health care for all clients. The solutions proposed in the commission's final report (President's Commission on Mental Health, 1978) reflect major themes of the 1970s—acknowledgement of limited resources and reemergence of individuals' responsibility for themselves. A primary focus of the commission's recommendations was the targeting of services to the neediest, most impaired groups, for example, the chronically mentally ill, minorities, children and adolescents, and the aged. Another substantive emphasis was coordination of existing community supports, including professional helpers and human service agencies, as well as the larger network of friends and family. Thus the National Institute of Mental Health initiated a Community Support Program through which they awarded contracts to states with the purpose of fostering deinstitutionalization by identifying community support systems. It is expected that in the 1980s a Mental Health Systems Act will further translate the commission's recommendations into federal policy.

Services to the Aged

The aged mentally ill fall within the bailiwick of both mental health programs and programs and services for the aged. As happens in these situations, neither system wants to be responsible for this problem group, yet neither wants to yield turf to the other. Thus many community service agencies would prefer not to deal with older adults who have psychiatric problems. However, at the same time, as the head of a state office on aging once remarked, "We don't need to work with the department of mental health. We take care of the mental health of our elderly with our programs at the nutrition centers." In order to discuss the mental health of older adults, therefore, we need to be concerned with the bureaucratic structures in both mental health and aging. Indeed, the history of supportive services for the aged has paralleled the history of community mental health programs.

Estes (1979) has suggested that the definition of problems and policies for the elderly has reflected the ups and downs of the economy over the past 20 years. The watchword emerging from the recession of the late 1950s was optimism. A focus on optimal functioning was reflected in the wording of the Older Americans Act of 1965 (Butler, 1975). As inflation and the costs of the Vietnam war grew, however, disillusionment replaced optimism. More modest goals and expectations became the rule, with an emphasis on coordination of already existing services to the detriment of direct services. At the same time, the resources of the family and the individual in countering the problems of later life were rediscovered (Shanas & Sussman, 1977). In what Lasch (1978) has called a period of diminishing expectations, the goals for social intervention in later life became muted.

The aged emerged as a special constituency when demographers began pointing out the changing age structure of the United States population. The year 1961 marked the establishment of the U.S. Senate Special Committee on Aging and the first White House Conference on Aging. These activities contributed to the legislative atmosphere that eventually produced the Social Security Amendments (Medicare and Medicaid) and the Older Americans Act in 1965.

Just as the Community Mental Health Centers Act of 1963 portrayed our national goals in the area of mental health, the Older Americans Act of 1965 represented a national commitment to improving the quality of life for older adults. The original act established a federal agency, the Administration on Aging, and gave it three programs to oversee: (a) grants to states for community service projects, (b) a research and demonstration program, and (c) a program to fund the training of personnel to serve the elderly. The act was amended in 1969, 1972, 1973, and 1978. In 1969, the states were given more responsibility for planning and coordinating services to the elderly. By 1972 programs coordinated through the Administration on Aging had reached only an estimated 1.1 million older adults, not even 5% of the elderly population (Butler, 1975). This limited success was partly responsible for the addition of nutrition programs to the community service projects in the 1972 amendments. In 1973 area agencies on aging were created as decentralized planning and coordination bodies on the local level. The 1978 amendments continued their coordinating role and required the Administration on Aging to coordinate its programs with other federal agencies. Thus the Older Americans Act embodied the decentralization theme of the 1970s, despite its enactment in the 1960s, an era of categorical programs that reflected a strong federal role in setting broad social goals (Estes, 1979).

While the Administration on Aging has been the focal point for coordination of services to the elderly, there have been other federal developments relating to older adults. Following the 1971 White House Conference on Aging, the National Institute on Aging was established in 1975 for the purpose of fostering basic research in the processes of aging. In 1976 the Center for Studies of the Mental Health of the Aging was established within the National Institute of Mental Health. Its mandate included support and coordination of activities in research, training, and technical assistance. Older adults have also been served through Title XX (Social Services) of the Social Security Act and through a variety of other age-targeted and nontargeted programs in federal departments such as Housing and Urban Development, Transportation, Labor, and Energy.

Limitations of the Existing System

The late 1970s presented opportunities for reflection and planning in the area of mental health and aging. In aging, the reauthorization of the Older Americans Act in 1978 provided the occasion for debate about current and future services for the elderly. The President's Commission on Mental Health undertook a national review of current efforts and future directions. The conclusion that emerged in both arenas was that previous efforts had not been successful in providing help to those most in need, but there has been little agreement regarding the sources of this failure.

Several explanations have been offered for the underutilization of mental health services by older adults. These explanations focus on the provider of services, the older adult recipient of services, and the mental health delivery system.

The attitudes and stereotypes of the therapist or mental health professional have often been cited as contributing to the exclusion of the elderly from services (Gaitz, 1974; Kastenbaum, 1978). "Professional ageism" (Butler & Lewis, 1977) encompasses a number of elements: (a) therapists' fears of their own old age, (b) therapists' conflicted feelings about their parents' aging, (c) a belief that aging means inevitable decline, (d) pessimism about the likelihood of change in the older adult client, and (e) a view that it is futile to invest effort in a person with limited life expectancy. Kahn (1975, p. 26) contended that the first two elements were simplistic and not useful as explanations, since they "would damn the aged to continued neglect so long as human beings have parents and so long as human beings die."[1] He sought instead explanations in the mental health system for the neglect of older patients.

A second interpretation of the elderly's underutilization of mental health services is that the current cohort of older adults are reluctant to consider their problems in psychological terms (Lawton, 1978). More generally, older adults are highly diverse culturally, large interindividual differences are common in many areas of functioning, and non-normative changes take on increasing importance in later life (Baltes & Danish, 1978). In addition, among older adults, health, financial, and legal needs are typically intertwined with mental health needs. And it is often family members or caretakers who seek aid.

Third, the insufficiency, inappropriateness, and expense of mental health services have all been cited as reasons why older adults have been underserved within the mental health system. Some have recommended increased budgets and numbers of professionals, pointing out that too few services have been available. Birren and Sloane (1977), for example, have suggested that by 1988 we will need a minimum of 2,000 clinical

---

[1] From R. L. Kahn, "The Mental Health System and the Future Aged," *The Gerontologist*, 1975, *15*, 24–31. Copyright © 1975 by the Gerontological Society. Reprinted by permission.

psychologists with training in aging. In addition, others have questioned the appropriateness of traditional psychological-intervention approaches, given the special characteristics and needs of older adults. Also the community mental health center may be physically inaccessible owing to distance or lack of transportation (Gaitz, 1974). Thus it has been proposed that in order to be effective, practitioners should offer nontraditional services in nontraditional settings (Lebray, 1979) and that community mental health centers should concern themselves with outreach, consultation, and mental health education (Kramer, 1978).

Finally, it has been suggested that older adults have not used those mental health services that were available because they could not afford them (Gaitz, 1974). Medicare and Medicaid have reimbursed only on a limited basis for psychological services. Amendments currently under congressional consideration would increase to $750 the annual coverage for outpatient mental health care; however, reimbursement for nontraditional services will remain problematic.

The solutions considered thus far have largely been aimed at fine tuning the service system. Other critics, however, have suggested that the inadequacies of current efforts in mental health and aging are inherent in the idea of "providing services." They argue that what is needed is a reconceptualization of the whole enterprise. This point of view has its proponents in both the mental health and aging fields. Two major themes emerge in this conceptual critique: (a) A service model that focuses primarily on the individual has the deleterious effect of placing the burden of change on the individual rather than on the social system; (b) an atmosphere of interest-group politics leads professionals to focus on protecting or enhancing their own self-interest.

Several authors have suggested that many of the problems of older adults are created or exacerbated by social factors such as economic trends, role loss, and negative stereotypes (Butler, 1975; Estes, 1979; Kuhn, 1978). To focus intervention on the individual, therefore, can lead only to failure. Furthermore, once the helping professionals have shifted their attention to the individual, the individual quickly becomes blamed for his or her own problems (Ryan, 1976). The links to the larger social context are forgotten.

In addition, the very act of problem definition, or translation into a serviceable problem, places a distance between the helper and the person being helped and leads to underestimation of the capacities of the older adult client (Moody, 1976). Thus, as Kahn (1975) notes, helping a person can, paradoxically, increase the impairment by inducing dependency, passivity, and a loss of the individual's sense of personal control. Along these lines, Blenkner, Bloom, Wasser, and Nielsen (1971) found that receiving more protective services may have accelerated decline and precipitated higher institutionalization rates. More generally, when any helping agent undertakes to decide what someone else needs, believing that it is in the client's best interest, it perpetuates an inequality that in the end defeats the helping agent's purpose (Gaylin, Glasser, Marcus, & Rothman, 1978).

In a service-provision system, the service provider is also enmeshed in a certain role. The increasing emphasis on professionalism within society as a whole (Sarason, 1977) and within clinical psychology in particular (Walsh, 1979) has contributed to interest in issues of professional territoriality. Providers have become an interest group lobbying for more of the services that they provide (Estes, 1979). It is, of course, in the interest of the profession to define older adults as needing mental health services. This is not to say that professionals are not genuinely concerned about the welfare of older adults. Most of them went into practice because they felt they could contribute to society and to their fellow citizens (Glasser, 1978). As Sarason (1977) has noted, however, they soon found severe limitations on the type and range of activities they could pursue under the banner of professional services. In addition, it should be no surprise that, having learned to do psychotherapy, clinical assessments, and case management, these professionals find older adults in need of just those kinds of mental health services.

Current Trends in Mental Health and Aging

As a result of increasing professionalism and its concomitant consumer dependency, the self-help movement emerged as a major influence in the human services field of the late 1970s. As Gartner and Reissman (1978) pointed out, two of the elements that contributed to this growth were an increasing distrust of the professional and a desire to return control to the individual consumer or client. The origins of the self-help movement also are part of the larger cultural heritage of an egalitarian belief and a commitment to help one's family and neighbors in times of stress (Levy, 1976).

This cultural heritage has also been the basis for the growing emphasis on community networks as support systems for those in distress. Professionals are urged to coordinate their efforts with informal care givers in the community, such as church groups and civic leaders (Pancoast, 1978). At the same time, a role has emerged for paraprofessionals as a linkage between formal and informal systems (D'Augelli, in press).

Reliance on the paraprofessional has grown because of the shortage of trained professionals. Albee (1959) observed that a one-to-one approach to treatment is too inefficient and that there will never be enough direct service professionals because the need will always outstrip our ability to train and support a professional cadre. While Albee provides the rationale, Reissman's (1965) helper-therapy principle may account for the continued attractiveness of the paraprofessional role in community networks. Reissman suggested that the helper derives at least as much, if not more, benefit from the helping as the person helped.

Older adults have seemed to many people to be an obvious source of personnel. They have functioned as paraprofessionals in two basic roles, community worker and peer counselor. The community worker role involves outreach, consultation, and education, including the fostering of self-help (Blonsky, 1973, 1974; Faulkner, 1975; Faulkner, Heisel, & Simms, 1975; Gatz, Tyler, Barbarin, & Hurley, 1979; Payne, 1977; Ruffini & Todd, 1979). Peer counselors provide direct service, usually individual or group counseling (Alpaugh & Haney, 1978; Becker & Zarit, 1978; Waters, Fink, & White, 1976). Volunteer programs that emphasize the beneficial effects on the volunteers, for example, foster grandparents or senior companions, have also been encouraged under the Older Americans Act.

Various demonstration projects have explored the prospects and limits of paraprofessional programs. Some of the problems include (a) balancing helper and helpee effects, (b) developing an intervention role that involves both solving the clients' immediate problems and building their competence, (c) relationships between paraprofessionals and other personnel, and (d) relationships between the paraprofessional program and other social-service organizations in the community. Santos (1978) and Gottesman and Saperstein (in press) have developed comprehensive models of training and community service emphasizing close liaisons with agencies and multiple levels of personnel. Without comprehensive approaches, paraprofessional programs will remain tangential parts of systems for providing mental health services.

While the themes of self-help, community networks, and paraprofessionals indicate an expanded conceptualization of the mental health system, rigorous evaluations of both past and current approaches often are lacking (Weber, 1977). Moreover, available data are more likely to involve process rather than outcome variables. For example, Butler (1975) noted that evaluations of the nutrition program of the Administration on Aging detail how many meals were provided for the elderly but say nothing about whether the program is meeting the nutritional needs of older Americans. The picture is similar for mental health. Attention has been focused on how many older adults need mental health services, how many are getting them, and how many professionals are providing them. Less time has been spent in documenting the effects of service delivery on the well-being of the older adult. In part, this evaluation approach is the result of the current political climate. As Binstock and Levin (1976) have pointed out, policymakers are most likely to develop and fund social programs that have quantifiable, short-term effects. The result is to focus accountability on process variables, or rates of utilization. Levine (1979) has suggested that federal regulations should state that provision of humane care is intended and that decency and dignity should be among the evaluation criteria even though other variables are easier to count.

Given this general lack of evaluative data on which to base program planning, two particular limits seem apparent: (a) Conceptualizations of current programs overlook some important demographic changes, and (b) the older adults' point of view has not yet been systematically incorporated into the planning of services. As Morris (1977), Laslett (1977), and Treas (1977) have suggested, several demographic elements may limit the family's ability to provide support for older adults in the years ahead. Examples of this changing family context include a drop in the average number of children born (which reduces the total number of children available as resources later), an increase in the number of couples choosing not to have children, an increase in the proportion of adults never married, the increasing tendency for woman to outlive their spouses, and the increasing number of serial divorces. All of these elements may interact to weaken the support system that the older adult can call on in time of need. As Hagestad (1979) and Smyer (1979) have pointed out, policies that rely on informal support should at least consider the possibility of changes in this resource.

In addition to this demographic element, Weber (1977) has commented on the striking absence of consumer satisfaction in the evaluation of community service programs and on the lack of involvement of consumers in decision making. The assertion of one older woman summarizes discontent at being a recipient of someone else's conception of a program: "If there is one thing I do not need at my age, it is to be trained."

Available evidence suggests that current services in both the mental health and aging sectors may, in fact, fail to focus on the major concerns of the elderly themselves. Lawton (1978) summarized a number of surveys of need for mental health counseling. Between

6% and 16% of older adults indicated a need for counseling. In addition, a consistently higher percentage felt that the services should be available for others. The attribution that others needed services could reflect a tendency for older adults to underreport their own needs and dissatisfactions in the absence of realistic prospects for their amelioration. Alternatively, many older adults play a significant role in the care and supervision of other impaired elderly—either family members or friends—and their survey responses may reflect felt needs for assistance in the caretaking role (Laurie, 1978).

Other surveys concerned with a range of human services to the aged have found striking discrepancies between needs as seen by providers and by recipients. The U.S. General Accounting Office (1977) study of elderly in Cleveland found that while the older adults indicated that their first need was for physical care in case of illness, the bulk of services provided by agencies focused on socialization activities. In another study, Berry and Stinson (1977) interviewed elderly consumers of services and local service providers. At the level of general statements, the goals of both groups were similar—providing supportive services to enhance the older person's independence and expanding the options of the older person. But their specific suggestions differed. The priorities of the older consumers were for particular direct services that would provide assistance when self-help was not enough, such as food stamps, educational programs on television, and materials at the library. In addition, they placed a greater priority than did providers on financial, employment, and transportation services. Providers, in contrast, emphasized more comprehensive programs, for example, group meals, which would serve a social function as well as providing food.

Estes (1979) captured a large part of the discrepancy between service recipients and service providers in her distinction between life-enhancing and life-supporting services. The purpose of life-enhancing services is to enlarge social networks and social opportunities for the elderly. In contrast, life-supporting services embody the basic elements necessary for survival, including the income, health, and housing requirements of the neediest elderly. Estes suggested that many of the Administration on Aging's efforts have been in the life-enhancing area. In this vein, a survey of participants and nonparticipants at a senior center (Hanssen, Meima, Buckspan, Henderson, Helbig, & Zarit, 1978) found that participants were largely attracted by the recreational focus. The center simply did not accommodate those elderly who were more limited physically or who were more depressed.

Similarly, planners of mental health services should recognize the link between physical health and mental health among the elderly (Butler & Lewis, 1977) and that services should be directed toward helping individuals and their families to cope better. Kuhn (1977, p. 197) pointed out the limitations of the socialization approach:

> How does this prepare anyone to deal with the angst that is within us all about growing old? The sheer terror of not having enough money, of acquiring some crippling disease, cannot be dispensed [of] with fun and games. One old man said to me, with some disgust, "My God, I've made ashtrays for everybody I know. Can I give you an ashtray?"[2]

Depression and Senility

Two of the most difficult mental health problems encountered by older adults and their families are depression and "senility." Depression is probably the most common psychiatric complaint among older adults (Bulter & Lewis, 1977). The importance of attending to depressive symptoms among the elderly is underscored by the high rate of suicide among older adults, particularly white males. Miller (1979) suggested that the actual number of geriatric suicides, including those not reported, may be at least 10,000 each year. Two aspects of depression in older adults make it particularly troublesome to treat. The first is that there are often real reasons for feeling depressed, for instance, personal losses that may trigger existential questions. Reflecting this aspect, Gurland (1976), in a review of several epidemiological studies, noted that the highest rates of depressive *symptoms* are found in persons above age 65. In contrast, the prevalence of depressive *disorders*, as diagnosed by psychiatrists, is highest between the ages of 25 and 65 and not among the older group. The second difficult aspect of depression is that family and friends do not enjoy being around depressed people. The depressed person tends to be dependent and demanding, thereby discouraging the very people who might be supportive. Thus, the families and caretakers need assistance, and the depressed older adults need interventions that will mobilize their resources while recognizing their concerns as valid.

If depression is the most common emotional problem of the elderly, senile dementia, or organic brain syndrome, may be the most feared. An 82-year-old retired pharmacist reflected the pain and anguish that

---

[2] From *Maggie Kuhn on Aging: A Dialogue Edited by Dieter Hessel.* Copyright © 1977 The Westminster Press. Used by permission.

often accompany dementia. His wife of 55 years is confined to their house; she has a chronic brain syndrome that has left her with delusions and disorientation:

It's not the physical decline I fear so much. It's becoming a mental vegetable inside of a healthy body. It's a shame that we can rehabilitate or treat so much of the physical ills, but when your mind goes, there's nothing you can do.

Neither the mental health system nor the aging network has developed adequate programs to identify and serve older adults with organic brain syndrome. This failure embodies a number of the limitations of current attempts to provide mental health services to the elderly. Of primary importance is the lack of research on the etiology and treatment of organic brain syndromes (see Task Panel on the Mental Health of the Elderly, President's Commission on Mental Health, 1978). A second element germane to the older adult with organic brain syndrome is the importance of coordinating psychological, social, and physical treatments. With the confused older adult, legal issues regarding competency are also raised. This underscores the complexity of the diagnostic and treatment task. Another element that hampers effective treatment for older adults with organic brain syndrome is that they become at once everybody's responsibility and nobody's responsibility. While this may be true for the mentally ill elderly in general, for the chronically impaired elderly it is particularly so. In addition, their needs are not well represented in the interest-group political process described by Estes (1979).

Perhaps most striking, though, is the discrepancy between the needs of mentally impaired older adults and available resources or services. As pointed out earlier, much of the effort in aging and mental health programs could be categorized as life-enhancing. In contrast, older adults with organic brain syndrome, and their caretakers, require life-supporting services. For example, respite care that allows families a break from their daily responsibilities seems essential (Robertson, Griffiths, & Cosin, 1977). A dilemma faced by the caretaker of any older adult with mental disorder—but especially one suffering from organic brain syndrome—is the decision regarding institutionalization. Unfortunately, the decision is most often made on the basis of what is available, rather than on what would be the best combination of treatment services for the particular patient. Many writers have pointed out the bias in the United States toward the institutional provision of services (Bell, 1973; Butler, 1975; Caro, 1973). The choice available for older

people and their families is often seen as an all-or-nothing contrast between an institutional setting with too many services or community maintenance with either no service or too few options available (Maddox, 1977; Pfeiffer, 1973). The problems faced by the caretakers of older adults with organic brain syndrome embody this dilemma of "fit" between the needs of the older person and the services available. As Kaplan (1972) suggested, our emphasis should be on developing choices for older adults and their families.

In summary, the problems of depression and senility reflect the current limitations of our efforts in aging and mental health and suggest areas for program development and research.

Future Prospects

In general terms, Kahn (1979) has characterized the next decade as the "sobering '80s." People will be under financial pressure, and they will expect more from self-help. They will also want services delivered at a reasonable cost with a minimum of red tape, although they are skeptical of the competence of the government to provide them. And Greenfield (1979) has commented that the country has moved into a time of "pluralism gone mad," in which each group speaks out for its own special interests, and no one in government helps to develop a consensus reflecting higher aims. These several themes, and the particular trends in mental health and in aging set in motion in 1978, will shape mental health efforts in the 1980s and into the years beyond. Taking these new directions into account, we next consider, in turn, the nature of the older adult population of the future, probable characteristics of the mental health delivery system, and some issues that will face the providers of mental health services to older adults. While disavowing any prescient powers, we suggest possible implications of various policies.

Older Adults in the Future

Demographic and cultural trends suggest that there will be greater demands for service, with more elderly seeking the types of psychological assistance currently offered. Future decades will see a major increase in sheer numbers of the elderly, even though the rate of growth of this segment of the population will not be as disproportionately large as it has been for several decades. Thus, even if we assume a constant percentage requiring and receiving mental health services, the strain on the mental health system will be great.

By several traditional indicators of deprivation associated statistically with greater mental health risk, the percentage of older adults needing treatment will probably also increase. For example, those aged 75 and over will form an increasing proportion of the elderly, and they are selectively at risk for problems such as senile dementia and suicide. In addition, the tendency toward single-person households is still on the increase, and with the sex difference in mortality also still increasing, an inordinate number of the elderly will be female. At the same time, despite their shorter life expectancy, the numbers of minority aged are growing even faster than the numbers of white aged.

What about the propensity or readiness of these elderly to seek treatment? An interesting clue for such forecasting was provided by the 1976 replication by Kulka and Tamir (1978) of the classic study, "Americans View Their Mental Health" (Gurin, Veroff, & Feld, 1960). During the 19 years between the two studies, the percentage of those 65 and over who had actually sought professional help for personal problems had risen from about 7% to 13%, a substantial increase, though the aged were still least likely among age groups to do so. However, Kulka and Tamir were also able to determine whether their respondents had defined a personal problem in mental health terms. Of all those who had, 67% of those 65 and over in 1976 had sought professional help, a percentage that did not differ appreciably from the comparable help-seeking rate of people of other ages. Kulka and Tamir's (1978) cohort analyses suggested stability or a mild increase in help-seeking attitudes and behavior within age cohorts over time. The implication is that today's adults of 20–49 years old, of whom about 44% defined problems in mental health terms, will be seeking assistance during their later lives at a much higher rate than today's 65+ cohort. While one cannot predict confidently the form that future demands for help will take, it seems reasonable that those forms that adults are now familiar with—traditional psychotherapy, self-help groups, and so on—will account for some of the help demanded.

Questions raised by these projections include, Who will provide these services? and How will these services be paid for? Much of our discussion below is devoted to these and related issues.

The Mental Health System of the 1980s

Based on the *Report to the President of the President's Commission on Mental Health* (1978) and on the proposed Mental Health Systems Act, we can expect that the future mental health system will feature community-based services, decentralization, planning and coordination, social-support systems and "linkage," targeting services to the most vulnerable, and prevention. While the general intent is to make efficient use of scarce service money, we consider below the potential unintended as well as intended consequences of each of these emphases:

1. Continuing the current service philosophy, emphasis will be on community-based services. However, there is still a tremendous lag between ideology and the implementation needed to create community-based alternatives for older adults, such as home-care services and group homes. In addition, there will always be a need for some institutional settings, and they will contain people in need of mental health consultation. Thus psychologists of the 1980s should focus on mental health consultation in a wide range of community-based and institutional sites currently staffed by a variety of paraprofessionals and professionals from other disciplines. Psychologists should infiltrate such settings as senior centers, congregate-housing and apartment buildings with large numbers of older adult residents, rape hotlines, social service agencies, and prisons.

2. The mental health system will be characterized by decentralization. This approach, embodied in the mental health catchment area and in the area agency on aging, has in the past had the positive effect of fostering continuity of care. While decentralization has been attractive to those concerned about the growing power of central government, it has also had the negative effect of allowing excessive latitude at the local level for the interpretation and implementation of national policy (Binstock & Levin, 1976). In addition, the focus of evaluation has quickly shifted from outcome to process. To avoid repeating this experience, those involved in shaping the enacting legislation (including lobbyists for psychologists) should focus on greater clarity in goals, including humane care, along with greater specificity of expected outcomes.

3. Continuing the decentralization theme, the proposed Mental Health Systems Act will provide planning and coordination money to the states. Estes (1979) has commented on the limited degree of success that planning and coordination strategies have had under the Older Americans Act. Her argument is that coordination is resisted by agencies that do not wish to lose autonomy. Estes also suggests that allocating money to coordination diverts it from the needs of the older adult to the professional planner. Furthermore, to the extent that policy continues to be segmented in various agencies at the federal level, local agencies will continue to receive overlapping mandates, thus thwarting coordinated service systems.

4. The emphasis on community support systems, which figured strongly in the report of the President's Commission on Mental Health, is reflected in the National Institute of Mental Health's Community Support Program and is translated by the Mental Health Systems Act into money for "linkage" with health and social service agencies. The potential positive effect of such emphases may be to eliminate the older adult's feeling of being treated as a series of fragmented problems rather than as a whole person (Kuhn, 1978). Potential negative effects, however, include the creation of more red tape rather than less and decreases in direct-service money because it is presumed that informal community support systems—families, churches, self-help groups—are providing for people's needs. Sarason and Lorentz (1979) have offered a creative alternative to "linkage" services in their concept of a resource-exchange network. The exchanges are made on the barter system, an attractive concept in an era of declining financial resources.

5. Services will be targeted to underserved populations and underserved areas. The intention is to direct scarce money to those most in need. Using federally assisted housing programs as an analogy, Lawton (1978) has pointed to the benefits of targeting for age. Prior to age-categorical programs, disproportionately low numbers of older adults were helped, and the housing was not appropriately designed for elderly residents. The main problem with targeted programs is that they stigmatize the targeted group. They also tend to pit various special interests (e.g., youth and elderly) against one another in a competition for scarce funds; "the crucial dilemma surrounding the politics of old age . . . is whether any disadvantaged group in society can gain access to the resource system without itself becoming a special interest" (Estes, 1979, p. 230). Butler's (1975) solution has been to favor age-specific services as an essential first step, enabling the elderly to obtain a more equitable share of federally subsidized services. Eventually, however, he would prefer to move away from age-specific programs, because they do implicitly reinforce age stereotypes. Rather than targeting age groups, Kastenbaum (1978) proposed the targeting of issues or transitions, such as bereavement, physical illness, or change of residence. Lawton (1978), too, has stated that this kind of problem-specific approach would probably be appealing to the current cohort of older adults. Estes (1979) also tended to favor targeting services to particular needs, pointing out that programs whose eligibility is determined solely by age tend to end up serving those who are better off rather than the most needy. Finally, Smyer and Gatz (1979) have argued for similar reasons against targeted training and the creation of a specialty of clinical geropsychology. They have noted, moreover, that an age-specific approach ignores the life span developmental context and that it mistakenly treats the problems of the aged as somehow fundamentally disparate. Instead, courses and practica that emphasize particular problems of older adults (e.g., dementia) can be superimposed on training in clinical, community, and life span developmental psychology.

6. The rhetoric of prevention will influence mental health legislation and policy statements of the 1980s. The final report of the President's Commission on Mental Health (1978) emphasized the importance of preventive approaches to disabling mental disorders. However, top priority was given to infants and young children, and not to older adults. Some additional considerations are suggested, therefore, for older adults in the 1980s. First, certainly, reducing stress and increasing coping skills and social support are relevant concepts for all ages, and a language optimizing human development is useful over the entire life span. Examples of optimizing strategies include (a) teaching coping skills, (b) providing counseling around predictable life crises (Danish, Smyer, & Nowak, in press), (c) maximizing person–environment fit through environmental design (Lawton & Nahemow, 1973), and (d) focusing on systemic factors associated with mental health, such as poverty or ageism. Second, a danger in adopting the prevention rhetoric is that the importance of direct, life-supporting services may be overlooked. As noted earlier, a constant theme is the need of the impaired elderly and their families for basic, direct services. The optimizing perspective allows one to place direct services in the same conceptual framework as activities usually considered preventive. In the past, many of our attempts have had the unintended consequence of putting the older adult in a passive dependent role, perhaps inducing a helpless stance or reducing the individual's stake in solving his or her own problems. Within an optimizing perspective, direct services should support, but not supplant, the capacities of older adults and their families. Kahn (1975) has referred to the concept of "minimal intervention"—intervention that is least disruptive of usual functioning in the usual setting. An important overriding element is the preservation of the individual's options (Iscoe, 1974).

Providers of Psychological Services to Older Adults in the 1980s

We return now to the consideration of who will provide mental health services and how those services will be paid for. We focus, first, on training programs and on the mental health personnel system and, second, on licensing and reimbursement.

1. The 1980s will see an emphasis on developing sufficient numbers of trained personnel to meet the mental health needs of older adults. However, concentrating on numbers of trained professionals alone is an inadequate approach. Very few programs provide doctoral training in mental health and aging, and the gap between the number of providers needed and the number available is already large and is expected to increase. Apart from this discrepancy, Albee (1959) suggested that we will never have enough trained personnel because the need for service will always outstrip training capacity. On this basis, he argued for preventive approaches and for the use of paraprofessionals. In 1978 the Task Panel on Mental Health Personnel of the President's Commission on Mental Health (1978) noted that any consideration of the supply of mental health personnel must take into account paraprofessionals and allied mental health professionals (e.g., counseling and guidance personnel, occupational therapists, vocational counselors, recreational therapists, pastoral counselors). They reported data from NIMH showing that in 1976 mental health workers with less than a BA degree accounted for 45.1% of the full-time-equivalent positions in United States public mental health facilities. In addition, 11.9% of positions were filled by allied professionals. Developing an effective personnel system should therefore incorporate various pyramid models (e.g., Seidman & Rappaport, 1974). For aging, Santos (1978) has suggested a three-tiered model that involves PhD professionals and coordinators, middle-level professionals, and paraprofessionals, including older adults. Doctoral curricula then would include training in program development, administration, consultation, program evaluation, and primary-prevention skills. In addition, more training opportunities are needed to permit existing providers to learn new skills. Given the mental health needs of the elderly and the dearth of providers, these steps seem particularly important.

2. With the rapidly increasing cost of health care in the United States, the expense of catastrophic illness has become a national concern. We expect that some form of national health insurance will be enacted in the 1980s. Whatever form it takes, it will have a major influence on mental health services for the elderly. Since older adults are major consumers of health care services, their needs will play a central role in shaping the coverage that is developed. Previous experience suggest that federal initiatives in this area will undoubtedly have unintended effects on services and recipients. Under Medicare and Medicaid, the growth of the proprietary nursing-home industry was one such unintended consequence. The community mental health program has often made the private psychiatric hospital, rather than the patient, the beneficiary of the scarce mental health dollar.

Placing mental health services within the national health-care package affects the service system's definition of the recipient, the provider, and appropriate treatments. In a medical framework, the older adult would be labeled ill and assume a patient role, thus increasing dependency. Moreover, since the mental health problems of older adults usually derive from a complex blend of biological, social, psychological, economic, and other elements, placing mental health care under national health insurance might limit the provider's ability and willingness to attend to this variety of elements, if for no other reason than reimbursement pressures.

On the treatment side, placing mental health services in the national health insurance scheme might result in overemphasis on traditional approaches and settings. Once again, the reimbursement pattern may design the service pattern. In addition, as Albee (1977) has warned, the mental health bureaucracy, despite its rhetoric, has a heavy investment in forestalling prevention. Indeed, Gerald Klerman, Director of the Alcohol, Drug Abuse, and Mental Health Administration, has suggested that health care should be focused on the disabled and diseased and that the promotion of mental health is beyond the domain of health care. As we have stated, both preventive and direct services are needed, and part of an agenda for the 1980s should be to seek funding mechanisms for mental health outside the health insurance system.

Third-party reimbursement and proposals for national health insurance have also influenced the organization and self-definition of a variety of health-providing groups, including psychologists, since it is likely that only licensed health-service providers will be eligible for reimbursement. These trends are reflected in the current debate on the credentialing of psychologists (Danish & Smyer, 1979; Wellner, 1978). Hogan (1979b), who has studied the philosophy and consequences of professional licensing, has concluded that "licensing laws regulating counselors and psychotherapists do little to protect the public, although they may be very helpful in establishing a profession's legitimacy and economic well-being" (Hogan, 1979a, p. 9).

The outcome of the licensure debate will have a number of significant effects on the delivery of mental health services to the elderly in the 1980s. The entry requirements may exacerbate professional shortages and may restrict the functioning of paraprofessionals, working against the types of pyramid models we have recommended. Licensure encourages private fee-for-service practice. Gottfredson and Dyer (1978), for example, reported that 54.7% of the time spent by psychologists in providing health services was in fee-for-service practice. And older adults have made minimal use of these types of services in the past. In addition, such a system might detract from the optimizing approaches to intervention that we have recommended. For these reasons, Hogan's proposed alternatives to restrictive licensure warrant consideration. In addition, Newbrough (1979) has argued that the public interest can be preserved only through systematic participation in professional organizations by consumers.

In the end, the older adult, the mental health system, and the provider must all be considered together. As the needs of older adults emerge in the 1980s, as public funds tighten, and as the number of professional groups focusing on the elderly increases, we can expect tension between the needs of the professional and the needs of the impaired older adult. We must be aware of our own self-interest in the plight of the elderly, lest we become like the missionaries of Hawaii who came to do good, and did well.

REFERENCES

Albee, G. *Mental health manpower trends.* New York: Basic Books, 1959.

Albee, G. Preventing prevention. *APA Monitor*, May 1977, p. 2.

Alpaugh, P., & Haney, M. *Counseling the older adult: A training manual for paraprofessionals and beginning counselors.* Los Angeles: University of Southern California Press, 1978.

Baltes, P. B., & Danish, S. J. Intervention in life-span development and aging: Issues and concepts. In R. R. Turner & H. W. Reese (Eds.), *Life-span developmental psychology: Intervention.* New York: Academic Press, 1978.

Becker, F., & Zarit, S. Training older adults as peer counselors. *Educational Gerontology*, 1978, *3*, 241–250.

Bell, W. G. Community care for the elderly: An alternative to institutionalization. *Gerontologist*, 1973, *13*, 349–354.

Berry, C. G., & Stinson, F. S. *Service consumption patterns and service priorities of the elderly* (Final report, Contract No. HEW-105-74-3104). Washington, D.C.: Administration on Aging, U.S. Department of Health, Education and Welfare, June 1977.

Binstock, R. H., & Levin, M. The political dilemmas of intervention policies. In R. H. Binstock & E. Shanas (Eds.), *Handbook on aging and the social sciences.* New York: Van Nostrand Reinhold, 1976.

Birren, J. E., & Sloane, R. B. *Manpower and training needs in mental health and illness of the aging* (Technical Report). Los Angeles: Ethel Percy Andrus Gerontology Center, University of Southern California, 1977.

Blenkner, M., Bloom, M., Wasser, E., & Nielsen, M. A research and demonstration project of protective services. *Social Casework*, 1971, *52*, 483–499.

Blonsky, L. E. An innovative service for the elderly. *Gerontologist*, 1973, *13*, 189–196.

Blonsky, L. E. Problems in development of a community action program for the elderly. *Gerontologist*, 1974, *14*, 394–401.

Bloom, B. L. *Community mental health: A general introduction.* Monterey, Calif.: Brooks/Cole, 1975.

Butler, R. N. *Why survive?* New York: Harper & Row, 1975.

Butler, R. N., & Lewis, M. *Aging and mental health.* St. Louis, Mo.: Mosby, 1977.

Caro, F. G. Designing systems of care—Planning and policy perspectives. In E. Pfeiffer (Ed.), *Alternatives to institutional care for older Americans: Practice and Planning.* Durham, N.C.: Center for the Study of Aging and Human Development, Duke University, 1973.

Danish, S. J., & Smyer, M. A. Licensing and the public interest. *Division of Community Psychology Newsletter*, 1979, *12*(3), 7–8.

Danish, S. J., Smyer, M. A., & Nowak, C. A. Developmental intervention: Enhancing life event processes. In P. B. Baltes & O. G. Brim, Jr., (Eds.), *Life-span development and behavior* (Vol. 3). New York: Academic Press, in press.

D'Augelli, A. R. Future directions for paraprofessionals in rural mental health, or How to avoid giving indigenous helpers civil service ratings. In P. A. Keller & J. D. Murray (Eds.), *Handbook of rural community mental health.* New York: Human Sciences Press, in press.

Dörken, H., & Webb, J. T. Licensed psychologists in health care: A survey of their practices. In C. A. Kiesler, N. A. Cummings, & G. R. VandenBos (Eds.), *Psychology and national health insurance: A sourcebook.* Washington, D.C.: American Psychological Association, 1979.

Dye, C. J. Psychologists' role in the provision of mental health care for the elderly. *Professional Psychology*, 1978, *9*, 38–49.

Estes, C. L. *The aging enterprise.* San Francisco: Jossey-Bass, 1979.

Faulkner, A. O. The black aged as good neighbors: An experiment in volunteer service. *Gerontologist*, 1975, *15*, 554–559.

Faulkner, A. O., Heisel, M. A., & Simms, P. Life strengths and life stresses. *American Journal of Orthopsychiatry*, 1975, *45*, 102–110.

Gaitz, C. M. Barriers to the delivery of psychiatric services to the elderly. *Gerontologist*, 1974, *14*, 210–214.

Gartner, A., & Reissman, F. *Self-help in the human services.* San Francisco: Jossey-Bass, 1978.

Gatz, M., Tyler, F. B., Barbarin, O., & Hurley, D. *The older adult as community worker.* Paper presented at the meeting of the Gerontological Society, Washington, D.C., Nov. 1979.

Gaylin, W., Glasser, I., Marcus, S., & Rothman, D. *Doing good.* New York: Pantheon Books, 1978.

Glasser, I. Prisoners of benevolence: Power versus liberty in the welfare state. In W. Gaylin, I. Glasser, S. Marcus, &

D. Rothman, *Doing good*. New York: Pantheon Books, 1978.

Gottesman, L. E., & Saperstein, A. The organization of an in-home services network. In M. P. Lawton & S. Hoover (Eds.), *Community housing alternatives for older Americans*. New York: Garland STPM Press, in press.

Gottfredson, G. D., & Dyer, S. E. Health service providers in psychology. *American Psychologist*, 1978, *33*, 314–338.

Greenfield, M. Pluralism gone mad. *Newsweek*, August 27, 1979, p. 76.

Gurin, G., Veroff, J., & Feld, S. *Americans view their mental health*. New York: Basic Books, 1960.

Gurland, B. J. The comparative frequency of depression in various adult age groups. *Journal of Gerontology*, 1976, *31*, 283–292.

Hagestad, G. O. *Problems and promises in the social psychology of intergenerational relations*. Paper prepared for a workshop on Stability and Change in the Family, National Research Council, Annapolis, Md., March 21–23, 1979.

Hanssen, A. M., Meima, N. J., Buckspan, L. M., Henderson, B. E., Helbig, T. L., & Zarit, S. H. Correlates of senior center participation. *Gerontologist*, 1978, *18*, 193–198.

Hogan, D. B. A position statement on licensing counselors and psychotherapists. *Division of Community Psychology Newsletter*, 1979, *12*(3), 9–12. (a)

Hogan, D. B. *The regulations of psychotherapists, Vol. 1. A study in the philosophy and practice of professional regulation*. Cambridge, Mass.: Ballinger, 1979. (b)

Iscoe, I. Community psychology and the competent community. *American Psychologist*, 1974, *29*, 607–613.

Kahn, H. Next decade will be the "Sobering '80s." *U.S. News and World Report*, August 20, 1979, p. 52.

Kahn, R. L. The mental health system and the future aged. *Gerontologist*, 1975, *15*, 24–31.

Kane, R. L., & Kane, R. A. Care of the aged: Old problems in need of new solutions. In P. H. Abelson (Ed.), *Health care: Regulation, economics, ethics, practice*. Washington, D.C.: American Association for the Advancement of Science, 1978.

Kaplan, J. An editorial. Alternatives to nursing home care: Fact or fiction. *Gerontologist*, 1972, *12*, 114.

Kastenbaum, R. Personality theory, therapeutic approaches, and the elderly client. In M. Storandt, I. C. Siegler, & M. F. Elias (Eds.), *The clinical psychology of aging*. New York: Plenum Press, 1978.

Kramer, J. A. Community mental health centers: Response and responsibility to the aged. In M. Gatz (Chair), *How can older adults be served by community mental health centers?* Symposium presented at the meeting of the American Psychological Association, Toronto, August 1978.

Kramer, M., Taube, C. A., & Redick, R. W. Patterns of use of psychiatric facilities by the aged: Past, present, and future. In C. Eisdorfer & M. P. Lawton (Eds.), *The psychology of adult development and aging*. Washington, D.C.: American Psychological Association, 1973.

Kuhn, M. E. *Maggie Kuhn on aging: A dialogue edited by Dieter Hessel*. Philadelphia, Pa.: Westminister Press, 1977.

Kuhn, M. E. An open letter. *Gerontologist*, 1978, *18*, 422–424.

Kulka, R. A., & Tamir, L. *Patterns of help-seeking and formal support*. Paper presented at the meeting of the Gerontological Society, Dallas, Texas, November 1978.

Lasch, C. *The culture of narcissism*. New York: Norton, 1978.

Laslett, P. In an aging world. *New Society*, 1977, *42*, 171–173.

Laurie, W. F. Employing the Duke OARS methodology in cost comparisons: Home services and institutionalization. *Center Reports on Advances in Research* (Center for the Study of Aging and Human Development, Duke University), 1978, *2*(2).

Lawton, M. P. Clinical geropsychology: Problems and Prospects. In *Master lectures on the psychology of aging*. Washington, D.C.: American Psychological Association, 1979. (Originally presented at the meeting of the American Psychological Association, Toronto, August 1978.)

Lawton, M. P., & Nahemow, L. Ecology and the aging process. In C. Eisdorfer & M. P. Lawton (Eds.), *The psychology of adult development and aging*. Washington, D.C.: American Psychological Association, 1973.

Lebray, P. E. Geropsychology in long-term care settings. *Professional Psychology*, 1979, *10*, 475–484.

Levine, M. Congress (and evaluators) ought to pay more attention to history. *American Journal of Community Psychology*, 1979, *7*, 1–17.

Levy, L. Self-help groups: Types of psychological processes. *Journal of Applied Behavioral Sciences*, 1976, *12*, 316–322.

Maddox, G. The unrealized potential of an old idea. In A. N. Exton-Smith & J. G. Evans (Eds.), *Care for the elderly: Meeting the challenge of dependency*. New York: Grune & Stratton, 1977.

Miller, M. *Suicide after sixty: The final alternative*. New York: Springer, 1979.

Mills, D. H., Wellner, A. J., & VandenBos, G. R. The National Register survey: The first comprehensive study of all licensed/certified psychologists. In C. A. Kiesler, N. W. Cummings, & G. R. VandenBos (Eds.), *Psychology and national health insurance: A sourcebook*. Washington, D.C.: American Psychological Association, 1979.

Moody, H. R. Philosophical presuppositions of education for old age. *Educational Gerontology*, 1976, *1*, 1–16.

Morris, R. *Family responsibility—implications of recent demographic and service trends for a natural helping system*. Paper presented at the 30th annual meeting of the Gerontological Society, San Francisco, November 1977.

National Institute of Mental Health. *Changes in the age, sex and diagnostic composition of the resident population of state and county mental hospitals, United States, 1965–1975* (Mental Health Statistical Note No. 146). Rockville, Md.: Author, 1978. (a)

National Institute of Mental Health. *Provisional data on federally funded community mental health centers, 1976–1977*. Rockville, Md.: Author, 1978. (b)

Newbrough, J. R. *Community psychology and the public interest*. Division 27 Presidential address presented at the meeting of the American Psychological Association, New York, September 1979.

Pancoast, D. L. *A method of assisting natural helping networks*. Paper presented at the meeting of the American Psychological Association, Toronto, August 1978.

Payne, B. P. The older volunteer: Social role continuity and development. *Gerontologist*, 1977, *17*, 355–361.

Pfeiffer, E. Designing systems of care—The clinical perspective. In E. Pfeiffer (Ed.), *Alternatives to institutional care for older Americans: Practice and planning*. Durham, N.C.: Center for the Study of Aging and Human Development, Duke University, 1973.

President's Commission on Mental Health. *Report to the President of the President's Commission on Mental Health*. Washington, D.C.: U.S. Government Printing Office, 1978.

Redick, R. W., Kramer, M., & Taube, C. A. Epidemiology of mental illness and utilization of psychiatric facilities among older persons. In E. W. Busse & E. Pfeiffer (Eds.), *Mental illness in later life*. Washington, D.C.: American Psychiatric Association, 1973.

Reissman, F. The helper therapy principle. *Social Work*, 1965, *10*, 27–32.

Robertson, D., Griffiths, R. A., & Cosin, L. Z. A community-based continuing care program for the elderly disabled: An evaluation of planned intermittent hospital readmission. *Journal of Gerontology*, 1977, *32*, 334–339.

Ryan, W. *Blaming the victim* (rev. ed.). New York: Vintage Books, 1976.

Ruffini, J. L., & Todd, H. F. A network model for leadership development among the elderly. *Gerontologist*, 1979, *19*, 158–162.

Santos, J. F. Mental health programs for the elderly: Much talk and little action. Paper presented at the symposium *Providing human services to older adults*, Antioch College, October 5, 1978.

Sarason, S. B. *Work, aging, and social change*. New York: Free Press, 1977.

Sarason, S. B., & Lorentz, E. *The challenges of the resources exchange network*. San Francisco: Jossey-Bass, 1979.

Seidman, E., & Rappaport, J. The educational pyramid: A paradigm for research, training, and manpower utilization in community psychology. *American Journal of Community Psychology*, 1974, *2*, 119–130.

Shanas, E., & Sussman, M. B. (Eds.), *Family, bureaucracy, and the elderly*. Durham, N.C.: Duke University Press, 1977.

Smyer, M. A. *Divorce and family support in later life: Emerging trends and issues*. Paper presented at the meeting of the American Psychological Association, New York, September 1979.

Smyer, M. A., & Gatz, M. Aging and mental health: Business as usual? *American Psychologist*, 1979, *34*, 240–246.

Storandt, M. Graduate education in gerontological psychology: Results of a survey. *Educational Gerontology*, 1977, *2*, 141–146.

Sue, S. Clients' demographic characteristics and therapeutic treatment. *Journal of Consulting and Clinical Psychology*, 1976, *44*, 864.

Treas, J. Family support systems for the aged: Some social and demographic considerations. *Gerontologist*, 1977, *17*, 486–491.

U.S. General Accounting Office. *Home health—the need for a national policy to better provide for the elderly*. Washington, D.C.: Author, 1977.

Wack, J., & Rodin, J. Nursing homes for the aged: The human consequences of legislation-shaped environments. *Journal of Social Issues*, 1978, *34*, 6–21.

Walsh, J. Professional psychologists seek to change roles and rules in the field. *Science*, 1979, *203*, 338–340.

Waters, E., Fink, S., & White, B. Peer group counseling for older people. *Educational Gerontology*, 1976, *1*, 157–170.

Weber, R. E. Evaluative research: Community mental health services for the aged. In J. E. O'Brien & G. F. Streib (Eds.), *Evaluative research on social programs for the elderly* (DHEW Publication No. (OHD) 77-20120). Washington, D.C.: U.S. Department of Health, Education, and Welfare, 1977.

Wellner, A. M. *Education and credentialing in psychology*. Washington, D.C.: American Psychological Association, May 1978.

Dolores Gallagher, Larry W. Thompson, and Sandra M. Levy

CHAPTER

2

Clinical Psychological Assessment of Older Adults

Psychological assessment, as traditionally done, has not been adequate for obtaining a valid profile of older people's functional status. What is needed in the 1980s is evaluation of systematically obtained data from a number of substantive domains (e.g., physical health, coping skills, cognitive functioning, affective status) and careful integration of these data to formulate intervention programs. Current assessment procedures frequently used with the elderly are reviewed critically, and specific directions for future research are recommended.

This chapter reviews problems, issues, and substantive areas related to clinical psychological assessment of the elderly. Assessment can be viewed as a systematic evaluative process that leads to specific judgments about a given person's (or group of people's) current and potential level of functioning in a variety of settings. These judgments, in turn, contribute to a decision-making process that can have significant impact on that person's subsequent life pattern. Psychological assessment should not, therefore, simply be equated with procedures of "psychometric testing," although standardized tests may be used in the assessment process. A number of prominent clinicians in the field of assessment have argued that psychological assessment is better conceptualized as more broadly oriented toward issues of problem solving (cf. Maloney & Ward, 1976). This is in contrast to the psychometric approach, with its more limited aim of providing descriptions of people's specific traits or dimensions, which relies heavily on objective standardized mea-

surement techniques. Thus psychological assessment should not be viewed as a set of specific procedures but should reflect a general process where actuarial, clinical, or any other types of data or observations are used in a hypothetico-deductive method of problem solving (Maloney & Ward, 1976). In a similar vein, Cronbach (1970) argues that psychological tests should be viewed as tools to aid in the collection of data and not as ends in themselves.

Numerous other workers in the area of assessment have offered specific alternatives to the traditional psychometric approach (cf. Bem & Allen, 1974; Bersoff, 1973; Goldfried & Kent, 1972). These include variations of a sequential branching model of assessment, in which measures are selected and sifted by the examiner to test specific hypotheses that emerge during the data collection or from the original referral questions. While not widely used, Kanfer and Saslow's (1969) work on functional analysis argues strongly that assessment must occur in a *specific* situational context. They feel that emphasis on the person in a situation or in numerous situations should be the focus of assessment, but they also admit that this way of evaluating

We wish to thank Mary Armen and Martha Moore for their technical assistance in preparing this manuscript. We particularly want to thank Margaret Gatz for her helpful editorial assistance.

This work was supported in part by NIMH Grants 5 T24 MH14811-03 and 1 R01 MH 32157-01 and by NIH Grant 5 P01 AG00133.

individuals requires considerable flexibility and creativity to make it operational.

Recently a number of researchers have begun to highlight problems encountered in the psychological assessment of the elderly (Arenberg, 1978; Crook, 1979; Kramer & Jarvik, 1979; Lawton, 1978; Schaie, 1978; Schaie & Schaie, 1977; Whelihan, 1978). In test construction and psychometric issues, representative problems include improper standardization, lack of normative data, poor reliability and external validity, absence of "ecologically valid" measures of functional capacity, ambiguous instructions, inappropriate content of items for older persons, and inability of tests to discriminate at lower levels of functioning. Evidence has also been presented to support the importance of noncognitive factors in test performance. These include an absence of "test taking set" and unfamiliarity with the rationale of standardized testing, increased susceptibility to fatigue factors, motivational difficulties, greater cautiousness, lower performance expectations, etc. With respect to assessment strategies, emphasis is placed on the need for integrative multidimensional approaches to minimize the high probability of misdiagnosis when the perspective and tools of only one discipline are used. There has also been increasing emphasis on determining the strengths and weaknesses of the older person's general psychological organization: These are too often overlooked when assessment focuses on description of psychopathology.

This burgeoning literature reflects a number of different theoretical perspectives. For example, gerontologically oriented psychologists such as Lawton and his associates organize assessment under the construct of competence, which emphasizes positive aspects of functional capabilities (cf. Lawton, 1971, 1972, 1978). Lawton (1972) has developed a useful model that conceptualizes behavior as falling within a number of domains, each of which contains behaviors of increasing levels of complexity. This model operationalizes "competence" in terms of both breadth and hierarchical function and is comprehensive enough so that most behaviors relevant to living in the real world can be placed within it. Lawton (1978) recognizes that in practice no single assessment technique or battery is capable of adequately measuring "competence" at this time. However, he describes this as the ideal aim of the art of assessment in the years to come.

A contrasting view, more consistent with the orientation of traditional clinical psychologists, embraces a pathology-oriented approach to the assessment of aging. This is perhaps best exemplified by the work of Gurland and his associates in the United States – United Kingdom Cross-National Project on psychopathology and symptomatic behavior in adult age groups (Gurland, Fleiss, Cooper, Sharpe, Kendall, & Roberts, 1970). Following their findings on cross-national differences in the frequency with which various psychiatric diagnoses were assigned in the age ranges below 65, Gurland, Copeland, Sharpe, and Kelleher (1976) designed the Geriatric Mental Status (GMS) Interview specifically for precision in differential diagnosis of elderly psychiatric patients. This semistructured interview schedule permits nearly 500 items pertinent to the individual's psychopathology to be rated with excellent reliability; the capacity of the GMS Interview to discriminate between organic brain syndrome and functional psychiatric disorder is discussed in detail in Fleiss, Gurland, and Des Roche (1976). The GMS contains questions on somatic concerns, cognitive function, affective states, and behavioral symptoms ratable from the interview; results are interpreted in light of additional data obtained on the patient, including a medical examination, informant's presentation of sociocultural history, and information about the older person's previous social adjustment.

Both of these positions have highly specific aims, and they approach the problem of assessment from very different directions. Nevertheless, they both emphasize the need for a comprehensive and multidimensional approach that cuts across a wide range of disciplines. This similarity between two such divergent positions clearly alerts clinicians to the importance of evaluating the contribution of situational influences (e.g., health, economics, social network, and other social and environmental variables) if they intend to carry out responsible psychological assessment with the elderly (see also Gaitz & Baer, 1970; Whelihan, 1979). Failure to consider the interdependent nature of processes in the elderly (e.g., by restricting observations to a single dimension) may lead to disappointments in attempting to formulate treatment plans (Comfort, 1978).

Psychologists appear to be the mental health professionals most likely to be able to provide a systematic evaluation of cognitive, behavioral, and emotional functioning in older adults. Psychologists may make a unique contribution to the multidisciplinary assessment process by focusing on developing accurate data on the individual older person's strengths as well as weaknesses. This contrasts with the medical model, which has tended to focus on disease and pathological processes. Here we are recommending an approach based on functional analysis of the person vis-à-vis the environment, similar to the ecological model of adaptation and aging developed by Lawton and Nahemow (1973). This approach suggests that within-person characteristics (such as health, sensorimotor skill, cognitive ability), outer environmental characteristics, and environmental characteristics *as perceived by* the individual contribute independently to behavior.

Most of the many strategies employed in psychological assessment fall into the categories of *quantitative* method (i.e., where scores in comparison to a normative sample are critical determinants of behavioral inferences) or *qualitative* approach (i.e., where it is the process of solving the problem that is of primary interest, rather than the scores obtained). This is a particularly important distinction to make in assessment of the elderly because of the widely acknowledged inadequacy of norms referred to earlier. Recent work by Albert and Kaplan (1980) and Butters (1980) stresses the importance of evaluating the process by which a person achieves a correct or incorrect solution to a test item or series of items.

We shall now bring these points to bear on the issues of what, why, how, and when to assess. Clearly these areas are interrelated, but for purposes of explication, they are discussed separately.

What to Assess

The specific emphasis may vary as a function of the referral question. The emphasis could range from traditional memory assessment to evaluation of the manner in which personality factors interact with environmental demands.

Traditionally the clinical psychologist has been prepared to evaluate intellectual and emotional processes, including orientation, attention, learning and memory, abstract reasoning, perceptual motor skills, motivation, personality organization, and psychopathology. As broad as this spectrum of functioning seems, however, such an assessment battery overlooks additional areas in need of assessment when dealing with an older person, including physical health, self-maintenance, leisure time use, life satisfaction and need for service, and environmental resources (Lawton, 1972; Whelihan, 1979).

Why to Assess

Assessment personnel need to be clear about the aim of the assessment process and the outcome or product that is being requested. For example, is the aim primarily to categorize the elderly person properly as a "major depressive disorder" or "organic brain syndrome," or is it to develop a notion of the person's competence? These are two very different questions and imply different procedures to obtain relevant in-

formation. As noted earlier, developing a comprehensive functional profile that includes multiple domains of strengths and weaknesses would seem to be the most appropriate goal. However, in clinical settings, which are typically short staffed and financially strapped, this ideal may not be practical. Nonetheless, the use to which the assessment information will be put will determine in large measure how the psychologist should proceed.

How to Assess

There are numerous ways to obtain information about individuals, their environment, and the interaction between them. Interpretation of the results of psychometric data is problematic owing to such factors as the increase in performance variability with age (cf. Heron & Chown, 1967), fatigue, sensory and physical impairments, distractibility, and difficulties establishing and maintaining rapport with elderly persons because of their anxiety about the purposes for which assessment data will be used. On the other hand, psychologists have underutilized observational data and judgments of family or significant others as potential sources of information about elderly individuals. Except in research settings, standard use of structured interview techniques (compared to nonstructured interviews) has also been limited, despite their superiority in establishing reliable diagnoses.

When to Assess

Assessment has historically been viewed as a "one-shot deal." However, with the recent advent of behavioral assessment procedures, emphasis has shifted to repeated evaluations over time to determine change in critical variables and to monitor client progress (particularly in intervention programs). Assessment should not be viewed as a static process but rather should go hand in hand with intervention of any kind, so that mental health professionals can continually evaluate their effectiveness.

The Context of Assessment

Finally, at the "meta" level, Levy (1980) has cautioned that assessment itself is a process of negotiation between the client and the assessment team. The nature of the data obtained is influenced to a greater or lesser degree by the nature of this implicit contract between client and assessor. This perspective emphasizes that there is no completely value-free assessment. The flavor of the interaction between client and assessor is influenced by expectations on the part of both parties, and the tone of the assessment report is colored by the needs of the referral system in combination with the clinician's values regarding age-related changes in functioning and age stereotypes. Levy's admonitions should serve to remind us that no matter how effective our tools of assessment are, they are never free of the limitations brought to bear on the assessment process by our own theoretical and social perspectives.

Recommended Assessment Domains

Measures of Physical Health Status

The elderly have by far the largest proportion of disease and illness in the population today, with heart disease, malignant neoplasms, and cerebrovascular diseases being the three top contributors to death in late adulthood in this country (Stahl, 1978). With respect to assessment, health has often been defined as the lack of illness or disease (Stahl, 1978), despite the fact that diseases may exist that are "asymptomatic"—for example, high blood pressure. Further, the disease or illness itself must be distinguished from the *impact* of the condition on the individual's ability to function (residual functional capacity). Use of medical services (frequency of hospitalizations and doctor's visits, etc.) is not recommended as an adequate indicator of health per se but may instead indicate attitudes toward and ability to gain and seek medical care. Therefore, in a comprehensive assessment of elderly individuals, the examiner must choose which definition of health to use (one based on illness and disease, or one based on residual functional capacity). There is the related issue of whose judgment should be obtained of the "health" of the individual patient—the physician's medical records, or the person's own subjective evaluation.

Self-report measures. When only a small number of health assessments are needed, physicians' assessments or reliance on medical records may be feasible. However, physicians' evaluations are expensive and often time-consuming; they are clearly not feasible when health status is a variable of interest in large-scale assessment surveys or for screening purposes at the time of initial assessment in most clinical settings.

In these instances the issue of whether self-reports of health can be substituted for clinical assessment is legitimate and has been the subject of extensive gerontological research. Self-ratings include a health index where information is obtained concerning the amount and kind of illness experienced by the subject

(Rosencranz & Pihlblad, 1970; Shanas, 1962); the determination of functional health capacities based on how restricted older people are in their activities because of physical condition (Markides & Martin, 1979; Rosow & Breslau, 1966); and simply rating one's own health on a scale of excellent, good, fair, or poor (Maddox & Douglass, 1973; Tissue, 1972).

For the most part, studies show a high correlation between subjective and objective assessments of older persons' health (Friedsam & Martin, 1963; Heyman & Jeffers, 1963; Suchman, Streib, & Phillips, 1958). Maddox and Douglass (1973) reported congruence of self-ratings and physicians' health ratings over a 15-year span; furthermore, self-ratings of health were a better predictor of future physicians' ratings than vice versa. Self-ratings of health are not merely another measure of morale or self-image but rather represent a summary statement about the way in which numerous subjective and objective aspects of health—such as health problems and functional capacity—are combined within the perceptual framework of the individual respondent (cf. Markides & Martin, 1979; Tissue, 1972).

Because of high stable correlations of self-ratings with physicians' ratings, the perceived health status of the elderly individual is an important factor to obtain in any assessment procedure. When there are specific questions related to issues of differential diagnosis, and when it is necessary to pinpoint the contribution of medical illness or disease more specifically to the psychosocial problems under evaluation, then more specialized scales may perhaps be warranted, such as Rosow and Breslau's (1966) Scale of Physical Capacity or Rosencranz and Pihlblad's (1970) Index of Illness and Disability, as discussed earlier, or actual physical examinations.

Medical evaluation. Frequently, the behavioral symptoms strongly indicate that additional medical consultation is in order. For example, in instances where test scores and observational data of elderly persons are suggestive of impaired functioning of the central nervous system, it is the clinician's responsibility to arrange for further medical evaluation to rule out acute or reversible conditions that could be treated effectively by medical means. Other examples of how various types of cerebral impairment manifest themselves on psychological measures are discussed below.

Clinical pharmacy evaluation. In assessing physical health status one must also examine the relation between prescription and over-the-counter medications and specific behavioral or intellectual problems noted. Cheung (1979), Cheung and Kayne (1975), Kapnick

(1978), and others have pointed out that the elderly are at high risk for adverse drug reactions because of their use of multiple physicians, their own tendency toward polypharmacy, and limited knowledge about drug interaction and adverse side effects in the elderly population. Yet the majority of adverse drug reactions are preventable (Williams, 1979). In addition, Salzman and Shader (1979) have reviewed numerous medications used by the elderly that may contribute to depression, such as the anti-hypertensives, which are frequently prescribed by physicians. Therefore, the integration of a clinical pharmacist into the assessment process whenever possible is recommended. In the absence of that capability, assessment can nevertheless include obtaining a careful drug history and consultation with a clinical pharmacist when questions arise (for various methods of obtaining this information, see Williams, 1979).

Intellectual Functioning and Cognitive Processes

Aside from health-related issues, age differences in cognitive functioning have probably received more attention than any other aspect of behavior. It would be impossible to do justice to this complex area of research in the limited space available; the aim here is to synthesize existing data and refer the reader to relevant primary sources.

Numerous studies have provided useful descriptions of age-related changes in virtually every cognitive dimension, ranging from simple reaction time (Birren, 1964) to abstract reasoning (Welford, 1958); yet reliable normative data for individual assessment purposes is uncomfortably sparse (Botwinick, 1977). Furthermore, the issue of adequate external validity on virtually all of these measures has been seriously called into question (Schaie, 1973, 1978); this question highlights the need to develop novel tests that call on the cognitive abilities actually used in everyday functioning (Krauss & Schaie, 1978). Despite the inadequacies of existing instruments, the need is so great that the clinician is forced to employ them in responding to clinical concerns. For example, a common presenting problem in older people is complaints about memory functioning. The typical questions raised are whether changes observed are to be expected as a result of the aging process (Wechsler, 1958), whether these changes reflect some unusually accelerated alteration in brain function (Reitan, 1955), or whether the problems can be accounted for by increased psychological distress (Miller, 1975).

Cognitive functioning. Knowledge of what to *expect* in terms of cognitive changes with advancing age is extremely important for clinicians if they are to assess the common presenting problems of the elderly adequately. In a review article that provides a useful starting point, Botwinick (1977) concludes that decline in intellectual ability is part of the normal aging process; however, he suggests that decline may start later in life than previously thought, may be smaller in magnitude, and may include fewer functions.

Cross-sectional studies using omnibus measures of intellectual functioning such as the Wechsler Adult Intelligence Scale (WAIS) (Wechsler, 1958) show evidence that, unlike verbal abilities, some performance abilities decline by the late 60s or early 70s (Doppelt & Wallace, 1955). This discrepancy has been found so consistently that it has been labeled the "classic aging pattern." Horn and Cattell (1967) obtained comparable results using measures other than those included in the WAIS. Their tests of fluid abilities (similar to the Performance subscales of the WAIS) showed a decline with age, whereas scores on their tests of crystallized functions (comparable to the Verbal subscales on the WAIS) held and even improved with age. Botwinick (1977) summarizes this cross-sectional literature by suggesting that speed of response and perceptual integration are the functions that decline.

Results obtained from longitudinal studies using the Primary Mental Abilities Test (PMA) (Thurstone & Thurstone, 1949) suggest that the onset of decline starts somewhat later—the late 70s or early 80s—but the general pattern of abilities affected agrees with that found in the cross-sectional studies (Schaie & Labouvie-Vief, 1974; Schaie & Strother, 1968). While there are methodological problems with both cross-sectional and longitudinal studies (Baltes, Schaie, & Nardi, 1971), the trends apparent are nevertheless consistent and compelling. A final point, however, is that these results leave unanswered the question of the relevance of these changes in abilities to the daily responsibilities of life in the later years.

This general pattern of decline has generated a strong and as yet unresolved controversy on whether elders' poor performance on certain kinds of intellectual activities reflects changes expected with normal aging or is due to organic brain syndrome or some other neuropathological process. Overall and Gorham (1972) and Goldstein and Shelly (1975) found that the pattern of change associated with normal old age is different from the pattern of deficit associated with brain syndrome in the elderly. In contrast, Reitan (1955) used cross-sectional data to conclude that older people's cognitive functioning significantly resembles that of organically brain-damaged younger persons (as validated against neurological and postmortem examinations).

An important caution to keep in mind here is that for most behavioral tests of brain damage, age-appropriate norms for the elderly have not yet been developed that are based on systematic comparisons of normal versus pathological performance of subjects in the upper age ranges. In the absense of these data, the majority of older normal subjects would be incorrectly classified as brain damaged if the Halstead-Reitan Neuropsychological Battery or other similar tests were the primary assessment devices used (see Davies, 1968, for illustration of this problem with respect to the Trailmaking test of the Halstead-Reitan Neuropsychological Battery).

Schaie and Schaie summarize this issue by noting that "substantial clinical ignorance" exists on how to diagnose brain status in the elderly from performance on intellectual tests (J. Schaie & Schaie, 1977; K. Schaie & Schaie, 1977). They point out that general adult norms for chronic diffuse loss simply cannot be used to assess brain damage in the elderly. Rather, whatever is characteristic of the brain-damaged elderly must be assessed against normal aging patterns. Therefore, until appropriate norms have been generated, optimal use of neuropsychological test batteries for purposes of differential diagnosis really cannot be made (Klisz, 1978).

In the interim, valid use of neuropsychological assessment procedures with the elderly would require an assessor with considerable sophistication in both developmental psychology and neuropsychology. Alternatively, one can search the literature for recommendations of specific tests that have demonstrated sensitivity for the assessment of compromised brain status in the elderly. For example, the Background Interference Procedure (BIP) of Canter and Straumanis (1969), when used with the Bender Gestalt Test, discriminates between chronic brain-syndrome patients and healthy elderly subjects.

It must also be remembered that intellectual-age performance functions reflect the operation of a multitude of antecedents and organism–environment interactions (Baltes & Labouvie, 1973). Cohort-specific factors such as education and occupational and ability levels must constantly be taken into account in assessing intellectual performance. All of these factors make it difficult to rely on a single score or even on a set of scores when making inferences about brain–behavior relations and their implications for everyday functioning. In fact, it may be extremely useful for clinical psychologists in the 1980s to examine the utility of augmenting, or even on occasion of replacing, psychometric approaches with more *qualitative* kinds of analyses (e.g., Kahn & Miller, 1978).

Butters (1980) and Albert and Kaplan (1980) show that close scrutiny of "process achievement"—performance in attempting to complete a task—can provide significantly more information about the *nature* of the problem the person is experiencing. Luria (1966, 1973) also stresses that this kind of approach enables the evaluator to determine not only the current level of cognitive functioning of the older person but also what *mechanisms* or neuropsychological processes underlie any less than optimal performance. Appropriate interventions can then be recommended to either reverse, slow down, or compensate for performance deficits (Golden, in press). The availability of Luria materials (Christensen, 1975a, 1975b), their standardization and validation (Golden, in press; Golden, Hammeke, & Purisch, 1978), and their use with elderly populations in the future will permit both a quantitative and qualitative analysis of performance. This approach holds promise for obtaining more precise information about cognitive processing in the elderly. However, future research and more extensive clinical use of these procedures are necessary to specify their relevance for early detection and evaluation of pathological processes in the elderly.

Cognitive screening measures. In the harried clinical world, where use of comprehensive cognitive-assessment techniques may be prohibitively expensive, there is a true need for brief "screening devices" that may give very rough initial estimates of the presence or absence of cognitive impairment in elderly individuals. A number of clinical scales appear in the literature that are used fairly widely for initial screening purposes. These include the Mental Status Questionnaire (MSQ) (Kahn, Goldfarb, Pollack, & Peck, 1960); the Face-Hand Test (Fink, Green, & Bender, 1952); the Short Portable Mental Status Questionnaire (SPMSQ) (Pfeiffer, 1975); the Clifton Assessment Scale (Pattie & Gilleard, 1975); and the Mini-Mental State (MMS) (Folstein, Folstein, & McHugh, 1975). Several studies have reported that Pfeiffer's SPMSQ predicted best to clinical organic syndrome, compared to some others in common use (cf. Haglund & Schuckit, 1976). However, Kahn, Zarit, Hilbert, and Niederehe (1975) report that when the MSQ and the Face-Hand Test are used together, they achieve excellent diagnostic differentiation.

These and other similar rating scales are reviewed in Kochansky (1979) and Levy (1980). Levy in particular has questioned the utility of these short clinical scales that attempt to predict a clinical diagnosis of organicity, since the proportion of variance accounted for may be lower than desirable, and since these tests may contribute little additional information to that derived from clinical interview. There is also the danger of "false negatives" if these tests are the sole assessment indicators of impairment in cognitive function, since they tend to miss people with mild cognitive impairment who are able to score well because of such other factors as education and socioeconomic status (Kramer & Jarvik, 1979; Pfeiffer, 1975).

Memory assessment. In view of the high frequency of memory complaints among the elderly, it is surprising that so little attention has been given to development of adequate assessment devices. The Wechsler Memory Scale (Wechsler, 1945) or modifications of this scale (Gilbert, Levee, & Catalano, 1968)—the most common tests in use—have come under repeated criticism (Erickson & Scott, 1977). Two nonverbal tests of memory involving the reproduction of designs are also used frequently. These are the Benton Visual Retention Test (Benton, 1974) and the Graham-Kendall Memory for Designs Test (Graham & Kendall, 1960). In both of these tests, however, memory performance is confounded with constructional skills, and these latter skills also are affected by age. Erickson, Poon, and Walsh-Sweeney (1980) have outlined a number of weaknesses of memory tests used with the elderly and have provided some recommendations for the design of future tests. A major challenge for assessment in the 1980s will be in the development of age-appropriate memory-assessment devices that incorporate the wealth of experimental data now available regarding age-related changes in memorial processes (Craik, 1977; Poon, Fozard, Cermak, Arenberg, & Thompson, 1980). A number of related areas in need of further work for clinical assessment include evaluation of memory complaints (Poon, Fozard, & Treat, 1978; Zelinski, Gilewski, & Thompson, 1980); learning skills (Arenberg & Robertson-Tchabo, 1977); and tests of attention and concentration (Kramer & Jarvik, 1979; Welford, 1980; Wingfield & Sandoval, 1980).

Finally, the psychologist assessing elderly persons must keep in mind that scores on measures of intellectual functioning or cognitive status or both can affect (and are affected by) a number of other factors, including personality style and affective status. For example, Costa, Fozard, McCrae, and Bosse (1976) found small but significant relations between personality and cognitive ability factors that could not be accounted for by education or social class. Similarly, Miller and Lewis (1977) found significant relations among attention, concentration, and level of affective status (in this case, depression) on a signal detection task. Clearly, further research is needed to study the impact and relative contribution of these and other "individual difference" variables on cognitive functioning in the later years.

Affective Status and Psychopathology

It is difficult to obtain reliable information from respondents of any age about their feelings and levels of distress. However, this problem is intensified in older populations because self-report indices are subject to a number of age effects, including increased social-desirability response set (Klassen, Homstra, & Aderson, 1975), response inhibition (Botwinick, 1973), anxiety (Crook, 1979), and difficulty understanding instructions and completing the forms themselves (Plutchik, 1979). Also there may be areas of psychopathology unique to the elderly that are missing from self-rating scales developed primarily for younger adults. McNair (1979) questioned whether there is sufficient empirical research on the reliability of test responses of the elderly compared with those of younger adults. In general, he concluded that sophisticated consideration of comparative choices among self-rated measures is precluded by the lack of multimethod, multitrait data establishing their validity.

A related issue concerns the validity and reliability of observer-related scales of psychopathology in the elderly. Kochansky (1979) commented on the dearth of comparison between self-ratings and observer ratings for assessing various affective states. In this section we first review problems with self- and observer-rating scales for the specific affects of depression and anxiety; this is followed by a review of multidimensional measures of affective state and psychopathology.

Depression. Depression constitutes a serious mental health problem for persons 65 years of age and older. Epstein (1976) reported that the prevalence of affective disorders in older persons (in the community and in hospitals) ranges between 10% and 65%. Gurland (1976) presented data from the United States – United Kingdom Cross-National Project indicating that only 5% of patients over age 65 were diagnosed as depressed by the study psychiatrists but that many more patients gave themselves high depression ratings on a symptom checklist. Gurland suggests that older people may be less frequently diagnosed as clinically depressed because they may be subject to a higher incidence of transient depressive episodes (often precipitated by external events). In addition, diagnostic criteria are unclear and tend to vary across the mental health professions.

It appears that depression in the elderly is complex, confusing, and difficult to diagnose. According to Salzman and Shader (1979), the most common symptoms of clinical depression in this age group may include helplessness, despair, feelings of worthlessness, apathy, pessimism, suicidal thoughts, and, less frequently, guilt over real or imagined past failures. However, it is unclear whether physical complaints should also be viewed as symptoms of depression in the elderly. For example, Salzman and Shader (1979) point out that typical physical symptoms of depression (e.g., sleep and appetite disturbances) may result from a variety of diseases or any number of medications frequently prescribed to older people.

Raskin (1979) summarizes the state of the art on depression measures in his remark that as of now we do not know which signs and symptoms of depression are unique to elderly clients or which are found in all elderly persons (normal as well as depressed). Even in those studies that make comparisons between depression indices in normal young adults and normal old adults, or between young and old depressed patients, the authors seldom clarify the criteria used to reach the diagnosis of clinical as opposed to normal dysphoric feelings. Add to this the fact that we do not know how to distinguish between "justified" and "unjustified" physical complaints (so that psychologists are unclear on the interpretation of endorsed somatic items on various depression measures), and we can understand the confusion in accurate assessment.

A related problem is the differentiation of depressive symptomatology from dementia associated with cerebral pathology. Severe depression can cause symptoms of dementia, and dementia often is accompanied by depressive signs (Libow, 1977; Post, 1972, 1975). A useful scale for assessing depressive symptoms in older adults would consist of items that focus on symptoms characteristic of depression in this age group and would be able to differentiate those symptoms from the dementias of old age. To the best of our knowledge, there exists no single scale (either self-rated or observer rated) that adequately accomplishes this task!

Self-rating scales. The more common self-rating scales include the Zung Self-Rating Depression Scale (SDS) (Zung, 1965); the Beck Depression Inventory (BDI) (Beck, Ward, Mendelson, Mock, & Erbaugh, 1961); and the Depression scale of the Minnesota Multiphasic Personality Inventory (MMPI) (Hathaway & McKinley, 1943). Because these tests were designed for and validated on younger samples, they must be interpreted cautiously when used with the elderly. The problem is aptly illustrated with research on the SDS. Zung (1967) reported that normal subjects over age 65 tended to have higher total scores, which he interpreted as support for a higher incidence of depression in older people. However, additional research suggested that the somatic items of this scale may provide a larger contribution to the total score than do the affective items (Zung, 1967). The somatic items may also have a different meaning for the old than for the young, and they are not well correlated with either well-being or psychological distress items on this scale (Blumenthal, 1975; Gallagher, McGarvey, Zelinski, & Thompson, 1978). There is an added problem in

that the SDS may not be reliable with individuals over age 70 (Gallagher et al., 1978).

Similar issues exist with regard to the BDI (Zemore & Eames, 1979) and the MMPI Depression scale (Harmatz & Shader, 1975). A promising self-report measure that merits further research and clinical application is the Depression subscale of the Hopkins Symptom Checklist (SCL-90) (Derogatis, Lipman, Rickels, Uhlenhuth, & Covi, 1974). It contains items focused on dysphoric mood per se, with only few somatic items included. Gallagher (1979) found this measure to be sensitive to change when used with elderly depressed clients in a psychotherapy outcome study.

Observer-rating scales. Kochansky (1979) notes that no observer-rating scales of depression have been developed specifically for the elderly but that the Hamilton Psychiatric Rating Scale (Hamilton, 1967) has been used in a number of studies involving older patients (Sakalis, Gershon, & Shopsin, 1974). Zung developed a Depression Status Inventory (Zung, Gianturco, Pfeiffer, Wang, Whanger, Bridge, & Potkin, 1974) to supplement the self-rating scale, but it has been used less extensively with older people. Other scales, such as the Phenomena of Depression Scale (Grinker, Miller, Sabahin, Nunn, & Nunnally, 1961) and the NIMH Collaborative Depression Mood Scale (Raskin, 1965) have not yet been used with older individuals.

Another kind of observer rating is based on a structured interview. Raskin (1979) recommends exploration of more standardized criteria for assessing the presence of clinical levels of depression, such as are found in the Research Diagnostic Criteria (RDC) of Spitzer, Endicott, and Robins (1978). Current work (Dessonville & Finnell, 1980; Lewinsohn & Finnell, 1979) suggests that the RDC is an appropriate schema for classification of depression in the elderly. Preliminary analysis of data collected on over 100 depressed and nondepressed elderly people showed clearly differing symptom patterns. Typically the RDC diagnoses are reached through administration of the Schedule for Affective Disorders and Schizophrenia (SADS) (Spitzer & Endicott, 1977), a structured interview technique designed to give "pure" classifications based on clearly defined criteria. According to Endicott and Spitzer (1978), the use of the SADS technique enables RDC diagnoses to be made with high reliability (*r*'s in the .80s). However, with older persons the SADS/RDC approach must be supplemented by inclusion of screening measures for organic dysfunction, along with appropriate health screening measures. The latter are necessary so that any physiological symptoms endorsed by the elderly person can be assessed in light of perceived health or actual physical health status. With these cautions in mind, the SADS/RDC approach seems to hold promise for reducing ambiguity in the diagnosis of depression in older adults.

Anxiety. There has been no thorough review of self-report anxiety measures used with the elderly since that of Chown (1968). Most of the studies at that time viewed anxiety in terms of "neuroticism." Only a few evaluated anxiety in subjects over age 60; their results were inconclusive about whether there is increased prevalence of anxiety with advancing age. Kral and Papetropoulus (1965) noted that only a small number of elderly patients can be appropriately diagnosed as having phobic anxiety reactions; Lehmann and Ban (1969) suggest that intrapsychic conflicts are rarely central to the anxiety seen in the elderly. Raskin (1979) too has suggested that anxiety in the elderly generally does not take the same form as anxiety in younger persons; in older adults it is often associated with some physical disorder. On the other hand, anxiety may even be considered adaptive in old age (Jarvik & Russell, 1979).

Neither self-report measures nor observer rating scales to measure anxiety have been designed specifically for the elderly. Self-report measures that have been used include the Manifest Anxiety Scale (Taylor, 1955); the Tension Factor of the Profile of Mood States (McNair, Lorr, & Droppleman, 1971) and the Self-Rating Anxiety Scale (Zung, 1971). For observer rating scales, Kochansky (1979) recommends that the Hamilton Anxiety Scale (Hamilton, 1959) and the Zung Anxiety Status Inventory (Zung, 1971) may have some utility. Researchers may want to be guided by Verwoerdt's (1976) schema for understanding and classifying anxiety reactions in the elderly; development of measures that are conceptually based would be welcome additions in the field.

Other forms of psychopathology. Schizophrenia and paranoid reactions may be difficult to assess adequately in older individuals. The scales that have been developed for use with a general psychiatric population often fail to sample the kinds of delusions or hallucinations seen in elderly patients (Raskin, 1979). A number of unique factors may play a role in the development of psychopathology in the elderly. For example, Post (1973) pointed out that patients who believe that talk is being directed at them from nearby often have significant hearing loss; Post thinks this may be the most common form of paranoid symptomatology in the elderly. In addition, Roth's (1955) clinically descriptive diagnostic category of "late paraphrenia"—which refers to onset of schizophrenic symptoms for the first

time in the latter decades of life—is unfortunately not in common use in the United States, despite its apparent validity for the elderly and its frequent diagnostic use in the United Kingdom. This construct relates to the diagnosis of schizophreniform disorder that has been incorporated into the newly revised system of psychiatric nomenclature (see below); therefore, description and diagnosis of severe psychopathology in the elderly may become more precise in the future.

Multi-dimensional scales for affect and psychopathology. Although the MMPI is the best known of the omnibus self-report measures (Hathaway & McKinley, 1943), its internal consistency and test–retest reliability with the elderly have not been determined, nor has adequate validity been demonstrated (McNair, 1979). Yet practitioners continue to use the MMPI with elderly persons as if young-adult norms or the age-corrected norms provided in Dahlstrom, Welsh, and Dahlstrom (1972) were appropriate. Bernal, Brannon, Belar, Lavigne and Cameron (1977) provide the best review to date of the various scales with which age changes have been found, but cohort effects on the MMPI have not even been addressed in the literature. Pfeiffer (1977) reports some preliminary findings with a short version of the MMPI known as the Mini-Mult (Kincannon, 1968), which may be useful for diagnostic purposes with the elderly because of its brevity. However, Fillenbaum and Pfeiffer (1976) noted three consequences when the Mini-Mult was used in a survey of community-residing elderly: significant sex- and race-related differences, somewhat unstable scale scores, and unduly elevated scores.

The norms for other self-report multidimensional scales, such as the Hopkins SCL-90 (Derogatis et al., 1974) and the Profile of Mood States (McNair et al., 1971) have also been standardized on younger adult populations. Scattered reports of their potential utility with elderly clients appear in the literature, but their actual clinical validity remains to be determined. For example, the Obsessive-Compulsive Factor of the SCL-90 includes items on memory complaints that may load on different factors for different ages (Gatz, 1978).

Observer-rated omnibus scales have been used with elderly inpatient and outpatient populations: the Brief Psychiatric Rating Scale (BPRS) (Overall & Gorham, 1962), the Inpatient Multidimensional Psychiatric Rating Scale (Lorr & Klett, 1966), and the Sandoz Clinical Assessment-Geriatric Scale (Shader, Harmatz, & Salzman, 1974). Kochansky (1979) recommended the BPRS, at least for the collection of geriatric psychopharmacological research data, because of its brevity and apparent sensitivity to drug effects. Other observer rating scales used to evaluate hospitalized geriatric patients (primarily for research purposes) include the Geriatric Rating Scale (Plutchik, Conte, Lieberman, Bakur, Grossman, & Lehrman, 1970) and the Nurses Observation Scale for Inpatient Evaluation (NOSIE) (Honigfeld, Gillis, & Klett, 1966). However, as has been noted repeatedly, no specific scale exists for rating psychopathology in elderly outpatients; this topic requires considerably more research effort.

Personality Measures

The paucity of theory regarding adult psychosocial developmental processes unfortunately limits the possibility of theory-based personality-assessment devices. Nor has the usefulness of personality tests for purposes of diagnosis and assessment been established (Lawton, Whelihan, & Belsky, 1980). Issues have been raised regarding the suitability of outdated norms for omnibus personality questionnaires (K. Schaie & Schaie, 1977; Schaie & Marquette, 1972), willingness of older people to respond openly regarding personal matters (Lawton et al., 1980), problems with increased social-desirability response set with age (Klassen et al., 1975), and many other problems mentioned earlier with regard to assessing psychopathology.

Omnibus self-report measures. Cross-sectional studies evaluating age differences in personality using available measures have suggested that personality organization may be relatively stable across the middle and late adult years (see Neugarten, 1977, for a review of these findings). For the most part, an increase in introversion in the second half of life is the only consistently replicated finding. Longitudinal studies using the Sixteen Personality Factor Questionnaire (16 PF) (Cattell, Eber, & Tatsuoka, 1970) also support a picture of stability of personality across a 10-year period in older adults. Costa and McCrae (1978) concluded from their cluster analysis of the 16 PF and other scales that objectively measured personality traits of anxiety, openness, and extraversion are meaningful and stable dimensions of individual differences that can be measured from adulthood through the eighth decade.

Lawton et al. (1980) have evaluated a number of the self-report scales of personality including the 16 PF, the Edwards Personal Preference Schedule (Edwards, 1953), the Maudsley Personality Inventory (Eysenck, 1959), and the Guilford-Zimmerman Temperament Survey (Guilford & Zimmerman, 1949). They recommend use of the Maudsley Personality Inventory because a short form is available, age differences associated with it appear to be few, and it appears useful in its

ability to measure neuroticism in a clinical situation. In contrast, they point out that nothing in the literature suggests how the 16 PF could be useful clinically with older adults.

Lawton et al. (1980) also reviewed various measures of personality characteristics that may be termed "personality style," including such traits as locus of control (Rotter, 1966), psychological differentiation (Witkin, Lewis, Hertzman, Machover, Meissner, & Wapner, 1954), and repression-sensitization (Byrne, 1964). In addition, age differences in behavioral rigidity have been evaluated by Schaie and Parham (1975) and norms developed for adult males and females through the eighth decade. While these constructs are of potential interest, both the discriminant validity and the clinical utility of these scales are essentially untested.

Although performance measures of personality have appeal because of their objectivity, their usefulness with older persons is at present quite limited (Hundlevy, 1973). Chown's (1961) use of behavioral measures of rigidity illustrates how performance measures can supplement self-report instruments, but the latter will most probably continue to be the chief source of objective data on adult personality.

Projective techniques. Kahana (1978) reviewed a number of strengths as well as weaknesses to consider when deciding whether or not to use projective tests with the elderly. In their favor, projective tests avoid many of the problems that confront the elderly in multiple-choice paper-and-pencil testing: Projective stimuli are more readily understood; they do not require complex verbal discrimination; there is less need to be "testwise" in the sense of figuring out complex formats or instructions; and finally, projectives allow the examiner the opportunity to observe the aged respondent closely, since they must be administered in a face-to-face interview. Projective tests also permit flexibility in mode of administration and allow the respondent to avoid gracefully areas that are embarrassing or painful. Kahana also commented on the incongruity between elderly subjects' willingness to complete various projective techniques and the clinician's unwillingness to use projective tests in a consistent way. Again, this seems to be an area with very little systematic research at the present time. There is the general problem of validating performance on projective tests with respect to specific personality dimensions or dynamics, but this is no less a problem with older respondents than with younger. However, projective techniques may be able to reveal personality dynamics not reachable through objective means.

The Thematic Apperception Test (TAT) (Murray, 1938) is the most frequently used projective technique for which reports are available on age differences.

Chown (1968) reviewed that TAT literature, including modifications on the original cards and scoring procedures for use with elderly persons. More recently, Lawton et al. (1980) reported several studies in which the TAT instructions needed to be modified in order to obtain responses beyond a descriptive level. Alternative apperceptive tests now available include the Gerontological Apperception Test (Wolk & Wolk, 1971) and the Senior Apperception Test (Bellak, 1975; Bellak & Bellak, 1973). They portray age peers and typical life situations of older people. However, with all of these techniques there is no single generally accepted scoring system, nor are norms available.

Rorschach's (1942) early observations on the constriction, stereotyping, and low perceptual clarity of older persons' responses on his projective technique have generally been supported by several subsequent studies (Bernal et al., 1977). Ames, Learned, Metraux, and Walker (1954) and Ames, Metraux, Rodell, and Walker (1973) have provided the most thorough discussion of Rorschach responses in old age, and they report very few consistent findings dependent on age. Yet Oberleder (1964), Klopfer (1974), and Kahana (1978) point out that the Rorschach technique may be a useful assessment device because it does not require a mode of performance that penalizes aged persons whose speed of responses or coordination has declined. Still, the clinician must consider the relative contribution of factors such as poor physical health (cf. Eisdorfer, 1960, who reported that hearing loss was related to poor Rorschach scores) as well as sociocultural background and other factors that clearly influence an elderly person's performance on a task of this nature.

Other projective techniques such as the Holtzman Inkblot Test (Holtzman, Thorpe, Swartz, & Herron, 1961), the Draw-a-Person Test (Machover, 1952), and the Sentence Completion Test (Holsopple & Miale, 1954) are discussed at length in Kahana's (1978) review. However, these measures may be related more to cognitive functioning than to personality dynamics (Lawton et al., 1980). Nevertheless, use of projective techniques may provide a somewhat standardized, ecologically valid avenue for assessing functional status and a useful index of the person's response to unstructured situations. Projective techniques should, in our opinion, be considered for inclusion in any comprehensive assessment procedure undertaken with the elderly, particularly when there is little or no opportunity for more natural observation.

Stressful Events, Coping Skills, and Life Satisfaction

In most physiological and psychological theories of aging, the concept of stress plays an elemental role, as stressful events are assumed to increase with advancing age. Early work (e.g., Selye, 1956) stimulated a good deal of research on the role of life events (e.g., retirement, widowhood) as potential stressors in the development of physical and mental illness (Dohrenwend & Dohrenwend, 1974; Holmes & Rahe, 1967). No evaluation of an elderly person would be complete without careful attention to prior history and evaluation of the person's resources to cope with these events. However, these domains have received little systematic attention from clinical psychologists; for a review of research in this area, the reader is referred to Chiriboga and Cutler (Chapter 25 in this book).

The Social Readjustment Rating Scale (Holmes & Rahe, 1967) has been the major research instrument in this area; it evaluates the impact of life changes preceding onset of illness. Holmes and Masuda (1973) have done substantial research indicating that the higher the total score on this measure, the greater likelihood there is of developing physical illness; however, the effect of various life changes seems to be strongly influenced by the context in which these changes occur. Attempts to describe this context have focused on variables such as whether the event is "on time" or "off time" (Hultsch & Plemons, 1979; Neugarten, 1973); the extent to which the individual has control over the event (Schulz & Brenner, 1977); previous experience dealing with stress and coping resources available (Lazarus, 1979); degree of anticipatory preparation (Eisdorfer & Wilkie, 1977); and the number of events occurring simultaneously (Palmore, Cleveland, Nowlin, Ramm, & Siegler, 1979). Of these contextual factors, two may be particularly relevant in the assessment of the elderly: timeliness of events and their cumulative effect. For example, widowhood has been found to be more stressful in the young than in the old, where presumably the event is "off time" and there is little opportunity to prepare (cf. Ball, 1977, for discussion of negative impact of bereavement on the young, compared to Heyman and Gianturco's 1973 study of its impact on older people). In terms of the cumulative effects of stressful events, Palmore et al. (1979) reported that single events (e.g., retirement, widowhood, or severe physical illness) had surprisingly few negative effects on social psychological adaptation (as reported in a battery of self-report scales). But when several of these events occurred for the same person, they tended to cumulate in negative impact and to cause the most difficulty to older people with few psychological and social resources.

Study of the process of adaptation has led workers to look at a number of factors including health, psychological and social resources, behavioral styles of reducing anxiety, and cognitive methods of coping with stress. Several techniques for tapping coping strategies are reviewed by Kahana, Fairchild, and Kahana (1978). These include the Geriatric Coping Schedule (Quayhagan & Chiriboga, 1976), which elicits open-ended responses to stressful situations into which older individuals should project themselves, and the Elderly Care Research Center Scale (Kahana & Kahana, 1975), which asks people to select a number of possible coping strategies for the stressful situations presented. Future research with measures that define coping in terms of *how* elderly people solve problems may permit identification of useful behavioral and/or cognitive strategies that would provide the basis for designing intervention paradigms of specific utility to this age group.

Currently there is no single assessment device that takes into account elderly people's perceptions of the stressfulness of particular life events while at the same time providing some description of the nature and extent of the behavioral, cognitive, or environmental means employed or required to adapt to them. As a first step, one could use the Geriatric Scale of Recent Life Events developed by Kiyak, Liang, and Kahana (1976), which is a modification of the original Holmes and Rahe (1967) scale designed specifically for the elderly. While no direct test of validity for this scale is now available, it is easily administered to elderly respondents, since it can be given as a self-report measure or incorporated into an oral interview. To further improve assessment of these related domains one could use additional questions (possibly styled after Lazarus, 1979, or Siegler, Gatz, George, & Tyler, 1979) about prior coping history and likely coping responses to present difficulties.

In addition to the study of coping responses per se, clinicians need to evaluate another factor that influences the ability to cope adequately—that is, subjective happiness or well-being. Work in this area dates back to the well-known Life Satisfaction Index of Neugarten, Havighurst, and Tobin (1961). Life satisfaction or well-being is generally viewed as a multidimensional concept; Lawton (1972) reported extensive work on its definition and measurement, which led to development of the Philadelphia Geriatric Center Morale Scale (Lawton, 1975). Either of these scales can be recommended as a good measure of well-being for older individuals, and the two scales correlate well with each other (Linn, 1979).

Finally, the reciprocal relationship among the variables discussed in this section can be seen when one examines how they can converge to influence an elderly person's reaction to a significant life change. For example, the impact of retirement may be far less negative for a person who has a prior history of adequate adjustment to other significant life events and who currently has a high degree of life satisfaction or morale.

Conversely, if retirement occurs close in time to other meaningful life changes, and the person has a history of poor adaptation to change, inadequate or marginal coping skills, and current low morale, that person may be "at risk" for subsequent development of psychological distress. Clearly, studies are needed to shed further light on how these factors interrelate and on what can be predicted from knowledge of their respective contribution to the total clinical picture.

Functional Capacity

Another extremely important factor related to adjustment is the individual's capacity to carry out the essential activities of daily living. Of course, depending on other factors such as physical and mental health status, functional behavior can vary from simple toilet and eating skills to maintenance of an occupation. Different aspects of functional capacity would need to be evaluated for a patient housed in a total-care environment than for a worker being phased out of a job who needed to remain in the work force for economic or psychological reasons.

This diversity of situations—requiring different adjustment patterns for older persons—emphasizes the importance of individual differences in the later years. For example, one person may be in such a state of decline at age 60 that a constant-care environment is called for, whereas another may still have the capacity for effective functioning in a work setting at age 90. But frequently the policies of social institutions are not sensitive to these differences, because their primary index of capacity has been chronological age. These differences argue strongly for measurement of "functional age," in contrast to chronological age, as a primary determinant of decisions pertaining to retirement and other living conditions (Schaie, 1977). Krauss (in press) reviews these arguments and presents examples of how functional age can be made operational for employers. Age-appropriate test materials, with adequate criterion validity, remain to be developed to enable measurement of the capacity to function in a work situation.

Activities of daily living. While the area is in need of development, both conceptually and empirically, a number of assessment devices dealing with activities of daily living are available. These have been used primarily in inpatient settings where there is a direct relation between deficits in self-care and the amount of care required from the institution. The Instrumental Activities of Daily Living Scale (IADL) (Lawton & Brody, 1969), the most widely used self-report measure of this type, covers a variety of activities relevant to everyday life ranging from self-care (e.g., bathing, hair care) to instrumental activities (e.g., shopping skills, ability to handle money, ability to transport oneself independently). Assessment of self-care and of instrumental activities is helpful in planning institutional care and living arrangements outside the institution. Lawton's (1972) broadened notion of functional assessment—including such additional factors as physical health, social roles and activities, morale, life satisfaction, and psychiatric status—can be measured through use of his revised IADL scale (Lawton, 1975).

For assessing functional capacity of impaired elderly samples, a number of behavioral rating scales are designed for and used with inpatient populations. Salzman, Kochansky, Shader and Cronin (1972) reviewed scales available for specific use with geriatric patients. Additional comprehensive reviews are found in Smith (1979) and Levy (1980). These reviewers recommend the Geriatric Rating Scale (Plutchik et al., 1970), the Physical and Mental Impairment of Function Evaluation (Gurel, Linn, & Linn, 1972) and the Nurses Observation Scale for Inpatient Evaluation (Honigfeld et al., 1966).

Community adjustment. A dimension related to functional capacity is the community adjustment of older people, including evaluation of their social adjustment (role, behavior, conformity to social expectations) and personal adjustment (subjective contentment, well-being). Linn (1979) reviewed a number of existing scales to assess these two dimensions of adjustment, but none were designed specifically with the geriatric community in mind. The Katz Adjustment Scale (Katz & Lyerly, 1963) is the best known and most widely used community adjustment scale; a unique feature is that information can be obtained from both the client and a designated "significant other." This scale takes advantage of the helpful information that significant others often provide to the psychologist, supplementing the psychologist's impression of the client's everyday functional capabilities.

Social and family networks have traditionally not been evaluated systematically by psychologists; social workers have been far more sensitive than psychologists to evaluating the impact of these networks on current problem situations. However, relevant data are beginning to emerge. Lowenthal and Chiriboga (1973) stressed the importance of the presence of a confidant for maintaining mental health during the crisis of bereavement; Niederehe (1978) reported significant relations between depression and the inadequacy of the social network (defined as frequency of contact, type of contact, and quality of relationship reported by the individual). Niederehe's work also represents an initial attempt to scale social network. Pattison's (1977) Psycho-Social Kinship Inventory is a more qualitative measure designed to describe degree of intimacy, reciprocity, and degree of positive emotion present in relationships reported by various client groups, although the measure has not yet appeared in articles describing interactions of the aged, with their families.

In addition, evaluation of the social network and the quality of the social support system can be necessary to the design of treatment interventions. For example, in behavioral types of therapy where potent reinforcers need to be identified in order for the intervention to be effective, knowledge of the social network can be invaluable in organizing behavioral programs. As Kanfer and Saslow (1969) emphasized, psychological symptoms are maintained by sets of antecedent and consequent conditions, meaning that they are a product of the interaction between the individual and the "network." This suggests that the network has to be involved in procedures designed to create behavioral change.

Multidimensional Assessment Batteries Designed for Screening Purposes

Throughout this chapter we have emphasized the need for comprehensive, multidimensional evaluation of the potential contribution of a variety of factors that interact and affect an elderly person's current status. Although we have approached this by reviewing a number of single domains (and their associated measures) and have recommended specific measures, we now wish to mention several limitations that obtain when various measures are used singly or are put together in piecemeal fashion. Several available integrated assessment "packages" have been designed specifically for the elderly which may be particularly useful at the screening stage, when it is impossible to do an in-depth evaluation of every domain recommended.

Most measures developed to assess the specific domains discussed have sprung from differing theoretical perspectives and therefore reflect conceptual orientations to aging and clinical issues that may not always be convergent. Also, some measures and techniques reviewed may not be ideal for clinical use. While they may index a given variable adequately for research purposes, they have not typically been designed for inclusion in a comprehensive assessment package, or for application to clinical problem solving. Consequently, several batteries have recently been developed that permit evaluation of how specific factors interrelate in the elderly. Their use at the initial screening stage may provide an economical and thorough way to begin the assessment process and to set the stage for later in-depth assessment of specific domains appropriate for a given individual. In addition, these batteries, since they were designed to bridge the gap between evaluation and treatment, may provide a more sensitive lead-in to intervention programming than does piecemeal administration of a number of discrete measures.

Two multidimensional batteries are the Older Americans Resources Services Questionnaire (OARS) (Pfeiffer, 1976) and the Comprehensive Assessment and Referral Evaluation (CARE) (Gurland, Kuriansky, Sharpe, Simon, Stiller, & Birkett, 1977–78).

The OARS technique, developed for the Duke University longitudinal study, is an interview with forced-choice responses that permits ratings of social resources, economic resources, mental health, and physical health. Interrater reliability on the OARS instrument has recently been found adequate by Fillenbaum, Smyer, and Pruchno (1979). This is critical when deciding whether or not to use the OARS, since its parts are designed to be completed by a multidisciplinary team working independently (e.g., psychiatrist and psychologist).

The CARE battery is a new and reliable assessment technique designed to elicit, rate, and classify information on the health and social problems of the older person. The CARE approach is useful in determining whether an elderly person should be referred for services; it can also be readministered to evaluate the effectiveness of the services rendered. The interview guide is so designed that symptoms may be examined further to help determine (a) the nature of the disturbance, (b) the factors contributing to the symptoms being reported, and (c) whether the symptoms have clinical significance. For example, if elderly clients report symptoms of depression, further questioning is done in a standard manner to ascertain the physical, psychological, or social determinants of those symptoms. Interrater reliability on this instrument is adequate, and the CARE has the advantage that, as with the OARS, sections of it can be administered by various members of a multidisciplinary team. Gurland et al. (1977–78) recommend its use in community surveys to identify older persons in need of assistance, in community health settings, and in research projects where effectiveness of interventions is to be measured. Application of the CARE technique to clinical settings has recently been recommended by Gurland (1979). In fact, a screening schedule has been designed to detect "pervasive depression" or "pervasive dementia" with maximal specificity and sensitivity. The screening scale has been adequately validated and may provide a useful alternative to the currently available mental-status screening devices discussed earlier. In addition, careful scoring procedures enable the trained clinical psychologist to diagnose and assess levels of severity for functional, organic, and social disorders. The instrument is quite promising and may well become useful in applied settings.

DSM-III Classification System

The need for a comprehensive multidimensional approach to assessment will become abundantly clear in clinical work with all age groups in the 1980s as the DSM-III classification system becomes more commonly used. The American Psychiatric Association's (1980) new *Diagnostic and Statistical Manual of Mental Disorders*, developed by its Task Force on Nomenclature and Statistics, is an innovative system that emphasizes multiaxial classification. This feature requires each individual to be evaluated on five independent dimensions that are conceptually compatible with the assessment domains discussed earlier in this chapter. The five dimensions are clinical psychiatric syndrome, personality disorders, physical disorders, severity of psychosocial stressors, and previous level of adaptive functioning. This multiaxial framework requires that each of the axes be assessed in some way. This approach builds in the notion that other factors may be potentially relevant to the understanding or management of a given individual and it provides clear criteria for assigning clinical diagnoses that should considerably increase the reliability of the diagnostic process across clinicians. In addition, DSM-III makes use of some diagnostic categories that may be particularly relevant with older adults (e.g., schizophreniform disorder, which refers to symptoms of schizophrenia present for a duration of less than six months).

Given the various methodological problems of assessment described throughout this chapter, the appropriate use of the DSM-III system with the elderly is a rather large task. In addition, the scales proposed for assessing the fourth and fifth axes do not fully reflect the complexities of measuring stress and coping discussed earlier. At the moment, then, it represents an ideal to aim for rather than a system to embrace. However, it may provide a constructive impetus to the assessment arena in the future.

Conclusions

The primary focus of this chapter has been on instruments of assessment within single domains of interest. However, in addressing the problems of the elderly the clinician should attend to the configuration of test results both within and across the various domains. Since practical limitations do not permit the assessment of all of the variables that may have some bearing on a given problem, the clinician must seek the highlights and then determine an assessment plan that will provide information of major importance for diagnosis and formulation of a treatment program. Any such plan of assessment should be sufficiently flexible to permit branching into subsequent areas of assessment as new information is obtained. Assessment can then be viewed as a hypothesis-testing process (cf. Maloney & Ward, 1976).

If assessment is to proceed smoothly and efficiently, it is important for the clinician to become familiar with the kinds of problems encountered when working with the elderly. For illustrative purposes, we would like to review four general disorders seen frequently by the clinician and to mention briefly some of the highlights to look for in the assessment process. These include (a) complaints of memory loss and general cognitive decline, (b) organic pathology and/or dementia, (c) depressive reaction, and (d) paranoid reaction.

One of the most frequent complaints of older people is that they cannot remember things as well as they used to and that they are unable to concentrate. This problem is usually accompanied by considerable psychological distress. As already mentioned, the clinician is immediately confronted with the questions of whether there is a justifiable basis for the complaint, whether that basis is consistent with normal age changes, and whether it is suggestive of organic pathology or may be due to an affective disorder. Specifically, with respect to memory function, recent work has directed our attention to the intricate interrelations of depression, memory complaints, and memory performance (Kahn et al., 1975; Zarit, Cole, Gallagher, Guider, & Kramer, 1978). Careful measurement of all three factors will be useful in attempting to solve the presenting problem. Basically, four configurations of these three factors occur with some regularity:

1. If the patient is complaining intensely of a memory problem, has an elevated level of depression, and yet performs within the normal range on an objective evaluation of memory performance, then this would argue strongly that the current memory problem may be due to an affective disturbance. An appropriate treatment program here might be time-limited psychotherapy accompanied by pharmacotherapy if that is indicated.

2. If memory complaints are intense in the face of relatively normal performance and minimal depression, then other intervening variables may be important. For example, anxiety may be a significant problem, or the patient may have a mild or minimal brain impairment. If brain impairment is suggested, other laboratory findings may be helpful, though frequently they are negative on first examination. Repeated assessments over time can be useful in this instance.

3. The most typical problem to be seen by the clinician is one where the complaints of memory function and the level of depression are both high, and performance measures on objective tests are poor. In this case, the issue is to determine whether the problem is due to brain impairment, depression, or a combination of the two. A detailed workup, including an array of other psychological tests and neurological and medical evaluations, is usually called for in order to develop an appropriate intervention program. Serial testing may be helpful to distinguish the relative contributions of brain impairment and depression.

4. Instances in which memory performance is poor, memory complaints are low, and depression scores are also low are consistent with a picture of serious brain impairment, and additional laboratory tests are indicated to rule this out. Typically such patients are unaware of their cognitive problems and do not acknowledge accompanying dysphoria.

However, the clinician should be alerted that the impact of depression on cognitive functioning in the elderly can become so extreme that patients may look as if they have serious brain impairment. Post (1975) and Libow (1977) labeled this condition "pseudodementia," and as the name indicates, the major determinant of the problem is assumed to be psychological. Appropriate treatment of the depression can at times have astounding effects in improving the cognitive function of these patients.

A second common assessment problem is the need to determine the presence and severity of impairment due to organic pathology. In some instances, this assessment process is included in response to the questions raised in the third configuration above. In other instances the client may have obvious symptoms of organic brain damage and may already carry a preliminary diagnosis of "chronic brain syndrome" or "senile dementia." In either case, the alternative may be either to assist in developing a final diagnostic formulation or to evaluate the strengths and weaknesses of the client's cognitive function in order to develop a rehabilitation program. The clinician should evaluate the overall level of cognitive functioning and compare the results with normative data for appropriate age groups. Identification of discrepancy patterns in various abilities that are compatible with a diagnosis of brain impairment is an essential step in the assessment process. Evidence of focal impairment can at times be extremely helpful in establishing a diagnosis. Referral for more detailed neuropsychological evaluation, including sensory and motor function, is frequently indicated.

While complex cognitive tests can often be helpful in formulating a diagnostic picture, their crudity is such that frequent false-positive errors can occur if the clinician relies too heavily on available normative data or has limited neuropsychological training. The clinician should be cautious in making or confirming a diagnosis of cerebral pathology unless a number of positive signs are apparent. In this particular situation, the clinician should be attentive to the distinction between acute and chronic brain damage. Acute brain syndrome may be reversible if the appropriate treatment is introduced.

Libow (1977) has detailed a number of causes of acute mental changes in the elderly that can possibly be reversed, such as problems with medications, imbalance in metabolic function, depression, nutritional problems, and other medical problems involving the breakdown of major systems such as the pulmonary or cardiovascular systems. In all instances of dementia, whether acute or chronic, families should be encouraged to pursue the diagnostic process until all possible causes of dementia that can be treated have been ruled out. Even in instances where the individual has a history of chronic mental changes, there may be some treatable problems, such as Vitamin B deficiency, treatable vascular complications, and longstanding severe depression, that have gone undetected. Low-pressure hydrocephalus is another cause of dementia that may be treatable. Persons with low-pressure hydrocephalus usually have a dementia of fairly rapid onset, accompanied by motor problems and incontinence. This is a rare problem, and elaborate medical and laboratory studies are needed to confirm positive evidence.

Depressive episodes are a third condition frequently seen by the clinician. Interview plus self-report measures can usually identify the presence of an affect disturbance. Further, it is important to ascertain the level of hopelessness and the likelihood of a suicide attempt before embarking on a treatment plan. It is important to remember that depressive symptomatology can be associated with a number of neurological and medical diseases. Salzman and Shader (1979) have provided a detailed list of medical conditions that are present with depressive symptomatology. They have also outlined a number of medications that can precipitate depressive episodes. A frequent problem can be seen in the use by old people of antihypertensives containing reserpine. Determining whether a picture of depression is associated with a medical problem or is drug related is important for the development of an adequate plan of therapy. While short-term therapy is typically the treatment of choice for depression in the elderly, this may not be indicated if the depression is a concomitant of a particular disease or drug.

A final problem pertains to the elderly person with a paranoid reaction. Frequently these people do not volunteer to come for psychological assessment but are brought in by other family members or are referred from a legal clinic. In some instances the bizarre nature of the delusional material in combination with the cognitive pattern may lead the clinicians to the erroneous conclusion that the patient is experiencing severe brain impairment. In this situation it is particularly important to attend to the patient's social network and community adjustment. Many of these people are living in relative isolation with only minimal contacts with a constructive support system. In some people, preoccupation with the delusional material can become so compelling as to seriously impair their ability to process information.

In addition, the development of delusional material sometimes has some basis in reality, and a detailed search can often be helpful in developing a therapy program. For example, a 68-year old Lithuanian immigrant was concerned that the FBI and his church were conspiring to deport him from the United States. Evaluation of his cognitive picture showed moderate problems in abstract reasoning and judgment, but his memory and fund of information were still adequate. A review of his support network revealed that the client had been living alone for several years. Recently his house had been broken into several times and coincidentally his pastor had admonished him repeatedly to get more involved in church affairs. The coincidence of these events, his isolation, and actual past experiences with Russian secret police in Lithuania provided a backdrop for the development of what appeared to be an extremely bizarre delusional system, accompanied by cognitive difficulties suggestive of cerebral impairment. A change in the social support system provided a remission from the delusion and subsequent improvements in cognitive function. This is an example of nontraditional intervention that psychologists will probably be called on to use more often in the future as assessment proceeds more carefully and psychosituational factors are more closely evaluated (see Chapter 3 in this volume for other examples of novel intervention strategies).

Summary and Future Prospects

Despite the numerous problems that have hampered clinical assessment of the elderly in the past, concrete steps are now available that can improve the assessment process substantially in future years. Development of comprehensive multimodal assessment programs with appropriate normative data should be implemented. Increased use of items that have "task relevance" for the elderly should address the problem of ecological validity. The concept of functional age could be extremely useful if suitable tests are employed to implement it in the assessment process. The use of a qualitative approach in analysis of performance is still underutilized and could provide meaningful insights into the diagnostic process. Finally, greater attention to situational determinants should improve the generality of test results. Should we meet the challenge of this mandate, the future for assessment in the 1980s should be bright indeed.

REFERENCES

Albert, M. S., & Kaplan, E. F. Organic implications of neuropsychological deficits in the elderly. In L. W. Poon, J. Fozard, D. Arenberg, L. Cermak, & L. W. Thompson (Eds.), *New directions in memory and aging: Proceedings of the George A. Talland Memorial Conference*. Hillsdale, N.J.: Lawrence Erlbaum, 1980.

American Psychiatric Association. *Diagnostic and statistical manual of mental disorders* (3rd ed.) Washington, D.C.: Author, 1980.

Ames, L. B., Learned, J., Metraux, R., & Walker, R. *Rorschach responses in old age*. New York: Harper, 1954.

Ames, L. B., Metraux, R., Rodell, J., & Walker, R. *Rorschach responses in old age* (rev. ed.). New York: Bruner-Mazel, 1973.

Arenberg, D. Introduction to a symposium: Toward comprehensive intervention programs for memory problems among the aged. *Experimental Aging Research*, 1978, *4*, 233.

Arenberg, D., & Robertson-Tchabo, E. A. Learning and aging. In J. E. Birren & K. W. Schaie (Eds.), *Handbook of the psychology of aging*. New York: Van Nostrand Reinhold, 1977.

Ball, J. F. Widow's grief: The impact of age and mode of death. *Omega*, 1977, *7*, 307–333.

Baltes, P. B., & Labouvie, G. Adult development of intellectual performance: Description, explanation, and modification. In C. Eisdorfer & M. P. Lawton (Eds.), *The psychology of adult development and aging*. Washington, D.C.: American Psychological Association, 1973.

Baltes, P., Schaie, K. W., & Nardi, A. Age and experimental mortality in a seven-year longitudinal study of cognitive behavior. *Developmental Psychology*, 1971, *5*, 18–26.

Beck, A. T., Ward, C. H., Mendelson, M., Mock, J. E., & Erbaugh, J. An inventory for measuring depression. *Archives of General Psychiatry*, 1961, *4*, 561–571.

Bellak, L. *The TAT, CAT, and SAT in clinical use* (3rd. ed.). New York: Grune & Stratton, 1975.

Bellak, L., & Bellak, S. S. *Manual for the Senior Apperception Test (SAT)*. Larchmont, N.Y.: C.P.S., 1973.

Bem, D. J. & Allen, A. On predicting some of the people some of the time: The search for cross-situational consistencies in behavior. *Psychological Review*, 1974, *81*, 506–520.

Benton, A. L. *The Revised Visual Retention Test* (4th ed.). New York: Psychological Corporation, 1974.

Bernal, G. A. A., Brannon, L. J., Belar, C., Lavigne, J., & Cameron, R. Psychodiagnostics of the elderly. In W. D. Gentry (Ed.), *Geropsychology: A model of training and clinical service*. Cambridge, Mass.: Ballinger, 1977.

Bersoff, D. N. Silk purses into sow's ears: The decline of psychological testing and a suggestion for its redemption. *American Psychologist*, 1973, *28*, 892–899.

Birren, J. E. *The psychology of aging*. Englewood Cliffs, N.J.: Prentice-Hall, 1964.

Blumenthal, M. D. Measuring depressive symptomatology in a general population. *Archives of General Psychiatry*, 1975, *32*, 971–978.

Botwinick, J. *Aging and behavior*. New York: Springer, 1973.

Botwinick, J. Intellectual abilities. In J. E. Birren & K. W. Schaie (Eds.), *Handbook of the psychology of aging*. New York: Van Nostrand Reinhold, 1977.

Butters, N. Potential contributions of neuropsychology to our understanding of the memory capacities of the elderly. In L. Poon, J. Fozard, D. Arenberg, L. Cermak, & L. W. Thompson (Eds.), *New directions in memory and aging: Proceedings of the George A. Talland Memorial Conference*. Hillsdale, N.J.: Lawrence Erlbaum, 1980.

Byrne, D. Repression-sensitization as a dimension of personality. *Progress in Experimental Personality Research*, 1964, *1*, 169–220.

Canter, A., & Straumanis, J. Performance of senile and healthy aged persons on the BIP Bender Test. *Perceptual Motor Skills*, 1969, *28*, 695–698.

Cattell, R. B., Eber, H. W., & Tatsuoka, M. M. *Handbook for the sixteen personality factor questionnaire*. Champaign, Ill.: Institute for Personality and Ability Testing, 1970.

Cheung, A. Drugs for the aging: Use and Abuse. In A. Reinhardt & M. Quinn (Eds.), *Current practice in gerontological nursing* (Vol. 1). St. Louis: C. V. Mosby, 1979.

Cheung, A., & Kayne, R. An application of clinical pharmacy services in extended care facilities. *California Pharmacist*, 1975, *23*, 22–43.

Chown, S. M. Age and the rigidities. *Journal of Gerontology*, 1961, *16*, 353–362.

Chown, S. M. Personality and aging. In K. W. Schaie (Ed.), *Theory and methods of research on aging*. Morgantown: West Virginia University Press, 1968.

Christensen, A. L. *Luria's neuropsychological investigation*. New York: Spectrum Publications, 1975. (a)

Christensen, A. L. *Luria's neuropsychological investigation: Manual*. New York: Spectrum Publications. 1975. (b)

Comfort, A. Non-threatening mental testing of the elderly. *Journal of the American Geriatrics Society*, 1978, *26*, 261–262.

Costa, P. T., Fozard, J., McCrae, R., & Bosse, R. Relation of age and personality dimensions to cognitive ability factors. *Journal of Gerontology*, 1976, *31*, 663–669.

Costa, P. T., & McCrae, R. R. Objective personality assessment. In M. A. Storandt, I. C. Siegler, & M. F. Elias (Eds.), *The clinical psychology of aging*. New York: Plenum Press, 1978.

Craik, F. I. M. Age differences in human memory. In J. E.

Birren & K. W. Schaie (Eds.), *Handbook of the psychology of aging*. New York: Van Nostrand Reinhold, 1977.

Cronbach, L. J. *Essentials of psychology testing* (3rd ed.). New York: Harper & Row, 1970.

Crook, T. H. Psychometric assessment in the elderly. In A. Raskin & L. F. Jarvik (Eds.), *Psychiatric symptoms and cognitive loss in the elderly*. Washington, D.C.: Hemisphere, 1979.

Dahlstrom, W. G., Welsh, G. S., & Dahlstrom, L. E. *An MMPI handbook. Vol. 1, Clinical interpretation* (rev. ed.). Minneapolis: University of Minnesota Press, 1972.

Davies, A. D. M. Measures of mental deterioration in aging and brain damage. In S. M. Chown & K. F. Riegel (Eds.), *Interdisciplinary topics in gerontology* (Vol. 1). Basel: S. Karger, 1968.

Derogatis, L., Lipman, R. S., Rickels, K., Uhlenhuth, E. H., & Covi, L. The Hopkins Symptom Checklist (HSCL): A measure of primary symptom dimensions. In P. Pichot (Ed.), *Psychological measurements in psychopharmacology: Modern problems in pharmacopsychiatry* (Vol. 7). Basel: S. Karger, 1974.

Dessonville, C., & Finnell, C. *Application of SADS interview to depressed and normal elderly populations*. Paper presented at the meeting of the American Psychological Association, Montreal, Quebec, Canada, September 1980.

Dohrenwend, B. S., & Dohrenwend, B. P. (Eds.), *Stressful life events*. New York: Wiley, 1974.

Doppelt, J., & Wallace, W. Standardization of the Wechsler Adult Intelligence Scale for older persons. *Journal of Abnormal and Social Psychology*, 1955, *51*, 312-330.

Edwards, A. L. *Manual for the Personal Preference Schedule*. New York: Psychological Corporation, 1953.

Eisdorfer, C. Developmental level and sensory impairment in the aged. *Journal of Projective Technique*, 1960, *24*, 129-132.

Eisdorfer, C., & Wilkie, F. Stress, disease, aging and behavior. In J. E. Birren & K. W. Schaie (Eds.), *Handbook of the psychology of aging*. New York: Van Nostrand Reinhold, 1977.

Endicott, J., & Spitzer, R. L. A diagnostic interview: The schedule for affective disorders and schizophrenia. *Archives of General Psychiatry*, 1978, *35*, 837-844.

Epstein, L. J. Symposium on age differentiation in depressive illness: Depression in the elderly. *Journal of Gerontology*, 1976, *31*, 278-282.

Erickson, R. C., Poon, L. W., & Walsh-Sweeney, L. Clinical memory testing of the elderly. In L. W. Poon, J. Fozard, L. Cermak, D. Arenberg, & L. W. Thompson (Eds.), *New directions in memory and aging: Proceedings of the George A. Talland Memorial Conference*. Hillsdale, N.J.: Lawrence Erlbaum, 1980.

Erickson, R. C., & Scott, M. L. Clinical memory testing: A review. *Psychological Bulletin*, 1977, *84*, 1130-1149.

Eysenck, H. J. *Manual of the Maudsley Personality Inventory*. London: University of London Press, 1959.

Fillenbaum, G., & Pfeiffer, E. The mini-mult: A cautionary note. *Journal of Consulting and Clinical Psychology*, 1976, *44*, 698-703.

Fillenbaum, G., Smyer, M., Pruchno, R. *A validity and reliability study of the Older Americans Resources Services Questionnaire*. Unpublished manuscript, Duke University, 1979.

Fink, M., Green, T., & Bender, M. The Face-Hand Test as a diagnostic sign of organic mental syndrome. *Neurology*, 1952, *2*, 46-58.

Fleiss, J., Gurland, B., & Des Roche, P. Distinctions between organic brain syndrome and functional disorders: Based on the geriatric mental state interview. *International Journal of Aging and Human Development*, 1976, *7*, 323-330.

Folstein, M. F., Folstein, S. E., & McHugh, P. R. "Mini-Mental State": A practical method for grading the cognitive state of patients for the clinician. *Journal of Psychiatric Research*, 1975, *12*, 189-198.

Friedsam, H., & Martin, H. A comparison of self and physicians' health ratings in an older population. *Journal of Health and Human Behavior*, 1963, *4*, 179-183.

Gaitz, C. M., & Baer, P. E. Diagnostic assessment of the elderly: A multi-functional model. *Gerontologist*, 1970, *10*, 47-52.

Gallagher, D. *Behavioral group therapy with the elderly*. Paper presented at the meeting of the American Psychological Association, New York, August 1979.

Gallagher, D., McGarvey, W., Zelinski, E. M., & Thompson, L. W. *Age and factor structure of the Zung Depression Scale*. Paper presented at the 31st annual meeting of the Gerontological Society, Dallas, Texas, November 1978.

Gatz, M. *Measures of change in the assessment of psychotherapy with older adults*. Paper presented at the 31st annual meeting of the Gerontological Society, Dallas, Texas, November 1978.

Gilbert, J. G., Levee, R. F., & Catalano, F. L. A preliminary report on a new memory scale. *Perceptual and Motor Skills*, 1968, *27*, 277-278.

Golden, C. J. A standardized version of Luria's neuropsychological tests. In T. Boll & S. Filskov (Eds.), *Handbook of clinical neuropsychology*. New York: Wiley, in press.

Golden, C. J., Hammeke, T. A., & Purisch, A. D. Diagnostic validity of a standardized neuropsychological battery derived from Luria's neuropsychological tests. *Journal of Consulting and Clinical Psychology*, 1978, *46*, 1258-1265.

Goldfried, M. R., & Kent, R. N. Traditional versus behavioral personality assessment: A comparison of methodological and theoretical assumptions. *Psychological Bulletin*, 1972, *77*, 409-420.

Goldstein, G., & Shelly, C. Similarities and differences between psychological deficit in aging and brain damage. *Journal of Gerontology*, 1975, *30*, 448-455.

Graham, F. K., & Kendall, B. S. Memory for Designs Test: Revised general manual. *Perceptual Motor Skills*, 1960, *11*, 147-188.

Grinker, R. R., Miller, J., Sabahin, M., Nunn, R., & Nunnally, J. C. *The phenomena of depressions*. New York: Hoeber, 1961.

Guilford, J. P., & Zimmerman, W. S. *The Guilford-Zimmerman tempermant survey: Manual of instructions and interpretations*. Beverly Hills, Calif.: Sheridan House, 1949.

Gurel, L., Linn M. W., & Linn, B. S. Physical and mental impairment-of-function evaluation in the aged: The PAMIE scale. *Journal of Gerontology*, 1972, *27*, 83–90.

Gurland, B. J. The comparative frequency of depression in various adult age groups. *Journal of Gerontology*, 1976, *31*, 283–292.

Gurland, B. J. Personal communication, July 1979.

Gurland, B., Copeland, J., Sharpe, L., & Kelleher, M. The Geriatric Mental Status Interview (GMS). *International Journal of Aging and Human Development*, 1976, *7*, 303–311.

Gurland, B., Fleiss, J., Cooper, J., Sharpe, L., Kendall, R., & Roberts, P. Cross-national study of the diagnosis of mental disorders: Hospital diagnoses and hospital patients in New York and London. *Comprehensive Psychiatry*, 1970, *11*, 18–25.

Gurland, B., Kuriansky, J., Sharpe, L., Simon, R., Stiller, P., & Birkett, P. The Comprehensive Assessment and Referral Evaluation (CARE)—Rationale, development, and reliability. *International Journal of Aging and Human Development*, 1977–78, *8*, 9–42.

Haglund, R., & Schuckit, M. A clinical comparison of tests of organicity in elderly patients. *Journal of Gerontology*, 1976, *31*, 654–659.

Hamilton, M. The assessment of anxiety states by rating. *British Journal of Medical Psychology*, 1959, *32*, 50–55.

Hamilton, M. Development of a rating scale for primary depressive illness. *British Journal of Social and Clinical Psychiatry*, 1967, *6*, 278–296.

Harmatz, J., & Shader, R. Psychopharmacologic investigations in healthy elderly volunteers: MMPI Depression Scale. *Journal of American Geriatrics Society*, 1975, *23*, 350–354.

Hathaway, S. R., & McKinley, J. C. *The Minnesota Multiphasic Personality Inventory Manual*. Minneapolis: University of Minnesota Press, 1943.

Heron, A., & Chown, S. *Age and function*. Boston: Little, Brown, 1967.

Heyman, D., & Gianturco, D. Long term adaption by the elderly to bereavement. *Journal of Gerontology*, 1973, *28*, 359–362.

Heyman, D., & Jeffers, F. Effect of time lapse on consistency of self-health and medical evaluations of elderly persons. *Journal of Gerontology*, 1963, *18*, 160–164.

Holmes, T. H., & Masuda, M. Life change and illness susceptibility. In J. P. Scott & E. C. Senay (Eds.), *Symposium on separation and depression* (Publ. No. 94). Washington, D.C.: American Association for the Advancement of Science, 1973.

Holmes, T. H., & Rahe, R. H. The social readjustment rating scale. *Journal of Psychosomatic Research*, 1967, *11*, 219–225.

Holsopple, J., & Miale, F. *Sentence completion—a projective method for the study of personality*. Springfield, Ill.: Charles C Thomas, 1954.

Holtzman, W. H., Thorpe, J. S., Swartz, J. D., & Herron, E. W. *Inkblot perception and personality: Holtzman inkblot technique*. Austin: University of Texas Press, 1961.

Honigfeld, G., Gillis, R. D., & Klett, C. J. NOSIE-30: A treatment-sensitive ward behavior scale. *Psychological Reports*, 1966, *21*, 65–71.

Horn, J. L., & Cattell, R. B. Age differences in fluid and crystallized intelligence. *Acta Psychologica*, 1967, *26*, 107–129.

Hultsch, D. F., & Plemons, J. K. Life events and life-span development. In P. B. Baltes & O. G. Brion, Sr. (Eds.), *Life-span development and behavior* (Vol. 2). New York: Academic Press, 1979.

Hundlevy, J. D. The measurement of personality by objective tests. In P. Kline (Ed.), *New approaches in psychological measurement*. New York: Wiley, 1973.

Jarvik, L. F., & Russell, D. Anxiety, aging, and the third emergency reaction. *Journal of Gerontology*, 1979, *34*, 197–200.

Kahana, B. The use of projective techniques in personality assessment of the aged. In M. Storandt, I. C. Siegler, & M. F. Elias (Eds.), *The clinical psychology of aging*. New York: Plenum Press, 1978.

Kahana, E., Fairchild, T., & Kahana, B. Adaptation. In W. A. Petersen, D. J. Mangen, & R. Sanders (Eds.), *The development of an instrument bank: Assessment of available instruments and measurement scales for the study of aging and the elderly*. Kansas City, Mo.: Midwest Council for Social Research in Aging, University of Missouri, 1978.

Kahana, E., & Kahana, B. *Strategies of coping in institutional environments* (Summary Progress Report, NIH Grant MH 24959-02). Detroit, Mich.: Wayne State University, 1975.

Kahn, R. L., Goldfarb, A. I. Pollack, M., & Peck, A. A brief objective measure for the determination of mental status of the aged. *American Journal of Psychiatry*, 1960, *117*, 326–328.

Kahn, R., & Miller, N. Assessment of altered brain function in the aged. In M. Storandt, I. Siegler, & M. E. Elias (Eds.), *The clinical psychology of aging*. New York: Plenum Press, 1978.

Kahn, R. L., Zarit, S. H., Hilbert, N. M., & Niederehe, G. Memory complaint and impairment in the aged. *Archives of General Psychiatry*, 1975, *32*, 1569–1573.

Kanfer, F., & Saslow, G. Behavioral diagnosis. In C. Franks (Ed.), *Behavioral therapy: Appraisal and status*. New York: McGraw-Hill, 1969.

Kapnick, P. Organic treatment of the elderly. In M. Storandt, I. Siegler, & M. F. Elias (Eds.), *The clinical psychology of aging*. New York: Plenum Press, 1978.

Katz, M. M., & Lyerly, S. B. Methods of measuring adjustment and social behavior in the community. *Psychological Reports*, 1963, *13*, 503–535.

Kincannon, J. C. Prediction of the standard MMPI scale scores from 71 items: The Mini-Mult. *Journal of Consulting and Clinical Psychology*, 1968, *32*, 319–325.

Kiyak, A., Liang, J., & Kahana, E. *Methodological inquiry into the schedule of recent life events*. Paper presented at the meeting of the American Psychological Association, New York, August 1976.

Klassen, D., Homstra, R. K., & Aderson, P. B. Influence of social desirability on symptom and mood reporting in a community survey. *Journal of Consulting and Clinical Psychology*, 1975, *43*, 448–452.

Klisz, S. Neuropsychological evaluation in older persons. In M. Storandt, I. Siegler, & M. F. Elias (Eds.), *The clinical psychology of aging*. New York: Plenum Press, 1978.

Klopfer, W. G. The Rorschach and old age. *Journal of Personality Assessment*, 1974, *38*, 420–422.

Kochansky, G. E. Psychiatric rating scales for assessing psychopathology in the elderly: A critical review. In A. Raskin & L. F. Jarvik (Eds.), *Psychiatric symptoms and cognitive loss in the elderly*. Washington, D.C.: Hemisphere, 1979.

Kral, V. A., & Papetropoulus, D. Treatment of geriatric patients. In N. S. Kline & H. E. Lehmann (Eds.), *International Psychiatry Clinics psychopharmacology*. Boston: Little, Brown, 1965.

Kramer, N., & Jarvik, L. Assessment of intellectual changes in the elderly. In A. Raskin & L. F. Jarvik (Eds.), *Psychiatric symptoms & cognitive loss in the elderly*. Washington, D.C.: Hemisphere, 1979.

Krauss, I. Assessment for retirement. In P. K. Ragan (Ed.), *Work and retirement: Policy issues*. Los Angeles: University of Southern California Press, in press.

Krauss, I., & Schaie, K. W. *Five novel tasks for the assessment of cognitive abilities in older adults*. Paper presented at the XIth International Congress of Gerontology, Tokyo, 1978.

Lawton, M. P. The functional assessment of elderly people. *Journal of the American Geriatrics Society*, 1971, *19*, 465–481.

Lawton, M. P. The dimensions of morale. In D. P. Kent, R. Kastenbaum, & S. Sherwood (Eds.), *Research planning and action for the elderly*. New York: Behavioral Publications, 1972.

Lawton, M. P. The Philadelphia Geriatric Center Morale Scale: A revision. *Journal of Gerontology*, 1975, *30*, 85–89.

Lawton, M. P. *What is the good life for the aging?* Kesten Lecture, University of Southern California, Ethel Percy Andrus Gerontology Center, October 19, 1978.

Lawton, M. P., & Brody, E. M. Assessment of older people: Self-maintaining and instrumental activities of daily living. *Gerontologist*, 1969, *9*, 179–188.

Lawton, M. P., & Nahemow, L. Ecology and the aging process. In C. Eisdorfer and M. P. Lawton (Eds.), *Psychology of adult development and aging*. Washington, D.C.: American Psychological Association, 1973, pp. 619–674.

Lawton, M. P., Whelihan, W. M., & Belsky, J. K. Personality tests and their uses with older adults. In J. Birren (Ed.), *Handbook of mental health and aging*. Englewood Cliffs, N.J.: Prentice-Hall, 1980.

Lazarus, R. S. *Ipsative-normative, process-oriented research on stress, coping and adaptation*. Symposium presented at the annual meeting of the Western Psychological Association, San Diego, April 1979.

Lehmann, H. E., & Ban, T. A. Chemotherapy in aged psychiatric patients. *Canadian Psychiatric Association Journal*, 1969, *14*, 361–369.

Levy, S. M. The psychosocial assessment of the chronically ill geriatric patient. In C. Phokopp & C. Bradley (Eds.), *Medical psychology: A New perspective*. New York: Academic Press, 1980.

Lewinsohn, P. M., & Finnell, C. Workshop on assessment of depression in the elderly. University of Southern California, Los Angeles, March 1979.

Libow, L. S. Senile dementia and "pseudo-senility": Clinical diagnosis. In C. Eisdorfer & R. O. Friedel (Eds.), *Cognitive and emotional disturbance in the elderly*. Chicago: Year Book Medical Publishers, 1977.

Linn, M. W. Assessing community adjustment in the elderly. In A. Raskin & L. F. Jarvik (Eds.), *Psychiatric symptoms and cognitive loss in the elderly*. Washington, D.C.: Hemisphere, 1979.

Lorr, M., & Klett, C. J. *Inpatient Multidimensional Psychiatric Scale* (rev. ed.). Palo Alto; Calif.: Consulting Psychologists Press, 1966.

Lowenthal, M. F., & Chiriboga, D. Social stress and adaptation: Toward a life-course perspective. In C. Eisdorfer & M. P. Lawton (Eds.), *The psychology of adult development and aging*. Washington, D.C.: American Psychological Association, 1973.

Luria, A. R. *Higher cortical functions in man*. New York: Basic Books, 1966.

Luria, A. R. *The working brain*. New York: Basic Books, 1973.

Machover, K. *Personality projection in the drawing of the human figure*. Springfield, Ill.: Charles C Thomas, 1952.

Maddox, G. L., & Douglass, E. B. Self-assessment of health: A longitudinal study of elderly subjects. *Journal of Health and Social Behaviors*, 1973, *14*, 87–93.

Maloney, M., & Ward, M. P. *Psychological assessment: A conceptual approach*. New York: Oxford University Press, 1976.

Markides, K. S., & Martin, H. W., Predicting self-related health among the aged. *Research on Aging*, 1979, *1*, 97–112.

McNair, D. M. Self-rating scales for assessing psychopathology in the elderly. In A. Raskin & L. F. Jarvik (Eds.), *Psychiatric symptoms and cognitive loss in the elderly*. Washington, D.C.: Hemisphere, 1979.

McNair, D. M., Lorr, M., & Droppleman, L. F. *Profile of mood states: Manual*. San Diego: Educational and Industrial Testing Service, 1971.

Miller, E., & Lewis, P. Recognition memory in elderly patients with depression and dementia: A signal detection analysis. *Journal of Abnormal Psychology*, 1977, *86*, 84–86.

Miller, W. Psychological deficit in depression. *Psychological Bulletin*, 1975, *82*, 238–260.

Murray, H. A. *Explorations in personality*. New York: Oxford University Press, 1938.

Neugarten, B. L. Personality change in late life: A developmental perspective. In C. Eisdorfer and M. P. Lawton (Eds.), *The Psychology of adult development and aging*. Washington, D.C.: American Psychological Association, 1973.

Neugarten, B. L. Personality and aging. In J. E. Birren & K. W. Schaie (Eds.), *Handbook of the psychology of aging*. New York: Van Nostrand Reinhold, 1977.

Neugarten, B. L., Havighurst, R. J., & Tobin, S. S. The

measurement of life satisfaction. *Journal of Gerontology*, 1961, *16*, 134–143.

Niederehe, G. *Psychosocial network correlates of depression in later life*. Paper presented at the 31st annual meeting of the Gerontological Society, Dallas, Texas, November 1978.

Oberleder, M. Effects of psychosocial factors on test results of the aging. *Psychological Reports*, 1964, *14*, 383–387.

Overall, J. E., & Gorham, D. R. The Brief Psychiatric Rating Scale. *Psychological Reports*, 1962, *10*, 799–812.

Overall, J. E., & Gorham, D. R. Organicity versus old age in objective and projective test performance. *Journal of Consulting and Clinical Psychology*, 1972, *39*, 98–105.

Palmore, E., Cleveland, W. P., Nowlin, J. B., Ramm, D., & Siegler, I. C. Stress and adaptation in later life. *Journal of Gerontology*, 1979, *34*, 841–851.

Pattie, A., & Gilleard, C. A brief psychogeriatric assessment schedule: Validation against psychiatric diagnosis and discharge from hospital. *British Journal of Psychiatry*, 1975, *127*, 489–493.

Pattison, E. M. A theoretical-empirical base for social-system therapy. In E. F. Foulks, R. M. Wintrob, J. Westermyer, & A. R. Favezza (Eds.), *Current perspectives in cultural psychiatry*. Jamaica: N.Y.: Spectrum Publications, 1977.

Pfeiffer, E. A short portable mental status questionnaire for the assessment of organic brain defect in elderly patients. *Journal of the American Geriatric Society*, 1975, *23*, 433–441.

Pfeiffer, E. Multidimensional functional assessment: The OARS methodology. Durham, N.C.: Duke University, Center of the Study of Aging and Human Development, 1976.

Pfeiffer, E. Psychopathology and social pathology. In J. E. Birren & K. W. Schaie (Eds.), *Handbook of the psychology of aging. New York:* Van Nostrand Reinhold, 1977.

Plutchik, R. Conceptual and practical issues in the assessment of the elderly. In A. Raskin & L. F. Jarvik (Eds.), *Psychiatric symptoms and cognitive loss in the elderly*. Washington, D.C.: Hemisphere, 1979.

Plutchik, R., Conte, H., Lieberman, M., Bakur, M., Grossman, J., & Lehrman, N. Reliability and validity of a scale for assessing the functioning of geriatric patients. *Journal of the American Geriatrics Society*, 1970, *18*, 491–500.

Poon, L. W., Fozard, J., Cermak, L., Arenberg, D. & Thompson, L. W. (Eds.). *New directions in memory and aging: Proceedings of the George A. Talland Memorial Conference*. Hillsdale, N.J.: Lawrence Erlbaum, 1980.

Poon, L. W., Fozard, J. L., & Treat, N. J. From clinical findings on memory to intervention programs. *Experimental Aging Research*, 1978, *4*, 235–253.

Post, F. The management and nature of depressive illnesses in late life: A follow-through study. *British Journal of Psychiatry*, 1972, *121*, 393–404.

Post, F. Paranoid disorders in the elderly. *Postgraduate Medicine*, 1973, *53*, 52–56.

Post, F. Dementia, depression, and pseudo-dementia. In D. F. Benson & D. Blumer (Eds.), *Psychiatric aspects of neurological disease*. New York: Grune & Stratton, 1975.

Quayhagen, M., & Chiriboga, D. A. *Geriatric coping scale applied to patients in convalescent hospitals*. Paper presented at the annual meeting of the Gerontological Society, New York, August 1976.

Raskin, A. *NIMH Collaborative Depression Mood Scale*. Rockville, Md.: National Institute of Mental Health, 1965.

Raskin, S. Signs and symptoms of psychopathology in the elderly. In A. Raskin & L. Jarvik (Eds.), *Psychiatric symptoms and cognitive loss in the elderly*. Washington, D.C.: Hemisphere, 1979.

Reitan, R. M. The distribution according to age of psychologic measure dependent upon organic brain functions. *Journal of Gerontology*, 1955, *10*, 338–340.

Rorschach, H. *Psychodiagnostics*. New York: Grune & Stratton, 1942.

Rosencranz, H. A., & Pihlblad, C. T., Measuring the health of the elderly. *Journal of Gerontology*, 1970, *25*, 129–133.

Rosow, I., & Breslau, N. A Guttman health scale for the aged. *Journal of Gerontology*, 1966, *21*, 556–559.

Roth, M. The natural history of mental disorders in old age. *Journal of Mental Science*, 1955, *101*, 281–301.

Rotter, J. B. Generalized experiences for internal vs. external control. *Psychological Monographs*, 1966, *80*, 1–28.

Sakalis, G., Gershon, S., & Shopsin, B. A trial of Gerovital-H-3 in depression during senility. *Current Therapeutic Research*, 1974, *16*, 59–63.

Salzman, C., Kochansky, G., Shader, R., & Cronin, D. Rating scales for psychotropic drug research with geriatric patients: II. Mood ratings. *Journal of the American Geriatrics Society*, 1972, *2*, 215–221.

Salzman, C., & Shader, R. I. Clinical evaluation of depression in the elderly. In A. Raskin & L. F. Jarvik (Eds.), *Psychiatric symptoms and cognitive loss in the elderly*. Washington, D.C.: Hemisphere, 1979.

Schaie, J. & Schaie, K. W. Psychological evaluation of the cognitively impaired elderly. In C. Eisdorfer & R. Friedel (Eds.), *Cognitive and emotional disturbances in the elderly*. Chicago: Year Book Publishers, 1977.

Schaie, K. W. Methodological problems in descriptive developmental research on adulthood and aging. In J. Nesselroade & H. Reese (Eds.), *Life-span developmental psychology: Methodological issues*. New York: Academic Press, 1973.

Schaie, K. W. Functional age and retirement. In U. Lehr (Chair), *Social and biological aspects of retirement age*. Symposium presented at the 4th Biennial Congress of the International Society for the Study of Behavioral Development, Pavio, Italy, September 21, 1977.

Schaie, K. W. External validity in the assessment of intellectual development in adulthood. *Journal of Gerontology*, 1978, *33*, 695–701.

Schaie, K. W., & Labouvie-Vief, G. Generational versus ontogenetic components of change in adult cognitive behavior: A fourteen-year cross-sequential study. *Developmental Psychology*, 1974, *10*, 305–320.

Schaie, K. W., & Marquette, B. W. Personality in maturity and old age. In R. M. Dieger (Ed.), *Multivariate personality research: Contributions to the understanding of personality in honor of Raymond B. Cattell*. Baton Rouge, La.: Claitor's, 1972.

Schaie, K. W., & Parham, I. A. *Manual for the test of be-*

havioral rigidity (2nd rev. ed.). Palo Alto, Calif.: Consulting Psychologists Press, 1975.

Schaie, K. W., & Schaie, J. Clinical assessment and aging. In J. Birren & K. W. Schaie (Eds.), *Handbook of the psychology of aging*. New York: Van Nostrand Reinhold, 1977.

Schaie, K. W., & Strother, C. R. A cross-sequential study of age changes in cognitive behavior. *Psychological Bulletin*, 1968, *70*, 671–680.

Schulz, R., & Brenner, G. Relocation of the aged: A review and theoretical analysis. *Journal of Gerontology*, 1977, *32*, 323–333.

Selye, H. *The stress of life*. New York: McGraw Hill, 1956.

Shader, R. I., Harmatz, J. S., & Salzman, C. A. A new scale for clinical assessment in geriatric populations: Sandoz Clinical Assessment-Geriatric Scale (SCAG). *Journal of the American Geriatrics Society*, 1974, *22*, 107–113.

Shanas, E. *The health of older people*. Cambridge, Mass.: Harvard University Press, 1962.

Siegler, I. C., Gatz, M., George, L. K., & Tyler, F. B. *Aging competently* (Final report, Grant 90-A-1022). Washington, D.C.: Administration on Aging, U.S. Department of Health, Education, and Welfare, 1979.

Smith, J. M. Nurse and psychiatric aide rating scales for assessing psychopathology in the elderly: A critical review. In A. Raskin & L. F. Jarvik (Eds.), *Psychiatric symptoms and cognitive loss in the elderly*. Washington, D.C.: Hemisphere, 1979.

Spitzer, R. L., & Endicott, J. *Schedule for Affective Disorders and Schizophrenia—Life-Time Version (SADS-L)*. New York State Psychiatric Institute, 1977.

Spitzer, R. L., Endicott, J., & Robins, E. Research diagnostic criteria: Rationale and reliability. *Archives of General Psychiatry*, 1978, *35*, 773–782.

Stahl, S. M. Measures of health, In W. A. Peterson, D. J. Mangen, & R. Sanders (Eds.), *The development of an instrument bank: Assessment of available instruments and measurement scales for the study of aging and the elderly*. Kansas City, Mo.: Midwest Council for Social Research in Aging, University of Missouri, 1978.

Suchman, E., Streib, G., & Phillips, B. An analysis of the validity of health questionnaires. *Social Forces*, 1958, *36*, 223–232.

Taylor, J. A personality scale of manifest anxiety. *Journal of Abnormal and Social Psychology*, 1955, *48*, 285–290.

Thurstone, L., & Thurstone, T. *SRA Primary Mental Abilities*. Chicago: Science Research Associates, 1949.

Tissue, T. Another look at self-rated health among the elderly. *Journal of Gerontology*, 1972, *27*, 91–94.

Verwoerdt, A. *Clinical geropsychiatry*. Baltimore: Williams & Wilkins, 1976.

Wechsler, D. A standardized memory scale for clinical use. *Journal of Psychology*, 1945, *19*, 87–95.

Wechsler, D. *The measurement and appraisal of adult intelligence* (4th ed). Baltimore: Williams & Wilkins, 1958.

Welford, A. T. *Aging and human skill*. Oxford: Oxford University Press, 1958.

Welford, A. T. Memory and age: A perspective view. In L. W. Poon, J. Fozard, L. Cermak, D. Arenberg, & L. W. Thompson (Eds.), *New directions in memory and aging: Proceedings of the George A. Talland Memorial Conference*. Hillsdale, N.J.: Lawrence Erlbaum, 1980.

Whelihan, W., *Psychological assessment in geriatric settings*. Paper presented at the annual meeting of National Association of Joint Hospital Accreditation, New Orleans, February 1978.

Whelihan, W. *Dynamics of the team interaction in geriatric assessment*. Paper presented at the Conference on Geriatric Assessment, VA Medical Center, St. Louis, March 1979.

Williams, B. *Psychopharmacology of aging: Drug interactions*. Paper presented at the Seminar in Clinical Aspects of Aging: Multimodal Assessment, University of Southern California, Andrus Gerontology Center Summer Institute, August 1979.

Wingfield, A., & Sandoval, A. W. Perceptual processing for meaning. In L. W. Poon, J. Fozard, L. Cermak, D. Arenberg, & L. W. Thompson (Eds.), *New directions in memory and aging: Proceedings of the George A. Talland Memorial Conference*. Hillsdale, N.J.: Lawrence Erlbaum, 1980.

Witkin, H. A., Lewis, H. B., Hertzman, M., Machover, K., Meissner, P., & Wapner, S. *Personality through perception*. New York: Harper & Row, 1954.

Wolk, R. L., & Wolk, R. B. *The Gerontological Apperception Test*. New York: Behavioral Publications, 1971.

Zarit, S., Cole, K., Gallagher, D., Guider, R., & Kramer, N. *Memory concerns of the aging: Cognitive and affective interventions*. Paper presented at the XIth International Congress of Gerontology, Tokyo, 1978.

Zelinski, E., Gilewski, M., & Thompson, L. W. Do laboratory tests relate to self-assessment of memory ability in the young and old? In L. Poon, J. Fozard, D. Arenberg, L. Cermak & L. W. Thompson (Eds.), *New directions in memory and aging: Proceedings of the George A. Talland Memorial Conference*. Hillsdale, N.J.: Lawrence Erlbaum, 1980.

Zemore, R., & Eames, N. Psychic and somatic symptoms of depression among young adults, institutionalized aged and noninstitutionalized aged. *Journal of Gerontology*, 1979, *34*, 716–722.

Zung, W. W. K. A self-rating depression scale. *Archives of General Psychiatry*, 1965, *12*, 63–70.

Zung, W. W. K. Depression in the normal aged. *Psychosomatics*, 1967, *8*, 287–291.

Zung, W. W. K. A rating instrument for anxiety disorders. *Psychosomatics*, 1971, *12*, 371–379.

Zung, W. W. K., Gianturco, D., Pfeiffer, E., Wang, H. S., Whanger, A., Bridge, T. P., & Potkin, S. G. Pharmacology of depression in the aged: Evaluation of Gerovital-H3 as an antidepressant drug. *Psychosomatics*, 1974, *15*, 127–131.

Sandra M. Levy, Leonard R. Derogatis, Dolores Gallagher, and Margaret Gatz

CHAPTER

3

Intervention With Older Adults and the Evaluation of Outcome

Common forms of disorder found in older adults are discussed within a biopsychosocial framework, and interventions that seem to make a difference in quality of functioning are examined. Promising research directions for outpatient treatment include analysis of change mechanisms within cognitive intervention strategies and examination of essential parameters of outcome variables, such as time to criterion for successful therapeutic outcome. Research directions for inpatient treatment include examining commonalities across effective treatments, such as the enhancement of a sense of control, and a further examination of factors affecting person–environment fit. Questions concerning process and outcome research design, as well as methodology, are also considered.

Writings concerned with the psychological treatment of the aged often express a certain righteous indignation over the state of the art and its supporting science. Smith (1979) points out that the elderly are portrayed as "aimless, apathetic, debilitated, disruptive, hypochondriacal, insecure, . . . out of control, sluggish, seclusive, and temperamental" (p. 333). The neglect of this population in terms of psychological intervention has been well documented and will not be reviewed again here (Knight, 1978–79; Sparacino, 1978–79; Storandt, Siegler, & Elias, 1978).

This chapter discusses important contributions to the clinical treatment of the aged that have occurred in the late 1970s and highlights future directions in research and practice resting on the base of these current developments. The introductory section constructs a framework within which to view the elderly patient and examines the issues related to pathology and treatment of both the elderly living in the community and those who are institutionalized. Summaries at the end of the first and second major sections of the chapter highlight important issues for empirical examination during the decade ahead. The final section concerns issues in therapy process and outcome research that appear to be unique to this population.

A Holistic View of Human Functioning

It is important when studying human behavior that a framework be drawn within which to understand the varieties of functioning. While space does not allow for extensive elaboration in this respect, mention should be made of the biopsychosocial model that is currently gaining acceptance in medicine as well as in the behavioral sciences (Engel, 1977; Schwartz & Weiss, 1978; Weiner, 1977). Taking a holistic view of human functioning, Rosen and Wiens (1979) argue that all health problems can be regarded as having an essential

I would like to thank Leon H. Levy for his helpful editorial criticism in the preparation of this chapter. Leonard R. Derogatis contributed the section on pharmacology and aging, Dolores Gallagher contributed to the section on individual and group treatment of older adults in the community, and Margaret Gatz contributed to the section concerned with evaluation of psychotherapy outcome; Margaret Gatz also provided valuable editorial criticism in the final preparation of this work.

psychological component. Although the mediating mechanisms by which psychosocial stimuli affect biological change are unclear at this point, it seems probable that psychological and environmental factors predispose, trigger, and maintain disease (Weiner, 1977).

Clearly, this holistic model of human functioning is a shift away from dualism, although dualism is deeply engrained in Western thought. For the balance of this chapter, this view of human structure—in which the *psyche* and *soma* are conceived as a single gestalt integrated within an environmental context—will provide the framework for our discussion of intervention with older adults. And because we are concerned here with psychological contributions to gerontology, little attention will be given to organic disorders per se. Rather, attention will be directed toward the social and environmental "side" of the dialectical process, and interventions that seem to make a difference in quality of functioning will be examined.

Treatment Targets: The Person and the Environment

Biological shifts and decrements (such as sensory and hormonal changes) and an eventual waning of energy are apparently essential aspects of human aging. Major therapeutic aims for the psychologist treating the elderly are, therefore, the remediation of excess disability (dysfunction over and above physiological necessity) and the facilitation of coping within the environmental context.

Taking an environmental approach, Lawton (1972) defined adaptation as the balance between environmental demands and organismic possibility. Optimally, a person–environment fit should be sought that supports the functioning of the increasingly frail geriatric patient. As Mechanic (1974) pointed out, the relation between social structure and personal adaptation has until recently been largely neglected. Because decrement is inevitable for the older patient, a major concern here is the context as a potentially prophylactic milieu.

The Community

Pathology in the Community: Response to Life's Normal Vicissitudes

In a perceptive writing, Blythe (1979) characterizes the current generation of old people as the first to live out the classic three score years and ten. In earlier generations, it was exceptional for individuals to live "to see their time out." It is a modern phenomenon

that the problems of the old have become a social burden, because it is only now that large numbers of elderly are remaining alive to burden the social conscience.

The still vital old people who live in the community are faced with losses that are, at least in part, imposed by the larger social context.

> Old age is not an emancipation from desire for most of us; that is a large part of its tragedy. The old want (but their sensible refusal to put such wants into words suggests to us that they have given up wanting) their professional status back, or their looks, or their circle—which is now a lot of crossed-off names in the address book—or sex, or just a normal future-oriented existence. Most of all they want to be wanted. It crashes in on them like a nightmare, the leaden fact they are eighty, and now it is often not so much a matter of their being incapable of having some of the things they want, as there being laws and conventions preventing their access to them.[1]

Most older adults live in the community and function in a relatively independent manner. Cross-culturally, only about from 2% to 4% of people over the age of 75 are bedfast at home, and about the same percentage are bedfast in institutions (Shanas, 1974).

Intrinsic decrements in physiological capacities do occur with age. For example, Stare (1977) has described physiological changes in digestion with age, including reductions in salivation, taste and olfactory receptor-cell sensitivity, and the quantity of digestive enzymes. These physiological changes, in addition to social factors such as isolation and frequent depression and apathy, contribute to physical malnourishment in many elderly. And this malnutrition can, in turn, produce behavioral and mood changes, such as confusion, depression, irritability, and the inability to make decisions (Sherwood, 1973). These manifestations of semistarvation may be presumed to be typical of old age or may earn the geriatric patient the diagnosis of chronic brain syndrome.

Aging also brings many decrements other than physical ones. These include role loss, the absence of normative structure accompanied by a growing sense of anomie, and the loss of reference groups. Ernst, Beran, Safford, and Kleinhauz (1978) reviewed research on both animal and human behavior related to the effects of social isolation, and suggested a circular relation between social isolation and decrements leading to cognitive dysfunction. Decreased sensitivity of the sensory receptors leads to a decrement in the amount of stimuli reaching the brain, which in turn

---

[1] From *The View in Winter*. Copyright © 1979 by Ronald Blythe. Reprinted by permission of Harcourt Brace Jovanovich, Inc.

might lead to cellular atrophy of brain tissue. This atrophy is reflected in loss of memory and general ability, eliciting signs of confusion, anxiety, and numerous specific fears. The resulting feelings of vulnerability lead the elderly further into depression, apathy, and withdrawal, increasing the isolation and general decrement in sensory stimulation and continuing the downward spiral of dysfunction. However speculative the interrelations in this cycle may be (and clearly, the relations are complex and undoubtedly bidirectional in nature), the effects of isolation for both the community and the institutionalized elderly are both negative and serious.

Rowland (1977) reviewed the literature concerned with life events that predict death in the elderly. Of the major events considered, only loss of a spouse and environmental relocation seem to be significantly associated with mortality in the old, and there were qualifying limits to these conclusions. The only well-designed relocation studies were carried out within an institutional setting, and only the seriously physically and psychiatrically ill were at greater risk when moved within those facilities. Also, death following loss of spouse appeared to occur mostly for males who were themselves ill and who lost their sources of care with the loss of their spouses. However, conclusions drawn from a recent epidemiological study suggest the possibility of an increased death rate of some 25,000 Americans annually as a direct result of significant personal losses (U.S. Department of Health, Education, and Welfare, 1979). While it may be true that bereavement is associated with a higher incidence of illness and death, systematic studies clearly need to be carried out examining the impact of bereavement on those who suffer such losses.

Apart from bereavement following death of significant others and reactive depression following a variety of losses, chronic depression in general appears to be more prevalent in the old (Epstein, 1976). In addition, an atypical pattern of "masked" depression is commonly found in the aged. In that pattern, the clinical presentation is one of somatic complaints, apathy, withdrawal, and functional slowness. For example, the reluctance to respond to questions during an interview is frequently attributed to "just old age," when the lack of communication is really a sign of significant depression.

According to Lipton (1976), psychopharmacological evidence suggests that depression in older age is associated with alterations in the synthesis, storage, release, and utilization of chemical neurotransmitters. Enzymes involved in these processes alter with age and are under genetic control. At a period of life where psychological stresses are generally high, interactions of negative life events and these biological changes produce the clinical state of depression. It is thought that a late-life onset of depression, without previous history of disorder, is indicative of a greater environmental and a smaller genetic component (Mendlewicz, 1976). And while the clinically depressed aged respond well to tricyclic drugs, real potential exists for side effects when psychopharmacological agents are used with the elderly. This area of psychopharmacological treatment of the elderly is dealt with further on in this chapter when treatment of the institutional aged is considered.

Additionally, while it is true that masked depression in the geriatric patient is often expressed through somatic concern, signs of depression can also be produced by infections or other physical disorders. As Epstein (1976) pointed out, it is frequently hard to determine whether physical complaints are based on somatic pathology or are primarily psychological in nature, or are both. Physical illness in the aged often develops in an insidious and progressive fashion, and it may be that a somatic disease process underlies the mood state. On the other hand, hypersomatic focus can prompt the report of symptoms resembling cases of cerebral vascular disease, angina pectoris, or other diseases (Epstein, 1976). Because behavioral manifestations (such as sleep disturbance) and somatic complaints (such as loss of appetite)—traditionally thought to reflect depressive mood—are also manifestations of actual physical disorders that frequently afflict the elderly, a depression scale, such as Beck's (1967) or Zung's (1965), that reflects the importance of physical complaints in mood disturbance may not be a valid measure of depression in the elderly. (See Chapter 2 of this volume for a further discussion of this validity issue.)

Two behavioral manifestations of depression among elderly people living in the community are alcoholism and suicide. Schuckit and Miller (1975) estimated that alcohol problems probably affect from between 2% and 10% of the whole population of the old, with even higher rates for widowers and the chronically ill within this population. Causes of alcohol abuse include feelings of uselessness and dependency (Bergman & Amir, 1973), poverty, and feelings of loss of status (Pascarelli & Fischer, 1974).

Finally, although the elderly represent only 18.5% of the American population, people over 60 years of age commit 23% of the suicides in this country (Miller, 1978). Miller has pointed out that suicides are generally underreported and has speculated that a conservative estimate is that at least 10,000 Americans aged 60 and older kill themselves each year. Most elderly suicides are men, and in fact, between the ages of 65 and 69, male suicides outnumber female suicides 4 to 1, but by age 85, the ratio increases to about 12 to

1 (Bromley, 1966; Weiss, 1968). As to the role of the physician as potential rescuer, Miller (1978) reported that three fourths of the men in his sample who killed themselves had visited a physician within the month before their suicides. Apparently the physicians either did not recognize the suicide potential or did not act on that recognition. Kucharski, White, and Schratz (1979) report a reluctance on the part of MDs to refer elderly patients for psychological or psychiatric help. Although they based their conclusions on responses to vignettes differing in patients' reported ages—a method of investigation that has been criticized on grounds of internal validity—their findings are consistent with general clinical experience with referral patterns.

Finally, a group at particular risk in the community is elderly women (Ross, 1974; Uhlenberg, 1979). The Task Panel on Mental Health and American Families (1978) of the President's Commission on Mental Health emphasized their at-risk status, particularly because of widespread poverty among older females in our society. The portrait of the elderly female of this cohort that emerged from a workshop on the older woman sponsored by the National Institute of Mental Health and the National Institute on Aging (USDHEW, 1979) was of a woman whose life is marked both by the continuities of working in the home and maintaining emotional connections with family, children, and peers and by the discontinuities of interrupted career and a large number of losses (departure of children and loss of spouse). She is faced with an unflattering stereotype and with poverty, poor access to transportation, loneliness, and isolation. She is three times as likely as her male peer to live in a nursing home. There is a real possibility that she will become an invalid or a pauper. Jackson (1972) has also referred to the "triple jeopardy" of being older, female, and a minority group member. Despite these disadvantages, the elderly woman of this cohort possesses great strength and potential, as witnessed by her ability to survive (Datan, 1977; Levy, in press; USDHEW, 1979).

A national survey conducted by the Social Security Administration (SSA) (Levy, 1979) also found that women across all age categories (ages 18–66) were significantly more distressed than males when rated on Langner (1962) item scores. These results correspond to the psychiatric, epidemiological findings reported by Dohrenwend and Dohrenwend (1974) and appear to be almost a universal phenomenon. The SSA survey also revealed that severe distress increased for both sexes in older age categories (except in the very oldest group, aged 65 and above), but again, the proportion of the sample experiencing (or at least reporting) the greatest disturbance occurred among females in every age category.

This psychological risk status for midlife and post-midlife women was also found in the cross-sectional community study of Lowenthal, Thurnher, and Chiriboga (1976) as well as in the longitudinal study of middle-aged women by Livson (1976). In the Livson study, traditionally feminine women were found to maintain their psychological health with relative equilibrium throughout the mid-years, while atypical women reported experiencing life constriction early in midlife but improved in psychological health after emerging from the mothering role. In the former study, Lowenthal et al. found striking sex differences across the life span of development and noted that middle-aged females, in particular, were a group at great psychological risk because of their general dissatisfaction with life.

The weight of the evidence, therefore, indicates both that women in our society experience more stress than men and that this stress increases at least until late midlife or older. Contributing to this stress are widowhood (Burkhauser, 1979; Glick, Weiss, & Parkes, 1974; Holden, 1979), retirement (Atchley, 1976; Fox, 1977; Levy, in press), and factors related to these statuses, such as poverty and social isolation (Morgan, 1976).

Treatment in the Community

This section examines particularly important current issues related to individual and group treatment, focusing especially on evidence supplied by controlled outcome studies, when available. Broader reviews of psychotherapy or of psychological intervention with the elderly can be found in Gottesman, Quarterman, and Cohn (1973), Eisdorfer and Stotsky (1977), Knight (1978–79), Sparacino (1978–79), Storandt, Siegler, and Elias (1978), and Brink (1979).

Professionally administered. Psychopharmacological intervention, which is mentioned briefly here, is dealt with in more depth in the discussion of the elderly in institutional settings. Because older patients metabolize psychopharmacological agents differently than do their younger counterparts (e.g., much lower dosages are necessary for the same biochemical effect), because of potential side effects, and because the elderly are typically prescribed multiple drugs for multiple chronic illnesses, Weissman (1979) and others have argued that for disturbances such as depression, psychological intervention appears to be safer and probably more effective. This may be especially true for the reactive depressions where the source of the disorder is frequently social loss. However, drug treatment is often presented as the intervention of choice. For example, a recent text entitled *Genesis and Treatment of Psychologic Disorders in the Elderly* (Gershon & Raskin, 1975) is devoted exclusively to physical treatments, including psychopharmacological intervention.

In a community study of drug-taking behavior, Guttmann (1977) listed the four most frequently prescribed categories of drugs given to the elderly: tranquilizers, diuretics, cardiovascular prescriptions, and sedatives/hypnotics. He also found a strong reliance on alcohol and over-the-counter preparations. According to Gutmann, while friends and relatives are frequently believed to be the source of drugs, his study found that almost all the elderly drug users (98.7%) obtained their antidepressants and sedatives from their family doctors and took them as prescribed. Guttmann concluded that although most of the elderly in his sample took the drugs legally and appropriately, a real danger existed from multiple drug ingestion. Underscoring the extent of the problem is his finding that less than 5% of the community elderly abstained completely from drugs and that roughly half used prescribed drugs in combination with both over-the-counter medications and alcohol. The major point here, however, is that physicians were the major source of drug prescriptions and that a sizeable proportion of the elderly were at high risk for damaging overmedication.

While this potential danger is serious among the elderly living in the community, institutionalized geriatric patients are apparently also at risk for side effects from overprescription—perhaps more so because of their physical frailty.

Individual psychotherapy. While it is commonly believed that the aged are not referred for individual treatment, the lack of understanding of the empirical complexity of the topic is reflected in a recent authoritative handbook on psychotherapy and behavior change (Garfield & Bergin, 1978). Garfield, in a chapter devoted to patient variables that affect therapeutic outcome, based his discussion of both sex and age effects on a few empirical studies that found no relation between age and rate of successful outcome. What Garfield did not mention is that therapy has not, in general, been considered a viable option for the elderly (Knight, 1978–79; Sparacino, 1978–79). Thus, in the studies that he reviewed, those older patients who came into therapy and continued to any outcome can hardly be considered a representative sample of the elderly. In addition, many studies that report outcome data with the "elderly" do not have really elderly subjects as patients. For example, in an outcome study of dynamic therapy with ghetto residents, Lerner (1972) studied outpatients ranging in age from 16 to 57!

The point is that we do not yet understand how age differences affect therapy processes or outcome, but at the least, Garfield's conclusion of no age effects on outcome is premature. Hoyer (1978) and others have pointed out that the high degree of interindividual variability encountered when working with the aged makes broad generalizations about the efficacy of particular treatments problematic. The reviews by Garfield (1978) and Smith and Glass (1977) show that at least *some* older adults can benefit from psychotherapy within the present system, certainly in short-term gain. However, even that modest conclusion may be premature, because variation in such factors as systematic diagnosis, level of measurements employed, techniques utilized, and therapist's skill preclude comparison across studies.

Discussions have recently appeared in the literature of therapists' reluctance to treat older patients (Garfinkel, 1975; Kastenbaum, 1964; Knight, 1978–79; Sparacino, 1978–79). For example, a recent national survey (Settin, 1979) has revealed a definite age bias in the therapy setting, reflected in descriptions of aged clients as significantly more severely pathological than younger clients matched for symptoms. Since organic pathology was diagnosed more frequently for the elderly, "usefulness of intervention" was endorsed significantly less for that group. Again, because of referral and treatment modality bias, few elderly are available for systematic, process and outcome outpatient studies, and most of the evidence of "success" for individual treatment with community elderly is anecdotal.

Generally, although a number of gerontologists (Butler & Lewis, 1977; Goldfarb, 1969) have argued for the potential benefit of individual psychotherapy in response to an older person's need for a significant primary relationship, the aged have historically been considered inappropriate for psychoanalytic and related insight-oriented psychotherapies. This position is based on the presumed rigidity, insufficient energy, and stored-up "well" of unconscious material that would need to be uncovered during the therapy process. Meerloo (1971) and Safirstein (1972), among others, have reported modifications of procedure with beneficial results in their case studies. However, again, there are mostly anecdotal data to support this view; for the most part, controlled studies of individual forms of dynamic or supportive psychotherapy are absent in the literature.

A specific therapeutic method used with older persons is that of the life-review process (Boylin, Gordon,

& Nehrke, 1976; Lewis, 1971). This process involves the use of reminiscence to reorganize and integrate the person's life as a totality. While beneficial results have been reported for both individual and group modalities within this framework (Romaniuk, 1979), there has been little systematic research comparing results of individual versus group participation in the life review. Methodological difficulties in past research on the life-review process have included failure to distinguish between spontaneous and elicited memories and between forms or functions of reminiscence, bias introduced by investigators during the course of "unstructured interviews," and different characteristics of subjects and circumstances surrounding the collection of data. These difficulties limit the comparability of the findings as well as the external validity of the results. The safest conclusion to be drawn on the function of reminiscence is that many important parameters are yet to be explored, and current understanding of this therapy technique is tentative at best.

The same situation exists with regard to behavior therapy. Most controlled research on behavioral interventions has been done with inpatient or institutional samples, where successful use of operant procedures has resulted in modification of a variety of target behaviors (the pertinent literature is discussed below). And while there are some case reports that describe successful behavioral intervention with, for example, depressed elderly people (Cautella & Mansfield, 1977), controlled research with elderly outpatients has been minimal. For example, careful reading of Cautella and Mansfield's chapter on behavioral techniques applied to the elderly reveals case reports but not a single controlled outcome study with elderly outpatients.

On the whole, differential effectiveness of two or more modalities of treatment for the *same* clinical phenomenon has not been addressed in the therapy outcome literature—and certainly not with older adults as patients. It is a technically difficult question to address, since suitable control conditions must be included and subject variables measured carefully. This means, among other things, that a fairly large number of subjects are needed to permit both appropriate statistical handling of the data and generalizability of results. Yet these kinds of questions need to be studied (Eisdorfer & Stotsky, 1977) in order to provide reliable guidelines for clinicians who will be treating an ever-increasing proportion of older persons in the community.

In a recent theoretical chapter on the linkage between major personality theories and modes of intervention, Kastenbaum (1978) discusses forms of cognitive personality theories and related forms of explanation for psychopathology. Within that framework, he discusses Kelly's (1955) personal construct theory and Seligman's (1975) notion of perceived helplessness

generating negative affect and dysfunctional behavior. Although Kastenbaum does not link these theories with controlled therapy research, they would seem to be applicable to an older population—particularly patients in that group suffering from reactive depression. However, some innovative relevant research currently under way (see Thompson & Gallagher, 1979–81) provides a controlled study of individual treatments, comparing behavioral and cognitive modes of intervention for severe depression in community elderly.

In Thompson and Gallagher's research, pilot data have been collected on the comparative effectiveness of two short-term, highly structured psychotherapies (behavioral and cognitive) compared to a short-term relatively unstructured relational control condition. Preliminary analysis of outcome data on 27 persons indicated that more elderly patients discontinued either behavioral or relational treatments than cognitive intervention. On the whole, clients reported a significant reduction in their levels of depression, regardless of conditions, upon completion of the 16 scheduled appointments. This finding was also supported by independent ratings by a trained observer as well as by therapists' evaluations of change.

The fact that the cognitive approach was well received by clients (that is, all clients who started in that condition completed the course of treatment) suggests its particular utility with this older cohort. Thompson and Gallagher suggest that while Beck's rationale for recording patients' dysfunctional thoughts and finding alternative forms of thinking about their situations seem to take continual practice for the treatment to be effective, the opportunity afforded for cognitive reappraisal of common life decrements (i.e., physical decline, etc.) may be the most appropriate and realistic therapeutic approach. When the elderly were able to perceive treatment as an educational experience designed to teach or reinforce existing coping skills, the therapy outcome seemed to be most successful.

The research described above is merely a rare example of careful, systematically controlled outcome research with an older patient group. It is hoped that it will provide a stimulus and a model for future studies of individual, as well as group, psychotherapy with older adults.

In sum, one yearns to say something more about individual, outpatient psychotherapy with the elderly. While much has been written from a clinical perspective, there is little definitive evidence that speaks to the issue. George Bernard Shaw once said something to the effect that Christianity has not failed, it has simply never been tried. While individual treatment of the elderly seems humane and potentially clinically appropriate, it ought not only to be tried, but also to be systematically studied.

Group treatment. Although group techniques with the elderly are becoming widely accepted, we still lack carefully controlled studies to determine the efficacy of various approaches. Further, most of the research in this area has taken place within an institutional setting. Theoretically, at least, it makes great sense to treat elderly clients within a group framework. Group therapy would seem particularly appropriate for older persons whose social identity may be greatly undermined by role loss as employment and even spouse and friends become unavailable for support and self-confirmation. Sharing experiences and interacting with peers should provide at least a sense of emotional security and might enhance personal dignity as coping abilities increase.

While the research in this area is still sparse, some studies on group process effectiveness have been reported in the literature. For example, Barrett (1978) compared the effects of self-help, consciousness-raising, confidant-support, and wait-list control groups in a study involving community-dwelling widows ranging in age from 32 to 74. The consciousness-raising form of intervention was reported to be the most effective, with women in that group reporting improvement in health and self-esteem while becoming less "other" oriented. Another study, reported by Keller and Croake (1975), compared rational-emotive group psychotherapy with a control condition and reported a significant decrease in irrational thinking and anxiety in the experimental group.

As seen in Thompson and Gallagher's (1979–81) preliminary findings, differential improvement is less frequently reported than are nonspecific effects. For example, Ingersoll and Silverman (1978) compared the effects of a "there-and-then," reminiscence-oriented outpatient group to a "here-and-now," behaviorally oriented form of group intervention. While the authors reported that the there-and-then, insight-oriented group showed greater overall improvement, only one measured difference between groups—somatic behavior—was statistically significant. These authors note, however, that the behavioral techniques employed in the here-and-now group required more time for the elderly to learn than the study permitted. A second controlled research effort, reported by Gallagher (1979), comparing behavioral group therapy with nondirective group therapy, showed that older persons were capable of responding to both forms of treatment. Although subjects in the behavioral group improved more in verbal interaction in the group setting, neither self-report measures of depression nor interpersonal behavior indicated a differential treatment effect.

Two conclusions can be drawn from the controlled studies of group therapy in elderly outpatients. In general, group intervention effectively alleviates psychological stress for at least some elderly persons, but outcome measures are not sufficiently refined to distinguish specific, treatment-linked response from general, nonspecific symptom change. While the response may not be tied to any specific treatment modality, it would be premature to conclude that was true until more refined outcome designs and measures are developed.

Family therapy and intermediate care facilities. Caring for a frail parent is a psychological reversal of patterns of dependency within a family, but there seem to be few cultural norms in today's society for guiding behavior in this area of intergenerational relationships. Middle-aged (and themselves aging) lay people and professionals alike are frequently disturbed and puzzled over how to care for their aging parents. Basically, the problems encountered here seem to be couched within the psychologically larger issues surrounding the management of the role shifts and reversals that occur between parent and child across the life course, but these problems have yet to be studied in depth.

If we can assume that for the 1980s the continued maintenance of the elderly by their families will be an increasing problem, then interventions aimed at fostering independent or semi-independent functioning in the community must be developed. One promising approach to such intervention is family therapy.

Eisdorfer and Stotsky (1977) suggest that although family therapy is increasingly considered appropriate for aged patients and their families, the support for this approach has until now remained largely speculative. For example, two recent texts devoted to psychological intervention with the elderly (Brink, 1979; Herr & Weakland, 1979) treat family therapy as a major focus of intervention. Both of these works, however, are practical guides to treatment and report no research related to the efficacy of this form of intervention. Garrison and Howe (1976) described an approach they call network building for the elderly, utilizing network sessions involving all significant others in the life of the patient. The aim of these sessions is to rebuild or cement interpersonal relationships for these elderly, but again no empirical support is provided for this mode of intervention.

A variety of other arrangements have been developed in recent years for maintaining the elderly in the community, in order to forestall the iatrogenic deterioration, dependency, and excess disability that may accompany premature institutionalization (Tobin & Lieberman, 1976). These arrangements include day-care facilities, communal living arrangements, foster home care, and planned intermittent hospitalization. While space does not permit a detailed discussion of each of these, a general issue might be raised for consideration (see Sherwood, 1975, for a more thorough discussion). As a result of various legislation passed in recent years (the Kerr-Mills Act, Medicaid, and Title XIX of Public Law 89–97), elderly psychiatric patients have been kept "in the community" by being placed in extended-care facilities. Since many of these facilities were incapable of providing any treatment other than custodial, the solution to the "problem" was in many cases no better than the original condition. Careful evaluation of the actual effects of alternative arrangements is needed. For example, Bradshaw, Vonderhaan, Keeney, Tyler, and Harris (1976) found that foster-home operators tended to retain residents who had become bedfast and hence in need of extensive nursing care, because they had developed emotional ties with the residents and did not want to institutionalize them. In a closer examination of the nature of the interpersonal ties within the foster-care arrangement, Newman and Sherman (1979–80) concluded that foster homes were, in fact, serving as surrogate familial environments in which integration and participation occurred, rather than merely serving as mini-institutions. But as Bradshaw et al. suggested, the special nature of this relationship of caretaker with elderly dependent patient may result in such additional effects as delay in referring the patient for more substantial care beyond the time when such a referral might be warranted.

Results from these two surveys highlight the general need to examine clinically based assumptions empirically—for example, that being "part of a family" is better than being "institutionalized." Adult foster care is only part of a continuum of sheltered housing for the old—and each segment must be evaluated in terms of its impact on the patient. Elderly patients clearly differ demographically and psychologically; they differ also in chronic disease site and stage of illness. And these major patient variables interact with the character of the immediate and larger social system within which the care context is located. Not only do the individual segments along the continuum of care need to be evaluated but decision patterns need to be examined that in effect move the patient from one segment to another. The reasons for and the effects of premature movement (such as Tobin and Leiberman argue against), as well as delayed movement (as Bradshaw et al. discovered) need to be systematically addressed in future research.

Alternatives to professionally administered treatments: The self-help group movement. As Butler, Gertman, Oberlander, and Schindler (1979–80) noted in a recent article, the phenomena of self-care and self-help have exploded onto the physical and mental health arena. These and other writers point out that this growing trend in consumer control of care delivery is couched within larger social phenomena of political activism, the humanistic growth movement, and public suspicion directed toward professional authority (Gartner & Riessman, 1977; Levy, 1976). For the elderly, such groups as the Gray Panthers, SAGE, and various widow-to-widow programs have increased in popularity within recent years. In addition, other self-help groups aimed at assisting those that are chronically ill—such as Make Today Count, ostomy clubs, or Mended Hearts Clubs—would also seem to be appropriate for the elderly who are often subject to these chronic conditions. Butler et al. (1979–80) suggest that mutual aid and self-help efforts could benefit the lonely, isolated, impoverished, bewildered, retired, or grieving elderly in the community. Although this observation is probably true, self-help groups are, in general, notoriously difficult to evaluate in terms of outcome effectiveness, and this, as well as other related issues, has been discussed by Lieberman (1978), Levy (1976), and others. It is appropriate here, however, simply to indicate that for some elderly—particularly those living independently in the community—groups such as SAGE (Senior Actualization and Growth Exploration) may prove to be viable sources of alternative therapeutic experience. The task of defining and measuring both appropriate process and outcome variables remains a future challenge.

Treatment in the Community: A Research Challenge for the 1980s

In a holistic view of human functioning, it seems reasonable to assume that environmental and social-psychological support provided to an increasingly frail older person might provide a stimulus for continued growth and optimal survival.

Reactive depression in the face of decrement and loss is a major problem in the elderly which seems to be amenable to psychological intervention. Alternatives need to be developed to drug treatment, and controlled "clinical trials" of psychological treatment modalities need to be tested. Within the promising approach of cognitive change strategies, specific change mechanisms need to be isolated, for example, modeling of alternative thought content (Meichenbaum, 1977) versus the ferreting out of thought fragments and fantasies (Beck, 1976). In addition, group versus individual modes providing the same type of treatment need to be systematically compared.

In regard to intergenerational relationships, research needs to be directed to issues such as role shifts and role reversals between middle-aged children and their aging parents, and new forms of family or multi-generational therapy need to be developed and tested for effectiveness. Again, alternative models of intervention need to be compared. For example, when the presenting family problem is an increasingly forgetful elderly family member with multiple chronic physical conditions that require strict adherence to a medical regimen, would "network" therapy be as effective as teaching the behavioral skills required to comply with multiple regimens? Would the design and implementation of a prosthetic environment, bypassing family intervention patterns, be most effective of all? Related to the above clinical issues, the decision process underlying institutionalization versus alternative arrangements needs to be more carefully examined, including the identification of sources of variance in differential decision outcome for patients matched for physical status.

Finally, although of a different order of concern, not only must the content of process and outcome variables unique to the old be understood and measured validly, but distinctive parameters of these variables must be thoroughly understood by researchers engaged in this area of inquiry. For example, within a behavioral treatment framework, time to criterion may simply be longer in the elderly. If this is not appreciated by the investigator, failure of target attainment may be incorrectly attributed to the patient.

Although the above is hardly an exhaustive list of important clinical and research directions for the 1980s, this aggregate of questions represents promising possibilities for advancement in the years ahead in the area of psychological treatment of the elderly living in the community.

The Institution

When the incapacitated elderly patient can no longer manage—or be managed in—any of the alternative living arrangements in the community ranging from "senior" housing to foster home and day-care placement, the next, and frequently final, move is to an extended-care facility or a nursing home. Today, there are nearly 25,000 nursing homes in the United States housing nearly two thirds of all institutionalized elderly (USDHEW, 1974). Total institutionalization represents the ultimate personal failure for both the elderly and their families. Most of the old view institutions as the least desirable of all the alternatives possible, a reflection of final surrender in giving up. Entry into an extended-care facility normally follows increasing mental or physical incapacity or both in the absence of the social support that might otherwise have enabled the person to remain in the community (Hendricks & Hendricks, 1977; Tobin & Lieberman, 1976).

There is a widespread belief among gerontologists that from only 4% to 5% of the old are in institutions. However, Kastenbaum and Candy (1973), as well as others (Ingram & Barry, 1977; Lesnoff-Caravaglia, 1978–79), have demonstrated that from 20% to 30% of the elderly in this country die in institutions and have argued that if the geriatric patients died there, they have also lived there. Although it may be that many of these elderly are not transferred to a total institution until they are terminally ill, nevertheless, it is clear from the figures that for an elderly person who lives long enough, the probability of ending up in a long-term care facility is rather high.

Pathology in the Institution: Neurological Deficit and Excess Disabilities

The hospitalized geriatric patient presents a particularly challenging assessment and treatment task for the psychologist. Cognitive and behavioral deficits are typically present, although the source of dysfunction is rarely clear. Severe cognitive and mood disturbance (referred to as dementia in the medical literature) is clinically quite heterogeneous (McDonald, 1969; Settin, 1978). Nearly 100 reversible conditions may mimic a few irreversible brain disorders (such as Alzheimer's disease or cerebral arteriosclerosis). Many cognitive and behavioral manifestations of "senility" may in fact be (a) secondary to acute medical conditions (such as malnutrition, mentioned earlier), (b) iatrogenically caused by treatments of all kinds—from improper medication to physical restraint (Covert, Rodrigues, & Solomon, 1977; Howard, Strong, Strong, & String, 1977), or (c) functional in origin, reflecting severe depression (Butler & Lewis, 1977; Libow, 1977). For example, a careful assessment would need to be made of confusion in a hospitalized elderly cancer patient. Clinically, patients in that group—particularly the very old—appear disoriented and unable to communicate. To be able to distinguish between functional symptoms due to distress and unfamiliarity of surroundings and symptoms due to brain metastases or neurological degeneration clearly requires extensive knowledge in the areas of both neuropsychology and gerontology. (For a more complete discussion of neurological deficits, see Eisdorfer & Cohen, 1978; Gershon & Raskin, 1975; and Chapter 2 in this volume).

Finally, some controversy exists in regard to the effects of institutionalization itself on the elderly patient's functioning. Although Tobin and Lieberman (1976) and Rodstein, Savitsky, and Starkman (1976) concluded that gross dysfunction did not seem to result from institutionalization itself but rather was present prior to admission into the long-term care facility, others (Kasl, 1972; Kent, 1963) have found significant physical changes occurring after hospitalization, particularly in patients who exhibited confusion and pronounced depression. Clearly, whether significant physical and psychological deterioration are directly attributable to the institutionalization itself needs to be further examined.

The notion of "excess disability" is important for consideration in the treatment of hospitalized elderly. Brody, Kleban, Lawton, and Silverman (1971) defined excess disability as the gap between existing and potential function in persons diagnosed (presumably validly) as having organic brain dysfunction. Since the answer to the question of how much the visible impairment of function is the result of organic impairment can range from total to none, the question is basically an empirical one. For the purpose of this chapter, we will not presume the nature or extent of neurological impairment but will simply apply the concept of "excess disability" to all cognitive and behavioral dysfunctions that are reversible.

Pharmacological Treatment Within the Institution

Pharmacotherapy of the elderly patient must be approached with caution, particularly when more than one compound (polypharmacy) is involved. Briefly, a number of important physiological modifications that take place with age—such as increasingly inefficient excretion by renal function—have general effects on the body's capacity to process and metabolize medications. And several specific alterations occur that necessitate changing normal prescription patterns in treating the elderly patient. These age factors in drug metabolism—for example, changes in gastric chemistry and intestinal circulation that affect drug absorption—work in a complex and interrelated fashion to render older persons much more sensitive to the clinical effects of most psychotherapeutic drugs. These effects are further enhanced by an increased responsiveness of the central nervous system to psychotropics, which is definitely age related and may be a function of changing neuron/glial cell ratios. For example, a significant class of side effects of the major neuroleptics are those that impair cholinergic mechanisms. Typically, these effects can involve constipation, vertigo, loss of ocular accommodation, urinary retention, and dry mouth. In the older patient, urinary retention may become particularly problematic in men with prostatic hypertrophy, and paralytic ileus may result from constipation. In addition, increased intraocular pressure may aggravate glaucoma.

More than occasionally, a confused state may develop in the elderly psychotic patient that is not a manifestation of psychopathology but rather is drug induced. In many of these instances, a phenothiazine drug has been given in conjunction with an antiparkinsonian agent, and a synergistic combination of anticholinergic effects from the two drugs produce a centrally acting anticholinergic toxicity (Smith, 1979).

Given the dangers inherent in the treatment of the old with pharmacological agents, it is not surprising that iatrogenic disorders related to drug treatment occur in institutionalized populations. Recently, investigators have studied medication procedures within long-term care facilities and have found rather widespread abuse related to this treatment modality (Covert et al., 1979; Howard et al., 1977; Miller, 1975). For example, in a study of the medication of 98 patients in a proprietary nursing home, Howard et al. found that a total of 536 drugs had been prescribed for the 98 patients. The drugs prescribed came to an average of 5.5 per patient. Twenty-two patients were receiving 8 or more drugs, one patient was receiving a total of 16 different drugs, and the average number of PRN (*pro re nata*, as needed) drug orders left by physicians was 3.2 per patient. Howard et al. noted that PRN orders were left for a variety of medications (psychotropic, cardiovascular, and hypnotic drugs, for example), and in fact some of the medications were ordered PRN inappropriately, with essentially little or no medical follow-up.

In addition to chemical restraints on patient behavior, mechanical restraints are not infrequently employed in these facilities: For example, patients may be strapped into wheelchairs and left to "watch" TV for hours at a time. Side effects from such procedures include impaired circulation, skin abrasions, and kineseopathologic sequelae (Covert et al., 1977; Miller, 1975). Covert et al. suggested alternative interventions for these "management" problems—such as exercise, remotivation therapy, and sensory stimulation—and some of the more promising alternatives are discussed below. A concluding point to be made here, however, is one made by Gutmann (1977) in his survey of drug taking by the elderly in the community. The mass media, physicians, families of patients, and the pharmaceutical industry are all locked into a tendency to "medicalize" all problems arising from the human condition. While this is an endemic problem in our whole society, for the frail geriatric patient, the dangers of overmedicating rather than psychologically intervening are very real. (For a general consideration of pharmacokinetics and the elderly, see Eisdorfer & Fann, 1976; Friedel, 1977; and Kapnick, 1978.)

Psychological Treatment Within the Institution

Space does not permit a complete discussion of all of the varieties of intervention that are currently found in the literature ("pet therapy," physical fitness therapy, companionship therapy, etc.). Here we will raise important issues concerning individualized treatment of excess disabilities, the use of familiar and "normal" past experience—such as wine drinking or dancing to music—to enhance well-being, and the creation of a sense of control in those who have ceased to have any over their lives. In addition, the notion of behavioral prosthetics is discussed, and promising possibilities for the operant "shaping" of prosocial behavior are highlighted.

Brody et al. (1971) reported short-term success in reducing "excess disabilities" by tailoring highly individualized behavioral, psychosocial, and medical treatment for a group of hospitalized geriatric patients. These authors reported a reduction in excess disabilities (but not medical impairments) in comparison with a control group, although these gains were not maintained at a nine-month follow-up (Brody, Kleban, Lawton, & Moss, 1974). Their conclusion that the reduction of excess disabilities in daily functional activities cannot be maintained without substantial effort is consistent with other findings. In fact, the weight of the evidence for other current lay-administered and didactically oriented forms of individual and group intervention with the institutionalized elderly (e.g., remotivation therapy and reality orientation therapy) is not encouraging with respect to long-term effectiveness. Admittedly, most of the patients involved in these studies are severely regressed, both cognitively and behaviorally. But in addition to methodological flaws in the various studies, it appears that a massive effort on the part of the staff does not "pay off" in terms of long-range change in the patients (Barnes, 1974; Citrin & Dixon, 1977; Thralow & Watson, 1974).

It may be that at least some patients benefit from intensive reality orientation or remotivation therapy, but the state of the evidence does not now support wholesale application of these small-group approaches to institutionalized older patients. Storandt (1978) has suggested that future research should attempt to identify effective change elements within these group processes in order to determine major sources of variance in behavioral outcome. For example, Brook, Degun, and Mather (1975) manipulated presence or absence of therapist in two groups of reality-orientation patients, both of which were provided the same "reality." The patients were rated by nurses who were blind to treatment conditions, and the researchers reported continued improvement only in the group with continuous therapist contact over the course of treatment. The effective source of change in this case was apparently the quality of the patient–therapist relationship.

Notwithstanding the potential for ferreting out ef-

fective parameters for some patients, perhaps as researchers we should take a step back and survey the total evidence. It is just conceivable that the promise of reversing excess disabilities in the severely regressed elderly—by group motivation and individual "drill"—is more than can be delivered. Perhaps the direction of future efforts should be toward the utilization of more behavioral and environmental approaches, as discussed below.

Some success in the enhancement of feelings of well-being and an increase in normal socialization patterns have been reported through the use of familiar, acculturated symbolic expressions of communication in community—wine or beer drinking and musical expression (Chien, Stotsky, & Cole, 1973; Mishara, Kastenbaum, Baker, & Patterson, 1975; Shapiro, 1969). Results from Kastenbaum and Slater's (1964) study suggested that although both wine and juice (provided at a social hour) enhanced group participation, patients in the wine group showed significantly greater group involvement. As these researchers pointed out, wine has social meaning for many and may have considerably less deleterious physical effects than other chemical agents. Shapiro (1969) reported that an opportunity for musical expression with a variety of familiar instruments provided not only physical exercise but social stimulation, with accompanying increased postive mood. Although the latter was not a controlled study, intuitively it makes sense that at least those elderly who are not severely dysfunctional would benefit experientially from a reintroduction of the familiar, with entrenched social meaning, into their institutional routine. Future research might be directed toward teasing out and examining the most relevant aspects of these familiar experiences in order to enhance their therapeutic effects. For example, with music, what is the relative contribution to positive affect and physical well-being of expressive involvement as compared to the experience of familiar melodies? Do the familiar melodies evoke reminiscence, and is that indiscriminately beneficial? In a single cohort, would music from a particular historical period—say, from the time when a group of 75- to 80-year olds were young parents—be more effective by evoking their youth than would music that evokes experience from later in their lives? For future investigators interested in enhancing the quality of life for those who have no other alternative but institutional existence, the effective parameters of these forms of non-noxious interventions should be carefully examined.

An issue that also arises in the outpatient treatment of depression is whether elderly patients show some improvement no matter what form of intervention is provided. Nahemow (1978) reached that conclusion, and Kahn and Zarit (1974) suggested that this may be true for the elderly in institutions as well. An increase in "life satisfaction" has been reported for insight-oriented treatment (Ingersoll & Silverman, 1978), group discussions (Williams, Kriauciunas, & Rodriguez, 1970), arts and crafts classes (Wagner & Lerner, 1968), task groups (Moran, 1978), and physical therapy (Morrison, 1969). In a refinement of this conclusion, Schultz (1976) suggested that any therapy, if controlled by the geriatric patient or offered at predictable intervals, would be potentially effective. In an experimental study in which patients controlled or were able to predict when therapeutic visits would occur, they improved in functioning, mood, and physical health. However, on follow-up, Schultz and Hanusa (1978) found no long-term effects attributable to the intervention. In fact, those who had initially benefited from the control and predictability-enhancing manipulations of the original study showed clear decrements in physical health and morale, while those in the original control group remained stable at follow-up.

Aside from the demonstration of an "A-B-A" effect (although not technically intended as such), two issues need to be raised. First, for institutionalized elderly, seriously deteriorated either physically or cognitively, long-term positive effects of discrete interventions appear not to occur. Specifically, in the Schultz and Hanusa study, when the control ceases, no benefit remains. Their finding is related to the second point: Serious ethical issues are related to experimental manipulation in field settings. Long-term effects, including those arising from cessation of the demonstration procedure, must be taken into account by investigators.

Behavioral prosthetics, operant conditioning, and the environmental setting. In an important chapter on behavioral prosthetics and the elderly, Lindsley (1964) discussed the usefulness of a free-operant conditioning laboratory to be used for diagnostic purposes with geriatric patients. Testing the functional parameters of environmental stimuli in a highly controlled setting would allow the psychologist to predict behavioral possibilities and potential change, implement controlling stimulus contingencies, and assess resulting patient behavior. Prosthetic environments are those that supply artificial devices in order to optimize and extend potential functioning. For example, Lindsley suggested that a response device that would amplify force such as needed to open automatic doors could be provided to enhance the geriatric patient's range of potential functioning. Interdisciplinary research efforts to design and study the effects of such mechanical enhancements of function offer a rich field of possibilities for gerontologists and engineering psychologists to pursue in the future.

Patient behavior appears also to be a function—at least in part—of the architectural structure of a facility (Cluff & Campbell, 1975), and even the arrangement of furniture has the effect of facilitating or impeding social interaction (Lipman & Slater, 1977). More generally, although the alteration of a total milieu obviously requires money, effort, and staff participation, certain physical as well as psychosocial aspects of the environment may have a profound effect on the patient's behavior within a total institution. An example of an environmental manipulation involving geriatric patients was reported by Cornbleth (1977). Wandering and nonwandering patients were assigned to "protected" (locked) or unprotected wards. The nonwanderers decreased in physical function (range of motion) on the locked ward and improved in the less protected environment. On the other hand, wanderers improved on the physical measure in the protected ward environment only. Mishara (1978) also found differential response to either a token-economy manipulation or a supportive milieu arrangement. In the token-economy condition, patients improved who were characterized as "less institutionalized," who were motivated to engage in target behaviors, and who were in better physical condition. In the milieu condition, geriatric patients who did not respond in the initial interview, and who were generally passive, showed more improvement.

Curiously, in Mishara's study, there was no improvement in *verbal* behavior under either condition. Generally, patients did not talk to one another, Lubinski (1978–79) pointed out in a review of recent research on verbal communication among the elderly that there is a paucity of communication among institutionalized and chronically ill elderly and also that there is generally little staff interest shown in whether patients talk or not. Barton (1978) reported lack of reinforcement contingencies for forms of social behavior among nursing-home patients, and in a report of the results of an attempt to condition the verbal behavior of geriatric patients by operant technique, Hoyer, Kafer, Simpson, and Hoyer (1974) also concluded that changing social behavior in aged residents is a low priority for staff.

Most of the carefully controlled studies done with the elderly within an operant framework have been carried out on the institutionalized old (see Cautella & Mansfield, 1977; Richards & Thorpe, 1978). Mishara, Robertson, and Kastenbaum (1973) outlined a five-step behavioral intervention strategy involving observation, reflection, intervention, assessment, and follow-up. They also discussed the need to be very careful in assessing *what* the behavior is that is being modified. For example, they presented a case of a patient who stopped ingesting foreign objects—the target behavior to be eliminated—but who was later discovered to have learned also "not to ingest ·anything, including food!" Clearly, an important issue is the meaning of the total intervention for the patient. For example, Richards and Thorpe, in a chapter on behavioral approaches with the elderly, included the case of a 67-year-old woman who had shown no "self-maintenance" behavior (she did not feed herself) for a period of five weeks. Verbal prompting, stimulus control, and immediate reinforcement with other tangible reinforcers were instigated as well as a time-out procedure in which the experimenter "turned her back" when the patient refused to eat. Within an A-B-A reversal design, baseline conditions were reestablished, and a "concomitant decrease in self-feedings" occurred. Unfortunately, the patient died "before the treatment condition could be reinstated" (Richards & Thorpe, 1978, p. 263). Ethically, one has to wonder about what if anything the experimental manipulation meant to the patient.

Another example of a similar dilemma is exemplified in the report of Fordyce, Fowler, Lehmann, and DeLateur (1973). These writers spoke of rearranging the contingencies for "pain" behavior—reinforcement for "well talk," time-contingent rather than pain-contingent medication schedules, etc. Again, the rationale for eliminating such pain behavior—to encourage the patient to attend once more to productive, environmental demands and become less focused on the limiting demands of the body—is humanistic and therapeutic. However, it would seem important to examine systematically the phenomenological impact on the patient experiencing the manipulation of contingencies and, again, to determine what it is that is actually being learned.

These interventions may also be viewed from a framework of staff expectancy and the negotiation of possibilities. Goldstein (1971) observed that patients tended to act passively ill in order to be taken care of, while staff tended to "push for" independence of functioning. There was a tacit agreement, however, between staff and patients that as long as the patients were "good," the staff would not be "mean" and withhold basic social sustenance from them. Gatz, Siegler, and Dibner (1979–80), in their study of the development of a therapeutic community, found similar processes occurring in staff–patient relations. Strauss (1978), in an excellent chapter concerned with silent bargains between staff and patients on geriatric wards, amplifies these findings. Owing to lack of funding and adequate personnel, patients tend to be managed on a tight schedule, and elderly patients are both in frequent pain and also socially isolated. The silent bargain to which Strauss refers involves the patients' willingness to tolerate pain at intervals and to fit their needs into staff routine in return for small favors and social contact. These negotiations are important not only as two-way exchanges but also as one-way behavioral shaping processes.

Of course, all of these issues seem related: staff inattention to prosocial and verbal behavior, operant shaping of self-management behavior, the elimination of "pain talk" as well as "pain behavior," and the negotiation of social needs through silent bargaining. We have raised these issues here to generate a broader reflection (a) on the meaning of the social environment for patients as well as staff, and (b) on the creation of environmental tone, rules, and expectancies either as fall-out from explicit intervention or as a naturally occurring and unreflected-upon creation of all the participants.

Humanizing Dying: Future Research Needs

Kalish (1978) has concluded that while the literature is filled with advice on how to die and how to work with the dying, there is a dearth of careful, relevant analysis based on systematically gathered data. And while it is true that dying is not unique to the elderly, it is a clinical issue that has particular relevance for patients at this end of the life continuum. Medical attitudes and practices have changed in recent years relative to prolongation of support systems for the dying and communication about dying with patients and families (Agate, 1973; Cassell, 1973; Committee on Medicine in Society, 1973; Noyes, Jochimsen, & Travis, 1977). Although it would seem important to examine the effects on patients and families of these changing trends, very little research has been done to date.

Among the many researchable issues in the area of psychological treatment and supportive care for the dying geriatric patient are the following: (a) environmental parameters that might make a difference in the dying process, for example, effects of a hospice environment (Saunders, 1973; Woodson, 1978); (b) the decision-making process on the part of the physician, nurse, patient, and patient's family—for example, congruent and incongruent decisions to terminate life support for the patient, and the effects of, say, incongruency on staff and patient stress levels (Miller, 1971); and (c) the use of indigenous groups, such as the Shanti volunteers (Garfield & Clark, 1978), as potentially effective care providers for some who are dying. The list given above obviously does not exhaust potential research issues. Clearly the published research available does not reflect the importance of this area. If, indeed, nearly 20% to 30% of the population die in institutions (Kastenbaum & Candy, 1973)—and from 70% to 80% die somewhere else—humanizing the dying process by exploring social and environmental parameters that make a difference remains an important area for future exploration.

Treatment in the Institution: Future Research Directions

A number of issues will need to be addressed in the decade ahead. First, the place of psychopharmacological intervention in the treatment of older adults is not a question of "either-or," and finer diagnostic discriminations need to be made concerning complementary biochemical and psychological interventions for specified clinical problems. Clearly, however, alternatives to psychopharmacological intervention— particularly for mood disorder—need to be developed. The evidence suggests that *control* over events, particularly positive ones, might be a major factor in fostering a sense of well-being in the institutionalized elderly. Another salient variable appears to be a continuous patient–therapist relationship. Enhancement of social behavior through the provision of cultural symbols and expressions of community is not only intuitively plausible but is also supported by some evidence.

To the extent that it is true that most older patients respond positively—no matter what form of supportive intervention is provided—researchers could also turn that seemingly nonspecific result into an issue for analysis. That is, what variables are common to interventions that seem to have a positive effect? Perhaps the element that is common to maintenance of personal control, a continuous patient–therapist relationship, and provision of cultural symbols is a return to the patients of a familiar, "normal" social space where expectancies for social exchange are supported by predictable experience.

Second, much more work needs to be done in the area of person–environment fit. Research examining the impact on both staff and residents of architectural and organizational structure has begun to bear fruit, and interdisciplinary cross-fertilization on problems of mutual concern would seem most appropriate. Researchers have begun to examine not only the effects of spatial structure but characteristics of the environment, such as its open or closed quality, that appear to interact with the physical and mental status of the aging patient with very different cognitive and behavioral effects.

Third, and related to the last research area, is the need to examine the impact of staff attitudes and expectancies on patient functioning in order ultimately to reshape these "therapist" variables in order to change patient behavior. The work of Moos, Gauvain, Lemke, Wax, and Mehren (1979) and others on social-organizational perceptions represents an important breakthrough in the analysis of the effects of differential expectancies on behavior and morale of both staff and residents. Person and environment perception, congruence–incongruence of expectancy, and the sociology of negotiation between participants remain important areas for investigation.

Major Research Controversies: What to Measure and How

With a model of the kind provided by Orlinsky and Howard (1978), variables to be assessed in therapy research include input (history of the participants, including expectancies brought to the therapy process), patient variables, therapist variables, and output (impact of the outcome on the patient's social environment). While none of these is more important than the others, perhaps the variable that is most salient here is the output, or target behavior to be changed. This is what brings the patient into contact with the change agents, this is what is measured or assessed during the process of intervention, and this is the variable of outcome that matters. As has been briefly discussed, the nature of pathology in the elderly—that is, the target of change—is a complex biopsychosocial issue. Crippling depression, isolation and withdrawal, lack of social competence, agitated manifestations of serious distress, etc., are all clearly forms of dysfunction and amenable to psychological intervention. But beyond the agreed-upon forms of psychological disturbance, other questions emerge for which there are no answers at present. Is there a continuity of pathology across the life span? A position held by many gerontologists, and supported by clinical experience at least, is that an intact and "healthy" personality early in life augurs well for adjustment in old age and that the elderly who do become dysfunctional manifested forms of dysfunction earlier in life. However, research from a variety of sources (Greer, Pettingale, & Morris, 1979; Tobin & Lieberman, 1976) suggest that, for example, paranoia and aggression have survival value in late life and can therefore not simply be labeled as maladaptive. If, in fact, this association proves to be valid, it would be important to consider mediating mechanisms on a biochemical level between affect and physical status. It has been suggested (Derogatis, Abeloff, & Melisaratos, 1979) that both the endocrine and the immune systems are responsive to psychosocial factors, and links between survivorship and individual response in the face of stress need to be carefully considered.

Related to the question of continuity is its inverse: Are there unique forms of disorder that arise only late in life (aside from organically based dysfunction)? For example, does the inevitable experience of bereavement, loss, and physical illness at the end of life create a unique form of pathology (reactive, yet intransigent) in terms of content and symptoms? Is there something unique about these losses for those in the later decades of their life? If the meaning, manifestation, and course of at least some forms of depression differ for older patients, then target goals and related outcome measures must clearly reflect that difference.

Obviously, we cannot talk about outcome apart from process. Are therapy processes such as life review and insight, which may terminate in either personal integrity or despair, unique to the elderly? Certainly, depth analysis involves, for example, "life review," no matter the age of the patient. Is there a unique quality—other than a longer life to review and hence a larger store of memories—to the process in the old? Personality theorists such as Jung and Erikson posit such a tendency in the aging human, but there is little systematically gathered evidence for its presence, necessity, or unique qualities. Until that is determined, valid and reliable measures of life-review occurrence and effects cannot be developed.

Certainly there is no dispute regarding the unique quality of the therapist–patient relationship in treating the old. The therapist is typically young enough to be the elder's child. A frequent assumption is that this

Table 3-1 Suggested Measures to Evaluate Psychotherapy Outcome With Older Patients

Domains change	Vantage point			
	Self	Therapist	Independent evaluator	Relative
Predominantly focused on symptomatology	**Symptoms** Hopkins Symptom Check List (Derogatis et al., 1974)	Face sheet	Psychiatric Status Schedule (Spitzer et al., 1970)	
	Functional capacity Activities of daily living (Lawton & Brody, 1969)			Activities of daily living
	Idiographic goals Goal Attainment Scale (Kiresuk & Sherman, 1968)	Goal Attainment		Goal Attainment Scale
Predominantly focused on adjustment	**Life satisfaction and life review** Life Satisfaction Index (Neugarten et al., 1961) Affect balance (Bradburn, 1969) Self esteem (Rosenberg, 1979) Developmental task accomplishment (Wolk & Telleen, 1976)			Personal Adjustment and Role Skills Scale (Ellsworth, 1975)
	Sense of control Desired Control Measure (Ziegler & Reid, 1979)			
	Coping strategies Geriatric Coping Scale (Quayhagen & Chiriboga, 1976) Behavioral attributes of psychosocial competence (Tyler, 1978)			
	Person–environment fit Environmental Perception, Preference, and Importance Scales (Nehrke et al., 1979)			

Note. The framework for this table is derived from Waskow and Parloff (1975) and from Gatz (1978).

state elicits conflicts in both participants. Whether one wants to couch conflict in psychoanalytic terms and discuss transference and countertransference issues, or whether one wants to speak of the generalization of role-reversal conflicts with one's own parents to the therapy exchange, special qualities inherent in this interaction must exist. Hence the crucial need to study these relationship variables systematically. What parameters make a difference? Does the same sex in patient and therapist mitigate the conflict or enhance it? Does the intergenerational conflict, whatever its nature, disappear when patient and therapist are of a different race, for example? Is there a critical age range for both participants in which these conflicts are maximal?

The design of psychotherapy outcome studies must take into account the types of issues raised in this chapter. For example, Table 3-1 uses a framework developed by Waskow and Parloff (1975) and proposes a set of measures for evaluating outcome with older adults. The measures (a) encompass the viewpoints of the client, the therapist, and "society" (Gomes-Schwartz, Hadley, & Strupp, 1978); (b) encompass both symptomatology and social role functioning, reflecting internal states as well as behaviors; (c) take into account both nomothetic and idiographic considerations (Lieberman & Bond, 1978); and (d) include measures used with other age groups as well as measures of issues unique to older adults. In designing a study, one would want to draw selectively from the table and include meaures of cognitive and medical aspects as appropriate (again, see Chapter 2 of this book for fuller treatment of assessment approaches with this population).

Hoyer (1978) has argued for the use of single-subject designs on the grounds that the wide range of intra-individual and interindividual variability found in older adults may otherwise mask individual change. Instead of an exclusive focus on between-group designs, he suggested the use of approaches such as Markov chain analysis (Gottman & Notarius, 1978) to analyze the process and outcome of therapy for single patient–therapist pairs.

A final note concerning outcome measurement is related to negative outcome or nonsignificant change. The design of outcome studies and measures used must clearly allow for possible negative outcome (Bergin & Suinn, 1975) as well as for the reliable measurement of rate of decline. For older adults, especially those manifesting cortical impairments, the appropriate goal of therapy may be to arrest or slow down decline.

In summary, although many writers have suggested that little or no progress has been made in understanding the effects of psychological treatment on the elderly, it is obvious that some real progress has been made. For example, we know that reactive depression in the elderly living in the community is responsive to cognitive interventions. We know that control is an important variable for inpatients, and we know something about person–environment parameters. But there is a lot that we do not know about specific change mechanisms, about the long-term effectiveness of interventions, and about pharmacological compared to psychosocial approaches. We hope that by the end of the 1980s the substance of what is known will be even more impressive.

REFERENCES

Agate, J. Care of the dying in geriatric departments. *Lancet*, 1973, *17*, 365–366.

Atchley, R. Selected social and psychological differences between men and women in later life. *Journal of Gerontology*, 1976, *31*, 204–22.

Barnes, J. Effects of reality orientation classroom on memory loss, confusion, and disorientation in geriatric patients. *Gerontologist*, 1974, *14*, 138–142.

Barrett, C. Effectiveness of widow's groups in facilitating change. *Journal of Consulting and Clinical Psychology*, 1978, *46*, 20–31.

Barton, E. *Apparent staff reinforcement contingencies for nursing home resident behavior*. Paper presented at the meeting of the American Psychological Association, Toronto, Ontario, Canada, 1978.

Beck, A. *Depression: Causes and treatment*. Philadelphia: University of Pennsylvania Press, 1977.

Beck, A. *Cognitive therapy and the emotional disorders*. New York: International Universities Press, 1976.

Bergin, A., & Suinn, R. M. Individual psychotherapy and behavior therapy. In M. R. Rosenzweig & L. W. Porter (Eds.), *Annual Review of Psychology* (Vol. 26). Palo Alto, Calif.: Annual Reviews, 1975.

Bergman, S., & Amir, M. Crime and delinquency among the aged in Israel. *Geriatrics*, 1973, *28*, 149–157.

Blythe, R. *The view in winter*. New York: Harcourt Brace Jovanovich, 1979.

Boylin, W., Gordon, S., & Nehrke, M. Reminiscing and ego integrity in institutionalized elderly males. *Gerontologist*, 1976, *16*, 118–124.

Bradburn, N. M. *The structure of psychological well-being*. Chicago: Aldine, 1969.

Bradshaw, B., Vonderhaan, W., Keeney, V., Tyler, L., & Harris, S. Community-based residential care for the minimally impaired elderly: A survey analysis. *Journal of the American Geriatric Society*, 1976, *24*, 423–429.

Brink, T. *Geriatric psychotherapy*. New York: Human Sciences Press, 1979.

Brody, E., Kleban, M., Lawton, M., & Moss, J. A longitudinal look at excess disabilities in the mentally impaired aged. *Journal of Gerontology*, 1974, *29*, 79–84.

Brody, E., Kleban, M., Lawton, M., & Silverman, H. Excess disabilities of mentally impaired aged: Impact of individualized treatment. *Gerontologist*, 1971, *11*, 124–133.

Bromley, D. *The psychology of human aging*. Baltimore: Penguin, 1966.

Brook, P., Degun, G., & Mather, M. Reality orientation, a therapy for psychogeriatric patients: A controlled study. *British Journal of Psychiatry*, 1975, *127*, 42–45.

Burkhauser, R. Are women treated fairly in today's social security system? *Gerontologist*, 1979, *19*, 242–249.

Butler, R., Gertman, J., Oberlander, P., & Schindler, L. Self-care, self-help, and the elderly. *International Journal of Aging and Human Development*, 1979–80, *10*, 95–119.

Butler, R., & Lewis, M. *Aging and mental health*. St. Louis: C. V. Mosby, 1977.

Cassell, E. Learning to die. *Bulletin of the New York Academy of Medicine*, 1973, *49*, 1110.

Cautela, J., & Mansfield, L. A behavioral approach to geriatrics. In W. Gentry (Ed.), *Geropsychology: A model of training and clinical service*. Cambridge, Mass.: Ballinger, 1977.

Chien, C., Stotsky, B., & Cole, J. Psychiatric treatment for nursing home patients: Drug, alcohol, and milieu. *American Journal of Psychiatry*, 1973, *130*, 543–548.

Citrin, R., & Dixon, D. Reality orientation: A milieu therapy in an institution for the aged. *Gerontologist*, 1977, *17*, 39–43.

Cluff, P., & Campbell, W. The social corridor: An environmental and behavioral evaluation. *Gerontologist*, 1975, *15*, 516–523.

Committee on Medicine in Society. Statement on measures to prolong life. *Bulletin of the New York Academy of Medicine*, 1973, *49*, 349–351.

Cornbleth, T. Effects of a protected hospital ward area on wandering and nonwandering geriatric patients. *Journal of Gerontology*, 1977, *32*, 573–577.

Covert, A., Rodrigues, T., & Solomon, K. The use of mechanical and chemical restraints in nursing homes. *Journal of the American Geriatric Society*, 1977, *25*, 85–89.

Datan, N. *The lost cause: The aging woman in American feminism*. Invited address presented at the Women's Studies Program, Indiana University, Bloomington, October 1977.

Derogatis, L., Abeloff, M., & Melisaratos, N. Psychological coping mechanisms and survival time in metastatic breast cancer. *Journal of the American Medical Association*, 1979, *242*, 1504–1508.

Derogatis, L., Lipman, R., Rickels, K., Uhlenhuth, E., & Covi, L. The Hopkins Symptom Checklist (HSCL). In P. Pichot (Ed.), *Psychological measurements in psychopharmacology*. Basel: S. Karger, 1974.

Dohrenwend, B., & Dohrenwend, B. Social and cultural influences on psychopathology. *Annual Review of Psychology*, 1974, *15*, 417–454.

Eisdorfer, C., & Cohen, D. The cognitively impaired elderly: Differential diagnosis. In M. Storandt, J. Siegler, & M. Elias (Eds.), *The clinical psychology of aging*. New York: Plenum Press, 1978.

Eisdorfer, C., & Fann, W. (Eds.). *Psychopharmacology and aging*. New York: Plenum Press, 1976.

Eisdorfer, C., & Stotsky, B. Intervention, treatment, and rehabilitation of psychiatric disorders. In J. Birren & K. Schaie (Eds.), *Handbook of aging and human development*. New York: Van Nostrand Reinhold, 1977.

Ellsworth, R. Consumer feedback in measuring the effectiveness of mental health programs. In M. Guttentag & E. Struening (Eds.), *Handbook of evaluation research* (Vol. 2). Beverly Hills, Calif.: Sage Publications, 1975.

Engel, G. L. The need for a new medical model: A challenge for biomedicine. *Science*, 1977, *196*, 129–136.

Epstein, L. Symposium on age differentiation in depressive illness: Depression in the elderly. *Journal of Gerontology*, 1976, *31*, 278–282.

Ernst, P., Beran, B., Safford, F., & Kleinhauz, M. Isolation and the symptoms of chronic brain syndrome. *Gerontologist*, 1978, *18*, 468–474.

Fordyce, W., Fowler, R., Lehmann, J., & DeLateur, B. Operant conditioning in the treatment of chronic pain. *Archives of Physical Medicine and Rehabilitation*, 1973, *54*, 399–408.

Fox, J. Effects of retirement and former work life on women's adaptation in old age. *Journal of Gerontology*, 1977, *32*, 196–202.

Friedel, R. Pharmacokinetics of psychotherapeutic agents in aged patients. In C. Eisdorfer & R. Friedel (Eds.), *Cognitive and emotional disturbance in the elderly*. Chicago: Yearbook Medical Publishers, 1977.

Gallagher, P. *Comparative effectiveness of group psychotherapies for the reduction of depression in elderly outpatients*. Paper presented at the meeting of the American Psychological Association, New York, August 1979.

Garfield, S. Research on client variables in psychotherapy. In S. Garfield & A. Bergin (Eds.), *Handbook of psychology and behavior change* (2nd ed.). New York: Wiley, 1978.

Garfield, S., & Bergin, A. (Eds.). *Handbook of psychotherapy and behavior change: An empirical analysis* (2nd ed.). New York: Wiley, 1978.

Garfield, C., & Clark, R. A community model of psychosocial support for patients and families facing life-threatening illness: The Shanti project. In C. Garfield (Ed.), *Psychosocial care of the dying patient*. New York: McGraw-Hill, 1978.

Garfinkel, A. The reluctant therapist. *Gerontologist*, 1975, *15*, 138–141.

Garrison, J., & Howe, J. Community intervention with the elderly: A social network approach. *Journal of the American Geriatric Society*, 1976, *24*, 329–333.

Gartner, A., & Riessman, T. *Self-help in the human services*. San Francisco: Jossey-Bass, 1977.

Gatz, M. *Measures of change used to assess psychotherapy with older adults*. Paper presented at the annual meeting of the Gerontological Society, Dallas, Texas, November 1978.

Gatz, M., Siegler, I., & Dibner, S. Individual and community: Normative conflicts in the development of a new therapeutic community. *International Journal of Aging and Human Development*, 1979–80, *10*, 249–263.

Gershon, S., & Raskin, A. *Genesis and treatment of psychologic disorders in the elderly.* New York: Raven Press, 1975.

Glick, F., Weiss, R., & Parkes, C. *The first year of bereavement.* New York: Wiley, 1974.

Goldfarb, A. Institutional care of the aged. In E. Busse & E. Pfeiffer (Eds.), *Behavior and adaptation in late life.* Boston: Little, Brown, 1969.

Goldstein, S. A critical appraisal of milieu therapy in a geriatric day hospital. *Journal of the American Geriatric Society*, 1971, *8*, 693–699.

Gomes-Schwartz, B., Hadley, S., & Strupp, H. Individual psychotherapy and behavior therapy. In M. R. Rosenzweig & L. W. Porter (Eds.), *Annual Review of Psychology* (Vol. 29). Palo Alto, Calif.: Annual Reviews, 1978.

Gottesman, L., Quarterman, C., & Cohn, G. Psychosocial treatment of the aged. In C. Eisdorfer & M. P. Lawton (Eds.), *The psychology of adult development and aging.* Washington, D.C.: American Psychological Association, 1973.

Gottman, J., & Notarius, C. Sequential analysis of observational data using Markov chains. In T. R. Kratochwill (Ed.), *Single subject research: Strategies for evaluating change.* New York: Academic Press, 1978.

Greer, S., Pettingale, K., & Morris, T. Psychological response to breast cancer: Effect on outcome. *Lancet*, 1979, 785–787.

Gutmann, D. *A survey of drug-taking behavior of the elderly* (National Institute on Drug Abuse, Services Research Administrative Report). Washington, D.C.: National Institute on Drug Abuse, 1977.

Hendricks, J., & Hendricks, C. *Aging in mass society.* Cambridge, Mass.: Winthrop Publishers, 1977.

Herr, J., & Weakland, J. *Counseling elders and their families.* New York: Springer, 1979.

Holden, K. The inequitable distribution of OASDI benefits among homemakers. *Gerontologist*, 1979, *19*, 250–256.

Howard, J., Strong, K., Strong, K., & String, H. Medication procedures in a nursing home: Abuse of PRN orders. *Journal of the American Geriatric Society*, 1977, *25*, 83–84.

Hoyer, W. *Design considerations in the assessment of psychotherapy with the elderly.* Paper presented at the meeting of the Gerontological Society, Dallas, Texas, November 1978.

Hoyer, W., Kafer, R., Simpson, S., & Hoyer, F. Reinstatement of verbal behavior in elderly mental patients using operant procedures. *Gerontologist*, 1974, *14*, 149–152.

Ingersoll, B., & Silverman, A. Comparative group psychotherapy for the aged. *Gerontologist*, 1978, *18*, 201–206.

Ingram, D., & Barry, J. National statistics on deaths in nursing homes. *Gerontologist*, 1977, *17*, 303–308.

Jackson, J. Black aged: In quest of the phoenix. In *Triple jeopardy: Myth or reality?* Washington, D.C.: National Council on Aging, 1972.

Kahn, R., & Zarit, S. Evaluation of mental health programs for the aged. In P. Davidson, F. Clark, & L. Hamerlynck (Eds.), *Evaluation of behavioral programs in community, residential and school settings.* Champaign, Ill.: Research Press, 1974.

Kalish, R. A little myth is a dangerous thing: Research in the service of the dying. In C. Garfield (Ed.), *Psychosocial care of the dying.* New York: McGraw-Hill, 1978.

Kapnick, P. Organic treatment of the elderly. In M. Storandt, I. Siegler, & M. Elias (Eds.), *The clinical psychology of aging.* New York: Plenum Press, 1978.

Kasl, S. Physical and mental health effects of involuntary relocation and institutionalization on the elderly: A review. *American Journal of Public Health*, 1972, *62*, 377–380.

Kastenbaum, R. The reluctant therapist. In R. Kastenbaum (Ed.), *New thoughts on old age.* New York: Springer, 1964.

Kastenbaum, R. Personality theory, therapeutic approaches, and the elderly client. In M. Storandt, I. Siegler, & M. Elias (Eds.), *The clinical psychology of aging.* New York: Plenum Press, 1978.

Kastenbaum, R., & Candy, S. The four per cent fallacy: A methodological and empirical critique of extended care facility population statistics. *International Journal of Aging and Human Development*, 1973, *4*, 15–21.

Kastenbaum, R., & Slater, P. Effects of wine on the interpersonal behavior of geriatric patients: An exploratory subject. In R. Kastenbaum (Ed.), *New thoughts on old age.* New York: Springer, 1964.

Keller, J., & Croake, J. Effects of a program in rational thinking on anxieties in older persons. *Journal of Counseling Psychology*, 1975, *22*, 54–57.

Kelly, G. *The psychology of personal constructs.* New York: Norton, 1955.

Kent, E. Role of admission stress in adaptation of older persons in institutions. *Geriatrics*, 1963, *18*, 133–136.

Kiresuk, T., & Sherman, R. Goal-attainment scaling: A general method for evaluating comprehensive community mental health programs. *Community Mental Health Journal*, 1968, *4*, 443–453.

Knight, R. Psychotherapy and behavior change with the non-institutionalized aged. *International Journal of Aging and Human Development*, 1978–79, *9*, 221–236.

Kucharski, L., White, R., & Schratz, M. Age bias, referral for psychological assistance and the private physician. *Journal of Gerontology*, 1979, *34*, 423–428.

Langner, T. A twenty-two item screening score of psychiatric symptoms indicating impairment. *Journal of Health and Human Behavior*, 1962, *3*, 269–276.

Lawton, M. Assessing the competence of older people. In D. Kent, R. Kastenbaum, & S. Sherwood (Eds.), *Research planning and action for the elderly.* New York: Behavioral Publications, 1972.

Lawton, M. P., & Brody, E. M. Assessment of older people: Self-maintenance and instrumental activities of daily living. *Gerontologist*, 1969, *9*, 179–186.

Lerner, B. *Therapy in the ghetto.* Baltimore: Johns Hopkins University Press, 1972.

Lesnoff-Caravaglia, G. The 5 per cent fallacy. *International*

Journal of Aging and Human Development, 1978–79, *9*, 187–192.

Levy, L. Self-help groups: Types and psychological processes. *Journal of Applied Behavioral Science*, 1976, *12*, 310–322.

Levy, S. *Psychiatric distress in the disabled and the non-disabled: The demoralization syndrome.* Paper presented at the meeting of the American Statistical Association, Washington, D.C., August 1979.

Levy, S. The adjustment of the older women: Effects of chronic ill health and attitudes toward retirement. *International Journal of Aging and Human Development*, in press.

Lewis, C. Reminiscing and self-concept in old age. *Journal of Gerontology*, 1971, *26*, 240–243.

Libow, L. Senile dementia and "pseudosenility": Clinical diagnosis. In C. Eisdorfer & R. Freidel (Eds.), *Cognitive and emotional disturbance in the elderly: Clinical issues.* Chicago: Yearbook Medical Publishers, 1977.

Lieberman, M. *Methodological issues in the evaluation of psychotherapy with older adults.* Paper presented at the meeting of the Gerontological Society, Dallas, Texas, November 1978.

Lieberman, M., & Bond, G. Self-help groups: Problems of measuring outcome. *Small Group Behavior*, 1978, *9*, 211–241.

Lindsley, O. Geriatric behavioral prosthetics. In R. Kastenbaum (Ed.), *New thoughts on old age.* New York: Springer, 1964.

Lipman, A., & Slater, R. Status and spatial appropriation in eight homes for old people. *Gerontologist*, 1977, *17*, 250–255.

Lipton, M. Age differentiation in depression: Biochemical aspects. *Journal of Gerontology*, 1976, *31*, 293–299.

Livson, F. Patterns of personality development in middle-aged women: A longitudinal study. *International Journal of Aging and Human Development*, 1976, *7*, 107–116.

Lowenthal, M., Thurnher, M., & Chiriboga, D. *Four stages of life.* San Francisco: Jossey-Bass, 1976.

Lubinski, R. Why so little interest in whether or not old people talk: A review of recent research on verbal communication among the elderly. *International Journal of Aging and Human Development*, 1978–79, *9*, 237–245.

McDonald, C. Clinical heterogeneity in senile dementia. *British Journal of Psychiatry*, 1969, *115*, 267–271.

Mechanic, D. Social structure and personal adaptation: Some neglected dimensions. In G. Coelho, D. Hamburg, & J. Adams (Eds.), *Coping and adaptation.* New York: Basic Books, 1974.

Meerloo, J. Psychotherapy with the aged. *Nederlands Tijdschrift voor Gerontologie*, 1971, *2*, 160–169.

Meichenbaum, D. *Cognitive-behavior modification.* New York: Plenum Press, 1977.

Mendlewicz, J. The age factor in depressive illness: Some genetic considerations. *Journal of Gerontology*, 1976, *31*, 300–303.

Miller, M. Decision-making in the death process of the ill aged. *Geriatrics*, 1971, *26*, 105–116.

Miller, M. Iatrogenic and neurisgenic effects of prolonged immobilization of the ill aged. *Journal of the American Geriatrics Society*, 1975, *23*, 360–369.

Miller, M. Geriatric suicide: The Arizona study. *Gerontologist*, 1978, *18*, 488–495.

Mishara, B. Geriatric patients in token economy and milieu treatments. *Journal of Consulting and Clinical Psychology*, 1978, *46*, 1340–1348.

Mishara, B., Kastenbaum, R., Baker, F., & Patterson, R. Alcohol effects in old age: An experimental investigation. *Social Science Medicine*, 1975, *19*, 535–547.

Mishara, B., Robertson, B., & Kastenbaum, R. Self-injurious behavior in the elderly. *Gerontologist*, 1973, *13*, 311–314.

Moos, R., Gauvain, M., Lemke, S., Wax, W., & Mehren, B. Assessing the social environments of sheltered care settings. *Gerontologist*, 1979, *19*, 74–82.

Moran, J. A. *The effects of insight-oriented group therapy and task-oriented group therapy on the coping style and life satisfaction of nursing home elderly.* Unpublished doctoral dissertation, University of Maryland, 1978.

Morgan, L. A re-examination of widowhood and morale. *Journal of Gerontology*, 1976, *31*, 687–695.

Morrison, M. Rehabilitation of the elderly patient. *Physiotherapy*, 1969, *55*, 190–197.

Nahemow, L. Discussion. In M. Storandt (Chair), *Methodological issues in the evaluation of psychotherapy with older adults.* Symposium presented at meeting of the Gerontological Society, Dallas, Texas, 1978.

Nehrke, M. F., Morganti, J. B., Whitbourne, S. K., Hulicka, I. M., Turner, R. R., & Cohen, S. H. *An empirical test of a person-environment congruence model: Cross validation of the EPPIS.* Paper presented at the meeting of the Gerontological Society, Washington, D.C., 1979.

Neugarten, B. L., Havighurst, R. J., & Tobin, S. S. The measurement of life satisfaction. *Journal of Gerontology*, 1961, *16*, 134–143.

Newman, E., & Sherman, S. Foster-family care for the elderly: Surrogate family or mini-institution? *International Journal of Aging and Human Development*, 1979–80, *10*, 165–177.

Noyes, R., Jochimsen, P., & Travis, T. The changing attitudes of physicians toward prolonging life. *Journal of the American Geriatric Society*, 1977, *25*, 470–474.

Orlinsky, D. E., & Howard, K. I. The relation of process to outcome in psychotherapy. In S. L. Garfield & A. E. Bergin (Eds.), *Handbook of psychotherapy and behavior change: An empirical analysis* (2nd ed.). New York: Wiley, 1978.

Pascarelli, E., & Fischer, W. Drug dependence in the elderly. *International Journal of Aging and Human Development*, 1974, *5*, 347–356.

Quayhagen, M., & Chiriboga, D. A. *Geriatric coping scale applied to patients in convalescent hospitals.* Paper presented at meeting of the Gerontological Society, New York, 1976.

Richards, W., & Thorpe, G. Behavioral approaches to the problems of later life. In M. Storandt, I. Siegler, & M. Elias (Eds.), *The clinical psychology of aging.* New York: Plenum Press, 1978.

Rodstein, M., Savitsky, E., & Starkman, R. Initial adjustment to a long-term care institution: Medical and behavioral aspects. *Journal of the American Geriatrics Society*, 1976, *24*, 65–71.

Romaniuk, M. *The function of reminiscence for older adults.* Paper presented at the meeting of the American Psychological Association, New York, September 1979.

Rosen, J., & Wiens, A. Changes in medical problems and use of medical services following psychological intervention. *American Psychologist*, 1979, *34*, 420–431.

Rosenberg, M. *Conceiving the self.* New York: Basic Books, 1979.

Ross, C. Geriatrics and the elderly woman. *Journal of the American Geriatrics Society.* 1974, *22*, 230–239.

Rowland, K. Environmental events predicting death for the elderly. *Psychological Bulletin*, 1977, *84*, 349–372.

Safirstein, S. Psychotherapy for geriatric patients. *New York State Journal of Medicine*, 1972, *72*, 2743–2748.

Saunders, C. The need for in-patient care for the patient with terminal cancer. *Middlesex Hospital Journal*, 1973, *72*, 1–6.

Schuckit, M., & Miller, P. Alcoholism in elderly men: A survey of a general medical ward. *Annals of New York Academy of Sciences*, 1975, *273*, 551–571.

Schultz, R. The effects of control and predictability on the physical and psychological well-being of the institutionalized aged. *Journal of Personality and Social Psychology*, 1976, *33*, 563–573.

Schultz, R., & Hanusa, B. Long-term effects of control and predictability-enhancing interventions: Findings and ethical issues. *Journal of Personality and Social Psychology*, 1978, *36*, 1194–1201.

Schwartz, G., & Weiss, S. Behavioral medicine revisited: An amended definition. *Journal of Behavioral Medicine*, 1978, *1*, 249–251.

Seligman, M. *Helplessness on depression, development, and death.* San Francisco: W. H. Freeman, 1975.

Settin, J. Some thoughts about diseases presenting as senility. *Gerontologist*, 1978, *18*, 71–72.

Settin, J. *Client age, gender and class as determinants of clinician's perceptions: A study of labeling bias.* Unpublished abstract, 1979.

Shanas, E. Health status of older people: Cross-national implications. *American Journal of Public Health*, 1974, *3*, 261–264.

Shapiro, A. A pilot program in music therapy with residents of a home for the aged. *Gerontologist*, 1969, *9*, 128–133.

Sherwood, S. Sociology of food and eating: Implications for action for the elderly. *American Journal of Clinical Nutrition*, 1973, *26*, 1108–1110.

Sherwood, S. (Ed.), *Long-term care.* New York: Spectrum, 1975.

Smith, C. Use of drugs in the aged. *Johns Hopkins Medical Journal*, 1979, *145*, 61–64.

Smith, M., & Glass, G. Meta-analysis of psychotherapy outcome studies. *American Psychologist*, 1977, *32*, 752–760.

Sparacino, J. Individual psychotherapy with the aged: A selective review. *International Journal of Aging and Human Development*, 1978–79, *9*, 197–220.

Spitzer, R., Endicott, J., Fleiss, J., & Cohen, J. The psy-chiatric status schedule. *Archives of General Psychiatry*, 1970, *23*, 41–55.

Stare, F. Three score and ten plus more. *Journal of the American Geriatric Society*, 1977, *25*, 529–533.

Storandt, M. Other approaches to therapy. In M. Storandt, I. Siegler, & M. Elias (Eds.), *The clinical psychology of aging.* New York: Plenum Press, 1978.

Storandt, M., Siegler, I., & Elias, M. (Eds.), *The clinical psychology of aging.* New York: Plenum Press, 1978.

Strauss, A. *Negotiations: Varieties, contexts, processes, and social order.* San Francisco: Jossey-Bass, 1978.

Task Panel on Mental Health and American Families. General issues and adult years (No. 040-00-00-392). In President's Commission on Mental Health, *Report to the President of the President's Commission on Mental Health.* Washington, D.C.: U.S. Government Printing Office, 1978.

Thompson, L., & Gallagher, D. Psychotherapy for depression in the elderly (NIMH Grant 1R01 MH32157-01). Unpublished research, April 1979–March 1981.

Thralow, J., & Watson, C. Remotivation for geriatric patients using elementary school students. *American Journal of Occupational Therapy*, 1974, *28*, 469–473.

Tobin, S., & Lieberman, M. *Last home for the aged: Critical implications of institutionalization.* San Francisco: Jossey-Bass, 1976.

Tyler, F. B. Individual psychosocial competence: A personality configuration. *Educational and Psychological Measurement*, 1978, *38*, 309–323.

Uhlenberg, P. Older women: The growing challenge to design constructive roles. *Journal of Gerontology*, 1979, *19*, 236–241.

U.S. Department of Health, Education, and Welfare, Public Health Service. *Health resources statistics: Health manpower and health facilities, 1974.* Washington, D.C.: Author, 1974.

U.S. Department of Health, Education, and Welfare, Public Health Service. *Special report on aging: 1979* (NIH Publication No. 79-1907). Washington, D.C.: Author, September 1979.

Wagner, A., & Lerner, S. Art therapy in the psychiatric hospital. *Journal of the American Geriatric Society*, 1968, *16*, 867–873.

Waskow, I., & Parloff, M. (Eds.) *Psychotherapy change measures.* Rockville, Md.: National Institute of Mental Health, 1975.

Weiner, H. *Psychology and human disease.* New York: Elsevier-North Holland, 1977.

Weiss, J. Suicide in the aged. In H. L. P. Resnik (Ed.), *Suicidal behaviors: Diagnosis and management.* Boston: Little, Brown, 1968.

Weissmann, M. *Depression in women: Progress and gaps in understanding treatment.* Paper presented at an NIMH-sponsored Conference on Women and Psychotherapy, Washington, D.C., March 1979.

Williams, S., Kriauciunas, R., & Rodriguez, A. Physical, mental, and social rehabilitation for elderly and infirm patients. *Hospital and Community Psychiatry*, 1970, *21*, 130–132.

Wolk, S., & Telleen, S. Psychological and social correlates of life satisfaction as a function of residential constraint. *Journal of Gerontology*, 1976, *31*, 89–98.

Woodson, R. Hospice care in terminal illness. In C. Garfield (Ed.), *Psychosocial care of the dying patient*. New York: McGraw-Hill, 1978.

Ziegler, M., & Reid, D. Correlates of locus of desired control in two samples of elderly persons: Community residents and institutionalized persons. *Journal of Consulting and Clinical Psychology*, 1979, *47*, 977–979.

Zung, W. A self-hating depression scale. *Archives of General Psychiatry*, 1965, *12*, 63–70.

SECTION
2

Neuropsychological Issues

Marilyn S. Albert, *Section Editor*

Introduction

The practice of neuropsychology includes three areas of activity: diagnosis, intervention (i.e., counseling and rehabilitation), and research. Since neuropsychology is a relatively young science, it is not surprising that its early stages of inquiry have been preoccupied with broad clinical issues, such as the following: What areas of the brain contribute to adequate language production? What functions are lateralized in the brain? What brain structures are essential for competent acquisition, storage, and retrieval of material? Progress in addressing these and other such questions has led to many practical applications of the knowledge gained. This is particularly reflected by the fact that a field of neuropsychological rehabilitation is beginning to emerge. The present chapter emphasizes the interrelations of such counseling and rehabilitation programs with advances in research and diagnosis and the implications of this process for the neuropsychology of aging. New directions in research are also discussed in order to indicate their ultimate relevance for the care of individual patients. The thorough investigation of brain-behavior relations in the elderly is not an abstract task without clinical relevance. Recent experience teaches us that such an endeavor may permit the development of intervention programs and may thereby affect the everyday life of aging individuals.

Interrelation of Research, Diagnosis, and Intervention

Information regarding the behavioral correlates of brain dysfunction has progressed to the point where this knowledge is now being put to practical use. Two representative programs from the area of neuropsychology illustrate the recent impact of research findings on rehabilitation techniques.

Aphasia

In the past the efficacy of speech therapy in aphasia (i.e., a disorder of language that is not secondary to disturbances in the mechanical process of articulation) has been unclear. Claims of success have been numerous, but actual proof has been limited. Nevertheless, investigators have continued to search for better treatment techniques, since the presence of aphasia among survivors of strokes severely reduces the possibility of adequate social adjustment in these patients. Neuropsychologists and aphasia therapists at several institutions have recently been attempting to develop methods of language retraining that are based on a careful analysis of the salient features of aphasic disorders. Melodic intonation therapy (Sparks, Helm, & Albert, 1974) represents one such attempt. This therapy program involves embedding short phrases and sentences in a simple, nonlinguistically loaded, melodic intonation pattern (i.e., a chant). As the aphasic patient improves, the melodic aspect of the program is phased out. The return of expressive language in the aphasic patients of the original study (Albert, Sparks, & Helm, 1973) was particularly striking because individuals with severe, long-standing, stable language deficits had been specifically selected for treatment.

Patients who had been unable to communicate through language were able to express themselves orally.

The theoretical foundation for this technique lay in the findings that the right hemisphere is dominant for melodic intonation (Milner, 1962). Albert et al. (1973) hypothesized that if melodic intonation could be attached to propositional language, the relative influence of the healthy right hemisphere on the bilateral contributions to language might be increased and therefore reduce the deleterious effects of the damaged left hemisphere. The contribution of research to intervention therapy, in this instance, is clear. Without the knowledge gained from a careful analysis of the neural mechanisms underlying human behavior, melodic intonation therapy might only have occurred serendipitously.

Closed Head Injury

A rehabilitation program designed for patients with closed head injuries (at Bar Ilan University, Ramat Gan, Israel) reflects the same interaction between research and therapeutic techniques. A careful analysis of the behavior of these patients (Gross, 1979) indicated that their most debilitating impairments were related to disturbances in attentional mechanisms. Tasks that required divided attention (either between two input sources or between input and holding or holding and responding), such as dichotic listening tasks, presented great obstacles to the brain-damaged subjects. They had difficulty focusing attention on the relevant details of a task so that organization could be imposed on incoming information. Their limited ability to perceive the critical dimensions of a situation thus restricted their ability to restructure their perceptions and thereby to evaluate an event or problem from more than one point of view.

Since these impairments were evident in both abstract neuropsychological tests and real-life situations, the rehabilitation program that was developed sought to retrain individuals through both means. Subjects were asked to perform tasks that required divided attention. For example, they were required to perform a visual letter-cancelation task while monitoring a series of auditory letters for a repeated letter. Initially patients tended to concentrate on one task while performance on the other deteriorated markedly. With practice, brain-damaged patients improved their ability to cope with both tasks simultaneously.

At the same time, group therapy sessions that involved role playing were conducted, which dealt with the impact of similar attentional deficits on everyday living. For example, the patient had to act as a mediator between two persons who had, for didactic purposes, contradictory points of view. In order to succeed in the role of mediator, the subject had to be able to listen to one person while thinking of the needs of another. This is an obvious lifelike example of a situation in which one must pay attention to two things simultaneously.

Related Clinical Issues

Given our increasingly detailed knowledge of brain-behavior relations and the possible implications of these for treatment as described above, neuropsychologists in the field of aging should not be content to investigate function in broad categories of people (e.g., impaired vs. unimpaired, organic vs. psychotic, acute vs. chronic), especially since recent biochemical studies indicate that there are distinctive neuroendocrine differences between subgroups of these people as well. In the field of mental illness, for example, genetic and pharmacological factors are becoming increasingly important in differentiating among this heterogeneous group of disorders. Recent studies point to the importance of catecholamines, particularly norepinephrine, in the pathogenesis of affective disorders (Kety, 1970). This is not the case for nonaffective disorders, such as schizophrenia. The increasing evidence for the heterogeneity of these and other illnesses with regard to symptomatology, etiology, and biochemical dysfunction makes imperative the precise diagnosis of patients who will be included in any investigation.

That is not to say that there is no great need for tests that can reliably make distinctions between broad categories of patients. There are clinical settings where large numbers of seriously impaired individuals need to be screened quickly. For this purpose, a short, easily administered, valid test of dysfunction is extremely useful. The Mental Status Questionnaire of Kahn, Goldfarb, Pollack, and Peck (1960), the Mini-Mental State questionnaire of Folstein, Folstein, and McHugh (1975), and the recently developed Neuropsychiatric Mental Status Examination of Eisdorfer, Cohen, and Keckich (1979) are examples of test instruments designed for this purpose.

Nevertheless, the enormous growth of evidence in the neurosciences regarding the specificity of function in the brain indicates that appropriate intervention techniques will be most successful if designed for specific subgroups of people. The neuropsychological data demonstrate that numerous psychological processes are served by anatomical "systems" in the brain. These processes may be vulnerable at a number of different points, some of which may be widely separated. Spoken language, for example, can be altered by damage to several cortical and subcortical areas. Such data were, in fact, used against the early localizationists. It is now apparent, however, that both lesion volume and lesion localization influence the specific pattern of impairment (Geschwind, 1965). The nature of the impairments will depend on either the particular part of the system that is damaged or the connections that have been disrupted, or both. Since each part contributes something characteristic to the whole, it is necessary to look carefully at the nature of the changes in order to understand them. This knowledge will, in turn, indicate which therapeutic techniques are likely to be effective.

Furthermore, it is essential for the development of such techniques that the multiple significance of task performance is appreciated. Impaired test performance may be the expression of a diversity of deficits. The analysis of the Tactual Performance Test (TPT) scores of elderly subjects in Chapter 5 demonstrates this point beautifully. Such multifactorial tasks (in which, for example, spatial memory, psychomotor ability, and visuospatial processing are all factors) need to be carefully examined in order to determine the impaired functions that are contributing to the observed behavior.

Even in tasks where fewer factors determine performance, it is important to be aware that a given solution can be arrived at by a variety of means. One must examine the process by which a given solution (correct or incorrect) is achieved in order to understand the underlying deficit. This notion has been summarized by numerous investigators but bears repeating.

A test response is not a score; scores, where applicable, are abstractions designed to facilitate intraindividual and interindividual comparisons and, as such, they are extremely useful in clinical testing. However, to reason or do research only in terms of scores or score patterns is to do violence to the nature of the raw material. The scores do not communicate the responses in full. (Shapiro, 1951)

The method the subject uses in tackling a problem will in general provide more information as to the character of a skill or of a psychological deficit than will the knowledge as to the subject's success or failure. (Elithorn, 1965)

If the focus is only on the final product and the quantitative score (i.e., the achievement rather than the process), valuable information may be lost and, in fact, we may even be misled. (Kaplan, in press)

Two examples from neuropsychological evaluations of healthy and brain-damaged persons serve to illustrate these points.

Patients with alcoholic Korsakoff's syndrome (who are amnesic as a result of chronic alcohol abuse and thiamine deficiency) and patients with Huntington's Chorea (who have a genetically transmitted dementing disorder in which they undergo progressive motor and intellectual deterioration) are both impaired on short-term memory tasks. If the Korsakoff's and Huntington's patients are presented with three words (e.g., apple, pen, roof) and are then required to count backward from 100 by two's to prevent rehearsal, they will be impaired in the recall of the three words after only 9 or 18 seconds of such counting activity. However, the underlying deficits that contribute to this task performance in the two groups of patients appear to be different (Butters, 1979). Manipulation of proactive interference, cues, and rehearsal time can improve the Korsakoff's patients' performance on this distractor task, but such changes in the experimental conditions have virtually no effect on the Huntington's patients' ability to recall materials. If one were to examine only the final test score, one might conclude that the memory disturbance in these subjects was the same when, in fact, only the test scores were equivalent.

Similarly, aphasic patients and healthy elderly subjects both show impairments on tests of naming to confrontation, when the stimulus items are line drawings of objects (Goodglass, in press). Preliminary data indicate that the errors of the elderly may result from misperceptions of the stimuli (Goodglass, in press; Thomas, Fozard, & Waugh, 1977), whereas the anomia of the aphasic patient emanates from an inability to find the appropriate target word for the object depicted. The naming score of an aphasic patient with a lesion in the left hemisphere may thus be identical to the score achieved by an elderly "normal" person, but the quality and source of the errors are very different. This again demonstrates the misunderstanding that might arise if only achievement scores are considered in a neuropsychological evaluation.

Finally, neuropsychological investigations of the elderly should attempt to ascertain not only the presence of dysfunction but the relative degree of disability, since this also has implications for treatment programs and support systems. Recent progress in the study of amnesic patients illustrates this point clearly. In the past, neuropsychological studies of mixed groups of amnesic patients were conducted because it was thought that amnesia was a unitary disorder. This was thought to be true despite amnesia's association with a number of etiologies (e.g., vascular, alcohol, viral, trauma) and brain sites (e.g., hippocampus, mammillary bodies, midline thalamus).

Recently, two sets of investigators have addressed this problem by comparing populations of alcoholic

Korsakoff's subjects and postencephalitic (i.e., herpes simplex encephalitis) patients (Albert, Butters, & Levin, in press; Lhermitte & Signoret, 1972). They report that a double dissociation exists between tests of anterograde and retrograde amnesia in these two groups of amnesic persons. The Korsakoff's patients have more severe short-term memory deficits but a less severe loss of remote memories than the postencephalitic subjects. Furthermore, these differences are reflected in the living situations that are necessary for these patients. Although the postencephalitic subjects are amnesic (as defined by their having a severe memory defect with no general intellectual decline), their short-term memory is sufficiently intact that they can write notes to remind themselves about tasks that need to be done. This enables some of them to live alone. One patient has, in fact, gone back to work as a secretary, even though her memory of events from the past does not extend beyond her late childhood. The alcoholic Korsakoff's patients, on the other hand, despite a significantly less severe loss of remote memory, must live in a protected environment, such as a nursing home, because of the severity of their short-term memory defect. Evidence for such double dissociations should be sought in studies of subgroups of impaired elderly persons for their theoretical, as well as practical, implications.

It is encouraging to see that attempts at remedial intervention therapy have recently begun in the field of aging (Birkhill & Schaie, 1975; Furry & Baltes, 1973; Labouvie-Vief & Gonda, 1976; Plemons, Willis, & Baltes, 1976; Sanders, Sterns, Smith, & Sanders, 1975). In order to be successful, such programs must derive direction from a thorough knowledge of the spared and impaired aspects of healthy and diseased elderly subjects. The nature of the deficits may preclude certain forms of therapy altogether or may make some methods appear more advantageous than others. If one is attempting to develop appropriate support systems for the elderly, it is imperative that the relative strengths and weaknesses of these individuals be understood so that the strengths can be exploited and maximized.

New Directions in Research

The technological advances of recent years have provided a multiplicity of sophisticated noninvasive methods for assessing brain function. These include electroencephalography (EEG), evoked potentials (EPs), event-related potentials (ERPs), topographic mapping and display of EP and EEG, regional cerebral blood flow (rCBF), computerized tomography (CT scans), and positron emission tomography. Since each of these techniques varies in temporal and geographical resolution, they supplement one another.

EPs and ERPs provide data at a molecular level. (See Chapter 4 for a discussion of these techniques in determining age-related change.) If such recordings are made over the entire surface of the skull, however, so much informaton is produced that it cannot be easily grasped and assimilated by visual inspection alone. Topographic mapping of EP and EEG data represents an attempt to translate these measurements of separate neural events into visual displays that communicate the more molar changing pattern of activation in the cortex. To date it has been used in the diagnosis of tumors (Duffy, Burchfiel, & Lombroso, 1979), in the diagnosis of brain lesions (Gotman, Gloor, & Roy, 1975), and in a study of dyslexic children (Duffy, Denckla, & Sandini, in press) and will shortly be employed in a study of healthy and dementing elderly subjects. Since rCBF reflects increased metabolic activity within a cortical region, it also yields valuable information about molar changes in geographically contiguous areas. However, it integrates these changes over a period of time (i.e., at present, rCBF can only measure an activity carried out for from 2 to 3 minutes in succession), whereas topographic mapping of EPs and EEGs records responses for closely spaced events. Thus, rCBF extracts phenomena that are characteristic over time for a given region but does not show changing patterns of activation from moment to moment. This may or may not be an advantage in the study of cognitive processes, since one might argue that cognition is, by nature, integrative and sustained. At the moment, it seems that both tools promise to reveal exciting and unexpected relations between brain function and behavior. (The January 1980 issue of *Brain and Language* is devoted to recent applications of the inhalation rCBF technique.)

CT scans provide a detailed, but static, picture of the brain which appears to complement the less detailed but more dynamic data provided by the mapping of brain electrical activity and rCBF. Since these scans are actually visualizations of brain density measurements that are stored in digital form, the advent of computer programs to evaluate these data directly represents exciting progress in a burgeoning field. Chapter 6 in this section describes these techniques in detail and their application to neuropsychological studies of the elderly.

The use of positron emission scanning in such investigations seems more remote. Although this scanning system provides complex images of localized metabolic activity (i.e., a combination of CT scans and rCBF), it still requires the injection of radioactive material. This may therefore prevent its application to large numbers of human subjects. In addition, the present scanners can measure only activity sustained for from 20 to 60 minutes, thereby limiting their application to many important phenomena of shorter duration. Nevertheless, it is virtually certain that technology will eliminate these shortcomings and that this technique will soon be used to study complex cognitive processes. As Feinberg et al. point out in Chapter 4, these technological advances present a great challenge to the ingenuity of neuropsychologists in their attempt to narrow the gap between behavior and neural events.

In order to get maximum benefit from the application of these tools to the study of the elderly, a number of obstacles need to be overcome. To begin with, any such study must be interdisciplinary in nature. The equipment and the professional expertise required obviously span several disciplines. At its best, the interaction of psychologists, neurologists, psychiatrists, internists, and statisticians can be mutually beneficial, conceptually and methodologically. Certain risks are inherent, however, in such a large-scale enterprise. Chapter 4 details many of these.

In addition, a broad neuropsychological battery that evaluates individual aspects of cognitive ability should be administered to large numbers of aging persons. This will permit investigators to assess the range of performance in older subjects, uncomplicated by the effects of disease. Such a battery should ideally be supplemented by tests that have concurrent validity (i.e., that measure performance in tasks of daily life dependent on the same abilities that are assessed by the test battery), since this should be the ultimate concern of the clinician and researcher alike. After all, it is possible that, compared to young and middle-aged subjects, elderly subjects may be impaired on neuropsychological tasks and still perform well daily activities that utilize these same abilities. The development of such tasks has already begun (e.g., Crook, Ferris, & McCarthy, 1979) and clearly needs to be continued.

It would also be beneficial to administer to these same subjects rating scales that evaluate such things as psychiatric status and mood. Few studies exist in which this has been done, and the relation is still unclear between neuropsychological test scores and the rating scales used so often in clinical settings.

Clinical Assessment

The greatest difficulty facing the clinician who wishes to assess neuropsychological function in the elderly is that most neuropsychological tests currently used with elderly subjects do not have adequate norms for individuals over 60 years of age. Since these tests were originally designed to differentiate between normal and pathological function in adults who were primarily between the ages of 20 and 60, it is not surprising that one cannot blindly apply them to aging subjects (See the data of Price, Fein, and Feinberg in Chapter 5 for an illustration of this problem). On the other hand, certain cognitive functions appear to be maintained with age (e.g., Digit Span Forward), and young adult norms may well be appropriate in many instances. At present, the clinician clearly has little choice but to use the current measures and to keep in mind the limitations of their application.

Several recent reviews discuss tests available for assessment of cognitive function and present current knowledge regarding the performance of the elderly (Albert & Kaplan, 1980; Eisdorfer & Cohen, 1978; Kramer & Jarvik, 1979). The ultimate selection of the tests to be used must, of course, depend on the purpose of the evaluation, the problems of the patient, and the constraints of time.

Conclusion

The coming decade offers much promise for the neuropsychological assessment of the elderly. A systematic and comprehensive analysis of cognition and related biological processes in aging persons, such as that described above and in the following chapters, should enable the researcher not only to document the presence or absence of impairment but also to understand the factors that contribute to it. A more detailed comprehension of the manner in which these impairments affect the individual should, in turn, aid in designing appropriate support systems for the rapidly increasing population of older persons.

REFERENCES

Albert, M. L., Sparks, R., & Helm, N. Melodic intonation therapy for aphasia. *Archives of Neurology*, 1973, *29*, 130–131.

Albert, M. S., & Kaplan, E. Organic implications of neuropsychological deficits in the elderly. In L. W. Poon, J. L. Fozard, L. S. Cermak, D. Arenberg, & L. W. Thompson (Eds.), *New directions in memory and aging: Proceedings of the George Talland Memorial Conference.* Hillsdale, N.J.: Erlbaum, 1980.

Albert, M. S., Butters, N., & Levin, J. Memory for remote events in chronic alcoholics and alcoholic Korsakoff patients. In H. Begleiter & B. Kissen (Eds.), *Alcohol intoxication and withdrawal*, New York: Plenum Press, in press.

Birkhill, W. R., & Schaie, K. W. The effect of differential reinforcement of cautiousness in intellectual performance among the elderly. *Journal of Gerontology*, 1975, *30*, 578–582.

Butters, N. Amnesic disorders. In K. M. Heilman & E. Valenstein (Eds.), *Clinical neuropsychology.* New York: Oxford University Press, 1979.

Crook, T., Ferris, S., & McCarthy, M. The misplaced objects task: A brief test for memory dysfunction in the aged. *Journal of the American Geriatrics Society*, 1979, *27*, 284–287.

Duffy, F. H., Burchfiel, J. L., & Lombroso, C. T. Brain electrical activity mapping (BEAM): A method of extending the clinical utility of EEG and evoked potential data. *Annals of Neurology*, 1979, *5*, 309–321.

Duffy, F. H., Denckla, M. B., & Sandini, G. Dyslexia: Regional differences in brain electrical activity by topographical mapping. *Annals of Neurology*, in press.

Eisdorfer, C., & Cohen, D. The cognitively impaired elderly: Differential diagnosis. In M. Storandt, I. Siegler, & M. Elias (Eds.), *The clinical psychology of aging.* New York: Plenum Press, 1978.

Eisdorfer, C., Cohen, D., & Keckich, W. *A Neuropsychiatric Mental Status Examination for the aged with dementing illness.* Paper presented at the meeting of the Gerontological Society, 1979.

Elithorn, A. Psychological tests. An objective approach to the problem of task difficulty. *Acta Neurologica Scandinavica*, 1965, Suppl. 13, 661–667.

Folstein, M. F., Folstein, S., & McHugh, P. R. "Mini-Mental State": A practical method for grading the cognitive state of patients for the clinician. *Journal of Psychiatric Research*, 1975, *12*, 189–198.

Furry, C. A., & Baltes, P. B. The effect of age differences in ability-extraneous performance variables on the assessment of intelligence in children, adults and the elderly. *Gerontology*, 1973, *28*, 73–80.

Geschwind, N. Disconnexion syndromes in animals and man. *Brain*, 1965, *88*, 237–294; 585–644.

Goodglass, H. Naming disorders in aging and aphasia. In L. K. Obler and M. L. Albert (Eds.), *Language and communication in the elderly.* Lexington, Mass.: D. C. Heath, 1980.

Gotman, J., Gloor, P., and Roy, W. F. A quantitative comparison of traditional reading of the EEG and interpretation of computer-extracted features in patients with supratentorial brain lesions. *Electroencephalography and Clinical Neurophysiology*, 1975, *38*, 623–639.

Gross, Y. *Cognitive rehabilitation.* Paper presented at the Boston VA Medical Center, July 1979.

Kahn, R. L., Goldfarb, A. I., Pollack, M., & Peck, A. Brief objective measures for the determination of mental status in the aged. *American Journal of Psychiatry*, 1960, *117*, 326–328.

Kaplan, E. Changes in cognitive style with aging. In L. K. Obler and M. L. Albert (Eds.), *Language and communication in the elderly.* Lexington, Mass.: D. C. Heath, 1980.

Kety, S. S. The biogenic amines in the central nervous system: Their possible roles in arousal, emotion and learning. In F. O. Schmitt (Ed.), *The Neurosciences: Second study program.* New York: Rockefeller University Press, 1970.

Kramer, N., & Jarvik, L. Assessment of intellectual change in the elderly. In P. Raskin & L. Jarvik (Eds.), *Psychiatric symptoms and cognitive loss in the elderly.* New York: Halstead Press, 1979.

Labouvie-Vief, G., & Gonda, J. N. Cognitive strategy training and intellectual performance in the elderly. *Journal of Gerontology*, 1976, *31*, 327–332.

Lhermitte, F., & Signoret, J. L. Analyse neuropsychologique et différenciation des syndromes amnésique. *Revue Neurologique*, 1972, *126*, 161–178.

Milner, B. Laterality effects in audition. In V. B. Mountcastle (Ed.), *Interhemispheric relations and cerebral dominance.* Baltimore: Johns Hopkins University Press, 1962.

Plemons, J. K., Willis, S. L., & Baltes, P. B. *Challenging the theory of fluid intelligence: A training approach.* Unpublished manuscript, College of Human Development, Pennsylvania State University, 1976.

Sanders, J. A. C., Sterns, H. L., Smith, M., & Sanders, R. E. Modification of concept identification performance in older adults. *Developmental Psychology*, 1975, *11*, 824–829.

Shapiro, M. B. Experimental studies of a perceptual anomaly. I: Initial experiments. *Journal of Mental Science*, 1951, *97*, 90–100.

Sparks, R., Helm, N., and Albert, M. L. Aphasia rehabilitation resulting from melodic intonation therapy. *Cortex*, 1974, *10*, 303–316.

Thomas, J. C., Fozard, J. L. and Waugh, N. C. Age-related differences in naming latency. *American Journal of Psychology*, 1977, *90*, 449–509.

Irwin Feinberg, George Fein, Leonard J. Price, Terry L. Jernigan, and Thomas C. Floyd

CHAPTER

4

Methodological and Conceptual Issues in the Study of Brain–Behavior Relations in the Elderly

There has been considerable recent progress in the development of noninvasive techniques for the study of human brain physiology and structure. Concurrent measurement of brain and behavioral variables in a defined group of elderly subjects is proposed as one method for evaluating age-related change, and an ongoing study of this nature is described. The practical and conceptual issues encountered include the selection and size of sample, the choice of biological and psychological measures, and the problems of statistical inference when many variables are studied in relatively few subjects.

The main goal of neuropsychology is to determine the effects of variations in the state of the brain on behavior, especially on those behaviors that reflect information-processing capacities. In the field of aging, this goal has both basic and clinical elements. On the level of basic science, the neuropsychologist attempts to measure the changes in information processing associated with age. On the clinical level, the neuropsychologist seeks to establish levels of information-processing skills required for (or correlated with) the ability to function adequately in society; stated more directly, the neuropsychologist attempts to devise tests that are diagnostic of senility.

Until quite recently, neuropsychologists concerned with the behavioral consequences of brain aging had

few measures by which this variable could itself be assessed directly. The clinical EEG shows relatively small quantitative changes with age: Several investigators have found that between the ages of 20 and 65 years, there occurs only about a 10% reduction in mean alpha frequency (see Feinberg, 1976). Direct measurement of cerebral blood flow (CBF) and oxygen consumption ($CMRO_2$) in human subjects became possible with the development of the Kety-Schmidt nitrous oxide method (Kety & Schmidt, 1948). However, this technique requires venous sampling from the jugular bulb and therefore could not be widely applied. Moreover, overall CBF and $CMRO_2$ showed virtually no change between young adulthood and healthy old age (Dastur, Lane, Hansen, et al., 1963), although both were significantly reduced in senile patients (Freyhan, Woodford, & Kety, 1951; Lassen, Feinberg, & Lane, 1960). Thus, neuropsychologists seeking to find relations between altered behavior and the brain changes produced by normal aging had only chronological age to use as an index of the changes.

This situation has changed dramatically over the

This research was supported by the Veterans Administration.

past two decades. A number of new techniques demonstrate large changes in brain variables as a function of age in cross-sectional studies. These include measures of sleep EEG, which, over the range from 20 to 65 years, change by an order from of from 20% to 150% (Feinberg, 1976). Some aspects of event-related potentials (ERPs), which can now be readily measured by computer averaging, also show substantial changes with age (Dustman & Beck, 1969) and have been said to distinguish between normal and senile groups (Gerson, John, Bartlett, & Koening, 1976).

The development of computed tomography (CT scans) permits, for the first time, noninvasive visualization of brain tissue. Elderly persons often (although by no means invariably) show evidence of increased fluid, usually indicative of brain atrophy, which can be quantified by computer as well as rated visually.

There have also been new developments in measurement of cerebral circulation and metabolism which stem directly from the principles worked out by Seymour Kety. Determination of CBF has been greatly simplified by external measurement of the clearance of a radioactive gas, xenon[133]. This permits estimates to be obtained noninvasively for specific brain regions and for grey and white matter separately (Obrist, Thompson, Wang, & Wilkinson, 1975). (The original Kety-Schmidt method provided only a weighted average for gray and white matter per 100 grams of brain tissue for both CBF and $CMRO_2$). Quite recently, a method has been developed to measure noninvasively the glucose utilization rate of specific brain regions. Positron emission tomography (PET) scans, which combine the principles of computed tomography with those of the deoxyglucose method of Sokoloff et al. (1977), now permit measurement of glucose metabolism noninvasively, in conscious subjects at rest or carrying out various mental operations (Phelps, 1977).

Thus, the neuropsychology of aging has moved from a condition of scarcity to an embarrassment of riches with respect to the availability of measures of brain physiology and structure that can be studied in relation to the changes in information-processing abilities that occur in normal and pathological aging. Existing techniques will doubtless be refined and supplemented as additional measures (perhaps reflecting in vivo biochemical and enzymatic states of the brain) are produced by a vigorous and fertile neuroscience. It seems clear that a major task of neuropsychology in the next decades will be to establish the functional implications of the brain changes associated with age that have now become measurable.

Such a contribution by neuropsychology is required for the understanding and practical application of these new brain measures. For example, although we can measure large changes in the sleep EEG with age, we do not know whether these changes are related to altered information-processing capacities and, if so, to which ones. Our present state of knowledge does not rule out the possibility that changes in sleep EEG reflect alteration in the metabolic state of the periphery or are secondary to brain changes not importantly related to information processing. We are even confronted with similar problems of interpretation with such apparently face-valid measures of brain integrity as computed axial tomography. As Jernigan et al. note in Chapter 6 of this book, we are not yet certain whether some of the milder degrees of apparent atrophy often found in the CT scans of the normal elderly actually reflect loss of brain tissue.

While neuropsychology must contribute to the understanding of these new biological measures of brain states, the converse should also be true: The availability of these measures can be expected to accelerate our psychological understanding and our ability to dissect the intellectual operations required for the performance of complex tasks. Thus, instead of simply studying cognition as a function of chronological age, we can study intellectual function in the elderly in relation to localized or diffuse atrophy, normal or diminished sleep spindles, normal or altered sleep cycle patterns, etc. By reducing the biological heterogeneity of our samples, we should increase our opportunity to detect correlations betwen specific brain changes on the one hand and specific cognitive functions on the other. Such data should allow us to design more effective methods of cognitive assessment.

In any investigation of brain and behavioral variables in the elderly, a number of methodologic, practical, and conceptual issues must be confronted. The decisions made on these issues will determine the conclusions that can be drawn; typically, the investigator must adopt strategies that are optimal for obtaining certain kinds of information at the expense of other data. Compromises may also be required between the demands of scientific rigor and practical constraints such as amounts of time and funding available. If the neuropsychological study of aging during the coming decade is to take full advantage of the technological advances in brain research, the implications of decisions regarding sample selection, size, and age must be thoroughly and explicitly considered. In the remainder of this chapter, we describe these and other general issues raised by an extensive multidisciplinary study of this sort.

Methodological and Conceptual Issues

The main goal of the study was to determine whether EEG sleep variables in the normal elderly are correlated with information-processing capacities. The underlying premise was not that cognitive function is *normally* related to sleep EEG patterns (i.e., such a relation would not be expected in young adults). Instead, it was hypothesized that cognitive impairment would be correlated with degree of abnormality (by young adult standards) of the EEG in the elderly. Even if significant correlations are observed between sleep EEG and cognitive measures, a causal relation cannot be assumed. The brain and behavioral variables could have been jointly affected by some third factor or factors. But if the two sets of variables have been measured with adequate validity and precision, failure to find significant correlations would argue strongly against the possibility that sleep processes, or other such variables, directly reflect or are causally involved in information processing. The same logic would apply to other brain-behavior variables.

In a cross-sectional study such as this, a major problem becomes immediately apparent; one cannot measure *decrement* in intellectual function directly. Instead, such decrement must be inferred from certain aspects of the current level of performance. It is sometimes overlooked that the same problems exist for biological measures. For example, the degree to which current measures of sleep EEG represent change from young adult levels in any individual is uncertain. Nevertheless, the magnitude of the changes in sleep from young adult levels found in most elderly subjects is so great as to suggest that a preponderant amount of this variance is produced by age.

Choice of Sample

In a group of elderly persons, one can reasonably assume that current performance on cognitive tests depends on several "traits," including original endowment (IQ), education, occupational experience, socioeconomic class (especially as it affects intellectual stimulation and availability of health care), health status, and degree of brain aging. A study aimed at determining the effects of brain aging on biopsychological measures should attempt to maximize the variance contributed by brain aging and to minimize other sources of variability. If the goal of the study is to determine the level of selected brain or behavioral measures in the entire elderly population, one must examine a representative cross-section of the aging community for health status, education, cultural background, and so forth. That approach would require an extremely large sample, which would be impractical for labor-intensive biological measures such as sleep studies.

Since our goal was to determine the effects of brain aging on biopsychological measures, we attempted to maximize the proportion of variance contributed by brain aging in our sample. To do this, we decided to study a group of retired elementary and high school teachers who were members of the California Retired Teachers Association (CRTA). This group was reasonably homogeneous in socioeconomic status, education, and lifetime vocational experience. But they nevertheless showed substantial variation, especially in the last two variables. Their educations ranged from the BA to the PhD degree. Actual teaching experience ranged from a lifetime spent in teaching kindergarten or the early elementary grades to teaching highly technical subjects in high school. Some teachers became full-time administrators as elementary and high-school principals. These differences were evident as the sample was recruited. It would not have been practical, however, to restrict the sample further, because it would have required a larger subject pool than was available.

Several "state" variables can also be expected to influence test results. Especially important, we believe, is degree of motivation. The unnatural aspects of the test situation for the average elderly individual have been discussed by numerous authors. Unfamiliar tasks and situations may make the subject feel uneasy and inadequate. The possible impact of these factors on the population selected for study should be evaluated so that the validity of the measures under investigation is not compromised by "state" variables of this sort.

In this regard, the selection of retired teachers seems, in retrospect, to have been inspired. They appeared to give their best performance through an extensive and sometimes arduous series of tests. Over a complex three-week test schedule, the 50 subjects tested to date never missed an appointment and were only rarely late. The reasons for this high level of motivation seemed to include the subjects' ability to understand thoroughly the goals of the study and their roles in achieving these goals; the long familiarity and acceptance by the subjects of the testing of mental abilities; a desire on the part of the subjects to acquit themselves well ("get good grades"); and last but not least, a desire to "do good works," that is, to make a useful contribution to society in their remaining years. We have found such idealism to be quite characteristic of the elderly.

Two other "state" variables, economic and medical "state," require mention. Elderly subjects may be under acute economic pressure and sometimes agree to participate in studies for which they are unmotivated solely to obtain the monetary compensation. This is always a problem with volunteers, especially those with low income. In our study, none of the subjects was experiencing serious economic pressure.

Medical status contributes to both "trait" and state.

One can include subjects with a variety of medical traits (i.e., ranging from those who are optimally healthy to those with chronic systemic degenerative diseases including diabetes, atherosclerosis, etc.). Including such a range of medical conditions enables the researcher to classify subjects as "optimally healthy" or "with systemic disease" as was done in the NIMH multidisciplinary study of aging (Birren, Butler, Greenhouse, Sokoloff, & Yarrow, 1963). Such a sample would permit an analysis of the effects of medical status on biopsychological measures. On the other hand, one generally wishes to exclude subjects experiencing acute changes in medical state (such as severe respiratory infections, uncontrolled diabetes, etc.) that might transiently affect performance. In the present study, we had intended to include subjects with chronic diseases. As it turned out, however, most subjects were optimally healthy and, in retrospect, it would have been better to eliminate the few with clearcut chronic systemic disease, since their number was insufficient to permit an analysis of the contribution of these conditions to the dependent variables.

In summary, we emerged with a white, middle-to-upper class sample of highly motivated volunteers who, as a group, were in remarkably good health. The psychometric performance of our subjects was in the superior range. There seems little doubt that the more impaired elderly members of the CRTA did not choose to volunteer for our study or else were eliminated during the initial medical screening.

Choice of Age Range

At least three main considerations may affect the choice of age range. First, one would choose to study subjects in an age range where a significant amount of brain aging could reasonably be presumed to have occurred. For many neurophysiological and anatomical measures there are unfortunately no clear guidelines on which to base such a decision. For example, some sleep EEG variables, such as Stage 4, show substantial age changes from young adulthood on; others, such as REM, show little change until extreme old age (Feinberg & Carlson, 1968). Senile plaques and neurofibrillary tangles become apparent in middle age though they do not become numerous until the sixth or seventh decade. Our choice was ultimately based on tradition and clinical judgment. We decided to set 65 years as the lower age limit.

A second issue is the age range to be included. The wider the range, the greater the possibility that nonspecific cohort differences or other non-brain-related concomitants of aging will influence the results. For this reason, our original goal was to select subjects within an extremely narrow range (2–3 years). This proved impractical because of the limited size of the subject pool. The actual age range of our first 50 subjects was from 66.5 to 78.3 years.

If a follow-up study after 3–5 years is planned, a third consideration with respect to age is that the subjects be young enough so that a reasonable number can be expected to survive for later evaluation. We had hoped to set the upper age limit at 75 years; again, limited availability led us to include subjects up to 78 years old.

Follow-up studies of an elderly cohort may permit one to obtain economically some of the more valuable information provided by longer term longitudinal investigation. The rate of brain aging appears to be greatly accelerated during and after the seventh decade; repeated observations during these years should offer the opportunity to study cognition as a function of relatively large changes in brain measures within the same subjects over a short period of time.

Choice of Size

The size of the sample required is obviously dependent on the underlying strength of the relations being investigated, the alpha level adopted for statistical significance, and the number of variables involved. Some guidance in determining sample size can be obtained through the power-analysis procedures recommended by Cohen and Cohen (1975). The present study employed four major and three secondary independent (predictor) variables (IVs). With an alpha level equal to .01 and a strength of effect (R^2) equal to .16 (set of four IVs accounting for 16% of the variance), a sample size of 85 subjects would have a power of .8 (i.e., would have 8 chances in 10 of demonstrating a relation if one was indeed present). We therefore set a target size of 90 subjects for our sample.

There are also nonstatistical considerations that influence the decision of size of sample. As a practical matter, funding agencies are often unwilling to support extensive data collection. Part of their caution undoubtedly stems from the very real difficulties of completing successfully a large and ambitious project. Funding agencies also seem reluctant to support, in the area of neuropsychology, the kinds of studies that are frequently supported in medicine. Large-scale medical studies are usually undertaken to obtain answers of immediate practical importance, such as to isolate causal factors in disease or to compare efficacy of treatment. However, it may be necessary to apply the same logic to *earlier* stages of neuropsychological investigation, that is, to studies aimed at isolating variables that play an important role in or are highly correlated with pathophysiological processes, even though the causal implications of these variables may be uncertain and their practical significance more remote. The use of the cooperative-studies approach, in which a number of laboratories adopt the same experimental design and pool their results, may prove effective. Cooperative studies, which were pioneered by the Veterans Administration, are now widely employed in medicine. The VA Hospital system would be uniquely suited for such investigations in the field of aging.

Another factor that affects the quality of a large-scale study is staff morale. An arduous schedule for a small staff can produce diminished morale (or "burnout") if data are to be collected over several years. With present and foreseeable fiscal constraints, it is not likely that this problem can be overcome by the use of larger staffs collecting the data in a more leisurely and comfortable fashion. Rotation of the staff might prove helpful.

Choice of Sex

Since women and men differ in longevity and in the apparent rate of other aspects of aging (e.g. rate of development of arteriosclerotic disease), adequate numbers of both men and women are required to make possible an analysis by sex. The population we sampled was unsatisfactory in this regard. There were few males in the CRTA, and it was not possible to obtain an adequate number of men from this group. It may become necessary for us to select additional males from a traditional male occupation with equivalent educational level, such as certified public accountants. In selecting any occupational subsample of the elderly for study, the investigator should be aware of the effects of sexist practices on both the occupational role and the sex ratio that will be obtained.

Choice of Biological Measures

The biological measures one may choose for a study such as this are enormously varied and ever increasing, as previously indicated. Since in a cross-sectional study one cannot measure decrement from previous levels directly, such impairment must be inferred from certain aspects of current level of performance. For example, sleep patterns in young adults differ so widely from those found in elderly subjects as to suggest that much of this variance is due to age. Obviously, the interpretation that "aged" sleep patterns result from brain aging would be more plausible if it were supported by other brain measures that change with age. We

therefore included CT scans and event-related potentials as two such measures, even though the functional significance of their change with age is not known. The biological measures selected for the present study were as follows:

1. Sleep EEG: Five nights of uninterrupted sleep recording, including one night of extended sleep (subjects in bed 12 hours) and a recovery night. Analysis of sleep stages, eye movement, and cycle patterns by visual scoring (Feinberg, Koresko, & Heller, 1967) and measurements of EEG waveforms by period and amplitude analyses.

2. CT scans: Visual analysis by "blind" ratings of ventricular and sulcal enlargement and computer estimates of total and regional intracranial fluid (see Chapter 6 of this book by Jernigan et al.). Collaboration with L. Zatz, Chief, Radiology Service, VA Medical Center, Palo Alto, California.

3. Event-related potentials: Visual, auditory, and visual-auditory ERPs were obtained following the procedures of Dustman and Beck (1969) and Gerson et al. (1976). In these procedures, subjects are passive. Collaboration with Ron Herning, University of California at San Francisco (UCSF).

4. Clinical EEG: Clinical ratings of abnormality will be carried out by Michael Aminoff, Chief of EEG at UCSF. Fourier analyses to be carried out by Ron Harper, University of California at Los Angeles.

5. Medical history, physical and neurological examinations: Carried out by M. Aminoff, UCSF.

6. Laboratory screen: Complete blood count; urinanalysis; tests of thyroid function; blood chemistries.

7. Psychiatric interview and life-history review: The goals of this interview, carried out prior to testing, were (a) to become acquainted with the subject's life history, and (b) to rule out past or present mental disorder. Five subjects were excluded from the study on the basis of interview findings; diagnoses included alcoholism, reactive depression (death of spouse), and paranoid schizophrenia.

While it is tempting to maximize the number of measures to be obtained, there are serious costs when studies are expanded beyond the testing of a few major hypotheses. As the number of biological variables increases—each one contributing several measures—the number of subjects required for adequate assessment of their interrelations increases. Each added study demands incremental effort from the staff and adds to the burden of the entire study. Moreover, such expansion reduces the rate at which data can be collected and analyzed. A delay in analysis runs the risk that faults or equipment malfunctions that degrade the data will not be discovered until it is too late to correct them. Inevitably one works more closely with some collaborators than others. For areas in which collaboration is more distant or delayed, data collection tends to flag. Considerable restraint and realism are required when embarking on multi-disciplinary investigations in order to avoid including so many variables that the quality of the entire enterprise is degraded.

Choice of Cognitive Functions Assessed

The methods available for assessment of cognitive function in the elderly have been the subject of several recent reviews (Eisdorfer & Cohen, 1978; Kramer & Jarvik, 1979; Schaie & Schaie, 1977) and are not discussed at length here. Our approach to this problem was to test intensively those cognitive functions that are recognized clinically and by self-report as being adversely affected by age. Thus, we employed several tests of new learning for both verbal and nonverbal material. We also used multiple tests of recent memory and of retrieval from long-term memory: Difficulties in such retrieval were among the most frequent complaints of our subjects. Tests of language function, word fluency, selected neuropsychological tests, and two widely used tests of adult intelligence, the Weschler Adult Intelligence Scale (WAIS) and the Progressive Matrices, completed the formal battery.

To obtain information regarding idiosyncratic and intermittent complaints of intellectual deficits, we developed a self-assessment questionnaire. Most workers in gerontology recognize that some complaints about intellectual deficit are unique to the individual and also that some of the complaints, especially those related to memory retrieval, are intermittent rather than constant. It therefore seemed desirable to obtain subjective reports. While such ratings are obviously of uncertain value, they might help to determine whether some measures of current performance do, in fact, reflect degree of impairment. Thus one can compare the memory-test results of subjects who complain of specific deficits in memory with those of subjects who do not; significant differences between such subgroups would add to one's confidence that performance on these tests actually reflects age-related impairment.

Choice of Statistical Analysis

The more tests one runs of statistical significance, the greater the probability of making Type 1 errors. This problem was especially acute in our study. When one considers that each of the biological measures yields a number of scores (for example, from the visually analyzed sleep EEG we obtain about 50 scores in addition to 13 computer measures), the problem of multiple tests seems insurmountable. In a sense, of course, it is: Conservative statistical procedures can minimize but not eliminate the risks of Type 1 errors.

The approach we adopted established several main hypotheses to be tested by confirmatory statistics. The size of our sample sharply limited the number of confirmatory tests we could carry out. We therefore divided the independent variables (IVs—those used to predict performance on the cognitive test, which constitute the dependent variables—DVs) into groups, hierarchically arranged with regard to their importance to the main hypotheses. Arranging the variables in hierarchical groups helps minimize the "experiment-wise" Type 1 error, since the significance of individual variables is tested only when the F value for the entire group is significant (Cohen & Cohen, 1975, analogue of Fisher's protected t test).

Obviously, this is only one of several conservative statistical methods. But it is important to emphasize that while sophisticated statistical techniques can guide scientific thinking, they cannot replace it. Interpretations of the findings in any study must ultimately depend on the strengths of the relations obtained, their internal consistency, and their plausibility, that is, their consistency with what is already known about brain and cognitive changes with age.

If findings emerge that meet the criteria of statistical and scientific inference, one can be gratified but not complacent. Even compelling results will require confirmation on an independent sample. The need for independent verification of positive findings is an aspect of behavioral science that is less appreciated than in other disciplines. Part of the reason for this must lie in the expense and the time-consuming nature of behavioral studies: One is usually reluctant to spend years of effort to prove (or disprove) what someone else has already reported. Yet precisely such efforts will be required if we are to construct a scientifically adequate and clinically useful neuropsychology of aging.

REFERENCES

Birren, J. E., Butler, R. N., Greenhouse, S. W., Sokoloff, L., & Yarrow, M. R. *Human aging: A biological and behavioral study.* Washington, D.C.: U.S. Government Printing Office, 1963.

Cohen, J., & Cohen, P. *Applied multiple regression/correlation analysis for the behavioral sciences.* New York: Wiley, 1975.

Dastur, D. K., Lane, M. H., Hansen, D. B., Kety, S. S., Butler, R. N., Perlin, S., & Sokoloff, L. Effects of aging on cerebral circulation and metabolism in man. In J. E.

Birren et al. (Eds.), *Human aging: A biological and behavioral study*. Washington, D.C.: U.S. Government Printing Office, 1963.

Dustman, R. W., & Beck, E. C. The effects of maturation and aging on the wave form of visual evoked potentials. *Electroencephalography and Clinical Neurophysiology*, 1969, *26*, 2–11.

Eisdorfer, C., & Cohen, D. The cognitively impaired elderly: Differential diagnosis. In M. Storandt, I. Siegler, & M. Elias (Eds.), *The clinical psychology of aging*. New York: Plenum Press, 1978.

Feinberg, I. Functional implications of changes in sleep physiology with age. In R. D. Terry & S. Gershon (Eds.), *Neurobiology of aging*. New York: Raven Press, 1976.

Feinberg, I., & Carlson, V. R. Sleep variables as a function of age in man. *Archives of General Psychiatry*, 1968, *18*, 239–250.

Feinberg, I., Koresko, R. L., & Heller, N. EEG sleep patterns as a function of normal and pathological aging in man. *Journal of Psychiatric Research*, 1967, *5*, 107–144.

Freyhan, F. H., Woodford, R. B., & Kety, S. S. Cerebral blood flow and metabolism in psychoses of senility. *Journal of Nervous and Mental Diseases*, 1951, *113*, 449.

Gerson, I. M., John, E. R., Bartlett, F., & Koening, V. Average evoked response (AER) in the electroencephalographic diagnosis of the normally aging brain: A practical application. *Clinical Electroencephalography*, 1976, *7*, 77–90.

Kety, S. S., & Schmidt, C. F. The nitrous oxide method for the quantitative determination of cerebral blood flow in man: Theory, procedure and normal values. *Journal of Clinical Investigation*, 1948, *27*, 476–484.

Kramer, N., & Jarvik, L. Assessment of intellectual change in the elderly. In *Psychiatric symptoms and cognitive loss in the elderly*. New York: Halstead Press, 1979.

Lassen, N. A., Feinberg, I., & Lane, M. H. Bilateral studies of cerebral oxygen uptake in young and aged normal subjects and in patients with organic dementia. *Journal of Clinical Investigation*, 1960, *39*, 491–500.

Obrist, W. D., Thompson, H. K., Wang, H. S., & Wilkinson, W. E. Regional cerebral blood flow estimated by ^{133}Xe inhalation. *Stroke*, 1977, *6*, 245–256.

Phelps, M. E. Emission computed tomography. *Seminars in Nuclear Medicine*, 1977, *7*, 337–365.

Schaie, K. W., & Schaie, J. P. Clinical assessment and aging. In J. E. Birren, & K. W. Schaie (Eds.), *Handbook of the psychology of aging*. New York: Van Nostrand Reinhold, 1977.

Sokoloff, L., Reivich, M., Kennedy, C., Des Rosiers, M. H., Patlak, C. S., Pettigrew, K. D., Sakaurada, O., & Shinohara, M. The ^{14}C-deoxyglucose method for the measurement of local cerebral glucose utilization: Theory, procedure and normal values in the conscious and anesthetized albino rat. *Journal of Neurochemistry*, 1977, *28*, 897–916.

Leonard J. Price, George Fein, and Irwin Feinberg

CHAPTER

5

Neuropsychological Assessment of Cognitive Function in the Elderly

The lack of valid norms for the elderly on specialized neuropsychological tests mandates a cautious approach by clinicians interpreting apparently pathological task performances in the aged. Our data on a group of highly intelligent and socially active elderly subjects emphasize this deficiency. There is a need for a more exhaustive description of cognitive function in the normal elderly rather than comparisons with young adult functioning. This strategy has been applied to a pattern of performance highly suggestive of brain damage in young adults but of limited clinical significance in the elderly.

The primary goal of the neuropsychology of aging is to differentiate between normal and pathological functions in the elderly. Accurate differential diagnosis is clearly necessary for determining appropriate intervention and counseling procedures. Yet a large number of neuropsychological tests in use today are based on the performances of young and middle-aged adults. It is becoming increasingly clear that norms for some of these tests may not be adequate for elderly populations (Crook, 1979; Schaie & Schaie, 1977). The objective of this chapter is to outline the shortcomings associated with applying such norms to aged individuals and to suggest possible alternatives to the difficulties described. Two widely administered test protocols, the Wechsler Adult Intelligence Scale (WAIS) and portions of the Halstead-Reitan Neuropsychological Battery (HRNB), have been selected to illustrate the need for developing procedures that can more reliably differentiate between "normal" or expected aging and

neuropathology. The problems associated with these tests are not unique but are used to illustrate a major difficulty in the neuropsychological assessment of the elderly.

Data were gathered in conjunction with a multidisciplinary, cross-sectional study of aging. The participants in this study were highly intelligent, socially active, elderly individuals. They were all members of the California Retired Teachers Association (CRTA), and most had a minimum of 17 years of education (i.e., a master's degree). They were not only highly educated but also exceptionally motivated and healthy (see Chapter 4 of this book). Such a population might reasonably be expected to perform at optimal level, and in fact, their IQs ranged from superior to very superior. Nevertheless, they showed a pattern of performance on the WAIS and on the HRNB that would be suggestive of brain dysfunction if the normative criteria were strictly observed. An anomalous pattern of performance on the Tactual Performance Test (TPT) of the HRNB was particularly striking in this regard. These findings, and possible explanations for them, are discussed in some detail in the following sections. The analysis of the TPT performance, in particular, has been included to emphasize the contribution that a detailed study of cognition in the elderly can make to an understanding of successful task performance.

This research was supported by the Veterans Administration Research Service.

In general, these data suggest that test scores of the type described should be used with great caution. In addition, clinicians should consider augmenting standard batteries with a variety of experimental cognitive paradigms so that the nature and maximal extent of any deficit may be better evaluated.

Wechsler Adult Intelligence Scale Norms

The WAIS (Wechsler, 1958) is a well-established, widely used test for assessing cognitive function. Its popularity owes much to the extensive normative data provided by Wechsler's nationwide standardization samples, from 16 to 64 years of age. This instrument assesses cognitive function through two comparisons: First, raw scores are converted to scaled scores by reference to Wechsler's young reference group at their so-called "peak" of mental development; second, summed scaled scores are converted to IQ scores with reference to the age-correct IQ conversion tables. While IQ scores for individuals up to age 64 are based on age-corrected norms from the nationwide sample, IQ scores for individuals past 64 years of age rest on a far less solid foundation of standardization data. Standardization of WAIS scores in the elderly was carried out on a sample of 352 elderly subjects in Kansas City (Doppelt & Wallace, 1955). On the basis of these results, Doppelt and Wallace created conversion scores so that, as in the nationwide norms for younger samples, Verbal and Performance IQs in a normal elderly sample would be equal and would average 100. Since numerous studies have shown that elderly subjects show a Verbal–Performance discrepancy on the WAIS (i.e., Performance scores are lower than Verbal scores), adequate age-correction factors for the Performance tests should be greater than those required for the Verbal tests in order for the Verbal and Performance IQ scores to be equivalent in a group of normal elderly subjects.

Figure 5-1 shows that this result was not obtained for the 36 females in the CRTA sample. While Performance scaled scores are lower than Verbal scaled scores, which is to be expected for elderly subjects, the same relationship also holds true with regard to the IQ scores [$t(35) = 4.74$, $p < .001$]. The pattern of Verbal–Performance IQ differences on the WAIS for the 13 men in the CRTA sample was virtually identical to that found for the women ($t(12) = 4.23$, $p < .01$). Thus the sex of the subjects is not likely to be responsible for the Verbal–Performance IQ difference shown in Figure 5-1. Although the CRTA sample is highly selected with regard to education and work experience—which may contribute to the relatively higher Verbal IQs—our data add to the results of others in

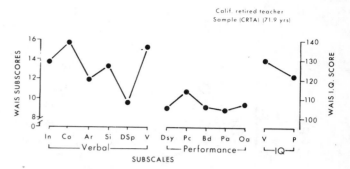

Figure 5-1. Weschler Adult Intelligence Scale (WAIS) Verbal and Performance subscales and IQ scores for elderly sample of 36 female retired California teachers (mean age = 71.9 years) (Abbreviations: In = Information; Co = Comprehension; Ar = Arithmetic; Si = Similarities; DSp = Digit Span; V = Vocabulary; Dsy = Digit Symbol; Pc = Picture Completion; Bd = Block Design; Pa = Picture Arrangement; Oa = Object Assembly; V = Verbal; P = Performance).

raising questions about the Doppelt and Wallace norms. Figure 5-2 shows that, excluding the standardization sample, six of the seven samples of elderly subjects examined by other investigators show lower Performance than Verbal IQs (Birren, Butler, Greenhouse, Sokoloff & Yarrow, 1963; Blusewicz, Schenkenberg, Dustman, & Beck, 1977; Eisdorfer & Cohen, 1961; Norman & Daley, 1959; Overall & Gorham, 1972).

These results suggest that the Doppelt and Wallace norms are not generally applicable and that their age corrections for the Performance subscales are too small. Eisdorfer and Cohen (1961) have suggested (a) that one source of this low estimate may be sampling bias resulting from inclusion in the normalization group of only those subjects who completed the WAIS, and (b) that because this group was a superior and unrepresentative elderly sample, the age correction, especially for the Performance tests, may have been inadequately low. Still other sources of bias in the normalization sample may have a regional basis related to social class, occupation, education, religion, or other factors. However, these sources of bias do not fully explain the differences in Verbal and Performance IQs displayed in Figure 5-2. For both the Norman and Daley (1959) study and the CRTA study, the samples are, if anything, more skewed toward higher intelligence than the Doppelt and Wallace standardization sample, and yet these two groups also show higher Verbal than Performance IQs.

The practical importance of a more appropriate age correction depends on the degree to which clinicians regard Verbal–Performance discrepancies in the

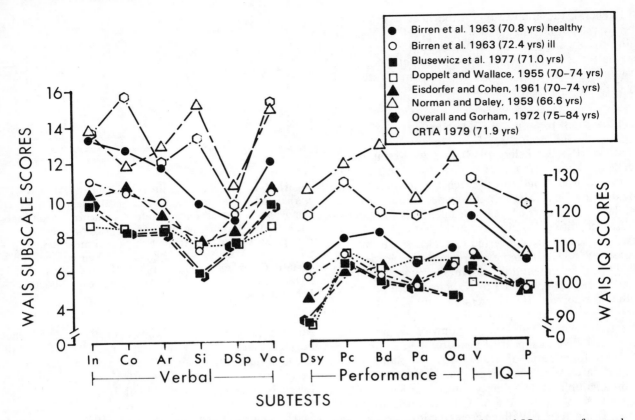

Figure 5-2. Weschler Adult Intelligence Scale (WAIS) Verbal and Performance subscales and IQ scores of several elderly samples (Abbreviations: In = Information; Co = Comprehension; Ar = Arithmetic; Si = Similarities; DSp = Digit Span; V = Vocabulary; Dsy = Digit Symbol; Pc = Picture Completion; Bd = Block Design; Pa = Picture Arrangement; Oa = Object Assembly; V = Verbal; P = Performance).

elderly as evidence of brain impairment. In a clinical assessment, one usually rules out other factors, such as lifetime occupational experience, which may inflate scores on one versus the other section of the WAIS (e.g., it would not be inconsistent with normal brain functioning for an architect to show a Performance IQ 15 points higher than a Verbal IQ). Once such variables have been ruled out, a 10-point or greater difference in IQs is often thought to suggest the presence of a form of cerebral dysfunction. The clinician then looks for other signs that would be consistent with this possibility. The clinical-inferential process is sufficiently challenging without the clinician's having to correct for deficient norms in evaluating brain-behavior relations. The need for such a reconsideration was suggested years ago by the work of Eisdorfer and Cohen (1961). Our data emphasize the importance and urgency of this issue to the neuropsychologist who examines elderly subjects.

Reports of changes in the factor structure of the WAIS in aging individuals are relevant to these findings (Berger, Bernstein, Klein, Cohen & Lucas, 1964;

Cohen, 1957). The typical factor structure includes first, a verbal-comprehension factor measured by Verbal IQ subscales; second, a spatial-organization factor measured by Performance subtests of the WAIS; and a third factor with highest loadings on the Digit Span subtest (Berger et al., 1964; Dennerell, Broeder, & Sokolov, 1964; Landsell & Smith, 1975; Riegel & Riegel, 1962; Russell, 1972). This third factor has been variously labeled a "memory" factor (Balinisky, 1942; Birren, 1952), a "freedom from distractibility" factor (Cohen, 1952), or an "attention and concentration" factor (Hover, 1950). Cohen (1957) reported that while the structure of intellectual functioning is stable between the ages of 18 and 54, that may not be true for subjects above age 60. Cohen found a change in the memory factor that "spreads over several new tests," which led him to suggest a "change in intellectual organization in the elderly, with memory playing a far more important role in determining individual differences in test performance" (p. 289). Similarly, Berger et al. (1964) found that for subjects over 60 years of age, memory "coalesces with Verbal skills, together forming a joint factor" (p. 205). Riegel and Riegel (1962) reported no change in factor structure on the WAIS with aging. This divergence could be due to differences in the populations evaluated or to the different methods of extraction and rotation used in developing the factor structures. Further analyses need to be carried out to assess whether memory and ability to maintain sustained concentration play a greater role in determining the performance of the elderly, as compared to younger individuals, on tests such as the WAIS.

Halstead-Reitan Neuropsychological Battery Norms

A number of investigators have emphasized the importance of adequate age correction for neuropsychological assessment in the elderly to avoid false-positive diagnosis of brain impairment.

Reed and Reitan (1963) found older subjects (mean age = 53 years) to be markedly inferior to young subjects (mean age = 28 years) on tests judged to require complex problem-solving operations such as the Categories Test or the Tactual Performance Test. Prigatano and Parsons (1976) studied the effects on the Halstead-Reitan Neuropsychological Battery of variables not related to brain damage, including age, education, occupation, and emotional state. They reported that in the group without brain damage, age was negatively correlated with performance on all tests. Vega and Parsons (1967), in their attempt to validate the Halstead-Reitan Neuropsychological Battery, found a significant negative correlation (r = −.57) between age and overall performance. They concluded that the clinician must be aware of the normal ranges of performance one can expect from older compared to younger populations. Failure to do so invariably results in increased false-positive diagnostic formulations concerning brain dysfunction. Cauthen (1978) cautions against applying neuropsychological cut-offs for brain damage developed on young populations when diagnosing the presence or absence of brain dysfunction in the elderly. He looked at performance on the Tactual Performance Test (TPT) at three different age levels between 20 and 60 years of age for three different IQ levels. Significant differences in performances attributable to age and IQ were found for the dominant, nondominant, and total-time scores, as well as for memory and location of blocks (see below for a description of the TPT task). Davies (1968) found that while only 20% of young subjects tested fell below Reitan's cut-off criteria on the Trails tests, 90% of subjects tested between ages 70 and 79 were misclassified. Thus, cut-off criteria derived on young sam-

Table 5-1 Percentages of CRTA Elderly Classified as Impaired According to Halstead's (1947) and Russell et al.'s (1970) Cut-Off Criteria for the Tactual Performance Test

Variable	Females (N = 36)	Males (N = 13)	Total sample (N = 49)
Total time	88.9	92.3	89.8
Dominant-hand time	55.6	84.6	63.3
Nondominant-hand time	88.9	92.3	89.8
Both-hands time	94.4	84.6	91.8
Memory of block shape	11.1	18.2	12.2
Location of blocks on board	75.4	84.6	77.6

Note. Sample consisted of volunteers from the California Retired Teachers Association (CRTA).

ples could give seriously misleading results if applied to older groups.

The implications of lower levels of performance among the elderly are important for the clinical neuropsychologist. The inevitable question is, Do pathological levels of performance have the same implications for central nervous system functioning in the elderly as they do in younger people?

The importance of this issue is clearly demonstrated by the data of the CRTA study, which tested a group of highly selected people who functioned at a superior level. This was reflected not only in their WAIS performances, but in their high level of functioning in daily life. Nevertheless, their neuropsychological test performances placed many of them within the "brain impaired" range (Halstead, 1947; Russell, Neuringer, & Goldstein, 1970). Table 5-1 shows the percentages of male and female subjects whose performance on the Tactual Performance Test was indicative of brain

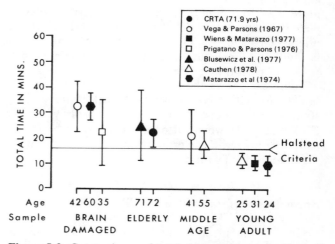

Figure 5-3. Comparisons of total time scores on the Tactual Performance Test for various groups according to Halstead's (1947) cut-off criteria for brain impairment.

Table 5-2 Percentages of CRTA Elderly Classified as Impaired by Halstead's (1947) and Russell et al.'s (1970) Cut-Off Criteria for Tasks on the Halstead-Reitan Neuropsychological Battery

Variable	Females (N = 36)	Males (N = 13)	Total sample (N = 49)
Finger Oscillation Task			
Dominant-hand taps	58.3	69.2	61.2
Nondominant-hand taps	38.9	69.2	49.0
Trails Test			
Part A (numeric)	47.2	38.5	44.9
Part B (alpha-numeric)	44.4	53.8	46.9
Perceptual errors	19.4	23.1	20.4
(imperceptions and suppressions)			
Average impairment rating	50.0	69.2	56.3

Note. Sample consisted of volunteers from the California Retired Teachers Association (CRTA).

damage according to Halstead's and Russell et al.'s criteria.

Only on the TPT memory measure do the majority of elderly subjects perform in the normal range. On all the remaining measures, substantial proportions—up to 90% in many cases—were in the abnormal range. It is quite possible, if not probable, that the subjects falling above the cut-off criteria do have a degree of brain impairment associated with aging that is substantially greater than other subjects in the sample. But none of this was reflected in "clinical" impairment, which is what the tests are supposedly designed to reflect.

Figure 5-3 graphically displays means and standard deviations on the TPT, as reported by six other investigators. As expected, all brain-damaged subjects took more than 15.6 minutes (the cut-off criterion) to complete the task. But so did many of the elderly as well as middle-aged subjects. Only young subjects, more similar in age to normative samples, fell within normal ranges of performance time.

Table 5-2 shows that on several other tasks of the Halstead-Reitan Neuropsychological Battery, substantial proportions of the normal healthy elderly CRTA subjects would also be classified as brain impaired. However, these proportions are generally lower than those found with the TPT.

Anomalous Performance on the TPT

One of the most interesting of the cognitive-test findings in the current study was the appearance of a particularly aberrant pattern of performance on the Tactual Performance Test. A brief description of this task will illustrate the nature of the impaired performance. This task requires that the subject, while blindfolded, place 10 geometrically shaped blocks into spaces on a board. Performance is then timed at this task, first with the dominant hand, then with the nondominant hand, and, finally, with both hands. After completing the last trial, the board and blocks are removed from sight, so that the subject has seen neither the block shapes nor their correct locations. The blindfold is removed and the subject is asked to draw the different shaped blocks, which provides a score for spatial memory, making sure to draw the blocks in their correct locations relative to the board and other blocks, which provides a "location" score. Early in the study it was noticed that a surprisingly high number of subjects performed the nondominant-hand trial at a slower rate than in the first, dominant-hand trial. This constitutes a reversal in the normal expected pattern of improvement in performance from the first to the second trial (by from 30% to 40%) and is usually interpreted as evidence suggesting dysfunction in the contralateral hemisphere.

Such deviant patterns of task performance are as crucial in clinical neuropsychological assessment as are absolute levels of performance. On the basis of known association of such deviant behavioral "signs" with particular types of brain dysfunction, clinical neuropsychologists make inferences about the nature, course, extent, and location of underlying cortical dysfunction (Reitan & Davison, 1974). This kind of assessment can be made only by those with extensive accumulated experience with the test battery. As the number of internally consistent, pathognomonic "signs" of deficit within a battery accumulate, a more specific and accurate diagnostic picture emerges concerning the nature of brain dysfunction that underlies the test pattern (Russell, Neuringer, & Goldstein, 1970). Thus it is important for neuropsychologists to become familiar with aberrant patterns of test performance that are commonly associated with particular pathological conditions, in order to reduce the false-positive and false-negative errors in neuropsychological assessment. By the same token, it is just as crucial to identify and examine instances where well-defined groups of otherwise normal subjects, such as the elderly, show patterns of performance that appear pathological at unexpectedly high levels. If there is no continuity in the brain-behavior relations throughout the age range (even with adjustment in the cut-off criteria), what then is the significance of pathognomonic patterns for senescent changes?

The reversal on the TPT shown by the CRTA subjects was investigated in an attempt to isolate the basis of the divergent performance. Four possible explanations seem likely: The reversal may represent (a) an impairment in spatial memory, (b) a primary psychomotor impairment of the nondominant hand, (c) a difficulty in organization of spatial relations, or (d) a combination of two or more of these disabilities.

To explore this intriguing pattern, a CRTA subgroup of four males and eleven females who showed the reversal pattern were compared to another subgroup that showed the normal expected pattern of performance. Subjects were matched on age, total TPT time, and, in all but one case, sex. The subgroup with the expected "normal" pattern showed improvement at each trial, though the improvement was not as large as is seen in young subjects. The level of improvement between first and last trial of the reversal subgroup (8.7%) was far lower than that of the matched group (39%). In fact, the second (nondominant hand) trial of the normal subgroup was equal to the reversal subgroup's third, and final, trial, (where both hands are used).

The upper portion of Table 5-3 shows the performance of these subgroups on the finger-oscillation task and the Trails Tests. The performances on these psychomotor tasks are equivalent, suggesting that the TPT performance differences between the groups are not the direct result of psychomotor slowing. The bottom half of the table compares the subgroups on measures sensitive to spatial memory and organization, including the number of block shapes the subject draws correctly (TPT memory) and their correct positioning in relation to the board and other blocks (TPT location). A prorated Performance IQ score, made up of the Block Design and Object Assembly subtests

from the WAIS is also presented. Russell et al. (1970) use this measure to assess spatial relations.

The two subgroups did not differ significantly on the measure for memory of block shapes (Memory). As a group, the CRTA members performed this part of the TPT best, with only 12% of the sample's scores falling into brain-damaged regions. On the other hand, the reversal subgroup seemed to have greater difficulty in remembering the *position* of the blocks on the board (Location). The two subgroups were also differentiated by Russell's spatial organization measure. IQ comparisons showed Verbal IQ scores to be equivalent, whereas Performance IQ scores were significantly higher for the matched subgroup. Comparisons between the subgroups on computer tomography measures of brain atrophy (see Chapter 6 of this book) failed to show significant differences between them.

Goldstein and Braun (1974) also report increases in the reversal of the normal expected pattern of improvement between Trials 1 and 2 on the TPT. Over 75% of their 70- to 79-year-old group (n = 12) reversed the expected pattern on the TPT, compared to under 19% of subjects age 30 to 40 years old (n = 75). Goldstein and Brown also report no differences between young and old groups in reversal rates (between dominant and nondominant hand) on the finger-oscillation task. They suggest that the TPT reversal pattern may reflect a "more rapid degeneration of interhemispheric connective fibres than of the cortical hemispheres themselves" (p. 1144). Their alternative explanation is that the TPT reversal pattern in the elderly may reflect dysfunction of the right hemi-

Table 5-3 Comparison between subgroup showing reversal of the expected pattern of TPT performance and subgroup of elderly matched on age and total TPT time

Comparison	Reversal subgroup		Matched subgroup		F	p
	M	SD	M	SD		
Psychomotor tasks						
Finger Oscillation (no. taps averaged over 5 trials)						
Dominant hand	45.7	6.5	45.7	7.3	.0	ns
Nondominant hand	40.5	5.9	43.2	7.0	1.26	ns
Dominant minus nondominant	5.2	4.3	2.6	2.8	4.01	ns (.055)
Trails Test						
Part A	33.8	9.0	31.9	8.0	.39	ns
Part B	90.3	43.2	81.1	20.5	.56	ns
Spatial organization						
Tactual Performance Test (no. blocks correctly reproduced)						
Memory for shapes	6.7	1.0	7.2	1.6	.93	ns
Location on board	2.1	1.8	3.9	2.2	6.16	<.02
Wechsler Adult Intelligence Scale (WAIS)						
Russell's spatial scaled score	42.0	6.2	48.3	7.9	5.92	<.03
WAIS IQ scores						
Verbal IQ	129.5	11.8	131.6	13.0	.22	ns
Performance IQ	118.7	6.5	123.7	6.4	6.5	<.04

sphere. This is suggested because the task requires internalized visualization and organization of spatial relations, a right-hemisphere function. In addition, the impaired *nondominant* hand in right-handed individuals, which was impaired on the TPT, is mediated by the right hemisphere. The lack of differences between the CRTA matched subgroups on the CT measures, however, appears to indicate that gross structural anomalies cannot account for the reversed TPT pattern.

Our results suggest that the reversal pattern of TPT performance in the elderly may be the result of a decreased ability to organize and synthesize spatial relations on this complex task, rather than psychomotor slowing or memory deficits per se. The significance of the impaired performance of some of the subjects on the TPT, and in fact on many psychometrics, is unclear. The subjects are functioning at very high levels, as indicated by high Verbal and Performance IQ scores, which, even for the reversal group, are 130 and 119, respectively. It may be that the cognitive basis of the reversal pattern is not identical for brain-damaged and normal elderly subjects. The implication of these patterns for underlying brain pathology is very interesting and needs to be studied further.

Concluding Remarks

The lack of valid age norms for neuropsychological tests is apparent and emphasizes the need for caution by clinicians in interpreting neuropsychological test scores of the elderly. Many other researchers have made similar points in the past, but the continued inadequacy of norms remains a problem, as is clearly demonstrated by the performance of the CRTA subjects. They are especially well-functioning, active, and involved elderly citizens who show little, if any, clinical evidence of neuropathology. Yet their performance on the WAIS and the Halstead-Reitan Neuropsychological Battery may be conventionally interpreted as indicating brain damage. While most normal elderly may in fact have significant brain impairment compared with young adults, the behavioral manifestations of such impairment are not usually clinically meaningful in terms of the decisions that neuropsychologists have to make about elderly individuals. If we wish to use neuropsychological procedures in assessing the elderly, we need a more thorough understanding of cognitive function in the aged. In order to accomplish this, a wide range of cognitive abilities in healthy, aging individuals needs to be evaluated, so that a pattern of spared and impaired functions can be established. Then the investigator can focus on determining the impaired mental operations responsible for inadequate

performance on specific tasks (as in the preceding analysis of the TPT test). One must determine the range of performance that can be expected from healthy elderly subjects before the boundaries between normal and pathological behavior can be demarcated. Above all, emphasis should be shifted away from describing "deficits" in the aged when young performances are the implicit standard of comparison. Instead, a realistic and representative evaluation of cognitive functions is needed. This will not only allow a more accurate definition of "pathology" but will define pathological performance in the elderly on their terms and not solely in terms of deviance from young-adult norms.

REFERENCES

Balinsky, B. An analysis of mental factors in various age groups from nine to sixty. *Genetic Psychology Monographs*, 1941, *23*, 191–234.

Berger, L., Bernstein, A., Klein, E., Cohen, J., & Lucas, G. Effects of aging and pathology on the factorial structure of intelligence. *Journal of Consulting Psychology*, 1964, *28*, 199–207.

Birren, J. E. A factorial analysis of the Wechsler Bellview Scale given to elderly populations. *Journal of Consulting Psychology*, 1952, *16*, 399–405.

Birren, J. E., Butler, R. N., Greenhouse, S. W., Sokoloff, L., & Yarrow, M. R. *Human aging: A biological and behavioral study* (DHEW Publ. No. 986). Washington, D.C.: U.S. Department of Health, Education, and Welfare, 1963.

Blusewicz, M. W., Schenkenberg, T., Dustman, R. E., & Beck, E. C. WAIS performance in young normal, young alcoholic, and elderly normal groups: An evaluation of organicity and mental aging indices. *Journal of Clinical Psychology*, 1977, *33*, 1149–1153.

Cauthen, N. Normative data for the Tactual Performance Test. *Journal of Clinical Psychology*, 1978, *34*, 456–460.

Cohen, J. A factor-analytically based rationale for the Wechsler Bellview. *Journal of Consulting Psychology*, 1952, *16*, 272–277.

Cohen, J. The factorial structure of the WAIS between early adulthood and old age. *Journal of Consulting Psychology*, 1957, *21* 283–290.

Crook, T. Psychometric assessment of the elderly. In A. Raskin & L. F. Jarvik (Eds.), *Psychiatric symptoms and cognitive loss in the elderly*. New York: Halstead Press, 1979.

Davies, H. D. M. The influence of age on Trail Making Test performance. *Journal of Clinical Psychology*, 1968, *24*, 96–98.

Dennerill, R., Broeder, J., & Sokolov, S. WISC and WAIS factors in children and adults with epilepsy. *Journal of Clinical Psychology*, 1964, *26*, 236–240.

Doppelt, J. E., & Wallace, W. L. Standardization of the Wechsler Adult Intelligence Scale for older persons.

Journal of Abnormal and Social Psychology, 1955, *51*, 312–330.

Eisdorfer, C., & Cohen, L. D. The generality of the WAIS standardization for the aged: A regional comparison. *Journal of Abnormal and Social Psychology*, 1961, *64*, 520–527.

Goldstein, S. G., & Braun, L. S. Reversal of expected transfer as a function of increased age. *Perceptual and Motor Skills*, 1974, *38*, 1139–1145.

Halstead, W. C. *Brain and intelligence*. Chicago: University of Chicago Press, 1947.

Hover, G. L. *An investigation of differences in intellectual factors between normal and neurotic adults*. Unpublished doctoral dissertation, University of Michigan, 1950.

Landsell, H., & Smith, F. J. Asymmetrical cerebral function for two WAIS factors and their recovery after brain injury. *Journal of Consulting and Clinical Psychology*, 1975, *43*, 923.

Matarazzo, J. D., Wiens, A. N., Matarazzo, R. G., & Goldstein, S. G. Psychometric and clinical test-retest reliability of the Halstead impairment index in a sample of healthy, young, normal men. *Journal of Nervous and Mental Disease*, 1974, *158*, 37–49.

Norman, R. D., & Daley, M. F. Senescent changes in intellectual ability among superior older women. *Journal of Gerontology*, 1959, *14*, 457–464.

Overall, J. E., & Gorham, D. R. Organicity versus old age in objective and projective test performance. *Journal of Consulting and Clinical Psychology*, 1972, *45*, 412–416.

Prigatano, G. P., & Parsons, O. A. Relationship of age and education to Halstead test performance in different patient populations. *Journal of Consulting and Clinical Psychology*, 1976, *44*, 527–533.

Reed, H. B. C., & Reitan, R. M. The significance of age in the performance of a complex psychomotor task by brain-damaged and non-brain-damaged subjects. *Journal of Gerontology*, 1963, *18*, 177–179.

Reitan, R. M., & Davison, L. A. *Clinical neuropsychology: Current status and applications*. New York: Winston/Wiley, 1974.

Riegel, R. M., & Riegel, K. F. A comparison and reinterpretation of factor structure of the W-B, the WAIS, and the Hawie on aged persons. *Journal of Consulting Psychology*, 1962, *26*, 31–37.

Russell, E. W. WAIS factor analysis with brain-damaged subjects using criterion measures. *Journal of Consulting and Clinical Psychology*, 1972, *69*, 133–139.

Russell, E. W., Neuringer, C., & Goldstein, G. *Assessment of brain damage: A neuropsychological key approach*. New York: Wiley, 1970.

Schaie, K. W., & Schaie, J. P. Clinical assessment and aging. In J. Birren & K. W. Schaie (Eds.), *Handbook of the psychology of aging*. New York: Van Nostrand Reinhold, 1977.

Vega, A., & Parsons, O. A. Cross validation of the Halstead Reitan tests for brain damage. *Journal of Consulting Psychology*, 1967, *31*, 619–623.

Wechsler, D. *The measurement and appraisal of adult intelligence*. Baltimore: Williams & Wilkins, 1958.

Wiens, A. N., & Matarazzo, J. D. WAIS and MMPI correlates of the Halstead-Reitan neuropsychology battery in normal male subjects. *Journal of Nervous and Mental Disease*, 1977, *164*, 112–121.

Terry L. Jernigan, Leslie M. Zatz, Irwin Feinberg, and George Fein

CHAPTER

6

Measurement of Cerebral Atrophy in the Aged by Computed Tomography

Computed tomography (CT) is an exciting new technique that allows researchers literally to peer into the living brain. It will contribute much to the study of cerebral atrophy and its functional consequences in aging. In this chapter some recently developed techniques are outlined for measuring the volume of fluid in the brain from CT scans. The problems inherent in such measurements are noted and their effects on the measures described. To illustrate the use of these techniques for clinical and experimental purposes, some early findings in a group of normal elderly women are presented. Finally, issues that bear on the limitations and proper interpretations of this research are discussed.

One of the most difficult problems neuropsychologists face is the lack of a useful anatomic validation criterion for their models of clinico-anatomic relations. Neurological examinations, including arteriography and pneumoencephalography, have proven inadequate for most purposes, and evidence from pathology comes too late and too infrequently. Not surprisingly, when computerized tomographic (CT) brain scans became available, interest in this new technique grew rapidly in the neuropsychological community. CT provides a noninvasive method for obtaining relatively high resolution images of the intracranial contents in vivo. The minimal radiation risk associated with the technique allows its use with a variety of different clinical groups and makes it feasible to examine normal subjects and to examine subjects repeatedly.

This technique and other new tomographic procedures, such as positron-emission tomography, provide a challenging opportunity for neuropsychologists in the next decade. Their task will be to establish the usefulness of this newly acquired anatomic information for improving the diagnosis and care of their patients. More generally, the data will be used to enrich current models of the contributions that different brain structures make to various psychological processes. This chapter describes one approach to these goals. Some recently developed techniques are outlined for measuring the volume of fluid in the brain from CT scans. The problems inherent in such measurements are noted and the effects of such problems on the measures are described. To illustrate the use of these measures for clinical and experimental purposes, some early findings in a group of normal elderly women are presented. Finally, issues that bear on the limitations and proper interpretation of this research are discussed.

Measurement of CSF Volume from CT Scans

The CT Images

Figure 6-1 illustrates the degree of differentiation between brain, cerebrospinal fluid (CSF), and bone

This research was supported by the Medical Research Service of the Veterans Administration.

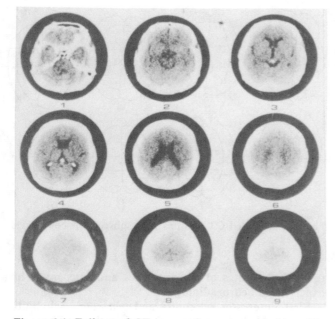

Figure 6-1. Full set of CT images from normal subject. The scans are numbered from the base to the apex of the skull.

Model and Calculations

The following method for measuring CSF volume utilizes a simple model that requires certain assumptions. The first is that the contents of the cranium are composed of only two materials: brain and CSF. Second, normal brain and CSF are assumed to have characteristic attenuation values, a_b and a_f, respectively. The third assumption is that although the attenuation values for normal brain and CSF may vary due to artifacts, their difference is constant. With these assumptions we can say that for a given volume of tissue,

$$a_o = p_b a_b + p_f a_f \qquad (1)$$

where a_o is the observed attenuation value for that volume of tissue, and p_b and p_f are the proportions of brain and CSF, respectively. Now

$$p_b = 1 - p_f, \qquad (2)$$

so in order to estimate p_f, estimates of a_f and a_b must be obtained. We obtain an estimate of a_b by sampling

that is obtained in the CT images. The gray areas of the scan are brain, the black areas are CSF, and the white areas are bone, or calcification. A full examination usually consists of 9 to 12 sections, each of which is approximately 1 cm thick. Each of the images is obtained by applying a gray scale to the range of values in an underlying attenuation matrix. This matrix is made up of rows and columns of numbers (256×256 in our scanner), each of which is an estimate of the degree of x-ray attenuation that occurred in a particular small volume of tissue. This volume of tissue measures 1 mm² times the 1-cm depth of the section. These dimensions vary somewhat for different scanners. The fact that the information in CT scans is in digital form is fortunate for those who would adapt the technique to research purposes.

In the following discussion, we describe a set of techniques developed for quantifying certain features of the CT scans. These techniques are particularly useful for the study of cerebral atrophy because they provide estimates of the CSF content in the brain. For our purposes, the term *atrophy* is used to refer to increases over normal of CSF volume in the cranium, in the absence of obstructive processes. As is illustrated in Figure 6-2, atrophic processes in the brain appear as dilatation of the ventricles (Section c compared to Section a) and/or as widening of the cortical sulci (Section d compared to Section b). Both changes result in local increases in the amount of CSF present.

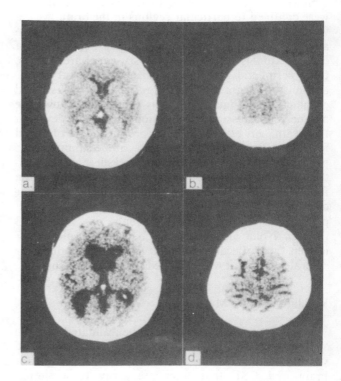

Figure 6-2. Set of CT images showing the appearance of cerebral atrophy. A normal brain is shown in Sections a and b. Sections c and d are from an atrophied brain at the levels of a and b, respectively.

an area of the section where there are no signs of pathology and no sulci, cisterns, or streak artifacts. This is called the normal brain sample. The sample should include as much white matter as possible. This is because the attenuation values of white and gray matter differ slightly, and sampling in gray matter tends to inflate the estimated CSF volume. Note that a separate normal brain sample is taken for each section. Since we previously found the average difference between normal white matter and CSF to be 13 attenuation units (Jernigan, Zatz, & Naeser, 1979) we estimate a_r to be $a_b - 13$. This difference will vary from scanner to scanner and must be experimentally determined. Solving for p_r yields

$$p_r = (a_b - a_o)/13. \qquad (3)$$

With this formula, the proportion of CSF in each hemisphere, each section, and over particular sets of sections is obtained. The procedure is described in detail in Jernigan et al. (1979).

Subsegmental Measures

Since we were interested in increases in CSF that were confined to particular regions in the brain, we devised an algorithm for segmenting the CT sections into an arbitrary set of subsegments. Each hemisphere of each section is segmented into six equal-area zones, three peripheral and three medial. The output of this automated segmentation algorithm is illustrated graphically in Figure 6-3. This figure also shows the number codes assigned to sections at various levels in the brain. An estimated CSF proportion is obtained for each of these small zones and can be summed over particular sets of them. For our measurement of ventricular dilatation we obtained a total CSF proportion for all medial segments on Sections 3 through 7. For our measure of sulcal widening we computed the CSF proportion in peripheral segments on Sections 3 through 7 plus all of Section 8, since only sulcal CSF is seen there. Because Section 9 was not obtained for several subjects, it was excluded from this measure.

Validation of the Measures

Ideally, the measures should be validated using a "phantom" of the head with realistically shaped ventricles and sulci, an actual skull, and materials for brain and CSF that attenuate x-ray to a similar degree. Each of these features influences the outcome of the analysis described above. Unfortunately, such a phantom has not yet been acquired. We have, however, attempted to validate the measures by comparing them

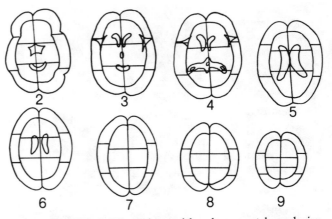

Figure 6-3. Coded CT sections with subsegment boundaries indicated.

to clinical ratings of the ventricles and sulci made by experienced neuroradiologists.

First, interrater reliability and test–retest reliability were established for the clinical ratings. The ventricular ratings of 30 scans by two neuroradiologists were compared using Spearman's rho, and a coefficient of .68 was obtained. The correlation for the sulcal ratings was .93. Two ventricular ratings by the senior neuroradiologist, made one week apart, gave a correlation of .85; and the sets of sulcal ratings gave a correlation of .81.

The correlation of the medial, or ventricular, automated measure with the clinical ventricular rating was .83. However, the correlation of the peripheral automated measure with the clinical sulcal rating was only .51. At first, we feared that the artifactual elevation of CT values near bone, which is an inherent problem in CT scans, was reducing the accuracy of the peripheral measures and that this accounted for the lack of agreement with the clinical rating. To test this hypothesis, we obtained a clinical rating of the peripheral area only, on Section 8. The medial area was blacked out. Section 8 was chosen because sulci appear in the periphery at this level. When this rating was compared to the automated peripheral CSF proportion from Section 8, the correlation was .84. This was as high as the test–retest correlation for the clinical sulcal rating, suggesting that the visible variations in peripheral CSF volume were being measured fairly accurately with the automated measure.

It appears that the low correlation between the clinical rating and the automated measure of the sulci was due to at least two factors. The first was the inflation of CT values as a function of their proximity to the skull. This caused the CT values obtained for CSF in peripheral areas to approach the higher CT value for the normal brain sample (which is taken medially).

Therefore, while a given volume of CSF can be estimated fairly accurately if it is in the medial area, the same volume is given a much lower estimate if it is in the periphery. If two such estimates of fluid volume, one from the periphery and one from the medial area, are summed, the sum is little higher than the medial value alone, although their true volume is about twice the medial value. This effectively weights the medial values much more heavily than the peripheral ones. Note that the peripheral CSF proportion may measure interindividual variation in peripheral fluid volume quite accurately, as appears to be the case from the analysis of Section 8 described above. However, a combined measure does not average the CSF volumes from both areas accurately, as neuroradiologists attempt to do in their visual rating. The sensitivity of the peripheral CSF measure is truncated, because, when CT values from areas where some fluid is present are so inflated that they equal the normal brain value, no fluid is detected.

A second reason for the low correlation of the automated measure with the clinical rating of the sulci was that more weight was placed on some areas than others by the neuroradiologist's visual rating. Particular attention was directed to areas where the neuroradiologist expected to find evidence of sulcal widening. The automated measures weight all areas within the specified set of subsegments equally. Thus the CSF proportion in the peripheral area of Section 9 alone correlated with the overall clinical rating of the sulci at .75, whereas that of Section 3 alone correlated at only .20, although the variances of these two CSF measures were quite close. Assuming that the reliabilities of the two measures are comparable, the neuroradiologist's rating may have been based more on the CSF variations in the periphery of Section 9 than on those in Section 3.

Future investigators will find that the artifactual inflation of peripheral CT values imposes a major limitation on automated measures of the sulci from CT scans, as described above. This is a problem for most scanners and must be taken into account in the interpretation of the results. The technique of segmenting the medial and peripheral areas, as we have done, provides a way to minimize the effects of this artifact. The two measures can be entered separately into the data analysis, for example, or their standardized scores can be combined to yield a more valid overall score.

Another way in which the bone artifact can cause problems is by inflating the CT values of the normal brain sample (a_b). To avoid this distortion, the sample should be taken in white matter areas as far away from the skull as possible. We prefer to take the sample from the region just lateral to the third ventricle on lower sections, just lateral to the lateral ventricles above these, and in the center of the centrum semiovale on high sections.

CSF Measures from Elderly Women

Analysis of the Global Measures

One application of this automated CT scan analysis to the neuropsychology of aging lies in establishing the degree of correlation between cognitive functions and cerebral atrophy in the normal elderly. A study with this aim is currently under way by the present authors and is described in greater detail in Chapters 4 and 5 of this book. A subset of the group described in those chapters, 30 of the female subjects, were given cognitive tests and CT scans. The initial phases of this investigation have highlighted a number of methodological and conceptual problems that must be considered by any researcher examining the relation between CT scan analyses and neuropsychological test performance. To begin with, it has been very difficult to formulate an adequate test of the hypothesized relation between these two sets of variables. The number of subjects studied in the present study was much smaller than the number of measures of cognitive function we collected. Furthermore, because we found few data in the literature that were relevant to the expected findings in such a select group, we were unable to reduce the number of cognitive variables on empirical grounds. A statistical test of the relation that included a large number of cognitive variables in combination would have lacked power with so small a sample size. A test that involved multiple analyses, each with a small number of variables, would have increased the "experiment-wise" Type I error above acceptable limits. The analysis selected was an "all possible subset" regression (Furnival & Wilson, 1974) described in Mosteller and Tukey (1977). The subtest scores from the Wechsler Adult Intelligence Scale (WAIS) were entered into four multiple regression analyses. In each, the criterion variable was one of the following: the clinical rating of the sulci, the automated CSF proportion for the peripheral (primarily sulcal) areas, the clinical rating of the ventricles, and the automated medial (primarily ventricular) CSF proportion. The WAIS subtests were selected for several reasons: They are relatively well standardized, their use is widespread, and they include measures of most of the cognitive abilities of greatest interest to us.

The results of the "best subset" regressions were not interpreted unless the F for the regression with all 11 variables in the equation was significant. This is a very conservative significance criterion, but it was necessary to reduce the likelihood of spurious findings due to test

Table 6-1 Best Subset Regression Results

Variable	Regression coefficient	t	p
Digit Span	−.0080	−5.12	<.01
Similarities	.0075	3.90	<.01
Constant	.055		

Note. For the Regression with 11 subtests, $F = 3.21$ ($p < .05$).

multiplicity. The criterion was met in only one of the regression analyses, the one with the automated medial CSF measure. The subset of the subtests that best predicted this measure consisted of the Digit Span and the Similarities subtests. The results of this analysis are summarized in Table 6-1. The regression coefficient for the Digit Span score was slightly higher than that for the Similarities score and was negative. The *t* statistics for the regression coefficients had 18 degrees of freedom, as specified by the method of Fisher's protected *t*, and were both significant at the .01 level. To obtain another estimate of their stability, a jackknifing technique was carried out by which the variability of the regression coefficients was estimated directly. This method is described in Mosteller and Tukey (1977). The regression coefficients obtained with this method were also significant.

Discussion

This result is interpreted to mean that Digit Span performance is adversely affected by ventricular enlargement in this population. The simple correlation of Digit Span with the medial CSF proportion was −.52 ($p < .01$). Also, the proportion of variability in the medial atrophy measure that can be predicted from Digit Span performance is significantly increased when a measure of initial intellectual endowment, Similarities, is added. This interpretation of the contribution of the Similarities subtest is made more convincing by the fact that the second and third best subsets of two variables included the Vocabulary and Information subtests, respectively, instead of Similarities. Both of these subtests are considered to tap so-called "crystallized" intellectual abilities, that is, functions that are relatively unaffected by aging. Other authors have suggested that structural brain changes can best be predicted by using difference scores computed from tests of resistant and of vulnerable abilities (Russell, Neuringer, & Goldstein, 1970; Wechsler, 1958). Our results support this contention and emphasize the importance of obtaining measures of original intellectual level in studies of brain function.

Although the overall *F* for the regression of the WAIS subtests with the clinical rating of the ventricles was not quite significant, the best subset selected in this analysis was very close to that given above. It consisted of the Digit Span, Digit Symbol, and Similarities subtests, the first two of which had negative coefficients.

The failure to find a significant relation between either of the sulcal measures and the WAIS subtests may have been due to the relative lack of power in these analyses. Because the CSF volumes from the medial and peripheral areas are combined in the automated sulcal measure, its validity is probably low. Although a better-designed automated sulcal measure might agree more closely with the clinical rating, several problems remain. First, the effects of the bone artifact on the sensitivity of even the visual sulcal rating may have reduced its predictive power sufficiently to produce a false negative result. Second, the range of variation in sulcal widening present in this group may have been too small for the effects of these changes to be detected with so few subjects. And third, the scores from the WAIS that we examined may simply not have been adequate measures of those cognitive functions that are affected most by sulcal widening.

Analysis of the Subsegmental Measures

One question that arises, of course, is whether the different areas within the medial zone contribute differently to the correlation between ventricular dilatation and Digit Span performance. Unfortunately, the investigation of this possibility poses even more difficult statistical problems. The following is a summary of some further analyses that we performed on the subsegmental measures and their relation to the Digit Span subtest. These analyses should be considered purely exploratory in nature and the results only suggestive of the underlying relations.

An arbitrary test statistic, described below, was computed to measure the relation between the set of medial subsegment scores and the Digit Span score. An approximate randomization test method was used to perform a distribution-free test of the significance of this statistic (Edgington, 1969; Jernigan & Ahumada, in preparation).

Using the actual data, the Digit Span score was correlated with each of the 30 medial subsegment scores from Sections 3 through 7. Then the eight subsegments with the highest negative correlations were entered into a multiple regression analysis with the Digit Span score. The obtained R^2 was taken as the test statistic. For the randomization test, the entire analysis was performed 20 times, and in each case the subsegment scores of each subject were randomly assigned to the Digit Span score of another. The statistics obtained in the randomized runs were compared to that obtained in the experimental analysis. The results are summarized below.

R^2 for the Digit Span regression with 8 variables: .54
R^2 for the 20 randomized simulations:

.31	.30	.15	.37
.20	.04	.46	.27
.11	.11	.18	.15
.06	.13	.12	.26
.35	.21	.26	.26

p = no. results as large as actual result/no. analyses = .048.

The R^2 obtained in the nonrandomized analysis was .54, and no randomized analysis produced as large a statistic. The probability of this event is less that .05. Figure 6.4 shows the locations of the eight subsegments entered into the regression analysis with the Digit Span score.

Discussion

The results of the stepwise regression suggest that the frontal areas in particular may be involved in the Digit Span performances, possibly those on the left more than those on the right. No significant improvement in the prediction of Digit Span scores was provided by adding posterior or right-hemisphere segments to the left frontal segments on Sections 3 and 6 (i.e., no variables had a significant F to enter at Step 2 of the regression). Interestingly, in studies of cerebral blood flow in elderly and demented subjects, higher correlations were found between left-sided measures and psychometric indices than between those indices and right-sided measures (Feinberg, Lane, & Lassen, 1960; Lassen, Feinberg, & Lane, 1960).

The validity of this pattern among the subsegment correlations, however, would be impossible to establish at this point. A replication of the pattern should be obtained before it can be considered meaningful. Furthermore, the interpretation of such a pattern must take into account certain other factors. For example, a pattern like this one may occur partly because variability in the CSF measures is only occurring to a sufficient degree in certain subsegments of the brain. In a group of stroke patients, for example, there could be considerable variability in the CSF proportion in areas where little occurs in the normal aged. This variability could be even more significant for their Digit Span performance than that in the left medial frontal segments was for Digit Span performance in the aged subjects. The relative variances observed in the measures, then, must be considered if general brain-behavior inferences are to be drawn. It is also important to know the established validity and reliability of the individual subsegment measures. If either validity or reliability is significantly different for different subsegment measures, then the pattern obtained may be due to this factor rather than to the underlying structures' contributing unequally to the cognitive function.

A few further comments are in order about analyses of the subsegment measures. Both the bone artifact and possible technical artifacts render simple comparisons of the mean CT values from different areas of the scan (or any measures computed from them) even more difficult to interpret than the correlation methods described above. This is because systematic differences in the shape of the adjacent skull, or in the proximity of the sampled regions to the skull, may produce significant differences in the mean CT values when the underlying tissues themselves are apparently identical. It is inappropriate, for example, to compare actual CT values from anterior peripheral areas to those from posterior peripheral areas. Differences between frontal and posterior areas, and from one hemisphere to another, may result from technical artifacts or the shape of the skull (Lemay, 1976). It should be possible, however, to establish differences between different areas by showing disparities in their relations to criterion variables, such as age, so long as artifacts and statistical issues are considered. Skull idiosyncracies might also produce differences between CT values from the same area in different subjects, but this effect should be smaller and the differences should tend to cancel each other.

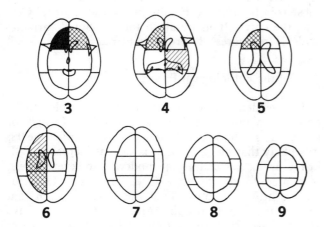

Figure 6-4. Locations of the eight subsegments with the highest negative Pearson correlations with the Digit Span score. Diagonal lines indicate areas with r's in the outer 5% of the distribution, cross-hatching indicates those with r's in the outer 1%, and black areas are those with r's in the outer .1%. The patient's right is on the reader's right.

Problems of Interpreting "Atrophy" in CT Scans

In the study with elderly women described above, the negative findings are perhaps as striking as the positive ones. No evidence was found for an association between degrees of apparent cerebral atrophy and performance on many cognitive tasks. We have tried above to point out some measurement issues that may have led to this result. The following paragraphs discuss some more general issues related to the nature and consequences of cerebral atrophy, issues that may also be relevant to our findings.

Increased CSF as Evidence of Brain Atrophy

Recent research has called in question the traditional interpretations of apparent cerebral atrophy. Previously the most likely cause for gradual increases in ventricular size was believed to be neural degeneration, probably in white-matter tracts that surround the ventricles. Similarly, increases in CSF on the cortex were thought to reflect loss of neurons in the adjacent cortical gyri. The following studies suggest that these changes may not, in some instances, be due to cell loss at all.

In an early CT study of anorexia nervosa (Enzmann & Lane, 1977), enlargement of the cortical sulci was found in three out of four patients examined. In a second study, by Heinz, Martinez, and Haenggeli (1977), sulcal widening and ventricular enlargement were found in four anorexia nervosa patients and one Cushing's patient. Repeat scans, however, showed apparent reversal of the atrophy in one of the anorexia nervosa patients and in the Cushing's patient. The study was notable in that the investigators were among the first to question the neural basis for the atrophy and to invoke possible explanations such as electrolyte and protein changes that might alter cranial fluid content.

Soon after these reports, Bentson, Reza, Winter, and Wilson (1978) reported similar findings in patients receiving steroid treatments. Both ventricular and sulcal enlargement were noted. In two cases in which repeat scans were obtained after reduction or cessation of steroid use, the apparent atrophy had decreased. The authors pointed out the possibility that changes resembling atrophy may be a nonneural concomitant of the poorly understood action of steroids on the brain. Reversed cerebral atrophy was also reported in a study of patients undergoing chemotherapy for cancers (Enzmann & Lane, 1978). Four of 32 patients were shown to have reduced ventricular and sulcal enlargement on repeat scans.

Most of the patients studied in these investigations were children or young adults. However, similar changes have also been reported in older adults. Carlen, Wortzman, Holgate, Wilkinson, and Rankin (1978) published a controversial report of increased ventricular size and considerably widened sulci in the CT scans of eight alcoholic patients. These findings were corroborated by two other studies in which atrophy was found in approximately 75% of the CT scans of alcoholics (Cala, Jones, Mastaglia, & Wiley, 1978; von Gall, Becker, Artmann, Lerch, & Nemeth, 1978). In repeat scans made after eight months of abstinence, four patients showed less atrophy, particularly in the form of narrower sulci (Carlen et al., 1978). Hill and Mikhael (1979) have challenged these findings, contending that measurement error is the most likely source of the reductions obtained. The reported interrater reliabilities for the CT measurements given by Carlen et al. are high and argue against this explanation, however.

None of the studies reviewed here can be taken as definitive, since the methods and designs were often crude and the number of subjects examined was small. The findings are suggestive, however, and several of these results have implications for the study of cerebral atrophy in the elderly. First, increases in CSF over the levels found in young subjects, especially slight increases, cannot be assumed to reflect neural changes. Second, when a difference is found between repeated measures of atrophy, it cannot be assumed to reflect a monotonic increase. Neither can the absence of a difference be interpreted as no change, especially when non-CNS pathology requires temporary chemotherapy or steroid treatments. Finally, if reversible atrophy exists, the correlations obtained for functional variables with CT measures will probably be reduced.

Rate of the Pathological Process

The incidence and magnitudes of reversible effects on CSF volume are unknown at this time. In light of numerous pathological studies done over many years, it is likely that much of what is seen as increased CSF in the brain, particularly at moderate to severe levels, is related to degenerative CNS processes. Unfortunately, little is known about the type of lesion that results in cerebral atrophy. Microscopic studies have shown that certain cellular changes occur with greater frequency in the brains of older people, and particularly in those of demented patients (Morel & Wildi, 1952; Scheibel & Scheibel, 1975; Tomlinson & Henderson, 1976). It is tempting to assume that these changes are causally related to the gross shrinkage of the brain so often noted on post-mortem examination of old people. However this relation has not been established, although some circumstantial evidence has been offered, such as the frontotemporal distribution of both cellular and gross changes (Brody, 1955; Morel & Wildi, 1952; Scheibel & Scheibel, 1975). Even if degenerative cellular changes prove to be linked to global atrophy, however, their consequences for the function of the affected areas remain undescribed.

Ample evidence in the animal literature suggests that the functional consequences of multiple lesions in the brain are often dependent on the time course of the causative process. For example, lesions made simultaneously may result in more striking deficits than identical lesions made in several stages (Finger, Walbran, & Stein, 1973). It is not known whether the functional effects of cerebral atrophy are more similar to simultaneous or to staged lesions, but the latter seems more likely.

Perhaps more relevant are the findings in human neuropsychological studies that cognitive effects of acutely destructive or rapidly progressive lesions are different from those of gradually progressive lesions. The deficits seen in the gradual lesions are generally milder, more factorially complex, and more difficult to localize (Fitzhugh, Fitzhugh, & Reitan, 1961; Reitan, 1966; Russell et al., 1970). All of these effects argue against the success of naive clinico-anatomic hypotheses in studies of the elderly. It may be of considerable value in these studies to obtain a measure of the rate of brain deterioration when possible—for example, when repeat scans are feasible.

Conclusion

In the preceding sections, numerous methodological and theoretical problems have been described. As always, unexpected complexities have emerged that temper the original enthusiasm over this new technique and its potential uses. However, the data obtained in the study described here are encouraging. It now seems likely that, given the caveats reviewed here, the relation of specific deficits occurring in the elderly to specific sites of cerebral degeneration may be revealed with this technique. In the near future, technological progress will make available higher resolution, lower radiation scans, and cheaper, and more accessible scanning units. In addition, other tomographic techniques will be used to provide data that will complement the results from the improved CT scans. With careful analysis and accurate interpretation of these data will come significant increases in our understanding of the processes of normal and pathological aging.

REFERENCES

Bentson, J., Reza, M., Winter, J., & Wilson, G. Steroids and apparent cerebral atrophy on computed tomography scans. *Journal of Computer Assisted Tomography*, 1978, *2*, 16–23.

Brody, H. Organization of the cerebral cortex. III. A study of aging in the human cerebral cortex. *Journal of Comparative Neurology*, 1955, *102*, 511–556.

Cala, L. A., Jones, B., Mastaglia, F. L., & Wiley, B. Brain atrophy and intellectual impairment in heavy drinkers. A clinical psychometric and computerized tomography study. *Australia and New Zealand Journal of Medicine*, 1978, *8*, 147–153.

Carlen, P. L., Wortzman, G., Holgate, R. C., Wilkinson, D. A., & Rankin, J. G. Reversible cerebral atrophy in recently abstinent chronic alcoholics measured by computed tomography scans. *Science*, 1978, *200*, 1076–1078.

Edgington, E. S. *Statistical inference: The distribution-free approach.* New York: McGraw-Hill, 1969.

Enzmann, D. R., & Lane, B. Cranial computed tomography findings in anorexia nervosa. *Journal of Computer Assisted Tomography*, 1977, *1*, 410–414.

Enzmann, D. R., & Lane, B. Enlargement of subarachnoid spaces and lateral ventricles in pediatric patients undergoing chemotherapy. *Journal of Pediatrics*, 1978, *92*, 535–539.

Feinberg, I., Lane, M. H., & Lassen, N. A. Senile dementia and cerebral oxygen uptake measured on the right and left sides. *Nature*, 1960, *188*, 962–964.

Finger, S., Walbran, B., & Stein, D. G. Brain damage and behavioral recovery: Serial lesion phenomena, *Brain Research*, 1973, *63*, 1–18.

Fitzhugh, K. B., Fitzhugh, L. C., & Reitan, R. M. Psychological deficits in relation to acuteness of brain dysfunction. *Journal of Consulting Psychology*, 1961, *25*, 61–66.

Furnival, G. N., & Wilson, R. W. Regression by leaps and bounds. *Technometrics*, 1974, *16*, 499–511.

Heinz, E. R., Martinez, J., & Haenggeli, A. Reversibility of cerebral atrophy in anorexia nervosa and Cushing's syndrome. *Journal of Computer Assisted Tomography*, 1977, *1*, 415–418.

Hill, S. Y., & Mikhael, M. Computed tomography scans of alcoholics: Cerebral atrophy? *Science*, 1979, 1237–1238.

Jernigan, T. L., & Ahumada, A. J. *A randomization test method for assessing multivariate relationships in neuropsychology.* Manuscript in preparation.

Jernigan, T. L., Zatz, L. M., & Naeser, M. A. Semiautomated methods for quantitating CSF volume on cranial computed tomography. *Radiology*, 1979, *132*, 463–466.

Lassen, N. A., Feinberg, I., & Lane, M. H. Bilateral studies of cerebral oxygen uptake in young and aged normal subjects, and in particular with organic dementia. *Journal of Clinical Investigation*, 1960, *39*, 491–500.

LeMay, M. Morphological cerebral asymmetries of modern man, fossil man, and nonhuman primate. *Annals of the New York Academy of Sciences*, 1976, *280*, 349–366.

Morel, F., & Wildi, E. General and cellular pathochemistry of senile and presenile alterations of the brain. *Proceedings of the First International Congress of Neuropathology*, 1952, *2*, 347–374.

Mosteller, F., & Tukey, J. W. *Data analysis and regression*. Reading, Mass.: Addison Wesley, 1977.

Reitan, R. M. A research program on the psychological effects of brain lesions in human beings. In N. R. Ellis (Ed.), *International review of research in mental retardation*, 1. New York: Academic Press, 1966.

Russell, E. W., Neuringer, C., & Goldstein, G. *Assessment of brain damage: A neuropsychological key*. New York: Wiley-Interscience, 1970.

Scheibel, M. E., & Scheibel, A. B. Structural changes in the aging brain. In H. Brody, D. Harman, & J. M. Ordy (Eds.), *Aging* (Vol. 1). New York: Raven Press, 1975.

Tomlinson, B. E., & Henderson, G. Some quantitative cerebral findings in normal and demented old people. In R. D. Terry & S. Gershon (Eds.), *Aging* (Vol. 3). New York: Raven Press, 1976.

von Gall, M., Becker, H., Artmann, H., Lerch, G. & Nemeth, N. Results of computer tomography on chronic alcoholics. *Neuroradiology*, 1978, *16*, 329–331.

Wechsler, D. *The measurement and appraisal of adult intelligence*. Baltimore: Williams & Wilkins, 1958.

Psychophysiological Issues: Brain Evoked Potentials

Stephen W. Harkins, *Section Editor*

Introduction

The following four chapters are concerned with recent applications of event-related-potential techniques in the study of normal and abnormal aging. Event-related potentials (ERPs) are the spatial-temporal pattern of brain electrical activity that is synchronized to the onset of an afferent stimulus or that follows an expected event. Because of the poor signal-to-noise ratio inherent in spontaneous electroencephalographic (EEG) activity, individual ERPs are generally not observable after any single stimulus presentation. ERPs, however, are assumed to be time-locked to stimulus presentation, while background EEG activity is assumed to be random in time with respect to stimulus presentation. Thus, by use of computers or summation devices, it is relatively easy to obtain ERPs averaged over a number of stimulus presentations.

The study of ERPs to discrete afferent stimulation is becoming commonplace in human psychophysiology. Substantial gains in ERP research are likely to occur in the coming decade because ERPs make it possible to evaluate physiological processes that may be related to sensory, perceptual, and cognitive functioning. The increased availability of low-cost signal-averaging equipment and microprocessors will have an obvious impact on the quantity of ERP studies in the near future. In gerontological research, there is a critical need for studies that address specific issues relevant to normal and abnormal aging, rather than for increasing numbers of purely empirical observations. The relation of evoked brain potentials to well-documented age changes in performance or in the evaluation of elderly persons with specific dementing illnesses are two areas obviously in need of thoughtful investigation.

ERP research has been limited by the following circumstances: (a) With few exceptions, the neural sites of origin of particular components of the ERP have not been defined, (b) the physiological mechanisms that give rise to ERPs are poorly understood, and (c) there is a poorly established relation between clinical states and changes in ERPs. Nevertheless, a relation has been found between properties of the ERP and psychological processes such as attention, speed of motor response, expectation, and complex cognitive behavior. Since it is these psychological processes that appear to undergo major changes with senescence, the future of ERPs in aging research appears promising, particularly since ERPs provide a noninvasive procedure for evaluating physiological concomitants and psychological processes of aging.

A recent advance in ERP research is the discovery that certain very short-latency, low-amplitude brain responses to auditory and somatosensory stimuli reflect sequential activation of brainstem nuclei. The clinical implications of these evoked potentials have been recognized (Starr, 1978). This discovery has led to the distinction between far-field and near-field brain electrical potentials, a distinction that is growing in importance. Far-field potentials refer to the volume conduction of electrical activity over a relatively large distance. Near-field potentials refer to electrical activity the source of which is comparatively close to the recording electrode (Jewett, 1970). Far-field brain potentials are widely distributed over the scalp. They cannot be recorded from bipolar recordings if the electrodes are only a short distance apart. Far-field potentials are, with few exceptions, not influenced by subject factors such as attention, alertness, cognitive load, or expectation. They provide an excellent example of obligatory brain responses to discrete afferent stimulation. As such, they permit, for the first time, evaluation of peripheral factors influencing characteristics of later or more rostrally occurring ERPs.

Chapter 7 discusses recent findings using far-field or brainstem auditory evoked potentials (BAEPs) in the study of normal and abnormal aging. This chapter presents findings that BAEPs may not change with normal aging per se but, rather, may reflect the degree of high-frequency hearing loss due to presbycusis. Latency shifts in these brainstem potentials appear in the presenile dementia patient, and Harkins and Lenhardt suggest that the BAEP may be useful in early diagnosis of such patients.

No studies to date have systematically evaluated far-field somatosensory evoked potentials in relation to aging, although evidence exists that these brainstem potentials may be related to sensory-perceptual experience (Harkins & Dong, 1979). This may be a particularly promising area for further research.

Near-field or cortical potentials are characterized by large differences in amplitude and polarity, with relatively small changes in electrode position. They are usually maximal in amplitude over a limited area of the scalp or cortex. These potentials are greatly influenced by subject factors. The relation between near-field or cortical ERPs in patients with clinical diagnoses of dementia is explored in Chapter 9. Squires and his associates report significant increases in latency of a particular component, the P_3 wave, in such patients. Their chapter discusses the feasibility of using this brain response to provide an objective means for distinguishing between normal and abnormal changes in age-related cognitive functioning. Squires et al. focus particularly on neurological diseases associated with advancing age. Their chapter highlights a need for future research to specify the diagnostic utility of ERPs in well-defined groups of cognitively impaired elderly patients. Well-controlled ERP study comparing Alzheimer's-type dementia patients with multi-infarct dementia patients is an obvious example.

Age changes in near-field potentials is also the sub-ject of Chapter 8, which focuses on a special subgroup of the elderly—the very healthy. Ford and Pfefferbaum report that ERPs reflect deficits in memory acquisition or encoding speed and motor time but not in memory scanning or retrieval time. Their chapter summarizes several years of research activities in this area and points to the relations between brain and behavioral responses in the very healthy elderly.

Chapter 10 reviews most of the research on brain potentials and aging. Smith, Thompson, and Michalewski present not only the historical context of this research but also future directions, particularly those with theoretical and clinical implications for the psychophysiology of aging.

There are several major issues in aging research for the coming decade that may not be unique to ERP studies, including both methodological and theoretical concerns that will be difficult to ignore. Where age differences are observed for some dependent measure, the question must be asked, whether this difference is due to age or to some factors of the methodology itself. For example, observed age differences in the contingent negative variation (CNV)—a very late brain response to expected events—may be due not to the effects of age on the underlying physiological processes giving rise to these potentials but rather to situational factors that differentially distract the elderly subject (Harkins, Moss, Thompson, & Nowlin, 1976). The research by Tecce and his colleagues is an excellent example of sensitivity to such factors and also illustrates the importance of evaluating topographical differences in ERPs, in old as compared to young people (Tecce, Yrchik, Meinbresse, Dessonville, & Cole, in press). In cases where such methodological issues are controlled and an age effect is apparent, attempts to specify the source of the effect are appropriate. For example, age differences in sensory potentials may be due as much to peripheral factors as to central processes. The impact of presbycusis on auditory potentials—even of relatively low-frequency acoustic stimulation—and subclinical peripheral neuropathies can influence both far-field and near-field somatosensory potentials. Finally, when the above issues are defined to the greatest degree possible, the question of concern becomes whether the age differences are due to the processes of age *qua* age or to disease, since the probability of disease increases with age. Only when disease processes are ruled out can the effects of age per se be evaluated.

The direction of ERP research in the coming decade must not only focus on the above issues but must do so on a firm theoretical basis. This will necessitate both studies to evaluate well-defined behavioral processes that are known to change with age, such as speed, and analysis of ERPs during task performance. The challenge of the coming years will be to develop paradigms that are theoretically based and that will allow parametric evaluation.

REFERENCES

Harkins, S. W., Moss, S. F., Thompson, L. W., & Nowlin, J. B. Relationship between central and autonomic nervous system activity: Correlates of psychomotor performance in elderly men. *Experimental Aging Research*, 1976, *2*, 409–423.

Harkins, S. W., & Dong, W. K. Averaged evoked potentials and sensory experience. In D. R. Kenshalo (Ed.), *Sensory functions of the skin of humans*. New York: Plenum Press, 1979.

Jewett, D. Volume-conducted potentials in response to auditory stimuli as detected by averaging in the cat. *Electroencephalography and Clinical Neurophysiology*, 1970, *28*, 609–618.

Starr, A. Sensory evoked potentials in clinical disorders of the nervous system. In W. Cowan, Z. Hall, & E. Kandel (Eds.), *Annual Review of Neuroscience*, 1978, *1*, 103–127.

Tecce, J. J., Yrchik, D. A., Meinbresse, D., Dessonville, B. A., & Cole, J. O. Age-related diminution of CNV rebound: I. Attention functions. In L. Deeke & H. H. Kornhuber (Eds.), *Motivation, motor and sensory processes of the brain: Electrical potentials, behavior and clinical use. Progress in brain research* (Vol. 54). Amsterdam, The Netherlands: Elsevier, in press.

Stephen W. Harkins and Martin Lenhardt

CHAPTER

7

Brainstem Auditory Evoked Potentials in the Elderly

Event-related potentials originating in specific relay nuclei of the auditory and somatosensory afferent tracts can be recorded from humans using scalp electrodes. In response to appropriate acoustic stimuli (up to seven waves), the brainstem auditory evoked potentials (BAEPs) occur within 8 msec of sound onset. Latency of these responses is influenced by stimulus intensity and rate as well as by the integrity of the brainstem auditory pathways.

In this chapter, the effects of age on the BAEP in the later years of life are discussed. The findings to date suggest that there is little change in these waves in healthy elderly persons that cannot be accounted for by presbycusis. One exception is an amplitude reduction in the healthy elderly in more rostral components. The effects of disease processes on the BAEP are reviewed, and data are presented suggesting that presenile dementia of the Alzheimer's type is associated with increased central nervous system transmission time.

Brainstem auditory evoked potentials (BAEPs) recorded from humans using surface skin electrodes were first reported by Sohmer and Feinmesser (1967) and subsequently were described in greater detail by Jewett and Williston (1971). The extensive and growing literature that has followed these reports reflects the emerging importance of these sensory evoked potentials. The BAEP is of particular interest to gerontologists because it allows measurement of both peripheral function and central neural activity in the auditory relay nuclei of the brainstem. The present chapter reviews recent findings concerning these evoked potentials and examines their utility in the study of normal and abnormal aging.

Site of Origin of Brainstem Auditory Evoked Potentials (BAEPs)

Figure 7-1 illustrates a BAEP obtained from a young adult with normal hearing. Following the convention established by Jewett and Williston (1971), we have labeled the individual waves of the BAEP with roman numerals. To obtain this sensory evoked potential, electroencephalographic (EEG) electrodes were attached to vertex and the right mastoid region, and a ground electrode was placed on the right ear. The evoking stimuli were clicks presented monaurally to the right ear at a rate of 10 per second and at an intensity of 70 dB equivalent hearing level (HL). The BAEP in Figure 7-1 and those in all subsequent figures were obtained by summing 1,024 or more individual responses.

There is greater consensus for where each wave of the BAEP originates than for any other scalp-recorded evoked potential. The sites of generation of Waves I through V have been associated with neural activity of the acoustic portion of the eighth cranial nerves (Wave I), the cochlear nuclei (Wave II), the superior olivary

The authors would like to thank Teresa McEvoy, Molly Warner, and Monte Scott for their attention to detail in data collection and reduction, Bruce Weber for his critical review of an early draft of this chapter, and Jodi Teitelman for her editorial assistance.

Research support was provided by National Institute on Aging Grants AG 02290 and AG 00573.

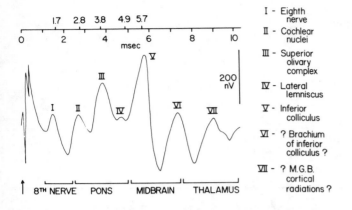

Figure 7-1. Brainstem auditory evoked potential (BAEP). The BAEP is typically composed of from 5 to 7 waves in the nanovolt range that occur within 8 to 10 milliseconds (msec) after onset of an appropriate acoustic stimulus. In this instance, the stimulus was an unfiltered or broadband transient (click) presented at 70 dB SL at an interstimulus interval of 100 msec. The putative site of origin of each wave is given on the right-hand side of the figure. Latency of peaks based on data from 11 young subjects are given for Waves I to V at the top of the time line. Clicks were delivered via Telephonics TDH 049 earphones with MX-41AR cushions and were generated by a Grason-Stadler click generator. Positivity at vertex produces an upward deflection (see test for recording details). Sweeptime in this and the following figures is 10.24 msec.

nuclei (Wave III), the lateral lemnisci or the nuclei lateral lemnisci (Wave IV), and the inferior colliculi (Wave V), as denoted in Figure 7-1. Waves VI and VIII may originate from the brachium of inferior colliculi and from the medial geniculate body, respectively. The origins of Waves I and II are fairly well accepted, but further investigation is needed to define the precise location of Wave III and the potentials following it. It is possible that the more rostral originating components of the BAEP reflect physiological responsiveness of the site specified, in addition to neural activity from the more caudal portions of the auditory afferent pathways. Interpretation of sites of origin is based on lesion studies in cats (Buchwald & Huang, 1975), topographic studies in humans (Hashimoto, Ishiyama, & Tozuka, 1979; Jewett & Williston, 1971; Van Olphen, Rodenburg, & Verwey, 1978), and correlations with confirmed sites of brainstem lesions in humans (Sohmer, Feinmesser, & Szabo, 1974; Starr, 1978; Starr & Achor, 1975, 1978; Starr & Hamilton, 1976; Stockard & Rossiter, 1977). While there is agreement on the site of origin for Waves I through V, it must be recognized that this remains tentative, particularly for the later waves. Nevertheless, it is well ac-

cepted that these waves reflect the physiological response of the classic brainstem auditory pathways.

Stability of the BAEP

Compared to other sensory evoked potentials, the BAEP is extremely stable when recorded from people with normal hearing, as is apparent in Figure 7-2. In this figure, eight repeated BAEPs from the same subject are overlapped. Wave IV, typically the most variable and smallest of the BAEP components, is buried in the trough between Waves III and V. Variations of peak latency for Wave V that exceed from .1 to .15 msec between repeated averages for one subject suggest artifacts in the recording system or the presence of an unacceptably high level of muscle activity. The within-subject stability of peak latencies of major components of the BAEP allows for some degree of confidence in calculating interwave latencies. Indeed, it is this feature that makes these responses of particular interest in the assessment of physiological integrity of the brainstem and in gerontological research.

Laboratories that report the interwave latency between Waves I and V have almost universally found it to be approximately 4.0 msec. If there was an increase in interwave latency in an elderly subject without apparent neurological deficits, it could be interpreted as a change in conduction along central nervous system (CNS) neurons or age changes in synaptic processes.

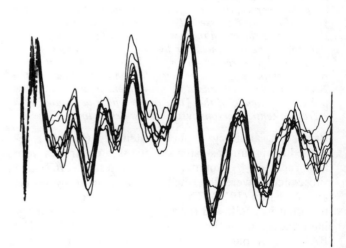

Figure 7-2. Stability of the brainstem auditory evoked potential (BAEP). Eight repeated BAEPs are overlapped to illustrate within-subject stability of the response. Recordings were from a young subject, as in Figure 7-1. Positivity at vertex produces an upward deflection. The click artifact is apparent in the first .7-msec period.

Such a slowing of brainstem transmission, even on the order of .3 msec, would be indicative of a CNS processing change with age. It would be important to explore this latency in regard to age-related deficits in more complex processes, such as the cognitive and psychomotor speed deficits often seen in elderly persons. The effects of normal and abnormal age changes on the BAEP are discussed in detail below.

Effect of Stimulus Intensity on the BAEP

As the stimulus intensity is decreased, there is a progressive increase in peak latency of all components of the BAEP. This increase is accompanied by a loss of resolution of the early waves. Waves VI and VII sometimes fail to be observed at low-intensity stimulation. Wave V, in turn, is often observed almost to subjective threshold. Figure 7-3 illustrates the effects of click intensity on the BAEP.

From instances where Waves I and V can be resolved at near-threshold intensities, it appears that interwave latency between these waves remains constant with changing stimulus intensity. Even at low intensities, Wave V follows Wave I by approximately 4 msec in the healthy young ear, indicating that intensity-dependent latency shifts in Wave V are due to receptor processes and subsequent changes in Wave I latency. Simultaneous recording of the electrocochleogram, which depends on the response of the auditory nerve, and Wave I of the BAEP show that they are equally responsive to intensity of acoustic stimuli (Eggermont, Odenthal, Schmidt, et al., 1974; Sohmer & Feinmesser, 1967). The electrocochleogram is recorded by placing an electrode in the external auditory canal close to the tympanic membrane or by surgically piercing the tympanic membrane and placing an electrode directly on the promontory of the medial wall of the middle ear. Latency of the electrocochleogram and Wave I of the BAEP reflect activation of the cochlea and auditory nerve without involvement of an intervening synapse (Davis, 1976), supporting the view that receptor responsiveness is the source of shifts in latency of all components of the BAEP as a function of stimulus intensity.

The effect of stimulus intensity on latency of the BAEP is summarized in Figure 7-4. This figure presents the latency of Wave V in three young men with normal hearing, except for subject BP, who had unusually acute hearing. Latency of Wave V is plotted between 5 and 80 dB HL. The regression equations for each subject are given in the upper right-hand corner. The y-intercept is an estimate of "threshold" for the BAEP. The slope (40 μsec/dB) observed here is con-

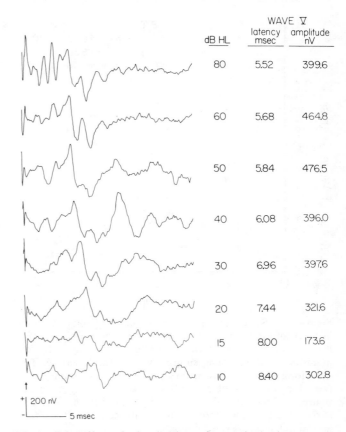

Figure 7-3. Effect of stimulus intensity on the brainstem auditory evoked potential (BAEP). Raw data from one young subject with normal hearing illustrate the effects of click intensity on latency and amplitide of components of the BAEP. (Interstimulus interval = 100 msec.) Note the progressive loss of resolution of the early waves with decreasing click intensity. Latency of Wave V faithfully follows intensity, changing approximately .04 msec/dB. Amplitude of Wave V is not reliably related to stimulus intensity. Stimulus and recording conditions are as in Figure 7-1 (see text).

sistent with that reported elsewhere (Galambos & Hecox, 1977).

The lowest-level stimulus that elicits a clearly detectable response can be of value in estimating hearing level and degree of hearing impairment by extrapolation for BAEP threshold (Weber & Fujikawa, 1977). One phenomenon that we have observed in from 17% to 20% of subjects is also illustrated in Figure 7-4. In subject BP there is a change in the responsiveness of Wave V between 25 and 35 dB. We have generally observed this occurring between 45 to 50 dB in young subjects and between 50 to 55 dB in the elderly. It is interesting to speculate that this type of response over the range of a few decibels may reflect CNS interac-

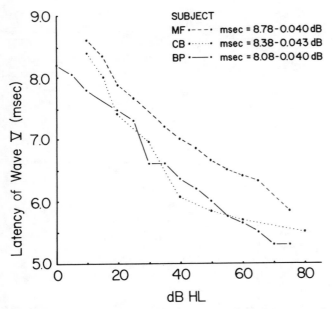

Figure 7-4. Summary of effects of intensity on latency of Wave V of the brainstem auditory evoked potential (BAEP). Latency of Wave V of the BAEP is plotted against click intensity for three young subjects with normal hearing. The data for subject CB are from Figure 7-3. Regression equations for each subject are presented at the top right of the figure. Subject BP had exceptionally acute hearing, and this is reflected in the y-intercept but not in the slope. Recording and stimuli as in previous figures.

tion between high-threshold (inner hair cells) and low-threshold units (outer hair cells), as postulated by Davis and Hirsh (1977).

Unlike latency, amplitude of BAEP waves correlates poorly with stimulus intensity. Upon reexamination of Figure 7-3, it is apparent that amplitude of Wave V (defined at the positive peak to the subsequent negative trough) is not reliably related to click intensity. In fact, waves other than Wave V are difficult, if not impossible, to identify at the lowest intensities.

Effects of Interstimulus Interval on the BAEP

The rate at which clicks or tone pips are presented affects both amplitude and latency of the waves of the BAEP. The effects of decreasing interstimulus interval (ISI) on the BAEP from a healthy young ear is illustrated in Figure 7-5. In this figure a line is drawn through the peak of Wave V. As ISI decreased from 100 msec (10 clicks/sec) to 7.5 msec (133 clicks/sec), there was a progressive increase in the latency of Wave V. Figure 7-6 illustrates change in peak latencies of Waves I, II, III, and V, based on values from 11 young

subjects. There is a consistent increase in the latency of all components with decreasing ISI, particularly below an ISI of 30 msec (33 clicks/sec). Since Wave I latency increased, it is possible that changes in Wave V with decreasing ISI are due to peripheral adaptation and/or fatigue, not to changes in CNS activity. Adaptation does occur at the peripheral level in the auditory system. For example, Eggermont et al. (1974)

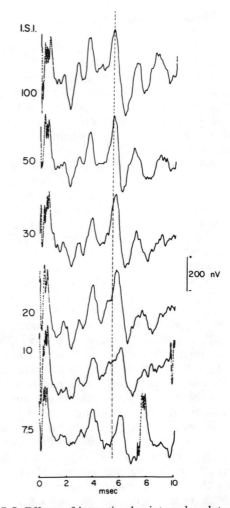

Figure 7-5. Effects of interstimulus interval on latency of the brainstem auditory evoked potential (BAEP). The effects of decreasing interstimulus interval (ISI), in msec, on BAEPs from one young subject with normal hearing are illustrated. A dashed line is drawn through the peak of Wave V to clicks with 100 ISI. Note the progressive shift in latency of this wave with decreasing ISI. (From "Effects of Interstimulus Interval on Latency of the Brainstem Auditory Evoked Potential" by S. W. Harkins, T. M. McEvoy, and M. L. Scott, *International Journal of Neuroscience*, 1979, *10*, 7–14. Copyright 1979 by Gordon and Breach Science Publishers Ltd. Reprinted by permission.)

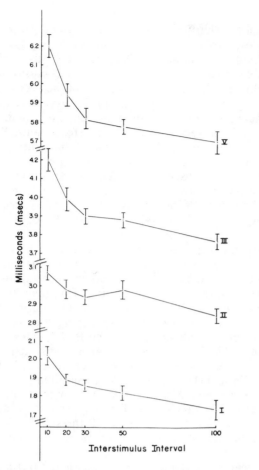

Figure 7-6. Mean latency in msec of each major component of the BAEP for 9 young subjects across various ISIs. Bars represent one standard error of the mean. (From "Effects of Interstimulus Interval on Latency of the Brainstem Auditory Evoked Potential" by S. W. Harkins, T. M. McEvoy, and L. M. Scott, *International Journal of Neuroscience*, 1979, *10*, 7–14. Copyright 1979 by Gordon and Breach Science Publishers Ltd. Reprinted by permission.)

report a .29-msec increase in the electrocochleogram between ISIs of 128 msec and 7 msec. This is consistent with the observed change in Wave I, illustrated in Figure 7-6, which was .29 msec between ISI 100 msec and ISI 10 msec. Evaluation of the changes in interwave latency with changing click rate allows estimation of central effects, if any.

The rate-dependent changes in interwave latency from Waves I to V (V minus I), from Waves II to V (V minus II), and from Waves III to V (V minus III) are plotted in Figure 7-7. As is apparent, there is a shift in the interwave latency between Waves I and V, indicating a CNS effect of click rate. An increase in the interwave latency between Waves I and V, how-

ever, is nonspecific, indicating a change between the level of the cochlear nuclei and the inferior collicular level. Changes in latency between Waves I and III would be more specific, suggesting change in activity at the medullary-pontine region. An increase in latency between Waves III and V would, in turn, indicate an effect at the pontine to tectal or midbrain level. The increase in latency between Waves II and V was significant, but the shift between Waves III and V was not (see Figure 7-7).

On the basis of these results, it appears that decreasing ISI has a dual effect on the latency of the BAEP, the first being a peripheral effect (as reflected by Wave I; see Figure 7-6) and the second, a CNS effect (as reflected in interwave latency between Waves II to V). The peripheral effect is probably due to the same phenomenon observed by Eggermont et al. (1974). It is interesting that the shift in Wave I (Figure 7-6) between ISI 100 msec and ISI 10 msec (.29 msec) was identical to that observed by Eggermont et al. (1974) for the electrocochleogram. The central effect, in turn, is very likely due to changes in synaptic processes with decreasing ISI, not to changes in conduction velocities of CNS elements (Harkins, McEvoy, & Scott, 1979).

Amplitude of the BAEP also changes reliably with

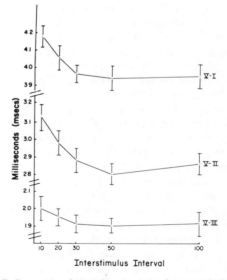

Figure 7-7. Interwave latencies or central transmission times between various components of the BAEP. Latency between components is on the ordinate and ISI on the abscissa (units on both axes in msec). (From "Effects of Interstimulus Interval on Latency of the Brainstem Auditory Evoked Potential" by S. W. Harkins, T. M. McEvoy, and L. M. Scott, *International Journal of Neuroscience*, 1979, *10*, 7–14. Copyright 1979 by Gordon and Breach Science Publishers Ltd. Reprinted by permission.)

decreasing ISI. Scott and Harkins (1978) report a progressive decrease in amplitude of Waves I, II, and III with decreasing ISI between 100 msec and 7.5 msec. Wave V exhibited an increase in amplitude between ISIs of 100 and 30 msec, but at ISIs shorter than 30 msec a decrease in Wave V amplitude was observed.

Subject Factors Influencing the BAEP

The major subject factors influencing the BAEP are hearing impairment, postnatal development of the central nervous system, and neurological disorders. Conductive, cochlear, and retrocochlear disorders generally result in prolonged latency, decreased amplitude, and elevation of thresholds for BAEPs. Wave V latency, because of its prominence and sensitivity to stimulus intensity, is the component of the BAEP most frequently used for clinical purposes.

In conductive hearing loss, Wave V latency to air-conduction clicks or tone-pips will show clinically relevant delays, but bone-conduction BAEPs will produce a Wave V within normal limits. BAEPs to bone conduction have been successfully recorded in a number of studies, and norms for particular laboratories are available (Maudlin & Jerger, 1979). In conductive hearing loss, the function relating latency of Wave V and stimulus intensity may simply be displaced above normal limits. In the case of sensorineural hearing loss with abnormal intensity recruitment, the response may be delayed at low intensities but may be within normal limits at higher intensities (Picton, Woods, Baribeau-Braun, & Healey, 1977).

The effect of cochlear damage on the BAEP is receiving increased attention. Of particular interest are attempts to relate characteristics of audiological findings to the BAEP, particularly with regard to identification of cochlear pathology. Such investigation rests on better control over the evoking stimulus. Broadband or unfiltered clicks are too nonspecific to allow the identification of frequency-specific hearing impairment. In the elderly, where progressive, high-frequency hearing loss (presbycusis) is the rule, improvement of stimulation parameters is obviously a factor of some concern. Behavior thresholds to unfiltered clicks, for example, may not change significantly with age, since the elderly person with even moderate presbycusis may be responding to the lower-frequency components of such stimuli. In such elderly persons, however, Wave V may show grossly increased thresholds (i.e., lowest intensity at which the response can be observed reliably) and prolonged latency at high intensity. This increased threshold may occur because the BAEP appears to arise from events originating in the high-fre-quency region (basal turn) of the cochlea (Galambos & Hecox, 1977).

Evidence indicates that the BAEP is due to synchronous activation of the basal portion of the cochlear hair (nerve) cells, mainly in the 1000- to 4000-Hz region (Coats & Martin, 1977; Don, Eggermont, & Brackmann, 1979; Picton et al. 1977; Picton & Smith, 1978). With regard to cochlear determinants, Wave V latency appears to depend on both integrity of appropriate receptors, in response to the traveling wave, and presence or absence of intensity recruitment in the transduction process (Picton et al., 1977). Combination of BAEPs with longer-latency auditory evoked potentials, such as the sustained potential P_3, or the contingent negative variation (Picton et al., 1977; see also Chapters 8 and 9 in this volume), may allow differentiation of patients with organic hearing loss from patients suspected of having nonorganic hearing loss.

Despite the success of the BAEP in identifying persons with middle-ear or cochlear deficits, little progress has been made in specifying the audiometric curve of the individual from the BAEP. Most authors report BAEPs to clicks or other transients, and, as noted, the frequency selectivity of unfiltered clicks is very limited (Davis, 1976). A recent attempt was made by Jerger and Maudlin (1979) to predict the audiogram in 275 ears with different types of hearing levels by correlation analysis of BAEP threshold and latency with behavioral audiometric indices. The results confirmed the importance of acuity in the 1000- to 4000-Hz region, as suggested by Coats and Martin (1977). The audiometric curve over this area is best predicted by multiplying the slope coefficient of the linear regression equation by the BAEP threshold for Wave V. The average pure-tone threshold (1.2 and 4 kHz) is most accurately predicted by multiplying the threshold of Wave V by .6. However, the standard error for such a calculation is 15.8 dB. Thus for a predicted pure-tone behavioral average of 55 dB, the probability is .67 that the actual value is between 40 and 71, and the probability is .95 for the threshold being between 25 and 86 dB. This offers little advantage in specifying pure-tone audiograms. Also, BAEP latency in the 70- to 90-dB HL range increased about .2 msec for each 30-dB increase in the sharpness of the audiogram between 1 and 4 kHz. The audiometric shape thus appears to be more important than absolute high-frequency hearing in determining Wave V latency. The subjects in the Jerger and Maudlin (1979) study ranged in age from 7 to 83 years, but no specific reference was made to aging as such.

Don et al. (1979) attempted to reconstruct behavior audiograms using high-pass masking noise in combination with broad-band clicks, and this may have implications for evaluation of individuals with presbycusis. At low intensities (down to 10 dB HL) the investigators found the BAEP to arise from the midfrequency regions between 1000 and 4000 Hz. At higher intensities (30 dB HL and above) contributions from lower frequency (500 Hz) as well as relatively high-frequency (up to 8,000 Hz) portions of the cochlea become apparent. The technique employed by Don et al. (1979) involves serial subtractions of the responses elicited to clicks in combination with high-pass masking noise from responses to unfiltered clicks. Using this derived BAEP procedure, Don et al. (1979) identified contributions to the BAEP originating from specific frequency regions of the cochlea with center frequencies at 500, 1000, 2000, 4000, and 8000 Hz in subjects with normal hearing. They found a high correlation between the amount of hearing loss, as indicated by conventional pure-tone audiometry, and derived BAEPs to low-level stimulation. Don and his associates are currently evaluating the derived BAEP technique in a large number of patients with peripheral hearing impairment, and the results of that study, if successful, may have significant effects on the use of the BAEP in evaluation of presbycusis in elderly people. This type of procedure indicates the limited value of using only unfiltered clicks in the study of BAEPs. Such stimuli, even at moderate intensities, stimulate nearly the whole cochlea. The derived BAEP high-pass masking technique may also be a productive approach to studying neural transmission time in uncooperative demented patients, either when auditory-input processing is desired for its own sake, or where the major interest is in analysis of transmission time over the central brainstem-auditory pathways in relation to disease processes.

A number of studies have evaluated the influences of postnatal development of the nervous system on the BAEP (Hecox & Galambos, 1974; Liberman, Sohmer, & Szabo, 1973; Salamy & McKean, 1976; Salamy, McKean, & Buda, 1975; Schulman-Galambos & Galambos, 1975). The results of these studies indicate that (a) BAEP component amplitudes increase with postgestational age, probably because of maturation and increase of neural elements; (b) BAEP response thresholds decrease with age because of maturation of the cochlea and neural elements; and (c) peak latencies decrease, probably owing to myelination of peripheral and central axons. The decrease in latency of the BAEP waveforms may also be due, in part, to maturational changes at the cochlea (Hecox, 1975). The BAEP appears to be a promising technique in assessment of auditory processes in infants and as a screening tool for children at risk for learning disorders due to peripheral hearing disorders.

The use of the BAEP as an assessment tool in clinical neurological disorders is relatively new (Starr, 1978). The BAEP is becoming increasingly important in evaluation of acoustic neuromas (Brackman & Selters, 1977; Terkildsen, Huis in't Veld, & Osterhammel, 1977; Thornton & Hawkes, 1976), in assessment for brainstem tumors (Starr & Achor, 1975; Stockard & Rossiter, 1977), and in certain degenerative and demyelinating disorders (Robinson & Rudge, 1975, 1977). Starr (1976) has suggested use of the BAEP as an index of brain death. Demyelination diseases such as multiple sclerosis can also result in prolongation of the interwave latencies of BAEP components (Robinson & Rudge, 1975, 1977; Shannon, Gold, Himmelfarb, & Carasso, 1979). The clinical usefulness of the BAEP in such cases derives from its effectiveness in distinguishing between peripheral and CNS disorders.

Effects of Aging on the BAEP

Only a few studies have evaluated the effects of age in the later years of life on the BAEP. Age differences or changes in the BAEP may be due to conductive, cochlear, or retrocochlear impairment. Latency changes due to age *qua* age can be identified only after complementary audiometric evaluation. The latency-intensity relation of Wave V in the elderly person with a conductive hearing loss may simply be shifted by an amount equivalent to such loss. Such people would probably show normal response latencies if tested with bone-conduction techniques (Maudlin & Jerger, 1979; Picton & Smith, 1978), and the interwave latency between Waves I and V would likely be normal.

Rowe (1978) evaluated normal variability of the BAEP in 25 young (age range from 17 to 33 years) and 25 elderly (age range from 51 to 75 years) subjects with no history of hearing impairment or neurological disease. Audiometric evaluation consisted of testing thresholds to the click stimuli employed to study the BAEP. The young group had behavioral thresholds within 6 dB of laboratory norms, while the elderly group was within 15 dB of norms. Ranges of the behavior thresholds within groups or other measures of central tendency were not reported. Stimuli were presented for both the behavioral testing and the BAEP studies in the ambient background noise of the laboratory. The click stimuli were delivered at 30 and 60 dB sensation level (SL); the monaural clicks at 60 dB SL were presented at 100-msec and 30-msec ISIs, while the 30-dB click was presented at a 33-msec ISI. Peak latencies were determined to the nearest .1 msec for Waves I to VII, and amplitude of Wave V was determined as the positive peak to negative trough. The interwave latency between the various peaks was computed in order to estimate the effects of age on both peripheral factors (Wave I latency) and CNS conduction times (e.g., Wave I to Wave V interval).

Rowe (1978) found that stimulation rate affected interpeak conduction times. The 30-per-second stimulation rate resulted in an increase in the interwave latency of Waves I to III, and Waves I to V, regardless of age. Peak latencies in all subjects increased with decreasing intensity at both click rates. Interpeak latencies were not affected by stimulus intensity, but peak latencies were increased in elderly compared to young subjects. Elderly subjects also exhibited longer interwave latencies between Waves I and II, but not between Waves III and V. The delay with age in the interwave latency between Waves I and III was interpreted as reflecting age changes in the pontine-medullary portion of the afferent auditory pathways. As indicated in Figure 7-1, Waves II and III are thought to be due to neural activity at the cochlear nuclei and the superior olivary complex, respectively. The absence of an effect on interwave latency between Waves III and V with age was interpreted as reflecting integrity of the midbrain-pontine region with normal aging. Amplitude of Wave V was found to be too variable a measure of the BAEP waveform to allow evaluation of the effects of age on response amplitude.

Beagley and Sheldrake (1978) evaluated BAEPs in 70 healthy subjects between the ages of 14 and 79 years. These authors were particularly interested in the possibility of increased interwave latencies between major components of the BAEP as a function of age. Subjects were divided into seven age groups, each representing the span of one decade. There were five males and five females in each group, all having normal age-adjusted audiograms. Intensity of the clicks was adjusted to compensate for loss at 3,000 Hz for individuals with a high-frequency hearing loss (presbycusis). The BAEP was recorded to monaural, unfiltered clicks at 80 and 60 dB SL (ISI of 50 msec) and at 70 dB SL (ISI of 100 msec) in a sound-attenuated booth. Beagley and Sheldrake observed only a minimal (nonsignificant) increase in peak latency of Wave V as a function of age. Most important, the interwave latency of approximately 4 msec between Waves I and V remained stable across all age decades. The authors concluded that there is no appreciable prolongation of response latency with age between 11 and 79 years. They also stressed the need for further evaluation in elderly people without presbycusis.

Beagley and Sheldrake (1978) found that the amplitude of Wave V tends to decrease with age. The authors suggest that this amplitude reduction may be due to age changes in tissue impedance or to decreases in response synchrony with increasing age. It is clear that the BAEP depends upon synchronized activity in the cochlea and brainstem (Davis, 1978), and age changes in both latency and amplitude of evoked potentials can be due to a loss of response synchrony. Substantiation of loss of synchrony with age would imply changes in temporal and spatial summation at the postsynaptic level and might be informative about signal-to-noise changes with age.

Fujikawa and Weber (1977) have also evaluated the latency of Wave V in a group of infants (1–2 months), a group of young adults (18–24 years) and a group of elderly adults (69–81 years). All of their subjects were female. Pure-tone audiograms were obtained for all of the adults, and the elderly evidenced signs of mild to moderate presbycusis. Stimuli were unfiltered clicks presented at ISIs of from 77 to 15 msec at 50 and 70 dB SL. Of particular interest to Fujikawa and Weber was the effect of click rate on the BAEP. Varying stimulus repetition has been employed as one means of evaluating "fatigability" of the afferent auditory system as reflected in amplitude and latency of the BAEP (Harkins et al., 1979; Hecox, 1975; Scott & Harkins, 1978). Fatigability or response adaptation has been shown to be greater in the immature than the mature nervous system (Myslivecek, 1970; Rose & Ellingston, 1970). It is as yet unclear whether the rate of adaptation in the healthy elderly population changes, but the results from Fujikawa and Weber (1977) suggest a dramatic increase in latency of Wave V in the senescent ear compared with the young ear. This issue is discussed below.

Further Empirical Findings

In a series of studies, we have evaluated the effects of stimulus intensity and rate on the BAEP in young and elderly subjects. A complete audiometric evaluation was performed on the elderly participants, including pure-tone thresholds, the Short Increment Sensitivity Index, speech discrimination, and stapedial reflexes. Subjective thresholds for the clicks were essentially the same for elderly and young groups. Preliminary results indicate that members of the elderly group had what could be considered subclinical auditory deficits, and the latency of Wave V reflected this impairment of hearing.

Figure 7-8 illustrates the effects of stimulus intensity on Wave V latency in a group of young ($n = 16$; mean age = 23) and a group of elderly ($n = 20$; mean age = 72) subjects. The stimuli consisted of unfiltered clicks presented at an ISI of 100 msec. Two BAEPs were obtained at each intensity (HL) and, if they did not differ by more than .1 msec, the two were averaged. If between-wave variability for Waves I, III, and V was

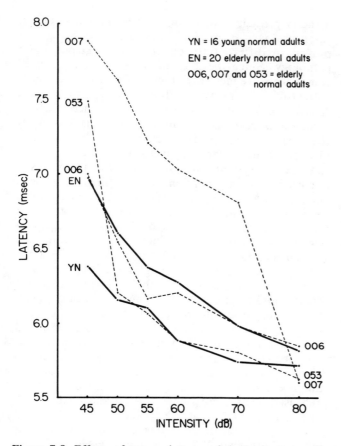

Figure 7-8. Effects of age on latency of the brainstem auditory evoked potential (BAEP). (Interstimulus interval = 100 msec.) In both elderly normals (solid line, EN) and young normals (solid line, YN), latency of Wave V decreases with increasing click intensity. Note that the latency for elderly normal adults at 55 dB is equivalent to latency of young adults at 45 dB. This is consistent with the magnitude of the hearing loss in the elderly and suggests that the prolonged latency of Wave V in the elderly is likely a concomitant of presbycusis and is therefore peripheral in origin. At higher intensities of click stimulation, particularly at 80 dB, the latency difference between the age groups was not statistically significant. Evaluation of latency-intensity response for each individual suggests that a subgroup of the elderly were evidencing intensity recruitment. This is illustrated by elderly Subjects #053 and #007. Elderly Subject #006 did not evidence abnormal intensity growth. (See text.)

greater than .1 msec, the runs were repeated. Owing to various artifacts, mainly myogenic activity, many of the elderly had to return to the laboratory as many as three or four times. All sessions were conducted in a sound-attenuated, electrically shielded chamber, with the subjects in a relaxed position in a reclining lounge chair with head and neck supported.

Figure 7-8 shows that the elderly normal (EN) volunteers were characterized by a delay in peak latency of Wave V at all intensities compared to the young subjects (YN). This was significant ($p < .01$) at all points, except at 70 dB ($p > .05$) and 80 dB ($p > .1$). It is important to observe that the peak latency curves of Wave V in the young and elderly are converging at 80 dB. Individual responses across intensity for three elderly subjects (#007, #053, and #006) are also plotted in this figure. Detailed audiological evaluation showed that Subject #007 had evidence of intensity recruitment with moderate presbycusis. Subjects #053 and #006 showed no clinical evidence of recruitment but some suggestion of presbycusis. These results point to the BAEP as a potentially sensitive index of cochlear and retrocochlear function in the elderly. To date information is lacking on the relations among the BAEP and audiometric findings, particularly for the elderly. From the results presented in Figure 7-8 it is clear that Wave V alone is an insufficient descriptor of age changes in neural conduction in the afferent auditory pathways, since it is influenced by conductive, cochlear, and retrocochlear factors.

Future studies of BAEP changes with age must attempt to define interwave latencies between major BAEP components in elderly persons with better than normal hearing (Beagley & Sheldrake, 1978; Rowe, 1978). While the evidence for intensity recruitment in Subject #007 was weak, the results presented in Figure 7-8 suggest that the age effect on Wave V is due to cochlear dysfunction with age, not to slowing in the central portions of the brainstem auditory pathways. Evaluations of central transmission time, as indexed by interwave latencies, are in progress. Such studies are methodologically difficult because of the lack of resolution of early components of the BAEP at lower intensities. This is particularly true in the elderly, in whom even mild presbycusis plus increased myogenic activity appear to decrease the signal-to-noise ratio. Figure 7-9 represents this problem graphically.

In Figure 7-9 two repeated (overlapped) BAEPs are presented from a young normal subject (YN) and an elderly normal (EN) subject. Stimuli were at 70 dB HL at an ISI of 100 msec. Note that all components are identifiable in the young subject but that Wave I in the elderly subject is ambiguous. The other components, even Wave IV, are easily identifiable in the young and elderly normal subjects. It has been our experience that multiple tests are often necessary to obtain high-quality recordings of BAEPs from elderly subjects, particularly at low stimulus intensities or short ISIs.

Use of the BAEP is now established as a comple-

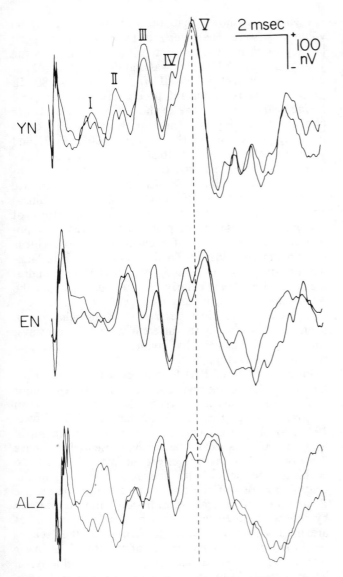

Figure 7-9. Brainstem evoked potentials (BAEPs) as a function of age and dementia. (Interstimulus interval = 100 msec.) Two overlapped BAEPs from a young normal (YN), an elderly normal (EN), and a patient clinically diagnosed as suffering from presenile dementia of the Alzheimer's type (ALZ) are presented. Each BAEP is in response to 1,024 click stimuli presented at a rate of 10/sec and an intensity of 70 dB HL. This figure demonstrates the difficulty in observation of early components, particularly Wave I, in elderly normals. A line is drawn through the peak of Wave V for the young subject to dramatize the latency shift in this wave in both the elderly normal subject and the Alzheimer's patient. Specification of the source of such a shift in Wave V rests on a complete audiometric evaluation and identification of the peak latency of Wave I.

mentary procedure in audiometric evaluation and clinical neurology. Increasingly the BAEP is being employed to differentiate cochlear and retrocochlear pathology. Since the sites of origin of many BAEP components are identified, they can be useful in the localization of brainstem disorders. As mentioned earlier, the BAEP is sensitive to the presence of demyelination diseases such as multiple sclerosis, tumors of the posterior fossa, infratentorial neoplasm, and olivopontocerebellar degeneration (Starr, 1978). Latency changes are also observed in experimentally impaired brain myelination in rats (Shah, Bhargava, Johnson, & McKean, 1978). The fact that the BAEP is sensitive to impaired brain myelination suggests that it might be useful in the study of age-related degenerative diseases such as Alzheimer's-type presenile and senile dementia.

The effects of abnormal aging on the BAEP are also illustrated in Figure 7-9. The third pair of overlapped traces comes from a patient diagnosed clinically as suffering from presenile dementia of the Alzheimer's type. This patient was 57 at the time of diagnosis and 59 at the time the BAEPs were recorded. Alzheimer's-type dementia is recognized as a primarily neural degenerative disease. The clinical diagnosis is presumptive and, in the present case, was based on a comprehensive neurological examination and history with congruent psychological, electroencephalographic, and brain scan studies. Such a diagnosis involves elimination of all other possible dementing illnesses.

The Alzheimer's-disease patient (ALZ in Figure 7-9) had a longer latency Wave V response than either the young or the elderly normal subjects. A line is drawn though the peak of Wave V in the young normal (YN) to dramatize this effect. From these data, however, it is unclear whether the latency shift is due to the effects of the degenerative disease or simply to a conductive or sensorineural hearing loss in the dementia patient. In order to explore this question, a group of young and elderly normal subjects were equated on the basis of Wave I latency with a group of senile and presenile dementia patients. Any group differences found in the more rostral components would then presumably be due to central processes.

Figure 7-10 illustrates that the significant ($p < .01$) shift in Wave V latency was observed in the group of patients suffering from Alzheimer's-type dementia compared to either young or elderly healthy volunteers. Amplitude of Wave V was also reduced ($p < .01$) in these patients. These results indicate the possibility that the BAEP may be a useful clinical tool in early diagnosis of dementing illnesses in late middle and old age. It is also apparent from this figure that the elderly normal (EN) group evidenced a slight increase in Wave V latency compared to the young normal group, but this latency shift was not significant. Peak-to-trough amplitude of Wave V was significantly reduced in the EN compared to the YN group (see Figure 7-10). These results are consistent with those of Beagley and Sheldrake (1978). It thus appears that in the healthy elderly with good hearing, there is no significant shift in interwave latencies of the BAEP if the young and elderly are equated for receptor function (i.e., latency of Wave I as well as pure-tone audiograms) but that response amplitudes are lower in elderly than in young normals. However, there appears to be a significant increase in central transmission time in Alzheimer's disease.

The BAEP represents "hard-wired" properties of the afferent auditory system. The individual components reflect sequential activation of brainstem structures as the acoustic message ascends to cortical levels.

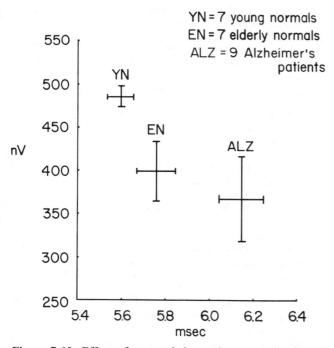

Figure 7-10. Effect of age and dementia on amplitude and latency of Wave V of the brainstem auditory evoked potential (70 dB, ISI = 100 msec). In this figure data are presented for young normal (YN), elderly normal (EN), and Alzheimer's-type dementia patients (ALZ). Since groups did not differ in latency of Wave I, the Wave V latency can be considered to reflect group differences in CNS transmission time. The results suggest a significant latency shift in central transmission time in the ALZ group compared to the young and elderly normal groups. Bars represent one standard error of the mean. Mean ages were 25 for YN, 67 for EN, and 58 for ALZ.

Alzheimer's-type dementia is neuropathologically characterized by diffuse cortical atrophy with enlargement of the ventricles and cortical sulci and a high occurrence of senile plaques and neurofibrillary tangles. Thus, upon first inspection, it is surprising that changes in BAEPs are observed in such patients (see Figure 7-10). Latency is prolonged and amplitude reduced in components of the BAEP in Alzheimer's-disease patients, which suggests that the pathological processes associated with this disease may not be restricted to cortical and immediately subcortical structures. Cellular atrophy in primarily sensory relay nuclei may not be greatly reduced in this disease, but impaired physiological function due to compromise of the intracellular neurotubular system may be present. No studies to date have systematically evaluated ultramicroscopic changes in afferent brainstem nuclei in Alzheimer's disease. Changes in postsynaptic dendritic processes and presynaptic endings, if present, would be consistent with the reduced physiological responsiveness observed in Alzheimer's-disease patients.

The reduced response amplitude of Wave V in elderly normals and presenile dementia patients may be related to decreased output at various levels of the neuroaxis due to cellular atrophy. Konigsmark and Murphy (1970), however, report that cell counts of the ventral cochlear nucleus (VCN) of humans do not change with age. They do note a significant decrease in volume of the VCN in the elderly, resulting in a significant increase in cell density (Konigsmark & Murphy, 1972). The increased cellular packing density was found to be due to loss of myelinated fibers. While few well-controlled cytological studies of brainstem pathways in elderly brains exist, Dublin (1976) reports considerable variability in the involvement of these structures with hearing impairment in elderly persons. Changes observed by Dublin (1976) include marked gliosis in the high-frequency region of the VCN (dorsal zonal involvement) as well as loss of neuronal elements. He reports nonspecific nerve cell degeneration and glia disruption of the laminated pattern of the inferior colliculi. Changes in ultrastructure of nerve and glial cells are a likely source of reduced BAEP amplitudes in senescent persons. In Alzheimer's-disease patients, the observed combination of reduced amplitude and increased response latencies suggests a decrease in afferent signal strength due to a reduction in physiologically intact neuronal elements as well as a change in conduction velocities and/or synaptic delays.

Psychophysical Correlates

Of particular relevance to changes in information processing with age is the relation between brainstem evoked potentials and sensory-perceptual experience. Only one study (Pratt & Sohmer, 1977) has studied this question systematically and only in young subjects. Pratt and Sohmer presented clicks, ranging from 30–75 dB HL in 5-dB steps, to 22 adults (aged 16 to 30 years). A magnitude-estimation procedure was used to obtain behavioral responses to the various click intensities. The individual and pooled psychophysical functions compared favorably to those of Stephens (1975) and Logue (1976). As expected, the latency of the major components of the BAEP decreased with increasing stimulus intensity. The BAEP-latency and click-intensity functions were not consistently related to the psychophysical functions. The brainstem responses failed to show either the intersession or intersubject variability observed in the psychophysical estimates. This suggests a more central mechanism for loudness estimation than the mechanisms giving rise to brainstem auditory evoked responses. These brainstem responses may reflect properties of a rather specific information channel with highly consistent exponents within and between subjects. Recently this model has been extended to brainstem somatosensory evoked potentials with better results.

Like the BAEP, brainstem somatosensory evoked potentials (BSEPs) have been demonstrated in rats (Weiderholt & Iragui-Madoz, 1977), cats (Iragui-Madoz & Wiederholt, 1977), and humans (Harkins & Dong, 1979). In these studies various components of the somatosensory far-field response or BSEP have been associated with volume conduction of activity from peripheral nerve, dorsal columns, dorsal column nulcei, lateral and medial thalamic nuclei, and sensorimotor cortical areas (Dong, Harkins, & Ashleman, 1980). Harkins and Dong (1979) reported that amplitude of components of the far-field and early near-field somatosensory evoked potential was best described as a power function of stimulus intensity. Slope of these functions was consistent with those observed for magnitude estimation. The basic issue of whether averaged evoked potentials measured from the scalp in humans are directly related to sensory-perceptual experience, in contrast to being reflections of global, nonspecific operations, is as yet unclear. Nevertheless, the BSEP may allow a more direct evaluation of conduction over the lemniscal system than is presently available. This possibility, together with direct evaluation of peripheral nerve-conduction velocity, may provide interesting physiological correlates of age changes in the skin senses.

The future of far-field or brainstem evoked potentials in aging research rests on demonstration of (a) their utility in separating peripheral from central deficits, (b) their relation to sensory-perceptual functioning, and (c) their differential responsiveness to the processes of aging per se versus disease processes, the probability of which increases with age. Input–output functions for these primitive brain responses may be predictive of the slowing of complex behavioral functions and information processing often observed in the elderly. In turn, the processes of aging may have only slight impact on primary afferent pathways at the level of the brainstem, and such minimal changes, beyond the receptor level, may have little consequence for higher level information processing changes with age. These are empirical issues that will be resolved in the coming years.

REFERENCES

Beagley, H. A., & Sheldrake, M. B. Differences in brainstem response latency with age and sex. *British Journal of Audiology*, 1978, *12*, 69–77.

Brackman, D., & Selters, W. A. Acoustic tumor detection with brainstem electrical response audiometry. *Archives of Otolaryngology*, 1977, *103*, 181–187.

Buchwald, J. S. & Huang, C. M. Far-field acoustic response: Origins in the cat. *Science*, 1975, *189*, 382–384.

Coats, A. C., & Martin, J. N. Human auditory nerve action potential and brainstem evoked response: Effects of audiogram shape and lesion location. *Archives of Otolaryngology*, 1977, *62*, 605–622.

Davis, H. Principles of electric response audiometry. *Annals of Otology, Rhinology, and Laryngology*, 1976, *85* (Suppl. 28), 1–96.

Davis, H. Basic and clinical aspects of brainstem recording in humans. In R. F. Naunton and C. Fernandez (Eds.), *Evoked electrical activity in the auditory nervous system.* New York: Academic Press, 1978.

Davis, H., & Hirsh, S. K. Brainstem electric response audiometry (BSERA). *Acta Otolaryngologica, Stockholm*, 1977, *83*, 136–139.

Don, M., Eggermont, J. J., & Brackman, D. E. Reconstruction of the audiogram using brain stem responses and high-pass noise masking. *Annals of Otology, Rhinology, and Laryngology*, 1979, *88* (Suppl. 57), 1–20.

Dong, W. K., Harkins, S. W., & Ashleman, B. T. *Origins of somatosensory far-field and early near-field evoked potentials.* Manuscript submitted for publication, 1980.

Dublin, W. B. *Fundamentals of sensorineural auditory pathology.* Springfield, Ill.: Charles C Thomas, 1976.

Eggermont, J. J., Odenthal, D. W., Schmidt, P. H., et al. Electrocochleography: Basic principles and clinical applications. *Acta Otolaryngologica, Stockholm*, 1974, *316*.

Fuijikawa, S. M., & Weber, B. A. Effects of increased stimulus rate on brain stem electric response (BER) audiometry as a function of age. *Journal of the American Audiology Society*, 1977, *3*, 147–150.

Galambos, R., & Hecox, K. Clinical applications of the brain stem auditory evoked potentials. In: J. E. Desmedt (Ed.), *Auditory evoked potentials in man: Psychopharmacology correlates of evoked potentials.* Basel: S. Karger, 1977.

Harkins, S. W., & Dong, W. K. Averaged evoked potentials and sensory experience. In D. R. Kenshalo (Ed.), *Sensory functions of the skin of humans.* New York: Plenum Press, 1979.

Harkins, S. W., McEvoy, T. M., & Scott, M. L. Effects of interstimulus interval on latency of the brainstem auditory evoked potential. *International Journal of Neuroscience,* 197, *10,* 7–14.

Hashimoto, I., Ishiyama, Y., & Tozuka, G. Bilaterally recorded brain stem auditory evoked responses. *Archives of Neurology,* 1979, *36,* 161–167.

Hecox, K. Electrophysiological correlates of human auditory development. In L. B. Cohen & P. Salapatek (Eds.), *Infant perception: From sensation to cognition* (Vol. II). New York: Academic Press, 1975.

Hecox, K., & Galambos, R. Brain stem auditory evoked responses in human infants and adults. *Archives of Otolaryngology,* 1974, *99,* 30–33.

Iragui-Madoz, V. J., & Wiederholt, W. C. Far-field somatosensory evoked potentials in the cat: Correlation with depth recording. *Annals of Neurology,* 1977, *1,* 569–574.

Jerger, J., & Maudlin, L. Prediction of sensorineural hearing loss from brainstem evoked responses. *Archives of Otolaryngology,* 1978, *104,* 456–461.

Jewett, D. L., & Williston, J. S. Auditory-evoked far fields averaged from the scalp of humans. *Brain,* 1971, *94,* 681–696.

Konigsmark, B. W., & Murphy, E. A. Neuronal populations in the human brain. *Nature,* 1970, *228,* 1135–1136.

Konigsmark, B. W., & Murphy, E. A. Volume of the ventral cochlear nucleus in man: Its relationship to neuronal population and age. *Journal of Neuropathology and Experimental Neurology,* 1972, *31,* 304–316.

Liberman, A., Sohmer, H., & Szabo, G. Standard values of amplitude and latency of cochlear audiometry (electrocochleography) responses in different age groups. *Arch. Klim. exp. ohr. Nas. u. Kehlk. Heilk.,* 1973, *203,* 267–273.

Logue, A. W. Individual differences in magnitude estimation of loudness. *Perception & Psychophysics,* 1976, *19,* 279–280.

Maudlin, L., & Jerger, J. Auditory brainstem auditory evoked responses to bone conducted signal. *Archives of Otolaryngology,* 1979, *105,* 656–661.

Myslivecek, J. Electrophysiology of the developing brain: Central and eastern European contributions. In W. Himwich (Ed.), *Developmental neurobiology.* Springfield, Ill.: Charles C Thomas, 1970.

Picton, T. W., & Smith, A. D. The practice of evoked potential audiometry. *Otolaryngology Clinics of North America,* 1978, *11,* 263–282.

Picton, T. W., Woods, D., Baribeau-Braun, J., & Healey, T. M. G. Evoked potential audiometry. *Journal of Otolaryngology,* 1977, *6,* 90–119.

Pratt, H., & Sohmer, H. Correlations between psychophysical magnitude estimates and simultaneously obtained auditory nerve, brain stem and cortical responses to click stimuli in man. *Electroencephalography and Clinical Neurophysiology,* 1977, *43,* 802–812.

Robinson, K., & Rudge, P. Auditory evoked responses in multiple sclerosis. *Lancet,* 1975, *1,* 1164–1166.

Robinson, K., & Rudge, P. Abnormalities of the auditory evoked potentials in patients with multiple sclerosis. *Brain,* 1977, *100,* 19–40.

Rose, G., & Ellingston, R. J. Ontogenesis of evoked responses. In W. Himwich (Ed.), *Developmental neurobiology.* Springfield, Ill.: Charles C Thomas, 1970.

Rowe, M. J. Normal variability of the brain stem auditory evoked response in young and old adult subjects. *Electroencephalography and Clinical Neurophysiology,* 1978, *44,* 459–470.

Salamy, A., & McKean, C. M. Postnatal development of human brainstem potentials during the first year of life. *Electroencephalography and Clinical Neurophysiology,* 1976, *40,* 418–426.

Salamy, A., McKean, C. M., & Buda, F. B. Maturational changes in auditory transmission as reflected in human brain stem potentials. *Brain Research,* 1975, *96,* 361–366.

Schulman-Galambos, C., & Galambos, R. Brain stem auditory-evoked responses in premature infants. *Journal of Speech and Hearing Research,* 1975, *18,* 456–465.

Scott, M. L., & Harkins, S. W. Amplitude of the brainstem auditory evoked response: The effect of interstimulus interval. *International Journal of Neuroscience,* 1978, *8,* 147–152.

Shah, S., Bhargava, V., Johnson, R. C., & McKean, C. M. Latency changes in brain stem auditory evoked potentials associated with impaired brain myelination. *Experimental Neurology,* 1978, *58,* 111–118.

Shannon, E., Gold, S., Himmelfarb, Z. H., & Carasso, R. Auditory potentials of cochlear nerve and brain stem in multiple sclerosis. *Archives of Otolaryngology,* 1979, *105,* 505–508.

Sohmer, H., & Feinmesser, M. Cochlear action potentials recorded from the external ear in man. *Annals of Otology, Rhinology, and Laryngology,* 1967, *76,* 427–435.

Sohmer, H., Feinmesser, M., & Szabo, G. Sources of electrocochleographic responses as studied in patients with brain damage. *Electroencephalography and Clinical Neurophysiology,* 1974, *37,* 663–669.

Starr, A. Auditory brainstem responses in brain death. *Brain,* 1976, *99,* 543–554.

Starr, A. Sensory evoked potentials in clinical disorders of the nervous system. *Annual Review of Neuroscience,* 1978, *1,* 103–127.

Starr, A., & Achor, J. Auditory brainstem responses in neurological disease. *Archives of Neurology,* 1975, *32,* 761–768.

Starr, A., & Achor, J. The generators of the auditory brainstem potentials as revealed by brainstem lesions in both man and cat. In R. F. Naunton & C. Fernandez (Eds.), *Evoked electrical activity in the auditory nervous system.* New York: Academic Press, 1978.

Starr, A., & Hamilton, A. Correlation between confirmed sites of neurological lesions and far-field auditory brainstem responses. *Electroencephalography and Clinical Neurophysiology,* 1976, *41,* 595–608.

Stephens, S. D. The loudness function for click stimuli. *Journal of Auditory Research,* 1975, *15,* 95–105.

Stockard, J. J., & Rossiter, V. S. Clinical and pathological correlates of brain stem and auditory response abnormalities. *Neurology*, 1977, *27*, 316–325.

Terkildsen, K., Huis in't Veld, F., & Osterhammel, P. Auditory brain stem responses in the diagnosis of cerebellopontine angle tumors. *Scandinavian Audiology*, 1977, *6*, 43–47.

Thornton, A. R. D., & Hawkes, C. H. Neurological application of surface recorded electrocochleography. *Journal of Neurology and Neurosurgical Psychiatry*, 1976, *39*, 586–592.

Van Olphen, A. F., Rodenburg, M., & Verwey, C. Distribution of brain stem responses to acoustic stimuli over the scalp. *Audiology*, 1978, *17*, 511–518.

Weber, B. A., & Fujikawa, S. M. Brainstem evoked responses (BER) audiometry at various stimulus presentation rates. *Journal of the American Audiological Society*, 1977, *3*, 59–62.

Wiederholt, W. G., & Iragui-Madoz, V. J. Far-field somatosensory potentials in the rat. *Electroencephalography and Clinical Neurophysiology*, 1977, *42*, 456–465.

Judith M. Ford and Adolf Pfefferbaum

The Utility of Brain Potentials in Determining Age-Related Changes in Central Nervous System and Cognitive Functioning

Experiments employing event-related potentials (ERPs) reveal neurological and cognitive differences between young and old subjects. We found ERPs useful in selective-attention experiments, sensitive to age-related neurological differences, and especially revealing when used with reaction time to mark the timing of mental events. Our findings suggest a significant role for the use of ERPs in research on the cognitive changes due to aging.

Since 1975 we have been investigating neurophysiologic differences between young and old people. We have found that event-related brain potential (ERP) data provide functional information that augments data gathered from structural (brain scans) and behavioral (reaction times) measures. The power of the ERP technique derives from three characteristics:

1. ERPs can be recorded during the deliberate manipulation of attention and can be used to assess alterations of this psychological phenomenon.

2. ERPs can be recorded from totally passive subjects from whom no overt task is required. In fact, the subjects can be demented, asleep, or reading a book, and it is still possible to assess neural and sensory functioning.

3. ERPs can be used to supplement reaction time (RT) data to estimate the timing of mental events. As

a relative measure of when a decision was made, we have used latency of the P3 wave of the ERP (described in Chapter 9 of this volume). This information, together with RT, can be used to estimate the timing of several cognitive processes and to suggest hypotheses about strategies adopted by subjects to perform a task.

We have exploited each of these advantages in several experiments on healthy young and *healthy* elderly subjects. We emphasize the health of our subjects because of our interest in age and not in the diseases that often accompany age. Diagnosed or undiagnosed disease can cause performance deficits that are due to specific pathologies and not to the general variable of age. As Squires et al. describe in Chapter 9, these specific pathologies cause changes in the ERP. Because we wanted to avoid studying the effects of pathology, we recruited women who were subjectively and by medical history and physical examination in exceptionally good health. None had active symptoms of

---

This research was supported by the Medical Research Services of the Veterans Administration and Grant MH 31072 and was performed at the Palo Alto VA Medical Center.

cardiovascular, neurological, respiratory, renal, gastrointestinal, or endocrine disease. Audiometry excluded subjects with more than a 30-dB hearing loss at 500 Hz. The ages of the elderly subjects were between 71 and 89 years, and those of the young subjects were between 20 and 30 years. All scored a 29 or 30 on the Mini-Mental State (MMS) of Folstein, Folstein, and McHugh (1975), a test of mental status also used by Squires et al. (Chapter 9 of this book).

Experiments on Attention

It is often observed that elderly people have more difficulty performing tasks requiring high levels of attention than do young people. Explanations for such difficulty range from underarousal (Davies & Davies, 1975), inability to focus attention on the task-relevant input channel (Craik, 1965), and difficulty in adopting expectancies appropriate to the stimulus probabilities (Rabbitt, 1965a, 1965b; Rabbitt & Birren, 1967).

Until recently it has been difficult to test these ideas because traditional measures of arousal, channel selection, and probability selection are not necessarily independent of each other, and furthermore, behavioral measures are unable to directly and reliably measure responses to stimuli that are to be ignored. The ERP offers a solution to these problems, since ERPs can be measured for both attended and ignored stimuli.

The paradigm we used is identical to that developed by Hillyard, Hink, Schwent, and Picton (1973) in which the N1 component of the ERP is sensitive to both channel selection and arousal (Hink & Hillyard, 1976; Naatanen, 1967; Picton, Hillyard, & Galambos, 1977; Schwent, Hillyard, & Galambos, 1976a, 1976b) and the P3 component is sensitive to the probability structure of stimuli within an attended and unattended channel (Ford, Roth, & Kopell, 1976; Roth, 1973; Squires, Donchin, Herning, & McCarthy, 1977). Details of the method and results are available elsewhere (Ford, Hopkins, Pfefferbaum, & Kopell, 1979). Subjects heard a series of high tones—1500 Hz, 30 dB sensation level (SL)—in one ear and low tones—800 Hz, 30 dB SL—in the other. Ten percent of the time the pitch of either tone was raised slightly (to 1560 Hz or 840 Hz), and these rare pitch changes were called "infrequents." Thus there were two different tones in each ear: a "frequent" and an "infrequent"—four tones in all. The tones were presented in random order every 200–800 msec. The subject listened to the sequence twice. On one run, the higher pitched infrequent tone in the right ear was designated as the target and was to be counted. The second condition was identical except that the higher pitched infrequent tone

in the left ear was designated as the target. The subject reported her count at the end of each run.

The ERPs to each tone were averaged separately. The means for N1 amplitude and P3 amplitude and latency are plotted in Figure 8-1. As can be seen in the

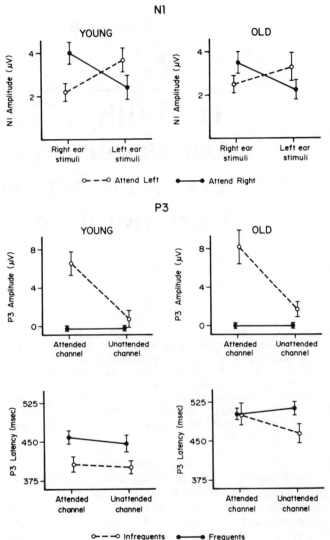

Figure 8-1. Top: Means and one standard error of the mean for N1 amplitude to frequent tones presented to the right ear and to the left ear during attention to infrequent tones in the right ear and in the left ear. Bottom: Means and one standard error of the means for P3 amplitude and latency to frequent and infrequent tones in the attended channel (collapsed across right and left ears) and unattended channel (also collapsed across right and left ears). (From "Age Effects of Brain Responses in a Selective Attention Task" by J. M. Ford, W. F. Hopkins III, A. Pfefferbaum, and B. S. Kopell, *Journal of Gerontology*, 1979, *34*, 388–395. Copyright 1979 by the Gerontological Society. Reprinted by permission.)

top of Figure 8-1, the overall amplitudes of N1 were not significantly different for the young and old subjects during our selective-attention task. It has been shown repeatedly that N1 amplitude can increase with concentration of attention (Naatanen, 1967). Thus the N1 data suggest that the task brought both groups up to a similar level of general attention to auditory stimuli. Also evident in the top of Figure 8-1 is the effect of the manipulation of attention on N1 amplitude. This effect was not different for the young and old subjects; the frequent tones evoked larger N1 peaks in the attended ear than in the unattended ear. Both young and old subjects were apparently attending selectively to the relevant channel of stimuli (Hillyard et al., 1973; Schwent & Hillyard, 1975; Schwent, Snyder, & Hillyard, 1976).

The lower part of Figure 8-1 shows that the P3 amplitude, which is an index of probability selection, did not discriminate between the old and the young subjects. This result suggests that subjects in both groups used stimulus probability information equally well, an interpretation that is consistent with the report of Sanford, Griew, and O'Donnell (1972), who showed that elderly subjects perform a probability match just as quickly and accurately as young subjects.

The lower part of Figure 8-1 shows a significant difference between young and old subjects in the latency of P3: P3 to the target stimuli is 80 msec later for the aged than for the young. Such a latency effect has been observed by others (Goodin, Squires, Henderson, & Starr, 1978; Marsh & Thompson, 1972). Recent work suggests that P3 latency reflects the amount of time necessary to make a decision (Ford et al., 1976; Kutas, McCarthy, & Donchin, 1977; Ritter, Simson, & Vaughan, 1972; Roth, Ford, & Kopell, 1978; Squires, Donchin, & Squires, 1977). If this is true, old subjects may be slower at deciding whether a stimulus is indeed a target. This is consistent with the suggestion of Rabbitt (1965b) that the elderly are slower at deciding whether information is irrelevant. Specific slowing in the elderly is discussed in more detail in the section describing experiments combining RT and ERP latency measures.

Old subjects did not count the targets as well as did the young, since the count reported by the old was significantly lower than the actual number of targets delivered. The elderly apparently either lost count or were poor at detecting targets. In a replication of this experiment, with the additional requirement that subjects press a button each time they heard a target, preliminary results showed the elderly again very poor at detecting targets—even though they were able to discriminate the target pitch from the standard pitch in the attended ear during training. During the experimental run, when tones occurred in both ears, most elderly subjects responded to fewer than half of the targets. Nevertheless, they all showed a strong selective-attention effect in the N1 amplitude data. These findings indicate that although they were not able to perform the ultimate behavioral task, the elderly were still attending selectively to the relevant channel of stimuli.

Experiments with Passive Subjects

We also have used ERPs to assess age-related neurophysiologic alterations in subjects who were assigned no task or whose attention was distracted from the stimulus sequence. Although our subjects were not demented or otherwise incapacitated, such a procedure might be of value for assessing neurophysiologic functions in patients unable or unwilling to cooperate with a behavioral task.

Details of the methods and results are described in Pfefferbaum, Ford, Roth, Hopkins, and Kopell (1979). The stimuli consisted of 500-Hz tones of four different intensities, 500 msec in duration, presented in a random order every 1500 msec. The sensation threshold was determined for each subject, and the stimuli were adjusted individually to be 60, 70, 80, and 90 dB above threshold. During the stimulus presentation the subjects read a large-print book.

Three major peaks (P1, N1, P2) and the late sustained potential (SP) were identified for each subject for each ERP. The P1 (mean latency = 39 msec), N1 (92 msec), and P2 (170 msec) peaks were identified by a computer algorithm. The SP was derived by computing the mean deviation from baseline for the 300–450 msec epoch of the ERP.

In Figure 8-2 the P1, N1, P2, and SP amplitudes are plotted. The N1 component shows little difference between the elderly and the young subjects, but the P1 component was enhanced for old subjects. The SP amplitudes were greatly diminshed for the elderly. As Figure 8-3 shows, the latency for P2 was greater in the elderly subjects than in the young. The amplitude of P2 (see Figure 8-2) revealed a disturbance in the orderly response to the range of intensities in the elderly compared to the young subjects. This complicated pattern suggests that the changes are not merely a nonspecific degradation of physiological processes. However, a single mechanism can be suggested to account for the increased positivity at P1 and the decreased negativity (i.e., increased positivity) at SP. Although the SP is most evident after about 250 msec, it may begin much sooner and be obscured by the earlier components. If it began as early as P1, the significantly smaller P1 and the larger (but not significantly so) N1 seen in the young group as compared to the old could be due to the influence of the SP. The larger negative SP for young subjects could "pull down" or decrease their P1 and increase their N1 negativity. It could also account for the smaller P2 seen in the young, especially at the low intensities (see Figure 8-2, Fz, 60 dB). Additional analyses were performed on the P1 to N1 amplitude and the N1 to P2 amplitude to investigate this hypothesis. While the absolute amplitude

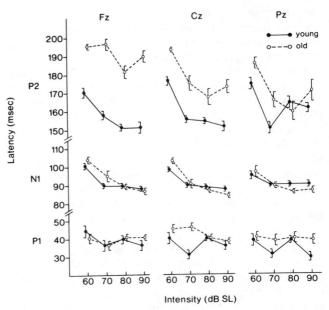

Figure 8-3. Means and one standard error of the mean for latency of P1, N1, and P2 components of ERPs to stimuli of 60, 70, 80, and 90 dB SL recorded from frontal (Fz), central (Cz), and parietal (Pz) electrode placements in old and young subjects. (From "Event-Related Potential Changes in Healthy Aged Females" by A. Pfefferbaum, J. M. Ford, W. T. Roth, W. F. Hopkins III, and B. S. Kopell, *Electroencephalography and Clinical Neurophysiology*, 1979, *46*, 81–86. Copyright 1979 by Elsevier Scientific Publishing Co. Reprinted by permission.)

from baseline to P1 was significantly larger for the old subjects, the P1 to N1 amplitude was not. The N1 to P2 amplitude measure, however, was affected by intensity differently for the different groups, as was the case with the baseline to P2 measure. Thus the influence of the SP might explain the P1 amplitude difference but cannot account for the P2 intensity-function differences between the two groups.

We have suggested that the diminished negativity over the frontal area of the brain might result from a loss in dendritic mass (Pfefferbaum et al., 1979). Scheibel and Scheibel (Scheibel, Lindsay, Tomiyasu, & Scheibel, 1975; Scheibel & Scheibel, 1975) have presented histologic evidence for the progressive loss of the horizontal dendritic system as a function of both age and senility, and they observed that considerable loss can occur without noticeable clinical results. If the frontally distributed slow waves, such as the SP, do have their origins in dendritic networks, our observations of reduced SP in elderly subjects would be consistent with the histological data. The lack of an orderly function relating stimulus intensity and response amplitude in the aged group is more difficult to account

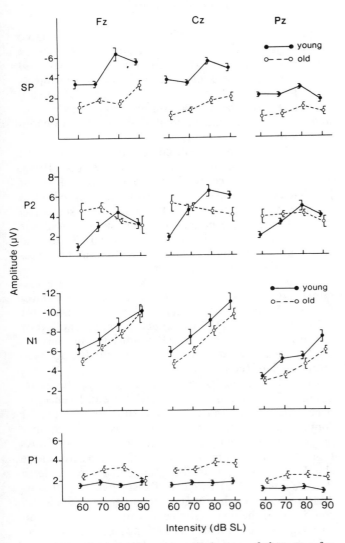

Figure 8-2. Means and one standard error of the mean for amplitude of P1, N1, P2, and SP components of ERPs to stimuli of 60, 70, 80, and 90 dB SL recorded from frontal (Fz), central (Cz), and parietal (Pz) electrode placements for old and young subjects. (From "Event-Related Potential Changes in Healthy Aged Females" by A. Pfefferbaum, J. M. Ford, W. T. Roth, W. F. Hopkins III, and B. S. Kopell, *Electroencephalography and Clinical Neurophysiology*, 1979, *46*, 81–86. Copyright 1979 by Elsevier Scientific Publishing Co. Reprinted by permission.)

for, however. The SP does have an algebraic influence on P2 but cannot completely explain the group difference seen in P2.

Experiments Combining RT and ERP Latency Measures

One of the most pervasive manifestations of aging is the slowing of many responses. Behavioral techniques have been used to identify specific stages in the sequence of information processing where age-related slowing might occur. We have added the tool of ERP latency information to the study of this question.

The latency of P3 has been used together with RT to estimate the timing of mental events (Donchin, 1979; Kutas et al. 1977). Specifically, it has been suggested that P3 reflects the timing of stimulus evaluation and can be used as a relative indicator of how long it takes to evaluate a stimulus in different situations. Thus with P3 latency as a marker of decision time and RT as a marker of the ultimate response, in the first experiment we gathered data suggesting age-related differences in strategies. In a second experiment we used P3 latency together with RT to estimate separately the time taken by young and elderly subjects in several stages of processing in a memory search task.

Choice RT Task Results

Twelve elderly women (mean age, 78) and 12 young women (mean age, 22) were subjects in a choice reaction-time task designed to elicit P3. Details of the methods and results are described in Pfefferbaum, Ford, Roth, and Kopell (in-press-a). The paradigm involved the presentation of tones of 500, 1000, and 2000 Hz, 40 msec in duration, with a 1000-msec interstimulus interval. The 1000-Hz tone occurred 80% of the time, whereas the 500- and 2000-Hz tones each occurred 10% of the time. The subjects were instructed to press an RT key whenever one of the 10% tones occurred (e.g., "press to the high-pitched tone only"). This design produced three classes of stimuli: frequent, infrequent target (requiring a key press), and infrequent nontarget. The EEG was sampled from frontal (F_z), central (C_z), and parietal (P_z) electrode sites, referenced to linked ears. Both the target and non-target infrequent tones produced ERPs with a prominent P3 component.

There were several significant differences when the ERPs of the young and old subjects were compared. The latency of P3 for both the target and nontarget stimuli was markedly prolonged for the aged subject. The scalp distribution of P3 also differed significantly between the two groups. For the young subject, P3 was maximal at P_z and smallest at F_z. The old subjects had a similar but less pronounced distribution for the target stimuli and almost equal amplitude P3 at F_z, C_z, and P_z for the nontarget stimuli. As a result of these distribution differences, the old subjects had larger P3 amplitudes than the young at the frontal scalp site but smaller P3 amplitudes than the young at the parietal location. Tecce, Yrchik, Meinbresse, Dessonville, and Cole (in press) presented data that demonstrated a similar age-related change in P3 amplitude distribution.

The slow wave (SW), which may begin earlier but is best observed after the P3, also revealed significant amplitude and distribution differences when the old and young subjects were compared. For the young subjects, the SW was negative at the frontal site and positive at the parietal. The SW in the aged subjects was also maximal over the parietal area but was positive at all three electrode sites.

It is possible that the differences in amplitude and distribution of P3 that appear when aged subjects are compared to young subjects are not due solely to changes in the P3 itself. The SW may have an effect on the observed P3 amplitude, and age-related changes in P3 may be due in large part to the age-related alterations in the SW.

Using the adaptive filter technique of Woody (1967), which allows the observation of single trials, we calculated the trial-by-trial latency of P3. The hypothesis that the P3 amplitude difference between old and young subjects at P_z is due to an increase in latency variability in the old subjects was not supported. The application of the adaptive filter produced equivalent increases in amplitude for both groups. A greater amplitude increase would have been expected for the old if their P3s were smaller than those of the young because of increased single-trial latency variability.

As was suggested above, an age-related decrease in the SP may explain some alterations in the amplitude of positive components (i.e., P1 and P2). A similar effect is postulated here to explain the change in amplitude of P3 with age, especially at F_z: Since P3 amplitude is influenced by the additive contributions of P3 and SW, then the marked diminution of SW frontal negativity may result in an increase in P3 amplitude.

The low negativity of the old subjects compared to the young, which is also seen following P2 to the frequent tones, suggests that it is not dependent on the continuous presence of the stimulus (i.e., the SP) as we had previously suggested above and in Pfefferbaum et al. (1979). It could be due to a decrease in expectancy (similar to a contingent negative variation, or CNV) in the old subjects, but the performance data do not provide any evidence for this assertion. A more likely explanation lies in the structural alterations seen in aged brains (i.e., loss of dendritic branches, Scheibel et al., 1975) which result in a decrease in the development of slow electronegative activity.

The P3-RT correlations were similar for the old and young subjects; their reaction times and overall accuracy were also not different. Both groups appear to have used a similar strategy with equal success. The similarity of P3-RT correlations also suggests a similar strategy, stressing accuracy more than speed (Duncan-Johnson, 1978; Kutas et al., 1977). An accuracy strategy is also supported by the relatively long reaction times for both groups. The occurrence of P3 relative to RT, however, differed considerably for the two groups; mean P3 preceded the mean RT for 11 of the 12 young subjects, but for only 5 of the 12 old subjects. Thus the young subjects fitted the prediction of an accuracy strategy suggested by Kutas et al. (1977), but the majority of the old subjects did not. Direct manipulation of strategy will be required to clarify the value of the relative P3 and RT timing for inferring the strategy used by a subject and the interaction of the P3-RT relation with age.

Memory Search Task

This paradigm uses the task developed by Sternberg (1966) to measure the speed of retrieval of items from short-term memory. The ERPs that accompany normal performance of this task had been investigated in our laboratory previously (Roth, Kopell, Tinklenberg, Darley, Sikora, & Vesecky, 1975; Roth, Tinklenberg, & Kopell, 1977). In this paradigm, the subject was presented with a memory set consisting of from 1 to 4 target digits. They were presented consecutively with a 1-sec interval between them. The digits define a memory set with 1, 2, 3, or 4 members. One second after the memory set was ended, a .5-sec warning tone (60 dB SL, 1000 Hz) came on. One second after the warning tone went off, the probe digit appeared. Subjects then pushed one of two telegraph keys to indicate whether the probe was in or out of the memory set. Target and probe stimuli were the digits 0–9 presented for 1 sec on an oscilloscope. Eight averages could be formed, defined by memory set size (4) and whether the probe was in or out of the set (2). Each average comprised about 22 trials, with only correct trials included. Although we evaluated many components of ERPs to the various stimuli (Ford, Roth, Mohs, Hopkins & Kopell, 1979), we found that the P3 following the probe seemed to be the most interesting. It was located by computer as the maximum positive peak between 200 and 800 msec from probe onset.

The P3 and RT data are summarized in Figure 8-4. RT is plotted as a function of memory set size. As can be seen, RT was a linear function of memory set size. This was true for both in-set and out-of-set probes. According to Sternberg's (1969) serial model, the intercept of this function represents the sum of time to encode the probe and the time to make the motor response. The slope of this function represents the time to scan memory for a single digit. As evident in the number below the graph, the RT slope was greater in old than in young subjects, as had been reported previously (Anders & Fozard, 1973). RT intercepts were also greater in the old than in the young. The latency of P3 to the probe did not follow the pattern, however, as can be seen in the center panel of Figure 8-4. Slopes listed below the graph indicate that P3 latencies did increase with set size, but the slope of this increase was the same for young and old. Also, the intercepts were larger for old than young but were in both cases much shorter than RT intercepts. Ford, Roth, Mohs, Hopkins, and Kopell (1979) postulated that P3 latency is a relative measure of how long it takes to decide whether a probe stimulus is a member of the memory set. Assuming a serial model, they also postulated that the time lapse between P3 and the RT may be taken up by processes following the decision, such as motor preparation and execution time. The RT-P3 latency functions are plotted in the right panel of Figure 8-4. Ford et al. further postulated that the intercept of the P3 latency function represents encoding time and that the intercept of the difference between RT and P3 latency is a measure of motor time alone. If motor time were constant for each set size, the slope of the RT-P3 latency versus set size would be zero. In fact, the slope of this function is 53.1 msec per digit for the old and 15.7 msec per digit for the young. This greater gap between P3 and RT for greater set sizes in the elderly may represent an increasing slowness in responding after increasingly difficult decisions. Squires, Squires, and Hillyard (1975) reported that P3 amplitude varied with confidence. Although the amplitude of P3 is smaller for old than for young subjects in this task (Pfefferbaum, Ford, Roth & Kopell, in-press-b), the amplitude did not decrease with more difficult decisions for the elderly.

Jordan and Rabbitt (1977) reported some interesting data that are relevant to this discussion. They found that as task difficulty was increased, the RTs of the old subjects slowed more than did the RTs of the young subjects. However, with practice this effect disappeared, leaving just an age lag constant between P3 and RT instead of an age differential, which is to say that perhaps the factor that dissociated P3 from RT could be reduced or eliminated with practice.

In summary, the general conclusions to be drawn from our study were that old subjects moved much

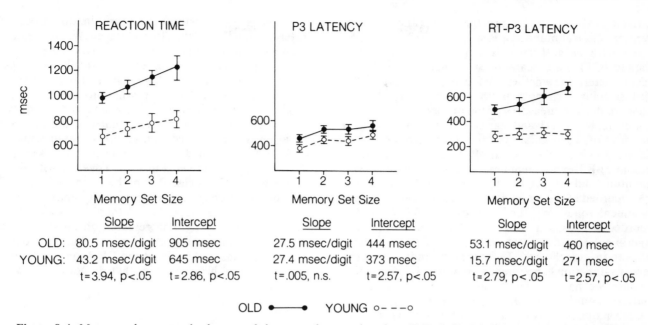

Figure 8-4. Means and one standard error of the mean for reaction time (RT) (left), P3 latency (center), and RT-P3 latency (right) as a function of memory set size for old and young subjects. P3 latencies are collapsed across electrode location and response type; RTs are collapsed across response type. Linear equations describing these RT-P3 latency measures were fitted by the method of least squares; *t* tests comparing young to old subjects were performed on the slope and intercept data. Below each figure is a table of the slope and intercept of that function for old and young subjects. The value of the *t* test comparing young and old subjects and an indication of whether it exceeded the *p* < .05 level of significance appear below the values of the slopes and intercepts. (From "Event-Related Potentials Recorded From Young and Old Adults During a Memory Retrieval Task" by J. M. Ford, W. T. Roth, R. C. Mohs, W. F. Hopkins III, and B. S. Kopell, *Electroencephalography and Clinical Neurophysiology*, 1979, *47*, 450–459. Copyright 1979 by Elsevier Publishing Co. Reprinted by permission.)

more slowly, encoded somewhat more slowly, scanned memory at the same speed, but were considerably less confident about more difficult decisions, than young subjects. Our conclusion that old and young subjects scan memory at the same speed differs from that of Anders and Fozard (1973) because we based our conclusion on P3 latency, whereas they used RT. We maintain that P3 latency is another tool that can be used with RT to gain more information about cognitive processes. It was especially useful here in allowing us to elaborate the RT finding of Anders and Fozard.

In a further analysis of those data we investigated the trial-by-trial relation between P3 latency and RT (Pfefferbaum et al., in-press-b). This was accomplished using an adaptive filter technique of Woody (1967) described above. Single-trial data show a high correlation between P3 latency and RT for young subjects but not for old. Because high correlations between P3 and RT are associated with an accuracy strategy (Kutas et al., 1977), this result implies that young people may wait for complete stimulus evaluation before initiating the response. That strategy does not appear to have been used by most of the elderly subjects, who probably took

a different approach. The P3-RT correlations for the elderly subjects varied with the size of the memory set. For the largest memory-set size, where elderly subjects had especially low P3-RT correlations, they also had more false alarms, which suggests that for that condition they adopted a strategy of speed over accuracy (Kutas et al. 1977). Similarly, in a condition where the elderly data showed an especially high P3-RT correlation, the data also showed more *omissions*. This suggests a strategy emphasizing accuracy with some RTs slow enough (> 2000 msec) to be tallied as omissions.

CT Scans and ERP Measures

The presence of these age-related ERP differences in a group of extraordinarily healthy and active subjects lends support to the assertion that these differences are due to age rather than to specific pathological states. However, occult pathology must always be considered as a possible contributor to the findings. ERPs offer a noninvasive method for assessing age-related neurophysiological changes before the appearance of concomitant clinical manifestation.

We are now gathering data from computed tomographic (CT) brain scans on a similar group of subjects to determine whether ERP changes are associated with structural changes in the brain. From the CT scans we derived measures of the proportion of fluid to tissue in the frontal and parietal cortex, as well as a measure of ventricular volume (Jernigan, Zatz, & Naesser, 1979). From the ERP data recorded during the choice-RT experiment described above, we chose P3 amplitude and latency recorded from all leads and the SW recorded at the Fz lead, to the target and nontarget infrequent tones. We further chose the SP amplitude recorded at Fz, Cz, and Pz, from the intensity function experiment also described above. Seven of the elderly subjects in our choice-RT experiment and 8 from the intensity-function experiment also were given CT scans. Because we have so few subjects, the results of our analyses should be considered preliminary.

Correlational analyses indicated that increases in the ratio of fluid to brain tissue in the frontal area are associated with later target P3s ($r = .73$, frontal; $r = .66$, central; $r = .73$, parietal) and more negative slow waves recorded over the frontal area ($r = -.81$). A group of findings that approached significance suggested that more positivity is associated with ventricular widening—that is, more positive P3s at frontal and central locations, more positive SPs also at frontal and central locations, and more positive SWs at the frontal lead. In light of the finding of Roberts and Caird (1976) that ventricles increase in size with age, and our finding that SP and SW are more positive in the elderly, it is not surprising that larger ventricles might be associated with more positive SW and SPs. On the other hand, it is somewhat surprising that P3 amplitude at frontal and central sites is not significantly increased in these elderly subjects, since P3 amplitude increases with ventricular widening. Perhaps the structural changes that *often* accompany age are better predictors of P3 amplitude than age itself. As such, the change in P3 amplitude may be a functional reflection of structural brain alterations.

SUMMARY

The results of these experiments indicate the power of ERPs in assessing neurological and cognitive differences between young and old subjects. Using a combination of ERP and behavioral techniques, we were able to demonstrate that elderly subjects can focus attention on a selected channel of input, even though they cannot always perform the discrimination task accurately or quickly within that channel. We arrived at this conclusion by using the ERP to assess the amount of attention being paid to events not requiring attention. In another experiment we demonstrated the sensitivity of a passive ERP paradigm to neurophysiological differences between young and old subjects. The strength of this paradigm is that it could be performed on demented, sedated, or otherwise unresponsive subjects. In a third set of experiments, we used the ERP as a marker of events in time. Together with RT, the latency of P3 suggested hypotheses for differences in performance observed between young and old subjects. These findings suggest that there is a significant role for the use of ERPs in research on the cognitive changes with aging. We also have preliminary data from brain scans that indicate the ERP may be sensitive to structural brain changes that do not always accompany age.

REFERENCES

Anders, T. R., & Fozard, J. L. Effects of age upon retrieval from primary and secondary memory. *Developmental Psychology*, 1973, *9*, 411–416.

Craik, F. I. M. The nature of the age decrement in performance of dichotic listening tasks. *Quarterly Journal of Experimental Psychology*, 1965, *17*, 228–240.

Davies, A. D. M., & Davies, D. R. The effects of noise and time of day upon age differences in performance at two checking tasks. *Ergonomics*, 1975, *18*, 321–336.

Donchin, E. Event-related brain potentials: A tool in the study of human information processing. In H. Begleiter (Ed.), *Evoked brain potentials and behavior. Vol. 2, Downstate Series of Research in Psychiatry and Psychology.* New York: Plenum Press, 1979.

Duncan-Johnson, C. C. *The P300 component of the cortical event-related potential as an index of subjective probability and processing duration.* Unpublished doctoral dissertation, University of Illinois, 1978.

Folstein, M. F., Folstein, S. E., & McHugh, P. R. "Mini-Mental State:" A practical method for grading the cognitive state of patients for the clinician. *Journal of Psychiatry Research*, 1975, *12*, 189–198.

Ford, J. M., Hopkins, W. F., III, Pfefferbaum, A., & Kopell, B. S. Age effects of brain responses in a selective attention task. *Journal of Gerontology*, 1979, *34*, 388–395.

Ford, J. M., Roth, W. T., & Kopell, B. S. Auditory evoked potentials to unpredictable shifts in pitch. *Psychophysiology*, 1976, *13*, 32–39.

Ford, J. M., Roth, W. T., Mohs, R. C., Hopkins, W. F., III, & Kopell, B. S. Event-related potentials recorded from young and old adults during a memory retrieval task. *Electroencephalography and Clinical Neurophysiology*, 1979, *47*, 450–459.

Goodin, D. S., Squires, K. C., Henderson, B. H., & Starr, A. Age-related variations in evoked potentials to auditory stimuli in normal human subjects. *Electroencephalography and Clinical Neurophysiology*, 1978, *44*, 447–458.

Hillyard, S. A., Hink, R. F., Schwent, V. L., & Picton, T. W. Electrical signs of selective attention in the human brain. *Science*, 1973, *172*, 1357–1369.

Hink, R. F., & Hillyard, S. A. Auditory evoked potentials during selective listening to dichotic speech messages. *Perception & Psychophysics*, 1976, *20*, 236–242.

Jernigan, T. C., Zatz, L. M., & Naesser, M. A. Semiautomated methods for quantitating CSF volume on cranial computed tomography. *Radiology*, 1979, *132*, 463–466.

Jordan, T. C., & Rabbitt, P. M. A. Response times to stimuli of increasing complexity as a function of aging. *British Journal of Psychology*, 1977, *68*, 189–201.

Kutas, M., McCarthy, G., & Donchin, E. Augmenting mental chronometry: The P300 as a measure of stimulus evaluation time. *Science*, 1977, *197*, 792–795.

Marsh, G. R., & Thompson, L. W. Age differences in evoked potentials during an auditory discrimination task. *Gerontologist*, 1972, *12*, 44.

Naatanen, R. Selective attention and evoked potentials. *Annals of the Finnish Academy of Science*, 1967, *151*, 1–226.

Pfefferbaum, A., Ford, J. M., Roth, W. T., Hopkins, W. F., III, & Kopell, B. S. Event-related potential changes in healthy aged females. *Electroencephalography and Clinical Neurophysiology*, 1979, *46*, 81–86.

Pfefferbaum, A., Ford, J. M., Roth, W. T., & Kopell, B. S. Age-related changes in auditory event-related potentials. *Electroencephalography and Clinical Neurophysiology*, in press. (a)

Pfefferbaum, A., Ford, J. M., Roth, W. T., & Kopell, B. S. Age differences in P3-reaction time associations. *Electroencephalography and Clinical Neurophysiology*, in press. (b)

Picton, T. W., Hillyard, S. A., & Galambos, R. Habituation and attention in the auditory system. In W. D. Keidel and W. E. Heff (Eds.), *Handbook of sensory physiology*, Vol. V: *Auditory system*. Berlin; Springer-Verlag, 1977.

Rabbitt, P. M. A. Age and discrimination between complex stimuli. In A. T. Welford & J. E. Birren (Eds.), *Behavior, aging and the nervous system*. Springfield, Ill.: Charles C. Thomas, 1965. (a)

Rabbitt, P. M. A. An age-decrement in the ability to ignore irrelevant information. *Journal of Gerontology*, 1965, *20*, 233–238. (b)

Rabbitt, P. M. A., & Birren, J. E. Age and responses to sequences of repetitive and interruptive signals. *Journal of Gerontology*, 1967, *22*, 143–150.

Ritter, W., Simson, R., & Vaughan, H. G., Jr. Association cortex potentials and reaction time in auditory discrimination. *Electroencephalography and Clinical Neurophysiology*, 1972, *33*, 547–555.

Roberts, M. A. & Caird, F. I. Computerized tomography and intellectual impairment in the elderly. *Journal of Neurology, Neurosurgery, and Psychiatry*, 1976, *39*, 986–989.

Roth, W. T. Auditory evoked responses to unpredictable stimuli. *Psychophysiology*, 1973, *10*, 125–138.

Roth, W. T., Ford, J. M., & Kopell, B. S. Long-latency evoked potentials and reaction time. *Psychophysiology*, 1978, *15*, 17–23.

Roth, W. T., Kopell, B. S., Tinklenberg, J. R., Darley, C. F., Sikora, R., & Vesecky, T. B. The contingent negative variation during a memory retrieval task. *Electroencephalography and Clinical Neurophysiology*, 1975, *38*, 171–174.

Roth, W. T., Tinklenberg, J. R., & Kopell, B. S. Ethanol and marihuana effects on event-related potentials in a memory retrieval paradigm. *Electroencephalography and Clinical Neurophysiology*, 1977, *42*, 381–388.

Sanford, A. J., Griew, S., & O'Donnell, L. Age effects in simple prediction behavior. *Journal of Gerontology*, 1972, *27*, 259–264.

Scheibel, M. E., Lindsay, R. D., Tomiyasu, U., & Scheibel, A. B. Progressive dendritic changes in aging human cortex. *Experimental Neurology*, 1975, *47*, 392–403.

Scheibel, M. E., & Scheibel, A. B. Structural changes in the aging brain. In H. Brody, D. Harman, & J. M. Ordy (Eds.), *Aging* (Vol. 1). New York: Raven Press, 1975.

Schwent, V. L., & Hillyard, S. A. Evoked potential correlates of selective attention with multi-channel auditory inputs. *Electroencephalography and Clinical Neurophysiology*, 1975, *38*, 131–138.

Schwent, V. L., Hillyard, S. A., & Galambos, R. Selective attention and the auditory vertex potential. I: Effects of stimulus delivery rate. *Electroencephalography and Clinical Neurophysiology*, 1976, *40*, 604–614. (a)

Schwent, V. L., Hillyard, S. A., & Galambos, R. Selective attention and the auditory vertex potential. II: Effects of signal intensity and masking noise. *Electroencephalography and Clinical Neurophysiology*, 1976, *40*, 614–622. (b)

Schwent, V. L., Snyder, E., & Hillyard, S. A. Auditory evoked potentials during multichannel selective listening: Role of pitch and localization areas. *Journal of Experimental Psychology*, 1976, *2*, 313–325.

Squires, K. C., Donchin, E., Herning, R. I., & McCarthy, G. On the influence of task relevance and stimulus probability on event-related potential components. *Electroencephalography and Clinical Neurophysiology*, 1977, *42*, 1–14.

Squires, N. K., Donchin, E., & Squires, K. C. Bisensory stimulation: Inferring decision-related processes from P300 component. *Journal of Experimental Psychology: Human Perception and Performance*, 1977, *3*, 299–315.

Squires, K. C., Squires, N. K., & Hillyard, S. A. Decision related cortical potentials during an auditory signal detection task with cued observation intervals. *Journal of Experimental Psychology: Human Perception and Performance*, 1975, *104*, 268–279.

Sternberg, S. High-speed scanning in human memory. *Science*, 1966, *153*, 652–654.

Sternberg, S. Memory-scanning: Mental processes revealed by reaction-time experiments. *American Scientist*, 1969, *57*, 421–457.

Tecce, J. J., Yrchik, B. S., Meinbresse, A. A., Dessonville, B. A., & Cole, J. O. Age-related diminution of CNV rebound: I. Attention functions. In L. Deecke & H. H. Kornhuber (Eds.), *Motivation, motor and sensory processes of the brain: Electrical potentials, behavior, and clinical use. Progress in brain research* (Vol. 54). Amsterdam, The Netherlands: Elsevier, in press.

Woody, C. D. Characterization of an adaptive filter for the analysis of variable latency neuroelectric signals. *Medical & Biological Engineering*, 1967, 5, 539–553.

Kenneth C. Squires, Thomas J. Chippendale, Kathy S. Wrege, Douglas S. Goodin, and Arnold Starr

CHAPTER

9

Electrophysiological Assessment of Mental Function in Aging and Dementia

The feasibility of using the endogenous P3 component of the auditory evoked potential as an objective means of evaluating cognitive function in aging and dementia was examined. A systematic increase in the latency of the P3 component was found as a function of increasing age in normal subjects. For patients with neurological diseases producing dementia, the latency of the P3 component substantially exceeded the normal age-matched value in 80% of the cases. The P3 latencies for neurological and psychiatric patients without dementia did not differ from normal, except for patients with a history of serious brain trauma. In those patients who were followed serially over periods of time during which there were changes in mental status, the P3 latency and clinical status correlated. These results suggest that the P3 latency may provide a sensitive means for evaluating changes in cognitive function resulting from normal aging and neurological dysfunction.

In response to sensory stimulation, a variety of evoked potential components can be recorded from the intact human scalp by using signal-averaging techniques. For heuristic purposes these components may be classified as either "exogenous" or "endogenous" (Donchin, 1975). The earliest exogenous components appear within a few milliseconds of stimulus onset and, depending upon the stimulus modality, form a sequence of waves extending for 100 or 200 msec. Their characteristics (amplitude and latency) are primarily determined by the physical characteristics of the eliciting stimulus, and it is presumed that they reflect the ascension of stimulus information up the sensory pathways. For detailed discussions of these components the reader is referred to recent reviews by Goff, Allison, and Vaughan (1978) and Hillyard, Picton, and Regan (1978).

The endogenous potentials, on the other hand, are largely independent of the physical characteristics of the sensory input and depend rather on the state of the subject and the context in which the stimulus is presented. A number of endogenous components have been reported, each of which is sensitive to psychological manipulation and may reflect a particular type or stage of cognitive activity. For detailed discussions of these components the reader is referred to recent reviews by Donchin, Ritter, and McCallum, (1978), Hillyard, Squires, and Squires (1979), and Picton and Stuss (1979).

Within the past decade one of the most striking trends in the study of evoked potentials has been the application of the exogenous components to clinical problems. As a result, evoked potential laboratories are now a common hospital feature. The reasons for this are several. First, the characteristics of the ex-

This research was supported by U.S. Public Health Service Grant NS11876.

ogenous components provide direct measures of sensory-pathway *function*. Their use thus supplements the standard physical examination for evaluating central nervous system function and complements the use of radiographic techniques, which evaluate brain *structure*. Second, recent technical developments have made it possible to monitor sensory transmission throughout much of the auditory, somatosensory, and visual pathways. Thus the level at which dysfunction occurs within the central nervous system can be defined with considerable precision. Third, evoked potential recording is noninvasive and the results may obviate the need for more invasive radiographic procedures. Fourth, the results are objective because they are independent of a behavioral response by the patient. Consequently, many patients who lack the ability or desire to respond can be evaluated. A recent review of the techniques and clinical applications of evoked potential recording is presented by Starr (1978).

Although evaluation of the central nervous system by recording exogenous evoked-potential components has repeatedly proven its value, there remain many patients about whom these procedures provide little direct information. These are patients whose sensory systems remain relatively intact while serious deficits appear in higher cognitive functions. As a consequence of the increasing numbers of older people in our population, the prevalence of illnesses that produce such variations in mental status is becoming an increasingly serious clinical problem. For the clinician, differentiating such patients with dementia due to organic causes from those with functional problems, such as depression, or from patients who are limited in their ability to interact with the examiner because of motor or language deficits, has classically been a difficult and highly subjective task. An objective measure of mental function that circumvents such obstacles of communication and cooperation would thus be a valuable addition to the clinician's armamentarium.

For this reason we have chosen to investigate the endogenous components of the evoked potential in neurological disease. Since there is a well-documented basis for ascribing variations in endogenous potentials to variations in cognitive processing in normal subjects, it seemed reasonable that a similar approach might provide a means for objectively evaluating mental function in patients suspected of having dementia. The ultimate expression of such an approach would be a series of tests that use the endogenous components to evaluate objectively various levels of cognitive processing, just as the exogenous components are currently used to evaluate the various levels of the sensory pathways.

In this presentation we concentrate on the most prominent and best characterized of the endogenous potentials, the P3 or P300 component (Sutton, Braren, Zubin, & John, 1965; Sutton, Tueting, Zubin, & John, 1967). Several recent review articles have spotlighted the P3 component and discussed its psychological correlates (Donchin et al., 1978; Picton, Campbell, Baribeau-Braun, & Proulx, 1978; Tueting, 1978). In brief, the amplitude of the P3 component elicited by an attended stimulus of any modality appears to be inversely related to the degree to which the subject expects the stimulus to be presented (Duncan-Johnson & Donchin, 1977; Roth, Ford, Lewis, & Kopell, 1976; Squires, Wickens, Squires, & Donchin, 1976; Squires, Squires, & Hillyard, 1975; Tueting, Sutton, & Zubin, 1971), and the latency of the P3 component appears to be directly correlated with the time required for the subject to perceive and categorize the stimulus according to a prescribed set of rules (Kutas, McCarthy, & Donchin, 1977; Ritter, Simson, & Vaughan, 1972; Ritter, Simson, Vaughan, & Friedman, 1979; Roth, Ford, & Kopell, 1978; Squires, Donchin, Squires, & Grossberg, 1977).

Age and the P3 Component

In the early stages of this work, it became apparent that the age of the patient had significant effects on the evoked potential waveform and particularly on the endogenous components. Effects of age on the exogenous components have been reported on numerous occasions and are reviewed by Klorman, Thompson, & Ellingson (1978). Age-related effects on the P3 component have also been previously reported by Marsh and Thompson (1972) and by Brent et al. (cited in Klorman et al. 1978). Ford and Pfefferbaum (Chapter 8 of this volume) discuss in detail several effects of normal aging on endogenous potentials and on behavioral responses (reaction time). The primary difference between the studies described by Ford and Pfefferbaum and those described here lies in the simplicity of our procedure, a constraint dictated by the intended application of the procedures to patients with diminished mental function.

The effects of normal aging were evaluated by testing 40 subjects between the ages of 15 and 76 years (Goodin, Squires, Henderson, & Starr, 1978). The subjects were considered normal if they had no history of neurological disease, were attending school, or were fully employed. For subjects who were retired, a score of at least 29 out of 30 points on the Mini-Mental State (MMS) exam of Folstein, Folstein, and McHugh (1975) was adopted as the criterion for normal mental status in place of full employment.

Trains of tonal stimuli—50 msec, 60 dB above normal threshold (HL)—were presented binaurally through earphones at a rate of one every 1.5 sec; 85% of the tones had a frequency of 1000 Hz, and 15% had a frequency of 2000 Hz. The sequence of tones was random, with the constraint that no two rare (2000 Hz) tones occurred in succession. The subjects were asked to count silently the occurrence of the rare tones and report the number at the end of a block of 400 tones. Separate averaged evoked-potential waveforms were obtained for the rare and frequent tones from three electrode sites on the scalp (F_z, C_z, P_z), referred to linked mastoids. A simultaneous averaged response was obtained from a pair of electrodes situated near the right eye in order to monitor eye-related potentials. The total duration of the averaging epoch was 768 msec, beginning at the onset of the tone.

The evoked potentials recorded at the vertex (C_z) for one subject are shown in Figure 9-1. All waveforms were characterized by the exogenous N1 and P2 components of the vertex potential. In addition, the rare tone was associated with a prominent P3 component, attributable to the differential cognitive processing of the rare tone. The effects of age on the rare-tone evoked-potential waveform are illustrated in Figure 9-2, where data are presented for six subjects between the ages of 15 and 71 years. The primary result was that the latency of the P3 component increased systematically with increasing age. This can be seen by comparing the peak latencies of the P3 components with the dashed line representing a latency of 300 msec. The P3 latency data for all subjects are presented in Figure 9-3. For young subjects the mean P3 component latency was approximately 300 msec (310 msec at age 15), and it increased at the rate of

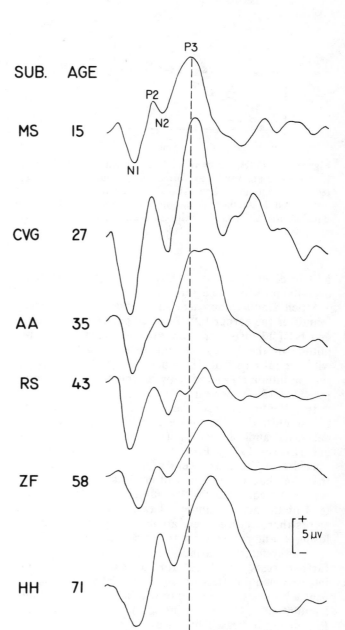

Figure 9-2. Rare-tone evoked-potential waveforms for six normal subjects shown in order of increasing age (top to bottom). The dashed line represents 300-msec poststimulus onset. (Data are from Squires, Goodin, & Starr, 1979).

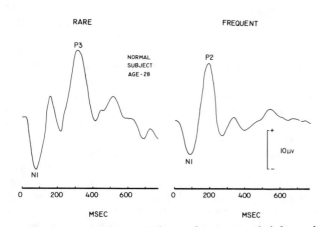

Figure 9-1. Evoked-potential waveforms recorded from the vertex (C_z) for one normal subject, age 28. Separate averaged waveforms are presented for the rare (left) and frequent (right) tones. (Data are from Squires, Goodin, & Starr, 1979).

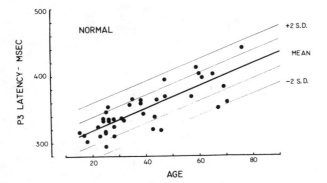

Figure 9-3. Latencies of the P3 components from the rare-tone evoked-potential waveforms for normal individual subjects as a function of age. Also shown are the regression line and 1 and 2 standard deviation (*SD*) bands describing the data. (Data are from Goodin, Squires, Henderson & Starr, 1978.)

1.64 msec per year (*p* < .001), reaching a latency of over 400 msec by the eighth decade.

Much smaller increases in latency with age were found for the earlier P2 (.74 msec per year, *p* < .001) and N1 (.13 msec per year, *ns*) components. The amplitude of the P3 component also decreased slightly with age (at a rate of .18 μv per year, *p* < .005), as did the amplitude measured between the N1 and P2 components (.15 μv per year, *p* < .01).

In order to interpret these results, it was necessary to establish that they were due to aging and not to decreased auditory sensitivity, which is common with age (Corso, 1971). Prior to testing, all subjects reported that the tones were well above threshold and that they had no difficulty discriminating between the rare and frequent tones. All subjects counted within 2 or 3 of the actual number of rare tones (60), and the errors that occurred were attributed by the subjects to losing count rather than to perceptual errors. There was no systematic variation in error rate with age. In further tests of three normal subjects, stimulus intensity had no effect on the latency of the P3 component until it was decreased to within 15 dB of threshold (simulating a 45-dB hearing loss), at which point the P3 latency increased by an average of only 15 msec. However, the latency of the N1 component in those tests increased by an average of 40 msec. In contrast, the mean increase in the N1 latency with age over the entire 60-year span studied here was only 6 msec, while the increase in P3 latency was over 100 msec. Since the effects of aging and decreased auditory sensitivity can be distinguished, it is unlikely that hearing deficts contributed significantly to the results. In fact, the effects of presbycusis would more likely be opposite those shown here, since differential changes in loudness at

1000 and 2000 Hz would result in an increase in the discriminability of the tones (Corso, 1971). Furthermore, these results are remarkably consistent with those reported by Ford, Roth, Mohs, Hopkins, and Kopell (1979) for vision.

Within the framework provided by a variety of studies of young normal subjects in which variations in the difficulty or complexity of a task were used to prolong processing time, and hence the P3 latency (Kutas et al., 1977; Ritter et al., 1972, 1979; Roth, Ford, Lewis, & Kopell, 1976; Squires et al., 1977), these data can reasonably be interpreted as demonstrating a slowing of cognitive processing with increasing age. Ford and Pfefferbaum (Chapter 8 of this volume) reach the same conclusion on the basis of their studies. The rate of increase in the P3 latency found here is relatively mild (1.64 msec per year) and would not serve to differentiate people of similar ages. However, as can be seen, the cumulative effect over the normal life span is an increase in P3 latency of approximately 100 msec to a value which is more than 30% greater than the increase found in the midteens. It is possible that many of the benign effects of age on cognitive function can be accounted for by accumulations of such latency prolongations across various stages of information processing.

Age, Task Difficulty and the P3 Component

A second study was conducted to pursue investigation of age-related variations in the P3 component through manipulation of task difficulty. Two sequences of 1000-Hz tones were presented at a rate of 1 per sec through earphones to 44 normal subjects between the ages of 8 and 82 years. In one condition, the rare tone (*p* = .15) had an intensity of 40 dB HL and the frequent tone (*p* = .85) had an intensity of 60 dB HL (easy condition). In the other condition, the rare and frequent tones had intensities of 57 dB HL and 60 dB HL, respectively (difficult condition). As in the previous study, the subjects were instructed to count the occurrences of rare tones. The order of presentation of the easy and difficult conditions was randomized among the subjects.

The primary result was that while the latency of the P3 component increased with age in both the easy and difficult conditions, the magnitudes of the increases differed from that found in the previous study and also varied according to the difficulty of the discrimination. The slope of the function for P3 latency versus age for the easy condition was .79 msec per year (*p* < .05), and for the difficult condition it was 1.49 msec per year (*p* < .001). A separate analysis of the difference in P3 latency between the easy and difficult conditions also yielded a significant effect of age ($p < .05$). Thus there was a significant interaction of task difficulty and age in the latency of the P3 component, with more difficult tasks producing increasingly long P3 latencies with advancing age. In terms of the previous hypothesis, it would then appear that the timing of the perceptual processes associated with the difficult discrimination were more susceptible to age than those for the easy discrimination.

Mental Function and the P3 Component

The objective of these studies has been to determine whether the P3 latency might be a useful means for evaluating mental function in clinical populations. Toward this end, a total of 151 patients have been tested. A portion of these data have been reported previously (Goodin, Squires, & Starr, 1978; Squires, Goodin, & Starr, 1979).

Three primary groups of patients were studied: 58 neurological patients diagnosed as demented as a result of organic causes, 33 psychiatric patients with no known deficits in mental function, and 60 neurological patients with no known deficits in mental function. The mental status of the patients was established by clinical evaluation and, when possible, by neuropsychological testing. The mental status of each patient was further quantified by us at the time of evoked-potential testing with the Mini-Mental State (MMS) examination (Folstein et al., 1975). A score of 25 or less on the MMS examination was adopted as the criterion for defining dementia.

The diagnoses and MMS scores for the three groups of patients are shown in Table 9-1. The mean MMS score for the demented patients was 19.6, for the psychiatric patients it was 28.7, and for the nondemented neurological patients it was 28.9.

The evoked-potential testing procedure was the same as that used in the initial study of aging described above. The patients were asked to count the occurrences of rare tones. This task was within the capability of most of the patients, though some of the demented patients had to be reminded frequently of the task, and their counts were not accurate. All patients were cooperative for the period of time required to complete the tests (approximately one-half hour), and the instructions appeared to have the desired effect of inducing the patients to attend to the tonal sequence. Operationally, the success of the procedure was demonstrated by the presence of P3 components in the rare-tone evoked-potential waveforms for nearly all of the patients, indicating differential processing of the rare and frequent tones. In tests of normal subjects it has been shown that the P3 component is relatively

Table 9-1 Diagnoses and Mini-Mental State (MMS) Examination Scores of the Three Groups of Patients

Diagnosis	Number	MMS score	ΔP3 (SD)
Demented patients			
Alzheimer's-type dementia	13	17.6[a]	2.79[b]
Metabolic encephalopathy	11	16.7	4.09[b]
Hydrocephalus	7	21.2	2.84
Cerebrovascular disease	8	21.3	4.98[c]
Brain tumor	4	19.0	4.20
Multiple sclerosis	2	23.5	8.19
Herpes simplex encephalitis	1	20.0	−.29
Uncertain etiology	12	21.7[a]	3.17
Mean	58	19.6	3.61
Psychiatric patients			
Depression	12	28.9[d]	−.22
Manic-depression	6	29.0	.16
Acute schizophrenia	4	28.3	−.23
Paranoid schizophrenia	11	28.4	−.30[b]
Mean	33	28.7	−.18
Nondemented neurological patients			
Multiple sclerosis	6	29.5	−.42
Cerebrovascular disease	7	29.3	−.41
Parkinson's disease	5	29.0	.50[b]
Hydrocephalus	5	29.0[a]	.87
Brain tumor	8	29.7[a]	−.52
Trauma	3	28.3	.41
Miscellaneous	17	28.3	.02[b]
Mean	51	28.9	−.03

[a] One patient could not be tested and is not included in the calculations.
[b] One patient could not be assigned a P3 latency and is not included in the calculations.
[c] Two patients could not be assigned a P3 latency and are not included in the calculations.
[d] Two patients were not tested and are not included in the calculations.

unaffected by the subject's approach to the task, so long as the stimuli are attended (Duncan-Johnson & Donchin, 1977; Squires et al., 1975).

The P3 component latencies for the neurological patients with dementia are presented in the top panel of Figure 9-4. Also shown are the 1- and 2-standard deviation (SD) limits derived from the data for the normal subjects. A distinct P3 component could be identified for all but four of these patients.

The P3 component latencies for the group of psychiatric patients are shown in the bottom panel of Figure 9-4, and those for the nondemented neurological patients are shown in the top panel of Figure 9-5. In these groups, only three patients were tested for whom a reliable P3 component could not be identified.

The distributions of the P3 latencies for the patients in the psychiatric and nondemented neurological groups were essentially identical to the distribution obtained for the normal subjects. For the demented pa-

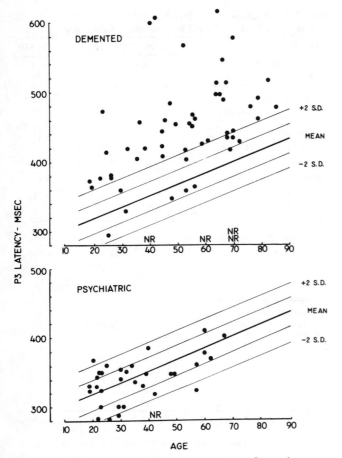

Figure 9-4. Latencies of the P3 components from the rare-tone evoked-potential waveforms for individual demented and nondemented psychiatric patients as a function of age. Also shown are the regression line and 1 and 2 *SD* bands derived from the data for normal subjects.

tients, however, the P3 latencies were more prolonged than for the majority of the normal subjects. On the average, the P3 latency for the demented patients exceeded the age-related mean value obtained for normal subjects by 3.61 *SD*, whereas for the psychiatric and nondemented patients the mean P3 latency closely matched that for the normal subjects (−.18 and −.03 *SD*, respectively). On the basis of these data, a reasonable criterion for defining dementia electrophysiologically for those patients with clearly defined P3 components would be a latency that exceeds the normal value by 2.0 *SD*. By this criterion, 80% of the demented patients would be categorized correctly, with false positive rates of 3% and 4% for the psychiatric and nondemented neurological patients, respectively. A similar diagnostic sensitivity obtains if the data for all patients, including those without identifiable P3 components, are included in the analysis, with the ad-

Table 9-2 Diagnoses and Mini-Mental State (MMS) Examination Scores of the Nondemented Neurological Patients with Residual P3 Latency Prolongations

Diagnosis	Number	MMS score	ΔP3 (*SD*)
Trauma	4	29.5	4.76
Surgery	3	27.3	3.19
Trauma/surgery	2	28.0	3.52[a]
Mean	9	28.4	4.02

[a] One patient could not be assigned a P3 latency and is not included in the calculations.

ditional criterion that the absence of a P3 component is indicative of dementia (81% correct detections of dementia, with a 6% false positive rate for both groups of nondemented patients).

The consistency of the P3 latency as a measure of mental status across diagnostic categories is illustrated in the last column of Table 9-1. For the demented patients, the mean P3 latency obtained for each diagnostic category except one exceeded the criterion value of 2 *SD* (the exception is discussed below), whereas for the two groups of nondemented patients, the mean P3 latency for each diagnostic category fell well within the

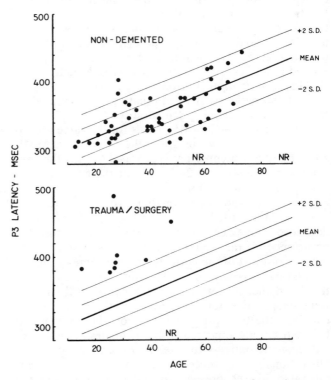

Figure 9-5. Latencies of the P3 components from the rare-tone evoked-potential waveforms for individual nondemented and nondemented trauma or surgery patients as a function of age. Also shown are the regression line and 1 and 2 *SD* bands derived from the data for normal subjects.

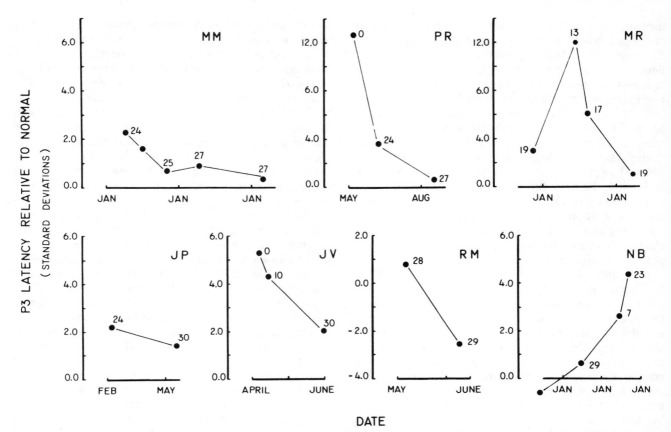

Figure 9-6. Latencies of the P3 components relative to the age-matched normal value (in *SD* units) for the rare-tone evoked-potential waveforms for seven neurological patients as a function of time during which there were variations in mental status. Also shown are the Mini-Mental State examination scores where available.

normal limits. For the demented patients, there were no systematic differences in P3 latency among the diagnostic categories.

The consistency with which the P3 latencies exceeded the normal limits for the various etiologies of dementia evaluated here suggests that a slowing of cognitive processing, as indexed by the P3 latency, is a common feature of many neurological diseases producing dementia. There are, however, diseases that produce diminished mental status that are not amenable to detection by this technique. A cardinal example is provided by the one subject tested here who exhibited an essentially pure amnestic syndrome secondary to herpes simplex encephalitis. This patient (age 31, Figure 9-4, top panel, and Table 9-1, 1st section) had a memory span of less than two minutes but had no difficulty in processing information so long as a memory component was not involved. In this case the P3 latency, which is a measure of the speed of cognitive processing, did not reveal the deficit.

Questions also remain regarding the remaining 10 patients who were classified as demented by neu-

rological evaluation and the MMS examination score but who had P3 latencies within the normal range. There is no consistent way to characterize these patients by etiology, and, in fact, a majority of them had uncertain diagnoses. There also was no consistency in their test scores or distribution of responses on the MMS examination. Many of these patients, however, had scores near the upper end of the range defining dementia (25 out of 30 points). In some of these cases the lack of correspondence between the electrophysiological measure, P3 latency, and the patient's mental status may be due to a weakness inherent in the brief mental status examination used here and might be eliminated by more comprehensive neuropsychological testing.

While it was impossible to resolve all of the inconsistencies between the behavioral and electrophysiological measures of mental status, it was possible to isolate one subgroup of patients in which the inconsistencies might be explained. This group consisted of nine patients with no indications of dementia but who exhibited prolonged P3 latencies and had a history of either severe brain trauma (often resulting in prolonged coma) or major neurological surgery. The diagnoses and MMS examination scores for these patients are presented in Table 9-2, and the individual P3 latencies are plotted in the bottom panel of Figure 9-5. For these patients, the prolonged P3 latency can be interpreted as an indication of residual alterations in brain function due to insults that had occurred as much as 18 months earlier, even though at the time of testing there was behavioral recovery to the point where the patients were apparently normal. It remains to be seen whether the deficits revealed by the electrophysiological test would be evident in a comprehensive neuropsychological examination. In either case, the sensitivity of the P3 latency in revealing subtle changes in brain function is a further indication of its potential clinical utility.

A further indication of the clinical usefulness of the P3 latency in evaluating mental status appears when patients are observed repeatedly. We have followed a few patients for periods ranging from months to years in which there were marked variations in mental status, due either to their clinical treatment or to the progression of their disease. The results of these studies are presented in Figure 9-6. Where available, the MMS examination score at the time of evoked-potential testing is presented next to the data point for the test session. For four of the patients there was a progressive recovery toward a normal mental status (MM, hydrocephalus; PR, anoxia; JP, medicine toxicity; JV, metabolic encephalopathy) and an associated decrease in P3 latency that eventually reached a normal or near-normal value. At the time of initial testing, one patient (RM, metabolite disturbance) had recovered to the point of having an essentially normal mental status and normal P3 latency but showed further clinical improvement and an additional shortening of the P3 latency over the next month. Another patient (MR, hydrocephalus) experienced a severe setback accompanied by a prolonged P3 latency and a subsequent recovery accompanied by a decrease in P3 latency to within normal limits. And another patient (NB, multiple sclerosis) showed a progressive decline in mental status combined with a progressive increase in P3 latency.

Discussion

These studies illustrate that aging and variations in mental status due to neurological disease are highly correlated with variations in the latency of the endogenous P3 component of the auditory evoked potential. When these data are compared with the results of

earlier studies of young normal subjects for whom correlations between P3 latency and the timing of cognitive processes have been demonstrated by direct manipulation of task difficulty or complexity, both aging and certain forms of dementia seem to show a slowing of cognitive processing. The effects of aging and dementia are clearly different, however, and can be distinguished by their differential effects on the earlier exogenous potentials (Goodin, Squires, & Henderson, 1978). A detailed analysis of the effects of normal aging on the various components of the evoked-potential waveform is presented in Chapter 8 of this volume.

From a clinical point of view it is important to note that the effects of various types of dementia on the P3 latency are consistent and substantial enough for diagnoses to be made on an individual basis. In the sample of patients studied here, 80% of the demented patients could be classified correctly. Perhaps more important, patients with functional rather than organic disorders rarely had P3 latencies that exceeded the normal range. Likewise, neurological patients without mental status deficits generally had P3 latencies within the normal range. These results suggest that the P3 latency can provide a sensitive, and perhaps specific, measure for differentiating organic dementia from functional disorders such as depression and schizophrenia, as well as for differentiating dementia from disorders of movement or linguistic skills that may give the appearance of reduced mental status. In clinical neurological practice, such differential diagnoses are often difficult to make and depend on subjective evaluation, even when time-consuming and expensive neuropsychological tests are employed. We feel that the procedures described here will provide an important adjunct to the clinical examination that can guide the clinician in the selection of further neuropsychological or radiological procedures.

The latency of the P3 component was also found to correlate closely with dynamic variations in the mental status of individual patients and thus may be useful as a guide in the therapeutic management of patients with neurological disease, as well as in defining the progression of the disease. On the other hand, for some patients who had experienced severe brain trauma, the P3 latency continued to be prolonged while mental status improved and thus provided an indication of residual variations in brain function lasting for periods of many months. Thus in the use of these procedures to evaluate mental status, the patient's past history must be carefully considered.

The distinctions made here among individual patients could not be based on analysis of the exogenous components of the evoked potential such as the N1 and P2 components. The reason is probably that in many forms of dementia the sensory pathways are relatively unaffected. In any case, it seems reasonable for mental function to be evaluated better from evoked-potential components that reflect cognitive processing than from those stemming from the primary sensory systems. Attempts to evaluate individual patients by some characteristic of the P3 component other than latency—such as P3 amplitude or scalp distribution—proved unsatisfactory. Thus, judging from these studies, the latency of the P3 component seems to be the most effective electrophysiological measure for evaluating variations in mental status associated with aging and neurological disease.

REFERENCES

Corso, J. Sensory processes and age effects in normal adults. *Journal of Gerontology*, 1971, *26*, 90–105.

Donchin, E. Brain electrical correlates of pattern recognition. In G. F. Inbar (Ed.), *Signal analysis and pattern recognition in biomedical engineering*. New York: Wiley, 1975.

Donchin, E., Ritter, W., & McCallum, W. C. Cognitive psychophysiology: The endogenous components of the ERP. In E. Callaway, P. Tueting, & S. Koslow (Eds.), *Event-related brain potentials in man*. New York: Academic Press, 1978.

Duncan-Johnson, C., & Donchin, E. On quantifying surprise: The variation of event-related potentials with subjective probability. *Psychophysiology*, 1977, *14*, 456–467.

Folstein, M., Folstein, S., & McHugh, P. "Mini-Mental State": A practical method for grading the cognitive state of patients for the clinician. *Journal of Psychiatry Research*, 1975, *12*, 189–198.

Ford, J. M., Roth, W. T., Mohs, R. C., Hopkins, W. F. III, & Kopell, B. S. Event-related potentials recorded from young and old adults during a memory retrieval task. *Electroencephalography and Clinical Neurophysiology*, 1979, *47*, 450–459.

Goff, W., Allison, T., & Vaughan, H. The functional anatomy of event-related potentials. In E. Callaway, P. Tueting, & S. Koslow (Eds.), *Event-related brain potentials in man*. New York: Academic Press, 1978.

Goodin, D., Squires, K., Henderson, B., & Starr, A. Age-related variations in evoked potentials to auditory stimuli in normal human subjects. *Electroencephalography and clinical neurophysiology*, 1978, *44*, 447–458.

Goodin, D., Squires, K., Starr, A. Long latency event-related components of the auditory evoked potential in dementia. *Brain*, 1978, *101*, 635–648.

Hillyard, S., Picton, T., & Regan, D. Sensation, perception and attention: Analysis using ERPs. In E. Callaway, P. Tueting, & S. Koslow (Eds.), *Event-related brain potentials in man*. New York: Academic Press, 1978.

Hillyard, S., Squires, K., & Squires, N. The psychophysiology of attention. In D. Sheer (Ed.), *Attention: Theory, brain functions and applications*. Hillsdale, N.J.: Erlbaum, 1979.

Klorman, R., Thompson, L., & Ellingson, R. Event-related brain potentials across the life span. In E. Callaway, P. Tueting, & S. Koslow (Eds.), *Event-related brain potentials in man*. New York: Academic Press, 1978.

Kutas, M., McCarthy, G., & Donchin, E. Augmenting mental chronometry: The P300 as a measure of stimulus evaluation. *Science*, 1977, *197*, 792–795.

Marsh, G., & Thompson, L. Age differences in evoked potentials during an auditory discrimination task. *Gerontologist*, 1972, *12*, 44.

Picton, T., Campbell, K., Baribeau-Braun, J., & Proulx, G. The neurophysiology of human attention: A tutorial review. In J. Regan (Ed.), *Attention and performance* (Vol. 7). Hillsdale, N.J.: Erlbaum, 1978.

Picton, T., & Stuss, D. The component structure of the human event-related potentials. In H. Kornhuber & L. Deecke (Eds.), *Progress in brain research: Electrical potentials related to motivation, motor and sensory processes of the brain*. Amsterdam: Elsevier, 1979.

Ritter, W., Simson, R., & Vaughan, H. Association cortex potentials and reaction time in auditory discrimination. *Electroencephalography and clinical Neurophysiology*, 1972, *33*, 547–555.

Ritter, W., Simson, R., Vaughan, H., & Friedman, D. A brain event related to the making of a sensory discrimination. *Science*, 1979, *203*, 1358–1361.

Roth, W., Ford, J., & Kopell, B. Long latency evoked potentials and reaction time. *Psychophysiology*, 1978, *15*, 17–23.

Roth, W., Ford, J., Lewis, S., & Kopell, B. Effects of stimulus probability and task relevance on event-related potentials. *Psychophysiology*, 1976, *13*, 311–317.

Squires, K., Goodin, D., & Starr, A. Event related potentials in development, aging and dementia. In D. Lehman & E. Callaway (Eds.), *Human evoked potentials*. New York: Plenum, 1979.

Squires, K., Wickens, C., Squires, N., & Donchin, E. The effect of stimulus sequence on the waveform of the cortical event-related potential. *Science*, 1976, *193*, 1142–1146.

Squires, N., Squires, K., & Hillyard, S. Two varieties of long-latency positive waves evoked by unpredictable auditory stimuli in man. *Electroencephalography and Clinical Neurophysiology*, 1975, *38*, 387–401.

Squires, N., Donchin, E., Squires, K. & Grossberg, S. Bisensory stimulation: Inferring decision-related processes from the P300 component. *Journal of Experimental Psychology: Human Perception and Performance*, 1977, *3*, 299–315.

Starr, A. Sensory evoked potentials in clinical disorders of the nervous system. *Annual Review of Neuroscience*, 1978, *1*, 103–127.

Sutton, S., Braren, M., Zubin, J., & John, E. R. Evoked potential correlates of stimulus uncertainty. *Science*, 1965, *150*, 1187–1188.

Sutton, S., Tueting, P., Zubin, J., & John, E. R. Information delivery and sensory evoked potentials. *Science*, 1967, *155*, 1436–1439.

Tueting, P. Event related potentials, cognitive events and information processing. In D. Otto (Ed.), *Multidisciplinary perspectives in event related potential (ERP) research.* Washington, D.C.: U.S. Government Printing Office, 1978.

Tueting, P., Sutton, S., & Zubin, J. Quantitative evoked potential correlates of the probability of events. *Psychophysiology*, 1971, *7*, 385–394.

David B. D. Smith, Larry W. Thompson, and Henry J. Michalewski

CHAPTER

10

Averaged Evoked Potential Research in Adult Aging— Status and Prospects

Recently the averaged evoked potential (AEP) technique has been applied to the study of the aging central nervous system (CNS). This research, which has been largely descriptive, has revealed age-associated amplitude, latency, and topography changes in brainstem and sensory AEPs and in those slow potentials that reveal information processing in the CNS. CNS models are presented as a conceptual framework for interpreting AEP changes with age. For example, topographical data are presented that support differential aging in the CNS, possibly involving the frontal cortex. Future topography studies of the AEP, combined with neuropsychological measures and neurological assessment, could help resolve the issue of selective cortical aging. Though provocative, such CNS/aging interpretations are based on ad hoc reasoning and are in need of direct empirical support. Other studies have related the AEP to information processing and performance changes with age. Though parallels exist, it has been difficult to demonstrate the nature of this relation. It is proposed that future studies combine AEP and performance measures using more complex and realistic tasks and so that stimuli in the task are used to elicit the AEP. Also, individual differences among older ages should be studied.

That an electrical event accompanying sensory stimulation is recordable from the brain has been recognized since the time of Caton (1875). However, the value of this knowledge for brain research could not be realized for a long time. Though single evoked potentials (EP) recorded directly from cortical areas are readily observable, these potentials ar so attenuated at the surface of the scalp as to be impossible to detect consistently in the larger background activity of the ongoing electroencephalogram (EEG).

In the late 1940s Dawson (1947) demonstrated that this signal-to-noise problem could be circumvented by superimposing a number of segments of the EEG that were time-locked to the presentation of discrete sensory stimuli. This was soon followed by use of the averaging technique and the averaging computer (Dawson, 1954). The subsequent quarter century of research has revealed that a complex series of scalp potentials occur before, during, and after any stimulus event, whether sensory, motor, or cognitive. The potentials in this series presumably represent the activity of neural generators at progressively higher levels in the central nervous system (CNS), from the brainstem to the association areas of the cortex.

Although the averaged evoked potential (AEP) has become the method of choice for studying the CNS in intact organisms, especially from scalp recordings in humans, it is only recently that this technique has been applied to the investigation of the aging nervous system. The relevance of such research is obvious for understanding the processes of human aging where changes in neural function may have psychological and psychophysiological correlates representing some of the most critical consequences of adult aging.

This chapter reviews the AEP research that has focused on adult aging and proposes some conceptual models to explain the age-associated differences observed. When appropriate, findings from related research in the fields of gerontology, neurophysiology, and electrophysiology, as well as relevant gerontological theory, are incorporated into the discussion. Overall, this chapter considers the current status of the study of averaged potentials and aging and provides some directions for further research.

Description of Averaged Evoked Potentials with Aging

On the basis of existing research it is possible to outline a reasonably detailed picture of age-related AEP changes. Considering the variety of experimental procedures used in this research, these changes are remarkably consistent and robust.

Sensory Averaged Evoked Potentials

An evoked potential can be obtained to any discrete auditory, visual, or somatosensory stimulus, and the subject need not be attending to or apparently aware of the stimulus (Libet, Alberts, Wright, & Feinstein, 1972). These responses occur in the first few hundred milliseconds following stimulus onset and are sometimes referred to as transient potentials. Our use of the term *sensory evoked* reflects the fact that components of this response arise from cortical and subcortical neural centers that are largely specific to the sensory modality involved. It is convenient to divide sensory AEPs into three sequential segments: early (brainstem), middle, and late components. Though traditional, this division is somewhat arbitrary; however, it is still useful, since age-related changes correspond to this temporal sequencing.

Early (brainstem) components. An area of research that is rapidly gaining attention involves the recording of very early AEPs related to the initial stages of auditory processing. These brainstem auditory evoked potentials (BAEP), or far-field potentials, are recorded from the scalp, are of short latency and submicrovolt size, and are believed to reflect neural generators deep within the brainstem (Jewett, Romano, & Williston, 1970; Picton, Hillyard, Krausz, & Galambos, 1974; Thornton, 1976). Figure 10-1 presents a characteristic BAEP waveform consisting of seven peaks (I–VII). The origin of many of the BAEP peaks is still controversial, but evidence from both animal and human studies has indicated the likely neural generators. These and their respective peaks are (I) the acoustic

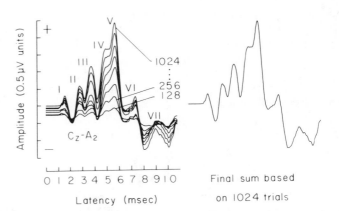

Figure 10-1. Sample brainstem auditory evoked potentials (BAEP) collected at a click intensity of 70 dB (SL) and a rate of 15 per second from a young subject (23 years, female) with normal hearing. The development of the BAEP components over blocks of 128 click-trials for eight successive blocks is shown on the left; the final BAEP waveform based on the sum of 1024 click presentations is shown on the right. Binaural stimulation was used. Lead derivation C_z to A_2.

nerve, (II) the cochlear nuclei, (III) the superior olivary complex and fibers crossing the midline, (IV) the lateral lemniscus, (V) the inferior colliculus, (VI) possibly the medial geniculate, and (VII) possibly the auditory radiations (Buchwald & Brown, 1977; Buchwald & Huang, 1975; Jewett, 1970; Sohmer & Feinmesser, 1967; Starr & Achor, 1975; Starr & Hamilton, 1976; Stockard & Rossiter, 1977).

The presumed association between the various peaks of the BAEP and structures within the brainstem has led to a clinical application of these potentials (Gibson, 1978; Hecox & Galambos, 1974; Starr, 1977). Extensive research has investigated the effects of stimulus parameters, particularly intensity and rate (Pratt & Sohmer, 1976; Scott & Harkins, 1978; Stockard, Stockard, & Sharbrough, 1978; Wolfe, Skinner, & Burns, 1978). Brainstem tumors and demyelinating diseases are said to produce abnormal responses, while hearing impairments increase BAEP latencies and alter amplitudes (Starr & Achor, 1975).

Michalewski, Patterson, Thompson, Bowman, and Litzelman (in preparation) have studied the relation of BAEPs to factors of aging. Twenty subjects (10 male, 10 female) from each of three age groups participated: young (20–39), middle-aged (40–59), and old (60–79). Stimuli consisted of brief auditory clicks presented binaurally at levels of 60, 70, and 80 dB (SL) above individual thresholds at rates of 5, 10, and 15 clicks per second. A number of effects resulted, including age and sex effects (Michalewski, Thompson, Patterson, Bowman, & Litzelman, 1980). Significant age effects were most apparent for Waves I, II, III, and IV; the latencies of these peaks were longer in the older group than in either young or middle-aged groups, particularly for older males. While latencies for Wave V and beyond were generally longer for the older group, differences did not reach significance. Short-latency components similar to the BAEP may be recorded from the somatosensory modality (Cracco & Cracco, 1976), but analogous components in vision have yet to be identified. (See Chapter 7 in this volume for additional information on short-latency waves and their potential and future relevance for adult-aging research.)

Middle-latency components. Following the early components, and within the first 50 to 100 msec, there

occurs a series of negative and positive deflections designated the middle components.

For all three sensory modalities (visual, auditory, and somatosensory) one or more AEP components in this latency range have been found to increase in the elderly vis-à-vis young subjects (Brent, Smith, & Michalewski, 1977; Drechsler, 1978; Dustman & Beck, 1969; Pfefferbaum, Ford, Roth, Hopkins, & Kopell, 1979; Schenkenberg, 1970; Straumanis, Shagass, & Schwartz, 1965). For visual and somatosensory stimuli the middle components are increased in peak latency with age, possibly by as much as 25 msec (Celesia, 1978; Celesia & Daly, 1977a; Drechsler, 1978; Dustman & Beck, 1966; Schenkenberg, 1970; Visser, Stam, Van Tilburg, Op den Velde, Blom, & De Rijke, 1976). In contrast, latency increases have not generally been observed for the middle components of the auditory AEP (Brent et al., 1977; Pfefferbaum et al., 1979; Schenkenberg, 1970; Smith, Tom, Brent, & Ohta, 1976). These changes in the AEP with age are illustrated in Figures 10-2, 10-3, and 10-4.

Late components. For the sensory AEP the late components occupy the recording epoch from 100 msec to approximately 400 msec poststimulus. The late components have been reported to decrease in amplitude with age for visual, somatosensory (Dustman & Beck, 1966; Schenkenberg, 1970), and auditory stimuli (Brent et al., 1977). Age differences in latency became progressively more pronounced in the late components (compared to the middle components), lengthening to 50 msec and more. Similar evidence of slowing has also been reported for visual and somatosensory AEPs (Drechsler, 1978; Dustman & Beck, 1969; Schenkenberg, 1970) and the vertex potential to auditory stimuli (Brent et al., 1977; Goodin, Squires, Henderson, & Starr, 1978; Ford, Hink, Hopkins, Roth, Pfefferbaum, & Kopell, 1979). Figures 10-3 and 10-4 illustrate these age-associated changes in the late components for auditory stimuli.

Slow Potentials

If a stimulus is given task significance, or novelty, it elicits a group of slow positive and negative waves (SPs) that are a major focus in current AEP research. It is important to distinguish between sensory AEPs as just discussed, which may occur to any stimulus, and those SPs that are present when stimuli take on informational value. The former are relatively brief in duration, are sensitive to physical parameters of the evoking stimulus, and are highly specific to the modality concerned. In contrast, SPs may last for seconds, are largely invariant to changes in physical

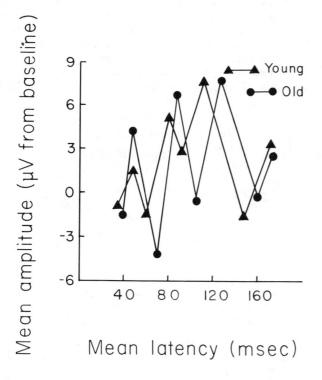

Figure 10-2. Mean amplitude versus latency plots for middle-latency components of the visual AEP comparing 18 old (63 years or older) and 18 young (19–45 years) subjects. Amplitudes are baseline to peak, and latency is from stimulus onset to peak amplitude. Elderly subjects have significantly greater amplitudes for Components 1, 2, and 5, and longer latencies for Components 1 through 6. (From "Visually Evoked Cerebral Response Changes Associated With Chronic Brain Syndromes and Aging" by J. S. Straumanis, C. Shagass, and M. Schwartz, *Journal of Gerontology*, 1965, *20*, 498–506. Copyright 1965 by the Gerontological Society. Reprinted by permission.)

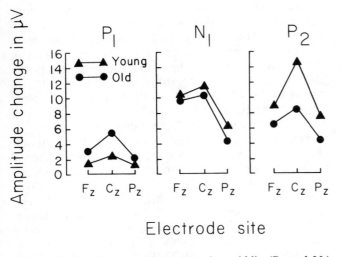

Figure 10-3. Mean amplitude plots for middle (P₁ and N₁) and late (P₂) components of the auditory AEP for 10 old (mean age = 71.1 years) and 10 young (mean age = 21.3 years) subjects at three electrode sites. Old subjects had significantly greater P₁ amplitude (mean latency = 66 msec), no difference in N₁ amplitude (mean latency = 115 msec), and a significantly smaller amplitude for P₂ (mean latency = 215 msec). Age differences in scalp distribution of P₂ amplitude were present. The elderly showed a relatively uniform P₂ amplitude at the three electrode sites, while young subjects showed a larger wave at vertex (C_z) compared to frontal (F_z) and parietal (P_z) sites.

parameters of the eliciting stimulus, and are less modality-specific than the sensory AEP. Thus, all of the early age-related studies that used nonsignal stimuli are confined to information concerning the sensory AEP (Dustman & Beck, 1966, 1969; Kooi & Bagchi, 1964; Schenkenberg, 1970; Straumanis et al., 1965; Tamura, Lüders, & Kuroiwa, 1972).

Late potential complex (LPC). Prominent among SPs is a late negative-positive complex comprising a brief negative wave (N_2 or N_{200}) followed immediately by a large positive wave (P_3 or P_{300}). Functionally, both waves are closely associated with one another and, therefore, are sometimes referred to as the N_{200}-P_{300} complex.

Brent et al. (1977) reported no age-related changes in N_{200} amplitude for the vertex potential using auditory stimuli. However, both Brent et al. (1977) and Goodin et al. (1978) reported a longer latency for N_{200} with age. The N_{200} wave is often partly obscured by the surrounding components of the AEP and, along with P_{300}, can be seen more clearly if a subtraction method is used or, even better, if the LPC, rather than being evoked by a stimulus, is elicited when an otherwise ex-

pected stimulus is deleted (Simpson, Vaughan, & Ritter, 1976, 1977). This latter stimulus paradigm has not been used in age-related research to date but may prove useful in clarifying age differences in the LPC.

Brent et al. (1977) reported that the P_{300} wave to a rare, unexpected tone was significantly smaller in older than in younger subjects at both central (C_z) and parietal (P_z) recording sites. Using similar stimuli and recording procedures, Goodin et al. (1978) reported an analogous decrease with age in the N_{200}-P_{300} peak-to-peak amplitude. However, other studies have not found these amplitude differences in P_{300} (Ford et al., 1979; Smith et al., 1976). An explanation offered for this discrepancy comes from studies indicating separate varieties of late positive P_{300} waves (Smith, Brent, Thompson, & Michalewski, 1978). Several investigators have reported that P_{300} waves following novel stimuli that were embedded in a repetitive stimulus sequence were largest over frontal and central regions, while the P_{300} following task-relevant stimuli were largest over central and parietal locations; the former were associated with aspects of orienting, while the latter were associated with perceptual decisions about the stimulus (Courchesne, 1978; Squires, Squires, & Hill-

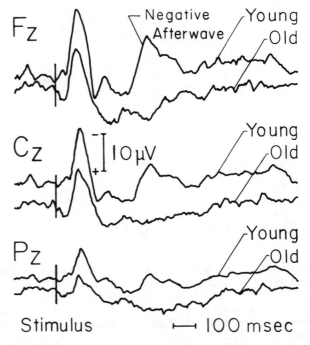

Figure 10-4. Illustration of the auditory AEP for one young and one elderly subject at frontal (F_z), vertex (C_z), and parietal (P_z) sites. Note the longer latency with age for components greater than 100 msec. The young subject showed a large negative afterwave at F_z and C_z which is largely absent in the elderly.

yard, 1975). Studies observing age differences (Brent et al., 1977; Goodin et al., 1978) have used stimuli likely to elicit a P_{300} wave associated with orienting, whereas those failing to observe such differences (Ford et al., 1979; Smith et al., 1976) used stimuli appropriate for the P_{300} wave of perceptual decision processes. Such an explanation would be consistent with anterior-posterior topographical differences in the AEP with age, as discussed elsewhere in this chapter. However, this explanation for different results for P_{300} amplitude is based on post hoc reasoning and remains in need of direct verification.

Many of the studies just cited concur that the P_{300} wave is significantly delayed in the elderly. Goodin et al. (1978), in a study of 40 subjects ranging in age from 15 to 75 years, determined the rate (by regression analysis) of increased P_{300} latency to be 1.8 msec per year over this age range.

Slow wave (SW). Rare, novel, or complex stimuli frequently elicit an SW that may persist for one second or more following the evoking stimulus (Loveless, 1976; Rohrbaugh, Syndulko, & Lindsley, 1978; Squires et al., 1975). Over the frontal scalp this wave has a prominent negative component (the negative afterwave) with a peak amplitude of from 10 to $20\mu V$. For more posterior recording sites (e.g., over the parietal cortex), the SW is less distinct and less negative in polarity. Like the LPC, the SW appears to comprise several waves rather than a single wave. Rohrbaugh et al. (1978), using a principal-components analysis, identified both an early (500–650 msec) and later (500–700 msec) SW. The early wave reflected a negative-to-positive gradient from frontal to more posterior electrodes, while the later component showed a negative focus at the vertex.

Figure 10-4 illustrates that the negative afterwave in frontal recordings for elderly subjects is either absent or markedly reduced (Smith et al., 1976, 1978). In addition, this absence of the negative afterwave with aging means an absence of the negative-to-positive gradient (Pfefferbaum et al., 1979; Smith et al., 1978) that characterizes the younger subject. This is illustrated in Figure 10-5.

Contingent negative variation (CNV). When two stimuli are paired ($S_1 - S_2$), so that the first acts as a warning signal for the second, a sustained negative slow potential of from 5 to 20 μV appears in the $S_1 - S_2$ interval. Since the initial report of it (Walter, Cooper, Aldridge, McCallum, & Winter, 1964), this averaged potential has received considerable attention (Otto, 1978; Tecce, 1972).

It now appears that the CNV may represent a less unique SP than was previously thought. If the $S_1 - S_2$

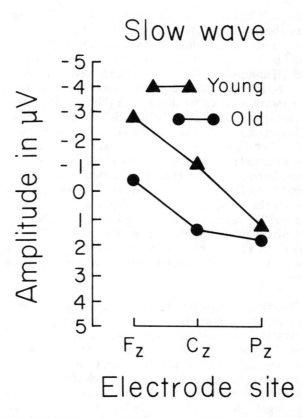

Figure 10-5. Mean amplitude plots of the slow wave (SW), comparing 10 young and 10 elderly subjects at midline recording sites F_z, C_z, and P_z. Young subjects show a significant negative-to-positive gradient from anterior (F_z) to posterior (P_z) sites. This gradient is much reduced in the elderly subjects.

interval is extended beyond 1 or 2 seconds, two negative components compose the CNV (Loveless & Sanford, 1974). The earlier of these, the so-called "O" wave, which depends on the properties of S_1, is maximal over frontal sites and is very likely an instance of the negative afterwave (see above) to S_1. The second wave, the "E" wave, begins 1 or 2 seconds before S_2 and reaches maximal negativity just prior to the end of the interval. This wave reflects the process of motor preparation (Kok, 1978) and is probably an instance of the readiness potential (see below). Which unique properties the traditional CNV has that are not accounted for independently by the negative afterwave or readiness potential remain to be determined.

In any case, a number of CNV studies have investigated age-related changes in this SP. In studies that have used short $S_1 - S_2$ intervals, where the CNV appears as a unitary wave, no substantial age differences have been noted (Harkins, Moss, Thompson, & Nowlin, 1976; Loveless & Sanford, 1974; Marsh & Thompson, 1973; Thompson, Marsh, & Zelinski in press; Thompson & Nowlin, 1971). However, for longer $S_1 - S_2$ intervals the preparatory component (E wave) is reported to be either diminished (Nakamura, Fukui, Kadobayashi, & Kato, 1978b; Schaie & Syndulko, 1978) or absent in the elderly (Loveless & Sanford, 1974). Schaie and Syndulko reported no differences in the amplitude of the early O wave but did find a delayed latency for the elderly. This latter report concerning the O wave is not consistent with our expectations if this component and the negative afterwave are one and the same. However, it is known that the negative afterwave is relatively insensitive to visual stimuli (Gaillard, 1977), which Schaie and Syndulko used, and this may account for their failure to observe age differences.

Readiness potential. This potential consists of a slowly increasing negative shift, 1 or 2 seconds prior to movement, that subsides rapidly with a positive deflection after the start of movement. The readiness potential comprises at least two components, a bilateral and symmetrical negativity (the Bereitschafts potential) that has a maximal amplitude at vertex (Deecke, Grozinger, & Kornhuber, 1976) and a lateralized negativity (the motor potential) that is maximal over the prerolandic cortex, contralateral to the side of stimulation (Grünewald, Grünewald-Zuberbier, Netz, Hömberg, & Sander, 1979).

Deecke, Englitz, and Schmitt (1978) reported that the Bereitshaftspotential (BP) was of relatively constant amplitude up to middle age (age 39) and then declined gradually. Positive BPs occurred occasionally in central and parietal sites for subjects over 60 years, while similar positive BPs were found for young adults only in frontal leads. In contrast to the BP, the motor potential was essentially constant across ages. These findings for the BP are therefore consistent, to some degree, with its relation to the E wave of the CNV. Further research is needed on the component waves of the CNV (E and O waves) and readiness potential to confirm and clarify the nature of age-associated changes in these SPs.

Temporal Characteristics

AEPs are influenced by the temporal and prior characteristics of stimulation (Davis, Mast, Yoshie, & Zerlin, 1966). In general, AEP amplitudes increase with longer interstimulus intervals and decrease with stimulus repetition. However, there are various qualifi-

cations to this conclusion, and the reader is referred to Callaway (1975) for details.

Interstimulus interval (ISI). Very short intervals between stimuli have been studied under the rubric of the "recovery cycle." The effects are a reduction in amplitude for the second of two stimuli presented temporally close in time (Allison, 1962). The recovery cycle, or time for the amplitude of a second stimulus to recover to the amplitude of the first, is shorter for earlier components of the AEP and progressively longer for later components. Shagass (1972) reported recovery cycles with age for somatosensory AEPs. For early and middle AEP components and ISIs from 2.5 to 120 msec, there were significant age differences, with faster amplitude recovery and slower latency recovery for the elderly. Comparable results have been reported by Floris, Morocutti, Amabile, Bernardi, and Rizzo (1968) for visual stimuli.

The temporal effects associated with ISIs longer than those investigated under the recovery cycle have been referred to as "fast habituation" (Callaway, 1975). Fast habituation occurs primarily to long latency components of the AEP for ISIs up to 10 seconds or more and is influenced by modality, subject, and task variables. The phenomena of fast habituation has been useful in investigating individual differences (Callaway, 1975) and cognitive processing related to cerebral lateralization (Shucard, Shucard, & Thomas, in press). To date, no studies have examined age as a function of these longer ISIs.

Stimulus repetition. Stimuli presented to an organism cease to evoke a reaction when repeated in identical form (Sokolov, 1963). Such "habituation" occurs at both physiological and behavioral levels. For the AEP, repetition of an unchanging stimulus produces a decrement in some component amplitudes, even when intertrial intervals are very long and subjects are alert and attentive (Öhman & Lader, 1972).

Brent et al. (1977) have reported age effects of repetition for the auditory AEP components N_1, P_2 and N_2 from a vertex recording site. On an initial trial block (30 repetitions), young subjects showed larger component amplitudes than the elderly, with a steeper decline in the later trial blocks. Repetition tended to reduce amplitude age differences in later trials and make the AEP more nearly similar for the two age groups. The authors noted that it seemed as if the older subjects were already partly habituated at the beginning of the experiment. This observation parallels Obrist's (1965) findings of age-related differences in alpha blocking with stimulus repetition. These results for habituation may have importance for interpreting

AEPs with age and are discussed in further detail later in this chapter.

Scalp Distribution

It is well known that different recording sites on the scalp yield AEPs differing in amplitude, latency, and component characteristics. These differences have been used in general AEP research to determine the locus of intracranial generators and to evaluate the possibility of cortical specialization. Age comparisons in scalp topography have been reported occasionally but seldom as the primary focus of research.

Drechsler (1978), studying the well-known contralateral asymmetry of the somatosensory AEP, found that the enhancement of middle latency components with age was more marked over the left then over the right central cortex. Conversely, Dustman and Beck (1969) observed no asymmetrical age differences in the sensory AEP to visual, auditory, or somatosensory stimuli. In the case of SPs, Marsh (1975), recording from sites C_5 and C_6, found support for left-right hemispheric differences with age in P_{300} amplitude but not in latency. The young had a larger amplitude P_{300} over the right hemisphere (C_6) whereas the elderly showed no difference between the hemispheres.

Anterior-posterior differences have consistently distinguished young from old subjects. In contrast to younger subjects, who exhibit a larger AEP in central and parietal regions for auditory and somatosensory stimuli, older subjects have a more equipotential distribution of amplitude across the whole scalp (Drechsler, 1978; Goodin et al., 1978; Smith et al., 1978). Age differences along the midline have also been reported for the latency of P_{300} (Marsh, 1975). During the latter half of the auditory evoked-potential epoch (500–1000 msec poststimulus onset), young subjects show a marked negative-to-positive gradient from frontal to parietal recording sites (Squires et al., 1975); this gradient is reduced or absent in elderly subjects (Smith et al., 1978). Figures 10-4 and 10-5 provide graphic illustration of these anterior-posterior age differences.

Interpretation of Averaged Evoked Potentials and Aging

Most of the research on the AEP with aging has been descriptive in nature. Only recently have efforts been made to test hypotheses concerning the origin of AEPs and their functional relations with age. Therefore our interpretation of age-related AEP changes is necessarily a post hoc application of descriptive data to some conceptual models, based on parallels drawn from behavioral or physiological observations.

Three approaches are used here in interpreting age-related AEP changes: first, an examination of possible methodological explanations and issues; second, a speculative application of AEP data to CNS aging models; and third, presentation of AEP and age studies related to an information-processing/performance approach.

Methodology

In few areas of research is methodology more critical than in that of AEPs. (For detailed discussions of AEP recording and other methodological procedures, the reader is referred to recent reviews by Otto, 1978, and by Venables and Christie, 1975). A similar complexity exists in experimental design for aging research and interpretation (Schaie, 1977).

Extracerebral factors. There is little doubt that the AEP is fundamentally of CNS origin. Still, there is considerable opportunity for nonneural potentials and other factors associated with averaging and recording to contaminate the data.

Since intracranial EPs are of considerably greater voltage than scalp EPs, any age-related alteration in the conductive properties of the overlying tissue and bone might be involved in AEP differences. However, in groups where large anatomical differences exist (men vs. women, children vs. adults) no correlation between anthropometric skull measurements and AEP characteristics has been demonstrated (Buchsbaum, Henkin, & Christiansen, 1974; Dustman & Beck, 1965). In addition, conductive changes should affect *all* AEP components with age and not specific characteristics, as has been noted. Though not conclusive, such evidence suggests that conductive properties are not involved significantly in AEP age changes.

Eye movements and blinking produce particularly large potentials over frontal and central recording sites, and the elderly engage in a significantly greater frequency of blinking than normal young people (Tecce, Savignano-Bowman, & Cole, 1978). While recent studies have controlled for eye movements and blinking, it is not clear whether myogenic responses of the neck and ear and the startle response have been similarly considered. Muscle contamination is important especially because of its selective character. For example, muscle potentials of the neck and ear affect middle-latency components of auditory and visual AEPs, while the startle response intrudes upon later components. Exacerbating the problem is the well-known difficulty the elderly have in inhibiting reflex motor responses and the increased significance of myogenic contamination in naive and anxious persons.

The pupillary reflex and peripheral nerve-conduction velocity—two other noncerebral factors known to change with age—have been considered by several authors who have excluded them as an explanation (Dustman & Beck, 1969; Shagass & Schwartz, 1965; Straumanis et al., 1965).

The weight of this evidence, both direct and indirect, indicates that extracerebral factors cannot reasonably account for age-related changes in the AEP. Nevertheless, the potential for contamination by extracerebral factors remains great in elderly subjects, and careful control of these factors in research cannot be overemphasized.

Recording procedures. Although most AEP studies of aging have used unipolar recordings, several have employed the bipolar method (Celesia & Daly, 1977a, 1977b; Drechsler, 1978; Straumanis et al., 1965; Visser et al., 1976). A comparison of studies using the two different montage methods yields no fundamental differences in age-related results. Of greater concern are the band-pass characteristics of the amplifier used and the length of the averaging epoch. Components of the AEP are present in different parts of the frequency spectrum, and SPs may extend for one or more seconds following the eliciting stimulus. Duncan-Johnson and Donchin (1979) have demonstrated how much the different band-pass characteristics commonly found in the literature can influence the amplitude and waveform of SPs. These same authors have emphasized the importance of selecting band-pass characteristics appropriate to the AEP components under study. Their admonition is especially relevant to age comparisons, where rather large differences may exist in the frequency characteristics of AEPs.

Response stability. The averaging technique assumes stability in the single-trial potentials that make up the average. Several lines of evidence indicate that satisfaction of this assumption may vary significantly with age. For latency stability, qualitative observations of the AEP wave form (Brent et al., 1977) and a statistical index of stability (Buchsbaum, et al., 1974) have suggested that individual EPs may not be as closely time-locked to stimuli for the elderly as at younger ages. This would have strong implications for interpretation, since it is known that latency stability can account for differences in component amplitude (Brazier, 1964). For amplitude, the assumption of stability is likely to be violated in most AEP research, though it may be critical when studying individual dif-

ferences. That amplitude stability may be a factor of concern is suggested by a study reviewed earlier on age-related differences in the effects of stimulus repetition on components of the vertex AEP (Brent et al., 1977). These findings indicate that age differences for the nonhabituated individual EP may be greater than is implied by the AEP comprising the usual 50–100 single-trial potentials.

The most direct method for dealing with this issue involves several procedures that have been developed for viewing single-trial data (Ruchkin, 1968; Ruchkin & Glaser, 1979; Woody, 1967). Although in their present state these techniques impose limitations, the techniques appear to be essential for future research on age differences in EPs. Indeed, single-trial analysis may be used for all future EP research. Equally important is the possibility that within-subject response variability, from whatever source, may have biological and psychological correlates unique to older subjects. Variability of the AEP has been shown to be related at younger ages to attentional factors and intellectual ability (Shucard & Callaway, 1974), and to mental health (Callaway, Jones, & Donchin, 1970).

CNS-Aging Models

Apart from methodological issues, an explanation of AEP changes can, in general, take one of two approaches: Such changes may be linked to physiologically based constructs such as inhibition, cortical reactivity, or physiological pathology, or they may be associated with behaviorally oriented processes such as attention, perception, and response speed. In this section several firmly established physiological and neurophysiological conceptual models are offered for the interpretation of AEP age-related changes. The subsequent section uses an information-processing/performance approach.

Inhibition. Theories of cerebral functioning designate inhibition as a basic property of the CNS that can be elicited in the motor or sensory cortex by direct cortical stimulation (Creutzfeldt, Innocenti, & Brooks, 1974; Serkov, Yanovskii, & Tal'nov, 1975) as well as by thalamocortical and peripheral afferent stimulation (Creutzfeldt, Watanabe, & Lux, 1966; Mountcastle & Powell, 1959). Mountcastle and Powell hypothesized that inhibition is the major mechanism to control excitation spread in sensory pathways in the cortex.

It is now generally accepted that the surface cortical EP primarily reflects some combination of excitatory and inhibitory postsynaptic potentials present in cortical pyramidal neurons; however, it has been difficult to correlate the positive and negative components of surface EPs and intracellular inhibitory and excitatory states (Goff, Allison, & Vaughan, 1978). Nevertheless, it has been shown that cerebral lesions outside specific sensory pathways result in enlarged EPs, whereas those in sensory tracts cause reduced ones (Cantor & Ilbag, 1973; Walker, Wolff, Halstead, & Case, 1944). This enhancement of the EP, resulting from nonspecific cerebral lesions, has been attributed to reduced inhibitory control of afferent stimulation. On this basis, the enlarged EPs observed in some neurological conditions have been interpreted as arising from deficits in central inhibition (Callner, Dustman, Madsen, Schenkenberg, & Beck, 1978; Lee & Blair, 1973).

As indicated earlier, for all three sensory modalities one or more AEP components in the middle-latency range are significantly larger in older than in young subjects. Straumanis et al. (1965) thought this difference might be due to greater excitation in the neuronal pool or, more likely, to a reduction in inhibitory activity. Subsequently, this latter explanation has been given by other authors (Dustman & Beck, 1969; Schenkenberg, 1970.)

Drechsler (1978) has argued that AEP age changes reveal an inhibitory deficit from another perspective. For young controls, the middle-latency components of the somatosensory AEP are limited to central and parietal regions of the cortex and are very attenuated in occipital regions. In contrast, Drechsler observed that the somatosensory AEP for aging persons appeared to be comparable in amplitude over the whole ipsilateral hemisphere. He attributed this to a loss of inhibitory processes producing a spread of cortical excitability that encompassed the whole hemisphere. The basis of this conclusion—the equipotential amplitude over the scalp of certain AEP components—is apparently a reliable finding (Goodin et al., 1978; Smith et al., 1978; see also Chapter 8 in this volume).

The evidence from AEP studies for a deficit in inhibition with age, while provocative, is based on ad hoc reasoning and perhaps should not be taken seriously without more direct evidence. The AEP differences observed can probably be explained in equally plausible ways. For example, Pfefferbaum et al. (1979) have suggested that some age-related changes in AEP amplitude might reflect an interaction of transient and SP components. Also, Buchsbaum et al. (1974) have pointed out the parallel between low circulating levels of gonadal hormone in the elderly and children and the enhanced AEP amplitudes in both groups compared to young persons. As yet, no attempts have been made to link AEP, age-related changes to independent measures of inhibition.

Reactivity. Behavioral decline in the elderly is popularly attributed to differences in cortical reactivity or arousal. The concept of arousal, as indicative of CNS excitability, comes from early experimental demonstration of the relation between the ascending reticular activating system and both EEG and behavioral arousal (Lindsley, Schreiner, & Magoun, 1949; Moruzzi & Magoun, 1949).

Early behavioral applications tended to conceptualize arousal as a unitary process and thus to view cortical, autonomic, and behavioral measures as parallel indices reflecting the general level of the organism's reactivity. Subsequent research has seriously questioned this unidimensional view of arousal. For example, behavioral arousal does not invariably accompany EEG arousal (Lindsley, 1960), and even EEG arousal exhibits both a short-duration phasic component and a longer-duration tonic component (Sharpless & Jasper, 1956). It is now clear that several forms of arousal can be separated functionally and anatomically and that many variables influence arousal both within and between forms (Lacey, 1967).

Marsh and Thompson (1977) have reviewed the controversial literature on age and arousal and have suggested that a multidimensional and situational view may help explain the seemingly contradictory findings. Such a view is consistent with the AEP data found in the elderly.

When stimulated passively or required to perform simple tasks, elderly people show AEP differences consistent with reduced cortical excitability, for example, a decrease in amplitude, an increase in latency, and a differential habituation for specific AEP response components. This concurs with similar studies of the EEG in older populations which indicate that with underarousal, mean alpha frequency and amplitude decline progressively, slow waves (1–7 Hz) are increasingly present (Drechsler, 1978), and EEG reactivity decreases (Obrist, 1965).

However, studies that have required active subject involvement and have measured the AEP (Ford et al., 1979; Marsh, 1975; Smith et al., 1976) or the CNV (Harkins et al., 1976; Marsh & Thompson, 1973; Thompson et al., in press; Thompson & Nowlin, 1971) indicate that the elderly are not necessarily underaroused and can exhibit levels of cortical excitability similar to those of younger persons. A parallel situational specificity is found with autonomic nervous system measures of arousal (Marsh & Thompson, 1977).

Although this evidence is consistent with a situational specificity that has considerable precedent in psychophysiological and gerontological research, it may also indicate greater variability in arousal for the elderly or perhaps difficulty in sustaining arousal levels without adequate external stimulation. In the future, research might profit by investigating AEPs and aging with experimental manipulation of arousal level.

Persistence. The bulk of evidence indicates that the nervous system processes information *as if* it were a single channel of limited capacity. This is manifested in a limitation on temporal resolution of stimuli. Thus for stimuli closely spaced in time, the reaction to the second stimulus is different in some way from the reaction to the first. This "refractory character" of the temporal response seems to be amplified with age, and as a result, there is a disproportionate slowing with age for continuous or closely spaced signals.

Axelrod (1963) has proposed that the senescent nervous system may show an increased persistence of neural activity from an initial stimulus, thus slowing or modifying the response to a second stimulus. Botwinick (1978), in reviewing the considerable behavioral data on stimulus fusion, masking, after-images, and illusions that pertain to a persistence model in aging, notes that much of the data is consistent with this model.

A possible physiological mechanism for persistence is suggested by recent electrophysiological evidence of age-related impairment in the capacity of synapses in the rat hippocampus to respond to repetitive stimulation (Landfield & Lynch, 1977). This neurophysiological observation is supported by neurochemical evidence of age-related impairment of brain-transmitter metabolism (Ordy & Kaack, 1975) and neuroanatomical evidence of age-dependent degeneration of synaptic elements in cortical tissue (Geinisman, Bondareff, & Dodge, 1977).

There is evidence for the AEP of age-related findings that correspond to this persistence hypothesis. For example, it is well known that flicker and click fusion occur at lower repetition rates for older than for younger persons (Botwinick, 1978). Celesia and Daly (1977b) studied the cortical frequency of photic driving (CFPD), the electrophysiological counterpart of critical flicker fusion. CFPD, defined as the highest frequency at which a photic driving response could be obtained as measured by steady-state potentials, decreased from 72 flashes per second for persons between 20 and 25 years of age to 60 flashes per second for those 60 years of age and above.

Also relevant to a persistence model are the recovery cycle experiments of Shagass (1972) mentioned earlier. While his finding of a faster amplitude recovery with age is not predictable from persistence theory, the slower latency recovery could be expected from the model. Future studies of the recovery cycle might profit by using longer ISIs than those used by Shagass so that the effects on SP components of the AEP could then be evaluated.

Qualitatively, the form of the AEP for the elderly shows a persistence of electrical positivity during the SW phase of the response, in comparison with the AEP at younger ages (see Figure 10-3). Such SW positivity is generally associated with a decrease in neural reactivity, while SW negativity is thought to be associated with heightened reactivity.

Visual masking, which has played an important part in evaluating the nature and timing of sensory processes, appears to offer a paradigm appropriate for use with AEP techniques. Several experiments confirm that old people are more susceptible to masking than younger people (Kline & Szafran, 1975; Walsh, 1976). Visual masking has also been studied in AEP research, but not with aging factors incorporated as a variable (Andreassi, de Simone, & Mellers, 1976). The fact that the AEP is elicited by discrete stimuli and is sensitive to the temporal features of stimulation would seem to make it a useful measure to evaluate persistence theory.

Cortical localization. Several lines of evidence suggest that parts of the CNS are more sensitive to, or become involved earlier in, the aging process than others. It is not unreasonable to expect differential rates of aging in the nervous system, for it is well established in gerontology that aging is not a uniform process, either between or within persons. Bondareff (1977), in a discussion of neuronal atrophy with age, cautions against the view of a generalized neuronal loss, stating that such "loss is a more exclusive process involving only selective parts of the brain" (p. 163).

Recent neuropsychological studies support a differential model of aging in the CNS. Halstead-Reitan tests of right hemispheric damage discriminate normal older subjects better than tests of left hemispheric or diffuse brain damage (Goldstein & Shelly, 1975; Overall & Gorham, 1972). Farver (1975), using tests that discriminate more circumscribed cortical areas, suggested a unique involvement of the right parietal lobe. Albert and Kaplan (1980) in reviewing the relevant literature, have concluded that perceptual and performance deficits in the elderly are most consistent with involvement of the frontal cortex and specifically the right frontal cortex.

While selective aging may involve several unique parts of the brain, the "frontal system" described by Nauta (1971) is a likely candidate for involvement. The frontal lobes form a unique and complicated system, with reciprocal connections to the parietal and temporal association cortices and to the limbic system and subcortical structures in the thalamus and reticular formation. As noted earlier, there are indications of anterior-posterior age differences in SP activity that can be interpreted as reflecting changes in this frontal system (Smith et al., 1978) and may be related to a diminished performance capacity with age. (See Chapter 8 in this volume for some additional data supporting specific frontal lobe involvement with aging.) This evidence suggests that topographical studies of the AEP, combined with neuropsychological measures and possibly with neurological assessment, may be important in resolving the issue of selective cortical aging.

Health status. There are variables correlated with aging, but presumably not synonymous with it, that profoundly affect the ability to specify the course of normal adult development from middle to old age (Birren & Schaie, 1977). Perhaps the most widely acknowledged example in gerontology concerns the age-related increase in physiological pathology and its direct and indirect consequences (Hertzog, Schaie, & Gribbin, 1978).

All the AEP age changes referred to in this chapter have come from so-called "normal and healthy" older subjects. Procedures used to screen for health have included the experimenter's subjective judgment, in some cases a medical history, and in a few cases a physical exam and other medical and mental tests. In general, studies have not reported in detail the procedures used in subject health screening, nor has there been any attempt to correlate health status and AEPs.

There can be little doubt that the incidence of renal, gastrointestinal, respiratory, cardiovascular, and other diseases increases in the later years (Moriyama, Kruegar, & Stamler, 1971; Timiras, 1972). The most important disease processes correlated with chronological age are those of the cardiovascular system—that is, coronary artery disease, hypertension, and cerebral vascular disorders. Both clinical and subclinical evidence of cardiovascular disease have been shown to correlate with age changes in psychomotor performance (Abrahams & Birren, 1973; Botwinick & Storandt, 1974; Light, 1975; Spieth, 1965) and measures of intellectual functioning (Birren, Butler, Greenhouse, Sokoloff, & Yarrow, 1963; Hertzog et al., 1978; Wilkie & Eisdorfer, 1973).

The exact mechanisms by which disease processes mediate behavior changes with age are undetermined, but they most likely involve primary changes in the CNS. Diffuse slowing of the EEG has been reported to be associated with diseases of the cardiovascular system, decreased blood flow, and impaired mental functioning (Obrist, 1965). Obrist (1972) has proposed a vascular insufficiency model to account for the inter-

relations of these three factors. According to this model, disease of the cardiovascular system causes reduced cerebral blood flow and chronic hypoxia. Over some period of time this condition leads to neuronal loss, followed by decreased mental functioning and EEG slowing. We are unfamiliar with any substantive evidence in the AEP literature, for any age, indicating the relation of the AEP to cerebral blood flow, EEG slowing, or other measures of cardiovascular and cerebral vascular function. Since the AEP is proving useful in various neurological assessments of the CNS, it is reasonable to anticipate that it may reflect changes associated with cardiovascular and cerebrovascular disease, especially when these are manifest in performance change in the elderly.

Information Processing and Performance

The recognition in the mid-1960s that certain components of the AEP vary reliably with task parameters has made it popular to conceptualize general AEP research in terms of information processing and performance. Chapter 8 of this volume demonstrates the potential of this approach for the future study of aging. Here we consider only the two areas of our own research involvement, those of response slowing and orienting.

Response slowing. A slowing of response and timing with age is a pervasive observation demonstrated in numerous experimental contexts (Welford & Birren, 1965). While changes in sense organs, muscles, and tendons, or a lack of motivation, may play a sizeable role in more infirm older individuals, only changes in central processes are sufficient to account for the progressive slowing observed in normal adult aging (Welford, 1977). The possibility of directly assessing this central slowing has led to a number of studies comparing SPs and response time (RT).

The amplitude of the CNV is thought to be related positively to efficient performance, as measured by RT. Marsh and Thompson (1973) first studied the question of whether age differences in the CNV might be associated with performance decrements in the elderly. They used a pitch discrimination task in which subjects were asked to judge whether the second of two tones (S_2) was higher or lower in pitch than a preceding tone (S_1). Both difficult and easy discriminations were required. Difficult trials produced longer RTs than easy trials, and younger subjects had faster RTs than the elderly; however, these age–RT differences were not reflected in CNV amplitude.

Harkins et al. (1976) studied the CNV and RT in 12 males between the ages of 64 and 77 years. Fast RT trials were compared with slow RT trials within subjects. The CNV amplitude was significantly related to response speed, but since no comparison group was used, age differences were not noted.

Marsh (1975) used the memory scanning task of Sternberg (1969) to compare P_{300} latency with the effect of memory load on RT. Consistent with prior research, RT increased with increased memory load, and this was correlated with an increase in P_{300} latency and a decrease in P_{300} amplitude. However, although older subjects had significantly longer RTs than young subjects at all levels of memory load, these age differences in RT were not reflected in P_{300} latency or amplitude.

Loveless and Sanford (1974) investigated whether poorer preparation for response by the elderly is involved in their behavioral slowing. They manipulated the foreperiod (.5, 1.0, 3.0, 6.0, and 15 sec) of a reaction-time task for a group of young and a group of older subjects. As expected, RT increased with foreperiod length and predictability, and the elderly were especially slow at the longest foreperiods. While different foreperiods influenced CNV amplitude, the main effect of age was not significant. When CNV form was considered, however, the elderly were found to lack the anticipatory E wave when the foreperiods were long. The authors concluded that the poor performance of the elderly at long foreperiods did not involve a failure to maintain preparation for response so much as an inability to initiate preparation at an appropriate time.

In a follow-up of Loveless and Sanford's work, Schaie and Syndulko (1978) attempted to correlate components of the CNV (O and E waves) with response time. They compared young and old subjects on a warned RT task with interstimulus intervals of 2, 4, and 8 seconds. They found no significant correlations between O or E wave amplitude of the CNV and RT for any of the three age groups studied (young, young-old, and old-old) and at any of the interstimulus intervals. There was an increase in O-wave latency with age, but its relation to RT was not indicated.

A recent report by Nakamura, Fukui, Kadobayashi, and Kato (1978a) provided evidence for a significant relation between the CNV, RT, and age. They compared three groups, ages 20–24, 51–62, and 68–76 years. When a motor response to S_2 was required, CNV decreased and RT increased with age. The relation was not observed when subjects merely attended to stimuli or verbally indicated a discrimination to S_2.

On the basis of behavioral evidence that older persons perform poorly in tasks when their attention or concentration is disturbed (Botwinick, 1978; Craik, 1977), Michalewski, Thompson, Smith, Patterson, Bowman, Litzelman, and Brent (in press) compared older and younger individuals in a divided-attention procedure using the CNV, RT, and heart rate as indices of distraction. Typically, events or tasks that distract the subject's concentration away from the $S_1 - S_2$ interval reduce CNV amplitude, lengthen RTs, and elevate cardiac activity (McCallum & Walter, 1968; Tecce & Cole, 1976; Tecce & Hamilton, 1973; Tecce, Savignano-Bowman, & Meinbresse, 1976; Tecce & Scheff, 1969). Three experimental conditions, administered to a group of elderly and a group of young subjects, included a recall, a no-recall, and a control, or no-letters, condition. In the recall or distraction-inducing condition, spoken consonant-vowel-consonant (CVC) letters were introduced into the CNV interval and were recalled after each trial. The no-recall condition was similar to the recall condition, except that recall of the CVCs was not required. The no-letters condition presented a standard $S_1 - S_2$ CNV situation.

The results of the distraction condition indicated that the CNV amplitudes were reduced when measured near the S_2 signal for both older and younger subjects. Longer RTs and higher heart rates were also noted for both groups during distraction. While no overall age differences in the amplitudes of the CNV were observed between the two groups at vertex (C_z) and parietal (P_z) placements, frontal (F_z) amplitudes in the elderly were found to be generally smaller than in the younger subjects, regardless of the experimental condition considered. The pooled averages for the older and younger groups are shown in Figure 10-6. In this figure the reduced CNVs for the elderly at the frontal location are apparent across the experimental conditions, in contrast to the younger subjects. The finding of reduced frontal activity in the CNV in the aged individual is consistent with the anterior-posterior age differences in SP activity discussed earlier, and it may be related to a diminished performance capacity, as indicated in response speed, for older subjects.

This series of studies on the CNV and RT provides only suggestive evidence that the CNV reflects processes associated with response slowing in the elderly. Perhaps this should be expected. Surely, observed response slowing involves a complexity of motor, cognitive, and sensory functions, while any single aspect of averaged potentials may reflect only a small part of this sequence of processes. In much research, frequent dissociation is evident between performance and amplitude/latency measures of the AEP. In spite of the clear parallels between age-associated RT changes and AEPs, it is unlikely that a simple relation between these two measures will be found.

Orienting. The orienting reflex is thought to prepare the organism for more efficient stimulus reception and information processing (Sokolov, 1963). Experimental

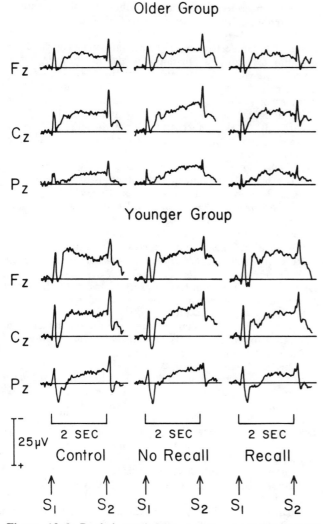

Older Group

Fz

Cz

Pz

Younger Group

Fz

Cz

Pz

25μV

| 2 SEC | 2 SEC | 2 SEC |

Control   No Recall   Recall

S₁   S₂   S₁   S₂   S₁   S₂

Figure 10-6. Pooled contingent negative variation (CNV) averages derived from individual records for the older (*n* = 11) and younger (*n* = 12) groups during recall (distraction), no-recall, and no-letters (control) conditions. The reduced CNVs for the elderly at the frontal location are apparent across conditions in comparson to younger subjects.

evidence appears to link orienting with elevated levels of activation and enhanced vigilance performance, and it is generally acknowledged that more intense orienting responses are related to better performance in attention-demanding tasks (Raskin, 1973).

Brent et al. (1977) examined a group of old and young subjects for stimulus orientation, repetition, and task relevance. They used a novel stimulus task that consisted of brief tones, all identical in pitch and intensity, except for an infrequent change in pitch. By instruction, the subjects sometimes ignored the tones (read a book) and at other times attended to (counted)

them. Novel tones produced a P₃₀₀ wave in both groups that was substantially smaller for the elderly whether the stimuli were attended to or not.

Goodin et al. (1978), also using a novel stimulus paradigm to investigate AEPs over the age range of 6 to 76 years, observed an essentially linear decrease in amplitude with age for the LPC to novel stimuli. Smith et al. (1978) reported that the negative afterwave present in frontal recordings in young subjects and thought to be associated with orienting (Rohrbaugh et al., 1978) is reduced or absent in older subjects.

While these studies strongly indicate that older people are deficient in CNS correlates of orienting, in so far as P₃₀₀ and the negative afterwave reflect it, they provide no direct evidence that such AEP changes are related to significant changes in information processing and performance. This criticism is not limited to these studies but is true for the large majority of AEP and aging research. As the previous section on response slowing indicates, the relation between AEP changes and diminished performance in the elderly has been difficult to demonstrate, and in any case is probably not a simple one. More aging studies with combined AEP and performance measurements are needed, and wherever possible, stimuli in the subjects' task should be used to elicit the EP. Equally important may be the use of more complex and realistic tasks and comparisons made not only across the adult life span but also in terms of individual differences among the elderly themselves.

REFERENCES

Abrahams, J. P., & Birren, J. E. Reaction time as a function of age and behavioral predisposition to coronary heart disease. *Journal of Gerontology*, 1973, *28*, 471–478.

Albert, M. S., & Kaplan, E. F. Organic implications of neuropsychological deficits in the elderly. In L. W. Poon, J. Fozard, L. Cermak, D. Arenberg, & L. W. Thompson (Eds.), *New directions in memory and aging: Proceedings of the George A. Talland Memorial Conference.* Hillsdale, N.J.: Lawrence Erlbaum, 1980.

Allison, T. Recovery functions of somatosensory evoked responses in man. *Electroencephalography and Clinical Neurophysiology*, 1962, *14*, 331–343.

Andreassi, J. L., de Simone, J. J., & Mellers, B. W. Amplitude changes in the visual evoked cortical potential with backward masking. *Electroencephalography and Clinical Neurophysiology*, 1976, *41*, 387–398.

Axelrod, S. Cognitive tasks in several modalities. In R. H. Williams, C. Tibbits, & W. Donahue (Eds.), *Processes of aging* (Vol. 1). New York: Atherton Press, 1963.

Birren, J. E., Butler, R. N., Greenhouse, S. W., Sokoloff, L., & Yarrow, M. R. Interdisciplinary relationships: Interrelationships of physiological, psychological and psychiatric findings in healthy elderly men. In *Human aging: A biological and behavioral study* (USPHS Publ. No. 986). Washington, D.C.: U.S. Government Printing Office, 1963.

Birren, J. E., & Schaie, K. W. (Eds.) *Handbook of the psychology of aging.* New York: Van Nostrand Reinhold, 1977.

Bondareff, W. The neural basis of aging. In J. E. Birren & K. W. Schaie (Eds.), *Handbook of the psychology of aging.* New York: Van Nostrand Reinhold, 1977.

Botwinick, J. *Aging and behavior.* New York: Springer, 1978.

Botwinick, J., & Storandt, M. Cardiovascular status, depressive affect, and other factors in reaction time. *Journal of Gerontology,* 1974, *29,* 543–548.

Brazier, M. A. B. Evoked responses recorded from the depths of the human brain. *Annals of the New York Academy of Science,* 1964, *112,* 33–59.

Brent, G. A., Smith, D. B. D., & Michalewski, H. J. Differences in the evoked potential in young and old subjects during habituation and dishabituation procedures. *Psychophysiology,* 1977, *14,* 96–97.

Buchsbaum, M. S., Henkin, R. I., & Christiansen, R. L. Age and sex differences in averaged evoked responses in a normal population, with observations on patients with gonadal dysgenesis. *Electroencephalography and Clinical Neurophysiology,* 1974, *37,* 137–144.

Buchwald, J. S., & Brown, K. A. The role of acoustic inflow in the development of adaptive behavior. *Annals of the New York Academy of Science,* 1977, *290,* 270–283.

Buchwald, J. S., & Huang, C. M. Far-field acoustic response: Origins in the cat. *Science,* 1975, *189,* 382–384.

Callaway, E. *Brain electrical potentials and individual psychological differences.* New York: Grune & Stratton, 1975.

Callaway, E., Jones, R. T., & Donchin, E. Auditory evoked potential variability in schizophrenia. *Electroencephalography and Clinical Neurophysiology,* 1970, *29,* 421–428.

Callner, D. A., Dustman, R. E., Madsen, J. A., Schenkenberg, T., & Beck, E. C. Life span changes in the averaged evoked responses of Down's syndrome and nonretarded persons. *American Journal of Mental Deficiency,* 1978, *82,* 398–405.

Cantor, F. K., & Ilbag, F. Facilitation of photic response by focal lesions. *Electroencephalography and Clinical Neurophysiology,* 1973, *34,* 77–79.

Caton, R. In J. B. Hamilton (Ed.), *Transactions of the International Medical Congress, Ninth Session,* 1875, *3,* 246. (Quoted in M. A. B. Brazier, *A history of the electrical activity of the brain.* London: Pitman, 1961.)

Celesia, G. G. Visual evoked potentials in neurological disorders. *American Journal of EEG Technologists,* 1978, *18,* 47–59.

Celesia, G. G., & Daly, R. F. Effect of aging on visual evoked responses. *Archives of Neurology,* 1977, *34,* 403–407. (a)

Celesia, G. G., and Daly, R. F. Visual electroencephalographic computer analysis (VECA). *Neurology,* 1977, *27,* 637–641. (b)

Courchesne, E. Changes in P_3 waves with event repetition:

Long-term effects on scalp distribution and amplitude. *Electroencephalography and Clinical Neurophysiology,* 1978, *45,* 754–766.

Cracco, R. Q., & Cracco, J. B. Somatosensory evoked potential in man: Far field potentials. *Electroencephalography and Clinical Neurophysiology,* 1976, *41,* 460–466.

Craik, F. I. M. Age differences in human memory. In J. E. Birren & K. W. Schaie (Eds.), *Handbook of the psychology of aging.* New York: Van Nostrand Reinhold, 1977.

Creutzfeldt, O. D., Innocenti, G. M., & Brooks, D. Vertical organization in the visual cortex (area 17) in the cat. *Experimental Brain Reserach,* 1974, *21,* 315–336.

Creutzfeldt, O. D., Watanabe, S., & Lux, H. D. Relations between EEG phenomena and potentials of single cells. I. Evoked responses after thalamic and epicortical stimulation. *Electroencephalography and Clinical Neurophysiology,* 1966, *20,* 1–18.

Davis, H., Mast, T., Yoshie, N., & Zerlin, S. The slow response of the human cortex to auditory stimuli: Recovery process. *Electroencephalography and Clinical Neurophysiology,* 1966, *21,* 105–113.

Dawson, G. D. Cerebral responses to electrical stimulation of peripheral nerve in man. *Journal of Neurosurgical Psychiatry,* 1947, *10,* 134–140.

Dawson, G. D. A summation technique for the detection of small evoked potentials. *Electroencephalography and Clinical Neurophysiology,* 1954, *6,* 65–84.

Deecke, L., Englitz, H. G., & Schmitt, G. Age dependence of the Bereitschaftspotential. In D. Otto (Ed.), *Multidisciplinary prospectives in event-related brain potential research.* Washington, D.C.: U.S. Environmental Protection Agency, 1978.

Deecke, L., Grozinger, B., & Kornhuber, H. H. Voluntary finger movements in man: Cerebral potentials and theory. *Biological Cybernetics,* 1976, *23,* 99–119.

Drechsler, F. Quantitative analysis of neurophysiological processes of the aging CNS. *Journal of Neurology,* 1978, *218,* 197–213.

Duncan-Johnson, C. C., & Donchin, E. The time constant on P300 recording. *Psychophysiology,* 1979, *16,* 53–55.

Dustman, R. E., & Beck, E. C. The visual evoked potential of twins. *Electroencephalography and Clinical Neurophysiology,* 1965, *19,* 570–575.

Dustman, R. E., & Beck, E. C. Visually evoked potentials: Amplitude changes with age. *Science,* 1966, *151,* 1013–1015.

Dustman, R. E., & Beck, E. C. The effect of maturation and aging on the wave form of visually evoked potentials. *Electroencephalography and Clinical Neurophysiology,* 1969, *26,* 2–11.

Farver, P. *Performance of normal older adults on a test battery designed to measure parietal lobe functions.* Unpublished master's thesis, Sargent College of Allied Health Professions, Boston University, 1975.

Floris, V., Morocutti, C., Amabile, G., Bernardi, G., & Rizzo, P. A. Recovery cycle of visual evoked potentials in normal, schizophrenic and neurotic patients. In N. S. Kline & E. L. Laska (Eds.), *Computers and electronic devices in psychiatry.* New York: Grune & Stratton, 1968.

Ford, J. M., Hink, R. F., Hopkins, W. F. III, Roth, W. T.,

Pfefferbaum, A., & Kopell, B. S. Age effects on event-related potentials in a selective attention task. *Journal of Gerontology*, 1979, *34*, 388–395.

Gaillard, A. W. K. The late CNV wave: Preparation versus expectancy. *Psychophysiology*, 1977, *14*, 563–568.

Geinisman, Y., Bondareff, W., & Dodge, J. T. Partial deafferentation of neurons in the dentate gyrus of the senescent rat. *Brain Research*, 1977, *134*, 541–545.

Gibson, W. P. R. *Essential of clinical electric response audiometry*. London: Churchill Livingstone, 1978.

Goff, W. R., Allison, T., & Vaughan, H. G., Jr. The functional neuroanatomy of event related potentials. In E. Callaway, P. Tueting, & S. H. Koslow (Eds.), *Event-related brain potentials in man*. New York: Academic Press, 1978.

Goldstein, G., & Shelly, C. H. Similarities and differences between psychological deficit in aging and brain damage. *Journal of Gerontology*, 1975, *30*, 448–455.

Goodin, D. S., Squires, K. C., Henderson, B. H., & Starr, A. Age-related variations in evoked potentials to auditory stimuli in normal human subjects. *Electroencephalography and Clinical Neurophysiology*, 1978, *44*, 447–458.

Grünewald, G., Grünewald-Zuberbier, E., Netz, J., Hömberg, V., & Sander, G. Relationships between the late component of the contingent negative variation and the Bereitschaftspontential. *Electroencephalography and Clinical Neurophysiology*, 1979, *46*, 538–545.

Harkins, S. W., Moss, S. F., Thompson, L. W., & Nowlin, J. B. Relationship between central and automomic nervous system activity: Correlates of psychomotor performance in elderly men. *Experimental Aging Research*, 1976, *2*, 409–423.

Hecox, K., & Galambos, R. Brainstem auditory evoked responses in human infants and adults. *Archives of Otolaryngology*, 1974, *99*, 30–33.

Hertzog, C., Schaie, K. W., & Gribbin, K. Cardiovascular disease and changes in intellectual functioning from middle to old age. *Journal of Gerontology*, 1978, *33*, 872–883.

Jewett, D. L. Volume-conducted potentials in response to auditory stimuli as detected by averaging in the cat. *Electroencephalography and Clinical Neurophysiology*, 1970, *28*, 609–618.

Jewett, D. L., Romano, M. N., & Williston, J. S. Human auditory evoked potentials: Possible brainstem components detected on the scalp. *Science*, 1970, *167*, 1517–1518.

Kline, D. W., & Szafran, J. Age differences in backward monoptic visual noise masking. *Journal of Gerontology*, 1975, *30*, 307–311.

Kok, A. The effect of warning stimulus novelty on the P300 and components of the contingent negative variation. *Biological Psychology*, 1978, *6*, 219–233.

Kooi, K. A., & Bagchi, B. K. Visual evoked responses in man: Normative data. *Annals of the New York Academy of Sciences*, 1964, *112*, 254–269.

Lacey, J. I. Somatic response patterning and stress: Some revisions of activation theory. In M. H. Appley & R. Trumbull (Eds.), *Psychological stress: Issues and research*. New York: Appleton-Century-Croft, 1967.

Landfield, P. W., & Lynch, G. Impaired monosynaptic potentiation *in vitro*: Hippocampal slices from aged, memory-deficient rats. *Journal of Gerontology*, 1977, *32*, 523–533.

Lee, R. G., & Blair, R. D. G. Evolution of EEG and visual evoked response changes in Jakob-Creutzfeldt disease. *Electroencephalography and Clinical Neurophysiology*, 1973, *35*, 133–142.

Libet, B., Alberts, W. W., Wright, E. W., & Feinstein, B. Cortical and thalamic activation in conscious sensory experience. In G. G. Somjen (Ed.), *Neurophysiology in man*. Amsterdam: Excerpta medica, 1972.

Light, K. C. Slowing of response time in young and middle-aged hypertensive patients. *Experimental Aging Research*, 1975, *1*, 209–227.

Lindsley, D. B. Attention, consciousness, sleep and wakefulness. In J. Field, H. W. Magoun, & V. E. Hall (Eds.), *Handbook of physiology. Vol. 3: Neurophysiology*. Washington, D.C.: American Physiological Society, 1960.

Lindsley, D. B., Schreiner, L. H., & Magoun, H. W. An electromyographic study of spasticity. *Journal of Neurophysiology*, 1949, *12*, 197–205.

Loveless, N. E. Distribution of responses to non-signal stimuli. In W. C. McCallum & J. R. Knott (Eds.), *The responsive brain*. Bristol: John Wright, 1976.

Loveless, N. E., & Sanford, A. J. Effects of age on the contingent negative variation and preparatory set in a reaction-time task. *Journal of Gerontology*, 1974, *29*, 52–63.

Marsh, G. R. Age differences in evoked potential correlates of a memory scanning process. *Experimental Aging Research*, 1975, *1*, 3–16.

Marsh, G. R., & Thompson, L. W. Effects of age on the contingent negative variation in a pitch discrimination task. *Journal of Gerontology*, 1973, *28*, 56–62.

Marsh, G. R., & Thompson, L. W. Psychophysiology of aging. In J. E. Birren & K. W. Schaie (Eds.), *Handbook of the psychology of aging*. New York: Van Nostrand Reinhold, 1977.

McCallum, W. C., & Walter, W. G. The effects of attention and distraction on the contingent negative variation in normal and neurotic subjects. *Electroencephalography and Clinical Neurophysiology*, 1968, *25*, 319–329.

Michalewski, H. J., Patterson, J. V., Thompson, L. W., Bowman, T. E., & Litzelman, D. *Age-related changes in the auditory brainstem potential*. Manuscript in preparation.

Michalewski, H. J., Thompson, L. W., Patterson, J. V., Bowman, T. E., & Litzelman, D. Sex differences in amplitudes and latencies of the human auditory brainstem potential. *Electroencephalography and Clinical Neurophysiology*, 1980, *48*, 351–356.

Michalewski, H. J., Thompson, L. W., Smith, D. B. D., Patterson, J. V., Bowman, T. E., Litzelman, D., & Brent, G. Reduced frontal activity in the elderly: Age differences in the contingent negative variation (CNV). *Journal of Gerontology*, in press.

Moriyama, I. M., Kruegar, & Stamler, J. *Cardiovascular diseases in the United States*. Cambridge, Mass.: Harvard University Press, 1971.

Moruzzi, G., & Magoun, H. W. Brain stem reticular formation and activation of EEG. *Electroencephalography and Clinical Neurophysiology*, 1949, *1*, 455–473.

Mountcastle, V. B., & Powell, T. P. S. Neural mechanisms subserving cutaneous sensibility, with special reference to the role of afferent inhibition in sensory perception and discrimination. *Johns Hopkins Hospital Bulletin*, 1959, *105*, 201–232.

Nakamura, M., Fukui, Y., Kadobayashi, I., & Kato, N. A comparison of the CNV in young and old subjects: Its relation to memory and personality. *Electroencephalography and Clinical Neurophysiology*, 1978, *46*, 345–350. (a)

Nakamura, M., Fukui, Y., Kadobayashi, I., & Kato, N. The effect of motor-response-deprivation on contingent negative variation (CNV): The morphology. *Folia Psychiatrica et Neurologica Japonica*, 1978, *32*, 237–247. (b)

Nauta, W. J. H. The problem of the frontal lobe: A reinterpretation. *Journal of Psychiatric Research*, 1971, 8, 167–187.

Obrist, W. D. Electroencephalographic approach to age changes in response speed. In A. T. Welford & J. E. Birren (Eds.), *Behavior, aging and the nervous system*. Springfield, Ill.: Charles C Thomas, 1965.

Obrist, W. D. Cerebral physiology of the aged: Influence of circulatory disorder. In C. M. Gaitz (Ed.), *Aging and the brain*. New York: Plenum Press, 1972.

Öhman, A., & Lader, M. Selective attention and "habituation" of the auditory averaged evoked response in humans. *Physiology and Behavior*, 1972, 8, 79–85.

Ordy, J. M., & Kaack, B. Neurochemical changes in composition, metabolism and neurotransmitters in the human brain with age. In J. M. Ordy & K. R. Brizzee (Eds.), *Neurobiology of aging*. New York: Plenum Press, 1975.

Otto, D. (Ed.). *Multidisciplinary perspectives in event-related brain potential research*. Washington, D.C.: U.S. Environmental Protection Agency, 1978.

Overall, J. E., & Gorham, D. R. Organicity versus old age in objective and projective test performance. *Journal of Consulting and Clinical Psychology*, 1972, *39*, 98–105.

Pfefferbaum, A., Ford, J. M., Roth, W. T., Hopkins, W. F., III, & Kopell, B. S. Event-related potential changes in healthy aged females. *Electroencephalography and Clinical Neurophysiology*, 1979, *46*, 81–86.

Picton, T. W., Hillyard, S. A., Krausz, H. I., & Galambos, R. Human auditory evoked potentials I: Evaluation of components. *Electroencephalography and Clinical Neurophysiology*, 1974, *36*, 179–190.

Pratt, H., & Sohmer H. Intensity and rate functions of cochlear and brainstem evoked responses to click stimulation in man. *Archives of Otorhinolaryngology*, 1976, *212*, 85–92.

Raskin, D.C. Attention and arousal. In W. F. Prokasy & D. C. Raskin (Eds.), *Electrodermal activity in psychological research*. New York: Academic Press, 1973.

Rohrbaugh, J. W., Syndulko, K., & Lindsley, D. B. Cortical slow negative waves following non-paired stimuli: Effects of task factors. *Electroencephalography and Clinical Neurophysiology*, 1978, *45*, 551–567.

Ruchkin, D. S. Analysis of nonhomogeneous sequences of evoked potentials. *Experimental Neurology*, 1968, *20*, 275–284.

Ruchkin, D. S., & Glaser, E. M. Simple digital filters for examining CNV and P300 on a single-trial basis. In D. Otto (Ed.), *Multidisciplinary perspectives in event-related brain potential research*. Washington, D.C.: U.S. Environmental Protection Agency, 1978.

Schaie, J. P., & Syndulko, K. Age differences in cortical activity associated with preparation to respond. *International Journal of Behavioral Development*, 1978, *1*, 255–261.

Schaie, K. W. Quasi-experimental research designs in the psychology of aging. In J. E. Birren & K. W. Schaie (Eds.), *Handbook of the psychology of aging*. New York: Van Nostrand Reinhold, 1977.

Schenkenberg, T. *Visual, auditory and somatosensory evoked responses of normal subjects from childhood to senescence*. Unpublished doctoral disseration, University of Utah, 1970.

Scott, M. L., & Harkins, S. W. Amplitude of the brainstem auditory evoked response: The effect of interstimulus interval. *International Journal of Neuroscience*, 1978, *8*, 147–152.

Serkov, F. N., Yanovskii, E. Sh., & Tal'nov, A. N. Monosynaptic inhibitory post synaptic potentials of cortical neurons. *Neurophysiology*, 1975, *7*, 351–358.

Shagass, C. *Evoked brain potentials in psychiatry*, New York: Plenum Press, 1972.

Shagass, C., & Schwartz, M. Age, personality, and somatosensory cerebral evoked responses. *Science*, 1965, *148*, 1359–1361.

Sharpless, S., & Jasper, H. Habituation of the arousal reaction. *Brain*, 1956, *79*, 655–680.

Shucard, D. W., & Callaway, E. Auditory evoked potential amplitude and variability-effects of task and intellectual ability. *Journal of Comparative and Physiological Psychology*, 1974, *87*, 284–294.

Shucard, D. W., Shucard, J. L., & Thomas, D. G. Auditory evoked potentials, habituation and cerebral lateralization of cognitive processing. *Science*, in press.

Simpson, R., Vaughn, H. G., Jr., & Ritter, W. The scalp topography of potentials associated with missing visual or auditory stimuli. *Electroencephalography and Clinical Neurophysiology*, 1976, *40*, 33–42.

Simpson, R., Vaughan, H. G., Jr., & Ritter, W. The scalp topography of potentials in auditory and visual discrimination tasks. *Electroencephalography and Clinical Neurophysiology*, 1977, *42*, 528–535.

Smith, D. B. D., Brent, G., Thompson, L., & Michalewski, H. Age related differences in habituation, orientation and attentional state as indicated by the average evoked potential. *Abstracts of the XIth International Congress of Gerontology*. Tokyo: Scimed Publications, 1978.

Smith, D. B. D., Tom, C. E., Brent, G. A., & Ohta, R. J. *Attention, evoked potentials and aging*. Paper presented at the 56th Annual Meeting of the Western Psychological Association, Los Angeles, April 1976.

Sokolov, Y. E. *Perception and the conditioned reflex*. New York: Macmillan, 1963.

Sohmer, H., & Feinmesser, M. Cochlear action potentials recorded from the external ear in man. *Annals of Otology, Rhinology, and Laryngology*, 1967, *76*, 425–435.

Spieth, W. Slowness of task performance and cardiovascular

diseases. In A. T. Welford and J. W. Birren (Eds.), *Behavior, aging and the nervous system*. Springfield, Ill.: Charles C Thomas, 1965.

Squires, N., Squires, K., & Hillyard, S. A. Two varieties of long-latency positive waves evoked by unpredictable auditory stimuli in man. *Electroencephalography and Clinical Neurophysiology*, 1975, *38*, 387–401.

Starr, A. Clinical relevance of brain stem auditory evoked potentials in brainstem disorders in man. In. J. E. Desmedt (Ed.), *Auditory evoked potentials in man. Psychopharmacology correlates of evoked potentials. Progress in clinical neurophysiology*. (Vol. 2). Basel: Karger, 1977.

Starr, A., & Achor, J. Auditory brainstem responses in neurological disease. *Archives of Neurology*, 1975, *32*, 761–768.

Starr, A., & Hamilton, A. E. Correlation between confirmed sites of neurological lesions and abnormalities of far-field auditory brainstem responses. *Electroencephalography and Clinical Neurophysiology*, 1976, *41*, 595–608.

Sternberg, S. Memory-scanning: Mental processes revealed by reaction-time experiments. *American Scientist*, 1969, *57*, 421–456.

Stockard, J. J., & Rossiter, V. Clinical and pathologic correlates of brainstem auditory response abnormalities. *Neurology*, 1977, *27*, 316–325.

Stockard, J. J., Stockard, J. E., & Sharbrough, F. W. Nonpathologic factors influencing brainstem auditory evoked potentials. *American Journal of EEG Technology*, 1978, *18*, 177–209.

Straumanis, J. J., Shagass, C., & Schwartz, M. Visually evoked cerebral response changes associated with chronic brain syndromes and aging. *Journal of Gerontology*, 1965, *20*, 498–506.

Tamura, K., Lüders, H., & Kuroiwa, Y. Further observations of the effects of aging on the wave form of the somato-sensory cortical evoked potential. *Electroencephalography and Clinical Neurophysiology*, 1972, *33*, 325–327.

Tecce, J. J. Contingent negative variation (CNV) and psychological processes in man. *Psychological Bulletin*, 1972, *77*, 73–108.

Tecce, J. J., & Cole, J. O. The distraction-arousal hypothesis, CNV, and schizophrenia. In D. I. Mostofsky (Ed.), *Behavior control and modification of physiological activity*. Englewood Cliffs, N.J.: Prentice Hall, 1976.

Tecce, J. J., & Hamilton, B. T. CNV reduction by sustained cognitive activity (distraction). *Electroencephalography and Clinical Neurophysiology*, 1973, Suppl. 33, 229–237.

Tecce, J. J., Savignano-Bowman, J., & Cole, J. O. Drug effects on contingent negative variation and eyeblinks: The distraction-arousal hypothesis. In M. A. Lipton, A. DiMascio, & K. F. Killam (Eds.), *Psychopharmacology: A generation of progress*. New York: Raven Press, 1978.

Tecce, J. J., Savignano-Bowman, J., & Meinbresse, D. Contingent negative variation and the distraction-arousal hypothesis. *Electroencephalography and Clinical Neurophysiology*, 1976, 41, 277–386.

Tecce, J. J., & Scheff, N. M. Attention reduction and suppressed direct-current potentials in the human brain. *Science*, 1969, *164*, 331–333.

Thompson, L. W., Marsh, G. R., & Zelinski, L. Topographical distribution of cortical potentials as a function of verbal or spatial processing set. *Experimental Aging Research*, in press.

Thompson, L. W., & Nowlin, J. B. Cortical slow potential and cardiovascular correlates of attention during reaction time performance. In L. Jarvik, C. Eisdorfer, & J. Blum (Eds.), *Aging: Psychological and somatic changes*. New York: Springer, 1971.

Thornton, A. R. D. Properties of auditory brainstem responses. *Revue de Laryngology*, 1976, *97*, 591–601.

Timiras, D. S. *Development, Physiology, and Aging*. New York: Macmillan, 1972.

Venables, P. H., & Christie, M. H. (Eds.). *Research in psychophysiology*. London: Wiley, 1975.

Visser, S. L., Stam, F. C., Van Tilburg, W., Op Den Velde, W., Blom, J. L., & De Rijke, W. Visual evoked response in senile and presenile dementia. *Electroencephalography and Clinical Neurophysiology*, 1976, *40*, 385–392.

Walker, A. E., Wolff, J. I., Halstead, W. C., & Case, T. J. Photic driving. *Archives of Neurology and Psychiatry*, 1944, *52*, 117–125.

Walsh, D. A. Age differences in central perceptual processing: A dichoptic backward masking investigation. *Journal of Gerontology*, 1976, *31*, 178–185.

Walter, W. G., Cooper, R., Aldridge, V. J., McCallum, W. C., & Winter, A. L. Contingent negative variation: An electric sign of sensorimotor association and expectancy in the human brain. *Nature*, 1964, *203*, 380–384.

Welford, A. T. Causes of slowing of performance with age. *Interdisciplinary Topics of Gerontology*, 1977, *11*, 43–51.

Welford, A. T., & Birren, J. E. (Eds.). *Behavior aging and the nervous system*. Springfield, Ill.: Charles C Thomas, 1965.

Wilkie, F. L., & Eisdorfer, C. Systemic disease and behavioral correlates. In L. F. Jarvik, C. Eisdorfer, & J. E. Blum (Eds.), *Intellectual functioning in adults: Psychological and biological influences*. New York: Springer, 1973.

Wolfe, J. A., Skinner, P., & Burns, J. Relation between sound intensity and the latency and amplitude of the brainstem auditory evoked response. *Journal of Speech and Hearing Research*, 1978, *21*, 401–407.

Woody, C. D. Characterization of an adaptive filter for the analysis of variable latency neuroelectric signals. *Medical and Biological Engineering*, 1967, *5*, 539–553.

Psychopharmacological Issues

Gail R. Marsh, *Section Editor*

Introduction

This section concerns the identification of physiological mechanisms involved in age-dependent changes in memory and other cognitive functions. In the past decade substantial progress has been made in neurochemistry. This research has provided considerable insight into how certain neurotransmitters and neuropeptides modulate behavior. At the same time, studies show that there are significant changes in neurotransmitter and neuroendocrine function in late life in the healthy old animal (Finch, 1977) and human (Samorajski, 1977). Furthermore, these changes appear more pronounced and may be predisposing factors in persons suffering from various clinical disorders such as Parkinson's disease (McGeer & McGeer, 1976b) and senile dementia of the Alzheimer's type (Bowen, Smith, White, & Davison, 1976; Perry, Perry, Blessed, & Tomlinson, 1977). Implicit in these observations is the assumption that if age-dependent changes in neurotransmitter or neuropeptide function are responsible for the cognitive impairments, then identification of the functional loss could lead to the development of appropriate therapeutic treatment.

An Overview of Peptide and Cholinergic Drug Effects on Memory and Related Psychological Functions

To establish a common ground for the following chapters, a brief review of the current concepts of memory functions in human and animal models is presented. This is followed by a more general discussion of the chapters in this section.

Current Concepts of Memory Function

Several recent works have reviewed how human memory functions are affected by aging (Botwinick & Storandt, 1974; Craik, 1977; Siegler, 1980). Of the theories advanced, those using the information-processing approach have assumed a dominant position. This has led to a reconsideration of how memory functions are measured and conceptualized. Three-stage models are typical, and their essential characteristics are as follows: The first stage holds information for very short periods (e.g., less than .5 sec for the visual store). The second stage holds information that is currently in consciousness, has capacity limitations, and has been called "short-term," "primary," or "working" memory by various theorists. The last stage is the permanent store, which seems of unlimited capacity and has been called "long-term" or "secondary" memory. There is little indication that the first stage of memory is altered by aging processes. There is every indication that the third stage is altered by aging. The evidence for the second stage remains controversial, as indeed do the functions that are assigned to it. It has been argued by Waugh and Norman (1965) that the second stage ("primary" memory in their terminology) shows perfect retention as long as its capacity is not exceeded and the items to be remembered are kept in mind (i.e., rehearsed). If either of these two requirements is not met, it is assumed that the primary memory must reobtain the necessary information from long-term storage ("secondary" memory in their terms). Thus any information obtained from secondary memory would reflect the operating characteristics of that memory store. If aging decreases the capacity of primary memory or causes the older person to be diverted more easily from current memory contents, then an age decrement would be expected.

Watkins (1974) has estimated that primary memory capacity is from 2.6 to 3.4 items. There appears to be little or no age-related decline in this memory store (Craik, 1977). Digit span—the number of digits a person can repeat back to the experimenter without error—has often been used to measure primary memory capacity. However, digit span may be a poor measure, since it typically reveals that from 5 to 7 items can be repeated back without error. With that many items it would appear that the measure depends to some extent on secondary memory. It is likely that this partial reliance on secondary memory is responsible for the slight reduction in performance that has been reported for the elderly on digit span (Botwinick & Storandt, 1974).

Many cognitive functions have been shown to decline with age (Arenberg & Robertson-Tchabo, 1977; Botwinick, 1977; Rabbitt, 1977). The inability of older subjects to perform as well as younger subjects at tasks requiring some sort of mental manipulation at the time the items are either being placed in memory or recalled has blurred the distinction between memory and other cognitive abilities. For example, the elderly are impaired on tasks requiring the sorting of stimuli before reporting them. This task likely confounds measurement of memory with other cognitive processes. Such "memory" scores will be depressed by the extent to which other cognitive processes have declined with age.

It is well accepted that there are age decrements in secondary memory. Secondary memory can be tested in a number of ways. For example, the subject can be instructed to attempt to remember 20 or more items. Another alternative is to give a smaller number of items but to prevent rehearsal of the items by involving the person in a second task for the duration of the retention interval. If the testing situation gives many cues to be used in retrieval of the memory, then the age decline is far less. Thus recognition tests show the elderly performing almost as well as the young (Botwinick & Storandt, 1974; Schonfield & Robertson, 1966). However, all age decrements in secondary memory function should not be ascribed to difficulties in retrieval. Initial storage of the memory trace also

seems to be poorer in the elderly (Drachman & Leavitt, 1972). How this deficit arises is not clear, but it has been characterized as a failure to use "organization" or to "process the material in depth." This leads to a weaker transfer of the material into secondary memory (Craik, 1977; Craik & Lockhart, 1972; Hultsch, 1974).

As for the last major item in memory function, forgetting, there appears to be a slight increase with age. One line of evidence has been provided by the testing of "remote" memories. These memories, which permit assessment of retention for material learned from 10 to as many as 60 years earlier, show that retention is about equal for all age groups exposed to the material (Botwinick & Storandt, 1980), with a slight loss reported for the elderly in some studies (Squire, 1974).

On any single test of retention the elderly may perform poorly. That is, they retrieve fewer items, and their recall of material is more variable. Buschke (1974) has shown that the elderly have greater variability than the young in that on one recall trial some items may be recalled, while on the next trial they will not, only to be recalled again on a later trial. This is likely to be the result of a faulty retrieval mechanism rather than "forgetting," since the material is always there but just not retrieved on every trial. Thus the evidence is weak that there is "decay" of memory traces over time or that such decay is accelerated in the elderly.

Recent evidence (Craik, 1977) indicates that there is not more rapid forgetting in the elderly owing to interference (i.e., conflicts between old memories and newly acquired material). Performance among the elderly is poorer on tasks where retrieval is made more difficult. For example, retrieval is made more difficult when a number of items in a list of words are all from the same category (e.g., tree: oak, pine, birch). The elderly are more affected by such manipulations of category size (Hultsch, 1975). The elderly may show impaired retrieval because a larger number of items are stored under a given retrieval cue (Kausler, 1970).

With the move to the information-processing model, integration of the material from memory and cognitive experiments is possible, but it becomes necessary to redefine some of the concepts. For instance, this model has fostered the reliance on latency of response as the primary measure of memory function, instead of the former reliance on errors or omissions as the principal measure. Several studies have shown that the time required to search a memorized list, or to match a digit to a memorized list, is longer in the elderly (Anders & Fozard, 1973; Anders, Fozard, & Lillyquist, 1972; Waugh, Thomas, & Fozard, 1978). Unfortunately, the move to the information-processing approach makes it more difficult to bridge the gap between human and animal models of memory.

Thus far, I have concentrated on human experimentation. Experimentation on animals has provided a complementary model for memory. However, comparison between animal and human studies cannot always be straightforward. The literature based on animal studies has not developed theoretical models based on verbal mediation of memory or cognitive abilities. At the same time, there is a paucity of data on memory or cognitive function of the human using tests that have no verbal component. Similarly, the procedures used in animal studies have no true analogue to recall, as it is used in the human literature, but only to recognition. Perhaps a more fundamental problem encountered in comparing studies based on animals with those based on humans is the denotative meaning of the terms applied. Occasionally, identical terms (e.g., "recent memory") have a different meaning. Finally, the consolidation model, which has dominated research in animals, has not been used often in human research, except for the use of electroconvulsive shock on patients. Thus, parallel development to bridge this gap in work on humans and animals would be particularly welcome.

For extensive review of the work on memory consolidation, many sources are available (e.g., Carlton & Markiewicz, 1973; Deutsch, 1973). The basic premise is that it takes time for a "permanent" memory trace to form. A corollary is that a memory is more easily disrupted early in its development. "Early" is usually defined in terms of a few hours, not in terms of seconds or days. In the same vein, "short-term" when used in this literature refers to minutes or hours, not milliseconds. By comparison, in human work short-term memory could be translated as "in the focus of attention," rather than simply in terms of passage of time. Thus, comparison of human and animal work has often been flawed because, even in the design stage, the experiments were not developed to test the same concepts.

Deutsch (1971, 1973) showed that the memory trace continued to build strength for several days after training and that the neuronal system involved was cholinergic. The system proved to be quite sensitive to the level of neurotransmitter present, for both an overabundance or a scarcity of acetylcholine (ACh) at the postsynaptic receptor sites was detrimental to memory function. From these observations Deutsch developed a model of the cholinergic synapse in memory function (Deutsch, 1971, 1973; Deutsch & Rogers, 1979). The impact of this model has been and should continue to be a very positive one. It has many heuristic features and should help to draw the work in humans and animals together on a common theoretical ground.

For instance, Drachman (1976, 1977; Drachman & Leavitt, 1974) showed that treatment of young adult humans with the ACh antagonist scopolamine (a receptor blocker) makes their behavior on memory tests similar to that observed with the elderly. This effect was reversible with the ACh agonist physostigmine, but not with a stimulant (amphetamine) that could overcome any possible sedative action of scopolamine. The data from these experiments have been interpreted as indicating that memory formation is apparently accompanied by increased "sensitivity" of the synapses, and not by increased numbers of synapses. However, this point still remains somewhat speculative. The implications of this model for the effects of aging on memory are explored in Chapters 11 and 12 in this volume.

General Discussion

The chapters in this section illustrate the utility of the psychopharmacological approach to the investigation of memory and the changes it undergoes with age. The theoretical model of the cholinergic synapse serving as the principal site of memory (Deutsch, 1971, 1973; Deutsch & Rogers, 1979) has stimulated a fruitful line of research. In this model the "sensitivity" of the synapse is controlled by a large number of factors including availability of the substrate and enzymes to synthesize the neurotransmitter, release and degradation of the neurotransmitter at the synapse, number and affinity of receptors for the transmitter, and availability of the "second messenger" in the neuron that is triggered into action when the receptor is stimulated. Thus there are multiple factors that could affect the function of the synapse and could be affected by aging processes. Reviews of recent work in neurotransmitters and neuromodulators with some references to aging processes are available (Davis & Berger, 1979; Finch, 1977; Iversen, Nicoll, & Vale, 1978; Liebeskind & Dismukes, 1978; McGeer & McGeer, 1976a; Samorajski, 1977).

Despite the large body of work in memory, there is still not a sufficient flow of ideas back and forth from human to animal studies, and vice versa, to keep the terminology evolving along the same lines of meaning. However, the chapters in this section reveal that common mechanisms may underlie the behavioral changes observed in aging animals and humans. Mohs, Davis, and Darley (in Chapter 12) and Sitaram, Weingartner, and Gillin (1978), working with humans, and Bartus (in Chapter 11), working with monkeys, all find that their subjects vary widely in sensitivity to physostigmine. Since underdosage produces no facilitation and overdosage actually produces poor retention, only a narrow range of dose levels is facilitatory for memory, and the dose must be "individualized" (e.g., what is ideal for one subject may be ineffective or disruptive for another). There is also the possibility that the cholinergic system in some older persons has deteriorated (e.g., decreased in number of receptors) to the point that neither short-term nor long-term treatment can overcome the deficit (Drachman, 1977). Also, Alzheimer's patients, who show drastic and progressive losses in memory function, have decreased choline acetyltransferase activity (the rate-limiting enzyme in acetylcholine production) in the caudate, putamen, frontal cortex, and hippocampus (Bowen et al., 1976; White, Hiley, Goodhart, Carrasco, Kent, Williams, & Bowen, 1977). These patients also show a decrease in the number of ACh receptors in hippocampal neurons, though no such changes were noted in other brain areas (Reisine, Yamamura, Bird, Spokes, & Enna, 1978). It should be noted that hippocampal neurons in the normal elderly have been shown to keep growing and increasing their area of contact with other hippocampal neurons. Alzheimer's patients do not show this continued growth (Buell & Coleman, 1979).

It is a hopeful sign that several laboratories (see Chapters 11, 12, and 13, in this section) are searching for an animal model to study aging effects on memory and that a variety of species have been investigated—mice, monkeys, and three strains of rats. In general, the findings reported in these chapters are congruent. Older animals learn and retain less well than young animals in one-trial-learning situations. Multiple-trial learning, to a high criterion, shows either no age differences or only small ones. Extinction is more rapid in the older animal. The finding of impaired learning or registration of the material in the older animal is certainly comparable to the same finding in humans. These chapters also point the way toward some of the work that must be done if we are to establish a link between animal and human studies. Theories of human memory are based largely on normal, young volunteers usually tested on recall of verbal material in a nonthreatening atmosphere, whereas animal models test young animals for recognition of nonverbal stimuli, often in situations where the motivation is painful shock, sickness, or highly alluring appetitive stimuli. Clearly we need more data on how humans perform on nonverbal material and on material that cannot easily be matched to verbal mediators. It would also be helpful to have more data on animals undergoing training with little stress. The factor of stress varies widely between experiments, often with little attention paid to it. For instance, it is difficult to know the exact extent of illness in the flavor-aversion procedure. Similarly, the level of shock varies widely between experiments and laboratories and could contribute disproportionately to differences in stress or other factors. Studies comparing performance across widely varying age groups may be especially susceptible to difficulties in the interpretation of their data resulting from such uncontrolled variables.

The strength of animal studies is in the ability to seek out the biological foundation of the behavioral functions observed. If some of the concepts from the human memory models could be tested in animals, both the human and animal models would benefit. Studies with drugs may allow a better confluence of findings in both humans and animals, since drugs provide a relatively mild and temporary intervention into central nervous system (CNS) functions and are therefore feasible in human as well as animal studies. Currently, some pathological states, such as depression and Alzheimer's disease, have no animal model. Models of such pathologies may be difficult to develop but would be very useful.

Most studies using drugs to investigate age-related differences in CNS mechanisms have not focused on the dramatic age differences that may exist in drug metabolism and excretion. It must be kept in mind that in addition to CNS factors, a number of peripheral changes also occur that can result in altered response to drug treatment. It is generally accepted that changes in the body's physiology with age affect concentration of a drug in the blood as well as delivery to the target tissue. Such changes include decreased intestinal absorption, plasma albumin concentration, lean body weight, total body water, renal function, and activity of the drug-metabolizing enzyme systems (Bender, 1970; Gillette & Hinsen, 1978; Gorrod, 1974; Levy, 1978; Richey & Bender, 1977). Thus the extent to which such factors could contribute to the results of aging studies must always be considered.

Some of the experiments in these chapters lead to the conclusion that both older humans and animals learn less rapidly or less intensely and thus have poorer memory traces later for recall. The neuropeptides tested by Jensen et al. and Cooper et al. (Chapters 13 and 14) may function to strengthen weak memory traces and aid in the formation or retrieval of memories. The methods used for training and for assessing retention may be crucial in testing this possibility. The problem is to equate the initial learning across the age groups. Extensive training before testing retention could result in "ceiling" or "floor" effects when learning and retention are assessed. Perhaps more meaningful comparison can be made between young and old subjects if low levels of training are employed (e.g., one-trial passive-avoidance learning, or learning a maze to a low criterion level). Cooper et al. (Chapter 14) demonstrate the problem of floor effects in their series of studies on flavor aversion. Both young and old animals given several training trials completely avoided the novel-tasting solution during the initial recovery period. However, after only one training session, both young and old animals consumed some of the novel solution. There was an age difference in that the old consumed more of the solution than did the young.

In Chapter 13 Jensen et al. suggest that opiate peptides may be acting at two different brain sites during memory formation. They report differential age effects on these brain sites. Effects of naloxone (a receptor blocker for these peptides) on learning are reported here, but retention tests have not yet been attempted. Also, studies that use opiate receptor stimulants for tests of memory and learning in old animals have not yet appeared. Using test procedures similar to those of Jensen et al., Cooper et al. (Chapter 14) show that the pituitary peptide vasopressin also influences memory function in rats. These findings may be mediated through the same system, in that the drug used by Jensen et al., naloxone, could affect ACh activity (Sitaram & Gillin, 1979) and thereby ACTH and vasopressin secretion, since ACh is known to effect release of these hormones. Similarly, some of the behavioral effects of vasopressin may be mediated through this hormone's facilitating effect on ACTH release (Yates, Russell, Dallman, Hedge, McCann, & Dhariwal, 1971). Clearly, the interaction among these various hormones/neurotransmitters will be a growing concern in the near future. Sleep is thought to affect the consolidation process (Hartmann, 1973). Sitaram and Gillin (1979) have pointed out that the neurotransmitter systems involved in sleep seem to interact with the cholinergic system, thus providing a possible biological model for linking sleep processes to this system.

Jensen et al. also note a sex difference in response to naloxone treatment in their old animals. While there is only a hint of a parallel to these results in the study of human memory and aging (Botwinick & Storandt, 1974, 1980), the sex differences have always been explained in terms of social rather than biological factors. Thus the sex difference in the Fischer rat must be examined in other strains and other contexts to assure its validity and generality. Perhaps this effect is related to a possible sex difference in pain threshold. Vasopressin does not have a differential effect on the CNS. Cooper et al. used both male and female rats in the flavor-aversion studies and obtained comparable results in both sexes. Some peptides have obvious sex-related functions, such as oxytocin for milk release in the female. This peptide is present in males and seems to have effects on cognitive function opposite to those of vasopressin (de Wied, 1974). Neither the mecha-

nism of action nor the possible differential sex responsiveness to this peptide has been studied.

All of the chapters in this section dealing with animal studies agree that the older animals are not handicapped in remembering by having inferior sensory systems. Bartus (Chapter 11) reports that old monkeys were able to see the stimuli as well as young monkeys, and Jensen et al. and Cooper et al. (Chapters 13 and 14) show older rats to perceive shock as well as younger rats. Thus, initial registration of the stimuli is not hampered by decreased sensory input. The arousal level of the old animals was also found not to be the difficulty in retrieving memories, for stimulants made retrieval worse. Bartus points out that reducing arousal via blockade of the dopamine and adrenergic systems does affect performance, but these effects do not grow as the retention interval is increased, as would be expected of a memory effect.

The difficulty of testing retention without involving other factors is demonstrated in the experiments described by Cooper et al. in which extinction rate was used to test retention. Extinction involves inhibiting the performance of an old learned response while at the same time learning to perform a new and different (often opposite) response. It is not a simple "forgetting" of the former response (Deutsch, 1971). When drug treatment given during extinction produces a change in extinction rate, the question becomes whether the effect was on the learning of the inhibitory response or on the retrieval mechanism. The results of Cooper et al. showed that the drug effect was likely on retrieval. Drug treatments were spaced four days apart, and each treatment returned the animal's response to the level seen on the first day of extinction. Subsequent to each of those treatments, the extinction curve seemed to begin anew rather than to return immediately to control levels on the following day. Thus it appears that the neuropeptide in some way selectively strengthened the weaker (or more distant) memory traces.

Chapter 11 also illustrates the difficulty of comparing human and animal experiments. Bartus used a delayed response method, both with and without distractor stimuli, to test immediate recall of which of nine keys had been illuminated. This method has been widely used in animal experiments to assess retention. However, human experiments, based on the human memory model, would likely be interpreted in terms of both memory and attentional functions, rather than strictly in terms of retention. The use of a second task to prevent rehearsal, as is common in human work on memory, could be used to advantage in the animal model to ascertain whether the poorer performance in older animals at longer delay intervals is best interpreted as an attention or a retention deficit.

The work of Bartus and that of Mohs et al. (Chapters 11 and 12) seem quite complementary. The ability of cholinergic blocking agents to produce memory defects in young adult humans and animals reinforces the adequacy of the animal model. Perhaps most promising is the finding that dietary treatment aimed at maintaining the CNS cholinergic system, if started early, may be able to offset aging effects on memory function. Similar results for the catecholine system have also been found (Cooper & Walker, 1979). Testing for similar effects in humans will obviously take a very long time. Further work on the physiological mechanisms involved with dietary treatment should be undertaken in animals to acquire a better understanding of the variables before human tests are started.

In summary, there are wide gaps in both theory and knowledge of the psychobiology of memory, and even more in aging effects on this system. Both human and animal models of memory have been developed, and while they diverge on some aspects, there are many points of convergence. Studies of aging effects on memory show great promise of significant gains in understanding in the coming decade. The application of pharmacological and neurochemical techniques should be one of the most fruitful avenues of approach to this question.

REFERENCES

Anders, T. R., & Fozard, J. L. Effects of age upon retrieval from primary and secondary memory. *Developmental Psychology*, 1973, 9, 411–415.

Anders, T. R., Fozard, J. L., & Lillyquist, T. D. The effects of age upon retrieval from short-term memory. *Developmental Psychology*, 1972, 6, 214–217.

Arenberg, D., & Robertson-Tchabo, E. A. Learning and aging. In J. E. Birren & K. W. Schaie (Eds.), *Handbook of the psychology of aging*. New York: Van Nostrand Reinhold, 1977.

Bender, A. D. The influence of age on the activity of catecholamines and related compounds. *Journal of the American Geriatric Society*, 1970, 18, 220–232.

Botwinick, J. Intellectual abilities. In J. E. Birren & K. W. Schaie (Eds.), *Handbook of the psychology of aging*. New York: Van Nostrand Reinhold, 1977.

Botwinick, J., & Storandt, M. *Memory, related functions and age*. Springfield, Ill.: Charles C Thomas, 1974.

Botwinick, J., & Storandt, M. Recall and recognition of old information in relation to age and sex. *Journal of Gerontology*, 1980, 35, 70–76.

Bowen, D. M., Smith, C. B., White, P., & Davison, A. N. Senile dementia and related abiotrophies: Biochemical studies on histologically evaluated human postmortem species. In R. D. Terry & S. Gershon (Eds.), *Neurobiology of aging*. New York: Raven Press, 1976.

Buell, S. J., & Coleman, P. D. Dendritic growth in the aged human brain and failure of growth in senile dementia. *Science*, 1979, 206, 854–856.

Buschke, H. Two stages of learning by children and adults. *Bulletin of the Psychonomic Society*, 1974, 2, 392–394.

Carlton, P. L., & Markiewicz, B. Studies of the physiological bases of memory. In E. Stellar & J. M. Sprague (Eds.), *Progress in physiological psychology*. New York: Academic Press, 1973.

Cooper, R. L., & Walker, R. F. Potential therapeutic consequences of age-dependent changes in brain physiology. In W. Meier-Ruge (Ed.), *CNS aging and its neuropharmacology: Experimental and clinical aspects*. Basel: S. Karger, 1979.

Craik, F. I. M. Age differences in human memory. In J. E. Birren & K. W. Schaie (Eds.), *Handbook of the psychology of aging*. New York: Van Nostrand Reinhold, 1977.

Craik, F. I. M., & Lockhart, R. S. Levels of processing: A framework for memory research. *Journal of Verbal Learning and Verbal Behavior*, 1972, 11, 671–684.

Davis, K. L., & Berger, P. A. *Brain acetylcholine and neuropsychiatric disease*. New York: Plenum Press, 1979.

Deutsch, J. A. The cholinergic synapse and the site of memory. *Science*, 1971, 174, 788–794.

Deutsch, J. A. (Ed.). *The physiological basis of memory*. New York: Academic Press, 1973.

Deutsch, J. A., & Rogers, J. B. Cholinergic excitability and memory: Animal studies and their clinical implications. In K. L. Davis & P. A. Berger (Eds.), *Brain acetylcholine and neuropsychiatric disease*. New York: Plenum Press, 1979.

de Wied, D. Pituitary-adrenal system hormones and behavior. In F. O. Schmitt & F. G. Worden (Eds.), *The neurosciences; Third study program*. Cambridge, Mass.: MIT Press, 1974.

Drachman, D. A. Memory and cholinergic function. In W. S. Fields (Ed.), *Neurotransmitter function*. New York: Statton International Medical Book, 1976.

Drachman, D. A. Memory and cognitive function in man: Does the cholinergic system have a specific role? *Neurology*, 1977, 27, 783–790.

Drachman, D. A., & Leavitt, J. Memory impairment in the aged: Storage versus retrieval deficit. *Journal of Experimental Psychology*, 1972, 93, 302–308.

Drachman, D. A., & Leavitt, J. Human memory and the cholinergic system. *Archives of Neurology*, 1974, 30, 113–121.

Finch, C. E. Neuroendocrine and autonomic aspects of aging. In C. E. Finch & L. Hayflick (Eds.), *Handbook of the biology of aging*. New York: Van Nostrand Reinhold, 1977.

Gillette, J. R., & Hinsen, J. A. Biotransformation of drugs. In J. Roberts, R. C. Adelman, & V. J. Cristofalo (Eds.), *Pharmacological intervention of the aging process*. New York: Plenum Press, 1978.

Gorrod, J. W. Absorption, metabolism and excretion of drugs in geriatric subjects. *Gerontologia Clinica*, 1974, 16, 30–42.

Hartmann, E. L. *The functions of sleep*. New Haven: Yale University Press, 1973.

Hultsch, D. F. Learning to learn in adulthood. *Journal of Gerontology*, 1974, *29*, 302–308.

Hultsch, D. F. Adult age differences in retrieval: Trace-dependent and cue-dependent forgetting. *Developmental Psychology*, 1975, *11*, 197–201.

Iversen, L. L., Nicoll, R. A., & Vale, W. W. (Eds.). Neurobiology of peptides. *Neurosciences Research Program Bulletin*, 1978, *16*, 211–370.

Kausler, D. H. Retention—forgetting as a nomological network for developmental research. In L. R. Goulet & P. B. Baltes (Eds.), *Life-span developmental psychology*. New York: Academic Press, 1970.

Levy, G. Pharmacokinetic assessment of the effect of age on the disposition and pharmacologic activity of drugs. In J. Roberts, R. C. Adelman, and V. J. Cristofalo (Eds.), *Pharmacological intervention of the aging process*. New York: Plenum Press, 1978.

Liebeskind, J. C., & Dismukes, R. K. (Eds.), Peptides and behavior: A critical analysis of research strategies. *Neurosciences Research Program Bulletin*, 1978, *16*, 490–635.

McGeer, E., & McGeer, P. L. Neurotransmitter metabolism in the aging brain. In R. D. Terry & S. Gershon (Eds.), *Neurobiology of aging*. New York: Raven Press, 1976. (a)

McGeer, P. L., & McGeer, E. G. Enzymes associated with the metabolism of catecholamines, acetylcholine and GABA in human controls and patients with Parkinson's disease and Huntington's chorea. *Journal of Neurochemistry*, 1976, *26*, 65–76. (b)

Perry, E. K., Perry, R. H., Blessed, G., & Tomlinson, B. E. Necropsy evidence of central cholinergic deficits in senile dementia. *Journal of Neurological Science*, 1977, *34*, 247–265.

Rabbitt, P. Changes in problem solving ability in old age. In J. E. Birren & K. W. Schaie (Eds.), *Handbook of the psychology of aging*. New York: Van Nostrand Reinhold, 1977.

Reisine, T. D., Yamamura, H. I., Bird, E. D., Spokes, E., & Enna, S. J. Pre- and post-synaptic neurochemical altera-tions in Alzheimer's disease. *Brain Research*, 1978, *159*, 477–481.

Richey, D. P., & Bender, A. D. Pharmacologic consequences of aging. *Annual Review of Pharmacology and Toxicology*. 1977, *17*, 49–65.

Samorajski, T. Central neurotransmitter substance and aging: A review. *Journal of the American Geriatrics Society*, 1977, *25*, 337–348.

Schonfield, D., & Robertson, E. A. Memory storage and aging. *Canadian Journal of Psychology*, 1966, *20*, 228–236.

Siegler, I. C. The psychology of adult development and aging. In E. W. Busse & D. G. Blazer (Eds.), *Handbook of geriatric psychiatry*. New York: Van Nostrand Reinhold, 1980.

Sitaram, N., & Gillin, J. C. Acetylcholine: Possible involvement in sleep and analgesia. In K. L. Davis & P. A. Berger (Eds.), *Brain acetylcholine and neuropsychiatric disease*. New York: Plenum Press, 1979.

Sitaram, N., Weingartner, H., & Gillin, J. C. Human serial learning: Enhancement with arecoline and impairment with scopolamine correlated with performance on placebo. *Science*, 1978, *201*, 274–276.

Squire, L. R. Remote memory as affected by aging. *Neuropsychologia*, 1974, *12*, 429–435.

Watkins, M. J. Concept and measurement of primary memory. *Psychological Bulletin*, 1974, *81*, 645–711.

Waugh, N. C., & Norman, D. A. Primary memory. *Psychological Review*, 1965, *72*, 89–104.

Waugh, N. C., Thomas, J. C., & Fozard, J. L. Retrieval time from different memory stores. *Journal of Gerontology*, 1978, *33*, 718–724.

White, P., Hiley, C. R., Goodhardt, M. J., Carrasco, L. H., Kent, J, P., Williams, I. E., & Bowen, D. M. Neocortical cholinergic neurons in elderly people. *Lancet*, 1977, *1*, 668–671.

Yates, F. E., Russell, S. M., Dallman, M. F., Hedge, G. A., McCann, S. M., & Dhariwal, A. P. S. Potentiation by vasopressin of corticotropin release induced by corticotropin-releasing factor. *Endocrinology*, 1971, *88*, 3–15.

Raymond T. Bartus

Cholinergic Drug Effects on Memory and Cognition in Animals

An important role of central cholinergic dysfunction in age-related cognitive impairment is corroborated by three independent lines of evidence: (1) psychopharmacological data demonstrating that disruption of normal cholinergic mechanisms in young monkeys and humans produces a memory impairment uniquely and qualitatively similar to that occurring naturally in aged animals of the same species; (2) neurochemical tests of animal and human brain demonstrating that age-related decreases in presynaptic and postsynaptic cholinergic function are generally more severe than those occurring in other neurotransmitter systems; and (3) direct neurophysiological recordings of cholinoceptive neurons in aged, memory-impaired rats, demonstrating a marked decrease in responsiveness to acetylcholine but not to glutamate. These data collectively suggest that (a) significant changes occur in the central nervous system with age which disturb normal cholinergic function, (b) these cholinergic mechanisms normally play an important role in mediating some aspects of memory impaired by age, and (c) the functional disruption observed in cholinergic mechanisms of aged subjects is partially responsible for the loss of memory observed with advanced age. While several studies attempting to improve memory in aged animals and humans through pharmacological manipulation of the cholinergic system have reported little success, there is evidence that some form of effective cholinergic manipulation may eventually be developed. This chapter suggests that future studies be directed toward the identification of specific age-related cholinergic dysfunctions and the interaction of these changes with those occurring in other neurotransmitter systems.

One of the most commonly reported clinical symptoms of aging is a gradual deterioration in memory func-

tions (Botwinick, 1975; Drachman & Hughes, 1971). One popular approach to alleviating these memory impairments involves using drugs to try to correct undefined neurochemical or metabolic deficiencies in the aged brain. A serious problem with this approach has been that until recently, little etiological data existed.

Within the last decade, however, increasing information has accumulated that central cholinergic neurotransmitter mechanisms may be particularly impaired with age and may be partly responsible for the age-related memory deficits. In fact, these data have stimulated an increasing number of clinical trials aimed at improving geriatric cognition through manipulation of the cholinergic system (see, e.g., Chapter 12 in this volume). However, despite the apparent logic of this approach, relatively little therapeutic success has been achieved thus far. For this reason, it seems necessary to review the rationale on which this approach is based and to examine the preclinical empirical findings and interpretations. From this overview, it may be possible to identify probable reasons for the disappointing clinical results and possible directions for further research aimed at ultimately improving the therapeutic effects.

The notion that central cholinergic mechanisms play a critical role in memory impairments of the aged is derived from several scientific disciplines, including animal and human psychopharmacology, biochemistry, and electrophysiology. However, for purposes of illustration and example, I will initially focus on my own and my co-workers' psychopharmacological work with young and aged monkeys and discuss related work from other disciplines when appropriate. This work with nonhuman primates provides certain advantages for this overview of the cholinergic rationale, because the entire series of behavioral and pharmacological studies was performed in the same test apparatus and under the same general procedures. Thus comparisons across studies will presumably be more meaningful and less dependent on unsupported assumptions. To simplify this summary, a brief description of the methods used for these primate studies is presented first.

Methods for Primate Behavioral and Psychopharmacological Studies

Two groups of Rhesus monkeys (*M. mulatta*) were used. One group was estimated to be between 5 and 6 years old at the time of testing, while the other group was estimated to be at least from 19 to 23 years old.

All testing for this series of studies was conducted in the Automated General Experimental Device (AGED) illustrated in Figure 11-1. Because the AGED and its application to geriatric research have been described in detail previously (Bartus, Fleming, & Johnson, 1978; Bartus & Johnson, 1976), only a brief description is provided here. The AGED consists basically of a 3 × 3 matrix of stimulus-response (S-R) panels on which color or pattern stimuli can be projected. Each S-R panel is hinge mounted directly in front of a reinforcement well so that when a panel is pushed the response is automatically recorded and a reinforcement well is simultaneously exposed. A stimulus observation window separates the monkey from the S-R matrix. It is equipped with a photocell and infrared light source to detect when the monkey's head is oriented toward the stimuli; this allows the procedure to be paced by the subject, and increases the likelihood that the monkey will begin to process the stimuli at the start of each trial. Because it has been demonstrated that experimenter-paced tasks produce spuriously low estimates of performance by aged subjects (Arenberg, 1965; Botwinick, 1973; Canestrari, 1963), this feature of the apparatus helps ensure that the estimation of age-related deficits is conservative. A one-way viewing screen can be inserted automatically between the S-R matrix and the monkey. When this screen is backlit, it allows the monkey to view but not respond to the S-R panels; when it is not backlit, it is opaque and visually isolates the S-R matrix from the monkey.

Basically, the same general test requirements were used for all studies. However, by subtly varying the procedure, significantly different behavioral paradigms

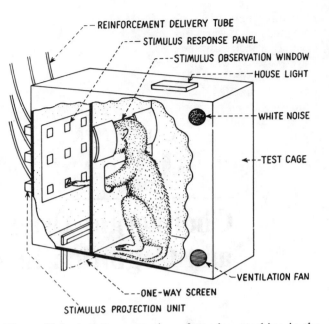

Figure 11-1. Artist's conception of monkey working in the Automated General Experimental Device (AGED) used in the primate studies reviewed here. The important features of the apparatus are labeled, including a stimulus observation window (through which the monkeys look to initiate each trial), a 3 × 3 matrix of stimulus-response panels (to which the monkey must respond to obtain a food reinforcement), and a one-way viewing screen (which serves to visually and/or physically isolate the monkey from the stimulus-response matrix, depending on its position and the amount of backlighting).

could be used that presumably measured different types of behavioral functions. For all procedures, each trial was subject paced and began as soon as the monkey placed its face into the observation window, which caused one or more stimuli to be flashed onto one of the nine S-R panels. For studies involving tests of memory, the monkey was allowed to respond only after the stimulus was extinguished. For studies not concerned with memory, the stimuli persisted after the one-way screen was lowered. Once the opportunity occurred, the monkey responded by pushing one of the nine S-R panels. If a correct response was made, a reinforcement pellet was delivered to the exposed reinforcement well. If the response was incorrect, a buzzer sounded for 500 msec and the screen was quickly raised to obstruct further responding.

Behavioral Profile of Aged Monkeys

As an important prerequisite to using the aged monkey as a model for tests of geriatric psychopharmacology, we conducted a series of studies designed to determine which behaviors are most severely affected by the aging process (Bartus, 1979a). This research was intended to provide some insight into the similarities and differences in age-related behavioral changes between monkeys, humans, and rodents, as well as to allow us to select an appropriate behavioral task for use in future psychopharmacological studies.

On the basis of these studies, it became clear that aged monkeys do indeed suffer quite dramatic behavioral deficits, but just as important, other functions appear to remain relatively unimpaired. Most impressive in this respect was the deficit in memory for recent stimulus events. This deficit was best exemplified using an automated delayed-response task. It was found that aged monkeys suffer a severe deficit in their ability to remember accurately the location of the stimulus at retention intervals as short as 15 sec (Bartus et al., 1978). Further, this impairment was shown to be rather specific to memory mechanisms, for the aged monkeys performed quite accurately under control conditions in which little or no memory was required (see Figure 11-2). Finally, altering the motivational level of the young monkeys by feeding them immediately before testing did not produce results that mimicked the aged monkeys; this demonstrates that age-related differences in motivation do not provide a very likely explanation of these results.

Subsequent experiments evaluated the extent to which probable dysfunctions in sensory processing might be responsible for the age-related memory impairment (Bartus et al., 1978). This test was performed by manipulating either the number of times the stimulus was flashed (from 1 to 8) or the duration of a single stimulus flash (from 100 to 500 msec) before the retention interval was initiated. The rationale of these tests was that if the aged monkeys performed more poorly on the memory task because of age-specific difficulties in perceiving the stimulus, then their performance should be more readily impaired by reductions in stimulus exposure and somewhat improved by increasing stimulus exposure. However, the results of these studies demonstrated that increasing the amount of stimulus exposure (either by repetition or by longer duration) did not differentially facilitate performance in the older monkeys. Similarly, although accuracy for both groups generally suffered when the stimulus availability was reduced, no measurable age-related differences were found. This same result was observed at all retention intervals.

These data, therefore, imply that the age-related deficiencies in sensory processing are neither a necessary nor a sufficient condition to account for the rather severe and specific memory impairments suffered by

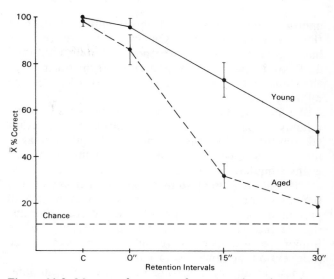

Figure 11-2. Mean performance of young and aged monkeys on different retention conditions of a delayed-response task. In this particular comparison, all monkeys were tested on the same retention intervals after 3 months of experience on the delayed-response procedure. In the continuous-information condition, the stimuli remained on during the opportunity to respond; in the other three conditions, the monkeys had to respond in the absence of a previously presented stimulus. Note the progressively greater deficits in the aged monkeys as the time between viewing the stimulus and the opportunity to respond increases. Chance performance is 11.1% (i.e., 1/9) in this procedure. Vertical bars represent standard errors of the mean (SEM). (Adapted from Bartus et al., 1978.)

the aged monkeys. In sum, the inability of the aged monkeys to perform accurately on the longer retention intervals appears to reflect a genuine dysfunction in mnemonic mechanisms involved with the storage or retrieval of information. Because of other controls equating past experience and current living conditions between age groups, these nonhuman primate data suggest that a fundamental biological dysfunction is at least partly responsible for the impairment in the aged animals. In addition, the data demonstrate that aged monkeys suffer impairments in memory that seem analogous to those reported for elderly humans. This finding supports the idea that aged monkeys might serve as a useful empirical model for those neurobehavioral dysfunctions.

To extend the evaluation, the two age groups were also compared for the degree to which irrelevant stimulus events presented during the retention interval differentially impaired memory (Bartus & Dean, 1979). This experiment used a minor variation of the same delayed-response procedure described in the earlier experiments. That is, on some of the trials an irrelevant red light was randomly flashed on one panel and then another every 500 msec during the entire duration of the retention interval. On the other trials, the backlights and stimulus-response panels remained dark, as in the prior experiments. As in other tests, the stimulus that was to be remembered was green on all trials.

We found that although the young monkeys were not reliably impaired by the presentation of irrelevant stimulation during the retention interval, the aged monkeys suffered a significant impairment when irrelevant stimulation was presented. In contrast to these results, a subsequent (unpublished) experiment from our laboratory revealed that similar irrelevent stimuli presented simultaneously with the correct stimulus (before the initiation of the retention period) did not impair performance as reliably in the same aged monkeys on the same memory task.

These results demonstrate that, like aged humans, aged monkeys are less able than young ones to suppress irrelevant stimuli from interfering with retention or retrieval of recently stored information (Broadbent & Heron, 1962; Bruning, Holzbauer, & Kimberlin, 1975; Caird, 1966; Taub, 1966, 1968). Thus these results support the notion that one factor contributing to the memory deficiencies of the elderly may involve irrelevant stimuli disrupting on-going mnemonic or decision-making processes.

As a further evaluation of the two age groups of monkeys, their ability to form new associations, to remember these associations over a period of weeks, and to modify old associations was compared (Bartus, Dean, & Fleming, 1979). The behavioral procedure was the same, except that two stimuli (one correct and the other incorrect) were presented during each trial, and both stimuli remained on after the screen was lowered. Thus, in order to obtain consistent reinforcement, the monkeys had to learn which of the two stimuli was correct. Because the stimuli remained on when the opportunity to respond occurred, the requirement of memory (of the type operationally defined and measured in the earlier studies) was eliminated. A series of such problems was given to each monkey of each age group. Although certain aged monkeys seemed to have greater difficulty on certain discrimination problems, no consistent or statistically reliable age-related deficits were observed, even on the most difficult problems. Thus, in the present test situation, which used a subject-paced procedure and other features designed to optimize stimulus control and efficient sensory processing, the notion that learning ability (i.e., the ability to form new associations) becomes seriously impaired with advanced age was not supported. Further, no age-related differences were observed in the ability to remember these discrimination problems over a period of from two to three weeks.

However, when the aged monkeys were trained on the reversal of previously learned discrimination problems (i.e., previously correct stimulus was now incorrect), highly reliable and consistent impairments were observed in the aged groups. Since no acquisition deficits were observed on any of the original color- or pattern-discrimination problems at any level of problem difficulty, the impairment observed during reversal learning suggests that aged monkeys suffer a greater deficit in modifying previously learned habits than in forming new ones. Once more, the data are consistent with the observations from other species of aged mammals, including humans, in demonstrating increased perseveration or response rigidity with old age (Botwinick, 1973; Elias & Elias, 1976).

In summary, the series of behavioral studies performed with these monkeys demonstrated that although not all behavioral functions are reliably impaired with age, highly reliable impairments in memory for recent stimulus events do occur. Significant deficits were also observed on tasks requiring the inhibition of attention to irrelevant sensory stimulation and the modification of previously established associations. As such, these data are consistent with much of the human behavioral data. Because the memory impairments were the most severe and consistent behavioral deficit observed in the aged monkeys—and are also most conceptually similar to the major clinical complaint of the elderly—the remaining pharmacological studies used this task to evaluate possible neuropharmacological mechanisms involved in the memory impairments that occur in old age.

Pharmacological Evidence for an Important Cholinergic Role

One of the most consistent and robust pharmacological phenomena observed on this memory task is that young monkeys injected with the cholinergic receptor-blocker scopolamine (from .01 to .03 mg/kg) exhibited a deficit that appeared strikingly similar to that occurring naturally in the aged monkeys (Bartus & Johnson, 1976). That is, no impairment occurred on the control condition, which required no memory for recent events, and increasingly greater impairments were observed as the duration of the retention interval was increased. Furthermore, this deficit in memory was clearly dose-related, with higher doses of scopolamine producing greater impairments, especially at the longest retention interval (see Figure 11-3). Because similar deficits are not observed with the quaternary form of scopolamine (an electrically charged molecule that does not affect the central nervous system because it passes the blood-brain barrier in only

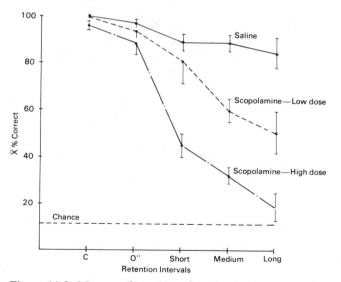

Figure 11-3. Mean performance of young monkeys on a delayed-response task under two doses of the anticholinergic scopolamine (low dose = from .01 to .015 mg/kg; high dose = from .20 to .30 mg/kg) and under a saline control condition. Note the progressive, dose-related impairment that occurs as the retention interval increases; this mimics the naturally occurring deficit found in aged monkeys. Even though accuracy under these doses was quite poor on the longest retention interval, apparent nonmnemonic effects were minimal and all monkeys easily completed the test session. Vertical bars represent SEM. (Adapted from Bartus & Johnson, 1976.)

minute quantities), it seems likely that the deficit is due to some disruption of central nervous system (CNS) functioning. These scopolamine—induced memory impairments have been independently corroborated in humans (Drachman & Leavitt, 1974) and provide further evidence that the deficits in young adults appear to be qualitatively similar to those occurring naturally in the elderly.

Subsequent studies in our primate laboratory demonstrated that the amnesia produced by scopolamine can be partially, but reliably, reduced by the anticholinesterase physostigmine (Bartus, 1978a). Similar beneficial effects were not observed with the central-nervous stimulant methylphenidate. In fact, methylphenidate potentiated the behavioral impairment of scopolamine at doses that normally produce no measurable effects (Figure 11-4). Earlier pilot work showed that higher doses of methylphenidate produced even greater impairments when given concurrently with scopolamine. Thus it is very unlikely than any dose of methylphenidate could be expected to reverse the scopolamine-induced amnesia. Because the primary effects of methylphenidate are on the central nervous system—exerting relatively weak peripheral

autonomic effects (Crook, Ferris, Sathananthan, Raskin, & Gershon, 1977)—and the scopolamine-induced amnesia is central in nature, it is unlikely that other stimulants even less specific to the central nervous system would be any more effective in reversing the scopolamine-induced memory deficit.

Once more, the conclusions derived from these data have been independently corroborated by recent human studies; these studies demonstrate not only that physostigmine can partially reverse the scopolamine-induced deficit but that the CNS stimulant amphetamine exacerbates the deficit (Drachman, 1977). Thus it is unlikely that the retention deficit induced by scopolamine in either humans or nonhuman primates can be related to its more general effects on arousal and attention or to similar sedative-like effects. These data reinforce the likelihood that the amnesia induced by scopolamine is due to a specific disruption of memory-related cholinergic mechanisms. As such, they suggest an important functional relation between normal aging and cholinergic malfunctioning.

To what extent may other classical neurotransmitters play an equally important role in age-related memory impairments? Recent biochemical evidence confirms that significant changes in other neurotransmitter systems, particularly dopaminergic and nor-

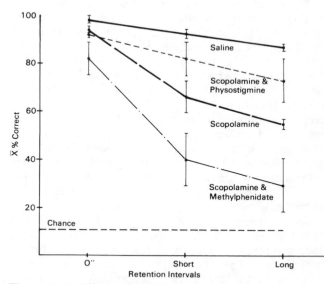

Figure 11-4. Effects of combinations of scopolamine (from .105 to .02 mg/kg), physostigmine (from .02 to .03 mg/kg) and methylphenidate (.0125 mg/kg) on performance of delayed-response task. Concurrent administration of physostigmine partially but reliably reversed the scopolamine-induced deficit, while concurrent administration of methylphenidate potentiated the deficit, at a dose of methylphenidate that produced no measurable effects when given alone (not shown). Vertical bars represent SEM. (Adapted from Bartus, 1978a.)

adrenergic, occur with old age. For example, substantial age-related decreases in the dopaminergic enzyme DOPA decarboxylase, as well as in the primary metabolite of dopamine, homovanillic acid (HVA), have been reported (Bowen, White, Flack, Smith, & Davison, 1974; Gottfries, Gottfries, & Roos, 1969; Gottfries, Rosengren, & Rosengren, 1965; McGreer & McGeer, 1976). In fact, the levels of HVA have been shown to correlate with the degree of dementia better than with the chronological age of the subject (Gottfries et al., 1969). Significantly fewer beta-adrenergic receptors have also been observed in the brains of aged animals (Maggi, Schmidt, Ghetti, & Enna, 1979). These data certainly raise the possibility that dysfunctions in either or both of these neurotransmitter systems may play important roles in the etiology of age-related memory impairments. However, one prerequisite for a dopaminergic or noradrenergic involvement, which had not been adequately tested, is whether disruption of these systems does, in fact, result in impairments qualitatively similar to those observed in aged subjects. The next study was therefore directed toward this question. Young, healthy monkeys were tested under varying conditions of dopamine or noradrenergic blockade with the same apparatus and procedure described for the other experiments.

The effects of dopamine blockade were evaluated by testing the monkeys' ability to perform the memory task under a wide range of doses (.006 mg/kg to .05 mg/kg) of the dopaminergic receptor-blocker haloperidol (Bartus, 1978b). The results demonstrated a general and progressive deterioration in performance as the dose of haloperidol was raised. Most conspicuously absent, however, was a selectively greater effect of haloperidol as the retention duration was increased. In other words, in contrast to the effects of cholinergic blockade, little or no evidence was found for a selective effect of dopaminergic blockade as the information was held for longer durations (see Figure 11-5). In another study from our laboratory (unpublished), very similar results were obtained with beta-adrenergic blockade. That is, propranolol also failed to mimic the highly specific impairments on the longer retention intervals that are observed naturally with aging and pharmacologically with scopolamine.

Thus, these data do not support the notion that dopamine or noradrenalin play a direct or critical role in the type of memory most severely impaired with age. Certainly the effects of dopamine and noradrenalin blockade are not as specific as those previously obtained via scopolamine-induced cholinergic-receptor blockade. At the same time, the data show that subtle changes in catecholaminergic mechanisms that may have been induced by scopolamine are not sufficient to produce the memory impairments observed; the data also offer additional support for a relatively critical role for cholinergic mechanisms in mediating memory.

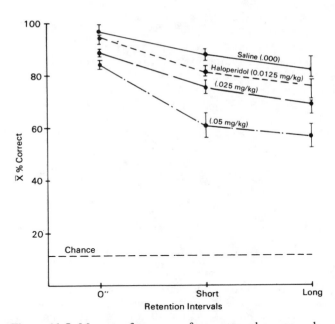

Figure 11-5. Mean performance of young monkeys on a delayed-response task under several different doses of the anti-dopaminergic haloperidol. Note that even at the highest dose (.05 mg/kg), performance did not drop to chance levels, even though the general disruptive effects of the drug were so great that no monkey completed the test session and all monkeys exhibited some impairment on the 0-sec control condition. Similar effects were obtained with the beta-adrenergic blocker propranolol (not shown). Vertical bars represent SEM. (Adapted from Bartus, 1978b.)

The data reported here also imply that the significant changes that occur in the dopaminergic and noradrenergic systems with age may be unrelated to the profound memory changes that have been observed with older humans and in the laboratory with aged, nonhuman primates. It seems logical that if a disruption in these neurotransmitter systems plays an important role in the etiology of the memory deficit seen with advanced age, selectively blocking their activity should produce qualitatively similar deficits in young subjects. The fact that such selective deficits were not produced under any of several doses of haloperidol or propranolol suggests that a critical role for dopamine or norepinephrine in the etiology of this behavioral dysfunction is unlikely. The additional fact that deficits that were qualitatively similar to those observed in aged monkeys have been consistently observed in young, scopolamine-injected monkeys renders a necessary catecholaminergic role that much more untenable.

A question that emerges, therefore, is what role, if

any, might the significant changes observed in the dopamine and noradrenalin systems play in aged behavior. The high correlation between extrapyramidal Parkinsonian symptoms and loss of cognitive function (Kristensen, Olsen, & Theilgaard, 1977), as well as that between depression and age (Kahn, Zarit, Hilbert, & Niederehe, 1975), attests to the likelihood that these systems are involved in important, age-related changes in brain function. In addition, it may be that these systems are involved in certain cognitive functions that are related to, but not directly involved with, memory impairment. This possibility would account for the correlation reported between decreases in HVA and severity of dementia.

In summary, although the specific relation between age-related changes in catecholaminergic function and possible behavioral impairments awaits further study, an important role of cholinergic dysfunctions and age-related memory deficits is already beginning to emerge. The nonhuman primate studies reviewed here demonstrate that of all the behaviors evaluated with the aged monkeys in this general test procedure, the most severe and consistent deficits occurred on tasks requiring memory for relatively recent events. At the same time, of all the classes of drugs tested with the memory paradigm, anticholinergics produced deficits most closely mimicking natural, age-related memory impairments. Thus, when considered with the corroborating human results, these data collectively suggest that disruption of normal cholinergic mechanisms produces a relatively specific inability to perform accurately on tasks requiring memory. They also offer circumstantial evidence that a dysfunction in cholinergic mechanisms may be involved in age-related memory impairments.

Biochemical and Neurophysiological Evidence for Cholinergic Changes

In addition to these pharmacological results in monkeys and humans, data from other disciplines and species also suggest that specific impairments in cholinergic mechanisms may play a particularly important role in the age-related memory impairments. For example, recent biochemical findings have revealed changes in central cholinergic activity as a function of age. Significant decreases in the activity of the synthesizing enzyme choline acetyltransferase (CAT, which is presumed to serve as a marker for presynaptic cholinergic activity) have been reported in normal aged brain (McGeer & McGeer, 1976; Perry, Perry, Gibson, Blessed, & Tomlinson, 1977). Even greater decreases have been observed in the brains of Alzheimer's patients (where memory impairments are

severe) (Perry, Tomlinson, Blessed, Bergmann, Gibson, & Perry, 1978; White, Goodhart, Kent, Hiley, Carrasco, Williams, & Bowen, 1977). The changes in CAT in Alzheimer's patients' brains have been shown to be positively correlated with the two major neurodegenerative symptoms of the disease, neurofibrillary tangles (Davies & Maloney, 1976) and senile plaques, as well as with the degree of cognitive impairment (Perry et al., 1978). Further, these changes contrast with the lack of measurable changes in the gamma amino butyric acid (GABA) synthesizing enzyme, glutamic acid decarboxylase, assayed from the same brains (Bowen, Smith, White, & Davison, 1976; Perry et al., 1978; Spillane, White, Goodhardt, Flack, Bowen, & Davison, 1977).

Changes in cholinergic receptors have also been evaluated in normal aging and in Alzheimer's patients, but these results remain somewhat confusing. For example, several authors compared Alzheimer's patients with normal age-matched controls and found no difference in number of receptors (Davies & Verth, 1978; Perry, Perry, Blessed, & Tomlinson, 1977). However, because brains from younger control subjects were not assayed, little can be said about the effects of age per se on the number of cholinergic receptors. White et al. (1977) reported that the number of cholinergic receptors decreases significantly with age in the nondemented elderly but that these changes are no greater in Alzheimer's patients. More recently, however, it has been reported that reliable decreases in the number of cholinergic receptors do in fact occur in Alzheimer's patients but that these changes are restricted primarily to the hippocampus (Reisine, Yamamura, Bird, Spokes, & Enna, 1978). Clearly, more work is needed to clarify these apparent differences and to develop a common consensus regarding the age-induced changes that do occur.

A more general question that remains to be answered is to what degree the changes observed in Alzheimer's patients are qualitatively different from those found in the normal elderly. Because most human biochemical data are derived from Alzheimer's patients, with little use of young (nonaged) controls, questions of this nature cannot be answered adequately from the existing literature. The animal literature, by its very nature, cannot easily settle issues pertaining to differences between normal aging and Alzheimer's disease because there is no animal model for Alzheimer's disease. It is notable that some neurochemical laboratories have reported significant decreases in both CAT (Vijayan, 1977) and number of cholinergic receptor sites (James & Kanungo, 1976; Lippa et al., 1980; Strong et al., 1980) in the same regions in which changes in human brain have been observed. One possibility that seems to be emerging is that with normal aging there occurs a loss in postsynaptic cholinergic-receptor sites in specific brain regions, in addition to a small decrease in CAT activity. In some patients with Alzheimer's disease, changes in cholinergic mechanisms continue to occur and lead to a substantial decrease in CAT activity. Possibly, the large changes in cholinergic function in Alzheimer's patients are manifested as the large cognitive deficits observed with this disease state compared with normal aging. However, these initial suggestions need to be confirmed by additional research with larger subject populations that involve a greater number of demented and nondemented age groups. Additional cholinergic and noncholinergic neurochemical processes—other than those reflected by CAT activity and muscarinic receptor binding—need to be scrutinized simultaneously to determine definitively changes between different phases of neurotransmission in the aged animal and human brain. For example, with regard to the cholinergic system, choline uptake is believed to be an important rate-limiting step in the acetylcholine synthesis (Cohen & Wurtman, 1975; Haubrich, Wang, Clody, & Wedeking, 1975) and yet

has not been assessed systematically in Alzheimer's patients or in the brains of normal aged animals or humans. And equally important postsynaptic processes involving possible changes in receptor turnover, membrane fluidity, and cyclic nucleotide-coupling mechanisms also need to be evaluated between young and aged adults, as well as with Alzheimer's patients in several neurotransmitter systems.

Clearly, the specific nature of the age-related neurochemical changes is currently obscure, and many neurochemical mechanisms have yet to be investigated. Yet it is apparent that significant decreases in cholinergic function do occur in the elderly, and these changes seem to be even greater in patients suffering from Alzheimer's disease, where age-related memory impairments are even more severe. However, neither these biochemical studies, which are merely correlative, nor the pharmacological studies summarized earlier, which offer circumstantial evidence only, provide direct evidence for a cholinergic basis for any functional impairment that might be found in the brains of old animals. For this reason, a recent interdisciplinary study (performed in collaboration with A.

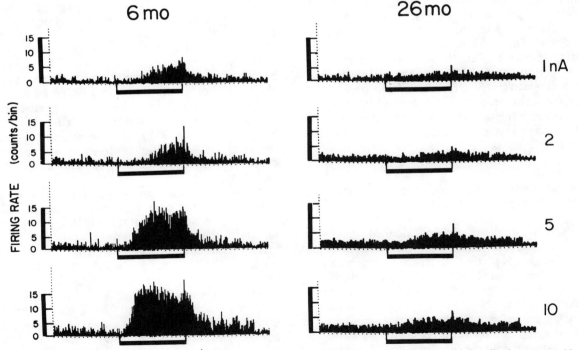

Figure 11-6. Histograms of unit activity from representative hippocampal pyramidal cells in young (6 months) and aged (26 months) rats. The horizontal bar under each histogram depicts the time during which acetylcholine was microiontophoretically applied. Note the progressively greater firing rate as current level was increased (from 1 to 10 nanoamperes) and the markedly dampened effect in the 26-month-old rat. (From "Brain Cholinergic Function and Memory in Aged Rats" by A. S. Lippa, R. W. Pelham, B. Beer, D. J. Critchett, R. L. Dean, and R. T. Bartus, *Neurobiology of Aging*, 1980, *1*(1), 10–16. Copyright 1980 by ANKHO International, Inc. Reprinted by permission.)

Lippa and R. Pelham) addressed the question of whether changes in the function of cholinergic neurons occur in memory-impaired aged animals (Lippa et al., in press). Because a number of practical problems occur when young and old nonhuman primates are used for study, young (5–6 months) and aged (24–26 months) Fischer 344 rats were used instead. We had previously shown that, like aged monkeys, aged Fischer 344 rats suffer specific behavioral impairments that involve severe deficits in retention of recent events and increased perseveration (or behavioral rigidity); this finding fulfilled an important prerequisite for this study.

Each rat was acutely implanted with 5-barreled micropipettes in the dorsal hippocampus. The hippocampus was chosen for this study because it is reported to suffer particularly severe neurodegeneration with aging and dementia (Scheibel & Scheibel, 1975), and its cholinergic system has been identified as exhibiting relatively large age-related neurochemical alterations (Reisine et al., 1978). It receives a major cholinergic input from cells originating in the medical septum (Blas, 1979). Microniontophoretic administration of acetylcholine stimulates the firing of hippocampal pyramidal cells, and this effect is antagonized by muscarinic antagonists (Bird & Aghajanian, 1976). Furthermore, damage to hippocampus has been reported to produce memory disturbances in several species, including humans (Drachman & Hughes, 1971).

Acetylcholine and glutamate were ejected through the side barrels of the pipette with several current levels (1, 2, 5, and 10 nanoamperes) in an attempt to measure dose-response functions. Neural activity from hippocampal pyramidal cells (identified by their slow-bursting firing pattern and their ability to be stimulated by acetylcholine and glutamate) was recorded from the center barrel. Both acetylcholine and glutamate stimulated pyramidal-cell firing rate in a dose-related manner. An analysis of covariance for the acetylocholine data yielded a significant effect of age as well as a significant Age × Current interaction (see Figure 11-6). Similar effects were not observed with the glutamate data. Acetylcholine produced significantly less neuronal stimulation at 1, 5, and 10 nanoamperes (nA) in cells recorded for old rats than in cells recorded from young rats. In addition, glutamate stimulated young cells (see Figure 11-7). This ability of glutamate to stimulate old cells argues against a generalized age-related decrease in neuronal sensitivity. Rather, the present results may be considered direct evidence for a selective, functional impairment of hippocampal cholinergic mechanisms.

At the end of the electrical recording session, brains were removed and stored at −60°C for subsequent

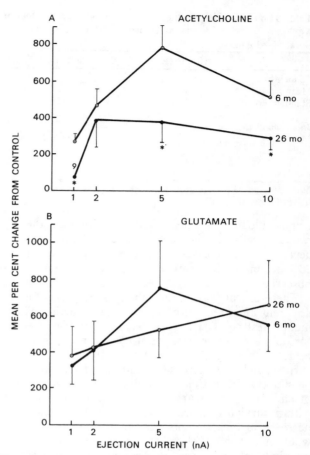

Figure 11-7. Mean percentage of change in firing rate of hippocampal neurons when acetylocholine (A) and glutamate (B) were iontophoretically applied. Note the significant increase in firing rate in all cases when the current level was increased and the significantly dampened effect in aged neurons to acetylcholine only. Vertical bars represent SEM. (From "Brain Cholinergic Function and Memory in Aged Rats" by A. S. Lippa, R. W. Pelham, B. Beer, D. J. Critchett, R. L. Dean, and R. T. Bartus, *Neurobiology of Aging*, 1980, *1*(1), 10–16. Copyright 1980 by ANKHO International, Inc. Reprinted by permission.)

biochemical evaluations. Quantification of the number and affinity of muscarinic receptors was performed on the same area (i.e., dorsal hippocampus) on which acetylcholine-stimulated electrical activity was recorded.

Biochemical determinations revealed a small but significant ($p < .05$, paired t test) decrease in the number of muscarinic receptors in the dorsal hippocampus of old rats (measured via 3H-QNB binding). However, no age-related differences were found in the presumed affinity of the neurotransmitter for its receptor (see Table 11-1). At present is is not clear how the changes in the number of muscarinic receptors relate to the elec-

Table 11-1 3H-QNB Binding in Rat Hippocampus: Effect of Age on Affinity and Receptor Density as Determined by Scratchard Analysis

Age	Affinity (K_D)	Receptor density (B_{max})
6–8 months		
Mean	.263	1580
Standard error	.013	50
26–29 months		
Mean	.279	1333
Standard error	.031	40
P (*t* test)	.343	.0036

Note. N = 5 rats per category. K_D = nM. B_{max} = protein. (Data are from Lippa et al., 1980.)

trophysiological results. That is, although the pyramidal cells in the aged brains exhibited a 50% decrease in responsiveness to acetylcholine, less than a 20% decline in the number of muscarinic receptors was observed.

There are at least three salient possibilities for this apparent anomaly, all of which require further experimental testing. The first is that it might be necessary for only a small percentage of muscarinic receptors to be lost for a significant biological impairment to occur. Second, the decrease in number of receptors may be simply a reflection of the decrease in total number of cholinoceptive neurons and not a loss of receptors within surviving neurons. If this were the case, the decrease in receptor number observed in these brains would not even be related to the decrease in functional reactivity of the surviving neurons from which these electrophysiological recordings were taken. Third, the loss of a fairly low percentage of muscarinic receptors may indeed be due to morphological changes in surviving neurons but may still be unimportant to whether the neuron ultimately fires. It is now apparent that binding of the neurotransmitter to the appropriate receptor represents only one step in a complex chain of events ultimately leading to an action potential. Thus it is conceivable that the modest decrease in number of receptors reflects a small, late degenerative phase in cholinergic decline and that the decreased neuronal responsiveness to acetylcholine may be due to an earlier, more serious disturbance in other, equally important postsynaptic mechanisms. For example, possible changes in acetylcholine-stimulated cyclic nucleotide-coupling mechanisms, and/or decreases in postsynaptic membrane fluidity and ionic permeability, could have produced the same change in responsiveness to acetylcholine.

Whichever possibility proves to be most tenable, it is clear that there still remains the task of eventually defining the specific nature of the age-related changes that occur in the cholinergic system and the ways in which they may contribute to memory impairments. At the same time, these results provide direct evidence that a functional decline in the cholinergic system occurs with advancing age. When considered with the psychopharmacological and biochemical studies discussed earlier, the data suggest that specific cholinergic impairments may indeed play a role in the age-related memory disturbances. Thus, one viable approach to treating these impairments may involve pharmacological manipulation of the cholinergic system.

Effects of Physostigmine on Memory in Aged Subjects

Because of the solid evidence supporting the notion that dysfunctions in cholinergic mechanisms may be responsible for the age-related memory impairments observed in humans, rats, and monkeys, we evaluated the effects of the anticholinesterase physostigmine on primate performance in the memory task described earlier (Bartus, 1979b).

Two different age groups of rhesus monkeys were used: One consisted of four young, unimpaired monkeys and the other of eight aged, memory-impaired monkeys. Six different doses of physostigmine (from .0013 to .04 mg/kg) were given to each monkey, according to a randomized block design. Performance under each of the doses was then compared to well-defined, individual baseline-control levels of performance. The accuracy of the young monkeys under physostigmine resembled that of young adult humans (see Chapter 12 of this volume). No reliable changes from baseline performance were observed with doses below .01 mg/kg, but some improvement was found at doses of .01 and .02 mg/kg. Finally, all four young monkeys performed less well under the highest dose (i.e., .04 mg/kg; see Figure 11-8). Thus the very steep dose-response function previously reported for young adult humans was also found in young monkeys, and the same relative doses produced the greatest improvement and most reliable impairment in both species.

Although most of the aged monkeys exhibited reliable improvement at about the same dose levels, their overall response as a group was much more variable than the younger animals. A few aged monkeys exhibited significant impairments at the lowest doses, at which both young monkeys and humans appear unaffected by physostigmine. Further, three of the eight aged monkeys exhibited a striking improvement at the highest dose, at which young monkeys and humans are typically impaired. Finally, three aged monkeys did not benefit from physostigmine at all, even though their impairment on the memory task was qualitatively similar to the other five monkeys who did exhibit improvement.

The experimental design and procedure used provide reasonable confidence that chance variations in base-

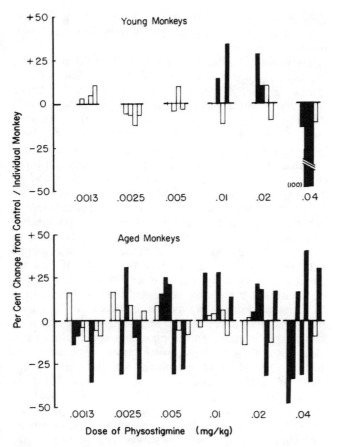

Figure 11-8. Performance on memory-dependent delayed-response trials by four young (top) and eight aged (bottom) rhesus monkeys injected with physostigmine. Each bar respresents an individual monkey's drug score compared with that monkey's own baseline performance level. Individual statistical confidence limits (*p* = .01) based on the control scores were used to determine whether a change in performance under any dose of physostigmine reflected a realiable change from baseline performance for that particular monkey (solid bars). Note the marked increase in variability to physostigmine on the memory test between aged monkeys.

line performance were not responsible for these peculiar drug effects in the aged monkeys, particularly since similar variability was not seen under saline control conditions. This variability is similar to several preliminary reports of different cholinomimetic agents in aged humans, in which the high degree of variability between subjects has sometimes been attributed to various method and measurement problems in the geriatric clinic (Boyd, Graham-White, Blackwood, Glen, & McQueen, 1977; Etienne, Gauthier, Dastoor, Collier, & Ratner, 1978; Etienne, Gauthier, Johnson, Collier, Mendis, Dastoor, Cole, & Muller, 1978). However, in the present automated laboratory situa-

tion, which utilized test-sophisticated subjects as their own controls and an objective measure of memory performance, problems of this sort should have been effectively controlled or eliminated. Yet higher intersubject variability under physostigmine was still observed in the aged subjects. Thus these data imply that the differences between age groups reflect a genuine age-specific change in response to physostigmine, presumably involving some variable relevant to the mediation of memory. However, little can at present be offered in the way of specific explanation. One possibility may be that the increased variability reflects day-to-day changes in individual sensitivity of pharmacological cholinergic manipulation, perhaps related to continuously shifting imbalances in cholinergic function. Or some undefined, age-related changes in response to physostigmine may exist in certain (but not all) aged subjects. Careful examination of the data revealed that differences in the degree of impairment among the aged subjects could not explain their individual differences in response to physostigmine.

Other possible explanations may exist that do not involve changes in central cholinergic mechanisms. For example, age-related changes in absorption and metabolism of physostigmine, or subtle undetected differences in susceptibility to side effects, could also have contributed to the differences in variability between age groups. Whatever the reason for these differences, however, the data indicate that careful individual titration of doses of physostigmine and other cholinomimetics might be necessary to enhance the chances of finding significant improvement in aged subjects. In fact, more recent findings by Davis and colleagues (see also Chapter 12, this volume) confirm the increased variability in aged human subjects and the fact that quite different doses may be most effective in different subjects.

At the same time, the lack of consistent facilitation should not be considered contradictory to the idea that cholinergic mechanisms are important in age-related memory impairments. Even if one accepts that some cholinergic dysfunction is partly responsible for the deficits, it might be naive to expect physostigmine to reverse the impairments in all aged subjects. Many aspects of cholinergic synthesis and transmission may become impaired during the aging process, all of which could ultimately produce a behavioral deficit in memory. Thus, simply increasing levels of acetylcholine, via physostigmine, may by insufficient or ineffective in some cases of behavioral impairment that result from what, at this point, remains an undiscovered cholinergic dysfunction. It may be necessary, therefore, to modify cholinergic function at more than one point in the metabolic pathway (e.g., precursor uptake, transmitter synthesis and/or degradation) or to restore the balance between two or more age-altered neurotransmitter systems, before a consistently positive effect on memory can be obtained. Nevertheless, these results indicate that (a) reliable changes in performance on this memory task do occur under physostigmine, (b) certain age-related differences in these effects also exist, and (c) aged monkeys vary widely (and significantly more than young subjects) in the dose level that yields significantly superior performance.

Although these results do not provide strong support for the use of physostigmine as a reliable therapeutic agent for cognition, they do provide additional circumstantial evidence for an important cholinergic role in age-related memory impairments. More important, they provide an objective rationale for believing that an appropriate pharmacological manipulation of the cholinergic system (perhaps in conjunction with other neurotransmitter systems) may eventually be developed to alleviate some of the cognitive declines associated with advanced age.

Precursor Manipulation of the Cholinergic System

Another approach to alleviating cognitive impairments in the aged might be through precursor manipulation of the cholinergic system. It has recently been shown that the availability of choline (the neurochemical precursor for acetylcholine) is an important rate-limiting step in acetylcholine synthesis. For example, Haubrich et al. (1975) and Cohen and Wurtman (1975) have independently demonstrated that acute injections of choline chloride temporarily but significantly increased brain acetylcholine in the guinea pig and the rat. It was later shown that increasing dietary choline chloride (Cohen & Wurtman, 1978) or lecithin (the normal dietary source of choline) (Hirsch & Wurtman, 1978) also significantly increases brain acetylcholine. Although some investigators have since reported difficulty in replicating the increase in brain acetylcholine levels (Flentge & Van den Berg, 1979; Haubrich, Wang, Chippendale, & Proctor, 1976; Wecker & Dettbarn, 1979; Wecker & Schmidt, 1979), most seem to agree that the cholinergic system is indeed stimulated by increased choline availability, even though this stimulation may not be reflected in levels of acetylcholine. In fact, review of the literature leaves little doubt that increased choline availability has a positive effect on central cholinergic function. In addition to the possible increase in levels of acetylcholine in several brain regions, some laboratories have also reported increases in nicotinic receptors (Morley Robinson, Brown, Kemp, & Bradley, 1977), choline acetyltransferase activity (Fernstrom & Wurtman, 1979; Hirsch, Growdon, & Wurtman, 1977), and cholinergic-stimulated dopaminergic activity (Haub-

rich & Pfleuger, 1979; Ulus, Scally, & Wurtman, 1977; Ulus & Wurtman, 1979) with increased precursor availability.

Despite this rather compelling evidence that increasing plasma choline levels can, in fact, enhance central cholinergic activity, few definitive clinical effects have been reported for geriatric patients. The scattered articles reporting mild or occasional effects in some aged subjects offer hope that this approach may ultimately provide limited relief to a subpopulation of geriatric patients. Yet numerous negative reports have appeared (e.g., see Ferris et al., 1979; Mohs et al., 1980), and no hard evidence exists that the effects observed are any more substantial than those reported for numerous other experimental therapies with lesser known mechanisms of action. Although available laboratory data on animals are still sparse, a preliminary study using aged rats also failed to substantiate the utility of this approach. In this study, aged Fisher 344 rats (from 20 to 32 months) were shown to suffer deficits on retention of a single-trial, passive-avoidance task (see Figure 11-9). Three additional groups of 24-month-old rats were administered either saline piracetam or choline chloride for a period of one week prior to training and testing. The dose of piracetam was selected on the basis of previous learning/memory studies. The dose of choline chloride (100 mg/kg) exceeded the minimum dose required to induce significant increases in central cholinergic activity in young rats. However, no reliable changes were observed in retention of the passive-avoidance task under choline chloride, even

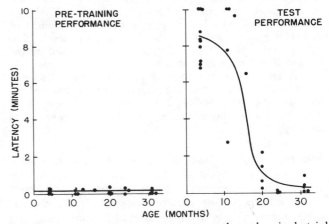

Figure 11-9. Performance on a step-through, single-trial passive-avoidance task across the life span of Fischer 344 rats. Note the gradual deterioration in retention (as reflected by the decrease in response latency on the test day) as the ages of the rats increase. (From "Brain Cholinergic Function and Memory in Aged Rats" by A. S. Lippa, R. W. Pelham, B. Beer, D. J. Critchett, R. L. Dean, and R. T. Bartus, *Neurobiology of Aging*, 1980, *1*(1), 10–16. Copyright 1980 by ANKHO International, Inc. Reprinted by permission.)

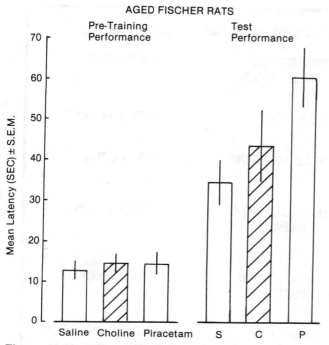

AGED FISCHER RATS

Figure 11-10. Effects of choline chloride (100 mg/kg), piracetam (100 mg/kg), and saline administered for one week prior to testing on passive-avoidance retention in aged rats. Vertical bars represent SEM.

though the task situation was sensitive to the facilitating effects of piracetam, a drug exhibiting marginal efficacy in the geriatric clinic (see Figure 11-10). Thus, at the present time the hope that precursor manipulation of the cholinergic system can be used to improve geriatric memory has no direct empirical support and rests solely on a rationale developed from other indirect lines of evidence. Indeed, the neurochemical evidence supporting this precursor rationale has yet to be confirmed (or tested) on brains from aged subjects. It is certainly possible that the mechanisms responsible for choline's being taken up into the presynaptic sites for conversion to acetylcholine might be markedly impaired with age. This problem, when considered with the established, age-related decrease in choline acetyltransferase activity discussed earlier may produce a condition in the aged brain in which increased availability of choline is no longer sufficient to induce a reliable or substantial change in cholinergic activity.

Because in clinical trials applying this approach it has been assumed that choline and lecithin produce the same functional changes in aged brain as in young brain, it would seem worthwhile to substantiate this assumption empirically. Certainly the possibility should be considered that a major reason that the clinical trials have been disappointing so far is that sup-

plemental choline and lecithin simply do not increase cholinergic activity in aged brain as they may in young brain. If this is true, and if the reasons can be identified, it might eventually be possible to combine choline with proper pharmacological treatment to enhance the therapeutic effects of precursor manipulation.

At the same time, other heuristically interesting possibilities should also be examined. For example, if age-related changes in the cholinergic system are at least partly responsible for the age-related memory impairments, and if dietary manipulation of available choline significantly affects cholinergic function, then it might be possible to modulate the rate at which the memory impairments occur with age by varying the availability of dietary choline. In other words, even though it might be difficult to reverse existent age-related neurochemical dysfunctions with choline or lecithin, it might be possible to retard the onset of these changes by proper stimulation of the cholinergic system while it is still operating efficiently. This approach necessarily requires that the subjects be given altered amounts of choline before the onset of the age-related behavioral deficits (and the presumed cholinergic deficiencies) and that this regimen be continued for durations extending into a meaningful part of the life span.

Because of this and other practical considerations, we selected the C57B1/6j mouse as a suitable species for testing this hypothesis. Before the test was performed, however, we conducted a series of studies on several age groups of this strain of mouse in order to sample a wide spectrum of behaviors across the life span of this subject (Dean et al., 1980). We found that of a dozen different behaviors measured, the most reliable and severe age-related impairment occurred on retention of a passive-avoidance learning task (see Figure 11-11). Because this deficit was also conceptually most similar to the severe memory loss reported in aged monkeys and humans, the passive-avoidance task was used to assess the effects of choline intake on age-related behavioral deficits. Two other behaviors were also measured—motor activity and psychomotor coordination—both of which were also impaired in aged mice but are presumably less related to memory loss.

Retired breeder mice (8.5 months old at the start of this study) were placed on purified diets (Bioserve, Inc.) which were either deficient in free choline (less than 1.0 mg/gm of food) or enriched (12 to 15 mg/gm of food). (The normal diet contains from 1.5 to 1.75 mg choline/gm of food.) From our previous studies across several age groups of these mice, we knew that little or no reliable change in these behaviors would be expressed by this age. Therefore, presumably, little relevant neurochemical change would yet have occurred.

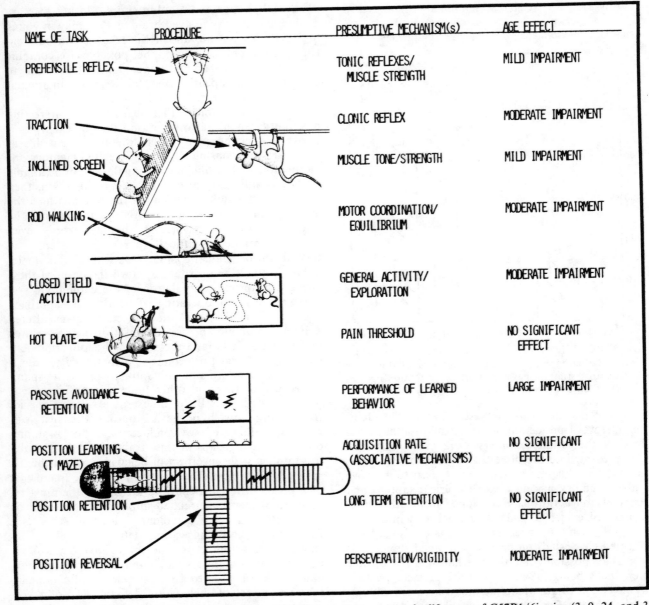

NAME OF TASK	PROCEDURE	PRESUMPTIVE MECHANISM(s)	AGE EFFECT
PREHENSILE REFLEX		TONIC REFLEXES/ MUSCLE STRENGTH	MILD IMPAIRMENT
TRACTION		CLONIC REFLEX	MODERATE IMPAIRMENT
INCLINED SCREEN		MUSCLE TONE/STRENGTH	MILD IMPAIRMENT
ROD WALKING		MOTOR COORDINATION/ EQUILIBRIUM	MODERATE IMPAIRMENT
CLOSED FIELD ACTIVITY		GENERAL ACTIVITY/ EXPLORATION	MODERATE IMPAIRMENT
HOT PLATE		PAIN THRESHOLD	NO SIGNIFICANT EFFECT
PASSIVE AVOIDANCE RETENTION		PERFORMANCE OF LEARNED BEHAVIOR	LARGE IMPAIRMENT
POSITION LEARNING (T MAZE)		ACQUISITION RATE (ASSOCIATIVE MECHANISMS)	NO SIGNIFICANT EFFECT
POSITION RETENTION		LONG TERM RETENTION	NO SIGNIFICANT EFFECT
POSITION REVERSAL		PERSEVERATION/RIGIDITY	MODERATE IMPAIRMENT

Figure 11-11. Summary of behaviors measured and the effects of age across the life span of C57B1/6j mice (3, 9, 24, and 31 months old). The most reliable and robust behavioral effect of age was observed on retention of a single-trial passive-avoidance task (see also Figure 11-12).

The diets were given ad lib for a period of 4.5 months, after which time the mice were tested for effects on retention of the passive-avoidance task as well as for psychomotor coordination and closed-field activity. Although little or no difference was observed on psychomotor coordination or general activity, a striking effect was observed on retention of the inhibitory avoidance task (Bartus, Dean, Goas, & Lippa, 1980). In fact, mice fed the choline-enriched diet performed as well as young, 3-month-old mice, whereas mice fed the choline-deficient diet performed as poorly as mice 23 months and older (see Figure 11-12).

The data are even more interesting when one considers that the most serious behavioral impairment in the aged mice occurred on this same task and that this deficit is also conceptually most similar to the memory loss observed in the aged monkeys and humans. At the same time, two other behaviors (motor and psychomotor activity) that also exhibited reliable changes with age but are presumably less closely related to memory loss were not affected by choline manipulations in this study.

The results of this study suggest that chronic manipulation of cholinergic precursor availability can significantly alter behavior and that these behavioral changes are similar to those that occur across the life span of the mouse. As such, the data offer the heuristically interesting possibility that certain changes in behavior that occur with age can, in fact, be modulated through appropriate precursor control.

These findings were confirmed and extended in another independent test of this hypothesis. Once again retired breeder C56B1/6j mice were used, but this time all of the mice were fed the same purified diet, deficient in choline. Choline was then supplemented in the water for the control group (1.5 mg choline per ml water), and the enriched group (4.0 mg choline per ml water). In this way, caloric intake between diet groups could be more easily controlled and choline intake more carefully monitored. Also, by reducing the amount of choline the enriched group received (about 2.7 times normal amounts), we could evaluate the effects of altering supplemental choline within nutritionally relevant levels.

For each of three months following the initiation of this study, mice from each of the three groups were removed from the colony and tested for retention on the passive-avoidance task. These tests demonstrated that after the first month (i.e., at 10 months of age), the choline-deficient mice had already begun to suffer reliable impairments of passive-avoidance retention compared to the control mice. Further, these deficits became more severe and more consistent over the next 2 months. Although the choline-enriched mice showed only a small improvement over the control mice after the first month, the difference continued to grow during the next two months. Thus by the end of the third month and continuing into the fourth, a reliable beneficial effect of the enriched diet was apparent (i.e., at 12 months of age).

The results of these studies provide the first clear evidence that manipulation of cholinergic precursor availability can significantly alter behavior. Further, these behavioral changes are qualitatively and quantitatively similar to those that occur naturally across the life span of the mouse. As such, they offer the heuristically interesting possibility that certain age-related changes in behavior can be modulated by chronic control of precursor availability. An important question concerns how long into the life span of the mouse, or of other mammals, increased choline may retard the onset of age-related retention losses. Similarly, it remains to be seen whether chronic precursor treatment

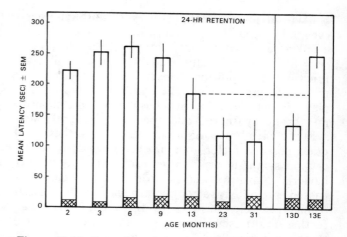

Figure 11-12. Retention of the single-trial passive-avoidance task across the life span of C57B1/6j mice. Retention is expressed as latency to reenter the shock chamber 24 hours after the aversive experience. Note the highly significant and progressive decrease in latency in the older mice. Because no consistent age difference in latencies was observed on the training day (cross-hatched bars), it is resonable to assume that this behavioral deficit is not due to differences in activity or responsiveness but more likely reflects an impairment in retention of the training trial. The two right-hand bars depict the reliable difference in retention of 13-month-old mice maintained on diets either deficient (D) or enriched (E) in choline for 4.5 months. Once again, no reliable differences existed between training and trial latencies. Note that the 13-month-old mice maintained on the choline-deficient diet performed as poorly as the 23-month-old, whereas the 13-month-old mice maintained on the choline-enriched diet performed as well as the 6-month-old mice. The vertical lines within each bar represent the standard error of the mean for each group. (From ''Age-Related Changes in Passive Avoidance Retention and Modulation With Chronic Dietary Choline'' by R. T. Bartus, R. L. Dean, J. A. Goas, and A. S. Lippa, *Science*, 1980, *209*, 301–303. Copyright 1980 by the American Association for the Advancement of Science. Reprinted by permission.)

subjects, for reversing existent deficits in the elderly may be more difficult than retarding the onset of deficits in mid-aged subjects. If it is true that the aged brain is relatively incapable of responding to additional precursor stimulation (in the same manner the younger brain may), then the most effective means of reducing these deficits through cholinergic precursor control might be to intervene before the behavioral impairments and neurochemical dysfunctions fully develop.

An issue of certain importance concerns what neurochemical changes may have been induced by the choline manipulations that ultimately produce the retention alterations. Certainly, sufficient literature exists to suggest that alterations in central cholinergic function should have occurred and that these alterations should have played a significant role in the behavioral impairments. However, this hypothesis eventually needs to be confirmed, for many changes could have occurred under chronic choline manipulation that are not directly related to central cholinergic function. In addition to serving as a necessary precursor for acetylcholine synthesis, choline also plays important roles in phospholipid metabolism, membrane synthesis, and (possibly) general post-synaptic membrane responsiveness. Thus these and other possible factors not directly related to acetyl-choline synthesis could have contributed to the behavioral changes observed. Although the data discussed previously strongly suggest an important cholinergic role, answers to these questions await further multidisciplinary research directed toward these specific issues.

At the same time, the data provide clear evidence for the notion that dietary choline manipulation can exert important modulating effects on the development of specific age-related behavioral impairments. By examining the relation between these changes and those occurring naturally with age (and the corresponding neurochemical changes in each condition), we come closer to gaining some additional insight into why the age-related neurobehavioral impairments occur and how they might ultimately be alleviated.

Summary and Synthesis

The preclinical studies reviewed here provide corroborating support that impaired cholinergic mechanisms are partly responsible for the memory impairments associated with old age and senile dementia. Although it would be overly simplistic to assume that the cholinergic system exclusively is involved in this behavioral impairment, it is not unreasonable to postulate that central cholinergic mechanisms play an important role and that correcting age-related malfunctions in the system might produce a substantial reduction in the degree of deficit or in the rate of further deterioration.

Preliminary attempts to improve geriatric memory via cholinomimetics have so far not been successful. However, they do provide some hope that this approach may ultimately lead to meaningful pharmacological relief. At the same time, invaluable insight into the etiology of this deficit should result from studies on (a) the specific nature of the cholinergic dysfunction, (b) its relation to changes in other neurological functions and neurotransmitter systems, and (c) the role these changes play in age-related memory loss. Ultimately, this information should aid the search for a truly effective pharmacological therapy.

REFERENCES

Arenberg, D. Anticipation interval and age differences in verbal learning. *Journal of Abnormal Psychology*, 1965, *70*, 419–425.

Bartus, R. T. Evidence for a direct cholinergic involvement in the scopolamine-induced amnesia in monkeys: Effects of concurrent administration of physostigmine and methylphenidate with scopolamine. *Pharmacology, Biochemistry, and Behavior*, 1978, *9*, 833–836. (a)

Bartus, R. T. Short-term memory in the Rhesus monkey: Effects of dopamine blockade via acute haloperidol administration. *Pharmacology, Biochemistry and Behavior*, 1978, *9*, 353–357. (b)

Bartus, R. T. Effects of aging on visual memory, sensory processing, and discrimination learning in a nonhuman primate. In J. M. Ordy & K. Brizzee (Eds.), *Sensory systems and communication in the elderly*. New York: Raven Press, 1979. (a)

Bartus, R. T. Physostigmine and recent memory: Effects in young and aged non-human primates. *Science*, 1979, *206*, 1087–1089. (b)

Bartus, R. T., & Dean, R. L. Recent memory in aged non-human primates: Hypersensitivity to visual interference during retention. *Experimental Aging Research*, 1979, *5*, 385–400.

Bartus, R. T., Dean, R. L., & Fleming, D. L. Aging in the rhesus monkey: Effects on visual discrimination learning and reversal learning. *Journal of Gerontology*, 1979, *34*, 209–219.

Bartus, R. T., Dean, R. L., Goas, J. A., & Lippa, A. S. Age-related changes in passive avoidance retention and modulation with chronic dietary choline. *Science*, 1980, *209*, 301–303.

Bartus, R. T., Fleming, D., & Johnson, H. R. Aging in the rhesus monkey: Effects on short-term memory. *Journal of Gerontology*, 1978, *33*, 858–871.

Bartus, R. T., & Johnson, H. R. Short-term memory in the rhesus monkey: Disruption from the anticholinergic scopolamine. *Pharmacology, Biochemistry and Behavior*, 1976, *5*, 31–39.

Bird, S., & Aghajanian, G. K. Neuropharmacology of hippocampal pyramidal cells. *Neuropharmacology*, 1976, *15*, 273–282.

Blas, T. V. P. Synaptic plasticity in the hippocampus. *Trends in Neurosciences*, 1979, *2*, 42–45.

Botwinick, J. *Aging and behavior*. New York: Springer, 1973.

Botwinick, J. Behavioral processes. In S. Gershon & A. Raskin (Eds.), *Aging* (Vol. 2). New York: Raven Press, 1975.

Bowen, D. M., Smith, C. B., White, P., & Davison, A. N. Neurotransmitter-related enzymes and indices of hypoxia in senile dementia and other abiotrophies. *Brain*, 1976, *99*, 459–496.

Bowen, D. M., White, P., Flack, R. H. A., Smith, C. B., & Davison, A. N. Brain-decarboxylase activities as indices of pathological change in senile dementia. *Lancet*, 1974, *1*, 1247–1249.

Boyd, W. D., Graham-White, J., Blackwood, G., Glen, I., & McQueen, J. Clinical effects of choline in Alzheimer senile dementia. *Lancet*, 1977, *2*, 711.

Broadbent, D. E., & Heron, A. Effects of a subsidiary task on performance involving immediate memory by younger and older men. *British Journal of Psychology*, 1962, *53*, 189–198.

Bruning, R. H., Holzbauer, I., & Kimberlin, C. Age, word imagery and delay interval: Effects on short-term and long-term retention. *Journal of Gerontology*, 1975, *30*, 312–318.

Caird, W. K. Aging and short-term memory. *Journal of Gerontology*, 1966, *21*, 295–299.

Canestrari, R. E. Paced and self-paced learning in young and elderly adults. *Journal of Gerontology*, 1963, *18*, 165–168.

Cohen, E. L., & Wurtman, R. J. Brain acetylcholine: Increase after systematic choline administration. *Life Sciences*, 1975, *16*, 1095–1102.

Cohen, E. L., & Wurtman, R. J. Brain acetylcholine: Control by dietary choline. *Science*, 1976, *191*, 561–562.

Crook, T., Ferris, S., Sathananthan, G., Raskin, A., & Gershon, S. The effect of methylphenidate on test performance in the cognitively impaired aged. *Psychopharmacology*, 1977, *52*, 251–255.

Davies, P., & Maloney, A. J. F. Selective loss of central cholinergic neurons in Alzheimer's disease. *Lancet*, 1976, *2*, 1403.

Davies, P., & Verth, A. Regional distribution of muscarinic acetylcholine receptor in normal and Alzheimer's-type dementia brains. *Brain Research*, 1978, *138*, 385–392.

Dean, R. L., Goas, J. A., Regan, B., Beer, B., & Bartus, R. T. *Age-related changes in behavior across the lifespan of C57B1/6j mice.* Manuscript submitted for publication, 1980.

Drachman, D. A. Memory and cognitive function in man: Does the cholinergic system have a specific role? *Neurology*, 1977, *27*, 783–790.

Drachman, D. A., & Hughes, J. R. Memory and the hippocampal reflexes. III. Aging and temporal EEG abnormalities. *Neurology*, 1971, *21*, 1–14.

Drachman, D. A., & Leavitt, J. Human memory and the cholinergic system. *Archives of Neurology*, 1974, *30*, 113–121.

Elias, P. K., & Elias, M. F. Effects of age on learning ability: Contributions from the animal literature. *Experimental Aging Research*, 1976, *2*, 165–186.

Etienne, P., Gauthier, S., Dastoor, D., Collier, B., & Ratner, J. Lecithin in Alzheimer's disease. *Lancet*, 1978, *1*, 1206.

Etienne, P., Gauthier, S., Johnson, G., Collier, B., Mendis, T., Dastoor, D., Cole, M., & Muller, H. F. Clinical effects of choline in Alzheimer's disease. *Lancet*, 1978, *1*, 508–509.

Fernstrom, M. H., & Wurtman, R. J. Increase in striatal choline acetyltransferase activity after choline administration. *Brain Research* 1979, *165*, 358–361.

Ferris, S. H., Sathananthan, G., Reisberg, B., & Gershon, S. Long-term choline treatment of memory-impaired elderly patients. *Science*, 1979, *205*, 1039–1040.

Flentge, E., & Van den Berg, C. J. Choline administration and acetylcholine in brain. *Journal of Neurochemistry*, 1979, *32*, 1331–1333.

Gottfries, C. G., Gottfries, I., & Roos, E. The investigation of homovanillic acid in the human brain and its correlation to senile dementia. *British Journal of Psychiatry*, 1969, *115*, 563–574.

Gottfries, C. G., Rosengren, A. M., & Rosengren, E. The occurrence of homovanillic acid in human brain. *Acta Pharmacologia Toxica*, 1965, *23*, 36–40.

Haubrich, D. R., & Pflueger, A. B. Choline administration: Central effect mediated by stimulation of aetylcholine synthesis. *Life Sciences*, 1979, *24*, 1083–1090.

Haubrich, D. R., Wang, P. F. L., Chippendale, T., & Proctor, E. Choline and acetylcholine in rats: Effect of dietary choline. *Journal of Neurochemistry*, 1976, *27*, 1305–1313.

Haubrich, D. R., Wang, P. F. L., Clody, D, E., & Wedeking, P. W. Increase in rat brain acetylcholine induced by choline or deanol. *Life Sciences*, 1975, *17*, 975–980.

Hirsch, M. J., Growdon, J. H., & Wurtman, R. J. Increase in hippocampal acetylcholine after choline administration. *Brain Research*, 1977, *125*, 383–385.

Hirsch, M. J., & Wurtman, R. J. Lecithin consumption increases acetylcholine concentrations in rat brain and adrenal gland. *Science*, 1978, *202*, 223–225.

James, T. C., & Kanungo, M. S. Alterations in atropine sites of the brain of rats as a function of age. *Biochemical and Biophysical Research Communications*, 1976, *72*, 170–175.

Kahn, R. L., Zarit, S. H., Hilbert, N. M., & Niederehe, G. Memory complaint and impairment in the aged: The effect of depression and altered brain function. *Archives of General Psychiatry*, 1975, *32*, 1569–1573.

Kristensen, V., Olsen, M., & Theilgaard, A. Levodopa treatment of presenile dementia. *Acta Psychiatrica Scandinavica*, 1977, *55*, 41–51.

Lippa, A. S., Pelham, R. W., Beer, B., Critchett, D. J., Dean, R. L., & Bartus, R. T. Brain cholinergic function and memory in aged rats. *Neurobiology of Aging*, 1980, *1*(1), 10–16.

Maggi, A., Schmidt, M. J., Ghetti, B., & Enna, S. J. Effect of aging on neurotransmitter receptor binding in rat and human brain. *Life Sciences*, 1979, *24*, 367–374.

McGeer, E., & McGeer, P. L. Neurotransmitter metabolism in the aging brain. In R. D. Terry & S. Gershon (Eds.), *Neurobiology of aging.* New York: Raven Press, 1976.

Mohs, R. C., Davis, K. L., Tinklenberg, J. R., & Hollister, L. E. Choline chloride effects on memory in the elderly. *Neurobiology of Aging*, 1980, *1*(1), 17–21.

Morley, B. J., Robinson, G. R., Brown, G. B., Kemp, G. E., & Bradley, R. J. Effects of dietary choline on nicotinic acetylcholine receptors in brain. *Nature*, 1977, *266*, 848–850.

Perry, E. K., Perry, R. H., Blessed, G., & Tomlinson, B. E. Necropsy evidence of central cholinergic deficits in senile dementia. *Lancet*, 1977, *1*, 189.

Perry, E. K., Perry, R. H., Gibson, P., Blessed, G., & Tomlinson, B. E. A cholinergic connection between normal aging and senile dementia in the human hippocampus. *Neurosciences Letters*, 1977, *6*, 85–89.

Perry, E. K., Tomlinson, B. E., Blessed, G., Bergmann, K., Gibson, P. H., & Perry, R. H. Correlation of cholinergic abnormalities with senile plaques and mental test scores in senile dementia. *British Medical Journal*, 1978, *2*, 1457–1459.

Reisine, T. D., Yamamura, H. I., Bird, E. D., Spokes, E., & Enna, S. J. Pre- and postsynaptic neurochemical alterations in Alzheimer's disease. *Brain Research*, 1978, *149*, 477–481.

Scheibel, M. E., & Scheibel, A. B. Structural changes in the aging brain. In H. Brody, D. Harman, & J. M. Ordy (Eds.), *Aging* (Vol. 1), New York: Raven Press, 1975.

Spillane, J. A., White, P., Goodhardt, M. J., Flack, R. H., Bowen, D. M., & Davison, A. N. Selective vulnerability of neurons in organic dementia. *Nature*, 1977, *266*, 558–559.

Strong, R., Hicks, P., Hsu, L., Bartus, R. T., & Enna, S. J. Age-related alterations in rodent brain cholinergic system and behavior. *Neurobiology of Aging*, 1980, *1*(1), 51–55.

Taub, H. A. Visual short-term memory as a function of age, rate of presentation and schedule of presentation. *Journal of Gerontology*, 1966, *21*, 388–391.

Taul, H. A. Age differences in memory as a function of rate of presentation, order of recent and stimulus organization. *Journal of Gerontology*, 1968, *23*, 159–164.

Ulus, I. H., Scally, M. C., & Wurtman, R. J. Choline potentiates the trans-synaptic induction of adrenal tyrosine hydroxylase by reserpine, probably by enhancing the release of acetylcholine. *Life Sciences*, 1977, *21*, 145–148.

Ulus, I. H., & Wurtman, R. J. Choline administration: Activation of tyrosine hydroxylase in dopamine neurons of rat brain. *Science*, 1976, *194*, 1060–1061.

Vijayan, V. K. Cholinergic enzymes in the cerebellum and the hippocampus of the senescent mouse. *Experimental Gerontology*, 1977, *12*, 7–11.

Wecker, L., & Dettbarn, W.-D. Relationship between choline availability and acetylcholine synthesis in discrete regions of rat brain. *Journal of Neurochemistry*, 1979, *32*, 961–967.

Wecker, L., & Schmidt, D. E. Central cholinergic function: Relationship to choline administration. *Life Sciences*, 1979, *25*, 375–384.

White, P., Goodhardt, M. J., Kent, J. P., Hiley, C. R., Carrasco, L. H., Williams, I. E., & Bowen, D. M. Neocortical cholinergic neurons in elderly people. *Lancet*, 1977, *1*, 668–671.

Richard C. Mohs, Kenneth L. Davis, and Claire Darley

CHAPTER

12

Cholinergic Drug Effects on Memory and Cognition in Humans

This chapter summarizes recent attempts to improve normal memory functioning and to alleviate age-related memory deficits by administering drugs that affect transmission at cholinergic synapses. In young adults, a low dose of physostigmine, a short-acting cholinesterase inhibitor, enhanced storage of information in long-term memory. Higher doses of physostigmine impaired all aspects of memory. Choline chloride, a precursor to acetylcholine, did not have a substantial effect on memory in a series of four studies with young and elderly adults. It has been difficult to conduct studies of elderly patients suffering from memory loss because of wide individual variations in baseline cognitive abilities and in dose-response curves for cholinergic drugs. A preliminary study utilizing methods that allow for such individual differences indicates that physostigmine can also improve memory in these patients.

This chapter presents the results of a recent series of studies conducted in our laboratory on the cognitive effects of cholinomimetic drugs. One goal of these studies has been to increase our understanding of cholinergic mechanisms in human memory functioning. A second goal has been to determine whether it is possible to alleviate some age-related memory deficits by administering drugs that increase transmission at cholinergic synapses. Several kinds of evidence indicate that cholinergic mechanisms play an important role in normal memory functioning and age-related memory loss. Some of the evidence from psychopharmacological and neuropathological studies is discussed briefly in the sections that follow. These studies provide the necessary background and theoretical rationale for our own studies, which are described later.

Although this chapter primarily concerns the effects of cholinergic drugs on memory functioning, it is useful to bear in mind that cholinergic mechanisms are involved in a variety of other psychological and behavioral processes. Particularly susceptible to fluctuations in central cholinergic activity are mood (Janowsky, El-Yousef, Davis, & Sekerke, 1973) and the control of movement (Davis, Hollister, Barchas, & Berger, 1976a; Klawans & Rubovits, 1972). As a consequence, drugs that affect the cholinergic system may have other psychological and behavioral effects in addition to their effects on memory. The psychological changes observed in any particular study of the effects of cholinergic drugs will depend on a variety of factors including drug, drug dose, the subjects participating, and the psychological assessment procedures used.

This research was supported by the Medical Research Service of the Veterans Administration. Part of the research reported in this chapter was performed while the first two authors were at the VA Medical Center, Palo Alto, California, and at the Stanford University Medical Center, Stanford, California.

Psychopharmacological Studies

Investigation of the effects of cholinergic drugs indicates that fluctuations in central cholinergic activity cause substantial changes in memory performance. When given to normal adults, anticholinergic drugs such as scopolamine impair the ability to store new information in long-term memory (Drachman, 1977; Drachman & Leavitt, 1974; Peterson, 1977). These drugs have much smaller effects on the ability to retrieve information from long-term memory and have no effect on the capacity of short-term memory (Drachman, 1977; Peterson, 1977). Interestingly, the kinds of performance deficits produced by scopolamine are very similar to those observed in elderly patients suffering from age-related memory loss (Drachman & Leavitt, 1974). Anticholinergic amnesia is not a result of the sedative properties of these drugs but rather is specifically associated with their effects at cholinergic synapses. This is indicated by the fact that amphetamine, a stimulant that releases catecholamines from central nervous system (CNS) neurons, does not reverse anticholinergic amnesia, while physostigmine, a cholinesterase inhibitor, does (Drachman, 1977).

The role of the cholinergic system in memory has also been supported by an extensive series of experiments with animals on the effects of cholinergic drugs on time-dependent changes in the memory trace. In these experiments animals are first trained to respond correctly in some task. At intervals ranging from minutes to weeks following training a cholinergic drug is administered and the animal is then tested for retention of the learned response. Both anticholinergic and cholinomimetic drugs have effects on memory retrieval that depend on the age of the memory trace. Cholinomimetics improve the retrieval of old, and presumably weak, memory traces but tend to impair the retrieval of newer, stronger memory traces. Anticholinergics almost always impair retrieval, but the impairment is greatest for older, weaker traces. These results are important because they are difficult to explain in terms of changes in attention or motivation. If cholinergic drugs affected memory performance by changing the animal's motivation or attention, we would expect them to affect retrieval of all memory traces uniformly. The fact that drug effects depend on the age of the memory trace suggests that memory traces are formed, at least in part, by time-dependent changes at cholinergic synapses. The results of these animal studies have been reviewed in detail by Deutsch (1971), who has also discussed their implications for studies of cholinergic mechanisms in human memory (Deutsch & Rogers, 1979).

Cholinergic Deficit in Dementia

Neuropathologic studies indicate that aging is associated with a specific loss of central cholinergic activity and that this loss is exacerbated in patients with senile dementia of the Alzheimer's type. Alzheimer's type dementia is now recognized to be the most prevalent cause of severe dementia in people over age 55 (Bowen, Smith, White, & Davison, 1976; Tomlinson, Blessed, & Roth, 1970). Neurohistologically this disease is characterized by large numbers of senile plaques and neurofibrillary tangles (Tomlinson et al., 1970); behaviorally it is characterized by a steady deterioration of memory and other cognitive functions (Roth & Hopkins, 1953). Although the neurohistological and behavioral sequelae of this disorder have been known for some time, the neurochemical changes occurring in Alzheimer's patients have only been described in the last few years. In patients dying of nonneurological causes, the activity of choline acetyltransferase (CAT), an enzyme that catalyzes the synthesis of acetylcholine, decreases with age for patients between 20 and 50 (McGeer & McGeer, 1976). After age 60 there is no significant correlation between age and CAT activity, but there is a negative correlation between CAT activity and the degree of neurohistological change characteristic of Alzheimer's disease; specifically, the number of senile plaques and the number of neurofibrillary tangles are inversely related to CAT activity (Bowen et al., 1976; Bowen, Spillane, Curzon, Meier-Ruge, White, Goodhardt, Iwangoff, & Davison, 1979). When they are compared with nondemented, age-matched controls, Alzheimer's patients are found to have significantly lower CAT activity (Bowen et al., 1979; Perry, Tomlinson, Blessed, Bergman, Gibson, & Perry, 1978). In addition memory loss measured by psychometric testing prior to death is correlated with loss of CAT activity in pa-

Table 12-1 Infusion Procedures for the Physostigmine Study

Time (minutes)	Procedure
−30	Two learning trials on list of 15 concrete nouns
−16	Methscopolamine (.5 mg subcutaneous)
0	Start infusion (1.0 mg physostigmine or saline)
+9	Digit span
+18	Two recall trials on list of 15 concrete nouns
+30	Six learning trials on list of 20 categorized nouns
+42	Memory-scanning task
+60	End infusion
+80	Two recall trials on list of 15 concrete nouns

tients with histologically verified Alzheimer's disease but not in nondemented, age-matched controls (Perry et al., 1978). Analyses of enzymes associated with the neurotransmitters dopamine, GABA, norepinephrine, and serotonin indicate (a) that activities of these enzymes decline with age but to a lesser degree than does CAT activity, and (b) that their activity is not further reduced by senile changes of the Alzheimer's type (Bowen et al., 1976, 1979; Davies & Maloney, 1976; Perry et al., 1978). These neurochemical studies suggest quite strongly that a loss of central cholinergic activity is the primary neurochemical abnormality in patients with Alzheimer's disease. They also imply that drugs that increase central cholinergic activity might help alleviate the memory deficits that occur with age and Alzheimer's disease.

Cholinomimetic Drugs and Memory

Physostigmine in Normal Subjects

Our attempts to improve memory performance with cholinomimetics began with two studies in which physostigmine was given to normal young adults. Physostigmine is a drug that temporarily inhibits acetylcholinesterase thereby slowing the destruction and increasing the concentration of acetylcholine at the synapse (Koelle, 1975). In our first study (Davis, Hollister, Overall, Johnson, & Train, 1976b) we gave young adults saline and either 2 or 3 mg of physostigmine intravenously on separate days. Results indicated that both doses impaired performance on a test of memory retrieval, a test of new learning, and the digit-span task. In addition, a few subjects became nauseated. Since nauseous subjects are unlikely to show memory improvements and because it is possible that high doses of cholinesterase inhibitors can actually block cholinergic transmission (Koelle, 1975), a second study was done with a lower dose of physostigmine administered by intravenous infusion over one hour (Davis, Mohs, Tinklenberg, Hollister, Pfefferbaum, & Kopell, 1978).

The test procedures presented in Table 12-1 were administered to 19 young adult males during the infusion of saline and during the infusion of 1 mg of physostigmine. Prior to the start of both infusions, methscopolamine, an anticholinergic that does not cross the blood-brain barrier, was given to minimize physostigmine's peripheral effects. Short-term memory functions were evaluated with the digit-span task and Sternberg's (1969) memory-scanning task. Performance on both tasks was nearly identical on the two test days, which indicated that the drug had little or no

effect on short-term memory. Retrieval from long-term memory was tested by having subjects try to recall, during the infusion, a list of 15 concrete nouns on which they received two learning trials prior to the infusion. Figure 12-1 presents the number of words recalled in this task. On the two preinfusion learning trials, recall scores were nearly identical on physostigmine and saline days. During the infusion, subjects were able to recall more words on physostigmine days than on saline days, although the difference was significant only at 80 minutes after the start of the infusion. At least two explanations are possible for the larger difference at 80 minutes than at 30 minutes after the start of the infusion. One is that the dose of physostigmine was more appropriate at 80 minutes than at 30 minutes. Deutsch's (1971) studies with animals suggest a second possibility—that physostigmine's effects on retrieval depend on the age of the memory trace. At the present time we cannot distinguish between these possibilities.

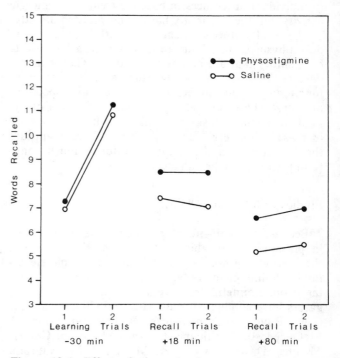

Figure 12-1. Effect of physostigmine on retrieval. Average number of words recalled on a test of retrieval in the low-dose physostigmine study. (From "Physostigmine: Improvement of Long-Term Memory Processes in Normal Subjects" by K. L. Davis, R. C. Mohs, J. R. Tinklenberg, L. E. Hollister, A. Pfefferbaum, and B. S. Kopell, *Science*, 1978, *201*, 272–274. Copyright 1978 by the American Association for the Advancement of Science. Reprinted by permission.)

Physostigmine's effects on learning were tested by having subjects learn a list of 20 nouns from a single semantic category during each infusion. Figure 12-2 presents the number of words recalled on this test. Subjects recalled more words in the physostigmine condition than in the saline condition. An analysis of variance demonstrated that this difference was highly significant. An experiment by investigators at the National Institute of Mental Health (NIMH) demonstrated similar improvement in learning produced by a low dose of the cholinergic agonist arecoline (Sitaram, Weingartner, & Gillin, 1978b). The NIMH study also found reliable individual differences in susceptibility to the effects of drugs acting on the cholinergic system. Specifically, it was found that the subject's improvement when given arecoline was positively correlated with the impairment produced when those same subjects were given scopolamine. Furthermore, the improvement produced by arecoline was inversely related to baseline memory performance. At present there is no satisfactory explanation for these differences. One reasonable hypothesis is that they are due to individual differences in baseline central cholinergic activity, but the possibility has not been tested directly.

The results of experiments with both high- and low-dose physostigmine indicate that this drug has effects on memory that are biphasic with dose. That is, a low dose of the drug can improve some aspects of memory functioning, while higher doses impair all aspects of memory. The results also give some indication of the kinds of memory tasks most likely to be improved by increased cholinergic activity. Specifically, it appears that the storage and retrieval of information in long-term memory can be enhanced.

Studies with Choline Chloride

Because the half-life of physostigmine or arecoline in plasma is only about 30 minutes (Koelle, 1975), these drugs are not very useful for the chronic elevating of cholinergic activity. In the search for a long-acting cholinomimetic drug, we and several other investigators have conducted trials with oral choline chloride (e.g., Boyd, Graham-White, Blackwood, Glen, & McQueen, 1977; Etienne, Gauthier, Johnson, Collier, Mendis, Dastoor, Cole, & Muller, 1978; Sitaram, Weingartner, Caine, & Gillin, 1978a). Choline is the precursor from which acetylcholine is synthesized in the tissues. It is normally obtained in the diet, and increases in dietary choline have been shown to increase brain acetylcholine concentrations in rats (Cohen & Wurtman, 1976; Haubrich, Wang, Clody, & Wedeking, 1975). The results of four studies done in our laboratory are summarized in Table 12-2. Two

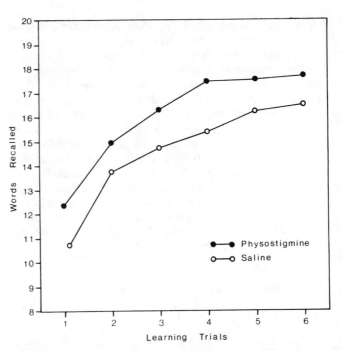

Figure 12-2. Effect of physostigmine on storage. Average number of words recalled on a test of learning in the low-dose physostigmine study. (From "Physostigmine: Improvement of Long-Term Memory Processes in Normal Subjects" by K. L. Davis, R. C. Mohs, J. R. Tinklenberg, L. E. Hollister, A. Pfefferbaum, and B. S. Kopell, *Science*, 1978, *201*, 271–274. Copyright 1978 by the American Association for the Advancement of Science. Reprinted by permission.)

studies involved young adults who had participated in the low-dose physostigmine study (Davis, Mohs, Tinklenberg, Hollister, Pfefferbaum, & Kopell, 1980), and two involved nondemented adults over 55 years of age (Mohs, Davis, Tinklenberg, Hollister, Yesavage, & Kopell, 1979). In all four studies subjects were given memory tests similar to those that we found sensitive to the effects of physostigmine. Both 2- and 4-gm doses were administered four times per day (QID). In none of the four studies was there a statistically significant difference between choline and placebo conditions on either learning or retrieval tests. Only at the lower dose was there even a trend toward better performance in the choline condition. One intriguing result emerged when we used only the data from those subjects involved in both the present study and our previous study with low doses of physostigmine. For those subjects it was possible to calculate performance differences between physostigmine and saline conditions for the physostigmine study, and between choline and placebo conditions for the choline studies. Correlating these differences, we found that subjects who improved most on physostigmine tended to show decreased per-

Table 12-2 Summary of Studies With Choline Chloride

Subjects	No. days of drug treatment	Dose (in gm/QID)	Effect		
			Learning	Retrieval	Correlation
Young adults from physostigmine study ($n = 13$)	3	4	none	none	negative with physostigmine
Young adults from physostigmine study ($n = 9$)	3	2	none	none	positive with physostigmine
Nondemented elderly ($n = 8$)	7	4	none	none	—
Nondemented elderly ($n = 11$)	21	2	none	none	—

formance when they were given 16 gm of choline per day and increased performance when they were given 8 gm of choline per day. In the absence of a statistically reliable drug effect on average performance, these correlations can only be regarded as suggestive that a population exists in whom choline could produce a significant improvement in performance. These findings are consistent with the results from the NIMH studies, which reported reliable individual differences in response to drugs acting on the cholinergic system (Sitaram et al., 1978b). At present, however, we would not even know how to select the subjects most likely to show a response to choline or any cholinergic drug.

Physostigmine in Elderly Patients

Since we were unable to demonstrate a substantial effect of choline on memory in most subjects, we have resumed our studies with physostigmine and are now testing elderly patients, some demented and some not. These studies attempt to deal with the problems of drug dose and individual differences that not only complicated our previous studies but could even make the results of a trial in elderly patients uninterpretable. As our previous studies have shown, physostigmine improves memory only in a fairly narrow low-dose range, while higher doses cause severe memory impairments. Furthermore, it is possible that the dose that produces maximum improvement may vary across subjects.

Evidence that elderly subjects vary considerably in their response to cholinomimetics comes from a series of studies on young and aged monkeys by Bartus (1979; see also Chapter 11 in this volume). Initially he gave each animal an extensive series of baseline memory tests so that the normal variability in memory performance could be determined for each animal. He then administered several doses of physostigmine and constructed dose-response curves for individual animals. For young monkeys, memory performance

improved at low doses but was impaired at high doses, just as we found in our studies with human subjects. For aged animals, however, dose-response curves were considerably more variable. Some aged animals did not improve at any dose, and for others the dose that produced maximum improvement varied from .0025 mg/kg to .04 mg/kg, a much greater range than was found for young animals.

These results have clear implications for the design of clinical trials to evaluate the effects of cholinomimetics in elderly patients. They indicate that the dose of physostigmine that improves memory performance in one patient could actually impair performance in another. Consequently, a study involving only one drug dose could show no effect on average performance, even if the drug caused substantial changes in individual subjects. To circumvent this difficulty we test each patient at four doses of physostigmine that cover the range of doses over which improvements might be expected to occur. To ensure that any improvement over placebo is not simply a reflection of random variation in performance, we then replicate the dose that produces the best performance along with the saline dose.

A second problem in these studies arises because there are substantial differences in baseline cognitive abilities among elderly patients. Tasks that are relatively easy for nondemented elderly subjects are often incomprehensible to patients with Alzheimer's disease. In addition, patients with Alzheimer's disease often differ substantially from one another in their cognitive abilities. Presumably, these differences result from the progressive nature of Alzheimer's disease, and a patient's cognitive abilities depend on the extent of the neuropathological changes that have occurred (Roth, 1955; Tomlinson et al., 1970). Because there are differences in baseline abilities, it is difficult to develop a single set of memory tests that are appropriate for evaluating the effects of cholinomimetic drugs in all patients. The difficulty can be illustrated by the results presented in Table 12-3 from three patients with Alzheimer's disease and a group of normal elderly patients. Each person was given three memory tests involving storage and retrieval of information in long-term memory, and the digit-span task to assess the capacity of short-term memory. On the picture-recognition test subjects first studied 12 pictures and then were asked to identify the studied pictures when they were presented along with 12 new pictures. The word-recognition test used similar study and test procedures; 12 high-frequency words were used as study items and as distractor items on the recognition test. Subjects responded *yes* to identify words previously shown, and *no* for new (distractor) words. Word recall was measured with a free-recall task in which subjects were presented with a list of 20 high-frequency nouns, at the rate of 1 word per 2 seconds and were then asked to recall the entire list.

As Table 12-3 indicates, the picture-recognition test was extremely simple for normal subjects, but two of three Alzheimer's patients consistently made errors, while the third usually obtained a perfect score. On the word-recognition test normal subjects usually obtained perfect scores while two of three Alzheimer's patients rarely scored above chance (12 of 24). The third Alzheimer's patient made some errors but consistently scored above chance. On a test of word recall, none of the Alzheimer's patients was able to recall any words, while normal elderly subjects recalled an average of about 12 words from a 20-word list. These results indicate that none of these tests would be an appropriate measure of drug effects on memory in all of these patients. For Alzheimer's patients the word-recall task was so difficult that even with considerably improved memory capabilities they might not be able to recall any words. Conversely, the recognition tasks are so simple for nondemented subjects that they could suffer

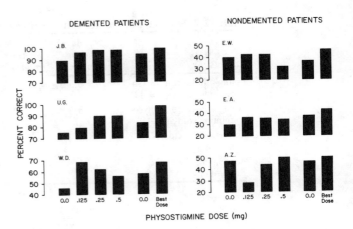

Figure 12-3. Average percentages correct on a test of storage into long-term memory for three demented and three nondemented patients tested during six infusions of physostigmine and saline. Results from the initial infusions of four doses given in randomized order are presented at the left of each panel. At the right of each panel are results obtained when saline and the dose of physostigmine that produced the best learning performance were replicated. Nondemented patients were given a word-recall task, and demented patients were given a picture-recognition task.

considerable memory impairment before performance on these tasks would begin to decline.

To be useful for evaluating drug effects, a test should be easy enough for patients to be able to demonstrate some learning and memory functioning but difficult enough so that the subject makes some errors (Mohs & Davis, 1979). This ensures that the test can measure both improvements and decrements due to the drug. Our own current strategy is to select such a test for each patient after a series of baseline measures are taken. In practice, one or more of the tests shown in Table 12-3 appear to be appropriate for most patients.

Memory-test results from six patients who received six infusions of physostigmine and saline are presented in Figure 12-3. The results from these patients are also reported in Davis, Mohs, and Tinklenberg (1979). Three of the patients were nondemented females, two were males with Alzheimer's disease, and one was a demented male with Huntington's disease. Huntington's is an inherited disease characterized by progressive loss of movement control and dementia; relative cholinergic underactivity has been implicated in this disorder (Davis et al., 1976a; Klawans & Rubovits, 1972). Initially, each patient was given memory tests during infusions of saline and during infusions of .125 mg, .25 mg, and .5 mg of physostigmine administered at a constant rate over 30 minutes. The order of infusions was randomized and all testing was double

Table 12-3 Memory-Test Results for Demented and Nondemented Elderly

Group	No. obser- vations	Average score (and range)			
		Digit span	Word recall	Word recognition	Picture recognition
Demented elderly					
Mr. A.	4	1.25 (1–2)	0 (0–0)	12.0 (11–13)	17.75 (15–21)
Mr. B	4	3.0 (2–4)	0 (0–0)	11.0 (11–11)	17.75 (16–20)
Mr. C	4	3.0 (2–4)	0 (0–0)	15.25 (13–19)	23.25 (22–24)
Normal elderly	15	6.0 (4–6)	10.7 (8–14)	23.8 (22–24)	24.0 (24–24)

blind. The tests given each patient were determined by the patient's baseline cognitive ability. For the nondemented patients a 24-word free-recall task was used to assess learning, while for the demented patients a recognition-memory test for 12 pictures was used. After the fourth infusion an investigator who had no knowledge of the drug conditions selected the day on which the best learning performance occurred. The dose given on that day and the placebo infusion were then replicated. The scores in Figure 12-3 are the percentages correct averaged across three trials for each patient.

During the initial four infusions, the dose that produced the best memory performance varied across patients, but no patient performed best on placebos. From our previous studies with young adults, we would expect to see individual dose-response functions looking like at least a portion of an inverted U. That is, we expect a subject's performance to improve steadily up to an optimal dose of physostigmine and then to level off or to decline at higher doses. We would not observe a high-dose decrement if the subject's best dose were at least as high as our maximum dose. What our previous results would not lead us to expect would be dose-response functions that show decreased performance at low doses and improved performance at high doses. At least five patients show a dose-response function consistent with the inverted U hypothesis. One patient (A. Z.) appears to show a decrement at the .125- and .25-mg doses, followed by an improvement at the .5 mg dose. We have no way of explaining this dose-response pattern other than to assume that some uncontrolled variables, such as the patient's motivational state, were having a greater effect on performance than was physostigmine. When the best dose and the saline infusion were replicated, all patients performed better during the physostigmine infusion than during the saline infusion.

Discussion

Memory Improvement by Cholinomimetics

Our studies with physostigmine in young adults demonstrate that cholinomimetics can improve memory performance at low doses but impair memory at high doses. Preliminary results from a study of physostigmine's effects in demented and nondemented elderly patients suggest that similar results can be obtained in these populations. It appears, however, that the dose of physostigmine that produces the maximum improvement is subject to greater individual variation in an elderly population than in healthy young adults.

Trials with two doses of oral choline chloride in both young and elderly adults did not demonstrate any significant effects on memory. The most plausible explanation for these negative results is that although oral choline does raise concentrations of acetylcholine in the brain, it may not increase the rate of transmission at cholinergic synapses (Jenden, 1979; Wurtman & Growdon, 1979). Another possibility is that choline increases transmission only in the striatum, a brain region not directly involved in memory functioning (Jenden, 1979). Although cholinergic neurons are distributed throughout the brain, a reasonable hypothesis is that cholinergic involvement in memory functioning is mediated primarily by the hippocampus. Cholinergic neurons are abundant in the hippocampus (Lewis & Shute, 1978), and neuropathological studies indicate that the loss of cholinergic activity in Alzheimer's patients is most pronounced in the hippocampus (Bowen et al., 1976; Davies & Maloney, 1976). In addition, it is known that patients with hippocampal lesions are unable to store new information in long-term memory (Milner, 1970). Presumably, an agent that is effective in alleviating the memory deficit in Alzheimer's patients would do so by increasing cholinergic activity in the hippocampus.

Specificity of Cholinergic Effects

Our results are consistent with the view that cholinergic mechanisms are involved primarily in a specific aspect of memory functioning, namely, the storage of information in long-term memory. The distinction between short- and long-term memory is an essential feature of many current psychological theories of memory (e.g., Anderson & Bower, 1973; Atkinson & Shiffrin, 1968, 1971; Baddeley, 1976) and has been supported by studies of patients with hippocampal lesions (Milner, 1970; Warrington & Weiskrantz, 1973). These theories assume that the human memory system comprises two functionally distinct memory stores. Short-term memory is a limited-capacity store used to hold small amounts of information for limited periods of time, while long-term memory is a store of essentially unlimited capacity where information is stored permanently. Our results with physostigmine, as well as the results of previous studies with anticholinergic drugs, indicate that cholinergic activity mediates the storage of information in long-term memory. Anticholinergics impair the learning of information that exceeds the capacity of short-term memory but have no measurable effect on tasks, such as digit span, that measure the capacity of short-term memory (Drachman, 1977; Peterson, 1977). Physostigmine also has no effect on tasks involving only short-term memory but, when given in a low dose, enhances learning of information that exceeds the capacity of short-term memory (Davis et al., 1978). Both anticholinergics and cholinomimetics have much smaller effects on retrieval of information from long-term memory (Davis et al., 1978; Drachman, 1977). Results of studies with animals suggest that improvements in retrieval will occur only for relatively weak memory traces (Deutsch, 1971; Deutsch & Rogers, 1979). In humans there have been no direct tests of the hypothesis that cholinergic drug effects on retrieval depend on the strength of the memory trace.

A potential source of confusion in comparing results from studies of cholinergic drug effects in humans and animals is the different terminology used by researchers in these two areas to describe memory performance. In this chapter we have used the term *short-term memory* to designate a memory store of limited capacity used to hold information for short periods of time. The term is used in a similar way by most other researchers.

In some instances, particularly among researchers who use animals as subjects, *short-term memory* is used to refer to any memory process that occurs over a short period of time. For example, the delayed-response paradigm used by Bartus, Fleming, and Johnson (1978) to assess cholinergic and other drug effects is usually referred to as a short-term memory paradigm. In this paradigm an animal is shown a display with an array of food wells. Initially the display is out of the animal's reach. A stimulus, such as a light, indicates which food well contains a reward. Then after a delay of variable duration, the animal is allowed to open one of the trays. The probability of choosing the rewarded tray correctly decreases as the delay increases. In addition, cholinergic drugs affect performance in this task when responses are delayed but not when animals are allowed to respond immediately. Since the maximum delay is usually less than 60 seconds, these results have been called effects on short-term memory. However, according to most theories of short-term memory, any delay would enable some storage of information in long-term memory, and as the delay increased, performance would be more likely to depend on information stored in long-term memory (Atkinson & Shiffrin, 1968, 1971; Baddeley, 1976).

The paradigm is analogous, in this respect, to the Brown-Peterson paradigm (Peterson & Peterson, 1959) in which humans are asked to recall a consonant trigram after a delay during which they must perform another task. Recall of the trigram decreases rapidly as the delay interval is increased from 0 to 60 seconds. Two-store models of memory assume that this decrease is due to the rapid loss of information from short-term memory (Atkinson & Shiffrin, 1968, 1971; Baddeley, 1976) and that, as the delay increases, recall depends primarily on the amount of information

stored in long-term memory. This analysis indicates that results obtained by Bartus (1979) on the effects of cholinergic drugs in monkeys are not inconsistent with our view that cholinergic transmission is involved primarily in the storage of information beyond the capacity of short-term memory.

Interactions with Other Neurochemical Systems

Acetylcholine does not, of course, exist in isolation from other neurotransmitters and neuromodulators. The cholinergic system is intimately connected with other neurotransmitter systems and with the neuroendocrine system. In all likelihood some of the effects of cholinergic manipulations on memory are mediated by neurochemical changes other than those at cholinergic synapses. At present, investigators have only started to explore these interconnections. However, some preliminary information is available on the interactions between acetylcholine and some other neurochemical mechanisms thought to be involved in age-related memory change.

Evidence from neuroendocrine studies indicates that the release of vasopressin is under cholinergic control. Nicotine, which stimulates the nicotinic but not the muscarinic receptors of the cholinergic system, causes the release of vasopressin when given intravenously (Cadnapaphornchai, Boykin, Berl, McDonald, & Schrier, 1974) or when injected directly into the ventricles (Castro de Souza & Silva, 1977). In animal models of learning and memory, vasopressin has been shown to improve both storage and retrieval of information (see e.g., Chapter 14 of this volume and de Wied, Bohus, Gispen, Urban, & van Wimersma Greidanus, 1978). These results suggest that some of the effects of cholinergic drugs on memory may be secondary to their effects on the release of vasopressin. To our knowledge no studies have addressed this question directly.

There are also connections between the cholinergic system and the brain's opiate system. Cholinomimetics, including physostigmine, enhance the analgesic effects of morphine and other opiates (see Sitaram & Gillin, 1979). Naloxone, an opiate antagonist, stimulates release of acetylcholine in guinea pig ileum (Sitaram & Gillin, 1979). Administration of naloxone has also been shown to affect memory storage processes in animals, although the effects differ for young and old animals (see Chapter 13 of this volume). These results suggest that changes in cholinergic transmission are often accompanied by changes in the activity of opiate receptors and that these opiate effects may play a role in memory storage and retrieval. However, the relations between these two systems have not been explored in sufficient detail to warrant any specific hypothesis about their interaction in memory processes.

REFERENCES

Anderson, J. R., & Bower, G. H. *Human associative memory*. Washington, D.C.: V. H. Winston, 1973.

Atkinson, R. C. & Shiffrin, R. M. Human memory: A proposed system and its control processes. In K. W. Spence & J. T. Spence (Eds.), *The psychology of learning and motivation: Advances in research and theory* (Vol. 2). New York: Academic Press, 1968.

Atkinson, R. C., & Shiffrin, R. M. The control of short-term memory. *Scientific American*, 1971, *225*, 82–90.

Baddeley, A. D. *The psychology of memory*. New York: Basic Books, 1976.

Bartus, R. T. Physostigmine and recent memory: Effects in young and aged nonhuman primates. *Science*, 1979, *206*, 1087–1089.

Bartus, R. T., Fleming, D., & Johnson, H. R. Aging in the rhesus monkey: Debilitating effects on short-term memory. *Journal of Gerontology*, 1978, *33*, 858–871.

Bowen, D. M., Smith, C. B., White, P., & Davison, A. N. Neurotransmitter-related enzymes and indices of hypoxia in senile dementia and other abiotrophies. *Brain*, 1976, *99*, 459–496.

Bowen, D. M., Spillane, J. A., Curzon, G., Meier-Ruge, W., White, P., Goodhardt, J. J., Iwangoff, P., Davison, A. N. Accelerated ageing or selective neuronal loss as an important cause of dementia? *Lancet*, 1979, *1*, 11–14.

Boyd, W. D., Graham-White, J., Blackwood, G., Glen, I., & McQueen, J. Clinical effects of choline in Alzheimer senile dementia. *Lancet*, 1977, *2*, 711.

Cadnapaphornchai, P., Boykin, J. L., Berl, T., McDonald, K. M., & Schrier, R. W. Mechanism of effect of nicotine on renal water excretion. *American Journal of Physiology*, 1974, *227*, 1216–1220.

Castro de Souza, E. M., & Silva, M. R. E. The release of vasopressin by nicotine: Further studies on its site of action. *Journal of Physiology*, 1977, *265*, 297–311.

Cohen, E. L., & Wurtman, R. J. Brain acetylcholine: Control by dietary choline. *Science*, 1976, *191*, 561–562.

Davies, P., & Maloney, A. J. F. Selective loss of central cholinergic neurons in Alzheimer's disease. *Lancet*, 1976, *2*, 1403.

Davis, K. L., Hollister, L. E., Barchas, J. D., & Berger, P. A. Choline in tardive dyskinesia and Huntington's disease. *Life Sciences*, 1976, *19*, 1507–1516. (a)

Davis, K. L., Hollister, L. E., Overall, J., Johnson, A., and Train, K. Physostigmine: Effects on cognition and affect in normal subjects. *Psychopharmacology*, 1976, *51*, 23–27. (b)

Davis, K. L., Mohs, R. C., Tinklenberg, J. R. Enhancement of memory in the elderly by physostigmine. *New England Journal of Medicine*, 1979, *301*, 946.

Davis, K. L., Mohs, R. C., Tinklenberg, J. R., Hollister, L. E., Pfefferbaum, A., & Kopell, B. S. Physostigmine: Improvement of long-term memory processes in normal subjects. *Science*, 1978, *201*, 272–274.

Davis, K. L., Mohs, R. C., Tinklenberg, J. R., Hollister, L. E., Pfefferbaum, A., & Kopell, B. S. Cholinomimetics and memory: The effect of choline chloride. *Archives of Neurology*, 1980, *37*, 49–52.

Deutsch, J. A. The cholinergic synapse and the site of memory. *Science*, 1971, *174*, 788–794.

Deutsch, J. A., & Rogers, J. B. Cholinergic excitability and memory: Animal studies and their clinical implications. In K. L. Davis & P. A. Berger (Eds.), *Brain acetylcholine and neuropsychiatric disease*. New York: Plenum Press, 1979.

de Wied, D., Bohus, B., Gispen, W. H., Urban, I., & van Wimersma Greidanus, Tj. B. Hormonal influences on motivational learning, and memory processes. In E. J. Sachar (Ed.), *Hormones, behavior, and psychopathology*. New York: Raven Press, 1976.

Drachman, D. A. Memory and cognitive function in man: Does the cholinergic system have a specific role? *Neurology*, 1977, *27*, 783–790.

Drachman, D. A., & Leavitt, J. Human memory and the cholinergic system. *Archives of Neurology*, 1974, *30*, 113–121.

Etienne, P., Gauthier, S., Johnson, G., Collier, B., Mendis, T., Dastoor, D., Cole, M., & Muller, H. F. Clinical effects of choline in Alzheimer's disease. *Lancet*, 1978, *1*, 508–509.

Haubrich, D. R., Wang, P. F. L., Clody, D. E., & Wedeking, P. W. Increase in rat brain acetylcholine induced by choline or deanol. *Life Sciences*, 1975, *17*, 975–980.

Janowsky, D. S., El-Yousef, M. K., Davis, J. M., & Sekerke, H. J. Parasympathetic suppression of manic symptoms by physostigmine. *Archives of General Psychiatry*, 1973, *28*, 542–547.

Jenden, D. J. The neurochemical basis of acetylcholine precursor loading as a therapeutic strategy. In K. L. Davis & P. A. Berger (Eds.), *Brain acetylcholine and neuropsychiatric disease*. New York: Plenum Press, 1979.

Klawans, H. L., Rubovits, R. Central cholinergic-anticholinergic antagonism in Huntington's chorea. *Neurology*, 1972, *22*, 107–116.

Koelle, G. B. Anticholinesterase agents. In L. S. Goodman & A. Gilman (Eds.), *The pharmacological basis of therapeutics* (4th ed.). New York: Macmillan, 1975.

Lewis, P. R., & Shute, C. C. D. Cholinergic pathways in CNS. In L. L. Iversen, S. D. Iversen, & S. H. Snyder (Eds.), *Handbook of psychopharmacology. Chemical pathways in the brain* (Vol. 9). New York: Plenum Press, 1978.

McGeer, E., & McGeer, P. L. Age changes in the human for some enzymes associated with metabolism of catecholamines, GABA, and acetylcholine. In J. M. Ordy & K. R. Brizzee (Eds.), *Neurobiology of aging*. New York: Raven Press, 1976.

Milner, B. Memory and the medial temporal regions of the brain. In K. H. Pribram & D. E. Broadbent (Eds.), *Biology of memory*. New York: Academic Press, 1970.

Mohs, R. C., & Davis, K. L. Cholinomimetic drug effects on memory in young and elderly adults. In A. I. M. Glen &

L. J. Whalley (Eds.), *Alzheimer's disease: Early recognition of potentially reversible deficits*. London: Churchill Livingston, 1979.

Mohs, R. C., Davis, K. L., Tinklenberg, J. R., Hollister, L. E., Yesavage, J. A., & Kopell, B. S. Choline chloride treatment of memory deficits in the elderly. *American Journal of Psychiatry*, 1979, *136*, 1275–1277.

Perry, E. K., Tomlinson, B. E., Blessed, G., Bergman, K., Gibson, P. H., & Perry, R. H. Correlation of cholinergic abnormalities with senile plaques and mental test scores in senile dementia. *British Medical Journal*, 1978, *2*, 1457–1459.

Peterson, R. C. Scopolamine induced learning failures in man. *Psychopharmacology*, 1977, *52*, 283–289.

Peterson, L. R., & Peterson, M. J. Short-term retention of individual verbal items. *Journal of Experimental Psychology*, 1959, *58*, 193–198.

Roth, M. The natural history of mental disorder in old age. *Journal of Mental Science*, 1955, *101*, 281–301.

Roth, M., & Hopkins, B. Psychological test performance in patients over 60. Senile psychosis and affective disorders of old age. *Journal of Mental Science*, 1953, *99*, 439–453.

Sitaram, N., & Gillin, J. C. Acetylcholine: Possible involvement in sleep and analgesia. In K. L. Davis & P. A. Berger (Eds.), *Brain acetylcholine and neuropsychiatric disease*. New York: Plenum Press, 1979.

Sitaram, N., Weingartner, H., Caine, E. D., & Gillin, J. C. Choline: Selective enhancement of serial learning and encoding of low imagery words in man. *Life Sciences*, 1978, *22*, 1555–1560. (a)

Sitaram, N., Weingartner, H., & Gillin, J. C. Human serial learning: Enhancement with arecoline and impairment with scopolamine correlated with performance on placebo. *Science*, 1978, *201*, 274–276. (b)

Sternberg, S. Memory scanning: Mental processes revealed by reaction-time experiments. *American Scientist*, 1969, *57*, 421–457.

Tomlinson, B. E., Blessed, G., & Roth, M. Observations on the brains of demented old people. *Journal of Neurological Sciences*, 1970, *11*, 205–242.

Warrington, E. K., & Weiskrantz, L. An analysis of short-term and long-term memory deficits in man. In J. A Deutsch (Ed.), *The physiological basis of memory*. New York: Academic Press, 1973.

Wurtman, R. J., & Growdon, J. H. Dietary control of central cholinergic activity. In K. L. Davis & P. A. Berger (Eds.), *Brain acetylcholine and neuropsychiatric disease*. New York: Plenum Press, 1979.

Robert A. Jensen, Rita B. Messing, Joe L. Martinez, Jr., Beatriz J. Vasquez, and James L. McGaugh

CHAPTER
13

Opiate Modulation of Learning and Memory in the Rat

Under some conditions, aged rats show a deficit in memory processes. These deficits appear to be task specific and are best seen following one-time-only learning experiences or when memory consolidation time is limited. Treatment with the opiate-receptor antagonist naloxone, given after training, produces memory facilitation in young rats but impairs retention in aged male rats. This effect may occur because aged male rats have decreased opiate-receptor densities in the frontal poles, anterior cortex, and striatum and also increased binding affinity in the frontal poles. A research strategy that combines behavioral and pharmacological studies with measurements of receptor properties may yield important new information about the neurobiological bases of memory impairment in the aged.

It is clear that one of the most debilitating consequences of advancing age is a decline in the efficiency of memory processes. This decline is seen in only a small percentage of the population, but in those people that are affected, the effects are often severe and prevent efficient functioning in the environment. However, until recently, the task of identifying those neurobiological changes that underlie impaired memory in the aged has received little attention from behaviorally oriented researchers. Yet the need for data about the physiological and psychological bases of senile dementia will become progressively more acute in the coming years because an ever-increasing proportion of our population will be comprised of people over 60 years of age and potentially at risk.

The disorders of memory associated with behavioral senescence are generally not recognized as national health problems, in contrast to diseases such as cancer or cardiovascular disorders; but in terms of the number of affected individuals, and economic, social, and emotional costs, behavioral senescence will surely come to be recognized by the public as a major problem in health care. Therefore, gaining an understanding of the neurobiological processes underlying age-related impairments in memory and cognitive functioning must be a primary goal of researchers in the 1980s. Only with a foundation of knowledge provided by basic research can effective and rationally based therapies for the disorders of memory associated with advanced age be developed.

The decline in the efficiency of memory processes in the aged has been extensively documented, and a number of excellent articles and reviews describing many aspects of this deficit are available (Botwinick, 1973; Botwinick & Storandt, 1974; Craik, 1977; Strehler, 1976; Talland, 1968; Thatcher, 1976). The magnitude of the decline in memory processes in the aged is not uniform and is dependent not only on which aspect of memory function is being measured but also on the type of assessment techniques employed. It appears that memories in the aged may be more vulnerable to interference effects (Broadbent & Heron, 1962; Inglis & Caird, 1963). However, studies that have attempted to directly measure differences between young and aged subjects in their susceptibility to retroactive and proactive interference have not yielded clear findings (Arenberg & Robertson-Tchabo, 1977).

From a psychological standpoint, the nature of the memory deficit in the aged is unclear. It can be interpreted as being a decrease in mental flexibility, a deficit in information-processing power, a storage deficit, a retrieval deficit, or a simple decrease in effective mental capacity (Craik, 1977). It is also quite possible that it results from a variety of interactions among several of these explanations.

The picture is similarly unclear when viewed from a psychobiological standpoint. With very few exceptions, the chronologies of age-related changes in the brain are unknown. There are at least three hypothetical time courses that could result in the pathologies of aging. First, these pathologies may be the result of a sudden decline in some measure from a stable level of function that was maintained throughout adulthood. Reports of sudden declines of this type are common: for example, the decrease in neuron number seen in the aged mouse (Johnson & Erner, 1972) and the aged human (Brody, 1970). Second, behavioral senility could result from biological processes that proceed to a limiting optimal level and then recede from that plateau to a new and lower level. This would result in an inverted U-shaped function for that psychological or neurobiological characteristic. This type of process has been observed in a number of physiological and behavioral measures, and processes that mature late in development appear to decline first with age. For example, in several species the capacity for efficient inhibitory (passive) avoidance learning appears later in development than the capacity for active avoidance learning (Davis & Jensen, 1976; Riccio, Rohrbaugh, & Hodges, 1968), while deficits in inhibitory avoidance performance appear in old rats at an age at which active avoidance behavior is still comparable to that of young adult animals (Jensen, Martinez, McGaugh, Messing, & Vasquez, 1980). A third possibility is that many of the manifestations of advanced age are simply the result of normal developmental trends that continue in a linear fashion throughout life. This interpretation implies that aging results from the steady accumulation of the effects of normal development, effects that become deleterious with time.

Although the causes of aging are not well understood, a large number of well-documented changes occur in the nervous system with advancing age (Brizzee, Harkin, Ordy, & Kaack, 1975; Brody & Vijayashankar, 1977; Corsellis, 1976; Scheibel, Lindsay, Tomiyasu, & Scheibel, 1975; Scheibel & Scheibel, 1976). Some of these changes, of course, must be related to impaired memory. However, most of the alterations seen in the brains of patients with senile dementia are also seen in aged people with normal levels of intellectual function. Thus, brain functions associated with memory and cognition appear to be organized in a sufficiently redundant way to permit normal behavior in many people, even after fairly extensive anatomical deterioration. There is a fairly well-defined pattern of neurological change in patients with senile dementia of the Alzheimer's type, but even these patients show occasional periods of lucidity in the less advanced stages of the disease, which indicates that the deficit may not be irreversible. The loose correlation between the anatomical and behavioral sequelae of aging, coupled with the difficulties of performing manipulative neurobiological research and exploratory pharmacological studies on aged humans, make the development and use of appropriate animal models of aging imperative within the next few years.

In our laboratory, and in many others as well, the senescent rodent is proving its value as a model for behavioral, physiological, and pharmacological research. The aged rat and the aged human both show similar deficits in a number of neural systems. However, none of the reported anatomical, physiological, or chemical changes seen in the senescent rat have yet been causally related to behavioral deficits.

There is a substantial body of behavioral data characterizing the age-related changes in memory processes in experimental animals. In one early study Oliverio and Bovet (1966) reported that acquisition of maze learning and shuttle-box avoidance is impaired in young (21-day-old) and mature (6-month and 1-year-old) mice compared to young-adult (60-day-old) mice. The older animals showed greater forgetting between the daily training sessions. Similarly, Freund and Walker (1971) reported that the rate of acquisition of shuttle-box avoidance learning was faster in 3- to 5-month-old mice than it was in mice aged 9 to 15 months. However, many behavioral studies with aged rodents have yielded findings that permit no clear conclusions to be drawn when the results are compared with those of other studies. For example, in experiments that employed avoidance tasks or maze-learning situations, some investigators reported no change in performance with increased age (Birren, 1962; Botwinick, Brinley, & Robbin, 1963; Kay & Sime, 1962; Wolthuis, Knook, & Nickolson, 1976), while others reported performance deficits in aged animals that became more substantial with increased task complexity (Doty, 1966; Goodrick, 1972; Verzar-McDougall, 1957). Some of the problems in reconciling these disparate results may be due to the substantial differences in the ages of the animals employed as aged subjects in these studies. Clearly, though, more research is needed to adequately characterize the differences in memory processes between mature and aged rodents.

During the last several years, research in our laboratory has focused on gaining an understanding of the neurobiological bases of age-related changes in memory processes. One aspect of this research centered around the development of an animal model of behavioral senility. This model has provided the basis for studies of pharmacological treatments that alter memory processes in these animals. In the development of this model, a variety of behavioral tests were used to assess differences in retention between adult and aged animals.

Early in this research program, Gold and McGaugh (1975) found that old rats show deficits in retention of an inhibitory-avoidance task compared to young adult animals. The aged rats displayed rapid forgetting, and when a low-intensity footshock was used (.2 mA, .4 sec), the retention deficit in these animals was apparent as early as 6 hours after training. This finding of impaired retention in aged Fischer 344 rats has been confirmed by researchers in other laboratories (Brizzee & Ordy, 1979; Ordy, Brizzee, Kaack, & Hansche, 1978) as well as in Sprague-Dawley rats (McNamara, Benignus, Benignus, & Miller, 1977) and random-bred rats (Rigter, Martinez, & Crabbe, in press). Taken together, these findings indicate that the impaired retention of an inhibitory-avoidance response in aged rats is a general phenomenon not dependent on genetic factors.

Recently we replicated and extended this basic finding in a study directed at characterizing the differences in retention between young and senescent rats. In the first phase of this research we used an inhibitory-avoidance task with three footshock levels, animals of both sexes and varying ages, and three different training-testing intervals. Data obtained from 3-month-old and 15-month-old male Fischer (F344) rats are shown in Table 13-1. In this study a 500-μA footshock was not sufficient to produce measurable retention in either the young or old animals. The 1000-μA shock produced good learning in both the young and old animals, but the 15-month-old rats showed a significant retention deficit compared to the young animals at the 7-day train-

ing-testing interval. The 1500-μA shock produced strong learning in all groups, and forgetting was not evident even at the 7-day training-retention testing interval. Although the 15-month-old rats used in this study cannot be considered to be senescent, their impaired retention performance suggests that accelerated forgetting appears at a younger age than some other measures of aging.

In a second study, an active avoidance task was employed with 3- and 15-month-old rats. Each rat was given 8 training trials and then a retention test of another 8 trials 1, 3, or 7 days later. In contrast to the findings observed with these animals in the inhibitory-avoidance task, the older rats generally showed better performance than young rats at all retention-test intervals. A summary of these findings is shown in Figure 13-1. The results of the inhibitory-avoidance study and the active-avoidance study taken together suggest that the memory deficit observed in aged rats is dependent on the nature of the training task and that aging does not produce a uniform impairment in memory processes. An important point here is that only 1 training trial was given in the inhibitory-avoidance task, while 8 training trials were administered in the active-avoidance task. This may indicate that older animals have difficulty with tasks that require that associations be made with a single event. This deficit in retention for one-time-only events is also seen in very young animals, while memories of multitrial events are retained quite well.

It is interesting, in this regard, that familiarization with the experimental apparatus prior to training attenuates the retention deficit of the young animals (Jensen & Davis, 1978). It is possible that prior experience in the apparatus allows the animal to learn something about its environment so that new memories, such as the administration of shock in a particular place, can be encoded more efficiently. Whether the same is also true of the aged animals remains to be determined. However, if this proves to be the case, then it would suggest that the deficit in the aged animals may be one of memory consolidation processes—that is, some memories are simply not encoded well enough to provide adequate retention over time.

The hypothesis of impaired memory-storage processes was further supported in another study performed in this laboratory. This experiment employed a swim-escape task (Birren & Kay, 1958) with young (3-month-old) and aged (24-month-old) male F344 rats. Each rat was placed in a large tub of water in a corner opposite a pole, and latency to climb the pole was recorded. Two training trials a day were given with a 30.0-sec intertrial interval. The results are shown in Figure 13-2. The young animals learned the task in one

Table 13-1 Median Retention Latencies (sec) for the Inhibitory Avoidance Task

Age and shock level	Training-testing interval		
	1-day	3-day	7-day
3-month-old males			
500 μA	19.5 (10)	36.8 (8)	10.8 (10)
1000 μA	600. (10)	600. (9)	600. (11)
1500 μA	600. (10)	495.6 (10)	527.6 (9)
15-month-old males			
500 μA	6.9 (7)	17.7 (6)	6.5 (6)
1000 μA	600. (6)	310.2 (7)	9.1 (7)
1500 μA	386.0 (7)	600. (7)	600. (7)

Note. Numbers in parentheses indicate the sample sizes of each group of rats.

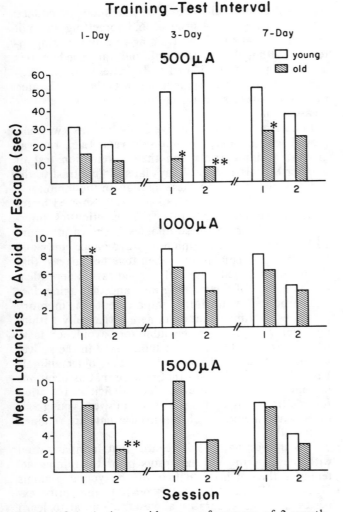

Figure 13-1. Active-avoidance performance of 2-month- and 15-month-old F344 male rats. Each bar represents the mean latencies of 6 animals to escape or avoid the shock on training day (Session 1) and on test day (Session 2) at three different shock levels. Note that the 15-month-old animals were consistently superior to the younger animals in this task (**p < .001; *p < .05).

trial, while the aged rats did not show acquisition until the second day. Again, an impairment in memory-storage processes is indicated by these findings. A similar deficit in acquisition performance with massed training trials in aged rats was previously reported by Doty (1966).

Because shock was used as the motivating stimulus in the active- and inhibitory-avoidance tasks, we felt that it was important to determine whether the observed differences in performance were due to changes in shock sensitivity with age. Neither flinch nor jump thresholds to shock were altered by aging.

When considered as a whole, these findings indicate that memory impairment with age is not general but is task specific. The poor retention performance of the aged rats in the inhibitory-avoidance task and their good retention in the active-avoidance task indicates that the deficit is probably in the memory-storage process itself. The active-avoidance task involves multiple training trials, while the inhibitory-avoidance task employs only a single discrete training trial. The good retention in the well-learned active-avoidance task suggests that the rate of forgetting in the old animals may not be faster than that seen in the young rats. The single training trial of the inhibitory-avoidance task produces poor memory encoding in the aged animals and, therefore, poor retention.

These findings and others raise the question of the nature of the changes in the aging brain that underlie these behavioral deficits. Changes in the number of neurons (Brody, 1976; Corsellis, 1976; Roberts & Goldberg, 1976), alterations in neuronal processes (Scheibel et al., 1975), and hypertrophy of astroglia (Landfield, Rose, Sandles, Wohlstadter, & Lynch, 1977; Tomlinson & Henderson, 1976) have all been well documented. Each of these changes results in a decrease in the capacity of neurons to interact with one another, and some are likely to be the cause of a number of behavioral alterations seen in old age, such as impaired memory.

Behavioral changes in the aged may also be the result of alterations in neurotransmitter metabolism. In the aging brain there are complex patterns of change in neurotransmitter synthesis, metabolism, and postsynaptic receptors. These changes are regionally specific and cannot be accounted for simply by loss of cells or general deterioration. In a very important program of research, McGeer and McGeer (1976) studied the decline with age of a number of neurotransmitter enzymatic systems in humans. They found that enzyme

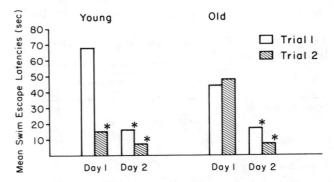

Figure 13-2. Swim-escape performance of young (3-month) and aged (24-month) F344 male rats. Each bar represents the mean escape latency of 7 animals (*p < .05 compared to the first trial).

activities generally decline rapidly from ages 5 to 20 years, and then slowly continue to decrease until age 50, which was the oldest age studied. They reported substantial declines in the activities of tyrosine hydroxylase, dopa decarboxylase, choline acetylase, acetylcholine esterase, and glutamic acid decarboxylase. These decreases occurred in some brain regions but not in others, and the regions where changes were observed were different for the various enzymes. In contrast, the activities of degradative enzymes, such as monoamine oxidase and catechol-o-methyl transferase, appear to increase in aged human brains (for a review, see Domino, Dren, & Giardina, 1978). It should be emphasized that these findings again indicate that aging does not simply produce a generalized neural deterioration; rather, with age, highly specific changes occur in various neural systems.

One area of research that is showing great promise in providing a connection between neuroanatomical deterioration, neurochemical alterations, and behavioral changes in the aged is the investigation of postsynaptic processes. Studies of changes in receptor systems may provide important information in the next decade for a number of reasons. First, changes in postsynaptic receptor systems provide a sensitive and quantitative index of the degree of synaptic deterioration. Second, measures of both receptor number and receptor binding affinity for neurotransmitters and neuromodulators can be obtained. Third, changes in receptor plasticity can be studied. Investigation of changes in receptor plasticity with age may provide evidence of very subtle alterations in membrane properties. Fourth, an abundance of neuropharmacological techniques already available makes it possible to relate changes in postsynaptic receptor systems to specific behaviors. For example, it may be possible to predict differential behavioral responsiveness of old and young animals to various drugs. This can be done if it is known that a particular behavior is at least partly mediated by a specific neurochemical system and if it is also known that there are differences in the receptor properties of this system in old and young animals. In addition, a different pattern of behavioral responses to a given drug in aged animals compared to young animals may well provide information about the neurobiological substrate of that behavior. It is our judgment that this research strategy holds great promise for the years to come.

Recently our laboratory initiated a program of research aimed at investigating changes in opiate receptors and the behavioral responses to opiates of aged rats. We chose to study opioid systems for a number of reasons. First, there is a growing awareness that peptide systems, particularly the opioid peptides, are important in the modulation of behavior and physio-

logical functions, and there is also a large and growing pharmacopoeia, as well as other research tools, available for the study of their functions. Second, although the identification of the endogenous ligands for opiate receptors is relatively recent, there is already more information available on opioid peptides than on other central nervous system peptides. In addition, some of the neuroanatomical loci that mediate their effects are already known. Thus, opiate analgesia is thought to be mediated by receptors in the periaqueductal gray, spinal cord, substantia gelatenosa, and possibly the striatum (Liebeskind, Giesler, & Urca, 1976). In contrast, the medial thalamus and striatum appear to be involved in the expression of opiate tolerance and withdrawal symptoms (Lal, 1975; Teitelbaum, Catravas, & McFarland, 1974), while the nucleus accumbens appears to be involved in the stimulant effects on locomotion of low doses of opiates (Pert & Sivit, 1977). Finally, as further discussed below, forebrain structures, such as the amygdala and the area surrounding the lateral ventricles, appear to be important in mediating the effects of opiates on learning and memory processes.

We initially found that naloxone given to young rats after training enhances retention performance in a one-trial inhibitory-avoidance task (Messing, Jensen, Martinez, Spiehler, Vasquez, Soumireu-Mourat, Liang, & McGaugh, 1979). These results are shown in Figures 13-3 and 13-4. In this study, two injections of naloxone were given, one immediately after training and a second 30 minutes later. We felt that two injections would be necessary because of the relatively short duration of action of naloxone and because memory consolidation occurs over a considerable period of time (McGaugh & Herz, 1972). A single injection of naloxone given immediately after training had no effect. The memory enhancement produced by naloxone is probably mediated by opiate receptor systems because its effect is antagonized by morphine. Further, when given in a single injection immediately after training, morphine in doses of either 1.0 or 3.0 mg/kg impaired retention (Jensen, Martinez, Messing, Spiehler, Vasquez, Soumireu-Mourat, Liang, & McGaugh, 1978). We also demonstrated that naloxone enhances retention in an active-avoidance task. Again, it was necessary to administer two injections of the drug, immediately before training and again 30 minutes later.

It is possible that it was necessary to administer two injections of naloxone because the duration of action of the drug is quite short. However, we made two additional observations that are difficult to explain by this assumption. While a moderate dose of naloxone, administered in two injections, facilitated retention performance in the inhibitory-avoidance task, higher doses had no effect. Even more anomalously, adminis-

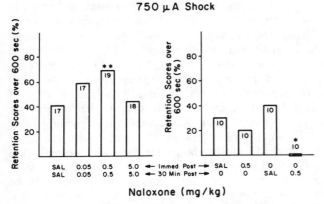

Figure 13-3. percentage ceiling retention latencies of rats given naloxone following training in a one-trial inhibitory-avoidance task (750-μA shock). Rats were injected (1 ml/kg, ip) and tested for retention 24 hours later. Numbers inside the bars are the numbers of animals in each group. Left panel: Rats were given either naloxone or .9% saline (SAL) in equally divided doses immediately after training and again 30 minutes later. Right panel: Rats were given naloxone or saline, either immediately or 30 minutes after training. (*p < .05; **p < .01, compared to the appropriate saline-injected control group.)

tration of naloxone in a single injection, given 30 minutes after training, impaired retention performance in this task. Therefore, the basis of the two-injection effect is not yet understood.

We next compared the effect of naloxone on memory in old and young F344 rats (Jensen et al., 1980; Vasquez, Jensen, Messing, Martinez, Rigter, & McGaugh, 1979). Old (26 month) and young (5 month) rats were trained on two tasks: inhibitory avoidance (500 μA; .5-sec footshock) and swim escape. Naloxone was given intraperitoneally (ip) in two equally divided doses, immediately after training and 30 minutes later, in both tasks. When retention was tested, we found that naloxone improved performance of the inhibitory-avoidance and swim-escape tasks in the young animals, while it impaired retention performance in the aged rats (see Figures 13-5 and 13-6). Determination of flinch and jump thresholds to electric shock showed that naloxone did not influence either shock sensitivity or reactivity in either age group, which indicates that these effects on retention are unlikely to be due to drug-induced changes in shock sensitivity.

In a recent replication and extension of these studies with the inhibitory-avoidance task, we found that the direction of the naloxone effect is dependent on the level of footshock. With a higher footshock (750 μA; .5 sec), naloxone enhanced retention performance in both young and aged rats. It thus appears that the response of aged rats to naloxone in the memory tasks

may differ from that of young animals in some conditions. These findings again emphasize that the direction of the memory-modulatory effects of naloxone are dependent on a number of factors such as age, footshock level, or injection schedule (Messing et al., 1979).

These findings are consistent with our hypothesis (Jensen et al., 1980) that changes in learning and memory with age are best observed when animals are subjected to a behavioral challenge, such as the one-trial inhibitory-avoidance task, or challenge by a pharmacological agent, such as naloxone, coupled with a one-trial task. The idea that pharmacological challenge may be a useful research strategy for future studies of the behavioral biology of aging is supported by several lines of research evidence. For example, aged rats show a marked reduction in brain acetylcholine activity after moderate doses of amphetamine, an effect not seen in younger animals (Vasko, Domino, & Domino, 1974). In addition, chlorpromazine administered shortly after avoidance training retards retention performance in both mature and aged rats. However, if injection of chlorpromazine is given 2 hours after training, only aged animals are affected (Doty & Doty, 1964). In another study (Doty & Doty, 1966), amphetamine enhanced the retention performance of aged rats when given 1 or 4 hours after training. However, amphetamine was ineffective when given to young rats at these long intervals. In each of these studies, the difference in memory processes between young and old animals was not apparent until

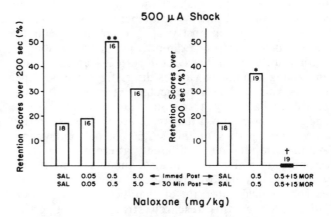

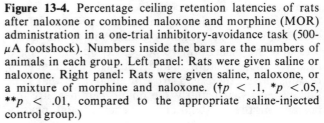

Figure 13-4. Percentage ceiling retention latencies of rats after naloxone or combined naloxone and morphine (MOR) administration in a one-trial inhibitory-avoidance task (500-μA footshock). Numbers inside the bars are the numbers of animals in each group. Left panel: Rats were given saline or naloxone. Right panel: Rats were given saline, naloxone, or a mixture of morphine and naloxone. (†p < .1, *p < .05, **p < .01, compared to the appropriate saline-injected control group.)

the animals were challenged with a pharmacological agent.

Concurrent with our behavioral experiments focusing on the effects of opiate drugs on learning and memory in young and aged animals, we are investigating differences in both opiate-receptor binding affinity and the number of opiate receptors in various brain regions of young and aged rats. We hope that these studies may shed light on the neurobiological substrate underlying the differences in effects of opiate drugs in young and old animals. Thus far we have completed measurements of the binding of tritiated dihydromorphine in a number of brain regions of young and aged male and female rats. These data show changes in both numbers and apparent affinities of opiate receptors with age, but these changes are regionally specific. In addition, there are differences between males and females. In aged female rats (Messing, Vasquez, Spiehler, Martinez, Jensen, Rigter, & McGaugh, 1980), there are decreases in receptor densities in the thalamus and midbrain. Also, young female rats exhibit two apparent binding sites for ^{3}H-dihydromorphine in the anterior cortex, while the old animals show only a single binding site. No differences were observed in other brain areas.

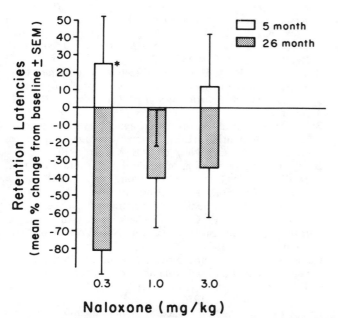

Figure 13-5. Mean percentage of change from baseline for young (5-month) and aged (26-month) rats that received one of three doses of naloxone immediately after inhibitory-avoidance training. At the .3-mg/kg dose, naloxone facilitated retention performance of the young animals, while it impaired the performance of the aged animals. (*$p < .05$, young-old difference.)

In the male rats, the situation is quite different (unpublished data from our laboratory). Receptor densities are reduced in old rats in the frontal poles, anterior cortex, and striatum. In addition, in the frontal poles, perhaps owing to some compensatory mechanism, the opiate binding sites of the aged male rats had a higher affinity for dihydromorphine than the younger animals. No differences were observed in opiate-receptor densities or binding affinities in any other brain regions of the aged male rat.

Thus the question arises whether there may be a relation between altered memory-modulatory effects of opiates and altered opiate receptors in aged rats. We feel that it is too early to give an affirmative answer to this question or to spell out the nature of the relation. However, we do think that a connection between the differences in the effects of opiate drugs in young and aged animals and the alterations in opiate receptor properties is very likely, and that one possible relationship in particular deserves further investigation.

Several laboratories, in addition to ours, have reported memory-modulatory effects of opiate alkaloids, opioid peptides, and opiate receptor antagonists. (For a review, see Messing et al., 1979). Two reports are particularly important. First, Gallagher and Kapp (1978) reported that nanomolar doses of the opiate-receptor agonist levorphanol, administered after training into the amygdalae of rats, impaired inhibitory-avoidance retention performance. On the other hand, naloxone enhanced retention, an effect that was blocked by levorphanol. In contrast to the findings of Gallagher and Kapp, Belluzzi and Stein (1977) reported that somewhat higher doses of morphine than those used by Gallagher and Kapp infused into the lateral ventricles after inhibitory-avoidance training improved retention performance. They suggested, as did Gallagher and Kapp, that the effect of these doses on memory was mediated by opiate receptors because it was antagonized by systemic administration of naloxone.

Thus there appear to be at least two anatomically distinct loci in the cerebral hemispheres in which opiate administration modifies learning and memory processes. These are the amygdala, where opiate agonists impair and antagonists enhance retention performance, and a periventricular area, where agonists enhance performance. Therefore, it may be reasonable to speculate that different brain regions mediate the memory enhancing or impairing actions of the systemically administered naloxone and morphine that we observed in young and aged rats. Thus, in the aged rats, regional changes in opiate-receptor density and affinity could alter the net effect of naloxone. The basis of the differences in opiate-receptor binding between aged male and female rats is not clear. It is possible that endocrine influences may be acting to produce different patterns of aging in males and females, but again, research is needed to clarify this question.

This research is still in its formative stages. Yet we feel that our strategy of relating changes with age in the properties of postsynaptic systems to the differential effects of pharmacological challenge on learning and memory offers excellent prospects for gaining an understanding of the biological bases of behavioral senility. As noted earlier, there is an increasing need for fundamental knowledge about the behavioral and neural biology of aging, for without this kind of research it is unlikely that effective therapies for the disorders of memory can be readily developed to meet the immediate needs of this decade.

REFERENCES

Arenberg, D., & Robertson-Tchabo, E. A. Learning and aging. In J. E. Birren & K. W. Schaie (Eds.), *Handbook of the psychology of aging.* New York: Van Nostrand Reinhold, 1977.

Belluzzi, J. D., & Stein, L. Enkephalin- and morphine-induced facilitation of long-term memory. *Society for Neuroscience Abstracts,* 1977, *3,* 230.

Birren, J. E. Age differences in learning a two-choice water maze by rats. *Journal of Gerontology,* 1962, *17,* 207–213.

Birren, J. E., & Kay, H. Swimming speed of the albino rat: I. Age and sex differences, *Journal of Gerontology,* 1958, *13,* 374–377.

Botwinick, J. *Aging and behavior.* New York: Springer, 1973.

Botwinick, J., Brinley, J. F., & Robbin, J. S. Learning and reversing a four-choice multiple Y-Maze by rats of three ages. *Journal of Gerontology,* 1963, *18,* 279–282.

Botwinick, J., & Storandt, M. *Memory-related functions and age.* Springfield, Ill.: Charles C Thomas, 1974.

Brizzee, K. R., Harkin, J. C., Ordy, J. M., & Kaack, B. Accumulation and distribution of lipofuscin, amyloid, and senile plaques in the aging nervous system. In H. Brody, D. Harman, & J. M. Ordy (Eds.), *Aging: Vol. 1. Clinical, morphologic, and neurochemical aspects in the aging nervous system.* New York: Raven Press, 1975.

Brizzee, K. R., & Ordy, J. M. Age pigments, cell loss and hippocampal function. *Mechanisms of Ageing and Development,* 1979, *9,* 143–162.

Broadbent, D. B., & Heron, A. Effects of a subsidiary task on performance involving immediate memory in younger and older men. *British Journal of Psychology,* 1962, *53,* 189–198.

Brody, H. Structural changes in the aging nervous system. In H. T. Blumenthal (Ed.), *Interdisciplinary topics in gerontology (Vol. 7).* New York: S. Karger, 1970.

Brody, H. An examination of cerebral cortex and brainstem aging. In R. D. Terry & S. Gershon (Eds.), *Neurobiology of aging.* New York: Raven Press, 1976.

Brody, H., & Vijayashankar, N. Anatomical changes in the nervous system. In C. E. Finch & L. Hayflick (Eds.), *Handbook of the biology of aging.* New York: Van Nostrand Reinhold, 1977.

Corsellis, J. A. N. Some observations on the Purkinje cell population and on brain volume in human aging. In R. D. Terry & S. Gerschon (Eds.), *Neurobiology of aging.* New York: Raven Press, 1976.

Craik, F. I. M. Age differences in human memory. In J. E. Birrin & K. W. Schaie (Eds.), *Handbook of the psychology of aging.* New York: Van Nostrand Reinhold, 1977.

Davis, J. L., & Jensen, R. A. Developmental aspects of active and passive avoidance learning in the cat. *Developmental Psychobiology,* 1976, *5,* 175–179.

Domino, D. F., Dren, A. T., & Giardina, W. J. Biochemical

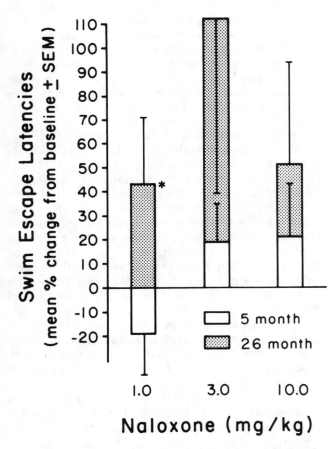

Figure 13-6. Mean percentage of change from baseline for young (5-month) and aged (26-month) rats that received one of three doses of naloxone immediately after training in the swim-escape task. A dose of 1.0 mg/kg naloxone impaired the retention performance of the aged animals (longer latencies), while it facilitated the performance of the young animals. (*p < .05, young-old difference.)

and neurotransmitter changes in the aging brain. In M. A. Lipton, A. DiMascio, & K. F. Killam (Eds.), *Psychopharmacology: A generation of progress.* New York: Raven Press, 1978.

Doty, B. A. Age differences in avoidance conditioning as a function of distribution of trials and task difficulty. *The Journal of Genetic Psychology*, 1966, *109*, 249–254.

Doty, B. A., & Doty, L. A. Effect of age and chlorpromazine on memory consolidation. *Journal of Comparative and Physiological Psychology*, 1964, *57*, 331–334.

Doty, B. A., & Doty, L. A. Facilitative effects of amphetamine on avoidance conditioning in relation to age and problem difficulty. *Psychopharmacologia*, 1966, *9*, 234–241.

Freund, G., & Walker, D. W. The effect of aging on acquisition and retention of shuttle box avoidance in mice. *Life Sciences*, 1971, *10*, 1343–1349.

Gallagher, M., & Kapp, B. S. Opiate administration into the amygdala: Effects on memory processes. *Life Sciences*, 1978, *23*, 1973–1978.

Gold, P. E., & McGaugh, J. L. Changes in learning and memory during aging. In J. M. Ordy & K. R. Brizzee (Eds.), *Neurobiology of aging*. New York: Plenum Press, 1975.

Goodrick, C. L. Learning by mature-young and aged Wistar albino rats as a function of test complexity. *Journal of Gerontology*, 1972, *27*, 353–357.

Inglis, J., & Caird, W. K. Modified digit spans and memory disorder. *Disorders of the Nervous System*, 1963, *24*, 46–50.

Jensen, R. A., & Davis, J. L. Inhibitory avoidance learning in young rats effected by previous familiarization with the apparatus. *Bulletin of the Psychonomic Society*, 1978, *11*, 247–248.

Jensen, R. A., Martinez, J. L., Jr., McGaugh, J. L., Messing, R. B., & Vasquez, B. J. Psychobiology of aging. In G. J. Maletta & F. J. Pirozzolio (Eds.), *The aging nervous system*. New York: Praeger, 1980.

Jensen, R. A., Martinez, J. L., Jr., Messing, R. B., Spiehler, V. R., Vasquez, B. J., Soumireu-Mourat, B., Liang, K. C., & McGaugh, J. L. Morphine and naloxone alter memory in rats. *Society for Neuroscience Abstracts*, 1978, *4*, 260.

Johnson, H. A., & Erner, S. Neuron survival in the aging mouse. *Experimental Gerontology*, 1972, *7*, 111–117.

Kay, H., & Sime, M. E. Discrimination learning with old and young rats. *Journal of Gerontology*, 1962, *17*, 75–80.

Lal, H. Narcotic dependence, narcotic action and dopamine receptors, *Life Sciences*, 1975, *17*, 483–496.

Landfield, P. W., Rose, G., Sandles, L., Wohlstadter, T. C., & Lynch, G. Patterns of astroglial hypertrophy and neuronal degeneration in the hippocampus of aged, memory-deficient rats. *Journal of Gerontology*, 1977, *32*, 3–12.

Liebeskind, J. C., Giesler, C. J., & Urca, G. Evidence pertaining to an endogenous mechanism of pain inhibition in the central nervous system. In Y. Zotterman (Ed.), *Sensory functions of the skin in primates with special reference to man*. Oxford: Pergamon Press, 1976.

McGaugh, J. L., & Herz, M. J. *Memory consolidation*. San Francisco: Albion, 1972.

McGeer, E., & McGeer, P. L. Neurotransmitter metabolism in the aging brain. In R. D. Terry & S. Gerschon (Eds.), *Neurobiology of aging*. New York: Raven Press, 1976.

McNamara, M. C., Benignus, G., Benignus, V. A., & Miller, A. T. Active and passive avoidance learning in rats as a function of age. *Experimental Aging Research*, 1977, *3*, 3–16.

Messing, R. B., Jensen, R. A., Martinez, J. L., Jr., Spiehler, V. R., Vasquez, B. J., Soumireu-Mourat, B., Liang, K. C., & McGaugh, J. L. Naloxone enhancement of memory. *Behavioral and Neural Biology*, 1979, *27*, 266–275.

Messing, R. B., Vasquez, B. J., Spiehler, V. R., Martinez, J. L., Jr., Jensen, R. A., Rigter, H., & McGaugh, J. L. ^{3}H-dihydromorphine binding in brain regions of young and aged rats. *Life Sciences*, 1980, *26*, 921–927.

Oliverio, A. & Bovet, D. Effects of age on maze learning and avoidance conditioning of mice. *Life Sciences*, 1966, *5*, 1317–1324.

Ordy, J. M., Brizzee, K. R., Kaack, B., & Hansche, J. Age differences in short-term memory and cell loss in the cortex of the rat. *Gerontology*, 1978, *24*, 276–285.

Pert, A., & Sivit, C. Neuroanatomical focus for morphine and enkephalin-induced hypermotility. *Nature*, 1977, *265*, 645–647.

Riccio, D. C., Rohrbaugh, M., & Hodges, L. A. Developmental aspects of passive and active avoidance learning in rats. *Developmental Psychobiology*, 1968, *1*, 108–111.

Rigter, H., Martinez, J. L., Jr., & Crabbe, J. C., Jr., Forgetting and other behavioral manifestations of aging. In D. Stein (Ed.), *Psychobiology of aging*. Amsterdam: Elsevier, in press.

Roberts, J., & Goldberg, P. B. Some aspects of the central nervous system of the rat during aging. *Experimental Aging Research*, 1976, *2*, 531–542.

Scheibel, M. E., Lindsay, R. D., Tomiyasu, U., & Scheibel, A. B. Progressive dendritic changes in aging human cortex. *Experimental Neurology*, 1975, *47*, 392–403.

Scheibel, M. E., & Scheibel, A. B. Structural changes in the aging brain. In R. D. Terry & S. Gerschon (Eds.), *Neurobiology of aging*. New York: Raven Press, 1976.

Strehler, B. L. Introduction: Aging and the human brain. In R. D. Terry & S. Gerschon (Eds.), *Neurobiology of aging*. New York: Raven Press, 1976.

Talland, G. *Human aging and behavior: Recent advances in research and theory* (Vol. 1). New York: Academic Press, 1968.

Teitelbaum, H., Catravas, G. N., & McFarland, W. L. Reversal of morphine tolerance after medial thalamic lesions in the rat. *Science*, 1974, *185*, 449–451.

Thatcher, R. W., Electrophysiological correlates of animal and human memory. In R. D. Terry & S. Gerschon (Eds.), *Neurobiology of aging*. New York: Raven Press, 1976.

Tomlinson, B. E., & Henderson, G. Some quantitative cerebral findings in normal and demented old people. In R. D. Terry & S. Gershon (Eds.), *Neurobiology of aging*. New York: Raven Press, 1976.

Vasko, M. R., Domino, L. E., & Domino, E. F. Differential effects of d-amphetamine on brain acetylcholine in young, adult, and geriatric rats. *European Journal of Pharmacology*, 1974, *27*, 145–147.

Vasquez, B. J., Jensen, R. A., Messing, R. B., Martinez, J. L., Jr., Rigter, H., & McGaugh, J. L. Naloxone impairs memory in aged rats. *Pharmacologist*, 1979, *21*, 269.

Verzar-McDougall, E. J. Studies in learning and memory in ageing rats. *Gerontologia*, 1957, *1*, 65–85.

Wolthuis, O. L., Knook, D. L., & Nickolson, V. J. Age-related acquisition deficits and activity in rats. *Neuroscience Letters*, 1976, *2*, 343–348.

Ralph L. Cooper, M. Colleen McNamara, W. Gary Thompson, and Gail R. Marsh

CHAPTER
14
Vasopressin Modulation of Learning and Memory in the Rat

Shock-motivated passive-avoidance and conditioned flavor-aversion procedures were used to compare the performance of young adult and old rats. Old animals were found to be impaired in both these test conditions. Systemic treatment with lysine vasopressin improved the old rats' performance when administered one hour prior to the retention test in the passive-avoidance task. Vasopressin treatment was also found to improve the performance of old rats by slowing the rate of extinction in the conditioned flavor-aversion procedure. These results suggest that age-dependent changes in endogenous vasopressin synthesis and/or secretion underlie some of the behavioral deficits observed in the older animal.

A number of studies have shown that as rodents approach old age, their performance on a variety of learning and memory tasks deteriorates (for reviews, see Arenberg & Robertson-Tchabo, 1977; Elias 1978; Elias & Elias, 1977). These studies have been primarily descriptive in nature and provide limited insight into the mechanisms underlying such behavioral change. However, significant advances have been made in our understanding of the neurochemical processes that mediate behavior in the young adult animal (Barchus, Akil, Elliot, Holman, & Watson, 1978; Gispen, van Ree, & de Wied, 1977; Prange, Nemeroff, Lipton, Breeze, & Wilson, 1978). In particular, the pituitary hormones adrenocorticotropin (ACTH) and vasopressin, as well as a number of related peptide fragments, have been shown to significantly affect the performance of adult animals on a wide variety of tasks. Our interest in one of these hormones, vasopressin, was stimulated by reports of age-dependent changes in

the ability of the old animal to synthesize and secrete this hormone (Turkington & Everitt, 1976); such observations suggest that some behavioral impairments may be related to decreased availability of vasopressin in old animals.

In this chapter we briefly review studies that demonstrate vasopressin's role in regulating specific behavioral responses in young adult animals. We then summarize recent studies of aged rats in our laboratory which suggest that treatment of the aged animal with synthetic vasopressin can reverse some age-dependent changes in behavior.

Vasopressin: Its Involvement in Regulation of Behavior

Vasopressin (or antidiuretic hormone) is a posterior pituitary hormone involved in the conservation of body water by reducing the amount of water excreted by the kidney. Vasopressin has also been reported to elevate blood pressure in mammals; however, there is no satisfactory evidence that it normally plays any role in the regulation of vasculature tone or blood pressure, since more vasopressin is required for this effect on blood pressure than is normally released by the intact animal (Turner & Bagnara, 1976).

This research was supported by National Institute on Aging (NIA) Research Grant AG00566 to Ralph L. Cooper and by NIA Training Grant AG00029. The authors acknowledge the skillful technical and editorial assistance of Karen Wacome and Susan Dakin.

Two forms of vasopressin are found among mammals: arginine vasopressin (AVP), the most widely distributed form, and lysine vasopressin (LVP), identified to date only in pig posterior pituitary (Turner & Bagnara, 1976). Considerable evidence has accumulated suggesting that in addition to the above effects, vasopressin is involved in the regulation of behavior by its action on the central nervous system (CNS). Decreasing the amount of endogenous vasopressin by removing the entire pituitary (hypophysectomy) or only the posterior lobe (posterior lobectomy) causes a number of behavioral deficits in the young adult rat (de Wied & Gispen, 1977). In such animals, treatment with vasopressin alone ameliorates impaired learning of a shuttlebox-avoidance response (Bohus, Gispen, & de Wied, 1973), increases resistance to extinction of shuttlebox- and pole-jump avoidance behavior (de Wied, 1965, 1971), and prolongs the retention of passive-avoidance behavior (Bohus, Ader, & de Wied, 1972).

Additional evidence for this hormone's involvement in memory and learning processes comes from studies using the Brattleboro rat. These animals have hereditary diabetes insipidus because they lack the ability to synthesize vasopressin, and they demonstrate marked memory deficits in both active- and passive-avoidance procedures (Bohus, van Wimersma Greidanus, & de Wied, 1975; de Wied, Bohus, Urban, & van Wimersma Greidanus, 1975). Subcutaneous treatment with low doses of vasopressin restores the behavior of these rats to that of the controls. Infusion of antivasopressin serum into the lateral ventricle of normal rats produces the same severe disturbances in passive-avoidance behavior found in the Brattleboro rat (van Wimersma Greidanus, Dogterom, & de Wied, 1975). Infusion of the antiserum either 30 minutes before or immediately after a single learning trial in a passive-avoidance task results in a loss of the passive-avoidance response in animals tested 24 or 48 hours after the learning trial. Similar results are found when the antiserum is injected 1 hour prior to the retention test, whereas injection from 6 to 8 hours after the initial learning trial has no effect on subsequent retention scores (van Wimersma Greidanus & de Wied, 1976).[1] These findings would argue that memory

processes, rather than learning itself, may have been disturbed, since the critical timing of the infusion reveals restricted periods during which the effects can be reproduced. The impaired retention seen in animals that have been treated with a memory-blocking agent is usually interpreted as retrograde amnesia (McGaugh, 1966).

Further supporting the argument that vasopressin is involved in both memory consolidation and recall, Rigter, Elgertse, and Van Riezen (1975) found that vasopressin, when administered either prior to acquisition or prior to the retention test, antagonizes carbon-dioxide-induced amnesia in a passive-avoidance task. Similar results have been reported for puromycin-induced amnesia in the mouse (Lande, Flexner, & Fleyner, 1972) and for pentylenetetrazol-induced amnesia in the rat (Bookin & Pfeifer, 1977). In their study, Bookin and Pfeifer argue that since it is unlikely that memory consolidation could be influenced 23 hours after the injection of the amnesic agent, vasopressin acts on recall rather than on memory consolidation.

Although the studies discussed above have used aversively motivated responses, this hormone's effect is not restricted to tasks involving aversive conditioning. Hostetter, Jubb, and Kozlowski (1977) showed that vasopressin injections given 20 minutes before each experimental session prolonged extinction of a food-reinforced T-maze discrimination task, and Bohus (1977) found that treatment with vasopressin after each acquisition session prolonged extinction of a sexually rewarded T-maze task.

Age-Dependent Changes in Behavior: Possible Role of Vasopressin

The investigation of age-dependent changes in learning and memory is fraught with methodological problems that are safely ignored (or readily controlled) by those who restrict their investigations to the young adult animal. For example, How does one equate young and old animals with respect to motivation? Do young and old animals perceive the task stimuli equally? Could age differences in general activity levels influence the outcome, and is the health of the old animals a factor? These problems have been reviewed in detail elsewhere (Arenberg & Robertson-Tchabo, 1977; Elias & Elias, 1977) and are mentioned here because they underscore the need to consider a wide range of factors that are thought to be of minimal importance and can be readily controlled in investigations restricted to young adult animals.

For example, several studies have shown that aged animals are deficient in aversively motivated tasks. A

---

[1] The fact that intraventricular infusion of the antiserum to vasopressin will disrupt memory processes substantiates the argument that the behavioral effects of this hormone are mediated by its action on the brain and not through changes in pituitary-adrenal function, water balance, or blood pressure. This argument is also supported by studies using the vasopressin analog desglycinamide lysine vasopressin (DG-LVP): Treatment with DG-LVP has the same behavioral effects as treatments with LVP, yet DG-LVP is devoid of pituitary-adrenal, water balance, or pressor effects (Lande, Witter & de Wied, 1971).

primary concern with regard to such age differences in avoidance learning is the possibility that the threshold for the aversive stimulus (usually shock) is altered by age. Shock thresholds have been reported to increase, to decrease, and not to change with age. Paré (1969) reported a decreased sensitivity to shock in old rats and attributed this change to a possible age-related decrease in skin conductivity or a loss of sensory receptors. Furchtgott and Wechkin (1962) found no correlation between shock threshold and speed of acquisition of an avoidance response in young and old rats, while Gordon, Scobie, and Frankl (1978) reported a series of studies that demonstrated increased sensitivity to shock (i.e., lower threshold) in older rats. Arenberg and Robertson-Tchabo (1977) point out, however, that under certain circumstances, the performance of young and old rats on shock-motivated tasks can be compared.

Such conditions were met in a series of studies by Doty (1966a, 1966b). Using "simple" and "discrimination" avoidance tasks, Doty found no differences between young and old rats in the number of trials to criterion in either task, indicating that the shock stimulus was equally effective in both age groups. However, age differences were noted when young and old animals were tested in a delayed-discrimination avoidance task. In the standard discrimination task, the rat was presented with a light in one of two escape compartments. If the rat failed to move into the lighted compartment within 5 sec, it received a 10-sec footshock. In the delayed-discrimination avoidance task, the light was presented in one of the compartments for 5 sec, but the animal was prevented from moving to the "safe" compartment for 3 sec after the light was turned off. Thus, at a constant shock intensity, the performance of young and old rats differed only when the task was made more complex by forcing the animal to hold pertinent information for a short period before acting.

We must also consider the possibility that studies using active avoidance are confounded by differences in activity levels of the different age groups. The old animals may have lower activity levels during the shock or a greater tendency to freeze during the avoidance period. If the older rat had a greater tendency to freeze or was less active, one would expect that in a passive-avoidance situation, performance would be superior to that of younger animals. This is not the case: Old animals perform worse than young adult animals in a passive-avoidance task (McNamara, Benignus, Benignus, & Miller, 1977; see also Chapter 13 of this volume). In summary, studies employing aversive-conditioning techniques demonstrate that the old animal is deficient on such tasks and that this deficiency is not due simply to an impaired ability to perceive the task stimulus or to a reduction in general activity level.

Shock-Motivated Passive Avoidance

Recent studies in our laboratory support the conclusion that aged animals are deficient in aversively motivated tasks. Using a one-trial step-through passive-avoidance procedure, we found differences in performance between young and old rats (Thompson & Cooper, 1979). Each rat was placed in a well-illuminated, white-walled compartment; a sliding door opened to provide access to an unlit, black-walled compartment. The compartments shared the same grid floor. During the acquisition trial, young and old animals entered the dark compartment shortly after the door was opened (median latencies: young = 11.6 sec, old = 18.3 sec). The door was then closed, and each animal was given a .5-sec footshock and returned to its home cage. A retention test was given 1 day or 1 week after the initial acquisition trial. The retention test consisted of once again placing each animal in the illuminated compartment and recording its latency to enter the dark compartment. If the animal did not enter the dark compartment within 5 minutes, it was removed and given a score of 300 sec.

In the first study, three different shock intensities were used; the results of the 1-week retention test are shown in Figure 14-1. With the lowest shock intensity (80 μA), neither young nor old animals avoided the unlit chamber, which suggests that this intensity was below shock-escape threshold for both age groups. With a shock intensity of 250 μA, the retention scores of young and old differed significantly (median latencies: young = 300 sec, old = 29.3 sec; Mann-Whitney U Test, $p < .005$). When a higher intensity footshock (350 μA) was administered, maximal latency scores (300 sec) were attained by both groups.

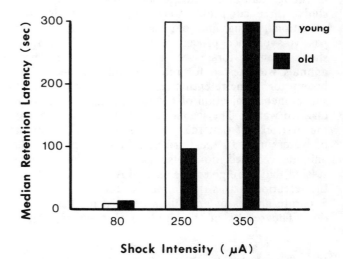

Figure 14-1. Median 1-week retention latencies in young and old rats at different current intensities.

One possible explanation of these data is that older rats do not perceive a given intensity of shock as well as do young rats. However, this interpretation seems unlikely for at least two reasons. First, we found that the intensity of footshock necessary to produce a lifting of the forepaws off the grid (shock-detection threshold) does not differ with age (both groups respond at 80 μA $\pm$ 10 μA) but does appear to be negatively correlated with the rat's body weight regardless of age (heavier rats required lower shock intensities to elicit a behavioral response). Second, the median latency score of old rats tested one day after training with the 250-μA footshock was 300 sec. These findings suggest that the old animals not only perceived the 250-μA shock but also made the association between the dark compartment and the shock.

It appears, therefore, that the impaired performance of the old animals after 1 week was due to a memory deficit. This interpretation is based on the observation that when tested after an interval of 1 day, the young and old animals' retention scores were not different. However, since both young and old animals had reached the maximum latency allowed, it is impossible to know how much longer the animals would have waited before entering the chamber. Had we let the animals remain in the test apparatus longer, the older animals might have entered the darkened chamber sooner than the young.

In an attempt to clarify these results, we performed another study. We reasoned that if a memory deficit was responsible for the impaired performance of the old animals that received the 250-μA footshock, then perhaps treatment with exogenous vasopressin could restore their performance to the level of the young animals. As mentioned above, treatment with LVP 1 hour prior to the retention test increases the retention scores of young adult animals deficient in vasopressin. In our study, three conditions were employed. In the first condition, young and old rats were trained in the passive-avoidance procedure using the 250-μA footshock intensity for .5 sec, as described above. These animals were tested for retention after 1 week. One hour prior to the retention test, the animals received a subcutaneous injection of LVP (.5 μg/kg, dissolved in distilled water). The second condition was the same as the first, except that these animals received injections of water only. In the third condition young and old animals received no footshock during the training session, but were given the same dose of LVP prior to the retention test as the animals in the first condition. Separate groups of animals were used in each condition. The results of this study are shown in Figure 14-2.

The old animals shocked and treated with LVP (Condition 1) had significantly longer retention scores

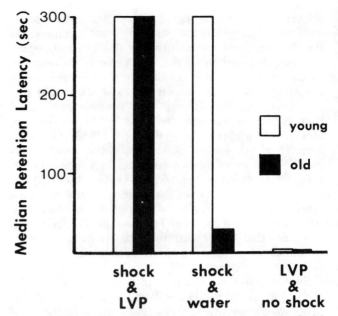

Figure 14-2. Median 1-week retention latencies obtained with rats shocked and treated with lysine vasopressin (LVP) (Condition 1), shocked and treated with water (Condition 2), or not shocked but treated with LVP (Condition 3).

(Mann-Whitney U test, $p < .05$) than did the old animals shocked and treated with water (Condition 2). The median retention score of the old rats in Condition 2 was significantly shorter (Mann-Whitney U test, $p < .05$) than that of the young rats. The latencies of the animals in Condition 3 were short and not different from those observed during the initial exposure to the apparatus. LVP treatment did not alter the median retention score of the young animals, which was maximum (300 sec) in Conditions 1 and 2. The dose of .5 μg/kg LVP used in this study was the most effective dose level found in a series of pilot studies in which young animals received doses of LVP ranging from .25 to 8.75 μg/kg It was noted in those pilot studies that doses higher than 2.5 μg/kg decreased the retention scores. However, some studies have reported improved performance on such tasks following doses of LVP (or DG-LVP) equal to or greater than those used in our studies (Bohus et al., 1972; Bookin & Pfeifer, 1977; Rigter, Van Riezen, & de Wied, 1974).

We view our findings as important for two reasons. First, the reversal of the age difference by LVP treatment supports the hypothesis that the old animal is deficient in memory retrieval. Second, the old animals tested in the passive-avoidance task behave like the Brattleboro rat—which is devoid of vasopressin—and like the young-adult hypophysectomized (or posterior lobectomized) rats that are deficient in vasopressin. Since the ability of the aged rat to synthesize and secrete vasopressin is also impaired, the present findings suggest that the impaired retention of the old animal occurs as a consequence of decreased availability of this posterior pituitary hormone and that this behavioral impairment can be overcome with LVP treatment.

In summary, we found age-dependent changes in the rat's behavior in a passive-avoidance task. This behavioral impairment could be ameliorated by using high footshock intensities, which indicates that the strength of the stimulus affects the subsequent behavior. We also found that the behavioral impairment in old rats could be overcome by treatment with LVP, which indicates that there is also a memory deficit, since old animals can recall this information if provided the appropriate endocrine milieu.

Conditioned Flavor Aversion

In another series of studies, we used the conditioned flavor-aversion procedure (Garcia, Hankins & Rusiniak, 1974) to investigate age differences in behavior. The basic premise of the conditioned flavor-aversion paradigm is that if an animal becomes ill following ingestion of a novel substance, it will ingest less of that substance upon subsequent presentation. In the past, the flavor-aversion procedure has been thought by most investigators to differ in many of its characteristics from traditional shock-induced passive-avoidance procedures. However, Logue (1979), in a detailed review of the literature comparing the flavor-aversion paradigm with traditional learning models, concluded, "In virtually all cases the same principles are sufficient for describing taste aversion and traditional learning data" (p. 289). We find this paradigm desirable for three reasons: (1) it involves a natural behavior (feeding or drinking), (2) the animal must make an association between its external environment (food or water) and internal environment (sickness) in order to maintain internal homeostasis, and (3) the animal's survival depends on accurate use of this information. Thus this paradigm allows evaluation of processes basic to the animal's survival and also an assessment of how such processes may change with age.

In our first study (McNamara & Cooper, 1979b), male rats 3, 6, 10, and 19 months of age were trained with a procedure similar to that described by Carey (1973), which pairs ingestion of a .1% saccharin solution with intraperitoneal injection of amphetamine (.5 mg/kg, ip). (Amphetamine was selected as the averting agent because we were concerned that the usual choice, lithium chloride, might be lethal to the older animals.) During the acquisition phase, the rats were restricted to 30 minutes per day access to either water

or saccharin. Three saccharin-amphetamine pairings were given, spaced 3 days apart. Only water was available on the two interim days. Three days after the last saccharin-amphetamine pairing, the animals were given a 30-minute two-bottle preference test, during which both saccharin and water were presented. On the first day saccharin was presented, saccharin consumption (ml saccharin/100 g of body weight) did not differ significantly among the age groups (Friedman 2-way analysis of variance, $p = .8$) (see Figure 14-3). Throughout the acquisition phase, intake of the saccharin solution decreased in all age groups at a similar rate after each successive amphetamine treatment. Water intake on interim days did not differ across ages for either the control of saccharin-amphetamine paired animals. Three days after the last saccharin-amphetamine pairing, the animals were given a 30-minute two-bottle preference test, during which both saccharin and water were presented. All four groups avoided the saccharin solution equally. Control animals given access

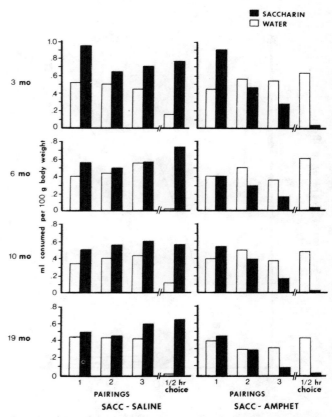

Figure 14-3. Consumption of water or saccharin solution (expressed as ml/100 g of body weight) during three saccharin-amphetamine or saccharin-saline pairings. The ½-hour choice test performed 3 days after the last day of acquisition is also shown at the right of each panel.

to a saccharin solution paired with .9% saline injections during the acquisition period showed a strong preference for the saccharin solution during the 30-minute choice tests.

In contrast to the similar behavior of the age groups during the acquisition phase, the extinction rate of the oldest rats was significantly faster than that of the younger groups. This occurred whether the animals were allowed ad lib access to saccharin and water (Figure 14-4) or were on a restricted access schedule with both fluids available for only 30 minutes per day (Figure 14-5). The restricted schedule resulted in faster extinction of the flavor aversion in all age groups (McNamara & Cooper, 1979a).

It might be argued that the more rapid extinction in the older group was due to age differences in the animals' ability to taste saccharin. However, this explanation is unlikely, because in a subsequent study we presented 3- and 19-month old rats with a series of two-bottle choice tests, pairing water with one of five different saccharin concentrations (.01%, .1%, .2%, 1.0%, and 5.0% solutions), and found the saccharin

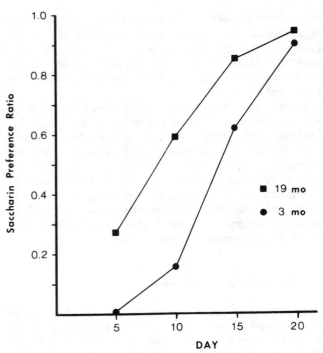

Figure 14-5. Saccharin preference ratios observed in 3- and 19-month-old rats during recovery from a conditioned flavor aversion. In this study the rats were provided restricted (30 minutes) access to saccharin and water each day. Note the difference between the saccharin preference ratios observed on this schedule and those shown in Figure 14-4.

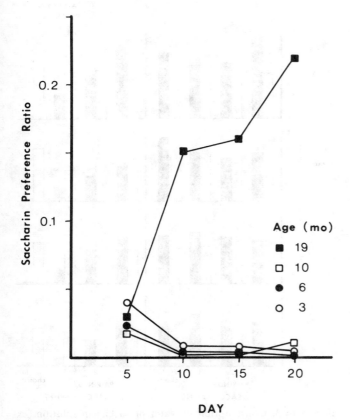

Figure 14-4. Saccharin preference ratios of four age groups during extinction of a conditioned flavor aversion. All rats were provided with 24-hour access to water and saccharin solution.

preference ratio (saccharin solution consumed/saccharin solution plus water consumed) to be the same in both age groups at all concentrations. More important, the two age groups showed their highest preference for saccharin at the .1% concentration. (See Figure 14-6).

Another factor in the faster extinction scores of the older animals during recovery from the flavor aversion might have been that the aversive affects of amphetamine were less severe in the older rats. This also seems unlikely, since old animals are more sensitive to the effects of amphetamine than are young animals (Bender, 1970). In fact, other studies in our laboratory of the anoretic effect of amphetamine in young and old rats demonstrated that the suppression of food intake in the old rat is significantly greater than that observed in young animals following the same dose of amphetamine (.5 or 1.0 mg/kg, injected ip).

Whether age differences in the extinction rate were due to age differences in learning, strength of the memory trace, or ability to recall could not be determined from the study just described. Since saccharin intake during the acquisition phase and the saccharin preference scores during the early recovery period were essentially the same in all age groups, it could be argued that the faster extinction rates in the older animals reflected impaired retention or recall. On the other hand, the strength of aversion (i.e., learning) in the older animals may have been weaker, but because the use of repeated saccharin-amphetamine pairings completely eliminated saccharin consumption in both groups, this "floor effect" in the data may have masked age differences in acquisition of the aversion. To determine which of these possibilities was correct, we performed the following studies.

The hypothesis that some aspect of the retention process was impaired was tested by subjecting old rats (19 months old) to the same aversive conditioning procedure described above (three .1% saccharin-amphetamine pairings). During the recovery phase, half of the group was given a daily two-bottle choice test beginning 24 hours after the last saccharin-amphetamine pairing. The remaining animals were provided with water only (30 minutes per day) for 9 days; beginning on the 10th day, these animals were given a daily two-bottle choice test. The rationale was that if the older animals lost information from memory faster than the younger animals, then after a 9-day delay older animals should drink more saccharin solution than would similar-aged animals on the 1st day of extinction. Contrary to our expectation, the saccharin preference score of these animals after a 9-day wait was essentially the same as that observed in the old animals tested 24 hours after completing the conditioning procedure (Figure 14-7). The course of extinction from that point on essentially paralleled that of the first group. Thus the hypothesis that older animals simply forget information rapidly was not supported. This

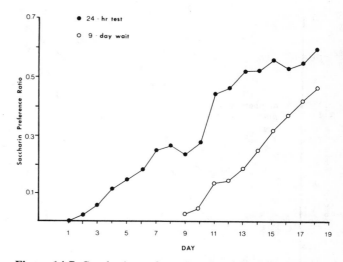

Figure 14-7. Saccharin preference ratios during the recovery from a conditioned flavor aversion for 19-month-old rats tested either 1 day or 9 days after the saccharin-amphetamine pairings.

result parallels the reports in the human literature (Craik, 1977).

We then examined the possibility that age differences in the strength of aversion may underlie the age differences in extinction scores. In this study, young and old rats received only a single .1% saccharin-amphetamine pairing and were provided a daily two-bottle preference test beginning 24 hours later. The extinction rates of both young and old animals in this experiment were significantly faster than in our previous study, in which three saccharin-amphetamine pairings were administered (Figure 14-8). However, as in the previous study, the extinction rate of the old rats was significantly faster than that of the young. This difference was clear in the first preference test: The saccharin preference score of the old rats was twice that of the young, which suggests that the age difference in extinction was most likely due to a difference in the strength of the association that developed in response to the aversive stimulus.

These studies demonstrated differences in performance between young and old animals subjected to a conditioned flavor-aversion procedure. Studies in young adult rats reveal that recovery from a flavor aversion is prolonged if the animals are treated with ACTH or ACTH 4-10 during the recovery period (Rigter & Popping, 1976; Smotherman & Levine, 1978). Because pilot studies in our laboratory revealed that vasopressin treatment of young adult animals may also prolong recovery from a conditioned flavor aversion, the following study was undertaken.

Male rats 3 and 19 months of age were subjected to

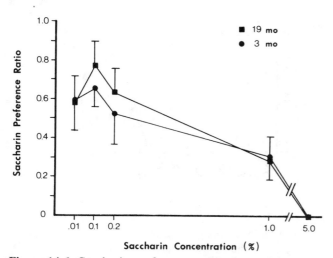

Figure 14-6. Saccharin preference ratios observed in young and old rats with paired presentation of five different saccharin concentrations.

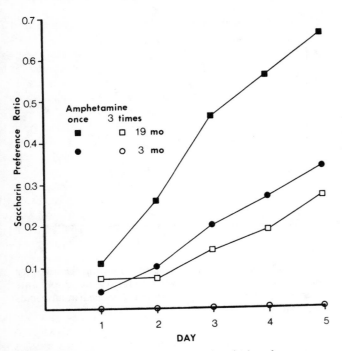

Figure 14-8. Saccharin preference ratios during the recovery from a conditioned flavor aversion for 3- and 19-month-old rats given one of three saccharin-amphetamine pairings.

three saccharin-amphetamine pairings as described above. Starting 3 days after the final pairing, the animals were given a daily two-bottle choice test. Starting on the 5th day, half of the animals in each group received an ip injection of lysine vasopressin (1 µg/kg in .5 cc of distilled water) 1 hour before the two-bottle choice test, while the remaining animals in the group received an injection of water (.5 cc). The injections were repeated every 4th day for 28 days. Figure 14-9 shows the results of this study. As in our earlier study, old control rats showed a faster extinction rate than did young control animals. Vasopressin was found to delay extinction in both young and old animals, compared with their age-matched controls. Comparisons between the old and young vasopressin-treated animals revealed that on the first four treatment days, age differences were eliminated (saccharin consumption in both age groups was minimum). Thereafter, saccharin consumption increased steadily, and subsequent vasopressin treatments were without effect. As a control, the saccharin preference scores of the two age groups were compared on the day before each vasopressin treatment. The saccharin preference scores of the old rats were significantly higher than those of the young on all but Day 16 (the day before the fourth vasopressin treatment).

It should be noted that this dose of vasopressin had no observable effect on water consumption of the

averted animals in either age group, nor did it influence water or saccharin consumption in other non-averted animals. Finally, saccharin-vasopressin pairings on the same schedule used for saccharin-amphetamine pairings did not have averting properties.

We have shown that recovery from a conditioned flavor aversion can be significantly prolonged in both young and old animals by treatment with LVP. More important, the similarity of the saccharin preference scores of the two age groups on the treatment days suggests that the old animals actually benefited more from this treatment than did the young and supports the hypothesis that age-dependent changes in behavior may result in part from age-dependent changes in the availability of vasopressin. Furthermore, the results of

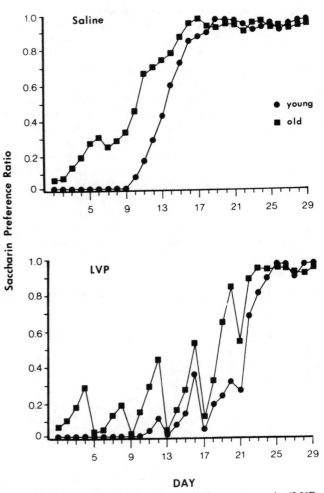

Figure 14-9. The effect of saline or lysine vasopressin (LVP; 1 µg/kg) on the saccharin preference ratios of 3- and 19-month-old rats during the recovery from a conditioned flavor aversion. Vasopressin or saline was injected on the days indicated by the numbers on the abscissa.

this experiment suggest that vasopressin in some way serves to maintain the learned response.

Studies in young animals which show that ACTH and ACTH 4–10 prolong recovery from a conditioned flavor aversion (cited above) suggest that these compounds may also benefit the old rat. The effects of ACTH or ACTH 4–10 on the behavior of the old rat during this procedure remain to be determined. Finally, since our studies reveal that the initial strength of aversion is weaker in old rats than in young, treatment with vasopressin or ACTH at the time of aversion may improve the old rats' subsequent performance. In fact, preliminary evidence indicates that this is the case. Treatment with LVP 1 hour prior to the injection of amphetamine slows the extinction rate in old animals exposed to a single saccharin-amphetamine pairing.

The observation that vasopressin influences the behavior of young and old animals has significant implications for our understanding of the physiological mechanisms underlying age-dependent changes in behavior. Studies using young adult animals show that vasopressin, as well as ACTH and particular peptide fragments of ACTH, can influence the animal's performance in a variety of tasks, particularly tasks using aversive conditioning (de Wied & Gispen, 1977). Studies of old rats reveal consistent age differences in performance in such aversive conditioning procedures. Together these observations indicate that the behavioral differences between young and old animals could be, in part, the consequence of age differences in the availability of such pituitary peptide hormones.

The regulatory effect of both vasopressin and ACTH on the rat's behavior is demonstrated in studies using the conditioned flavor-aversion procedure: When injected during recovery from a conditioned flavor aversion, vasopressin, ACTH (Levine, Smotherman, & Hennessy, 1977), and ACTH 4–10 (Rigter & Popping, 1976) prolong extinction. However, extinction eventually occurs despite continued treatment (see Figure 14-9). The importance of ACTH secretion at the time of conditioning also has been demonstrated. Marked elevations in serum corticosterone (and presumably its trophic hormone, ACTH) have been observed in response to lithium chloride injections paired with the presentation of a novel flavor (Smotherman, Hennessy, & Levine, 1976). If the animal is pretreated with dexamethasone to block ACTH secretion in response to lithium chloride, acquisition of the aversion is not blocked. However, the aversion is weaker, as reflected by more rapid extinction and elevated preference scores during the initial recovery period. Similar findings have been reported for hypophysectomized animals following the pairing of the novel substance with the toxic effect of X-irradiation (Garcia &

Kimeldorf, 1960). Thus, although vasopressin and ACTH are not necessary for the formation of a conditioned flavor aversion, the strength of the aversion appears to be affected by the amount of these hormones present at the time of conditioning, which thus influences the animal's response during both the acquisition and recovery phases of this procedure.

It should be noted that vasopressin has also been found in the anterior pituitary (Chateau, Marchetti, Burlet, & Boulange, 1979) and appears to play a role in normal ACTH release. Vasopressin has been reported to act on the ACTH-secreting cells (corticotrophs) of the anterior pituitary to increase their responsiveness to the corticotropin-releasing factor (Yates, Russell, Dallman, Hedge, McCann, & Dhariwal, 1971). The significance of such vasopressin–ACTH interactions for age-dependent changes in behavioral performance remains to be determined. However, since age-dependent changes in ACTH secretion have been noted in the rat (Tang & Phillips, 1978), and since vasopressin injections increase pituitary ACTH release (Yates et al., 1971), the possibility that the behavioral effects noted in our studies may have been the result of alterations in the ACTH secretion needs to be evaluated.

In summary, by using the conditioned flavor-aversion procedure, we found a significant age-related difference in behavior. Since this difference is readily identifiable in both male and female rats of at least two strains (Long Evans and Sprague Dawley), it provides a good behavioral tool for investigating the physiological mechanisms involved in age-dependent changes in behavior. More important, these studies substantiate the hypothesis that behavioral deficits in the old animal are reversible and provide the framework for addressing a variety of questions concerning pituitary hormone secretion, aging, and behavior. Some important questions to be addressed include: How does vasopressin act to bring about these changes in behavior? Are age-dependent changes in vasopressin availability secondary to some age-dependent change in CNS transmitter function?

Stimulation of acetylcholine (ACh) receptors has been shown to result in a release of vasopressin (as well as ACTH). Age-dependent decreases in CNS ACh and choline acetyl transferase (CAT) have been reported (McGeer & McGeer, 1975; Meek, Bertilsson, Cheney, Zsilla, & Costa, 1977). These observations suggest that the decrease in pituitary vasopressin release is associated with a decrease in CNS cholinergic function. In fact, pilot studies in our laboratory indicate that treatment of old rats with physostigmine, a drug that inhibits the breakdown of ACh, is as effective as treatment with LVP in reversing the behavioral age difference in the conditioned flavor aversion task. However, feeding old rats a diet supplemented with choline (50 and 100 mg/100 g of food) has no effect on their behavior in this task. These results are similar to those of Mohs (see Chapter 12 of this volume) that describe the effect of choline-supplemented diets versus physostigmine treatment on the behavior of elderly humans. Other studies (see Chapter 11 of this volume) suggest that placing animals on a choline-enriched diet at an early age may benefit their performance later in life. Thus, while choline-supplemented diets may not be beneficial if introduced later in life, they may be beneficial if initiated at an earlier age. Similar observations have been reported by Cooper (1977) and by Cooper and Walker (1979). They found that the catecholamine precursor L-tyrosine would reinstate ovarian function in aged rats. This effect in the old animals was prolonged and enhanced when L-tyrosine had been introduced as a dietary supplement relatively early in the female's life.

Conclusion

The observation that behavioral deficits can be ameliorated through exogenous hormone treatment indicates that neural systems sensitive to various types of hormonal stimulation remain functionally competent in the older animal. This observation also raises the possibility that procedures may be developed to prevent age-dependent changes in the neuroendocrine axes, resulting in the maintenance of behavioral function as the organism ages. Obviously, a good deal of research is needed before we understand the nature of age-dependent endocrine changes, the mechanism by which they influence the organism's behavior, and the extent to which they can be delayed or reversed. However, the studies reviewed in this section indicate that this approach to understanding the physiological processes involved in age-dependent changes in behavior should prove most useful in future gerontological research.

REFERENCES

Arenberg, D., & Robertson-Tchabo, E. A. Learning and aging. In J. E. Birren & K. W. Schaie (Eds.), *Handbook of the psychology of aging*. New York: Van Nostrand Reinhold, 1977.

Barchus, J. D., Akil, H., Elliot, G. R., Holman, R. B., & Watson, S. J. Behavioral neurochemistry, neuroregulators and behavioral states. *Science*, 1978, *200*, 964–973.

Bender, D. A. The influence of age on the activity of catecholamines and related therapeutic agents. *Journal of the American Gerontological Society*, 1970, *18*, 220–232.

Bohus, B. Effect of desglycinamide-lysine vasopressin (DG-LVP) on sexually motivated T-maze behavior of the male rat. *Hormones and Behavior*, 1977, *8*, 52–61.

Bohus, B., Ader, R., and de Wied, D. Effects of vasopressin on active and passive avoidance behavior. *Hormones and Behavior*, 1972, *3*, 191–197.

Bohus, B., Gispen, W. H., and de Wied, D. Effect of lysine vasopressin and ACTH 4-10 on conditioned avoidance behavior of hypophysectomized rats. *Neuroendocrinology*, 1973, *11*, 137–143.

Bohus, B., van Wimersma Greidanus, T., & de Wied, D. Behavioral and endocrine response of rats with hereditary hypothalamic diabetes insipidus (Brattleboro strain). *Physiology and Behavior*, 1975, *14*, 609–615.

Bookin, H. B., & Pfeifer, W. D. Effect of lysine vasopressin on pentylenetetrazol-induced retrograde amnesia in rats. *Pharmacology, Biochemistry and Behavior*, 1977, *7*, 51–54.

Carey, R. J. Long-term aversion to a saccharin solution induced by repeated amphetamine injections. *Pharmacology, Biochemistry and Behavior*, 1973, *1*, 265–270.

Chateau, M., Marchetti, J., Burlet, A., & Boulange, M. Evidence of vasopressin in adenohypophysis: Research into its role in corticotrope activity. *Neuroendocrinology*, 1979, *28*, 25–35.

Cooper, R. L. Reinstatement of ovarian cycles in aged female rats fed L-tyrosine supplemented diets. *Gerontologist*, 1977, *17*, 49.

Cooper, R. L., & Walker, R. F. Potential therapeutic consequences of age-dependent changes in brain physiology. *Interdisciplinary Topics in Gerontology*, 1979, *15*, 54–76.

Craik, F. I. M. Age differences in human memory. In J. E. Birren & K. W. Schaie (Eds.), *Handbook of the psychology of aging*. New York: Van Nostrand Reinhold, 1977.

de Wied, D. The influence of the posterior and intermediate lobe of the pituitary and pituitary peptides on the maintenance of a conditioned avoidance response in rats. *International Journal of Neuropharmacology*, 1965, *4*, 157–167.

de Wied, D. Long-term effect of vasopressin on the maintenance of a conditioned avoidance response in rats. *Nature*, 1971, *232*, 58–60.

de Wied, D., Bohus, B., Urban, I., & van Wimersma Greidanus, T. B. Memory deficit in rats with diabetes insipidus. *Brain Research*, 1975, *85*, 152–156.

de Wied, D., & Gispen, W. H. Behavioral effects of peptides. In H. Gainer (Ed.), *Peptides in neurobiology*. New York: Plenum Press, 1977.

Doty, B. A. Age and avoidance conditioning in rats. *Journal of Gerontology*, 1966, *21*, 287–290. (a)

Doty, B. A. Age differences in avoidance conditioning as a function of distribution of trials and task difficulty. *Journal of Genetic Psychology*, 1966, *109*, 249–254. (b)

Elias, M. F. Aging studies of behavior with Fischer 344, Sprague-Dawley, and Long-Evans rats. In D. C. Gibson, R. C. Adelman, & C. Finch (Eds.) *Development of the rodent as a model system of aging*. Washington, D.C.: U.S. Department of Health, Education and Welfare, 1978.

Elias, M. F., & Elias, P. K. Motivation and activity. In J. E. Birren & K. W. Schaie (Eds.), *Handbook of the psychology of aging*. New York: Van Nostrand Reinhold, 1977.

Furchtgott, E., & Wechkin, S. Avoidance conditioning as a function of prenatal x-irradiation and age. *Journal of Comparative and Physiological Psychology*, 1962, *55*, 69–72.

Garcia, J., Hankins, W. G., & Rusiniak, K. W. Behavioral regulation of the milieu interne in man and rat. *Science*, 1974, *185*, 824–831.

Garcia, J., & Kimeldorf, D. J. Some factors which influence radiation-conditioned behavior of rats. *Radiation Research*, 1960, *12*, 719–727.

Gispen, W. H., van Ree, J. M., & de Wied, D. Lipotropin and the central nervous system. *International Review of Neurobiology*, 1977, *20*, 209–250.

Gordon, W. C., Scobie, S. R., & Frankl, S. E. Age-related differences in the electric shock detection and escape thresholds in Sprague-Dawley albino rats. *Experimental Aging Research*, 1978, *4*, 23–35.

Hostetter, G., Jubb, S. L., & Kozlowski, G. P. Vasopressin affects the behavior of rats in a positively-rewarded discrimination task. *Life Sciences*, 1977, *21*, 1323–1328.

Lande, S., Flexner, J. B., & Flexner, L. B. Effects of corticotropin and desglycinamide 9 lysine vasopressin on suppression of memory by puromycin. *Proceedings of the National Academy of Science*, 1972, *69*, 558–560.

Lande, S., Witter, A., & de Wied, D. An octapeptide that stimulates conditioned avoidance acquisition in hypophysectomized rats. *Journal of Biological Chemistry*, 1971, *246*, 2058–2062.

Levine, S., Smotherman, W. P., & Hennessy, J. W. Pituitary-adrenal hormones and learned taste aversion. In L. H. Miller, C. A. Sandman, and A. J. Kastin (Eds.), *Neuropeptide influences on the brain and behavior*. New York: Raven Press, 1977, 163–177.

Logue, A. W. Taste aversion and the generality of the laws of learning. *Psychological Bulletin*, 1979, *86*, 276–296.

McGaugh, J. L. Time dependent processes in memory storage. *Science*, 1966, *153*, 1351–1358.

McGeer, E. G., & McGeer, P. L. Age changes in the human for some enzymes associated with metabolism of catecholamines, GABA and acetylcholine. In J. M. Ordy & K. R. Brizzee (Eds.), *Neurobiology of aging*. (Vol. 16). New York: Plenum Press, 1975.

McNamara, M. C., Benignus, V. A., Benignus, G., & Miller, A. T., Jr. Acquisition and retention of active and passive avoidance learning in rats as a function of age. *Experimental Aging Research*, 1977, *3*, 3–16.

McNamara, M. C., & Cooper, R. L. *Age differences in conditioned taste aversion: Possible role of vasopressin*. Paper presented at the meeting of the Society for Neuroscience, Atlanta, Georgia, November 1979. (a)

McNamara, M. C., & Cooper, R. L. *Development and retention of conditioned taste aversion learning in rats of different ages*. Paper presented at the meeting of the American Physiological Society, New Orleans, Louisiana, October 1979. (b)

Meek, J. L., Bertilsson, L., Cheney, D. L., Zsilla, G., & Costa, E. Aging-induced changes in acetylcholine and serotonin content of discrete brain nuclei. *Journal of Gerontology*, 1977, *32*, 129–131.

Paré, W. P. Interaction of age and shock intensity on acquisition. of a discriminated conditioned emotional response. *Journal of Comparative and Physiological Psychology*, 1969, *68*, 364–369.

Prange, A. J., Nemeroff, C. B., Lipton, M. A. Breeze, G. R., & Wilson, I. C. Peptides and the central nervous system. In L. L. Iversen, S. D. Iversen, & S. H. Snyder (Eds.), *Handbook of pharmacology: Biology of mood and antianxiety drugs* (Vol. 13). New York: Plenum Press, 1978.

Rigter, H., Elgertse, R., & Van Riezen, H. Time dependent anti-amnesic effect of ACTH 4-10 and desglycinamide-lysine vasopressin. *Progress in Brain Research*, 1975, *42*, 163–171.

Rigter, H., & Popping, A. Hormonal influences on the extinction of conditioned taste aversion. *Psychopharmacologia*, 1976, *46*, 255–261.

Rigter, H., Van Riezen, H., & de Wied, D. The effects of ACTH and vasopressin analogs on CO2 induced retrograde amnesia in rats. *Physiology and Behavior*, 1974, *133*, 381–388.

Smotherman, W. P., Hennessy, J. W., & Levine, S. Plasma corticosterone levels as an index of the strength of illness induced taste aversions. *Physiology and Behavior*, 1976, *17*, 903–908.

Smotherman, W. P., & Levine, S. ACTH and ACTH 4-10 modification of neophobia and taste aversion responses in the rat. *Journal of Comparative Psychology and Physiological*, 1978, *92*, 22–23.

Tang, F., & Phillips, J. G. Some age-related changes in pituitary-adrenal function in the male laboratory rat. *Journal of Gerontology*, 1978, *33*, 377–382.

Thompson, W. G., & Cooper, R. L. *The effects of age and vasopressin on passive avoidance responding in rats*. Paper presented at the meeting of the Gerontological Society, Washington, D.C., 1979.

Turkington, M. R., & Everitt, A. V. The neurohypophysis and the aging, with special reference to the antidiuretic hormone. In A. V. Everitt and J. A. Burgess (Eds.), *Hypothalamus, pituitary, and aging*. Springfield, Ill.: Charles C Thomas, 1976.

Turner, C. D., & Bagnara, J. T. *General endocrinology*. Philadelphia: Saunders, 1976.

van Wimersma Greidanus, T., & de Wied, D. Modulation of passive avoidance behavior of rats by intracerebroventricular administration of antivasopressin serum. *Behavioral Biology*, 1976, *18*, 325–333.

van Wimersma Greidanus, T., Dogterom, J., & de Wied, D. Intraventricular administration of antivasopressin serum inhibits memory in rats. *Life Science*, 1975, *16*, 637–644.

Yates, F. E., Russell, S. M., Dallman, M. F., Hedge, G. A., McCann, S. M., & Dhariwal, A. P. S. Potentiation by vasopressin of corticotropin release induced by corticotropin-releasing factor. *Endocrinology*, 1971, *88*, 3–15.

Steven H. Ferris, Barry Reisberg, and Samuel Gershon

CHAPTER

15

Neuropeptide Modulation of Cognition and Memory in Humans

Neuropeptides are a new class of compounds that play a significant role in brain function. Neuropeptides related to adrenocorticotropic hormone (ACTH) and vasopressin have been evaluated for possible positive effects on memory and cognition in the elderly. Studies with normal subjects suggest that ACTH analogs may improve human attention, arousal, or motivation, but studies with elderly subjects and patients with senile dementia have not demonstrated clinical efficacy. Preliminary results with vasopressin, which may have more direct effects on memory, appear to be more promising. Future research should elucidate the potential role of neuropeptides in treating the cognitive deficits of aging and dementia.

It is well-known that elderly people commonly complain of reduced cognitive ability, especially in the process that clinicians refer to as recent memory and that cognitive psychologists call secondary or long-term memory (LTM). Laboratory studies have generally confirmed the effects of aging on many aspects of mental function (Birren & Schaie, 1977; Botwinick, 1978).

Although cognitive decline related to normal aging may not significantly impair a person's activities in daily living, such deficits may compound the usual psychological, social, and economic problems of the elderly. In senile dementia, however, which afflicts about 10% of our elderly citizens (and 30% of those over the age of 80), there is a profound, progressive deterioration in cognitive processes, especially in memory function. There is currently no treatment of

proven clinical value for improving impaired cognition (Reisberg, Ferris, & Gershon, 1980). The challenge for geriatric psychopharmacology in the 1980s will be to identify and develop pharmacological intervention strategies that will reduce or prevent the cognitive decline of normal aging and senile dementia.

The study of neuropeptides is one of several promising areas of research that may lead to treatments for improving age- or dementia-related cognitive decline. It has been known for a long time that the peripheral hormones of the endocrine system play an important regulatory role in human physiology and behavior. In recent years, it has been discovered that many pituitary peptide hormones, or short-chain peptide fragments of these hormones, are present in the brain and have direct central nervous system (CNS) effects (Guillemin, 1978). It is now believed that these neuropeptides are either synthesized in the brain or transported there directly from the hypothalamus (Krieger & Liotta, 1979). Furthermore, evidence has been accumulating which suggests that these neuropeptides function in the brain either as neurotransmitters or as modulators of neurotransmitters (Guillemin, 1978; Krieger & Liotta, 1979). Most well-known among this new class of substances are the endorphins and enkephalins. Of particular relevance to the processes of attention, memory, and the cognitive deficits of aging are neuropeptides related to adrenocorticotropic hormone (ACTH) and vasopressin (antidiuretic hormone, or ADH) (Beckwith & Sandman,

1978; de Wied, 1973, 1977; van Wimersma Greidanus & de Wied, 1977). In this chapter we review the growing literature on the effects of these peptides in humans, emphasizing studies in our laboratory and elsewhere that have involved either normal or cognitively impaired elderly subjects. We then attempt to reach at least a tentative conclusion on whether or not these interesting compounds are of value for treating cognitive decline in aging.

ACTH Fragments (alpha-MSH, ACTH 4-10, ACTH 4-9)

The pituitary hormone ACTH has a major effect on behavior, particularly on the regulation of fear and stress responses (Miller, Sandman, & Kastin, 1977). However, a short-chain fragment of the ACTH molecule (the 4th to the 10th amino acids, H-Met-Glu-His-Phe-Arg-Trp-Gly-OH) produces some of the behavior effects of ACTH, despite a lack of peripheral hormonal effects. This fragment, ACTH 4-10, facilitates both avoidance and appetitive animal learning and improves resistance to extinction. It also reduces amnesias due to electroconvulsive shock (ECS), inhalation of CO_2 to unconsciousness, or antibiotic injection. The effects are short term, that is, restricted to the period following ACTH 4-10 injection.

Results with ACTH 4-10 in human trials have been less dramatic than those in the animal literature. The studies with cognitively normal volunteers are summarized in Table 15-1.

Studies with Normal Subjects

The earliest human studies with ACTH fragments were reported at the beginning of the 1970s. In an EEG study, Endröczi, Fekete, and de Wied (1970) that ACTH 1-10 produced some recovery of a previously habituated EEG arousal response to sensory stimulation. A similar postinjection recovery and persistence of a previously habituated EEG arousal to novel stimulation was subsequently reported for ACTH 4-10 (Miller, Kastin, Sandman, Fink, & Van Veen, 1974). The resting EEG, however, is apparently not affected by ACTH 4-10 (Sannita, Irvin, & Fink, 1976). In a study to evaluate possible behavioral effects of a portion of the melanocyte-stimulating hormone (alpha-MSH), which contains the same amino-acid sequence as ACTH 4-10, Kastin, Miller, Gonzalez-Barcena, Hawley, Dyster-Aas, Schally, Parra, and Velasco, (1971) found that alpha-MSH increased the amplitude of averaged somatosensory evoked potentials. This was also the first study to examine possible cognitive effects of this peptide sequence. There was no effect on verbal memory, but visual memory on the Benton Visual Retention Test (BVRT) was significantly improved.

The cognitive effects of ACTH 4-10 were first examined in the Miller et al. (1974) study. In addition to the EEG arousal effects noted above, visual retention on the BVRT was improved to a small, marginally significant extent. There was also a small reduction in level of anxiety.

The Miller, Sandman, and Kastin group have inter-

Table 15-1   Summary of Clinical Studies with ACTH 4-10: Normal Subjects

Authors	Design (N)	Dosage[a]	Results
Endröczi et al. (1970)	Crossover (16)	1 mg, 2 mg ACTH 1–10 (IV)	Improved dishabituation of EEG hypersynchrony
Kastin et al. (1971)	Crossover (5)	10 mg αMSH (IV)	Improved visual attention
Miller et al. (1974)	Parallel (20)	10 mg (IV)	Improved attention
Gaillard & Sanders (1975)	Parallel (18)	30 mg	Reduced deficit in continuous RT (prevented fatigue or loss of motivation)
Sandman et al. (1975)	Parallel (20)	15 mg (IV)	Concept-shift learning improved
Dornbush & Nikolovski (1976)	Crossover (10)	30 mg	Impaired complex task (increased general arousal)
Sannita et al. (1976)	Crossover (12)	5–96 mg	No consistent EEG changes
Miller et al. (1976)	Crossover (20)	30 mg	CPT task improved, increased attention
Sandman et al. (1977)	Crossover (11)	15 mg (IV)	Inconsistent effects on attention tasks
Wagenaar, Timmers et al. (1977)	Parallel (40)	30 mg	Inconsistent effects on concept-shift performance
Wagenaar, Truijens et al. (1977)	Parallel (34)	30 mg	Improved long-term memory retrieval
Vieth et al. (1978)	Parallel (33) (women only)	30 mg	Improved paragraph memory, impaired concept-shift learning
Miller, Fischer et al. (1977)	Parallel (20)	30 mg	No effects on CAR extinction

Note. Abbreviations: IV = intravenously; RT = reaction time; CPT = continuous performance task; CAR = conditioned avoidance response.
[a] Subcutaneous injection of ACTH 4-10, unless otherwise indicated.

preted the results of their MSH/ACTH 4-10 studies as suggesting an enhancement effect on attentional processes. Results of subsequent human studies generally have been consistent with this interpretation. However, a clear distinction has not been made experimentally between the hypothesized effect on focused attention or vigilance and an alternative explanation of an effect on general arousal or motivational level. Thus, Gaillard and Sanders (1975) examined the effect of ACTH 4-10 on a 30-minute continuous reaction time (RT) task. The peptide had no effect on initial RTs but tended to reduce the usual decline in performance on this long, fatiguing task. The authors interpreted their results as suggesting an increase in the maintenance of motivation. A study by Dornbush and Nikolovski (1976) provided results consistent with a more general motivational or arousal effect. In order to examine the possible specificity of ACTH 4-10 for effects on short-term memory (STM), three simple tasks (auditory-verbal, visual-verbal, and visual-nonverbal STM) and one complex task (bisensory simultaneous STM) were examined. There were no drug effects on any of the simple STM tasks, but ACTH 4-10 produced a clear-cut deficit on the complex task. Since an improvement in concentration and focused attention should improve performance on this difficult task, the authors interpreted their results as suggesting that the compound increased general arousal level rather than attention. Since the relation between arousal level and performance is presumed to be an inverted U-shaped function, increasing arousal in highly motivated subjects should impair performance.

However, an explanation for the action of ACTH 4-10 in terms of general arousal is not consistent with the results of some other studies that examine the attention process more closely. Miller, Harris, Van Riezen, and Kastin (1976) evaluated the effects of ACTH 4-10 on the continuous-performance task (CPT), a measure of attention and vigilance. Although a ceiling effect tended to obscure possible treatment differences, ACTH 4-10 improved performance when the attentional demands were maximized. In addition, memory improved on the BVRT and the Wechsler Memory Scale, as did performance on the Digit Span and Digit Symbol Substitution subtests of the Wechsler Adult Intelligence Scale (WAIS). All of these effects are consistent with an interpretation of enhancement in focused attention.

Several other studies have also shown positive changes on memory-retrieval performance (Wagenaar, Truijens, Vunderink, Sanders, & Gaillard, 1977; Vieth, Sandman, George, & Stevens, 1978). However, these presumed "attention" effects on memory tasks can be alternatively interpreted as being caused by an enhancement of motivation. It is also of interest

that the memory-retrieval paradigm, which in animals has consistently demonstrated ACTH 4-10 effects—namely, resistance to extinction of a conditioned avoidance response (CAR)—failed to show any drug-related changes when applied to human subjects (Miller, Fischer, Groves, Rudrauff, & Kastin, 1977).

Another experimental procedure often used to evaluate attention is a concept-learning task in which a new formula for solving the task at hand must be acquired following a sudden shift from a previously learned interfering formula. Several studies have used this type of task to evaluate the effects of ACTH 4-10. Sandman et al. (1975) found that ACTH 4-10 biased the subjects toward staying with the concept or formula for solving problems rather than shifting to trying new formulas. They also reported a reduction in anxiety and improvements on the attention-sensitive BVRT and Rod and Frame Test. However, in a subsequent experiment (Sandman, George, McCanne, Nolan, Kaswan, & Kastin, 1977), ACTH 4-10 had less consistent effects on concept-shift learning. In addition, the neuropeptide appeared to impair simple sensory detection, while it improved more complex sensory detection and failed to improve visual memory on the BVRT.

Wagenaar, Timmers, and Frowein (1977) have also examined the effects of ACTH 4-10 on concept-shift learning. In three separate experiments, they found an enhancement of shift-learning performance, an improvement for "introverts," and then a complete failure to replicate the results of either of the first two studies. Finally, Vieth et al. (1978) found that ACTH 4-10 impaired rather than improved concept-shift learning in female subjects.

In summary, the results of studies with normal human subjects have an inconsistent array of generally small but often statistically significant effects on a variety of cognitive tasks. The interpretation of these effects has been either in terms of enhancement of focused attention or in terms of a stimulantlike effect on general arousal or motivation. Changes in memory-task performance have sometimes been demonstrated, usually involving retrieval from visual, nonverbal memory. These changes are believed to reflect an apparent improvement in attention or motivation rather than a primary effect on memory storage or retrieval.

Pribram (1977) has suggested a possible explanation for these often conflicting or inconsistent findings and interpretations in terms of a three-process model of attention/arousal. According to this model, there is an arousal system, which is phasic, involves brief responses to input, and controls the "stopping" of behaviors; an activation or readiness system, which is tonic, is longer acting, and controls "starting" and sensorimotor activity or motor sets; and an effort system, which controls general arousal anxiety, coordinates the interaction between the arousal and the activation systems, and controls complex behaviors and evokes shifts to new activities. If it is hypothesized that ACTH 4-10 has a direct modulating influence on the effort system, and thereby has only indirect effects on arousal or readiness, the inconsistent experimental findings on arousal and attention may become more comprehensible. Thus one cannot isolate behavioral measures related to any one of these three systems and expect always to obtain consistent results. The effect of the peptide on particular tasks and in particular subject groups may vary considerably depending on the endogenous states of these three systems and on the nature of their mutual interactions.

It follows from this line of reasoning that a possible limitation of the studies with normal subjects is that these subjects perform maximally, that is, they are fully aroused, motivated, and focused on the tasks. Since this may not be the case for normal elderly or senile dementia patients, it might be predicted that ACTH 4-10 would have greater behavioral effects in impaired subjects than in young normal subjects.

Studies with Cognitively Impaired Subjects

A number of studies have been conducted to examine the possible efficacy of ACTH 4-10 in subjects with some degree of cognitive impairment. These include five studies involving either normal elderly subjects or patients with mild to moderate symptoms of senile dementia. These clinical studies are summarized in Table 15-2.

Only one of the studies with young impaired subjects demonstrated a consistent peptide-related effect. Sandman, George, Walker, Nolan, and Kastin (1976)

reported improved concept-shift learning in mentally retarded adults. However, Rapoport, Quinn, Copeland, and Burg (1976) failed to find cognitive changes in hyperactive, learning-disabled children. Similarly, Draper and Haughton (1978) obtained negative results with alcoholics who had been withdrawn from alcohol. In psychiatric patients treated with electroconvulsive therapy (ECT), Small, Small, Milstein, and Dian (1977) found a marginal improvement in visual retrieval after only one ECT session but no effects if the drug was administered following several ECT sessions. A variety of memory and attentional measures were administered in these three studies.

In a study using normal elderly subjects, Dornbush and Volavka (1976) compared several dosages of ACTH 4-10 with a placebo and found a dose-related improvement in RT. However, measures of STM and perceptual-motor performance were unchanged. An evaluation of ACTH 4-10 in cognitively impaired elderly subjects was conducted in our laboratory (Ferris, Sathananthan, Gershon, Clark, & Moshinsky, 1976). Single injections of 15 mg, 30 mg, or a placebo were administered to 24 patients on separate days in a crossover design. An extensive cognitive test battery was administered before and after the injection on each test day. The results were largely negative in that all but two measures failed to show any treatment effects. There was a slowing of RT following the 30-mg dosage and a slight improvement in visual memory retrieval on the day following the 30-mg injection. There were no significant effects on either EEG or mood.

The results of other studies with elderly subjects have also been predominantly negative. Will, Abuzzahab, and Zimmerman (1978) found no consistent cognitive changes in elderly community residents with

Table 15-2 Summary of Clinical Studies with ACTH 4-10: Cognitively Impaired Patients

Author	Population	Design (N)	Dosage	Results
Sandman et al. (1976)	Mentally retarded adults	Parallel (20)	15 mg (IV)	Impaired concept-shift learning
Ferris et al. (1976)	Elderly impaired	Crossover (24)	15, 30 mg	Slight slowing of RT and improvement in day-later recall
Branconnier et al. (1979)	Elderly impaired	Crossover (18)	30 mg	Slight improvement in mood, antifatigue effect
Dornbush & Volavka (1976)	Elderly normals	Crossover (4)	15, 30, 45, 60 mg	Improvement in RT, no changes in STM
Will et al. (1978)	Elderly normals	Parallel (44)	15 mg	No consistent changes
Rapoport et al. (1976)	Hyperactive, LD children	Crossover (30)	30 mg	No changes
Small et al. (1977)	ECT inpatients	Parallel (20, 30)	15, 30 mg	Slight improvement in visual memory after one ECT
Draper & Haughton (1978)	Alcoholics	Crossover (60)	30 mg	No effects
Willner et al. (1979)	Elderly impaired	Crossover (40)	30 mg	Improvement in "conceptually organized retrieval"

Note. Abbreviations: IV = intravenously; ECT = electroconvulsive therapy; RT = reaction time; STM = short-term memory; LD = learning disabled.

objective complaints of declining memory ability. Branconnier, Cole, and Gardos (1979) also failed to demonstrate significant cognitive changes. However, they did confirm the earlier report of Gaillard and Sanders (1975) of a marginal improvement in serial RT, which possibly reflected an attenuation of the effects of fatigue. In this study there were some positive effects on mood, as measured by a self-rating scale, the POMS. Specifically, there was a reduction in depression, anger, and confusion, and an increase in vigor. In another study with mild senile dementia patients, Willner, Rabiner, and Feldmar (1979) reported an improvement in the conceptual organization of semantic category retrieval but no significant changes on an assortment of other cognitive and behavioral measures.

Overall, these studies have failed to confirm a clinical utility for ACTH 4-10. In general, the findings for cognitively impaired subjects, including the elderly, are consistent with, but are even less impressive than, the results for young normal subjects.

Oral ACTH 4-9

A serious practical limitation of ACTH 4-10 is that it remains behaviorally active only if administered intravenously or subcutaneously. Thus, even if it were effective, it would be impractical for routine clinical use. Because of the difficulty of administration, only single-dose effects of ACTH 4-10 have been evaluated. It is possible that chronic treatment would produce quite different or more efficacious results. Therefore the availability of ACTH 4-9, a synthetic, orally active analogue of ACTH 4-10, was greeted with great expectations. This new peptide (H-Met[O]-Glu-His-Phe-D-Lys-Phe-OH) was synthesized by replacing several

amino acids in the ACTH 4-10 chain with different amino acids (de Wied, 1973). In animal studies, the behavioral effects of this synthetic peptide are quite similar to the effects of ACTH 4-10, but at 1/1000th the dosage of ACTH 4-10. The results of some recent human studies with this orally active peptide are summarized in Table 15-3.

Unfortunately, the potential clinical utility of this more practical compound has not as yet been substantiated. Gaillard and Varey (1977) examined the effects on young normal subjects of single doses of ACTH 4-9 on a wide array of cognitive measures. As was previously found for ACTH 4-10, the drug reduced the usual decline in performance in a 30-minute serial RT task. Thus the peptide had antifatigue or motivational effects. However, there were no changes on other cognitive tasks, including supraspan STM, closure flexibility, nonverbal abstraction, and verbal learning. Similarly, there were no changes in mood.

In another study with normal young subjects, Fink and Irwin (1978) examined the effects of four days of treatment. There were no significant changes in EEG, critical flicker frequency, attention as evaluated by CPT, and a variety of memory tasks. Gaillard (1978) failed to find a significant single-dose effect on the serial RT task in hypophysectomized patients. In a study with mentally retarded adults, Walker and Sandman (1979) failed to replicate with ACTH 4-9 the previously reported improvement with ACTH 4-10 in concept-shift learning.

Two studies have now been conducted using mildly to moderately impaired senile dementia patients. Branconnier and Cole (1977) examined the effects of 7 days of treatment. Their results for an extensive cognitive battery failed to reveal any consistent drug-related effects. In another study recently completed in our lab-

Table 15-3 Summary of Clinical Studies with Oral ACTH 4-9

Author	Population	Design (N)	Dosage	Results
Gaillard & Varey (1977)	Normal volunteers	Crossover (26)—single dose	5, 10, 20 mg	Reduced decline in serial RT performance (increased "motivation") no change in other tasks
Fink & Irwin (1978)	Normal volunteers	Crossover (12)—4 days	20 mg	No change in EEG, CFF, mood (small decrease in verbal learning, increase in remote memory)
Gaillard (1978)	Hypophysectomized patients	Parallel (19)—single dose	10 mg	No changes (trend, improvement in continuous RT)
Walker & Sandman (1979)	Mentally retarded adults	Parallel (24)—single dose	5, 20 mg	No changes (slight increase in concept-shift learning)
Branconnier & Cole (1977)[a]	Mild senile dementia	Parallel (40)—7 days	5, 10, 20 mg	No changes (slight increase in paired-associate learning)
Ferris et al. (1979)[a]	Mild senile dementia	Crossover (50)—single dose and 14 days	5, 10, 20 mg	Slowed RT with 10-mg single dose, reduced depression after 14 days

Note. Abbreviations: RT = reaction time; CFF = critical flicker frequency.
[a] Elderly subjects.

oratory (Ferris, Reisberg, & Gershon, 1979), a total of 50 mildly to moderately impaired senile dementia outpatients completed the project. The patients' degree of cognitive impairment was documented by means of our usual screening procedures, including an extensive history, medical-neurological evaluation, psychiatric evaluation, and standardized psychometric testing. These patients were, at best, below average for their age and WAIS vocabulary level on the Guild Memory Test. Based on the overall evaluation, patients were assigned a Global Deterioration Scale (GDS) rating of 1 (normal) through 7 (very severe). Participation in this study was limited to patients with a GDS rating of 2 (very mild) to 5 (moderately severe). Patients were excluded if they had a history of psychosis, alcoholism, head injury, or neurological disease; if they had a Hamilton Depression Scale total score greater than 20; or if they were taking concomitant psychotropic medication.

The study was designed as a double-blind multiple crossover so as to provide for an evaluation of the effects of both single-dose and chronic treatment for four different dosages and a placebo. In order to evaluate single-dose effects, patients received Treatment A on Day 1 and Treatment B on Day 2. In order to evaluate the effects of 2 weeks of treatment, Treatment B was continued for Days 3–15, followed by a return to Treatment A for Days 16–29. Treatment A and B were either a particular dosage and a placebo, or two different active dosages. Only 20 of the 50 subjects received a placebo as one of their two treatment conditions. The four dosages used were 20 mg or 10 mg given as single doses, or 10 mg or 5 mg given both morning and night.

Comprehensive behavioral and cognitive assessments were administered on the acute-treatment days and following each 2-week treatment period. The behavioral evaluations included a self-rating mood scale and several geriatric rating scales completed by a psychiatrist. The cognitive battery included a wide variety of memory tasks and perceptual-motor performance tasks.

The results were not encouraging. The statistical analyses for each measure involved a comparison of each dosage versus the placebo for both acute and chronic treatment. Only two of the cognitive measures showed statistically significant treatment effects ($p < .05$). Digit Span Forward, a measure of primary memory and often a reflection of degree of attention, showed significant impairment after 2 weeks of treatment at the highest dose (20 mg), and at the lowest dose (5 mg given twice per day).

Further, simple and disjunctive RT, which also reflect attention as well as sensorimotor processing and central speed, were significantly slowed ($p < .05$) by acute treatment with the intermediate dosage (10 mg). However, there were no effects on RT after 2 weeks of treatment. This slowing of RT by a single dose is consistent with a similar finding in our earlier acute study of ACTH 4-10 (Ferris et al., 1976). Thus, overall, there was no improvement in cognitive functioning, only the suggestion of a mild deficit in attention.

There were, however, positive effects on mood, as reflected by statistically significant changes ($p < .05$) on the patient self-rating mood scale. Scores on the Depression mood factor were significantly reduced after a 2-week treatment with three of the four dosage regimens (5 mg, 5 mg; 10 mg; and 20 mg), and the Competence mood factor was increased for these same treatments. For the 5-mg, 5-mg dosage, scores on the Anxiety factor were also reduced. Thus, the 2-week treatment with ACTH 4-9 appears to have had antidepressant effects. This apparent effect on mood with chronic treatment is consistent with a similar antidepressant effect previously reported for acute ACTH 4-10 in elderly subjects (Branconnier et al., 1979). Interestingly, the scores on the Fatigue factor were significantly increased after the acute 10-mg dosage. Since this same acute dosage slowed RT, there is consistency between cognitive and fatigue effects for the acute administration of the intermediate dose.

In summary, the effects on cognition of ACTH 4-9 appear to be weaker than those of ACTH 4-10. This orally active peptide does not appear to be of clinical value for the treatment of the cognitive decline found with aging and dementia, at least at the dosages evaluated. However, the possibility of positive effects on mood with chronic treatment may warrant further evaluation of this interesting peptide.

Vasopressin

Vasopressin is synthesized and secreted by the anterior hypothalamus via the posterior pituitary (van Wimersma Greidanus & de Wied, 1977). It has peripheral effects on blood pressure (when given in large doses) and water balance (via its normal action on the kidney) and is therefore also known as an antidiuretic hormone. Animal studies, including work with vasopressin analogs having minimal peripheral activity, have shown that this neuropeptide facilitates learning and increases resistance to extinction for both avoidance and appetitive behavior (de Wied, 1977; van Wimersma Greidanus & de Wied, 1977). It also antagonizes experimentally induced retrograde amnesias, and animals that lack vasopressin (hereditary diabetes insipidus) show impairment of learning and memory. It is apparent that vasopressin has direct CNS effects in animals (see Chapter 14 of this volume). It is believed to exert long-term effects on the consolidation of memory, as opposed to the short-duration behavioral effects of ACTH analogs.

There have now been a number of vasopressin studies in humans. Waggoner, Slonim, and Armstrong (1978) treated seven children suffering from diabetes insipidus in a 4-week open trial with the analog arginine vasopressin (DDAVP). A parent questionnaire revealed an improved "psychological status." Oliveras, Jandali, Timsit-Berthier, Remy, Benghezal, Audibert, and Moeglen (1978) treated four amnesic patients with an analog, lysine vasopressin, for at least several weeks. One alcoholic patient got worse, but three head-trauma patients showed marked improvement in memory, as revealed by clinical evaluation. The most compelling results have been reported by Legros, Gilot, Seron, Claessena, Adam, Moeglen, Audibert, and Berchier (1978). Twenty-three elderly, inpatient volunteers received either a dosage of 16 IU of lysine vasopressin (intranasally) or a placebo for 3 days. Vasopressin produced statistically significant improvement on all psychometric tests in a cognitive battery including tests of concentration, attention, and memory. Although these results are quite encouraging, it is unclear whether the subjects were normal or impaired.

A vasopressin trial in a single Korsakoff-syndrome patient was conducted by LeBoeuf, Lodge, and Eames (1978). Treatment for 8 weeks with a dosage of 22.5 IU per day of lysine vasopressin reduced depression in hospitalized psychiatric patients (Gold, Weingartner, Ballenger, Goodwin, & Post, 1979). The possibility that the cognitive changes produced by vasopressin could be secondary to changes in depression must therefore be considered. Furthermore, since vasopressin can release ACTH, the antidepressant activities of ACTH analogs and of vasopressin may be related.

Although the positive results reported for vasopressin are based largely on small subject samples or uncontrolled trials, the results seem promising. And they certainly warrant further well-designed studies in both normal and cognitively impaired elderly subjects.

Discussion

It is clear that the neuropeptides discussed in this chapter do have some cognitive effects. However, the specificity of these agents for the particular cognitive processes that decline with aging and dementia has not yet been well defined. For ACTH analogs, the studies conducted thus far have failed to demonstrate significant clinical benefit. The preliminary findings with vasopressin analogs seem more promising, but further research is needed to substantiate these initial results.

The human research with neuropeptides also serves to highlight some of the current problems in the psychopharmacology of aging. Issues revealed in reviewing this research include the problems of dosage and the selection of test measures. A variety of dosages have been used, but in most studies only a single dosage is evaluated. The variability and inconsistency in the results may be due to some extent to the dosage variations. That some of the treatment effects found in our studies with ACTH 4-10 and ACTH 4-9 were dose specific is consistent with this possibility. Unfortunately, since these neuropeptides produce neither side effects nor gross behavioral effects, the determination of optimal dosages in future research may prove to be difficult.

The studies reviewed have also used a wide variety of cognitive test measures. Interpretations of the nature of the peptide effects would be greatly facilitated by the use of objective evaluation measures with greater specificity for particular components of memory and other cognitive processes. Another issue concerns defining the distinction between small, statistically significant improvements on cognitive tasks and genuine clinical efficacy. This problem will need to be addressed as new compounds with more substantial effects are developed.

Even though the particular peptides discussed in this chapter have failed to show clinical utility, other peptides may eventually be shown to have useful effects. Many of the neuropeptides are interrelated, and some share certain core structures. For example, the structures of ACTH 4-10, vasopressin, methionine enkephalin, and leucine enkephalin are all part of the structure of beta-lypotropin. Furthermore, ACTH 4-10 and leucine enkephalin have the same core amino-acid sequence, and vasopressin and methionine enkephalin share a different core sequence. Interestingly, Rigter (1978) has shown that in rats, lucine enkephalin and ACTH 4-10 have similar effects in reducing CO_2-induced amnesia. Analogously, the nature of the effects of methionine enkephalin and vasopressin are quite similar. An enormous amount of basic research is currently being conducted to probe the nature of and functional significance of neuropeptides. As we learn more about the specificity of action of these substances, new pharmacological intervention strategies may emerge for improving cognitive function in aging.

REFERENCES

Beckwith, B. E., & Sandman, C. A. Behavioral influences of the neuropeptides ACTH and MSH: A methodological review. *Neuroscience and Biobehavioral Reviews*, 1978, *2*, 311–338.

Birren, J. E., & Schaie, K. W. (Eds.). *Handbook of the psychology of aging*. New York: Van Nostrand Reinhold, 1977.

Botwinick, J. *Aging and Behavior* (2nd ed.). New York: Springer, 1978.

Branconnier, R. J., & Cole, J. O. *A preliminary data analysis of the effects of Org 2766 on mild senile organic brain syndrome*. Unpublished report, Boston State Hospital, 1977.

Branconnier, R. J., Cole, J. O., & Gardos, G. ACTH 4-10 in the amelioration of neuropsychological symptomatology associated with senile organic brain syndrome. *Psychopharmacology*, 1979, *61*, 161–165.

de Wied, D. Pituitary-adrenal system hormones and behavior. In F. O. Schmitt, & F. G. Warden (Eds.), *The neurosciences* (Vol. 3). Cambridge, Mass.: MIT Press, 1973.

de Wied, D. Peptides and behavior. *Life Sciences*, 1977, *20*, 195–204.

Dornbush, R. L., & Nikolovski, O. ACTH 4-10 and short-term memory. *Pharmacology, Biochemistry and Behavior*, 1976, *5*(Suppl. 1), 69–72.

Dornbush, R. L., & Volavka, J. ACTH 4-10: A study of toxicological and behavioral effects in an aging sample. *Neuropsychobiology*, 1976, *2*, 350–360.

Draper, R., & Haughton, H. *Double-blind clinical trial of Org O.I. 63: Effects on performance of chronic alcoholics in the withdrawal period*. Unpublished Organon report, Oss, Holland, 1978.

Endröczi, K., Fekete, T., & de Wied, D. Effects of ACTH on EEG habituation in human subjects. *Progress in Brain Research*, 1970, *32*, 254–266.

Ferris, S. H., Reisberg, B., & Gershon, S. *Neuropeptide effects on cognition in the elderly*. Paper presented at the meeting of the American Psychological Association, New York, September 1979.

Ferris, S. H., Sathananthan, G., Gershon, S., Clark, C., & Moshinsky, J. Cognitive effects of ACTH 4-10 in the elderly. *Pharmacology, Biochemistry and Behavior*, 1976, *5*(Suppl. 1), 73–78.

Fink, M., & Irwin, P. *Effect of Org 2766 on EEG, behavior and memory in normal male volunteers*. Unpublished report, Department of Psychiatry, School of Medicine, State University of New York at Stony Brook, 1978.

Gaillard, A. W. K. *Some effects of Org 2766 on serial reaction time in hypophysectomy patients*. Unpublished report, Institute for Perception, TNO, Soesterberg, Holland, 1978.

Gaillard, A. W. K., & Sanders, A. F. Some effects of ACTH 4-10 on performance during a serial reaction task. *Psychopharmacologia*, 1975, *42*, 201–208.

Gaillard, A. W. K., & Varey, C. A. *Some effects of Org 2766 on various performance tasks*. Unpublished report, Institute for Perception, TNO, Soesterberg, Holland, 1977.

Gold, P. W., Weingartner, H., Ballenger, J. C., Goodwin, F. K., & Post, R. M. Effects of 1-desamino-8-D-arginine vasopressin on behavior and cognition in primary affective disorder. *Lancet*, November 1979, p. 10.

Guillemin, R. Peptides in the brain: The new endocrinology of the neuron. *Science*, 1978, *202*, 390–402.

Kastin, A. J., Miller, L. H., Gonzalez-Barcena, D., Hawley, W. D., Dyster-Aas, K., Schally, A. V., Parra, M. L. V., & Velasco, M. Psychophysiologic correlates of MSH activity in man. *Physiology and Behavior*, 1971, *7*, 893–896.

Krieger, D. T. & Liotta, A. S. Pituitary hormones in brain: Where, how and why? *Science*, 1979, *205*, 366–372.

LeBoeuf, A., Lodge, J., & Eames, P. G. Vasopressin and memory in Korsakoff syndrome. *Lancet*, Dec. 23, 1978, p. 1370.

Legros, J. J., Gilot, P., Seron, X., Claessena, J., Adam, A., Moeglen, J. M., Audibert, A., & Berchier, P. Influence of vasopressin on learning and memory. *Lancet*, 1978, i, pp. 41–42.

Miller, L. H., Fischer, S. C., Groves, G. A., Rudrauff, M. E., & Kastin, A. J. MSH/ACTH4-10 influences on the CAR in human subjects: A negative finding. *Pharmacology, Biochemistry and Behavior*, 1977, *7*, 417–419.

Miller, L. H., Harris, L. C. Van Riezen, H., & Kastin, A. J. Neuroheptapeptide influence on attention and memory in man. *Pharmacology, Biochemistry and Behavior*, 1976, *5*(Suppl. 1), 17–21.

Miller, L. H., Kastin, A. J., Sandman, C. A. Fink, M. & Van Veen, W. J. Polypeptide influences on attention, memory and anxiety in man. *Pharmacology, Biochemistry and Behavior*, 1974, *2*, 663–668.

Miller, L. H., Sandman, C. A. & Kastin, A. J. *Neuropeptide influences on the brain and behavior*. New York: Raven Press, 1977.

Oliveros, J. C., Jandali, M. K., Timsit-Berthier, M., Remy, R., Benghezal, A., Audibert, A., & Moeglen, J. M. Vasopressin in amnesia. *Lancet*, 1978, i, p. 42.

Pribram, K. H. Peptides and the protocritic processes. In L. H. Miller, C. A. Sandman, & A. J. Kastin (Eds.), *Neuropeptide influences of the brain and behavior*. New York: Raven Press, 1977.

Rapoport, J. L., Quinn, P. O., Copeland, A. P. & Burg, C. ACTH 4-10: Cognitive and behavioral effects in hyperactive children. *Neuropsychobiology*, 1976, *2*, 291–296.

Reisberg, B., Ferris, S. H., & Gershon S. Pharmacotherapy of senile dementia. In J. O. Cole (Ed.), *Psychopathology in the aged*. New York: Raven Press, 1980.

Rigter, H. Attenuation of amnesia in rats by systematically administered enkephalin. *Science*, 1978, *200*, 83–85.

Sandman, C. A., George, J., McCanne, T. R., Nolan, J. D., Kaswan, J., & Kastin, A. J. MSH/ACTH 4-10 influences behavioral and physiological measures of attention. *Journal of Clinical Endocrinology and Metabolism*, 1977, *44*, 884–891.

Sandman, C. A., George, J. M., Nolan, J. D., Van Riezen, H., & Kastin, A. J. Enhancement of attention in man with ACTH/MSH 4-10. *Physiology and Behavior*, 1975, *15*, 427–431.

Sandman, C. A., George, J., Walker, B. B., Nolan, J. D. & Kastin, A. J. Neuropeptide MSH/ACTH 4-10 enhances attention in the mentally retarded. *Pharmacology, Biochemistry and Behavior*, 1976, *5*(suppl. 1), 23–28.

Sannita, W. G., Irwin, P., and Fink, M. EEG and task performance after ACTH 4-10 in man. *Neuropsychobiology*, 1976, *2*, 283–290.

Small, J. G., Small, I. F., Milstein, V., & Dian, D. A. Effects of ACTH 4-10 on ECT-induced memory dysfunctions. *Acta Psychiatrica Scandanavia*, 1977, *55*, 241–250.

van Wimersma Greidanus, T. B., & de Wied, D. The physiology of the neurohypophyseal system and its relation to memory processes. In A. N. Davison (Ed.), *Biochemical correlates of brain structure and function*. New York: Academic Press, 1977.

Vieth, J. L., Sandman, C. A., George, J. M., & Stevens, V. C. Effects of MSH/ACTH4-10 on memory, attention and endogenous hormone levels in women. *Physiology and Behavior*, 1978, *20*, 43–50.

Wagenaar, W. A., Timmers, H., & Frowein, H. *ACTH 4-10 and adaptive learning*. Unpublished report, Institute for Perception, TNO, Soesterberg, Holland, 1977.

Wagenaar, W. A., Truijens, C. L., Vunderink, R. A. F., Sanders, A. F., & Gaillard, A. W. K. *Three experiments on the effect of ACTH 4-10 on human learning*. Unpublished report, Institute for Perception, TNO, Soesterberg, Holland, 1977.

Waggoner, R. W., Slonim, A. E., & Armstrong, S. H. Improved psychological status of children under DDAVP therapy for central diabetes insipidus. *American Journal of Psychiatry*, 1978, *135*, 361–362.

Walker, B. B. & Sandman, C. A. Influences of an analog of the neuropeptide ACTH 4-9 on mentally retarded adults. *American Journal of Mental Deficiency*, 1979, *83*, 346–352.

Will, J. C., Abuzzahab, F. S., & Zimmermann, R. L. The effects of ACTH 4-10 versus placebo in the memory of symptomatic geriatric volunteers. *Psychopharmacology Bulletin*, 1978, *14*, 25–27.

Willner, A. E., Rabiner, C. J., & Feldmar, G. G. *Effect of ACTH 4-10 upon semantic and phonetic retrieval in elderly subjects with memory problems*. Paper presented at the Second International Neuropsychological Society European Conference, Noordwijkerhout, Holland, June 27–30, 1979.

Cognitive Issues: Advances in the Cognitive Psychology of Aging

Anderson D. Smith, *Section Editor*

Introduction

Cognitive psychology deals with an old question: How can we describe and understand human functioning? It attempts to answer this question by specifying the processing involved in sensing, perceiving, encoding, remembering, and restructuring information. The cognitive approach implies an active, strategy-equipped organism whose complex behavior can only be understood by attacking the complexity directly, armed with theoretical constructs, intervening variables, and models of the structures and processes being investigated.

Some information processing seems to be "automatic," that is, not under the control of the subject. Other processing is controlled by the specific cognitive strategies used by the subject, with strategy choice influenced by experience, context, motivation, and the nature of the information itself. Better understanding of these types of information processing will probably be the legacy of cognitive psychology.

It is now well documented by studies from the experimental and psychometric laboratories, in addition to our observations of everyday functioning, that older persons process information and behave differently from younger persons. The literature suggests that older persons are different while attending to, perceiving, encoding, and remembering information, processes involved in tasks ranging from simple perceptual decision making to complex problem solving. Whether you are dealing with psychometric measures of cognitive ability or with experimental laboratory performance, age differences are found more often than not. However, the chapters presented here also describe conditions in which age differences are not found. These exceptions pose problems for hypotheses of a single, general decline. The role of cognitive psychology, therefore, is to define and understand the differences, when found, in terms of the structures and processes posited by the conceptual framework on which cognitive psychology is based.

Cognitive psychology is covered in two sections of this book. The present section deals with basic research in cognitive processing, and the following section focuses on speed of behavior, a specific topic that generated a great deal of research in the 1970s. The five chapters in the present section review the conceptual issues of the 1970s and suggest new directions and prescriptions for research in the 1980s. Four of these five chapters deal with the four major areas of cognitive psychology: attention and perception, learning and memory, concept formation and problem solving, and intelligence and cognitive ability. The fifth chapter is James Fozard's 1979 presidential address to the Division of Aging and Adult Development of the American Psychological Association. Fozard's chapter serves as a bridge between the present section and the section on speed of behavior that follows it. In addition, Fozard specifically suggests directions for intervention programs and applications for the research findings being developed. In most cases, the chapters in the present section reflect robust research endeavors

223

that evidence significant progress in the recent past and a great deal of hope for the future. This progress and hope are generated by the unifying information-processing framework with which this section is concerned. In fact, as Hoyer and Plude suggest in Chapter 16, the conceptual distinctions between the various topics covered in this section are becoming more and more artificial.

Because of the common conceptual framework, there are shared concerns for the future expressed in the different chapters. First, it is apparent even to the casual observer of these research areas that the methodologies and research paradigms are becoming more sophisticated and more conceptually adequate. Part of this, of course, is because the theoretical formulations and questions are becoming more refined. This conclusion is reached in all of the papers. Giambra and Arenberg (Chapter 18) aptly point out that methodology is shaped by the theoretical ideas current in the field. In addition to the methodological and theoretical sophistication provided by experimental psychology, significant advances have been made in life span developmental psychology. The issue of determining "true age" effects, for example, is discussed by Hartley, Harker, and Walsh in Chapter 17 and is the primary focus of Willis and Baltes in Chapter 19.

In addition, the chapters propose that we expand our methodological repertoire. Hoyer and Plude suggest better use of the recent developments in sensory and perceptual measurement that have taken place in the experimental laboratory. Giambra and Arenberg hope for more idiographic studies that use the "thinking aloud" procedure used by Newell and Simon in their research. Three of the chapters call for more naturalistic observation to develop a catalog of the cognitive processes as they occur in the various natural contexts in which people of different ages find themselves. This plea has been given recent impetus by the work of James Fozard.

Such a behavior catalog may show differences in the nature of the cognitive processes required by subjects of different age groups. Willis and Baltes aptly remind us that our psychometric instruments are based on the activities of young adults. In addition, our laboratory cognitive tasks often simulate the academic activities predominant in the lives of young adults. Hartley, Harker, and Walsh describe results showing that when tasks are used that are more familiar and more closely aligned to the day-to-day activities of older adults, age differences may be attenuated or even eliminated.

This plea for greater "ecological validity" is logically concomitant with the turn away from the "deficit" model of cognitive aging. Research discussed in all of the chapters suggests that the differences and changes we observe could well reflect adaptive changes

in performance based on strategies and experiences used by subjects of different ages. A single, definitive "deficit" hypothesis does not seem capable of surviving the weight of all the evidence. The significant interactions between age and experimental treatment, and the success of intervention and training procedures, suggest a more complex explanation. A ubiquitous deficit with a neurological cause does not seem capable of explaining all of what Willis and Baltes refer to as the "plasticity" in cognitive performance seen in perceptual, memory, problem-solving, and psychometric laboratories.

This issue is probably the major one in the cognitive psychology of aging: the extent to which some age differences and changes are specific, adaptive changes in strategy and the extent to which others are irreversible, neurological deficits. This issue goes by many names: neurological versus experiential; deficit versus adaptive change; competence versus performance; production deficit versus mediation deficit. The extent to which age effects are not irreversible deficits but changes in cognitive strategy used to perform the task should be determined before applications of cognitive findings can be pursued.

Finally, there is the realization that cognitive behavior is multivariate in nature. Investigators are abandoning the conceptually limiting strategy of addressing hypothetical dichotomies. Questions of the 1970s included, Is perceptual slowing peripheral or central? Is the memory deficit due to storage or retrieval? Is the difference due to chronological age or cohort effects? While these distinctions are theoretically important, it is becoming clear that no single hypothesis will be able to account for our findings. More often than not, effects are influenced by many factors and involve both prongs of the dichotomies. For example, slowing probably involves the entire information-processing system, both peripheral and central, as James Birren points out in the next section of this book (see Chapter 21). If "processing deficits" are found on learning and memory tasks, then both acquisition and retrieval should be influenced by these deficits. As most of the following chapters suggest, rarely is all the variance accounted for by a single hypothesis. Designs are more and more addressing the extent to which several factors affect age differences and age changes, a reflection of the multivariate nature of our field of study.

Jenkins (1979) reminds us that we must consider four basic factors when doing research in cognitive psychology, and these factors are equally applicable when age is studied. These factors are described in the figure. Cognitive research involves a particular group of subjects of specific characteristics, such as age and intelligence; some particular criterion task to

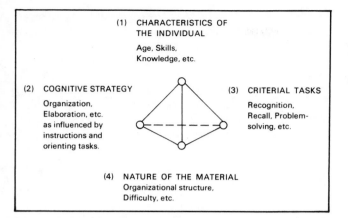

(1) CHARACTERISTICS OF
THE INDIVIDUAL

Age, Skills,
Knowledge, etc.

(2) COGNITIVE STRATEGY

Organization,
Elaboration, etc.
as influenced by
instructions and
orienting tasks.

(3) CRITERIAL TASKS

Recognition,
Recall, Problem-
solving, etc.

(4) NATURE OF THE MATERIAL
Organizational structure,
Difficulty, etc.

A conceptual model for doing research in cognitive psychology (adapted from Jenkins, 1979).

perform, such as recognition memory or solving cryptoarithmetic problems; some specific materials to be processed, such as a list of words or a discourse passage; and particular cognitive strategies used to perform the task, such as elaborative processing or si-

multaneous scanning. While these factors seem intuitively obvious, we must not forget to consider all four simultaneously in any research program. Each is related to every other, and any interaction between two factors could be modified by a change in one of the others. Cognitive research in the 1980s will reflect a better understanding of these complexities because there will be a better appreciation that information processing occurs in a contextual milieu. The greatest changes accompanying aging are the contexts in which people function. Understanding human functioning, therefore, is predicated on understanding the contextual nature of all cognitive processing. This is the task for the 1980s, and the five chapters in this section provide some guidance for accomplishing this goal.

REFERENCE

Jenkins, J. J. Four points to remember: A tetrahedral model of memory experimemts. In L. S. Cermak & F. I. M. Craik (Eds.), *Levels of processing in human memory.* Hillsdale, N.J.: Lawrence Erlbaum, 1979.

William J. Hoyer and Dana J. Plude

Attentional and Perceptual Processes in the Study of Cognitive Aging

This chapter highlights some recent trends and proposes some future directions in the study of attentional and perceptual processes in adulthood and old age. The internal processes that serve to organize immediate experience and behavior at several levels of analysis (e.g., sensory, perceptual, selective attentional, cognitive) are emphasized. Specific topics covered include stimulus persistence, perceptual noise, masking, sequential integration, effortful versus automatic processing, sustained versus transient visual information-processing channels, and "top-down," "bottom-up," and "middle-out" sequences of perceptual organization.

The field of perceptual aging is rapidly progressing in at least three directions. One of these, the sensory level of analysis, reflects the general tendency of scientific inquiry to become increasingly reductionistic. Perceptual and sensory functions can now be studied more anatomically and with greater technological precision than ever before. Increasingly, research in perceptual aging is drawing on the methodological and technological advancements of mainstream perception research. At the same time many more "basic" experimental psychologists are taking an interest in aging research and are including adult age comparisons as one aspect of their research programs. Basically, the research issues being addressed at the sensory level concern how we take in information presented very briefly. Specifically what happens to our capacity to perceive new information as we grow older? Are physiological aging processes responsible for changes in perceptual functioning?

Recent evidence suggests that older persons are at a disadvantage in tasks requiring the processing of brief information (e.g., Kline & Orme-Rogers, 1978; Walsh, 1976), but each new bit of data seems to raise new questions. For example, many researchers are now directing their efforts at *localizing* age-related changes in the structures and functions of perception. How investigators approach the task of localizing age-related changes in sensory and perceptual functioning necessarily reflects their own implicit model of human information processing. First, information processing can be viewed as a continuous flow of input from receptors at the periphery to the brain. Many researchers in perceptual aging have been guided by the central-versus-peripheral distinction. Others have tended to view information processing as a hierarchical sequence of functions or stages (e.g., encoding, sorting, selecting). More recently, a third view of human information processing has emerged, which can be traced to Kahnemen's (1973) work on attention and mental effort. The issue is how and where in the in-

Preparation of this chapter was supported in part by BRSG Grant S07 RR07068-14 awarded by the biomedical Research Support Grant Program, Division of Research Resources, National Institutes of Health to Syracuse University. We gratefully acknowledge the helpful comments made by Edward Blatt, John Dineen, Audrey Fullerton, Donald Kline, Daniel Smothergill, and Wayne Watson. This chapter represents the equal and shared contribution of both authors.

formation-processing system the individual allocates fixed-capacity resources (see Craik & Simon, 1980; Navon & Gopher, 1979).

A second frontier of perceptual aging research addresses the sorting and selecting aspects of information processing. The empirical revival of the concept of attention in mainstream experimental psychology has served to enhance interest in the question of adult age differences in selective attention—the ability to separate relevant from irrelevant information. Evidence supporting an age-related, selective-attention deficit has been found in several studies using different paradigms (see Hoyer, Rebok, & Sved, 1979; Kausler & Kleim, 1978; Rabbitt, 1965). Based on a review of a wide range of research (from neuroanatomical to cognitive), Layton (1975) proposed the "perceptual-noise" hypothesis as a summary heuristic for the general trend toward increased distractibility with advancing age. While the perceptual noise metaphor has been generally useful, the nature of the "noise" remains to be specified.

The third general line of investigation of perceptual aging concerns the higher order mechanisms that control sensory and perceptual processing. Basically, the research issue is how and to what extent subjects voluntarily control their perceptions. Although there are relatively few adult developmental investigations of "top-down" processing, the advances made by nondevelopmental researchers in this area point to its importance to the understanding of perceptual aging.

In the sections that follow, we briefly highlight the specific findings in each of these three areas of perceptual aging research. We are considering these areas simply as current lines of inquiry. It is important to point out that we are *not* proposing a multistage model of perceptual aging. On the contrary, our view is that age-related changes both at the most basic sensory levels and at higher cognitive voluntary levels affect one's perceptual experiences. Thorough analysis of perceptual aging involves the understanding of changes throughout the information-processing system. We begin with discussion of the factors that affect the processing of briefly presented visual information. Since relatively more is known about the relations among sensory processes and higher processes in the domain of vision, our focus is on the visual processing system.

Processing Limitations and Aging

All perceptual processes take time, and therefore *time* constitutes one type of limitation to perceptual processing. A second type of limit to processing is *space*, which has to do with how much information can be handled at any one moment. Where in the sequence of processing information do age-related limitations occur?

Most conceptualizations of human information processing represent the flow of information as proceeding through a sequence of stages, each of which is characterized by progressively higher levels of abstraction. The first and most peripheral level of analysis is located at the site of the sensory receptors. Information from the environment is translated into some kind of internal code, which is then transmitted to "higher" levels of processing. At some point subsequent to sensory coding, perceptual processes operate on the transformed information, and attentional mechanisms guide, at least to some extent, the processing of that information.

Though the distinctions between sensation, perception, and attention are somewhat arbitrary, age-related limits on processing have been reported at each of these levels of analysis. Several writers have already reviewed the research on age-related changes in pre-retinal structures (e.g., Corso, 1971; Fozard, Wolf, Bell, McFarland, & Podolsky, 1977). There are two important structural changes that affect visual processing: The diameter of the pupil decreases, and the crystalline lens thickens and yellows with advancing age. Both of these changes impose limits on the amount of light reaching the retina. It has been argued that these preretinal changes contribute to the observed rise in absolute threshold with age (Weale, 1963). Similarly, much of the age-related decrease in fusion threshold for critical flicker frequency can be attributed to structural change in the lens and pupil (Weale, 1965). Other age-related structural changes impose limitations on processing too, and the reader is referred to the thorough review of this material by Fozard et al. (1977).

Age-Related Limitations on Perceptual Processing

Investigations of age-associated limitations in perceptual processing have centered mainly on temporal rather than spatial constraints. In particular, much research has been devoted to age differences in the rate of processing visual information (see, for example, Plude, Blatt, Hoyer, & Dineen, 1980). In the past decade the two experimental paradigms that have dominated the study of age-related changes in temporal processing are stimulus masking and sequential stimulus integration. Two other lines of perceptual research that have received relatively less attention over the past decade concern age differences in susceptibility to aftereffects and illusions. Excellent reviews of the aging literature concerning these latter phenomena are available in Comalli (1970), Fozard et al. (1977), and Pollack and Atkeson (1978). Another research area that has received relatively less attention, but which has important implications for a two-process view of attention (discussed later), involves adult age differences in the serial versus the parallel nature of preattentive processes. In a sense, this issue concerns spatial constraints on information processing, and it supplements our understanding of age-related temporal processing limits (see Lindsay & Norman, 1972; Solso, 1979).

Before addressing the research on age-related, temporal processing constraints, it is useful to examine the distinction between peripheral and central components of visual information processing. There are two very different perspectives on the peripheral–central distinction. The older view follows from the traditional neurophysiological distinction between peripheral and central nervous system function. Here, the lateral geniculate and primary visual cortex (i.e., retrochiasmal structures) are taken as central. The more recent perspective follows from information-processing models (e.g., Turvey, 1973) in which structures up to and including the primary visual cortex are viewed as peripheral. Often the disagreement among researchers on which effects are "central" and which are "peripheral" relates only to which definition is used.

Related to the central–peripheral distinction is the use of various stimulus presentation techniques to assess their respective effects. Three types of presentation conditions can be employed in studying visual processing: (a) monoptic—in which stimuli are presented to one eye only, (b) dichoptic—in which stimuli are presented alternately to each eye, and (c) binocular—in which stimuli are presented to both eyes simultaneously. Many investigators have suggested that dichoptic viewing reflects central-processing effects because two stimuli, each presented to a different eye, can interact only at or subsequent to the site of convergence (e.g., Kline & Birren, 1975; Walsh, 1976). However, it may be inappropriate to argue for a central processing locus exclusively. Recently, Sakitt (1975, 1976) found evidence for a robust persistence effect at the level of retinal photoreceptors that may account for dichoptic viewing effects. The argument centers on the storage and transmission characteristics of photoreceptor cells in the retina. For example, if retinal storage persists for 500 msec, the photoreceptors of one eye may send a 500-msec signal to the site of binocular interaction. During this time, if a second stimulus impinges on the other eye, a second, separate signal will be transmitted to the retrochiasmal site and there will be sufficient time for the signals to interact. Thus, convergence of the independent stimuli is made possible not necessarily by storage characteristics at the converging (central) site but rather by storage mechanisms localized in the retinal (peripheral) system. Long (1979) provides a good discussion of the dichoptic viewing procedure and its associated problems.

Though the distinction between central and peripheral processing limitations is not well delineated, the emphasis on component visual mechanisms has served a heuristic function in research on perceptual processing.

Masking. When two stimuli are flashed in rapid succession, their visual traces interact. When the first stimulus obscures the second, the phenomenon is called forward masking; when the second stimulus obscures the first, it is called backward masking. In either case the interference results because the visual system takes some amount of time to clear or to recover from stimulation. The longer this signal processing takes, the greater is the opportunity for masking to occur. Susceptibility to masking effects is usually indexed by the critical period required to escape masking effects. When this period is measured from the offset of the first signal to the onset of the second, interstimulus interval (ISI) is the dependent variable. When the critical interval is measured from the onset of the first signal to the onset of the second, stimulus-onset asynchrony (SOA) is the dependent variable. In both instances the emphasis is on the time required to escape masking. The duration of this critical period has been used to provide estimates of signal clearing time in the central nervous system, as well as to help isolate the relative contributions of central and peripheral components in visual processing (Turvey, 1973).

In older age groups, there is an increase in the critical period required to escape masking effects. For example, Kline and Szafran (1975) used a backward monoptic masking paradigm to show that elderly subjects (M = 68.2 years) suffered from a visual noise mask at significantly longer ISIs than did young subjects (M = 23.3 years). In order to maintain criterion performance, older adults required longer ISIs than did younger adults at all target durations tested. Kline and Szafran (1975) concluded that "there is, with increasing adult age, a significant increase in the time needed to process completely a single perceptual event" (p. 311). In addition, the authors suggested that this slowing limits the number of perceptual events that the senescent visual system handles per unit of time. Similar results were obtained in a follow-up study by Kline and Birren (1975).

Walsh (1976) focused on SOA in order to assess age-related differences in signal processing. Following Turvey's distinction between central and peripheral masking effects, Walsh not only manipulated target durations and ISIs but also varied target intensities and SOA in order to delineate age-related differences in the rate of visual information processing. Older subjects (M = 64.2 years) required significantly longer ISIs to escape masking than did younger adults (M = 19.5 years), which is consistent with the findings of Kline and Birren (1975). Walsh showed that his older subjects needed 24% longer SOAs than did young adults in order to escape the effects of masking. The lack of an interaction between age and the other experimental factors on SOA was taken to suggest that "no qualitative differences in central perceptual processes exist between the age groups employed in this investigation" (Walsh, 1976, p. 183). Thus, while the rate of processing may decline with age, the stages of processing appear relatively age-invariant in adulthood.

Finally, in two recent investigations involving monoptic backward-masking paradigms, Walsh, Till, and Williams (1978) and Till (1978) found evidence of age-related slowing in peripheral visual processing. The data in both studies conformed to Turvey's (1973) formula for describing peripheral masking effects. In both investigations there was a constant increase with age in the time required to escape masking. This was attributed to a slow-down in peripheral processing accompanying age.

All of these masking investigations have produced results supporting the notion that there is a definite age-associated slowing in the rate of processing visual information. While the precise locus of the slowing remains unclear, the trend toward systematic manipulations of parameters affecting the magnitude of masking effects will likely produce more definitive evidence bearing on the central-peripheral distinction. Perhaps the inferred neural mechanisms underlying age-related slowing pervade the entire information-processing system (Pollack, 1978).

Sequential integration. Eriksen and Collins (1967) modified the typical backward-masking paradigm by eliminating the necessity for a mask to interfere with processing a target stimulus. Instead of setting up a condition in which performance was hindered by interacting visual signals, they devised a task in which interacting signals actually facilitated detection accuracy. The procedure involved sequentially flashing two halves of a stimulus pattern and requiring subjects to identify the stimulus contained in the integrated halves. As expected, longer ISIs produced poorer detection performance, while shorter ISIs yielded higher levels of accuracy, exactly the opposite of masking paradigms.

Recently, Kline and Baffa (1976) used the Eriksen and Collins paradigm to investigate age-related differences in temporal processing. Young (M = 21.3 years) and elderly (M = 55.6 years) adults were required to identify stimulus words that were presented sequentially in two halves separated by variable ISIs. It was hypothesized that the slower rate of processing in the senescent visual system would facilitate performance at longer ISIs. But young adults outperformed older adults at all ISIs.

In a follow-up study, Kline and Orme-Rogers (1978) recognized that temporal luminance summation and contrast reduction may have influenced the Kline and Baffa (1976) findings. Eriksen (1966) and others (e.g., Eriksen & Lappin, 1964; Pollack, 1973) have shown that background luminances, as well as target stimuli, are summated temporally. This reduces the contrast ratio of a given target stimulus to its ground, making the target less detectable. Kline and Orme-Rogers suggested that perhaps older adults are more susceptible to the effects of luminance summation and contrast reduction, owing to their slower rate of processing visual information. In order to attenuate summated-contrast reduction, the authors used stimuli consisting of white figures against black backgrounds. In line with their expectations, older adults (M = 68.0 years) outperformed younger adults (M = 18.9 years) as ISI increased.

These studies of sequential integration support the notion of age-associated limitations in visual information processing. Futher, these studies have made apparent the need to specify precisely the stimulus conditions sufficient for producing differential age-related performance in perceptual processing. The locus of age-related slowing has not as yet been specified, and the aim of recent work has been to identify some of the neural substrates underlying visual processing. Before considering some of the explanations of age-related slowing that have grown out of this line of research, we turn to the study of age-associated limitations on perceptual capacity.

Serial versus parallel perceptual processing. Spatial limits on perceptual processing impose constraints on the quantity of information that can occupy the system at any given time. When information is handled one unit (or one channel) at a time, then processing is said to be serial. If multiple units (or channels) can be handled simultaneously, then processing is parallel in nature. Since Sperling's (1960) preliminary investigations of visual short-term storage, there have been numerous attempts to replicate and further define the nature of parallel perceptual processing (cf. Abel, 1972; Averbach & Coriell, 1961; Bjork & Murray, 1977; Shiffrin & Gardner, 1972).

In one test of the serial-parallel issue, Watson

(1978) found equivalent magnitudes of response competition in a task requiring selective attention to a single position in a display of several items. Reaction time (RT) was equivalent, whether a target was presented alone or was flanked by response-compatible items. When response-incompatible items bordered the target, RT was slowed, but subjects ranging in age from 20 to 65 years showed equivalent RT slowing. Watson argued that these findings were attributable to the parallel processing of displays by all ages tested, even when target-location cues were provided. Thus even "unwanted" stimuli gained access to the perceptual system due to the parallel and nonselective nature of this early perceptual process.

There is some evidence to suggest that the processing of briefly presented visual information takes place in parallel throughout adulthood. More research is needed to clarify this point. More clearly, it appears that the rate of processing during perception undergoes age-related slowing. One major explanation of this slowing is the stimulus-persistence hypothesis.

Stimulus persistence "refers to the possibility that the neural representation of a stimulus persists for some time after offset of the physical energy impinging on the receptor surface" (Haber & Standing, 1969, p. 43). The stimulus-persistence hypothesis proposes that the senescent visual system is slowed in rate of processing owing to the extended refractory period of aged neurons.

The stimulus-persistence hypothesis encompasses a diverse literature concerning adult age differences in visual information processing (cf. Botwinick, 1978, Chapter 11). However, in terms of its explanatory potential it fails to provide a clear understanding of the mechanisms or the locus of age-related slowing. Thus, while the stimulus-persistence hypothesis has served a useful descriptive purpose over the past decade, its usefulness as a guide to research in the 1980s is questionable (Plude et al., 1980).

Perceptual aging: Where to next? That there are age-associated temporal limitations on visual perception is well documented (e.g., Botwinick, 1978; Fozard et al., 1977; Welford, 1977). This slowing has been shown to persist over a variety of task demands and experimental paradigms. Yet relatively little is known with precision about the nature and locus of these age-related constraints.

The use of direct rather than indirect assessment techniques may provide insight into the nature of age-associated differences in visual processing (see Haber & Standing, 1969). Recently, Walsh and Thompson (1978) used one of Haber and Standing's direct methods to assess age-related differences in the persistence of a form. They found that the short-term visual

storage of young adults ($M = 24.0$ years) persisted 15% longer than that of elderly subjects ($M = 67.0$ years). However, it may be asked to what extent summated contrast reduction can account for these findings (Kline & Orme-Rogers, 1978). Further research using direct-assessment techniques is warranted to clarify these results.

Future investigations of age-related processing limitations should identify precisely the kind of temporal constraint being assessed. Recently, Hawkins and Shulman (1979) provided two definitions of persistence in visual perception that may clarify some inconsistencies in the literature. According to these authors, Type I persistence is "the temporal disparity between the objective and phenomenal durations of a stimulus," whereas Type II persistence "relates to the duration of the aftereffect rather than to the duration of the stimulus itself" (Hawkins & Shulman, 1979, p. 348). Haber and Standing's (1969) direct techniques and studies of critical flicker frequency apply mainly to Type I persistence. Studies of positive afterimages and Eriksen and Collins's (1967) sequential integration paradigm examine Type II persistence. Perhaps the pattern of age-related slowing is different for different types of persistence.

Finally, as noted above, perceptual aging research in the 1980s will benefit from hypotheses that link age-related processing limits to underlying mechanisms and specific loci. An example of such hypothesizing is found in Pollack's (1978) extension of the general stimulus-persistence notion. Based partly on the work of Sakitt (1976), Pollack suggested that the locus of age-related slowing is in the photoreceptors of the retina. Perhaps gradual decreases in the metabolic efficiency of thin afferent fibers in the retina during aging are responsible for these age-related changes (McFarland, 1968).

Further refinement of Pollack's hypothesis might incorporate a distinction between sustained and transient channels in visual processing. At the neurophysiological level it has been suggested that the visual system is composed of two physiologically and anatomically distinct processing channels. These have been labeled the X and Y systems (Brooks & Jung, 1973; Rowe & Stone, 1977). Both systems originate in the retina in the X-type and Y-type receptive fields of retinal ganglion cells. Functionally, the X system can be viewed as providing highly accurate pattern information to the striate system via a sustained response channel. The Y system provides information about changes in visual fields to the tectal system via a fast transmission channel. Developmentally, aging processes may act differentially on the X and Y systems, since the two systems may have different maintenance demands on their cell bodies.

At present the X-Y model, while lacking specification of direct physiological-cognitive links, provides a useful heuristic. For example, spatial (Campbell, 1973; Campbell & Robson, 1968) as well as temporal (Robson, 1966) modulation paradigms could be employed for mapping specific age-related changes in the two systems. Additionally, experimental paradigms taken from contemporary cognitive psychology (e.g., Breitmeyer & Ganz, 1976) could serve to map age-related changes in information processing, based on attentional and pattern demands. In short, the X-Y model can serve both to generate developmental hypotheses and to stimulate the use of new experimental methods in perceptual aging research.

Age-related Limitations on Attention

Current interest in the study of attention can be traced to the publication of Broadbent's *Perception and Communication* in 1958. This book, along with a change in focus of research toward to study of limited-capacity short-term systems (see Brown, 1958; Peterson & Peterson, 1959), helped to lay the foundation for the currently useful information-processing approach to cognition (Erdelyi, 1974; Lachman, Lachman, & Butterfield, 1979). Kahneman (1973) noted that Broadbent's (1958) model and other early models of attention were "bottleneck" models. Theorists differed on where the bottleneck or the selective-filtering mechanism was assumed to be located in the sequence of processing information (Deutsch & Deutsch, 1963; Keele, 1973; Norman, 1968; Treisman, 1964). Broadbent's (1958, 1977) *single-filter* theory, as well as other single-channel theories (e.g., Welford, 1977), have been able to account for the general effects of information load on processing time. However, other variables in addition to the quantity of information and its rate of presentation have been shown to affect attentional performance. Some of these factors are stimulus and response repetition (Biederman, 1972), familiarity (Kreuger, 1975), speed–accuracy demand characteristics (Pew, 1969), perceptual organization (Garner, 1974), and practice (Schneider & Shiffrin, 1977).

The main assumption of single-channel attentional theories is that processing limitations involve difficulties in translating and moving information from the sensory buffer to long-term memory. Treisman's (1964) shadowing study—in which it was shown that an ignored stimulus actually activates information in long-term storage at the same time another stimulus is being processed—posed serious problems for single-channel theory. Alternatively, it has been suggested that more than one signal has unimpaired parallel access to long-term memory and that selective attention occurs at the memory level (aided by cues such as memory location) and not at the sensory level (e.g., Deutsch & Deutsch, 1963; Norman, 1968). One currently important theory-generated research question is whether more than one signal has simultaneous and unimpaired access to information already stored in memory.

In contrast to the bottleneck models, recent formulations of attention have emphasized the *capacity limitations* of attention (e.g., Kahneman, 1973). Hasher and Zacks (1979) noted that information-processing operations often vary in their attentional requirements. Some operations (called *automatic*) use very little of the person's limited capacity for attention, whereas other operations (labeled *effortful*), such as active rehearsal, require much attentional capacity. Hasher and Zacks's (1979) distinction between automatic and effortful attentional processing was based on earlier work by Shiffrin and Schneider (1977) and others (e.g., LaBerge & Samuels, 1974; Posner & Snyder, 1974). Before discussing the very recent evidence pertaining to the distinction between automatic and effortful processing in old age (e.g., Hasher & Zacks, 1979; Madden & Nebes, in press; Plude & Hoyer, 1980), the findings on adult age difference in effortful or controlled processing are presented briefly.

Selective attention. Several authors have suggested that there is an age-associated deficit in the ability to extract relevant from irrelevant information (e.g., Layton, 1975; Rabbitt, 1977; Schonfield, 1974). This observation has been derived from various experimental paradigms applied to the study of age-related effects of irrelevant information. We will consider some of the prominent methods that have been used in studying age-related limitations on the selectivity of attention.

Rabbitt (1965) used a visual search paradigm to investigate the apparent age decrement in the ability to ignore irrelevant information. Generally, as the number of nontarget items in a display increases, the more difficult it becomes to detect a target within that display. This has been termed the *display-size effect*. The magnitude of the display-size effect is attributed to the subject's inability to ignore irrelevant display items while searching for relevant ones. Rabbitt (1965) demonstrated that the magnitude of the display-size effect was larger for elderly than for young adults. A card-sorting procedure was used in which old (M = 67.4 years) and young (M = 19.0 years) adults performed in two conditions of relevancy. The first condition required a two-choice sort on the basis of whether one of two targets was detected; in the second condition there were eight targets to be discriminated. In both conditions targets appeared individually within four levels of irrelevancy: none, one, two, or eight distractor letters. The results implicated age as a significant factor, but its interaction with the amount of target information did not reach significance. Thus, while young adults sorted more rapidly overall than did older subjects, both groups were slowed equivalently by having to search for eight targets instead of two. Importantly, there was a significant Age × Irrelevancy interaction which indicated that older subjects were disproportionately slowed as the number of distractors increased. Rabbitt (1965) concluded that older people have more difficulty ignoring irrelevant stimuli than do younger adults.

Wright and Elias (1979) recently questioned whether nontargets in visual-search tasks are truly "irrelevant." Since irrelevant stimuli have to be discriminated from relevant stimuli in visual search, age differences in visual search may reflect difficulties in *discriminating* relevant from irrelevant information, not in *ignoring* the irrelevant stimuli. In order to assess the age-related differences in the processes of ignoring versus discriminating irrelevant information Wright and Elias (1979) modeled their study after Eriksen and Eriksen's (1974) nonsearch detection task. Young (18–25 years) and older (60–82 years) adults were required to respond on the basis of a (relevant) target presented in the center of a horizontal display. On some trials, other (irrelevant) items bordered the target position. Both age groups were slowed by the presence of "neutral" irrelevant information, but the elderly were not differentially slowed by this factor.

Wright and Elias (1979) used a *selective-filtering* task. In contrast, visual-search tasks like Rabbitt's (1965) can be classified as *selective-search* tasks. In the filtering task, a subject must ignore or filter out information that is irrelevant to task performance, whereas in the search task, irrelevant stimuli must be discriminated from relevant stimuli. Perhaps the pattern of age-associated limitations on attentional selectivity differ for the two kinds of task.

Farkas and Hoyer (1980) recently conducted two experiments that relate to the filtering–search distinction. In both experiments the interfering effects of background (irrelevant) information either did or did not contrast with the orientation of targets. In the first experiment (selective search), the position in a display of a target varied over cards in a deck. In the second study (selective filtering), the position of a target did not vary over cards. In the first task, elderly (60–81 years), but not middle-aged (37–58 years) or young (18–30 years), adults were slowed by the presence of contrasting irrelevant information. All three age

groups were slowed by the presence of irrelevant information in the same orientation as the target. In the second study, no age group was slowed by contrasting irrelevant information, and only the oldest group was slowed by the presence of similar irrelevant information. These findings support the view that irrelevant information may have different age-associated effects depending on the nature of the attention demands of the task. The reader is referred to Chapter 18 in this book and to Rabbitt (1977) for a discussion of how age-associated changes in attentional selectivity affect other cognitive processes (e.g., problem solving).

Age-related limits on attentional capacity. Investigations of age-related differences in the *capacity* of attention are concerned with the quantity of information to which attention can be allocated at any given moment. Adult age differences are found on tasks requiring attention to be divided (a) between two input sources, (b) between stimulus input and rehearsal, and (c) between rehearsing and retrieving or responding (see Craik, 1977; Craik & Simon, 1980).

One of the clearest demonstrations of adult age differences in divided attention was reported by Kirchner (1958). Subjects in two age groups, young (18–24 years) and elderly (60–84 years), observed a display of 12 lights, and the subjects' job was to press a switch below the light when the light came on. Pressing the switch turned off that light and turned on another light. In this phase of the task older subjects performed at levels comparable to young subjects. However, when the task was made more complicated (i.e., to press the key corresponding to the previous light), an age deficit was obtained. Older subjects made more errors, which indicates an inability to allocate attention between memory for the light and response.

Layton (1975) reviewed much of the research on adult age differences in attention and proposed the perceptual-noise hypothesis. Layton argued that aging is accompanied by a decrement in the ability to suppress internal and external irrelevant stimulation. Layton's hypothesis, unlike "neurological noise" (Gregory, 1959) and "stimulus persistence" (Botwinick, 1978), does not require links to underlying neural mechanisms for its validation. Instead, "it deals with observed and manipulable environmental noise rather than with inferred and nonmanipulable physiological noise" (Layton, 1975, p. 876). Although Layton presented evidence supportive of the perceptual-noise view of aging, conditions exist under which there appears to be no age-related increase in perceptual noise (e.g., Wright & Elias, 1979). Thus it is important that future investigations determine the particular conditions yielding age-related increases in perceptual noise. One approach that appears well suited for this undertaking centers on the distinction between automatic and effortful processing, discussed earlier.

Age-related limits on effortful and automatic processes. According to the two-process view of attention, some processes require attention for their operation and other processes require little or none of the limited capacity of attention. The former have been variously termed *effortful* (Hasher & Zacks, 1979), *controlled* (Schneider & Shiffrin, 1977), and *conscious* (Posner & Snyder, 1974), whereas the latter have been called *automatic* (Hasher & Zacks, 1979; Schneider & Shiffrin, 1977) and *unconscious* (Posner & Snyder, 1975). If there is an age-related decrease in the capacity of attention, then tasks requiring effortful processing are likely to yield greater magnitudes of age-associated decline than tasks that can be performed automatically. Thus it is important to distinguish between age-related limits in effortful versus automatic processing.

In order to assess age differences in effortful and automatic processing, researchers have adopted paradigms employed in contemporary cognitive psychology. For example, Schneider and Shiffrin (1977) used a hybrid memory-search/visual-search paradigm to show that young subjects who developed an automatic target detection strategy were uninfluenced by manipulations of information load (i.e., target-set size and display size), while subjects who had to rely on controlled processing (i.e., scanning and selective attention) showed typical decrements as a function of load. The critical manipulation determining whether processing was controlled or automatic centered on the consistency of stimulus-to-response mapping during an extensive training period. Subjects given consistent stimulus mapping developed an automatic processing mode, while those given varied mapping continued to rely on capacity-limited control processes (see Schneider & Shiffrin, 1977; Shiffrin & Schneider, 1977).

Recently, Plude and Hoyer (1980) investigated adult age differences in visual search using a card-sorting task. Young (M = 23.6 years) and elderly (M = 75.0 years) subjects searched either for an unchanging memory set (consistent mapping) or for changing memory sets (varied mapping) in displays containing a target letter and either none, three, or eight distractor letters. The main finding was that under the varied-mapping condition, the traditional pattern of age-associated decrement in search was obtained. In the consistent-mapping condition, adult age differences in the processing of irrelevant information were not found. This finding was taken as evidence that age-related decrements in visual search can be eliminated or at least minimized when the demand on effortful processing is lessened via consistent stimulus mapping.

In a related study, Madden and Nebes (1980) examined the acquisition of automaticity by young (18–25 years) and elderly (61–74 years) subjects. Again, a hybrid memory-search/visual-search paradigm was used, but here display was kept constant at two items. Search was conducted for fixed memory sets containing one, two, or three targets. It was found that the slopes of the set-size functions for both age groups decreased at equivalent rates over sessions. This was taken as evidence that elderly and young adults acquire automaticity at equivalent rates (see also Hasher & Zacks, 1979; Hoyer & Plude, 1980).

The significance of the automatic–effortful distinction with regard to perceptual aging is in terms of the allocation of attention. Examples can be found of highly efficient attentional allocation in executing well-practiced skills. Often these skills require no "mental effort" or "concentration." Air-traffic controllers, computer technicians, surgeons, and trial lawyers may all be able to carry out aspects of their jobs without the degree of concentration orginally required when these skills were being acquired. Perhaps the degree of age-imposed limitation on such skills is minimal in comparison to unpracticed skills.

Attention and aging: Where to next? In discussing the literature on adult age differences in attentional selectivity, we noted the need for investigators to distinguish procedurally between the task of ignoring irrelevant stimuli and that of discriminating irrelevant from relevant stimuli. It appears that the pattern of age-related differences in selectivity may be different under these conditions.

We also noted the importance of distinguishing between tasks requiring *effortful* and *automatic* processing. The pattern of age-associated decrement in performance appears to depend on the degree to which effortful processing is involved.

The study of adult age differences in the effects of familiarity on attention also deserves further investigation. It has been shown that familiarity plays an important role in determining the magnitude of age-related decline in memory-scanning rate (Thomas, Waugh, & Fozard, 1978) and naming latency (Poon & Fozard, 1978). In many respects, the acquisition of automaticity (Madden & Nebes, 1980) is analogous to the development of familiarity. The extent to which familiarity facilitates the acquisition of automaticity and whether familiarity factors interact with age are important questions for future investigation.

Higher Order Perceptual Processing

Contemporary theories of visual information processing differ with regard to the hypothesized order of processing. The three current positions are *top-down*, *bottom-up* and *middle-out* (Kinchla & Wolf, 1977). Evidence for a top-down sequence of processing comes from studies with college-age adults which show that the identification of a higher order object or form facilitates the recognition of lower order components. In contrast, in bottom-up sequence of processing the lower order features lead to the recognition of the object. For example, in the early stages of reading development, the child's recognition of letters leads to the recognition of words (LaBerge & Samuels, 1974; Wheeler, 1970). It is likely that a well-practiced perceiver relies on a top-down sequence or at least a middle-out sequence of processing. A middle-out sequence suggests that objects having a familiar size or spatial frequency are processed first, with subsequent processing taking place at both higher and lower levels (see Kinchla & Wolf, 1979).

Several types of paradigms (e.g., Aderman & Smith, 1971; Miller, 1979) have been used to show that our perceptions are influenced by what we expect to see and by what we have just seen. Several current models of perceptual processing allow for the influence of instructions, expectations, and other cognitive factors. In Bruner's (1957) model, for example, perception was considered as a process of categorizing stimulus inputs; prior experience and contextual factors were seen as affecting perception by determining the type and availability of categories. More recently, Rummelhart's (1977) interactive model emphasized the notion that sensory events and the contents of memory are simultaneously interacting.

The most recent evidence in young adulthood seems to give precedence to "global" features over "local" features (Broadbent, 1977; Navon, 1977). That is, we see first the "forest" and then the "trees." However, such research rarely takes into account the individual's perceptual past history and individual differences in adaptive-regulative functions. A developmental view in which emphasis is given to the age-related or age-accumulated experiences of the perceiver is needed in order to test the generalizability as well as the "external validity" of these findings. Whether the sequence of information processing is top down, bottom up, or middle out is likely to depend on what is being perceived and on the individual's unique previous experience with that information (see Hoyer, in press).

Toward an Integrated Theory of Perceptual Aging

The last decade has witnessed an upsurge of interest in broadening theory and research on perception (e.g., Neisser, 1976; Pick & Saltzman, 1978). Such expansion efforts will probably continue through the next decade. Contemporary models of human information processing leave room for differential psychologists to fill in the data on interindividual differences and intraindividual change. But it is possible that research and theory on perceptual aging can yield more than a quantitative "filling in" of the parameters of perception. Current knowledge, as well as what is yet to be known about aging processes, is likely to contribute to our general understanding of perception. If the field of perceptual aging is to develop significantly in the next decade, it will need to reflect more than a broadening of the general experimental work.

The focus of perceptual aging research thus far has been on the study of adult age differences in the ability to take in new information and to attend selectively to this new information. We have already given coverage to the recent advances in our understanding of age-related limitations in perceptual processing. This work can be seen as one general component of perception. A second component—which reflects a developmental–functionalist orientation to perception—has to do with how people continuously and voluntarily allocate their perceptual resources. We need to understand more about *how* the content of perceptual experience changes as we grow older. Factors (e.g., attitudes, expectancies) influencing age-related interindividual differences in the perception of external events deserve research consideration, but as yet there is no uniform concept of "perceptual style"—personality-based strategies for processing information.

Researchers are becoming increasingly interested in ways of cataloging interindividual differences in perceiver strategies (Erdelyi, 1974). It is reasonable to propose that there is a greater degree of voluntary personal control over perceptual organization as we grow older. Neisser (1976) refers to the old joke of the optimist who perceives the object as doughnut and the pessimist who sees the hole; neither is mistaken and neither sees the whole object. Similarly, as we grow older it may be easier to perceive a cup of tea or mug of beer as either half-full or half-empty. Pick and Saltzman's (1978) discussion of modes of perceiving and processing information, and chapters by Posner, Nissen, and Ogden (1978) and Shaw and Pittenger (1978) in that same volume highlight some of the directions to be taken toward this topic.

In summary, several recommendations can be made in the hope of enhancing the symbiosis between the experimental work on perception and the field of cognitive aging. First, it is suggested that perceptual aging involves the interaction of a changing perceiver and an active environment. Although the environment may be structurally static, eye movements and body movements present the environment to the visual system differently from moment to moment. The processing of perceptual experiences with advancing age is influenced by changes within the information-processing sequence and by higher order cognitive controls (e.g., needs, expectancies). It has been suggested that the individual's familiarity with the information to be processed influences the extent to which effortful or automatic processes are involved.

Many of the processes we label perception, memory, attention, and learning, to name a few, greatly overlap. It is expected that many of the artificial distinctions will blur in the future. In their place, research paradigms leading to the specification of functionally distinct components of perceptual processing will emerge. For example, it is likely that the relation between short-term memory and perception will be reconceptualized.

Finally, it is important to emphasize that while some perceptual processes may exhibit age-related decline in adulthood, other processes, such as higher order selectivity, may come to play a more significant role in accounting for perceptual experience. We hope that the emerging models of perceptual aging will incorporate the uniqueness of the aging individual's perceptual experience.

REFERENCES

Abel, M. *The visual trace in relation to aging.* Unpublished doctoral dissertation, Washington University, 1972 (cited in Botwinick, 1978).

Aderman, D., & Smith, E. E. Expectancy as a determinant of functional units in perceptual recognition. *Cognitive Psychology*, 1971, *2*, 117–129.

Averbach, E., & Coriell, H. S. Short-term memory in vision. *Bell System Technical Journal*, 1961, *40*, 309–328.

Biederman, I. Human performance in contingent information-processing tasks. *Journal of Experimental Psychology*, 1972, *93*, 219–238.

Bjork, E. L., & Murray, J. T. On the nature of input channels in visual processing. *Psychological Review*, 1977, *84*, 472–484.

Botwinick, J. *Aging and behavior.* New York: Springer, 1978.

Breitmeyer, B. G., & Ganz, L. Implications of sustained and transient channels for theories of visual pattern masking, saccadic suppression, and information processing. *Psychological Review*, 1976, *83*, 1–36.

Broadbent, D. E. *Perception and communication.* London: Pergamon, 1958.

Broadbent, D. E. The hidden preattentive processes. *American Psychologist*, 1977, *32*, 109–118.

Brooks, B., & Jung, R. Neuronal physiology of the visual cortex. In R. Jung (Ed.), *Handbook of sensory physiology*, (Vol. 8). Berlin: Springer-Verlag, 1973.

Brown, J. Some tests of the decay theory of immediate memory. *Quarterly Journal of Experimental Psychology*, 1958, *10*, 12–21.

Bruner, J. S. On perceptual readiness. *Psychological Review*, 1957, *64*, 123–152.

Campbell, F. The transmission of spatial information through the visual system. In F. Schmitt & F. Worden (Eds.), *The neurosciences: Third study program.* Cambridge, Mass.: MIT Press, 1973.

Campbell, F., & Robson, J. Application of Fourier analysis to the visibility of gratings. *Journal of Physiology*, 1968, *197*, 551–556.

Comalli, P. E., Jr. Life-span changes in visual perception. In L. R. Goulet & P. B. Baltes (Eds.), *Life-span developmental psychology: Research and theory.* New York: Academic Press, 1970.

Corso, J. F. Sensory processes and age effects in normal adults. *Journal of Gerontology*, 1971, *26*, 90–105.

Craik, F. I. M. Age differences in human memory. In J. E. Birren & K. W. Schaie (Eds.), *Handbook of the psychology of aging.* New York: Van Nostrand Reinhold, 1977.

Craik, F. I. M., & Simon, E. The roles of attention and depth of processing in understanding age differences in memory. In L. W. Poon, J. L. Fozard, L. S. Cermak, and L. W. Thompson (Eds.), *New directions in memory and aging: Proceedings of the George A. Talland Memorial Conference.* New Jersey: Lawrence Erlbaum, 1980.

Deutsch, J. A., & Deutsch, D. Attention: some theoretical considerations. *Psychological Review*, 1963, *70*, 80–90.

Erdelyi, M. H. A new look at the new look: Perceptual defense and vigilance. *Psychological Review*, 1974, *81*, 1–25.

Eriksen, B. A., & Eriksen, C. W. Effects of noise letters upon the identification of a target in a nonsearch task. *Perception & Psychophysics*, 1974, *16*, 143–149.

Eriksen, C. W. Temporal luminance summation effects in backward and forward masking. *Perception and Psychophysics*, 1966, *1*, 87–92.

Eriksen, C. W., & Collins, J. F. Some Temporal characteristics of visual perception. *Perception and Psychophysics*, 1967, *74*, 476–484.

Eriksen, C. W., & Lappin, J. S. Luminance summation-contrast reduction as a basis for certain forward and backward masking effects. *Psychonomic Science*, 1964, *1*, 313–314.

Farkas, M. S., & Hoyer, W. J. Processing consequences of perceptual grouping in selective attention. *Journal of Gerontology*, 1980, *35*, 207–216.

Fozard, J. L., Wolf, E., Bell, B., McFarland, R. A., Podolsky, S. Visual perception and communication. In J. E. Birren & K. W. Schaie (Eds.), *Handbook of the psychology of aging.* New York: Van Nostrand Reinhold, 1977.

Garner, W. R. *The processing of information and structure.* Potomac, Md.: Lawrence Erlbaum, 1974.

Gregory, R. L. Increases in "neurological noise" as a factor in aging. *Proceedings of the Fourth International Congress on Gerontology*, 1959, *1*, 314–324.

Haber, R. N., & Standing, L. G. Direct measures of short-term visual storage. *Quarterly Journal of Experimental Psychology*, 1969, *21*, 43–54.

Hasher, L., & Zacks, R. T. Automatic and effortful processes in memory. *Journal of Experimental Psychology: General*, 1979, *108*, 356–388.

Hawkins, H., L., & Shulman, G. L. Two definitions of persistence in visual perception. *Perception and Psychophysics*, 1979, *25*, 348–350.

Hoyer, W. J. Information processing, knowledge acquisition, and learning: Developmental perspectives. *Human Development*, in press.

Hoyer, W. J., & Plude, D. J. *Aging and the attentional components of visual information processing*. Paper presented at the symposium on Aging and Human Visual Function, National Academy of Sciences, Washington, D.C., 1980.

Hoyer, W. J., Rebok, G. W., & Sved, S. M. Effects of varying irrelevant information on adult age differences in problem solving. *Journal of Gerontology*, 1979, *34*, 553–560.

Kahneman, D. *Attention and effort*. Englewood Cliffs, N.J.: Prentice-Hall, 1973.

Kausler, D. H., & Kleim, D. M. Age differences in processing relevant versus irrelevant stimuli in multiple-item recognition learning. *Journal of Gerontology*, 1978, *33*, 87–93.

Keele, S. W. *Attention and human performance*. Pacific Palisades, Calif.: Goodyear, 1973.

Kinchla, R. A., & Wolf, J. The order of visual processing: "Top-down," "bottom-up," or "middle-out." *Perception & Psychophysics*, 1979, *25*, 352–358.

Kirchner, W. K. Age differences in short-term retention of rapidly changing information. *Journal of Experimental Psychology*, 1958, *55*, 352–358.

Kline, D. W., & Baffa, G. Differences in the sequential integration of form as a function of age and interstimulus interval. *Experimental Aging Research*, 1976, *2*, 333–343.

Kline, D. W., & Birren, J. E. Age differences in backward dichoptic masking. *Experimental Aging Research*, 1975, *1*, 17–25.

Kline, D. W., & Orme-Rogers, C. Examination of stimulus persistence as the basis for superior visual identification performance among older adults. *Journal of Gerontology*, 1978, *33*, 76–81.

Kline, D. W., & Szafran, J. Age differences in backward monoptic masking. *Journal of Gerontology*, 1975, *30*, 307–311.

Kreuger, L. E. Familiarity effects in visual information processing. *Psychological Bulletin*, 1975, *82*, 949–974.

LaBerge, D., & Samuels, S. J. Toward a theory of automatic information processing in reading. *Cognitive Psychology*, 1974, *6*, 293–323.

Lachman, R., Lachman, J. L., & Butterfield, E. C. *Cognitive psychology and information processing: An introduction*. Hillsdale, N.J.: Lawrence Erlbaum, 1979.

Layton, B. Perceptual noise and aging. *Psychological Bulletin*, 1975, *82*, 875–883.

Lindsay, P. H., & Norman, D. A. *Human information processing*. New York: Academic Press, 1972.

Long, G. M. The dichoptic viewing paradigm: Do the eyes have it? *Psychological Bulletin*, 1979, *86*, 391–403.

Madden, D. J., & Nebes, R. D. Aging and the development of automaticity in visual search. *Developmental Psychology*, in press.

McFarland, R. A. The sensory and perceptual processes in aging. In K. W. Schaie (Ed.), *Theory and methods of research on aging*. Morgantown: West Virginia University Press, 1968.

Miller, J. Cognitive influences on perceptual processing. *Journal of Experimental Psychology: Human Perception and Performance*, 1979, *5*, 546–562.

Navon, D. Forest before trees: The precedence of global features in visual perception. *Cognitive Psychology*, 1977, *9*, 353–383.

Navon, D., and Gopher, D. On the economy of the human-processing system. *Psychological Review*, 1979, *86*, 214–255.

Neisser, U. *Cognition and reality*. San Francisco: Freeman, 1976.

Norman, D. A. Toward a theory of memory and attention. *Psychological Review*, 1968, *75*, 522–536.

Peterson, L. R., & Peterson, M. J. Short-term retention of individual items. *Journal of Experimental Psychology*, 1959, *58*, 193–198.

Pew, R. The speed-accuracy operating characteristic. *Acta Psychologica*, 1969, *30*, 16–26.

Pick, H. L., & Saltzman, E. (Eds.). *Modes of perceiving and processing information*. Hillsdale, N.J.: Lawrence Erlbaum, 1978.

Plude, D. J., Blatt, E. R., Hoyer, W. J., & Dineen, J. T. *Age-related differences in the processing of brief visual information: Is stimulus persistence enough?* Unpublished manuscript, Syracuse University, 1980.

Plude, D. J., & Hoyer, W. J. *Adult age differences in visual search as a function of stimulus mapping and information load*. Unpublished manuscript, Syracuse University, 1980.

Pollack, I. Interaction effects in successive visual displays: An extension of the Eriksen-Collins paradigm. *Perception and Psychophysics*, 1973, *13*, 367–373.

Pollack, R. H. A theoretical note on the aging of the visual system. *Perception and Psychophysics*, 1978, *23*, 94–95.

Pollack, R. H. & Atkeson, B. M. A life-span approach to perceptual development. In P. B. Baltes (Ed.), *Life-span developmental psychology* (Vol. 1). New York: Academic Press, 1978.

Poon, L. W., & Fozard, J. L. Speed of retrieval from long-term memory in relation to age, familiarity, and datedness of information. *Journal of Gerontology*, 1978, *33*, 711–717.

Posner, M., Nissen, M. J., & Ogden, W. C. Attended and unattended processing modes: The role of set for spatial location. In H. L. Pick & E. Saltzman (Eds.), *Modes of perceiving and processing information*. Hillsdale, N.J.: Lawrence Erlbaum, 1978.

Posner, M., & Snyder, C. R. R. Attention and cognitive control. In R. L. Solso (Ed.) *Information processing and cognition: The Loyola Symposium.* Potomac, Md.: Lawrence Erlbaum, 1974.

Rabbitt, P. M. A. An age-decrement in the ability to ignore irrelevant information. *Journal of Gerontology,* 1965, *20,* 233–238.

Rabbitt, P. M. A. Changes in problem solving ability in old age. In J. E. Birren & K. W. Schaie (Eds.), *Handbook of the psychology of aging.* New York: Van Nostrand Reinhold, 1977.

Robson, J. Spatial and temporal contrast-sensitivity functions of the visual system. *Journal of the Optical Society of America,* 1966, *56,* 1141–1142.

Rowe, M., & Stone, J. Naming of neurones. Classification and naming of cat retinal ganglion cells. *Brain Behavior and Evolution,* 1977, *14,* 185–216.

Sackitt, B. Locus of short-term visual storage. *Science,* 1975, *180,* 1318–1319.

Sackitt, B. Iconic memory. *Psychological Review,* 1976, *83,* 257–276.

Schneider, W., & Shiffrin, R. M. Controlled and automatic information processing: I. Detection, search, and attention, *Psychological Review,* 1977, *84,* 1–66.

Schonfield, D. Translations in gerontology—from lab to life: Utilizing information. *American Psychologist,* 1974, *29,* 796–801.

Shaw, R., & Pittenger, J. Perceiving change. In H. L. Pick & E. Saltzman (Eds.), *Modes of perceiving and processing information.* Hillsdale, N.J.: Lawrence Erlbaum, 1978.

Shiffrin, R. M., & Gardner, G. T. Visual processing capacity and attentional control. *Journal of Experimental Psychology,* 1972, *93,* 72–83.

Shiffrin, R. M., & Schneider, W. Controlled and automatic human information processing: II. Perceptual learning, automatic attending, and a general theory. *Psychological Review,* 1977, *84,* 127–190.

Solso, R. L. *Cognitive psychology.* New York: Harcourt Brace Jovanovich, 1979.

Sperling, G. Information available in brief visual presentations. *Psychological Monographs,* 1960, *74,* (Whole No. 11).

Thomas, J. C., Waugh, N. C., & Fozard, J. L. Age and familiarity in memory scanning. *Journal of Gerontology,* 1978, *33,* 528–533.

Till, R. E. Age-related differences in binocular backward masking with visual noise. *Journal of Gerontology,* 1978, *33,* 702–710.

Treisman, A. M. Monitoring and storage of relevant messages in selective attention. *Journal of Verbal Learning and Verbal Behavior,* 1964, *3,* 449–459.

Turvey, M. On peripheral and central processes in vision: Inferences from an information-processing analysis of masking with patterned stimuli. *Psychological Review,* 1973, *80,* 1–52.

Walsh, D. Age differences in central perceptual processing: A dichoptic backward masking investigation. *Journal of Gerontology,* 1976, *31,* 178–185.

Walsh, D., & Thompson, L. W. Age differences in visual sensory memory. *Journal of Gerontology,* 1978, *33,* 383–387.

Walsh, D., Till, R. E., & Williams, M. Age differences in peripheral visual processing: A monoptic backward masking investigation. *Journal of Experimental Psychology: Human Perception and Performance,* 1978, *4,* 232–243.

Watson, W. E. *Inadvertent processing of irrelevant information: Age equivalences and differences.* Paper presented at the meeting the Gerontological Society, Dallas, Texas, November 1978.

Weale, R. A. *The aging eye.* New York: Harper, 1963.

Weale, R. A. On the eye. In A. T. Welford & J. E. Birren (Eds.), *Behavior, aging, and the nervous system.* Springfield, Ill.: Charles C Thomas, 1965.

Welford, A. T. Motor performance. In J. E. Birrent & K. W. Schaie (Eds.), *Handbook of the psychology of aging.* New York: Van Nostrand Reinhold, 1977.

Wheeler, D. D. Processes in word recognition. *Cognitive Psychology,* 1970, *1,* 59–85.

Wright, L. L., & Elias, J. W. Age differences in the effects of perceptual noise. *Journal of Geronotology,* 1979, *34,* 704–708.

Joellen T. Hartley, Judith O. Harker, and David A. Walsh

CHAPTER

17

Contemporary Issues and New Directions in Adult Development of Learning and Memory

Information-processing investigations of age-related memory differences examine the capacities of different memory stores and the operation of acquisition and retrieval functions on them. Research has proceeded along three lines: differences in acquisition or retrieval processes, differences in organizational processes, and differences in depth of processing. Deficient processing strategies do not seem to account for all age-related memory differences. Explanations involving processing speed are also problematic. This chapter raises the question of ecological validity and generality of list-memory findings and discusses new directions for research in discourse processing and acquisition of spatial information.

Aging is a process almost always accompanied by a perceived decline in the ability to acquire and remember information. The apparent regularity and permanence of this decline makes an understanding of age-related changes in learning and memory an area of major importance for developmental investigations. Since the study of learning and memory has traditionally been within the purview of experimental psychology, what we know about learning and memory in old age and how we attempt to explain it have been influenced by theoretical models developed in this field. Associationism and information processing have provided the most influential theoretical models for the developmental study of learning and memory processes. These paradigms have dictated both the specific questions to be addressed and the methodologies

used to answer the questions. Since research on learning and memory is currently dominated by the information-processing view of the world, our discussion is restricted to the issues in aging research that have been addressed by this tradition. For the reader who is interested in reviewing the research conducted in the tradition of associationism, we recommend the excellent reviews by Kay (1959) and Jerome (1959) for some of the earliest work on aging and memory, the detailed review of the empirical literature by Botwinick (1973), and Kausler's (1970) review of interference theory as applied to aging phenomena.

A general characteristic of the work considered in this chapter is that the effects of age on behavior have been assessed between groups rather than within groups. This reliance on a cross-sectional method has resulted in research findings that describe *age differences* rather than *age changes*. A rather large literature exists that points out the difficulties in interpreting data obtained from cross-sectional studies (for a recent review of research methodologies, see Schaie, 1977; cf.

Preparation of this chapter was supported in part by Postdoctoral Fellowship AG05114 from the National Institute on Aging to the first author, Postdoctoral Fellowship MH07552 from the National Institute of Mental Health to the second author, and Career Development Award AG00017 from the National Institute on Aging to the third author.

also Adam, 1978). Briefly, with cross-sectional methods, the effects of a person's chronological age cannot be unambiguously distinguished from the effects of that person's sociocultural age (cohort differences). There are at least three important reasons, however, why cross-sectional methods are useful and appropriate.

First, the study of learning and memory is continually undergoing change in theoretical and empirical orientation. Investigators who attempt longitudinal investigations with a current method may find their results of limited theoretical interest some 10 or 15 years later when the study is completed.

Second, it seems useful to identify those areas of performance where current cohorts of older and younger people differ in important ways and to find theoretically based and empirically supported explanations of the behavioral differences. Whether these differences result from cohort or ontogenetic change can be evaluated, to some extent, on a rational consideration of the types of variables found to be related to the differences. Furthermore, at the applied level, the sorting of causes into cohort or ontogenetic categories is probably unimportant, compared to identifying the mechanisms responsible for these behaviorally important differences.

Third, in the broad view, a person's "true" age is necessarily determined by chronological and sociocultural events. Therefore, cross-sectional experimental methods, combined with pertinent information about an individual's life pattern, offer rich sources of information about factors that are important in determining cognitive performance across the life span.

Information-Processing Approaches

The information-processing model assumes that the learner participates actively, rather than passively, in acquiring and remembering information; therefore, the learner's cognitive activities and their effectiveness for learning and remembering are central questions. Because of its emphasis on deliberate cognitive activity and memory capacity, this model has been a rich source of hypotheses regarding the locus of age differences in memory. Craik (1977), in his review of the literature since 1959 on human memory and aging, notes that the majority of the research grew from information-processing ideas.

Primary Memory

Early information-processing studies comparing older and younger people were concerned with estimating the relative capacity of the hypothesized memory stores. Since long-term memory was assumed to be an unlimited store, much of the research dealt with short-term memory. If it had been possible to detect age differences in this hypothetical early stage of the information-processing sequence in memory (thereby creating a "bottleneck"), then an important step would have been taken in understanding the cause of age differences in memory. Craik (1977) has suggested a distinction between primary and secondary memory (Waugh & Norman, 1965) rather than one between short-term and long-term memory when dealing with these issues, in order to avoid confusion with retention-interval concepts. We will follow Craik's suggestion in our discussions.

The memory-span task has been used frequently to estimate the capacity of primary memory: How many letters, words, or digits can a person recall in correct serial order? The studies of span estimation reported by Botwinick and Storandt (1974), Craik (1968), and Talland (1965, 1968) are representative of the results of this line of research; namely, these studies showed that age differences are not usually found and that when they are, they are small in magnitude. After reviewing this literature, Craik (1977) has concluded that age differences in primary memory *capacity* are minimal. The ambiguities in the literature on primary memory in older people have been attributed by Craik (1977; Craik & Simon, 1980) to the degree to which the tasks used have required manipulation of information in primary memory or have required division of attention during information input. To the extent that attention cannot be focused exclusively on performance of the memory span task, or that organization of the material is required or encouraged by the task, older people perform at a lower level than younger people. Thus, the frequently voiced conclusion that primary memory is not impaired in older adults may require some qualification. Under undemanding conditions primary memory capacity does not seem to be reduced in older adults. But primary memory capacity under conditions that require cognitive manipulation for restructuring or reorganizing the input may, in fact, be effectively reduced and may result in substantial age differences in the amount of information available for storage in subsequent secondary-memory stages.

Secondary Memory

One of the clearest findings in the field of aging and memory research is that once the amount of material to be remembered exceeds the span of primary memory, older people are unable to recall as much of the material as younger people. Consequently, the majority of recent research on aging and memory has concentrated on understanding the nature and causes of age-related deficits in secondary memory. Researchers have found it useful to differentiate between acquisition, storage, and retrieval operations when formulating hypotheses about age differences in secondary memory (Melton, 1963). This distinction between separate stages of memory has guided several major lines of research. Since there is little evidence that retention is impaired in older people, few researchers now consider the storage stage of memory as a possible locus of age-related deficits (Craik, 1977; Smith, 1975). Instead, interest has focused on acquisition and retrieval stages.

One approach to the investigation of age differences in secondary memory has attempted to specify whether memory decrements in older people reflect mainly an acquisition deficiency (in which the information is not available in memory) or a retrieval deficiency (in which the information is available but is not accessible at the time of recall). The strategy in this research has been to compare performance of older and younger groups on tasks that are assumed either to minimize retrieval requirements (recognition or cued-recall tasks) or to maximize them (free-recall tasks). Some early studies implicated the retrieval stage of memory as the primary locus of age-related memory deficits. Schonfield and Robertson (1966) found that age differences were absent when recognition of words was tested, even though age differences were found in free recall of the same material. Laurence (1967b) reported no age differences when category cues were presented at the time of recall of a list of categorizable words. However, other investigators have since shown that age differences occur even with recognition procedures (e.g., Botwinick & Storandt, 1974; Erber, 1974; Wickelgren, 1975). Erber's study suggested that the difficulty of the recognition task was an important factor in the recognition performance of older subjects and that earlier studies had employed a task too simple to allow the observation of possible age differences. Similarly, further studies on the effects of retrieval cues have shown that age deficits are not always eliminated when cues are provided (Drachman & Leavitt, 1972; Hultsch, 1975; Smith, 1977). The rather extensive literature on this problem has been reviewed by Craik (1977) and by Smith (1980). Both reviewers concluded that retrieval difficulty, though one of the causes of age differences in recall of information, is probably not the sole cause. Clearly the original assumption of this research approach—that retrieval could be studied independently of acquisition—is not tenable. For example, studies by Tulving and Thomson (1973) on the principle of encoding specificity provide evidence for the interdependence of the acquisition and retrieval stages of memory. There is also accumulating evidence (see Craik & Simon, 1980; Smith, 1980) that older and younger people do not encode information the same way, which makes it even more difficult to examine retrieval independently.

A second approach to understanding age differences in secondary memory has focused on organizational processes in older and younger learners. The impetus for this line of research derives from two sources: (1) evidence of a high correlation between amount recalled in a free-recall task and the degree of organization detected in the recall protocols (Mandler, 1967; Tulving, 1962), and (2) evidence that older people do not spontaneously use mediators in paired-associate learning (e.g., Canestrari, 1968; Hulicka & Grossman, 1967). If a failure to use mediational strategies indicates a general failure to seek or use relations between items on a verbal list, then older learners might be particularly impaired in free-recall tasks where organization is important for high levels of recall. Attempts to substantiate organizational deficiency as an explanation of age differences in free recall have used three strategies: (1) direct measurement of organization in the recall protocols of older and younger learners, (2) manipulation of the amount of organization inherent in the list, and (3) instructions to organize.

The measurement of organization has not produced consistent results. Laurence (1966), using the measure developed by Tulving (1962), assessed subjective organization (SO) by having children, young adults, and older adults provide verbal recall of pictorial material. Laurence found no differences in SO between the two adult groups, even though there was a substantial recall difference. But Hultsch (1974), who used a different measure of subjective organization, one that presumably did not penalize younger subjects for increases in number of words recalled from trial to trial, found that older subjects did not organize as much as younger subjects.

Laurence (1967a) used the second strategy in a study with lists of either unrelated words or words that were related conceptually. While older adults scored lower than younger adults on free recall, the age differences were less with the related words. The interaction between age and material suggested that the older subjects made use of organization to enhance recall, once the basis of organization was obvious, but they apparently did not organize spontaneously.

The third strategy was used by Hultsch in several experiments (Hultsch, 1969, 1971). Each of these studies found a significant beneficial effect for older and younger subjects when organization was encouraged by the experimental manipulations (a sorting task similar to that used by Mandler, 1967). However, in only one study (Hultsch, 1971) was the magnitude of the age difference in recall reduced by the manipulation of organizational factors.

Thus, attempts to support a hypothesis of organizational deficiency in older adults have not been uniformly successful. Certainly, more evidence is required in order to assess this hypothesis, especially since organizational differences are offered frequently as an explanation for age differences in secondary memory. Studying age differences with various direct measures, such as subjective-organization measures or category-clustering measures, might resolve some of the present ambiguities. If measured organization is not found to differ, perhaps the recall difficulties experienced by older subjects are related to the appropriateness of the organization developed for the support of retrieval, rather than to the amount of organization. For example, if older people form higher-order memory units that are not necessarily organized around an effective retrieval plan, the benefit of the organization for recall may be reduced. Or if they attempt to organize the elements on the word list with information that already exists in memory, it may become difficult to separate information acquired in the present episode from information acquired in previous episodes.

A third major line of research on aging and memory examines encoding processes more directly and takes as its point of departure the levels-of-processing approach outlined by Craik and Lockhart (1972). An orienting task is used to direct the type of encoding a subject engages in during an incidental learning task. The relative effectiveness with which each type of encoding promotes recall of the incidentally learned material is then measured. The major construct of the levels-of-processing approach is "depth of processing," with semantic processing assumed to be deeper than other types of processing (e.g., orthographic, phonemic). A second construct, "elaboration," refers to the amount and breadth of cognitive work that has been done on an event within a given level of processing. Memory for an event (or for a word) is assumed to be a function of the amount and depth of cognitive work done on the event at the time of encoding. Events that have been processed deeply and elaborately are assumed to be recalled more readily than events that have been processed less deeply or less elaborately.

As applied in the study of age differences in memory, the primary hypothesis stemming from the levels-of-processing approach is that when left to their own mnemonic devices, older people do not process information as deeply as younger people do. Instructions to learn generally evoke certain strategies for processing in the learners, and this is where older learners are seen to be at the greatest disadvantage: They are assumed to be less likely to engage in elaborate semantic processing. However, the requirements of a semantic-orienting task should guarantee that semantic processing occurs and should therefore reduce age differences in recall. Experimental tests of this hypothesis have been reviewed by Craik and Simon (1980) and by Smith (1980). The results of this research have been surprising: Age differences in free recall are generally found to be *larger* with semantic orienting tasks (deeper processing) than with nonsemantic tasks (shallower processing) and of the same magnitude as those observed with intentional-learning instructions. These results suggest that the processing deficit in older persons may not be just a failure to engage in semantic processing, but rather an inability to maximize the mnemonic benefits of semantic processing. This conclusion must be modified somewhat by the finding that age differences are minimized when a semantic-orienting task is followed by a recognition test (White, as reported in Craik, 1977; Perlmutter, 1979). As Craik and Simon (1980) concluded, the key seems to be that while semantic encoding leads to more effective acquisition, it does not necessarily guarantee retrieval of the information. When retrieval requirements are minimized, as in a recognition test, the superiority of semantic encoding can be observed. On the other hand, a study by Mason (1979) found both recall and recognition to be more impaired in older adults than in younger, when semantic processing was required by the orienting task. Clearly, locating the source of these inconsistencies will require further investigation. Future research may also enable us to understand how encoding and retrieval processes interact and how encoding can be guided to maximize the probability of retrieval in older people.

Current Issues and Explanations

Most of the research surveyed here has assumed that age differences in memory result from differences in the way older and younger people process information and that this so-called "processing deficiency" of older learners can be overcome by "correct" strategies. However, the manipulation of processing strategies (e.g., organizational factors, depth of processing) has not generally eliminated age differences in performance. Further, although training studies have been conducted to improve the memory techniques of elderly subjects, with a few exceptions these programs, which stress the use of "effective" processing strategies, have not succeeded in bringing older persons to the same level of performance as young persons (for a review see Poon, Walsh-Sweeney, & Fozard, 1980). Thus, although processing deficiency may account for some of the age-related differences in memory performance, it does not seem to account for the whole deficit.

A strong position in favor of a physiologically based explanation of age differences in memory has been taken recently by Waugh and Barr (1980) and by Salthouse (1980). These authors have disagreed with the notion that processing strategies under the learner's control are the key to age differences in memory; instead, they suggest an explanation based on a general slowing in the speed of behavior as a result of changes in the nervous system. In this formulation, the elderly are viewed as employing the same types of processing strategies as younger people, and the limiting factor in memory performance is seen as the rate at which these operations can be accomplished by the central nervous system. Birren (1974; Chap. 21, this book) has proposed similar hypotheses for the impact on behavior of age-related slowing in speed of processing and has implicated slowing to explain age-related differences in memory.

For three reasons we believe that the speed-of-processing explanation is an unproductive research hypothesis for memory investigations. First, within the framework of existing models of memory (e.g., Atkinson & Shiffrin, 1968; Norman & Rumelhart, 1970), the speed-of-processing explanation predicts large age differences in primary memory, predictions that are not supported by much memory research. Second, the proponents of speed-of-processing explanations have not articulated the secondary memory mechanisms that would be affected adversely by slower processing. Third, the stages of memory processing that show the greatest slowing also show the least memory impairment, and the stages that show the greatest memory impairment show the least slowing. We will elaborate these points in more detail.

Walsh has reported a series of investigations that clearly document major age differences in the speed of peripheral and central perceptual processes (Walsh, 1976; Walsh, Till, & Williams, 1978; Walsh, Williams & Hertzog, 1979). These investigations show that older adults require 30% more processing time than younger people to construct a sensory memory representation of visual input. Furthermore, Walsh and Thompson (1978) have demonstrated that visual sensory memory persists for a shorter duration in old than in young adults. Finally, Walsh and Prasse (1980) have reported that older adults require as much as 80% longer processing times to extract information from sensory memory and recode it into primary memory. Thus there is substantial evidence for large amounts of slowing in memory-related mechanisms. Within the framework of current models of memory, a speed-of-processing explanation predicts substantial age-related differences in the next hypothesized stage of information processing, specifically, primary memory. But the vast literature on aging and primary memory, reviewed above, provides little or no support for this prediction.

In the typical primary-memory task, capacity of the system is seldom found to differ as a function of age. However, the critical experiments may not yet have been conducted. If there is any validity to the speed-of-processing explanation, then brief tachistoscopic presentations should produce large age differences in primary memory span for digits, even though the same subjects, using standard presentation rates may show no age differences in memory span.

While causal relations can be spelled out which predict that a slowing in the speed of processing should adversely affect primary memory in older adults, the manner in which slowing can affect secondary-memory stages has not been made clear. It contributes little to suggest that slowing causes age differences in secondary memory in the absence of a task-specific model of memory operation that would specify the impact of slowing on particular memory mechanisms. Furthermore, detailed specifications must be provided on how these affected memory mechanisms might result in less information stored or retrieved from secondary memory. This concern can be clarified by a simple computer metaphor. Two computers may differ by 100% in the speed with which they execute hardware instructions, although each will store and retrieve identical amounts of information when executing the same program. Slower processing does not in itself mean that less information is stored or retrieved.

Before we leave the computer metaphor, another point can be made. Longer processing times do not always mean slower processing. The same computer may take different lengths of time to execute a program on different days, depending on the concurrent processing demands at program execution time. Thus, a time-sharing computer (an appropriate methaphor for human functioning) may require more time to complete the same series of instructions when other processing demands must be dealt with. This metaphor suggests an important hypothesis that has received little attention. Rather than proposing that older people remember less because they process slower, this hypothesis suggests that they may divert their processing resources to concurrent processing demands and thus never complete the operations necessary for efficient encoding and retrieval of information from secondary memory. We will return to this issue later.

A third problem with the speed-of-processing explanation is that the pattern of age differences in memory is the reverse of the pattern of age differences in speed of information processing. There is strong evidence of age differences in the speed of processing at early stages of information input where memory performance does not differ as a function of age. However, there is little or no evidence of any substantial slowing at higher stages where the greatest differences in memory performance are seen. For example, there is no change with advancing age in speed of retrieval from semantic memory (Eysenck, 1975), for picture naming (Poon & Fozard, 1978), or for naming latencies (Waugh & Barr, 1980). Speed-of-processing explanations of memory must address these paradoxes and inconsistencies if they are to contribute to our understanding of age-related differences in memory.

While much recent research has explored age differences in encoding and retrieval processes, an older notion concerning age differences in attentional factors has received little experimental or theoretical scrutiny. The negative effect of divided attention on the performance of a number of tasks by the elderly has long been known (e.g., Welford, 1958; see also Craik, 1977, for a summary of the literature). Craik and Simon (1980) have also hypothesized that age-related decrements in attentional factors contribute to the memory deficits observed in older people and that the impact of attentional deficits increases when the memory load is large and requires deeper and more elaborate encoding. In a sense, a learning task with a supraspan list has many of the characteristics of a divided-attention task: The learner must simultaneously hold newly presented items in primary memory and retrieve old information in order to carry out those cognitive operations that are most likely to guarantee later retrieval of the incoming events (e.g., elaboration of the individual stimulus, organization of groups of stimuli, generation of visual images). In other words, the learner must attend to both external and internal events. With stimuli presented rapidly, the attentional demands become quite large. Craik and Simon (1980) have suggested that because aging is associated with a reduction in "processing resource," older people are particularly likely to perform poorly on tasks that require much cognitive energy. A reduction in processing resource, they point out, would explain why elderly subjects are not able to benefit as much as younger subjects from semantic encoding instructions. If older people find this deeper level of processing more difficult or demanding, they may simply do less of it than younger people. This new focus on attentional factors and constraints on performance imposed by available processing resources opens up an area rich in testable hypotheses. However, as our computer metaphor suggested, the older adults may not have lost processing resources but rather may be dealing with higher concurrent processing demands.

The Question of Ecological Validity

The common characteristic of the work surveyed here, and indeed of most research on age differences in learning and memory, is its concern with memory for lists of words acquired in a laboratory situation. As the evidence has revealed, age differences observed with these tasks are pervasive and substantial. But to what extent can we reach general conclusions about age differences in memory on the basis of list-memory findings? A frequent criticism holds that the typical laboratory word-list tasks tap a kind of learning that is not relevant to the learning and remembering that people do in their daily lives. Consequently, a trend has been developing to seek "ecological validity" in the tasks required of subjects, and particularly in the study of adult age differences in learning and memory.

The question of ecological validity is also important for memory-intervention techniques. Without exception, the mnemonic techniques that have been the basis of memory-improvement studies (e.g., visual-imagery methods) are concerned primarily with memory for lists, though the importance of list memory in the daily lives of adults is not known. Thus, we may question whether techniques for remembering lists have any effect on improving the overall memory functioning of older adults, or on reducing their complaints about memory.

While the need for ecological validity in psychological research is frequently expressed (e.g., Neisser, 1976; Walsh & Baldwin, 1977), we do not know how relevant or how ecologically valid various experimental tasks are to adult life. There has been no systematic examination of the kinds of learning required in the typical adult's daily life. What cognitive demands are actually made on adults? What kinds of learning behaviors do adults engage in? What changes in cognitive demands and learning behaviors occur at different stages of adulthood? Are different cognitive demands made on persons in different occupations, and do these demands ultimately affect their patterns of cognitive development? When a few of these questions are answered, we will have some notion of ecological validity based on fact rather than the beliefs or hopes of researchers. The answers to these questions may require the application of methodologies borrowed from other disciplines. Specifically, the techniques employed by ethnography could perhaps be extended to accomplish this task.

Recently, investigators have successfully adapted ethnographic techniques to educational and developmental questions: for example, to the development of nonverbal communication (Knott, 1979) or the learning of social rules in classrooms (Green & Wallat, 1979). We believe that ethnographic methods would be useful in describing the range of adult activities and would allow us to focus on those activities that involve learning, memory, and language. The first stage of such an analysis would yield a list of general categories of the behavior that adults engage in. The second stage would be to discover the amount of time that different groups of adults spend on the different subcategories—adults of different ages, of both sexes, from different occupational and socioeconomic groups. The third stage would group the behaviors in terms of the cognitive abilities people draw on to accomplish them. Since the purposes of ethnographic studies are normally quite different from those proposed here, adaptation of ethnographic techniques needs to be done with care.

Clearly, this is an extensive project to propose. However, parts of the problem could be approached by undertaking studies of limited scope, for example, in-depth studies of a small sample of adults across all their activities, or a study of behaviors in a narrow environment, such as a business office, factory, or home. These descriptions would allow researchers interested in adult development of learning and memory to make more intelligent decisions about the direction of their research efforts and to bring ecological validity to their research.

In the absence of an empirically based description of adult learning and memory activities, however, researchers must continue to rely on intuition and introspection to guide their research questions and choice of tasks. Intuition tells us that there may be large disparities between the life demands of adults and the current thrust of research in adult development of learning and memory. And some thoughtful introspection suggests that, unlike memorizing lists of words, acquisition and recall of information presented in discourse are activities that most adults do on a daily basis. Information as diverse as dietary guidelines and spatial directions might be spoken or written in a discourse format. Evidence of remembering might be demonstrated by the subjects' ability to carry out dietary instructions or to find their way in a given spatial environment.

Discourse Processing

Age differences in memory for information contained in discourse have received the attention of only a few researchers. The existing studies can be grouped according to three related questions: (1) Are there age differences in the acquisition of information not explicitly stated in the text? (2) Are there age differences in comprehension of discourse? (3) Are there age differences in the free recall or utilization of information presented in a text? After a brief review of the existing literature we will outline the characteristics of discourse that we believe can provide a framework to guide future research in adult development of learning and memory.

Age differences in memory for information not explicitly stated in a text have been addressed by Walsh and Baldwin (1977) and by Till and Walsh (1980). The Walsh and Baldwin study used the linguistic-abstraction paradigm (Bransford & Franks, 1971) and found no age differences in people's tendency to integrate a series of partial information statements into a holistic representation of the ideas contained across the parts. Till and Walsh (1980) had older and younger subjects read sentences from which an implication could be drawn. The sentences were read under several conditions of encoding (shallow or deep). Free recall of the sentences did not differ as a function of age, but younger subjects outperformed older subjects when recall was cued by an implication that could be derived from each sentence. However, this was not due to the inability of older adults to draw implications. When an implication was demanded at the time of the original reading, and recall was then tested with an implicational cue, the elderly subjects recalled as many sentences as did the younger. More interesting is the fact that the implicational cue given was one selected by the experimenter and was not necessarily the one drawn by the subject when reading the sentence. Apparently the major factor governing the results was the *activity* of drawing implications from the sentences, rather than the encoding of specific retrieval cues. In each of these studies, the major interest was in the extraction of information from single sentences (Till & Walsh, 1980) or groups of single sentences (Walsh & Baldwin, 1977), rather than from sentences connected into typical discourse. In a recent investigation, however, Cohen (1979, Exp. 1) reported that older subjects were less able than younger ones to make correct inferences after reading 60–75-word passages. Cohen concluded that with highly educated subjects, the failure to make correct inferences could not be attributed to memory deficiencies, since the older and younger participants performed equivalently on questions that tapped explicit information from the passages. These results are consistent with the findings of Till and Walsh (1980) and suggest that some aspects of discourse comprehension may be impaired in older adults.

Taub (1976, 1979) has examined the question of age differences in discourse comprehension using both 957-word and 215-word passages. In each of these studies, comprehension was measured with a series of multiple-choice questions concerning the materials in the texts. Age differences in comprehension were observed in both studies, with the older persons performing less well than the younger. However, Taub (1979) found age differences in comprehension only for adults whose Weschler Adult Intelligence Scale (WAIS) Vocabulary scores were in the "average verbal ability" range.

Older and younger persons with WAIS Vocabulary scores in the "bright average" range did not differ from each other in the measurement of comprehension. And in a recent report, Finkle and Walsh (1979) reported age differences in discourse comprehension for a group of highly educated elderly people (16 years of education) who were compared with a younger student group (14.6 years of education). Since Finkle and Walsh did not obtain a measure of verbal intelligence in their sample it is difficult to compare their results with those of Taub (1976, 1979). However, the Finkle and Walsh sample was drawn from a college-educated volunteer pool that consistently obtained high scores on standardized vocabulary tests. Clearly the extent and nature of age differences in discourse comprehension have not been resolved. Since verbal intelligence apparently plays a major role in data interpretation, these measures should be obtained routinely so that valid comparisons can be made between the results from different laboratories.

Several investigations have been concerned with age differences in the free recall of information presented in prose. Typically the subject is asked to read the text and then to reproduce as accurately as possible the material read. Emphasis is usually placed on the amount recalled, and paraphrasing is encouraged when necessary. The findings to date seem to be characterized chiefly by their inconsistency from laboratory to laboratory.

Gordon and Clark (1974) were among the first investigators to attempt a systematic study of age differences in memory for prose. Older and younger subjects read a 300-word passage once and then free-recalled it orally. Recall was scored using an informal, intuitive idea count, with a maximum possible score of 18 ideas. Age differences in number of ideas recalled were found at both immediate and 1-week retention intervals, and the superiority of recall of the younger subjects was even greater with delayed recall. Older adults also made lower recognition scores at both retention intervals, a result that Gordon and Clark interpreted as evidence for a storage deficit in the elderly. Taub and Kline (1978) also found that multitrial, oral, free recall for prose material was impaired in the elderly, but the age differences were not apparent until the third or fourth trial when learning 60-word passages. At a point in learning equivalent to Gordon and Clark's test trial (after one study trial), Taub and Kline's older and younger groups did not differ. In their experiment, recall was scored for the presence of key words, their synonyms, or "correct ideas." A score of 26 points was possible for each of the 60-word passages.

There are two obvious differences between the studies reported by Gordon and Clark (1974) and by Taub and Kline (1978). First, the two scoring systems differed in the amount of information required in the recall protocols in order to achieve a maximum score on the passages. The Taub and Kline system would have been *more* sensitive to any differences that existed, since the shorter passages were divided into smaller units for scoring. But Taub and Kline did not observe age differences after one trial with their passage, whereas Gordon and Clark did. The two studies differed also in the length of the passages used. Apparently, with short passages, older and younger persons are able to extract and retain for reproduction an equivalent amount of information on first reading. With longer passages, or with additional trials on shorter passages, the older learner is less able either to acquire or to retrieve as much information as the younger learner. It is not possible to choose between acquisition and retrieval on the basis of these studies, although Gordon and Clark's results strongly implicate acquisition failure as at least part of the difficulty in the recall of prose by older persons. Furthermore neither of these investigations examined the recall protocols in a manner that allows the locus of the recall deficit to be specified—whether gist, details, or logical connections. In assessing memory for prose material, it is important to determine the kinds of information most susceptible to loss in order to understand which processes (e.g., comprehension or memory) are responsible for age differences.

We are aware of four studies that have attempted to look at age differences in recall of prose with a finer-grained analysis. Cohen (1979, Exp. 3) reported that a highly educated older group recalled fewer summary propositions and fewer modifier propositions from a 300-word story than did a highly educated younger group. In this experiment, the story was presented orally at a slow rate and recall was also oral. The class of information that Cohen grouped into the general category of "modifier proposition" included logical connectives as well as locative, temporal, qualitative, and comparative information. No attempt to identify differences with the general class of modifiers was reported.

Meyer and her associates have conducted the most systematic work on adult age differences in prose recall that is available to date (Meyer, Rice, Knight, & Jessen, 1979a, 1979b). In their first study relatively short passages (139 or 205 words) were presented to young, middle-aged, and older subjects. Reading a passage was followed by written recall. The subjects were then asked to give a one-sentence summary of the passage and to complete a partly-filled outline of the passage. There were no age differences on any of the tasks: Free recall did not differ, summarizing was equivalent, and the outline listing of main ideas was equivalent. These results are not consistent with those of Cohen (1979, Exp. 3). A second study (Meyer et al., 1979b) is also inconsistent with Cohen's results. In the second study a longer passage (641 words) was used, and recall was scored for idea units that had been identified in a 17-level hierarchical analysis of the structure of the text (see Meyer, 1975, for details of the structural analysis of this text). Young, middle-aged, and older adults read the text and then produced written recall. Again there were no overall age differences in text recall, but the younger subjects tended to be more sensitive to the levels of information in the text. While recall for all age groups was higher for top-level information, recall from the younger subjects fell off more sharply on lower level propositions than did recall for either the middle-aged or older groups. The older subjects, on the other hand, tended to remember more of the lower level information than did the younger subjects.

In attempting to resolve the disparities between the Meyer studies (Meyer et al., 1979a, 1979b) and the Cohen study (Cohen, 1979, Exp. 3), certain characteristics of the procedures and materials appear to differ sufficiently to warrant discussion. Cohen used both spoken presentation and recall, whereas Meyer et al. used written presentation and recall. Thus, in the Cohen study, there was no opportunity for the subject to glance back at previous information, as might well have occurred in the Meyer et al. studies. The role of recursions in reading is uncertain, but they may have been an important influence on the performance differences in these studies. For example, Cohen has interpreted her results in terms of age differences in processing capacity—an interpretation similar to that of Craik and Simon (1980)—according to which older people are penalized when they must attend to the incoming surface meaning of the message while simultaneously attempting to integrate that information into the general meaning structure of the text. If a passage is presented orally, simultaneous processing is necessary. If a passage is *read*, however, the information needed for integration of new input continues to be available on the page, and the input of new information can be delayed until the reader is able to process it. These comments are speculative and will need empirical verification.

One final study should be mentioned. Zelinski, Gilewski, and Thompson (1980) investigated the relation between metamemory and several laboratory memory tests, including prose recall. The recall protocols were scored using an adaptation of the system developed by Meyer (1975). These investigators found no age differences in recall of propositions at the most superordinate level, but older subjects recalled fewer propositions at each of the subordinate levels included in the passage. This study stands in contrast to both the Meyer et al. studies (1979a, 1979b) and the Cohen (1979, Exp. 3) study.

While the existing studies on age differences in discourse processing have been mainly exploratory, and certainly conflicting, they serve as an important first step. Future studies will undoubtedly reflect the influence of the growing body of knowledge in the general literature concerning basic discourse processes. In attempting to understand how the human mind processes the information contained in a discourse, researchers have focused on the properties of discourse itself—its *propositional content* (or microstructure), its *cohesion*, and its overall *logical organization* (or macrostructure). These unique characteristics of discourse have been shown to determine what is remembered from discourse rather than the characteristics that are known to affect word-list recall. For example, Meyer (1975), Marshall and Glock (1978), and Harker (1979) have demonstrated that the serial position of information in a narrative has little to do with the probability of its being recalled. Rather, the hierarchical organization of the discourse predicts which information will be recalled.

The basic meaning of the information contained in discourse is its propositional content. A key methodological problem encountered in research on discourse was the lack of an objective, well-defined way to describe the content of a discourse passage. Such a description was needed as a basis for describing and evaluating the recall protocols produced by subjects. Solution of this problem was attempted in several fields in the early 1970s: linguistics (Grimes, 1975; Leech, 1970), artificial intelligence and computer simulation (Schank, 1972; Simmons, 1973; Winograd, 1972), and cognitive psychology (Crothers, 1972; Frederiksen, 1975; Kintsch, 1972; Meyer, 1975; Rumelhart, Lindsay & Norman, 1972).

To date, Meyer's (1975) representational system is apparently the only one that has been used in adult developmental studies (Meyer et al., 1979b; Zelinski, Gilewski, & Thompson, 1980). The system developed by Kintsch (1974) could also be useful in explaining age differences in memory for prose. For example, Cohen (1979, Exp. 3) found large age differences in the recall of a rather heterogeneous group of modifier propositions. Using the system developed by Kintsch, these same propositions could be separated into several types of modifiers, as well as into a class of connective propositons that capture the logical relations between elements in a text. This distinction would permit a closer analysis of the nature of age differences in discourse processing and memory. A further advantage of a formal representational system is that it would allow researchers in a number of different laboratories to communicate more effectively with each other when describing age differences in prose recall. This would reduce the difficulty in interpreting what an "idea" is in various informal systems (cf. Gordon & Clark, 1974; Taub & Kline, 1978).

Cohesion refers to several features of discourse that make it seem "connected" (Halliday & Hasan, 1976). Lexical cohesion is present when lexical content recurs throughout a discourse, as when the same term or its synonym appears in several different propositions. Anaphora is another type of cohesion that includes pronoun substitution and ellipsis. Comprehending this type of structure requires a "low" level of inference and coordination of information across at least two different propositions. To the extent that processing resources are diminished in older persons (Cohen, 1979; Craik & Simon, 1980), the type of cohesion present in a text may be an important factor in comprehension. When anaphora is used, memory load and processing resource must be diverted to the task of identifying the referent. With lexical cohesion, the referent is immediately identified, and comprehension should be facilitated.

There are currently two different yet complementary views of macrostructure. Crothers (1978) and Frederiksen, Frederiksen, Humphrey, and Ottesen (1978) have developed a "bottom-up" view in which macrostructure is seen as consisting of connections that unite individual propositions into an organized whole. These connections may include logical, causal, temporal, comparative, or other relations that connect two or more propositions and form structural links and hierarchies among different parts of the text. Frederiksen (1977) has shown that these structures function as processing units for acquisition and recall of information. Further evidence of the psychological reality of bottom-up processing has been found by Meyer (1977) and McKoon (1977). The development of a bottom-up macrostructure appears to rely on the reader's ability to keep track of the logical relations among pieces of information, separating the relevant from the irrelevant. A number of investigations have shown that older persons may have difficulty ignoring irrelevant information (e.g., Hoyer, Rebok, & Sved, 1979; Rabbit, 1965, 1977). Thus older persons may be less able to extract a macrostructure in the bottom-up view of the concept.

A "top-down" view of macrostructure states that discourse has levels of structure in addition to those described by microlevel propositional systems. The reader or listener brings knowledge of structure, known as a schema, to the body of discourse to be understood. The importance of top-down schemata for recall has been shown by a number of researchers (Kintsch & van Dijk, 1978; Mandler, 1978; Rumelhart, 1975; Stein & Nazworski, 1978; Thorndyke, 1977). We might expect that older persons would perform well on comprehension and recall of texts that could be organized according to some well-learned schema. Since the organization determined by a schema is external to the text and relatively fixed, little attention should be demanded in using it.

Spatial Information

Our introspections on the cognitive demands placed on adults of all ages suggested that the learning and remembering of spatial information is also an important area for future investigations. In a typical day most of us make trips outside our homes to retrieve a wide variety of goods and services, to engage in employment, and to seek entertainment. For most of us these demands seem trivial, but a moment's reflection reveals a complex set of behaviors supported by a wealth of information and sophisticated processing abilities. For example, traveling to one's favorite restaurant for dinner might include knowledge about its location, knowledge about a series of paths by which it can be reached, and the ability to remember the location of significant landmarks at which changes in direction must occur (cf. Walsh, Krauss, & Regnier, in press). Furthermore, most of us demonstrate the ability to find an alternative path when we encounter a traffic detour. Even more amazing is our ability to try another person's favorite restaurant for dinner, and to locate it from a set of verbal instructions. The latter task involves all of the knowledge and processes of the former, in addition to the ability to encode the linguistic instructions, recode them into a spatial representation, and then carry out a new set of spatial behaviors.

Three questions seem to us to deserve major research efforts. First, developmental differences in the acquisition of spatial information need to be examined. Are there changes across the life span in the ability to acquire spatial information as a function of the mode of processing (i.e., observing one's movement through an environment, examining a map, processing verbal instructions presented in a discourse format)? Second, developmental patterns in the form of spatial information storage deserve special attention. Are young adults more or less likely than older adults to retain coordinated "images" of the familiar environmental spaces? Is aging associated with an increase or decrease in the use of verbal propositions to represent spatial information? Third, researchers need to explore the effectiveness with which spatial information is utilized by adults. Are adults of all ages equally effective in navigating familiar environments? Are the young more or less competent than the aged in generating novel paths to new or familiar locations? Do changes in an environment (the addition or deletion of landmarks) disrupt the way-finding behavior of young or aged adults differently? These questions outline some major issues for future investigations of adult development of learning and memory. They also underline the restricted scope of much of the current and past literature on the development of learning and memory capacities.

How Much is Enough?

Most of our accumulated knowledge about the adult development of learning and memory grows out of investigations that collect small samples of behavior from large samples of subjects. The differences these investigations report may be statistically reliable, but their generality across larger samples of behavior (e.g., extended practice on the same task) may be questionable. An intuition shared by many of us is that it is easier to learn new information about a topic and retain it longer as our knowledge about the topic increases. Furthermore, the processes and strategies that support new learning may be very different in the later stages of learning than in the earlier stages. For example, the performance of adults learning to play chess goes through a series of qualitatively different stages. The novice learns first the possible moves of each playing piece. The need and method for defending one's important pieces and attacking those of the opponent must also be mastered. Eventually, the more talented players learn to perceive the playing board as sets of configurations. The advanced player learns complicated strategies that begin with the first move and unfold across longer periods of play. Clearly, the nature of the learning process changes dramatically as one's experience with chess increases. Most of the current literature examines only the early acquisition phase of simple learning tasks. Future research in the adult development of learning and memory needs to examine the rate of shift from inefficient to more efficient processing strategies with extended practice and the increase (or decrease) in learning capacity as a function of accumulated knowledge in a content area.

Conclusion

While much progress has been made in the past decade toward delineating the nature and extent of age-related deficits in learning and memory, many important questions remain to be examined. As noted in this chapter, questions remain unanswered about age differences in organizational processes, other elaborative processes, and the relation between encoding and retrieval. Definitive research is needed in these areas. Further, since age-related differences in the use of efficient processing strategies cannot account for the entire performance deficit seen in standard laboratory tasks, how shall we attempt to explain the remaining deficit? Speed-of-processing differences have been proposed as a general explanatory concept for cognitive deficits related to aging, including deficits in memory processes, but to date this explanation has not received convincing support. The concept of age-related differences in processing capacity has also emerged as a potentially important factor in explaining age differences in memory performance. Each of these ideas can be evaluated only in the context of its ability to explain and predict the full range of deficiencies in memory skills that are observed in older adults. This task remains to be accomplished.

In considering areas for future investigation of adult development of learning and memory, we have suggested discourse comprehension as an important area for research. Discourse represents one of the major sources from which adults of all ages acquire information; but there are other modes of acquiring information that may be important for specific types of information. For example, discovery, observation, and participation may be critical for learning of procedures or skilled movements. In opening up new areas of investigation, researchers must take care to restrict their generalizations about patterns of adult development to the format in which the information was learned (word list, discourse, observation, participation) and to the method by which remembering was assessed (verbal recall, performance of instructions, utilization of information). Learning and memory performance probably changes along a number of dimensions across the life span. Therefore, the careful development of new research approaches could expand our current knowledge base significantly.

REFERENCES

Adam, J. Sequential strategies and the separation of age, cohort, and time-of-measurement contributions to developmental data. *Psychological Bulletin*, 1978, *85*, 1309–1316.

Atkinson, R. C., & Shiffrin, R. M. Human memory: A proposed system and its control processes. In K. W. Spence and J. T. Spence (Eds.), *The psychology of learning and motivation* (Vol. 2). New York: Academic Press, 1968.

Birren, J. E. Translations in gerontology—from lab to life: Psychophysiology and speed of response. *American Psychologist*, 1974, *29*, 808–815.

Birren, J. E. *Age and speed of behavior: An old and young*

issue. Paper presented at the 87th meeting of the American Psychological Association, New York, September 1979.

Botwinick, J. *Aging and behavior.* New York: Springer, 1973.

Botwinick, J., & Storandt, M. *Memory, related functions and age.* Springfield, Ill.: Charles C Thomas, 1974.

Bransford, J. D., & Franks, J. J. The abstraction of linguistic ideas. *Cognitive Psychology,* 1971, *2,* 331–350.

Canestrari, R. E. Age changes in acquisition. In G. A. Talland (Ed.), *Human aging and behavior.* New York: Academic Press, 1968.

Cohen, G. Language comprehension in old age. *Cognitive Psychology,* 1979, *11,* 412–429.

Craik, F. I. M. Short-term memory and the aging process. In G. A. Talland (Ed.), *Human aging and behavior.* New York: Academic Press, 1968.

Craik, F. I. M. Age differences in human memory. In J. E. Birren & K. W. Schaie (Eds.), *Handbook of the psychology of aging.* New York: Van Nostrand Reinhold, 1977.

Craik, F. I. M, & Lockhart, R. S. Levels of processing: A framework for memory research. *Journal of Verbal Learning and Verbal Behavior,* 1972, *11,* 671–684.

Craik, F. I. M. & Simon, E. Age differences in memory: The roles of attention and depth of processing. In L. W. Poon, J. L. Fozard, L. S. Cermak, D. Arenberg, & L. W. Thompson (Eds.), *New directions in memory and aging: Proceedings of the George Talland Memorial Conference.* Hillsdale, N.J.: Lawrence Erlbaum, 1980.

Crothers, E. J. Memory structure and the recall of discourse. In R. O. Freedle & J. B. Carroll (Eds.), *Language comprehension and the acquisition of knowledge.* Washington, D.C.: V. H. Winston, 1972.

Crothers, E. J. Inference and coherence. *Discourse Processes,* 1978, *1,* 51–78.

Drachman, D., & Leavitt, J. Memory impairment in the aged: Storage versus retrieval deficit. *Journal of Experimental Psychology,* 1972, *93,* 302–308.

Erber, J. T. Age differences in recognition memory. *Journal of Gerontology,* 1974, *29,* 177–181.

Eysenck, M. W. Retrieval from semantic memory as a function of age. *Journal of Gerontology,* 1975, *30,* 174–180.

Finkle, T. J., & Walsh, D. A. *Sentence and discourse comprehension in young and old adults.* Paper presented at the 87th meeting of the American Psychological Association, New York, September 1979.

Frederiksen, C. H. Representing logical and semantic structure of knowledge acquired from discourse. *Cognitive Psychology,* 1975, *7,* 371–458.

Frederiksen, C. H. Semantic processing units in understanding text. In R. O. Freedle (Ed.), *Discourse production and comprehension.* Vol. 1 in the series: *Discourse processes: Advances in research and theory.* Norwood, N.J.: Ablex, 1977.

Frederiksen, C. H., Frederiksen, J. D., Humphrey, F. M., & Ottesen, J. *Discourse inference: Adapting to the inferential demands of school texts.* Paper presented at an American Educational Research Association Symposium, Toronto, Canada, April 1978.

Gordon, S. K., & Clark, W. C. Application of signal detection theory to prose recall and recognition in elderly and young adults. *Journal of Gerontology,* 1974, *29,* 64–72.

Green, J. L., & Wallat, C. Social rules and communicative contexts in kindergarten. In J. L. Green (Ed.), "Communicating with young children." *Theory into Practice,* 1979, *18,* (4).

Grimes, J. E. *The thread of discourse.* The Hague: Mouton, 1975.

Halliday, M. A. K., & Hasan, R. *Cohesion in English.* London: Longman, 1976.

Harker, J. O. *Factors affecting children's acquisition of knowledge from discourse.* Unpublished doctoral dissertation, University of California, Berkeley, 1979.

Hoyer, W. J., Rebok, G. W., & Sved, S. M. Effects of varying irrelevant information on adult problem solving. *Journal of Gerontology,* 1979, *34,* 553–559.

Hulicka, I. M., & Grossman, J. L. Age group comparisons for the use of mediators in paired-associate learning. *Journal of Gerontology,* 1967, *22,* 46–51.

Hultsch, D. F. Adult age differences in the organization of free recall. *Developmental Psychology,* 1969, *1,* 673–678.

Hultsch, D. F. Adult age differences in free classification and free recall. *Developmental Psychology,* 1971, *4,* 338–342.

Hultsch, D. F. Learning to learn in adulthood. *Journal of Gerontology,* 1974, *29,* 302–308.

Hultsch, D. F. Adult age differences in retrieval: Trace-dependent and cue-dependent forgetting. *Developmental Psychology,* 1975, *11,* 197–201.

Jerome, E. A. Age and learning—experimental studies. In J. E. Birren (Ed.), *Handbook of aging and the individual: Psychological and biological aspects.* Chicago: University of Chicago Press, 1959.

Kausler, D. H. Retention-forgetting as a nomological network for developmental research. In L. R. Goulet & P. B. Baltes (Eds.), *Life-span developmental psychology.* New York: Academic Press, 1970.

Kay, H. Theories of learning and aging. In J. E. Birren (Ed.), *Handbook of aging and the individual.* Chicago: University of Chicago Press, 1959.

Kintsch, W. Notes on the semantic structure of memory. In E. Tulving & W. Donaldson (Eds.), *Organization of memory.* New York: Academic Press, 1972.

Kintsch, W. *The representation of meaning in memory.* Hillsdale, N.J.: Lawrence Erlbaum, 1974.

Kintsch, W., & van Dijk, T. A. Toward a model of text comprehension and production. *Psychological Review,* 1978, *85,* 363–394.

Knott, G. P. Nonverbal communication during early childhood. In J. L. Green (Ed.), "Communicating with young children." *Theory Into Practice,* 1979, *18* (4).

Laurence, M. W. Age differences in performance and subjective organization in the free recall of pictorial material. *Canadian Journal of Psychology,* 1966, *20,* 388–399.

Laurence, M. W. A developmental look at the usefulness of list categorization as an aid to free recall. *Canadian Journal of Psychology,* 1967, *21,* 153–165. (a)

Laurence, M. W. Memory loss with age: A test of two strategies for its retardation. *Psychonomic Science,* 1967, *9,* 209–210. (b)

Leech, G. N. Towards a semantic description of English. Bloomington: Indiana University Press, 1970.

Mandler, G. Organization and memory. In K. W. Spence & J. T. Spence (Eds.), *The psychology of learning and motivation* (Vol. I). New York: Academic Press, 1967.

Mandler, J. M. A code in the node: The use of a story schema in retrieval. *Discourse Processes*, 1978, *1*, 14–35.

Marshall, N., & Glock, M. Comprehension of connected discourse: A study into the relationships between the structure of text and the information recalled. *Reading Research Quarterly*, 1978, *14*, 10–56.

Mason, S. E. The effects of orienting tasks on the recall and recognition performance of subjects differing in age. *Developmental Psychology*, 1979, *15*, 467–469.

McKoon, G. Organization of information in text memory. *Journal of Verbal Learning and Verbal Behavior*, 1977, *16*, 247–260.

Melton, A. W. Implications of short-term memory for a general theory of memory. *Journal of Verbal Learning and Verbal Behavior*, 1963, *2*, 1–21.

Meyer, B. J. F. *The organization of prose and its effects on memory*. Amsterdam: North Holland Publishing Co., 1975.

Meyer, B. J. F. What is remembered from prose: A function of passage structure. In R. O. Freedle (Ed.), *Discourse production and comprehension*. Norwood, N.J.: Ablex Publishing Co., 1977.

Meyer, B. J. F., Rice, G. E., Knight, C. C., & Jessen, J. L. *Differences in the type of information remembered from prose by young, middle, and old adults* (Research Report No. 5, Prose Learning Series). Tempe: Arizona State University, Department of Educational Psychology, College of Education, Summer 1979. (a)

Meyer, B. J. F., Rice, G. E., Knight, C. C., & Jessen, J. L. *Effects of comparative and descriptive discourse types on the reading performance of young, middle, and old adults* (Research Report No. 7, Prose Learning Series). Tempe: Arizona State University, Department of Educational Psychology, College of Education, Summer 1979. (b)

Neisser, U. *Cognition and reality*. San Francisco: Freeman, 1976.

Norman, D. A., & Rumelhart, D. E. A system for perception and memory. In D. A. Norman (Ed.), *Models of human memory*. New York: Academic Press, 1970.

Perlmutter, M. Age differences in adults' free recall, cued recall, and recognition. *Journal of Gerontology*, 1979, *34*, 533–539.

Poon, L. W., & Fozard, J. L. Speed of retrieval from long-term memory in relation to age, familiarity, and datedness of information. *Journal of Gerontology*, 1978, *33*, 711–717.

Poon, L. W., Walsh-Sweeney, L., & Fozard, J. L. Memory skill training for the elderly: Salient issues on the use of imagery mnemonics. In L. W. Poon, J. L. Fozard, L. S. Cermak, D. Arenberg, & L. W. Thompson (Eds.), *New directions in memory and aging: Proceedings of the George Talland Memorial Conference*. Hillsdale, N.J.: Lawrence Erlbaum, 1980.

Rabbitt, P. An age-decrement in the ability to ignore irrele-

vant information. *Journal of Gerontology*, 1965, *20*, 233–238.

Rabbitt, P. Changes in problem solving ability in old age. In J. E. Birren & K. W. Schaie (Eds.), *Handbook of the psychology of aging*. New York: Van Nostrand Reinhold, 1977.

Rumelhart, D. E. Notes on a schema for stories. In D. G. Bobrow & A. Collins (Eds.), *Representation and understanding*. New York: Academic Press, 1975.

Rumelhart, D. E., Lindsay, P. H., & Norman, D. A. A process model for long term memory. In E. Tulving & W. Donaldson (Eds.), *Organization of memory*. New York: Academic Press, 1972.

Salthouse, T. A. Age and memory: Strategies for localizing the loss. In L. W. Poon, J. L. Fozard, L. S. Cermak, D. Arenberg, & L. W. Thompson (Eds.), *New directions in memory and aging: Proceedings of the George Talland Memorial Conference*. Hillsdale, N.J.: Lawrence Erlbaum, 1980.

Schaie, K. W. Quasi-experimental research designs in the psychology of aging. In J. E. Birren, & K. W. Schaie (Eds.), *Handbook of the psychology of aging*. New York: Van Nostrand Reinhold, 1977.

Schank, R. C. Conceptual dependency: A theory of natural language understanding. *Cognitive Psychology*, 1972, *3*, 552–631.

Schonfield, D., & Robertson, E. A., Memory storage and aging. *Canadian Journal of Psychology*, 1966, *20*, 228–236.

Simmons, R. F. Semantic networks: Their computation and use for understanding English sentences. In R. C. Schank & K. M. Colby (Eds.), *Computer models of thought and language*. San Francisco: Freeman, 1973.

Smith, A. D. Aging and interference with memory. *Journal of Gerontology*, 1975, *30*, 319–325.

Smith, A. D. Adult age differences in cued recall. *Developmental Psychology*, 1977, *13*, 326–331.

Smith, A. D. Age differences in encoding, storage, and retrieval. In L. W. Poon, J. L. Fozard, L. S. Cermak, D. Arenberg, & L. W. Thompson (Eds.), *New directions in memory and aging: Proceedings of the George Talland Memorial Conference*. Hillsdale, N.J.: Lawrence Erlbaum, 1980.

Stein, N. L., & Nazworski, T. The effects of organization and instructional set on story memory. *Discourse Processes*, 1978, *1*, 177–194.

Talland, G. A. Three estimates of the word span and their stability over the adult years. *Quarterly Journal of Experimental Psychology*, 1965, *17*, 301–307.

Talland, G. A. Age and the span of immediate recall. In G. A. Talland (Ed.), *Human aging and behavior*. New York: Academic Press, 1968.

Taub, H. A. Method of presentation of meaningful prose to young and old adults. *Experimental Aging Research*, *1976, 2*, 469–474.

Taub, H. A. Comprehension and memory of prose by young and old adults. *Experimental Aging Research*, 1979, *5*, 3–13.

Taub, H. A., & Kline, G. E. Recall of prose as a function of age and input modality. *Journal of Gerontology*, 1978, *5*, 725–730.

Thorndyke, P. W. Cognitive structures in comprehension and memory of narrative discourse. *Cognitive Psychology*, 1977, *9*, 77–110.

Till, R. E., & Walsh, D. A. Encoding and retrieval factors in adult memory for implicational sentences. *Journal of Verbal Learning and Verbal Behavior*, 1980, *19*, 1–16.

Tulving, E. Subjective organization in free recall of "unrelated" words. *Psychological Review*, 1962, *69*, 344–354.

Tulving, E., & Thomson, D. M. Encoding specificity and retrieval processes in episodic memory. *Psychological Review*, 1973, *80*, 352–373.

Walsh, D. A. Age differences in central perceptual processes: A dichoptic backward masking investigation. *Journal of Gerontology*, 1976, *31*, 178–185.

Walsh, D. A., & Baldwin, M. Age differences in integrated semantic memory. *Developmental Psychology*, 1977, *13*, 509–514.

Walsh, D. A., Krauss, I. K., & Regnier, V. A. Spatial ability, environmental knowledge, and environmental use: The elderly. In L. Liben, A. Patterson, & N. Newcombe (Eds.), *Spatial representation and behavior across the life span*. New York: Academic Press, in press.

Walsh, D. A., & Prasse, M. J. Iconic memory and attentional processes in the aged. In L. W. Poon, J. Fozard, L. S. Cermak, D. Arenberg, & L. W. Thompson (Eds.), *New directions in memory and aging: Proceedings of the George Talland Memorial Conference*. Hillsdale, N.J.: Lawrence Erlbaum, 1980.

Walsh, D. A., & Thompson, L. W. Age differences in visual sensory memory. *Journal of Gerontology*, 1978, *33*, 383–387.

Walsh, D. A., Till, R. E., & Williams, M. V. Age differences in peripheral perceptual processes: A monoptic backward masking investigation. *Journal of Experimental Psychology: Human Perception and Performance*, 1978, *4*, 232–243.

Walsh, D. A., Williams, M. V., & Hertzog, C. K. Age-related differences in two stages of central perceptual processes: The effects of short duration targets and criterion differences. *Journal of Gerontology*, 1979, *34*, 234–241.

Waugh, N., & Barr, R. Memory and mental tempo. In L. W. Poon, J. L. Fozard, L. S. Cermak, D. Arenberg, & L. W. Thompson (Eds.), *New directions in memory and aging: Proceedings of the George Talland Memorial Conference*. Hillsdale, N.J.: Lawrence Erlbaum, 1980.

Waugh, N. C., & Norman, D. A. Primary memory. *Psychological Review*, 1965, *72*, 89–104.

Welford, A. T. *Ageing and human skill*. London: Oxford University Press, 1958.

Wickelgren, W. A. Age and storage dynamics in continuous recognition memory. *Developmental Psychology*, 1975, *11*, 165–169.

Winograd, T. Understanding natural language. *Cognitive Psychology*, 1972, *3*(1), entire issue.

Zelinski, E. M., Gilewski, M. J., & Thompson, L. W. Do laboratory memory tests relate to everyday remembering and forgetting? In L. W. Poon, J. L. Fozard, L. S. Cermak, D. Arenberg, & L. W. Thompson (Eds.), *New directions in memory and aging: Proceedings of the George Talland Memorial Conference*. Hillsdale, N.J.: Lawrence Erlbaum, 1980.

Leonard M. Giambra and David Arenberg

CHAPTER

18

Problem Solving, Concept Learning, and Aging

Studies of problem solving and aging published since 1974 are briefly reviewed and are categorized according to the task studied: (a) concept learning, (b) problem solving other than concept learning, and (c) training to improve problem-solving performance. Some prescriptions for aging research in this area in the next decade include the following proposals: (a) to design aging studies within the framework of theories of problem solving that have been fruitful with young adults; (b) to avoid studying problems that have not been thoroughly investigated with young adults; (c) to adopt "thinking-aloud" procedures; and (d) to study a small number of individuals over many problems. The goal of research in this next decade should be to predict individual performance as a function of age.

Problem solving and concept learning in geropsychology were last reviewed by Rabbitt (1977). Rabbitt's references are dated 1974 or earlier; therefore, the overview that follows includes few papers published before 1975. Furthermore, while there is a continuous but thin stream of research investigating the fate of logical-concept attainment in old age from the standpoint of Jean Piaget and his theories, no attempt is made to summarize or evaluate that research here. An excellent summary and evaluation has been provided by Hooper and Sheehan (1977), who include papers through 1976. Two papers relating Piagetian theory to adult development are known to have appeared between 1977 and 1979. One topic not addressed by Hooper and Sheehan concerns the possible existence of a "fifth stage" of cognitive development

that emerges in adulthood (see Arlin, 1975, 1976; Cropper, Meck, & Ash, 1977; Fakouri, 1976).

Overview

The separation of published studies into those concerned with problem solving and those concerned with concept learning is artificial, somewhat strained, but very convenient. To some investigators, concept learning is simply problem-solving activity of a specific type. However, the experimental procedures and materials of concept learning are much more standardized than are other areas of problem solving. Thus the concept-learning literature tends to be more coherent and less fragmented. Herein lies the convenience of reviewing the concept-learning literature separately from the problem-solving literature, which is taken here to include all the problem-solving research not concerned with concept learning.

In general, concept learning involves a well-defined universe of objects that is partitioned into two subsets according to some rule; one subset contains exemplars of the concept, the other, nonexemplars. Concept learning is said to occur when a subject can categorize or label objects of the universe as exemplars or nonexemplars of the concept. Typically, the subject is also asked to explicate the rule that correctly partitions the universe. The problem-solving literature reviewed represents a heterogeneous mixture of procedures and material highly resistant to organization and synthesis.

One of the prominent research issues of the 1970s was whether the problem-solving performance of the old, given that it is typically inferior to that of the young adult, could be improved by training and if so, by what kinds of training. Some other research issues of the 1970s identified by Rabbitt (1977) were (a) the roles of memory and organizational strategies in the effects of aging on problem-solving performance; (b) the effects of "shift" (i.e., changing the solution of a problem after some criterion has been attained) on age differences (failure to switch is sometimes described as rigidity, i.e., continuing to respond in a manner no longer appropriate when conditions change); and (c) the effects of age differences in rate of information processing on problem-solving performance.

Problem Solving

Four papers dealing with problem solving and aging have appeared since 1974 (Hayslip, 1977; Heyn, Barry, & Pollack, 1978; Kesler, Denney, & Whitely, 1976; Lee & Pollack, 1978), and all were cross-sectional in design. Hayslip (1977), using three age groups (17–26, 39–51, 59–76) and anagram problems, found that only 2 of 13 measures of anagram difficulty were significantly correlated with likelihood of solution in all age groups and thus were valid indicators at all age levels. Hayslip's elaborate discussion relating fluid and crystallized intelligence measures to anagram performance is too complex and speculative to be dealt with in this review. Age comparisons of performance were presented in a subsequent paper (Hayslip & Sterns, 1979), and no age differences were noted.

Lee and Pollack (1978) compared performance on Witkin's Embedded Figures Test for females in each of the age decades from the twenties to the seventies. They found a substantial decrement in performance during the fifties, an outcome unchanged when visual acuity and IQ were taken into account. Each person's strategy, determined by posttest interview, on the Embedded Figures Test was ascertained, but no differential strategic approach was discernible between the women under and over age 50.

Heyn et al. (1978) used 20 problems taken from the problem-solving literature with three age groups and found that the 40–50-year-old group solved the most problems, with the 20–30- and 60–70-year-old groups solving an equal number of problems. Analysis of types of errors showed that of the three age groups, the 60–70-year-olds made the most errors of omission (giving no solutions to problems), while the 20–30-

year-olds made the most errors of commission (giving incorrect solutions). However, it was found that the 40–50-year-old group had significantly more education than the other two equally educated age groups. No attempt was made to partial out this educational confound from the performance measures.

Kesler et al. (1976), using a most diverse set of problem-solving tasks with 30–50- and 65–81-year-old groups, attempted to account for observed age differences using the variables of education, occupation, and nonverbal intelligence. The broad range of problem-solving tasks used in their study makes it one of the more important in the recent aging literature. Using regression analyses, Kesler et al. found that education and nonverbal intelligence contributed significantly to the prediction of problem-solving performance but that age did not. Age was significant, however, in the Age × Sex analyses of variance of the problem-solving performance measures. This outcome led Kesler et al. to argue that they had accounted for the individual differences in performance by using individual-specific measures that, if left uncontrolled, would lead spuriously to an age-difference conclusion. However, their recoding of age into a binary variable, which thereby reduced its precision and hence its potential contribution in the multiple regression, makes their conclusion statistically weak. Furthermore, because this is essentially a correlational study, there is a need to replicate their study with an experimental design in which education and nonverbal intelligence are blocked variables, assuming, of course, the validity of a measure of nonverbal intelligence over the adult life span.

Concept Learning

Five papers involving concept-type problem solving and aging have appeared since 1974 (Hayslip & Sterns, 1979; Hoyer, Rebok, & Sved, 1979; Mack & Carlson, 1978; Rogers, Keyes, & Fuller, 1976; West, Odom, & Aschkenasy, 1978). In addition, two papers that appeared in 1974 but were not reviewed by Rabbitt (1977) are also included (Brinley, Jovick, & McLaughlin, 1974; Offenbach, 1974).

Using the Category Test of the Halstead-Reitan Neurological Battery, Mack and Carlson (1978) concluded that 60–80-year-old bright normal subjects performed in a manner like that of 15–77-year-old patients with suspected neurological dysfunction. The performance of a 20–37-year-old normal group was superior to the performance of both the old group and the neurologic group. Mack and Carlson, however, failed to separate their neurologic patients into age groups matching those of the young and old normal subjects; as a result, any comparisons with the neurologic group are difficult to interpret.

In their attempt to link the psychometric and experimental approaches to the study of cognitive processes and aging, Hayslip and Sterns (1979) have made an important contribution. With individuals of an adult life span sample, they obtained psychometric measures of crystallized and fluid intelligence, as well as experimentally derived measures of anagram problem solving and unidimensional concept learning. The expected age differences were found on concept learning and on the fluid-intelligence measure; but no age differences occurred on the crystallized-intelligence measure or on the anagram problems. Hayslip and Sterns applied complex correlational analysis involving psychometric and experimental measures in an attempt to show how the relative contributions of fluid and crystallized intelligence to anagram problem solving and unidimensional concept learning differ in the young, the middle-aged, and the old. The results led Hayslip and Sterns to question the utility of the fluid–crystallized ability distinction in predicting age-related trends in problem-solving tasks.

The effects of age and at least one other variable in concept-identification performance were reported in three studies: (a) Brinley et al. (1974) varied the memory requirements; (b) Hoyer et al. (1979) varied the amount of irrelevant information; and (c) West et al. (1978) investigated the degree of perceptual salience of the stimuli in the to-be-learned concept. The concept-learning literature based on college students indicates that all of these variables can influence concept-learning difficulty.

Brinley et al. studied memory requirements by manipulating the availability of past stimuli, the amount of information to be stored and retained, the positive or negative nature of the information, and the recodability of the information into chunks. Within the task limits of these variables, it was determined that *only* the recoding potential interacted with age. With highly recodable stimulus sequences, the decrease in mean number of problems solved as the age of the groups increased (from 21–35 to 36–50 to 51–65 to 66+) was much more gradual than it was for stimulus sequences that were less recodable. The 21–35-year-old group was not affected by recodability.

Hoyer et al., using unidimensional concept-learning problems, found that as the number of irrelevant dimensions increased, the oldest age group (62–85 years) made disproportionately more errors on the concept problems than did either the young (18–21 years) or the middle-aged (42–56 years) groups. Unexpectedly, the middle-aged group made the fewest errors.

Response times increased disproportionately more with age when the number of irrelevant dimensions was increased. Hoyer et al. interpreted the relation between the error and the response-time data as indicating that the middle-aged group traded time for accuracy successfully while the elderly either did not or could not. However, the better error scores for the middle-aged subjects may have been due to their mean of 16.6 years of education, compared with only 13.8 years for the young and 10.8 years for the elderly. A step-wise multiple-regression analysis found that age increased the variance accounted for by only 1% when entered *after* years of education, whereas age accounted for 4% of the variance when entered *before* years of education; for years of education the percentages were 3% *after* and 5% *before* the age entry. It should be noted, however, that the relation between age and performance was not linear; as a result, the proportions of variance attributed to the age variable in the multiple-regression analyses—which were based on linear components—were reduced.

West et al., using conjunctive concept problems, found for all three age groups in their study that when the solution involved the two least salient stimulus dimensions, the mean number of trials to criterion and mean percentage of errors were greater than when the solution involved the two most salient dimensions. There was no Age × Saliency interaction. The younger adults (18–22 years) were superior to the children (10–14 years) and the older adults (60–78 years), and there was no difference between the children and the older adults with either dependent measure. West et al. pointed out that the differences between the means of the young adults on the least salient dimensions and those of the children and older adults on the most salient dimensions were not statistically significant, and from this concluded that the conceptual abilities of the three age groups were similar. This conclusion seems unwarranted, since in the high-saliency condition, the performance of the young adults was superior to that of the children and the elderly. To conclude that the conceptual abilities of the three groups are similar, it must be shown that at some level of saliency the performances are equivalent. The equality of children's and older adults' performance is consistent with the ontogenetic-biological regression view of intellectual development across adulthood that appears in the Piagetian aging literature.

Offenbach (1974) used a procedure that permitted him to determine which hypothesis, in a unidimensional concept problem, a subject was entertaining on any trial. This procedure was administered to samples consisting of children in Grades 1, 3, and 5 and to adults who were college sophomores or older adults

(65–87 years). Some of Offenbach's findings are intriguing. Not only was the performance of the older group poorer than that of any other age group but the older subjects were *least* likely to retain a hypothesis after a correct response and *most* likely to retain a hypothesis after an incorrect response. According to Offenbach, (1974)

> The elderly's data seemed to indicate that even if they chose the correct cue [hypothesis], they did not recognize it as such, and therefore, did not then learn. . . . Their behavior appeared less systematic and more random. It is as though the elderly utilized an information processing strategy during the tasks similar to a "zero-memory" solution. Thus they responded to each trial independent from the previous trials. (p. 490)

Rogers et al. (1976) analyzed the behavior of 57–85-year-old adults when the solution was shifted without the subject's knowledge during a unidimensional concept problem. The shift came after a criterion of solution was reached and was either a reversal (same dimension) or a nonreversal (another dimension) shift. This was an attempt to ascertain the degree to which the elderly exhibit perseveration or rigidity in keeping a previously effective, but now ineffective, solution hypothesis. Regardless of the type of reversal, it took from one to six trials before the elderly discarded their now incorrect, but previously correct, hypothesis. The mean was 2.4 trials, which is evidence for very little perseverative behavior. Unfortunately, with no comparison group of younger adults, this small effect may be unrelated to age. However, Offenbach's (1974) finding that the elderly were less likely than the young to shift after an error supports an age-rigidity hypothesis.

Thus the 1970s presented a confusing and contradictory picture of the relation of aging to the processes of concept learning and problem solving. Subject variables such as visual acuity and education acted to confound any clear and consistent age effects, with both linear and nonlinear age effects produced. The research provided little insight into how information-processing components or inferential/inductive skills might be changing, and in many of these studies, little was found to indicate *which* skills were altered.

Training to Improve Performance

The generally poorer performance of the elderly on concept-learning and problem-solving tasks has led to the use of intervention techniques that are intended to improve performance and demonstrate that the deficits are not immutable—that is, that there is "plasticity" in the cognitive performance of the elderly. The earlier literature (see Rabbitt, 1977) demonstrated that training of various sorts can enhance performance immediately after training. Denney and Denney (1974) and Denney, Jones, and Krigel (1979) again demonstrated short-term effectiveness. Sanders, Sanders, Mayes, and Sielski (1976) and Sanders, Sterns, Smith, and Sanders (1975) also attempted to improve performance through training. However, both of the Sanders et al. studies appear to have had confounds that make questionable the equivalence of the tasks undertaken by the trained and untrained groups: The training seems to change the task from complete learning or attribute identification to rule learning, which is usually an easier task. Two recent studies (Labouvie-Vief & Gonda, 1976; Sanders & Sanders, 1978) have been designed to deal with the extent to which the enhanced performance continues in the long term.

Sanders and Sanders investigated the effect of two training procedures with a more difficult concept-identification task 1 year after training on an easier task, whereas Labouvie-Vief and Gonda determined the effect of two training procedures 2 weeks later on an identical and on a transfer task. Sanders and Sanders found that only one training procedure produced long-term effects; Labouvie-Vief and Gonda found that one type of training produced long-term effects on the original task, and the other type of training produced long-term effects on the transfer task. In the Sanders and Sanders study, the two training conditions differed only in that the ineffective one had a token-reward system associated with it. Training involved a programmed-learning sequence designed to promote a systematic testing strategy. Their post hoc hypothesis, which accounts for the simultaneous success and failure of two essentially similar types of training in terms of extrinsic and intrinsic rewards, requires more evidence to be convincing. Labouvie-Vief and Gonda found that a simple practice control group (called "unspecific training") also showed long-term effects on the original and transfer tasks equal in magnitude to those produced by the two types of training involved. One type was cognitive training in the form of planning and self-guidance. The other was cognitive training plus instructions on how to reduce task anxiety. These authors interpreted the outcome as indicating that practice probably allowed their elderly subjects to develop their own effective strategies and that these strategies were more likely to be retained than strategies taught in the training groups. Furthermore, to these authors and to us as well, this is a more optimistic outcome; it indicates that the elderly can, when given sufficient opportunity to develop their skill and gain additional experience with unfamiliar tasks and problems, improve their performance without outside intervention.

A Course for the Geropsychology of Problem Solving and Concept Learning in the 1980s

On a bicycle, the back wheel must follow the front wheel. The geropsychology of problem solving and concept learning is the back wheel to the front wheel of the psychology of problem solving and concept learning. One might define the geropsychology of problem solving and concept learning as the study of the influence of age on theories, principles, and laws of problem solving and concept learning in the adult. Thus it is clear to us that the geropsychology of problem solving and concept learning will make important and significant advances only when the psychology of problem solving and concept learning has itself made significant advances. The course of the geropsychology of problem solving and concept learning in the next decade would be profoundly altered by adherence to this position. Let us examine some of the consequences of that adherence.

The Age-Replication Consequence

This consequence would have geropsychologists attempt to replicate with older adults those experiments and procedures that have proven most fruitful in leading to coherent and relatively general theories of problem solving and concept learning in the young adult. Thus, for example, geropsychology stands to gain much by emulating the information-processing approach of Newell and Simon (1972).

Newell, Simon, and their colleagues have studied problem solving in several areas and have developed an information-processing theory that allows for extensive and detailed verification. An information-processing theory of problem solving permits translation to computer programs that simulate the problem solver's behavior on specific problems. Clearly, then, we should study the problems that Newell and Simon have studied (cryptoarithmetic, logical theorem proving, making chess moves, etc.), using the methods they have used ("thinking aloud," eye-movement recording, etc.) on persons representative of the adult life span. As a first step, we should be able to observe where Newell and Simons's problem-solving theory incorrectly predicts the problem-solving behavior of older people—or perhaps at what ages the predictions become erroneous. As a second step, we should look at the ways in which their information-processing theory might be modified to include the parameter of age or its functional/behavioral concomitant. Finally, we might then reconstitute their theory so that simulation could be carried out to verify the age-dependent components of the theory.

The Prohibition-Against-Aging-Studies Consequence

This consequence would have geropsychology demand that age *not* be included as an independent variable in any study of problem solving and concept learning in which the concepts and problems studied have received little prior investigation in the young adult. Furthermore, even if a concept or a problem has received extensive study with young adults, it should *not* be studied in older adults until a sufficiently verified theory has been developed that accounts for the young adults' performance. That is, it is of little use to look at age differences or changes on a concept-learning or problem-solving task if no sufficiently powerful and explicit theory exists to account for the performance on that task of the "standard" young adult group. Viewed from another perspective, this Prohibition-Against-Aging-Studies consequence would help move us out of the "Gee-whiz, look at the age difference" mentality (which represents the least taxing, thoughtful, and useful of all mentalities) to an insistence that age differences or changes be explained by specifying the nature of the modifications that must be made to theories that account for the standard (young adult) age group's performance. To achieve this rise in consciousness, we, in the geropsychology of problem solving, must look disapprovingly at studies of such "unexplained" problems or concept tasks within the framework of the old mentality. Furthermore, we must look approvingly at those who study the solution of a "problem" only within the standard age group, so that they may contribute to the development of a verified theory or explanation of performance on that problem.

Some Further Prescriptions for the Next Decade

Adopt the "thinking-aloud" procedure. The "thinking-aloud" procedure requires problem solvers to make their thoughts public. While solving a problem the subjects must verbalize all the thoughts they are aware of and that are pertinent to solving the problem. Thinking aloud is *not* introspection, since it does not require the problem solver to evaluate and analyze the thoughts, mental events or ideas. Thinking aloud provides the experimenter with informationally dense (Simon, 1979) subject-produced outputs that are unlike the informationally sparse outputs resulting from the common practice of using only a few dependent measures to reflect performance on a problem-solving task (e.g., trials to solution or number of errors). Newell and Simon have used the thinking-aloud procedure in developing a successful theory of problem solving in a special subset of problems. They have developed methods for translating the thinking-aloud protocols into statements that permit a detailed identification of the processes and knowledge each subject found necessary to solve the problems.

One of the ideas implicit in using the thinking-aloud procedure is that a successful theory must be able to predict what an *individual* (not group) will do (or can do) *at any point* in a problem. The thinking-aloud protocols provide a rich account of an individual's behavior at any point in a problem. We know from the psychological literature that a mean group performance is usually not very predictive of an individual's performance. Furthermore, the literature in concept learning strongly suggests that there may be at least three different individual strategies used in learning a concept or solving a problem. Thus the thinking-aloud protocols of many individuals will permit the experimenter to specify and catalogue the several—but probably not numerous—problem-solving strategies utilized so that the full richness of human thinking behavior might be incorporated into a general theory of thinking or problem solving. Of course, to be most useful, this method must be capable of providing a theory that can discriminate one type of strategy from another before a solution is attempted or early in the attempt at solution.

It must now be evident that the thinking-aloud procedure is essentially idiographic in orientation and runs counter to the generally prevailing nomothetic approach dominant in psychology today and over the past four decades. Furthermore, since the thinking-aloud method produces such informationally rich data, the study and analysis of such data on each individual is an extremely time-consuming venture. Experience, both personal and as reported by Newell and Simon, has also shown this approach to be most arduous for the experimenter. Therefore, studies using this method will most likely use relatively small numbers of subjects, with the result that the experimenter must continually deal with questions related to the generality of the findings. Nonetheless, it is our firm belief that the question of generality must not prevent this approach from being implemented; its use will account for and predict the problem-solving approach of at least some subsets of the population. Generality of the findings will be determined by replication by other experimenters studying the problem on their small number of individuals. Thus the burden of generality will be borne not college of experimentalists concerned with problem solving.

Study each individual over many problems. By this prescription it is meant that each individual subject should be studied (a) on a particular problem type to the point of reaching maximum or near-maximum proficiency, and (b) on many different kinds of problems, that is, on problems that differ in verbal description but require the same "methods" for solution—called isomorphs (Hayes & Simon, 1977)—and on problems that may require different methods for solution.

To study people until they reach their highest levels of proficiency on a particular type of problem would provide us with valuable information on such important aspects of problem-solving behavior as how problem-solving strategies differ under conditions of minimal and maximal familiarity or experience with the problem. Furthermore, any observed progressive changes in strategy would provide valuable information on how individuals develop their problem-solving strategies and thus learn to solve problems. There is a large class of problems that most individuals may not be able to solve until they have had extensive experience with those problems. Under minimal experience, this could result in thinking-aloud protocols that defy analysis or reflect quickly changing or incoherent strategic approaches to the problem. In this situation subjects would be required to work problems until they were able to solve them and thus would have developed a coherent strategy inferrable from their protocol.

Studying an individual on a family of problems that required the same skills would provide us with information on how people come to understand a problem and how that understanding may lead to a generalization of one strategy or a consolidation and assimilation of several (specialized) strategies. This kind of information is noticeably sparse in both the psychology and geropsychology of problem solving.

Rabbitt (1977) advocated the analysis of complex problem-solving behavior to reveal the component processes and the relative contributions of those processes to performance and to age differences in performance. Some progress in that direction was made during the 1970s, and it seems likely that some of the nomothetic research of the 1980s will continue in that direction. However, in our judgment, the greater contributions in that direction will come from the more idiographic research.

We believe that to make significant advances in the 1980s, the geropsychology of problem solving and concept learning ought to follow the course spelled out above. The studies reviewed earlier, through their minimal progress in providing insight into the processes of problem solving as related to aging, speak emphatically for the recommended change in experimental emphasis. Surely, if real progress had been made then we would not constantly be faced with the results of studies with ambiguous evidence on the experimental hypotheses leading to ad hoc and uninformative explanations of the unexpected equivocal results. The idiographic paradigm advocated in this paper should provide the experimenter with a rich harvest of specific and precise information about what his or her subjects are doing and consequently with the means to account for the commonly obtained equivocal outcomes; for example, failures in training procedures could be precisely specified. The present course (a) is essentially independent of the main stream of the psychology of problem solving, (b) represents only a group-mean mentality, and (c) is based on experimental procedures that produce informationally sparse output. To continue on this course is to guarantee that the minimal advances in understanding achieved in the 1970s will continue into the 1980s.

REFERENCES

Arlin, P. K. Cognitive development in adulthood: A fifth stage? *Developmental Psychology*, 1975, *11*, 602–606.

Arlin, P. K. Toward a metatheoretical model of cognitive development. *International Journal of Aging and Human Development*, 1976, 7, 247–253.

Brinley, J. F., Jovick, T. J., & McLaughlin, L. M. Age, reasoning and memory in adults. *Journal of Gerontology*, 1974, *29*, 182–189.

Cropper, D. A., Meck, D. S., & Ash, M. J. The relation between formal operations and a possible fifth stage of cognitive development. *Developmental Psychology*, 1977, *13*, 517–518.

Denney, N. W., & Denney, D. R. Modeling effects on the questioning strategies of the elderly. *Developmental Psychology*, 1974, *10*, 458.

Denney, N. W., Jones, F. W., & Krigel, S. H. Modifying the questioning strategies of young children and elderly adults with strategy-modeling techniques. *Human Development*, 1979, *22*, 23–36.

Fakouri, M. E. "Cognitive development in adulthood: A fifth stage?": A critique. *Developmental Psychology*, 1976, *12*, 472.

Hayes, J. R., & Simon, H. A. Psychological differences among problem isomorphs. In N. S. Castellan, Jr., D. B. Pisoni, & G. R. Potts (Eds.), *Cognitive theory* (Vol. 2). Hillsdale, N.J.: Lawrence Erlbaum, 1977.

Hayslip, B., Jr. Determinants of anagram problem solution in adulthood. *Experimental Aging Research*, 1977, *3*, 147–163.

Hayslip, B., Jr., & Sterns, H. L. Age differences in relationships between crystallized and fluid intelligences and problem solving. *Journal of Gerontology*, 1979, *14*, 404–414.

Heyn, J. E., Barry, J. R., & Pollack, R. H. Problem solving as a function of age, sex and the role appropriateness of the problem content. *Experimental Aging Research*, 1978, *4*, 505–519.

Hooper, F. H., & Sheehan, N. W. Logical concept attainment during the aging years: Issues in the neo-Piagetian research literature. In W. F. Overton & J. M. Gallegher (Eds.), *Knowledge and development. Vol. 1, Advances in research and theory*. New York: Plenum Press, 1977.

Hoyer, W. J., Rebok, G. W., & Sved, S. M. Effects of varying irrelevant information on adult age differences in problem solving. *Journal of Gerontology*, 1979, *14*, 553–560.

Kesler, M. S., Denney, N. W., & Whitely, S. E. Factors influencing problem solving in middle-aged and elderly adults. *Human Development*, 1976, *19*, 310–320.

Labouvie-Vief, G., & Gonda, J. N. Cognitive strategy training and intellectual performance in the elderly. *Journal of Gerontology*, 1976, *31*, 327–332.

Lee, J. A., & Pollack, R. H. The effect of age on perceptual problem-solving strategies. *Experimental Aging Research*, 1978, *4*, 37–54.

Mack, J. L. & Carlson, N. J. Conceptual deficits and aging: The category test. *Perceptual and Motor Skills*, 1978, *46*, 123–128.

Newell, A., & Simon, H. A. *Human problem solving*. Englewood Cliffs, N.J.: Prentice-Hall, 1972.

Offenbach, S. I. A developmental study of hypothesis testing and cue selection strategies. *Developmental Psychology*, 1974, *10*, 484–490.

Rabbitt, P. Changes in problem-solving ability in older age. In J. E. Birren & K. W. Schaie (Eds.), Handbook of the psychology of aging. New York: Van Nostrand Reinhold, 1977.

Rogers, J. C., Keyes, B. J., & Fuller, B. J. Solution shift performance in the elderly. *Journal of Gerontology*, 1976, *31*, 670–675.

Sanders, J. A. C., Sterns, H. L., Smith, M., & Sanders, R. E. Modification of conceptual identification performance in older adults. *Developmental Psychology*, 1975, *11*, 824–829.

Sanders, R. E., & Sanders, J. A. C. Long-term durability and transfer of enhanced conceptual performance in the elderly. *Journal of Gerontology*, 1978, *33*, 408–412.

Sanders, R. E., Sanders, J. A. C., Mayes, G. J., & Sielski, K. A. Enhancement of conjunctive concept attainment in older adults. *Developmental Psychology*, 1976, *12*, 485–486.

Simon, H. A. Information-processing models of cognition. *Annual Review of Psychology*, 1979, *30*, 363–396.

West, R. L., Odom, R. D., & Aschkenasy, J. R. Perceptual sensitivity and conceptual coordination in children and younger and older adults. *Human Development*, 1978, *21*, 334–345.

Sherry L. Willis and Paul B. Baltes

CHAPTER
19

Intelligence in Adulthood and Aging: Contemporary Issues

Issues in the study of psychometric intelligence are discussed from a life span developmental perspective. A first set of issues involves questions of developmental design aimed at valid identification of ontogenetic life span change; a second set of issues deals with proper assessment of intellectual behavior in older adults; and a third set of issues relates to explanatory-causal work on intellectual aging and the role of intervention paradigms. As a framework of causal-explanatory research, a trifactorial model of influences on life span development is presented which identifies three categories of influences—age-graded, history-graded, and non-normative—assumed to interact in producing regularities and variations in life span development. During the last decade, clarification of these isssues has resulted in a major reevaluation of the traditional evidence on intellectual aging. Whereas general decline was traditionally considered the primary characteristic of intellectual aging, it appears that intellectual aging in current cohorts is much more plastic and heterogeneous than past research with limited methodologies would have implied. It it suggested that future research emphasizing the issues outlined will result in a view of intellectual aging that is differential rather than normative and dynamic rather than static.

The area of adult intelligence has received considerable attention in the gerontological literature during the past decade. Contributing to this context of renewed interest, and sometimes controversy (Baltes & Schaie, 1976; Horn & Donaldson, 1976, 1977; Schaie & Baltes, 1977), has been a focus on a series of methodological issues dealing with questions of design and control necessary for valid measurement of developmental change. While such methodological issues may apply to various aspects of developmental aging, it has been in the study of psychometric intelligence that they have been most fully examined. Moreover, findings from data sets employing such methods have suggested the need for possible revisions and extensions in our theories and models of intellectual aging.

This chapter discusses several of these issues that gained considerable attention in the 1970s and that may have important implications for the study of adult intelligence in the coming decade. First, several issues dealing with the assessment of change in intellectual behavior are examined. It is suggested here that the methodologies used to assess intellectual aging relate directly to questions regarding the timing, directionality, and pervasiveness of such change and that consideration of intellectual aging within a life span context may provide a broader perspective of such change than has been obtained within a narrow age period approach. Second, two issues related to the definition and measurement of intelligence are explored. The differential patterns of intellectual aging suggested by cohort-sequential research have led some researchers to suggest the need for (a) age/cohort-rele-

An earlier version of the ideas contained in this chapter was published in F. Hoffmeister and C. Müller (Eds.), *Brain Function in Old Age: Evaluation of Changes and Disorders.* (New York: Springer-Verlag, 1979). Grant support from the National Institute on Aging (5 R01 AG00403) for a project entitled "Cognitive Modifiability in Aging" to Pennsylvania State University and Paul B. Baltes and Sherry L. Willis (co-investigators) is acknowledged.

vant intelligence measures, and (b) consideration of intraindividual variability (plasticity) as a dimension of intellectual assessment. Finally, the need for an explanatory as well as a descriptive approach to the study of intellectual aging is considered. A multicausal model identifying three possible sets of influences is outlined as a heuristic scheme for interpretation of existing data and the design of future research.

One additional comment is needed. Adult intelligence has been defined in many ways (e.g., Botwinick, 1977; Resnick, 1976; Sternberg & Detterman, 1979). In general, two major approaches to the study of intellectual behavior have been identified. The psychometric approach has been the more dominant of the two, both from a historical perspective and in terms of the volume of theory and research stemming from a given perspective. Psychometric concepts of intelligence have been developed largely in connection with intelligence testing, prediction, and the concept of human abilities (e.g., Cattell, 1971; Guilford, 1967; Horn, 1978; Thurstone, 1938). A second major approach is related to the study of intelligence as cognition, involving processes of perception, learning, memory, and problem solving (Kintsch, 1970; Sternberg & Detterman 1979). While the other four chapters in this section deal with aspects of the cognitive approach, the issues to be discussed in the present chapter have been primarily associated with the psychometric approach to the study of intelligence. Since this chapter focuses on identifying and discussing some of the current salient issues in the field, it does not provide a comprehensive review of the gerontological literature in this area. Several such reviews are available for the interested reader (Baltes & Labouvie, 1973; Botwinick, 1977; Horn, 1978; Labouvie-Vief, 1977; Schaie, 1979).

Developmental Change in Intellectual Aging

Assessment of Change

Longitudinal and cohort-sequential designs. During the past decade considerable attention has been given to clarifying the relation between various forms of age-developmental methods of data collection, such as the cross-sectional and longitudinal methods (Baltes, 1968; Baltes, Reese, & Nesselroade, 1977; Nesselroade & Baltes, 1979; Riley, 1979; Schaie, 1965, 1970; Schaie & Baltes, 1975). It is now recognized that the basic descriptive task of any developmental approach (including the study of aging) consists of the proper identification of two components of variability: (1) intraindividual variability, and (2) interindividual differences in intraindividual variability. Unless designs permit the clear separation of these two components of variability, misidentification of development change and of developmental differences in change will result. In fact, up to a few years ago, much of the literature on intelligence in old age suffered from this methodological flaw.

For a given birth cohort (individuals born at a specified time, say, in 1900), only the longitudinal method can provide for direct information on both intraindividual change and interindividual differences in such change. In a strict sense, the cross-sectional method is never an appropriate substitute for longitudinal (repeated measurement) investigation. However, intellectual aging research is further complicated by possible biocultural changes affecting the course of life span development for individual cohorts. An example of such biocultural changes are cohort effects.

If such biocultural changes exist, single-cohort longitudinal information on change is not sufficient, and developmental designs must consider two additional components of variability: (3) between-cohort differences in intraindividual variability, and (4) between-cohort differences in interindividual differences in intraindividual variability. As a consequence, if biocultural change in intellectual behavior is obtained, findings from single-cohort longitudinal studies cannot tell the entire story about intellectual aging. The reason is that a single-cohort longitudinal study is but a sample from a population of cohort-specific longitudinal studies, and therefore its results cannot be generalized to other cohorts. To what degree the life span development observed in one cohort can be generalized to another is a matter of empirical demonstration.

In psychology, and especially in the area of psychometric intelligence, it has been established that such generalization across cohorts is not possible for current aging cohorts living in the Western world. Cohort-sequential studies, for example, by Schaie and his colleagues (e.g., Nesselroade, Schaie, & Baltes, 1972; Schaie, 1979) in the United States, or by Rudinger (1976) in Germany—the latter based on data from the Bonn Longitudinal Study—represent powerful and persuasive cases. In Schaie's longitudinal sequential study begun in 1956, age changes in intellectual performance on Thurstone's Primary Mental Abilities Test have been examined for several cohorts of adults over a 14- to 21-year period (Schaie, 1970, 1979). Age changes were measured at 7-year intervals, 1956, 1963, 1970, and 1977. With such a design it is possible to examine age/cohort relations for the five primary abilities. In addition, the inclusion at each 7-year assessment interval of random samples of individuals from the same birth cohorts allows comparison

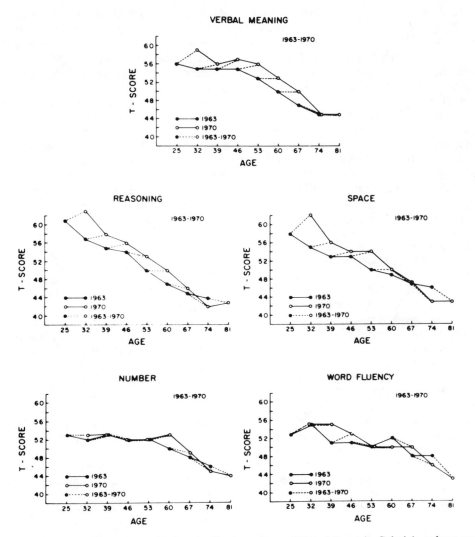

Figure 19-1. Comparison of cross-sectional with longitudinal gradients (dotted lines) in Schaie's cohort-sequential research on adult intelligence. (From "Generational Versus Ontogenetic Components of Change in Adult Cognitive Behavior: A Fourteen-Year Cross-Sequential Study" by K. W. Schaie and G. Labouvie-Vief. *Developmental Psychology*, 1974, *10*, 305–320. Copyright 1974 by the American Psychological Association. Reprinted by permission.)

of the selective longitudinal sample with independently drawn random samples from the same population.

Figure 19-1, which shows 7-year longitudinal age changes (from 1963 to 1970) on the five primary abilities for eight birth cohorts, highlights some of the general trends of age/cohort relations (Schaie & Labouvie-Vief, 1974). With regard to longitudinal age changes (dotted lines), no significant decrement in performance on any ability was noted before the late 60s. Significant increments across the 7-year period were noted at earlier ages (20s, 30s) for Verbal Meaning and Space. Moreover, significant cohort differences favoring younger cohorts are evident for some abilities,

notably Verbal Meaning, Reasoning, and Space. The data suggest both cohort effects varying by abilities and the relatively late and limited occurrence of ontogenetic decrement in such healthy, well-educated populations, as represented in longitudinal research.

Control groups. Findings from these data must be tempered, however, by consideration of a number of perspectives. First, it is in the nature of cohort effects (and biocultural change in general) that they are not fixed. On the contrary, their direction and magnitude change. As a consequence, the pattern depicted in Figure 19-1 is specific to the cohorts and historical times studied. In fact, Schaie's (1979) summary presentation of results from additional data points (1956, 1963, 1970, 1977) makes it apparent that cohort change in the mental abilities studied is rarely linear.

Second, there is the effect of selective attrition on longitudinal samples. Discrepancies between members of the longitudinal sample and independent samples from the parent population tend to increase over time. In Schaie's work, data from the two samples seem to differ primarily in level of function and, for some abilities, in the age range of onset of reliable decrement (Schaie, Labouvie, & Buech, 1973). The attrited longitudinal sample then appears more representative of a stable population of healthy, well-educated, middle-class individuals, whereas the independent sample appears to be more representative of less well-educated, lower-middle-class populations. Differences in data between the two samples may be most important when considering the magnitude of age changes in intelligence. Following Riegel's earlier work, Botwinick (1977) has recently discussed this issue in more detail.

The issue of control groups in longitudinal research is an important one and has received increasing attention in research on psychometric intelligence. Control groups are necessary for at least three sets of possible sources of error in research on aging (see Baltes et al., 1977; Schaie, 1977). A first set deals with changes in the parent population (e.g., birth cohort) itself, from which longitudinal samples are drawn. Biological mortality, if it is correlated with the dependent variable under study, is the classical example. A second set of sources of error that require design control involves changes in experimental samples due to initial selective sampling and selective drop-out. In general, the findings are that biological survivors, longitudinal participants, and longitudinal survivors score higher and show less aging decrement in psychometric intelligence than those who die, fail to participate, or leave a longitudinal study before it is completed.

A third set of control issues relates to questions of measurement validity and measurement equivalence. Examples are the problem of retest effects associated with reactive measures and the possibility of changes in the validities of tests when they are given to different ages and cohorts. In the area of psychometric intelligence, each of these three sets of design problems has been shown to be relevant in empirical work (e.g., Baltes, Schaie, & Nardi, 1971; Blum, Clark, & Jarvik, 1973; Eisdorfer & Wilkie, 1973; Riegel & Riegel, 1972; Rudinger, 1976; Schaie, 1979).

Summary of descriptive evidence and prospects. It is difficult to draw firm conclusions from present evidence on intellectual aging, which has been collected via application of cohort-sequential methodology, given a number of design and measurement limitations.[1] However, in our view there are enough results to suggest the following points about current cohorts:

1. Chronological age per se accounts for a relatively modest amount of the variance observed in intellectual aging during late adulthood up to the 60s or early 70s. Differences between cohorts, up to ages 60–70, equal or exceed in importance chronological age differences (Schaie & Parham, 1977). Chronological age gains in prominence, however, as age reaches the 70s.

2. Interindividual differences (including cohort differences) in intellectual aging are large and suggest differential (heterogeneous) rather than homogeneous patterns of aging.

3. There appear to be marked differential changes for various intellectual abilities (e.g., Verbal Meaning, Number) with regard not only to age but also to cohort.

The findings from longitudinal and cohort-sequential research suggest that intellectual change be examined from a differential aging perspective. Key features of this approach would be variability, multidirectionality, and multidimensionality (Baltes & Willis, 1979; Labouvie-Vief & Chandler, 1978). Such an approach, emphasizing intra- and interindividual variability in intellectual aging, contrasts somewhat with the more traditional approach to change in intellectual aging that has sought to identify a normative or "classical" pattern of change. Moreover, some evidence is beginning to appear that there may also be differential cohort/ability relationships in terms of level of functioning.

A differential aging perspective, however, is not restricted to *interindividual* variability in development, with cohort differences as one aspect of such interindividual variability. In addition, focusing on differential aging also suggests concern with *intraindividual* variability. The range of intraindividual variability (plasticity), both long-term and short-term, appears not to have received as much attention as interindividual variability and requires further exploration. Recent cognitive intervention studies are one mecha-

---

[1] Botwinick's (1977) thoughtful review presents perhaps the best reasoned case for maintaining a position that includes decline in intellectual abilities (small and differential in late adulthood, general and large in old age) as the major feature of intelligence in adulthood and old age. For the data base covered, Botwinick's interpretation has many strengths. However, in our view (see, e.g., Baltes & Willis, 1979), Botwinick does not pay sufficient attention to issues of aging-fair measurement and questions of plasticity. These issues are discussed later in this chapter.

nism for examining short-term intraindividual variability and are discussed later in this chapter.

In any case, such an emphasis on variability (both inter- and intraindividual) suggests that intellectual aging must be viewed as a dynamic rather than a static phenomenon. Researchers in the area need to be sensitive to the need for continual reexamination not only of their perspectives on intellectual aging but also of the change in evidence that occurs in conjunction with biocultural variation.

Definition and Measurement of Adult Intelligence

The differential aging perspective suggested by recent cohort-sequential studies also has implications for the definition and measurement of adult intelligence. Such an approach questions the validity of measurement systems developed for younger age groups for assessing age- and cohort-relevant dimensions of adult intelligence. In addition, the wide range of variability shown in intellectual functioning in adulthood suggests consideration of intraindividual plasticity as a further dimension of intellectual assessment.

Age- and Cohort-Relevant Intelligence Measures

When research on adult and gerontological intelligence began, it was common practice to use existing psychometric tools as a framework to define and measure intelligence. However, this strategy is at best a shortcut.

Earlier psychometric research on intelligence with children and young adults was based on careful analyses of the tasks and settings related to intellectual behavior in those age groups. The historical giants of the field of psychometric intelligence, such as Binet and Thurstone, spent considerable time developing appropriate task material and age-appropriate models of intelligence. Researchers interested in late adulthood and old age, however, have a tendency simply to apply the methods of psychometric intelligence that have been developed for younger age populations. Thus we find longitudinal studies into late adulthood based on the Army Alpha tests, developed largely in the context of the military services, or on the Primary Mental Abilities Test, constructed for research with college students. Note that such intelligence tests, in terms of their content and predictive validity, were designed primarily for forecasting successful performance in

academic and professional settings characteristic of early adult life.

As a consequence, as suggested earlier by Demming and Pressey (1957) and more recently by Schaie (1978; Schaie & Schaie, 1977), what we know about psychometric intelligence in the older adult is based on instruments and models developed for the young. In other words, we know how to compare the older person with the young in youth-oriented tasks and settings. But we have relatively few instruments that can tell us much about the unique nature of intellectual behavior and its predictive validity in the older adult. Although this critical view of existing measurement instruments was expressed rather persuasively some time ago, the effort invested in counteracting this deficiency has been amazingly meager. Moreover, some of the most aggressive proponents of a trait conception of intellectual aging, which is often associated with positions of marked decline (e.g., Horn, 1978; Horn & Donaldson, 1977), base their own research and interpretation almost exclusively on the use of test instruments developed in the context of young adults, where academic performance served as the major validation criterion.

If a representative assessment of gerontological intelligence is at stake, a youth-oriented approach does not appear defensible, at least not as the primary strategy of assessment. What is imperative in future research on adult and gerontological intelligence is to make the intellectual behavior of older adults and their ecologies the guides for content, predictive, and construct validation. Linking the intellectual behavior of older persons to that of younger ones by using youth-oriented instruments may remain a part of our search for life span knowledge and life span bridges connecting intellectual development. But, in order to produce balance in assessment methods and models of intelligence, future work on gerontological intelligence will need to be life span and old age centered. It will need to consider problems of task analysis and validation that reflect the intellectual demands on the older person and the recognition of multiple-age (or developmental) and multiple-setting criteria as references for validation (Schaie, 1978).

For example, if intelligence is a construct aimed at measuring successful adaptation in particular settings and task situations that are changing as life span development progresses, we need to know what settings and tasks related to intellectual behavior are unique to the older person (Clement, 1977; McClelland, 1973). What are the intellectual tasks of advancing adulthood and how are these tasks related to the task systems of earlier life? To what degree may it be necessary for the older adult to unlearn (rather than passively forget) knowledge and skills acquired in the first part of life? It seems fair to conclude that on this score, research on gerontological intelligence is truly in its infancy, some notable exceptions notwithstanding (e.g., Clayton & Birren, in press; Gardner & Monge, 1977; Schaie, 1977–78).

Average Performance (Trait) Versus Intraindividual Variability (Plasticity)

A second theme of the dominant approach to the study of psychometric intelligence in late adulthood has been an extraordinary preconception of viewing abilities as largely invariant and fixed, "as attributes that have many of the properties of a trait, as this concept is used in general biology. That is, . . . defined as an enduring characteristic by means of which one person can be distinguished from another" (Horn, 1977, p. 140). This general trait approach is reflected in the usual observational scheme associated with psychometric intelligence, which involves an average performance per individual based on a static, single-occasion measurement of intellectual performance in a variety of tasks. Note that averaging is based on averaging of tasks given on one occasion, rather than on consideration of a developmental (longitudinal) time continuum or the individual's adaptive capacity to different life situations. An additional feature of age-comparative research on psychometric intelligence is that assessment has been conducted under standard fixed conditions, with all persons participating in the same observational procedure, independent of their life (pretest) history.

Obviously, such an average performance- and trait-oriented approach does not lead to information on the *range* (limits) of behavior (Baltes & Baltes, 1980). In the study of psychometric intelligence, the implied premise is that single-occasion observations on a variety of intellectual tasks (with testing conditions held constant) lead to general information about the performance of an individual. This can be true only for the limited case represented by the testing situation. Recognizing this limitation is particularly important if assessment of intelligence is seen as an indicator not only of performance but of capacity or potential. In fact, in the gerontological literature, performance measures in static situations are often taken as measures of what the elderly person is capable of doing in principle (intelligence as capacity or competence). This is a highly questionable inference (see Botwinick, 1977), because it involves generalization from performance in test situations to unobserved

settings and to possible treatment benefits and thereby neglects intraindividual variability.[2]

It is rarely recognized that information on intraindividual variability and on the conditions for such variability (e.g., as a function of pretest history or concurrent treatment conditions) is an important ingredient of a comprehensive theory of psychometric intelligence. Historically, the concept of testing the limits had been introduced exactly for the purpose of obtaining information on intraindividual variability or the possible range of performance. The available evidence on gerontological intelligence, however, is thoroughly lacking in knowledge about plasticity or intraindividual variability, whether seen in a short-term (concurrent) or long-term (developmental) framework. Short-term, or concurrent, plasticity refers to the range of performance that a given person can display at any given developmental time, if subjected to different treatment conditions. Long-term, or developmental, plasticity refers to range of performance, not at any given point in time, but in regard to the nature of developmental functions (Wohlwill, 1973) or developmental behavior-change processes as they extend over longer segments of the life course.

Thus we do not know what aged persons could do. All we know is what they do, if they live in the context of the current social ecology, if they are not exposed to varying biological and environmental conditions (whether construed as facilitative or interfering) before assessment begins, and if they are asked to participate in one mode of assessment, one dictated by procedures and models developed in the life context of the young adult. With such evidence, it is not possible to make statements about aspects of intellectual potential but only, to use a statistical analogue, about a "fixed level" of performance delivered in a highly specific setting.

Baltes and his colleagues (Baltes & Danish, 1980; Baltes & Willis, 1977) discuss the importance of intervention research for exploring the possible range of psychological aging in greater detail and in a more general context. There is beginning to be research to counteract the traditional preconception of average performance (trait) in psychometric intelligence (for a review, see Labouvie-Vief, 1976, 1977). The most di-

---

[2] In the literature on abnormal cognition in geriatric medicine, the issue of separating competence from performance deficits has a counterpart problem. A distinction between "true" senility, presumed to be biologically based, and various forms of pseudosenilities is discussed by medical researchers and practitioners (e.g., Libow, 1977). The methodological requirement of testing and studying the limits of performance presented in this chapter applies equally well to that forum of research and diagnosis.

rect line of inquiry is based on intervention research. Intervention research is aimed at examining the role of various behavioral intervention programs and so-called ability-extrinsic performance factors affecting the intraindividual range of intellectual performance. Such intervention work is aimed not only at assessing what older persons do but what they could do if conditions were different. In general, the relevant data are not yet rich enough to warrant firm conclusions. In our own research, however, the evidence for much more intraindividual plasticity in gerontological intelligence than has been acknowledged by most researchers in the field appears impressive (Hofland, Willis, & Baltes, 1980; Plemons, Willis, & Baltes, 1978; Willis, Blieszner, & Baltes, 1980).

In considering the magnitude of such preliminary findings on the responsiveness (plasticity) of older adults to various performance-enhancing treatments, it becomes apparent why research on the conditions for intraindividual variability in intellectual performance is so critical for an understanding of old age. If, for example, the hypothesis (Labouvie, Hoyer, Baltes, & Baltes, 1974) is correct that the majority of older persons generally live (a) in a cognitively deprived environment, and (b) in one which deemphasizes youth-oriented tasks involving academic and occupational achievement, then our current assessment of the intellectual capacity of older persons by means of psychometric instruments is terribly deficient and aging biased. The current assessment focus is on static assessment of intellectual behavior in specific settings, settings that are likely to be unrepresentative or even dysfunctional for the elderly. Appropriate assessment should include examining the range of intellectual behavior and the conditions under which performance variability is obtained.

To prevent a possible misunderstanding, we would like to emphasize here that findings on intraindividual plasticity need not be taken as implying that there is no decline at all in intellectual performance with aging, or that older persons benefit more from cognitive training than younger adults. What the evidence suggests is only that many older persons do benefit from intellectual experiences if (a) they are presented with supportive conditions, and (b) they attend to the tasks involved. The question of whether intellectual "capacity" remains at the same level from adulthood into old age is an open question at this point. In fact, we acknowledge that the basic intellectual capacity may not remain invariant but is likely to show decline, especially in very advanced old age and in the face of brain-related health problems. However, we tend to believe also that intellectual capacity can be "practiced" and, in addition, exhibits a kind of reserve that can be "activated" if necessary (Baltes & Willis, in preparation). Such a perspective on intelligence is similar to the biological concept of reserve which states that mature organs have a larger capacity than is necessary for regular functioning (Fries, 1980). Intervention research, with its focus on studying the conditions for intraindividual variability (plasticity), is the kind of inquiry that permits further examination of such questions.

Adult and Gerontological Intelligence: Toward Explanation

Thus far our discussion has focused primarily on issues associated with a descriptive approach to intellectual aging. In this section, progression toward an explanatory approach is examined.

What is the current explanatory evidence on the aging of psychometric intelligence? First of all, we now know that the explanatory task is not a simple one, because the picture of descriptive change in psychometric intelligence is not a simple, normative age function. Intelligence is not a unitary construct but involves several dimensions of ability; there is little interindividual homogeneity; there is multidirectionality; and there is emerging evidence for intraindividual plasticity (both in terms of individual life courses and momentary variability). In other words, the descriptive pattern of intellectual aging is one of much complexity and little apparent parsimony.

Such a pluralistic outcome can be taken as evidence that research on psychometric intelligence is not one of the royal roads to understanding processes of aging. Or, if one were to take Comfort's (1964) evolutionary perspective, one could argue that there is little universality and parsimony in aging per se, because the evolutionary process has not led to a specific genetic program for that component of life. According to Comfort, this may be so because aging, as part of the postreproductive phase of life, is only tangentially related to species survival in the evolutionary sense. Such interpretations, while perhaps premature and discouraging, are reasonable alternatives that need consideration (Baltes & Baltes, 1980).

However, there are a few observations that involve constructive implications for explanatory-causal research design. First of all, the key conclusion is that, except for perhaps advanced old age, there is not too much to be gained in explanatory research on psychometric intelligence by focusing on chronological age and age-associated mechanisms alone. For the most part, at least up to the early 70s, chronological age accounts for less variance than such subject variables as cohort, education, social-occupational status, and health (Granick & Friedman, 1973; Green, 1969; Rudinger, 1976; Schaie & Willis, 1978). Second, because of multidimensionality and multidirectionality, there is not much promise in research using a unitary construct of general intelligence. These observations also imply that for much of late adulthood (but not for advanced old age), age-correlated average biological changes in health are not sufficient either to affect intellectual functioning at the level of group analysis (Eisdorfer, 1977; Eisdorfer & Wilkie, 1973) or to remain uncounteracted by the plasticity of the aging persons, their living environment, or other forms of behavioral and medical intervention.

A Multicausal and Interactive Model of Influences on Aging

One option for future explanatory work is to forcefully expand our conception of causation, to go beyond age-associated determinants and mechanisms, and to include factors that, while affecting intelligence, cannot easily be isolated if one follows a methodological paradigm that is age based. In this spirit, Baltes and his colleagues (Baltes, 1979; Baltes, Cornelius, & Nesselroade, 1979; Baltes & Willis, 1979) have formulated a multicausal and interactive model of influence on life span development. This model is represented in Figure 19-2. It is not advanced as a theory of development but as a methodological paradigm potentially useful in the search for causal relations and determinants that make for intraindividual and differential development. Explicit recognition of the multiple influences represented may lead to a set of research enterprises that are structurally different from the research themes of the past.

Specifically, Figure 19-2 identifies three sets of influences that, mediated through the developing indi-

vidual, act and interact to produce development (aging) and developmental differences. The three sets of influences are age-graded influences, history-graded influences, and non-normative influences or critical life events. Each of these influences can be conceptualized as having biological and environmental correlates and as reflecting interactive processes.

Age-graded influences are defined as encompassing those biological and environmental determinants that exhibit (in terms of onset and duration) a fairly high correlation with chronological age. For the most part, they are fairly normative (general) and predictable. That is, their occurrence, timing, and duration are fairly similar for all individuals of a given set of aging cohorts. Examples of such age-graded influences are events and processes related to biological maturation and to age-graded socialization, including many aspects of education, the family life cycle, and occupation.

History-graded influences consist of those biological and environmental events that exhibit a fairly high correlation with historical change. Their degree of generality and predictability varies. Some of them, however, are fairly normative, in that they apply to most members of a given set of aging cohorts in similar ways, although the effects do not need to be identical for different age cohorts living at the same time. Examples of history-graded influences would be effect patterns associated with cohort differences, economic depressions, the impact of wars or major epidemics on the life course of individuals, or the long-term historical processes associated with such events as industrialization and the changing structures of family life.

Non-normative critical life events refer to determinants of development that do not occur in any age-graded or history-graded manner for most individuals, either in terms of their presence or, if they are present, in terms of timing and patterning. Therefore, they are fairly idiosyncratic and less predictable than age- and history-graded influences. Influences on life span development associated with rare opportunities (awards, foreign travel), medical trauma, accidents, temporary unemployment, divorce, or the death of a loved one are examples of such non-normative critical life events (see Schoenfeldt, 1973). In a general context, Hultsch and Plemons (1979) have presented a stimulating discussion of the role of life events in understanding human development. As to cognitive aging, Eisdorfer (1977) has recently explored possible relations between life events and cognitive functioning, using stress as the process by which such a linkage may be specified.

As we approach the explanatory study of intellectual

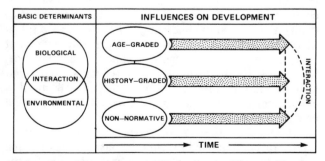

Figure 19-2. Three sources of influence on life-span development that cumulate and interact over time (adapted from Baltes, 1979; Baltes, Cornelius, & Nesselroade, 1979).

aging from the multicausal framework outlined in Figure 19-2, it may be possible to be more directed in our search by working from a converging framework of description and explanation (Baltes & Willis, 1979). Convergence between descriptive and explanatory efforts is possible, because the multicausal model outlined makes it possible to coordinate empirical findings on intellectual aging with their explanation. The findings of large interindividual differences and multidirectionality in psychometric intelligence, for example, appear less cumbersome if the assumed determining influences exhibit a corresponding pattern of differential and multiple causation. The definition and operation of history-graded influences, and particularly of non-normative critical life events, are aimed directly at a causal explanation of differences in development. By definition, non-normative life influences, while important in regulating intellectual behavior at the individual level, do not occur in identical ways for groups of individuals. Therefore, they are not expected to produce homogeneous outcomes at the level of interindividual aggregation.

To use a concrete example: If it is correct that much of the evidence on psychometric intelligence suggests little normative age decline prior to the 70s for the majority of healthy older adults, the primary explanation of change occurring in some persons might be found in non-normative life events such as health trauma or other forms of personal crisis. However, research on intellectual aging in advanced old age, which is assumed to exhibit more age-graded normative decline, would appropriately be oriented toward causal schemes that include a search for age-graded influences. Similarly, if one were to follow Botwinick's (1977) descriptive analysis of differential age-change patterns, for example, in verbal versus performance scores on the Wechsler Adult Intelligence Scale, comparable decisions could be made about the likelihood of success in explanatory work. If age-graded, history-graded, and non-normative influence models and associated search strategies are contrasted as methodological paradigms, diverse models of explanation could be identified and tested to account for the differences in aging patterns observed for distinct classes of intellectual behavior.

In many respects, a focus on age-graded, history-graded, and non-normative critical life events might be seen as posing new conceptual and methodological problems regarding the logical status and further refinement of each of these influences. This would be so if one treated the scheme as the beginnings of a theory rather than as a heuristic device. In that case, problems would arise, for example, because none of the influences would denote an exclusive category of antecedents or a specific process of behavior change.

At present, however, the three sets of influences denote search strategies rather than distinct theoretical constructs. As our knowledge about the importance of history-graded and non-normative influences develops, it will be necessary to explore whether it is possible to specify the processes and mechanisms associated with their occurrence and transaction in similar ways, as has been true for the elaboration of age-associated factors. Illustrative examples for such elaboration are the use of stress and adaptation (Eisdorfer, 1977) as the process by which critical life events operate in controlling intellectual behavior, or the use of operant paradigms (Baer, 1973; M. Baltes & Barton, 1977) in specifying the nature of the transaction (or interaction) between aging individuals and age-graded environmental influences.

At this time, it is not clear whether the three sets of influences will lead to distinct process formulations. Alternatively, identical processes (e.g., various types of learning) may be used to account for the operation of each of them, though with perhaps different emphases and different levels of analysis. In any case, however, elevating history-graded influences and non-normative critical life events to a level of explanatory power comparable to that of age-associated factors will mandate new perspectives on research design. For example, one of the methods that appears to be ideally suited for the identification of the processes inherent in the multicausal and interactive model outlined is that of structural equation analysis (Goldberger & Duncan, 1973; James & Singh, 1978; also see chapters by Jöreskog and Rogosa in Nesselroade & Baltes, 1979). This method, developed primarily by researchers in econometrics and sociology, permits the formulation and evaluation of multivariate systems of variables in terms of directional and interactive causality.

Process and Intervention Research Methodology

In an earlier part of this chapter, we emphasized that information on intellectual behavior should include statements about both average performance (trait) and intraindividual range of performance (plasticity). Both types of information are important not only to separate components of capacity (competence) from those of performance in intellectual aging but also to identify the conditions under which stability and change (incremental or decremental) in intellectual aging are obtained.

Process research of the experimental-psychology type is rather standard in work on basic processes such as learning, perception, attention, and cognition. In the area of psychometric intelligence, however, this type of explanatory work is relatively infrequent, although a number of articles have repeatedly called for it as a methodological paradigm (e.g., Anastasi, 1958, 1970; Baltes & Labouvie, 1973; Buss, 1973; Ferguson, 1954; Tryon, 1935). When does process research on intellectual aging attain particular relevance? There are two features of process research that research aimed at the explanation of aging should exhibit. These features go beyond those usually associated with the design advantages of experimentation per se.

First, for process research to be useful in the study of development (aging), it needs to take an observed developmental or aging phenomenon as the target for explanatory analysis. It is not sufficient to focus on any behavior change or any kind of interindividual variability as a dependent variable. The behavior change under consideration must have meaning in the context provided by a given developmental theory or model.

The requirement of a developmental approach to defining the target for description and explanation has been expressed most forcefully in writings by Birren and Renner (1977), Goulet (1973), Wohlwill (1973), and Baltes et al. (1977). In the context of gerontology, the same perspective applies to the selection of explanatory mechanisms. Not any explanatory effort is likely to be useful. From the viewpoint of developmental theory, those explanatory mechanisms are good candidates that focus on antecedent processes having meaning in the context of a given theory of development or aging. The need for selecting a theoretically meaningful behavior-change process as a target is most apparent when a life span approach to the study of aging is taken (Riley, 1979). This is so because life span developmental research on aging emphasizes aging as a lifelong process. As one attempts to delineate a given behavior-change process, it is important to recognize the limitations of past process research that has largely centered on age functions and age-associated mechanisms. Thus, process research that deals with history-graded and non-normative influences and functions as a guiding framework will benefit if it is oriented explicitly toward a theory-based approach to the definition and explanation of process.

Second, it is important to recognize the dual role of intervention in such process research on aging (Baltes & Danish, 1980; Baltes & Willis, 1977). In any research paradigm involving experimentation to understand process, direct or indirect manipulation of antecedents (and the creation of treatment effects due to such manipulation) is the key rationale. The strategy of experimentation, therefore, is intrinsically linked to some form of intervention. However, interventive work can go beyond the causal control of variability as observed in a given phenomenon prior to the experiment. Intervention can include the planned magnification or reduction of intraindividual and interindividual variability. Such a planned magnification or reduction of a phenomenon is particularly important if the ecology in which a given behavior-change process (the phenomenon) naturally occurs does not present conditions for variability or for certain segments of it, such as those necessary for optimal functioning.[3]

How does this view of intervention apply to the area of psychometric intelligence? Researchers have argued that the naturalistic conditions of behavior (life) of the old person, in general (M. Baltes & Barton, 1977) as well as in intellectual functioning (Labouvie et al., 1974), are not supportive of efficient behavior in the sense of optimization. If the naturalistic conditions for life with regard to aging are indeed restricted in scope, it is imperative to emphasize process research that incorporates the second role of intervention work, that of planned magnification or reduction of intraindividual and interindividual variability. Information collected on the basis of such intervention paradigms will not only lead to a fuller understanding of the conditions for varying outcomes of life span development, including differential aging in intelligence. It will also provide for the type of information necessary to make recommendations for changes in social policy and health care, where knowledge about the conditions for dysfunctional and optimal aging is a central question (Baltes & Danish, 1980; Baltes & Willis, 1979).

As mentioned before, the recent years have seen a nascent interest in exploring the usefulness of intervention paradigms with the goal of understanding the conditions for diverse and varying forms of intellectual aging. However, the bulk of past research on psychometric intelligence in old age is descriptive and is youth and status quo oriented. Therefore, not having much knowledge about the conditions for and the range of intellectual plasticity is the result of past neglect of appropriate methodology.

The concluding commentary offered on the need for interventive process research in the study of intellectual aging is another example of the critical role that established methodologies and conceptions play as a field evolves. In the area of psychometric intelligence, the conceptual approach to the study of intellectual aging will need to include some radical departures from the mainstream of past practice. Whether the same perspectives are applicable to other

---

[3] It is important to recognize that the identification of intervention conditions that produce variability in aging is not identical to the task of identifying the initial conditions responsible for a given phenomenon. The search for the origins of aging in nature requires additional steps aimed at external validation (Baer, 1973; Baltes et al., 1977). The distinction between sufficient and necessary conditions is helpful to understanding the logic of explanatory analysis in the context of developmental research, as is the concept of age or developmental simulation (Baltes & Goulet, 1971).

areas of psychological research on old age awaits further examination. However, it appears fruitful to venture such a hypothesis.

REFERENCES

Anastasi, A. Heredity, environment, and the question "How." *Psychological Review*, 1958, *65*, 197–208.

Anastasi, A. On the formation of psychological traits. *American Psychologist*, 1970, *25*, 899–910.

Baer, D. M. The control of the developmental process: Why wait? In J. R. Nesselroade & H. W. Reese (Eds.), *Life-span developmental psychology: Methodological issues*. New York: Academic Press, 1973.

Baltes, M. M., & Barton, E. M. New approaches toward aging: A case for the operant model. *Educational Gerontology*, 1977, *2*, 383–405.

Baltes, P. B. Longitudinal and cross-sectional sequences in the study of age and generation effects. *Human Development*, 1968, *11*, 145–171.

Baltes, P. B. Life-span developmental psychology: Some converging observations on history and theory. In P. B. Baltes & O. G. Brim, Jr. (Eds.), *Life-span development and behavior* (Vol. 2). New York: Academic Press, 1979.

Baltes, P. B., & Baltes, M. M. Plasticity and variability in psychological aging: Methodological and theoretical issues. In G. Gurski (Ed.), *Aging and the CNS*. Berlin: Schering, 1980.

Baltes, P. B., Cornelius, S. W., & Nesselroade, J. R. Cohort effects in developmental psychology. In J. R. Nesselroade & P. B. Baltes (Eds.), *Longitudinal research in the study of behavior and development*. New York: Academic Press, 1979.

Baltes, P. B., & Danish, S. J. Intervention in life-span development and aging: Issues and concepts. In R. R. Turner & H. W. Reese (Eds.), *Life-span developmental psychology: Intervention*. New York: Academic Press, 1980.

Baltes, P. B., & Goulet, L. R. Exploration of developmental variables by manipulation and simulation of age differences in behavior. *Human Development*, 1971, *14*, 149–170.

Baltes, P. B., & Labouvie, G. V. Adult development of intellectual performance: Description, explanation, and modification. In C. Eisdorfer & M. P. Lawton (Eds.), *The psychology of adult development and aging*. Washington, D.C.: American Psychological Association, 1973.

Baltes, P. B., Reese, H. W., & Nesselroade, J. R. *Life-span developmental psychology: Introduction to research methods*. Monterey, Calif.: Brooks/Cole, 1977.

Baltes, P. B., & Schaie, K. W. On the plasticity of intelligence in adulthood and old age: Where Horn and Donaldson fail. *American Psychologist*, 1976, *31*, 720–725.

Baltes, P. B., Schaie, K. W., & Nardi, A. H. Age and experimental mortality in a seven-year longitudinal study of cognitive behavior. *Developmental Psychology*, 1971, *5*, 18–26.

Baltes, P. B., & Willis, S. L. Toward psychological theories of aging and development. In J. E. Birren & K. W. Schaie (Eds.), *Handbook of the psychology of aging*. New York: Van Nostrand Reinhold, 1977.

Baltes, P. B., & Willis, S. L. Life-span developmental psychology, cognitive functioning, and social policy. In M. W. Riley (Ed.), *Aging from birth to death*. Boulder, Colo.: Westview Press, 1979.

Baltes, P. B., & Willis, S. L. Enhancement of intellectual functioning in old age: Penn State's Adult Development and Enrichment Project (ADEPT). In F. I. M. Craik & S. E. Trehub (Eds.), *Aging and cognitive processes*. New York: Plenum, in press.

Birren, J. E., & Renner, V. J. Research on the psychology of aging: Principles and experimentation. In J. E. Birren & K. W. Schaie (Eds.), *Handbook of the psychology of aging*. New York: Van Nostrand Reinhold, 1977.

Blum, J. E., Clark, E. T., & Jarvik, L. F. The New York State Psychiatric Institute Study of Aging Twins. In L. F. Jarvik, C. Eisdorfer, & J. E. Blum (Eds.), *Intellectual functioning in adults*. New York: Springer, 1973.

Botwinick, J. Aging and intelligence. In J. E. Birren & K. W. Schaie (Eds.), *Handbook of the psychology of aging*. New York: Van Nostrand Reinhold, 1977.

Buss, A. A conceptual framework for learning affecting the development of ability factors. *Human Development*, 1973, *16*, 273–292.

Cattell, R. B. *Abilities: Their structure, growth, and action*. Boston: Houghton Mifflin, 1971.

Clayton, V., & Birren, J. E. Age and wisdom across the life span: Theoretical perspectives. In P. B. Baltes & O. G. Brim, Jr., (Eds.), *Life-span development and behavior* (Vol. 3). New York: Academic Press, in press.

Clement, F. *Adaptation au milieu: Méthode et connaissance*. Paper presented at the World Conference on Aging, Vichy, France, April 1977.

Comfort, A. *Aging: The biology of senescence*. New York: Holt, Rinehart & Winston, 1964.

Demming, J. A., & Pressey, S. L. Tests "indigenous" to the adult and older years. *Journal of Counseling Psychology*, 1957, *4*, 144–148.

Eisdorfer, C. Stress, disease and cognitive change in the aged. In C. Eisdorfer & R. O. Friedel (Eds.), *Cognitive and emotional disturbance in the eldery*. Chicago: Year Book Medical Publishers, 1977.

Eisdorfer, C., & Wilkie, F. Intellectual changes with advancing age. In L. F. Jarvik, C. Eisdorfer, & J. E. Blum (Eds.), *Intellectual functioning in adults*. New York: Springer, 1973.

Ferguson, G. A. On learning and human ability. *Canadian Journal of Psychology*, 1954, *8*, 95–112.

Fries, J. F. *Health and aging in the year 2000*. Paper presented at the NOVA Conference on Behavioral Aging, Fort Lauderdale, Fla., January 1980.

Gardner, E. G., & Monge, R. H. Adult age differences in cognitive abilities and educational background. *Experimental Aging Research*, 1977, *3*, 337–383.

Goldberger, A. S., & Duncan, O. D. (Eds.). *Structural equation models in the social sciences*. New York: Seminar Press, 1973.

Goulet, L. The interfaces of acquisition: Models and methods for studying the active, developing organism. In J. R. Nesselroade & H. W. Reese (Eds.), *Life-span developmental psychology: Methodological issues*. New York: Academic Press, 1973.

Granick, S., & Friedman, A. S. Educational experience and the maintenance of intellectual functioning by the aged. In L. F. Jarvik, C. Eisdorfer, & J. E. Blum (Eds.), *Intellectual functioning in adults*. New York: Springer, 1973.

Green, R. F. Age-intelligence relationships between ages sixteen and sixty-four: A rising trend. *Developmental Psychology*, 1969, *1*, 618–627.

Guilford, J. P. *The nature of human intelligence*. New York: McGraw-Hill, 1967.

Hofland, B., Willis, S. L., & Baltes, P. B. *Fluid intelligence performance in the elderly: Retesting and intraindividual variability*. Unpublished manuscript, College of Human Development, Pennsylvania State University, 1980.

Horn, J. L. Personality and ability theory. In R. B. Cattell & R. M. Dreger (Eds.), *Handbook of modern personality theory*. New York: Halsted Press, 1977.

Horn, J. L. Human ability systems. In P. B. Baltes (Ed.), *Life-span development and behavior* (Vol. 1). New York: Academic Press, 1978.

Horn, J. L., & Donaldson, G. On the myth of intellectual decline in adulthood. *American Psychologist*, 1976, *31*, 701–719.

Horn, J. L., & Donaldson, G. Faith is not enough: A response to the Baltes-Schaie claim that intelligence does not wane. *American Psychologist*, 1977, *32*, 369–373.

Hultsch, D. F., & Plemons, J. K. Life events and life-span development. In P. B. Baltes & O. G. Brim, Jr. (Eds.), *Life-span development and behavior* (Vol. 2). New York: Academic Press, 1979.

James, L. R., & Singh, B. K. An introduction to the logic, assumptions, and basic analytic procedures of two-stage least squares. *Psychological Bulletin*, 1978, *85*, 1104–1122.

Kintsch, W. *Learning, memory, and conceptual processes*. New York: Wiley, 1970.

Labouvie, G. V., Hoyer, W. J., Baltes, P. B., & Baltes, M. M. Operant analysis of intellectual behavior in old age. *Human Development*, 1974, *17*, 259–272.

Labouvie-Vief, G. Toward optimizing cognitive competence. *Educational Gerontology*, 1976, *1*, 75–92.

Labouvie-Vief, G. Adult cognitive development: In search of alternative interpretations. *Merrill Palmer Quarterly*, 1977, *23*, 227–263.

Labouvie-Vief, G., & Chandler, M. Cognitive development and life-span developmental theories: Idealistic vs. contextual perspectives. In P. B. Baltes (Ed.), *Life-span development and behavior* (Vol. 1). New York: Academic Press, 1978.

Libow, L. S. Senile dementia and "pseudosenility": Clinical diagnosis. In C. Eisdorfer & R. O. Friedel (Eds.), *Cognitive and emotional disturbance in the elderly*. Chicago: Year Book Medical Publishers, 1977.

McClelland, D. C. Testing for competence rather than for "intelligence." *American Psychologist*, 1973, *28*, 1–14,

Nesselroade, J. R. & Baltes, P. B. (Eds.), *Longitudinal research in the study of behavior and development*. New York: Academic Press, 1979.

Nesselroade, J. R., Schaie, K. W., & Baltes, P. B. Ontogenetic vs. generational components of structural and quantitative change in adult cognitive behavior. *Journal of Gerontology*, 1972, *27*, 222–228.

Plemons, J. K., Willis, S. L., & Baltes, P. B. Modifiability of fluid intelligence in aging: A short-term longitudinal training approach. *Journal of Gerontology*, 1978, *33*, 224–231.

Resnick, L. B. (Ed.), *The nature of intelligence*. Hillsdale, N.J.: Lawrence Erlbaum, 1976.

Riegel, K. F., & Riegel, R. M. Development, drop and death. *Developmental Psychology*, 1972, *6*, 306–319.

Riley, M. W. (Ed.). *Aging from birth to death*. Washington, D.C.: American Association for the Advancement of Science, 1979.

Rudinger, G. Correlates of changes in cognitive functioning. In H. Thomae (Ed.), *Contributions to human development* (Vol. 3). Basel: Karger, 1976.

Schaie, J. P., & Schaie, K. W. Psychological evaluation of the cognitively impaired elderly. In C. Eisdorfer & R. O. Friedel (Eds.), *Cognitive and emotional disturbance in the elderly*. Chicago: Year Book Medical Publishers, 1977.

Schaie, K. W. A general model for the study of developmental problems. *Psychological Bulletin*, 1965, *64*, 92–107.

Schaie, K. W. A reinterpretation of age-related changes in cognitive structure and functioning. In L. R. Goulet & P. B. Baltes (Eds.), *Life-span developmental psychology: Research and theory*. New York: Academic Press, 1970.

Schaie, K. W. Quasi-experimental designs in the psychology of aging. In J. E. Birren & K. W. Schaie (Eds.), *Handbook of the psychology of aging*. New York: Van Nostrand Reinhold, 1977.

Schaie, K. W. Toward a stage theory of adult cognitive development. *Journal of Aging and Human Development*, 1977–78, *8*, 129–138.

Schaie, K. W. External validity in the assessment of intellectual performance in adulthood. *Journal of Gerontology*, 1978, *33*, 695–701.

Schaie, K. W. The primary mental abilities in adulthood: An exploration in the development of psychometric intelligence. In P. B. Baltes & O. G. Brim, Jr. (Eds.), *Life-span development and behavior* (Vol. 2). New York: Academic Press, 1979.

Schaie, K. W., & Baltes, P. B. On sequential strategies in developmental research: Description or explanantion? *Human Development*, 1975, *18*, 384–390.

Schaie, K. W., & Baltes, P. B. Some faith helps to see the forest: A final comment on the Horn and Donaldson myth of the Baltes-Schaie position on adult intelligence. *American Psychologist*, 1977, *32*, 1118–1120.

Schaie, K. W., Labouvie, G , & Buech, B. Generational and cohort-specific differences in adult cognitive functioning: A fourteen year study of independent samples. *Developmental Psychology*, 1973, *9*, 151–166.

Schaie, K. W., & Labouvie-Vief, G. Generational vs. ontogenetic components of change in adult cognitive behavior: A fourteen-year cross-sequential study. *Developmental Psychology*, 1974, *10*, 305–320.

Schaie, K. W., & Parham, I. A. Cohort-sequential analyses of adult intellectual development. *Developmental Psychology*, 1977, *13*, 649–653.

Schaie, K. W., & Willis, S. L. Life-span development: Implications for education. In L. S. Shulman (Ed.), *Review of educational research* (Vol. 6). Itasca, Ill.: Peacock, 1978.

Schoenfeldt, L. F. Life history subgroups as moderators in the prediction of intellectual change. In L. F. Jarvik, C. Eisdorfer, & J. E. Blum (Eds.), *Intellectual functioning in adults*. New York: Springer, 1973.

Sternberg, R. J., & Detterman, D. K. (Eds.), *Human intelligence: Perspectives on its theory and measurement*. Norwood, N.J.: Ablex, 1979.

Thurstone, L. L. *Primary mental abilities*. Chicago: University of Chicago Press, 1938.

Tryon, R. C. A theory of psychological components—an alternative to "mathematical factors." *Psychological Review*, 1935, *42*, 425–454.

Willis, S. L., Blieszner, R., & Baltes, P. B. *Training research in aging: Modification of intellectual performance on a fluid ability component*. Unpublished manuscript, College of Human Development, Pennsylvania State University, January 1980.

Wohlwill, J. F. *The study of behavioral development*. New York: Academic Press, 1973.

James L. Fozard

The Time for Remembering

Laboratory, psychometric, and impressionistic data indicate that pronounced age decrements occur in the capacity as well as the time required to remember newly learned information. In contrast, the capacity of older adults to remember information in short- and long-term memory is not decreased. While older adults require more time to retrieve information from short- and long-term memory, they appear more efficient in searching long-term memory. Numerous research and practical implications of these conclusions are discussed, and it is argued that greater research efforts be made to link age differences in memory to personality variations in motivation and to the effects of intervention into problems of memory.

The scope and quantity of the major accomplishments in the field of memory and aging over the past decade are significant for their scientific importance, their potential for practical application, and their implications for reformulating current concepts of memory for future research and application. This chapter selectively addresses each of these issues.

The phrase "the time for remembering" here refers first to the occasions for remembering and second to the time required to remember. In turn, the occasions for remembering refer first to laboratory-based analyses of memory and second to the roles played by individual differences in people and situations that affect our understanding of the relation between memory and aging. Throughout this chapter the implications of the major findings for future research and practical application are stressed.

"The time for remembering" also refers to my suggestions for plans for future activities, which are discussed in terms of a transactional analysis of the rela-

tions between memory and aging (Fozard & Thomas, 1975). The only novel aspect of this approach in the present chapter is the argument that knowledge in the area will be accrued most rapidly if the research conducted is carried out in the context of an active clinical intervention program (Fozard & Popkin, 1978).

First I shall provide a rapid overview of the major conclusions to set the stage for the more detailed discussion to follow. The bulk of research in the past decade has used an information-processing concept involving studies of age differences in the capacities of several hypothetical memory stores and the transfer of information among them. A nontechnical example of each of the memory stores discussed in this chapter is illustrated in Table 20-1, which uses the example of remembering names at a party.

Recalling one's own name from tertiary or long-term memory is an example of retrieving very well-learned information. At the other extreme, sensory, or iconic, memory is defined by the minimum time necessary to identify the letters in an unfamiliar name.

Primary and secondary memory go together (Waugh & Norman, 1965). Primary memory is an ephemeral, short-term store from which information is lost if it is not rehearsed. Secondary memory is the repository of newly learned information.

Working memory is related to secondary memory

This chapter is based in part on the Division 20 presidential address given at the 87th Annual Convention of the American Psychological Association, New York, September 1979. Research described in the paper was supported by the Veterans Administration Medical Research Service and by the National Institute on Aging.

Table 20-1 Examples of Remembering From Different Hypothetical Memory Stores at a Party

Sensory	Primary	Secondary	Working	Tertiary
Shortest time required to identify letters of new name	Recall new name just after hearing it	Recall new name after meeting 10 other people	Recall rule to use only first names at party	Recall own name

(Welford, 1980). It refers to the ability to adopt and remember a set of conventions for a particular cognitive task. In terms of the example, remembering only to use first names at a particular party might exemplify working memory.

Evidence for cross-sectional age differences and longitudinal age changes in the capacity of the various stores is summarized in Table 20-2. Three types of evidence are shown on the rows of the table. Anecdotal refers to my impressions gained from a decade of listening to many lay descriptions of age-related problems. Note that only in the case of secondary memory are the anecdotal impressions unequivocally supported by more objective evidence. Psychometric refers to findings from standardized psychological tests, and experimental refers to data from controlled laboratory studies. For efficiency, the references are almost all to secondary reviews from which the primary sources may in turn be identified.

Table 20-2 shows that the age-related decreases in sensory memory capacity are defined only by laboratory studies (Corso, 1977; Fozard, Wolf, Bell, McFarland, & Podolsky, 1977). There is no convincing evidence for age declines in primary memory (Craik, 1977). Relevant psychometric evidence is exemplified by the findings of no differences or changes in the Forward Digit Span (for a review see Botwinick, 1977).

All lines of evidence show an age-related decline in the capacity of secondary memory. Relevant psychometric data include the backward Digit Span and Digit Symbol test (Botwinick, 1977). The experimental evidence, both cross-sectional and longitudinal, is exemplified by the work on rote learning and the Benton Visual Retention Test by Arenberg and his colleagues (Arenberg & Robertson-Tchabo, 1977). The longitudinal evidence is particularly compelling because it includes a control for long-term practice effects.

The evidence for age differences in working memory comes from laboratory studies of problem solving and industrial gerontology exemplified by the research of Belbin and Belbin (1968) and others described by Welford (1958, pp. 193–198) and Rabbitt (1977, pp. 518–519). The tenor of the findings is that remembering the rules or plans for carrying out a task represents a major difficulty for older adults.

The negative evidence about age differences or changes in tertiary memory is now quite compelling, despite the common complaints of older persons that they cannot remember familiar information as well as when they were younger. Relevant psychometric evidence includes the lack of decline in vocabulary or in information or in other tests commonly used to assess crystallized intelligence (Botwinick, 1977). Selected experimental evidence is discussed more fully later.

The major conclusions on age and speed of memory processes are summarized in Table 20-3. Existing evidence is based on cross-sectional research. An observed response latency has two parts. The perceptual motor component is the time required to perceive the stimulus and prepare a response, once one has been selected; it is usually relatively constant in one experiment, and its role in age-related slowing is ubiquitous. Decision making is the time required to search

Table 20-2 Evidence for Age-Related Declines in Memory Capacity

Type of study and type of evidence	Memory store				
	Sensory	Primary	Secondary	Working	Tertiary
Cross-Sectional studies					
Anecdotal	—	Positive	Positive	Positive	Positive
Psychometric	—	Negative	Positive	—	Negative
Experimental	Positive	Negative	Positive	Positive	Negative
Longitudinal studies					
Anecdotal	—	—	—	—	—
Psychometric	—	Negative	Positive	—	Negative
Experimental	—	—	Positive	—	—

Table 20-3 Cross-Sectional Experimental Evidence for Age-Related Slowing of Memory Processes

Component affected	Memory store				
	Sensory	Primary	Secondary	Working	Tertiary
Perceptual motor	Positive	Positive	Positive	—	Positive
Decision making	—	Positive	Positive	Positive	Negative

memory, and it varies depending on what is being recalled from what store; the amount of its slowing with age is largest in secondary and smaller in tertiary and primary memory.

Although age-related slowing of simple and choice reaction time has been well documented over decades of research, the major empirical demonstrations of slowing of memory processes have occurred in the past decade. Although it is tempting to conclude with Rabbitt (1968), Waugh and Barr (1980), and Salthouse (1980) that slowing of mental processes with age is the major factor explaining age differences in memory, a satisfactory direct empirical demonstration is not yet at hand. A similar analysis applied to visual information processing, some aspects of which clearly involve memory processes (Fozard et al., 1977), suffers from the same problem; amassing instances that are compatible with the viewpoint do not themselves provide a direct test.

One major qualification to the hypothesis stems from the observation that age differences in speed of secondary memory process are different from those involving primary and tertiary memory (see, for example, Chapter 17 in this volume). Second, the body of evidence implicating age-related slowing of one or more of the information-processing stages—perceptual, decision-making, or motor—has employed so many different experimental tasks and subject populations that its overall impact is less compelling than it might have been had a more coherent approach been taken (Waugh & Barr, 1980; see also Chapter 21 in this volume). Because of the strong relation between task difficulty and reaction time, it is difficult to find a set of tasks that assess speed of primary, secondary, and tertiary memory processes and at the same time to use a common procedure for partitioning the decision-making and perceptual-motor aspects of the task.

Recent research provides three types of evidence that support the notion that age-related slowing of cognitive processes plays a major role in explaining age-related memory problems. First, research by Salthouse (1980) shows that speed of mental rehearsal improves ease of memorization and retention of paired associates, a task typically used to demonstrate age differences in secondary memory. Use of a divided-at-

tention task, as suggested by Wingfield and Sandoval (1980), provides an alternative approach to studying memorization in relation to cognitive speed. In a longitudinal analysis of age changes in peformance on the Owens Mental Ability Task, Cunningham (see Chapter 23 in this volume) and Witt and Cunningham (1979) demonstrated that the advantage in speeded tasks enjoyed by some young adults benefited them in older age as well. Similar conclusions from cross-sectional studies relating individual differences in personality with cognitive functioning were drawn by Costa and Fozard (1978), Fozard and Costa (in press), and Costa, Fozard, McCrae, and Bosse (1976). The logic of this type of evidence now requires that individual differences on acceptable tests of behavioral speed be used to predict speed of memory processes, both within and across age groups.

A second line of evidence is based on analyses by Salthouse (1977) and by Cerella, Poon, and Williams (see Chapter 24 in this volume) that the observed slower performance of old adults in comparison to young ones on a variety of tasks may be described by applying a constant multiplier to the scores of the younger adults. The rule applies across a variety of classifications of tasks so that the time required for the task by young adults, rather than its meaning in terms of an information-processing analysis, is the critical variable.

The third line of evidence comes from analysis of frequency distributions of reaction times for subjects representing different age groups. The results of these studies show that the age differences in two-choice reaction time are accounted for by the age difference in the perceptual-motor component of the task, rather than by the number and duration of the decision-making components. Moreover, the response times of older subjects are more variable than those of younger ones relative to their own mean reaction times, in easy and hard versions of similar tasks (Fozard, Thomas, & Waugh, 1976; Thomas, Waugh, & Fozard, 1978; Waugh, Fozard, & Thomas, 1978). The hypothesis of greater within-subject variability in response latencies in old age provides a biologically plausible explanation of slower mean response latencies and is also consistent with the finding of substantial individual differences in mean retention times among cohorts of elderly adults. As pointed out in Chapter 24 of this volume, the uniformity of the results of existing analyses of age difference in frequency distribution of response times is promising, but further refinements in the approach are required.

Tertiary Memory

Substantial and consistent research accomplishments have accrued over the past decade in the investigation of age differences in tertiary, or long-term, memory.

Two studies by my colleagues and I (Fozard & Poon, 1976; Fozard, Waugh, & Thomas, 1975) demonstrate that the rate of forgetting of pictures over 2½ years does not differ with age. The results are important because the materials were learned under laboratory conditions.

For material learned under natural conditions, Bahrick, Bahrick, and Wittlinger (1975), Schonfield (1972), and others (see Craik, 1977, for a review), have demonstrated good retention for similar faces and places and other information learned by adults some one to three decades previously. The ingenuity of the procedures used by these investigators insured that the information to be recalled was in fact known to the subjects.

But good long-term memory in old age is not restricted to material of idiosyncratic significance. Relevant data come from research studies of age differences in the ability to remember common expressions or names of well-known personalities that are more likely to be known to members of one age group than to those of another (see Poon, Fozard, Paulshock, & Thomas, 1979; Squire, 1980). Typically, older persons remember information known directly to both young and elderly adults as well as do young persons. They recall information unique to their cohort better than do young adults, who could only have known the same information second hand. Such findings dispel the widespread belief that good memory by older adults is restricted to material of idiosyncratic importance. (See also Perlmutter, 1980, and Walsh and Baldwin, 1977, for other lines of converging evidence for this generalization.)

The finding of good long-term retention by old adults raises the question of the relations between long-term memory and the amount of knowledge accumulated over the life span, and at the Talland Memorial Conference, Lachman and Lachman (1980) described research efforts relevant to the question. Their test material concerned movies, sports, current

events, and so forth. An example is, "What was the former name of Muhammed Ali?" To such questions adults representing three age groups either wrote the answer or indicated that they did not know or could not remember. The items not correctly recalled were then presented in a multiple-choice format. Subjects indicated their confidence for each of their selections on a scale bounded by the categories "definitely sure" and "wild guess."

The Lachmans found that total knowledge increased with age. The efficiency of remembering remained constant across age. Thus older people retrieved information from a larger base of information as efficiently as younger ones did from a smaller base.

Subjects in all age groups were equally accurate in estimating the degree of confidence in their knowledge. As shown in Figure 20-1 the percentage of correct recognitions increased with judged confidence equally for all adults.

The Lachmans also studied the time the subjects spent trying to remember. Recall that the subjects either gave the answer or responded that they did not know or did not remember it. Afterward some subjects judged each item on a four-point scale ranging from "definitely did not know answer," to "could recall it if given more time and a few hints." In a subsequent recognition test, it was found that adults in all age

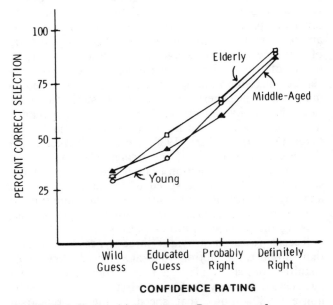

Figure 20-1. Recognition memory. Percentage of correct selections of multiple-choice alternatives, according to rated confidence in choice, by subjects in three age groups. Data are from Lachman and Lachman (1980).

groups spent the minimum time searching for answers to items they considered they did not know and the maximum for items they thought they could recall if given more time or a few hints. Typically, the times spent in such mental search were 5 seconds for the "do not know" and 9 seconds for the "could recall if given more time and a few hints." Such latencies could suggest memory difficulties to one using a nonobjective clinical assessment of memory function.

Given the small age differences in capacity of tertiary memory, the speed of retrieval of information from that store becomes a question of interest. Indeed, older adults commonly complain of taking a long time to recall the names of familiar people, places, and objects. The time taken to name pictured objects is one way to measure the speed of retrieving information from tertiary memory. The procedure developed by Oldfield and Wingfield (Wingfield, 1968) was adapted by Thomas, Fozard, and Waugh (1977). In Figure 20-2 naming latency refers to the time taken to name an object without any prompting. Presumably, the name is retrieved from long-term memory. In the "name picture match" condition, a word was presented just before each picture. When the word correctly named the picture the name was retrieved from primary rather than long-term memory, and as shown in the figure, the time required to name the picture was shorter. In contrast, the latencies for pictures preceded

by a word not matching the picture were similar to those observed when no word prompts were used.

In all three conditions the average time required to say the names of the pictured objects increased by the same amount over age, about .2 sec. The constant difference in performance between naming latency and picture matching indicated that the age effect is almost entirely attributable to slowness in the perceptual-motor component of the naming latency, not the memory-search component.

One of Thomas, et al.'s (1977) most important findings was that the familiarity of the word as evidenced by its frequency of occurrence in printed English was the most important determiner of speed. If so, the speed of retrieval by older persons for material with which they are relatively more familiar than younger adults should be faster, and vice versa, while the speed of retrieval for material equally familiar to both should be the same. This hypothesis was unequivocally supported in a variation of the naming-latency experiment reported by Poon and Fozard (1978).

The significance of the work on long-term memory summarized above is fourfold: (1) It clarifies a number of misconceptions about the capacity and quality of long-term memory in older adults; (2) it provides converging evidence that the age differences in the speed of retrieval from long-term memory cannot be attributed to slowness of searching through memory—if

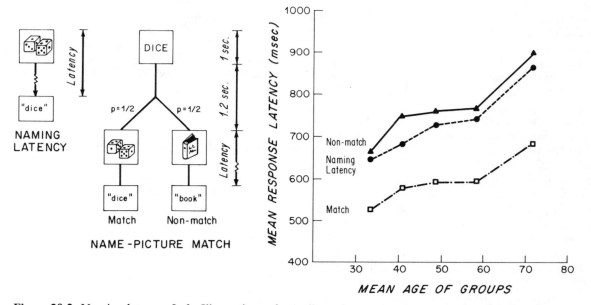

Figure 20-2. Naming latency. Left: Illustrations of paradigms for naming (no word name shown before picture), matching, and nonmatching (word name shown before picture). Right: Mean response latency for five age groups in the three conditions. (From "Age-Related Differences in Naming Latency" by J. C. Thomas, J. L. Fozard, and N. C. Waugh, *American Journal of Psychology*, 1977, *90*, 499–509. Copyright 1977 by the Board of Trustees of the University of Illinois. Reprinted by permission.)

anything, older persons are relatively more efficient in retrieval processes; (3) the methodology of the various studies provides an excellent basis for further research; and (4) the studies provide a clear-cut set of procedures for distinguishing between normal age changes in retrieving well-learned information and abnormal changes observed in clinical populations. Other research on long-term memory is reviewed by Hartley et al. in Chapter 17 of this volume and by Craik (1977).

Sensory Memory

A second area in which there have been major new findings is sensory memory, a very short-term store that is the respository of the most primitive translations of environmental information. The amount of time that information is available in visual sensory memory is the sum of the presentation time of the stimulus and the duration of an ephemeral positive afterimage. A backward-masking technique is used to limit the total amount of time that information is available in the store.

The results of several studies by Kline and Szafran (1975), Walsh (1976), and Walsh and Thompson (1978) have shown that the minimum time required to identify a single letter or numeral is greater for older than younger adults, and that the time required to identify items in a larger display is proportionately longer. Welford and Birren and others have speculated that the traces of stimuli may be relatively longer in older adults because of greater neural noise. However, direct psychophysical assessment of visual persistence does not support this view; Walsh and Thompson found estimated visual persistence in adults in their 70s to be about 40 msec shorter than that of 20-year-old adults.

Following Miller (1956), Sperling (1963) has shown that the maximum number of items that can be identified in the brief exposures that characterize sensory memory is about four. When from four to seven unrelated letters or numerals are presented in studies of sensory memory, the function relating stimulus duration to the number of letters identified typically increases rapidly up to about 50–60 msec, and then increases more slowly afterwards. Typical data for young adults are shown in Table 20-4, which summarizes some very recent data by Cerella, Poon, and Fozard. The time in which the seven letters were available ranged from 10 to 200 msec. Each presentation was preceded by a ready signal and followed by a mask. In comparison to young adults, older adults were worse at all exposures both in the initial level of performance and the amount of improvement in per-

Table 20-4 Number of Correct Letters at Various Target Durations

Age group	Duration (msec)						
	10	20	40	60	100	110	200
21	.8	1.6	2.3	2.8	3.2	3.7	3.6
71	.5	0.6	1.3	1.8	2.0	2.6	2.6

formance. The auxiliary data from the same experiment are entirely consonant with published data by Walsh and his colleagues, which indicates that the time required to identify a single letter was also greater for those adults.

The significance of the data on age differences in sensory memory is threefold. The first is the clear demonstration that the rate of assimilation of verbal information from this most primitive memory store is slower for older adults. The second is that the magnitude of the age-related slowing of mental process in sensory memory is different from that observed in primary and secondary memory. The relative difference in the speed of performance between older and younger adults in the experiment of Cerella, Poon, and Fozard is different from that reported for the speed of memory scanning, for example, by Anders, Fozard, and Lillyquist (1972).

The third implication is methodological. For the most part, the experimental procedures used in studies of sensory memory provide estimates of the speed of mental operations that do not themselves depend on measuring speed of responding to a signal. It is now recognized that the use of such procedures is critical to enlarging our understanding of age-related slowing of mental processes and its effect on the acquisition and retention of information (Crowder, 1980; Fozard et al., 1977).

Primary and Secondary Memory

The third area in which there have been significant advances is in the refinement of the well-known distinction between the effect of age on primary and secondary memory (Craik, 1968, 1977). The analysis by Smith (1975, 1980) of the acquisition, storage, and retrieval processes in secondary memory indicates that whatever retrieval problems exist simply compound the effects of poor memorization in accounting for the substantial deficits in performance observed in the elderly.

The analyses of Smith and others emphasize the need to study age differences in the memorization and forgetting of specific times in a list to be memorized.

In an effort to study forgetting of particular items in a list at various stages of memorization, Fozard and Poon (1978) varied the conventional paired-associate task. Each of 12 pairs of words was presented twice in a trial block, so that the number of other pairs between the first (T1) and second (T2) presentations of a pair could be varied. When T1 − T2 = 1, the item was presumably being retrieved from primary memory. When T1 − T2 was equal to 3 or 5, or when the item was presented for the first time in a block (T1), the information was more likely to be retrieved from secondary memory. The task continued until a subject could recite all the response words twice consecutively with no more than one error, or until 15 trials had been reached. "Learners"—those who achieved criterion within 15 trials—were given 5 blocks beyond the criterion, while "nonlearners" were given 5 blocks beyond the allotted 15.

As in other studies (Craik, 1977), the proportion of learners in each of three groups with median ages of 20, 52, and 63 years decreased with age, 100%, 72%, and 42%, respectively.

Figure 20-3 (upper panel) displays the number of trials required by learners in the three age groups to reach criterion for the different intervals. Only when a second item was presented immediately following the first (T1 − T2 = 1), and the subject was retrieving the word from primary memory, were subjects performing virtually without error. As the number of items separating the two presentations of a pair increased and thus the degree of involvement of secondary memory in recall increased, so did age-related differences in performance.

The lower panel of Figure 20-3 displays the mean response times for different intervals. For the learners, −1 on the abscissa refers to the trial just before the subject reached the learning criterion; C1 and C2 refer to the two criterion trials; and 1 through 5 refer to the five postcriterion trial. For the learners, the age differences in response latency for items in primary memory were small, as were the effects of practice. However, practice consistently affected the speed of recalling information from secondary memory in learners of all ages.

The mean response times of correct responses for the nonlearners in the last few trials are also displayed in the figure. It is clear that the difficulties experienced by the nonlearners affected the response times to items they had memorized successfully.

The significance of these findings is twofold. First, the data illustrate for the first time how short-term forgetting contributes to the overall age differences in rote-learning scores. The second implication is methodological. It is clear that the procedure outlined pro-

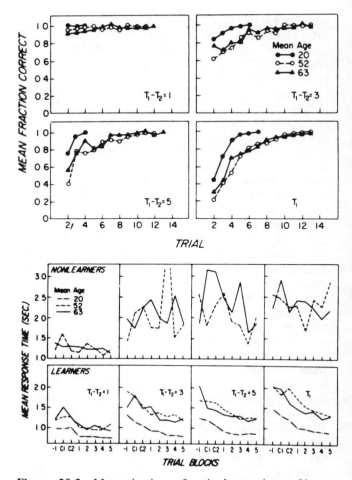

Figure 20-3. Memorization of paired associates. Upper panel: Percentage of correct anticipation of paired associates by adults in three age groups over 15 trials, according to separation between first (T1) and second (T2) presentations of a word pair. Lower panel: Mean response times for learners and nonlearners for correct response just before memorization (−1) at point of memorization (C1, C2) and in five post-criterion trials (1–5). Data are from Fozard and Poon (1978).

vides a method for identifying significant age differences in the ability to memorize. For example, the effect of relative massing or spacing of items to be memorized on the total number of trials can be studied, as can the effects of emphasizing or prompting learners on vexing items. Recall that Goodrick (1973) found that older rats learning a 14-unit maze benefited from massed training trials, while younger ones did not.

One of the striking findings in the study of memorization described earlier was the tremendous variability in the time required to recall items that were correctly memorized by subjects who were still learning the list, compared to those who had already mastered the list. In order to better show the relation between age and speed of retrieval of newly memorized material, two recent studies are described. The starting point for the research came partly from analyses by Welford (1969) and Birren (1974) in which they inferred that carry-over effects from one trial to the next may differ in young and elderly adults. Accordingly, age-related differences in "repetition effects," as described by Bertelson (1963), should be expected in choice reaction tasks. Older persons may require more time either (a) to identify the stimulus signal, (b) to decide which response goes with which signal, or (c) for a combination of the two.

To evaluate these possibilities, the conventional binary choice task was modified by Waugh et al. (1978). The subject pressed the left key whenever the digit displayed was the same as the immediately preceding one and the other key when it was not. Thus the subject's response was contingent on the relation between the current and preceding stimulus.

With respect to the previous event in the sequence, the average response times for 230 subjects increased, from shortest to longest, in all four conditions: (a) both the stimulus and response were the same; (b) stimulus same, response different; (c) both stimulus and response different; and (d) stimulus different and response same. In the two conditions in which the same kind of trial could occur three times in succession (a and d), practice effects were observed in all age groups. The reaction times of subjects in the oldest of the three groups exceeded those of the younger two by a constant amount under all conditions; there was no evidence that stimulus or response repetition interacted with age. The relative speeds of performance on the four conditions supported only the hypothesis that repeating a given signal is sufficient to produce the repetition effect in a choice reaction task.

The results of the preceding study suggest that in a binary-decision task in which subjects are given an explicit requirement to retain information from the preceding event, age-related differences in response latency will be much larger than in a conventional binary-decision task, in which all of the information necessary to select the correct response is presented on the current trial. Poon and Fozard provided a direct evaluation of this hypothesis.

In one of four experimental conditions, the subject was required to decide whether the current stimulus was the same or different from its immediate predecessor in the sequence. This condition represented a replication of the study of Waugh et al. (1978). In a second condition, the subject was required

to say whether his or her previous response was the same as that on the current trial. When a stimulus sign "same" was illuminated, the subject was to press the same response lever as on the previous trial; when "different" was illuminated the subject was to press the other lever.

In order to evaluate the hypothesis that the requirement to remember either the stimulus or the response was sufficient to result in an age-related slowing of the decision-making process, a conventional two-choice reaction task was also included in the experiment. Finally, a simple reaction-time control condition was included.

The data shown in Figure 20-4 are consistent with the hypothesis that an explicit requirement to remember the immediately preceding event in order to make a judgment is sufficient to cause age-related behavioral slowing.

There was no interaction between age and difference between simple and choice reaction time, but there was in the tasks in which there was an explicit memory requirement. The rank order of difficulty of different kinds of trials was the same as observed earlier by

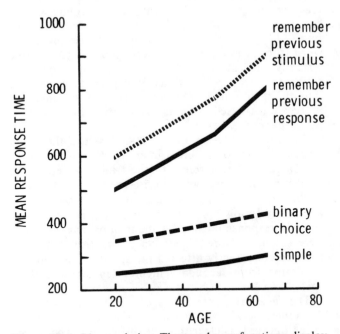

Figure 20-4. Binary choice. The two lower functions display mean response time by adults in three age groups when one (simple) or two (binary) known stimulus alternatives were employed. The two upper functions display response times when subjects judged whether the current stimulus or the current response matched or differed from its immediate predecessor in the sequence. Unpublished data by Poon and Fozard.

Waugh, Fozard, and Thomas. Again, there was no evidence for the idea of differential stimulus or response carry-over effects between young and old adults.

To probe further back into memory, Poon and Fozard (1980) studied continuous recognition memory. Each word was designated new on its first presentation and old on its second. As the number of intervening items between the first and second presentations increases from 0 to some larger number like 64, the probability that the item will be retrieved from primary memory decreases at the same time that the probability of retrieval from secondary memory increases.

Fifty-seven males (18–85 years) participated in the continuous-recognition memory task. High- or low-frequency words were presented every 3 seconds, and retention intervals were 3, 6, 12, 24, 48, 96, or 192 seconds.

There were no age differences in the accuracy of identifying words for the first time. Nor were any age-by-word frequency effects found in accuracy. Both the accuracy and latency data indicated a two-step function with a steep decay function for from 1 to 4 items followed by a more gradual decline.

The response latencies paralleled the results for accuracy and are summarized in Figure 20-5. No age differences occurred in the time taken to identify new words. There was a more rapid increase with age in

response times with increasing separation up to 4 items and a slower increase thereafter. There was no interaction between word frequency and age.

As with the naming latency data reported by Thomas et al. (1977), there were no differences with age in the effects of familiarity on speed of performance. When the estimated perceptual motor components of the task were subtracted out of each subject's performance, the age patterns in the results were unchanged.

The results of all of the experiments confirm that there is an age-related decrease in accuracy and retrieval time in secondary memory that is independent of differences in acquisition. There is no evidence for a differential carry-over effect of stimulus and response traces at the time of registration. The rate of forgetting and the time required to make a decision increase more rapidly with increasing age.

Intervention and New Directions

The present discussion of intervention and new directions in research is here linked to possibilities for intervention because of my conviction that such a link will guide research efforts more efficiently than will other more elegant and systematic approaches.

In the past 4 years there has been a substantial

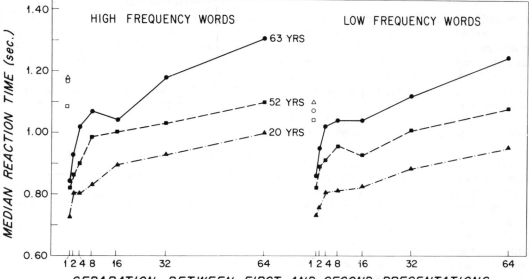

Figure 20-5. Continuous recognition memory. Age differences in typical response times to judge a word "old" on its second presentation, according to number of items between first and second presentation. Single unfilled points indicate time required to identify words as new on initial presentation. Data are from Poon and Fozard (1980).

upsurge of interest in the possibilities for intervention in the memory problems of the elderly, an effort to which I and my colleagues have devoted considerable attention (Costa & Fozard, 1978; Fozard & Popkin, 1978; Fozard & Costa, in press; Poon, Fozard, & Treat, 1978; Poon, Fozard, & Walsh-Sweeney, 1980; Treat, Poon, Fozard, & Popkin, 1978). Although the practical justifications for developing intervention possibilities seem self-evident, the scientific justification may not (Erickson, Poon, & Walsh-Sweeney, 1980). There are at least three reasons for research to be directed to this area.

Intervention will help set limits for generalizations about memory and aging. For example, the major limitations of standardized psychometric tests are related to the narrow range of behavior sampled. For example, the universally observed age-related decline in performance on the Digit Symbol test, wants, as Botwinick pointed out in 1967, a satisfactory psychological explanation. Twelve years later, only slight progress has been made on the effect on age of the simplest intervention, practice. Erber (1976) and later Grant, Storandt, and Botwinick (1978) found that practice, but not incentives, noticeably improves the performance of elderly subjects. Salthouse (1977) performed a single straightforward set of experiments which reduced by over half the competing explanations cited by Botwinick (1967) for the performance deficit associated with age. Such efforts are the exception to the rule rather than part of the everyday activity in the field.

Intervention will also provide a rapid, self-correcting approach to understanding noncognitive factors related to age differences in memory function. Transient motivational states, situational anxiety, and depression interact significantly with differences in task difficulty in ways that often provide a misleading picture of age deficits in memory function (see Kahn & Miller, 1978). At the very least, intervention can help establish the limits of behavior before and after adaptation to a task.

A third scientific reason for studying intervention is that it provides a necessary check on the validity of application of memory theory across the adult life span. All transactional theories of psychological development (Baltes & Baltes, 1979; Fozard & Thomas, 1975; Lawton & Nahemow, 1973) postulate that the relation between people and their particular environment changes over the adult life span. The postulated changes may affect differentially the significance to a subject of a task designed to test a hypothesis about memory. Cohort differences in education and background can well serve to exaggerate individual differences among researchers and subjects alike. One of the

most practical ways to short-circuit some of the conceptual difficulties posed by these issues is to include procedures that will clearly define the limits of expected behavior.

The ingredients of a program of intervention include a taxonomy of problems, a list of potential interventions, and a suitable transactional viewpoint. For clarity as well as parsimony, a specific discussion of pharmacological interventions is omitted (for a recent review, see Hines & Fozard, in press).

Three classes of intervention are shown on the rows of Table 20-5. Task redesign refers to operations, including many feedback procedures, that simplify the display of information, the making of a response, or the relation between the two.

Task redesign can improve speed in primary memory by reducing the number of items that must be reviewed mentally. The value of task redesign to working memory is based on studies by Arenberg (1974), Belbin and Belbin (1968), and Welford (1969) which show how changing the instructions helps performance.

Training improves secondary memory because it facilitates memorization. Poon et al. (1980) exhaustively reviewed the role of imagery and other mnemonics in reducing age differences in secondary memory through facilitation of learning. A variety of studies demonstrate that older adults can use mnemonic aids effectively, but they are less likely than younger persons to do so spontaneously.

The positive effects of cognitive-skill training are quite task specific, although Plemons, Willis, and Baltes (1978) have recently demonstrated a generalization gradient for a group of assessments of fluid intelligence over a 6-month period after the original training. Their study is unique because it conceptualizes generalization on the basis of a factor-analytically determined array of tasks.

Table 20-5 Possibilities for Diminishing Age Differences in Memory

Type of intervention	Primary	Secondary	Working	Tertiary
Capacity				
Task redesign	—	Poor	Good	Slight
Training	—	Good	Fair	Slight
Individual differences	—	Good	—	Fair
Speed				
Task redesign	Good	Slight	—	Slight
Training	Slight	Good	—	Slight
Individual differences	Fair	Fair	—	Fair

Training should include counseling and psychotherapy. Poon et al., (1978) have shown how counseling and therapy could include among their goals the alleviation of undue anxiety about memory problems and the maintenance of motivation to encourage elderly persons to undergo cognitive training.

Intervention needs to be based on individual differences in psychological traits because chronological age is a singularly poor basis for classifying people on many stable, measurable psychological characteristics, including memory function.

Robertson-Tchabo, Arenberg, and Costa (1979) correlated 6-year changes in scores on the Benton Visual Retention Test with traits measured by the Guilford-Zimmerman Temperament Survey. Men who maintained their performance base were more active, more energetic and productive, more responsible and self-restrained, and less impulsive and more task oriented. These results are particularly striking because they are independent of the age changes in the memory test scores.

Fozard and Costa (in press) examined the relation between traits measured by the Cattell Sixteen Personality Factor Questionnaire and tests of the speed of retrieval from memory. For secondary memory, better performance in older subjects was associated with greater impulsiveness, low control, increased arousal associated with anxiety, and greater openness. All of these traits define a typical way of responding to the environment that was favorable to older adults. In contrast, the presence of these same traits tended to interfere with the speed of retrieval from secondary memory by younger adults.

For speed of retrieval from primary and tertiary memory, greater impulsiveness was related to faster speed of retrieval, whereas greater imaginativeness was associated with slower speed of retrieval. These trends held over all age groups.

The results of these preliminary investigations suggest that intervention programs based on information about personality and interests are possible, but the empirical demonstrations need to be performed. The major value of the findings for future work stems from the observation that age interacts differently with different memory processes. In addition, research on the effects on memory of transient states such as depression and anxiety (Kahn & Miller, 1978) can be improved if researchers take into account individual differences in stable personality traits.

A program of intervention for memory problems of the elderly—including cognitive skill training, individual counseling, and the redesign of tasks—will reduce present limitation in our knowledge in at least four areas: (1) the interrelation in information obtained from formal assessments of memory and from problems of learning and memory in everyday life; (2) psychological assessments of memory and clinical procedures; (3) the potential for general ability and maintenance of cognitive skill training; and (4) responses of depression and transient emotional states to "normal" age-related problems.

With respect to diagnosis, it has been difficult for some time to establish a clear relation between self-reported complaints and memory functions (Erickson, 1978; Erickson & Scott, 1977). Kahn and his associates (see Kahn & Miller, 1978, for a review) have shown that elderly persons who manifest symptoms of depression are more likely to complain of memory problems than are nondepressed age peers with organic impairment. This clinical finding, along with others, has suggested that self-observed memory complaints are secondary to disease processes. The excellent work by Zarit and others on memory intervention programs has also failed to demonstrate a clear-cut relation between complaints and memory functioning. However, Zelinski, Gilewski, and Thompson (1980) have described an improved self-report instrument that helps the respondent define the situations in which memory problems occur and describe the steps normally taken to deal with them. With this instrument Zelinski et al. found that older adults are much better at identifying problems than previously believed.

Development of intervention will rapidly force us to deal with two subjects neglected in the past decade: the uses of memory and the constraints created by memory on the choices of activities at different stages of the life span. My clinical colleagues who read this are, I am sure, saying, "It's about time!" As Hultsch and Pentz (1980) said in a presentation at the Talland Memorial Conference, "Memory is a means to an end as well as an end it itself."

Since Freud's (1914/1956) classic analysis, it has been recognized that the phenomena of selectivity and motivation in remembering are at the core of most psychological diagnostic and treatment procedures and most everyday experiences of changes in memory.

Rod McKuen (1975, pp. 70–71) captures the relation between the selectivity of memory and human motives nicely in his poem "Room" from which the following two verses are quoted:

> I'd post a letter
> but I don't know
>   your address
>
> I'd call
> but how would I begin
> let alone maintain
>   a conversation?

Once I'd promised
to forget you
I ran backward
making sure
That I'd remember you
for always.

The observation of a positive relation between reminiscing and adjustment has been at the core of a great deal of clinical theory and practice (Pfeiffer, 1977), Butler's (1963, 1974) work on life review, or reconstruction of the past, being just one example. Partly as a reaction to the limitations of reality orientation for confused institutionalized elderly persons, Naomi Feil at the Cleveland Montefiore Home for the Aged has devised a therapy to help elderly persons use the remnants of the past to achieve meaningful existence in their last years. The ideas are presented in the film *Looking for Yesterday*.

An empirically based psychological analysis of the usefulness of and satisfaction with memory in old age is long overdue. The work of Giambra (1979) on age differences in daydreaming shows how content of motivational material differs with age. There are many implications for clinical practice and research in his findings.

Birren (1969) and Bromley (1974, pp. 326–329) have made some analyses of the role of memory in cognitive functioning at work. As to how motivational differences relate to memory and work, the writings of Simone de Beauvior in *The Coming of Age* (1972) provide a useful supplement to the conventional research literature. She cites examples that illustrate how the accumulation of experience may hinder the successful pursuit of careers by trapping people in outmoded ways of thinking and a desire to protect their accomplishments rather than to progress. She applied these principles to the writings of well-known persons in nonphysical occupations. According to her examples, scientists are particularly vulnerable to being trapped by their own past work. The weakness of the scientist may be the strength of the writer or philosopher, who works with a more self-contained, imaginary intellectual system. Painters and composers, whose artistic expression necessarily involves a more limited range of tools, are less susceptible to being victims of their own pasts.

Little is known about aging and memory in nonoccupational pursuits. Indirect evidence (Fozard & Popkin, 1978) is compatible with the idea that expectations for the future are a function of memory of past experiences in nonoccupational pursuits as well as in work. The decline in intensity and range of interests with older age has been well documented by Gordon

and Gaitz (1977). The relevance of memory is illustrated in Figure 20-6. In the analysis of age differences in self-reported involvement in four classes of leisure activity, participants in the Normative Aging Study consistently overestimated the level of involvement in their activities anticipated after retirement. The discrepancy is illustrated by the differences between the lower function in each panel, which shows present involvement, and the upper ones, which show the level anticipated after retirement. The cross-sectional trends reported by Fozard and Popkin (1978) are now supported by longitudinal evidence. The final points on the right of each function show the changes in actual level of involvement over a 5-year period by men who actually retired. The open circle shows their anticipated level of involvement just prior to retirement. Clearly, memory as a tool in future plans and hopes can be deceptive, and an empirical analysis of the issue should be an exciting one for psychology in the next decade.

The foregoing examples make me agree with Baltes and Willis (1979), Schaie and Schaie (1977) and Hultsch and Pentz (1980) that an age related taxonomy is needed of situations in which memory is used.

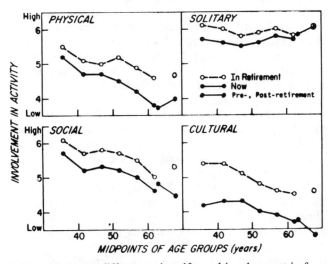

Figure 20-6. Age differences in self-rated involvement in four classes of activity by males currently employed (solid lines), and as anticipated by them in retirement (dotted lines). The open circles display the perceived involvement anticipated in retirement by a group of males shortly before their actual retirement. The two connected filled circles at the right of each function display the actual self-rated involvement as the same subjects perceived it before and after their retirement. (Unpublished data from the Veterans Administration Narrative Aging Study, courtesy of D. Ekerdt, C. Rose, and R. Bosse.)

The ecological analysis of adult development by Fozard and Thomas (1975) made it clear that one major consequence of aging is differential adaptation to specific environments. In environments to which an individual is well adapted, the cognitive load is eased because more memory information is carried in the environment. Much specific analysis is required to make these ideas useful.

The preceding reminiscence about the past decade of accomplishment in the area of memory and aging provides a basis for optimism about the future of research on memory and aging. If I have the opportunity to discuss the topic a decade from now, and provided I can remember what will probably have happened, it will most likely be a good story. But memory is a selective and constructive cognitive process (Bartlett, 1932; Neisser, 1967) for persons of all ages, and so the objectivity of such a review will require careful scrutiny.

Perhaps Rod McKuen put it best in his poem "Afterthought":

> Now the memory blurs
> You didn't feed it
> Not to worry,
> Not to worry,
> I'll keep filling the holes
> Until they're whole.

REFERENCES

Anders, T. R., Fozard, J. L., & Lillyquist, T. D. Effects of age upon retrieval from short-term memory. *Developmental Psychology*, 1972, *6*, 214–217.

Arenberg, D. A longitidunal study of problem solving in adults. *Journal of Gerontology*, 1974, *29*, 650–658.

Arenberg, D., & Robertson-Tchabo, E. A. Learning and aging. In J. E. Birren & K. W. Schaie (Eds.), *Handbook of the psychology of aging*. New York: Van Nostrand Reinhold, 1977.

Bahrick, H. P., Bahrick, P. O., & Wittlinger, R. P. Fifty years of memory for names and faces: A cross-sectional approach. *Journal of Experimental Psychology: General*. 1975, *104*, 54–75.

Baltes, P. B., & Baltes, M. M. *Plasticity and variability in psychological aging: Methodological and theoretical issues*. Paper presented at Symposium on Methodological Considerations in Determining the Effects of Aging on the CNS, Free University of Berlin, Berlin, West Germany, July 1979.

Baltes, P. B., & Willis, S. L. The critical importance of appropriate methodology in the study of aging: The sample case of psychometric intelligence. In F. Hoffmeister (Ed.). *The evaluation of old age-related changes and disorders of brain functions*. Heidelberg: Springer, 1979.

Bartlett, F. C. *Remembering*. Cambridge, England: Cambridge University Press, 1932.

Belbin, E., & Belbin, R. M. New careers in middle age. In B. L. Neugarten (Ed.), *Middle age and aging*. Chicago: University of Chicago Press, 1968.

Bertleson, P. Serial choice reaction time as a function of response versus signal and response repetition. *Nature*, 1963, *206*, 217–218.

Birren, J. E. Age and decision strategies. In A. T. Welford & J. E. Birren (Eds.), *Interdisciplinary topics in gerontology* (Vol. 4). Basel: S. Karger, 1969.

Birren, J. E. Translations in gerontology—From lab to life: Psychophysiology and speed of response. *American Psychologist*, 1974, *29*, 808–815.

Botwinick, J. *Cognitive processes in maturity and old age*. New York: Springer, 1967.

Botwinick, J. Intellectual abilities. In J. E. Birren & K. W. Schaie (Eds.), *Handbook of the psychology of aging*. New York: Van Nostrand Reinhold, 1977.

Bromley, D. B. *The psychology of human aging* (2nd ed.). Middlesex, England: Penguin Books, 1974.

Butler, R. N. The life review: An interpretation of reminiscence in the aged. *Psychiatry*, 1963, *26*, 65–76.

Butler, R. N. Successful aging and the life review. *Journal of the American Geriatric Society*, 1974, *22*, 529–535.

Corso, J. F. Auditory perception and communication. In J. E. Birren & K. W. Schaie (Eds.), *Handbook of the psychology of aging*. New York: Van Nostrand Reinhold, 1977.

Costa, P. T. & Fozard, J. L. Remembering the person: Relations of individual difference variables to memory. *Experimental Aging Research*, 1978, *4*, 291–304.

Costa, P. T., Jr., Fozard, J. L., McCrae, R. R., & Bosse, R. Relationships of age and personality type to cognitive ability factors. *Journal of Gerontology*, 1976, *31*, 663–669.

Craik, F. I. M. Short-term memory and the aging process. In G. A. Talland (Ed.), *Human aging and behavior*. New York: Academic Press, 1968.

Craik, F. I. M. Age differences in human memory. In J. E. Birren & K. W. Schaie (Eds.), *Handbook of the psychology of aging*. New York: Van Nostrand Reinhold, 1977.

Crowder, R. G. Age effects in echoic memory. In L. W. Poon, J. L. Fozard, L. S. Cermak, D. Arenberg, & L. W. Thompson (Eds.), *New directions in memory and aging: Proceedings of the George A. Talland Memorial Conference*. Hillsdale, N.J.: Lawrence Erlbaum, 1980.

deBeauvoir, S. *Coming of age*. (translated by Patrick O'Brian). New York: Putnam's, 1972.

Erber, J. T. Age differences in learning and memory on a digit-symbol substitution task. *Experimental Aging Research*, 1976, *2*, 45–53.

Erickson, R. C. Problems in the clinical assessment of memory. *Experimental Aging Research*, *1978, 4*, 255–272.

Erickson, R. C., Poon, L. W., & Walsh-Sweeney, L. Clinical memory testing of the elderly. In L. W. Poon, J. L. Fozard, L. S. Cermak, D. Arenberg & L. W. Thompson (Eds.). *New directions in memory and aging: Proceedings of the George A. Talland Memorial Conference*. Hillsdale, N.J.: Lawrence Erlbaum, 1980.

Erickson, R. C., & Scott, M. L. Clinical memory testing: A review. *Psychological Bulletin*, 1977, *84*, 1130–1149.

Fozard, J. L., & Costa P. T. Age differences in memory and decision-making in relation to personality, abilities, and endocrine function: Implications for clinical practice and health planning policy. In M. Marios (Ed.), *Aging: A challenge for science and social policy.* London: Oxford University Press, in press.

Fozard, J. L., & Poon L. W. *Age-related differences in long-term memory for pictures.* Paper presented at the meeting of the Gerontological Society, New York, October 1976.

Fozard, J. L., & Poon L. W. Speed and accuracy of recall from primary and secondary memory during and after memorization of unfamiliar verbal material. *Proceedings of the 11th International Conference of Gerontology (Tokyo)*, 1978, *2*, 185.

Fozard, J. L., & Popkin, S. J. Optimizing adult development: Ends and means of an applied psychology of aging. *American Psychologist*, 1978, *33*, 975–989.

Fozard, J. L., & Thomas, J. C. Psychology of aging: Basic findings and their psychiatric applications. In J. G. Howells (Ed.), *Modern perspectives in the psychiatry of old age.* New York: Brunner-Mazel, 1975.

Fozard, J. L., Thomas, J. C., & Waugh, N. C. Effects of age and frequency of stimulus repetitions on two-choice reaction time. *Journal of Gerontology*, 1976, *31*, 556–563.

Fozard, J. L., Waugh, N., C., & Thomas J. C. Effects of age on long-term retention of pictures. *Proceedings of the Tenth International Congress of Gerontology* (Jerusalem), 1975, *2*, 137. (abstract)

Fozard, J. L. Wolf, E., Bell, B., McFarland, R. A., & Podolsky, S. Visual perception and communication. In J. E. Birren & K. W. Schaie (Eds.), *Handbook of the psychology of aging.* New York: Van Nostrand Reinhold, 1977.

Freud, S. The psychopathology of everyday life. In A. A. Brill (Ed.), *The basic writings of Sigmund Freud* (Vol. IV). London: Hogarth, 1956. (Originally published, 1914)

Giambra, L. M. Sex differences in daydreaming and related mental activity from the late teens to the early nineties. *Aging and Human Development*, 1979, *10*, 1–34.

Goodrick, C. L. Maze learning of mature-young and aged rats as a function of distribution of practice. *Journal of Experimental Psychology*, 1973, *98*, 344–349.

Gordon, C., & Gaitz, C. M. Leisure and lives: Personal expressivity across the life span. In R. H. Binstock & E. Shanas (Eds.), *Handbook of aging and the social sciences.* New York: Van Nostrand Reinhold, 1977.

Grant, E. A., Storandt, M., & Botwinick, J. Incentive and practice in the psychomotor performance of the elderly. *Journal of Gerontology*, 1978, *33*, 413–415.

Hines, T. M., & Fozard, J. L. Memory and aging: Relevance of recent developments for research and application. In C. Eisdorfer (Ed.), *Annual review of gerontology and geriatrics* (Vol. 1). New York: Springer, in press.

Hultsch, D. F., & Pentz, C. A. Encoding, storage and retrieval in adult memory: The role of model assumptions. In L. W. Poon, J. L. Fozard, L. S. Cermak, D. Arenberg, & L. W. Thompson, (Eds.), *New directions in memory and aging: Proceedings of the George A. Talland Memorial Conference.* Hillsdale, N.J.: Lawrence Erlbaum, 1980.

Kahn, R. L., & Miller, N. E. Adaptational factors in memory function in the aged. *Experimental Aging Research*, 1978, *4*, 273–290.

Kline, D. W., & Szafran, J. Age differences in backward monoptic visual noise masking. *Journal of Gerontology*, 1975, *30*, 307–311.

Lachman, J. L., & Lachman, R. Age and the actualization of world knowledge. In L. W. Poon, J. L. Fozard, L. S. Cermak, D. Arenberg, & L. W. Thompson (Eds.), *New directions in memory and aging: Proceedings of the George A. Talland Memorial Conference.* Hillsdale, N.J.: Lawrence Erlbaum, 1980.

Lawton, M. P. & Nahemow, L. Ecology and the aging process. In C. Eisdorfer & M. P. Lawton, (Eds.), *The psychology of adult development and aging.* Washington, D.C.: American Psychological Association, 1973.

McKuen, R. *Collected poems.* New York: Simon & Schuster, 1975.

Miller, G. A. The magical number seven, plus or minus two: Some limits on our capacity for processing information. *Psychological Review*, 1956, *63*, 81–97.

Neisser, U. *Cognitive psychology.* New York: Appelton-Century-Crofts, 1967.

Perlmutter, M. An apparent paradox about memory and aging. In L. W. Poon, J. L. Fozard, L. S. Cermak, D. Arenberg, & L. W. Thompson (Eds.), *New directions in memory and aging: Proceedings of the George A. Talland Memorial Conference.* Hillsdale, N.J.: Lawrence Erlbaum, 1980.

Pfeiffer, E. Psychopathology and social pathology. In J. E. Birren & K. W. Schaie (Eds.), *Handbook of the psychology of aging.* New York: Van Nostrand Reinhold, 1977.

Plemons, J. K., Willis, S. L., & Baltes, P. B. Modifiability of fluid intelligence in aging: A short-term longitudinal training approach. *Journal of Gerontology*, 1978, *33*, 224–231.

Poon, L. W., & Fozard, J. L. Speed of retrieval from long-term memory in relation to age, familiarity and datedness of information. *Journal of Gerontology*, 1978, *33*, 711–717.

Poon, L. W., & Fozard J. L. Age and word frequency effects in continuous recognition memory. *Journal of Gerontology*, 1980, *35*, 77–86.

Poon, L. W., Fozard, J. L., Paulshock, D. R. & Thomas J. C. Questionnaire assessment of age differences in retention of recent and remote events. *Experimental Aging Research*, 1979, *5*, 401–411.

Poon, L. W., Fozard, J. L., & Treat, N. W. From clinical and research findings on memory to intervention programs. *Experimental Aging Research*, 1978, *4*, 235–254.

Poon, L. W., Fozard, J. L., & Walsh-Sweeney, L. Memory training for the elderly: Salient issues on the use of imagery mnemonics. In L. W. Poon, J. L. Fozard, L. S. Cermak, D. Arenberg & L. W. Thompson (Eds.), *New directions in memory and aging: Proceedings of the George A. Talland Memorial Conference.* Hillsdale, N.J.: Lawrence Erlbaum, 1980.

Rabbitt, P. M. A. Age and the use of structure in transmitted information. In G. A. Talland (Ed.), *Human aging and behavior.* New York: Academic Press, 1968.

Robertson-Tchabo, E. A., Arenberg, D., & Costa P. T. Temperamental predictors of longitudinal change in performance on the Benton Revised Visual Retention Test among seventy-year old men: An exploratory study. In F. Hoffmeister & C. Müller (Eds.), *Brain function in old age: Evaluation of changes and disorders*. New York: Springer-Verlag, 1979.

Salthouse, T. A. The role of memory in the age decline in digit symbol substitution performance. *Journal of Gerontology*, 1977, *33*, 232–238.

Schaie, K. W., & Schaie, J. P. Clinical assessment and aging. In J. E. Birren & K. W. Schaie (Eds.), *Handbook of the psychology of aging*. New York: Van Nostrand Reinhold, 1977.

Schonfield, D. Theoretical nuances and practical old questions: The psychology of aging. *Canadian Psychologist*, 1972, *13*, 252–266.

Smith, A. D. Aging and interference with memory. *Journal of Gerontology*, 1975, *30*, 319–325.

Smith, A. D. Age differences in encoding, storage, and retrieval. In L. W. Poon, J. L. Fozard, L. S. Cermak, D. Arenberg, & L. W. Thompson (Eds.), *New directions in memory and aging: Proceedings of the George A. Talland Memorial Conference*. Hillsdale, N.J.: Lawrence Erlbaum, 1980.

Sperling, G. A model for visual memory tasks. *Human Factors*, 1963, *5*, 19–31.

Squire, L. R. The neuropsychology of amnesia: An approach to the study of memory and aging. In L. W. Poon, J. L. Fozard, L. S. Cermak, D. Arenberg, & L. W. Thompson (Eds.), *New directions in memory and aging: Proceedings of the George A. Talland Memorial Conference*. Hillsdale, N.J.: Lawrence Erlbaum, 1980.

Thomas, J. C., Fozard, J. L., & Waugh, N. C. Age-related differences in naming latency. *American Journal of Psychology*, 1977, *90*, 499–509.

Thomas, J. C., Waugh, N. C., & Fozard, J. L. Age and familiarity in memory scanning. *Journal of Gerontology*, 1978, *33*, 528–533.

Treat, N. J., Poon, L. W., Fozard, J. L., & Popkin, S. J. Toward applying cognitive skill training to memory problems. *Experimental Aging Research*, 1978, *4*, 305–320.

Walsh, D. A. Age differences in central perceptual processing: A dichoptic backward masking investigation. *Journal of Gerontology*, 1976, *31*, 178–185.

Walsh, D. A., & Baldwin, M. Age differences in integrated semantic memory. *Developmental Psychology*, 1977, *13*, 509–514.

Walsh, D. A., & Thompson, L. W. Age differences in visual sensory memory. *Journal of Gerontology*, 1978, *33*, 383–387.

Waugh, N. C., & Barr, R. Memory and mental tempo. In L. W. Poon, J. L. Fozard, L. S. Cermak, D. Arenberg, & L. W. Thompson (Eds.), *New directions in memory and aging: Proceedings of the George A. Talland Memorial Conference*. Hillsdale, N.J.: Lawrence Erlbaum, 1980.

Waugh, N. C., Fozard, J. L., & Thomas, J. C. Age-related differences in serial binary classification. *Experimental Aging Research*, 1978, *4*, 433–442.

Waugh, N. C., & Norman, D. A. Primary memory. *Psychological Review*, 1965, *72*, 89–104.

Welford, A. T. *Aging and human skill*. London: Oxford University Press, 1958.

Welford, A. T. Age and skill: Motor, intellectual and social. In A. T. Welford & J. E. Birren (Eds.), *Interdisciplinary topics in gerontology* (Vol. 4). Basel: S. Karger, 1969.

Welford, A. T. Memory and age: A perspective view. In L. W. Poon, J. L. Fozard, L. S. Cermak, D. Arenberg, & L. W. Thompson, (Eds.), *New directions in memory and aging: Proceedings of the George A. Talland Memorial Conference*. Hillsdale, N.J.: Lawrence Erlbaum, 1980.

Wingfield, A. Effects of frequency on identification and naming of objects. *American Journal of Psychology*, 1968, *81*, 226–234.

Wingfield, A., & Sandoval, A. W. Perceptual processing for meaning. In L. W. Poon, J. L. Fozard, L. S. Cermak, D. Arenberg, and L. W. Thompson (Eds.), *New directions in memory and aging: Proceedings of the George A. Talland Memorial Conference*. Hillsdale, N.J.: Lawrence Erlbaum, 1980.

Witt, S. J., & Cunningham, W. R. Cognitive speed and subsequent intellectual development: A longitudinal investigation. *Journal of Gerontology*, 1979, *34*, 540–546.

Zelinski, E. M., Gilewski, M. J., & Thompson, L. W. Do laboratory memory tests relate to everyday remembering and forgetting? In L. W. Poon, J. L. Fozard, L. S. Cermak, D. Arenberg, & L. W. Thompson (Eds.), *New directions in memory and aging: Proceedings of the George A. Talland Memorial Conference*. Hillsdale, N.J.: Lawrence Erlbaum, 1980.

SECTION

5 Part II

Cognitive Issues:
Speed of Behavior

James E. Birren and M. Virtrue Williams, *Section Editors*

Introduction

The process of research in the psychology of aging has been one of collecting diverse particulars of behavioral differences. In a chapter on the theory of aging in Birren and Schaie's *Handbook of the Psychology of Aging*, Klaus Riegel suggested, aptly, that this state of affairs should be considered a failure of the investigators of the aging process to understand the unique principles of the process that they study. Anderson Smith, in his introduction to the chapters in Section 5, Part I of the present book, notes that a new freedom has been offered to researchers in the psychology of aging by recent advances in the theory of cognition and by new and powerful multivariate statistical techniques. It is our hope, and indeed our belief, that such freedom will lead to new and provocative advances in our understanding of the psychological impact of the aging process. At the same time, we are concerned that these new theories and techniques not shackle the researchers of the 1980s to the concepts and approaches employed by the experimental psychologists of the 1970s. We find ourselves, therefore, in agreement with Baltes and Willis (1977) in their concern for the unquestioning application to research on aging of techniques appropriate to young subjects. Beyond these concerns, however, is our belief that the application of theory in developmental research must make sense in a developmental framework. Few theories hold such promise. We have chosen to consider an appropriate, ecologically valid variable—speed of behavior—and a

sensible developmental theory—a general, progressive loss of cognitive speed.

The following chapters examine the issues and interrelations of cognitive processes, age, and speed of behavior. Observations of slowness of behavior in old persons and animals are among the most established of behavioral data. The interaction of slowness of behavior with cognition and the lack of fruitful hypotheses about the origins of the slowness, however, have not been apparent in the past. In this sense, the subject matter is not only old but also very young, in that the organizing or interpretive principles are just beginning to emerge.

Our intent was to present a diversity of approaches to the organizational-interpretive problem posed by the phenomenon of behavioral slowing with age. To this end the chapters in this section represent different approaches to explanations, organization, and development of theories and models. Generally these chapters can be contrasted on the extent to which they employ biological or behavioral principles.

Although they differ in approach, all address the highly significant topic of speed of behavior with age. Speed of behavior, along with memory, represent the two behavioral processes most consistently found to decline with age. For that reason both of them are fruitful areas for further study.

The first chapter, by Birren, Woods, and Williams, surveys a broad field of literature on many aspects of behavioral slowing, including its possible relation to memory. The chapter seeks to understand phenomena of behavioral slowing in terms of a single neurobiological process that exerts a pervasive influence on all behavior mediated by the central nervous system. The more complex the behavior, the greater the consequences of the slowing. In young organisms, the speed of behavior appears to be a consequence of specific aptitudes; in the old organism, slowness appears to emerge as a general property of behavior. The chapter by Stern, Oster, and Newport deals with reaction time as an expression of hemispheric dominance. The evidence is regarded from the point of view that the right hemisphere may suffer greater deterioration with age. The experimental evidence presented suggests that reaction time does not show a differential hemispheric effect. The evidence at this point suggests that decline in speed of behavior is a broad or general phenomenon not linked as yet with regional cerebral deterioration.

Cunningham's chapter looks at the ubiquity of slowness of behavior in the performance of complex aptitude tests. More and more intercorrelations among age and aptitude factors suggest an increasingly general impact of behavioral speed. Factor structure itself, however, appears consistent across age levels.

The fourth and last chapter, by Cerella, Poon, and Williams, examines the effect of task complexity on reaction time of the elderly. These authors found that the complexity effect can be explained by a generalized slowing of mental processes.

Collectively, where do these chapters lead us? Although cautiousness is always in order in the interpretation of convergence in psychological data, the chapters nonetheless show remarkable consistency on two points. First, the tendency for old adults to be slow in their behavior has become a widely accepted benchmark finding; second, this slowness has a diffuse or general quality about it that pervades many kinds of behavior. This situation has provided the authors with an opportunity, if a perplexing one, to attempt an explanation of the antecedents of the slowness and the reasons so many behavioral functions are influenced by it. One would judge that if the slowness in speed of behavior had readily fitted the paradigms of other areas of experimental or social psychology, such a major phenomenon would by now have achieved the status of a mature topic in the science of psychology. From its failure to do so, one may infer that some aspects of the changes in the organization of behavior with age have not yielded readily to concepts borrowed from established areas of investigation. As a problem area, slowness of behavior with age seems pregnant with research opportunities for specialists in other research areas as well as for those committed to the study of adult development and aging. The phenomenon is widely replicable, shows high variance relative to other variables, and pervades most, if not all, observable aspects of behavior.

REFERENCE

Baltes, P. B., & Willis, S. L. Toward psychological theories of aging and development. In J. E. Birren & K. W. Schaie (Eds.), *Handbook of the psychology of aging*. New York: Van Nostrand Reinhold, 1977.

James E. Birren, Anita M. Woods, and M. Virtrue Williams

CHAPTER

21

Behavioral Slowing With Age: Causes, Organization, and Consequences

In the matrix of relations between the physiology, anatomy, and behavior of the older nervous system, a particular vantage point is research on the slowness of behavior with age. A review of the evidence indicates that the slowing of behavior with age not only appears in motor responses and sensory processes but becomes more obvious with increasing complexity of behavior. For this reason the expression "slowness of behavior with age" is preferred to the more limited phrase "changes in reaction time with age." While there are probably both general and specific factors in behavioral slowing with age, the organization of a general factor of slowness raises some fundamental questions. Behavioral factors are apparently involved, but more recent emphasis has been placed on the role of neurobiological changes in the central nervous system.

Perhaps the most ubiquitous and significant change observed in the older organism is slowness of behavior. Slowness is not limited to motor responses or to peripheral sensory phenomena, as this chapter documents; instead, it appears to be even more evident the more complex the behavior observed and the higher the mediating neural structures in the nervous system. We have selected this feature of behavior for examination because it seems basic to other phenomena and it in turn offers the greatest possibility of being explained in terms of accompanying neurobiological changes. Except in narrow areas of research, the literature of present-day psychology can be described as particulate in nature. The psychology of aging is no exception, and there is a notable lack of theory with which to articulate the facts that are now so voluminous (Birren

& Schaie, 1977). Published research in the psychology of aging has not been notably additive, with the possible exception of behavioral slowing with age.

Evolution has provided us with a foundation for survival in the nervous system that is organized partly on the basis of our genetic heritage (brain stem) and partly on the basis of experience (cerebrum). The tantalizing aspect of the behavior of the whole organism is that behavior can shift quickly from one kind of determinant to another, with varying degrees of biological or learned determinism in between. One can shift from concentration in abstract thought to stereotypic rage within seconds. Such shifts in the dominant control mechanisms are of concern in aging, since the latencies, amplitudes, and duration of the regulatory mechanisms may themselves change with age.

With the increased emphasis being placed on the role of the central nervous system (CNS) in aging and in regulating important biological processes, the slowness of behavior with age takes on new significance. Measurement of the slowness of behavior seen in older organisms may offer both one of the best tools to assess aging of the CNS and a vantage point from which to gain understanding about the organization of age changes in behavior.

Historical Perspective

The earliest discussion of the speed of behavior and age that we have found appears in Quetelet's book of

293

1835 in which he mentions the "swiftness and length of stride of man," but laments that "the data for different ages are wanting" (p. 72). Quetelet had learned, in discussion with Babbage in the 1830s, that Babbage had been investigating how many times a man could do certain things in one minute, for example, how many strokes of oar or how many blows of a hammer. Quetelet was interested in the interrelations of the various physical and mental faculties of man and the lawfulness of development and aging.

Much later, in the 1870s, Galton gathered data from a health exposition and found a difference of about 13% in mean response speed between 60-year-olds and 20-year-olds (see Koga & Morant, 1923). This general finding has been replicated many times—to the point where slowing in simple reaction time with age is, perhaps, one of the most replicated findings of behavioral change with age. In a compendium of 26 studies of simple reaction-time experiments comparing young to old subjects, we found, on the average, a 20% difference in reaction time between 20-year-olds and 60-year-olds. Welford (1977), in a recent review, obtained identical results.

The most parsimonious of the major hypotheses to explain slowing seems to be one that proposes a general primary mechanism within the nervous system. Although the evidence is not conclusive, an impressive amount of data supports pursuing this hypothesis.

Behavioral Implications

In an early experiment designed to investigate the influence of effector mechanisms in a simple reaction-time experiment, Birren and Botwinick (1955) used three alternative responses to a simple auditory signal. A release response was used for the finger, jaw, and foot of each subject. The length of the neural pathway and the musculature of each of these responses are very different. The differences in reaction time for the age groups were significant (male subjects: 32 aged 18–36, and 32 aged 61–91). The important point was demonstrated that the three very different response modes all showed differences in slowing between young and old of about the same magnitude. There is little reason, therefore, to attribute much of the slowing with age to neural conduction velocity (see also Birren & Wall, 1956).

Another study that addressed the issue of general slowing in reaction time did so by varying stimulus conditions while keeping the response conditions the same for all trials (Birren, Riegel, & Morrison, 1962). This study used 22 stimulus conditions of varying complexity ranging from simple lights to a complex word-completion task. In all tasks the subject's responses were the same—pressing appropriate buttons.

A principal-components analysis of these data isolated five major factors for each age group (30 subjects aged 18–33; 23 subjects aged 60–80). In the first factor for the elderly, 44% of the variance was isolated. This component had high loadings for the elderly on tasks as disparate as movement time (.61), choice reaction time (.83), Digit Symbol (.85), and word association (.80). The young subjects, by contrast, showed only 29% loading of the variance on the first factor, with a movement-time loading of −.24.

In this study the determinants of the behavior of young and old subjects in this context are clearly different, with the older subjects distinguished by a large general speed factor. This general speed component is related not only to simple movements but also to tasks that contain a large element of cognition. The authors concluded that

> age differences in speed of responses are not limited to simple motor aspects of tasks but involve to an even greater extent verbal processes. . . . The results in general support the view that older subjects tend to show a characteristic slower response speed, whereas young adult subjects are more task specific in their response speed." (Birren et al., 1962, p. 16)

This conclusion embraces the entire conceptual thrust of the present chapter—that with age there is an emergent, limiting factor on speed of task completion—a general decline in speed of behavior.

Intelligence

Perhaps the most intriguing aspect of slowness of behavior with age is the ubiquity of its effect. While a decline in speed was noted first in simple stimuli and responses, its effect seems to spread to complex behaviors such as those expressed in measurements of intelligence.

Early studies of intellectual changes across adulthood generally indicated primarily a decline in abilities. Indeed, some researchers have reported a general decline in intellectual function beginning as early as adolescence and continuing in a linear fashion across the life span (e.g., Wechsler, 1939). This picture of intellectual decline is supported by a number of studies (Botwinick, 1967; Horn, 1970; Jones, 1959; see also Baltes & Labouvie, 1973). More recently, however, such a simple portrayal of the state of ontogenetic change has been called both inaccurate and overly simplistic. The phenomena of ontogenetic change may ultimately require a more complex model (Baltes & Schaie, 1976), particularly since a holistic linear decline model is outdated.

Ontogenetic Speed Effects

Several reports have pointed out the need to distinguish between ontogenetic effects and environmental effects on performance of cognitive tests. In particular, Schaie and his associates have argued that studies should be pursued that are designed to separate the effects of time of measurement, cohort, and ontogenetic change (Schaie, Labouvie, & Buech, 1973; Schaie & Labouvie-Vief, 1974; Schaie & Parham, 1977; Schaie & Strother, 1968). It is now apparent that any attempt to minimize the importance of the effect of cohort performance differences is at best wishful thinking. At the same time, to the extent that developmental psychologists find evidence of ontogenetic change, it is incumbent on them to report it. Schaie and his colleagues have emphasized the findings of their research that are unique—their quantification of what in other designs are inextricable confounds—cohort and time of measurement effects. The present chapter points to those areas of cognition that repeatedly show ontogenetic effects.

The Primary Mental Abilities subtests that show ontogenetic change most consistently are those that require speed. Results reveal that the first tests to show significant ontogenetic decline are invariably the tests of Spatial Visualization, Inductive Reasoning, and Word Fluency. In a study that tested cohort with ontogenetic effects in a cohort-sequential design, Schaie and Parham (1977) found decrements beginning at ages 67, 67, and 39 for Spatial Visualization, Inductive Reasoning, and Word Fluency, respectively. These results were obtained using independent samples rather than repeated measures. While these ages are later than those reported by Botwinick (1977), they are in accord qualitatively in that measures in Schaie's data show an order of decline similar to that in studies cited by Botwinick (see Figure 21-1).

General Speed Factor in Intelligence

The question of a general age-related speed factor in intelligence has been studied by Cunningham and Birren (1976), who used data from Owens's Army Alpha testing of university students (Owens, 1953, 1966). This is particularly relevant because Cunningham and Birren formally tested the hypothesis of factor invariance in a sequential design of intelligence testing. Using factor-analytic methods developed by Cliff (1966) and Jöreskog (1971; McGraw & Jöreskog, 1971), Cunningham and Birren tested for similarity of Varimax factor solutions, first between age-matched samples taken in 1973 and 1919 and then in a longitudinal sample of subjects 20, 50, and 60 years old.

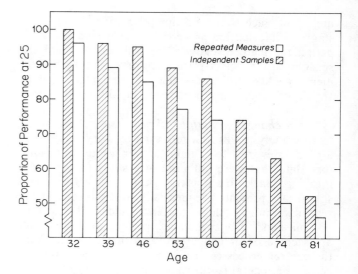

Figure 21-1. Age differences in verbal fluency in relation to performance at age 25. Data were obtained from a cohort-sequential analysis of adult intellectual development and revealed a trend with age for both repeated measurements of the same subjects and independent samples (data from Schaie & Parham, 1977).

They found that the 1973 sample of 20-year-olds more closely matched the 20-year-olds in 1919 than it did later testings of the same group, a fact that supports an ontogenetic interpretation of the subsequent findings.

The finding most relevant to the present discussion, however, was that cognitive factor structure, when tested in a confirmatory design, was not found to be invariant across age. To the contrary, an earlier report by Cunningham states,

> The general conclusion resulting from the data analysis so far is that the inter-relationships among cognitive variables, as represented in the factor structure, appeared to be changing with age, and that these differences were most pronounced for highly speeded variables." (Cunningham, 1974)

Information Processing

Speed changes in human performance with age are also evident in newer areas of investigation. A recent approach to the study of human cognition is the information-processing model proposed by Neisser (1967) and others, which has been suggested for the study of age effects (Birren, 1974). The information-processing approach divides cognitive processes into sequential steps, beginning with stimulus acquisition and ending with response. With this approach it becomes theoretically possible to compare the time required at each stage in the processing series. Five stages of information processing have been considered: peripheral feature analysis, central feature analysis, sensory store, short-term memory, and long-term memory. Age differences that can be interpreted as speed differences have been found in all five stages.

Speed changes in peripheral processing. Peripheral-feature analysis was first proposed by Turvey (1973) in a model designed to explain the apparently contradictory data that were gathered in a study of backward masking. Backward masking occurs when two visual stimuli are presented sequentially to a subject and the second stimulus occludes the first, which is then said to be "masked." The two stages, peripheral and central, are seen to occur concurrently, with the proviso that the central processes are contingent on the output of certain peripheral feature analyzers (Turvey, 1973).

A study by Walsh, Till, and Williams (1978) directly addressed the question of peripheral processing changes with age and used conditions of presentation such that peripheral masking would occur, that is, monoptic presentation with random noise masking stimuli (Turvey, 1973). Two age groups were tested (mean ages of 24.3 and 68.2 years). Significant slowing in peripheral processes was found between the two age groups, as indicated by a longer interstimulus interval to escape masking and a longer stimulus-onset asynchrony (SOA). The age differences in processing ranged from approximately 11 to 20 msec for different levels of target energy.

Central processing. Central perceptual processing occurs subsequent to peripheral processing; however, at very low target energies, peripheral processing may proceed so slowly that central processing is concurrent with it (Turvey, 1973). Investigations of central processing with age have shown significant differences in speed between young adults (18–30 years) and old adults (60–80 years) (Hertzog, Williams, & Walsh, 1976; Walsh, Williams, & Hertzog, 1979). Most illustrative of these studies is that of Walsh (1976), which replicates Turvey (1973) in a central masking design.

In central masking, as in peripheral masking, substantial age differences were found in processing speed. When the data in the Walsh (1976) study are collapsed across target duration for SOA, there is an approximately 23-msec difference between the young and old groups. This represents about a 31% increase in the time required for an old subject to escape masking over a young subject.

This typical finding of apparent slowing in perceptual processing speed with age has been found in adults by a number of investigators. Comparing the performance of young adults (19 years) to two groups of middle-aged adults (35 and 55 years), Welsandt, Zupnick, and Meyer (1973) found that the 55-year-old group performed at slower rates. Kline and Szafran (1975) and Kline and Birren (1975) found slowing with age in both monoptic and dichoptic presentations using backward masking. However, as neither study was designed for interpretation in the concurrent-contingent hypothesis of visual information processing, the exact locus of the slowing in information processing is ambiguous.

Speed changes in iconic memory. Age differences in the sensory storage or iconic stage of visual processing have been studied by Walsh and Thompson (1978). This stage of processing is just subsequent to that studied by the method of central masking. The icon is a holistic virtual image of the optic array that is not yet represented as a symbolic memory (Neisser, 1967). One method of estimating the duration of this image is by subjective judgment of the continuity of a form. The time between successive presentations of the same form is varied to determine the largest separation between presentations that the subject can tolerate and still perceive the form as continuous. The subject will perceive the form as continuous provided the sum of the duration of stimulus presentation plus the interstimulus interval is less than the subject's icon duration. Walsh and Thompson, using both monoptic and dichoptic stimulus presentation durations of 10, 50, and 90 msec, derived estimates of icon persistence of 289 msec for a young (20 years) group and 248 msec for an old (67 years) group, an age-related difference of 40 msec, or 12%. Mode of presentation did not affect icon persistence.

Shortening of the iconic image results in there being less time available in the older nervous system to generate memories of visual events. The iconic image is searched for items to be stored as memories (Neisser, 1967), and not all items in the iconic image are ultimately stored. Thus the individual must choose among them—only those specifically attended to are used to generate memories (Averbach & Coriell, 1961; Sperling, 1963). As the iconic image is foreshortened with age, it becomes critical how quickly such an image is searched and memories generated.

During the period of iconic memory, specific items from the icon are selected for attention. This selection will then include those items in short-term memory. Short-term memory has been shown to be confined to a small number of items and to have a specific capacity (Atkinson & Shiffrin, 1971). There has been no consistent demonstration of a reduction in the capacity of such memory with age (Craik, 1977). The review, or scan, of short-term memory does, however, seem to slow with age.

Speed changes in review of short-term memory. Scanning short-term memory is the apparent item-by-item sequential review of items in short-term store, as first demonstrated by Sternberg (1966). He showed that if a subject was required to determine whether a test item was a member of a set of immediately learned items, that the response latency was a linear function of the number of items in the learned set up to a maximum set size of seven. He suggested that the slope of such a function was an index of the rate at which the items in short-term memory (the immediately learned set) were scanned. He also, postulated that the intercept of such a function was an index of response-execution and nerve-conduction velocity.

Anders, Fozard, and Lillyquist (1972) used this method and found that as the age of the subjects increased, both the slope and the intercept of the scan function increased (see Figure 21-2). Anders et al. concluded that this indicates a slowing with age of the rate of scanning. This result has been replicated by Eriksen, Hamlin, and Daye (1973) and by Anders and Fozard (1973).

General Slowing in Perceptual Processes

Evidence for general slowing in information processing is less straightforward than that for intelligence. To date, only one study can be said to address this question. In this study by Williams (1978), three differing stages of information processing were studied with a within-subject design by means of visual backward masking. The first stage was central processing (Turvey, 1973), the second was persistence of iconic memory, and the third was one of semantic interaction.

Williams tested the subjects across a wide range of stimulus-onset asynchronies with three types of masks, each type designed to interrrupt processing at a different point in the sequence. Using a repeated-measures analysis of variance, he found that the masks did indeed show different patterns of interference, which indicated that different points of processing were being disrupted. Of particular interest, however, is the fact that the three age groups (20–30 years, 40–50 years, 60–70 years) showed a stable slowing of information processing across age groups and conditions. The older groups showed significant slowing compared to the young group; however, there was not an age-by-condition interaction. Inspection of the data indicated a constant lagging in speed of information processing across levels—a general decline of behavioral speed.

Speed changes and memory. Several studies indicate that the speed of behavior is related to memory ability. Though the data are limited to correlations of performance on two measures, these correlations appear consistent and high. Birren (1965) reports, for example, that the Wechsler Memory Scale and the speed of writing digits showed essentially no correlation (−.01) for young adults (18–32 years) but a significant correlation (.52) for older subjects.

It has been argued that speed is "motor" and that memory is "cognitive" and thus that the two are not related. However, in a study by Botwinick and Storandt (1974b) the timed Digit Symbol subtest of the Wechsler Adult Intelligence Scale was found to be correlated with scores on the Vocabulary subtest from the same scale. Botwinick and Storandt found, contrary to the notion that such tests were orthogonal, that the two tests showed correlations of .50; that is, 25% of the variance on one was explained by the other. To make these findings more impressive, the effect of age—a possible common variable to each—had been controlled by a partial correlational procedure.

In a subsequent study, Botwinick and Storandt (1974b), examined 10 men and 10 women in each decade from 20 to 70 years of age on a series of tests related to memory and associated psychological functioning. When the results of the memory tests were combined with the non-memory psychological tests and a factor analysis was performed, Botwinick and

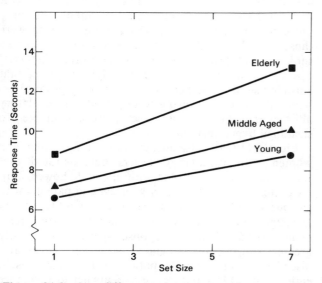

Figure 21-2. Age differences in response time to retrieve items in short-term memory in relation to size of the set of immediately learned items (data from Anders, Fozard, & Lillyquist, 1972).

Storandt identified four major factors. Of these factors, one had major loadings from the psychomotor speed measures (including copying digits, crossing off symbols, and slow writing) and also from tests of memory spans and memory for patterns. The factor on which the speed measures loaded accounted for 16% of the variance; only the first factor was equally large. Botwinick and Storandt concluded that memory tasks that require repeated sequential processing of information are most sensitive to changes in cognitive speed.

Both storage and retrieval processes appear to be potentially sensitive to behavioral speed. While until recently psychologists have emphasized the problems of retrieval and age (see Birren, 1974), the short spans of Botwinick and Storandt (1974b) seem more easily explained in terms of storage. This finding is of special interest in view of recent reports of anatomical changes in the paleocortex, which are discussed later.

The Relation of Speed Changes to Health

Although major evidence suggests that slowness of behavior with advancing age occurs as a result of a primary change in the nervous system, environmental differences and disease can interact with this process to modify its appearance and rate of change.

Birren (1965) has suggested the existence of at least two speed factors: a primary factor of aging at a subcortical level reflected in all or most processes mediated by the central nervous system, and a secondary factor of cortical integrity influenced by disease, particularly those diseases resulting in local cell loss, interference with circulation, and ischemia.

A study by Dirken (1972) illustrates the interaction of these proposed primary and secondary factors of aging. Dirken analyzed 150 psychological and physiological variables in a cluster analysis and found that somatic and mental aspects of aging were highly interdependent. He concluded that a large portion of the variance associated with aging is controlled by a general process influencing all subsystems simultaneously. Such evidence supports the theory that changes in central processing time with age may be the major independent variable in explaining much of the behavioral change with age. Furthermore, this timing appears to be dependent on other physiological factors that may result in an additive effect, especially the consequence of somatic disease.

Circulatory Status and Behavioral Slowing

Patients with hypertension or coronary heart disease typically perform less well than those with no vascular problems but better than brain-damaged patients of the same age on various perceptual and cognitive measures (Reitan, 1954). In a study by Spieth (1965), in which a battery of psychological performance tests was given to men aged 23 to 59, the results indicated that mild or moderate degrees of cardiovascular disorder were reliably associated with slow performance on psychomotor tasks; however, patients with cerebrovascular disorders showed even greater impairment in serial reaction time.

According to Spieth (1965), the slowness in performance was in the decision phase rather than the movement phase of the reaction process and could be attributed to consequences of disease processes such as circulatory insufficiency. Men in the mildly diseased group who were in nominally "normal" health showed slowed performance, even though they did not exhibit traditional symptoms of cerebrovascular impairment. Spieth also found that uncontrolled hypertension was related to slowed serial reaction time (RT) while medicated hypertension was not.

More recent data (Botwinick & Storandt, 1974a) have shown that subjects who reported more cardiovascular symptoms on the Cornell Medical Index also showed slowed simple auditory reaction times.

Another study, by Light (1975), on hypertensives under the age of 60 did not corroborate Spieth's finding regarding the beneficial effect of antihypertensive medication on serial reaction time. Light found that both drug treatment and type of hypertensive disorder—in this study indicated by plasma renin activity (PRA)—may be behaviorally important. Out of 180 hypertensive men and women, the only untreated subjects who showed unusual slowing were those with high PRA; slowing was found in treated subjects at all levels of PRA. Furthermore, substantial age-related slowing was observed. Light suggested that chronic use of antihypertensive drugs may produce behavioral side effects owing to impaired autoregulatory abilities in patients whose vasculature has adapted to sustained hypertension.

Light's (1978) subsequent study of 271 men and women with vascular disorders demonstrated that serial reaction time slowed with age and showed similar patterns for both healthy subjects and patients with various vascular problems. Her results confirmed that although both cardiovascular problems and drug-treatment variables affect response speed, significantly greater slowing is associated with cerebrovascular disorders. In other words, patients with transient ischemic attack (TIA) and stroke patients performed more slowly than treated and untreated hypertensives and patients with coronary heart disease. This suggests that transient cerebral ischemia may be associated with enduring behavioral impairment, even though neurologic signs of ischemia do not persist; indeed, transient ischemia may be responsible for much of the behavioral deficit observed in the "healthy" elderly as well.

Light's (1978) finding that most untreated hypertensives and patients with coronary heart disease show no substantial slowing may indicate that deficits in response speed in patients with mild cardiovascular disorders are not primarily related to heart or blood-pressure problems but to concomitant cerebrovascular problems. This hypothesis may account for the slowing seen in older, relatively healthy subjects, since the relation between age and atherosclerosis is well documented (Kral, 1964; Simonson, 1964; Simonson & McGavack, 1964).

A lack of oxygen in the brain may also result from conditions other than cerebrovascular disease, such as reduced cardiac output. A direct demonstration of this can be seen in the work of Lagergren (1974) and Lagergren and Levander (1975), who varied the pulse rate of a group of patients in whom artificial cardiac pacemakers had been implanted. The heart rate of the patients was varied externally and was set at either 70 or 45 beats per minute. At the slow pulse rate, the patients showed a significant slowing of reaction time and other indications of poor mental performance. An additional decrement in performance was noted in the reaction time when the patients were placed in a sitting position in contrast to the supine position. Given marginal cardiac output under the slow pulse-rate condition, the sitting posture apparently resulted in a further reduction of perfusion pressure across the brain and was accompanied by a further reduction in available oxygen, which was manifest in the additional slowness in reaction time.

These studies also reported that immediate recall of memory for verbal associations was poorer at the slow heart rate but that delayed recall after 1½ hours was not affected. This suggests that long-term memory is not influenced as much by metabolic processes as is the acquisition phase of memory.

Brain Damage

The idea that psychomotor reactions are sensitive indices of the integrity of the nervous system is not new in psychology (Hicks & Birren, 1970; King, 1965; Talland, 1965). Bruhn and Parsons (1977) found epileptic and brain-damaged groups to be significantly slower than control patients on median RT and also to have greater intraindividual variability. In particular, older epileptic subjects showed more RT variability than did younger ones.

The consistent finding has been that brain-damaged subjects respond more slowly than age-matched controls. Benton's (1977) study of behavioral slowing compared the combined effects of age and brain damage to the effect of each variable alone. He found a significant interaction of age and brain damage on simple reaction time. Thus, while young brain-damaged subjects were approximately 24 msec slower than young control subjects, old brain-damaged subjects were approximately 81 msec slower than old control subjects.

A study by Miller (1970) suggested parallels between the effects on reaction time of brain damage and aging. Miller found that young brain-damaged subjects showed significantly greater slowing than age-matched controls on both simple and choice reaction-time performance. This deficit was attributed to a slowing in the decision-making phase of information processing, since the relative difference in performance levels between the two groups increased with the complexity of the task. A similar deficit in central processing has been suggested as the underlying mechanism for reduced function in old age (see Figure 21-3).

Reaction-time tasks have been found to be especially sensitive to both diffuse and focal brain damage in nearly all areas of the brain (Hicks & Birren, 1970; Light, 1978), and slowed response time is associated with age as well as with known brain dysfunction.

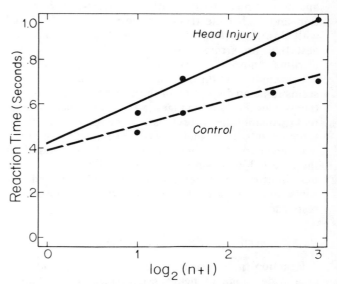

Figure 21-3. Differences in simple and choice reaction time in young adult subjects with head injuries in comparison with control subjects. The abcissa is given as the logarithm of the number of choices in the stimulus plus 1 (data from Miller, 1970).

The important role of simple reaction time as a reflection of overall cerebral status has also been demonstrated in a study on reaction time in unilateral cerebral disease (Benton & Joynt, 1958). Benton and Joynt showed that patients with cerebral lesions confined to a single hemisphere demonstrated slowing in the speed of reaction when both the ipsilateral and the contralateral hand were tested (see Figure 21-4). Apparently these focal lesions impair the general capacity of the organism to perform.

Although brain damage and age both may lead to decreased speed, they are not identical in effect. Ferris, Crook, Sathananthan, and Gershon (1976) found that disjunctive reaction time alone correctly distinguished the senile patients from the normal patients with 86% accuracy (see Figure 21-5). Both simple and disjunctive reaction times were slower in the senile patients, but the slowing in disjunctive reaction time was substantially greater. Thus, disjunctive reaction time appears to be a reliable index of disease-related mental decline.

Another view of the role of central processes in the behavioral slowing of brain-damaged subjects concerns the autonomic-somatic relations to reaction time proposed by Holloway and Parsons (1972). They found that nonpathological subjects had faster reaction times associated with greater heart rate deceleration and greater electrodermal responsivity during the preparatory interval prior to the reaction-time response. The brain-damaged group showed almost the opposite relation between reaction-time performance and autonomic activity—with later heart-rate deceleration and higher electrodermal responsivity associated with slower reaction time. Holloway and Parsons suggest that impairment of the central nervous system disrupts "normal" relationships between autonomic activity and reaction-time performance, although there seems to be no disruption of the underlying mechanisms themselves. Perhaps changes in the central nervous system (probably the cortex) disrupt the integration of autonomic activity in such a way that reactivity in brain-damaged persons becomes dissociated from demands of the external environment. Or such dissociated activity may interfere or compete with the brain-damaged person's ability to attend to or perform the appropriate response.

Parkinsonism, Depression, and Schizophrenia

Reaction-time measures are used as diagnostic tools in a wide range of neuropsychological testing situations. The following behavioral disorders are often characterized by a pronounced psychomotor slowing, which is thought to be influenced by central nervous system mechanisms.

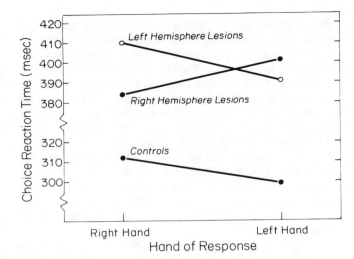

Figure 21-4. Choice reaction times of the right and left hands for control subjects and subjects with right- and with left-hemisphere brain damage (data from Benton & Joynt, 1958).

Parkinsonism. An important implication for understanding brain mechanisms involved in psychomotor speed is the relation of parkinsonism to aging. Parkinsonism is believed to be an age-related disease that displays dramatic defects in voluntary movement.

At the present time there are only contradictory results regarding the impairment of simple reaction-time performance in parkinsonism (Hicks & Birren, 1970). When the performance test requires a more complex response, however, there is little doubt that parkinsonians show a loss of speed, which suggests

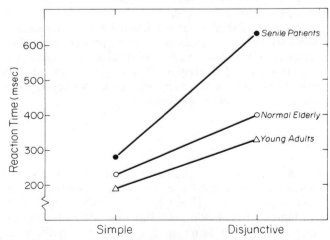

Figure 21-5. Differences in simple and choice reaction times for young and elderly subjects and patients classified as senile (data from Ferris, Crook, Sathananthan, & Gershon, 1976).

that this disorder is not simply "premature aging" with its concomitant general loss of speed (Hicks & Birren, 1970). Parkinsonians have been shown to perform less well than middle-aged, younger, and own-age matched controls on complex reaction-time tasks.

Research suggests that the subcortical structures associated with parkinsonism (e.g., the thalamus and basal ganglia) may be significantly involved in the activation and expression of the higher intellectual functions that are dependent on the integration of two or more sensorimotor modalities, contribution of cortical association areas, and the arousal system.

Depression. A slowing in response speed, or retardation of motor, perceptual, and cognitive functioning, is considered an important characteristic of depressive illness (Martin & Rees, 1966; Weckowicz, Nutter, Cruise, & Yonge, 1972). Weckowicz et al. proposed that the combined effects of age and depression on speed of performance of motor, perceptual, and cognitive tasks generally tend to be additive. Statistical analyses of his data yielded interaction effects, with depressive illness producing especially marked retardation in older subjects. Only the simple RT test, however, consistently differentiated the effect of depression from that of age, showing simple RT to be significantly longer in depressed subjects, regardless of age.

Schizophrenia. A substantial body of literature suggests that slowing of information processing may be a basic deficit in schizophrenia (Hemsley & Hawks, 1974; Slade, 1971). When responding at rates comparable to normal subjects, the schizophrenic patient appears to do so before the information is completely processed. This is supported by Hawks and Marshall (1971), who found that schizophrenics excluded the most irrelevant stimuli from consideration at any early stage in processing and that the responses they made were associated with the correct response and were not totally irrelevant to it.

Hemsley and Hawks (1974) tested two groups of schizophrenics, acute patients (mean age, 30 years) and chronic patients (mean age, 43 years). Experimental manipulation of response speed changed the number of errors made by both groups, with speeding resulting in more errors and slowing in fewer. When the effect of age and intelligence were removed statistically, the only remaining significant difference between the two schizophrenic groups was that chronic patients were slower than the acute patients on the digit-copying test.

Manic-Depressive Psychosis

Hemsley and Philips (1975) found that over a number of cycles in a single patient with manic-depressive psychosis, the frequency of slow RT responses increased with increasing depression, whereas during the manic episodes the number of slow responses was about the same as during the normal period. However, manic periods were characterized by an increased number of premature responses (i.e., responses made to the warning signal). The depressive phase of the illness appears to retard the mediating processes, while in the manic phase the patient's ability to inhibit responses is altered.

It appears, then, that old age, behavioral disorders, and brain damage may all have detrimental effects on psychomotor speed. The same mechanism in the central nervous system may underlie this slowing phenomenon in all three groups; indeed, behavioral evidence for a general speed factor that affects all areas of psychomotor performance in older persons shows up repeatedly in the literature (Birren, 1965; Birren et al., 1962).

Physical Fitness

Exercise, or activity level, has been manipulated in numerous studies designed to associate physical fitness with various psychological measures, including psychomotor speed. Botwinick and Thompson (1968) found that while response times of a group of older subjects were significantly slower than those of young athletes, they were not significantly slower than young men of the same age who were not athletes. This suggested that at least part of the slowness of older persons may be attributable to lack of physical fitness. However, a subsequent study by Botwinick and Storandt (1974a) found a correlation between amount of exercise and reaction time only in younger subjects, not in older subjects.

Barry, Steinmetz, Page, and Rodahl (1966) found that their elderly subjects (mean age 70 years) improved on some gross motor tasks and noncognitive psychological tasks after a 3-month exercise program. They attributed the changes to an altered physiological status, which in turn was thought to have influenced adaptation of some "neural regulatory mechanism" to a "higher level of functioning."

It has been proposed that exercise is associated with other psychological factors in various populations. Clement (1966) found that middle-aged habitual exercisers have faster reaction times than nonexercisers. Physical exercise has been shown not to affect certain cognitive tasks in normal older people (Barry et al.,

1966) but to improve cognitive performance in normal middle-aged persons (Powell & Pohndorf, 1971) and institutionalized geriatric patients (Powell, 1974). Other studies have shown some relation between physical fitness, as measured by activity level, and psychomotor performance in the aged (Ohlsson, 1976; Spirduso, 1975; Spirduso & Clifford, 1978). In these studies exercisers were compared with nonexercisers, and the "more fit" exercisers were found to have significantly faster reaction times than the nonexercisers.

Tredway (1978) used predicted maximum oxygen uptake (VO_2max) as a physical-fitness measure and found it to be significantly correlated with both reaction time and movement time in older persons; the higher the fitness level, the faster the reaction and movement times. These correlations were of a low magnitude, however, possibly owing to the small range of predicted VO_2max found in her homogeneous older sample.

Regarding the association between exercise and intellectual performance, de Vries (1970) has suggested that improvement in cognitive processes may result less from physical conditioning than from "central stimulation," that is, arousal of the central nervous system. Thus any increase in a subject's sensitivity and responsiveness would be a reflection of an increase in arousal. Psychomotor performance may be facilitated similarly, by heightening the subject's sensitivity and responsiveness.

The role that exercise may play in maintaining optimum cerebral physiology in older adults has yet to be studied in detail. Recent data show that mental activity results in increased regional blood flow; this suggests that oxygen and glucose requirements of cerebral tissues may be highly dynamic processes with occasions of transient ischemia that might temporarily embarrass mental functioning (Sokoloff, 1979). Exercise may, of course, alter the character of neural tissue itself. Retzlaff and Fontaine (1965) used forced exercise in old rats and found an increase in size of the spinal motor neurons. Still another pathway of influence may be by an adequate oxygen supply through respiration. This is suggested by the as-yet uninterpreted relations found in several studies between reaction time and forced expiratory capacity (Dirken, 1972; Heron & Chown, 1967). Surprisingly high correlations have been obtained between reaction time and respiratory function, which suggests that persons with large lung capacity may be more able to maintain a high level of oxygenation of the blood and circulation. Such a desirable combination of benefits could result from frequent periods of exercise. In any event, the prospect must be kept open that exercise may result in maintaining a high level of perfusion of the brain.

Implications and Interpretations of the Slowing of Behavior With Age

Behavioral Implications

There are three sets of implications of slowness of behavior: its causes, organization, and consequences. Behavior can be both a cause and an effect. It seems necessary, then, to discuss both the causes of slowness and the consequences of slowness of behavior. In either event, the organization of the behavioral slowing is of particular importance since it determines the ubiquity and manner of this phenomenon's manifestation.

Behavioral causes of slowing with age. If the slowness were dependent on specific cortical structures, one might expect to find some behaviors fast and others slow. For example, one might speak slowly but move quickly if a threatening object appeared; however, such is not the case, for the slowness of aging is not punctate but diffuse. One may ask what kind of a behavioral process could result in a generalized slowing. Botwinick (1978) has reviewed the evidence on cautiousness, which could potentially produce such a result. Cautiousness is a disinclination to respond quickly because of the importance attached to making a mistake. Botwinick concluded,

> While there is controversy whether or not the trade-off of speed for accuracy, and the omission error for the commission error, is volitional in nature, there is little doubt that older people do not tend to risk being wrong for the sake of being right or fast. (1978, p. 125)

One might assume that with advancing age, cautiousness generalizes across behaviors because of the learned consequences of responding quickly and wrongly, thus resulting in a "habit" of being slow. While some human behavior may be explained on this basis, it can hardly explain the slowness of behavior observed in other mammals (e.g., rats) living in artificial environments (Birren, 1955).

Transient mental sets may also contribute to slowness. In humans, the older adult tends to depend more on group opinion on which to base responses (Klein, 1972). However, a set that appears as a form of cautiousness can be reversed if the subjects are given ego-reinforcing information about their behavior (Klein & Birren, 1973). Other aspects of set in relation to aging have been discussed by Brinley (1965). Some of the set phenomena of aging appear reversible, while others seem more a necessary consequence of behavioral capacities. There remains a continuing discussion of the extent to which the older subject must be slow, wants to be slow, or has a set to be slow.

Organization of behavioral slowing. While cautiousness on a learned or set basis is seen as a partial explanation of the slowing of behavior with age, a large part of the slowing with age may be due to other causes. For example, repeated practice in swimming did not markedly improve the speed of swimming in older rats, though it did reduce their susceptibility to fatigue (Kary & Birren, 1958). Attempts have been made to improve reaction time in humans by giving mild electric shocks for slow responses (Botwinick, Brinley, & Robbin, 1959), with the result that both young and old subjects improve equally. These data were gathered using irregular anticipation intervals for the stimulus. When regular anticipation intervals were used, the age difference became smaller. Apparently, if the subjects can anticipate when the stimulus is to be given, older subjects are in a relatively better position to respond quickly. One might infer that the greater relative improvement of response speed in the older subject under regular stimulus-presentation conditions may involve attention rather than cautiousness.

In vigilance studies, old subjects seem to attend and perform like young subjects when the rate of information presentation is slow. Talland (1966) found that under fast conditions of presentation, the capacity to attend to a signal presented randomly in a series falls off in older subjects. He believed that the older subjects were slower both in scanning incoming signals and in deciding whether a particular signal matched the model. Such matters raise the paradoxical question of whether the low attention gives rise to the slowness or the slowness results in the lower attention.

Welford (1977), applying the concept of *neural noise* to aging, postulates that, if the strength of a signal is diminished relative to background noise, the older organism must take longer to perceive information and to respond appropriately. The difficulty with that explanation is less at the behavioral level, where it may have some heuristic value, than at the neurobiological level, since there is as yet no obvious or identifiable neural locus or mechanism that would increase the noise level of the older central nervous system.

It may be unreasonable to expect that there is *only one* form of slowing with advancing age. However, there is good reason to pursue the goal of identifying a common mechanism of neurobiological slowness observed at the behavioral level. To this core process may be added many specific forms of slowness that may have a wide range of causes. Perhaps one should envisage a primary ontogenetic slowing in a subcortical structure that can be influenced by additional processes, such as learned cautiousness, or localized tissue damage in a wide range of structures.

Consequences of behavioral slowing. Slowness affects a person's chances of survival when critical evasive action must be taken quickly, for example, when faced with a sudden, unanticipated environmental demand. However, at another level, an important theoretical implication of slowness is that the underlying mechanism(s) may limit complex thinking. This view reverses an often-held interpretation of slowing as a compensation for altered cognition, that is, one is slow because one's cognitive processes are changed. In contrast, the view held here is that cognition changes because the mediating processes are slow. Thus, slowness becomes an important limiting variable for a wide range of performance. If it takes too long to complete a task, one may not only forget the elements one is trying to integrate or to reason about but one may also forget the goal of the task itself.

Another implication of behavioral slowing is that since it may reflect vital physiological conditions of the organism, it can be used as an indicator of the integrity of the nervous system. Thus it seems appropriate to explore further the neurobiological substrate upon which the speed of behavioral events depends.

Neurobiological Implications

The understanding and conceptualization of increasing behavioral slowness with age has been paced by advances in neurobiology. Three areas of investigation bear on the slowing of behavior: neurobiology of motor output, micromorphology of discrete nuclei, and diffuse neuroendocrinology.

The data on reflex times do not reveal large age differences. Indeed, one study found no age difference in the patellar reflex (Clarkson, 1978), and the investigator concluded that perhaps the patellar stretch-reflex mechanism and its facilitation was unaffected by age and physical activity. In 1959 Magladery concluded that slowing with age became more impressive, the higher in the nervous system one studied. While there are are undoubtedly some alterations in the speed of peripheral effector and sensory afferent systems with age, they are not large in comparison to changes in speed of behavior mediated by the brain (Weiss, 1959).

Since the turn of the century, reports have cited a reduction with age of Purkinje cells in the cerebellum for humans (Ellis, 1920). Others have confirmed this for humans and other animals (Bondareff, 1959). Thus a contributor to the slowing of behavioral responses may well be the loss of cells in the extrapyramidal, or "fast," motor system. However, the behavioral evidence indicates that slowness is not restricted to the programming and executing of the motor response.

Neuron counts in different brain areas do not suggest uniform patterns of reduction with age. However, selective losses of neurons in nuclei that have diffuse connections could have important implications. Brody

(1976) has reported reduced cell counts in the locus ceruleus, a nucleus that radiates norepinephrine-secreting axons to the cerebrum and the cerebellum. Given the role of the ascending reticular system in enhancing or suppressing the excitability of many neurons, it is in a vital position to modulate responses to stimuli and contribute to the slowness of old age.

One of the more significant studies with implications for behavior is a report by Landfield and Lynch (1977) in which stimulation of hippocampal cells in brain slices showed that the older rat brain had less post-tetanic potentiation than the young rat brain. Ranking animals by the amount of synaptic potentiation (by a 9-Hz stimulus) and by retention of a two-choice avoidance response, Landfield and Lynch found a high degree of correlation ($r = .85$). The reduction in synaptic potentiation may be a result of the reduced synapses observed by Bondareff (1979). It begins to look as if morphological change can be associated with a slowness of neural events and with memory changes.

Electron microscope studies have shown a reduction of synapses in humans (Cragg, 1975). Bondareff and Geinisman (1976) reports a loss of synapses of about 27% per unit area in the senescent rat, with no change in tissue volume. Bondareff (1979) believes that it is unlikely that this reduction of synapses is a result of loss of neurons. Since the number of synapses per unit length of dendrite seems reduced, the loss of synapses is apparently not a consequence of earlier dendrite loss. Thus the older neuron need not be lost in order to influence function; it may show a significant reduction in its connections with other cells. A reduction of the neuronal dendritic tree with age seems well established for humans (Scheibel, Lindsay, Tomiyasu, & Scheibel, 1975, 1976) and rodents (Feldman & Dowd, 1975). It appears that a reduction in neuronal connectivity is a likely candidate for a general mechanism of slowing.

Neurotransmitter reductions in the brain may be expected to accompany the reduction with age in synaptic density, and such reductions have been reported. Reductions in dopamine, norepinephrine, and serotonin have been reported for senescent mouse brain (Samorajski, Friede, & Ordy, 1971). Gamma-aminobutyric acid has been found to be higher in senescent than in young rodents (Davis & Himwich, 1975). In addition, lower levels of acetylcholinesterase were found in the brains of senescent rats, which thus suggests a decrease in the activity of acetylcholine with age. One cannot say which comes first with age—an insufficiency of neurotransmitters, a loss of presynaptic vesicles, or a change in the level of neurophysiological activity resulting from stimulation.

A reduced axoplasmic transport in the fibers of senescent rats was suggested by Bondareff (1979).

Such reduction would impair the maintenance of distal synapses and reflect a reduction in axoplasmic transport of proteins from the cell body. Changes in presynaptic and postsynaptic membrane proteins could result, along with insufficient transmitter substances. Bennett and Bondareff (1977) have shown that vestibular nuclei (lateral) neurons dissected from old rats had a different binding pattern than those from young rats.

Evidence of other cerebral metabolic changes with age can be seen in the work of Patel (1977). He reported in vitro studies of senescent rat brain in which the oxidation of labeled glucose declined, as did 3-hydroxybutyrate and ketone bodies.

A more specific change with age was observed by Finch (1973) in a single type of cell, the dopaminergic cell. He reported a reduction in dopamine levels in old mice of 25% in the striatum, 35% in the median eminence, and 45% in the posterior pituitary. These fibers have a function in the regulation of biological vigor.

Along with other evidence about the nature of the changes in the nervous system with age, data on oxygen consumption and glucose utilization must be considered. Sokoloff (1979) presents evidence that elderly patients with chronic brain syndrome and psychosis show significantly lowered cerebral blood flow and cerebral metabolic rate. Also, studies of glucose utilization in young and middle-aged rats have indicated significant differences in regional metabolic activity. Notable is the reduction with age in glucose utilization in the sensory areas of the cortex and in the basal ganglia. Hicks and Birren (1970) implicated the basal ganglia in the slowing of behavior with age. Sokoloff (1979) found no difference with age in glucose utilization by the hippocampus, an area important to memory functions and one previously described in this review as showing functional changes with age.

Behavioral and Physiological Interactions in Aging

To a developmental psychologist, an ultimate criterion of behavioral effectiveness is survival. Behavioral speed may prove to be a predictor of longevity. Two studies have generated provocative data that suggest the efficacy of this use of speed of behavior. Jalavisto and her associates tested 130 women aged 44 to 93 (Jalavisto, Lindquist, & Makkonen, 1964) and used familial longevity as a variable to separate tests that were correlated with biological vigor from tests that were not. Among her behavioral and physiological measures was reaction time, which together with the sensory and intellectual tests showed a high correlation with chronological age. Most of the variance in her measurements was associated with the "aging factor," which in this study was a cluster of sensory, motor, and cognitive processes, reaction time, and vital capacity of the lungs. Why vital capacity should show a correlation with behavioral measures is puzzling. The investigators offered two alternatives: (1) that a large vital capacity might be a consequence of motivation and strong muscular exertion, and (2) that a low vital capacity might indicate a relative hypoxia.

In startlingly similar findings, Heron and Chown (1967) reported a factor loading of .73 for 1-second forced expiratory volume on the "aging factor," and Dirken (1972) reported .75. Heron and Chown's results were based on 540 men and women (about 50 men and 40 women in each decade from age 20 to the 70s). Dirken tested 316 male industrial workers, 8 for each year of age between 30 and 70 years. Dirken selected eight measures from a total of 150 to use as an index of functional age. These measurements, which correlated .87 with chronological age, included auditory pitch ceiling, figure comprehension, reaction time, multiple choice, accuracy in semantic categorization, maximum breathing frequency, maximum systolic tension, aerobic capacity, and forced expiratory volume. The close associations between age, reaction time, and respiratory functions suggest an important set of relations.

Conclusion

This chapter has reviewed evidence of a decline in speed of behavior with age and has presented preliminary arguments to suggest that this loss in speed is a reflection of a general mediating process in the central nervous system. This process appears to lead to a general slowing in speed of behavior, which in turn is reflected across a number of specific behaviors. While speed of behavior may appear to be a limited behavioral phenomenon, this facet of behavior appears to have consequences for a wide range of other behaviors and is therefore of general interest.

Since one property of the slowing appears to be a pervasive influence on all events mediated by the nervous system, it is well to expect neural correlates of the behavior either to be diffuse or else to reflect the action of specific nuclei so placed that they influence cortical, cerebellar, and brainstem functions simultaneously.

Reduction in synaptic density with age appears to come close to a reliably observed change that would slow the transmission of neurophysiological excitation. Should this reduction in synapses not be as widespread

as is now believed, there remains the prospect that it can influence several key areas, for example, the dentate gyrus of the hippocampus, which is associated with learning and memory.

Still another key set of nuclei are those that make up the reticular system. The reduction in cells in the human locus ceruleus reported with age has potentially great significance for behavior. As part of the ascending reticular system, the locus ceruleus influences the level of excitation of the cerebellum, cerebrum, and limbic system. Such a nucleus could play a central role in the slowing of behavior with age.

One should also pursue the alternative view that the structural changes are adaptive to the activity level of the nervous system. With age, not only may function follow structure but structure may follow function. Some of what now appears as a pattern of aging could in fact reflect diminished physical activity of the older organism. There may, of course, be some limit beyond which structural change following functional decline is no longer reversible. Attempts should be made to modify the slowness of aging by means of psychological stimulation, exercise, drugs, hormones, and nutrients.

Slowness offers an information bridge between the behavioral and biological sciences as they delve into phenomena of aging. However, since speed of behavior has been shown to be a function of the level of biological fitness of the individual—both general physical fitness as well as the presence or absence of pathology—speed of behavior may be of great practical use in determining the level of an individual's biological functioning.

This approach may be of use in investigating late-life ontogenetic changes, in that specific limiting behavioral functions may be reflected across many behaviors in older organisms. Greater theoretical understanding of the process of ontogenetic change in late life should be vigorously pursued. A good criterion of such theories might be their ability to predict individual survival.

REFERENCES

Anders, T. R., & Fozard, J. L. Effects of age upon retrieval from primary and secondary memory. *Developmental Psychology*, 1973, 9, 411–415.

Anders, T. R., Fozard, J. L., & Lillyquist, T. D. Effects of age upon retrieval from short-term memory. *Developmental Psychology*, 1972, 6, 214–217.

Atkinson, R. C., & Shiffrin, R. M. The control of short-term memory. *Scientific American*, 1971, 224, 82–90.

Averbach, E., & Coriell, H. S. Short-term memory in vision. *Bell Systems Technical Journal*, 1961, 40, 309–328.

Baltes, P. B., & Labouvie, G. V. Adult development of intellectual performance: Description, explanation, modification. In C. Eisdorfer & M. P. Lawton (Eds.), *The psychology of adult development and aging*. Washington, D.C.: American Psychological Association, 1973.

Baltes, P. B., & Schaie, K. W. On the plasticity of intelligence in adulthood and old age: Where Horn and Donaldson fail. *American Psychologist*, 1976, *31*, 720–725.

Barry, A. J., Steinmetz, J. R., Page, H. F., & Rodahl, K. The effects of physical conditioning on older individuals. II. Motor performance and cognitive function. *Journal of Gerontology*, 1966, *21*, 192–199.

Bennett, K. D., & Bondareff, W. Age-related differences in binding of Conconavalin A to plasma membranes of isolated neurons. *American Journal of Anatomy*, 1977, *150*, 175–184.

Benton, A. L. Interactive effects of age and brain disease on reaction time. *Archives of Neurology*, 1977, *34*, 369–370.

Benton, A. L., & Joynt, R. J. Reaction time in unilateral cerebral disease. *Confinia Neurologica*, 1958, *19*, 247–256.

Birren, J. E. Age differences in startle reaction time of the rat to noise and electric shock. *Journal of Gerontology*, 1955, *10*, 437–440.

Birren, J. E. Age changes in speed of behavior: Its central nature and physiological correlates. In, A. T. Welford & J. E. Birren, (Eds.), *Behavior, aging and the nervous system*. Springfield, Ill.: Charles C Thomas, 1965.

Birren, J. E. Translations in gerontology—from lab to life. Psychophysiology and speed of response. *American Psychologist*, 1974, *29*, 808–815.

Birren, J. E., & Botwinick, J. Age differences in finger, jaw, and foot reaction time to auditory stimuli. *Journal of Gerontology*, 1955, *10*, 429–432.

Birren, J. E., Riegel, K. F., & Morrison, D. F. Age differences in response speed as a function of controlled variations of stimulus conditions: Evidence of a general speed factor. *Gerontologia*, 1962, *6*, 1–18.

Birren, J. E., & Schaie, K. W. (Eds.). *Handbook of the psychology of aging*. New York: Van Nostrand Reinhold, 1977.

Birren, J. E., & Wall, P. D. Age changes in conduction velocity, refractory period, number of fibers, connective tissue space and blood vessels in sciatic nerve of rats. *Journal of Comparative Neurology*, 1956, *104*, 1–16.

Bondareff, W. Morphology of the aging nervous system. *In* J. E. Birren (Ed.), *Handbook of aging and the individual*. Chicago: University of Chicago Press, 1959.

Bondareff, W., & Geinisman, Y. Loss of synapses in the dentate gyrus of the senescent rat. *American Journal of Anatomy*, 1976, *145*, 129–136.

Bondareff, W. Synaptic atrophy in the senescent hippocampus. *Mechanisms of Aging and Development*, 1979, *9*, 163–171.

Botwinick, J. *Cognitive processes in maturity and old age*. New York: Springer, 1967.

Botwinick, J. Intellectual abilities. In J. E. Birren & K. W. Schaie (Eds.), *Handbook of the psychology of aging*. New York: Van Nostrand Reinhold, 1977.

Botwinick, J. *Aging and behavior*. New York: Springer, 1978.

Botwinick, J., Brinley, J. F., & Robbin, J. S. Modulation of speed of response with age. *Journal of Genetic Psychology*, 1959, *95*, 137–144.

Botwinick, J., & Storandt, M. Cardiovascular status, depressive affect, and other factors in reaction time. *Journal of Gerontology*, 1974, *29*, 543–548. (a)

Botwinick, J., & Storandt, M. *Memory, related functions and age*. Springfield, Ill.: Charles C Thomas, 1974. (b)

Botwinick, J., & Thompson, L. W. Age differences in reaction time: An artifact? *Gerontologist*, 1968, *8*, 25–28.

Brinley, J. F. Cognitive sets and accuracy of performance in the elderly. In A. T. Welford & J. E. Birren (Eds.), *Behavior, aging, and the nervous system*. Springfield, Ill.: Charles C Thomas, 1965.

Brody, H. An examination of cerebral cortex and brainstem aging. In R. D. Terry & S. Gershon (Eds.), *Neurobiology of aging*. New York: Raven Press, 1976.

Bruhn, P., & Parsons, O. A. Reaction time variability in epileptic and brain damaged patients. *Cortex*, 1977, *13*, 373–384.

Clarkson, P. M. The relationship of age and level of activity with the fractionated components of patellar reflex time. *Journal of Gerontology*, 1978, *33*, 650–656.

Clement, F. Effect of physical activity on the maintenance of intellectual capacities. *Gerontologist*, 1966, *6*, 91–92; 126.

Cliff, N. Orthogonal rotation of congruence. *Psychometrika*, 1966, *31*, 33–42.

Cragg, B. G. The density of synapses and neurons in normal, mentally defective and aging human brains. *Brain*, 1975, *98*, 81–90.

Craik, F. I. M. Age differences in human memory. In J. E. Birren & K. W. Schaie (Eds.), *Handbook of the psychology of aging*. New York: Van Nostrand Reinhold, 1977.

Cunningham, W. R. *Age changes in the factor structure of human abilities*. Unpublished doctoral dissertation, University of Southern California, 1974.

Cunningham, W. R., & Birren, J. E. Age changes in human abilities: A 28-year longitudinal study. *Developmental Psychology*, 1976, *12*, 81–82.

Davis, J. M., & Himwich, W. A. Neurochemistry of the developing and aging mammalian brain. In J. M. Ordy & K. R. Brizzee (Eds.), *Neurobiology of aging*. New York: Plenum Press, 1975.

de Vries, H. A. Physiological effects of an exercise training regimen upon men aged 52 to 88. *Journal of Gerontology*, 1970, *25*, 325–336.

Dirken, J. M. (Ed.). *Functional age of industrial workers*. Groningen: Wolters-Nordhoff, 1972.

Ellis, R. S. Norms for some structural changes in the human cerebellum from birth to old age. *Journal of Comparative Neurology*, 1920, *32*, 1–34.

Eriksen, C. W., Hamlin, R. M., & Daye, C. Aging adults and rate of memory scan. *Bulletin of the Psychonomic Society*, 1973, *1*, 259–260.

Feldman, M. L., & Dowd, C. Loss of dendritic spines in aging cerebral cortex. *Anatomy and Embryology*, 1975, *148*, 279–301.

Ferris, S., Crook, T., Sathananthan, G., & Gershon, S. Reaction time as a diagnostic measure in senility. *Journal of the American Geriatrics Society*, 1976, *24*, 529–533.

Finch, C. Catecholamine metabolism in the brains of aging mice. *Brain Research*, 1973, *52*, 261–276.

Hawks, D. V., & Marshall, W. L. A parsimonious theory of overinclusive thinking and retardation in schizophrenia. *British Journal of Medical Psychology*, 1971, *44*, 75–83.

Hemsley, D. R., & Hawks, D. V. Speed of response and associative errors in schizophrenia. *British Journal of Social and Clinical Psychology*, 1974, *13*, 293–303.

Hemsley, D. R., & Philips, H. C. Models of mania: An individual case study. *British Journal of Psychiatry*, 1975, *127*, 78–85.

Heron, A., & Chown, S. *Age and function*. London: J. & A. Churchill, 1967.

Hertzog, C. K., Williams, M. V., & Walsh, D. A. The effect of practice on age differences in central perceptual processing. *Journal of Gerontology*, 1976, *31*, 428–433.

Hicks, L. H., & Birren, J. E. Aging, brain damage, and psychomotor slowing. *Psychological Bulletin*, 1970, *74*, 377–396.

Holloway, F. A., & Parsons, O. A. Physiological concomitants of reaction time performance in normal and brain-damaged subjects. *Psychophysiology*, 1972, *9*, 189–198.

Horn, J. L. Organization of data on life-span development of human abilities. In L. R. Goulet & P. B. Baltes (Eds.), *Life-span developmental psychology: Research and theory*. New York: Academic Press, 1970.

Jalavisto, E., Lindquist, C., & Makkonen, T. Assessment of biological age. III: Mental and neural factors in longevity. *Annales Academiae Scientiarum Fennicae*, 1964, *106*, 3–20.

Jones, H. E. Intelligence and problem solving. In J. E. Birren (Ed.), *Handbook of aging and the individual*. Chicago: University of Chicago Press, 1959.

Jöreskog, K. G. Simultaneous factor analysis in several populations. *Psychometrika*, 1971, *36*, 409–426.

Kay, H., & Birren, J. E. Swimming speed of the albino rat: Fatigue, practice, and drug effects on age and sex differences. *Journal of Gerontology*, 1958, *13*, 378–385.

King, H. E. Psychomotor changes with age, psychopathology and brain damage. In A. T. Welford & J. E. Birren (Eds.), *Behavior, aging, and the nervous system*. Springfield, Ill.: Charles C Thomas, 1965.

Klein, R. L. Age, sex and task difficulty as predictors of social conformity. *Journal of Gerontology*, 1972, *27*, 229–236.

Klein, R. L., & Birren, J. E. Age, perceived self-competence and conformity. *Proceedings of the 81st Annual Convention of the American Psychological Association*, 1973, pp. 779–780. (Abstract)

Kline, D. W., & Birren, J. E. Age differences in backward dichoptic masking. *Experimental Aging Research*, 1975, *1*, 17–25.

Kline, D. W., & Szafran, J. Age differences in backward visual masking. *Journal of Gerontology*, 1975, *30*, 307–311.

Koga, Y., & Morant, G. M. On the degree of association between reaction times in the case of different senses. *Biometrika*, 1923, *15*, 346–372.

Kral, V. A. Localized cerebral ischemia, its incidence in senile and arteriosclerotic psychosis. In E. Simonson & T. H. McGavack (Eds.), *Cerebral ischemia*. Springfield, Ill.: Charles C Thomas, 1964.

Lagergren, K. Effect of exogenous changes in heart rate upon mental performance in patients treated with artificial pacemakers for complete heart block. *British Heart Journal*, 1974, *36*, 1126.

Lagergren, K., & Levander, S. Effects of changes in heart rate in different body positions upon critical flicker fusion threshold and reaction time performance in patients with artificial pacemakers. *Journal of Psychiatric Research*, 1975, *12*, 247.

Landfield, P. W., and Lynch, G. Impaired monosynaptic potentiation in *in vitro* hippocampal slices from aged, memory deficient rats. *Journal of Gerontology*, 1977, *32*, 523–533.

Light, K. C. Slowing of response time in young and middle-aged hypertensive patients. *Experimental Aging Research*, 1975, *1*, 209–227.

Light, K. C. Effects of mild cardiovascular and cerebrovascular disorders on serial reaction time performance. *Experimental Aging Research*, 1978, *4*, 3–22.

Magladery, J. W. Neurophysiology of aging. In J. E. Birren (Ed.), *Handbook of aging and the individual*. Chicago: University of Chicago Press, 1959.

Martin, I., & Rees, L. Reaction times and somatic reactivity in depressed patients. *Journal of Psychosomatic Research*, 1966, *9*, 375–382.

McGraw, B., & Jöreskog, K. G. Factorial invariance of ability measures in groups differing in intelligence and socioeconomic status. *British Journal of Mathematical and Statistical Psychology*, 1971, *24*, 154–168.

Miller, E. Simple and choice reaction time following severe head injury. *Cortex*, 1970, *6*, 121–127.

Neisser, U. *Cognitive psychology*. New York: Appleton-Century-Crofts, 1967.

Ohlsson, M. *Information processing related to physical fitness in elderly people* (Rep. No. 71). Stockholm: University of Stockholm, Institute of Applied Psychology, 1976.

Owens, W. A. Age and mental abilities: A longitudinal study. *Genetic Psychology Monographs*, 1953, *48*, 3–54.

Owens, W. A. Age and mental ability: A second follow-up. *Journal of Educational Psychology*, 1966, *57*, 311–325.

Patel, M. S. Age-dependent changes in the oxidative metabolism in rat brain. *Journal of Gerontology*, 1977, *32*, 643–646.

Powell, R. R. Psychological effects of exercise therapy upon institutionalized geriatric mental patients. *Journal of Gerontology*, 1974, *29*, 157–161.

Powell, R. R., & Pohndorf, R. H. Comparison of adult exercisers and nonexercisers on fluid intelligence and selected physiological variables. *Research Quarterly*, 1971, *23*, 70–71.

Quetelet, M. A. *Sur l'homme et le développement de ses*

facultés (2 vols.). Paris: Bachelier, Imprimeyr-Libraire, 1835.

Reitan, R. M. Intellectual and affective changes in essential hypertension. *American Journal of Psychiatry*, 1954, *110*, 817–824.

Retzlaff, E., & Fontaine, J. Functional and structural changes in motor neurons with age. In A. T. Welford & J. E. Birren (Eds.), *Behavior, aging and the nervous system*. Springfield, Ill.: Charles C Thomas, 1965.

Samorajski, T., Friede, R. L., & Ordy, J. M. Changes in behavior, brain, and neuroendocrine chemistry with age and stress in C57B1/10 male mice. *Journal of Gerontology*, 1971, *26*, 168–175.

Schaie, K. W., Labouvie, G. F., & Buech, B. U. Generational and cohort-specific differences in adult cognitive functioning: A fourteen-year study of independent samples. *Developmental Psychology*, 1973, *9*, 151–166.

Schaie, K. W., & Labouvie-Vief, G. Generational versus ontogenetic components of change in adult cognitive behavior: A fourteen-year cross-sequential study. *Developmental Psychology*, 1974, *10*, 305–320.

Schaie, K. W., & Parham, I. A. Cohort-sequential analysis of adult intellectual development. *Developmental Psychology*, 1977, *13*, 649–653.

Schaie, K. W., & Strother, C. R. A cross-sequential study of age changes in cognitive behavior. *Psychological Bulletin*, 1968, *70*, 671–680.

Scheibel, M. E., Lindsay, R. D., Tomiyasu, U., & Scheibel, A. B. Progressive dendritic changes in aging human cortex. *Experimental Neurology*, 1975, *47*, 392–403.

Scheibel, M. E., Lindsay, R. D., Tomiyasu, U., & Scheibel, A. B. Progressive dendritic changes in the aging human limbic system. *Experimental Neurology*, 1976, *53*, 420–430.

Simonson, E. Cerebral ischemia: Introduction. In E. Simonson & T. H. McGavack (Eds.), *Cerebral ischemia*, Springfield, Ill.: Charles C Thomas, 1964.

Simonson, E., & McGavack, T. H. *Cerebral ischemia*. Springfield, Ill.: Charles C Thomas, 1964.

Slade, P. D. Rate of information processing in a schizophrenic and a control group: The effect of increasing task complexity. *British Journal of Social and Clinical Psychology*, 1971, *10*, 152–159.

Sokoloff, L. Effects of normal aging on cerebral circulation and energy metabolism. In F. Hoffmeister & C. Müller (Eds.), *Brain function in old age: Evolution of changes and disorders*. New York: Springer-Verlag, 1979.

Sperling, G. A model for visual memory tasks. *Human Factors*, 1963, *18*, 275–278.

Spieth, W. Slowness of task performance and cardiovascular diseases. In A. T. Welford & J. E. Birren (Eds.), *Behavior, aging, and the nervous system*. Springfield, Ill.: Charles C Thomas, 1965.

Spirduso, W. W. Reaction and movement time as a function of age and physical activity level. *Journal of Gerontology*, 1975, *30*, 435–440.

Spirduso, W. W., & Clifford, P. Replication of age and physical activity effects on reaction and movement time. *Journal of Gerontology*, 1978, *33*, 26–30.

Sternberg, S. High-speed scanning in human memory. *Science*, 1966, *153*, 652–654.

Talland, G. A. Initiation of response, and reaction time in aging, and with brain damage. In A. T. Welford & J. E. Birren (Eds.), *Behavior, aging, and the nervous system*. Springfield, Ill.: Charles C Thomas, 1965.

Talland, G. A. Visual signal detection as function of age, input rate and signal frequency. *Journal of Psychology*, 1966, *63*, 105–115.

Tredway, V. *Mood effects of exercise programs for older adults*. Unpublished doctoral dissertation, University of Southern California, 1978.

Turvey, M. T. On peripheral and central processes in vision: Inferences from an information-processing analysis on masking with pattern stimuli. *Psychological Review*, 1973, *80*, 1–52.

Walsh, D. A. Age differences in central perceptual processing: A dichoptic backward masking investigation. *Journal of Gerontology*, 1976, *31*, 181–188.

Walsh, D. A., & Thompson, L. W. Age differences in visual sensory memory. *Journal of Gerontology*, 1978, *33*, 383–387.

Walsh, D. A., Till, R. E., & Williams, M. V. Age differences in peripheral perceptual processing: A monotonic backward masking investigation. *Journal of Experimental Psychology: Human Perception and Performance*, 1978, *4*, 232–243.

Walsh, D. A., Williams, M. V., & Hertzog, C. K. Age-related differences in two stages of central perceptual processes: The effects of short duration targets and criterion differences. *Journal of Gerontology*, 1979, *34*, 234–241.

Wechsler, D. *The measurement of adult intelligence*. Baltimore: Williams & Wilkins, 1939.

Weckowicz, T. E., Nutter, R. W., Cruise, D. G., & Yonge, K. A. Speed in test performance in relation to depressive illness and age. *Journal of the Canadian Psychiatric Association*, 1972, *17*, 241–250.

Weiss, A. D. Sensory functions. In J. E. Birren, (ed.), *Handbook of aging and the individual*. Chicago: University of Chicago Press, 1959.

Welford, A. T. Motor performance. In J. E. Birren & K W. Schaie (Eds.), *Handbook of the psychology of aging*. New York: Van Nostrand Reinhold, 1977.

Welsandt, R. F., Zupnick, J. J., & Meyer, P. A. Age effects in backward visual masking (Crawford paradigm). *Journal of Experimental Child Psychology*, 1973, *15*, 454–461.

Williams, M. V. *Age differences in the speed of perceptual processes: Comparison of three centrally acting masks*. Unpublished doctoral dissertation, University of Southern California, 1978.

J. A. Stern, P. J. Oster, and K. Newport

CHAPTER

22

Reaction Time Measures, Hemispheric Specialization, and Age

Decision and transit time components of reaction time were abstracted from left and right index-finger responses recorded as 240 participants (whose ages ranged from 7 to 79 years) performed nonverbal, visual detection tasks or a visual detection task conducive to verbal processing as well. For adults only, cerebral asymmetry effects were demonstrated. Faster left-hand decision time, and by inference more efficient right-hemisphere processing, was found for the nonverbal, visual detection tasks but not for the visual detection task conducive to verbal processing. The amount by which adults' left-hand decision times were shorter than their right-hand decision times in the nonverbal tasks did not change with age. This result places limitations on the generalization that the aging process has a more detrimental effect on nonverbal and presumably right-hemisphere processing than on verbal, sequential, and presumably left-hemisphere processing. Evaluation of transit time revealed significant age-dependent effects. While this result contradicts much of the literature, different findings may be a function of the tasks used. If tasks involve large-amplitude motor responses, there may be no differences as a function of aging, while if tasks, like those used here, involve small-amplitude precision movements of fingers, differences may emerge.

> An abundance of data may be worth less than even an indifferent theory but, at least, it can guard from premature theorizing. (Talland, 1965, p. 556)

The history of studies dealing with the effect of aging on response speed have gone through a number of transformations. The earliest research dating back to the 1800s suggested that age-related slowing was principally attributable to peripheral sensorimotor phenomena. The current era of research has demonstrated that the central nervous system (CNS) is the major contributor to response slowing associated with aging. Given the current interest in functional specialization of the two cerebral hemispheres, and the concern with identifying functions attributable to the nondominant, right hemisphere, a new era in reaction time (RT) studies in aging will begin to develop. Can RT studies be used to evaluate changes in hemispheric specialization during development? We believe they can, and we will present some data in support of this notion. This chapter is divided into four sections: first, the study of hemispheric differences using RT paradigms; second, the experimental procedure; third, the results and their implications; and finally, an attempt to speculate on viable areas of research in the evaluation of hemispheric differences and aging.

Hemispheric Specialization

The last two decades have produced cumulative evidence for functional lateralization of the cerebral hemispheres. The right hemisphere appears to be specialized for holistic, Gestalt processing and the left hemisphere for analytic or sequential processing, at least for right handed subjects (Dimond & Beaumont, 1974; Harnad, Doty, Goldstein, Jaynes, & Krauthamer, 1977; Levy, 1969; Swisher & Hirsh, 1972). This characterization of differences in hemi-

This research was supported in part by National Institute on Aging Research Grant 5 PO1 AG00535-03.

spheric function is superior to the verbal–nonverbal dichotomy springing from earlier literature, in which an isomorphism between verbal and nonverbal stimuli and the type of internal processing evoked was implicitly assumed. It also marks a change in emphasis from stimulus characteristics to task demands. However, for the sake of maintaining thematic clarity throughout the review and results sections of this presentation, we use the labels *verbal* and *nonverbal* to refer to the type of *processing* most efficiently carried out by the left and right hemispheres, respectively. We emphasize *efficiency* of hemispheric function because we are not suggesting that one hemisphere is silent during the performance of a given task or that a given task can be solved by only one hemisphere. What is suggested is that certain functions are performed more efficiently by one hemisphere and that most of us use similar strategies in solving relatively simple problems.

The major noninvasive techniques for determining hemispheric utilization in humans have included channeling stimulus information to selected visual and auditory pathways and studying variables such as detection threshold, as well as detection and perceptual accuracy (Kimura, 1973); recording eye and head turning that occur in response to questions involving thought (Kinsbourne, 1973); studying patients with brain damage or patients who have undergone commissurotomy (Sperry, 1974); and recording electrophysiological responses from contralateral sites on the skin surface. Investigators have also examined covariation between reaction time and measures abstracted from electroencephalographic (EEG) recordings to assess brain–behavior relations (Marsh, 1975).

Reaction Time in Measurement of Hemispheric Specialization

Efficiency of hemispheric function has increasingly come to be measured in terms of reaction time because it is sensitive to cerebral laterality effects even when response accuracy reveals no differences (Springer, 1977, pp. 329–330). As the literature on RT and cerebral laterality is voluminous, we have restricted ourselves to an illustrative review of studies that used visual inputs and manual responses and have emphasized issues particularly pertinent to the experimental results presented in this chapter.

The use of RT to assess relative efficiency in hemispheric processing capitalizes on the anatomy of the sensory and motor pathways. The nasal hemiretina of each eye projects to the contralateral hemisphere, and the temporal hemiretina to the ipsilateral hemi-

sphere. Movement of the left and right hands is controlled principally through contralateral pathways. Thus, where the task demands nonverbal processing, projection of stimuli to the left visual field (LVF) and left-hand response should produce the faster reaction time, because both the most efficient processing and the control of the left-hand movement are carried out in the right hemisphere. With stimulus presentation to the LVF, right-hand reaction time would include the extra time needed for transfer of information across the corpus callosum to the motor centers of the left hemisphere. When the same stimuli are projected to the right visual field (RVF), slower right-hand RT should be due to less efficient left-hemisphere processing in a nonverbal task, because control of right-hand movement rests in the left hemisphere and no transcallosal transfer of information preparatory to overt response is necessary. Demonstration of hemispheric lateralization using this method of hemifield projection rests on finding an effect of visual hemifield, an interaction of hemifield with task type (when RT is averaged across hands), or an interaction between hand, visual field, and task type when RT of each hand is entered into the analysis.

More recently, cerebral laterality effects have been obtained when visual stimuli are projected foveally (Haun, 1978). Under these circumstances there is no "hemisphere of prior entry." Assuming that both hemispheres can process the information with equal ease, there should be no difference between left- and right-hand RT. Demonstration of faster left- or right-hand RT, then, indicates greater efficiency of left- or right-hemisphere processing. However, when stimuli are not selectively projected to one hemisphere, the establishment of a Task Demands (verbal–nonverbal) × Hand interaction is essential to the demonstration of cerebral laterality effects. Where only one task type is used and superiority for, say, the left hand is found, there is no guarantee that the procedures would not yield a superior left-hand RT for any task, or that processing demands (as perceived by the subjects, not as intended by the experimenter) were nonverbal. In contrast, where a Task Type × Hand interaction is found, the adequacy of the task-demands manipulation is more assured.

The literature on cerebral laterality effects in the visual mode using RT as the dependent measure underscores the lack of any isomorphism between stimulus type and the type of processing evoked. While the superiority of the right hemisphere for visual matching or recognition of faces has been established in a number of studies (Broman, 1978; de Renzi, Faglioni, & Spinnler, 1968; Rizzolatti, Umilta, & Berlucchi, 1971), Patterson and Bradshaw (1975) have demonstrated, using schematic faces, that a left- or right-hemisphere superiority may be obtained, depending on manipulations of task demands. When subjects were to respond "same" when a target face (one of three) matched a face in memory, and the targets differed from the memory face on all features or were identical to the memory face, an LVF superiority was found for both "same" and "different" judgments. In a subsequent experiment in which the procedure was the same except that the test faces differed from the memory face on only one feature, judgments of difference were made faster than judgments of sameness and stimuli presented to the RVF (and thus the left hemisphere) were responded to faster than those presented to the LVF. It should be noted, however, that the former results fail to replicate those of Geffen, Bradshaw, and Wallace (1971, Exp. 1), who used similar stimuli and presentation procedures.

Davis and Schmit (1973) provided a similar demonstration for letters. They used a matching task similar to that of Posner and Mitchell (1967) in which subjects were to respond to graphic identity (AA, aa positive set; Aa, aA negative set) or to name identity (Aa, Bb positive set; AB, ab, Ab, aB negative set). Davis and Schmit reported that, for "same" judgments, reaction times for graphic identity were faster when both stimuli of a pair were projected to the right hemisphere, while for name identity, reaction time was faster when both stimuli were projected to the left hemisphere. Opposite results were obtained for "different" judgments. White and White (1975) replicated these results with one exception. They found a right-hemisphere superiority for name identity when the correct judgment was "same."

Moscovitch's (1972) results indicate that memory load may affect the hemisphere for which faster response is recorded. His procedure required subjects to maintain in memory a set of letters (one or six). Two seconds after presentation of the standard set, a test letter was presented visually to the left or right hemisphere. Subjects made a manual response (hand not specified) that signaled "same" or "different." When the letter "set" was a single letter, presentation of the test stimulus to the right hemisphere resulted in shorter RT than presentation of the test stimulus to the left hemisphere. When a multiple letter set had to be retained for comparison, there was a left-hemisphere superiority.

In general, where the task involves making simple decisions about graphic features of a display, the evidence suggests that processing of stimuli presented to the right hemisphere (a) is faster as long as the discriminations are relatively easy, (b) can be made on the basis of graphic features, and (c) is correctly responded to with the judgment of "same." Where the appropriate response is "different," the results are mixed, with a right-hemisphere superiority found in some studies (Geffen et al., 1971; Gross, 1972) and a left-hemisphere superiority in others (Davis & Schmit, 1973; Patterson & Bradshaw, 1975, Exp. 1, nonsignificant).

Where tasks have required analysis of semantic properties of the stimulus, the clinical evidence (Buffrey, 1974; Coughlan & Warrington, 1978) for an RVF superiority is persuasive, as is the experimental literature when procedural differences such as type of presentation (unilateral or bilateral) are taken into account (White, 1969, 1972).

One reason for inconsistent findings, such as Patterson and Bradshaw's (1975) failure to replicate the results of Geffen et al. (1971), is inattention to the type of manual response required. Geffen et al.'s subjects responded with the digits of one hand, while Patterson and Bradshaw required bimanual responses and used the faster response without identifying the hand. As two-handed coordinated movements are preprogrammed for simultaneous initiation and termination (Kelso, Southard, & Goodman, 1979), Patterson and Bradshaw's use of bimanual response would result in recording the RT produced by the slowest combination of visual field and hand. And in many RT studies subjects responded with digits of the preferred hand only. Thus, any RT advantage arising from the anatomy of the sensorimotor pathways alone is confounded with differential hemispheric processing efficiency for a given task.

Though the classical literature on crossed and uncrossed reaction times (Poffenberger, 1912) has been cited as indicating contralateral control of upper limb movement, current evidence suggests a more complex picture. Whole arm and hand movements can be controlled by both contralateral and ipsilateral projections from the motor cortex (Brinkman & Kuypers, 1973; Filbey & Gazzaniga, 1969), while independent hand and finger movements are controlled solely or principally by projections from the contralateral hemisphere (Brinkman & Kuypers, 1973). Thus, right–left RT differences obtained with finger responses (Geffen et al., 1971) are subject to different interpretation in the context of cerebral laterality than are those obtained with grosser whole-hand movements (Davis & Schmit, 1973) like those involved in the movement of a lever or joystick.

RT, Hemispheric Specialization, and Aging

The literature on alterations in intellectual functioning associated with age suggests that some functions show relatively little decline as a function of aging, while others demonstrate marked decline. For example, on tests of intellectual functioning such as the Weschler Adult Intelligence Scale (WAIS), tests tapping verbal functions generally demonstrate less of a decline than those tapping perceptual-motor functions and the processing of novel information. Horn and Cattell (1966, 1967) have developed tests presumed to measure "crystallized" and "fluid" intelligence. Crystallized intelligence is presumed to reflect prior learning and experience, and fluid intelligence to reflect manipulation of novel information. These authors have found fluid intelligence to decline with age while crystallized intelligence is well maintained.

Based on the pattern of declining performance on psychometric tests one could infer that there is a differential decline attributable to the aging process between left- and right-hemisphere functions, with the right-hemisphere functions declining more rapidly than those principally performed by the left. Klisz (1978), in her review of the literature on the neuropsychological deficits associated with aging, comes to the conclusion that "there is some evidence that the performance of normal older people resembles that of people with right hemisphere brain damage, *suggesting that in older people, there may be a greater decline of right hemisphere function than of left hemisphere functions*" (p. 83, italics hers). Klisz's conclusions are based principally on test results obtained with the Halstead-Reitan Neuropsychological Test Battery and on the studies of Overall and Gorham (1972) and Goldstein and Shelly (1975). The latter authors demonstrate that the psychological deficits of older persons do not resemble those seen in patients with diffuse brain damage. Schaie and Schaie (1977), on the basis of performance patterns of older subjects, also suggest that the pattern of older patients resembles that of patients with right-hemisphere dysfunction.

Though results of psychometric test data may suggest right-hemisphere impairment as a function of aging, more direct measures of CNS function, such as the EEG, provide little corroborative evidence. For example, Busse and Obrist (1963) reported that from 30% to 50% of elderly males demonstrate focal slowing in the left anterior temporal region that is not, however, related to alteration in psychological functions such as those measured by the WAIS (Obrist, 1971). Thus, inferences of hemispheric dysfunction based on neuropsychological measures need to be tempered by the lack of positive neurological measures suggestive of right-hemisphere damage. The lack of concordance between EEG and test-battery results should perhaps not be surprising.

As Elias and Kinsbourne (1974) have pointed out, psychometric tests are not designed to discriminate between deficiencies in verbal and nonverbal abilities. Tests of verbal and performance abilities, like the Vocabulary and Block Design sub-tests of the WAIS, differ in response requirements, stimulus familiarity, and task demands so as to preclude control or assessment of processing mode—verbal or nonverbal. Therefore, results of these tests, while suggestive, are inadequate for conclusions about decline in right- or left-hemisphere function.

Examining change in cerebral laterality with age could provide a useful experimental method for validating the inference from psychometric test data that there is a greater decline in right- than in left-hemisphere functions, and in nonverbal than in verbal abilities with age. If so, RT should be disproportionately slower in noverbal right-hemisphere tasks for old than for young subjects. Similarly, if as Elias and Kinsbourne's data suggest, women experience, with aging, a greater decline in the ability to process nonverbal stimuli than do men, the disproportionately slower response in nonverbal right-hemisphere tasks should be observed more for older women than for older men.

There have been few studies in aging research pertinent to tests of these expectations. Elias and Kinsbourne (1974) used controlled mode of response and minimized the role of long-term memory in evaluating the effects of age and sex on the ability to process verbal and nonverbal stimuli. Subjects were presented with verbal stimuli (the abbreviations DL, DR, UR, or UL for down and left, down and right, etc.), some consistent with the class "clockwise," and some not. The subjects were to indicate by releasing appropriate buttons when stimuli represented clockwise. For men the difference between the reaction times to verbal and to visual spatial stimuli remained relatively consistent over age, but for women the time to process visual-spatial stimuli increased disproportionately with age compared to the time to process verbal stimuli.

The Elias and Kinsbourne study has frequently been cited as demonstrating decline in visual-spatial as opposed to verbal abilities among women only. However, as the authors noted, their subjects were not constrained to use a particular coding strategy; verbal or visual coding strategies could have been used to process either arrows or letters. Since McGlone and Davidson (1973) had previously shown that processing orientation stimuli was more difficult for women and that women are more likely to use verbal coding, the Elias and Kinsbourne data are insufficient for drawing conclusions about the effect of age and sex on verbal and visual-spatial nonverbal processing abilities, per se.

The issue of change in verbal and nonverbal processing abilities with age has been extended to the auditory mode in only a few studies. Elias and Elias (1976) and Elias, Wright, and Winn (1977) attempted to extend the results of the Elias and Kinsbourne study to the auditory mode by using a paradigm appropriate to examination of laterality effects. In addition to testing for an Age × Sex interaction in the processing of verbal and nonverbal stimuli, they addressed directly the issue of differences in hemispheric function with age.

In the Elias and Elias study, verbal and nonverbal stimuli—words or tones of differing frequency—were presented monaurally, and subjects were asked to indicate whether successively presented tones or words matched. Since each cerebral hemisphere appears to receive auditory information primarily from the contralateral ear, a right-ear (left hemisphere) advantage for verbal stimuli and a left-ear (right hemisphere) advantage for tonal stimuli were predicted. However, type of stimulus, verbal or nonverbal, did not interact with ear of presentation in affecting reaction time. Hence Elias and Elias failed to demonstrate that their tasks (as opposed to stimuli) indeed required verbal and nonverbal processing. Moreover, no age-by-sex effects like those in the Elias and Kinsbourne study were found. The older subjects were generally slower in response to both tones and words. The paradigm used by Elias, Wright, and Winn was essentially the same, although words and vowel sounds served as verbal and nonverbal stimuli, and the results were again essentially negative. No interaction of stimulus type with ear of presentation was established for any age group. Moreover, Elias, Wright, and Winn employed no data analysis appropriate to the detection of an Age × Sex × Stimulus Type interaction; such an interaction would have to be present to replicate Elias and Kinsbourne's finding that women's processing of nonverbal stimuli declines disproportionately with age compared to men's.

In a more recent study, Johnson, Cole, Bowers, Foiles, Nikaido, Patrick, and Woliver (1979) used a dichotic listening procedure and did find an age and an age-by-sex effect in the processing of verbal stimuli only for the age range from 44 to 79. Series of digits were presented simultaneously to both ears, and subjects were instructed to write down the digits presented to one or the other ear first. A right-ear (left hemisphere) superiority for the verbal task was highly significant. Memory for dichotic materials presented to the left ear (right hemisphere) but not to the right ear (left hemisphere) was found to decline substantially with age. The age-by-sex effect was attributable to a significant decline with age in left-ear, right-hemisphere response for women only. However, the authors noted that the decline, while comparable for men, did not

reach significance, owing to the small number of men tested (19, as opposed to 54 women). In a second experiment, a right-hemisphere task involving memory for tone series presented dichotically was used, but no hemisphere asymmetry was established, which complicated interpretation.

We have, then, from Johnson et al. (1979) demonstration of decline with age in right- but not left-hemisphere efficiency in a left-hemisphere task. However, since subjects were required to write down their responses, the demonstration of left-hemisphere superiority may be attributable to response requirements and not to different efficiency of processing in left and right hemispheres. And the argument regarding decline in right-hemisphere function would have been more persuasive had a right-hemisphere task been used successfully.

The results of one other study on age and hemispheric asymmetry in the processing of auditory stimuli are relevant to further investigation in this area. Simon (1967) used a choice RT task in which tones were presented monaurally and compared the time for crossed (responding with the hand contralateral to ear of stimulation) and uncrossed (responding with the hand ipsilateral to ear of stimulation) responses. The difference in rapidity between crossed and uncrossed responses was greater and the crossed responses were slower for an older group and for women, but there was no Age × Sex interaction. Older women tended to have relatively slower crossed reactions, though the Age × Sex × Crossed vs. Uncrossed interaction was not significant. It should be noted that Simon's measure of RT was not comparable to decision time but rather included a transit-time component. Whether the faster responses of men are attributable to faster motor response or faster decision making cannot therefore be determined from the results of his study.

Simon's results do suggest that for the old more than for the young, the need for transfer of information across the corpus callosum slows response. If this result is replicable, it may point to an important locus of slowing with age. Unfortunately, in the Simon study, hemispheric asymmetry may have been confounded with attentional factors. A tone presented to either ear may produce an orienting response and a propensity to respond in the direction of stimulation.

In the aging literature, as in the literature on hemispheric specialization in general, little attention has been paid to the effect of response requirements on results. For example, Waugh, Fozard, Talland, and Erwin (1973) used left- and right-hand release responses to light stimuli to measure RT as a function of age. Their concern, however, was not to evaluate between-hand differences, and no data were provided on possible differences. Nebes (1978) also evaluated RT to light stimuli as a function of age and fortunately analyzed data on left- and right-finger release times. A significant effect was obtained, with left-hand response faster than right-hand response. Interestingly, Nebes made no comment on these differences (which were not age dependent). In general, most investigators who have examined RT differences with age have used the preferred hand only, or have used left and right hand responses, but for control purposes only and without reporting on them, or have reported the results but with no further discussion.

Present Experiment

Rationale

Investigation of hemispheric specialization could provide a powerful tool for illuminating brain–behavior relations associated with aging as well as sex-related aging effects. Our review suggested that recording reaction time from both hands in a series of simple tasks was an appropriate procedure for studying hemispheric functions. Unlike previous studies of aging in which letters and visual-spatial stimuli or words and tones (Elias & Elias, 1976; Elias & Kinsbourne, 1974) were used to define the verbal and nonverbal tasks, we used the same stimuli—the onset and offset of lights—throughout.

These stimuli were chosen for two reasons. Because there is little information on cerebral laterality and aging, while there are documented interactions between age, sex, and stimulus type (Elias & Kinsbourne, 1974), an experimental procedure using a simple light stimulus seemed a best first approach to assessing laterality differences across sex and age. Second, we wanted to manipulate task demands (verbal and verbal–nonverbal) through instructions. As Springer (1977, p. 327) has noted, "Obtaining different results with the same stimuli as a function of instruction is a powerful demonstration of the importance of task variables in determining the outcome of laterality studies." We used four tasks, three of which—the simple, bilateral, and choice RT tasks—were simple visual-perception tasks not necessitating or inviting verbal translation of stimulus information for their solution. These tasks require nonverbal processing, and a right-hemisphere superiority has been repeatedly shown for simple and two-choice reaction time to lights (Bradshaw & Perriment, 1970; Jeeves & Dixon, 1970; Kappauf & Yeatman, 1970) for college age subjects. In contrast, our reverse-choice RT task involved a verbal rule or verbal correction of the tendency to re-

spond with left hand to left light and right hand to right light. Anzola, Bertoloni, Buchtel, and Rizzolatti (1977) have reported diminished left–right hand differences for a reverse choice (their incompatible uncrossed condition, p. 299) as compared to a choice task (their compatible uncrossed condition, p. 299). These different task demands—nonverbal processing for the simple, bilateral, and choice reaction time tasks, and verbal and nonverbal for the reverse-choice task—should result in a Task Demands × Hand interaction, with the left hand faster for the tasks demanding nonverbal processing, and no left hand superiority for the task requiring verbal as well as nonverbal manipulation.

Other aspects of the experimental procedure and assessed responses were included in the design as a check on the validity of our cerebral-laterality results for age. We included a test for the validity of our RT measures and results that could be compared to the more traditional RT-aging literature. We assessed both decision and motor components of RT, with the expectation that only the decision component should reflect lateralization of function, that is, there should be a Task-Demands × Hand interaction for the decision component of RT only. A Task × Hand interaction for the motor component would indicate a spurious result. Moreover, the decision and motor-component results could be compared to past aging literature on this topic.

It should be noted that we did not expect significant differences between hands for the bilateral task, because two-handed coordinated movement is preprogrammed for simultaneity in initiation and termination (Kelso et al., 1979). The bilateral task was included in order to examine the development of concerted hemispheric control of coordinated movement from childhood to late maturity.

Method and Procedures

Data were collected for 40 (20 male and 20 female) 7-, 9-, and 11-year-old middle-class children of above-average intelligence, as measured with the Peabody Picture Vocabulary Test (Hoine, 1976, Newport, 1977) and for 20 (10 male, 10 female) subjects in each of six age groups for which the average ages were 20, 35, 45, 55, 65, or 75 years. Children were tested at their schools, and all adult subjects were volunteers who came to our laboratory. All subjects with one exception were right-handed as ascertained by self-report and the hand used to execute the crossing-out test.

Subjects sat before a simple display board composed of three high-intensity red light-emitting diodes and a response panel with four response pads. The left and right lights were placed 3 cm to the left and right of the central light. The response pads were 1 cm square, with the two proximal ones 2.5 cm apart. The distal ones were 7.5 cm apart and placed 3.5 cm from the proximal ones (center to center). It is therefore unlikely that increasing sensory threshold with distance of stimuli or response pads from the fovea would affect results. The stimulus panel was attached to the response panel and placed at a 135° angle with respect to it. Each subject arranged the location of the stimulus-response apparatus so that movement of the fingers from one response pad to the other was as comfortable as possible. Changes in electrical capacitance were used to record response-pad release and contact, and subjects were instructed to move their fingers from pad to pad by lifting them off the response board rather than by sliding them.

At the beginning of each trial, regardless of task, subjects were instructed to place their index fingers on left and right proximal (start) pads and were told that when the signal light (one was predesignated for each trial series) was turned on, they were to move the appropriate finger(s) as rapidly as possible to the corresponding distal target pad(s). Four measures were abstracted for each trial: (1) decision time forward (DTF)—time from light onset to release of the start pad; (2) transit time forward (TTF)—time from start pad release to contact of the target pad; (3) decision time reverse (DTR)—time from light offset to target pad release; and (4) transit time reverse (TTR)—time from target pad release to contact of the start pad. In the results section we emphasize findings for forward movement.

The following four tasks were used: simple (SRT)—in which in a given trial series only the left or only the right light would be illuminated and the subject was to release only the corresponding left or right pad; bilateral (BRT)—in which only the center light was illuminated, which signaled release of both left and right pads; choice (CRT)—in which either the left or the right light might be illuminated on any given trial and which signaled response with the corresponding hand; reverse choice (RCRT)—in which, again, either the left or right light might be illuminated, but the left light signaled a right-finger response and the right light a left-finger response. It should be emphasized that in the simple, bilateral, and choice RT tasks, the left light always signaled a left-finger movement and the right light always signaled right-finger movement. Only in the reverse-choice task were these contingencies reversed.

All participants proceeded through the four tasks in the following order: bilateral, simple, choice, and reverse choice. Half of the participants in each age-by-sex group performed the simple task with the left hand first, and half with the right hand first. At the introduction of each new task subjects were fully instructed about stimulus-response contingencies and were administered practice trials sufficient to demonstrate that they understood the instructions. Practice trials were followed, for each task, by 12 test trials for which left-digit and 12 test trials for which right-digit response was correct. Thus there were a total of 12 test trials for the bilateral, simple-left, and simple-right tasks, and a total of 24 trials each for the choice and reverse-choice tasks. To prevent subjects from anticipating onset or offset and thereby reducing their measured RT, interstimulus interval (ISI) and stimulus duration were varied between 4 and 8 sec. The duration of the light stimulus and ISI, as well as the order of left or right illumination in the choice and reverse-choice tasks, were randomized across trials within each task series.

Data Analysis

Decision and transit times were recorded as DC voltage shifts on magnetic tape and were submitted to computer analysis, which identified any anticipatory movements as well as other errors. Each participant's median left- and right-digit decision and transit times were calculated for each task for errorless trials only. The number of errors was too small to allow their separate analysis.

The data for children and for adults were first submitted to separate analyses of variance (ANOVAs) including the factors of Age, Sex, Task Demands, Hand, Decision versus Transit Time, and Direction of Movement (forward to target pads and return to start pads), with repeated measures on the last four factors. Additional ANOVAs, one for each RT component measure (DTF, TTF, DTR, TTR), were then conducted to help us interpret significant interaction effects identified in the overall analyses. These additional ANOVAs included only the factors of Age, Sex, Task Complexity, and Hand, with repeated measures on the last two factors. Simple effects were used to interpret significant interactions in these additional ANOVAs.

Validity of RT Component Measures Across Young and Adult Samples

Before looking at the data pertinent to the issue of change in relative efficiency of hemispheric function with age, let us briefly examine the validity of our measures and task-demand manipulations for both young and adult samples. There are two specific issues of concern. Of the two RT component measures, does decision time alone appear to reflect central processing for all age groups? Are responses to all three tasks characterized as nonverbal differentiated from responses to the nonverbal–verbal tasks (reverse choice) for both children and adults?

For adults, while task demand significantly affected both decision and transit time (see Table 22-1), it accounted for 40.0% of the variance in decision time and only .9% of the variance in transit time (by $\hat{\omega}^2$, Dodd & Schultz, 1973). For children, the corresponding figures were: 41.0% and .6%. A comparison of figures 22-1 and 22-2 shows that there was a disproportionately greater effect of task demand on decision time than on transit time for every age. These results, while confirming what common sense tells us—namely, that pure decision and motor components of RT cannot be experimentally isolated—also show that our measures do reflect principally decision making and motor implementation for children as well as for adults and thus lend credence to our expectation that cerebral laterality effects should be reflected in decision time, and not in transit time.

Two results are pertinent to the second issue. For adults, the task-demand effect for decision time (Figure 22-1) was attributable mainly to the difference in response between the reverse-choice task and all other tasks. The slopes of the lines depicting increases in decision time from the simple to the bilateral to the choice task are shallow and comparable for all adult

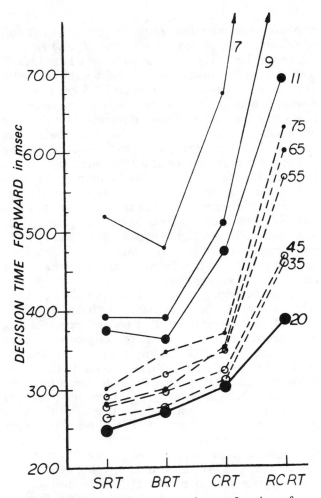

Figure 22-1. Decision time forward as a function of age. Numbers next to lines refer to average age of each group. SRT = simple reaction time; BRT = bilateral reaction time; CRT = choice reaction time; RCRT = reverse choice reaction time.

age groups, which suggests that for all adult samples, these three tasks involve the same simple type of decision process. An abrupt increase in the slope occurs for the reverse-choice task for all adult groups. Moreover, it is apparent from Figure 22-1 that only the slope depicting the relation between decision time and task demands for the choice and reverse-choice tasks becomes systematically steeper as we go from the youngest to the oldest adult group.

For children a similar case cannot be made. The effect of task demand is not due simply or even primarily to the effect of the reverse-choice task as compared to the three other tasks. The slope of the graph depicting the relation between decision time and task demands increases sharply from simple to choice

Table 22-1 Summary of F Ratios Obtained in the Four Analyses of Variance for Adults

Source	df	Decision time forward	Decision time return	Transit time forward	Transit time return
Age (A)	5	7.98***	.60	8.19***	6.39***
Sex (S)	1	1.82	1.46	39.11***	30.57***
A × S	5	2.45*	.74	2.81*	1.64
Participants (P)/AS	108				
Task Demands (T)	3	281.37***	54.42***	14.23***	14.73***
T × A	15	5.61***	1.08	.68	1.05
T × S	3	.39	.54	1.40	1.18
T × A × S	15	1.32	1.77*	1.28	.95
PT/AS	324				
Hand (H)	1	26.69***	.04	8.83**	1.97
H × A	5	2.16	2.54*	9.51***	8.06***
H × S	1	1.98	3.46	1.94	.31
H × A × S	5	1.63	1.38	1.82	1.26
PH/AS	108				
T × H	3	7.53***	4.66**	.45	1.80
T × H × A	15	1.14	1.29	.51	.71
T × H × S	3	.55	1.07	1.52	.88
T × H × A × S	324	1.85*	1.52	.77	1.08

*$p < .05$. **$p < .004$. ***$p < .0001$.

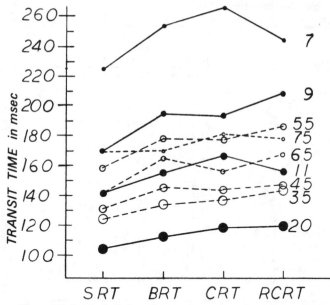

Figure 22-2. Transit time forward as a function of age. Numbers next to lines refer to average age of each group. SRT = simple reaction time; BRT = bilateral reaction time; CRT = choice reaction time; RCRT = reverse choice reaction time.

tasks. For children, unlike adults, the choice task is clearly not an easy task involving processing demands comparable to those for the bilateral and simple tasks.

Given this difference in the validity of equating bilateral, simple, and choice tasks with nonverbal processing, one could expect differences in the appearance of cerebral laterality effects for children and adults.

Hemispheric Specialization and Age

Adults. For the adult sample the Task Demand × Hand interaction was significant for decision time (Table 22-1), as depicted in Figure 22-3. Mean left-hand decision time was faster for all nonverbal tasks but not for the reverse-choice task, which involved both verbal and nonverbal operations. For the nonverbal tasks, the left-hand superiority was significant for the simple ($p < .01$) and choice ($p < .01$) tasks but not, as anticipated, for the bilateral task in which the two hands are constrained to simultaneous initiation of response (Kelso et al., 1979). For the task involving verbal as well as nonverbal processing (namely, reverse choice), the left hand was not faster ($p > .10$). (All tests of simple effects were conducted with 1 and 432 degrees of freedom.) The main effect for hand—that the left hand was faster—was due simply to the inclusion of

three tasks for which left-hand response should be faster.

The Task Demand × Hand interaction did not vary with age (see Task Demand × Hand × Age in Table 22-1), which indicates that the degree of cerebral laterality as measured in this study did not vary with age. Similarly there was no Task Demand × Hand × Sex interaction, which indicates that the degree of cerebral laterality did not vary significantly with sex, though the left-hand superiority for the nonverbal tasks was slightly greater for men than for women. Simple effects used to interpret the third-order interaction among task demand, hand, age, and sex revealed no readily interpretable variation in the Task Demand × Hand interaction at given levels of age and sex.

The absence of a Task Demand × Hand interaction

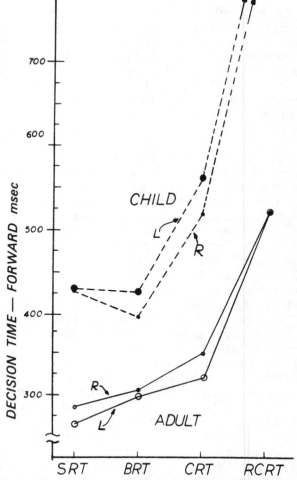

Figure 22-3. Decision time forward for children as a group (7–11-year-olds) and all adults (20–75-year-olds) for left (L) and right (R) hands.

for transit time confirmed our expectation that transit time would be insensitive to cerebral laterality effects. Regardless of task demand, transit time recorded from the preferred right hand was faster, which accounted for the significant hand effect. This result is not surprising, since motor implementation is generally faster with the dominant hand. Thus the general finding of faster RT with the right hand may occur because most studies do not discriminate between decision and motor times. We suspect that the larger the amplitude of the movement, the greater the apparent right-hand advantage. The Hand × Age effect for transit time (Table 22-1) was attributable to the magnitude of superiority of the right hand at age 20.

One other finding for transit time deserves mention. While there was no significant effect of sex for decision time, men's transit times were significantly faster than women's for every age group. This result suggests that inclusion of a large motor component in the measure of RT may influence results on cerebral laterality, especially when the data for men and women are analyzed separately. We found (incidental to demonstrating variation in results due to the RT measure used) that when the measure of RT was total time (decision plus transit time) and the data for men and women were treated separately, a Task Demand × Hand interaction was apparent for men only (Stern, Oster, & Newport, 1979).

Children. For children there was no Task × Hand interaction (Table 22-2) for decision time, whereas there was one for transit time. The reason for the lack of a Task × Hand interaction for children becomes clearer if one examines the effect of other variables on the decision time of children and contrasts the factors significantly affecting the decision times of adults and children (see Tables 22-1 and 22-2).

There was for children, as for adults, a significant main effect for hand. However children, unlike adults, made faster responses with the right hand (Figure 22-3). Moreover, children showed a significant Hand × Sex interaction (depicted in Figure 22-4). Males showed the pattern of our adult sample, with faster left- than right-hand decision times, though the difference between their left- and right-hand decision times was not significant ($p > .10$). For females the pattern was reversed: The faster decision time was with the right hand, and the difference between left and right hands was significant ($p < .01$). Left-hand decision time of the males was also significantly faster than that of the females ($p < .01$). For females only, there was a significant developmental trend toward faster left- than right-hand decision time with increasing age.

Why do children as a group show a right-hand advantage? Children may utilize a different "logic" in

Table 22-2 Summary of F Ratios Obtained in the Four Analyses of Variance for Children

Source	df	Decision time forward	Decision time return	Transit time forward	Transit time return
Age (A)	2	33.05****	31.70****	7.31**	10.94****
Sex (S)	1	.16	2.20	.38	1.92
A × S	2	.29	.56	.09	.04
Participants (P)/AS	109				
Task Demands (T)	3	609.07****	58.06****	6.45***	1.95
T × A	6	21.83****	2.22*	.74	1.66
T × S	3	2.47	.23	2.90	1.32
T × A × S	6	1.34	.77	.90	2.58*
PT/AS	327				
Hand (H)	1	4.42*	.45	.10	4.36*
H × A	2	.17	.60	.69	1.17
H × S	1	11.68***	.14	9.30**	.35
H × A × S	2	2.31	2.42	4.30*	1.04
PH/AS	109				
T × H	3	2.10	4.93**	4.27**	2.09
T × H × A	6	1.11	.41	1.12	2.12*
T × H × S	3	.19	1.29	.95	.16
T × H × A × S	6	.41	1.11	.87	.60
PTH/AS	327				

* $p < .05$. ** $p < .006$. *** $p < .0003$. **** $p < .00001$.

performing these tasks. They may, in the simple and choice tasks, for example, have to inhibit responding with the other hand more consciously than do adults. Such inhibition may bring into play left-hemisphere processing mechanisms and account for the lack of left-hand advantage. The right-hand advantage in these right-handed young subjects, like the right-hand advantage for adult's transit time, may in part be attributable to greater experience in using the right hand.

The cerebral laterality effects demonstrated in this study cannot be accounted for on the basis of an attentional model (Kinsbourne, 1973). For the simple RT tasks, selective activation of the left or right hemisphere could have developed, as response hand was designated before each test series; however, faster left-hand decision time was also found for the choice RT task in which presentation of stimuli to the left or right side, and therefore response with the left or right hand, was pseudorandomized across trials. Results also cannot be attributed to spatial compatibility of light stimuli and response hand. Anzola et al. (1977) demonstrated that spatial stimulus–response (S–R) compatibility affects choice, but not simple RT. However, as Anzola et al. noted, their manipulation of S–R correspondence for the choice RT task also altered the *type of processing* required for task execution.

Moreover, a faster left-hand response in simple RT tasks has been found in previous studies, especially where the task had not been extensively practiced. For example, Nebes (1978), using a simple RT task and a measure of RT identical to our DTF, found left-hand response significantly faster than right-hand response. Rabbitt's (1966) data on left-hand (LH) and right-hand (RH) responding also showed that LH responses were faster than RH responses in three out of three relevant comparisons. Dimond (1970), though reporting no significant difference in decision time between the left and right hands, presented mean values demonstrating that faster LH responses occurred with greater frequency than faster RH responses. The same was true for the results of Kelso et al. (1979). All of these studies, with the exception of that of Nebes (1978), used young adult subjects, and in none of them was faster left-hand response examined within the context of hemispheric specialization. It is apparent from our results that this pattern may be unique to adults, since children between 7 and 11 years old demonstrate a mixed pattern, with boys performing like adults, with left-hand responses faster than right (though not statistically reliable), but with a reversed and statistically reliable pattern for girls.

There are, however, two limitations to the generalizability of our results. First, instead of using tasks for which clear right- and left-hemisphere superiorities had been previously demonstrated, we used one nonverbal task and one task requiring both nonverbal and verbal processing. Our demonstration of cerebral laterality would have been more persuasive had the second task type produced a faster right-hand response. Second, stimuli were not projected to selected visual hemifields and thus to the left or right hemisphere. Though Haun (1978) has demonstrated cerebral laterality effects using foveal presentation, our

results should be replicated with a hemifield projection technique and systematic manipulation of verbal and nonverbal task demands. We are currently initiating such studies. While we found no greater decline in right-hemisphere function with age for women than for men, sex-related differences are more likely to emerge with use of more complex tasks. Systematic manipulation of task demands is essential for isolation of the kind of processing, if any, that distinguishes the performance of older men from that of older women. The need for replication is underscored by the paucity of studies in aging research devoted to cerebral laterality. Cerebral lateralization was not included among the topics covered in the last *Handbook in the Psychology of Aging* (Birren & Schaie, 1977), or in recent treatments of cognition (Botwinick, 1978) or sex-related differences (Cohen & Wilkie, 1979) in aging.

Concerted Hemispheric Control of Two-Handed Movement

Kelso et al. (1979) demonstrated that initiation and termination of movements in a bilateral RT task were simultaneous, even when the two digits traveled unequal distances or to targets of different sizes. Simultaneity under such conditions implies that concerted activity of the two hemispheres constrains symmetrically located, functional groupings of muscles to act as a unit. Moreover, that bilateral RT was longer than single-handed RT for the *same* movement (see Figures 22-1 and 22-2 and Kelso et al.) also argues for concerted activity of the hemispheres. Since movement of the digits is under the control of the contralateral hemisphere (Brinkman & Kuypers, 1973), coordinated, bilateral movement requiring interhemispheric communication would take longer than single-handed movement controlled by one hemisphere.

In contrast to the data of Kelso et al. and our data for adults, we found that children's decision times were faster for the bilateral than for the simple task. Seven-year-olds initiated movement in the bilateral task significantly faster than in the one-handed simple RT task ($p < .01$); 9- and 11-year-olds also performed faster in the bilateral task but not significantly so ($p > .10$). Moreover, the longer reaction times for children were associated with faster performance in the bilateral than in the one-handed task. Why should simultaneously lifting the left and right fingers be accomplished more rapidly by children than the lifting of a single finger?

It may be that in performing the simple task, the children, after registering the position of the signal light, had to make a decision about moving only the hand on that side. That is, for children the decision

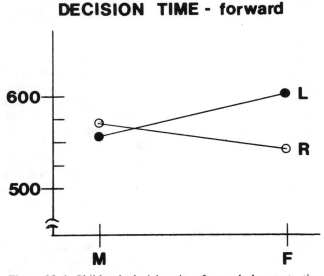

Figure 22-4. Children's decision time forward: demonstration of Sex × Hand interaction.

time in the simple task may be longer because it includes time for response inhibition, which would be unnecessary in the bilateral task. This interpretation is compatible with Luria's (1966) notion (a) that in early development, excitation created by stimulation spreads immediately to the motor system and creates diffuse somatic responses that interfere with the appropriate response, and (b) that development proceeds by increasing differentiation of the central nervous system so that for older children activation of the motor system is controlled to permit specific directed responses.

It could be objected that slower performance of the simple task by the children was attributable to interference effects. We can reject this possibility, because half of the subjects in each group performed the simple task with the left hand first, and half performed it with the right hand first. Interference effects attributable to bilateral performance should have exerted a greater effect on the simple task immediately following it. However, changing the order for the simple task produced no significant effect.

Another interesting phenomenon was revealed by a comparison of adult performance on the simple and bilateral tasks. With increasing age, bilateral RT was observed to increase more rapidly than one-handed RT, lending support to the idea that tasks involving transfer of information across the corpus callosum are performed more slowly by older adults than tasks that do not require such transfer (Simon, 1967), presumably because the transfer allows greater opportunity for information loss or distortion due to neural noise. However, while bilateral RT increased, simultaneity of initiation and termination in bilateral movement did not deteriorate (and in fact left–right hand differences decreased slightly) with advancing age. This is precisely what one would anticipate if simultaneity in bilateral movement reflects a motor automatism produced by concerted activity of the hemispheres. Apparently the CNS compensates for neural noise in the bilateral movement by responding more slowly and preserving simultaneity of movement initiation. We are currently pursuing the implications of these results (Oster, Stern, & Newport, 1980).

Age and RT

Because our results for age and age-related effects other than hemispheric specialization largely replicated or were compatible with past findings, we will summarize them here and comment briefly on novel aspects of our results.

1. For adults, with the exception of DTR, all RT component measures were influenced significantly by age. This result for DTR is not in general supported by the RT literature, where one of the most robust findings is that RT is significantly affected by age. How then can we account for the lack of significant effects on DTR in our study? Our evaluation of task-complexity demands suggests that for adults DTR involves the least complex of all the decisions faced by our subjects. The sole decision they had to make was to return the finger with which they had responded 3–5 seconds earlier to its initial resting place when the signal light went off. No decision had to be made about *which* hand to move or exactly *where* to place the finger. Since degree of impairment as a function of age is significantly related to task difficulty, it appears that at least one of our measures reflects a decision so simple as to be minimally affected by aging. We are not the first investigators to find RT components that are not, or are only minimally, affected by age. Botwinick and Thompson (1971) reported similar results for a simple DT component.

With children this extrapolation does not work; they showed significant age effects regardless of the decision that had to be made. We would like to suggest that for the young child, the decision about making a return movement is more complicated than it is for either older children or adults. We suspect that (a) the younger child's memory of finger location is more fragile than that of the older child, (b) the memory of the motor act that brought the finger from the proximal to the distal pad is also subject to rapid decay, and (c) younger children will have to more actively inhibit moving the proximal hand because of their more poorly developed inhibitory control system. The task faced by younger children is thus qualitatively different from that experienced by older children or adults.

2. For both adults and children, task demands affected transit as well as decision time (compare Figures 22-1 and 22-2). The effect for transit time, while small, was reliable. How can we account for this effect? Since, for other reasons, task complexity was not counterbalanced, this result may be attributable to fatigue or time-on-task effects. We would like to reject this possibility for two reasons. First, such an effect should develop more rapidly and be more severe for older subjects; however, the slope of transit time as a function of task complexity does not appear to be steeper for our older than for our younger subjects. Second, the listing of tasks on the abscissa of our graphs corresponds not to the temporal order in which the tasks were administered but rather to the ordering of tasks according to our conception of their difficulty. The BRT task was in fact the first task administered,

followed by SRT, CRT, and RCRT in that order. Nevertheless, it is apparent that for all adult groups, with the possible exception of the 75-year-old group, transit time is more rapid for SRT than for BRT. From this result we suspect that task difficulty is a more important determiner of transit-time differences than is time on task.

What the results of task-demand effects on DTR (for children) and TTF (for adults and children) suggest is that though one can attempt to logically tease apart "central" from "peripheral" processes, they may in fact interact and their interaction is reflected in both the decision- and transit-time measures.

3. The difference between the interactive influence of age and task demand on data for children and adults deserves some further comment. It is obvious from Figure 22-1 that the slope depicting the relation between CRT and RCRT becomes systematically steeper as we go from the young adult to the oldest adult group. As the reverse-choice task alone involved change of stimulus-response set and response inhibition, this result is compatible with the general finding that change in cognitive set affects older persons more than young adults (Brinley, 1961).

For children we see that the differences between CRT and SRT performance are consistently larger than for the young adult and older adult groups. Children took, on the average, 29% more time to perform the CRT than the SRT task. For the adult population the average increment is 11%, and there appears to be no increment attributable uniquely to aging. Thus simple two-choice decision time does not appear to be significantly more affected by the aging process than BRT or SRT performance. However, children 7–11 years old demonstrate significant increments in decision time for this task, as compared to simple reaction time. We suspect that task difficulty from the vantage point of the performer accounts for the greater performance differential of the children.

It is only when we look at the ratio of RCRT to CRT that we find both the youngest and oldest groups demonstrating similar increments. The 7- and 9-year-old groups demonstrate increments similar to the 55-, 65-, and 75-year-old groups; the 11-year-olds are comparable to the 35- and 45-year-old groups. Whether the larger increment in RT for the last task of the series is a function of "fatigue" or "attentional" variables or is attributable to alterations in information processing as a function of differential sensitivity of older subjects to poorer stimulus-response compatibility can only be answered indirectly from this study. Because of the lack of drastic changes in transit times, we suspect that the effect is not attributable to fatigue or attentional variables. Calculating the increment in

transit time from SRT to RCRT, we obtain ratios of 1.22 for the youngest group and 1.15, 1.12, 1.27, 1.0, and 1.06 for the 35-, 45-, 55-, 65-, and 75-year-old groups. It is the youngest group (without the 55-year-old group) that shows the greatest increment in movement time between early and last task performance. Though the evidence is admittedly indirect, it suggests that the larger increment in RT performance for the RCRT task is not attributable to greater time-on-task or fatigue effects for our older subjects but to stimulus-response incompatibility or perseverative effects.

There has been considerable debate in the reaction-time literature on whether age effects are more detrimental to the decision-making component or the motor component of RT. For example, Szafran (1951), Singleton (1954), and Spieth (1955) have concluded that DT is affected more by the aging process than by movement time. Though Welford (1969), when he says, "Broadly speaking very simple actions such as raising the finger when a signal is given, show virtually no slowing from the twenties to the sixties, and little beyond" (p. 2), bases his conclusions at least in part on a study by Pierson and Montoye (1958), our reading of that study found movement time (MT) to be as affected as RT (comparable to our DTF) by the aging process. Spirduso (1975) found a greater decrement in movement time than in decision time, which demonstrates significant increases in transit time with age. Our results demonstrated, not surprisingly, that whether MT or DT appears to be more affected by age depends on task parameters (see Figure 22-5). In tasks requiring simple decisions (SRT, BRT, CRT) and movements, MT appears to increase more than does DT with age. In tasks requiring more complex decisions (RCRT) and simple movements, DT appears to increase more than MT does with age.

Depicted in Figure 22-5 is a comparison of decision and transit time (forward) as a function of the aging process. For each measure and for each age group we expressed performance as a ratio of the performance of our 20-year-old group. (The 20-year-old group was selected as base because the RT literature and our results suggest that performance peaks at this age.) Thus, for example, for the 35-year-old group, DT is 6% slower than that of the 20-year-old group, while their transit time is 20% slower. It is only in our oldest age groups performing on the incompatible-choice RT task that the relative increment in transit time is smaller than the increment in decision time. Our conclusions contrast with Welford's (1959) conclusion that "at least until the forties or fifties and perhaps in some cases beyond, the actual time spent making movements does not rise, or rises very little with age. Slowing of performance occurs mainly during those por-

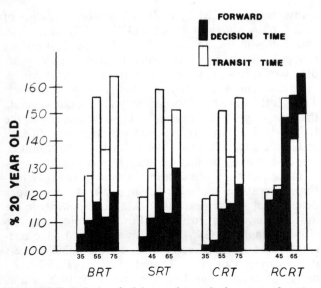

Figure 22-5. Relative decision and transit times as a function of age. In all cases percentage is computed with decision and transit times of the 20-year-old group as base. In all cases the first bar is for the 35-year-old group, the second bar for the 45-year-old group, the third bar for the 55-year-old group, the fourth bar for the 65-year-old group, and the fifth bar for the 75-year-old group.

tions of the task where signals are being perceived and responding actions are being prepared" (p. 581). The studies reviewed by Welford principally involved gross hand and arm movements. Our study utilized rather more restricted movements of the fingers. We suspect, therefore, that the type of movement required may be a major determinant of whether one does or does not see appreciable alterations in movement time as a function of age. Thus, whether transit time is more affected than decision time depends on the nature of both the decision and the motor response required. If the task involves large muscle movements, it may well be that decision time (which includes preparation for movement) is significantly affected by the aging process, while movement time does not discriminate between age groups. However, if the task involves small muscle movements, we find that both decision time and transit time are significantly affected by aging, the latter more detrimentally than the former, especially in simple tasks.

Some Projections for Future Research

Our results on left–right hand differences in decision time have a number of interesting implications for the hemispheric laterality issue. We suggest that respond-

ing faster with any one hand is a function of the nature of the task required of our subjects. Our hypothesis was that the left-hand advantage occurs when task demands are conducive to holistic, nonverbal processing carried out more efficiently by the right hemisphere. If the task is complicated, so that left-hemisphere functions are involved, the left-hand advantage disappears or is replaced by a right-hand advantage, depending on the degree to which verbal analytic processing is evoked. If these speculations prove to be correct, we will have another simple and noninvasive technique for studying aspects of hemispheric information processing. The validity of our findings should be reexamined using a procedure, like hemifield projection of stimuli, which allows control over the sensory pathway and thus the hemisphere to which stimuli are channeled, in conjunction with systematic manipulation of the difficulty of verbal and nonverbal tasks.

While use of the hemifield projection technique ensures prior entry to one hemisphere and therefore does much to clarify the interpretation of left–right hand RT data, the technique has not been used frequently in aging research. Only if the eye remains fixed on a point midway between left and right visual fields is projection to given areas of the retina certain. To ensure that eye movements to the field of projection do not influence results, investigators have typically presented visual stimuli for periods shorter than reaction time for eye movement to a stimulus presented in the periphery, or about 200 msec. But that method does not preclude the subject's making anticipatory or random (with respect to the timing of stimulus presentation) eye movements to the field of projection, and random eye movements may be spaced as closely as every 80 msec. Some evidence suggests that use of stimulus presentation periods too short to allow an eye movement to the field of projection may result in the inability of older persons to perform the task (Walsh, Williams, & Hertzog, 1979). An alternative control for eye movement—having subjects report items presented at the point of central fixation in addition to responding to items presented to the left and right visual fields—could complicate interpretation of results where performance of old and young groups are to be compared. Task complexity as well as left–right hemisphere differences could account for age-related results. Continuous recording of eye movements by means of electro-oculography, while not interfering with performance of the principal task, would allow one to exclude from analysis any trials on which eye movements occurred and thus to increase stimulus presentation to a suprathreshold duration. Though the suprathreshold stimuli may lead to a ceiling effect for errors, reaction-time data would still be sensitive to cerebral laterality effects. Thus one could obtain results on cerebral laterality that are not confounded by change in sensory threshold with age.

One aspect of our study not covered in this chapter suggests some further concerns. Though, in general, one finds progressive decrements in reaction-time measures as a function of aging, we found that the pattern for female subjects departed somewhat from this pattern. Females in the 50–59-year-old age group performed significantly more poorly, whether the measure was decision or transit time, than did the older females. Hormonal changes and perhaps changes in affect associated with menopause may be the major contributors to this phenomenon. There is some corroborative evidence from Fedor-Freybergh (1977), but again the finding needs replication. Most studies of aging prior to 1965 did not include women, and generally, where women were included, the constitution of age groups could have masked any effect of life phase change (Hodgkins, 1962; Panek, Barrett, Sterns, & Alexander, 1978).

With the current and apparently expanding interest in the nature of hemispheric specialization of function, the individual differences in preferred modes of information processing, and the knowledge that the aging process is significantly more detrimental to performance tasks that *presumably* tap right-hemispheric functions, we suspect that intrepid investigators will begin to look at the interrelations between these two "bits" of information. For example, one might ask whether persons whose preferred mode of information processing selectively overemphasizes use of right-hemispheric functions will show less impairment in such functions than those whose preferred mode emphasizes left-hemispheric processing. Or would more impairment result from their continued insistence on using a hemisphere that has lost some of its functional efficiency? We emphasize functional efficiency, since to our knowledge no neuroanatomical or electrophysiological evidence has been generated to account for impaired performance on tasks that engage right-hemisphere functions more than left-hemisphere functions.

This too might be a fruitful area of research, especially with the current interest in averaged evoked responses (Walrath & Hallman, 1979) and the application of sophisticated time-series analysis to electroencephalographic wiggles. These procedures applicable to the study of hemispheric specialization are, however, subject to a major constraint—namely, they do not allow us to evaluate directly which localized area of the brain is involved in the performance of a specific task. Electroencephalography and the subsidiary measure of averaged evoked responses are about as close as we can get to the direct measurement of central nervous system processes. Unfortunately, the evidence allowing inferences to be drawn about hemispheric specialization of function with these techniques is far from unequivocal (Donchin, Kutas, & McCarthy, 1977; Hillyard & Woods, 1979). Similarly, using more peripheral physiological measures such as electrodermal activity to discriminate between hemispheric utilization is fraught with pitfalls. Though Gruzelier and Venables (1973) and also Myslobotsky and Rattok (1977) have generated some evidence in support of the utility of bilateral electrodermal measures for such differentiation, the literature is not, on the whole, unequivocally supportive of their speculations (Gross & Stern, in press; Ketterer & Smith, 1977; LaCroix & Comper, 1979). Moreover, it is unclear whether electrical activity underlying the electrodermal response in the hands or feet is mediated via ipsilateral or contralateral pathways. Thus, interpreting differences in electrodermal activity within the context of hemispheric specialization is complicated.

We suspect that the development of newer and more sensitive physiological measures will allow us to look at more biological aspects of hemispheric specialization and information processing than has been true in the past. Two examples come to mind. The first deals with a new type of EEG procedure, namely, magnetoencephalography. The developers of this technique claim that it allows one to assess much more restricted areas of CNS function than is true of EEG and, in fact, makes it possible to discriminate between encephalographic recordings of motor responses made with the left and right hand.

The second procedure involves the use of radioactive tracer techniques to study regional cerebral blood flow as affected by cognitive activity. The assumption here is that if one hemisphere, or one restricted area of a hemisphere, is more intensely involved in processing a specified type of information, then that area of the brain requires more oxygen. An increase in oxygenation is accompanied by an increase in blood flow. Obrist, Thompson, Wang, and Wilkinson (1975) and Risberg and Ingvar (1973) have demonstrated an increase in cerebral blood flow associated with cognitive activity, and Lassen, Ingvar, and Skinhøj (1978) have demonstrated localized changes in blood flow associated with such tasks as reading. However, the first demonstration of alterations in regional cerebral blood flow associated with restricted types of information processing was published by Gur and Reivich (1980). It is this technique which, though expensive, holds a great deal of promise for investigating CNS activity associated with perception and cognition. These results are provocative but need to be replicated before this technique becomes *the* procedure for evaluating hemispheric activation.

REFERENCES

Anzola, G. P., Bertoloni, G., Buchtel, H. A., & Rizzolatti, G. Spatial compatibility and anatomical factors in simple and choice reaction time. *Neuropsychologia*, 1977, *15*, 295–302.

Birren, J. E., & Schaie, K. W. (Eds.), *Handbook of the psychology of aging*. New York: Van Nostrand Reinhold, 1977.

Botwinick, J. *Aging and behavior* (2nd ed.). New York: Springer, 1978.

Botwinick, J., & Thompson, L. W. Cardiac function and reaction time in relation to age. *Genetic Psychology*, 1971, *119*, 127–132.

Bradshaw, J. L., & Perriment, A. D. Laterality effects and choice reaction time in a unimanual two-finger task. *Perception & Psychophysics*, 1970, *7*, 185–188.

Brinkman, J., & Kuypers, H. G. J. M. Cerebral control of contralateral and ipsilateral arm, hand and finger movements in the split-brain rhesus monkey. *Brain*, 1973, *96*, 653–674.

Brinley, J. F. Cognitive sets, speed and accuracy of performance in the elderly. In A. T. Welford & J. E. Birren (Eds.), *Behavior, aging, and the nervous system*. Springfield, Ill.: Charles C Thomas, 1961.

Broman, M. Reaction-time differences between the left and right hemispheres for face and letter discrimination in children and adults. *Cortex*, 1978, *14*, 578–591.

Buffrey, A. W. H. Asymmetrical lateralization of cerebral functions and the effects of unilateral brain surgery in epileptic patients. In S. J. Dimond & J. G. Beaumont (Eds.), *Hemisphere function in the human brain*. New York: Wiley, 1974.

Busse, E. W., & Obrist, W. D. Significance of focal electroencephalographic changes in the elderly. *Postgraduate Medicine*, 1963, *34*, 179–182.

Cohen, D., & Wilkie, F. Sex-related differences in cognition among the elderly. In M. A. Wittig & A. C. Petersen (Eds.), *Sex-related differences in cognitive functioning. Developmental issues*. New York: Academic Press, 1979.

Coughlan, A. K., & Warrington, E. K. Word-comprehension and word-retrieval in patients with localized cerebral lesions. *Brain*, 1978, *101*, 163–185.

Davis, R., & Schmit, V. Visual and verbal coding in the interhemispheric transfer of information. *Acta Psychologica*, 1973, *37*, 229–240.

de Renzi, E., Faglioni, P., & Spinnler, H. The performance of patients with unilateral brain damage on face recognition tasks. *Cortex*, 1968, *4*, 17–34.

Dimond, S. Reaction times and response competition between the right and left hands. *Quarterly Journal of Experimental Psychology*, 1970, *22*, 513–520.

Dimond, S. J., & Beaumont, J. G. *Hemisphere function in the human brain*. New York: Wiley, 1974.

Dodd, D. H., & Schultz, R. F. Computational procedures for estimating magnitude of effect for some analysis of variance designs. *Psychological Bulletin*, 1973, *79*, 391–395.

Donchin, E., Kutas, M., & McCarthy, G. Electrocortical indices of hemispheric utilization. In S. Harnad, R. W. Doty, L. Goldstein, J. Jaynes, and G. Krauthamer (Eds.), *Lateralization in the nervous system*. New York: Academic Press, 1977.

Elias, J. W., & Elias, M. F. Matching of successive auditory stimuli as a function of age and ear of presentation. *Journal of Gerontology*, 1976, *31*, 164–169.

Elias, J. W., Wright, L. L., & Winn, F. J. Age and sex differences in cerebral asymmetry as a function of competition for "time" and "space" in a successive auditory matching task. *Experimental Aging Research*, 1977, *3*, 33–48.

Elias, M. F., & Kinsbourne, M. Age and sex differences in the processing of verbal and nonverbal stimuli. *Journal of Gerontology*, 1974, *29*, 162–171.

Fedor-Freybergh, P. The influence of oestrogens on the well being and mental performance of climacteric and postmenopausal women. *Acta Obstetricia et Gynecologica Scandinavica*, 1977, Supplement 64.

Filbey, R. A., & Gazzaniga, M. S. Splitting the normal brain with reaction time. *Psychonomic Science*, 1969, *17*, 335–336.

Geffen, G., Bradshaw, J. L., & Wallace, G. Interhemispheric effects on reaction time to verbal and nonverbal visual stimuli. *Journal of Experimental Psychology*, 1971, *87*, 415–422.

Goldstein, G., & Shelly, C. H. Similarities and differences between psychological deficit in aging and brain damage. *Journal of Gerontology*, 1975, *30*, 448–455.

Gross, J. S., & Stern, J. A. An investigation of bilateral asymmetries in electrodermal activity. *Pavlovian Journal of Biological Science*, in press.

Gross, M. M. Hemispheric specialization for processing of visually presented verbal and spatial stimuli. *Perception & Psychophysics*, 1972, *12*, 357–363.

Gruzelier, J., & Venables, P. H. Skin conductance responses to tones with and without attentional significance in schizophrenic and non-schizophrenic psychiatric patients. *Neuropsychologia*, 1973, *11*, 221–230.

Gur, R. C., & Reivich, M. Cognitive task effects on hemispheric blood flow in humans: Evidence for individual differences in hemispheric activation. *Brain and Language*, 1980, *9*, 78–92.

Harnad, H., Doty, R. W., Goldstein, L., Jaynes, J., & Krauthamer, G. (Eds.). *Lateralization in the nervous system*. New York: Academic Press, 1977.

Haun, F. Functional dissociation of the hemispheres using foveal visual input. *Neuropsychologia*, 1978, *16*, 725–733.

Hillyard, S. A., & Woods, D. L. Electrophysiological analysis of human brain function. Chapter 12 in M. S. Gazzaniga (Ed.), *Handbook of behavioral neurobiology: Neuropsychology* (Vol. 2). New York: Plenum Press, 1979.

Hodgkins, J. Influence of age on the speed of reaction and

movement in females. *Journal of Gerontology*, 1962, *17*, 385–389.

Hoine, H. *Motor overflow and the speed of reaction in children*. Unpublished doctoral dissertation, Washington University (St. Louis), 1976.

Horn, J. L., & Cattell, R. B. Age differences in primary mental ability factors. *Journal of Gerontology*, 1966, *21*, 210–220.

Horn, J. L., & Cattell, R. B. Age differences in fluid and crystallized intelligence. *Acta Psychologica*, 1967, *26*, 107–179.

Jeeves, M. A., & Dixon, N. F. Hemisphere differences in response rates to visual stimuli. *Psychonomic Science*, 1970, *20*, 249–251.

Johnson, R. C., Cole, R. E. Bowers, J. K., Foiles, S. V., Nikaido, A. M., Patrick, J. W., & Woliver, R. E. Hemispheric efficiency in middle and later adulthood. *Cortex*, 1979, *15*, 109–119.

Kappauf, W. E., & Yeatman, F. R. Visual on-and-off latencies and handedness. *Perception & Psychophysics*, 1970, *8*, 46–50.

Kelso, J. A. S., Southard, D. L., & Goodman, D. On the coordination of two-handed movements. *Journal of Experimental Psychology: Human Perception and Performance*, 1979, *5*, 229–238.

Ketterer, M. W., & Smith, B. D. Bilateral electrodermal activity, lateralized cerebral processing and sex. *Psychophysiology*, 1977, *14*, 513–516.

Kimura, D. The asymmetry of the human brain. *Scientific American*, 1973, *228*, 70–78.

Kinsbourne, M. The mechanism of hemispheric control of the lateral gradient of attention. In P. M. A. Rabbitt & S. Dornic (Eds.), *Attention and performance* (Vol. 5). New York: Academic Press, 1973.

Klisz, D. Neuropsychological evaluation in older persons. In M. Storandt, I. C. Siegler, & M. F. Elias (Eds.), *The clinical psychology of aging*. New York: Plenum Press, 1978.

LaCroix, J. M., & Comper, P. Lateralization in the electrodermal system as a function of cognitive/hemispheric manipulations. *Psychophysiology*, 1979, *16*, 116–129.

Lassen, N. A., Ingvar, D. H., & Skinhøj, E. Brain function and blood flow. *Scientific American*, 1978, *239*, 62–71.

Levy, J. Possible basis for the evolution of lateral specialization of the human brain. *Nature*, 1969, *224*, 614.

Luria, A. R. *Higher cortical functions in man*. New York: Basic Books, 1966.

Marsh, G. R. Age differences in evoked potential correlates of a memory scanning process. *Experimental Aging Research*, 1975, *1*, 3–16.

McGlone, J., & Davidson, W. The relation between cerebral speech processing of laterality and spatial ability with special reference to sex and hand preference. *Neuropsychologia*, 1973, *11*, 105–113.

Moscovitch, M. Choice reaction time study assessing the verbal behavior of the minor hemisphere in normal adult humans. *Journal of Comparative and Physiological Psychology*, 1972, *80*, 66–74.

Myslobotsky, M. S., & Rattok, J. Bilateral electrodermal

activity in waking man. *Acta Psychologica*, 1977, *41*, 273–282.

Nebes, R. D. Vocal versus manual response as a determinant of simple reaction time. *Journal of Gerontology*, 1978, *33*, 884–889.

Newport, K. *The relationships of decision-time, movement-time, and age on four reaction-time tasks*. Honors thesis, Washington University (St. Louis), 1977.

Obrist, W. D. *EEG and intellectual function in the aged*. Paper presented at the 25th annual meeting of the American EEG Society, Minneapolis, Minnesota, 1971.

Obrist, W. D., Thompson, H. D., Wang, H. S., & Wilkinson, W. E. Regional cerebral blood flow estimated by [113]Xenon inhalation. *Stroke*, 1975, *6*, 245–256.

Oster, P. J., Stern, J. A., & Newport, K. *Concerted hemispheric control of two-handed movement: Qualitative change in development*. Scheduled for presentation at the meeting of the American Psychological Association, Montreal, Quebec, Canada, September 1–5, 1980.

Overall, J. E., & Gorham, D. R. Organicity vs. old age in objective and projective test performance. *Journal of Consulting and Clinical Psychology*, 1972, *39*, 98–105.

Panek, P. E., Barrett, G. V., Sterns, H. L., & Alexander, R. A. Age differences in perceptual style, selective attention, and perceptual-motor reaction time. *Experimental Aging Research*, 1978, *4*, 377–387.

Patterson, K., & Bradshaw, J. L. Differential hemispheric mediation of nonverbal visual stimuli. *Journal of Experimental Psychology: Human Perception and Performance*, 1975, *1*, 246–252.

Pierson, W. R., & Montoye, H. J. Movement time, reaction time, and age. *Journal of Gerontology*, 1958, *13*, 418–421.

Poffenberger, A. T. Reaction time to retinal stimulation with special reference to the time lost in conduction through nerve centers. *Archives of Psychology*, 1912, *23*, 1–73.

Posner, M. I., & Mitchell, R. F. Chronometric analysis of classification. *Psychological Review*, 1967, *74*, 392–409.

Rabbitt, P. M. A. Times for transition between hand and foot response in a self-paced task. *Quarterly Journal of Experimental Psychology*, 1966, *18*, 334–339.

Risberg, J., & Ingvar, D. M. Patterns of activation in the gray matter of the dominant hemisphere. *Brain*, 1973, *96*, 737–756.

Rizzolatti, G., Umilta, C., & Berlucchi, G. Opposite superiorities of the right and left cerebral hemispheres in discriminative reaction time to physiognomial and alphabetical material. *Brain*, 1971, *94*, 431–442.

Schaie, K. W., & Schaie, J. P. Clinical assessment and aging. In J. E. Birren and K. W. Schaie (Eds.), *Handbook of the psychology of aging*. New York: Van Nostrand Reinhold, 1977.

Simon, J. R. Choice reaction time as a function of auditory S-R correspondence, age, and sex. *Ergonomics*, 1967, *10*, 659–664.

Singleton, W. T. The change of movement timing with age. *British Journal of Psychology*, 1954, *45*, 166–172.

Sperry, R. W. Lateral specialization in the surgically separated hemispheres. In F. O. Schmitt and F. G. Worden

(Eds.), *The neurosciences: Third study program*. Cambridge, Mass.: MIT Press, 1974.

Spieth, W. Slowness of task performance and cardiovascular disease. In A. T. Welford & J. E. Birren (Eds.), *Behavior, aging, and the nervous system*. Springfield, Ill.: Charles C Thomas, 1955.

Spirduso, W. W. Reaction time and movement time as a function of age and physical activity levels. *Journal of Gerontology*, 1975, *30*, 435–440.

Springer, S. P. Tachistoscopic and dichotic listening investigations of laterality in normal human subjects. In S. Harnad, R. W. Doty, L. Goldstein, J. Jaynes, & G. Krauthamer (Eds.), *Lateralization in the nervous system*. New York: Academic Press, 1977.

Stern, J. A., Oster, P. J., & Newport, K. *Hemispheric interference and age: Motor versus decision components of RT*. Paper presented at the 32nd annual meeting of the Gerontological Society, Washington, D.C. Nov. 25–29, 1979.

Swisher, L., & Hirsh, I. J. Brain damage and the ordering of two temporally successive stimuli. *Neuropsychologia*, 1972, *10*, 137–152.

Szafran, J. Change with age and with exclusion of vision in performance at an aiming task. *Quarterly Journal of Experimental Psychology*, 1951, *3*, 111–118.

Talland, G. A. Initiation of response, and reaction time in aging, and with brain damage. Chapter 26 in A. T. Welford & J. E. Birren (Eds.), Behavior, aging, and the nervous system. Springfield, Ill.: Charles C Thomas, 1965.

Walrath, L. C., & Hallman, L. E. *Age-related changes in visual ERP during memory storage and retrieval*. Paper presented at the meeting of the American Psychological Association, New York, August 31–September 5, 1979.

Walsh, D. A., Williams, M. V., & Hertzog, C. K. Age-related differences in two stages of central perceptual processes: The effects of short duration targets and criterion differences. *Journal of Gerontology*, 1979, *34*, 234–241.

Waugh, N. C., Fozard, J. L., Talland, G. A., & Erwin, D. E. Effects of age and stimulus repetition on two choice RT. *Journal of Gerontology*, 1973, *28*, 466–470.

Welford, A. T. Age and skill: Motor, intellectual and social. In A. T. Welford & J. E. Birren (Eds.), *Decision making and age*. New York: S. Karger, 1969.

White, M. J. Laterality differences in perception: A review. *Psychological Bulletin*, 1969, *72*, 387–405.

White, M. J. Hemispheric asymmetries in tachistoscopic processing. *British Journal of Psychology*, 1972, *63*, 497–508.

White, M. J., & White, K. G. Parallel-serial processing and hemispheric function. *Neuropsychologia*, 1975, *13*, 377–381.

Walter R. Cunningham

CHAPTER
23

Speed, Age, and Qualitative Differences in Cognitive Functioning

The stability of factor structure of intellectual abilities with age is considered. In one longitudinal study and three cross-sectional studies carried out by the author no change was found in the number of factors, nor were there any psychologically important changes in the pattern of factor loadings. Factor covariances tended to become larger with age, however, and this tendency became most pronounced for high-speeded demand tasks (e.g., perceptual speed measures). The absence of a reduction in the number of factors, even in the older group, precludes clear support for the dedifferentiation hypothesis. Although the increased factor covariances with age might be construed as supporting dedifferentiation, given these results, a greater interdependence of abilities in later life seems a more plausible explanation than outright dedifferentiation. Further avenues of research are proposed.

A topic of considerable importance for understanding the behavior of the aged and how behavior changes with age is speed and timing. In the psychology of aging, wherever we look, we see the importance of the speed of behavior (Birren, 1974). The principle of the slowing of behavior with age is ubiquitous. It appears in obvious places such as in studies of choice reaction time and psychomotor performance. In studies of learning and memory, whether one considers problems of acquisition or retrieval, speed of stimuli presentation and response emerge as critical factors in explaining psychological differences between the young and the old. Also, if we consider more complex, higher order behavior such as intelligence, the speed of behavior emerges as a critical variable of interest.

This generalizability of the importance of the speed of behavior is in no way limited to areas of psychological research. If we consider the performance of physiological or cellular systems, we again find that the speed of system response is an important variable in the understanding of age changes.

The importance of the speed of behavior is also found to be highly robust across different methods employed to carry out research on aging. For example, the issue of cohort differences and the discrepancies between cross-sectional and longitudinal results have produced a great deal of rethinking in a number of prominent formulations on changes in intelligence with age. The impact of sequential data, however, has been to emphasize rather than diminish the importance of the speed of behavior. For example, the longitudinal gradients of Schaie and Strother (1968) show greater

The research discussed here was supported by a National Institute of Child Health and Human Development predoctoral fellowship, AoA Grant 90-A-646, National Institute on Aging Grant R23 AGO 1162, and the Center for Gerontological Studies at the University of Florida. This support is gratefully acknowledged.

I would like to take this opportunity to acknowledge the assistance of a number of graduate students who labored long and hard on the massive data collection and data processing involved in the Florida study. To these students, Thomas Harbin, Patricia Richardson, Mary Opel, Sandra Witt, and Paul Chafetz, I extend my sincere gratitude.

decrements than the cross-sectional gradients for perceptual speed. Thus the conclusion has been that cross-sectional studies may actually underestimate the extent of slowing with age.

In addition to an impressive generalization across topic, discipline, and design, the importance of the speed of behavior emerges from a remarkable variety of ways of looking at data in a statistical sense. For example, most psychologists tend to emphasize the analysis of mean scores in the study of behavior. While there may be many good reasons for this approach, the subtleties of aging are often reflected in other statistical representations as well. For example, the speed of behavior manifests itself in considerations of variances and covariances. If we consider the variability of response within individual subjects in different kinds of reaction-time tasks, we find that variability of response is often larger in older subjects than in young ones. Rather often, in my view, hypotheses of considerable scientific merit can be tested more suitably by contrasting variances rather than mean scores.

My own research for several years now has concentrated on studying covariances among measures of intelligence and how these structures change with age. Detailed reports of these findings are available elsewhere (Cunningham, 1980, in press; Cunningham & Birren, in press; Cunningham & Richardson, 1978). Given the ubiquitous role of the speed of behavior in cognitive research with the aged, it should come as no surprise that it should manifest itself in this context as well.

Cunningham and Birren (in press) reanalyzed data from Owens's (1953, 1966) long-term longitudinal study which used the eight subtests of the Army Alpha Examination. In order to facilitate interpretations of the data, an additional time-lag comparison was included that compared factor structure of young people in 1919 on the first occasion of longitudinal measurement with the factor structure of young people in the 1970s. Changes in factor structure that are statistically highly significant were found in the longitudinal comparisons, with the changes most marked in the 60-year-old group. In the time-lag comparison, however, a strikingly similar factor structure was found for young people in 1919 and young people in the 1970s. In particular, a simultaneous model was found plausible in which the factor loading and factor covariance matrices were constrained to be identical across groups. It is somewhat unusual to find such similar structures across groups that vary systematically. Note that these groups differed in occasion of measurement and cohort by approximately 50 years. This result suggested that the effects of cohort and time on ability factor structure are negligible, and it therefore

rendered plausible an ontogenetic interpretation of the longitudinal changes. These general findings supported the stability of factor structure when age is held constant and further supported the hypothesis that factor structure changes systematically with age.

The most striking change in structure noted in Cunningham and Birren's results was the increased correlation between the Verbal factor and the Highly Speeded Relations factor. Thus in the young subjects the Speeded Relations factor and the Verbal Comprehension factor appear to be virtually independent, whereas in the oldest group they are highly correlated and share almost 50% of the variance across factors. The Verbal and Numerical factors also tended to be more highly correlated on the two later occasions of measurement than on the first occasion of measurement.

While this study was constructive in showing changes over long-term longitudinal comparisons within age-homogeneous groupings, it could have been improved by the use of a more extensive sampling of abilities. Increasing the number of variables has two advantages. First, short sets of subtests in the traditional group-intelligence tests are not ideal materials for factor-analytic investigations. While comparisons based on such tests may contribute to conclusions on whether the structures differ across age or cultural groups, they would not lead to very precise conclusions about the nature of such factor changes. This is because the factors are not as clearly marked as they might be with more numerous and more refined psychometrically developed measures. Also, from the perspective of variable sampling, it is clear that a more diverse and representative sample of intellectual tasks would be desirable.

Taking into account the limitations of the previous research, particularly the small variable sets and the modest samples involved, I designed a study to investigate factor-structure age differences, with a better sampling of the universe of abilities, and with substantially larger participant samples, in the hope of achieving more stable parameter estimates than had occurred in earlier work. The primary hypothesis was that age differences in factor structure would be greater for highly speeded tasks but would be less pronounced for tasks in which speed was not a critical feature.

There were four major reasons for carrying out this study: (1) to evaluate the comparative construct validity (both convergent and discriminate) across age groups; (2) for theoretical reasons, to shed further light on the viability of the dedifferentiation hypothesis i.e., is there a reduction in the number of factors—see Reinert, 1970, for a review; (3) to evaluate the plausibility of applying multivariate procedures (e.g., multivariate analysis of variance), which involve the assumption of homogeneity of covariance structures; and (4) to investigate the generality of factor structures developed in the young to elderly samples.

The young sample consisted of about 200 young men and women ranging in age from 15 to 32 years of age. For the older subjects the factors were organized into three batteries, with complete data being obtained on about 300 senior citizens for each battery. Within each battery, the subjects were divided into two subgroups of "younger old" and "older old," with about 150 persons in each group. Young subjects were recruited by newspaper advertisement in the local Gainesville, Florida area, while the older subjects were recruited in cooperation with the American Association of Retired Persons in approximately 30 cities throughout the state of Florida. The younger old ranged in age from about 59 to 68 years, while the older old ranged from about 69 to 88 years. These age ranges were very slightly different across batteries.

Factors and related variables were selected on the basis of well-replicated findings from the young adult psychometric literature (French, Ekstrom, & Price, 1963; Guilford, 1967). Ten factors (and 30 measures) were selected for the age-comparative study.

The various factors were organized into three batteries on the basis of the degree of speededness required for each factor. Battery I consisted of four factors, such as Perceptual Speed, in which the speed of carrying out the task was the most prominent characteristic of the test. Battery II contained five factors that were mixed with regard to speed demands. Battery III consisted of three factors for which speed requirements were considered minimal.

The specific hypotheses were (1) that age differences in factor structure would be obtained, (2) that larger differences would be found for the highly speeded battery, (3) that the observed differences would be primarily in terms of the factor covariance matrices (that is, the interrelations between factors), and (4) that some factor fusion would occur in the highly speeded battery (that is, the number of factors required to explain the interrelations would be reduced in the older samples). The data analyses involved simultaneous factor analysis using maximum likelihood techniques which yield chi-square goodness-of-fit measures to evaluate structural similarity (Jöreskog, 1971).

Across the whole study, it was found that the number of factors remained constant across all three batteries. Thus no factor fusion occurred. Although statistically highly reliable differences in factor loading patterns were obtained, these differences were in terms of the magnitude of the loadings, not in the pattern of

saliency. Thus even though significant differences in factor loading pattern were found, the differences did not alter the construct validity of the measures but rather merely indicated slightly different magnitudes of loadings. The primary differences in structure were manifested in the factor covariances. As expected, the changes in factor covariances were most dramatic for the highly speeded battery, with three of six factor covariances attaining such unusually high values that they were arbitrarily constrained to be .70. This was in keeping with the traditional psychometric practice of limiting the magnitude of interrelations in hand-rotated solutions, since it is well-known (Comrey, 1973) that a simple structure solution can almost always be improved by allowing factors to be ever more highly correlated. In my opinion, an analogous situation occurs in maximum likelihood modeling as well, and thus it makes sense to limit a priori the maximum value of interrelations that factors are allowed to attain, in order to avoid possible rotational artifacts. It is noted in passing that such high interrelations could provide a point of departure for reconsidering the number-of-factors problem, but in the data under consideration both chi-square tests and the Tucker reliability coefficients supported an equivalent number of factors across age groups.

Tables 23-1 through 23-4 show a summary of the factor covariance results. In general, throughout the analyses we attempted to keep the factors orthogonal, relying on a chi-square goodness-of-fit test, positive manifold, and simple structure to evaluate resulting structures. Orthogonal solutions with excellent simple structure and positive manifold were easy to obtain in the young sample. Orthogonal solutions were always rejected by the chi-square test in the older samples. In the highly speeded battery (as had been the case in the previous Cunningham and Birren study) factors tended to become considerably more interrelated with age. Because of variations in scale within and across studies, and also to simplify the fairly complex outcomes and their exposition, it seemed useful to group the factor covariances obtained into three groups: covariances at or near zero (that is, orthogonal or virtually so), intermediate covariances (probably greater

Table 23-1 Factor Covariances for the Cunningham and Birren Study

Degree of factor interdependence	Approximate age		
	20	50	60
Orthogonal or close to it	1	0	0
Intermediate	2	2	1
Fixed at about .7	0	1	2

Table 23-2 Factor Covariances for the Highly Speeded Battery of the Florida Study

Degree of factor interdependence	Approximate age		
	18–32	50–68	69–88
Orthogonal or close to it	6	0	0
Intermediate	0	6	3
Fixed at about .7	0	0	3

than zero but less than .7), and covariances that tended to be so high as to be fixed at a maximum value of .7. For the Cunningham and Birren study, and for Batteries I and II, a relation emerges between degree of factor covariance and age. For Battery III, the unspeeded battery, however, there is no clear-cut trend in the two older groups. Also, as hypothesized, the highest factor covariances were observed in Battery I, the highly speeded battery. Further, high covariances occurred earlier (for age) than in the other two batteries.

Certain caveats are appropriate with regard to the data presented in Tables 23-1 through 23-4. First, in order to present a simple and uncluttered overview of the results of four sets of age-comparative factor analyses, much detailed information was omitted. The general effect of this simplification was to emphasize the tendency toward greater factor covariances with age and to blur some inconsistencies in this pattern. For example, in the highly speeded battery, two factor covariances (of six) actually decreased slightly in the oldest age group compared to the younger old. Thus, in some ways, the tables presented make the results appear more consistent than they really were. Also, it is important to recognize that in any factor-analytic study, there are an infinite number of possible rotational solutions that can be applied. Other rotational schemes might conceivably yield different results. I believe, however, that the model-testing procedures employed are optimal (given the current state of the art) for evaluating the generality of ability factor structures previously developed in studies with young adults.

The Florida study was cross-sectional in design. It seems plausible, however, that the resulting age differences reflect age changes. Thus I am assuming that cohort differences in covariance structure are negligible. There are several reasons for this. First, there is no published evidence supporting cohort differences in covariance structure. Second, our longitudinal study results (Cunningham and Birren, in press) yield the same pattern of empirical findings as the cross-sectional results in the Florida study: same number of factors, very similar or identical factor loading patterns, with trends toward greater factor covariances with age, and with such trends being most pronounced in highly speeded tasks. Third, time-lag comparisons of interrelations among ability variables yield negligible differences (e.g., the remarkable fit in structure for young people in 1919 and young people in the 1970s).

Some other issues should be explicitly considered as well. For some variables in the Florida study, variances increased with age. It is logically possible that the increased covariances might reflect progressively greater heterogeneity (particularly of educational attainment) in each succeeding age group. This could conceivably be a sampling artifact or a genuine age change in variance that would account for the increased factor covariance. This hypothetical effect could be conceived of in the following way. It is well-known that restriction in range of scores diminishes the magnitude of correlation between variables. It is possible that increasing the variances of variables would increase the interrelations between variables; these increases would be reflected in the factor model as enlarged covariances.

There are several reasons to doubt this line of reasoning. First, some factors showed increased factor covariances when constituent variables showed negligible or no increased variances. Second, in the Cunningham and Birren longitudinal study, participants were constant across occasions of measurement, but uniformly scaled average variances (across variables, within occasions) actually decreased slightly with age. Moreover, if the increased covariances were reflective of increased educational heterogeneity, then one would expect strong effects for factors such as Verbal

Table 23-3 Factor Covariances for the Mixed Speeded Battery of the Florida Study

Degree of factor interdependence	Approximate age		
	18–32	50–68	69–88
Orthogonal or close to it	10	5	0
Intermediate	0	5	10
Fixed at about .7	0	0	0

Table 23-4 Factor Covariances for the Less Speeded Battery of the Florida Study

Degree of factor interdependence	Approximate age		
	18–32	50–68	69–88
Orthogonal or close to it	3	0	0
Intermediate	0	3	3
Fixed at about .7	0	0	0

Comprehension, which are known to be sensitive to educational variables, and weak effects for factors such as Perceptual Speed, which are less closely related to education. The observed pattern of results is just the reverse. Given these observations, the increase in covariances does not appear to be an artifact of selection or of age changes in range of ability.

The general conclusions were as follows. Owing to the relative stability of factor loadings across all of the studies considered, the age comparative construct validity of measures seemed to be well supported. We found no actual fusion of factors. Therefore there is no direct support for dedifferentiation. The fact that increased factor covariances were found raises the possibility that dedifferentiation may occur at much older ages or perhaps in senile samples (see, e.g., Dixon, 1965). But the age range in the Florida study was quite high. Thus these results suggest that the principle of dedifferentiation, if valid, may not be particularly important and may apply only to groups of really advanced age (older than 85?) or to the senile.

On the other hand, the finding of increased covariances appears reliable and has now been replicated across quite a number of different groups of factors. In my view the primary question at hand is, What can account for these differences in covariance structure? If abilities become more interdependent with age, it seems only logical to ask what is the source of this greater interdependence.

One possibility, which we are currently beginning to investigate in our laboratory, is the possibility that a slowing of memory processes or decrements in the efficiency of memory may account for these structural differences in intellectual functioning. There are, of course, other possibilities as well. Attentional deficits and health status also appear as plausible mechanisms for further investigation.

What further research appears useful on the basis of the results reported here? Many investigators are becoming interested in relations among cognitive processing variables and psychometric variables. Such interest is sometimes expressed in factor paradigms. It would be of interest to explore structural differences in cognitive processing variables generally to determine whether similar structural changes are associated with age at that level of analysis. Another area of interest concerns the stability of intelligence-test structure over cultural change. Although the weight of current evidence favors the notion of considerable stability, the amount of evidence available is, in absolute terms, quite modest. Therefore additional time-lag studies of

structure with test batteries suitable for factor-analytic techniques would be very useful. This is particularly true for time-lag comparisons in late life. Also, studies of test batteries with different characteristics than those employed in the work described here would be constructive. Note that the factors employed here are narrow and tightly defined. Broader common factors might yield greater qualitative differences than those obtained here, as was the case with our longitudinal research with the Army Alpha (Cunningham and Birren, in press). Clearly there is much to be done.

REFERENCES

Birren, J. E. Psychophysiology and speed of response. *American Psychologist*, 1974, *29*, 808–815.

Comrey, A. L. *A first course in factor analysis.* New York: Academic Press, 1973.

Cunningham, W. R. Ability factor structure differences in adulthood and old age. *Multivariate Behavioral Research*, in press.

Cunningham, W. R. Age comparative factor analysis of ability variables in adulthood and old age. *Intelligence*, 1980, *4*, 133–149.

Cunningham, W. R., & Birren, J. E. Age changes in the factor structure of intellectual abilities in adulthood and old age. *Educational and Psychological Measurement*, in press.

Cunningham, W. R., & Richardson, P. C. *Age differences in factor structure of highly speeded intelligence tests.* Paper presented at the meeting of the American Psychological Association, Toronto, Ontario, Canada, September 1978.

Dixon, J. C. Cognitive structure in senile conditions with some suggestions for developing a brief screening test of mental status. *Journal of Gerontology*, 1965, *20*, 41–49.

French, J. W., Ekstrom, R. B., & Price, L. A. *Manual for kit of reference tests for cognitive factors.* Princeton, N.J.: Educational Testing Service, 1963.

Guilford, J. P. *The nature of human intelligence.* New York: McGraw-Hill, 1967.

Jöreskog, K. G. Simultaneous factor analysis in several populations. *Psychometrika*, 1971, *36*, 409–426.

Owens, W. A. Age and mental abilities: A longitudinal study. *Genetic Psychology Monographs*, 1953, *48*, 3–54.

Owens, W. A. Age and mental ability: A second follow-up. *Journal of Educational Psychology*, 1966, *57*, 311–325.

Reinert, G. Comparative factor analytic studies of intelligence throughout the human life-span. In L. R. Goulet & P. B. Baltes (Eds.), *Life-span developmental psychology.* New York: Academic Press, 1970.

Schaie, K. W., & Strother, C. R. A cross-sequential study of age changes in cognitive behavior. *Psychological Bulletin*, 1968, *70*, 671–680.

John Cerella, Leonard W. Poon, and Diane M. Williams

CHAPTER
24

Age and the Complexity Hypothesis

The reaction-time literature was surveyed with respect to the hypothesis that more complex tasks result in greater performance deficits for the elderly. This hypothesis was supported by data from 18 studies encompassing a variety of information-processing tasks and appears to be a consequence of a proportional slowing of the mental functions of the elderly. Two levels of deficit were seen in the data, a slight slowing on sensorimotor tasks and a more severe slowing on tasks involving mental processing.

A study by Arnold and Farkas (1978) is typical of many experiments performed in the last three decades on the effects of age on information processing. The experiment centered around a carefully considered problem, the visual detection of target symbols, the solution of which involved the employment of a specific set of information processes. The task was administered to a group of college-age subjects and to a group of elderly subjects, and the average task-completion time for each group was measured. The left column of Table 24-1 shows completion times for a simple version of the task, the detection of target symbols embedded in clearly distinguishable background symbols. Target detection for young subjects was very rapid, 20 seconds per block of 12 trials, and for older subjects it was less rapid, 31 seconds per block, or 11 seconds over the time of the young subjects.

The right column of Table 24-1 shows processing times on a more difficult version of the task. Target symbols in this task were embedded in highly similar background symbols. The increased difficulty of detection is reflected in the young subjects' latencies, which were now 38 seconds per block. For older subjects,

latencies for the more difficult condition were 62 seconds per block, an increase of 24 seconds over young subjects. Thus the difference in performance times between the young and old subjects increased from the simpler to the more difficult condition.

Arnold and Farkas's study is typical in two ways: First, in format, dozens of studies in the last decades have compared young and old subjects' processing times on various information-processing tasks. Second, and more interesting, their study is typical in its results—not only was slowing found in the cognitive functions of the older subject, but, as we shall focus on in this chapter, the slowing increased significantly in the more difficult task; that is, the age deficit jumped from 11 to 24 seconds.

This pattern of results was noted early by theorists in the field. In 1965 Welford surveyed data suggesting a "linear increase" in the time taken by elderly subjects, compared to young subjects, to complete a task "as the task becomes more difficult." Birren, also in 1965, summarized age deficits in a similar vein: "Although present in simple skills, the slowing appears larger as one ascends a hierarchical ladder of the complexity of process" (p. 215).

Aside from the fact of slowing per se, the observation that the amount of slowing is related to the difficulty of the task may be one of the earliest general

---

Preparation of this chapter was supported by National Institutes of Health Grant AG00467 and the Veterans Administration Research Service. The authors are indebted to James L. Fozard, J. Jack McArdle, Lawrence C. Perlmuter, Timothy A. Salthouse, Alan T. Welford, and Michael Williams for their comments on earlier drafts.

Table 24-1 Search Time in Seconds for 12 Targets Embedded in Noise

Age	Confusability	
	Low	High
Young	20	38
Old	31	62

Note. Data are from Arnold & Farkas, 1978.

conclusions drawn from the gerontological literature on reaction times. This idea has not faded from view. Crowder (1980, p. 194) speaks of "a tendency for age effects to be larger in harder conditions," a tendency that he discusses in a wide-ranging review. Similarly, Barr (1980) uses this idea to analyze shape differences in aging functions that plot performance on various tasks as a function of decade of life.

The Complexity Hypothesis

Let us term the idea that the magnitude of the age difference in reaction times is proportional to the difficulty of the task, the *complexity hypothesis*. In this chapter we attempt to examine the complexity hypothesis in light of the experimental evidence of the 1950s, 1960s, and 1970s. The exercise of reevaluating data from different studies is filled with pitfalls ranging from variability in number of subjects employed, instructions, subject motivation, sampling procedures, and experimental conditions to differences in the reported data format. Nevertheless, we hope the case for the complexity hypothesis can be strengthened in three ways. First, if the complexity hypothesis indeed characterizes the aging process, its effects ought to be observed in any experiment that contrasts information-processing tasks. Second, although comparisons of conditions within individual experiments provide tests of the hypothesis, comparisons of conditions between experiments offer even more opportunities for evaluation. Thus the hypothesis should be able to rank order, in terms of the magnitude of the age difference, all of the conditions of all of the studies combined. Third, in addition to noting qualitatively whether or not a given study or pair of conditions shows a "complexity effect," we would like a quantitative measure of how well the data agree with the hypothesis.

The Measurement of Complexity

There seems to be one central obstacle to the realization of a more decisive test of the complexity hypothesis. We are in need of a generalized measure of task complexity, a measure that can assign a complexity score C_i to any information-processing tasks T_i—at least to any task with a conventional reaction-time format involving the presentation of a stimulus and the computation of a response. Some such measures have been advanced in the context of aging. Welford (1965) noted that

$$C_n = 1n_2(N)$$

provides a psychologically relevant measure of the complexity of the family of N-way choice reaction-time tasks. Birren and Botwinick (1951) found that

$$C_n = N$$

offers a complexity measure for sets of problems involving the addition of 2N digits. Neither of these measures, however, is sufficiently general to be applicable to an arbitrary task. Nor, we confess, are we able to offer a generalized complexity metric. We will propose instead an alternative.

How might a complexity measure be devised? Presumably one would start with an information-processing model able to decompose any task into a set of constituent processes. This of course is a goal of cognitive psychology, as typified in such texts as those by Lindsay and Norman (1977) and Glass, Holyoak, and Santa (1979), a goal hardly realized today. If psychologically relevant descriptions of information-processing tasks were available, some function would be advanced on ordered sets of information processes purporting to measure processing complexity. To evaluate such a function we would be inclined to compare the complexity scores assigned to a set of tasks to the actual processing times required by the tasks. We would object if a low complexity score were assigned to a task requiring a lengthy computation—or if a high complexity score were assigned to a task with a rapid execution time. In short, we would consider computation time decisive in fixing the difficulty of a task. But if processing time is assumed to define or at least to covary with task complexity, then we need no other measure of complexity.

We propose, therefore, that the processing time for a task be adopted as a measure of its complexity, where processing time is defined as the latency of the task itself minus a sensorimotor control latency. The control latency is usually obtained from a special version of the task in which the same stimulus presentation and the same motor response are involved but without an intervening computational requirement.

Table 24-2 Data Matrix

	Task	
Age	Control	Experimental
Young	A	B
Old	C	D

A Test of the Hypothesis

The form of a quantitative test of the complexity hypothesis can now be illustrated by a representative data matrix, pictured in Table 24-2. The matrix has the same structure as Table 24-1 in that A, B, C, and D represent average response times of young and old subjects on an experimental task and on a sensorimotor task. We wish to test the hypothesis that the age difference in a series of such data matrices will increase monotonically with task difficulty. As agreed upon above, task difficulty will be measured by the size of the task effect in the data matrix.

$$\text{Task difficulty} = \frac{B + D}{2} - \frac{A + C}{2}. \qquad (1)$$

That is, the larger the reaction times in the experimen-

tal task compared to the control task, the more difficult the task.

The age difference is given by the processing time for old subjects minus young subjects. The processing time in turn is given by the latency on the experimental task minus the control latency. Thus

$$\text{Age difference} = (D - C) - (B - A), \qquad (2)$$

which is the Age × Condition interaction effect in the data matrix.

In its general form, the complexity hypothesis states that the age difference will be monotonic with task difficulty, that is, as one increases, so will the other. Let us adopt the linear form of the general hypothesis in which the age difference will be directly proportional to task difficulty:

$$\text{Age difference } \alpha \text{ task difficulty.} \qquad (2a)$$

We can now formulate a quantitative version of the complexity hypothesis by substituting the definitions given by Equations 1 and 2 in the proportionality Equation 2a: Across any set of reaction time studies the prediction is made that

$$(D - C) - (B - A) = k\left[\frac{B + D}{2} - \frac{A + C}{2}\right]. \qquad (3)$$

Table 24-3 Experimental Data Used in Analysis

Type	Reference	No. of conditions	No. of age groups	Notes
Sternberg memory scanning	Anders & Fozard, 1973	6	2	
	Anders, Fozard, & Lillyquist, 1972	8	3	
	Erickson, Hamlin, & Daye, 1973	3	3	
	Thomas, Waugh, & Fozard, 1978	8	5	
Stimulus–response mapping	Kay, 1955 (cited in Welford, 1977)	3	6	
	Birren, Riegel, & Morrison, 1962	12	2	First 12 conditions only
	Simon, 1968	8	2	
Multiple choice RT	Goldfarb, 1941 (cited in Welford, 1977)	3	5	
	Griew, 1959	6	2	L1 and L2 series analyzed separately
	Suci, Davidoff, & Surwillo, 1960	4	2	
Alerting RT	Botwinick & Brinley, 1962	8	2	Irregular series not used
	Botwinick & Thompson, 1966	8	4	Premotor component only
Card-sorting	Botwinick, Robbin, & Brinley, 1960 (cited in Welford, 1977)	5	2	
	Crossman & Szafran, 1956	4	3	Experiment I only
	Rabbitt, 1964	8	2	
Line length discrimination	Birren & Botwinick, 1955	12	2	
Paired associate learning	Waugh, Thomas, & Fozard, 1978	3	4	Experiment I only
Stimulus–response recall	Fozard & Poon, 1976	4	3	

Ideally, a test of Equation 3 would encompass every aging study with reaction time as the dependent measure. It is doubtful that such an undertaking is practical. Failing this, one might select a subset of studies according to an objective rule. In this preliminary effort we have been guided only by the desire to include a diversity of information-processing tasks in the hope of ensuring the generalizability of the results. In Table 24-3 are assembled 18 studies on reaction time drawn from the gerontological literature from 1941 to 1978. The studies report data from a total of 54 groups of subjects, and from 99 experimental conditions ranging from choice reaction time to memory scanning.

Equation 3 was tested by constructing from each study in Table 24-3 a series of 2 × 2 matrices and systematically pairing the data from every experimental task and from every older age group with the data from a control task and a young age group. The "control task" for a study was identified as the task resulting in the lowest reaction times for the study; in practically every case this task had the same input–output requirement as the experimental task but no computational requirement. The "young age group" for a study was defined as the subject group in their 20s (data from younger subjects, if any, was not employed in the analysis) or occasionally if there was none, the subject group in their 30s. The 18 studies yielded 154 separate 2 × 2 matrices. The condition effect, Equation 1, and the interaction term, Equation 2, were computed for each matrix, and the results were normalized by dividing by the young subjects' control reaction time. Condition and interaction effects were thus expressed as a percentage of the basic sensorimotor time for the task. Normalized values were then entered as points in the plot of condition effects versus interaction effects, as shown in Figure 24-1.

The scatter of points in this plot shows that, in general, as condition effects increase, so do interaction effects, with an overall correlation between them of .89. In addition, a linear regression returns a negligible y-intercept

$$Y = 47X - .09. \qquad (4)$$

Because the X and Y terms in Equation 4 are not independent, the exact significance of the correlation .89 is difficult to assess. Nevertheless, the proportionality between the interaction effect and the condition effect is direct and serves as a strong support for the complexity hypothesis in this preliminary exploration.

Explaining the Complexity Hypothesis

A variety of explanations have been offered for complexity effects. In individual studies, these Age × Condition interactions are often referred to the content of the tasks, as Arnold and Farkas (1978) concluded from the data in Table 24-1. Those data show some decline in the basic processes of visual search with advanced age and, according to Arnold and Farkas, a much more serious decline in the particular processes involved in the discrimination of fine detail.

Comalli, Wapner, and Werner (1962) used similar reasoning in analyzing Stroop test latencies, which showed an interaction of age with color-compatible, and color-incompatible conditions. The word identification that is required on color-compatible trials is slightly compromised with age, Comalli et al. concluded, while the inhibition of the competing response required on color-incompatible trials is more seriously compromised and leads to the Age × Complexity interaction.

Fozard and Poon (1976) attributed the progressive decline in older subjects' performances across the several conditions of a choice reaction-time experiment

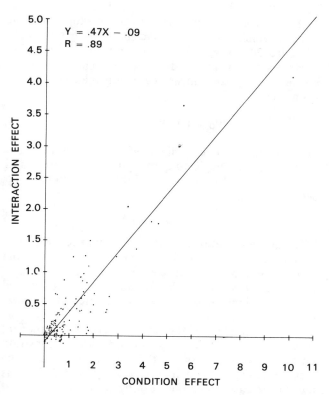

Figure 24-1. Data from old subjects and experimental tasks were compared with data from young subjects and control tasks. The comparison shows that the magnitude of the age effect on a task (i.e., the age × task interaction) is proportional to the difficulty of the task (i.e., the condition effect).

to the age-related decline in memory access requirement in the more complicated conditions. Fozard and Poon followed the logic of Welford (1964), who, in reviewing complexity effects in a variety of experiments, sought to isolate a general mechanism that would explain the individual cases. Welford noted decline in the short-term memory function of elderly subjects and reasoned that more complex tasks burden short-term memory in two ways: first, in the elaborateness of the "control programme" which must be stored to guide execution of the task, and second, in the amount of information requiring temporary storage in the course of a solution. On both accounts, short-term memory failure could cause a selective disadvantage for complex tasks. This disadvantage would be further aggravated by any reduction in the speed of processing because of the increased intervals of storage (Welford, 1958).

While these explanations deal adequately with individual effects, it seems unlikely that their aggregate effect would be systematic, as we have found in the data shown in Figure 24-1. One would expect that the size

of the interaction effect associated with a given condition effect would be arbitrary if each case had a different cause such as its particular short-term memory load; such data would plot as a broad horizontal band in Figure 24-1. The proportionality between interaction effect and condition effect that was in fact obtained suggests that some more general aging mechanism may be at work.

The regularity in condition and interaction effects led us to wonder if a similar regularity might not be found in the component reaction times themselves. Salthouse (1978) has described a simple method for assessing the effects of age on reaction times. A space is defined with young subjects' reaction times on one axis and old subjects' reaction times on the other. Each task for which an estimate of both young and old reaction times is available is plotted as a point in this space. The locus of these points will define the relation, or lack of relation, between young and old performances on tasks.

This method was applied to the data assembled in Table 24-3. Each young latency was paired with every older latency from the same task, and one was plotted against the other (see Figure 24-2). The distinction between control and experimental tasks disappears in the process, which results in 189 such pairs altogether.

Figure 24-2 suggests that a simple proportionality exists between young and old scores. This impression is confirmed in the linear regression relating old and young reaction times:

$$\text{Old} = 1.36 \text{ Young} - .07. \qquad (5)$$

The correlation here is high, .95, and the y-intercept term is small. Neglecting the y-intercept term, and rewriting in the notation of Table 24-2, Equation 5 becomes

$$D = kB, C = kA. \qquad (6)$$

The equation states that the performance of elderly subjects on a task is equal to the performance of young subjects on the task multiplied by a coefficient k that is the same across tasks. Elderly subjects are thus slowed by an invariant factor in the performance of information-processing tasks.

It seems likely that the relation between component reaction times enforced by Equation 6 may constrain possible relations between the age difference and the task difficulty defined in Equations 1 and 2. This is indeed the case, as can be seen by substituting kB and kA for D and C in these definitions. It will be seen that Equation 6 mathematically determines Equation 3. Thus, given Equation 6, Equation 3 follows by logical necessity.

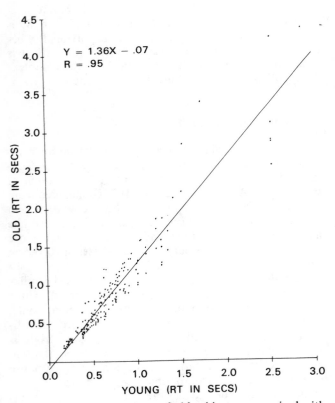

$$Y = 1.36X - .07$$
$$R = .95$$

Figure 24-2. Reaction times of old subjects were paired with reaction times of young subjects on 99 different tasks. The comparison shows that the reaction times of old subjects are approximately a linear function of those of the young subjects.

We believe that Equation 6 may provide an explanation of the complexity hypothesis, an explanation that is fundamentally different from task-specific theories. Whereas task-specific theories ascribe complexity effects to factors operating in difficult conditions that are not present in easy conditions—factors that put the elderly subject at a particular disadvantage—Equation 6 interprets complexity effects in terms of a single mechanism operating equally in difficult and easy conditions, the mechanism of performance slowing.

Refining the Explanation

It seems remarkable that the two parameters of Equation 5, which ignore every detail of the information processes involved, should be able to account for .95² or 90% of the old subjects' data assembled in Table 24-3. However, an important consideration mitigates the apparent success of the model. Two factors contribute to the overall variance in old subjects' scores: first, the task effects, which by themselves would predict that old scores would equal young scores, that is, old scores would lie along the diagonal in Figure 24-2, and second, the age effects, which would account for the elevation of the observed scores above the diagonal. In Figure 24-2, it is clear that the greater of the two factors is the task effects, and the smaller is the age effects. In fact, of the 90% overall variance that is explained, 77% is due to task (i.e., the prediction that Old = Young), and only 13% is due to age.

We can isolate the age effects in the data by replacing each old score with an old-minus-young difference score. How much of the variance of the age effects alone does Equation 5 account for? On this measure, the predictive accuracy of Equation 5 is not so high—only 40% of the age effects are explained.

We next asked the question, Can the predictions of Equation 5 be improved by taking into account further information about the subjects or the tasks? This question was pursued by introducing additional independent variables in the course of a stepwise multiple linear regression. In the sections to follow, the results of that analysis are reviewed.

Effects of age. In terms of its adequacy as a model of aging, Equation 5 glosses over a variable likely to be of considerable importance, the actual age of the older subjects whose data it attempts to predict. The young scores in Figure 24-2 were taken from subjects in their 20s; the old scores, on the other hand, were taken from subjects of widely different ages, covering every decade from the 30s through the 80s. It must surely be the case that the slowing coefficient is itself a function of age. To assess this factor, the points of Figure 24-2 were distinguished according to whether they were taken from subject groups whose average age was over 60 or under 60 (but over 30). The two regressions are presented in Table 24-4 (Part II, a,b).

Taking the age of an older subject group into account, even via the two-way classification ± 60, improves the percentage of age-specific variance accounted for from 40% to 78% and the percentage of overall variance accounted for from 90% to 96.4%. Would an additional breakdown of subject groups by age further improve the accuracy of the model? The

Table 24-4 Effects of Different Factors on Older Subject's Reaction Times

Independent variables	Interaction terms	Regression equations	Overall accountable variance (%)	Age-specific variance (%)
I. Standard RT		O = 1.36 Y − .07	90.2	40
II. Age and standard RT	a. Over 60	O = 1.62 Y − .13	96.4	78
	b. Under 60	O = 1.16 Y − .04		
III. Task and standard RT	a. Card sorting	O = 1.08 Y + .15	91.2	57
	b. Memory scanning	O = 1.40 Y − .16		
	c. S–R mapping	O = 1.32 Y + .03		
	d. Choice reaction time	O = 1.70 Y − .26		
	e. PI	O = 1.25 Y + .08		
	f. Miscellaneous	O = 1.50 Y − .12		
IV. Central/peripheral and standard RT	a. Sensorimotor	O = 1.14 Y − .01	91.7	61
	b. Mental	O = 1.62 Y + .00		
V. Age and central/ peripheral and standard RT	a. Mental over 60	O = 1.66 Y + .00	96.1	81
	b. Mental under 60	O = 1.14 Y + .02		
	c. Sensory over 60	O = 1.25 Y + .00		
	d. Sensory under 60	O = 1.18 Y − .07		

answer is no: Regressing older subject scores onto chronological age (rather than a binary variable) plus control scores plus the Age × Control interaction term does slightly less well (96.1%), perhaps because the relations involved are nonlinear.

Effects of task. We next ask the question, will the inclusion of task type improve the prediction of Equation 5? In Table 24-3, the 18 studies are grouped into five classes by experiment type (choice reaction time, memory scanning, etc.) to which we added a sixth "miscellaneous" class consisting of the last three studies in the table. Table 24-4, Part III shows separate regression lines for each task type. The slopes associated with the different tasks vary over the range from 1.08 to 1.70. It is this range of slopes, one might surmise, which embodies the effects of task type—choice reaction time slows by a factor of 1.7, while card sorting declines only .08, and so forth.

Table 24-4, Part III, thereby defines a six-equation, 12-parameter model that takes into account the effects of task type in predicting elderly subjects' performance. To what extent does consideration of type of task increase the accuracy of prediction? The answer, surprisingly, is virtually none at all. The 12-parameter model accounts for 91.2% of the old subjects' data, a gain of only one percentage point over the two-parameter model of Equation 5. Thus a knowledge of task type contributes almost nothing to the prediction of age effects, beyond the knowledge of the control score.

Central Versus Peripheral Effects

We will examine one more factor that could reasonably be thought to affect the performance of the elderly. Again the distinction involves type of task but at a more general level than was just considered. This is the distinction between sensorimotor processes and mental processes.

In order to examine this factor, it was necessary to separate sensorimotor times and mental processing times. Sensorimotor times were taken directly from those points in Figure 24-2 representing sensorimotor conditions. Mental processing times were derived from the remaining points in Figure 24-2, representing experimental conditions, by subtracting from each experimental latency the associated sensorimotor latency and thereby isolating the mental processing component of the overall latency.

The two regressions are given in Table 24-4, Part IV. Compared to the overall regression of Equation 5 (m = 1.36), mental processing times show a slightly higher slope (m = 1.62), and sensorimotor control

times a slightly lower slope (m = 1.14). The two equations represent a modest increase in overall variance accounted for (91.7%) over Equation 5 alone (90.2%), and a more substantial increase in age-specific variance (from 40% to 61%). We have thus some justification for concluding that sensorimotor functions and mental functions are differentially affected by age, with mental functions being slowed by a factor of 1.62 and sensorimotor functions by a factor of 1.14.

Combined Effects

Let us consider this matter in more detail by crossing the two factors that have been demonstrated to affect older subjects' reaction times—age and complexity. The two factors have two levels each, which leads to four regressions: the performance on sensorimotor and cognitive functions of subjects over 60 and subjects under 60. So far it has been established that an increase in the age of a subject group from under 60 to over 60 leads to an increase in the degree of slowing exhibited on all tasks taken together. It has also been established that a shift in the nature of the task from one that is primarily sensorimotor to one that is exclusively cognitive leads to an increase in the degree of slowing exhibited by all subject groups taken together. We ask now how these two factors interact.

The regression equations for a and b in Part V of Table 24-4 break down mental processing times by age. These equations can best be understood by contrasting them with the equations for a and b of Part II in Table 24-4, which depict the performances of subjects over 60 and subjects under 60 on all tasks combined. How is the prediction of performance on a task altered by the information that the task involves purely mental operations? The answer found by comparing these two pairs of equations is, almost none at all.

Regression equations for c and d of Part V in Table 24-4 break down sensorimotor times by age. Again we ask, how does the information that a task is sensorimotor affect predictions made on the basis of age alone? By contrasting these two equations with the equations for a and b of Part II, the answer is more interesting. While there is little difference contrasting the performance of the subjects under 60, subjects over 60 perform better on sensorimotor tasks than on all tasks combined.

Thus, by examining the central and peripheral reaction times in addition to the subject's age we have arrived at a model that accounts for 81% of the age-specific variance. Further, the model shows that mental components slow drastically with age, while sensorimotor components slow very little with age.

Conclusion

We have come full circle in our consideration of the age-related slowing phenomenon on information-processing tasks. We started with the hypothesis that more complex tasks resulted in greater deficits for the elderly. We then saw that the observations underlying this hypothesis could actually be accounted for by a uniform slowing of mental functions. Finally, a closer examination of the data revealed that there were in fact two levels of deficit—a slight slowing exhibited on sensorimotor tasks, and a more severe slowing on tasks involving mental transformations. The distinguishing factor seems not to be the difficulty of the task, because performance across the range of tasks on each level can be explained by a uniform deficit. Rather, the distinguishing factor seems to be the significant involvement of central as opposed to primarily peripheral processes. We have returned therefore to a complexity hypothesis, but one that distinguishes only central and peripheral levels.

Perhaps, on the other hand, our analyses have simply lacked the resolution to expose further factors. We have made one attempt to increase resolution by examining the age parameters of six different types of tasks separately. Distinguishing between types of task in this way did not improve the predictions of the model.

Let us summarize our preliminary effort in attempting to understand the complexity hypothesis with the qualification that the task may be filled with methodological pitfalls. Subjects in their 20s served as the baseline in our study. In comparison to this baseline, the latencies of subjects in their 40s and 50s are increased by a factor of about 1.2. This slowing is seen equally in sensorimotor functions and in purely mental functions. The sensorimotor times of subjects in their 60s and 70s are little further affected, holding at around 1.2. Their mental processing times, however, show a large additional decline, slowing to a factor of 1.6 or 1.7. This slowing appears to affect all mental processes equally and may account for the complexity effects observed in the data.

REFERENCES

Anders, T. R., & Fozard, J. L. Effects of age upon retrieval from primary and secondary memory. *Developmental Psychology*, 1973, *9*, 411–415.

Anders, T. R., Fozard, J. L., & Lillyquist, T. D. Effects of age upon retrieval from short-term memory. *Developmental Psychology*, 1972, *6*, 214–217.

Arnold, S., & Farkas, M. Age differences in speed and strategies of perceptual search. *Gerontologist*, 1978, *18*, 45. (Abstract)

Barr, R. Some remarks on the time-course of aging. In L. W. Poon, J. L. Fozard, L. Cermak, D. Arenberg, & L. W. Thompson (Eds.), *New directions in memory and aging: Proceedings of the George A. Talland Memorial Conference.* Hillsdale, N.J.: Lawrence Erlbaum, 1980.

Birren, J. E. Age changes in speed of behavior: Its central nature and physiological correlates. In A. T. Welford & J. E. Birren (Eds.), *Behavior, aging and the nervous system.* Springfield, Ill.: Charles C Thomas, 1965.

Birren, J. E., & Botwinick, J. The relation of writing speed to age and to senile psychoses. *Journal of Consulting Psychology*, 1951, *15*, 243–249.

Birren, J. E., & Botwinick, J. Speed of response as a function of perceptual difficulty and age. *Journal of Gerontology*, 1955, *10*, 433–436.

Birren, J. E., Riegel, K. F., & Morrison, D. F. Age differences in response speed as a function of controlled variations of stimulus conditions: Evidence of a general speed factor. *Gerontologia*, 1962, *6*, 1–18.

Botwinick, J., & Brinley, J. Aspects of RT set during brief intervals in relation to age and sex. *Journal of Gerontology*, 1962, *17*, 295–301.

Botwinick, J., & Thompson, L. W. Components of reaction time in relation to age and sex. *Journal of Genetic Psychology*, 1966, *108*, 175–183.

Comalli, P. E., Wapner, S., & Werner, H. Interference effects of Stroop color-word test in childhood, adulthood, and aging. *Journal of Genetic Psychology*, 1962, *100*, 47–53.

Crossman, E. R. F. W., & Szafran, J. Changes with age in the speed of information-intake and discrimination. *Experimentia Supplementum*, 1956, *4*, 128–135.

Crowder, R. Age effects in echoic memory. In L. W. Poon, J. L. Fozard, L. Cermak, D. Arenberg, & L. W. Thompson (Eds.), *New directions in memory and aging: Proceedings of the George A. Talland Memorial Conference.* Hillsdale, N.J.: Lawrence Erlbaum, 1980.

Eriksen, C. W., Hamlin, R. M., Daye, C. Aging adults and rate of memory scan. *Bulletin of the Psychonomic Society*, 1973, *1*, 259–260.

Fozard, J. L., & Poon, L. W. Decision making and aging I: Changes of decision speed with memory requirement. In L. W. Poon & J. L. Fozard (Eds.), *Design conference in decision making and aging* (Veterans Administration Technical Report 76-01). Boston, Mass.: Veterans Administration, 1976.

Glass, A. L., Holyoak, K. J., & Santa, J. L. *Cognition.* Reading, Mass.: Addison-Wesley, 1979.

Griew, S. Complexity of response and time of initiating responses in relation to age. *American Journal of Psychology*, 1959, *72*, 83–88.

Lindsay, P. H., & Norman, D. A. *Human information processing.* New York: Academic Press, 1977.

Rabbitt, P. M. A. Age and time for choice between stimulus and between response. *Journal of Gerontology*, 1964, *19*, 307–312.

Salthouse, T. A. *Age and speed: The nature of the relation-*

ship. Unpublished manuscript, Department of Psychology, Washington University (St. Louis), 1978.

Simon, R. J. Signal processing time as a function of aging. *Journal of Experimental Psychology*, 1968, *78*, 76–80.

Suci, G. J., Davidoff, M. D., & Surwillo, W. W. Reaction time as a function of stimulus information and age. *Journal of Experimental Psychology*, 1960, *60*, 242–244.

Thomas, J. C., Waugh, N. C., & Fozard, J. L. Age and familiarity in memory scanning. *Journal of Gerontology*, 1978, *33*, 528–533.

Waugh, N. C., Thomas, J. C., & Fozard, J. L. Retrieval time from different memory stores. *Journal of Gerontology*, 1978, *33*, 718–724.

Welford, A. T. *Aging and human skill*. London: Oxford University Press, 1958.

Welford, A. T. Experimental psychology in the study of aging. *British Medical Bulletin*, 1964, *20*, 65–69.

Welford, A. T. Performance, biological mechanisms and age: A theoretical sketch. In A. T. Welford, & J. E. Birren (Eds.), *Behavior, aging and the nervous system*. Springfield, Ill.: Charles C Thomas, 1965.

Welford, A. T. Motor performance. In J. E. Birren, & K. W. Schaie (Eds.), *Handbook of the psychology of aging*. New York: Van Nostrand Reinhold, 1977.

SECTION

6

Stress and Coping

David A. Chiriboga, *Section Editor*

Introduction

During the 1970s, research on stress exhibited a dramatic growth that owed much of its impetus to the Schedule of Recent Events (SRE), a measure of stress developed by Holmes and Rahe of the University of Washington at Seattle. Since its introduction in 1967, literally hundreds of studies have used either the SRE or one of its numerous permutations. The results have demonstrated convincingly the link between stress and both physical and mental health. Less convincing have been efforts to substantiate the proposal by Holmes and Rahe (1967) that stress can be defined in terms of life events and that the link between life events and health change is essentially a result of the cumulative readjustment necessitated by these events.

Perhaps in response to the many questions raised by research using SRE-type instruments, the middle to late 1970s saw an increasing concern with studies of the nature of stressful conditions, or stressors as they were first called by Selye (1956), and the reasons why such stressors are implicated in health changes. Current research is focusing not only on conditions of stress (including but not limited to life events) but on coping strategies employed to ameliorate these stresses and on approaches to defining the parameters of the stress response. Theoretical formulations also entered maturity as investigators such as Lazarus (1979), Cox (1978), Pearlin and Schooler (1978), Eisdorfer (1977), and Fiske (1980) went beyond the simple linear models of causality that dominated early conceptualization in the field. For stress research, the 1980s may well prove to be an age of complexity as investigators abandon the early simplistic models and methods in favor of those predicated on complex interactions between predisposing characteristics, mediate and immediate stressors, mediating resources, coping strategies, and a complex array of outcomes.

Gerontological interest in stress followed a different path during the past decade than did the mainstream of research. Rather than relying on event inventories, gerontologists turned toward the in-depth study of specific conditions, those generated, for example, by relocation, bereavement, and retirement, as well as by more esoteric situations such as the so-called "empty nest," divorce in the later years, and vulnerability to laboratory test conditions. While there is obvious value to these investigations, gerontologists may find it profitable to borrow from the methodologies existing in the general body of stress research. The life-events approach, for example, taps a broad range of stress experiences; in effect, it takes the stress temperature of the individual. Those who focus on single-stress conditions have in the past tended to ignore the possibility that the focal stressor may be occurring in the context of other stresses—just as focusing on life events alone may lead researchers to ignore the complexities represented by the individual life events included in their inventories.

Not only has its focus been different, but gerontological research on stress during the 1970s did not share in the general wave of excitement and growth evident in the mainstream of research. One consequence of this is that while there are now generally accepted life-events inventories for children, adolescents, graduate students, the hospitalized, navy personnel, and so forth, there are no generally accepted inventories available for use with the middle-aged or the aged. With some few exceptions, such as the recent interest in the impact of crime on the elderly, gerontological research on stress may have diminished rather than increased during the 1970s. Particularly lacking are longitudinal investigations into the nature and meaning of stress in later life, although studies at the Human Development and Aging Program at the University of California, San Francisco and those at the Duke University Center for the Study of Aging and Human Development represent exceptions.

The general paucity of research on stress and the elderly is surprising, not only because of the well-documented relation between stress and health among persons of all ages but also because of the particular vulnerabilities of the elderly. For example, not only are the social, physical and economic losses associated with the aging process stresses in themselves, but they also constitute decrements in the resources available to the older person to cope with subsequent stresses. These vulnerabilities have been recognized for some time, and Pfeiffer (1977), in a chapter in the latest *Handbook on the Psychology of Aging*, goes so far as to suggest that most mental pathology in later life is due to the failure of the older person to cope with the various stresses of later life. In the same volume, Eisdorfer and Wilkie (1977) emphasize the value of a fuller understanding of stress in later life for intervention on both behavioral and somatic levels. Clearly, research during the 1980s would do well to devote more attention to stress and the elderly.

In the following chapters of this section, several researchers present methods and models for studying stress and coping. Two chapters are concerned with specifying the characteristics of potentially stressful situations. Not content with the life-events approach to defining stress, these authors demonstrate the value of selected additional characteristics. Chiriboga and Cutler, for example, compare stresses identified with a comprehensive life span oriented life-events instrument, with the stresses identified from questions dealing with chronic stress, anticipations of stress, and even the nonoccurrence of life events. They conclude that research limited to the life-events method is likely to miss many of the critical stresses of later life, and they emphasize the importance of assessing how individuals perceive the stresses they experience.

Miller has gone in another direction in his quest for a fuller explication of the stresses impinging on people. Rather than focusing on those events directly experienced by the individual, Miller has studied community-wide events as reported in the mass media. His research orientation is similar to that of Brenner (1979), who has reported a strong association between socioenvironmental factors such as inflation, economic change, and rates of unemployment, on the one hand, and rates of first admission to mental hospitals, cardiovascular disease mortality, alcohol consumption, crime, and so forth, on the other. Of interest to gerontologists is Miller's finding that persons of different ages are affected by different kinds of community events. His work emphasizes the differential vulnerabilities of older and younger persons to the same environmental stimuli and, together with the findings of Chiriboga and Cutler, suggests the wide range of conditions that are potentially stressful to older persons.

The other two chapters take us away from the nature of the impinging stressor to a consideration of how individuals deal with these stressors. Research on coping, a subset of stress research, is at a very early stage of development. There is considerable disagreement, for example, as to whether coping is best defined in terms of basic personality predispositions, defense mechanisms, habitual styles of response, or discrete behaviors elicited in specific conditions. Cohen's research exemplifies an approach that characterizes coping in relatively global terms. In Cohen's research with Lazarus, as well as in her ongoing research on breast cancer, respondents are classified in terms of their overall stance toward health problems. The results are provocative: Denial, a defense style that would intuitively seem less effective as a coping strategy, was associated with more successful outcomes than the vigilant, problem-focused style that the classic work of Janis (1958) indicated to be most effective in postsurgical recovery.

Cohen suggests that in situations where little control over the stressor is possible, avoidance strategies may be quite effective. Her findings have an obvious relevance to the study and care of elderly persons, who not only are more likely than younger persons to suffer from health problems but also may exercise little control over the major losses they face. One result may be an increasing dependence on passive or avoidance strategies in later life. Moreover, not only do these strategies have a theoretical linkage with the concept of disengagement, as indicated by Cohen, but they seem to bear more than a coincidental similarity to ego-mastery styles characteristic of the elderly. Her findings suggest that the change in mastery style from an active, manipulative stance toward a more passive and accommodating style—which Gutmann (1977) found in the TAT protocols of individuals as they move from middle to later life—may be linked with changes in the coping strategies employed in real-life situations. Although little research has been done on the coping strategies of the elderly, there is some preliminary evidence that at least in institutional settings, they are not only more likely to employ passive than active strategies (Cutler & Chiriboga, 1976; Quayhagen & Chiriboga, 1976) but also to experience a greater sense of well-being when they do (Felton & Kahana, 1974).

The series of clinical and empirical studies reported by Horowitz and Wilner constitute an ambitious and sustained attempt to study the full spectrum of stress-related issues. Not only coping but also the stressors and the social pathologies that evolve from stressors represent the field of study at the Center for the Study of Neuroses at the Langley Porter Institute, University of California, San Francisco. Insofar as coping is concerned, Horowitz and Wilner provide an alternative to Cohen's relatively global assessment procedure: They use extensive lists of discrete and specific coping behaviors. Although the inventory of coping behaviors has produced some suggestive results, the clinical interviews conducted at the Center for the Study of Neuroses have at the same time suggested that the most important ways in which people cope with stress may be either unconscious or forgotten. It is hoped that the integration of clinical and empirical techniques possible in their research will lead toward some solutions to the questions of what coping is and how it can be measured.

Horowitz and Wilner provide several examples of the kinds of instruments and approaches that are relevant to the study of aging. Moreover, the research of Horowitz and his colleagues at the Center for the Study of Neuroses provides a working example not only of multidisciplinary clinical and empirical research but also of the successful integration of such research with service delivery. As is discussed in some detail in the epilogue to this book, linkages between research and service delivery are more conspicuous by their absence than by their presence. The researchers at the Center for the Study of Neuroses not only study stress and intervention but apply their research findings to treatment. One consequence of this integration of effort is a sophisticated approach to clinical assessment and treatment. For example, the short form of the stress inventory described by Horowitz and Wilner is routinely administered to outpatients at the large mental hospital with which the Center is affiliated. The results are machine scored and analyzed; attending psychiatrists and psychologists receive a printout of the patient's score and a notation if the incidence and severity of stress are abnormally large. This type of instrument may well be of value to those concerned with delivery of services to the elderly, for whom a brief but valid index of background stress may prove invaluable in decision making by staff concerning proper case disposition. Its development and application, within the context of a combined research and treatment center, presents a model for those interested in the problems of the elderly.

REFERENCES

Brenner, M. H. Influence of the social environment on psychopathology: The historic perspective. In J. E. Barrett (Ed.), *Stress and mental disorder*. New York: Raven Press, 1979.

Cox, T. *Stress*. Baltimore, Md.: University Park Press, 1978.

Cutler, L., & Chiriboga, D. *Coping process in the organically impaired elderly*. Paper presented at the 29th annual meeting of the Gerontological Society, New York, October 13–17, 1976.

Eisdorfer, C. Stress, disease and cognitive change in the aged. In C. Eisdorfer and R. O. Friedel (Eds.), *Cognitive and emotional disturbance in the elderly*. Chicago: Year Book Publishers, 1977.

Eisdorfer, C., & Wilkie, F. Stress, disease, aging and behavior. In J. E. Birren and K. W. Schaie (Eds.), *Handbook of the psychology of aging*. New York: Van Nostrand Reinhold, 1977.

Felton, B., & Kahana, E. Adjustment and situationally-bound locus of control among institutionalized aged. *Journal of Gerontology*, 1974, *29*, 295–301.

Fiske, M. Tasks and crises of the second half of life: The interrelationship of commitment, coping and adaptation. In J. E. Birren and R. Bruce Sloane (Eds.), *Handbook of mental health and aging*. Englewood Cliffs, N.J.: Prentice-Hall, 1980.

Gutmann, D. The cross cultural perspective: Notes toward a comparative psychology of aging. In J. E. Birren and K. W. Schaie (Eds.), *Handbook of the psychology of aging*. New York: Van Nostrand Reinhold, 1977.

Holmes, T. H., and Rahe, R. H. The social readjustment rating scale. *Journal of Psychosomatic Research*, 1967, *11*, 213–218.

Janis, I. L. *Psychological stress: Psychoanalytic and behavioral studies of surgical patients*. New York: Wiley, 1958.

Lazarus, R. S. The stress and coping paradigm. In C. Eisdorfer, D. Cohen, A. Kleinman, and P. Maxim (Eds.) *Theoretical bases in psychopathology*. New York: Spectrum Publications, 1979.

Pearlin, L. I., and Schooler, C. The structure of coping. *Journal of Health and Social Behavior*, 1978, *19*, 2–21.

Pfeiffer, E. Psychopathology and social pathology. In J. E. Birren and K. W. Schaie (Eds.), *Handbook of the psychology of aging*. New York: Van Nostrand Reinhold, 1977.

Quayhagen, M. P., and Chiriboga, D. *Geriatric Coping Schedule: Potentials and problems*. Paper presented at the 29th annual meeting of the Gerontological Society, New York, October 13–17, 1976.

Selye, H. *The stress of life*. New York: McGraw-Hill, 1956.

David A. Chiriboga and Loraine Cutler

CHAPTER
25

Stress and Adaptation: Life Span Perspectives

During the 1970s most research on stress followed the life-events approach of Holmes and Rahe. This chapter examines some current methodological concerns with the approach and reviews its contribution to knowledge from the perspective of adult development and aging. Research findings are then presented from a longitudinal study conducted on men and women who were between the ages of 16 and 67 when first contacted. The results suggest that life-events instruments can provide important information about stress and adaptation throughout life but that additional dimensions of stress also deserve study.

During the past decade, stress research has been strongly influenced by the life-events approach of Holmes and Rahe (1967). Their research instrument, the Schedule of Recent Events, which is quickly administered and easy to understand, draws on the theoretical premise that the source of stress is disruption of homeostasis and that degree of change is therefore a valid index of disruption. A unique feature of the instrument is its use of psychometrically derived standardized weights to assess degree of change for life events. Researchers using the Schedule of Recent Events, or one of its many variants, have found low-order but significant correlations with indicators of both physical and psychosocial distress in a variety of populations. Recent reviews of the extensive literature generated by the life-events approach can be found in Masuda and Holmes (1978), Rahe (1979), and Dohrenwend (1979).

Methodological and Substantive Issues

Despite its wide acceptance, the Schedule of Recent Events and similar instruments are meeting with growing dissatisfaction. The restricted range of potential stressors represented by the 42 life events in the schedule has raised questions about its content validity when applied to special populations such as minority groups or the aged (cf. Ander, Lindstrom, & Tibblin, 1974; Brown & Birley, 1968; Lowenthal & Chiriboga, 1973). The standardized weighting system has been criticized as ignoring the important factor of individual assessment (cf. Chiriboga, 1977; Lazarus, 1980; Lowenthal & Chiriboga, 1973; Sarason, Johnson & Siegel, 1978; Vinokur & Selzer, 1973). And the combining of positive and negative change into a single life-change-unit (LCU) score has diverted attention from the very different consequences of such changes for psychosocial functioning (cf. Chiriboga, 1977; Gerst, Grant, Yager, & Sweetwood, 1978; Lowenthal & Chiriboga, 1975; Lundberg & Theorell, 1976; Mechanic, 1975; Mueller, Edwards, & Yarvis, 1977; Ross & Mirowsky, 1979; Tennant & Andrews, 1978). Combin-

This research was supported by National Institute on Aging Grant AG00002, by National Institute of Child Health and Human Development Grants HD03051 and HD05941, and by National Institute of Mental Health Grant MH33713.

ing positive and negative change also ignores the multidimensionality of stress (cf. Chiriboga & Dean, 1978; Masuda & Holmes, 1978; Schwartz & Myers, 1977). Moreover, the conceptual restriction of stress to the acute, discrete onset conditions represented by so-called life events is an oversimplification of the topic. For example, an event-oriented methodology fails to recognize the importance of anticipatory stress (cf. Lieberman, Prock, & Tobin, 1968), chronic stress (cf. Lazarus, 1980), the nonoccurrence of events (Beeson & Lowenthal, 1975), and events that may be simply "off schedule" (Neugarten & Datan, 1972).

Life Events and the Adult Life Course

From the perspective of the life span social scientist, an additional cause for concern is how little is known, after more than 10 years of investigation, about the significance of life events for people at different stages of their life course.

The early and influential work on life-events methodology by Holmes and Rahe (1967) reported nearly universal agreement among people of different racial, class, educational, and age groups on the ranking of events according to life change. While the authors reported generally high overall correlation for rankings of events by various groups, they did not report group differences on the weightings for events. Later studies that reported both overall concordance and individual item differences found that while concordance levels continued to be high, item differences abounded, For example, Masuda and Holmes (1967) compared LCU rankings of white Americans with those of Japanese, and found differences on more than 40% of the events. Weights given by Europeans differed significantly from those by Americans on 48% of the items (Harmon, Masuda, & Holmes, 1970) and from those by black Americans on 62% (Komaroff, Masuda, & Holmes, 1968). Of particular relevance to the present chapter is that in a reanalysis of the initial Holmes and Rahe (1967) article, Masuda and Holmes (1978) report that weights given by those under age 30 differed from those given by people over age 60 on 54% of the items.

Perhaps because of the originally reported lack of age difference, much of the subsequent research has ignored the age variable, even when ages in the sample ranged over 20 or more years (see, for example, Cochrane & Robertson, 1973; Morrison, Hudgens, & Barchha, 1968; Reavley, 1974; Rubin, Gunderson, & Arthur, 1971; Wershow & Reinhart, 1974).

When life events are considered from a developmental perspective, however, some tentative conclusions can be drawn. One conclusion is that a general

decrease in the experiencing of life events comes with age (cf. Ander et al., 1974; Chiriboga & Dean, 1978; Dekker & Webb, 1974; Lowenthal & Chiriboga, 1973; Masuda & Holmes, 1978; Nelson, Mensh, Hecht, & Schwartz, 1972; Uhlenhuth, Lipman, Balter, & Stern, 1974). To what extent this decrease can be linked to theories of disengagement is unclear, but the second conclusion is suggestive: The degree of disruption potentially represented by various life events is rated as lower by older persons (cf. Horowitz, Schaefer, & Cooney, 1974; Jewell, 1977; Masuda & Holmes, 1978). In other words, not only are life events less frequent, but in a sense the older person puts more distance between the self and events that do intrude—or at least the older person perceives this to be the case. The third conclusion from existing studies is that the content validity of many life-events inventories is particularly suspect when dealing with wide age ranges: Some of the items included may be more appropriate to younger populations than to older ones (Ander et al., 1974; Lowenthal & Chiriboga, 1973).

Some attempts to improve the content validity of inventories have, unfortunately, raised more issues than they have solved. For example, Amster and Krauss (1974) added several items for use with older populations (including "losing drivers' license," "institutionalization," and "feeling of slowing down") and dropped several others. At least two of the added items, however, seem to invoke the possibility of a spurious relation with age: "reaching 65" and "reaching 70." A study by Gutmann (1978) employed an undefined "panel of experts" to decide which events were to be included in a 34-item life-events inventory for use with older people. Although the items themselves were not specified, the results raise questions about their relevance to later life. For example, the frequency distribution of life events for a community sample of men and women aged 60 and over was described as "indicating that vacations and trips are among the most important events in an older person's life" (Guttmann, 1978, p. 484).

Research from the Human Development and Aging Program

In 1969 the Human Development and Aging Program of the University of California, San Francisco, began a longitudinal study designed to address questions raised about the use of life events. The research grew out of earlier work on stress and coping in samples of community and institutionalized older persons (see Lowenthal, 1964; Lowenthal, Berkman, & Associates, 1967). At the initial contact, the sample consisted of 216 men and women facing one of four normative transition periods: departure from the parental home, birth of first child, departure of last child from the parental home, and retirement. In cross-sectional analyses of baseline data, it was found that knowing the individual's perceptions of stress contributed to the researcher's understanding of the relation of live events to adaptation (Lowenthal & Chiriboga, 1973, 1975). A more sophisticated instrument to measure stress was then developed in a collaborative research effort by Mardi Horowitz, Richard Rahe, and David Chiriboga.

The new instrument, the Life Events Questionnaire, expands the original 42 events included in the SRE to 138 and requires respondents to assess the impact of the event. Reliability estimates for the basic questionnaire were reasonably high (Horowitz, Schaefer, Hiroto, Wilner, & Levin, 1977), and follow-ups have been administered 5 and 7 years after the longitudinal study. In one subsequent analysis, four alternative approaches to weighting life events were compared. A subsample of events was coded (1) according to the LCU system of Holmes and Rahe (1967), (2) according to the standard weights derived from the averaged rating of nine psychiatrists (Horowitz, 1976), (3) by simple summation of the number of events, and (4) by the intensity of positive or negative assessments made by the respondents. The two standardized systems and the simple summated scores were highly intercorrelated and showed only minimal associations with self-reported physical health, psychiatric symptomatology, locus of control, morale, self-concept, income, and satisfaction with activities and goals (Chiriboga, 1977). However, measures based on the respondents' own assessments showed substantially stronger and more frequent correlations with criterion indices.

In another investigation, 11 dimensions of stress (marital/dating, family, finances, legal, etc.) were identified on the basis of a content analysis of items included in the Life Events Questionnaire. The same subjects were used as in the prior study. On nearly all dimensions, the younger respondents evidenced more stress than did the middle-aged and retirement groups. Women generally reported more stress on each dimension than men did (Chiriboga & Dean, 1978). Changes on a number of psychosocial indicators of adaptation were then computed for the 3-year period assessed by the stress instrument. It was found that (1) negative stresses were moderately to strongly associated with changes in psychosocial functioning; (2) the effect on adaptation of the several stress dimensions varied by life stage and sex; and (3) negative stress was not necessarily associated with poorer adaptation. In fact, negative stress correlated with improvement in one third of the significant associations.

New Directions in Stress Research

Although the literature on the life-events approach to the study of stress communicates a sense of energy and relevance, there is a disquieting sense that perhaps, in spite of its intuitive appeal, the life-events approach promises too much and delivers too little. As a matter of fact, in a growing number of studies that compare the standard weighting systems typical of the approach, weighted scores show a high correlation with simple counts of life events but do no better than simple counts in predicting adaptation (Chiriboga, 1977; Grant, Sweetwood, Gerst, & Yager, 1978; Ross & Mirowsky, 1979).

An alternative approach quantifies the individual's perceptions of life events, especially desirability and impact of the events, (cf. Chiriboga, 1977; Lowenthal & Chiriboga, 1973; Lundberg & Theorell, 1976; Masuda & Holmes, 1978; Mueller et al., 1977; Tennant & Andrews, 1978; Vinokur & Selzer, 1973; Yamamoto & Kinney, 1976). Researchers using the individual's assessment, however, may find themselves confronted by confounded results. For example, if the outcome measure is emotional distress of some sort (such as number of symptoms, anxiety, or depression), the same factors that lead a respondent to report greater emotional distress may also lead to reports of greater impact for stressors (cf. Dohrenwend, 1979; Rahe, 1979).

The extent to which factors such as current emotional state affect the assessment of stress is still in the early stages of appraisal. In one study that addressed the issue directly, subjects who were assigned to one of three mood conditions—elated, neutral, or depressed—were administered a life-events instrument before and during the experiment. A comparison of the results showed no evidence that mood affected subjects' assessments of life events (Siegel, Johnson, & Sarason, 1979). However, in the absence of replicated evidence, researchers interested in subjective assessments should be cautious in their interpretation of results, particularly when using cross-sectional or retrospective research designs.

The remainder of this chapter presents a series of analyses that explore some of the directions life span research on stress may take during the 1980s. The research is drawn from the Longitudinal Study of Transitions of the Human Development and Aging Program. This study (Lowenthal, Thurnher, Chiriboga, & Associates, 1975) combines a life span orientation with a long-term interest in stress and adaptation. Four sets of analyses are described: the direction of change in preoccupations with stress at different life stages, the prediction of change in stress preoccupations, identification of additional dimensions of stress, and the predictive value of combining life events with the additional dimensions of stress.

Analysis A: Changing Directions of Positive and Negative Stress Preoccupations

Although there is considerable evidence that older people experience fewer life events than younger people, previous research has been based on a cross section of ages and has not addressed the question of whether the apparent decrease in exposure to life events is a function of place in the life course or of cohort. Longitudinal data on stress experiences permit a comparison across life stages of the extent of change in stress preoccupations reported by respondents.

Sample. During follow-up interviews 5 and 7 years after the longitudinal study of transitions, 173 subjects completed the Life Events Questionnaire. These included subjects who, during the baseline contact, were high-school seniors (21 men and 24 women), newlyweds (20 men and 21 women), middle-aged par-

ents (21 men and 22 women), or people facing retirement (23 men and 21 women). A more complete description of the sample can be found in Lowenthal et al. (1975).

Method. In the Life Events Questionnaire (LEQ) respondents check off events that happened to them during the past year, how positively or negatively they felt about each event reported, and how much they thought about each event (i.e., how intrusive each was in their thoughts). Eleven categories of stress were developed from the items—work, marriage and dating, family, nonfamily relations, home, legal, financial, thoughts and feelings, personal, school, and health of family and friends. Since respondents evaluated the positive or negative quality of each event, it was possible to develop positive and negative stress-preoccupation measures for each category, as well as summated or overall scores, for each of the two contact points. Change scores were then computed.

Results. Systematic differences in stress experiences were found for men and women at different points along their life course. The middle-aged and retirement

Table 25-1 Mean Scores on Positive and Negative Stress Change Variables, with Associated Two-Way ANOVA Probabilities for Gender and Stage Effects

Stress change variables	Two-way ANOVA effects	Gender		High school		Newlyweds		Parents		Retirement	
		Men	Women	Men	Women	Men	Women	Men	Women	Men	Women
Overall negative stress	(S)	49.50	50.84	48.02	48.80	46.96	50.22	51.62	51.97	51.10	52.62
Health		102.58	101.67	101.76	101.88	103.00	100.38	102.24	101.86	103.26	102.52
Work	I	99.89	101.31	101.62	98.29	95.25	103.67	101.95	100.86	100.48	102.86
Thoughts		101.51	101.98	98.33	99.67	101.00	101.19	104.90	103.14	101.74	104.19
Marriage		102.25	100.03	103.57	97.79	102.80	99.24	101.52	101.54	101.22	101.81
Family	S	101.59	102.89	101.00	98.17	98.75	103.38	103.24	105.95	103.09	104.57
Nonfamily		99.12	101.30	95.76	100.92	99.55	100.57	99.76	101.64	101.22	102.10
Personal		100.35	99.84	99.67	98.50	98.25	99.81	100.05	98.95	103.09	102.33
Legal		99.81	100.09	99.14	99.71	99.45	100.14	100.76	100.54	99.87	100.00
Financial		99.84	100.86	98.28	100.83	101.10	101.38	100.00	100.95	100.00	100.28
Home		99.48	99.89	99.24	100.58	98.85	98.86	100.00	100.00	99.78	100.00
School		99.81	100.23	99.62	100.88	99.60	99.95	100.00	100.00	100.00	100.00
Overall positive stress	S, (I)	50.37	49.64	48.84	53.91	48.40	47.38	54.57	51.32	49.64	45.26
Health		102.02	100.85	103.14	104.38	97.35	97.14	105.10	100.00	102.26	101.43
Work		106.40	104.13	106.38	112.00	104.25	102.28	100.62	103.14	104.43	98.05
Thoughts		100.12	100.23	100.33	100.12	100.00	100.57	100.14	100.23	100.00	100.00
Marriage	S	102.00	100.98	105.81	102.54	96.60	98.43	106.57	103.54	99.04	99.05
Family		102.48	100.64	103.67	104.25	102.45	93.90	101.67	102.50	102.17	101.28
Nonfamily	(I)	101.36	102.31	97.57	104.86	104.90	100.38	102.95	103.77	100.30	99.76
Personal	(I)	103.98	105.02	102.48	106.96	100.85	101.71	108.00	111.91	104.39	98.90
Legal		100.18	100.00	100.00	100.00	100.00	100.00	100.71	100.00	100.00	100.00
Financial		100.99	100.72	100.95	103.46	100.90	100.71	100.91	99.91	101.26	98.43
Home		101.47	100.78	100.28	102.92	100.20	102.24	102.43	100.54	102.78	97.14
School	S	99.13	100.12	95.86	99.00	100.65	100.95	100.00	100.68	100.00	100.00
Number of respondents		85	88	21	24	20	21	21	22	23	21

Note. S and I indicates two-way analysis of variance (ANOVA) probabilities of stage or interaction effects ≤ .05. When letters are enclosed within parentheses, ≤ .10.

groups gave a larger overall measure of negative stress than did the two younger groups (see Table 25-1). In the 11 categories of negative stress that constitute the overall score, only one exhibited a significant stage difference: the family. High school and newlywed groups showed very little change in family stresses, but the two older groups—especially the middle-aged parents who were in the midst of the so-called "empty-nest" transition—reported a sizable increase in negative family stresses. Work stresses exhibited an interaction of group and sex: Newlywed and retirement-age women showed an increase in negative work stress, and newlywed men showed the greatest decrease.

For positive stress, the middle-aged parents showed the greatest overall increase, while the retirement men and women showed the greatest decline. In other words, the middle aged increased significantly in both overall positive and overall negative stress, while the retirement-age men and women had the misfortune to suffer an increase in negative and at the same time a decrease in positive stress. There was also a tendency toward an interaction effect for overall positive stress: While positive stress declined more in women than in men, the reverse was true among the (former) high school seniors—positive stresses increased more in women than in men.

The only positive changes of any significance among the 11 separate categories were for marriage. While subjects generally reported at least some increase in positive marital events, those who reported the most increases were the middle-aged parents, while the retirement and newlywed men and women showed some decline in this category. Taken together with the finding noted previously—that the middle aged experienced a considerable number of negative life events in the family category—the results in the marital category seem to be saying that the empty nest represents both crisis and challenge since it shows elements of both! In contrast, entry into the retirement phase of life appears to be associated with more pain than pleasure.

Discussion. The comparisons discussed above concern change, and they say nothing about preoccupation with stress. Since the older respondents were in general less likely than the young to report stress preoccupations at the 5-year follow-up (Chiriboga & Dean, 1978), the lack of life-stage differences suggests that for the most part the initial differences were simply maintained over the 2 years of the study. It is not clear how long it takes to detect major developmental shifts in the stress experiences of adults, if such shifts occur. A 10-year follow-up of the transitions study is now in preparation and may help to clarify the extent to which stress preoccupations ebb and flow along the life course.

Analysis B: Predicting Change in Stress Preoccupations

Since analysis A found stage of life and sex to be associated with changes in positive and negative stress preoccupations, and as such to be predisposing factors, Analysis B was designed to investigate whether psychosocial characteristics of the individual can be used to predict changes in stress preoccupations. Previous research had suggested that individuals differ markedly in what might be called "stress proneness," and that diverse life-styles may reflect people's different ways of coping with the world in general, and with stress in particular. One finding suggested that a dual model of adaptation—one that contrasted people's psychosocial resources and deficits—was associated with differences in exposure to various kinds of stimulation, including life events (Lowenthal & Chiriboga, 1975). For example, people with a high degree of both resources and deficits were found to manifest an active life-style characterized by complexity and breadth in their social relations, leisure activities, goals, and time perspective—in their lives in general. In contrast, people with a paucity of both resources and deficits seemed to prefer a simpler form of existence, one characterized not so much by activity as by regularity and relaxation.

Sample. The subjects employed for Analysis A were also employed for Analysis B.

Method. The measures of overall preoccupation with positive and negative stress described in Analysis A were used to construct a typology of change (the two measures were minimally associated: $r = .10$). Respondents were divided into those high and low on positive stress by means of a median split; respondents high and low on negative stress were similarly divided. The two dichotomies, combined, produce a fourfold typology: (1) *the avoiders*—people for whom both positive and negative stress have declined; (2) *the lucky*—persons for whom negative stress has declined and positive stress increased; (3) *the overwhelmed*—people for whom positive stress has declined and negative stress increased; and (4) *the stress-prone*—people for whom both positive and negative stress have increased.

The predictors of stress change were 20 baseline variables that either contributed to a resource-and-deficit model of adaptation or were significantly associated with it (see Lowenthal et al., 1975). These variables included measures of the number of different social roles, the number of friends, athletic activities, maintenance (i.e., shopping, cooking, house cleaning) activities, contemplative activities, solitary activities, awareness of social problems, satisfaction with goals and activities, number of years projected into the future, number of psychiatric symptoms, self-criticism, negative self-concept, positive self-concept, life satisfaction, the Bradburn Affect Scale (Bradburn, 1969), and ratings by a group of social scientists on life-course perspective, degree of perceived stress, feelings of being controlled or encroached upon by others, general satisfaction with one's way of life, and mutuality in social relations. In addition, age, socioeconomic status, and religious participation were included as definers of demographic status.

In order to predict stress type, the Statistical Package for the Social Sciences (SPSS) (Nie, Hull, Jenkins, Steinbrenner, & Bent, 1975) version of stepwise discriminant analysis was chosen as the appropriate statistic. The stopping rules adopted were an F-to-enter of less than 1.0 or a tolerance of less than .50. Four separate analyses were performed: for the younger (i.e., high-school and newlywed) men and women and for the older (i.e., parental and retirement) men and women.

Results: The younger men. As shown in Table 25-2, the stress-prone appeared to be the most distinct of the four stress types for the younger men. Examination of the mean scores for the variables entering most

strongly into the discriminant function suggests that the stress-prone had originally been the most restricted in projections into the future, the most restricted in overall perspective on their lives, but at the same time the most aware of social problems. The avoiders, in contrast, had originally manifested the greatest perspective on their past lives and a fairly lengthy projection into the future; they had scored lowest on evidence of mutuality in social relationships and were only moderately aware of social problems. The lucky had been the least aware and concerned with social problems, somewhat limited in future projections and in perspective on their past life, and yet the highest in mutuality. The overwhelmed had been more aware of social problems than the lucky, but less than the stress-prone; they had projected furthest into the future and manifested the greatest perspective on their past lives. They had, however, been fairly low in mutuality in social relations.

The younger women. Among the younger women, the two groups that were originally most distinct from each other were the overwhelmed and the lucky. Solitary activities were most favored by the overwhelmed, while at baseline the lucky had been the least likely to indulge in such activities. The reverse was true

Table 25-2 Results for Younger Men and Women of a Discriminant Analysis Using the Stress Typology as Criterion and Selected Baseline Variables as Predictors

	Younger men				Younger women			
Part of analysis	Avoiders	Lucky	Over-whelmed	Stress-prone	Avoiders	Lucky	Over-whelmed	Stress-prone
I. Means of discriminating variables								
Awareness of social problems	.54	.40	.67	1.17				
Extension in time	65.77	42.20	69.44	22.83				
Life-course perspective	.73	.16	.40	−.29				
Mutuality in social relations	−.89	.62	−.66	−.63				
Sports activities					56.33	56.69	47.78	54.93
Solitary activities					52.00	48.11	59.25	53.64
Positive self-concept					30.75	29.62	27.10	31.15
General satisfaction with self					−.32	.25	−.74	.09
II. F-ratio matrix (discriminant analysis)								
Lucky	4.14***				1.72			
Overwhelmed	.42	2.60*			3.28**	5.32***		
Stress-prone	8.90***	5.53***	6.53***		.49	1.35	3.64***	
df		(4, 31)				(4, 37)		
III. Statistics for final step								
Variables entered (with entry criterion)[a]	Awareness of social problems (158.75)**				Sports activities (145.56)			
	Extension in time (57.88)***				Solitary activities (83.59)**			
	Life-course perspective (101.95)***				Positive self-concept (114.86)*			
	Mutuality in social relations (200.32)**				General satisfaction with self (43.16)			
Wilk's lambda before analysis	.10***				.15***			
Wilk's lambda at final step	.30***				.50***			
Rao's V at final step	58.75				34.06			

[a] Rao's V, a generalized distance measure, was used as the criterion of entry.

* $p \leq .10$; ** $p \leq .05$; *** $p \leq .01$.

Table 25-3 Results for Older Men and Women of a Discriminant Analysis Using the Stress Typology as Criterion and Selected Baseline Variables as Predictors

Part of analysis	Older men				Older women[a]			
	Avoiders	Lucky	Over-whelmed	Stress-prone	Avoiders	Lucky	Over-whelmed	Stress-prone
I. Means of discriminating variables								
Sports activities	49.36	44.44	47.16	48.87				
Maintenance activities	39.47	37.69	49.54	46.05	51.93	57.14	56.15	58.29
Contemplative activities	48.72	42.67	51.13	45.81				
Extension in time	6.90	23.56	25.54	28.62				
Age (at baseline contact)					52.78	50.80	56.58	54.78
Socioeconomic status					2.67	1.90	2.25	2.11
Life satisfaction					30.22	30.00	29.67	25.33
II. F-ratio matrix (discriminant analysis)								
Lucky	4.38***				2.02			
Overwhelmed	3.66**	2.09			1.22	1.21		
Stress-prone	5.16***	1.17	0.59		2.58*	1.34	1.04	
df		(4, 36)				(4, 33)		
III. Statistics for final step								
Variables entered (with entry criterion)[b]	Sports activities (158.91)*				Age (84.12)			
	Maintenance activities (89.61)				Socioeconomic status (22.97)			
	Contemplative activities (119.94)*				Maintenance activities (45.63)			
	Extension in time (54.82)***				Life satisfaction (67.19)			
Wilk's lambda before analysis	.26***				.48			
Wilk's lambda at final step	.47***				.61			
Rao's V at final step	36.33				20.09			

[a] None of the variables to enter were sufficiently strong to meet the criteria set for the stepwise analysis. For purposes of comparison, the analysis was subsequently allowed to cycle four steps.
[b] Rao's V, a generalized distance measure, was used as the criterion of entry.
* $p \leq .10$; ** $p \leq .05$; *** $p \leq .01$.

for participation in athletic activities, where the lucky had the highest participation of all the types, and the overwhelmed the lowest. The lucky women had been the most satisfied with their way of life, while those overwhelmed at baseline had been the most dissatisfied. One variation: The overwhelmed originally identified themselves with the fewest positive adjectives in an adjective checklist, while the stress-prone identified with the most positive adjectives (the avoiders and the lucky fell in between).

The older men. Among the older men (see Table 25-3), the avoiders were originally the most distinct from the other stress types. Projections into the future proved to be the most effective discriminator—in fact, the length of time projected into the future at baseline differentiated among the four groups nearly as efficiently as the four variables included in the final step. The avoiders—those who declined in both positive and negative stress—projected the fewest years into the future, only an average of 7 years, whereas the remaining groups projected more than 20 years, on the average. The stress-prone projected the furthest. The avoiders also had been the most likely to participate in

athletic activities (they were followed closely by the stress-prone).

The older women. The variables to be entered into the prediction equation did not meet the criteria imposed for cycling. However, the analysis was allowed to run for four steps to identify possible predictors. The overall discrimination was nonsignificant, but there was a suggestion that the avoiders originally differed from the lucky in being slightly younger, of higher socioeconomic status, less likely to be involved in maintenance activities such as household chores and shopping, and generally happier with their lives.

Discussion. The results tend to bear out impressions derived from baseline data that people's life-styles may provide clues to how they manage stress. That is, some people seem to be stress avoiders, while others enjoy the stimulation and challenge of seeking out all kinds of new experiences, and still others attempt to be more selective in the kinds of experiences they face. There are also people who seem to manage stress relatively poorly, the overwhelmed. If we look back 7 years in the lives of these people who are experiencing a greater proportion of negative stress preoccupation, we see that a distinguishing characteristic was their tendency to have problems in social relations. This was particularly true for the younger men and women in the sample.

Although this foray into the predictive properties of a person's life-style is illuminating, particularly insofar as it suggests that "coping" is not necessarily best defined by the discrete and specific behavioral strategies now inventoried, the results are hardly conclusive (see, e.g., Lazarus, 1980; Quayhagen & Chiriboga, 1976). Of the many methodological issues raised, that of validity is perhaps the most problematic. Hultsch and Hickey (1978) have outlined a sequence of validity requirements that are appropriate for the type of research being presented (i.e., research based on a mechanistic metamodel). In their sequence, the first requirement is that the presumed cause must clearly precede the effect. The research design analyzed here seems to meet this requirement reasonably well. The predictor set of variables was obtained from the respondents 5 years before the initial application of the LEQ, and 7 years before the second application.

The second requirement is to demonstrate that the predictors are indeed causes of the changes in stress, and that no other explanations are plausible. This requirement appears nearly impossible to meet. Clearly, the causes of changes in stress are multiple, and the predictors employed in the analysis are a meager (albeit selected) sampling from the diverse factors that might be linked with changes in positive and negative stress preoccupation.

The third requirement is to demonstrate that the interpretation of the elements in the explanatory model is adequate. One approach to such a demonstration is concurrent validation, an approach that is currently being pursued. One series of analyses is considering variations in stress type across 18 dimensions of leisure activity. In general, the findings add to our understanding of what the stress types signify. For example, among the older women, 100% of the stress-prone, as opposed to 57% of the avoiders, were high on a dimension labeled Flamboyance. Ninety percent of the avoiders were high on a dimension labeled Peace and Quiet, as opposed to 18% of the overwhelmed. Ninety percent of the lucky, and 80% of the stress-prone were high on a Play dimension, as opposed to only 42% of the overwhelmed. Seventy percent of the stress-prone were high on Intellectual Challenge, as compared to 33% of the overwhelmed.

The fourth, and final, requirement is to demonstrate that the cause–effect relation can be generalized to other conditions. Although this requirement, which deals with external validity, has not been met, a 3-year follow-up study of divorcing men and women will provide the needed data. In this study, the LEQ and the predictor variables were administered during the baseline contact; the questionnaire is being administered at follow-up.

Analysis C: Additional Dimensions of Stress

Although the life-events approach represented by the work of Holmes and Rahe (1967) has received strong criticism, most of its critics continue to use some variation of the same approach. Whether they expand on the number of events or require respondents to assess the degree of distress or the amount of control associated with events, the result is still the same: a life-events approach. The Life Events Questionnaire is an example of such a not-so-radical departure, and while the information it provides has proved to be relevant for life span analyses and significantly related to adaptation, the fact remains that it defines stressors solely in terms of life events. In order to expand the definition, several open-ended questions and one structured instrument have been included in a follow-up interview; together they assess dimensions of stress suggested in the literature as being worthy of study.

Sample. During the 7-year follow-up interviews of the Longitudinal Study of Transitions, 163 respondents completed both the LEQ and the alternative measures of stress. The respondents included most of those who at baseline had been high-school seniors (22 men and 21 women), newlyweds (21 men and 19 women), middle-aged parents of high-school seniors (21 men and 20 women), or people facing retirement (20 men and 19 women).

Method. The LEQ asks respondents to indicate which of a list of events happened to them during the past year, how positively or negatively they felt about each event reported, and how much they thought about each event. For the purposes of this analysis, only negative preoccupation scores for the 11 categories of stress were included.

The additional 18 stress measures were based on a literature review which suggested the potential importance of anticipated stress (Chiriboga, 1972; Lazarus, 1966; Lieberman et al., 1968), being off-schedule (Elder & Rockwell, 1976; Neugarten & Datan, 1974), chronic stress or hassles (Lazarus, 1980), and the so-called "non-event" (Beeson & Lowenthal, 1975). A Hassles Inventory was developed which consists of 11 Likert-type questions dealing with the degree of hassles associated with work, parents, spouse, children, parents, friends, relatives, neighbors, health, finances, social activities, and time pressures. Other measures tapped whether experiences had made the respondents feel behind time, ahead of time, whether they had expected something to happen that had failed to, whether important experiences had been delayed or postponed, and whether they were anticipating some stressful experience. A final set of measures tapped how much control respondents exerted over the most stressful experience of the year and how severe their emotional response to the experience was.

The 11 categories of negative-stress preoccupation and the 18 additional stress measures were included in a factor analysis designed to yield a factorial matrix with maximum generalizability. The SPSS (Nie et al., 1975) factor program was used in the calculations. Alpha factoring provided the initial factor matrix, while an oblique rotation (Delta = 0) provided the final matrix.

Results. Ten factors met the criterion eigenvalue of 1.00 established for this exploratory analysis; together they accounted for 62% of the variance evidenced among all stress measures. Each factor is described briefly below; some are clearly based on the Life Events Questionnaire, some are based on the alternative approaches, and some are based on a mixture.

1. *Being Off Schedule.* As shown in Table 25-4, this factor loads highest on the variables reflecting delays in experiencing events or otherwise getting behind

Table 25-4 Factor-Pattern Matrix From Oblique Rotation of Alpha Factors

Stressor Measures	Factors									
	1	2	3	4	5	6	7	8	9	10
A. Negative preoccupation dimensions										
Habits								.64		
Work								.56		
Thoughts		−.44						.57		
Marital		−.34					−.28			
Family			.58							
Nonfamily		−.34	.28						.35	
Personal					.36					
Legal		−.52								
Financial	.28	−.39							.31	
Home								.80		
School								.67		
B. Hassles										
Work										−.36
Spouse					.71					
Children			.37		.65					
Parents	.34									
Friends										−.38
Relatives										−.58
Neighbors				−.54						
Health				−.62						
Financial	.49									
Social	.39		.32							
Time					.28					−.41
C. Scheduling										
Behind time	.68									
Ahead of time					.37					
Anticipation	.29				.31					
Delayed event	.51									
Nonevent					.39					
D. Major stress										
Control		−.28			.28	.34				
Emotion						−.80				

Note. Factors: 1 = Being Off Schedule, 2 = Negative Preoccupation, 3 = Family Stress Preoccupation, 4 = Health Hassles, 5 = Disharmony, 6 = Family Hassles, 7 = Major Stress Conditions, 8 = Stress of the Daily Routine, 9 = Home Preoccupations, 10 = General Hassles.

Table 25-5 Mean Scores on Stress Factors, by Life Stage and Sex

Stress factors[a]	Two-way ANOVA effects[b]	High school			Newlyweds			Empty nest			Retirement		
		Men	Women	Both	Men	Women	Both	Men	Women	Both	Men	Women	Both
1. Off Schedule	A, S	.36	.66	.51	.34	.57	.45	−.44	−.20	−.32	−.78	−.59	−.69
2. Negative Preoccupation	(S)	.06	−.23	−.08	.01	−.22	−.10	.18	−.13	.03	.22	.10	.17
3. Family Preoccupation	A, S	−.46	−.02	−.24	−.32	.00	−.16	.04	.33	.18	.07	.43	.25
4. Health Hassles	A	.13	.35	.24	.02	.21	.11	.07	−.08	−.00	−.37	−.37	−.37
5. Disharmony	A, (I)	.43	−.18	.13	.33	.32	.32	−.05	−.17	−.11	−.47	−.26	−.37
6. Family Hassles	A, S	−.70	.00	−.36	.29	.74	.51	.06	.20	.13	−.36	−.16	−.26
7. Major Stress		.10	.03	.07	.20	−.08	.06	−.02	−.15	−.08	.14	−.26	−.06
8. Daily Routine	(S)	.07	.19	.13	−.17	.40	.10	−.04	−.20	−.12	−.30	.07	−.12
9. Home Preoccupation	A, S	.38	.60	.49	−.15	.33	.08	−.43	−.29	−.36	−.34	−.13	−.24
10. General Hassles	A, S	.04	−.34	−.14	−.18	−.65	−.41	.19	−.04	.07	.70	.29	.50
Number of respondents		22	21	43	21	19	40	21	20	41	20	19	39

[a] A higher score indicates greater stress, save on Factors 2, 4, 7, and 10.
[b] A, S, and I indicate that two-way (ANOVA) effects for age, sex and interactions, respectively, are significant at $p = .05$. Letters enclosed in parentheses indicates $p \leq .10$.

schedule. The retirement respondents scored lowest on this factor, while the high school and newlywed respondents were more likely to report items reflecting this condition (Table 25-5). Women reported being more often off-schedule than men.

2. *Negative Preoccupation*. Made up entirely of LEQ measures, this factor includes negative preoccupation with legal affairs, inner events, finances, marriage and dating, and nonfamily relations. There were no significant stage or sex differences found, although women tended to report greater negative preoccupation than men did.

3. *Family Stress Preoccupation*. Negative family preoccupation loaded highest on this factor, which also included hassles with children and with social activities. The middle-aged parents and the retirement respondents showed greater family stress than did the two younger groups—a finding of some interest, since most research employing life-event approaches has found that older people report less stress. Women were more stressed than men in family matters at each of the four life stages.

4. *Health Hassles*. This factor loads highest on hassles dealing with personal health, although the presence of hassles with neighbors raises interesting questions about the influence of one's immediate social milieu on at least physical health! Older respondents, particularly those in retirement, reported more of this type of hassle.

5. *Disharmony*. On this factor, the highest loading measures concerned the nonoccurrence of events, feeling ahead of schedule, personal stress (such as changes in hobbies, change in political or religious beliefs, the experience of discrimination), and anticipations of impending stress. The retirement sample scored lowest

on this factor, while the data from high-school men were most likely to suggest this "off kilter" condition, followed, in decreasing order, by the newlyweds and middle-aged parents.

6. *Family Hassles*. While the Family Stress factor is concerned primarily with relatives and children, the Family Hassles factor draws from hassles with the spouse and children (the intercorrelation of the two factors is minimal: $r = .09$). There was a sex difference in the distribution of family hassles, with women reporting more hassles than men. There was also a stage difference: The newlyweds stood out as being more hassled in family matters than any other group. The retirement and high-school samples fell at the low end, while the middle-aged parents were in between.

7. *Major Stress Conditions*. This factor loads strongly only on the two variables that dealt with feelings of control over the most stressful experience of the preceding year and the severity of the emotional reaction to that experience. No stage or sex differences were found.

8. *Stresses of the Daily Routine*. Life-event measures dealing with the personal routine of life, work, and inner events contributed most to this factor. Again there were no stage differences, but women tended to report more stresses in daily routine of life.

9. *Home Preoccupations*. The major contributor to this factor was the LEQ dimension dealing with home-related stresses. However, school stresses were also important, and financial and nonfamily preoccupation asserted a modest influence. Generally this appears to be a young people's variable, especially with the influence of school, and it is therefore not surprising that the high-school seniors come out as highest on this factor. The middle-aged parents were the lowest, with the

retirement and newlywed respondents falling in between. Women were considerably more preoccupied by home/school events than were men.

10. *General Hassles*. Hassles with relatives, with time pressures, and to a lesser extent with friends and work make up this factor. Women reported being more hassled than men, and the only stage difference was that the retirement sample was the least hassled.

Discussion. The results demonstrated the advantage of considering stressors from a more differentiated perspective than that afforded by life events alone. There was, for example, only minimal overlap between the two sets of stress measures compared in the analyses. Of the 10 factors, only two included both types of stressors: Family Stress and Disharmony. Among the remainder, five were drawn solely from the alternative measures of stress, and three from life-events dimensions. Clearly, then, life events are but one of the many faces of stress.

With the increase in scope provided by the alternative measures, subtleties in the nature of stressors become apparent. For example, it has already been mentioned that older persons generally report fewer life events than younger people and consider them to be less disrupting. In the present analysis, older people re-

ported greater stress in two of the seven factors where stage of life exerted an influence on the distribution: Family Stress Preoccupation and Health Hassles. Coupled with the finding in Analysis A that the relative proportion of positive to negative stresses seems to shift in later life toward a more negative balance, the results reaffirm the suggestion of early research that older persons may, in fact, be more troubled by stress than are younger persons (cf. Langner & Michael, 1963; Lowenthal et al., 1967).

Analysis D: The Prediction of Adaptation by Multiple Dimensions of Stress

Since Analysis C dealt only with the interrelationship among stress measures, Analysis D was designed to determine whether the stress factors identified in Analysis C actually contributed to the prediction of changes in adaptive status.

Sample. The sample was the same as the one employed in Analysis C.

Method. The 10 stress factors were included as potential predictors in a series of stepwise multiple

Table 25-6 Stepwise Multiple Regression (MR) Prediction of Change in Four Measures of Adaptation for Younger Men (Former High School and Newlywed)

Change criterion	Predicting variables	Beta	Simple r	MR	Adjusted r²	Increase[a] in adjusted r²
Overall life satisfaction	Income	−.12	−.18	.57**	.21	+.16
	Education	−.20	−.27			
	Disharmony	−.30	−.41			
	Major stress[b]	.12	.29			
	Daily routine	−.25	−.31			
	Family preoccupation	.18	.08			
Doctor's visits	Income	−.11	−.30	.61***	.27	+.14
	Education	−.31	−.34			
	Health Hassles[b]	−.30	−.30			
	Off-schedule	.25	.30			
	Disharmony	−.22	−.28			
Depression	Income	.34	.24	.63***	.29	+.14
	Education	.12	.39			
	Major stress[b]	−.46	−.33			
	General hassles[b]	−.39	−.14			
	Negative preoccupation	−.25	−.18			
	Daily routine	−.17	−.12			
Emotional problems	Income	.35	.26	.65***	.32	+.19
	Education	.22	.35			
	Health hassles[b]	−.50	−.37			
	Negative preoccupation[b]	−.20	−.22			
	Major stress[b]	−.26	−.10			
	Family hassles	−.17	.02			

[a] Increase in adjusted r² when stressor measures are added to income and education.
[b] High score indicates *less* stress.
* $p \leq .10$; ** $p \leq .05$; *** $p \leq .01$.

Table 25-7 Stepwise Multiple Regression (MR) Prediction of Change in Four Measures of Adaptation for Younger Women (Former High School and Newlywed)

Change criterion	Predicting variables	Beta	Simple r	MR	Adjusted r²	Increase[a] in adjusted r²
Overall life satisfaction	Income	.05	.07	.50*	.14	+.19[c]
	Education	−.03	−.03			
	Negative preoccupation[b]	.32	.38			
	Family hassles	−.24	−.31			
	Major stress[b]	−.22	−.20			
Doctor's visits	Income	−.13	.19	.77**	.52	+.48
	Education	−.12	−.25			
	Home preoccupation	−.70	−.69			
	General hassles[b]	.26	.40			
	Health hassles[b]	.14	−.01			
Depression	Income	−.07	−.06	.39	.06	+.08[c]
	Education	.18	.15			
	Health hassles[b]	−.29	−.21			
	Major stress[b]	.28	.21			
Emotional problems	Income	.16	.16	.41	.07	+.10[c]
	Education	−.07	−.02			
	Disharmony	.29	.32			
	Daily routine	.21	.24			

[a] Increase in adjusted r² when stressor measures are added to income and education.
[b] High score indicates *less* stress.
[c] Adjusted r² sign for demographic variables alone was negative (−).
* $p \leq .10$; ** $p \leq .01$.

regression analyses, where four measures of change in adaptive status were the criteria: change in depression, change in emotional problems, change in life satisfaction, and change in the number of medical visits. Change was computed from the 5-year to the 7-year follow-up.

Separate analyses were computed for the younger (former high-school seniors and newlyweds) men and women and for the older (middle-aged parents and the retired) men and women. In order to minimize the development of trivial solutions, the stopping rules for the stepwise multiple regression included a cut-off for variables not in the solution: an F-to-enter of less than 1.00 or a tolerance of less than .50. In order to control for the effects of education and income, these two variables were included as first-entry, forced predictors. As shown in the column entitled "Increase in Adjusted r²" in Tables 25-6 through 25-9, education and income in general did not contribute in any strength to the variance accounted for in the prediction equations.

Results. The results, as shown in Tables 25-6 through 25-9, are quite complex and group-specific. The highlights are as follows.

First, change in at least one measure of adaptation was predicted at highly significant levels by the regression techniques in each group of respondents. Changes in the more problem-focused measures of depression, emotional problems, and medical visits were predicted in three out of four groups. Changes in overall satisfaction were successfully predicted only for the younger men, although trends were shown for the younger women and older men. It can be concluded that the experience of stress predicts change in functional status, especially when the measure of adaptation is problem focused.

Second, factors based primarily on the alternative measures of stress contributed at least as much to the predictive equations as did the factors based on life-events measures. In fact, alternative stress factors were one of the two major contributors to the prediction equations in all instances where the prediction reached a significant probability level. It can be concluded that knowledge of the less frequently studied stresses does enhance our understanding of the adaptive process.

Third, as was found in earlier data based solely on the life-events dimensions (Chiriboga & Dean, 1978), increased stress was associated with improved adaptation in a sizable proportion of the correlations. Some of these associations may be spurious. For example, more family stress and more family hassles were associated with improved morale and decreased emotional problems, respectively, among the younger men. However, it is important to note that those men who had not married or who had not had children were automatically lower on family stresses. If it is true that marriage and having children are associated with

Table 25-8 Stepwise Multiple Regression (MR) Prediction of Change in Four Measures of Adaption for Older Men (Middle-Aged Parent and Retirement)

Change criterion	Predicting variables	Beta	Simple r	MR	Adjusted r²	Increase[a] in adjusted r²
Overall life satisfaction	Income	−.04	−.10	.49*	.13	+.17[c]
	Education	−.02	−.09			
	General hassles[b]	.35	.35			
	Health hassles[b]	.32	.29			
	Negative preoccupation[b]	.20	.10			
Doctor's visits	Income	.03	−.04	.35	.05	+.07[c]
	Education	−.13	−.18			
	Health hassles[b]	.30	.33			
Depression	Income	.07	.06	.63**	.26	+.25
	Education	−.39	−.16			
	Family hassles	.17	.34			
	Disharmony	.40	.32			
	Health hassles[b]	−.21	−.16			
	Home preoccupation	−.25	−.20			
	Daily routine	.20	.30			
Emotional problems	Income	−.01	.07	.56**	.18	+.22[c]
	Education	.12	.10			
	General hassles[b]	−.27	−.38			
	Disharmony	−.45	−.26			
	Family hassles	.23	.20			
	Family preoccupation	.16	.20			

[a] Increase in adjusted r² when stressor measures are added to income and education.
[b] High score indicates *less* stress.
[c] Adjusted r² sign for demographic variables alone was negative (−).
* $p \leq .10$; ** $p \leq .05$.

Table 25-9 Stepwise Multiple Regression (MR) Prediction of Change in Four Measures of Adaptation for Older Women (Middle-Aged Parent and Retirement)

Change criterion	Predicting variables	Beta	Simple r	MR	Adjusted r²	Increase[a] in adjusted r²
Overall life satisfaction	Income	.00	.03	.47	.10	+.15[c]
	Education	.07	.07			
	Health hassles[b]	.23	.30			
	Negative preoccupation[b]	.33	.29			
	Major stress[b]	.20	.25			
Doctor's visits	Income	.33	.25	.85**	.63	+.62
	Education	.02	−.05			
	Home preoccupation	.80	.68			
	Health hassles[b]	−.26	−.20			
	Off-schedule	−.19	−.03			
	Family preoccupation	.18	.22			
	Daily routine	−.12	−.00			
	Disharmony	.12	.05			
Depression	Income	−.05	.01	.73**	.45	+.44
	Education	.12	.24			
	Off-schedule	.54	.53			
	Family preoccupation	.51	.45			
	Negative preoccupation[b]	.33	−.15			
	Major stress[b]	.23	.17			
Emotional problems	Income	−.08	−.15	.58*	.21	+.24[c]
	Education	−.12	−.13			
	Home preoccupation	.55	.41			
	General hassles[b]	−.43	.05			
	Family preoccupation	.38	.28			
	Health hassles[b]	.35	.00			

[a] Increase in adjusted r² when stressor measures are added to income and education.
[b] High score indicates *less* stress.
[c] Adjusted r² sign for demographic variables alone was negative (−).
* $p \leq .05$; ** $p \leq .01$.

improved adaptation among younger men, then much of the apparent association between family stress and adaptation may be simply a by-product of family status. On the other hand, some of the associations of stress with improved functioning may reflect the potential of stress as a growth agent. The benefits of stress (what Selye, 1976, calls "eustress") have been considered (cf. Elder, 1974; Vaillant, 1974), but little empirical evidence exists to substantiate the idea.

Discussion. Both the life-events measures and the more innovative measures aided in the prediction of change in adaptation. When considered separately, neither set of variables explained the significant portions of the variance in adaptive change that they did when considered together. In short, while the results do not suggest that the life-events approach be abandoned, they do suggest that workers in the field should pay heed to the complexities of stress instead of relying on the simple and more easily administered—but also more restrictive—life-events instruments.

Some Final Thoughts

Field research on stress conditions received a tremendous boost in 1967, when the original Schedule of Recent Events was first published. The major contribution of the Schedule of Recent Events then, as now, was its standardized weighting system, which at once simplified the task for the respondent and shortened administration time. During the next 8 to 10 years most studies employed the instrument without much questioning, although several major modifications soon appeared (cf. Dohrenwend, Krasnoff, & Askenasy, 1978; Horowitz et al., 1977; Hurst, Jenkins, & Rose, 1978; Paykel, Prusoff, & Uhlenhuth, 1971; Sarason et al., 1978). More recently, however, the number of articles critical of both the instrument and the approach has escalated until they now tip the balance. At this juncture even the developers of the instrument are openly discussing its problems (cf. Masuda & Holmes, 1978; Rahe, 1979).

What should replace the life-events approach or how it should be modified are still in doubt. One of the advantages of the Schedule of Recent Events has been its flexibility. However, since a substantial proportion of its users have added or subtracted items or procedures in order to increase its relevance to specific populations or research questions, replication has become difficult to achieve. If, like the Phoenix, a new life-events instrument emerges from the fire of criticism now enveloping it, it will certainly be a changed instrument. Insofar as life span research is concerned, these changes may well go in the direction of expanding the number of events, including an assessment of the desirability of events from the respondent's perspective, and perhaps including additional dimensions of stress such as those discussed in Analyses C and D. In this way the basic approach may sample the stress experiences of adults more adequately.

REFERENCES

Amster, L. E., & Krauss, H. H. The relationship between life crises and mental deterioration in old age. *International Journal of Aging and Human Development*, 1974, *5*, 51–55.

Ander, S., Lindstrom, B., & Tibblin, G. Life changes in random samples of middle-aged. In E. K. Gunderson and R. H. Rahe (Eds.), *Life stress and illness*. Springfield, Ill.: Charles C Thomas, 1974.

Beeson, D., & Lowenthal, M. F., Perceived stress across life course. In M. F. Lowenthal, M. Thurnher, D. Chiriboga, & Associates, *Four stages of life: A comparative study of women and men facing transitions*. San Francisco: Jossey-Bass, 1975.

Bradburn, N. *The structure of psychological well-being*. Chicago: Aldine, 1969.

Brown, G. W., & Birley, J. L. T. Crises and life changes and the onset of schizophrenia. *Journal of Health and Social Behavior*, 1968, *9*, 203–214.

Chiriboga, D. A. *The prediction of relocation stress among the aged: A comparative study*. Unpublished doctoral dissertation, University of Chicago, 1972.

Chiriboga, D. A. Life event weighting systems: A comparative analysis. *Journal of Psychosomatic Research*, 1977, *21*, 415–422.

Chiriboga, D. A., & Dean, H. Dimensions of stress: Perspectives from a longitudinal study. *Journal of Psychosomatic Research*, 1978, *22*, 47–55.

Cochrane, R., & Robertson, A. The life events inventory: A measure of the relative severity of psychosocial stressors. *Journal of Psychosomatic Research*, 1973, *17*, 135–139.

Dekker, D. J., & Webb, J. T. Relationships of the social readjustment rating scale to psychiatric patient status, anxiety, and social desirability. *Journal of Psychosomatic Research*, 1974, *18*, 125–130.

Dohrenwend, B. P. Stressful life events and psychopathology: Some issues of theory and method. In J. E. Barrett (Ed.), *Stress and mental disorder*. New York: Raven Press, 1979.

Dohrenwend, B. S., Krasnoff, L., & Askenasy, A. R. Exemplification of a method for scaling life events: The PERI life events scale. *Journal of Health and Social Behavior*, 1978, *19*, 205–229.

Elder, G. H., Jr. *Children of the great depression: Social change in life experience*. Chicago: University of Chicago Press, 1974.

Elder, G. H., Jr., & Rockwell, R. C. Marital timing in women's life patterns. *Journal of Family History*, 1976, *1*, 34–53.

Gerst, M. S., Grant, I., Yager, J., & Sweetwood, H. The reliability of the social readjustment rating scale: Moderate and long-term stability. *Journal of Psychosomatic Research*, 1978, *22*, 519–523.

Grant, I., Sweetwood, H., Gerst, M. S., & Yager, J. Scaling procedures in life events research. *Journal of Psychosomatic Research*, 1978, *22*, 525–530.

Gutmann, D. Life events and decision making by older adults. *Gerontologist*, 1978, *18*, 462–467.

Harmon, D. K., Masuda, M., & Holmes, T. H. The social readjustment rating scale: A cross-cultural study of western Europeans and Americans. *Journal of Psychosomatic Research*, 1970, *14*, 391–400.

Holmes, T. H., & Masuda M. Life change and illness susceptibility. In B. S. Dohrenwend and B. P. Dohrenwend (Eds.), *Stressful life events: Their nature and effects*. New York: Wiley, 1974.

Holmes, T. H., & Rahe, R. H. The Social Readjustment Rating Scale. *Journal of Psychosomatic Research*, 1967, *11*, 213–218.

Horowitz, M. J. *Stress response syndromes*. New York: Aronson, 1976.

Horowitz, M. J., Schaefer, C., & Cooney, P. Life event scaling for recency of experience. In E. K. E. Gunderson & R. H. Rahe (Eds.), *Life stress and illness*. Springfield, Ill.: Charles C Thomas, 1974.

Horowitz, M. J., Schaefer, C., Hiroto, D., Wilner, N., & Levin, B. Life event questionnaires for measuring presumptive stress. *Psychosomatic Medicine*, 1977, *39*, 413–431.

Hultsch, D. F., & Hickey, T. External validity in the study of human development: Theoretical and methodological issues. *Human Development*, 1978, *21*, 76–91.

Hurst, M. W., Jenkins, C. D., & Rose, R. M. The assessment of life change stress: A comparative and methodological inquiry. *Psychosomatic Medicine*, 1978, *40*, 126–141.

Jewell, R. W. *A quantitative study of emotion: The magnitude of emotion rating scale*. Unpublished medical thesis, University of Washington, 1977.

Komaroff, A. L., Masuda, M., & Holmes, T. H. The social readjustment rating scale: A comparative study of Negro, Mexican and white Americans. *Journal of Psychosomatic Research*, 1968, *12*, 121–128.

Langner, T. S., & Michael, S. T. *Life stresses and mental health*. New York: Free Press, 1963.

Lazarus, R. S. *Psychological stress and the coping process*. New York: McGraw-Hill, 1966.

Lazarus, R. S. The stress and coping paradigm. In C. Eisdorfer, D. Cohen, A. Kleinman, & P. Maxim (Eds.), *Theoretical bases in psychopathology*. New York: Spectrum, 1980.

Lieberman, M. A., Prock, V. N., & Tobin, S. S. Psychological effects of institutionalization. *Journal of Gerontology*, 1968, *23*, 343–353.

Lowenthal, M. F. *Lives in distress*. New York: Basic Books, 1964.

Lowenthal, M. F., Berkman, P. L., & Associates. *Aging and mental disorder in San Francisco: A social psychiatric study*. San Francisco: Jossey-Bass, 1967.

Lowenthal, M. F., & Chiriboga, D. Social stress and adaptation: Toward a life-course perspective. In C. Eisdorfer & M. P. Lawton (Eds.), *The psychology of adult development and aging*. Washington, D.C.: American Psychological Association, 1973.

Lowenthal, M. F., & Chiriboga, D. Responses to stress. In M. F. Lowenthal, M. Thurnher, D. Chiriboga, & Associates, (Eds.), *Four stages of life: A comparative study of women and men facing transitions*. San Francisco: Jossey-Bass, 1975.

Lowenthal, M. F., Thurnher, M., Chiriboga, D., & Associates. *Four stages of life: A comparative study of women and men facing transitions*. San Francisco: Jossey-Bass, 1975.

Lundberg, U., & Theorell, T. Scaling of life changes: Differences between three diagnostic groups and between recently experienced and nonexperienced events. *Journal of Human Stress*, 1976, *2*, 7–17.

Masuda, M., & Holmes, T. H. The social readjustment rating scale: A cross-cultural study of Japanese and Americans. *Journal of Psychosomatic Research*, 1967, *11*, 227–237.

Masuda, M., & Holmes, T. H. Life events: Perceptions and frequencies. *Psychosomatic Medicine*, 1978, *40*, 236–261.

Mechanic, D. Some problems in the measurement of stress and social adjustment. *Journal of Human Stress*, 1975, *1*(3), 43–48.

Morrison, J. R., Hudgens, R. W., & Barchha, R. G. Life events and psychiatric illness: A study of 100 patients and 100 controls. *British Journal of Psychiatry*, 1968, *114*, 423–432.

Mueller, D. P., Edwards, D. W., & Yarvis, R. M. Stressful life events and psychiatric symptomatology: Change or undesirability? *Journal of Health and Social Behavior*, 1977, *18*, 307–317.

Nelson, P., Mensh, I. N., Hecht, E., & Schwartz, A. N. Variables in the reporting of recent life changes. *Journal of Psychosomatic Research*, 1972, *16*, 465–471.

Neugarten, B. L. & Datan, N. The middle years. In S. Arieti (Ed.), *American handbook of psychiatry*, (2nd ed.). New York: Basic Books, 1974.

Nie, N. H., Hull, C. H., Jenkins, J. G., Steinbrenner, K., & Bent, D. H. *SPSS: Statistical package for the social sciences* (2nd ed.). New York: McGraw-Hill, 1975.

Paykel, E. S., Prusoff, B. A., & Uhlenhuth, E. H. Scaling of life events. *Archives of General Psychiatry*, 1971, *25*, 340–347.

Quayhagen, M. P., & Chiriboga, D. *Geriatric Coping Schedule: Potentials and Problems*. Paper presented at the 29th annual meeting of the Gerontological Society, New York, October 13–17, 1976.

Rahe, R. H. Life change events and mental illness: An overview. *Journal of Human Stress*, 1979, *5*(3), 2–10.

Reavley, W. The relationship of life events to several aspects of "anxiety." *Journal of Psychosomatic Research*, 1974, *18*, 421–424.

Ross, C. E. & Mirowsky, J. A., II. A comparison of life-event-weighting schemes: Change, undesirability, and effect proportional indices. *Journal of Health and Social Behavior*. 1979, *20*, 166–177.

Rubin, R. T., Gunderson, E. K., & Arthur, R. J. Life stress and illness patterns in the U.S. Navy. IV. Environmental and demographic variables in relation to illness onset in a battleship's crew. *Journal of Psychosomatic Research*, 1971, *15*, 277–288.

Sarason, I. G., Johnson, J. H., & Siegel, J. M. Assessing the impact of life changes: Development of the life experiences survey. *Journal of Consulting and Clinical Psychology*, 1978, *46*, 932–946.

Schwartz, C. C., & Myers, J. K. Life events and schizophrenia: Comparison of schizophrenics with a community sample. *Archives of General Psychiatry*, 1977, *34*, 1238–1241.

Selye, Hans. *Stress in health and disease*. Boston: Butterworths, 1976.

Siegel, J. M., Johnson, J. H., & Sarason, I. G. Mood states and the reporting of life changes. *Journal of Psychosomatic Research*, 1979, *23*, 103–108.

Tennant, C., & Andrews, G. The pathogenic quality of life event stress in neurotic impairment. *Archives of General Psychiatry*, 1978, *35*, 859–863.

Uhlenhuth, E. H., Lipman, R. S., Balter, M. B., & Stern, J. Symptom intensity and life stress in the city. *Archives of General Psychiatry*, 1974, *31*, 759–764.

Vaillant, S. E. Natural history of male psychological health: II. Some antecedents of healthy adult development. *Archives of General Psychiatry*, 1974, *31*, 15–22.

Vinokur, A., & Selzer, M. I. Life events, stress and mental distress. *Proceedings of the 81st Annual Convention of the American Psychological Association*, 1973, *8*, 329–330.

Wershow, H. J., & Reinhart, G. Life change and hospitalization—A heretical view. *Journal of Psychosomatic Research*, 1974, *18*, 393–401.

Yamamoto, K. J., & Kinney, O. K. Pregnant women's ratings of different factors influencing psychological stress during pregnancy. *Psychological Reports*, 1976, *39*, 203–214.

Mardi J. Horowitz and Nancy Wilner

CHAPTER

26

Life Events, Stress, and Coping

Rating scales have been developed to measure the degree of subjective distress from a particular life event and to assess coping strategies for adjusting to that event. Three such scales are described: the Life Events Questionnaire, for measuring cumulative stress over time; the Impact of Event Scale, for measuring periods of intrusion and avoidance after a stressful life event; and the Coping Inventory, for measuring the usefulness of various strategies for adapting to a serious life event. Illustrative data are presented to demonstrate that intensive clinical studies can lead to measurements useful in larger scale field investigations.

The connections between serious life events, predisposition in terms of coping and defensive styles, and reactions such as adaptation or morbidity, encompass an area of keen scientific interest. Because the issues involved in the study of interactions between personal, situational, and social concomitants of stress are complex, it is important to focus first on methodology. Our work in a special clinic for the treatment of stress-response syndromes after a serious life event enables us to examine a rich array of variables through individual case studies. Eventually, the findings from such studies may contribute to the development of methods that will be useful for larger scale studies of more general populations. Such methodological possibilities are discussed after a brief statement about our approach.

At the Center for the Study of Neuroses—one of 10 clinical research centers funded by the National Institute of Mental Health—the focus is on time-limited brief therapy for persons with post-traumatic stress disorders. We select for study cohorts of patients who have experienced the same life event, such as death of a parent or spouse. We are undertaking prevention studies in which we evaluate persons before serious life events occur, then evaluate the level of their distress if such events are experienced, and introduce prophylactic treatment in an effort to prevent chronic symptoms or other forms of morbidity. The basic research format includes independent clinical evaluations of persons before brief treatment and at various times after termination of therapy. We also examine contrast groups composed of volunteers who have experienced life events similar to those of our patients and who are willing to undergo the same battery of rating scales and evaluation interviews but who do not seek treatment.

Through clinical operations augmented by interviews that are audiotaped and videorecorded, we are accumulating an expanding archive of interviews and clinical summaries, as well as rating scales done by pa-

The authors would like to express their gratitude to Barbara Kent for data from the Cancer Rehabilitation Project (NCI-N01-CN-45061-05).

This research was conducted at the Center for the Study of Neuroses, Langley Porter Institute, University of California, San Francisco, under an MHCRC Grant from the National Institute of Mental Health (MH30899), a research grant from the National Institute of Child Health and Human Development (AG00002), and a University of California Biomedical Research Support Grant (570057).

tients, field subjects, evaluating clinicians, and psychotherapists. Studies based on these archives fall into three interrelated research paradigms: the descriptive, associational, and group-contrast modes of scientific design. The descriptive studies focus on intensive and systematic reviews of process and outcome variables in a single case and follow a method called configurational analysis (Horowitz, 1979; Horowitz, Marmar, & Wilner, 1979). This method of sequential clarification is used to examine problems, patient states, role-relation models, and information-processing styles as they change over time. The analysis involves a series of 10 steps. Step 1 requires a pretherapy problem list and a follow-up on the outcome of those same problems. Steps 2, 3, and 4 describe patient states, role relations, and information-processing styles at pretherapy evaluation. Steps 5, 6, and 7 describe those same three variables during therapy, and Steps 8, 9, and 10 describe them at follow-up.

Two independent teams, each consisting of three clinicians, review videotaped therapies and compare their results after they have completed each of the 10 steps required for configurational analysis. Differences are then resolved by further review of these videotaped materials, and a consensus report is produced. Descriptive studies also include individualized outcome assessment and use teams of clinicians to determine reliability, to seek consensual validation, and to analyze the patterns of ratings by different persons at various points in time.

Our findings to date indicate a fairly discrete entity of stress-response syndromes (Horowitz, 1976). This finding has been incorporated into the third edition of the American Psychiatric Association's (1980) *Diagnostic and Statistical Manual*. The stress-response syndrome includes a category of post-traumatic stress disorders defined in part by intrusive and repetitive thought, denial and numbing phases, and other signs and symptoms of stress. We have also found that brief therapy appears to be effective in reducing these signs and symptoms. These findings merit further, more systematic group-comparison studies, and such studies are planned for the immediate future.

Such basic clinical studies are, of course, concerned with the same variables found in field and experimental studies and with many more besides. We are interested in an assessment of a person for the seriousness of crisis, the degree of distress following crises (or life changes), and the habitual and current adaptive or maladaptive response processes. While participants are chosen because of a particular life event, such as personal injury or death, we are also interested in measuring cumulative stress based on other serious life events that they may have experienced before, during, or after treatment, since cumulative stress may be an important intervening variable.

We have also attempted to use our clinical experience to develop rating scales that measure the degree of subjective distress from a particular life event and to derive, in a preliminary way, a method for assessing coping operations. Discussions concerning the detailed interaction of multiple variables and clinical relevance are available in the literature (Horowitz, Wilner, & Alvarez, 1979; Horowitz, Wilner, Kaltreider, & Alvarez, 1980). Here we simply focus on three kinds of questionnaires. The discussion that follows indicates the degree of usefulness of these questionnaires for other studies, including those concerned with persons coping with stress at various stages of the life cycle.

Life Events Questionnaire

Our own approach to life-events questionnaires evolved during experimental studies of the hypothesis that traumatic perceptions presented in stress films would be followed, in those viewing such films, by episodes of intrusive and repetitive thoughts and visualizations of these perceptions (Horowitz, 1975; Horowitz & Wilner, 1976). In order to control for presumptive stress as an intervening variable, we needed to derive a score on life-change units for the subjects in the experiments. We investigated instruments like those of Holmes and Rahe (1967) but found them suitable only for scoring events within a fairly recent time period. This led us, by degrees, to begin to alter the questionnaires so as to include in a total presumptive stress score events that may have occurred in the past but that still have an enduring impact (such as the death of a parent during childhood). We also found that some events, such as those concerned with sexuality, were not included in the original Holmes and Rahe instruments. We thus decided to devise our own related instruments, using differential weights for recency or remoteness in time of particular events and including some internal events (such as being confused or angry for as long as 3 days) that are scored separately (Horowitz, Schaefer & Cooney, 1974; Horowitz, Schaefer, Hiroto, Wilner, & Levin, 1977).

We compiled two lists of life events, one short and one long. The short form, based on the life-events questionnaires of Holmes and Rahe (1967) and of Paykel, Prusoff, and Uhlenhuth (1971), differed from its precursors by having columns for five points in time and some items concerning change in sexual attachments. The subject could indicate whether an event had been experienced 1 week, 1 month, 6 months, 1 year, or 3 years earlier. Subjects thus had, for each discrete event, five columns in which to estimate presumptive stress according to the recency or remoteness of the event. The items were described at the top of the one-page short form as "life changes, both positive and negative, found stressful by some people."

The subjects' task was to estimate how stressful each event would be for them now if the event had occurred at a given time in the past. A 100-unit scale was used for the rating of current stress. On this scale, 1 indicated "no stress at all," and 100 indicated the highest degree of stress each person "could imagine experiencing," with equal intervals between. The first subjects to complete this form were 119 unpaid volunteers from medical center and university settings. Of these, 95 were under 30, and 24 were over 30. There were 53 males and 66 females. Subjects' presumptive stress scores for each individual event almost universally decreased in a gradual slope as time elapsed after an event.

On the long form, events were grouped into seven sets: deaths, separations, arguments with important persons, major threats to self or self-image, minor threats to self or self-image, threats to material well-being, and residual life changes or critical moments not otherwise categorized. For every set, remoteness and recency in time significantly affected the weights assigned. The decline in stress effects over time is an obvious finding; no one could fail to predict it. But less obvious findings concern potential differences in assignment of presumptive stress scores by sex, by age, and by individual persons, who vary in the experience of an event.

On all seven item sets, women rated events as more stressful than did men. This difference may arise from a variety of factors, but the two possibilities of central importance are mental set due to role characteristics and a "real" differential in responsiveness to stress. We believe this variation in assignment of weights is due substantially to social roles in which women are encouraged to admit the stress of life events while men are not. We do not believe the variation is due to greater vulnerability to stress on the part of women.

Younger persons tended to rate items as more stressful than did older persons on only three of the seven sets: deaths, separations, and major threats to self or self-image.

Indications of personal experience of an item made a significant difference for only two item sets—minor threats to self or self-image and threats to material well-being—and the effect was small. Those who had experienced such events rated them as more stressful than those who had not, with a relatively lower rate of descending level of stress over time.

While women generally rated individual items higher than men, and younger persons rated them higher than older persons, there was agreement among different subgroups on the degree of stress of particular life events. Men correlated with women in rank ordering items by assigning weights, and this correlation was high, positive, and significant (Spearman $r = .96$, $df = 33$, $p < .001$). Comparable correlations were also found between older and younger subjects ($r = .86$, $df = 33$, $p < .001$).

Judgments by psychiatrists of presumptive stress from life events were available from another study, and we compared their scores with those of the psychiatric outpatients and nonpatients described above. The psychiatrists had rated our longer and more inclusive list of 143 life events, which had been constructed in collaboration with Rahe and Chiriboga. Since 26 of the items were worded identically to items from the short-form list of life events used with the patients and nonpatients, scores assigned to these similar items by the diverse groups could thus be compared.

The three groups agreed substantially in assigning presumptive stress scores to the 26 items and had an overall concordance of .89 (by Kendall's coefficients, $df = 25$, $p < .001$). The correlation between nonpatients' and psychiatrists' weightings was .82; between patients' and psychiatrists' weightings, .76; and between patients' and nonpatients' weightings, .89.

The addition of a temporal dimension to life-events questionnaires permits derivation of a total current presumptive stress score for a person or group based not only on the incidence of events but on when they occurred. Using this approach, we found that persons with high levels of presumptive stress, derived from the sum of the weightings for external events on our Life Events Questionnaire (Short Form, see Appendix A), tended to be more emotionally responsive to stressful films shown as part of the experimental study.

In a later study of the first 66 patients treated in our clinic for stress-response syndromes, we found similar results. The correlation between presumptive stress derived from the Life Events Questionnaire and the total stress score on our specific measure of distress for a given life event—the Impact of Event Scale (described later in this chapter)—was positive, but low, and did not reach significance ($r = .17$). Presumptive stress from life events correlated with the Hopkins Checklist-90 subscales for anxiety ($r = 29$, $p < .01$), for anger ($r = .21$, $p < .05$), and for somatization ($r = .21$, $p < .05$), which suggests that cumulative stress is a relevant issue in the amount of distress experienced after a specific serious life event. In this study too, women assigned higher weights to life events than did men.

Impact of Event Scale (IES)

Perhaps of more interest, because it is an individualized measure of subjective distress (rather than a generalized measure of presumptive distress), is our Impact of Event Scale (revised version, see Appendix B). This scale was developed to measure the current degree of self-reported distress related to a specific event (Horowitz et al., 1979). In studies of psychological responses to stressful life events, common qualities of conscious experience were found among patients with different personality styles (Breuer & Freud, 1895; Horowitz, 1973, 1976; Janis, 1969; Lazarus, 1966). In our clinic two major types of response to these experiences—intrusion and avoidance—were abstracted from evaluation and psychotherapy interviews. Intrusion was characterized by unbidden thoughts and images, troubled dreams, strong waves or pangs of feelings, and repetitive behaviors. Avoidance responses included ideational constriction, denial of meanings and consequences of the event, blunted sensation, behavioral inhibition, counterphobic activity, and awareness of emotional numbness.

Items for this measure were derived from statements most frequently made by distressed persons who had experienced recent serious life events. The scale focuses on the form and quality of conscious experiences during the previous 7 days, and the event for the individual serves as a written referent on the scale itself. The 7-day time unit was found to be best for clinically valid reports of current subjective distress and states of mind related to a particular life event. Studies of reliability and validity led to reducing these items from 30 to 16, with two subscales that were both logically and empirically consistent. These subscales yield intrusion and avoidance subscores (Cronbach's alpha was .78 and .82 for these subscales, respectively; test–retest reliability for the instrument was .87). We also found that clinicians were able to establish "indifference points" for these scales. An "indifference point," or threshold, is loosely defined as that point on a particular measure where a patient who scores higher or lower is judged to be at a qualitatively different level of distress. In this way we have been able to establish two thresholds, one that separates low from medium levels of distress, and one that separates medium from high levels of distress.

As a brief illustration of findings on the Impact of Event Scale (IES), Table 26-1 presents the percentages of positive endorsement of intrusion and avoidance items during the week previous to testing by 66 patients who had experienced a serious life event an average of 6 weeks before their entry into the clinic and completion of the IES. (Tables 26-1 through 26-3 refer to the original IES. In the revised scale, given in Appendix B, some items have been reworded and some

Table 26-1 Impact of Event Scale Results of 66 Subjects With Stress Disorders

Scale item	Percentage of subjects positively endorsing item	Group M	SD
Intrusion items			
I had waves of strong feelings about it.	88	3.8	1.9
Things I saw or heard suddenly reminded me of it.	85	3.7	1.9
I thought about it when I didn't mean to.	76	3.3	2.2
Images related to it popped into my mind.	76	3.2	2.2
Any reminder brought back emotions related to it.	76	3.0	2.1
I have difficulty falling asleep because of images or thoughts related to the event.	64	2.6	2.4
I had bad dreams related to the event.	44	1.7	2.2
Avoidance items			
I knew that a lot of unresolved feelings were still there, but I kept them under wraps.	71	3.0	2.2
I avoided letting myself get emotional when I thought about it or was reminded of it.	70	2.8	2.1
I wished to banish it from my store of memories.	65	2.8	2.3
I made an effort to avoid talking about it.	61	2.2	2.0
I felt unrealistic about it, as if it hadn't happened or as if it wasn't real.	58	2.2	2.3
I stayed away from things or situations that might remind me of it.	53	2.2	2.3
My emotions related to it were kind of numb.	59	2.1	2.1
I didn't let myself have thoughts related to it.	50	1.8	2.2

Note. Scale of intensity for group mean (within past 7 days): 5 = severe, 3 = moderate, 1 = mild, and 0 = not at all.

Table 26-2 Comparison Between Two Groups' Mean Scores on Subscales of the Impact of Event Scale

Impact of Event Scale (entry level)	Parental bereavement		
	Patient subjects ($n = 31$)	Field subjects ($n = 36$)	p
Intrusion items	22	14	$<.001$
Avoidance items	21	10	$<.001$

omitted.) The patients included 16 men and 50 women between 20 and 75 years of age. The mean scores for each item were calculated separately for men and women, as well as for the total group. Women indicated a significantly higher level of endorsement than men on three items. These items were all in the avoidance category: "I was aware that I had a lot of feelings about it, but I didn't deal with them," "I avoided letting myself get upset when I thought about it or was reminded of it," and "It seemed to me that I was reacting less than would be expected." However, the total subjective stress scores, derived by adding the positive scores for each item, were not significantly affected by sex.

All items were endorsed frequently. Those most often endorsed—"Things I saw or heard suddenly reminded me of it," and "I had waves of strong feelings about it"—were acknowledged by 85% and 88% of the subject sample, respectively. Even the item with the lowest endorsement, "I had bad dreams related to the event," was acknowledged by 44% of the 66 subjects. All five of the most frequently endorsed items had a mean weighted score of 3 or more, indicating that *as a group*, these subjects experienced such episodes at a high level of frequency and intensity, even though the stressful event had usually been experienced several months earlier and the time frame of endorsement of any scale item was limited to the past 7 days.

Table 26-2 shows some preliminary data from our study of persons seen after the death of a parent; it contrasts a group who came for treatment with a second group, obtained by review of hospital death records and contact with next of kin, who were inter-

viewed but not treated. As one might expect (but as we were not sure we could expect before we did the study), the persons who came for treatment an average of 6 months after the event had significantly higher levels of distress related to the particular event than did the field subjects, who were seen an average of 2 months after the event.

As indicated earlier, at various points in time the amount of current distress from a particular event can be studied by asking the person about experiences during the past 7 days. The data in Table 26-3 for intrusion and avoidance items on the Impact of Event Scale indicate significant declines with time and treatment for a group of subjects who were previously given psychotherapy for post-traumatic stress disorders after various losses and injuries. The scores on intrusion items declined from a mean of 20 at entry to the clinic to a mean of 10 at the first follow-up (at least 8 months later). Avoidance scores declined from a mean of 17 at entry to a mean of 6 at the first follow-up.

Coping Inventory

If the Life Events Questionnaire is at least marginally useful for showing presumptive stress from total life crises of an external nature and if the Impact of Event Scale can indicate the degree of distress caused by a particular life event in a given time period, then it may be possible to examine what strategies a person finds helpful in adapting to serious life events. From our clinical experience we considered this an extremely "sticky" area. Most theories of coping and defense, including the one on which we based the questionnaire presented in the following section, classify outcomes of processes rather than processes themselves, since these processes function out of awareness, are probably not amenable to self-report, and are also very difficult for clinicians to report on in a reliable fashion. Our clinical evidence also suggests that some of the processes that have been most helpful to people are the ones that they have forgotten or were unaware of at the time they used them.

With a warning that the state of the art is not very advanced and that our Coping Inventory, like others in

Table 26-3 Impact of Event Scale Data Over Time and Treatment

Impact of Event Scale	Stress syndromes—data from completed therapies						
	Entry ($n = 45$)	Therapy hour 4 ($n = 25$)	p (t tests)	Therapy hour 8 ($n = 23$)	Therapy hour 12 (end of therapy) ($n = 45$)	Follow-up ($n = 45$)	p (t tests)
Intrusion items	20	16	$<.05$	12	11	10	ns
Avoidance items	17	12	$<.05$	12	8	6	$<.05$

the field, is only a preliminary instrument and may have only transitory usefulness, we present some sample data.

Purpose of the Instrument

The Coping Inventory (see Appendix C) was designed to obtain general information on the frequency and helpfulness of various operations commonly reported during clinical interviews as useful in coping with serious life events.

Instrument

Typical phrases used in clinical interviews served as a guide for the development of the 33-item Coping In-

ventory. We used the same design strategy as with the Impact of Event Scale: For each item, subjects were asked to indicate whether such a mode of response to the specific serious life event in question had been used and whether the process was helpful in reducing strain. This measure was then scored for the frequency of endorsement of each item, and for the frequency with which it was found helpful (the percentage of persons endorsing an item who also endorsed it as helpful).

Subjects

Three groups of subjects were derived from diverse population pools. One group (n = 56) was composed of cancer patients whose illness had been diagnosed an average of 7 weeks earlier. A second group (n = 37)

Table 26-4 Responses to Coping Inventory Items by Three Groups

Coping Inventory item	Percentage who used item			Percentage who used item and found it helpful		
	Stress patients	Cancer patients	Significant others	Stress patients	Cancer patients	Significant others
Turning to other attitudes and activities (5 of 11 items)						
I tried to concentrate on other things in my life.	86	55	43	40	40	51
I tried to find some other outlets, like sports, cooking, or gardening, to relieve some of the feelings I had.	71	25	27	32	36	52
I tried to devote myself to my work.	60	29	35	18	38	63
I spent more time in nature, listening to music, in art, or writing.	49	18	14	35	39	36
I sought increased consolation in philosophy and religion.	31	25	38	35	44	29
Working through the event (3 of 16 items)						
I tried to develop an attitude toward the event that would help me to deal with it.	94	75	81	39	45	23
I thought about events in my past life that might help me deal better with the present.	74	36	46	35	44	17
I tried to think about the good things that had happened in my life and weigh what had happened against them for a better perspective.	54	50	54	31	42	50
Socialization (all 6 items)						
I tried to talk about the event with others.	89	43	68	42	63	44
I looked for a person who could provide direction for me.	86	77	19	36	49	11
I sought increased emotional support from others.	77	32	35	64	50	54
I tried not to withdraw from other people.	57	73	54	25	79	35
I tried to be more useful to others.	54	30	41	31	37	34
I tried to find people who had experienced the same kind of event to see how they dealt with it.	31	27	32	45	33	16

Note. Stress patients, n = 35; cancer patients, n = 56; significant others of cancer patients, n = 37.

was composed of those who were "significant others" to these cancer patients. A third group (*n* = 35) consisted of persons who had come to our clinic for treatment of stress-response syndromes following a serious life event, and who completed the form at the termination of therapy (12th session). The form was usually completed an average of 3 months after the therapy began, or from 8 to 9 months after the serious life event occurred.

Items on the Coping Inventory were logically divided into three subjects for scoring: (1) Turning to Other Attitudes and Activities, (2) Working Through the Event, and (3) Socialization. All items were scored by from 14% to 100% of the subjects.

In order to present the coping items that were reported to be the most helpful, we have selected those items that were used and scored as helpful by over 33% of at least two of the three groups of subjects described above. The items have been separated into categories for ease of presentation. Also presented are some of the least helpful items, as well as the most helpful, in order to show what people *feel* is most or least helpful. These are not necessarily coping strategies that *are* actually the most or least helpful.

As noted in Table 26-4, of the 11 items in the category "Turning to Other Attitudes and Activities," the five most helpful were: "I tried to concentrate on other things in my life"; "I tried to devote myself to my work" (found helpful by the cancer patients and their significant others more frequently than by the group of persons with stress-response syndromes); "I tried to find some other outlets like sports, cooking, or gardening to relieve some of the feelings I had"; "I sought increased consolation in philosophy and religion"; and "I spent more time in nature, listening to music, in art, or writing." The least helpful item in this category, for the persons who were experiencing the event (the stress patients and the cancer patients) was: "I tried to put the event out of mind and just go on with my life." As one might expect, this coping item was reported as helpful by a larger proportion of the significant others to the cancer patients.

In the category of Working Through the Event, a subset of 16 items, only three were endorsed as helpful by over 33% of at least two groups: "I tried to develop an attitude toward the event that would help me deal with it"; "I tried to think about the good things that had happened in my life and weigh what had happened against them for a better perspective"; and "I thought about events in my past life that might help me deal better with the present." None of the items in this group stood out as particularly low in ratings of helpfulness.

In the group of six Socialization items, all six were of high utility to at least two of the three groups: "I

tried to talk about the event with others"; "I looked for a person who could provide direction for me"; "I sought increased emotional support from others" (the most helpful item in the entire scale, across the three groups); "I tried not to withdraw from other people"; "I tried to be useful to others"; and "I tried to find people who had experienced the same kind of event to see how they dealt with it."

Conclusions

By presenting some data illustrating the nature of our Life Events Questionnaire, Impact of Event Scale, and Coping Inventory, we hoped to suggest that intensive clinical studies can, by noting repetitive patterns, gradually lead to the kind of measurements that can be used in larger scale field investigations. Since the types of experiences endorsed on both the Impact of Event Scale and the Coping Inventory are vulnerable to distortion, data on these scales should always be supplemented by methods for obtaining convergent validity. It is noteworthy that no subject in any of our groups was unable to complete the scales. Our clinic uses clinicians' ratings of similar variables, as well as subsequent reviews of videotapes, for more complex independent clinical judgments. Nonetheless, our overall experience is that scores such as those on the intrusion and avoidance subscales of the Impact of Event Scale are quite useful and have good face validity for persons under stress.

Research in this field, described in the chapters of this section, suggests that we are gradually blocking out the relevant variables in the field of response to serious life events. If we are cautious and skeptical about the nature of our instruments for measuring these variables, we can improve scientific theory in this area. The types of variables that interest us in clinical treatment appear to be consistent with the types of variables that interest both investigators who study the various stages of the life cycle and those whose orientation is epidemiological, a fact that suggests convergent efforts on this important territory may be made in the future.

REFERENCES

American Psychiatric Association. *Diagnostic and statistical manual of mental disorders* (3rd ed.). Washington, D.C.: Author, 1980.

Breuer, J., & Freud, S. *Studies on hysteria* (2nd std. ed.). London: Hogarth Press, 1895.

Holmes, T. H., & Rahe, R. H. The social readjustment rating scale. *Journal of Psychosomatic Research*, 1967, *11*, 213–218.

Horowitz, M. Phase-oriented treatment of stress response syndromes. *American Journal of Psychotherapy*, 1973, *27*, 506–515.

Horowitz, M. Intrusive and repetitive thoughts after experimental stress: A summary. *Archives of General Psychiatry*, 1975, *32*, 1457–1463.

Horowitz, M. *Stress response syndromes*. New York: Aronson, 1976.

Horowitz, M. *States of mind*. New York: Plenum Press, 1979.

Horowitz, M., Marmar, C., & Wilner, N. Analysis of patient states and state transitions. *Journal of Nervous and Mental Disease*, 1979, *167*, 91–99.

Horowitz, M., Schaefer, C., & Cooney, P. Life event scaling for recency of experience. In E. Gunderson & R. H. Rahe (Eds.), *Life stress and illness*. Springfield, Ill.: Charles C Thomas, 1974.

Horowitz, M., Schaefer, C., Hiroto, D., Wilner, N., & Levin, B. Life event questionnaires for measuring presumptive stress. *Psychosomatic Medicine*, 1977, *39*, 413–431.

Horowitz, M., & Wilner, N. Stress films, emotion and cognitive response. *Archives of General Psychiatry*, 1976, *30*, 1339–1344.

Horowitz, M. J., Wilner, N., & Alvarez, W. Impact of event scale: A measure of subjective stress. *Psychosomatic Medicine*, 1979, *41*, 209–218.

Horowitz, M., Wilner, N., Kaltreider, N., & Alvarez, W. Signs and symptoms of post traumatic stress disorders. *Archives of General Psychiatry*, 1980, *37*, 85–92.

Janis, I. *Stress and frustration*. New York: Harcourt, Brace, Jovanovich, 1969.

Lazarus, R. S. *Psychological stress and the coping process*. New York: McGraw-Hill, 1966.

Paykel, E. S., Prusoff, B. A., & Ulenhuth, E. H. Scaling of life events. *Archives of General Psychiatry*, 1971, *25*, 340–347.

APPENDIX A

Life Events Questionnaire—Short Form (Center for the Study of Neuroses, U. of California, San Francisco

Short Form: Equivalent Weights (Combined Sex and Age Groups)

* The checklist below consists of events which are sometimes important experiences. Read down the list until you find events that have happened to you personally. Check box under the column which indicates how long ago the event happened. Check each event as many times as it happened. For deaths (the first three items) there are several boxes in each time period; mark the additional boxes if more than one occurred. For events which continued for a long period of time, such as pregnancy, check the beginning date and the ending date and then check the boxes in between. If you can't remember the exact dates, just be as accurate as you can.

	Weights				
	Within 0–1 mo.	Within 1–6 mo.	Within 6–12 mo.	Within 1–2 yr.	Over 2 yr.
Death of a child or spouse (husband, wife or mate)?	90	81	67	50	32
Death of a child or spouse (husband, wife or mate)? (2nd)	90	81	67	50	32
The death of a parent, brother or sister?	79	70	51	34	22
The death of a parent, brother or sister? (2nd)	79	70	51	34	22
The death of a parent, brother or sister? (3rd)	79	70	51	34	22
The loss of a close friend or important relationship by death?	70	53	36	22	12
The loss of a close friend or important relationship by death? (2nd)	70	53	36	22	12
Legal troubles resulting in being held in jail?	82	65	51	37	27
Financial difficulties?	60	43	26	13	7
Being fired or laid off?	68	46	27	16	8
A miscarriage or abortion (patient or spouse)?	71	53	31	18	11
Divorce, or a breakup with a lover?	76	63	45	29	16
Separation from spouse because of marital problems?	75	61	41	24	14
Court appearance for a serious violation?	70	41	23	13	5
An unwanted pregnancy (patient, wife or girlfriend)?	72	57	42	25	15
Hospitalization of a family member for serious illness?	69	46	26	14	8
Unemployment more than one month (if regularly employed)?	57	42	20	10	6
Illness/injury kept in bed for week or more, hosp. or emerg. room?	65	48	25	12	5
An extra-marital affair?	62	50	37	25	17
The loss of a personally valuable object?	47	26	13	8	5
Involvement in a lawsuit (other than divorce)?	61	41	23	13	7
Failing an important examination?	62	37	19	9	5
Breaking an engagement?	65	47	27	14	7
Arguments with spouse (husband, wife or mate)?	59	40	26	17	11
Taking on a large loan?	42	29	20	14	10
Being drafted into the military?	62	51	39	30	17
Troubles with boss or other workers?	50	23	9	4	3
Separation from a close friend?	49	36	24	16	10
Taking an important examination?	45	12	5	2	2
Separation from spouse because of job demands?	65	51	38	26	15
A big change in work or in school?	49	30	16	9	5
A move to another town, city, state or country?	46	32	20	10	5
Getting married or returning to spouse after separation?	60	45	34	23	18
Minor violations of the law?	31	15	7	3	2
Moved home within the same town or city?	25	13	7	3	2
The birth or adoption of a child?	52	39	26	18	15
Being confused for over 3 days?	62	34	15	10 ⎫	
Being angry for over 3 days?	52	25	10	5 ⎪ Internal	
Being nervous for over 3 days?	48	23	10	5 ⎬ Events	
Being sad for over 3 days?	46	24	12	6 ⎭	
Spouse unfaithful?	68	55	40	27	19
Attacked, raped or involved in violent acts?	72	57	42	25	18

* These are the instructions to subjects who just indicate occurrence and frequency of events. The numbers are the weightings later applied to these subjects' check marks. Scores for internal events and external events are added separately. Investigators interested only in external events could simply delete internal events.

APPENDIX B

Impact of Event Scale (Center for the Study of Neuroses, U. of California, San Francisco)

```
Code #_____
Date_____
Sex_____
Age_____
Rater_____
Interview_____
```
Do not write in this box

INSTRUCTIONS

Please fill in the INFORMATION section. Below that is a list of comments made by people after stressful life events. Please fill in the box for each item, indicating how frequently these comments were true for you *DURING THE PAST SEVEN DAYS*. If they did not occur during that time, please fill in the NOT AT ALL box. Please answer EACH item by filling in ONE of the boxes.

INFORMATION

About_____ago, I experienced_____.
　　(weeks)　　　　　　　　　　　　　　　(write in life event)

	NOT AT ALL	RARELY	SOME-TIMES	OFTEN
1. I thought about it when I didn't mean to.	1	2	3	4
2. I had trouble doing other things because the event kept coming into my mind.	1	2	3	4
3. I avoided letting myself get upset when I thought about it or was reminded of it.	1	2	3	4
4. I tried to remove it from memory.	1	2	3	4
5. I had trouble falling asleep or staying asleep because of pictures or thoughts about it that came into my mind.	1	2	3	4
6. I had waves of strong feelings about it.	1	2	3	4
7. I had dreams about it.	1	2	3	4
8. I stayed away from reminders of it.	1	2	3	4
9. I felt as if it hadn't happened or it wasn't real.	1	2	3	4
10. I tried not to talk about it.	1	2	3	4
11. Pictures about it popped into my mind.	1	2	3	4
12. Other things kept making me think about it.	1	2	3	4
13. I was aware that I still had a lot of feelings about it, but I didn't deal with them.	1	2	3	4
14. I tried not to think about it.	1	2	3	4
15. Any reminder brought back feelings about it.	1	2	3	4
16. My feelings about it were kind of numb.	1	2	3	4

APPENDIX C

Coping Inventory (Center for the Study of Neuroses, U. of California, San Francisco)

INSTRUCTIONS

| Code #_____ |
| Date_____ |
| Age_____ |
| Sex_____ |
| Rater_____ |
| Interview_____ |

Do not write in this box

About_____ ago, you experienced_____.
　　　　(weeks)　　　　　　　　　　　　　　　　(write in life event)

Below is a list of ways that other people sometimes use to cope with stressful life events. Please read each item on the list and decide whether it applies to you. If it does not, fill in the box under the DOES NOT APPLY column. If the statement does sound at least a little like something you did, then fill in the box in the DOES APPLY column. If it does apply and was VERY HELPFUL, fill in the box in that column. Please answer EACH item by filling in ONE of the boxes.

	DOES NOT APPLY	DOES APPLY	DOES APPLY AND WAS VERY HELPFUL
1. I tried to concentrate on other things in my life.	0	1	2
2. I tried to think through the meanings of the event for my life at present.	0	1	2
3. I tried to work out how the event related to things in my past.	0	1	2
4. I worked to revise my expectations of the future.	0	1	2
5. I tried to find a humorous or even tragi-comic element in the event or in life in general.	0	1	2
6. I tried to separate the rational from the irrational in my responses.	0	1	2
7. I tried to separate the possible from the unlikely consequences that occurred to me.	0	1	2
8. I sought increased emotional support from others.	0	1	2
9. I tried to find new interests.	0	1	2
10. I tried to experience all my feelings and work them through.	0	1	2
11. I tried to dose myself, to experience feelings sometimes, but put them out of mind at other times.	0	1	2
12. I tried to put the event out of mind and just go on with my life.	0	1	2
13. I sought consolation in philosophy or religion.	0	1	2
14. I spent more time in nature, listening to music, with art or writing.	0	1	2
15. I tried to devote myself to my work.	0	1	2
16. I tried to talk about the event with others.	0	1	2
17. I tried to find people who had experienced the same kind of event to see how they dealt with it.	0	1	2
18. I tried to figure out why the event evoked the feelings it did.	0	1	2
19. I tried not to be bothered by conflicting feelings in my reactions to the event.	0	1	2

(continued)

Coping Inventory (continued)

20. I tried to develop an attitude toward the event which would help me to deal with it.   [0] [1] [2]

21. I tried to clarify the choices I have in adjusting my present life to the effects of the event.   [0] [1] [2]

22. I tried not to withdraw from other people.   [0] [1] [2]

23. I welcomed some time alone to think about what had happened.   [0] [1] [2]

24. I tried to figure out what would happen in the future if I behaved one way, and what would happen if I behaved another way.   [0] [1] [2]

25. I tried not to make any decisions about the future until I was sure I was seeing things more clearly.   [0] [1] [2]

26. I tried to look at my present situation as realistically as possible.   [0] [1] [2]

27. I thought about events in my past life which might help me to deal better with the present.   [0] [1] [2]

28. I tried to find some other outlets, like sports, cooking, or gardening, to relieve some of the feelings I had.   [0] [1] [2]

29. I tried doing things impulsively, that I might have thought about before, if they made me feel better and didn't bother anyone else.   [0] [1] [2]

30. I tried to think about the good things that had happened in my life and weigh what had happened against them, for a better perspective.   [0] [1] [2]

31. I tried to be more useful to others.   [0] [1] [2]

32. I looked for a person who could provide direction for me.   [0] [1] [2]

33. I tried to remind myself that what has happened could have been worse.   [0] [1] [2]

Frances Cohen

27

Coping With Surgery: Information, Psychological Preparation, and Recovery

This chapter discusses research studies that have investigated the relation between coping and recovery from surgery. One study examined patients' avoidance of or vigilance toward information about the surgery. Contrary to predictions, vigilant patients had a more complicated recovery pattern. The second study provided interventions designed to involve patients actively in the recovery process. Treatment effects were found only in post-hoc analyses, which took into account the information given by the surgeon. The results suggest (a) that in certain health-care situations, avoidance may be an effective coping strategy, and (b) that it may be difficult to provide patients with a sense of active control.

A large body of literature deals with the relation between life events and physiological outcomes such as the development of physical illness (e.g., Dohrenwend & Dohrenwend, 1974; Gunderson & Rahe, 1974); however, the mechanisms that could link these factors are not well understood. It may be that the crucial factor relating life events and illness is not that an event has occurred, but, rather, how the event is appraised and what coping processes are mobilized in response. This chapter focuses on research studies that evaluate how people cope with the stressful event of surgery and on the relation between coping and recovery from the operation.

Physicians frequently note that despite similarities in

physical condition, surgical patients (as well as patients with a variety of illnesses) often differ greatly in the course of physical recovery. It has been thought that this variability may be due in part to differences in the ways patients cope with the stresses involved. Because of the greater incidence of health problems among those in their middle and later years, it is particularly important to determine what factors influence recovery and whether psychological interventions can improve the recovery process. Moreover, as the developmental literature suggests, there may be critical differences in the types of coping strategies used by people at different stages of the life cycle. These differences may influence intervention tactics. For example, if active modes of coping are less common among older patients and yet prove to be the most adaptive strategy, health professionals might plan special intervention programs with this population to influence the ways in which they cope.

In the search for links between psychological factors

The research described in this chapter was supported in part by a Research Grant MH-2136 from the National Institute of Mental Health, a predoctoral traineeship from the Rehabilitation Services Administration (Grant No. RH4), and a grant from the Chancellor's Patent Fund at the University of California, Berkeley.

and recovery from surgery, the assumption most often made is that people who are ill prepared for surgery or use maladaptive coping styles will become anxious, angry, or depressed in the postoperative situation. These negative feelings, especially anxiety, may be reflected in postoperative emotional episodes, may cause increased use of pain medications, or may decrease bodily resistance. The mechanisms that might link coping and these different aspects of recovery are discussed in more detail elsewhere (Cohen & Lazarus, 1979).

Many researchers have suggested that furnishing information can help prepare patients for coping in situations of threat (for reviews, see Auerbach & Kilmann, 1977; Cohen & Lazarus, 1979). Janis (1958) felt that information was necessary to prod people to do the "work of worrying." By gaining information about the threats to be faced, Janis thought a person could begin to develop effective means of coping with the subsequent events. In another study, Egbert, Battit, Welch, and Bartlett (1964) attempted to reduce postoperative pain by instructing patients in moving and in the use of coughing and deep breathing exercises. The patients who received this information were sent home earlier and took less pain medication than those not instructed. However, many health care professionals echo the belief that "ignorance is bliss" and that patients need only reassurance about their recovery. A review of the research in which preoperative psychological interventions were provided shows that information did not consistently result in improved recovery (Cohen & Lazarus, 1979). Studies by Andrew (1970), DeLong (1970), Auerbach, Kendall, Cuttler, and Levitt (1976), and Wilson (1977) suggest that there may be important interactions between the type of information presented and personality characteristics of the patient.

The theoretical framework presented by Lazarus and his colleagues (e.g., Lazarus, 1966; Lazarus, Averill, & Opton, 1970, 1974; Lazarus & Launier, 1978) suggests that the way people appraise a situation should have important consequences for the ways they cope and for their subsequent emotional, physiological, and behavioral reactions. This framework was used to investigate the relation between information and recovery from surgery in two studies. The first study assessed mode of coping—the patient's avoidance of or vigilance toward information about the surgery—and the relation between these coping modes and recovery. The second study, in which information was given to patients, assessed the impact of the different interventions on recovery and whether there were interactions between the information given and the patient's preoperative coping mode.

Mode of Coping and Recovery from Surgery

In the first study to be discussed, 59 hernia, gall bladder, and thyroid patients scheduled for elective surgery were interviewed the night before their operation (for details of the study, see Cohen & Lazarus, 1973). By means of a structured interview, patients were asked detailed questions about what they knew about their illness, surgery, and the postoperative course, and whether they had sought information from others. Avoidance and vigilance, as judged from the interview data, were treated as a dimension and rated on a 10-point scale. High ratings implied vigilant modes, low ratings implied avoidant modes, and a middle group included patients emphasizing neither one nor the other. The rating was made by listening to tape recordings of the interviews and by using detailed criteria for rating. An independent rater also rated the interviews; the reliability of rating was found to be high.

The avoidance and vigilance ends of the dimension were defined generally as follows. Avoidance: Patients who avoid or deny information about the operation, as evidenced by restriction of knowledge or awareness about their medical condition and the nature of the surgery and unwillingness to discuss their thoughts about it. Vigilance: Patients who seek out information about their medical condition or are knowledgeable about it, as evidenced by their knowing details about their medical problems and the nature of the surgery and by their readiness to discuss them. These patients are also especially alert to emotional or threatening aspects of the situation.

The avoidance–vigilance measure is a process, or episodic, measure of coping, rather than a dispositional measure. That is, the patient's behavior was assessed directly in the particular situation of threat, and the mode of coping was inferred. Dispositional measures assess a person's habitual tendencies to use one or another coping mode. Two dispositional measures were also used in this study, but since these measures showed low or nonsignificant relations with each other, with the process measures of coping, and with indicators of recovery, they are not discussed further here.

To measure recovery, four indicators were used: (1) length of hospital stay, (2) number of pain medications taken, (3) number of minor medical complications (including such problems as nausea, headache, and treatment for medical difficulties such as infection) weighted according to their severity, and (4) number of negative psychological reactions (evidence of emotional behavior such as anxiety, depression, or anger). These were also summed to give an overall recovery index. Because of the heterogeneity in the course of recovery for each operation, standard scores were employed. Transformations were made for each operation into a T-score distribution.

The results of this study were contrary to predictions. Those who knew the most about their operation—the vigilant group—had significantly more minor medical complications ($p < .05$) and a longer hospital stay ($p < .01$). There was also a trend for this group to have more negative psychological reactions and a more complicated overall recovery pattern. Patients using avoidant strategies generally did best in recovery, although their recovery scores were not significantly different from those of the middle group. One possible interpretation of these results is that vigilant copers use a strategy of actively trying to master the world by seeking information and trying to learn everything they can about the situation to be faced. In the postoperative hospital context, however, they may be unable to "master" the situation actively and be forced to be dependent and passive. This could produce lowered self-esteem and an increased sense of vulnerability, which might have a negative influence on the patient's recovery. Kornfeld, Heller, Frank, and Moskowitz (1974) expressed a similar view in explaining why patients who were dominant and self-assured had a greater incidence of postoperative delirium following open-heart surgery. Alternately, because vigilant patients not only had detailed information about the medical aspects of their surgery but were also aware of the possible negative complications, it is possible that knowledge of these threatening possibilities helped create their more complicated recovery. This process might be somewhat similar to the ways symptoms develop in "medical student" disease.

A third explanation focuses on the interpersonal transactions between physician and patient. Vigilant patients may act in ways that draw attention to their medical complaints and may indicate such concern about their medical condition that physicians decide to hospitalize them longer. We do not know enough about the determinants of each of the indexes of recovery, or about the decision process related to discharging a patient or assessing and treating complaints, to evaluate the extent to which an interpersonal-transactions explanation would apply.

Although the theoretical explanation for the findings is not clear, these results do suggest the possibility that knowledge of threatening details of surgery, if not tempered by denial, may result in more complicated recovery, and that avoidant-denial forms of coping may be effective in a medical situation where, although many threats are possible, few actually materialize.

To explore the results further, analyses were done relating age, life changes, and anxiety to the indicators

of recovery. Insofar as age is concerned, the study included only patients between 21 and 60 years of age and therefore covers only the young adult and middle-aged segments of the adult life course. Within the age range sampled, no significant relations were found between age and any of the recovery measures. That age itself did not directly influence recovery in this study, whereas coping did, suggests the power of coping processes in influencing recovery.

The Holmes and Rahe (1967) Schedule of Recent Experiences was also administered prior to surgery and its relation to recovery assessed. One might have anticipated from Holmes and Rahe's work (e.g., Rahe, Meyer, Smith, Kjaer, & Holmes, 1964) that patients with high life-change scores (more "stressed," according to their definition) would fare worse in recovery from surgery than those with few life changes. However, no significant relations were found between life-change scores for the previous 6 months or the previous 2 years and any of the indicators of recovery. This finding is consistent with other studies, which have found no significant main-effect relations between life-change scores and objective medical-outcome indicators (Nuckolls, Cassel, & Kaplan, 1972; Rundall, 1976). Cohen (1979) discusses some further limitations of the life-change approach.

Self-rated anxiety was found to be significantly related only to the incidence of negative postoperative psychological reactions ($p < .001$), with patients high in self-reported anxiety having more emotional difficulties. This is consistent with other studies, which have found a positive linear relation between preoperative anxiety level and postoperative negative emotional states (Johnson, Leventhal, & Dabbs, 1971; Sime, 1976; Wolfer & Davis, 1970) rather than a curvilinear relation (Janis, 1958).

Psychological Preparation, Coping, and Recovery

The second study was designed to investigate the influence of different types of psychological preparation on patients' recovery from surgery. Laboratory evidence had suggested that a subject's appraisal of a situation could be altered by presenting information that would deny or offer an intellectualization of the negative implications of that situation (Lazarus & Alfert, 1964; Speisman, Lazarus, Mordkoff, & Davison, 1964) and thus subsequently reduce physiological arousal. In previous studies of surgical patients, different types of psychological intervention had not been thoroughly tested in any one study; it seemed important also to explore the interaction between coping and personality factors and the effectiveness of each intervention.

Various researchers have suggested that coping strategies that give a person an active role to play in a threatening situation help to reduce stress, since they give the person a sense of mastery or control. Others have asserted that interventions would be most successful if they also provided information about what the person could *do*, behaviorally, to master a difficult situation. For example, Leventhal, Watts, and Pagano (1967) found that cigarette smokers trying to give up smoking did best if they were also given specific information on how to stop smoking (i.e., ways to avoid conditions conducive to smoking, etc.). Similar suggestions have also become more common in psychotherapy, especially in order to achieve short-term goals or behavioral changes.

However, although giving people a sense of control is thought to be adaptive, the relation between control and adjustment is not straightforward and depends on the meaning that control has for the person (Averill, 1973; Gal & Lazarus, 1975; Janis & Rodin, 1979). Efforts to gain control may be stress-inducing for some patients or in some situations where control is impossible.

The result of the Cohen and Lazarus (1973) study suggested that vigilant patients might benefit from receiving information about how they could participate actively in their own recovery and regain some sense of control. This would be more consistent with their self-image and might therefore improve their recovery. To test this possibility, the second study (for details of the study, see Cohen, 1975) used interventions designed to give patients information about how they could gain some sense of active participation or control in the postoperative setting. Two types of active-participant approaches were used: (1) telling the patients what they could *do* postoperatively (following Egbert et al., 1964), and (2) suggesting how patients could improve recovery by the way they *think* (a positive-thinking approach). In addition, a third approach emphasized a passive orientation and provided reassurance as to the benign nature of the procedure.

One hundred fifty-three gall bladder and hernia patients were interviewed preoperatively and classified into one of three groups, based on whether they showed avoidance, vigilance, or both kinds of coping behavior. After this classification was made, subjects were given one of three brief treatment interventions (none in the control group) designed to alter postoperative coping strategies. To assure that cells in the 3 × 4 design (Preoperative Coping Mode × Treatment Orientation) were filled proportionately, a preset formula was used. The *active participant-behavioral* orientation (AP-B), based on the information given by Egbert et al. (1964), attempts to involve patients as active participants in the recovery process by pointing

out what they can *do* to improve their recovery. It stresses the importance of moving, breathing, coughing, and so forth, and suggests how the patient may do these in the easiest and least painful way. The *active participant-cognitive* orientation (AP-C), based on the approach of Norman Vincent Peale (1952), involves patients as active participants in their own recovery processes in terms of the way they *think*. It stresses the importance of their attitude toward their own recovery and gives suggestions for ways to think positively and avoid focusing on unpleasant thoughts. The *benign-appraisal* orientation (BA) was a passive-reassurance approach, which focused on why the recovery period should be appraised as nonthreatening. It discusses the competence of the medical staff and why the patient should not be worried about the recovery period. Patients receiving either the AP-B or the AP-C orientations were also given a card that summarized the information presented.

The same four recovery indicators were used. A special correction was made in the recovery index for patients having slightly more complex operative procedures (see Cohen, 1975, for details), such as a cholecystectomy with common bile-duct exploration. Patients were also interviewed postoperatively, and process ratings were made of postoperative mode of coping, degree of active involvement in the recovery process, and postoperative reaction to the preoperative orientation.

During the course of the study it became apparent that there were substantial differences in the amount and kinds of information various doctors gave their patients. These differences were revealed through overhearing what certain physicians told their patients, as well as by noting that patients of particular doctors seemed, on the whole, more or less knowledgeable about details of their medical problems. Rather than ignore the variation in doctors' input, it appeared that it might be important to evaluate it systematically and determine the influence it had in combination with other variables under study. Thus, after all the patient data were collected, the surgeons whose patients had been included in the study were interviewed. In the interview the physicians were asked individually what they generally told patients about each type of operation and how various questions and types of patients were handled. The information from each physician was classified on the following 3-point scales: (1) amount of information given, (2) amount of reassurance given, and (3) amount of information given about the risks of the operation.

Results. The main hypotheses of the study were that there would be an interaction between treatment condition and preoperative mode of coping, as well as main effects for each dimension. It was specifically predicted that vigilant patients would show improved recovery if given one of the active participant orientations. However, contrary to predictions, the results showed no significant main effects and no significant interactions. The data tended to replicate the findings of the first study, reported earlier, on the minor medical-complications variable, only in a separate analysis carried out on the control group ($n = 37$). Since the varying treatment orientations provided may have affected recovery, a separate analysis on a group that had received no orientation was necessary to determine whether replication was achieved.

It was unclear why no treatment effects were found, since investigators who used similar orientations had found significant effects on some aspects of recovery (e.g., Egbert et al., 1964; Healy, 1968; Langer, Janis, & Wolfer, 1975; Lindeman & Van Aernam, 1971). While most of these previous studies contained serious methodological problems that raise doubts about their findings (see discussion in Cohen, 1975), the weak treatment effect was quite unexpected. First, it is possible that the treatments were too short or not sufficiently elaborate, thereby losing power. Second, information presented by a paramedical person in the context of an informed-consent research study may not have the impact that such information would have if given by medical personnel not identifying their research status. Most of the earlier studies, which were carried out before it was necessary to obtain informed consent for participating in psychological research, had the advantage of increased credibility of the information given. Surman, Hackett, Silverberg, and Behrendt (1974) suggest that this may have been why they were unable to achieve effects from their intervention with open-heart surgery patients.

Third, although the AP-B orientation systematically presented information about the importance of moving, coughing, and deep breathing, this information is now part of standard medical practice and thus is presented, though less systematically, to all patients postoperatively. Thus the AP-B information may have been utilized by all subjects, preventing any unique treatment effect.

Another possibility seems quite likely. As was discussed earlier, physicians varied considerably in the amount and types of information they gave to patients. If various doctors were presenting patients with information that was incongruent with the orientations presented, the effect of the treatment orientation would thus be confounded. For example, if patients were reassured there was nothing to worry about (BA), but their surgeon gave them much information about the risks of the operation, this information about risks would be incongruent with the orientation received. An evaluation of the incongruity of the information from physicians with each orientation was made, post-hoc analyses were run, and those patients who had received incongruous information were eliminated from the analysis. This reduced the subject sample to 70. In general, the analyses revealed that those in the control group stayed longer in the hospital, which suggests that any *consistent* psychological preparation may help to reduce hospital stay. Those in the AP-C group had more psychological problems postoperatively; this fact suggests that problems may arise when patients are instructed to think positively.

Finally, although many investigators have suggested that various extraneous factors, such as the physical condition of the patient, number of previous medical problems, age, sex, and length of the operation, could have a strong influence on the pattern of recovery after surgery, the results showed little support for this view. The physical condition of the patient (as measured by the anesthesiologist's preoperative risk rating), number of previous medical problems, and sex of the patient did not correlate with recovery outcomes. Analyses relating length of operation to outcome were run separately for hernia and gall-bladder patients. The only significant correlation was between length of the operation and length of hospital stay, but this was found for hernia patients only, not for gall-bladder patients. There was a significant correlation between age and number of days hospitalized ($r = .25$, $p < .01$). To determine whether people between age 60 and 65 accounted for most of this relation, an analysis was carried out eliminating all patients over 60 years of age. Results revealed a significant though somewhat reduced relation ($r = .19$, $p < .05$) on this variable.

It may be important that a relation to age was found on only one recovery indicator—number of days hospitalized. That the correlation was reduced when patients over 60 years of age were eliminated from the sample suggests that the over-60 group is a somewhat different subsample. Age should be considered in future studies, either by limiting the age range of the sample to be studied, checking for equal distribution among treatment groups of the over-60 group, or evaluating directly the effects of age on recovery indicators. Using a very wide age range (such as 15–90 years, as one study did), without evaluating the influence of age on recovery indicators, cannot be justified.

It is interesting to note that while age was correlated with the physical condition of the patient ($r = .36$, $p < .001$) and with the number of previous medical problems ($r = .46$, $p < .001$), neither of these two variables showed significant relations to any of the recovery indicators. Nor did age correlate with any indicator except the number of days hospitalized. Age thus did not appear to have specific influences on physical-outcome measures but rather on a measure that might tap some component of the surgeon/patient interaction concerning how long the patient should be hospitalized.

Conclusions

What conclusions can be drawn from the data presented in this chapter? First, the data suggest that when intervention studies are done, it is important to assess the other information the patient receives. If incongruent information is presented, the treatment effects may be muted. Thus in the intervention study, when the effects of other informational inputs were systematically taken into account, some significant treatment effects emerged.

Second, the results suggest that avoidance may be an effective coping strategy in certain health-care situations. These strategies may be especially useful in situations where a person cannot do anything directly to alter the threats that exist or where, although many threats are potential, few actually materialize. Avoidance may *not* be as effective in coping with serious medical procedures. For example, Layne and Yudofsky (1971) suggest that with open-heart surgery, preoperative denial may result in increased postoperative psychotic reactions, because the denial mechanism is inadequate to deal with the aftermath of the physical assault of such surgery and with the nature of the intensive-care-unit environment. However, Morse and Litin (1969) report the opposite result.

This issue was addressed in a study I did of women facing outpatient biopsies (two-stage procedure) to determine whether they had breast cancer. I hypothesized that avoidance would be a useful coping strategy for those women whose lumps were found to be benign, but not for those having malignancies. It seemed to me that avoidant strategies would prevent a woman from preparing for the possibility that she might have cancer and that if a malignancy were found, she would be overwhelmed as a result. Although the data for this study have not as yet been analyzed, my impression during the period of data collection was that patients using avoidant strategies did quite well psychologically and emotionally in coping at the time of the breast-biopsy procedure and also if a mastectomy were required. Those who were vigilant appeared to have more difficulty in coping at the biopsy and, for those with cancer, at the mastectomy stages. If these findings are confirmed when the data are systematically analyzed, this will be further support for the notion that avoidant strategies can be more effective for coping in health-care situations than was originally thought.

Third, these and other data raise a question of whether independence and autonomy—valuable attributes in dealing with ordinary life situations—may have negative consequences in medical situations where control of the situation is out of the patient's hands. As mentioned earlier, Kornfeld et al. (1974) found this kind of group to have a higher incidence of postoperative delirium following open-heart surgery. Women who are independent and autonomous (as measured with the Holtzman Inkblot Technique) show greater delay in seeking treatment for symptoms of breast or cervical cancer (Fisher, 1967; Hammerschlag, Fisher, DeCosse, & Kaplan, 1964). Tuberculosis patients who take an active role have difficulty adjusting to the hospital environment but do better in the community after discharge (Vernier, Barrell, Cummings, Dickerson, & Hooper, 1961). Thus independence and automony may aid in long-term rehabilitation from illness, though it may also result in emotional distress or difficulty in the early stages of the disease. It is important to point out that this distress may be only a short-term effect. Further study is needed to · determine in what situations these personality attributes have positive or negative consequences and whether intervention can be made to alter these relations.

Fourth, regarding interventions, two important questions can be raised. First, to what degree is it possible to give people a sense of active mastery or control in a medical setting? Can attempts to do so boomerang if the situation is one where very little control over negative events is possible? Second, what type of interventions would be effective in helping independent people to cope with negative medical procedures? One psychologist who had to undergo numerous painful surgeries as a result of severe burns stated that self-hypnosis was a valuable aid. Self-hypnosis gave him a sense of control in a situation where little else could be influenced. A challenge for researchers in the next decade is to develop different types of intervention strategies and to determine their usefulness for different types of patients. An important consideration will be whether different types of interventions will be most beneficial for people at different stages of the life course.

Implications

Illness and the need for surgical intervention are more common in the middle and later years. For helping an older population adjust to necessary medical procedures, it may be useful to intervene psychologically. The results reviewed here suggest that there is still much to be learned about the types of information that may aid adjustment to stressful medical procedures, as well as the usefulness of particular intervention strategies for different types of people. At different stages in the life cycle people may employ different coping techniques and benefit differentially from different types of interventions. These factors need to be explored systematically. Mages and Mendelsohn (1979) describe some of the coping issues that are salient for people at different stages of the life cycle who are informed that they have cancer. For example, they suggest that in the aged adult population, cancer often leads to an acceleration of aging processes such as disengagement from external investments, increased dependency, and need to review and integrate one's past. They have also found that patients at each life stage have different types of anger and that many of the older adults seem to face cancer with less anger than do patients who are younger.

> The young are angry because they may not ever have a chance to develop their lives; the mid-life adults are angry because their lives may be cut short before they can finish their tasks; the pre-retirement and retirement age group are angry because they may not be able to enjoy the leisure earned by a lifetime of work. But many of the older people, particularly those who have reviewed their past and feel they have lived their lives well, were able to deal with their illness with a greater degree of equanimity than the younger patients. They seem, by virtue of their age, to have faced their mortality, and so the issue of dying per se has less intensity than it does for younger and middle-aged adults. This, combined with generational differences, may well explain our finding that active modes of coping, as well as more overt and acute distress, are far more characteristic of younger than of older patients. (Mages & Mendelsohn, 1979, p. 277)

Their findings are consistent with data from my ongoing study of breast biopsy patients. In that study I looked at the differential coping strategies used by women at different stages of the life cycle. Many of the older women were not overly upset at the news that cancer had been diagnosed. One 70-year old woman, for example, stated that she "had always wondered what I would die from, and now I know." The data for this study have not been systematically analyzed as yet, but it appears that the younger women were the most anxious and upset about the need for a biopsy and about the cancer if cancer was diagnosed. In the intervention study reported on earlier, there was some evidence that older patients were more likely to use avoidant coping strategies. Although the correlation between age and the avoidance–vigilance rating was only $-.20$, which indicates a weak relation, it was nonetheless significant ($p < .05$). Thus it suggests that to some degree older people use less active coping processes.

More information is needed about the differential coping strategies that people use at different stages of the life cycle and the influence of these strategies on adaptive outcomes. Rather than ignore age as a variable, or try to limit the subject sample so as to restrict it to only certain stages of the life cycle, it is important for investigators to examine the relevance of age as it influences coping, the effectiveness of various interventions, and adjustment in medical situations.

REFERENCES

Andrew, J. M. Recovery from surgery, with and without preparatory instruction, for three coping styles. *Journal of Personality and Social Psychology*, 1970, *15*, 223–226.

Auerbach, S. M., Kendall, P. C., Cuttler, H. F., & Levitt, N. R. Anxiety, locus of control, type of preparatory information, and adjustment to dental surgery. *Journal of Consulting and Clinical Psychology*, 1976, *44*, 809–818.

Auerbach, S. M., & Kilmann, P. R. Crisis intervention: A review of outcome research. *Psychological Bulletin*, 1977, *84*, 1189–1217.

Averill, J. R. Personal control over aversive stimuli and its relationship to stress. *Psychological Bulletin*, 1973, *80*, 286–303.

Cohen, F. *Psychological preparation, coping, and recovery from surgery.* Unpublished doctoral dissertation, University of California, Berkeley, 1975.

Cohen, F. Personality, stress, and the development of physical illness. In G. C. Stone, F. Cohen, N. E. Adler, & Associates. *Health psychology—A handbook. Theories, applications, and challenges of a psychological approach to the health care system.* San Francisco: Jossey-Bass, 1979.

Cohen, F., & Lazarus, R. S. Active coping processes, coping dispositions, and recovery from surgery. *Psychosomatic Medicine*, 1973, *35*, 375–389.

Cohen, F., & Lazarus, R. S. Coping with the stresses of illness. In G. C. Stone, F. Cohen, N. E. Adler, & Associates. *Health psychology—A handbook. Theories, applications, and challenges of a psychological approach to the health care system.* San Francisco: Jossey-Bass, 1979.

DeLong, D. R. *Individual differences in patterns of anxiety arousal, stress-relevant information and recovery from surgery.* Unpublished doctoral dissertation, University of California, Los Angeles, 1970.

Dohrenwend, B. S., & Dohrenwend, B. P. Overview and prospects for research on stressful life events. In B. S. Dohrenwend & B. P. Dohrenwend (Eds.), *Stressful life events: Their nature and effects.* New York: Wiley, 1974.

Egbert, L. D., Battit, G. E., Welch, C. E., & Bartlett, M. K. Reduction of postoperative pain by encouragement and instruction of patients. *New England Journal of Medicine*, 1964, *270*, 825–827.

Fisher, S. Motivation for patient delay. *Archives of General Psychiatry*, 1967, *16*, 676–678.

Gal, R., & Lazarus, R. S. The role of activity in anticipating and confronting stressful situations. *Journal of Human Stress*, 1975, *1*(4), 4–20.

Gunderson, E. K. E., & Rahe, R. H. (Eds.). *Life stress and illness.* Springfield, Ill.: Charles C Thomas, 1974.

Hammerschlag, C. A., Fisher, S., DeCosse, J., & Kaplan, E. Breast symptoms and patient delay: Psychological variables involved. *Cancer*, 1964, *17*, 1480–1485.

Healy, K. Does preoperative instruction make a difference? *American Journal of Nursing*, 1968, *68*, 62–67.

Holmes, T. H., & Rahe, R. H. *Schedule of Recent Experiences*. Seattle: School of Medicine, University of Washington, 1967.

Janis, I. L. *Psychological stress: Psychoanalytic and behavioral studies of surgical patients*. New York: Wiley, 1958.

Janis, I. L., & Rodin, J. Attribution, control, and decision making: Social psychology and health care. In G. C. Stone, F. Cohen, N. E. Adler, & Associates. *Health psychology—A handbook. Theories, applications, and challenges of a psychological approach to the health care system*. San Francisco: Jossey-Bass, 1979.

Johnson, J. E., Leventhal, H., & Dabbs, J. Contribution of emotional and instrumental response processes in adaptation to surgery. *Journal of Personality and Social Psychology*, 1971. *20*, 55–64.

Kornfeld, D. S., Heller, S. S., Frank, K. A., & Moskowitz, R. Personality and psychological factors in postcardiotomy delirium. *Archives of General Psychiatry*, 1974, *31*, 249–253.

Langer, E. J., Janis, I. L., & Wolfer, J. A. Reduction of psychological stress in surgical patients. *Journal of Experimental Social Psychology*, 1975, *11*, 155–165.

Layne, O. L. Jr., & Yudofsky, S. C. Postoperative psychosis in cardiotomy patients. *New England Journal of Medicine*, 1971, *284*, 518–520.

Lazarus, R. S. *Psychological stress and the coping process*. New York: McGraw-Hill, 1966.

Lazarus, R. S., & Alfert, E. The short-circuiting of threat by experimentally altering cognitive appraisal. *Journal of Abnormal and Social Psychology*, 1964, *69*, 195–205.

Lazarus, R. S. Averill, J. R., & Opton, E. M., Jr. Towards a cognitive theory of emotion. In M. B. Arnold (Ed.), *Feelings and emotions*. New York: Academic Press, 1970.

Lazarus, R. S., Averill, J. R., & Opton, E. M., Jr. The psychology of coping: Issues of research and assessment. In G. V. Coelho, D. A. Hamburg, & J. E. Adams (Eds.), *Coping and adaptation*. New York: Basic Books, 1974.

Lazarus, R. S. & Launier, R. Stress-related transactions between person and environment. In L. A. Pervin & M. Lewis (Eds.), *Perspectives in interactional psychology*. New York: Plenum Press, 1978.

Leventhal, H., Watts, J. C., & Pagano, F. Effects of fear and instructions on how to cope with danger. *Journal of Personality and Social Psychology*, 1967, *6*, 313–321.

Lindeman, C. A., & Van Aernam, B. Nursing intervention with the presurgical patient—the effects of structured and unstructured preoperative teaching. *Nursing Research*, 1971, *20*, 319–332.

Mages, N. L., & Mendelsohn, G. A. Effects of cancer on patients' lives: A personological approach. In G. C. Stone, F. Cohen, N. E. Adler, & Associates. *Health psychology—A handbook. Theories, applications, and challenges of a psychological approach to the health care system*. San Francisco: Jossey-Bass, 1979.

Morse, R. M., & Litin, E. M. Postoperative delirium: A study of etiologic factors. *American Journal of Psychiatry*, 1969, *126*, 388–395.

Nuckolls, K. B., Cassel, J., & Kaplan, B. G. Psychosocial assets, life crisis, and the prognosis of pregnancy. *American Journal of Epidemiology*, 1972, *95*, 431–441.

Peale, N. V. *The power of positive thinking*. New York: Prentice-Hall, 1952.

Rahe, R. H., Meyer, M., Smith, M., Kjaer, G., & Holmes, T. H. Social stress and illness onset. *Journal of Psychosomatic Research*, 1964, *8*, 35–44.

Rundall, T. G. *Life change and recovery from surgery*. Unpublished doctoral dissertation, Stanford University, 1976.

Sime, A. M. Relationship of preoperative fear, type of coping, and information received about surgery to recovery from surgery. *Journal of Personality and Social Psychology*, 1976, *34*, 716–724.

Speisman, J. C., Lazarus, R. S., Mordkoff, A., & Davison, L. Experimental reduction of stress based on ego-defense theory. *Journal of Abnormal and Social Psychology*, 1964, *68*, 367–380.

Surman, O. S., Hackett, T. P., Silverberg, E. L., & Behrendt, D. M. Usefulness of psychiatric intervention in patients undergoing cardiac surgery. *Archives of General Psychiatry*, 1974, *30*, 830–835.

Vernier, C. M., Barrell, R. P., Cummings, J. W., Dickerson, J. H., & Hooper, H. E. Psychosocial study of the patient with pulmonary tuberculosis: A cooperative research approach. *Psychological Monographs*, 1961, *75*(6), 1–32.

Wilson, J. F. *Determinants of recovery from surgery: Preoperative instruction, relaxation training, and defensive structure*. Unpublished doctoral dissertation, University of Michigan, 1977.

Wolfer, J. A., & Davis, C. E. Assessment of surgery patients' preoperative emotional condition and postoperative welfare. *Nursing Research*, 1970, *19*, 402–414.

Francis T. Miller

Measurement and Monitoring of Stress in Communities

A panel of 42 rural North Carolina citizens was selected on the basis of the types of environmental events they considered to be stressful or reassuring. At the beginning of each of 9 months, panelists were asked to report the events of the previous month they considered as stressful or reassuring. Two weeks later they were asked to rate a composite list of the 25 most mentioned items. At the end of the 9-month period, the relationship of the stress ratings to measures of psychological casualty was studied. Admissions rates from the area to the state hospital and alcohol rehabilitation center, warrants issued, and probations revoked were plotted against stress measures. An increase in the casualty figures was found either in the same month that there was an increase in the stress measure or in the month after.

This chapter examines one of three classes of events that contribute to the experiencing of stress: the *pervasive*. The other two classes, *individual* and *shared*, have received considerably more attention. Individual events are those that may be unique to the experiencing individual. Included in that class might be illness in the family, changing jobs, or having a dependent in-law move into one's household. Spurred by the work of Holmes and Rahe (1967), a great deal of attention in the research literature of the past decade has focused on the relation of such events to physical and emotional disorder. Shared events are those experienced by collectives of individuals in a community who might share a common status (e.g., poverty, poor education, lack of job security) or a common place in the de-

velopmental life cycle (e.g., recent retirement, increased amount of unstructured time, decreased income, increased number of physical problems). More recently, increasing attention has been paid to life transitions or major turning points as sources of stress (Datan & Ginsberg, 1975; Hultsch & Plemons, 1979; Lowenthal & Chiriboga, 1973). Since 1950, at least 60 published articles have related such sociocultural variables to emotional disorder (Dohrenwend, 1979; Dohrenwend & Dohrenwend, 1974).

A pervasive event is one that has an impact on the total community. Relatively little attention has been placed on pervasive events at a day-to-day level and on their contribution to the experiencing of stress. Studies have been published on the impact of earthquakes (Blaufarb & Levine, 1972; Cohen, 1976), floods (Richard, 1974; Titchner, Kapp, & Winget, 1976), and tornados (Hartsough, Zarle, & Ottinger, 1974). Similarly, attention has been paid to the impact of the closing of an aerospace industry in Seattle and to cutbacks in program level at Cape Canaveral. Such major events led the National Institute of Mental Health to mandate the development of mental-health service plans for community disasters.

At a less dramatic but more prolonged level, we saw the oil crisis of 1973–1974, which started on October 18 and gradually escalated to long lines at gas stations and modified rationing in February and March. As this pervasive event continued and lines were longer and longer at the gas pumps on cold mornings, there was increased mental health fall-out. According to the Raleigh, North Carolina *News and Observer*, there were increases in the incidence of violence in the gas lines, increased cases of animal abuse and neglect, more family separations, more bank robberies, more state hospital admissions, and increases in other indicators of deterioration in the quality of life. As the gas lines extended, more and more people exceeded their tolerance limits for frustration. During the first week of December 1979 that same newspaper reported psychological fall-out from the Three Mile Island nuclear accident and mentioned that a team of psychologists was studying the phenomenon.

While the linkages between mental health casualty and major pervasive events have been demonstrated convincingly, there remains a need to evaluate the stress impact of the ebb and flow of day-to-day events in the community. Brenner (1971, 1973) found that fluctuations in the economy were related to increases and decreases in rates of heart disease mortality and mental illness over a period of years. So it would seem reasonable to postulate that the ebb and flow of other classes of events might have some impact on the experiencing of stress by individuals in the community.

Catalano (1975) developed a conceptualization of community stress based on aggregates of life cycle, economic, and miscellaneous random events, as studied by Theorell and Rahe (1971). Catalano (1975) suggested that the "variation over time in the total number of life change units experienced by a community, and manifested by the incidence of health and behavioral problems, could be considered as a function of the proportion of its population in high risk cohorts and the stability of its economy" (p. 307). This view emphasizes the role of the economy in psychological well-being.

The Catalano model focuses on important elements of the pervasive class of events but does not appear to include the impact of other classes of events such as social and political. I have been able to find only two empirical studies directly applicable to pervasive events as a class. One was conducted at the University of Texas School of Public Health at Houston under the leadership of C. Morton Hawkins. The other, under my leadership, was conducted by the Community Psychiatry Division of the University of North Carolina at Chapel Hill's Department of Psychiatry (Miller, Aponte, Bentz, Edgerton, & Hollister, 1974). The Hawkins effort carried out community-wide monitoring of behavioral problems and help-seeking behaviors to determine whether behavioral "outbreaks" or "epidemics" occur in a metropolitan area. They

planned to identify and describe potential precursor events to unusual increases of frequencies of community-wide behavioral responses. The Hawkins team approached the problem of monitoring pervasive events by focusing on newspaper and television reporting. Though they were able to monitor the events, they were unable to find an appropriate technique for evaluating the impact of events (Hawkins, 1976). They tried having community members score the impact of a news headline as high, medium, or low, but they abandoned that approach. They also attempted to evaluate the "exposure" of events across media; that is, they identified events that were reported by both newspapers and TV, but they found so many events that the approach was considered unworkable.

A number of potential behavioral sequelae of pervasive events were assessed (Ben Taub Hospital emergency visits, emergency ambulance calls, Jefferson Davis Hospital mental health visits, Jefferson Davis Hospital mental-health-related telephone calls, and crisis-hotline calls), and the team found that they could identify high activity dates. But they were not successful in linking media events to the behavior variables.

From 1970 to 1973, the Community Psychiatry Division of the University of North Carolina's Department of Psychiatry engaged in a series of studies to explore the impact of pervasive events on people in a rural community and to explore the relevance of such events to mental health casualty. The first assumption of these studies was that different people respond differently to pervasive events—that an event might be stressful for one individual and reassuring for another. The second assumption was that the people could be grouped on the basis of the way that they respond to pervasive events. To test those assumptions, 96 men and women, comprising a random sample from a rural county in North Carolina, were selected and interviewed on two occasions 1 month apart. At the first interview, each participant was presented with a list of 100 newspaper headlines representing international, national, state, and local events gathered during a single month from the two major newspapers serving the county. Approximately equal number in each category were identified as social, political, or economic events. Subjects were asked to rate each event on a 5-point scale from "very stressful" through a midpoint of "neutral" to "very reassuring." The second interview contained half the original list of events in order to test the reliability of the raters. The resulting median test–retest correlation was .71. A detailed examination of the correlations indicated that demographic factors did not predict reliability. The sharecropper was as likely as the bank officer to be a reliable rater of pervasive events (Brogan, 1971).

The ratings of the 100 items by the 96 rural residents were subjected to an inverse factor analysis, which yielded seven factors or groupings of people who responded differently to the newspaper headlines (Miller, Bentz, & Aponte, 1971). The groupings of people represented in the factors were tentatively named (1) the conservative, authority-centered segregationist versus the liberal antiestablishment integrationist, (2) system stability versus system instability, (3) the pocket-book concerned, nonactive liberal versus the profit-seeking separatist, (4) the proforma black-unity advocate versus the antiestablishment white supremacist, (5) antiauthority, proeconomic development versus proauthority, antieconomic development, (6) the self-satisfied, social-financial conservative versus the frustrated, antisystem liberal, and (7) the general good citizen versus the antieverything.

Four of the factors (3, 5, 6, and 7) were not linked to demographic variables. The other three factors were so linked and suggest that age, race, and sex play a part in people's sensitivity to life stresses. For example, the extremes of Factor 1 place the white, older housewife in opposition to the younger black laborer of either sex. People representing both extremes on this factor were particularly sensitive to local economic concerns, to segregation issues, and to the place of the poor in the social order. They evaluated 75 of the 100 life-event items in the questionnaire as stressful. Factor 2 places the 40–49-year olds in opposition to those older and those slightly younger. The 40–49-year-olds attributed high reassurance to events indicating that taxes were being collected smoothly, that there was a possibility of tax relief, and that the stock market was recovering. They tended to ignore or rate as neutral events connoting either economic threat or racial tension. Factor 4 placed the black unskilled worker or housewife with a median income of less than $6,000 against the white, skilled or semiskilled worker with an income above $6,000. The representatives of the opposing poles of this factor responded differentially to events pertaining to integration, black autonomy, instances of injustice to blacks, government intervention in local life, the nation's war involvement, and the farm economy.

Like the Hawkins group in Houston, the North Carolina team (Miller et al., 1974) found that even though news events reported by the media could be monitored, there was no reliable way to evaluate either the saliency or the impact of those events. An exploration of the relation of headline size to perceived stressfulness yielded a correlation low enough to suggest that the editor or layout person for the newspaper could not be utilized as an "expert" on community impact. Because of that finding and because of a growing realization that members of the community were having their awareness of pervasive events sharpened through diverse forms of both public and private communications, it was concluded that local citizens should be not only evaluators of the impact of events but also reporters of the events to be evaluated.

From the randomly selected 96 local residents mentioned above, a panel of 42 were selected. Selection was based on the factor-loading scores of individuals and on their test–retest reliability scores. The ideal panelist was one who had demonstrated high reliability and who had a high factor-loading score on only one factor. It was assumed that in interviews people would report as stressful or reassuring the types of events to which they were most sensitive. The opposite poles of the seven factors were each represented by three individuals. Interviews were conducted, but, in order to minimize the intrusion of the research into their lives, only two of the three individuals were interviewed in any given month.

The panel was selected in July and August of 1971 and began to function in August. At the beginning of each month a group of panelists who were to be active during that month were interviewed individually. Each was asked to recall events of the previous month that were stressful and those that were reassuring. Then the reporter's memory was "nudged" with the question, "How about at the international level?" Similar stimulus phrases inquired about national, state, and local events.

Interview items were classified according to level or location (international, national, state, and local) and according to type (social, political, economic). Events reported by the most panelists were considered as most salient. Each month the 20 most salient events were worded in a neutral manner, randomly ordered, and then presented to the panelists for rating in a second interview. Each event was rated on a 5-point scale from "very stressful" (1), through "neutral" (3), to "very reassuring" (5).

After the first 4 months, the events reported by each of the 14 groups of 3 panelists were studied in detail. It was found that reporters who represented five of the seven factors saw as stressful or reassuring the types of events predicted by the original factor structures (Miller & Aponte, 1972a). Of the remaining respondents, those representing Factor 2 reported many more events related to the local economy than would have been predicted by their responses to the 100-item questionnaire. Their concern with local events may have been an artifact of being asked each month, "How about at the local level?" Those representing Factor 7 showed an almost complete reversal from the anticipated response. Although in the original analysis respondents from one pole had rated 79 of the 100 items as reassuring, after 4 months 63% of the events reported by these respondents were perceived as stressful instead of reassuring. Even so, it was estimated that 80% of the items reported as stressful or reassuring by the entire panel of 42 were of the type and value predicted by the factor structure. Thus it was concluded that the factor groupings constituted a reasonably reliable approach to eliciting differential perceptions of pervasive events.

After 9 months the interviewing terminated, and the results were studied to determine whether variations in stress levels over time could be detected and whether any variations detected were related to changes in mental health casualty (Miller & Aponte, 1972b). The ratings of the panelists representing the opposite poles of each factor were compared first. T tests computed for the monthly ratings suggested that panelists representing opposite poles of the various factors did not differ significantly in their ratings of the 20 salient events for each of the 9 months. This finding was surprising, since representatives of opposite poles of the same factor had been identified as reporting different events as stressful or reassuring. An examination of the plots of the average ratings of the opposing groups was confirmatory, however. Raters representing one pole may have cast ratings somewhat higher or lower than raters at the other, but the plots tended to be parallel. That is, when a group representing one pole of a factor perceived an increase in stress or reassurance, the group at the other pole agreed. This pattern obtains across as well as within factor groups. When the ratings of the opposite-pole evaluators were summed, six of the seven factor groups perceived the months of November and March as the most reassuring. Similarly, all seven factor groups perceived August and December as most stressful, while three rated September as equally stressful. Four of the factor groups identified February and three identified April as moderately stressful. Thus, even though the factor groups tended to identify different events as stressful, they agreed in general about the months during which stress was highest. August–September and December were clearly identified as high-stress months by this measure.

The months in which different classes of events were rated as most stressful or most reassuring were also examined. The classes of events were political, social, and economic. Greatest agreement was found on stress ratings of economic events. All seven factor groups identified August–September and January, and six of the seven identified April, as high in stress. Social events received the next highest agreement. Evaluators in six of the seven factor groups identified August and September as high on social stress, and all of them identified December; five of the seven also named February. On political events, four groups identified October as high in stress and five identified December and January. Thus, although the times at which the different classes of events received high stress ratings might differ somewhat, they tend to covary. August–September, and December–January, along with April, appear to elicit the high-stress label.

In order to test the relevance of these measures to mental health casualty, data were obtained from the county on admissions rates to the state hospital and to the alcohol rehabilitation center, as well as counts of warrants issued and probations revoked in the county. Plots of each were developed. Three of the four measures of casualty were low for the first month, August, but in September three were high. Warrants issued and admissions to the alcohol rehabilitation center and state hospital increased in December and January. (It is perhaps not surprising that few probations were revoked during the holiday period.) All four outcome measures were high in March, although March was not identified by our stress indicators as a time of great disruption. However, two of the three periods that were so identified—September and December–January—were accompanied by increases in three of the four mental health casualty measures.

A second potential measure of pervasive stress was developed by assessing the difference between the mean ratings of persons representing the opposite poles of each factor. Such groups tend to polarize on events to which they are sensitive. That is, if an event is rated as very reassuring by those at one pole, it is usually rated as very stressful by those at the other. It was hypothesized that at times of greatest stress there would be the greatest disagreement between the raters at the opposite poles of the factor. This disagreement was measured by the difference in mean ratings of the polar opposite groups. The resulting measure was called conflict.

On the conflict measure, five of the seven factor groups agreed on September and December as high-stress months, and six of the seven agreed on March. These correspond closely to the months agreed on as reflecting high counts of mental health casualty. A composite conflict score, pooled across factor groups, yielded a picture of September–October, December, and March as high-stress months. Conflict appears to be more closely related to casualty than the average scores noted previously.

A third potential measure of stress, called thrust, was also computed. Thrust was developed on the idea that raters representing the opposite poles of each factor were expected to rate events differently—that an event perceived as stressful at one pole might be viewed as reassuring at the other. Therefore, the polarity of the ratings for one pole were reversed and added to those at the other. The result reflected the diversity of the factor groups. Two of the factor groups clearly found the 9-month period more stressful than the others. One clearly perceived more reassurance during the same period. Overall, the measures reflected a moderate level of stress in the county, but there were peaks. For example, five of the seven rater groups saw an increase in stress from November to December, with December representing the 9-month high. More of the rater groups reported August, November, December, and March to be of higher stress than any other months. These are the periods which correspond roughly to the casualty peaks reported earlier. However, the relation of thrust to casualty scores was not as clear-cut as it was for the other stress measures.

In summary, these exploratory studies of the relation of pervasive events to mental health casualty have been sufficiently promising to warrant further exploration. Although the studies have not specifically examined these effects with an elderly population, they offer a fruitful area of exploration to investigate the contribution of the environment to the psychological well-being of the elderly. It would be useful to replicate the studies reported here for a longer period of time and to compare the effectiveness of a random sample of reporter-evaluators with a panel constructed by the more elaborate approach involving attitude-set groups.

From the perspective of adult development and aging, it is reasonable to suggest that one's stage of life may be closely associated with which pervasive events are perceived as stressful and which are perceived reassuring, and these perceptions may have causal influence on physical and psychological well-being. In a series of studies I performed, under some conditions the middle-aged were found to view the world as generally reassuring, whereas older persons viewed events connoting social and economic change as particularly stressful. Researchers concerned with aging in the 1980s should pay particular attention to the adjustment of the older citizen at times when the flow of community events suggests an increase in the rate of change along social and economic dimensions. During periods of social change and particularly when the community is exhibiting a high potential for internal discord, older persons may be expected to manifest a heightened state of vulnerability. That state may in turn exert an influence on how they react to events at the more commonly studied individual and shared levels.

REFERENCES

Blaufarb, H., & Levine, J. Crisis intervention in an earthquake. *Social Work*, 1972, *17*, 16–19.

Brenner, M. H. Economic changes and heart disease mortality. *American Journal of Public Health*, 1971, *63*, 606–610.

Brenner, M. H. *Mental illness and the economy*. Cambridge, Mass.: Harvard University Press, 1973.

Brogan, D. *Factors which influence the repeatability of human judgments of stress produced by newspaper headlines*. Paper presented to the American Statistical Association, Atlanta, Georgia, 1971.

Catalano, R. Community stress: A preliminary conceptualization. *Man-Environment Systems*, 1975, *5*, 307–310.

Cohen, R. Postdisaster mobilization of a crisis intervention team: The manager's experience. In H. Parad, H. Resnik, & L. Parad (Eds.), *Emergency and disaster management*. Bowie, Md.: Charles Press, 1976.

Datan, N., & Ginsberg, L. H. (Eds.). *Life-span developmental psychology: Normative life crises*. New York: Academic Press, 1975.

Dohrenwend, B. P. Stressful life events and psychopathology: Some issues in theory and method. In J. E. Barrett et al. (Eds.), *Stress and mental disorder*. New York: Raven Press, 1979.

Dohrenwend, B. P., & Dohrenwend, B. S. Social and cultural influences on psychopathology. *Annual Review of Psychology*, 1974, *25*, 417–452.

Hartsough, D., Zarle, T., & Ottinger, D. Tornado recovery: The development of professional and paraprofessional response to a disaster. *Journal of Community Psychology*, 1974, *2*, 311–320.

Hawkins, C. M. *Detection of community outbreaks with community data* (Final report, NIMH Grant R01 MH 22915). University of Texas School of Public Health, Houston, January 1, 1976.

Holmes, T. H., & Rahe, R. H. The Social Readjustment Rating Scale. *Journal Of Psychosomatic Research*, 1967, *11*, 213–218.

Hultsch, D. F., & Plemons, J. K. Life events and life span development. In B. P. Baltes (Ed.), *Life span development* (Vol. 2). New York: Academic Press, 1979.

Lowenthal, M. F., & Chiriboga, D. Social stress and adaptation: Toward a life course perspective. In C. Eisdorfer and M. P. Lawton (Eds.), *The psychology of adult development and aging*. Washington, D.C.: American Psychological Association, 1973.

Miller, F. T., & Aponte, J. F. *A monitoring system for community stress*. Paper presented to the Southeastern Psychological Association, Atlanta, Georgia, 1972. (a)

Miller, F. T., & Aponte, J. F. *A system for evaluating stress in communities*. Paper presented at the meeting of the

American Psychological Association, Honolulu, Hawaii, September 1972. (b)

Miller, F. T., Aponte, J. F., Bentz, W. K., Edgerton, J. W., & Hollister, W. G. *Experiences in rural mental health: Measuring and monitoring stress in communities.* Chapel Hill: University of North Carolina, Department of Psychiatry, 1974.

Miller, F. T., Bentz, W. K., & Aponte, J. F. Stress-sensitive groups in a rural population. *Proceedings of the 79th Annual Convention of the American Psychological Association*, 1971, *6*, 731–732.

Richard, W. Crisis intervention services following natural disaster: The Pennsylvania Recovery Project. *Journal of Community Psychology*, 1974, *2*, 211–219.

Theorell, T., & Rahe, R. Psychosocial factors and myocardial infarction. *Journal of Psychosomatic Research*, 1971, *15*, 25–31.

Titchner, J., Kapp, F., & Winget, C. The Buffalo Creek syndrome: Symptoms and character changes after a major disaster. In H. Parad, H. Resnik, and L. Parad (Eds.), *Emergency and disaster management*. Bowie Md.: Charles Press, 1976.

SECTION
7

Environmental Issues

Joyce Parr, *Section Editor*

Introduction

During the 1970s there was a marked increase in concern for the way various environmental factors affect the behavior of older persons. Some of this interest arose from a recognition that many behaviors considered to be less than optimal may be a function of specific environments rather than of increasing age. Many requests for more information have come from practitioners faced with questions of designing housing, work situations, and social rehabilitation programs. Theoretical and research questions have come from the perspectives of architecture, ecological psychology, social gerontology, clinical psychology, and social work.

Two chapters in recent handbooks (Carp, 1977; Lawton, 1977) have provided broad reviews of studies conducted over the last 10 to 15 years. Throughout these reviews is the clear recognition of the importance of understanding how environmental features interact with characteristics of persons to influence behavior. There is also a consistent recognition that our ability to predict behavior based solely on our knowledge of personal characteristics such as personality measures or health status is limited. Moos (1973) reviewed a number of studies to demonstrate the increase in variance in behavior, which is explained when information about the environment is taken into account.

On the other hand, the literature is full of pleas for better ways of describing or classifying the important environmental features (see Howell in Chapter 31 of this volume; Koncelik, 1979; Lawton, 1977; Moos, 1973). In 1973 Moos stated that "it may be cogently argued that the most important task for the behavioral and social sciences should be the systematic description and classification of environments and their differential costs and benefits to adaptation" (p. 662). The three chapters in this section can be viewed as three types of responses to the frustration researchers experience as they try to find behaviorally meaningful ways to describe the environment.

Another way to understand the efforts of the authors in this section is to see their work as attempts to integrate more of the components of the complex behavioral system we call person–environment interaction.

Parr (in Chapter 29) argues for differentiating and defining as clearly as possible the separate components that participate in such interactions. She argues that this is important both for clarity in measuring variables and for interpreting research findings to environmental practitioners. Parr proposes that research studies be analyzed in terms of how inclusive they are of four classes of variables: person characteristics, environment characteristics, mediators, and behaviors. In the absence of well-explicated, general theories, Parr proposes that the best way to examine portions of a complex system without destroying its functional integrity is to choose one behavior at a time and then to investigate a variety of possible interactive influences on it.

Windley and Scheidt (Chapter 30) emphasize the importance of viewing interaction as a process. They state the principle that persons and environmental factors are always affecting each other in a "reciprocal" fashion. They emphasize the dynamic nature of the physical environment, consider the social and physical components of the environment as inseparable, and argue that the environment so "surrounds" the person that the person cannot be defined apart from environment.

Windley and Scheidt make a number of methodological suggestions to those who want to function from within a dialectical approach to research. Central to this effort is a typology of environmental attributes, proposed by the authors to provide a meaningful scheme from which to understand the process of person–environment interaction. The attributes are then used to organize a discussion of present knowledge and needed research.

For Howell (Chapter 31), environments are hypothetical constructs in the minds of individuals, which they use to compare current with previous situations. Howell illustrates the importance of memories and expectations by which people interpret the environments in which they find themselves and suggests that people act in and on their environments in terms of their past history. She further argues that, as researchers, we too often have investigated our own conceptualizations of environment to the neglect of the perspectives of the persons who function in it. Howell therefore proposes that we examine people's perceptions and behavior in light of their individual environmental histories.

Each of the following chapters describes and analyzes some of the limitations of present knowledge regarding person–environment interaction. Each argues for a particular approach to research in the future.

REFERENCES

Carp, F. M. Housing and living environments of older people. In R. H. Binstock & E. Shanas (Eds.), *Handbook of aging and the social sciences*. New York: Van Nostrand Reinhold, 1977.

Koncelik, J. A. Human factors and environmental design for the aging: Physiological change and sensory loss as design criteria. In T. O. Byerts, S. C. Howell, & L. A. Pastalan (Eds.), *Environmental context of aging—Lifestyles, environmental quality and living*. New York: Garland Press, 1979.

Lawton, M. P. Impact of the environment on aging and behavior. In J. E. Birren & K. W. Schaie (Eds.), *Handbook of the psychology of aging*. New York: Van Nostrand Reinhold, 1977.

Moos, R. Conceptualizations of human environments. *American Psychologist*, 1973, *28*, 652–665.

Joyce Parr

29

The Interaction of Persons and Living Environments

A four-component model of person–environment interaction is proposed for investigating potentially interactive influences on the behavior of elderly persons in their living environments. A strategy is outlined that limits the focus of studies while maintaining the interactive nature of variables. The usefulness of the model for analyzing the information available in the current literature is demonstrated. And, the argument is made that good research in person–environment interaction requires the sources of information, perspectives, and skills of both environmental practitioners and researchers.

There is an increasing recognition that characteristics of environments interact with characteristics of persons to produce behavior. It is also recognized, however, that much work is needed to develop meaningful ways to describe this interaction.

As in any relatively new field of analysis, a basic problem is finding a way to break down or organize in a *conceptually* meaningful way the important dimensions in a complex system. Such conceptualization is essential for theory development and to serve as a guide to research efforts. It is also important to a developing field that its concepts be clearly defined and tied to events that are *functionally* meaningful. This requires that concepts or descriptors point as clearly as possible to characteristics or occurrences of events thought to be important. This is particularly critical if the results of research are to be usable by practitioners. An understanding of person–environment in-

teraction is important both to researchers and practitioners, for both theoretical and applied reasons.

The goals of this chapter are to describe the limitations of available information regarding person–environment interaction, to propose a classification system or model that can serve as a guide to the development of future research studies, and to describe some promising approaches to research. Finally, it is proposed that the most constructive approach to person–environment research during the 1980s will be to address applied questions in real settings; to make the research interdisciplinary by bringing together the understandings of different perspectives, including those of practitioners; to take a whole-system view of research questions; and to aim toward the development of mini-, rather than general or overarching, theories of interaction.

Limitations of Present Knowledge

There are three basic reasons why our understanding of person–environment interaction is as limited as it is:

The author acknowledges, with appreciation, an increased understanding of the needs and insights of environmental practitioners gained through the opportunity to work with James Christison, Paul Wade, and John McRae. She also wishes to express appreciation to Marion Bunch, who served as reviewer of this chapter.

Too many of the concepts we have used have not had clear referents or have not been formulated with behavior in mind; parts of the person–environment system have been studied without adequate recognition of the interactive effects of other critical parts; and knowledge developed from one perspective has not been communicated or interpreted to persons functioning within other perspectives.

In the following discussion each of the limitations is analyzed, and proposals are made that are designed to help avoid such problems in future research. The chapter concludes with a discussion of the critical importance of interdisciplinary communication to research in person–environment interaction.

The analysis begins with the assumption that it is behavior in environments that is the primary interest of both theoreticians and practitioners. In other words, what we really want to know is how persons function in given settings. We also want to know as much as we can about why they function the way they do. The second question moves us into the area of theory development and testing. Answers to that question are also essential if we are to apply successfully knowledge gained in one setting to the design of other settings.

Problems With Concepts: Clarity and Behavioral Relevance

One basic problem with the concepts we have used is that it has not been clear what characteristics or behaviors they include. Sometimes a concept has been too global. When this has happened various investigators have disagreed on what should be included, and a multitude of different techniques have appeared, all presuming to measure the same concept. This has happened, for example, with the concept of life satisfaction. Its availability as a concept has propagated a great many studies. It has also resulted in the development of many different scales and has produced an enormous amount of conflicting data.

A large percentage of the research that has been done by behavioral scientists interested in environmental questions has focused on the kinds of settings in which people say they are satisfied. The correlates studied have included such physical features as number of rooms or the presence of a kitchen or balcony, larger environmental factors such as the distance to services or the frequency of crime in a neighborhood, or social characteristics such as the age-concentration of a building or neighborhood.

Sometimes researchers have considered satisfaction as a critical subjective variable and thus justifiable for study in and of itself. For others, however, satisfaction seems to have been used in lieu of more ardent efforts to develop specific behavioral criteria. Some may have used it in hope that it would absorb, reflect, or result from, in some additive manner, a whole variety of other possible criterion variables.

A second thing that happens with global concepts is that techniques designed to measure concepts are recognized to overlap with measures of other concepts. This has happened with life satisfaction, morale, adjustment, and developmental task accomplishment. More than 10 years ago Carp (1969) warned of some of the problems associated with using global criterion concepts such as adjustment. She suggested that "the variable inclusion of different aspects of criterion concepts into criterion measures contributes to the present state of confusion" (p. 341).

More recently, there has been some evidence in the literature of an increasing awareness of the problem of confusion associated with such global concepts. George (1979) expressed the need for reexamining the concept of life satisfaction and the psychometric characteristics of the available instruments. Cutler (1979) demonstrated both the multidimensionality of the concept of life satisfaction and that the dimensionality differs substantially across age groups. Larson (1978) presented a review of a variety of measures used to investigate the well-being of older persons. While he concludes that "within this multiplicity of related measures is a shared core of something that can be called subjective well-being" (p. 110), he cautions us against assuming that instruments measure the same thing in different populations. Larson cautions that such measures tell us little about individual informants and notes that "we have little idea how the construct permeates ongoing daily experience" (p. 112). The lack of specificity and its frequent use as a simple correlate with environmental features has resulted in very little information of use either for the design of environments or for the development of theories of person–environment interaction. A major contribution to the future of person–environment research would be to lay to rest, with proper eulogies and due expressions of appreciation for past contributions, the naive notion that simple correlation with any generalized measure of life satisfaction is an adequate criterion for evaluating an environment.

A third way in which the referents of a concept may be obscured is confusion regarding what kind of variable we are talking about. This problem has appeared in both the behavioral science and the architectural literature. The most common instance is a lack of clarity on whether a variable is being measured reasonably directly or is an indirect measure of something that is inferred to exist. For example, a health-perception questionnaire, the scores on which have correlated reliably with physicians' ratings, is an indirect measure. (The question of *which* of these two measures is more likely to be "real" is not at stake for the purposes of this argument.) On the other hand, we may be interested in a more direct measure of how persons perceive their health so that we can investigate the effect of that perception on choice of retirement housing. In that instance, correlation with physicians' ratings is relatively unimportant.

This is not simply a question of level of abstraction—of how far removed a measure is from the "real" thing. The argument is that both "real" and perceived measures may make significant contributions to our understanding of person–environment interaction. It is critical, however, to keep clearly in mind that they are different kinds of variables. It is critical to know which kind of variable we are trying to measure with a given instrument.

A major block to progress in person–environment research has been the lack of functionally meaningful ways of describing the environment (e.g., see Howell, Chapter 31, this volume; Koncelik, 1979; Lawton, 1977c; Moos, 1973). Sometimes in our efforts to devise techniques for describing the characteristics of environments, we have fallen into the trap of confusing environment with perceptions of environment. For example, some typologies consider "familiarity" as an attribute of environments. An investigator interested in that dimension may assume that if residents rate a particular environment as "familiar," the creation of another building similar to the first would be rated in like fashion. The investigator may not, however, have sufficient information or be able to specify what spatial or decorative characteristics make it "familiar." (The investigator also needs information about the persons who are doing the rating. That issue is discussed later in this chapter). Even concepts like "legibility" or "privacy" are fraught with the same dangers. This does not mean that we should not study these attributes, only that we must be aware of what kinds of measures we are using.

The differentiation between alpha and beta press makes the same distinction. Alpha press traditionally refers to the "actual" environment and beta press to the "perceived" environment. What seems to be happening in the field at the moment is that because meaningful categorizations of alpha press have been difficult to develop and because the typologies we have had have not led to efficient prediction of behavior, both behavioral scientists and architects are moving toward the exclusive investigation of beta press. The emphasis at the present time seems to be much more to look at people's perceptions of their environments as ends in themselves.

The danger in looking only at beta press is that we may fall into the trap of assuming that the perception

is the same as the physical environment. When we do that, we lose the ability to produce data that can directly influence the design of environments. When we confuse the variables or fail to compare residents' perceptions with actual environmental characteristics, we have very little to offer practitioners. Practitioners cannot build perceived environments. On the other hand, it is extremely important for designers and builders to know as much as possible about how environmental features contribute to the residents' perceptions.

This brings us back to the question of how to measure alpha press. One of the problems is that the measures typically used to described environments were not developed with behavior in mind. For example, square footage may be an obvious way to describe space, but unless there is some hypothesis regarding how square footage might affect specific behaviors, we should not expect it to correlate with measures of behavior. Behaviorally relevant environmental dimensions are most likely to be developed when practitioners and researchers work together. The importance of encouraging interactive efforts among persons of different perspectives and the value of what we can learn from each other are discussed later in this chapter. Some examples of recent efforts to describe the "actual" environment in behaviorally meaningful ways are presented.

The Person—Environment System

The second basic reason why understanding of person–environment interaction is limited is that we have typically considered only parts of the interactive system at any one time.

A Four–Component Model

Figure 29–1 presents a model of the essential parts of that system. The model is not intended to be a major theoretical statement. Rather, its purpose is to separate conceptually and outline the various components or classes of variables that need to be considered when questions of person–environment interaction are to be investigated. The model is subsequently used to assess the present status of knowledge by analyzing which components have been studied and which have been neglected. The point to be made is that as more of the components are considered in a single study, the understanding that is gained becomes more sensitive. Consideration of the model is suggested as a discipline and guide for planning future studies.

The four components or classes of variables are person characteristics (P), environmental characteristics

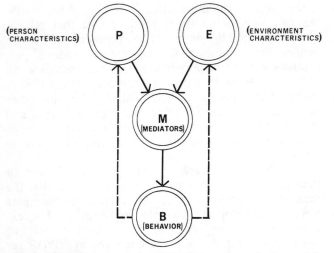

Figure 29-1. Person–environment interaction—basic model.

(E), mediators (M), and behaviors (B). Person characteristics include such things as abilities, desires or goals, health, and economic resources. Environmental characteristics include such things as distances, physical barriers, noise, presence of activity, spatial organization, availability of services, privacy, accessibility of information, and rules. At this level the environmental features should be measured as directly and objectively as possible (i.e., alpha press). Most of the discussions of research presented in this chapter deal with characteristics of the physical environment. Characteristics of the social environment should also be analyzed within this framework. Some discussion of the work of Moos and his associates on the social environment is included.

Mediating variables include such things as how people perceive the environment, the importance to them of environmental characteristics, what they expect to receive from the environment, how they expect to be able to change it, and the experience of matches or discrepancies between persons and environments. It is important to note that it is at the mediator level that interaction begins to occur. By definition, mediators show the influence of both personal and environmental characteristics.

Behavioral measures include actions from which the researcher infers competence and task accomplishment, the way the occupant uses or modifies the environment, or other peoples' or the user's self-evaluations of the appropriateness of behavior in the environment.

According to the model, (1) person and environmental characteristics interact through a set of mediators that moderate their individual or combined effects on behavior; (2) it is unlikely that characteristics of either persons or environments directly determine behavior; and (3) mediators such as the experience of congruence or expectations of being able to control events in one's life should not be considered as end products. The model clearly places a heavy emphasis on behavioral measures that occur in specific environmental contexts and are affected by personal and mediator variables; it suggests that analyses are needed to determine whether constructed mediating variables, such as expectancies based on past experience, improve our understanding of the interaction processes; and it suggests the need to define and explore mediating variables that have both person and environmental relevence (e.g., see discussions later in this chapter of the work of Reid, Haas, & Hawkings, 1977, and of Nehrke, Morganti, Whitbourne, Hulicka, Turner, & Cohen, 1979). The dotted arrows in Figure 29-1 from behavior to person and to environment characteristics indicate that one kind of meaningful behavior in an environment may be for the person to act on the environment, to change goals, or to increase skills.

The arrows drawn between the classes of variables are not considered exhaustive or exclusive. It is expected that the direction of influence may be conceptualized differently from one situation to another. This is not considered a problem for the model. The purpose of the presentation is to sensitize investigators who want to do research in person–environment interaction to the likelihood that at least these four kinds of variables will be operating simultaneously in whatever situation they study.

A Strategy: Limited but Interacting Variables

A number of theoretical approaches proposed to increase our understanding of person–environment interaction have appeared in the literature, but their very breadth has sometimes posed more of a dilemma than a tool for research (e.g., Kahana, 1975; Lawton & Nahemow, 1973; Moos, 1973; Pastalan & Carson, 1970; Rosow, 1967). For example, a broad theory like the one presented by Lawton and Nahemow (see also Nahemow & Lawton, 1973, and Lawton, 1975, for further elaboration of the theory) focuses on person–environment interaction as it affects adaptive behavior. It considers the person in terms of the competencies of health, sensation-perception, motoric behavior, and cognition, and the environment in terms of the demand-quality of resources and incentives. Personality style and environmental cognition are seen as mediators between changing adaptation and press levels and behavior. The concept of "adaptation level" also seems to be a mediator, describing the way in which abilities and press interact to affect behavior. Lawton (1972, 1977b) proposed a taxonomy for types of behaviors which includes seven components ranging from basic life maintenance (e.g., breathing and eating) to complex social role behaviors. He also proposed a taxonomy of kinds of environments which includes the physical, the personal, the supra personal, and the social (Lawton, 1978). The dilemma is that a theory designed to be so inclusive taxes us with developing and validating an overwhelming number of measures before the theory can be tested. This has no doubt discouraged research purporting to test the major theories. Such research would be beyond the time and commitment of all but a few investigators who could devote a lifetime to research in this area. On the other hand, knowledge in an area is more likely to increase as more persons are engaged in research efforts.

It is in response to this analysis of the present state of affairs that a strategy is offered for facilitating interactive research. It is proposed that in the absence of a well-explicated general theory specifying which variables are important and how they should interrelate, the best way to study a complex system without destroying its functional integrity is to choose one kind of behavior and to look at possible interactive influences on the occurrence or quality of that behavior. To the extent that we include measures representative of the other three kinds of variables, the wholeness or integrity of the interactive system remains intact. This strategy contrasts with those attempts to describe either persons or environments along a whole range of characteristics, such as in studies, for example, that devise what may be a very interesting description of a population along various personal or mediator dimensions but lack any understanding of how any one or all of those dimensions may interact with features of an environment. While the proposed strategy may not result in new general theories of behavior, it should be useful in developing minitheories that are testable.

An illustration may be helpful. A researcher interested in a particular kind of social interaction behavior may measure individual subjects' desire for or interest in social interaction (P). Either availability of space in a particular location or similarity of expressed interest on the part of other persons might be examined as the environmental (E) feature. The mediator variable (M) could be people's evaluations of the likelihood of finding other persons in the available space or the degree of satisfication with previous interactions with the available persons. The behavioral measure (B) might be actual contacts or descriptions of the kinds and frequencies of interaction that take place.

Howell (1978) studied the frequency of social behaviors (B) in the shared spaces (E) of four low-income, high-rise, urban elderly housing projects in Cambridge, Massachusetts. She used a variety of techniques to obtain information on use of shared space within each of the four buildings, including observations of behavior at various times of day. She concluded that the design features (E) that appeared to have an impact on social behavior (B) were the location and length of the primary path from the front entrance to the elevators; location, differentiation, and size of the social spaces; and visual connections between shared spaces. In discussing her findings, she gave thought to why particular types of residents (P) used space in certain ways. She proposed, for example, the concept of "defensive surveillance" (M) to help understand residents' behavior. She also hypothesized that Rosow's (1967) personality types might be useful for predicting the differential use of shared space. She noted that spending time in shared spaces with other elderly persons is a new experience for most elderly and suggested that they have to learn new behaviors appropriate to that situation. Thus the possible effects of previous learnings as well as the specific reinforcements (M) available to residents in the new situations were being considered as potentially important. Howell's chapter in this section indicates that she intends to pursue the study of the personal history of residents (P) and its effect on contextual meaning (M) as it relates to behavior (B) in living environments (E).

Although simple correlations of life satisfaction (M) with environmental characteristics (E) have not yielded much usable information, studies focusing on life satisfaction do illustrate the value of considering more components of the interactive system. Wolk and Telleen (1976), for example, found that different sets of person variables (P) predicted satisfaction (M) in settings with differing levels of constraint (E). Health for example, predicted satisfaction in a high constraining environment whereas perceived autonomy and self-concept predicted satisfaction in low constraining environments. Success at developmental tasks predicted satisfaction in both settings. Wolk and Telleen's study did not make a clear distinction between person and mediator variables, and the environmental and behavioral measures are weak, but the findings provide some interesting interactive information.

Markides and Martin (1979) demonstrated that not only does the variable health (P) influence life satisfaction (M) but that health influences activity (B), which serves as a mediator, and improves prediction to life-satisfaction measures. The alternative hypothesis, that life satisfaction might serve as a mediator between health and activity, was not tested. The potential significance of environmental factors, for example, in permitting activity is missing.

An important feature of Markides and Martin's study was the use of path analysis to demonstrate the direct and indirect effects through a mediator of one variable on another. This study illustrates the value of one of a growing number of design and analysis procedures grouped together under the label of causal modeling. Given the potential importance of mediators in our understanding of person–environment interaction, such procedures merit consideration in planning studies.

Conner, Powers, and Bultena (1979) found little direct relation between the number and types of social interactions (B) and satisfaction (M). They concluded that "concern should be focused more on identifying personal needs [P] that are met by interaction [B], the meanings attached to various social relationships [M], the extent to which social relationships are substitutable [probably M], and circumstances [M or E] under which substitution can and does occur" (p. 120). Even with their stated sensitivity to the problem of using different methods to measure social interaction, the authors still used the dependent variables of life satisfaction and adjustment interchangeably. Nevertheless, the conclusion that social behaviors need to be understood and predicted in terms of personal needs (P) and meanings (M) is helpful. Attention to the environment in which these needs, meanings, and behaviors occur should further increase our understanding of those events and contribute significantly to our understanding of person–environment interaction.

Support Versus Constraint: A Policy and Research Issue

The value has been expressed by policy makers, social scientists, and older persons themselves that persons are "better off" when they remain "independent" and "in control" as long as possible. How "better off," "independent," and "in control" should be defined has not been clear, however, and their correlation with environmental factors has not been demonstrated. The policy directive to provide "least restrictive environments" has been clearly stated. The question remains, however, as to which kinds of environmental characteristics provide support and which constrain different kinds of elderly people in their attempts to maintain control (see Parr, 1978, for an earlier discussion of this issue). Clearly, only research studies that provide understandings of how all four system components interact will be adequate to answer such questions.

The question is of concern particularly from the applied point of view, though findings will also be helpful for theory development in person–environment interaction. Some developers, architects, and managers of housing for the elderly have been sensitive to the impact that their decisions will have on the amount of control residents have or are encouraged to exercise (Christison, 1970; Gelwicks, 1977; Koncelik, 1976; McRae, 1975; Zeisel, Epp, & Demos, 1977).

The term *constraint* has been used in a variety of ways in the behavioral science literature. Lawton and Cohen (1974) have noted that elderly are more vulnerable to constraint. Kahana (1975) outlined three sources of constraint: restrictiveness in the environment (E), limited degrees of individual freedom (P), and internal perception of limited degrees of freedom (M). Constraint may be personal (P), as in the cases of health, lack of information, or limited economic resources; or architectural (E), as with stairs; or attitudinal (M), as in the expectation that exertion of independence will "not do any good."

Several investigators have reported greater life satisfaction (M) where fewer environmental constraints (E) were present (Lawton, Nahemow, & Teaff, 1975; Smith & Lipman, 1972). References to quite subtle kinds of environmental constraints have been discussed in the literature. Wolk and Telleen (1976) have asserted that settings that provide more supports for residents than are necessary can create constraints. Carp (1977) has stated that "an overly supportive environment [E] robs the individual of initiative and of the opportunity to exercise his/her adaptive ability" [B] (p. 264).

Such subtle forms of constraint are difficult to identify. What is constraining for one person may not be for another (P). For example, the extent to which distance (E) from friends or services is constraining depends upon ease of personal mobility (P), ability to conceptualize how to get there (P), and how much one wants the stimulation of "getting out" (P). The constraining effect of rules about the front door being locked at night in a congregate living site (E) depends upon whether persons like to go out or have guests in at night (P), whether their fingers are nimble enough to manipulate a key in a lock (P), and how secure they feel knowing that the building door is locked (M). Railings around toilets and emergency call systems (E) are viewed by some as a suggestion of their incompetence (M), and hence constraining, and by others as supportive (M).

Steinfeld (1977) observes that "an environment is not the same to all individuals because people experience it differently and have varying degrees of mastery over it" (p. 2). He notes that some people act on or toward their environments. On the other hand, some "become dependent on staff or tend to manipulate other people in order to satisfy their needs" (p. 13).

Anecdotal evidence suggests that the availablity of some kinds of supports (E) may encourage some persons (P) to become more dependent than they need to be (B) whereas for others the supports may provide a relief from psychological stress (M). For such persons, the knowledge that the supports are there if they need them allows them to be more independent and function with greater freedom (B) than if the supports were not there.

How the effects of design or managerial decisions are assessed will also depend on the outcome criterion that the researcher uses. The "right" thing may be different depending on whether the criterion is life satisfaction (M) or persons taking care of their own needs (B). For example, providing services in a building may please some occupants very much. On the other hand, providing assistance such as transportation to help them get services outside the building might encourage greater independence by developing confidence in functioning in the community. A study reported by Lawton (1977a) shed some light on the effects of providing services on-site. When he measured changes over time in both satisfaction and use of community resources, he found that over a 1-year period, residents in a facility with services became more satisfied but used community resources less than those who did not have services immediately available. What was still lacking, however, for interpretation of the significance of these findings for policy was information on the initial and changed personal characteristics of the residents living in the two buildings. For example, if health or social attitudes had contributed initially to the choice of place of residence, they might play a significant role in determining both degree of satisfaction expressed and use of community resources.

Some combination of (a) recognizing individual differences in the need for physical and social support, and (b) allowing or encouraging as much independence in individual exercise of choice as possible, seems to be indicated. But such formulas are not presently available. Fozard and Popkin (1978) reviewed available research on visual, memory, and learning processes as they relate to the design of environments for health, leisure, and work activities. They concluded that "the optimum in environments for the aging will promote independence of activity and provide challenges to the individual, not simply maximize physical comfort and safety." They further stated that "we should be concerned with providing environments which facilitate individual variations in behavior (an optimal strategy for any group)" (p. 976). Similar suggestions have been made by others (e.g., Byerts, 1978, 1979; Carp, 1977; Koncelik, 1979).

There seem to be several options. We can try to (a) match persons with specifically designed environments; (b) build in enough flexibility or a sufficiently wide range of options within a given living situation to be able to provide different environments for different types of residents as needed; or (c) encourage persons to develop their own environments based on their own needs and interests.

Information useful for making decisions on these options for elderly persons must be based on research that has investigated the interactions among all four kinds of variables. Anything less could result in inappropriate decisions for the persons who are our concern.

The concept of personal control is integrally related to the support–constraint issue. Some examples from the locus of control literature demonstrate the increased usefulness of findings as more of the system components are included. Locus of control is a mediator construct that refers to the degree to which people see the events occurring in their lives as contingent on their own efforts and abilities (for general reviews, see Lefcourt, 1976; Phares, 1976; Rotter, 1966).

Wolk and Kurtz (1975) found a correlation between locus of control (M) and adaptive behavior (B) but recognized that internal control may either have led to or have been a result of adaptive involvement. Wolk (1976) demonstrated that an environmental characteristic such as situational constraint can moderate the relation between locus of control (M) and developmental task accomplishment (B). On the basis of their findings, Pincus and Wood (1970) suggested that a person characteristic such as health status (P) can moderate the relation between perceived autonomy (M) and the exercise of autonomy (B). (The alternative hypothesis, that perceived autonomy could moderate between health status and behavior, was not proposed but is also a possibility.)

A study by Reid et al. (1977) found that consideration of the importance to a person of a particular event or outcome (P) increased the correlation between degree of expected control (M) and happiness and self-concept. They also found differences in the correlations by sex (P) and by whether people lived in institutional or noninstitutional settings (E). They found, for example, that for institutionalized males the relation between expected control and self-concept was particularly strong. No behavioral measures were examined, however. Reid et al. devised parallel measures of the importance of events and of expectancies for being able to control those events. The seven items used are descriptive of real situations likely to occur in the lives of the persons being studied. Some of the items are such that it would also not be difficult to develop parallel behavioral measures. These qualities should make the measures particularly useful for future research. Each of the last three locus-of-control studies included measures of three of the four system components. The inclusion of the fourth would have increased our understanding even more.

To summarize, the proposed strategy suggests that a single dimension or concept such as control can be studied in an interactive mode. The researcher need not even study a whole range of life events at once but can focus, for example, on the residents' control of privacy, or of personal possessions, or of their own time. If it is person–environment interaction we are interested in, then we should study the importance of control to persons, the extent to which the environment encourages or restricts control (spatially or by rules), and the extent of control that persons expect to have on the use or exertion of control.

Promising Approaches to the Study of Person—Environment Interaction

One study that has investigated all four system components and in which the findings are potentially very useful is that of Regnier, Walsh, and their associates at the University of Southern California. This group has been engaged over the last several years in a study of factors that influence the perception and use of neighborhoods by elderly residents. Regnier (in press) and Walsh, Krauss, and Regnier (in press) have recently described some of their methods and findings. Spatial abilities (P), actual characteristics of the environment such as distance, street relations, landmarks, and incidence of crime (E), environmental perception and knowledge (M), and environmental use (B) in elderly community residents have been interrelated. The research group has hypothesized that people's tested spatial abilities (P) will affect both their perceptions of neighborhoods (M) and the accuracy with which they can represent the neighborhoods (B), and that knowledge of the neighborhood (M) will mediate between spatial ability (P) and the use of services (B) in that neighborhood. With such data, it will be possible, for example, to compare the predictive value of length of residence in a neighborhood with that of spatial ability on the use of the neighborhood.

At the time of this writing the data are still under analysis. A number of quite interesting findings are beginning to emerge, however. The personal characteristics that predict the size of the area that people perceive as their neighborhood are not the same as those that predict the accuracy of people's judgment of distance to important landmarks. The amount of driving done and the ease of walking significantly predict neighborhood size (M) on hand-drawn maps (B). On the other hand, higher levels of education and good health were the primary predictors of accuracy of judgment of distance (B). One of the unique characteristics of this study is that neighborhood residents are being brought into the laboratory for testing of spatial abilities in order to elaborate personal characteristics. In the laboratory traditional and new psychometric procedures for measuring spatial abilities are being administered. This will provide the opportunity to compare paper-and-pencil procedures, which might easily be used in any setting, with the more complex laboratory procedures.

Another part of the study examines different procedures that people use in acquiring new spatial information. For this aspect they are comparing information learned from a simulated trip through an imaginary city (which appears to have been filmed from an automobile) with the opportunity to view a stationary model of that same community for a specified period of time. Preliminary results indicate that the ability to review the stationary model results in a significantly larger amount of environmental learning in elderly residents.

These investigators have been very careful in developing their measures. The referents are clear. The difference between actual and perceived environments is clear, and focusing on that difference has produced some very interesting comparisons, for example, actual versus perceived safety and security of neighborhoods (Regnier, in press). All four system components are included, and the study should result in some very useful findings.

Another interesting study is that of Nehrke et al. (1979), which was originally based on the congruence theory of Kahana (1975). Kahana proposed to compare the similarity or discrepancy between individual needs or preferences and perceived characteristics of the environment (beta press). She proposed seven dimensions, which are primarily social in nature and have to do with the people, staff, and rules within an institution. The only physical characteristics included were the dimensions of privacy and stimulation.

Some problems have been experienced in attempts to render the dimensions operational. Nehrke et al. (1979) and I, in some pilot work, have found low internal consistencies within the subscales purported to measure the dimensions. Nehrke used the same Environmental Characteristics Questionnaire items that had originally been developed for nursing-home populations. Parr had replaced some items in an attempt to make them more appropriate to elderly residents living more independently. Kahana (1979) is continuing the work on these dimensions and the techniques for measuring them.

Nehrke et al. (1979), in the meantime, have developed and are testing an Environmental Perception, Preference and Importance Scale (EPPIS), which measures 15 empirically derived dimensions. They use parallel measures of perceived environment (M), environmental preference (P), and the importance or salience of a characteristic to residents (M).

Congruence scores on each dimension are derived by subtracting preference ratings (P) from perception ratings (M) and multiplying the difference by the importance score (M). The value of determining how important the particular characteristic or activity is to a person was previously demonstrated in the locus-of-control literature (Reid et al., 1977).

Residents of four different living areas (E) within a Veterans Administration (VA) domiciliary have been tested with these scales. In addition, measures of morale and life satisfaction and staff ratings of adjustment were obtained.

Some interesting findings have emerged, in that congruence for various combinations of the 15 dimensions predicted differentially the well-being and adjustment measures in different living areas. Nehrke et al. feel that the EPPIS holds promise for the design of differential intervention procedures for groups of residents in different settings, depending on what behavior changes are targeted.

The authors recognize that the EPPIS has been used only with an elderly male VA population. On the other hand, the scale has shown sufficient reliability and usefulness in differentially predicting adjustment and well-being to merit further investigation. At present, work is progressing to check out the long-term stability of scores and the long-term predictive usefulness. Another step would be to characterize more specifically the residents and physical environments in different settings in an attempt to understand better why congruence on different dimensions was differentially predictive of adjustment. The work by Nehrke and his associates provides a demonstration of the value of considering all four classes of variables simultaneously.

A third study provides an interesting model for studying the interaction of individuals and their environments (Barbarin, Tyler, & Gatz, 1979). One purpose of the research was to study the interaction of individual and community competence. Extensive information was gathered regarding the characteristics of individuals, their perceptions of the resources within their communities, and their personal styles of coping in their communities.

Both age and racial differences (P) affected how residents perceived the communities (M) and how they coped within the communities (B). Elderly people characterized the effectiveness of their communities not only in terms of problems and deficits, as younger adults did, but also in terms of their abilities to generate their own solutions. For blacks, the experience of community life was related more to how active they were in using influential people to solve their problems; for whites, experience of community was related more to the ways they had to handle life problems and to their evaluation of formal resources available to them in their community. Correlations were also demonstrated between the amount of information persons had about their community and locus of control.

A second major purpose of the Barbarin et al. study was to use and evaluate intervention efforts designed to make community information more available (E) to residents. A number of interesting findings emerged regarding changes in perception and coping style following these intervention efforts. In this manner the findings demonstrated the way in which an environmental change—the availability of information—can modify perceptions (M), future behavior (B), and perhaps even future personal capabilities (P).

In terms of the four classes of variables, the Barbarin et al. study is the weakest in providing and evaluating actual environmental characteristics. The basic assumption that persons' perceptions of their communities was the important predictor of behavior was pervasive. Still in need of investigation are questions about whether changing the actual resources and services of the community or simply influencing people's knowledge and perceptions of community resources is the more constructive solution.

A fourth effort, by Moos and his associates, has concerned environmental determinants of behavior. Their investigations have focused particularly on characteristics of the social environment and have, in recent years, been extended to sheltered-care environments for the elderly. This effort has resulted in the most systematic set of procedures yet devised for describing and comparing various aspects of environments (Lemke, Moos, Mehren, & Gauvin, 1979; Moos & Lemke, 1979).

Five instruments comprise the Multiphasic Environmental Assessment Procedure (MEAP). The Physical and Architectural Features Checklist (PAF) measures nine dimensions. The Policy and Program Information Form (POLIF) describes characteristics along 10 dimensions. The Resident and Staff Information Form (RESIF) summarizes administrative information regarding residents and staff. The Rating

Scale (RS) is designed to be used by an outside observer. A Sheltered Care Environment Scale (SCES) focuses on resident and staff perceptions of the social environment. The SCES covers, with seven subscales, the three basic dimensions of social environments that Moos has studied in various settings—relationship, personal growth, and system maintenance and change. A particular value of this latter scale is its availability in three parallel forms. The same items can be used to describe how people feel things really are, to describe what they would like them to be, and to assess prospective staff and residents' expectations.

In terms of the four-component model, Moos's procedures provide many measures of the physical, social, policy, and program features of the environment. They also measure many potentially important mediators, particularly as they describe residents' experience of the social environment. One wishes for more parallel measures so that, for example, residents' experience of how important order and organization are in the facility could be compared with the existence of policies and regulations to create or enforce order. Another wish is for a measure of residents' experience of features of physical environments in order to compare them with the thorough descriptions of space and aids provided by the PAF.

The representation of measures of person and behavioral characteristics, by comparison, is minimal. They are described only by summaries derived from administrative records and estimates by staff of the numbers of residents who are capable of and do engage in various activities. While such estimates may provide interesting comparisons of staff across facilities, and the reliabilities are acceptable, one wonders how similar such estimates would be to what individual residents would report, for example, on how many times they watched television, wrote letters, visited friends, or went shopping.

Among the possible uses for the MPAP described by Moos and Lemke (1979) are evaluating environmental impact, enhancing clinical case descriptions, and increasing person–environment congruence. For each of these examples, Moos and Lemke suggest that additional measures of individual resident characteristics are needed for comparison with the characteristics summarized by the MEAP. Sociodemographic characteristics and functional ability levels are suggested as being important, as are such measures as morale and life satisfaction.

The Importance of Interdisciplinary Communication

Almost by definition, the study of person–environment interaction demands interdisciplinary effort. It requires skills in measuring behavior as it occurs in environments and skills in describing environments in behaviorally meaningful ways. The difficulties of interdisciplinary communication are not new, however. Koncelik (1976), a products designer who has written on nursing-home environments, notes that

The point of social and psychological data on environment . . . is that they should lead to better environments. To do this, the information must be interpretable by others who build, program, and deliver care. At present much information which could be used or applied is too riddled with jargon and unidisciplinary orientation to be of use in the design process. This problem could be ameliorated by having designers learn research techniques and participate in data collection. (p. 8)

Koncelik also notes that "if a balanced approach is to be achieved, the design process must be opened up to include other disciplines willing to share the responsibilities. This is hard to achieve because designing is a risk" (p. 8).

Parr, Christison, and Wade (1979) have discussed some of the reasons for such lack of communication and have made a strong plea for interdisciplinary research. One observation they made was that practitioners seem to have read more of the behavioral science literature than behavioral scientists have read of theirs. Much architectural literature, for example, exhibits sensitivity to the importance of how people perceive and use space. Fewer behavioral scientists, however, seem to understand how space is created and what the elements are that limit or permit the creation of space. Environmental practitioners can bring their experience of what has seemed to work and what has not. They can also provide the material for "real" experiments, which would not otherwise be accessible to behavioral scientists. Behavioral scientists, on the other hand, bring analytic skills, measurement techniques, and the recognition of the values and limitations of their data. With some promising exceptions, what now seems to be the state of affairs is that practitioners continue to base their judgments on their personal observation and on whatever information about elderly people they have been able to glean from the gerontological literature. Some interesting guidelines for design and typologies for describing the attributes of environments have been proposed, but not many hard data have appeared by way of follow-up. Behavioral scientists, meanwhile, have continued their research on life satisfaction and locus of control without reference to the environmental characteristics that are critical to the understanding of those concepts.

In the interest of better interdisciplinary communication, some efforts on the part of practitioners are mentioned here that might well be consulted by behavioral scientists considering doing research in the area of person–environment interaction. It is important for behavioral scientists to understand the ways in which visually and spatially oriented practitioners have been trying to deal with characteristics of the physical environment. They provide a good source for hypotheses that need testing.

The architect Gelwicks (1977) lists 16 directives or guidelines for the design of congregate living facilities. He presents each with a rationale and an example. It is hard to argue with any of the directives, though the rationales are stated as if they were based on thoroughly documented research, which is not the case. Nevertheless, the suggestions do seem constructive, and they comprise a good effort at putting partial information into a form that is understandable to practitioners. Behavioral scientists may wonder at some of Gelwick's generalizations, but they must also recognize the demands of practitioners who must make decisions about buildings and services. What researchers can do is first to read what the practitioners are saying in order to understand their problems better, then to design studies to test some of the assumptions, preferably in cooperation with a practitioner, and finally to come up with data that can be of value in establishing future guidelines.

Zeisel et al. (1977) prepared a monograph outlining guidelines for the design of low-rise buildings to house older people. This publication listed in detail design features with brief descriptions of the way in which older people might use those features. It was illustrated with examples selected from a design competition for elderly housing in Dracut, Massachusetts. After preparing that information, Zeisel et al. asked an expert panel of eight psychologists, sociologists, architects, and interior designers to rate each feature and the design suggestions in terms of whether there were any available data to support the analysis. Of the 123 features described, only 32 of them were thought by at least two of the eight experts to be backed by systematic data. For only eight of the features did three or more of the experts know of systematic data that would support the suggestions. Such findings illustrate rather well the lack of research data relevant to specific design features. Zeisel et al.'s recognition and documentation of that lack should help to encourage more research.

Several examples are available of practitioners' attempts to explore possible implications of behavioral theories for the design of environments. One is a discussion by Gelwicks and Newcomer (1974). Using Lawton and Nahemow's (1973) theory, they considered the implications for over- and undersupport in environments when planning housing for the elderly. They also explored the usefulness of Rosow's (1967)

description of personality types and proposed matches between preferred life-style and the age-concentration of a neighborhood. Howell (1978) also used Rosow's types to hypothesize the way in which people might use or perceive shared spaces in congregate housing projects. Zeisel (1975) has reiterated the importance of Barker's (1968) notion of the "behavior setting," which considers the environment as a social-physical unit. Zeisel notes,

> Describing behavior settings includes at least an understanding of what people generally do there, how people know what is expected of them there, how norms of behavior are established, which attributes of the physical environment tell potential users what is expected of them, and what the environment is like. (p. 11)

The typology proposed by Windley and Scheidt in Chapter 30 of this section provides a good example of efforts to describe behaviorally meaningful environmental attributes. Another is that of Koncelik (1979), who has proposed a classification system of "relationships" between persons and environments, in which he includes the four categories of warning, interpretation, negotiation, and responsiveness.

Pastalan and Carson (1970) developed the concept of the "loss-continuum" that accompanies aging. They suggest that varying environmental supports need to be provided, depending on those losses. This concept has been used by a number of practitioners. McRae (1975) notes that "stimulating the senses of older people is important to compensate for losses related to visual, auditory, tactile, vibratory, odoriferous,, and thermal factors of the near environment" (p. 13). Steinfeld (1977, p. 4) has suggested that "congruence between a point on the loss continuum and present living arrangements determines how well those arrangements meet the individual needs." Pastalan (1977) has gone further to develop the "empathic model," which describes techniques for increasing sensitivity to the needs of persons for whom one is designing.

The whole point to this discussion is that the techniques and concepts developed by practitioners to describe environments need to be considered in relation to the techniques available to describe persons and their behavior. One example that seems to hold special promise for research in person–environment interaction is McRae's (1975) notion of "seams." McRae (1975, p. 87) states that

> all successful spaces have carefully knitted seams connecting them. These invisible lines may also be thought of as the edges of a space. These edges are sometimes powerful psychological boundaries, establishing territories or domains.

What is particularly important about this concept is that it describes a characteristic of space that is measurable and that may be useful in understanding people's behavior in that space. We need to work cooperatively with practitioners to find more concepts like this one. There may already be other constructs in the heads of practitioners that would provide meaningful ways to understand physical space in the same way in which we use constructs to understand behavior. It would be ideal to identify psychological and spatial constructs directly relevant to each other whose interactive affects on behavior could be studied.

Parr and McRae (1980) are currently collaborating on an effort to relate McRae's architectural concepts of seams, edges, filters, couples, and locks (E) to the environmental options (M) they provide, to the person characteristic of desire for (P) and expectation of control over (M) environmental situations and events. These presumably interacting variables will be investigated for their effects on the choice behavior of residents (B) in middle- and upper-income congregate living sites.

Summary

A four-component model of person–environment interaction has been proposed for use in investigating potentially interactive influences on the behavior of elderly persons in their living environments. A strategy for limiting the focus of studies while maintaining the interactive nature of variables has been outlined, and a demonstration of the usefulness of the model for analyzing the information available in the current literature has been presented. Finally, the argument has been made that good research in person–environment interaction requires the sources of information, perspectives, and skills of both environmental practitioners and researchers. No claims are made that the model and strategy described represent an ultimate solution. They have been proposed, however, as a heuristic alternative to the limitations presented by less focused, interactive or interdisciplinary approaches.

REFERENCES

Barbarin, O., Tyler, F., & Gatz, M. *Individual and community competence: developing and integrating successful coping strategies over time* (Final report, HEW #90-A-520/01 and 02). College Park, Md.: University of Maryland, Center on Aging and Department of Psychology, January 1979.

Barker, R. *Ecological psychology: Concepts and methods for studying the environment of human behavior.* Stanford, Calif.: Stanford University Press, 1968.

Byerts, T. O. Toward a better range of housing and environmental choices for the elderly. In P. A. Wagner & J. McRae (Eds.), *Back to basics—Food and shelter, Proceedings of the Southern Gerontology Society*, Gainesville, Florida, 1978.

Byerts, T. O. Specialized environments. In T. O. Byerts, S. C. Howell, & L. A. Pastalan (Eds.), *Environmental context of aging—Lifestyles, environmental quality and living.* New York: Garland Press, 1979.

Carp, F. M. Compound criteria in gerontological research. *Journal of Gerontology*, 1969, *24*, 341–347.

Carp, F. M. Housing and living environments of older people. In R. H. Binstock & E. Shanas (Eds.), *Handbook of aging and the social sciences.* New York: Van Nostrand Reinhold, 1977.

Christison, J. A. *Emphasis on living.* Valley Forge, Pa.: Judson Press, 1970.

Conner, K. A., Powers, E. A., & Bultena, G. L. Social interaction and life satisfaction: An empirical assessment of late-life patterns. *Journal of Gerontology*, 1979, *34*, 116–121.

Cutler, N. E. Age variations in the dimensionality of life satisfaction. *Journal of Gerontology*, 1979, *34*, 573–578.

Fozard, J. L., & Popkin, S. J. Optimizing adult development. *American Psychologist*, 1978, *33*, 975–989.

Gelwicks, L. E. The congregate facility: An architectural program. In W. T. Donahue, M. M. Thompson, & D. J. Curren (Eds.), *Congregate housing for older people* (DHEW Publication No. (OHD) 77-20284). Washington, D.C.: U.S. Government Printing Office, 1977.

Gelwicks, L. E., & Newcomer, R. J. *Planning housing environments for the elderly.* Washington, D.C.: National Council on the Aging, 1974.

George, L. The happiness syndrome: Methodological and substantive issues in the study of social-psychological well-being in adulthood. *Gerontologist*, 1979, *19*, 210–216.

Howell, S.C. *Shared spaces in housing for the elderly.* Cambridge, Mass.: Laboratory of Architecture and Planning, Massachusetts Institute of Technology, 1978.

Kahana, E. A congruence model of person–environment interaction. In P. G. Windley, T. O. Byerts, & F. G. Ernst (Eds.), *Theory development in environment and aging.* Washington, D.C.: Gerontological Society, 1975.

Kahana, E. A congruence model of person–environment fit. In F. Carp (Chair), *Alternative conceptions of the person–environment interaction.* Symposium presented at the meeting of the Gerontological Society, Washington, D.C., 1979.

Koncelik, J. A. *Designing the open nursing home.* Stroudsberg, Pa.: Dowden, Hutchinson, & Ross, 1976.

Koncelik, J. A. Human factors and environmental design for the aging: Physiological change and sensory loss as design criteria. In T. O. Byerts, S. C. Howell, & L. A. Pastalan (Eds.), *Environmental context of aging—Lifestyles, environmental quality and living.* New York: Garland Press, 1979.

Larson, R. Thirty years of research on the subjective well-being of older Americans. *Journal of Gerontology*, 1978, *33*, 109–124.

Lawton, M. P. Assessing the competence of older people. In D. P. Kent, R. Kastenbaum, & S. Sherwood (Eds.), *Re-*

search, planning and action for the elderly. New York: Behavioral Publications, 1972.

Lawton, M. P. Competence, environmental press and the adaptation of older people. In P. G. Windley, T. O. Byerts, & F. G. Ernst (Eds.), *Theory development in environment and aging*. Washington, D.C.: Gerontological Society, 1975.

Lawton, M. P. Applying research knowledge to congregate housing. In W. T. Donahue, M. M. Thompson, & D. J. Curren (Eds.), *Congregate housing for older people* (DHEW Publication No. (OHD) 77-20284). Washington, D.C.: U.S. Government Printing Office, 1977. (a)

Lawton, M. P. Evaluation research in fluid systems. In J. E. O'Brien & G. F. Streib (Eds.), *Evaluative research on social programs for the elderly* (DHEW Publication No. (OHD) 77-20120). Washington, D.C.: U.S. Government Printing Office, 1977. (b)

Lawton, M. P. Impact of the environment on aging and behavior. In J. E. Birren & K. W. Schaie (Eds.), *Handbook of the psychology of aging*. New York: Van Nostrand Reinhold, 1977. (c)

Lawton, M. P. *The physical environment*. Paper presented at the Nova Behavioral Conference on Aging, Port St. Lucie, Florida, May 1978.

Lawton, M. P., & Cohen, J. The generality of housing impact on the well-being of older people. *Journal of Gerontology*, 1974, *29*, 194–201.

Lawton, M. P., & Nahemow, L. Ecology and the aging process. In C. Eisdorfer and M. P. Lawton (Eds.) *Psychology of adult development and aging*. Washington, D.C.: American Psychological Association, 1973.

Lawton, M. P., Nahemow, L., & Teaff, J. Housing characteristics and the well-being of elderly tenants in federally assisted housing. *Journal of Gerontology*, 1975, *30*, 601–607.

Lefcourt, H. M. *Locus of control*. New York: Wiley, 1976.

Lemke, S., Moos, R., Mehren, B., & Gauvin, M. *The multiphasic environmental assessment procedure: Handbook for users*. Palo Alto, Calif.: Social Ecology Laboratory, Veterans Administration Medical Center, and Stanford University School of Medicine, 1979.

Markides, K. S., & Martin, H. W. A causal model of life satisfaction among the elderly. *Journal of Gerontology*, 1979, *34*, 86–93.

McRae, J. *Elderly in the environment: Northern Europe*. Gainesville: University of Florida, College of Architecture and Center for Gerontological Studies and Programs, 1975.

Moos, R. Conceptualizations of human environments. *American Psychologist*, 1973, *28*, 652–665.

Moos, R., & Lemke, S. *Multiphasic environmental assessment procedure—Preliminary manual*. Palo Alto, Calif.: Social Ecology Laboratory, Veterans Administration Medical Center, and Stanford University School of Medicine, 1979.

Nahemow, L., & Lawton, M. P. Toward an ecological theory of adaptation and aging. *Environmental Design Research*, 1973, *1*, 24–32.

Nehrke, M. F., Morganti, J. B., Whitbourne, S. K.,

Hulicka, I. M., Turner, R. R., & Cohen, S. H. An empirical test of a person–environment congruence model: Cross validation of the EPPIS. In F. Carp, (Chair), *Alternative conceptions of the person–environment interaction*. Symposium presented at the meeting of the Gerontological Society, Washington, D.C., 1979.

Parr, J. *Support vs. constraint: A person–environment analysis of retirement housing*. Paper presented at the International Congress of Gerontology, Tokyo, Japan, August 1978.

Parr, J., Christison, J. & Wade, P. The interaction of persons and living environments: experience and research. In J. Parr & A. Small (Co-chairs), *Contemporary issues on older persons and their environments*. Symposium presented at the meeting of the American Psychological Association, New York, September 1979.

Parr, J., & McRae, J. *Optionality in living environments*. Paper presented at the Nova Conference on Enhancing the Quality of Life of Older Persons, Ft. Lauderdale, Florida, February 1980.

Pastalan, L. The empathic model: A methodological bridge between research and design. *Journal of Architectural Education*, 1977, *31*, 14–15.

Pastalan, L. A., & Carson, D. H. *Spatial behavior of older people*. Ann Arbor: University of Michigan–Wayne State University Institute of Gerontology, 1970.

Phares, E. J. *Locus of control in personality*. Morristown, N.J.: General Learning Press, 1976.

Pincus, A., & Wood, V. Methodological issues in measuring the environment in institutions for the aged and its impact on residents. *Aging and Human Development*, 1970, *1*, 117–126.

Regnier, V. Neighborhood images and use: A case study. In M. P. Lawton (Eds.), *Community housing choices for older Americans*. New York: Garland Press, in press.

Reid, D. W., Haas, G., & Hawkings, D. Locus of desired control and positive self-concept of the elderly. *Journal of Gerontology*, 1977, *32*, 441–450.

Rosow, I. *Social integration of the aged*. New York: Free Press, 1967.

Rotter, J. B. Generalized expectancies for internal versus external control of reinforcement. *Psychological Monographs*, 1966, *80* (1), Whole No. 609.

Smith, K., & Lipman, A. Constraint and life satisfaction. *Journal of Gerontology*, 1972, *27*, 77–82.

Steinfeld, E. *Acting toward the environment in old age*. Paper presented at the 5th Annual SAEE Conference, Buffalo, New York, October 1977.

Walsh, D., Krauss, I., & Regnier, V. Spatial abilities, environmental knowledge and neighborhood use of the elderly. In L. Liben, A. Patterson, & N. Newcombe (Eds.), *Spatial representation and behavior across the life span: Theory and application*. New York: Academic Press, in press.

Wolk, S. Situational constraint as a moderator of the locus of control-adjustment relationship. *Journal of Consulting and Clinical Psychology*, 1976, *44*, 420–427.

Wolk, S., & Kurtz, J. Positive adjustment and involvement during aging and expectancy for internal control. *Journal of Consulting and Clinical Psychology*, 1975, *43*, 173–178.

Wolk, S., & Telleen, S. Psychological and social correlates of life satisfaction as a function of residential constraint. *Journal of Gerontology*, 1976, *31*, 89–98.

Zeisel, J. *Sociology and architectural design*. New York: Russell Sage Foundation, 1975.

Zeisel, J., Epp, G., & Demos, S. *Low rise housing for older people* (HUD-483 (TQ)-76, U.S. Department of Housing and Urban Development). Washington, D.C.: U.S. Government Printing Office, 1977.

Paul G. Windley and Rick J. Scheidt

CHAPTER

30

Person – Environment Dialectics: Implications for Competent Functioning in Old Age

The position is taken that a dialectical perspective of person–environment relations can enhance understanding of the interactions of competence and environment for older populations. Two recent theoretical formulations of competence are evaluated against this position. A taxonomy of 11 environmental attributes is presented with strong dialectical implications and with an applied rationale and research context for each attribute. The criteria for competent functioning that guide current research are briefly reviewed. Illustrative case studies are offered that involve two attributes (accessibility and adaptability) which interact with the competence of older persons. Implications of the dialectical perspective, particularly for the development of criteria for effective responding, are discussed.

This chapter presents selected issues in the study of environment and aging that will occupy researchers in the 1980s, especially those concerned with competent functioning in older populations. In the following pages, we define and apply a particular perspective—the dialectical perspective—to the organization of our discussion of these issues. Further, we attempt to illustrate how this perspective can stimulate future research in this area (a) by making researchers more aware of the unexamined values guiding their activities; (b) by suggesting context-relevant taxonomic dimensions to classify specific behavioral and environmental events; (c) by aiding in the generation of criteria for competent functioning and planned interven-

tion; and (d) by lending to the study of concrete behavior episodes across environments of varying type and scale.

Recent Theoretical Formulations in Aging—Environment Relations

In recent years, the dialectical perspective or model has gained an increasing number of adherents, particularly among life span developmentalists and social psychologists (Datan & Reese, 1977; Rappoport, 1977; Riegel, 1976a, 1976b). Briefly, the dialectical perspective posited by Riegel (1976b) focuses on the study of change. Moreover, it rejects the use of traditional constructs in psychological thinking, such as competencies, traits, and abilities. It is particularly critical of assessment approaches that purport to reflect such universal and stable properties, which are considered abstract reifications of more "concrete events and episodes which characterize human actions" (Riegel, 1976b, p. 354). Consequently, changes in humans can be apprehended only by studying concrete psychol-

Part of the findings reported in this chapter were made possible by a Gerontological Society Summer Research Fellowship (1976) awarded to the first author.

ogical events in their interactions with events internal and external to the organism. The dialectical perspective assigns less importance to homeostasis, emphasizing instead progressive changes brought about by inner and outer contradictions (Hultsch & Hickey, 1976; Riegel, 1976a). Thus,

> it deals with conflicts which create asynchronies within or between any two of four dimensions of development: inner-biological, individual-psychological, cultural-sociological, and outer-physical. Development aims at synchronizing progressions along different dimensions. (Hultsch & Hickey, 1978, p. 81)

Intrinsic to this study of change is the assumption of reciprocal causality, each dimension affecting the others and simultaneously being affected by them. Thus, unidirectional (and linear) causal models that focus on antecedent → consequent events are incomplete.

Though the dialectical perspective has been viewed as an irritant by some researchers in other disciplines, it is generally compatible with the values, if not always the activities, of researchers in the environment–behavior domain (Cvetkovich, 1977). General examples include the work of Barker (1968), Rapoport (1975), Tuan (1974), and Willems (1973).

The similarities between recent formulations in environment–aging relations and the dialectical perspective are most clearly reflected in the 1974 conference on the development of theory in environment and aging held at Kansas State University (Windley, Byerts, & Ernst, 1975). Ittelson (1975) traces the history of the conceptualizations of person–environment relations, noting the historical origins of discrete characterizations of "man-the-responder" and "man-the-creator." He notes early 20th century behaviorism and its environmental extremism, as well as what modern-day trait and self-theorists owe to earlier faculty psychology. He believes in the inseparability of the person and the environment and implies reciprocal causation in his discussion of feedback models. Ittelson (1975) advocates that an adequate theory will

> take as its starting point the inseparability of man and environment and will recognize that neither man nor environment is ever encountered, nor can ever be defined, independent of the other. Such a theory will inevitably contain elements inimical to current approaches both in behavioral sciences and in the design field. (p. 8)

Broadly speaking, the theory that Ittelson calls for might easily be couched within a dialectical perspective.

But how compatible are existing theories of environment–aging relations with a dialectical point of view? It is helpful here to consider two of the most influential theories in this area, Kahana's person–environment congruence model and Lawton's adaptation theory. Our review of these theories is brief, and the reader is advised to consult Kahana (1975) and Lawton (1975a, 1977) for more detail.

Person–Environment Congruence Model

Kahana's congruence model characterizes the optimal environment as one that offers maximal congruence between individual needs and environmental press. Adaptive behavior is the mechanism through which such fit is achieved, and congruence leads to a sense of well-being, the primary outcome variable. Kahana states that relations between person–environment fit and well-being can be tested empirically in a cross-sectional study but that her congruence-adaptation model can be tested only in longitudinal studies. Study of adaptive strategies through time is, of course, consistent with the dialectical perspective, as would be any truly developmental perspective.

Kahana proposes three sets of alternate models: The first set considers instances in which mismatch is cumulative and continuous; the second set considers instances in which mismatch is problematic or detrimental beyond a certain critical point or range; the third is the optimal congruence model (based upon Helson's adaptation model), in which complete congruence is considered harmful and moderate deviations have positive effects. (Alternate conceptions of directionality are also posited within each set, e.g., zero difference, one-directional difference, two-dimensional difference.) The first two models or sets are based on a tension-reduction model in which mismatch has negative outcomes, while congruence is satisfying and represents the desired state of affairs. As such, they are not dialectical in orientation. The dialectical view places a positive value on asynchronies as sources of change and growth. Thus, it is a view more compatible with the optimal-congruence model. Either too much mismatch or complete congruence produces a negative outcome. A dialectical theorist might bristle at the assumption that complete congruence is ever more than a momentary occurrence (if that) or that extreme need-press mismatch is necessarily detrimental to the individual. But overall, the dialectical view acknowledges the progressive flux of synchronic and asynchronic relations between inner (biological, psychological) and outer (culture-sociological, physical) events.

Lawton's Adaptation Theory

Lawton and Nahemow (1973) elaborated a model of adaptation and aging based on an interactionist view of behavior (B = (f)P × E). "Competence" represents the person element (P) of the formula, and "environmental press," the environmental element (E). Adaptive behavior is the behavioral outcome (B) of interest (outer criterion), though Lawton also recognizes internal outcomes (level of morale, happiness). Competence is defined as a profile of a person's capacities, including biological health, sensation-perception, motor behavior, and cognition (Lawton, 1975a). Environmental press is observationally defined as challenges or "demands" that activate behavior in people. The theory specifies that those who operate at higher levels of competence can adapt to a wider range of environmental press and have greater likelihood of experiencing favorable adaptive outcomes. Those of lower competence will experience a greater range of press in negative terms, exhibiting a narrower range of adaptive behavior. This is but a sketch of Lawton's theory, and the reader should consult the Lawton and Nahemow (1973) and Lawton (1975a; 1977) treatises for a thorough review.

Lawton's adaptation theory has several dialectical elements. Competence and environmental press are presented as transactional terms. Lawton readily acknowledges that many aspects of the individual and of the environment are not accounted for in the theory. He takes pains to eliminate those individual characteristics that are less dynamic or too static, such as needs, traits, and so forth. Such constructs are viewed as being of unclear adaptive quality. The model delineates individual (or individual-psychological, inner-biological, to use Riegel's terms) processes to a greater extent than environmental press. The exclusion of greater emphasis on cultural-sociological and outer physical factors might be considered a dialectical weakness. In fact, Katz's (1975) critique of Lawton's theory strikes at a number of omissions of a dialectical nature; these include (a) the failure to focus on the dynamic nature of the environment and environmental changes; (b) the failure to specify the importance of time frames of special significance to older persons' behaviors; (c) the issue of how and by whom environments for older people are shaped and managed; and (d) questions regarding how societal attitudes toward older persons enter into the model.

A Dialectical Taxonomy of Environmental Attributes

This section attempts to address what Katz (1975) suggested was a significant weakness in both the Kahana and Lawton perspectives, that is, the failure to focus on the dynamic nature of the physical environment and on the dimensions of environmental change.

Some attempts have been made to assign dimensions to environments. Lawton and Nahemow (1973) and Frederiksen (1972) summarized several investigators' efforts to develop environmental taxonomies. Taxonomies ranged from social and psychological characteristics of settings (Krause, 1970; Pace, 1968; Sells, 1963) to physical attributes of settings (Harrigan, 1974; Lawton & Kleban, 1971), and some used a combination of both social and physical attributes (Anderson, 1963; Taietz, 1970). Notwithstanding considerable work here, each taxonomy was developed to suit the unique needs of the investigator and lacks empirical refinement and theoretical consensus (Lawton & Nahemow, 1973).

A central issue in taxonomic development is the distinction between taxonomies of *attributes* of environments and taxonomies of *environments* themselves. Taxonomies (or categories) of physical environments include schools, churches, commercial buildings, government buildings, neighborhoods, or on a smaller scale, kitchens, classrooms, and corridors. Attributes of environments include potential for privacy or social interaction, level of sensory stimulation and comfort, or degree of accessibility. We are arguing that a taxonomy that categorizes attributes of settings rather than settings themselves is more likely to suggest research questions relevant to designing environments in which people can function competently. Further, this taxonomy combines social and physical components rather than treating them separately. The rationale for this combination is threefold. First, as Ittelson (1970) has pointed out, the *environment surrounds*; it enfolds the individual, and therefore behavior cannot be studied separately from environment. Since environments are always multidimensional, it makes little sense to talk simply of categories of environments. For example, it is difficult to imagine how one would study the interaction of food preparation and "kitchen" defined as such. Kitchen must be defined by attributes such as light level, accessible distance to equipment, or square feet of work space.

Second, environment–behavior interactions *change over time*. Environmental attributes are more sensitive to change than are categories of environments. For example, bedrooms often become studies or sewing rooms when children move away, though such shifts in function are usually slow to occur. Attributes such as lighting level, or potential for privacy, may fluctuate hourly. To study environment–behavior interaction over time, dimensions of environment must keep pace with changes in behavior.

A third point concerns *scale of environment*. Taxonomies of environments are scale specific, that is, categories at the scale of housing are not the same as categories for neighborhoods, districts, or cities. For example, when studying the mobility patterns of the elderly across different environmental scales, it is difficult to link these patterns to categories of environment because of continually shifting frames of reference. Attributes, on the other hand, cut across all scales and all categories of environment. Degree of environmental accessibility may apply to architectural barriers for a dwelling unit as well as for the neighborhood or the city.

Because attributes are more easily linked to behavior, they accommodate more adequately three dialectical concerns: capturing reciprocal interaction of person and environment, identifying synchrony-asynchrony of such interactions, and being sensitive to change of interactions over time.

The 11 environmental attributes defined below are based on the work of Brill (1970), Spivak (1973), Steele (1973), and Weisman (1978). After each attribute is defined briefly, critical questions that need to be addressed in research are raised, followed by a short review of research exemplifying how the attributes relate to various aspects of elderly behavior that lead to critical issues for research in the 1980s. The list of attributes is neither exhaustive nor orthogonal. Each attribute can be assessed either objectively or subjectively. We agree with Lawton (1978) that since subjective and objective assessments of environment are correlated, both should be employed in aging/environment research.

Sensory Stimulation

What should the quality and intensity of environmental stimuli be? Research on sensory processes shows that as a person ages, the amount of environmental information received by the organism is reduced. Lawton and Nahemow (1973) indicate that each sensory domain (e.g., visual acuity, dark adaptation, auditory threshold, olfactory sensitivity) shows an age decrement. In addition, Eisdorfer (1968) has found that environmental information appears to be processed more slowly with increasing age. Research completed by Pastalan, Mautz, and Merrill (1973) mechanically simulated age-related sensory decrements. Research assistants wore specially prepared eye lenses and ear plugs and recorded their experiences and reactions as they negotiated settings common to older people. Researchers experienced a reduction and distortion of environmental information leading to increased cautiousness, disorientation, and decreased speed of activity. Elderly people often experience difficulty with ambiguous and intense stimuli, such as

those encountered in large buildings or while driving. Redundant cueing (presenting information via more than one sense modality) has been employed by designers as compensation—for example, allowing smells from the kitchen to penetrate the dwelling unit in addition to sounding a bell or buzzer announcing meal times. An important research question then becomes, To what extent and in what ways can environmental stimulation help to compensate for age changes?

Legibility

How can the organization and clarity of an environment be improved? Legibility is the degree to which a setting possesses spatial organization and incorporates the components of identity and structure (Lynch, 1960), that is, the extent to which a setting is perceptually understandable and facilitates orientation, predictability, and direction finding. Although Lynch's two characteristics of environmental legibility (identity and structure) were identified some 20 years ago, little research has been done with these characteristics in environments for the elderly. The degree to which an individual can identify and structure environmental components to form a functional internal representation or image is influenced by the way in which that information is packaged and portrayed to the organism, as well as how much incoming information the organism is equipped to receive and process from the environment. Given the elderly's reduced sensory capacity, they may receive a less differentiated image. This might lead to disorientation or fear in a setting resulting from inability to predict outcomes from certain actions. Environments that lack identifiable components, such as streets in a city or distinct hallways in a building, and that lack cohesiveness are likely to increase nonadaptive behavior.

Regnier (1975) found that services perceived to be within a 3-to 6-block radius from the dwelling were utilized more often than those 6 blocks away. This relatively small radial boundary is thought to reflect the shrinking home range of the elderly discussed by Stea (1970). He also found in a sample of elderly apartment dwellers in San Francisco that the size and shape of cognitive maps of neighborhoods drawn from memory were related to the use of neighborhood services. Ecological characteristics such as topography, traffic patterns, land-use patterns, bus routes, district designations, population density, and perceived crime rate affected the size and shape of neighborhood maps drawn by elderly residents. Thompson (1965), Stea (1969), and Lee (1970) concluded that for a nonelderly population, the following factors affected neighborhood cognition: (a) the relative attractiveness of trip origins, (b) the kind and number of barriers separating two points, (c) the familiarity of certain trips and areas, (d) the magnitude of the geographical distance between two points, and (e) the attractiveness of the connecting path between these points. The degree to which these factors affect the behavior of older people should occupy researchers in the 1980s.

Comfort

What environmental conditions contribute to subjective feelings of comfort and ease in task performance? Comfort includes the presence or absence of luminous, acoustic, thermal, and anthropometric properties of a setting. The review below illustrates only temperature and lighting.

Although there is consensus by most researchers that metabolic rate and sensory acuity diminish with age, research findings are inconclusive regarding the sensitivity of older people to high and low temperatures. Kenshalo (1977) found that no age differences occurred between old and young subjects in detection of temperature differences. In a study by Rohles (1969) 72% of his elderly sample judged 76°F to be comfortable while in a sedentary state. However, data from most such studies were obtained under laboratory conditions from relatively healthy older subjects. Krag and Kountz (1950) argue that although thermal comfort criteria may change very little with advancing age, the ability of the elderly temperature-regulating system to cope with extreme temperatures appears to be impaired.

Because of age-related visual pathology such as increasing lens opacity and lens thickening and yellowing, discomfort, eye strain, and irritation are experienced by many older people (Corso, 1971). Pastalan et al. (1973) have found that daily tasks ordinarily require three times as much lighting for an average older person as for the average 20-year-old. With an increase in lighting level, the probability of glare becomes greater. Wolf (1960) has demonstrated that sensitivity to glare for a sample of 80-year-olds is nearly twice that of 20-year-olds. Light–dark adaptation poses additional irritation and discomfort for many elderly. Koncelik (1976) noted that the adaptation rate for most 70-year-olds is nearly twice that for 20-year-olds. Two important research questions emerge here: In what ways do lighting and temperature conditions combine to produce problematic adjustment for older people engaging in different activities? What is the range of adaptation possible for older people in these conditions over time?

Privacy

To what extent do the features of a setting allow a person to control unwanted visual and acoustical stimuli from others and to others? Much of the theoretical foundation in this area has been developed by Altman (1974), Pastalan (1970), and Westin (1970). Altman considers privacy an interpersonal boundary regulation process in which the physical environment controls inputs from others and outputs to others. While Westin classifies privacy phenomena into four states (solitude, intimacy, anonymity, and reserve), Pastalan regards privacy as a manifestation of territoriality. Almost all researchers agree that the attainment of privacy is essential to maintaining positive self-regard, self-reflection, and autonomy and to providing emotional release. Lawton and Bader (1970) found among a sample of 839 subjects of varying ages that younger subjects were more likely to want private rooms if they were currently living in a private room and if they were living in the community rather than in an institution. Schwartz (1969) found among institutionalized aged that the desire for privacy correlated highly with length of time in the institutional setting. Lawton, Liebowitz, and Charon (1970) discovered among a small sample of mentally impaired elderly that both privacy behavior and mobility increased after the ward was remodeled from an open-bed arrangement to private rooms for each patient. Koncelik (1976) argues that the most important private space among institutionalized elderly is the resident's room, which he estimates should constitute 80% of the total rooms in a nursing home. Building on the ideas of Pressey (1973), Koncelik adds that for maximum privacy, resident rooms should be so located in a house-porch-street configuration that the semiprivate areas (e.g., lounges) all lie between the residents' rooms and the public areas (e.g., hallways). Some critical research questions for the future include the following: What is the relative importance of visual versus aural privacy to older people engaging in everyday behavior? What specific environmental arrangements are perceived by older people to be most effective in enhancing privacy in varied settings?

Adaptability

How easily can a setting be rearranged to accommodate new or different patterns of behavior? Older persons may require changes because of developmental of health factors. Others may find satisfaction in rearranging their settings to provide a different view. Beattie (1970) and Lawton (1970a) have argued that there are significant environmental factors that could be manipulated to help compensate for age-related changes. However, little research has gone beyond the theoretical stage here. Howell (1976) discovered in a study of elderly in congregate housing that some apartment designs accommodated large pieces of furniture more easily than did others. Carp (1966), in her study of Victoria Plaza, found that a movable storage closet enabled many elderly residents to alter their apartments to accommodate a wide range of functions. Windley (1977) found in 30 case studies of elderly people living in single-family dwellings that many rooms doubled for activities not originally intended and that many adaptations had been made in order to support increased dependency. Considerable work is needed to determine what kinds of environmental adaptations are successful in accommodating the most common needs of older persons.

Control (Territoriality)

To what degree does an environment facilitate personalization and convey individual ownership of space? How much jurisdiction do people actually have over spaces they use? The most comprehensive contribution on this attribute is the work of Newman (1972), who related such environmental characteristics as resident density, building height, building shape, surveillance potential, and corridor design to incidence of vandalism and crime, social isolation, sense of jurisdiction, feelings of security, and general appearance and upkeep of public housing. For example, Newman demonstrated that the fewer the tenants on a single floor, the more responsible they will be in questioning or reporting strangers. While Lipman (1967) found among residents in a home for the aged considerable verbal and physical defensive behavior toward chairs in a dayroom, DeLong (1967) discovered that territorial defense occurred less often among patients with private rooms. Sommer (1970) discussed the conflicting territorial needs of staff and residents in an institutional setting for older people. To reduce the incidence of territorial conflict, Koncelik (1976) argues for a biaxial room arrangement in two-patient rooms in nursing homes rather than an asymmetrical arrangement. The consensus among most researchers is that defensive behavior would probably decline with the provision of private space and room to display personal effects, and also with a reduction in the size and

an increase in the number of social-interaction spaces. This is still a research question in need of verification.

Sociality

To what extent do features of an environment encourage or discourage social contact among people? The study of the sociality of settings was pioneered by Osmond (1959), who developed the sociofugal-sociopetal dichotomy. By definition, sociofugal environments discourage social interaction, while sociopetal settings allow people to converse and interact at will. In a sample of 15 congregate housing sites, Lawton (1970b) found a correlation between a large number of building-centered social activities and greater proximity to resources in the larger community. Increased social activity was also found to be related to better health of the residents, a greater number of available social spaces in the building, and the degree to which tenants left their apartment doors ajar. Rosow (1967) found that social interaction among elderly apartment dwellers was a function of proportion of age peers in the setting. Friedman (1966) and Lawton and Simon (1968) found that residents in housing for the elderly are more likely to interact socially and maintain friendships with people living on their own floors and with those living next door than with those located farther away. Ittelson, Proshansky, and Rivlin (1970) found among institutionalized patients that social interaction increased as the number of beds in a room decreased, and Sommer (1970) found that social interaction increased in the lounge of a care facility when the elderly residents were seated around several small square tables rather than in straight rows against the walls. Lawton et al. (1970) discovered that when a senile patients' ward was remodeled to approximate a house-porch-street configuration (where patients' private rooms adjoined a semipublic space adjacent to a public corridor), mobility into public areas increased. Further research should consider the relative impact of population density, propinquity, spatial configuration, and furniture arrangement on social interaction in both institutional and noninstitutional environments for older people.

Accessibility

There are two interrelated concepts underlying the attribute of accessibility: the ease with which a person can traverse from Point A to Point B in a given setting, and the degree to which more stationary objects or products can be manipulated. Newcomer (1973) found among urban elderly that distance to services affected service utilization. Regnier (1975) argues, however, that other environmental characteristics temper the effects of distance on accessibility: topography, crime rate, land use, percentage of elderly, public transportation, ethnic identification, traffic patterns, and district designations. Schwartz (1975) states that the provision of signs, special lighting, and texture cues to warn elderly housing residents of dead-end corridors and approaching staircases would significantly increase accessibility and reduce general ambiguity. Paying particular attention to floor materials would eliminate hazardous conditions and increase ambulation by those in walkers and wheelchairs. Windley (1977) found among elderly living in a single-family dwellings that improperly designed stairways and thresholds in doorways made some areas inaccessible. Housing features, such as kitchen cupboards and bathroom fixtures, that required extensive bending and reaching or excessive muscular strength also significantly decreased accessibility. Koncelik (1976) has suggested excellent and innovative solutions to increase accessibility in nursing-home settings for the elderly. Future researchers should develop an operational definition of accessibility that would account for the cumulative effects of multiple barriers in any given setting. Perhaps the simple enumeration of barriers perceived by a sample of older people engaging in everyday tasks could serve as an index of accessibility for a setting.

Density

To what degree is a space perceived to be crowded either in absolute numbers of people, or in the proportion of elderly in a given setting? The classic study on the proportions of elderly in housing is Rosow's (1967) study, in which degree of social interaction and housing satisfaction among elderly apartment dwellers was a function of the proportion (about 60%) of age peers in the setting. Other researchers have obtained similar findings (Bultena & Wood, 1969; Messer, 1967). Kahana and Kahana (1970) found that institutionalized elderly placed on age-integrated wards improved more in social interaction than those placed on age-segregated wards. Barker and Barker (1961) demonstrated that when small-town environments are underpopulated, both in absolute population size and in number of available behavior settings, older people are forced into more active community participation. Important research questions here are What are the most effective ways to define population per square unit of space? Is there any significant difference in population per square mile, per acre, per block, or per dwelling

unit, in their respective abilities to predict behavior of older people? In what ways other than age proportion can social density be defined?

Meaning

To what degree does a setting hold meaning for people? Meaning is often symbolically attributed to concrete features of environments such as spires on religious facilities, McDonald's golden arches, or styles of buildings from times past. Environmental meaning also may be socially rooted, such as in memories of growing up in a special kind of house or neighborhood. Meaning or attachment to environment is one of the most elusive of attributes and is consequently difficult to measure. Moreover, almost no empirical work has been done in this area. In 30 case studies of elderly living in single-family dwellings, Windley (1977) found a high attachment to the dwelling, with length of residence the most explanatory variable. Physical settings are inseparable from life experiences and provide a historic backdrop from which older people evaluate current and future life events (Howell, 1979). To sort out those significant characteristics of settings most important to the development of meaning will require further empirical work.

Quality (Aesthetics)

This attribute deals with the aesthetic appeal of a setting from the user's point of view. It is well documented that architects' and planners' aesthetic criteria often differ substantially from those of the user (Altman, 1973; Goodman, 1971). Designers normally apply aesthetic principles such as rhythm, balance, mass-void relations, novelty, and so forth, to the geometry or configuration of a building, whereas users' judgments are more simplistic and varied. Nondesigners are more apt to judge buildings in terms of maintenance and upkeep, the presence or absence of vegetation, and size of apartment, and they depend on prior style experiences in their preference for new settings. To date there is no agreed-upon list of aesthetic principles that adequately assess the quality of designed environments for the elderly.

Criteria for Effective Functioning

The taxonomy we have just presented has some unique features that make it well suited to the study of environment–behavior relations of older persons. Each attribute provides a context for framing the interaction of internal individual (biological, psychological) and environmental (social, physical) processes. Each attribute also allows for both observer- and subject-based assessment to be made of these interactions at various levels. Foremost, in our view, is that the taxonomy provides a framework of some breadth for understanding the integrated aspects of behavioral responding. The primary rationale for the selection of these attributes (though not exclusive of other possible attributes) is that each of them suggests an aspect for understanding competent functioning. That is, each attribute frames research questions concerned with *how well* older individuals are getting along. Each provides a point of orientation for this primary concern, and yet each orients one to a specifically different type of individual–environmental interaction.

What specifically does the framework offer for developing specific criteria of effective functioning? How would such criteria differ from criteria developed by traditional approaches? To answer these questions, it is necessary to review illustrative conceptual and operational definitions of competence. At least two reasons justify such a review. First, such definitions guide the collection of information and thus determine the context of data collection. Second, many of these definitions serve as guiding criteria for intervention efforts to improve the competent functioning of older persons (Baltes & Labouvie, 1973; Baltes & Willis, 1977).

The criteria developed by the so-called "internal antecedents" approach (Goldfried & D'Zurilla, 1969) are perhaps most contrary to a dialectical view of competence. That approach places primary stress on intraorganismic processes and products as determinants of the production of effective behavior. Criteria of competence, from such a point of view, include such processes and abilities as reality orientation, active information search, frustration tolerance (Caplan, 1963; Moos & Tsu, 1977), adaptive flexibility (Adelson & Kalis, 1970), information processing (Insel and Moos, 1974), and cognitive and emotional locus of control (Caplan, 1963; White, 1960). These criteria have been derived largely from studies of "adaptive failures" and have focused on minimum standards for the integrative functioning of psychological and biological systems within the individual. The internal antecedent approach also encompasses phenomenological criteria, of course, where people's own standards or requirements for goal fulfillment are considered crucial for determining their own level of competent functioning (Lawton, 1975a).

Normative criteria have been heavily relied on also (Lawton, 1975b)—that is, the extent to which behavior meets society's expectations. Adopting a greater social

Figure 30-1. Steep and lengthy steps to the front entry make access to dwelling unit difficult.

flavor, criteria of the "normative approach" include social products and achievements (Phillips & Cowitz, 1953), social cognition (Flavell, Botkin, & Fry, 1968; O'Sullivan, Guilford, & de Mille, 1965), and role-enactment, including amount of time and energy spent in role activity (Sarbin, 1970). Socially oriented researchers have discussed dysfunctional conduct occurring as a result of being "ecologically misplaced," particularly when the individual has "unanswered or incorrectly answered ecological questions" (Sarbin, 1970, p. 94). For Sarbin, the criterion for effective responding resides in the "normative ecology," where the individual asks of self, "How well am I doing, enacting, or participating?" Others adopt criteria according to classifications of rule-breaking behavior (Goffman, 1963; Scheff, 1970).

The "interactionist approach" has generated criteria most clearly consistent with a dialectical position. This is because it combines behavioral and situational contexts of adaptive responding. Behavioral contexts are quite specific, often represented by specific classes of situations (Scheidt & Schaie, 1978). Interactionists have typically sought environmental or situational criteria of response effectiveness by advocating analysis of behavioral requirements of situations that must be negotiated by the individual. Response evaluation is based on how well these requirements are met, usually assigned by knowledgeable peers (Goldfried & D'Zurrilla, 1969), or on self-evaluations of those on whom assessments are desired (Scheidt & Schaie, 1978).

Thus, the most vexing question for researchers of the 1980s continues to be one that was asked but that has never reached clear resolution during the last decade: What is functionally adaptive or effective re-

Figure 30-3. Stair-riser height is divided in half by addition of intermediate-height wooden platform.

Figure 30-2. Excessive height of risers (11½ in., or 29 cm) and short treads make basement stairs dangerous and difficult to negotiate.

Figure 30-4. Discontinuous sidewalks hinder access to site for residents in low-rise elderly housing.

Figure 30-5. Extended toilet seat permits easy egress from fixture, but improper location of handrail makes leverage and grasping difficult.

sponding? As Mechanic (1962) and Lumsden (1975) have indicated, behavior has long-run as well as short-run significance; what is viewed as adaptive at one point in time may turn out to be ultimately maladaptive at another point. Also, actors and evaluators of behavior, when different persons, view action from different perspectives and thus "may not always agree on the validity of the label for a specific response outcome" (Lumsden, 1975, p. 217). Mechanic (1962) concludes that the pursuit of criteria for functionally adaptive responding poses a serious but perhaps not a soluble challenge, one that serves as "a sensitizing approach rather than a clearly defined and refined set of ideas that may be operationalized effectively" (p. 53).

The troublesome aspects of multiple perspectives for evaluating response effectiveness will continue to be problematic so long as the search for a narrow definitive set of criteria continues. We believe that a dialectical perspective, necessarily encompassing a wider

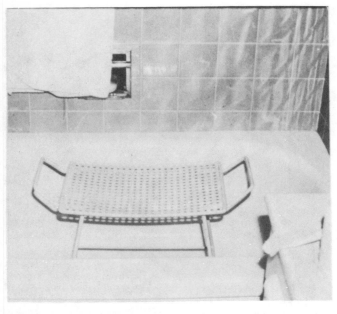

Figure 30-6. Portable seat in tub aids entry and egress and permits rinsing without being totally submerged in the water.

Figure 30-7. Many kitchens pose storage problems for those unable to reach top shelves without standing on stools.

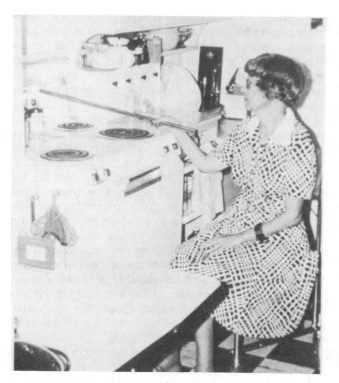

Figure 30-8. Many kitchen fixtures become inaccessible when ambulation is restricted.

specific determination of older person–environment situations that place demands on adaptive strategies but not to the point of overwhelming the individual. Such ranges and classes of asynchronies effectively encourage the active exercise of adaptive strategies, while simultaneously providing feedback on their success or failure. (This closely parallels what Lawton has termed the "zone of maximum potential.") Adjustments made by older persons in response to concrete asynchronies (exemplified by two taxonomic attributes presented in the next section) illustrate the flavor of this approach.

Taxonomic Attributes and Competent Functioning: Illustrative Examples

Two attributes (of the 11 presented)—accessibility and adaptability—illustrate the utility of the taxonomy for examining competence-environment relations for

range of criteria for response evaluation, is to the advantage of researchers here. It suggests alternatives to status quo research in this area. For example, the dialectical approach put forward by Riegel (1976a) rejects so-called entity or trait conceptions of abilities and competencies. Thus competency is better viewed as the adequacy with which older people have been able to resolve the concrete, momentary crises resulting from asynchronies between any of the four developmental planes. Such adjustments would be continually occurring, and the processes or strategies mediating resolution of such crises would themselves be modified over time. Such a view is consistent with Riegel's (1976b) premise that a dialectical approach emphasizes "continuous change brought about through the successive interaction of concrete events over time" (p. 394). Riegel does not completely reject homeostatic states or equilibrium but rather views the relations of inner (inner-biological, individual-psychological) and outer (social-cultural, outer-physical) dialectics as ever unsteady over the long course. In our view, a central task for researchers investigating well-being and competence is to identify what might be called "healthy asynchronies." Varying with the population of interest, this identification would entail a context-

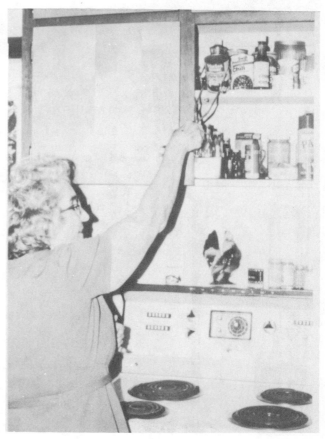

Figure 30-9. Easily purchased devices such as these tongs aid in retrieving hard-to-reach items.

older persons. These examples are derived from the case studies of older people conducted by Windley (1977) and mentioned earlier.

Two groups of 15 elderly persons each were sampled; the first group comprised persons who were about to move from their single-family dwelling because they felt they could no longer live independently in their current environment. The second group consisted of those who at one time contemplated a similar move but instead made alterations in their dwelling unit in order to remain. (It should be mentioned that although this discussion focuses primarily on physical environmental factors, lack of environmental support was not the only reason for moving. Financial problems, desire to live closer to family, and pressure from family were other factors mentioned.) The names for

Figure 30-10. A hospital cart on wheels replaces a section of base cabinet to permit easy access to needed kitchen materials.

each group were obtained through two county home-extension agents who were well acquainted with local elderly residents. Each respondent was then interviewed in a 2- to 3-hour session that included a personal tour of the dwelling, where environmental problems, as well as solutions, were identified and photographed.

Figures 30-1 and 30-2 provide an example of restricted access to and within a dwelling unit. Because of reduced muscular strength and balance, the elderly resident cannot negotiate these stairs unaided. Moreover, elderly friends are reluctant to visit her for similar reasons. Figure 30-3 shows how one resident improved dwelling access by dividing an otherwise high stair riser (11½ in., or 29 cm) in half by the addition of a wooden platform. Other elderly residents in the complex followed suit by making the same adaptation. Figure 30-4 shows how discontinuous side-walks in a low-rise housing project for the elderly hinder site accessibility for those in wheelchairs and walkers. Neighborly visiting from one complex to another is severely curtailed because of routes perceived by elderly residents to be inaccessible.

Figure 30-5 shows how the extention of a toilet seat can aid the egress process for those with reduced muscular strength in legs and torso. The handrail, however, is located too far back to act as a point of leverage for someone in a sitting position. Figure 30-6 illustrates one resident's tub adaptation. With the use of a detachable shower head, body rinsing is performed more easily while seated on this portable plastic-coated stool than during total immersion in the water. The mesh fabric allows for adequate drainage of water from the stool. Figures 30-7, 30-8, and 30-9 show kitchen accessibility problems encountered by many elderly. Being confined to a wheelchair or experiencing bending and reaching problems makes it necessary to employ adaptational aids such as the stick (to operate the oven) in Figure 30-8 and the tongs in Figure 30-9. Additional kitchen adaptations are shown in Figures 30-10 and 30-11. An ordinary hospital cart on wheels has replaced a bank of drawers (Figure 30-10), which permits easy storage and access of kitchen materials. Figure 30-11 illustrates a different kitchen-storage adaptation for a wheelchair resident, where dishes and cookware are placed one item deep at an accessible height, thus eliminating the need for frequent bending and reaching.

Although the figures show unsystematically derived examples of problems encountered by many of the elderly, environmental accessibility might be rendered systematically operational simply by counting the number of barriers encountered in a specific environment by a given subject during normal daily activities.

Figure 30-11. Dishes and cookware are within easy reach for wheelchair-bound resident.

The adaptability of the setting could be determined by the number of barriers easily eliminated and perhaps by the cost of such intervention. It should be clear that competence can be defined only in an environmental context and that person and context are in a continuous reciprocal interaction.

Implications for Future Research

In conclusion, we believe that a dialectical perspective has numerous implications for the conceptualization and conduct of environment–behavior research at several levels, including what should be studied and how information might be interpreted. We have attempted to show that the dialectical perspective is a broad, value-based world view for thinking about how

to theorize about behavioral events. Developmental and social psychological theoreticians have discussed these functions extensively (Altman, 1979; Baltes & Cornelius, 1977; Hultsch & Hickey, 1978; Rappoport, 1977). Researchers on competent functioning should be aware of these broad implications, which affect both content and explanatory features of research (Overton & Reese, 1973). In the previous pages, we have tried to illustrate how these concerns are of importance to environment–aging researchers in particular.

More specifically, the dialectical perspective provides an inherent conceptualization of environment. The four levels of events specified by Riegel (1976a) may be usefully conceived as four levels of environment (inner-biological, individual-psychological, social-cultural, outer-physical), though the boundaries are somewhat arbitrary. This conception prescribes a basic taxonomy that might be used to classify much research in the environment-aging field and by virtue of this, could sensitize us to currently existing gaps in our knowledge about the interaction of the four environmental planes. For example, Lawton's general theory of competence might be viewed as emphasizing synchronic and asynchronic relations among three dialectical planes—inner-biological and individual-psychological, which define competence, and the outerphysical, composed of environmental press (attributes). Further, much research in aging focuses on sensory deficits experienced by older people (inner-biological) and the asynchronies such changes imply in negotiating the everyday environment (outer-physical, social-cultural), with concomitant impact on self-esteem (individual-psychological).

It has been suggested that the dialectical perspective gives direction to the sequence one uses to establish the validity of empirical inferences when conducting research (Hultsch & Hickey, 1978). Specifically, in this view, one attempts first to satisfy external or ecological validity concerns; this is followed by an equal but later concern with internal validity issues. This reversal of the traditional sequence of validity concerns (Campbell & Stanley, 1966) has strong implications for environment–aging research. Those interested in assessing the well-being or competent functioning of the elderly might be concerned first with adequately representing the range of socio-physical environments relevant to everyday experiences of the selected elderly population and then with adequately identifying the range of functional-dysfunctional behaviors displayed in these settings (Scheidt & Schaie, 1978). This environment–behavior nexus would provide an ecologically valid taxonomic framework, with cells representing major environment–behavior attribute combinations.

Further, such taxonomic derivations should derive from time-sampling observational strategies, as well as "participant dialogues," involving the ongoing reflections and judgments of representatives of the population of interest. As in analytic induction (Denzin, 1970), the taxonomic framework would hopefully be educed to represent a model or grounded theory of adaptive behavior. Such an effort has not yet been made but is highly recommended for research in the 1980s.

Although much environment–behavior research recognizes a dialectical perspective, the research designs, data-gathering instruments, and methods of analysis are borrowed from traditional behavioral sciences. Traditional experimental design often links variables together artificially and separates "the variables controlling behavior from the fabric in which they are embedded, and this destroys the patterns of correlations between variables as they exist in natural situations" (Petrinovich, 1979, p. 375). Dependent measures are thus assumed to be unidirectional outcomes of independent influences. Because all environments are multidimensional, we recommend a multivariate approach to all research problems in which environmental attributes are combined with psychosocial dimensions of environments to predict behavioral outcomes. Such outcomes should then be monitored over time for their reciprocal effects on environmental attributes. We urge the use of more naturalistic methods in data collection, such as time-activity logs, behavior-setting analysis, and photographic recording of behavior. Such methods not only leave the setting intact but can be combined with more quantitative measures to triangulate or cross-validate measures, an often-suggested but heretofore neglected activity in the environment–behavior field.

We recommend an all-out effort to develop and refine a taxonomy of the physical and social environment. Few investigators have taken this challenge seriously. The taxonomy offered in this chapter serves as a beginning. Both self-evaluative and observer-based measures of these attributes are needed across the full range of environmental settings.

While there is disagreement about whether a dialectical perspective subsumes or stands alongside other theoretical perspectives, there is growing agreement that a dialectical model does not prescribe or necessitate new methodology (Baltes & Cornelius, 1977; Hultsch & Hickey, 1978); rather, dialectical thinking should have its biggest impact "at the level of synthesis, not analysis" (Cvetkovich, 1977, p. 689). Considerable past research in aging–environment relations could be reexamined dialectically. Studies that have focused on congruence might instead consider, in more detail, coping strategies of subjects during periods of incongruence. Finally, in studies in which patterns of behavior have emerged from sequential manipulations of environment, the reciprocal effects of those behaviors on environments should be studied. For excellent examples of this approach, see Sommer (1970) and Davis and Hathaway (1977).

REFERENCES

Adelson, D., & Kalis, B. L. *Community psychology and mental health: Perspectives and challenges.* Scranton, Pa.: Chandler, 1970.

Altman, I. Some perspectives on the study of man–environment phenomena. In W. F. E. Preiser (Ed.), *Environmental design research.* Stroudsberg, Pa.: Dowden, Hutchinson & Ross, 1973.

Altman, I. Privacy: A conceptual analysis. In D. H. Carson (Ed.), *Man–environment interactions: Evaluations and applications* (EDRA-5). Milwaukee, Wisc.: Environmental Design Research Association, 1974.

Altman, I. *Privacy regulation and social penetration: A dialectic analysis.* Division 8 presidential address at the meeting of the American Psychological Association, New York, September 1979.

Anderson, J. E. Environment and meaningful activity. In R. H. Williams, C. Tibbitts, & W. Donahue (Eds.), *Processes of aging* (Vol. 1). New York: Atherton, 1963.

Baltes, P. B., & Cornelius, S. W. The status of dialectics in developmental psychology: Theoretical orientation vs. scientific method. In N. Datan & H. Reese (Eds.), *Life-span developmental psychology: Dialectical perspectives of experimental research.* New York: Academic Press, 1977.

Baltes, P. B., & Labouvie, G. Adult development of intellectual performance: Description, explanation and modification. In C. Eisdorfer & M. P. Lawton (Eds.), *The psychology of adult development and aging.* Washington, D.C.: American Psychological Association, 1973.

Baltes, P. B., & Willis, S. Toward psychological theories of aging and development. In J. E. Birren & K. W. Schaie (Eds.), *Handbook of the psychology of aging.* New York: Van Nostrand Reinhold, 1977.

Barker, R. *Ecological psychology: Concepts and methods for studying the environment of human behavior.* Stanford, Calif.: Stanford University Press, 1968.

Barker, R. G., & Barker, L. S. The psychological ecology of old people in Midwest, Kansas and Yoredale, Yorkshire. *Journal of Gerontology*, 1961, *61*, 231–239.

Beattie, W. M. The design of supportive environments for the life span. *Gerontologist*, 1970, *10*, 190–193.

Brill, M. A systems approach to environmental design. *Environment: Planning & Design*, January 1970, pp. 38–41.

Bultena, G. L., & Wood, V. The American retirement community: Bane or blessing? *Journal of Gerontology*, 1969, *24*, 209–217.

Campbell, D. T., & Stanley, J. C. *Experimental and quasi-experimental designs for research.* Chicago: Rand McNally, 1966.

Caplan, G. Emotional crises. In A. Deutsch (Ed.), *The encyclopedia of mental health* (Vol. 2). New York: Franklin Watts, 1963.

Carp, F. M. *A future for the aged.* Austin: University of Texas Press, 1966.

Corso, J. F. Sensory processes and age effects in normal adults. *Journal of Gerontology*, 1971, *26*, 90–105.

Cvetkovich, G. Dialectical perspectives on empirical research. *Personality and Social Psychology Bulletin*, 1977, *3*, 688–696.

Datan, N., & Reese, H. *Life-span developmental psychology: Dialectical perspectives of experimental research.* New York: Academic Press, 1977.

Davis, A. J., & Hathaway, B. J. *Reciprocity in parent–child verbal interactions.* Paper presented at the meeting of the American Psychological Association, San Francisco, August 1977.

DeLong, A. *An outline of the environmental language of the older person.* Paper presented at the meeting of the American Association of Homes for the Aging, Atlanta, Georgia, November 1967.

Denzin, N. *The research act: A theoretical introduction to sociological methods.* Chicago: Aldine, 1970.

Eisdorfer, C. Arousal and performance: Experiments in verbal learning and a tentative theory. In G. Talland (Ed.), *Human aging and behavior.* New York: Academic Press, 1968.

Flavell, J. H., Botkin, P. J., & Fry, C. L. *The development of role-taking and communication skills in children.* New York: Wiley, 1968.

Frederiksen, N. Toward a taxonomy of situations. *American Psychologist*, 1972, *27*, 114–123.

Friedman, E. P. Spatial proximity and social interaction in a home for the aged. *Journal of Gerontology*, 1966, *21*, 566–570.

Goffman, E. *Stigma: Notes on the management of spoiled identity.* Englewood Cliffs, N.J., Prentice-Hall, 1963.

Goldfried, M. R., & D'Zurilla, T. A behavioral-analytic model for assessing competence. In C. D. Spielberger (Ed.), *Current topics in clinical and community psychology* (Vol. 1). New York: Academic Press, 1969.

Goodman, R. *After the planners.* New York: Simon & Schuster, 1971.

Harrigan, J. E. Human factors information taxonomy: Fundamental human factors applications for architectural programs. *Human Factors*, 1974, *16*, 432–440.

Howell, S. *Shared spaces in housing for the elderly.* Design Evaluation Project, Massachusetts Institute of Technology, October 1976.

Howell, S. *Environments as hypotheses in human aging research.* Paper presented at the meeting of the American Psychological Association, New York, September 1979.

Hultsch, D. F., & Hickey, T. External validity in the study of human development: Theoretical and methodological issues. *Human Development*, 1978, *21*, 76–91.

Insel, P., & Moos, R. The social environment. In P. Insel & R. Moos (Eds.), *Health and the social environment.* Lexington, Mass.: Lexington Books, 1969.

Insel, P. M., & Moos R. Psychological environments: Expanding the scope of human ecology. *American Psychologist*, 1974, *29*, 179–188.

Ittelson, W. H. *The perception of the large-scale environment.* Paper presented to the New York Academy of Sciences, New York, April 1970.

Ittelson, W. H. Some issues facing a theory of environment and behavior. In P. Windley, T. Byerts, & F. Ernst (Eds.), *Theory development in environment and aging.* Washington, D.C.: Gerontological Society, 1975.

Ittelson, W. H., Proshansky, H. M., & Rivlin, L. G. Bedroom size and social interaction of the psychiatric ward. *Environment and Behavior*, 1970, *2*, 255–270.

Kahana, B., & Kahana, E. Changes in mental status of elderly patients in age-integrated and age-segregated hospital milieus. *Journal of Abnormal Psychology*, 1970, *75*, 177–181.

Kahana, E. A congruence model of person-environment interaction. In P. Windley, T. Byerts, & F. Ernst (Eds.), *Theory development in environment and aging.* Washington, D.C.: Gerontological Society, 1975.

Katz, R. A discussion of Powell Lawton's paper on "Competence, environmental press, and the adaptation of older people." In P. Windley, T. Byerts, & F. Ernst (Eds.), *Theory development in environment and aging.* Washington, D.C.: Gerontological Society, 1975.

Kenshalo, D. R. Age changes in touch, vibration, temperature, kinesthesis and pain sensitivity. In Birren, J. E., & Schaie, K. W. (Eds.), *Handbook of the psychology of aging.* New York: Van Nostrand Reinhold, 1977.

Koncelik, J. A. *Designing the open nursing home.* Stroudsberg, Pa.: Dowden, Hutchinson & Ross, 1976.

Krag, C. L., & Kountz, W. B. Stability of body function in the aged. *Journal of Gerontology*, 1950, *5*, 227–235.

Krause, M. S. Use of social situations for research purposes. *American Psychologist*, 1970, *25*, 748–753.

Lawton, M. P. Assessment, integration and environments for the elderly. *Gerontologist*, 1970, *10*, 38–46. (a)

Lawton, M. P. Public behavior of older people in congregate housing. In J. Archea & C. Eastman (Eds.), *Proceedings of the 2nd Annual Environmental Design Research Association Conference.* Pittsburgh, Pa., October 1970, pp. 372–379. (b)

Lawton, M. P. Competence, environmental press and the adaptation of older people. In P. Windley, T. Byerts, & F. G. Ernst (Eds.), *Theory development in environment and aging.* Washington, D.C.: Gerontological Society, 1975. (a)

Lawton, M. P. *Planning and managing housing for the elderly.* New York: Wiley, 1975. (b)

Lawton, M. P. The impact of the environment on aging and behavior. In J. Birren & K. W. Schaie (Eds.), *Handbook of the psychology of aging.* New York: Van Nostrand Reinhold, 1977.

Lawton, M. P. The housing problems of community-resident elderly. In *Occasional papers in housing and community affairs* (Vol. 1, HUD-4970 PDR). Washington, D.C.: U.S. Dept. of Housing and Urban Development, December 1978.

Lawton, M. P., & Bader, J. Wish for privacy by young and old. *Journal of Gerontology*, 1970, *35*, 48–54.

Lawton, M. P. & Kleban, M. H. The aged resident of the inner city. *Gerontologist*, 1971, *11*, 277–283.

Lawton, M. P., Liebowitz, B., & Charon, H. Physical structure and the behavior of senile patients following ward remodeling. *Aging and Human Development*, 1970, *1*, 231–239.

Lawton, M. P., & Nahemow, L. Ecology and the aging process. In C. Eisdorfer & M. P. Lawton (Eds.), *The psychology of adult development and aging*. Washington, D.C.: American Psychological Association, 1973.

Lawton, M. P., & Simon, B. B. The ecology of social relationships in housing for the elderly. *Gerontologist*, 1968, *8*, 198–205.

Lee, T. Perceived distance as a function of direction in the city. *Environment & Behavior*, 1970, *2*, 40–51.

Lipman, A. Chairs as territory. *New Society*, April 1967.

Lumsden, D. Towards a systems model of stress: Feedback from anthropological study of the impact of Ghana's Volta River Project. In I. Sarason & C. D. Spielberger (Eds.), *Stress and anxiety* (Vol. 2). New York: Wiley 1975.

Lynch, K. *Image of the city*. Cambridge, Mass.: MIT Press, 1960.

Mechanic, D. *Students under stress: A study in the social psychology of adaptation*. New York: Free Press of Glencoe, 1962.

Messer, M. The possibility of an age-concentrated environment becoming a normative system. *Gerontologist*, 1967, *7*, 247–251.

Moos, R., & Tsu, V. D. The crisis of physical illness: An overview. In R. Moos (Ed.). *Coping with physical illness*. New York: Plenum Press, 1977.

Newcomer, R. *Housing services and neighborhood activities*. Paper presented at the meeting of the Gerontological Society, Miami, 1973.

Newman, O. *Defensible space*. New York: Macmillan, 1972.

Osmond, H. The relationship between architect and psychiatrist. In C. Goshen (Ed.), *Psychiatric architecture*. Washington, D.C.: American Psychiatric Association, 1959.

O'Sullivan, M., Guilford, J. P., & de Mille, R. *The measurement of social intelligence*. Report 34 from the Psychological Laboratory, University of Southern California, 1965.

Overton, W. F., & Reese, H. Models of development: Methodological implications. In J. R. Nesselroade & H. W. Reese (Eds.), *Life-span developmental psychology: Methodological issues*. New York: Academic Press, 1973.

Pace, C. R. The measurement of college environments. In R. Tagiuri & G. H. Litwin (Eds.), *Organizational climate: Explorations of a concept*. Boston: Harvard University, Graduate School of Business Administration, 1968.

Pastalan, L. A. Privacy as an expression of human territoriality. In L. A. Pastalan & D. H. Carson (Eds.), *Spatial behavior of older people*. Ann Arbor: University of Michigan, 1970.

Pastalan, L. A., Mautz, R. K., & Merrill, J. The simulation of age related sensory losses: A new approach to the study of environmental barriers. In W. F. E. Preiser (Ed.), *Environmental design research*. Stroudsberg, Pa.: Dowden, Hutchinson & Ross, 1973.

Petrinovich. L. Probabilistic functionalism: A conception of research method. *American Psychologist*, 1979, *34*, 373–390.

Phillips, L., & Cowitz, B. Social attainment and reactions to stress. *Journal of Personality*, 1953, *22*, 270–283.

Pressey, S. Age counseling: Crises, services, potential. *Journal of Counseling Psychology*, 1973, *20*, 356–360.

Rapoport, A. Toward a redefinition of density. *Environment and Behavior*, 1975, *7*, 133–158.

Rappoport, L. Symposium: Towards a dialectical social psychology. *Personality and Social Psychology Bulletin*, 1977, *3*, 678–680.

Regnier, V. Neighborhood planning for the urban elderly. In D. S. Woodruff & J. E. Birren (Eds.), *Aging: Scientific perspectives and social issues*. New York: D. Van Nostrand, 1975.

Riegel, K. F. The dialectics of human development. *American Psychologist*, 1976, *31*, 689–700. (a)

Riegel, K. F. From traits and equilibrium toward developmental dialectics. In J. K. Cole & W. J. Arnold (Eds.), *Nebraska Symposium on Motivation* (Vol. 24). Lincoln: University of Nebraska Press, 1976. (b)

Rohles, F. H. Preferences for the thermal environment by the elderly. *Human Factors*, 1969, *11*, 37–41.

Rosow, I. *Social integration of the aged*. New York: Free Press, 1967.

Sarbin, T. R. A role-theory perspective for community psychology: The structure of social identity. In D. Adelson & B. L. Kalis (Eds.), *Community psychology and mental health: Perspectives and challenges*. Scranton, Pa.: Chandler Publishing Co., 1970.

Scheff, T. *Being mentally ill: A sociological theory*. Chicago: Aldine, 1970.

Scheidt, R. J., & Schaie, K. W. A taxonomy of situations for an elderly population: Generating situational criteria. *Journal of Gerontology*, 1978, *33*, 848–857.

Schwartz, A. Perception of privacy among institutionalized aged. *Proceedings of the 77th annual meeting of the American Psychological Association*, 1969, *4* (Pt. 2), 727–728.

Schwartz, A. N. Planning micro-environments for the aged. In D. S. Woodruff & J. E. Birren (Eds.), *Aging: Scientific perspectives and social issues*. New York: D. Van Nostrand, 1975.

Sells, S. B. An interactionist looks at the environment. *American Psychologist*, 1963, *18*, 696–702.

Sommer, R. Small group ecology in institutions for the elderly. In L. A. Pastalan & D. H. Carson (Eds.), *Spatial behavior of older people*. Ann Arbor: University of Michigan Press, 1970.

Spivak, M. Archetypal place. *Architectural Forum*, 1973, *139*, 44–49.

Stea, D. Environmental perception and cognition: Toward a model for "mental maps." In G. J. Coates & K. M. Moffett (Eds.), *Response to environment*. Raleigh, N.C.: School of Design, North Carolina State University, 1969.

Stea, D. Home range and use of space. In L. A. Pastalan & D. Carson (Eds.), *Spatial behavior of older people*. Ann Arbor: University of Michigan Press, 1970.

Steele, F. *Physical settings and organization development*. Reading, Mass: Addison Wesley, 1973.

Taietz, P. *Community structure and aging*. Ithaca, N.Y.: Cornell University, Department of Rural Sociology, 1970. (Mimeo)

Thompson, D. L. New concept: Subjective distance. *Journal of Retailing*, 1965, *39*, 1–6.

Tuan, Y. F. *Topophilia: A study of environmental perception, attitude, and values*. Englewood Cliffs, N.J.: Prentice-Hall, 1974.

Weisman, G. *Behavioral concerns*. Manhattan, Kansas: Kansas State University, Department of Pre-Design Professions, 1978. (Mimeo)

Westin, A. *Privacy and freedom*. New York: Atheneum Press, 1970.

White, R. Competence and the psychosexual stages of development. In M. Jones (Ed.), *Nebraska Symposium on Motivation*. Lincoln: University of Nebraska Press, 1960.

Willems, E. P. Behavioral ecology as a perspective for man-environment research. In W. F. E. Preiser (Ed.), *Environmental design research* (Vol. 2). Stroudsberg, Pa.: Dowden, Hutchinson & Ross, 1973.

Windley, P. G. *Environmental intervention: Case studies in independent living among the rural elderly* (Summer Research Fellowship Program Report). Washington, D.C., Gerontological Society, 1977.

Windley, P. G., Byerts, T. O., & Ernst, F. G. *Theory development in environment and aging*. Washington, D.C.: Gerontological Society, 1975.

Wolf, E. Glare and age. *Archives of Ophthalmology*, 1960, *64*, 502–514.

Sandra C. Howell

CHAPTER
31
Environments as Hypotheses in Human Aging Research

Psychologists approach the problem of defining optimum living environments for aging people from several vantage points. Some choose to evaluate individual competencies in order to match the social, physical, and service environment to a given level of function. Others address the issue of personal control as a mediator in whether or not an individual functions well psychologically in any environment. This chapter considers the historical and contextual factors that may strongly influence the psychological well-being of older people in residential environments they have previously inhabited or in those they first experience. Physical characteristics of buildings and neighborhoods are seen as particularly salient variables in this approach, since it is hypothesized that familiar patterns of using space, as well as the meaning of past environmental experiences, support a sense of identity in older people.

Are there reasons to suspect that the physical environment affects the behavior and the phychological states of aging people? The discussion that follows suggests that there are, and it attempts to provide a theoretical framework in which the transactions between people as they age and the built environment may be analyzed. In recent years, gerontologists have mounted research to explore the physical attributes of environments that may be pertinent to individual and social psychological states. Reviews of this work can be found in Lawton and Nahemow (1973), Lawton (1977), and Howell (1980b). For the most part, the research recorded has been descriptive or quasi-experimental; only now is work in this area approaching the level of theoretical

organization of ideas (Kahana, 1975; Lawton & Nahemow, 1973; Schooler, 1975).

In psychology as a whole, the built environment (structures and spaces created by human intervention)—when it has been included in experimental paradigms at all—has been alluded to as if it were some vague intervening variable. When attempts have been made to specify measurable characteristics of the environment, the resultant attributes have tended to read like a list of stimuli in a verbal-learning task or like sensate phenomena to which clusters of responses can be correlated. Most frequently, clusters of physical, social, and demographic attributes of environments are pieced together in the hope that they constitute a valid collective variable that will prove explanatory, as in studies of responses to tall buildings (Newman, 1977). An alternative position holds that environments are true hypothetical constructs constituted in an individual's mind in response to historically dynamic interactions between that individual and physical settings over the course of a lifetime of events in place. This position sustains the MacCorquedale and Meehl (1948) differentiation in which hypothetical constructs have status as mini-theories while intervening variables remain as sets of experimental intrusions. If this position is further extended to the issue of context variability, those research elements we have labeled "variable" must also include experienced environments. To the extent that this hypothesis is verifiable, our current practice of measuring individual attitudes and behaviors of aging persons within a particular context may, in fact, obscure and distort our understanding of the developmental roles played by these environments (Proshansky, 1976) and thus provide us with limited information on which to build a psychology of aging.

Adaptation Reconsidered

What have we, as social scientists, used to measure our perceptions of relevance in the relation of environments to aging? A review of the literature suggests that we may have perseverated on psychosocial variables extraneous to the main cognitive-affective framework as well as bypassed those variables generated in the process of human aging vis-à-vis the physical environment (Baltes & Willis, 1977).

Vis-à-vis, we should note, is an operational term in social anthropology (McBride & Clancy, 1976) that connotes an interaction system, typically of people, in which the behavior of Actor A serves as feedback to Actor B, which in turn is used to modify the behavior of Actor B in an *adaptive* fashion (and vice versa for Actor A). Children are socialized predominately in vis-à-vis interactions. Bennett (1976a, 1976b) differentiates *adaptation* based on values and norms in human societies confronted by the dynamics of change from the more biologically derived, genetically determined fluctuations to achieve homeostasis that are seen in other organisms. He, and others in anthropology, contrast *adaptation*, as a long-run individual-social phenomenon, with *adjustment*, a short-run coping style required of an individual or group in a situation of an unanticipated or unfamiliar nature. *Adjustment*, as measured by indices of satisfaction, well-being, and behavior, may or may not prove *adaptive* to the individual or society.

In adult development and aging we have been treating adaptation more as Helson (1964) defined it—progressive accommodation between the individual and the physical-social setting—as if required by the conscious or unconscious awareness of competence, physiological or psychological (Kahana, 1975; Lawton & Nahemow, 1973). In existing paradigms, measures of personal competence and of change of competence over time have become the key to evaluating the appropriateness, or adaptivity, of the environment as a support (or reinforcer) for independence. Thus we tend to say that a person has adapted appropriately who has elected an environment that provides support relative to that person's level of competence. In parallel, we identify environments as positively (or negatively) reinforcing if elements of them provide an opportunity to maximize (or inhibit) the remaining competencies of

individual residents.[1] Thus, improperly illuminated corridors in residential or institutional settings operate in conflict with reduced visual acuity among the elderly and thereby result in behavioral "adaptations" at levels lower than could be expected, given the other-than-visual capacities of the individual. Residents are less mobile, ambulate more slowly and hesitantly, require more guidance, explore and interact with the environment and people less, and may even exhibit symptoms of confusion and paranoia when cues are unseen or misconstrued.

Current competency, as measured by psychological and physiological instruments (Kahana, 1975; Lawton & Nahemow, 1973), may not, however, implicate the entire gamut of cognitive-affective bases for environmental behaviors in aging. The argument presented here is that the concept of adaptation in aging theories needs to be refined. In terms of perceptions of self in the environment, the homeostasis quest, if it exists, may be a process more internal to the individual, and homeostasis may not be the organizing principle on which the individual relates to environments. Rather, it may be secondary reinforcement and novelty (which may seem at cognitive-affective odds) that govern the psychological perspectives of aging people with regard to the physical (built) environment.

In a society where humorists often convey the human condition more sensitively than do social scientists, I am reminded of several *New Yorker* cartoons I have collected. One shows a very Victorian brownstone with a figure peering from a lone, lighted second-story window and a sign in front of the building that asserts, "This building to be demolished (as soon as the old lady dies)." Another shows an old lady sitting straight up in her iron bed, gazing out her half-shaded window from a clearly dilapidated room, and yelling, "Good morning, Cross Bronx Expressway!" And a third depicts an obviously older, two-story suburban house, with its proud aging couple framed by the ubiquitous picture window in the living room. A sign on the front lawn that one might expect to read "FOR SALE." instead states, "We have lived here 35 years."

What if the transactions between aging people and whatever their current environment is were not merely what we observe as "adaptive" accommodation but rather were sets of responses to their nonrandom his-

---

[1] McIlvaine Parsons, in a personal communication, commented that "negatively reinforcing does not properly mean inhibiting; it means strengthing by reducing or avoiding aversive consequences." I fail to see the operational difference in human behavior when the strengthening of an accomodating behavior constitutes inhibition of potential independence.

tories of interactions with environments, as these cartoons suggest?

The Importance of Contextual Relevance

It must have been some (albeit naively intuitive) suggestion of this sort that led me in 1971 to postulate and test a hypothesis of the role of familiarity in the perceptual recognition of older persons (Howell, 1972), a hypothesis that Rabbitt (1977) acknowledged forced some questions about the role of stored experience in problem solving and about the adequacy of many of our current paradigms in geropsychology. As experimental stimuli I used photoreproductions of 1908 Sears and Roebuck catalogue items; as controls I used photos of neutral patterns and contemporary objects (pencils, buttons). The elderly in this cross-sectional study performed significantly better than expected in response to the experimental stimuli; in fact, they did as well as their younger comparison group. One woman, a retired pattern cutter in the textile industry, far outperformed both the other elderly and the young in the recognition of pure pattern cards. The absence of contextual relevance in studies of language recognition (Baumrin, 1974) is also important, since verbal labeling appears as a dependent variable in many of our paradigms involving environmental objects (Poon & Fozard, 1978).

The context variable has become a legitimate theoretical issue in psychology in that human memory and the actions it generates, in whatever stimulus arena, are governed by their contextual relevance to the person involved (Lachman, 1979). This has long been the central message of Gibson and of his colleagues and critics alike (Gibson, 1977; Jenkins, 1977; Shaw & Bransford, 1977; Verbrugge, 1977).

To argue that current context, as perceived and interacted with, is a function of both the measurable attributes (physical and social) of the presenting scene (Moos & Lemke, 1979) and the person-place-event history of the respondent is to provide a basis for better explanation and prediction of environment and aging behaviors. Rather than viewing this elaboration as further softening and unduly complicating psychology (although it *will* become complex), we should reach out with excitement to the new insights that a social science version of Feynman's "sum-over-histories" hypothesis for atomic particles could afford the field of environment and behavior (Feynman, Leighton, & Sands, 1965; Pribram, 1977). The sum-over-histories hypothesis assumes that all matter (including mind) cumulates and responds selectively to events over time. Of course, for constantly moving particles, the social meaning is irrelevant.

This chapter proposes that the behaviors of aging individuals, including perceptions, persistent attitudes, social interactions, and current uses of the physical environment, are based on (a) psychoenviornmental history, and (b) perceived comparison of past and present contexts (relevance). Further, it is argued that this contextual relevance is fundamental to self-perception and as such is a particularly powerful operation among the aged, for whom retention of identity is acknowledged to be critical. This proposition has considerable implications for the ways we do psychology in both the laboratory and the field and for both theoretical and applied work.

The issue of contextual relevance appears to be important even in measures of competency used on the more frail institutionally bound person. Elaine Brody of the Philadelphia Geriatric Center tells a story about an old woman who seeks counsel from a nurse so that when a mental status examiner comes around again, she won't disappoint him by not knowing the name of the place she's in or of the President of the United States: "If only he would ask where my grandchildren live, their names and what they are doing, I'm sure I could help him!" A number of critics have commented on the problematic nature of behavior modification in institutional environments, only incidentally noting the possible contextual irrelevance of such efforts to the institutionalized individuals' perceptions of their current environment in relation to past settings.

My major theme, then, is that built environments are integral to virtually all stimulus configurations that enter into social learning, personality, and cognitive development in modern humans. As such, environmental experiences "resonate" in memory storage and relate themselves to this or that purpose or context that the individual may entertain. Further, bits of psychoenvironmental history are utilized as hypothetical constructs in transactional measures with the current environment and serve to test "Who am I?" contextually.

My conviction that such a proposition has merit came about by the nearly simultaneous confluence of three experiences. The first was a frustration with aggregate data from a national study concerned with the well-being of older people in age-segregated, subsidized housing (Nahemow, Lawton, & Howell, 1977). We were learning very little about the transactions between people and environment, for we had gathered too little and quite disjointed information about the attributes of the settings. Further, hints appeared (in scatter-shot questions or open-ended responses) that Lawton and I had not theoretically framed our inquiry so that we might tap into the intrapsychic and interpersonal, not to mention the vis-à-vis, behaviors of our respondents within these environments. In addition, we gathered virtually no information on the housing histories of our subjects. That approximately 80% of our high-rise dwellers had resided in single-family or under four-unit multifamily settings most of their lives only whetted my intellectual appetite.

The second set of insights arose from data being gathered by my then-ancillary graduate student, Graham Rowles, a social geographer who was at that time, and still is, intrigued by how older people "structurize"[2] space, place, and time (Rowles, 1978). The third, and not incidental, event was the intimate experience I was having in tracking my 79-year-old mother's reentry into environments following a series of left-hemispheric cerebral hemorrhages and a profoundly negative brain scan. In my mother's recovery process I observed a remarkably literal recreation of mind and self. Within this recreation, historic transactions with environments were repeatedly generated, sometimes seemingly spontaneously and randomly and at other times as explicit responses to the context at hand.

How does the above discussion affect the ways that we now structure our paradigms in gerontology? From the standpoint of learning and memory, what is acquired in an initial environment–person transaction, later to be retrieved and applied to a subsequent environmental encounter, might best be seen as a "set to respond" rather than as a particularly learned interpretation of an environmental stimulus.

It seems doubtful that the retrieval of environmental memories is based on any single organization of individual or sequential person–environment translations, as would be the case if one assumed an information-processing stance. Rather it seems likely that the organization of past experiences serves a present purpose. In the case of environmental memory, rate of retrieval may not be its most functionally salient feature, since a person would typically have no adaptive reason to recover information about past transactions at any particular speed. Nor is the amount of information about the environment apparently as salient as the idiosyncratic choices made on the occasions of retrieval. And neither does it seem sensible to talk about "inappropriate or inefficient encoding" (Hultsch & Pentz, 1980) at the time of initial learning affecting environmental-information retrieval, since we cannot be sure what the intentions or the accessory contextual issues were at the time of acquisition or at subsequent retrieval times.

Thus, I conclude that what is important in environ-mental memory in the process of aging are (a) the qualitative rather than the quantitative nature of the information, and (b) the strategy of selection (i.e., intention), which, I argue, changes over time and with the context. It is these important influences of adaptation and context that lead me to consider the environment a hypothetical construct rather than an experimenter's intervening variable in aging research. When Hultsch and Pentz (1980) refer to the multistore models wherein information acquired is stored "in some meaningful way" (not otherwise elaborated), they hit the crux of the matter with regard to the role of environment in intrapsychic development and in behavioral manifestations of that development in old age!

Rather than continue to investigate retrievability and the conditions for it, geropsychologists can transform their study of environmental memories by raising the question of the personal relevance of an act of or the content of a particular retrieval. This brings us back to the issue of why an older person would elect to retrieve an environmental experience and its associated cues at all. At the present time we have no better theoretical explanation than J. J. Gibson's concept of "affordance," that is, that the retrieval serves some intrapsychic or intentional purpose.

Finally, it can be argued whether paradigms that make use of verbal or written materials are at all transferrable to visual-social experiences. The living environment, experienced as a behavior setting replete with visual, acoustic (sometimes language), and social inputs surely must be very differently encoded than the discrete words, sentences, or paragraphs used for verbal learning in the laboratory. It is difficult to conceptualize this as a hierarchical process, as suggested by Hultsch and Pentz (1980), but it does seem that the meaning of current events must be bounded by past environmental experiences and the multiple ways they were used by the individual.

Common Space

To return to the earlier question: In what ways and in what physical settings have aging people expressed their relationship to the built environment? A review of data (both quantitative and qualitative) that I and my colleagues collected in 1975 in a national study of elderly people in public housing led to a series of what I must call focused pilot explorations (Howell, 1980b). In these studies the buildings (physically classifiable) were the independent variables, tenants were sampled purposively by location within buildings, and reported and observed behaviors and attitudes, particularly as

---

[2] The somewhat awkward word "structurize" was chosen because it reflects the Piagetian developmental concept of "schema" as a restructuring process that is believed to be a lifelong cognitive dynamic.

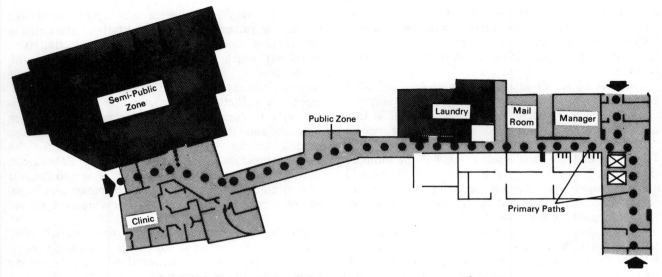

Figure 31-1. Site C, least penetrable access to communal space.

they related to social interaction, constituted the dependent variables.

In the national study a series of questions had been asked regarding the use made by residents of communal spaces within the designated buildings. Of these settings, among the 53 sites in the subsample that contained such spaces, approximately 40% of the respondents reported that they never or rarely participated in either formal or informal activities within the setting. If the *raison d'etre* for these spaces was to stimulate social interaction, resocialization, and new-friendship formation, the settings were not accomplishing the goals set for them. While the only historic evidence of the extent of social isolation among our national sample was a rough typology of former resi-

dences and reported frequencies of interaction with relatives and friends, the response tendencies suggested the need to probe further the social-behavioral effects of high-density designs for age-segregated housing.

Following this national study, four Cambridge, Massachusetts, sample sites were selected. Three of the four sites had high tenant homogeneity and were similiar in design; these facts were confirmed through analysis by an architecturally trained staff and by colleagues. The fourth building was selected predominantly for a pilot study of some density-behavior hypotheses. The physical characteristics (independent variables) that differentiated the three primary research environments and allowed testing of hypotheses were (a) the absolute distance between the main building entry and the elevator that provided access to all the

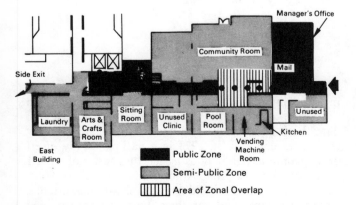

Figure 31-2. Site B, most penetrable access to communal space.

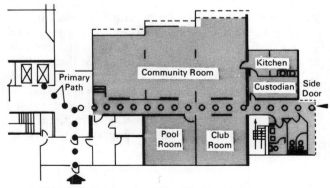

Figure 31-3. Site A, intermediate penetrability to communal space.

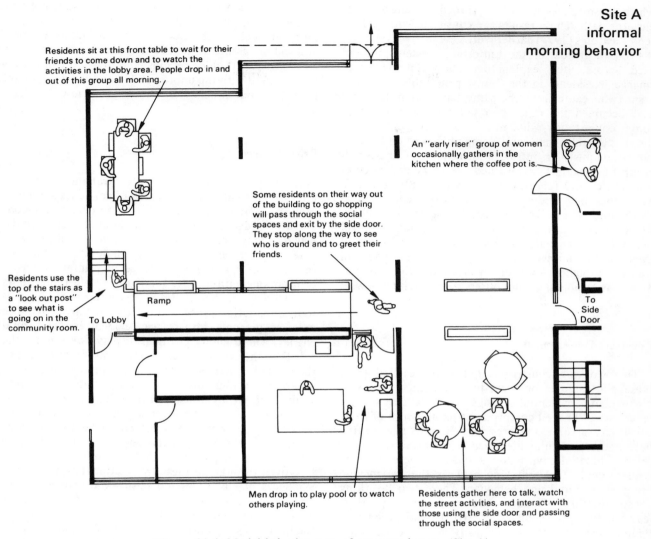

Site A
informal
morning behavior

Residents sit at this front table to wait for their friends to come down and to watch the activities in the lobby area. People drop in and out of this group all morning.

An "early riser" group of women occasionally gathers in the kitchen where the coffee pot is.

Some residents on their way out of the building to go shopping will pass through the social spaces and exit by the side door. They stop along the way to see who is around and to greet their friends.

Residents use the top of the stairs as a "look out post" to see what is going on in the community room.

Ramp

To Lobby

To Side Door

Men drop in to play pool or to watch others playing.

Residents gather here to talk, watch the street activities, and interact with those using the side door and passing through the social spaces.

Figure 31-4. Modal behavior map of communal space (Site A).

living units, (b) the location of planned communal spaces in relation to this critical circulation path, and (c) the degree of penetrability of the communal spaces from the main circulation path. (Penetrability was defined operationally according to degree of visual, auditory, and ambulatory accessibility.) These characteristics occur in all residential settings; at the low-density extreme of the single-family suburban home, the critical entry path is contained by the resident's property line, and the communal spaces are the public sidewalks and streets.

Sharing with my colleagues in gerontology various stereotypes of the elderly, I hypothesized that spaces (a) proximate to the heaviest circulation of people in and out of the building, and (b) most penetrable from this path would be the ones most frequently used and the ones used for the widest variety of informal social interaction. Hence the one building in which tenants were forced to move directly through a contiguous open lobby and common space to reach the elevator to their own living units was expected to show the greatest levels of observed and reported interaction (see Figure 31-1 through 31-3).

The pilot results were informative. Systematic behavior mapping, (Figure 31-4), supplemented by photography, showed less interaction and fewer informal group formations in two of the three buildings: the least penetrable building—in which the common spaces were located considerably off the entry to the elevator path—and the most penetrable building—in which these spaces literally absorbed the entry to the elevator path. These results are consistent with and extend Lawton's (1977) earlier work.

From a review of the uniform interview protocol used across sites, explanatory constructs began to emerge. Residents in the "most penetrable" environment (who came from the same tenant pool as those who occupied the other two settings) reported, with some consistency, discomfort at having to walk through a public showcase: Some remarked on the presumed cliquish or intrusive behaviors of the small group of "regulars" who lined the entry and circulation spaces and reported attempts generally to avoid, by timing and body behaviors, encounters in these semipublic spaces. In contrast, in the third building, which architecturally permitted more personal control over informal encounters while still allowing incidental awareness of immediate peripheral activity spaces in transit, a higher level of social interaction (Figure 31-4) was exhibited in both observation and interview.

Construct Development

Two working constructs that have resulted from these pilot studies on behaviors of aging persons in high-density residential settings are "offensive surveillance" and "limited commitment path." Both of these constructs assume that residents in the new setting have had a particular historical relationship with their prior residential environments and that there is a consequent contextual matching between the present and the past, in mind and behavior. These two "working constructs" are, of course, the researchers' hypothetical structures; the subjects' constructs, still to be investigated, are probably linguistically more mundane but descriptively richer.

The concept of offensive surveillance was suggested by Goffman's (1971) detailed discussion of the ways in which individuals attempt to maintain their privacy in public places, by Altman's (1975) explorations of perceived crowding and privacy as control of intrusions into one's personal space, and by Stokols's (1978) suggestion that residential density needs to be assessed in terms of antecedent environmental experiences, which transfer expectancies to new residential environments.

The concept of a limited commitment path is suggested by geropsychology literature that deals with risk taking by older persons in problem-solving tasks (Botwinick, 1973). The logic of transferring the concept of risk to the environmental sphere can be found in the fact that when entering an unfamiliar space, an individual must consider a series of possible encounters to be dealt with. The individual must, in fact, make a commitment to any of these encounters (including rejection and embarrassment) in the decision to proceed and enter a space. If older persons tend to avoid risk taking (i.e., dealing with the unpredictable and the unfamiliar) then their spatial behaviors should also show this characteristic.

Private Space

In sharp contrast to the architectural anonymity and impersonal treatment by tenants of corridors and common spaces in most moderate- to high-density age-congregate residential settings in the United States are the private living units, which tenants have anointed with determined statements of self, often in utter defiance of the rules of space use. Evidence of primary vis-à-vis transactions within these relatively sterile rental units was everywhere, and patterns began to emerge as photodocumentation proceeded across 55 apartments. The greatest personal impact was evident in (a) formal entries, where highly personal displays were more the rule than the exception, despite the uniform tokenism of the limited apartment entry area; (b) the simulation of separate sleeping rooms by the creation of furniture walls in efficiency units; and (c) primary behavior settings repeatedly created around what can be presumed from other gerontology research to be the principle communication and activity centers of the elderly in America, the telephone and the television.

Woven through all these transactional patterns were evidences of environmental pasts—the people, places, and objects of remembered selves—most notably, the widow's now functionally unnecessary double bed and the husband's high dresser (which public-housing space standards disallow). In the national study these bedroom items and the formal dining set were reported as the most frequently felt furnishing loss in moving to a smaller living unit. The formal dining set would have been "underutilized" even if it had fitted into the new environment, although the meaningfulness of 2/year family events is relevant!

Summary

This chapter has attempted to integrate newer thinking in cognitive psychology with efforts in gerontology to understand the transactions between aging people and the built environment. It has been proposed that the built environment is encoded, on encounter, as a hypothetical construct for which the individual has contextual and historical matches. The intraphysic processes and social behaviors of older people in various environments can thus be understood through exploring the nature of these constructs rather than by treating environments as experimenter–imposed intervening variables.

It is suggested, in addition, that environments (buildings and settings) can be used in hypotheses about behavioral aging as long as the definable properties of the environments are specified as either independent or intervening variables.

If we assume that we can operationally define those design and social attributes that are new (unfamiliar) to a populations' history, perceived adjustments to new environments may or may not be *adaptive* (in either psychological or social terms) to individuals or to a society, depending on the values and goals to which there is collective adherence.

Implications and Directions

The paradigms appropriate to investigating environment–behavior transactions across the life cycle may necessitate quite different language than that traditionally used in learning and memory studies. Although it is true that people can describe, in words, some aspects of their environmental feelings and experiences, those experiences have probably neither been acquired nor "stored" within verbal categories.

Evidence accumulating from research that has used "unobtrusive measures" (behavior mapping, photo-documentation) as well as structured interviews strongly indicates that older individuals become attached to particular environments and objects for reasons that are as yet unclear. In a verbal learning paradigm we seem to be able to make operational the variables of familiarity and meaningfulness. Environmental learning and memory paradigms will require the use of different operations (e.g., the number and intensity of subjective events linked to place rather than the replicability of a place-label in experimental time and context). Extension back into the generational (or cohort) environmental history of subjects (Poon & Fozard, 1978; Howell, 1972) may need to be an integral part of paradigms. This is the real meaning of context and the implication of contextual relevance.

I see the 1980s as a time of breakthrough in identifying those parts of the architectural (and neighborhood) environment that need to be preserved so that the personal histories of the current generation of elderly can be sustained and their intrapsychic adaptation supported. There is a unique art deco historic-preservation district in south Miami Beach that is a

prototype of identity in place. Inhabited now by a low-income migrant population of elderly New Yorkers, it represents their reminiscence and our cultural link with their place and time. Psychological research in aging should be able to assist planners in determining what elements of this physical environment to retain, or if they must be replaced, at what level of continuity with past architectural landscapes and settings.

A clearer understanding of environmental cognition may also provide us with necessary strategies to help aging people use their environmental experiences better in making decisions about housing.

REFERENCES

Altman, I. *The environment and social behavior.* Monterey, Calif.: Brooks/Cole, 1975.

Baltes, P. B., & Willis, S. L. Toward psychological theories of aging and development. In J. E. Birren & K. W. Schaie (Eds.), *Handbook of the psychology of aging.* New York: Van Nostrand Reinhold, 1977.

Baumrin, J. M. The perception of the relation of a silent interval in non-speech stimuli: A test of the motor theory of speech perception. *Journal of Speech and Hearing Research,* 1974, *17,* 294–309.

Bennett, J. W. Anticipation, adaptation and the concept of culture in anthropology. *Science,* 1976, *192,* 847–853. (a)

Bennett, J. W. *The ecological transition: Cultural anthropology and human adaptation.* New York: Pergamon, 1976. (b)

Botwinick, J. *Aging and behavior.* New York: Springer, 1973.

Feynman, R. P., Leighton, R. B., & Sands, M. (Eds.). *The Feynman lectures on physics* (Vol. 3). Reading, Mass.: Addision Wesley, 1965.

Gibson, J. J. The theory of affordances. In R. Shaw & J. Bransford (Eds.), *Perceiving, acting and knowing.* Hillsdale, N.J.: Lawrence Erlbaum, 1977.

Goffman, E. *Relations in public.* New York: Harper & Row, 1971.

Helson, H. *Adaptation level theory.* New York: Harper & Row, 1964.

Howell, S. C. Familiarity and complexity in perceptual recognition. *Journal of Gerontology,* 1972, *27,* 364–371. (Reprinted in D. B. Lumsden & R. Sherren (Eds.), *Experimental studies in adult learning and memory.* Washington, D.C.: Hemisphere, 1975.)

Howell, S. C. *Designing for aging: Patterns of use.* Cambridge, Mass.: MIT Press, 1980. (a)

Howell, S. C. Environment and aging. In C. Eisdorfer (Ed.) *Annual review of gerontology and geriatrics.* New York: Springer, 1980. (b)

Hultsch, D. F., & Pentz, C. A. Encoding, storage, and retrieval in adult memory: The role of model assumptions. In L. W. Poon, J. L. Fozard, L. S. Cermak, D. Arenberg, & L. W. Thompson (Eds.), *New directions in memory and aging: Proceedings of the George A. Talland Memorial Conference*. Hillsdale, N.J.: Lawrence Erlbaum, 1980.

Jenkins, J. J. Remember that old theory of memory? Well, forget it! In R. Shaw & J. Bransford (Eds.), *Perceiving, acting and knowing*. Hillsdale, N.J.: Lawrence Erlbaum, 1977.

Kahana, E. A congruence model of person-environment interaction. In P. Windley, T. Byerts, & F. Ernst (Eds.), *Theory development in environment and aging*. Washington, D.C.: Gerontological Society, 1975.

Lachman, M. E. *Ecological validity in the study of adult personality*. Paper presented at the symposium "Lab to Life" held at the meeting of the Gerontological Society, Washington, D.C., November 1979.

Lawton, M. P. The impact of the environment on aging and behavior. In J. E. Birren & K. W. Schaie (Eds.), *Handbook of the psychology of aging*. New York: Van Nostrand Reinhold, 1977.

Lawton, M. P., & Nahemow, L. Ecology and the aging process. In C. Eisdorfer & M. P. Lawton (Eds.), *Psychology of adult development and aging*. Washington, D.C.: American Psychological Association, 1973.

MacCorquedale, K., & Meehl, P. E. On the distinction between hypothetical constructs and intervening variables. *Psychological Review*, 1948, *55*, 95–107.

McBride, G., & Clancy, R. The social properties of places and things. In A. Rapoport (Ed.), *The mutual interaction of people and their built environment*. The Hague, Netherlands: Mouton, 1978.

Moos, R. H., & Lemke, S. *Assessing the physical and architectural features of sheltered care settings*. Palo Alto, Calif.: Social Ecology Laboratory, Veterans Administration Medical Center, and Stanford University Medical Center, 1979.

Nahemow, L., Lawton, M. P., & Howell, S. C. Elderly people in tall buildings: A nationwide study. In D. Conway (Ed.), *Human response to tall buildings*. Stroudsburg, Pa.: Dowden, Hutchison & Ross, 1977.

Newman, J. Perceptions of building height: An approach to research and some preliminary findings. In D. Conway (Ed.), *Human response to tall buildings*. Stroudsburg, Pa.: Dowden, Hutchison, & Ross, 1977.

Poon, L. W. & Fozard, J. L. Speed of retrieval from long-term memory in relation to age, familiarity, and datedness of information. *Journal of Gerontology*, 1978, *33*, 711–717.

Pribram, K. H. Some comments on the nature of the perceived universe. In R. Shaw & J. Bransford (Eds.), *Perceiving, acting and knowing*. Hillsdale, N.J.: Lawrence Erlbaum, 1977.

Proshansky, H. Environmental psychology and the real world. *American Psychologist*, 1976, *31*, 303–310.

Rabbitt, P. Changes in problem solving ability in old age. In J. E. Birren & K. W. Schaie (Eds.), *Handbook of the psychology of aging*. New York: Van Nostrand Reinhold, 1977.

Rowles, G. *Prisoners of space? Exploring the geographical experiences of older people*. Boulder, Colo.: Westview Press, 1978.

Schooler, K. K. Response of the elderly to environment: A stress-theoretic perspective. In P. G. Windley & G. Ernst (Eds.), *Theory development in environment and aging*. Washington, D.C.: Gerontological Society, 1975.

Shaw, R., & Bransford, J. (Eds.), *Perceiving, acting and knowing*. Hillsdale, N.J.: Lawrence Erlbaum, 1977.

Stokols, D. In defense of the crowding construct. In A. Baum, J. E. Singer, & S. Valins (Eds.), *Advances in environmental psychology. Vol. 1. The urban environment*. Hillsdale, N.J.: Lawrence Erlbaum, 1978.

Verbrugge, R. R. Resemblances in language and perception. In R. Shaw & H. Bransford (Eds.), *Perceiving, acting and knowing*. Hillsdale, N.J.: Lawrence Erlbaum, 1977.

Interpersonal Relations

Lillian E. Troll, *Section Editor*

Introduction

The interpersonal relations considered in the chapters of this section are almost all those among family members. This is not surprising. Our accumulated research on families of later life (see Troll, Miller, & Atchley, 1978) shows that the progressive disengagement from societal involvement characteristic of aging Americans is, in fact, disengagement into, not from, their families. How much of this age-related trend is a process of aging, however, and how much a characteristic mainly of today's cohorts of older people, we cannot say. Since the majority of today's older people are women—a high proportion of whom migrated to western cities from nonindustrialized areas, both within and outside this country—they are more likely to believe that close attachments to men, or even to other women who are not family members, threaten family loyalty and solidarity (Lopata, 1977).

Research to date has attended to a variety of questions about interpersonal relations in later life. Interest in demography has centered on possibilities for relationships, that is, on who is available. This has yielded information about family size, household composition, geographic propinquity, and age profiles of families, neighborhoods, and regions. Availability underlies all issues of interpersonal relations among older people, as demonstrated in each of the following chapters. The number of people one's own age and older colors attitudes toward the present and the future.

The recent interest in midlife transition, the topic of Cytrynbaum and his colleagues in Chapter 34, is a consequence of this heightened awareness of life's later years. Parents who are alive, even though they may be deteriorating physically, increase the likelihood of continuing some kind of parent–child relations over most of the years of adulthood if not into old age itself. Chapter 32, by Alpert and Richardson, would have ended with adolescent children if it had been written 10 or more years ago. Not only more children but also more adults now have grandparents who serve as models and interact with them in many ways, and the fact that many of the grandparents have only a few grandchildren around may increase the value of grandchildren to these grandparents (see Chapter 35 by Troll). Cicirelli (Chapter 33) points out that present cohorts of older people, who come from large families, are more likely to have siblings available than are cohorts in the past—and possibly in the future. Present cohorts are also more likely to have more siblings than other close associates available to them for relationships.

Related to issues of availability are those of interaction frequency. Studies in this domain have in some ways been more limited than studies of availability. Most have been survey investigations that have used self-report questionnaires. Further, most of these surveys compared findings without regard to availability denominators. That is, interactions with children, siblings, or even friends have not been customarily assessed in terms of how many children, siblings, or friends exist or are available for such interactions.

Many interaction studies have also focused only on helping interactions. For example, older respondents have been asked how readily they would seek help from various people listed rather than how they feel about these people or whether they find them important to the quality of their daily life.

During the past decade, some interest has been shown in the qualitative aspects of relationships, such as the functions they fulfilled, communality of values, and feelings involved. However, this area has received much less attention than more quantitative issues, as Alpert and Richardson note in Chapter 32. Also, too often, attention has been focused on life satisfaction, morale, or adequacy of functioning instead of on exploring the more basic and general questions of continuity and change in the dynamics of enduring relationships.

In general, research to date on the interpersonal relationships of older people has been atheoretical, pragmatic, and descriptive. One among many questions waiting to be asked concerns the conditions under which particular relationships, such as spouse, sibling, or parent, retain their importance over the length of life, as compared with the conditions under which they decrease or increase in importance. For example, do feelings about a sister or brother, who are perhaps more peripheral, remain relatively unchanged regardless of frequency of communication while feelings for more central people, such as a spouse or a child, change or develop? Many such questions might provide clues to the development of human relationships as such. What are the effects of people's egocentricity in perspective, or of their sharing or lack of sharing of their ongoing lives?

Another important issue is substitution. Is a close friend or relative lost in early life easier to replace than an equivalent friend or relative lost later in life? If so, why? Does the seeming absence of relationships among institutionalized older people speak to their social incompetence, their irreplaceable losses, or some selection factor that keeps people who have close ties out of institutions? Are interpersonal bonds cemented between members of some dyads or groups such that the death or loss of a member destroys the fabric of the group itself while relationships between members of another kind of group are more interchangeable and allow for replacement of lost members?

The chapters in this section show that we are beginning to ask many questions in this area of interpersonal relations in later life. In fact, the questions overshadow the occasional firm answers. Lest we be dismayed by this imbalance, however, we should recall that at the beginning of the 1970s, scarcely anyone had given thought to late-life interactions. Ten years ago,

our data consisted primarily of a body of survey findings on residential nearness of kin, on frequency of communication, and on amount of help exchanged (Troll, 1971). Many of our new questions have moved beyond counting and labeling to an examination of some of the complex processes involved.

Our understanding of interpersonal relationships over the life span must be based on individual development over the life span. From the perspective of the individual, we can trace an oscillation in salience between parent–child and husband–wife dyads—from parent–child to husband–wife to parent–child to husband–wife to parent–child—although the individual may shift from one pole of the parent–child dyad to the other. These shifts could be initiated by particular determining experiences, internal or external, biological or social. Each transition could be marked by a reorganization of behaviors involving suppression of those no longer appropriate, recovery of those once again appropriate, and development of new ones to fill new needs. Thus, an accumulation of biological and social events or processes can propel youth toward mating and then to childbirth—moving their focus from parent–child to husband–wife to parent–child dyads. After their children are grown, husband and wife may turn to each other again until such events as widowhood or deteriorating parents shift their focus once more. The obligatory nurturant behaviors called forth by the imperatives of needy, helpless children (or aging parents) can structure other feelings and behaviors, even to the point of suppressing those that do not fit. Removal or absence of such imperatives could release some suppressed or repressed feelings and behaviors, and the new, sometimes widened, set of behaviors can be fitted into a reorganized personality structure. Recent thinking about sex role shifts in middle age centers upon the move toward androgyny from an earlier rigid polarization in stereotypical masculinity or femininity.

Cytrynbaum and his colleagues suggest that shifts may also be determined by inner developmental processes. An individual's development in terms of egocentrism (focus on self versus focus on others), for example, could shape the extent of caring and responsibility for others that she or he would undertake. Findings by Nydegger and Mitteness (1979) about the differences in parenting behavior between older and younger fathers and between older and younger children are a case in point.

The timing of shifts or changes in modes of interpersonal behavior is affected not only by the demands of current situations, external and internal, but by preceding life experiences. Social learning theory (e.g., Mischel, 1970) stresses the uniqueness of life histories whose commonalities are consequences of common social conditions that have shaped common sequences of life experiences. But there is an alternative view in which the life span follows a more universally determined course: a general waxing of activities, relationships, and experiences followed by a general waning or contracting of all activities, relationships, and experiences. The latter theory has been presented by Jung (1969), Buhler (1968), and others. It has been supported by data from the Kansas City studies of disengagement (Cumming & Henry, 1961) and by the social network research of Fischer and his colleagues (Stueve & Fischer, 1978) in California. As noted earlier, however, family relationships do not seem to follow this waning pattern.

Function

The phrase "man is a social animal" implies that human beings need each other in a fundamental way. Yet functional analyses of interpersonal behavior are rare. Do different relationships serve different interpersonal purposes at different periods of life? Does a husband or wife serve a different function from a child, or from a parent, or from a friend or sibling? The question of other relationships' substituting for lost or missing relationships has been raised occasionally in the literature on aging, it is true, but except for Rosow (1967), the issue has not been addressed directly. Rosow found that neighbors do not substitute for distant children. Do children ever substitute for a missing spouse?

The research on helping behavior is indirectly associated to function. Hill and his colleagues (Hill, Foote, Aldous, Carlson, & Macdonald, 1970) found different quantities of aid and also different kinds of aid exchanged among parents, children, and adult grandchildren. All generations give some and get some. While young adults and grandparents are relatively greater recipients and the middle generation relatively greater donors, both in goods and services, no one generation comes off clearly as either giver or receiver when all types of aid are considered. The chapters on parenting and grandparenting refer to this issue briefly.

As for other functions of relationships, beyond the pioneer study on functions of friendship by Candy (1977), who found three major factors (in a factor-analytic investigation of adults of different ages)—Intimacy-Assistance, Status, and Power—little systematic attention has been given to this question. Would the same basic functions apply to other human relationships, perhaps in varying proportions? Candy found that while Intimacy-Assistance was primary at all ages, both Status and Power seemed to be less and less important for each age group older than adolescents—except for retirees, who ranked these reasons higher in their choice of friends than did younger persons (all of the subjects were students, teachers, or retired teachers). A related study was undertaken by Reedy (1977), who looked at age differences in the relative importance assigned to different aspects of marital love. Not surprisingly, sex was primary among newlyweds, and emotional security and loyalty were primary among older couples. Her cross-sectional data were replicated by retrospective reports of golden wedding couples (Parron, 1978).

Cicerelli's chapter points to variation in functions of different siblings, at least by sex, with sisters having an effect different from that of brothers. He also suggests that the nature of sibling interaction—rivalry and affection—changes with time. Incidental reports from family studies suggest that parents may see or contact one child daily and another only once a month. While geographic proximity plays a part in this difference, it is not unknown for parents to telephone a child who lives across the country in order to share some information and not mention it to another child who lives next door. One friend will be spoken with regularly, another only when the mood hits. Particular styles of grandparenting pertain to particular grandparents, and grandparents may use different styles for different grandchildren. Nydegger and Mitteness (1979) report that fathers diminish their authority relations with their children over the years of adulthood (of the children) but do not change their companionate-friendship functions.

Influence over another person is one kind of function; it is part of the power factor found by Candy (1977). Reciprocal influences of parent on child and of child on parent, as well as of grandparent on grandchild and grandchild on grandparent (Bengtson & Troll, 1978; Hagestad, 1978), reflect ongoing socialization functions in the interactions of later life. Other relationships may also serve such functions (Troll et al., 1978), as discussed by Cicerelli.

Research is contradictory with respect to the effect on mental health of interpersonal relationships in later life. Some studies show higher morale among older people whose children live at a distance than among those whose children are close at hand (Troll et al., 1978). At the same time, Lowenthal and Haven (1968) found that one confidant—any confidant—separated older people who were able to cope in "the community" from those who landed in a psychiatric ward. Clark and Anderson (1967), on the other hand, found that people who had always lived alone fared better than those who had had close ties that were severed;

isolation is not the same as desolation. Alpert and Richardson conclude that a nonlinear effect is operating here. We need more research on the past histories of older people in relation to their present relationships. Unfortunately, most current "social network" investigations ignore this issue.

Measurement

As noted in various chapters, our understanding of interpersonal relations in later life depends largely on self-reports and evaluations by clinicians. Both such sources are subject to distortion. Self-reports have led to many of our most blatant misconceptions. Young people typically report that their loved ones are complementary in character to themselves. Their apparent desire to achieve Plato's unity may blind them to the similarities that are found when both partners are questioned. (See Bengtson & Kuypers, 1971, for a discussion of "developmental stake" in such distortions.) The same kind of discrepancy has been found repeatedly in studies of "identification" based on young-adult children's descriptions of their parents. Egalitarian-minded husbands and wives both report (and believe) that they are sharing housework and child care, but in a time-motion study of couples' household participation, Walker (1970) found that even a wife who is employed puts in five times as many hours per day as her husband. Similarly, after retirement, husbands do not move into the home and take over half of the housework, even though it may seem that way to them (Troll et al., 1978). What they do is continue to perform "masculine" tasks to "help out," which is not the same as assuming responsibility for them.

I mentioned earlier that counts of interactions do not give information about quality of interactions. Grandparents who live in the same homes as their grandchildren are more likely to say that they want closer and more meaningful interactions than are those who live in separate households. Daily visits may be empty and bitter, whereas weekly phone calls may provide life-sustaining warmth. Members of golden wedding couples are able to tell you everything the other one is doing, even though their communication is largely nonverbal (Parron, 1979).

Effects of relationships, when measured by clinicians' judgments or tests of life satisfaction, morale, or adjustment, are almost all based on nosologies derived from pathology. Now that we are asking new questions, we should be able to come up with new ways to answer them. Not only does our information consist of descriptive data but most of our questions ask for *more* descriptive data. A few explanatory variables have been considered, however: availability, sex, social class, health, mobility, personality, strength of family boundaries, and major life events. The first and last of these have already been discussed. The following paragraphs briefly review the others.

Sex Differences

Sex differences permeate all interpersonal relationships of later life, perhaps as much as they do relationships of earlier life (Troll et al., 1978). Women seem to be more affiliative and more tied to their families than are men. Sisters are the closest of all siblings, as noted by Cicirelli. Grandparental influence is most apparent in the maternal line. Wives are likely to be the major confidants of most older men. The families of older women are usually parent–child systems; those of older men are usually husband–wife systems. Widows turn to other women: their daughters and daughters-in-law, their sisters, and their friends. Widowers remarry.

Social Class

Education and economic condition are interrelated: The more education, the higher the socioeconomic status. Both together affect survival, in that higher socioeconomic status is associated with longer survival. Lower socioeconomic status has also been associated with earlier marriage, larger number of offspring, and thus greater availability of kin in later life. In spite of more immediate kin among lower socioeconomic families, however, the habits and values of middle-class people, which include visiting and entertaining more than working-class people do, tend to equalize contact. Middle-class people also interact with friends and colleagues more than do working-class people (Troll, 1971; Troll et al., 1978); geographic separation is less of a handicap to middle-class relationships because transportation is more readily affordable.

Health

Failing health in old age can set in motion a complex set of interpersonal changes. There can be simultaneous or sequential increases in both interaction frequency and intensity on the part of some and decreases in frequency and intensity on the part of others. Failing health is usually a signal to others to provide increased attention and care. On the other hand, decreasing reserves of strength can lead to reduced social activities both within and outside the family. Frail older people may find boisterous family gatherings and very active children beyond their capacity to enjoy or even tolerate. Longitudinal studies may in future show some disengagement *from* the family too at the very end of life.

Mobility

We live in a mobile society. People move up or down in socioeconomic status and out and around geographically, often cutting out opportunities to build up meaningful new interpersonal relationships while attenuating meaningful old ones (Hess, 1972). Old people are presumed to be particularly affected by mobility. Most of our data, however, show that geographic separation from close family and friends is usually time limited, with a coming together at a later point in time (Troll et al., 1978). There is a possible progression in old age from living in one's own home near one's children to moving into the household of a child, to long-term care institution, to death in an acute-care hospital. Migration to the sun belt, for example, may produce only temporary separation, which may be ended by subsequent migration south of other family members and perhaps even friends or, alternatively, by the return of sun-belt dwellers to be near their children when their health deteriorates.

Personality

Some people are more sociable than others. This is true at all ages. Undoubtedly, some people are more selective in their interpersonal relationships than others. The typology of Maas and Kuypers (1974) suggests that being family-centered in old age is the consequence of being family-centered earlier in life. One might expect that people-oriented or family-centered people would be the "desolates" of old age, when losses by death decimate the ranks of friends and kin, but we have no data here, nor any about substitution of relationships. Most late-life relationships tend to be of long standing. Most old widowers marry people they have known for years (McKain, 1969). Is it possible for bereft older people to replace old friends with new, or old loves with new? We should try to find out.

Life Events

Cytrynbaum's chapter focuses on the supposed universal transition of midlife. This is seen as being ac-

companied by predictable shifts in interpersonal relationships. Following on this theme, we might predict other psychically driven changes in feelings and interactions at other major turning points of life. Research in the 1980s, it is hoped, will look at shifts in friendship and kinship relations as signal variables marking off significant turning points of life. Shifts in life satisfaction, morale, or mental health may be less meaningful indicators of important life transformations than are shifts in interpersonal interactions. Lowenthal and her colleagues, particularly Majda Thurnher and David Chiriboga (Lowenthal, Thurner, & Chiriboga, (1975) have been in the forefront of such explorations. Much more extensive and intensive research is called for here.

Family System

In my chapter on grandparenting, I allude to the heuristic construct of the family system for conceptualizing interpersonal relations in old age as well as in early life. Common themes, rituals, and heroes, for example, may be indicators of strength of family boundaries and family integration that can help us understand the social behavior of old people—and thus, we hope, shape helping policy for more significant intervention. At least it would be desirable to differentiate between older people from "tight" families and those from "loose" families. Providing substitute family relations may be appropriate for those who have lost important kin—if such relations can be substituted. More peerlike interactions may be more appropriate for people who were not socialized to strong kin attachments.

REFERENCES

Bengtson, V., & Kuypers, J. Generational difference and the generational stake. *Aging and Human Development*, 1971, *2*, 249–260.

Bengtson, V., & Troll, L. Youth and their parents: Feedback and intergenerational influence in socialization. In R. Lerner & G. Spanier (Eds.), *Child influences on marital and family interaction.* New York: Academic Press, 1978.

Buhler, C. The developmental structure of goal setting in group and individual studies. In C. Buhler & F. Massarik (Eds.), *The course of human life.* New York: Springer, 1968.

Candy, S. *A comparative analysis of functions of friendship in six age groups of men and women.* Unpublished doctoral dissertation, Wayne State University, 1977.

Clark, M., & Anderson, B. *Culture and aging.* Springfield, Ill.: Charles C Thomas, 1967.

Cumming, E., & Henry, W. *Growing old: The process of disengagement*. New York: Basic Books, 1961.

Hagestad, G. *Patterns of communication and influence between grandparents and grandchildren in a changing society*. Paper presented at the World Conference of Sociology, Upsala, Sweden, August 1978.

Hess, B. Friendship. In M. W. Riley, M. Johnson, & A. Foner (Eds.), *Aging and society. Vol. 3. A socialization of age stratification*. New York: Russell Sage Foundation, 1972.

Hill, R., Foote, N., Aldous, J., Carlson, R., & Macdonald, R. *Family development in three generations*. Cambridge, Mass.: Schenkman, 1970.

Jung, C. The stages of life. In *Structure and dynamics of the psyche* (R. F. C. Hull, trans.). Princeton, N.J.: Princeton University Press, 1969.

Lopata, H. The meaning of friendship in widowhood. In L. Troll, J. Israel, & K. Israel (Eds.), *Looking ahead: A woman's guide to the problems and joys of growing older*. Englewood Cliffs, N.J.: Prentice-Hall, 1977.

Lowenthal, M., & Haven, C. Interaction and adaptation: Intimacy as a critical variable. *American Sociological Review*, 1968, *33*, 20–30.

Lowenthal, M., Thurnher, M., & Chiriboga, D. *Four stages of life*. San Francisco: Jossey Bass, 1975.

Maas, H., & Kuypers, J. *From thirty to seventy*. San Francisco: Jossey-Bass, 1974.

McKain, W. C. *Retirement marriages* (Agriculture Experimental Station Monograph 3). Storrs: University of Connecticut Press, 1969.

Mischel, W. Sex-typing and socialization. In P. Mussen (Ed.), *Carmichael's handbook of child psychology* (Vol. 2). New York: Wiley, 1970.

Nydegger, C. & Mitteness, L. Transitions in fatherhood. *Generations*, 1979, *4*, 14–15.

Parron, E. *An exploratory study of intimacy in golden wedding couples*. Unpublished master's thesis, Rutgers University, 1978.

Parron, E. *Relationships in black and white golden wedding couples*. Unpublished doctoral dissertation, Rutgers University, 1979.

Reedy, M. *Age and sex differences in personal needs and the nature of love: A study of young, middle-aged, and older adult couples*. Unpublished doctoral dissertation, University of Southern California, 1977.

Rosow, I. *Social integration of the aged*. New York: Free Press, 1967.

Stueve, A., & Fischer, C. Social networks and older women. Presented at a Combined National Institute on Aging – National Institute of Mental Health Workshop on Older Women, Washington, D.C., September 1978.

Troll, L. The family of later life: A decade review. *Journal of Marriage and the Family*, 1971, *33*, 263–290.

Troll, L., Miller, S., & Atchley, R. *Families of later life*. Belmont, Calif.: Wadsworth, 1978.

Walker, K. Time spent by husbands in household work. *Family Economics Review*, June 1970, pp. 8–11.

Judith L. Alpert and Mary Sue Richardson

32

Parenting

In contrast to the more traditional focus on parental effects on the child, research and theory on the effects of parenting on parents are considered. Following delineation of significant demographic trends affecting family composition and structure and a critical review of family stage theory, research on the effects of parenting within each of five parenting stages is reviewed. These stages are (1) before becoming parents, (2) childbirth and postpartum, (3) early and middle years of parenting, (4) parenting with adolescent children, and (5) parenting with adult children. In addition, the effects of parenting on marital relationships and careers are considered.

There are two major approaches to the study of parenting. One concerns the effect of parenting on the parent. This focus on adults—largely multidisciplinary in orientation, engaging psychologists, sociologists, and economists, among others—was rare prior to the last decade. Although some researchers who focus on the adults involved in parenting believe that the well-being of parents is related to the well-being of their children, their concern, particularly if they have a life span developmental orientation, is with parenthood as a role in adult development. In this context socialization in adulthood is best conceptualized in terms of the roles adults enact (Brim, 1966). As a role, parenthood is a process that begins before the birth of the first child and continues throughout life. The nature of the role sets a framework for viewing continuity and change over the life cycle.

The earlier and more traditional approach to the study of parenting concerns the effects of parenting on the child. This has been the orientation of both developmental and other psychologists for at least half a century. For the most part child-focused experts do not consider the needs of parents. Here the literature is directed toward identification of parental behaviors associated with children's functioning (see Clarke-Stewart, 1978, for a review of the literature). More recently, given changes in family structure, those interested in parental effects on the child have had to broaden this definition of parenting. For example, increased employment of mothers outside the home has generated interest in the effects of maternal employment on children (Etaugh, 1974; Hoffman, 1974; Siegel & Hass, 1963; Wallston, 1973) and the effects of day care on children (Bronfenbrenner, 1975; Kagan, Kearsleg, and Zelazo, 1978; Kilner, 1977; Woolsey, 1977). A related consideration of the father's parental role has shifted from attention to such effects as fathers' absence on children, particularly on boys (Herzog & Sudia, 1968), to more direct attention to the effects of fathers as parents on children, including issues such as sex role identification, intellectual development, motivation to achieve, vocational choice, and mental health (Biller, 1971; R. Fein, 1978; Hamilton, 1977; Lynn, 1974).

Although, as we shall see, this simple dichotomy between children or parents as the dependent variable is theoretically limited and outdated, it provides a framework for focusing on the effects of parenting on

This chapter is based on a paper presented at the Social Policy Luncheon sponsored by the Bush Center in Child Development and Social Policy, Yale University, New Haven, Connecticut, September 28, 1979. The authors acknowledge the assistance of Hedy Bernstein for gathering library materials. A grant from the Bush Center in Child Development and Social Policy, Yale University, supported the writing of this chapter.

parents. Since parenting occurs in a family, it is affected not only by the individual personalities of the interacting parent–child dyads but also by the nature of the family system in which parenting takes place. Thus for a fuller understanding of parenting—which represents a nexus of psychological and sociological influences on individual development—we draw on research and theory in family sociology as well as in psychology, in particular on the research and theory generated by sociologists interested in developmental theories of the family. The questions these sociologists address most closely parallel the concerns of psychologists interested in parenting as an adult role (Hill & Mattessich, 1979).

The chapter comprises the following sections. First, the basic demographic data on changes in parenting roles and family structures set the context for our examination of parenting. Following is a section on family-stage theory in family studies, in which our rationale is developed for selecting the stages in which to organize the research on parenting effects on parents. Research related to parenting within each stage is then considered. Including all parenting stages rather than focusing specifically on those stages most relevant to aging reflects the state of the literature on parenting and our expectation that this will provide a better framework for considering effects of parenting at any life stage. The research base reviewed ranges from specific empirical and descriptive studies to more general, theoretically based research. Although we attempt to put some order into what might be considered a potpourri of findings, it is important to recognize that this situation reflects the state of knowledge about parenting. Throughout we emphasize the need for the generation of theoretical models addressed to issues of parenting. Finally we look at how parenting affects and interacts with other major roles in adults' lives across stages. Specifically, relations are considered between parenting and one aspect of marriage, *marital quality*, and one aspect of work, *role conflict*. Thus the chapter's organization reflects a perspective in which parenting is conceived as a life experience and a role with implications for adult development, both directly and in interaction with other major life roles. In the language of family sociology (Aldous, 1978), this chapter represents a synthesis of research on the parenting career in the parent–child subsystem of the family and on the effects of parenting on aspects of the marriage and work careers.

Some United States Demographic Trends

Given space limitations, this review is selective rather than exhaustive; too many demographic statistics are published for complete coverage. For example, the U.S. Department of Labor, U.S. Department of Commerce, and U.S. Department of Health, Education and Welfare report on such topics as marital and family characteristics of workers; labor force patterns of working, divorced, and separated women; and population characteristics of children in day-care and preschool settings. These data are available for various racial, social class, and other specialized groups. Glick (1977) provided an excellent review of changes over the last 80 years in family life-cycle patterns for women; other reviews have considered implications of recent changes (Hoffman, 1977; Van Dusen & Sheldon, 1976). In general, the picture is one of much change, at least in some characteristics.

The first change is a decline in the number of children people have or plan to have. After World War II, during the 1950s, there was a steady increase in family size. The 1970s saw a reversal of that trend. In 1965, for example, women who had ever been married, aged 30–34, bore an average of 3 children. In 1975 the same kind of woman had an average of 2.4 children (U.S. Bureau of the Census, 1978).

The second change is a decrease in the proportion of their lives that people spend in active child-rearing—if their children are closely spaced. The average woman in the 1970s will bear children for about 7 years (from age 23 to 30), as compared with 10 years (from age 23 to 33) for the early 1900s mother. Moreover the 1970s mother will have preschool-age children for a little over a decade (Glick & Norton, 1977). The corresponding change is the increase in the proportion of the adult life span remaining after the independence of children, with a concomitant increase in the significance of issues related to parenting with adult children.

The third change is a rise in one-parent families. The number of children under 18 living with only their mothers increased by 3 million from 1970 to 1978 (U.S. Bureau of the Census, 1978). This increase occurred despite the 5.4-million decrease in persons under age 18 from 1950 to 1977. During the year from 1977 to 1978 (Glick & Norton, 1979), the number of one-parent families increased by 9%.

The fourth change is an increase in women's employment outside the home. The increase is most notable (57% increase from 1960 to 1975) for mothers with preschool children. The labor-force participation rates for ever-married mothers with children less than age 6 were 18.2%, 25.3%, and 38.9% for 1955, 1965, and 1975, respectively (U.S. Department of Labor, 1976). Although women who are separated, divorced, or widowed have higher labor-force participation rates than those still married, approximately one third of ever-married mothers participated in the labor force in 1975. Thus, mothers at all stages are more frequently employed, with associated changes in family structure and the experience of parenting.

Obviously these demographic trends are related to each other and are due to a complex interaction of political, medical, economic, social, and psychological forces. In relation to family structures, it is clear that it is increasingly outdated to conceive of a nuclear family—with traditional division of labor by gender—as typical. Moreover, given extension of the life span and restriction of childbearing years, it is misleading to focus only on the childbearing stages of parental roles. The experience of later stages of parenting is both more common and more important than it used to be in its interaction with adult development.

Family Stage Theory

Family stages are generally considered as structurally and qualitatively distinct and as an organizing rubric for examining developmental issues. A number of stages have been formulated in family studies. These are usually multidimensional, based on criteria such as age of oldest child, duration of marriage, and employment status of father (Aldous, 1978; Duvall, 1977; Glick, 1977; Rodgers, 1973). Since stages represent a particular configuration of positions and roles, shifts from one stage to the next are precipitated by a clear break with early family structure and a change in positions and roles.

Associated with the concept of stages is the concept of family developmental tasks. As presented by Aldous (1978), a family developmental task operates as a bridge between the individual and society, in that the family must meet the developing needs of the individual and the needs of the society. Tasks proposed include, for example, physical maintenance of family members, maintenance of family members' motivation to perform family and other roles, and socialization. These tasks are modified and become more or less salient at different points in the life cycle. Magrabi and Marshall (1965) articulated the concept of limited linkage in which success with meeting tasks at one particular stage sets the boundaries for possible task performance at later stages.

In her review Aldous attests to the conceptual promise of stage and task formulations while recognizing that these formulations are mainly postulates with little empirical support. In a much more critical vein, other writers have noted that family stage theory is descriptive rather than explanatory, that the organismic assumptions of such developmental models (i.e., that development is linear rather than potentially regenerative) may not apply, and that the stage formulations available imply a nuclear family system, which ignores historical changes in normative family structures (Hill & Mattessich, 1979; Klein, Jorgensen, & Miller, 1978). The diverse family structures and situations delineated by Rapoport, Rapoport, and Strelitz (1977) include divorced parents, childless marriages, one-parent families, adoptive and foster parents, communal living, dual-worker families, and stepparenting. A family-stage model that does not incorporate these structures and situations is not useful. On a more empirical level, studies have indicated that multidimensional family-stage designations offer little if any explanatory power beyond the individual criteria for stages (Nock, 1979) or in comparison to other stratification schemes (Spanier, Sauer, & Larzelere, 1979).

In summary, then, despite the promise of family-stage models, they do not provide the comprehensive and empirically sound frameworks we need. A promising approach suggested by Broderick (1971) and Magrabi and Marshall (1965), which avoids the problem of stages, entails a decision or game-tree model on which development of individual families can be charted in terms of specific turning points. It may be that we need to reformulate the definition of family itself in order to generate a more universally applicable family-stage model.

Given the lack of any better family-stage model at present, we will focus on the subsystem of parent and child and, with the age of the oldest child as the sole criterion of stage, use a variation of the descriptive stage framework of Rapoport et al. (1977). The five stages considered here are (1) before becoming parents, (2) childbirth and postpartum, (3) early and middle years of parenting, (4) parenting with adolescent children, and (5) parenting with adult children. Obviously, in the presence of several children, particularly if they are widely spaced, a parent may experience several stages simultaneously.

Stages of Parenting

Before Becoming Parents

Decision making. Following worldwide concern about overpopulation, research on decisions about parenthood has borne fruit, as Kupinsky's (1977) and Safilios-Rothschild's (1977) reviews indicate. Inquiries have cut across national boundaries. In fact, much of the research has been by demographers and sociologists in developing and third-world countries. Psychologists have not been as centrally involved, although some psychological models for understanding fertility are available (Adler, 1979; Fawcett, 1973; Fishbein & Jaccard, 1973; Hoffman & Hoffman, 1973; Veevers, 1974).

Unfortunately variables such as parenthood motivation, values of children, satisfactions and costs of children, and attitudes toward children have been relatively unsuccessful in predicting fertility behaviors. Clearly there is a need for more psychological and sociological research and theory on such decision making, probably within an interdisciplinary framework, as Newman and Thompson (1976) suggest.

Studies of young men and women who are not parents show that their perceptions of the parent role are most positive when parent and work roles are combined (Alpert & Richardson, 1978; Alpert, Richardson, Perlmutter, & Shutzer, 1980; Richardson & Alpert, 1976, in press). These findings, based on variations of the Thematic Apperception Test (TAT), are in line with data reporting widespread plans of young people to combine family and occupational roles (e.g., Wilson, 1975). Generally these positive perceptions of the parent role are supported by societal expectations (Russo, 1976) and media portrayal (Kellmer, 1974). They contrast, however, with research showing the stress and problems of parenting and its negative consequence in relation to other adult roles (literature is reviewed later on parental stress and dissatisfaction, marital satisfaction over the family life cycle, and role conflict for employed parents). In general, this empirical literature does not seem to have reached most adults who decide to have a child. The popular literature generally focuses more on the "how to" of parenting; books entitled *Preparation for Parenthood* have more to do with parent-craft than with parenting (Rapoport et al., 1977). For the most part this literature indicates that people in our society have little idea of what is entailed when they make the decision to parent. The possibility that perceptions may become more realistic among those who postpone parenting to a later age has not been considered.

Pregnancy. Much of the literature on pregnancy and the prospective mother has been psychoanalytic in orientation. Earlier research with clinical samples concerned the woman's feeling of crisis, her level of psychosexual development, and her acceptance of her traditional female role (Deutsch, 1945). More recently the emphasis has shifted from pathology to a largely psychoanalytically based "developmental task" model with an attempt to predict "adaptation" to motherhood (e.g., Benedek, 1970; Bibring, 1959). While research associated with this literature generally involves small samples, is correlational in design, and suffers from a lack of reliable and valid instruments, there seem to be some cumulative and consistent results: (a) Pregnancy is frequently a period of developmental crisis or, at least, transition (Leifer, 1977); (b) Maternal feelings increase over time, and the feelings of the pregnant woman change toward mother, husband, and self (Albeit, 1975; Ballou, 1978, Leifer, 1977; Newton, 1955); and (c) Certain personality measures (e.g., anxiety, negative attitudes toward pregnancy, emotional stability), the quality of the relationship with husband and mother, and characteristics of the pregnancy predict emotional adjustment to pregnancy and to parenthood (Chester, 1979; Cohen, 1966; Colman & Colman, 1973; Davids & Holden, 1970; Davids, Holden, & Gray, 1963; Eichler, Winickoff, Grossman, Anzalone, & Gofseyeff, 1977; Flapan & Schoenfeld, 1972; Grimm & Venet, 1966; Zemlick & Watson, 1953).

The more recent studies are more sophisticated in design, eschewing retrospective data and pursuing a more complex order of relations among variables. In this regard the study by Eichler et al. (1977) is particularly interesting in its attempt to show multiple links between characteristics of the fetus and later infant and the mother's psychological and physical state. A completely different approach was taken by Ballou (1978), who used the case study method within a psychoanalytic framework to examine the experience of pregnancy for the mother.

There has been little research so far on the expectant father. Several studies indicate that men's attitudes and problems associated with pregnancy are similar to those expressed by their wives (Colman & Colman, 1973; Liebenberg, 1967; Soule, 1974) and that they sometimes experience also a reevaluation of their own parental relationship, in this case with their fathers (Gurwitt, 1976). Fein (1976) reviewed research in this area. Chester's (1979) data, however, showed a sex difference in the experience of pregnancy, with the likelihood that men are more concerned about role changes of parenting than are their wives during pregnancy.

Research is also needed on the psychosocial factors related to socialization for the parent role during the pregnancy stage, particularly in light of the literature on unrealistic expectation for parenting, reviewed previously, and the sociological literature indicating lack of any effective socialization for parenthood (Lopata, 1971). The experimental study by Taylor and Langer (1977), demonstrating an avoidance of pregnant women, particularly by men, raises questions about possible environmental and social strains during pregnancy. Research on childbirth and parent-preparation classes, which has typically focused on their effects on the childbirth experience or subsequent adaptation to parenting with inconsistent results (Doering & Entwisle, 1975; Parke & O'Leary, 1975; Wente & Crockenberg, 1976), might profitably consider effects on the parents' experience of pregnancy itself. Also to be considered is the relation between age and the experience of pregnancy.

Finally, it is striking that so little research has examined psychological correlates of hormonal changes during pregnancy. Rossi's (1977) review of this area indicates potentially promising directions, derived from animal research, for research on humans.

Childbirth and Postpartum

Childbirth. Research on psychological variables in childbirth is scarce, since, as Lamb (1976, 1978) pointed out, the childbirth experience has only recently been considered a natural rather than a medical or surgical experience. The most interesting research focuses on maternal or paternal bonding. Rossi (1977) has argued that the behavior of parents is of particular evolutionary significance, is critical in the care and development of children, and, because of biosocial factors, is more easily learned by mothers than by fathers. Research on bonding also has implications for obstetrical practices, which typically have interfered with the normal bonding process (Arms, 1975). Much of the research on bonding has studied only the mothers and has both described the specific maternal behavioral patterns evoked by infants (Klaus, Kennell, Plumb & Zuehike, 1970; Stern, 1974) and related them to variables such as maternal responsiveness at later stages (Leifer, 1977; Parlee, in press). Other research indicates that the experience of birth is a moving emotional experience for fathers as well as mothers (Greenberg & Morris, 1974; Klaus & Kennell, 1976), that fathers, like mothers, are eager to interact with their infants (Parke & Sawin, 1976, 1977), and that strong and salient attachments develop between fathers and infants from an early age (Lamb, 1977; Lamb & Lamb, 1976). Nydegger and Mittemas (1979) indicate that older fathers are particularly likely to be involved with their young children. Although the question of whether mothers form bonds with their infants more easily than fathers is unanswered, that fathers form strong, affective bonds with infants is well supported.

Postpartum. The traditional emphasis in the literature on the postpartum period has been on maladaptive states such as depression or psychosis, with attempts to predict premorbid characteristics (Davids, DeVault, & Talmadge, 1961; Gordon & Gordon, 1968). Although much of this literature is flawed by use of retrospective data, one of the better designed studies traced the depressive reaction following childbirth to women's problems in their own maternal identification (Melges, 1968). More recently, Turner and Izzi (1978) questioned whether interference with the early maternal bonding process may not precipitate depression.

While research on postpartum depression tends to focus only on the mother and is interested mainly in psychopathology, other studies have looked at social changes, particularly at the significance of the first child as a crisis or transitional event (Dyer, 1963; Hobbs & Cole, 1976; LeMasters, 1957; Rossi, 1968). It seems to be more difficult for mothers than for fathers (Hobbs, 1965) and more difficult for women who have had a career (Douglas, 1968). Chester's (1979) study suggests that mothers do not face the implications of role and social changes until after the birth, owing perhaps to their preoccupation with the physical aspects of pregnancy. Parlee (in press) and Rossi (1968) indicate that the social isolation experienced by new mothers may be a particular problem. There is evidence that the transition to parenthood precipitates a great deal of change in mothers' social support systems, change that is related to their psychological functioning (Richardson & Kagan, 1979).

Few studies have focused on problems in fathers' postpartum adaptation. Fathers describe their problems as loss of attention from wife and difficulty in developing a coherent role vis-à-vis wife and child (Fein, 1975). Weinberg (1979), using a multidimensional scaling procedure, identified similar dimensions of stress in parenting for both mothers and fathers. These difficulties concerned both care of child and adult life management. Further research is needed to examine more fully the sources of stress in the transition to parenthood and to identify factors related to parent adaptation.

Early and Middle Years of Parenting

This stage of parenting, according to Rapoport et al. (1977), is initiated when the child moves out of infant dependency and continues until the child reaches adolescence. They describe it primarily as a plateau with elements of strain, particularly in the early years because of the psychological demands of children and financial pressures.

With respect to psychological demands, research on women in a conventional nuclear-family structure has shown them to be "mothers at risk." Sociologists have documented the psychosocial deprivations of housewives confronted with the constant demands of young children. (See Rapoport et al., 1977, for a review of this literature.) For example, Oakley (1974) compared the housewife role in its monotony, fragmentation, and pressures for speed in performance to factory work. Caplow (1954) described the role as one of the few "occupations" that requires no training or experience, rewards inefficient behavior, and involves activities of low value. On a psychological level, some studies of depression show that married women with young children living at home are more depressed and anxious than men or other women (Brown, Bhrolchain, & Harris, 1975; Campbell, Converse, & Rodgers, 1976; Mazer, 1976; Radloff, 1975; Seiden, 1976). Not all studies support this conclusion, however. For example, Pearlin (1975) concludes that there is no difference between employed women and homemakers with regard to depression; rather, the meaning of their roles to the women involved must be taken into account in order to understand the incidence of depression.

Early and middle stages of parenting are also stages of financial pressure and a high level of occupational demand, stresses borne predominantly by men (Benson, 1967; Berger & Wright, 1978; Lynn, 1974) and evidenced in some by decreased job satisfaction (Wilensky, 1961, 1964). According to Rapoport et al. (1977), there are two potential sources of change in this pressure on men to perform in their occupational careers. One is their dissatisfaction with this traditional emphasis on occupational achievement, and the second is the positive value placed on parenting for men, as exemplified in the writings of Farrell (1974) and Fasteau (1974). A force militating against such change is the degree to which the structure of work continues to make stereotyped demands on men (Kanter, 1977a; Rosen & Jerdee, 1974).

The foregoing research assumes a conventional family structure, which our examination of demographic trends has shown to be decreasingly normative. Nevertheless, numerous authors (Gutmann, 1975; Hoffman & Manis, 1978; Lamb, 1978) have referred to the conservative impact of children on gender roles, accentuating the occupational role of the father and the child-rearing role of the mother. The extent to which this conservative impact is moderated by diverse family structures and situations is not known. On the one hand, data show that mothers who work outside the home are more likely than homemakers to share equally with their husbands in family decision making (Blood & Wolfe, 1960; Hoffman, 1977). On the other hand, available evidence documents that working mothers do most of the family work—that is, child care and housekeeping responsibilities (Pleck, 1977; Robinson, 1977)—which suggests a gender role differentiation similar to housewives. Single parents, having both job and home as sources of strain, should be under considerable stress during these years.

In contrast to the research on sources of strain, Hoffman and Manis (1978) reported on satisfaction and dissatisfaction with the parent role. Their results indicate that, despite data showing more tension and anxieties among young parents than parents at any other stage (Campbell et al., 1976), there is also greatest satisfaction at the preschool stage.

Parenting With Adolescents

Parenting with adolescents generally is described as a period of conflict and strain. Issues of conflict between parents and their adolescent children that are mentioned in the literature include sexuality, achievement, setting of limits, communications barriers, and values (Rapoport et al., 1977). Much of the literature is descriptive and provides little insight into the effects of adolescent children on parents beyond the fact of conflict. The conflict is frequently discussed in terms such as "generation gap," although some indicate that the extent of conflict may not be as great as is frequently assumed (e.g., Thurnher, Spence, & Lowenthal, 1974).

Other studies have taken a more theoretical approach to the issue of generational similarity and contrast, although most have assumed that change occurs predominantly in the younger generation. Others suggest that the direction of change in the context of generational contrast is reciprocal (Hagestad, 1977; Mead, 1970). Drawing on this literature, Bengtson and Troll (1978) developed one of the more sophisticated theoretical models, which elucidates the reciprocal influence of parents and their adolescent children. Their model addresses the question of generational change and continuity. They draw on the literature describing parent–child similarity in four areas, politics, religion, sex roles, and work-achievement orientation (e.g., Bengtson & Troll, 1978; Troll, Neugarten, & Kraines, 1969), and studies on the strength of parent–child affect (e.g., Bengtson & Black, 1978; Hagestad, 1977; Kalish & Knudtson, 1976; Troll & Smith, 1976). The model describes intergenerational influence in which the close emotional ties between parents and children provide a basis for reciprocal influence. In this model the bilateral influence between youth and parents is affected by family themes and historical processes. The model, with its supporting research, represents and depicts parents affected by major social and historical changes through interaction with their adolescent children. Moreover, by focusing on the degree of affect between parents and adolescent children, it puts into perspective the discussions of intergenerational conflict.

The seeds of another theoretical approach to parenting with adolescents can be seen in the brief comments in the literature on the interlocking of developmental tasks of both adolescents and their middle-aged parents (Aldous, 1978; Bengtson & Kuypers, 1971; Rapoport et al., 1977). Although this notion has not yet been fully articulated or developed, it offers another perspective on reciprocal influence of parents and adolescent children.

Parents of adolescents are often the children of aging parents. Blenkner (1965) has suggested that the development of filial maturity—that is, to be a resource for an aged parent without precipitating a dependent "role reversal"—is a critical task at this stage. Two contrasting images of these middle-aged parents are presented: (1) They are overburdened by demands of both younger and older generations (Brim, 1976; Hess & Waring, 1978; Vincent, 1972), or (2) they are a "comfortable" generation whose resources are not fully tapped (Fogarty, 1975). Clearly, parenting with adolescents is, to some extent at least, affected by the experience of being children of an older generation.

Parenting With Adult Children

The stage of parenting with adult children begins when children are presumed to achieve adult status and extends through the rest of life. Given longevity data, this period may cover a considerable time span. We do not include grandparenting here because it is dealt with elsewhere in this book (Chapter 35).

There is a dearth of literature on parenting in the later years (Chilman, 1968; Rapoport et al., 1977; Troll, 1971). Indicative of this neglect is the common term, *postparental*, applied to this stage (Troll, Miller, & Atchley, 1979). The notion that parenting is over once children are "launched" can be traced, in part, to some misconceptions about the isolation of the nuclear child-rearing family and a sense that adult children should be left on their own. Within this general picture of neglect, however, two areas have received attention: reactions to the "empty nest," and the nature of the ties between adult children and their parents.

The stereotype of the depressed and irritable middle-aged woman has typically been associated in the popular imagination with menopause. More recently, psychological symptomatology during middle age in women has been attributed to role change and role loss as children leave the home. In this vein, Pauline Bart's (1970) work on depression in middle-aged women is perhaps best known. Contrasting with this view is an emerging body of research indicating that the independence of children is greeted with relief and increased satisfaction by many women (Chilman, 1968; Harkins, 1978; Lowenthal & Chiriboga, 1972; Rollins & Feldman, 1970). There is some evidence that this may be particularly true for women who have

worked. Although there are some exceptions (Lowenthal, Thurnher, & Chiriboga, 1976), fathers' reactions to this role transition are generally not considered. This neglect appears to be particularly inappropriate in light of the studies that show an increasing family orientation among older men (Gutmann, 1975). Nydegger and Mittemas (1979) note that men who become fathers at later ages experience more companionship with their children throughout this stage than do those who are fathers at an earlier age.

Until recently the evidence on ties between adult children and their parents was restricted to descriptions of the degree of contact and patterns of mutual helping (Cantor, 1975; Hill, 1970; Shanas, 1973; Sussman, 1965, 1976). This research documented a surprisingly high level of both contact and helping, even when children and parents lived far apart. These factors were often assumed to imply a high level of positive affect. Hess and Waring (1978), however, questioned this assumption in their review of the literature and suggested that contact and giving help may not imply positive affect at all. Since current social policy absolves adult children of the onus of caring for their aging parents, ties are now essentially voluntary for both generations of adults and may be problem filled. Forces likely to impede positive parent–child ties in old age include the cohort differences due to historical change, constraints on the sharing and helping process, other heavy demands on the middle-aged children, and dislocating role transitions for both generations. On the positive side, forces pulling the generations together are essentially elements in the socialization process such as similarity in values and role modeling.

Despite the incompleteness of our knowledge about the bases for continuing familial interaction across generations, current research documents the inaccuracy of the prevailing stereotype depicting ill and aging parents as wanting to be dependent on their adult children (Shanas, 1973). Older parents for the most part express strong preferences for remaining independent of their children (Sussman, 1953; Yankelovich, Skelly & White, Inc., 1977).

Regarding the effect of ties with adult children on the well-being of the parents, evidence is meager and inconsistent (Hess & Waring, 1978), but there is some evidence that a moderate degree of contact between adult children and their parents is optimal (Kerchkoff, 1966; Stinnett, Collins, & Montgomery, 1970).

In sum, our understanding of the source, nature, and effects of ties between adult children and their parents is sketchy. One would expect these ties to change over time, given the long time span included in this stage for most parents. Although the conceptualization of filial maturity gives some focus to our understanding of adult children's relationship to their parents, the literature has not fully addressed the corresponding task of the older parents (Troll et al., 1979).

Marital Quality

The effect of parenting on adults' lives can be considered in terms of its impact on the marital relationship. Two ways of conceptualizing this relationship are in terms of marital stability and marital quality (Lewis & Spanier, 1979). This section focuses on marital quality as measured by satisfaction, integration, and adjustment, since these aspects of the marital relationship have generated most research. Marital quality has been defined, interpreted, and measured differently by different investigators. The most common research design adopted in studies of parenting effects on marital quality is cross-sectional post hoc, which is not conducive to the study of development. Groups differing on such variables as presence/absence, number, or age of children have been compared on marital adjustment, stability, or satisfaction. In addition, there are some longitudinal studies (e.g., Burgess & Wallin, 1953; Luckey & Bain, 1970) and some studies not relying on self-report data (e.g., Rosenblatt, 1974). These limitations in defining terms, identifying stages, and selecting methodology have been considered (Hoffman & Manis, 1978; Rollins & Galligan, 1978; Schram, 1979).

Despite the methodological problems, there are some clear trends, as a number of reviews indicate (Aldous, 1978; Christensen, 1968; Lewis & Spanier, 1979; Rollins & Feldman, 1970; Schram, 1979). General marital satisfaction decreases during the early years of child rearing, beginning with the arrival of the first child, but sometimes increases after the departure of children from the parental home. This U-shaped curve is believed to be very flat; only a limited variation in marital satisfaction is associated with family stages (Rollins & Cannon, 1974; Schram, 1979; Spanier, Lewis, & Cole, 1974).

The results need to be interpreted cautiously, given the many methodological problems in this area and, in many of the studies, the lack of control of important intervening variable such as ages of parents, number of years married, and occupational career. At least three factors could account for an upward trend in stated satisfaction during later parenthood: (1) a cumulative drop in dissatisfied couples over time, due to divorce; (2) still-married research participants' need to justify a long marital life together; and (3) role changes that covary with parental stages. Obviously the results are complicated here, and the drop in marital quality with

advent of children does not exist for all couples. One of the more interesting findings from Hoffman and Manis's (1978) study is that if children are planned and desired, they can strengthen rather than weaken a marriage. This accords with a hypothesis developed by Christensen (1968) to account for the inconsistent relation between number of children and marital satisfaction. According to Christensen, it is not the number of children in a family but the ratio of children born to the number desired that is related to marital satisfaction.

There are a number of research needs in this area. First, more research should take into account current demographic trends. With women's increasing educational attainment and labor-force participation, old results are becoming obsolete. Also, most of the research on marital satisfaction is based on married couples who are the children's biological parents. There is little or no research on the effect of the presence of children on relationship or marital satisfaction between unmarried adults living together or remarried couples when only one member is the biological parent of the child. Second, in-depth studies are needed to illuminate how marriage relations change as a function of children, rather than simply how children affect some index of marital quality. In a recent study Hoffman and Manies (1978) considered changes in marital power, division of labor, and husband–wife affectional relationships through the stage of parenting with adolescents. Particularly needed are studies on the effects of children on marriages in later life and studies on transitions in the family or in the parenting life cycle (Schram, 1979). Third, the reciprocal influence between the quality of marital life and the character and development of children should receive attention. Different types of children may have a differential impact on marital adjustment (Dyer, 1963). Finally, two promising approaches to theory building in this area are available. One is directed solely at the reciprocal interaction between parents and children over time (Rollins & Galligan, 1978); the second considers parenting stages as only one source of influence in a broad theoretical model of marital quality and stability (Lewis & Spanier, 1979).

Role Conflict

Much of the research on the relation between parent and work roles focuses on role conflict and considers primarily mothers (Rollins & Nye, 1979). Studies have drawn on role theory for their conceptualizations of conflict (Goode, 1962; Gross, Mason, & McEachern, 1958; Kahn, Wolfe, Quinn, Snoek, & Rosenthal, 1964; Secord and Backman, 1974) and have documented the incidence of role conflict among employed mothers (Heckman, Bryson, & Bryson, 1977; Johnson & Johnson, 1976; Nevill & Damico, 1975; Rapoport & Rapoport, 1969).

Additional research has examined correlates of conflict such as husbands' support of their wives' employment (Bailyn, 1970; Hawley, 1972; Kundsin, 1974) and wives' level of career commitment or involvement (Holahan & Gilbert, 1979a, 1979b; Pearlin, 1975), strategies for reducing conflict (Gilbert, Holahan, & Manning, 1979; Hall, 1972), and the effects of conflict (Cartwright, 1978; Kaley, 1971; Powell & Reznikoff, 1976; Stewart, 1978). Stewart's approach to this last issue highlights the complexity of the question. She distinguished between positive (e.g., life satisfaction) and negative (e.g., physical and psychological symptoms) index of mental health and found that combinations of work and family roles are more highly correlated to life satisfaction than to psychological symptoms. Rollins and Nye's (1979) review of this area supports the notion that employment of mothers is related to both positive and negative index of mental health and thus is not itself a good predictor.

The bulk of the literature on men's relationships with their families considers issues such as the effect of father's occupation on family socioeconomic status and their sons' educational and occupational aspirations (Aldous, Osmond, & Hicks, 1979). What is more remarkable, however, is that fathers are found to be more involved in family than in work roles (Adamek & Goudy, 1966; Rosenberg, 1957; Staines & O'Connor, 1979). Pleck's study (in press) demonstrates one implication of this involvement, in that for both men and women, family satisfaction contributes more to overall well-being than does job satisfaction.

If fathers are so highly involved in their family roles, one would expect to find role conflict among fathers as well as mothers. Indeed, equal levels of role conflict for men and women have been reported (Herman and Gyllstrom, 1977; Holahan & Gilbert, 1979a; Pleck, in press). It is difficult, however, to reconcile these data with previously cited studies on the lack of equivalent time spent by employed parents on family work: those studies show that employed mothers continue to do the major share of the family work. Perceptions of conflict are very likely affected by expectations, which probably differ by sex. That is, men may expect less conflict than women and may consequently perceive more conflict when it does occur.

Conceptual models developed by Safilios-Rothschild (1976) and Pleck (1977) have pointed to the structural incompatibilities between work and family systems as these affect men and women, and Kanter (1977b) noted that the social sciences have largely ignored the interaction between the two domains. She described

several valuable lines of inquiry that extend beyond the limited notion of role conflict.

Many of these studies were concerned primarily with the earlier stages of parenthood. Only one study systematically considered the effect of family life stage on the experience of conflict for adult women. Hall (1975) reported that conflict for women and the number of roles performed increases with each successive stage of parenting, at least through the stage of parenting with adolescent children. Thus role conflict is not specific to the early stages of parenting only.

Conclusion

Research and theory on parenting is an emerging area, rich in potential but limited in actual findings. With few exceptions, most studies reviewed used cross-sectional designs, which do not distinguish between the influences of historical change and cohort membership. We can have little confidence, therefore, that our conclusions about the nature and experience of parenting will be generalizable to other cohorts. For example, recent major changes in womens' work patterns strongly influence the literature on role conflict. The experience of the Depression and World War II, for members of the current older generations of parents, colors our knowledge about the later stages of parenting. The advancement of the field will be furthered by more widespread use of research designs capable of separating out these confounding influences. The models described by Schaie (1973) are exemplary in this respect.

We have mentioned that parenting does not always occur in conventional nuclear families. Given recent demographic changes and related changes in family structures, our research base becomes increasingly irrelevant. We need to examine both the experience of parenting in a broad range of family structures and the interaction of family structure and parenting.

The review of parenting research also reveals a paucity of theoretical models addressing major questions of interest. Troll and Bengtson's (1979) theory of generational change and influence is a good example of theory building in the area. As with this model, the trend in much of the recent literature emphasizes the interactional feedback patterns between parents and children and between the family system and the larger society of which it is a part. A number of these interactional approaches, with their corresponding methodological problems, are ably discussed by Klein et al. (1978). Another potentially valuable approach to the study of parenting draws on the stressful-life-events literature in a life span framework (Hultsch & Plemons, 1979). In view of the number of such events and transitions in the typical parenting career, this approach may be particularly valuable for identifying those factors that enhance or impede development.

From the developmental perspective, an interdisciplinary effort is critical to delineate and validate stages and related developmental tasks along the lines of Hill and Mattessich's (1979) work in this area. Until that happens, the application of developmental theory to parenting will be an unfulfilled promise. Specification of stages and tasks need to be considered for individuals, families, and parent and occupational roles. Models for each of these areas and integration among models will greatly enrich the context in which parenting is studied.

When the primary focus is on aging and the last stage of parenting, it becomes clear that a model delineating parenting stages by age of children is misleading. For example, combining middle-aged parents of adult children with aging parents of middle-aged to aging children obscures our understanding. Within an interactional, reciprocal framework, stage as well as age of children needs to be built into our conceptualization of parental stages. The major areas of interest in the literature on parenting of adult children seem to be the nature and the effect of parent–child ties and their possible shifts during old age. One might expect parent–child ties to increase in importance as involvement in other social roles and relationships terminates, for example, through retirement or death of a spouse. So far, parenting of adult children has largely been ignored as a significant adult role.

REFERENCES

Adamek, R., & Goudy, W. Identification, sex, and change in college major. *Sociology of Education*, 1966, *39*, 183–199.

Alder, N. E. Decision models in population research. *Journal of Population*, 1979, *2*, 187–202.

Albeit, S. A. *A study of women during their first pregnancy.* Unpublished doctoral dissertation, Yale University, 1975.

Aldous, J. *Family careers: Developmental change in families.* New York: Wiley, 1978.

Aldous, J., Osmond, M. W., & Hicks, M. W. Men's work and men's families. In W. R. Burr, R. Hill, F. I. Nye, & I. L. Reiss (Eds.), *Contemporary theories about the family* (Vol. 1). New York: Free Press, 1979.

Alpert, J. L., & Richardson, M. S. Conflict, outcome, and perception of women's roles. *Educational Gerontology: An International Quarterly*, 1978, *3*, 79–87.

Alpert, J. L., Richardson, M. S., Perlmutter, B., & Shutzer, F. Perceptions of major roles by college students. *Psychology of Women Quarterly*, 1980, *4*, 581–586.

Arms, S. *Immaculate deception: A new look at women and childbirth in America.* Boston: Houghton Mifflin, 1975.

Bailyn, L. Career and family orientations of husbands and wives in relation to marital happiness. *Human Relations*, 1970, *23*, 97–113.

Ballou, J. W. *The psychology of pregnancy.* Lexington, Mass.: Lexington Books, 1978.

Bart, P. Mother Portnoy's complaint. *Transaction*, 1970, *8*, 69–74.

Benedek, T. The psychobiology of pregnancy. In E. J. Anthony & T. Benedek (Eds.), *Parenthood: Its psychology and psychopathology.* Boston: Little, Brown, 1970.

Bengtson, V. L., & Black, K. D. Intergenerational relations and continuities in socialization. In P. Baltes and K. W. Schaie (Eds.), *Life-span developmental psychology: Personality and socialization.* New York: Academic Press, 1978.

Bengtson, V. L., & Kuypers, J. A. Generational differences and the developmental stake. *Aging and Human Development*, 1971, *2*, 249–260.

Bengtson, V. L., & Troll, L. Youth and their parents: Feedback and intergenerational influence in socialization. In R. M. Lerner & G. B. Spanier (Eds.), *Child influences in marital and family interaction.* New York: Academic Press, 1978.

Benson, L. *Fatherhood: A sociological perspective.* New York: Random House, 1967.

Berger, M., & Wright, L. Divided allegiance: Men, work, and family life. *Counseling Psychologist*, 1978, *7*, 50–52.

Bibring, G. L. A study of the psychological processes in pregnancy of the earliest mother-child relationship. In R. S. Eissler & A. Freud (Eds.) *The psychoanalytic study of the child* (Vol. 16). New York: International Universities Press, 1959.

Biller, H. B. *Father, child, and sex role.* Boston, Mass.: D. C. Heath, 1971.

Blenkner, M. Social work and family relationships in later life with some thoughts on filial maturity. In E. Shanas & G. Streib (Eds.), *Social structure and the family: Generational relations.* Englewood Cliffs, N.J.: Prentice Hall, 1965.

Blood, R. O., & Wolfe, D. W. *Husbands and wives: The dynamics of married living.* New York: Free Press, 1960.

Brim, O. G., Jr. Socialization through the life cycle. In O. G. Brim & S. Wheeler (Eds.), *Socialization after childhood: Two essays.* New York: Wiley, 1966.

Brim, O. G., Jr. Male mid-life crisis: A comparative analysis. In B. B. Hess (Ed.), *Growing old in America.* New Brunswick, N.J.: Transaction Books, 1976.

Broderick, C. B. Beyond the five conceptual frameworks: A decade of development in family theory. *Journal of Marriage and the Family*, 1971, *33*, 139–159.

Bronfenbrenner, U. *Research on the effects of day care.* Manuscript prepared for Advisory Committee on Child Development of the National Academy of Science, 1975.

Brown, G. W., Bhrolchain, M. N., & Harris, T. Social class and psychiatric disturbances among women in an urban population. *Sociology*, 1975, *9*, 225–254.

Burgess, E. W., & Wallin, P. *Engagement and marriage.* Philadelphia: J. B. Lippincott, 1953.

Campbell, A., Converse, C., & Rodgers, W. *The quality of American life.* New York: Russell Sage Foundation, 1976.

Cantor, M. Life space and the social support system of the inner city elderly of New York. *Gerontologist*, 1975, *15*, 23–27.

Caplow, T. *The sociology of work.* New York: McGraw-Hill, 1954.

Cartwright, L. I. Career satisfaction and role harmony in a sample of young women physicians. *Journal of Vocational Behavior*, 1978, *12*, 184–196.

Chester, N. L. *Pregnancy and new parenthood: Twin experiences of change.* Paper presented at the meeting of the Eastern Psychological Association, Philadelphia, 1979.

Chilman, C. S. Families in development at mid-stage of the family life cycle. *Family Coordinator*, 1968, *17*, 306.

Christensen, H. T. Children in the family: Relationship of number and spacing to marital success. *Journal of Marriage and the Family*, 1968, *30*, 283–289.

Clarke-Stewart, K. A. Popular primers for parents. *American Psychologist*, 1978, *33*, 359–369.

Cohen, M. B. Personal identity and sexual identity. *Psychiatry*, 1966, *29*, 1–12.

Colman, A., & Colman, L. *Pregnancy, the psychological experience.* New York: Seabury Press, 1973.

Davids, A., DeVault, S., & Talmadge, M. Psychological study of emotional factors in pregnancy. *Psychosomatic Medicine*, 1961, *23*, 93–103.

Davids, A., & Holden, R. Consistency of maternal attitudes and personality from pregnancy to eight months following childbirth. *Developmental Psychology*, 1970, *2*, 364–366.

Davids, A., Holden, R., & Gray, G. B. Maternal anxiety during pregnancy and adequacy of mother and child adjustment eight months following childbirth. *Child Development*, 1963, *34*, 993–1002.

Deutsch, H. *Psychology of women.* New York: Grune & Stratton, 1945.

Doering, S. G., & Entwisle, D. R. Preparation during pregnancy and ability to cope with labor and delivery. *American Journal of Orthopsychiatry*, 1975, *45*, 825–837.

Douglas, G. Some disorders of the puerperium. *Journal of Psychosomatic Research*, 1968, *12*, 101–106.

Duvall, E. M. *Marriage and family development* (5th ed.). Philadelphia: Lippincott, 1977.

Dyer, E. D. Parenthood as crisis: A restudy. *Marriage and Family Living*, 1963, *25*, 196–201.

Eichler, L. S., Winickoff, S. A., Grossman, F. K., Anzalone, M. K., & Gofseyeff, M. H. *Adaptation to pregnancy, birth and early parenting: A preliminary view.* Paper presented at the meeting of the American Psychological Association, San Francisco, August 1977.

Etaugh, C. Effects of maternal employment on children: A review of recent research. *Merrill-Palmer Quarterly*, 1974, *20*, 71–98.

Farrell, W. *Beyond masculinity.* New York: Random House, 1974.

Fasteau, M. F. *The male machine.* New York: McGraw-Hill, 1974.

Fawcett, J. T. *Psychological perspectives on population.* New York: Basic Books, 1973.

Fein, G. G. Children's sensitivity to social contexts at 18 months of age. *Developmental Psychology*, 1975, *11*, 853–854.

Fein, R. A. Men's entrance to parenthood. *Family Coordinator*, 1976, *25*, 341–350.

Fein, R. A. Research on fathering: Social policy and an emergent perspective. *Journal of Social Issues*, 1978, *34*, 122–136.

Fishbein, M., & Jaccard, J. Theoretical and methodological considerations in the prediction of family planning intentions and behavior. *Representative Research in Social Psychology*, 1973, *4*, 37–52.

Flapan, M., & Schoenfeld, H. Procedures for exploring women's childbearing motivations, alleviating childbearing conflicts, and enhancing maternal role development. *American Journal of Orthopsychiatry*, 1972, *42*, 389–397.

Fogarty, M. *Forty to sixty: How we waste the middle aged.* London: Bedford Square Press, 1975.

Gilbert, L. A., Holahan, C. K., & Manning, L. *Conflict with the parent role: Perceived cost of effective coping.* Paper presented at the meeting of the American Psychological Association, New York, September 1979.

Glick, P. C. Updating the life cycle of the family. *Journal of Marriage and the Family*, 1977, *39*, 7.

Glick, P. C., & Norton, A. J. Marrying, divorcing, and living together in the United States today. *Population Bulletin*, 1977, *32*(5). (Population Reference Bureau, Inc., Washington, D.C.)

Glick, P. C., & Norton, A. J. *1979 Update Population Bulletin*, February 1979, pp. 39–41. (Population Reference Bureau, Inc., Washington, D.C.)

Goode, W. J. Theory of role strain. *American Sociological Review*, 1962, *25*, 483–496.

Gordon, R., & Gordon, K. Factors in post-partum emotional adjustment. *American Journal of Orthopsychiatry*, 1968, *38*, 688–692.

Greenberg, M., & Morris, N. Engrossment: The newborn's impact upon the father. *American Journal of Orthopsychiatry*, 1974, *44*, 520–531.

Grimm, E., & Venet, W. The relationship of emotional adjustment and attitudes to the course and outcome of pregnancy. *Psychosomatic Medicine*, 1966, *28*, 34–48.

Gross, N., Mason, W. S., & McEachern, A. W. *Explorations in role analysis.* New York: Wiley, 1958.

Gurwitt, A. Aspects of prospective fatherhood: A case report. *Psychoanalytic Study of the Child*, 1976, *31*, 237–271.

Gutmann, D. Parenthood: A key to the comparative study of the life cycle. In N. Datan & L. H. Ginsberg (Eds.), *Life-span and developmental psychology.* New York: Academic Press, 1975.

Hagestad, G. D. *Role change in adulthood: The transition to the empty nest.* Unpublished manuscript, Committee on Human Development, University of Chicago, 1977.

Hall, D. T. A model of coping with role conflict: The role behavior of college adult women. *Administrative Science Quarterly*, 1972, *17*, 471–486.

Hall, D. T. Pressure from work, self, and home on the life stages of married women. *Journal of Vocational Behavior*, 1975, *6*, 121–132.

Hamilton, M. L. *Fathers' influence on children.* Chicago: Nelson-Hall, 1977.

Harkins, E. B. Effects of empty nest transition on self-report of psychological and physical well-being. *Journal of Marriage and the Family*, 1978, *40*, 549–558.

Hawley, P. Perceptions of male models of femininity related to career choice. *Journal of Counseling Psychology*, 1972, *19*, 308–313.

Heckman, N. A., Bryson, R., & Bryson, J. G. Problems of professional couples: A content analysis. *Journal of Marriage and the Family*, 1977, *39*, 323–330.

Herman, J. B., & Gyllstrom, K. K. Working men and women: Inter- and intrarole conflict. *Psychology of Women Quarterly*, 1977, *2*, 319–333.

Herzog, E., & Sudia, C. Fatherless homes: A review of research. *Children*, 1968, *15*.

Hess, B. B., & Waring, J. M. Parent and child in later life. In R. M. Lerner & G. B. Spanier (Eds.), *Child influences on marital and family interaction. A life-span perspective*. New York: Academic Press, 1978.

Hill, R. *Family development in three generations*. Cambridge, Mass.: Schenkman, 1970.

Hill, R., & Mattessich, P. Family development theory and life-span development. In P. B. Baltes & O. G. Brim, Jr. (Eds.), *Life-span development and behavior*. New York: Academic Press, 1979.

Hobbs, D. F. Parenthood as crisis: A third study. *Journal of Marriage and the Family*, 1965, *27*, 367–372.

Hobbs, D. F., & Cole, S. C. Transition to parenthood: A decade replication. *Journal of Marriage and the Family*, 1976, *38*, 723–731.

Hoffman, L. W. Effects of maternal employment on the child. A review of the research. *Developmental Psychology*, 1974, *10*, 204–228.

Hoffman, L. W. Changes in family roles, socialization, and sex differences. *American Psychologist*, 1977, *32*, 644–657.

Hoffman, L. W., & Hoffman, M. L. The value of children to parents. In J. T. Fawcett (Ed.), *Psychological perspectives on population*. New York: Basic Books, 1973.

Hoffman, L. W., & Manis, J. D. Influences of children on marital interaction and parental satisfactions and dissatisfactions. In A. M. Lerner and D. B. Spanier (Eds.), *Child influences on marital and family interaction: A life-span perspective*. New York: Academic Press, 1978.

Holahan, C. K., & Gilbert, L. A. Conflict between major life roles: Women and men in dual career couples. *Human Relations*, 1979, *32*, 451–467. (a)

Holahan, C. K., & Gilbert, L. A. Interrole conflict for working women: Careers versus jobs. *Journal of Applied Psychology*, 1979, *64*, 86–90. (b)

Hultsch, D. F., & Plemons, J. K. Life events and life-span development. In P. B. Baltes & O. G. Brim, Jr. (Eds.), *Life-span development and behavior* (Vol. 2). New York: Academic Press, 1979.

Johnson, F. A., & Johnson, C. L. Role strain in high commitment career women. *Journal of the American Academy of Psychoanalysis*, 1976, *4*, 13–36.

Kagan, J., Kearsley, R. B., & Zelazo, P. R. *Infancy: Its place in human development*. Cambridge, Mass.: Harvard University Press, 1978.

Kahn, R. L., Wolfe, D. M., Quinn, R. P., Snoek, J. D., & Rosenthal, R. A. *Organizational stress: Studies on role conflict and ambiguity*. New York: Wiley, 1964.

Kaley, M. M. Attitudes toward the dual role of the married professional woman. *American Psychologist*, 1971, *26*, 301–306.

Kalish, A., & Knudtson, F. W. Attachment versus disengagement: A life-span conceptualization. *Human Development*, 1976, *19*, 171–181.

Kanter, R. M. *Men and women of the corporation*. New York: Basic Books, 1977. (a)

Kanter, R. M. *Work and family in the United States: A critical review and agenda for research and policy*. New York: Russell Sage Foundation, 1977. (b)

Kellmer, P. M. *The needs of children*. London: Hutchinson, 1974.

Kerchkoff, A. C. Family patterns and morale in retirement. In I. H. Simpson & J. C. McKinney (Eds.), *Social aspects of aging*. Durham, N.C.: Duke University Press, 1966.

Kilner, S. *Infant-toddler group day care: A review of research* (ERIC Document Reproduction Service No. ED 156 308). Urbana, Ill.: ERIC Clearinghouse on Early Childhood Education, December 1977.

Klaus, M. H., & Kennell, J. H. *Maternal-infant bonding*. St. Louis: Mosby, 1976.

Klaus, M. H., Kennell, J. H., Plumb, N., & Zuehike, S. Human maternal behavior at first contact with her young. *Pediatrics*, 1970, *46*, 87–92.

Klein, D. M., Jorgensen, S. R., & Miller, B. C. Research methods and developmental reciprocity in families. In R. M. Lerner & G. B. Spanier (Eds.), *Child influences on marital and family interaction: A life-span perspective*. New York: Academic Press, 1978.

Kundsin, R. B. (Ed.). *Women and success: The anatomy of achievement*. New York: Morrow, 1974.

Kupinsky, S. The fertility of working women in the United States: Historical trends and theoretical perspectives. In S. Kupinsky (Ed.), *The fertility of working women: A synthesis of international research*. New York: Praeger, 1977.

Lamb, M. E. The role of the father: An overview. In M. E. Lamb (Ed.), *The role of the father in child development*. New York: Wiley, 1976.

Lamb, M. E. Father-infant and mother-infant interaction in the first year of life. *Child Development*, 1977, *48*, 167–181.

Lamb, M. E. Influence of the child on marital quality and family interaction during the prenatal, perinatal and infancy periods. In R. M. Lerner & G. B. Spanier (Eds.), *Child influences on marital and family interaction: A life-span perspective*. New York: Academic Press, 1978.

Lamb, M. E., & Lamb, J. E. The nature and importance of the father-infant relationship. *Family Coordinator*, 1976, *25*, 379–386.

Leifer, M. Psychological changes accompanying pregnancy and motherhood. *Genetic Psychology Monographs*, 1977, *95*, 55–96.

LeMasters, E. E. Parenthood as crisis. *Marriage and Family Living*, 1957, *19*, 352–355.

Lewis, R. A., & Spanier, G. B. Theorizing about the quality and stability of marriage. In W. R. Burr, R. Hill, F. I. Nye, & I. L. Reiss (Eds.), *Contemporary theories about the family* (Vol. 1). New York: Free Press, 1979.

Liebenberg, B. Expectant fathers. *American Journal of Orthopsychiatry*, 1967, *37*, 358.

Lopata, H. Z. *Occupation: Housewife*. New York: Oxford University Press, 1971.

Lowenthal, M. F., & Chiriboga, D. Transition to the empty nest: Crisis, challenge, or relief? *Archives of General Psychiatry*, 1972, *26*, 8–14.

Lowenthal, M. F., Thurnher, M., & Chiriboga, D. *Four stages of life: A comparative study of women & men facing transitions*. San Francisco, Calif.: Jossey-Bass, 1976.

Luckey, E. B., & Bain, J. E. Children: A factor in marital satisfaction. *Journal of Marriage and the Family*, 1970, *32*, 43–44.

Lynn, D. B. *The father: His role in child development*. Monterey, Calif.: Brooks/Cole, 1974.

Magrabi, F. M., & Marshall, W. H. Family developmental tasks: A research model. *Journal of Marriage and the Family*, 1965, *27*, 454–461.

Mazer, M. *People and predicaments*. Cambridge, Mass.: Harvard University Press, 1976.

Mead, M. *Culture and commitment: A study of the generation gap*. New York: Basic Books, 1970.

Melges, F. T. Postpartum psychiatric syndromes. *Psychosomatic Medicine*, 1968, *30*, 95–108.

Nevill, D., & Damico, S. Role conflict in women as a function of marital status. *Human Relations*, 1975, *28*, 487–498.

Newman, S. H., & Thompson, V. D. (Eds.). *Population psychology: Research and educational issues* (Publication No. (NIH) 76-574). Washington, D.C.: U.S. Department of Health, Education and Welfare, 1976.

Newton, N. *Maternal emotions*. New York: Paul B. Hoebes, 1955.

Nock, S. L. The family life cycle: Empirical or conceptual tool. *Journal of Marriage and the Family*, 1979, *41*, 15–26.

Nydegger, C., & Mittemas, L. Transitions in fatherhood. *Generations*, 1979, *4*, 14–15.

Oakley, A. *The sociology of housework*. London: Martin Robertson, 1974.

Parke, R. D., & O'Leary, S. Father-mother-infant interaction in the newborn period: Some findings, some observations, and some unresolved issues. In K. F. Riegel & J. Meacham (Eds.), *The developing individual in a changing world*. Vol. 2. *Social and environmental issues*. The Hague, The Netherlands: Mouton, 1975.

Parke, R. D., & Sawin, D. B. The father's role in infancy: A re-evaluation. *Family Coordinator*, 1976, *25*, 365–371.

Parke, R. D., and Sawin, D. B. *The family in early infancy: Social interactional and attitudinal analyses*. Paper presented to the Society for Research in Child Development, New Orleans, La., March 1977.

Parlee, M. Psychological aspects of menstruation, childbirth, and menopause: An overview with suggestions for further research. In R. Unger & F. Denmark (Eds.), *Women: Dependent or independent variable?* New York; Psychological Dimensions, in press.

Pearlin, L. I. Sex roles and depression. In N. Datan & L. H. Ginsberg (Eds.), *Life-span developmental psychology: Normative life crises*. New York: Academic Press, 1975.

Pleck, J. The work-family role system. *Social Problems*, 1977, *24*, 417–427.

Pleck, J. H. Men's "family work" role: three perspectives and some new data. *Family Coordinator*, in press.

Powell, B., & Reznikoff, M. Role conflict and symptoms of psychological distress in college-educated women. *Journal of Consulting and Clinical Psychology*, 1976, *44*, 473–479.

Radloff, L. S. Sex differences in depression: The effects of occupation and marital status. *Sex Roles*, 1975, *1*, 249–265.

Rapoport, R., & Rapoport, R. N. The dual career family. *Human Relations*, 1969, *22*, 3–30.

Rapoport, R., Rapoport, R. N., & Strelitz, Z. *Fathers, mothers, and society*. New York: Basic Books, 1977.

Richardson, M. S., & Alpert, J. L. Role perceptions of educated adult women: An exploratory study. *Educational Gerontology*, 1976, 171–185.

Richardson, M. S., & Alpert, J. L. Role perceptions: Variations by sex and role. *Sex Roles*, in press.

Richardson, M. S., & Kagan, L. *Social support and the transition to parenthood*. Paper presented at meeting of the American Psychological Association, New York, September 1979.

Robinson, J. P. *How Americans use time: A social-psychological analysis of everyday behavior*. New York: Praeger, 1977.

Rodgers, R. H. *Family interaction and transaction: The developmental approach*. New York: Prentice-Hall, 1973.

Rollins, B. C., & Cannon, K. L. Marital satisfaction over the family life cycle: A reevaluation. *Journal of Marriage and the Family*, 1974, *36*, 271–283.

Rollins, B. C., & Feldman, H. Marital satisfaction over the family life cycle. *Journal of Marriage and the Family*, 1970, *32*, 20–28.

Rollins, B. C., & Galligan, R. The developing child and marital satisfaction of parents. In R. M. Lerner & G. B. Spanier (Eds.), *Child influences on marital and family interaction: A life-span perspective*. New York: Academic Press, 1978.

Rollins, E. M., & Nye, F. I. Wife-mother employment, family, and society, In W. R. Burr, R. Hill, F. I. Nye, & I. L. Reiss (Eds.), *Contemporary theories about the family* (Vol. 1). New York: Free Press, 1979.

Rosen, B., & Jerdee, T. Sex stereotyping in the executive suite. *Harvard Business Review*, 1974, *52*, 45–48.

Rosenberg, M. *Occupations and values*. New York: Free Press, 1957.

Rosenblatt, P. C. Behavior in public places: Comparison of couples accompanied and unaccompanied by children. *Journal of Marriage and the Family*, 1974, *36*, 750–755.

Rossi, A. S. Transition to parenthood. *Journal of Marriage and the Family*, 1968, *30*, 26–34.

Rossi, A. S. A biosocial perspective on parenting. *Daedalus*, Spring 1977, *106*, 1–31.

Russo, N. F. The motherhood mandate. *Journal of Social Issues*, 1976, *32*, 143–154.

Safilios-Rothschild, C. Dual linkages between the occupational and family systems: A macro-sociological analysis. In M. Blaxall & B. Reagan (Eds.), *Women and the workplace*. Chicago: University of Chicago Press, 1976.

Safilios-Rothschild, C. The relationship between women's work and fertility: Some methodological and theoretical issues. In S. Kupinsky (Ed.), *The fertility of working women: A synthesis of international research.* New York: Praeger, 1977.

Schaie, K. W. Methodological problems in descriptive developmental research on adulthood and aging. In J. R. Nesselroade & H. W. Reese (Eds.), *Life-span developmental psychology: Methodological issues.* New York: Academic Press, 1973.

Schram, R. W. Martial satisfaction over the family life cycle: A critique and proposal. *Journal of Marriage and the Family*, 1979, *41*, 7–40.

Secord, P. F., & Backman, C. W. *Social psychology.* New York: McGraw-Hill, 1974.

Seiden, A. M. Overview: Research on the psychology of women. 1. Gender differences and sexual and reproductive life. *The American Journal of Psychiatry*, 1976, *133*, 995–1007.

Shanas, E. Family-kin networks and aging: A cross-cultural perspective. *Journal of Marriage and the Family*, 1973, *35*, 505–571.

Siegel, A. E., & Haas, M. B. The working mother: A review of reseach. *Child Development*, 1963, *34*, 513–542.

Soule, A. B. *The pregnant couple.* Paper presented at the meeting of the American Psychological Association, New Orleans, La., August 1974.

Spanier, G. B., Lewis, R. A., & Cole, C. L. Marital adjustment over the family life cycle: The issue of curvilinearity. *Journal of Marriage and the Family*, 1974, *37*, 263–275.

Spanier, G. B., Sauer, W., & Larzelere, R. An empirical evaluation of the family life cycle. *Journal of Marriage and the Family*, 1979, *41*, 27–38:

Staines, G. L., & O'Connor, P. *The relationship between work and leisure.* Unpublished paper, University of Michigan Survey Research Center, 1979.

Stern, D. Mother and infant at play: The dyadic interaction involving facial, vocal, and gaze behavior. In M. Lewis & L. Rosenblum (Eds.), *The effect of the infant on its caregiver.* New York: Wiley, 1974.

Stewart, A. *Role combination and psychological health in women.* Paper presented at the meeting of the Eastern Psychological Association, Washington, D.C., March 1978.

Stinnett, N., Collins, J., & Montgomery, J. E. Marital need satisfaction of husbands and wives. *Journal of Marriage and the Family*, 1970, *32*, 428–434.

Sussman, M. The help pattern in the middle class family. *American Sociological Review*, 1953, *18*, 23.

Sussman, M. Relationships of adult children with their parents in the United States. In E. Shanas & G. Streib (Eds.) *Social structure and the family.* Englewood Cliffs, N.J.: Prentice-Hall, 1965.

Sussman, M. The family life of old people. In R. Binstock & E. Shanas (Eds.), *Handbook of aging and the social sciences.* New York: Van Nostrand Reinhold, 1976.

Taylor, S. P., & Langer, E. J. Pregnancy: A social stigma? *Sex Roles*, 1977, *3*, 27–35.

Thurnher, M., Spence, D., & Lowenthal, M. F. Value conflict and behavioral conflict in intergenerational relations. *Journal of Marriage and the Family*, 1974, *36*, 308–319.

Troll, L. E. The family of later life: A decade review. *Journal of Marriage and the Family*, 1971, *33*, 263–290.

Troll, L., & Bengtson, V. Generations in the family. In W. R. Burr, R. Hill, F. I. Nye, & I. L. Reiss (Eds.), *Contemporary theories about the family* (Vol. 1). New York: Free Press, 1979.

Troll, L. E., Miller, S. J., & Atchley, R. C. *Families in later life.* Belmont, Calif.: Wadsworth, 1979.

Troll, L., Neugarten, B. L., & Kraines, R. J. Similarities in values and other personality characteristics in college students and their parents. *Merrill-Palmer Quarterly*, 1969, *15*, 323–336.

Troll, L., & Smith, J. Attachment through the life span: Some questions about dyadic bonds among adults. *Human Development*, 1976, *19*, 156–170.

Turner, M. F., & Izzi, M. H. The COPE story: A service to pregnant and postpartum women. In M. T. Notman & C. C. Nadelson (Eds.), *The woman patient: Medical and psychological interfaces* (Vol. 1). New York: Plenum Press, 1978.

U.S. Bureau of the Census. *Statistical abstract of the United States: 1978* (99th ed.). Washington, D.C.: Author, 1978.

U.S. Department of Labor. *Women workers today.* Washington, D.C.: Women's Bureau, 1976.

Van Dusen, R. A., & Sheldon, E. B. The changing status of American women: A life cycle perspective. *American Psychologist*, 1976, *31*, 106–116.

Veevers, J. E. Voluntarily childless wives: An exploratory study. In E. Peck & J. Senderowitz (Eds.), *Pronatalism: The myth of mom and apple pie.* New York: Crowell, 1974.

Vincent, C. E. An open letter to the "caught generation." *Family Coordinator*, 1972, *21*, 143–150.

Wallston, B. The effects of maternal employment on children. *Journal of Child Psychology and Psychiatry*, 1973, *14*, 81–95.

Weinberg, S. *Measurement of stressful life events associated with transition to parenthood.* Paper presented at meeting of the American Psychological Association, New York, September 1979.

Wente, A. M., & Crockenberg, S. B. Transition to fatherhood: Lamaze preparation, adjustment difficulty and the husband-wife relationship. *Family Coordinator*, 1976, *25*, 351–357.

Wilensky, H. Life cycle, work situation and participation in formal associations. In R. W. Kleemeier (Ed.), *Aging and leisure: Research perspectives on meaningful use of time.* New York: Oxford University Press, 1961.

Wilensky, H. L. Varieties of work experience. In H. Borow (Ed.), *Man in a world at work.* Boston: Houghton Mifflin, 1964.

Wilson, K. M. Today's women students: New outlooks and new challenges. *Journal of College Studies Personnel*, 1975, *16*, 378–381.

Woolsey, S. H. Pied piper politics and the child care debate. *Daedalus*, 1977, *106*, 127–146.

Yankelovich, Skelly & White, Inc. *Raising children in a changing society.* Minneapolis, Minn.: General Mills, 1977.

Zemlick, M., & Watson, R. Maternal attitudes of acceptance and rejection during and after pregnancy. *American Journal of Orthopsychiatry*, 1953, *23*, 570–578.

Victor G. Cicirelli

CHAPTER
33

Sibling Relationships in Adulthood: A Life Span Perspective

The course of sibling relationships throughout adulthood and old age is examined in detail. Three issues are considered: (1) whether the sibling relationship deteriorates with age or is reactivated in later life, (2) whether the sibling relationship in later life is characterized by rivalry and competition or by closeness and cooperation, and (3) whether observed sibling effects in old age are the result of early or contemporaneous influences. Emerging questions and new directions for further research are advanced.

Sibling relationships in childhood and adolescence are recognized as important to the child's cognitive and social development. Does the effect of siblings stop at adulthood, or does the sibling relationship remain an important influence throughout the entire life span?

Lifelong sibling influence is certainly possible, since sibling relationships can have the longest duration of any human relationship, and perhaps also can be the most egalitarian of all those within the family. The relationship begins with the birth of a second child and ends only with death. It is not uncommon today to find sibling relationships that have persisted for 80 to 90 years.

The situation in which the relationship between siblings takes place changes drastically over the life span, however. At the beginning it is one of intimate daily contact and sharing of most experiences, including the socializing influence of the same parents. Throughout the school years, siblings may have different teachers and different friends and peer groups, but they still have their home experiences in common. Later, when

they leave their parents' home to pursue a career or to marry and establish families of their own, they tend to separate from each other as well. They may live in different cities or even different countries. Contact becomes voluntary except on certain ritual occasions, and most life experiences are no longer shared. Still later, they may share the obligations of caring for their parents during their declining years. With the death of the parents, sibling contact returns to a more voluntary level until the end of life.

If for no other reason than its uniqueness and duration in time, sibling influence during adulthood and old age is worth studying. Do siblings modify each other's cognitive functioning, feelings, and behavior in either an immediate or a long-range way? Sibling relationships represent a subsystem of the total family system, perpetuated over the life span and reactivated periodically either in conjunction with or independently of other family subsystems.

Sibling Research in Adulthood and Old Age

Research on sibling relationships in adulthood and old age is very limited in comparison with the body of sibling research in childhood and adolescence. Three

Preparation of this chapter was assisted in part by a Summer Fellowship from the Institute of Aging, Portland, Oregon, Certain of the author's research was supported by a grant from the NRTA-AARP Andrus Foundation.

fundamental issues have emerged, which are considered in turn.

Is There a Decline or a Resurgence of the Sibling Relationship in Old Age?

Do siblings maintain an active relationship in adulthood and old age, or do they simply drift apart? Much of the literature on this issue derives from sociological or anthropological studies of the extended family in later life and has been summarized by Troll (1971), Troll, Miller, and Atchley (1978), and Riley and Foner (1968).

Table 33-1 summarizes a number of studies dealing with siblings of American adults. Adams (1968) studied young to middle-aged adults whose median age was 33 years. About 88% had at least one living sibling; the mean number of living siblings was 3.9. The number of people over age 65 with at least one living sibling was reported as 75%–80% by Shanas, Town-

send, Wedderburn, Friis, Milhoj, and Stehouwer (1968) and as 93% by Clark and Anderson (1967). Bild and Havighurst (1976) reported that from 46%–86% of their subsamples of Chicago elderly from residential hotels had a living sibling. Cicirelli (1979) found that 78% of older residents of a small midwestern city had at least one living sibling. Those in the 60–69 age group had a mean of 2.9 living siblings; those a decade older, 70–79, had a mean of 2.2; and those over age 80 had a mean of only 1.1.

Thus, although the number of living siblings declines with advancing age, even the oldest group still had one living sibling. What about their relationships?

Investigators who have asserted that sibling relationships decline with age have based their argument on geographic proximity and frequency of contact between them. (See Table 33-1.) Rosenberg and Anspach (1973) argue the case for decline most strongly, reasoning that for siblings' relationship to be viable, they should live near each other. In their study of blue-

Table 33-1 Existence, Proximity, and Frequency of Contact With Siblings at Various Ages

Study	Age range	N	Population	% subjects with living sib	Mean no. sibs	% subjects with sib within		% subjects with sib contact	
						Same city	100 miles	Week	Month
Adams (1968)[a]	33 (Mdn)	799	Subjects married 1–20 yr Greensboro, N.C.	88	3.9	29	60	69 (same city) 12 (100 miles)	93 65
Rosenberg & Anspach (1973)	45–79	1,360	Married subjects with kin in greater Philadelphia	—	—	75 (age 45–54) 64 (55–64) 49 (65–79)		68 (of 75%) 58 (of 64%) 47 (of 49%)	
Clark & Anderson (1967)	65+	435	Elderly in San Francisco	93	—	—	—	—	—
Shanas et al. (1968)	65+	2,500 each country	National probability sample in U.S., Denmark, U.K.	75–80	—	—	—	34 (males) 43 (females)	39 44
Bild & Havighurst (1976)	60	540	Elderly in 7 areas of Chicago	46–86 (hotel sample)	—	—	—	17–30 (visit) 31–43 (phone)	
Cicirelli (1979)[b]	60–96	300	Elderly in Lafayette, Ind.	78	2.9 (60–69); 2.2 (70–79); 1.1 (80+)	26	56	17	33

[a] Adams (1968) data refer to sibling closest to age.
[b] Cicirelli (1979) data refer to sibling with whom there is most contact.

collar Philadelphians, they found that 75% of people aged 45–54 had a sibling in the metropolitan area, as did 64% of those aged 55–64, but only 49% of those over age 65 had a sibling. Rosenberg and Anspach concluded, therefore, that for over half of those age 65 and older, siblings "effectively do not exist." For Adams's (1968) North Carolina young adults, 29% of the siblings closest in age lived in the same city, 60% within 100 miles. Since Adams asked about the sibling "closest in age" rather than about "any sibling," age comparisons cannot be made. Cicirelli (1979) asked a third kind of question, the residence of the sibling with whom older people had the most contact. He found that 26% lived in the same city and 56% within 100 miles. If the sibling most contacted can be equated to the sibling closest in age, the proximity data of Adams and Cicirelli are roughly comparable. All in all, it is not clear whether these data support Rosenberg and Anspach's position on availability.

With regard to frequency of contact, Adams (1968) found that although the frequency of visiting decreased with distance, 65% of siblings who lived within 100 miles of each other visited monthly or more often, whereas 69% saw siblings in the same city at least weekly. Rosenberg and Anspach (1973) found that of their subjects who reported siblings available to them in the greater Philadelphia area, 68% (of 75%) of those aged 45–54 had seen a sibling in the week preceding the interview, in contrast with 58% of those 55–64 and 47% of those over age 65. Shanas et al. (1968) found that from 34% to 43% of the American sample in their three-nation survey had contact with a sibling at least weekly; the amount of contact decreased with both age and distance. In Bild and Havighurst's (1976) seven groups of Chicago older people, from 17% to 30% saw siblings at least weekly. Cicirelli (1979) found that 17% of the older people he interviewed saw the sibling with whom they had the most contact at least once a week, while 33% had contact at least monthly and 56% had contact several times a year. (Frequencies of telephoning were similar to frequencies of visiting. Those with living siblings who neither visited nor telephoned kept in contact through letter writing. Only a few of the older respondents actually lost contact with any of their siblings. On the other hand, only 2% resided with a sibling.) From these data, one can conclude that although substantial numbers of adults maintain contact with their siblings, such contact does decrease with age.

An opposing view to Rosenberg and Anspach's is based on the criterion of feelings of closeness and affection rather than proximity and contact (Allan, 1977; Atchley, 1977; Cicirelli, 1979; Cumming & Schneider, 1961; Farber, 1966; Manney, 1975).

Manney observed that though some siblings tend to drift apart and communicate only indirectly through their parents during young adulthood and the child-rearing years, most tend to renew relationships as their children mature and leave home. They seem to become closer once again.

When children first leave home, they retain early feelings toward their siblings. Cicirelli (1980a) found that college women had very strong positive feelings for at least one sibling and felt as close to the "closest" sibling as to their mother and closer than to their father. Later-born women felt closer to their siblings than did earlier-born women; also they felt closer to siblings closer to them in age.

In another study Cicirelli (1979) that 65% of older people he studied felt "close" or "extremely close" to the sibling with whom they had the most contact. Only 5% reported not feeling close at all. Both men and women tended to name sisters and middle-born siblings as the "closest" sibling. Seven percent of those interviewed reported turning to a sibling as a primary source of psychological support. This is significant because most married older people regard their spouse as a primary support and conform to strong cultural norms favoring feelings toward their children.

Allan (1977) examined the qualitative nature of sibling relationships in later life. Even when contact was limited, involvement continued. Siblings kept in touch with each other's location, activities, and circumstances, and direct interaction was supplemented with indirect information gained through the family network. The enduring nature of this relationship has greater significance when one considers how easily ties with former neighbors, friends, or co-workers are broken. Even when negative feelings toward their siblings' spouses affected their interactions, they usually managed to maintain some kind of relationship. Frequent close companionship with siblings was more prevalent in working-class than middle-class families.

The strength and quality of sibling relationships also seems to depend on sex. Adams (1968) found stronger affectional ties between sisters than between brothers or cross-sex siblings. Not only did sisters tend to feel close, but more than half reported feeling closer in adulthood than they had when they were growing up. Adams attributes this to common interests in marriage and children. By contrast, ties between brothers were less close, particularly among working-class samples. Cross-sex pairs were intermediate in closeness. These findings replicate those of Cumming and Schneider (1961), who reported the sister–sister bond closer than other sibling ties in later life, followed by sister–brother, then brother–brother.

The question of whether sibling relationships deteriorate with age cannot be answered on the basis of present data, which lack consistency in criteria for proximity and frequency of contact and definition of which siblings are considered. On the other hand, for closeness, affection, value consensus, and commitment, the evidence seems to point in the direction of strong sibling relationships. But problems exist here too. Measures of closeness, affection, value consensus, and commitment have been relatively crude, with limited evidence for validity and reliability.

Using factor analysis, Cicirelli (1979) found that amount of visiting, amount of telephoning, feelings of closeness, and similarity in values were strongly correlated with each other (rs ranged from .76 to .92); proximity had a weaker correlation with the other variables (rs ranged from .30 to .41). This interdependence of measures might lend support to those who assert that sibling relationships decline with age. Sibling relationships at an advanced age, however, may be better assessed by their strength relative to other relationships within the family as well as with friends and neighbors. Loss of vigor with advancing age restricts visiting of all kinds. Unfortunately all the studies thus far have been cross-sectional, and there may be cohort differences that would account for apparent age differences in sibling relationships.

Rivalry or Cooperation?

The psychoanalytic school has placed considerable emphasis on sibling rivalry as a major aspect of the relationship between siblings, and this is supported by evidence that rivalry and competition between siblings exist in childhood and adolescence (Sutton-Smith & Rosenberg, 1970). Berezin (1977) observed frequent quarrels among siblings as they discussed the care of aged parents. He interpreted expressions of irrational, hostile attitudes as indicators of regression to earlier sibling relationships. According to Laverty (1962), who observed older people in clinical situations, feelings of rivalry as well as feelings of closeness to siblings tend to persist into old age and are reactivated in relevant situations. Rivalry may also be expressed subtly by using a sibling as a yardstick for one's own activities and achievement (Troll, 1975).

Rivalry, like closeness, appears to vary with sex. Adams (1968) found that in adulthood brothers reported more competitiveness, ambivalence, and jealousy in their relationships than did any other sibling combination. Such rivalry was particularly strong where there was a status difference between brothers. Allan (1977), however, found that sibling rivalry appeared to dissipate in adulthood. This conclusion was based on intensive interviews with adults, over a wide age range, from a "typical community." He suspected that such mellowing of the relationship was at least partly a function of the more limited kinds of interac-

tions that occur as siblings get older. On the other hand, he suggested that old tensions and conflicts might reemerge if siblings were forced to live together again (or became closely intertwined due to family responsibilities).

As noted earlier, Cicirelli's (1979) data overwhelmingly show positive bonds among older siblings. Possible variations in sibling relationships have not been considered as yet. One can be very close with one sibling and rivalrous with another. It is also possible that there are both functional and dysfunctional aspects of the sibling relationships, both closeness and rivalry. In fact, situations involving greater closeness between siblings may increase the possibility of greater rivalry as well. There may be a love–hate ambivalence throughout the life span, perhaps even dialectical in process, leading to new levels of maturity or immaturity in sibling relationships. Or rivalry may appear under some circumstances (e.g., inheritance) and closeness under others (e.g., major illness).

Early Influence or Contemporaneous Effects?

An issue that has not been well defined thus far is whether sibling behaviors observed in later life are merely persistent effects of early influences or whether siblings continue to influence each other directly in adulthood and old age. One view of sibling effects is that behaviors in adulthood result from differential parental treatment in childhood (Rothbart, 1971, demonstrated differential parental treatment of preschool children). A second view is that children in the family influence each other early in life through intimate daily interactions that depend on birth order, age and age spacing, and sex (Cicirelli, 1976; Sutton-Smith & Rosenberg, 1970). Although a large number of outcome variables have been associated with such family structural characteristics (for a review, see Sutton-Smith & Rosenberg, 1970), demonstrations of siblings as direct causal agents of each other's behavior are rare. A study by Cicirelli (1972) found not only that first-grade children interacted differently with siblings than with familiar matched peers when the older child taught a concept to the younger, but that the amount of concept learning depended on whether the "teacher" was a sibling. There is as yet no similar causal evidence in later life. When relationships are found between older persons' characteristics or behaviors and such sibling structure variables as family size, birth order, sex, age, and age spacing, there is a question about whether the effects should be attributed to contemporaneous influence of siblings or to early influences of differential parental treatment or sibling interaction, or both.

Walter Toman's (1976) work illustrates the position

that childhood sibling effects determine the course of later life. Toman hypothesized that the more nearly a marital partner duplicated sibling relationships, the more successful and free from conflict the marriage would be. For example, the most successful match for the oldest sister of brothers would be the youngest brother of sisters. Toman described the characteristics of people from different positions in the family constellation and presented clinical data in support both of these portraits and of the duplication theorem. Toman's duplication theorem has been widely cited, but there is little supporting evidence.

Another kind of birth order study using college students (e.g., Schachter, 1959) investigated the effects of birth order on affiliation and conformity. Sutton-Smith and Rosenberg's (1970) review of these studies concluded that there is support for a conclusion that firstborns manifest stronger affiliative needs than later borns, and that firstborn males are more conforming than later-born males. Harris (1964), in his study of eminent firstborn and later-born sons, suggested many personality characteristics that differentiated the two groups. Schooler's (1972) critical review of birth-order studies is recommended to readers interested in pursuing this topic. He concluded, after examining scores of bias in previous studies, that reported birth-order effects are largely spurious if other sibling-structure variables are not controlled.

Studies of long-range effects on intellectual abilities and achievement in adulthood are largely confined to studies of eminent personalities (Sutton-Smith & Rosenberg, 1970; Zajonc & Markus, 1975). Most studies support the superiority of the firstborn. Zajonc's "confluence model" suggests that the rate of intellectual development is dependent on the average intellectual environment of the family (both parents and siblings) during the formative years, and that early-born children profit by tutoring younger siblings. If the confluence model survives mounting criticism, and if siblings continue to provide social and intellectual stimulation for each other in later life, then perhaps an extension of the confluence model could be applied to explain changes in intellectual ability in old age in terms of contemporary sibling influence. Such a possibility may seem speculative at this point, but it becomes more plausible in view of the very special position of sibling relationships throughout life. Also, effects of birth order and other sibling variables are strongly associated with age from birth to maturity (Cicirelli, 1967; Zajonc, Markus, & Markus, 1979). It is not unreasonable to suspect that sibling effects may continue to be age dependent in maturity.

In a recent study of family variables related to locus of control in subjects aged 60–90, Cicirelli (1980b) found that subjects with more living brothers were more likely to have an external locus of control. On the other hand, subjects who saw their siblings more often, agreed with them more, and felt closer to them were more likely to have an internal locus of control. The fact that this relationship held for all the living siblings and with measures of ongoing sibling relationships may support the hypothesis that siblings continue to exert an influence in later life. Further support for such a hypothesis comes from a different investigation (Cicirelli, 1977), which examined the problems and concerns of 64 men and women between 65 and 88. Sisters had a greater influence than brothers, but the form of the influence differed with the sex of the subject. The more sisters an older man had, the happier he felt and the less threatened by economic or social insecurities. In contrast, the more sisters an older women had, the more concerned she was with maintaining social skills, social relationships outside the family, helping others in the community, and being able to deal with criticism by younger people. Thus, whereas sisters give older men emotional security, they seem to challenge older women. As noted earlier, relationships with sisters in adulthood are stronger than those with brothers, and sisters take a major role in preserving family relationships and providing emotional support to their siblings. Indeed, after the death of their mother, a sister may take on the mother's role in looking after her brothers, or she may assume a brother's deceased wife's caretaking role (Townsend, 1957; Troll, 1971).

Much further research, at least some of it experimental, is needed if the issue of early or contemporaneous sibling effects is to be resolved. Longitudinal experimental studies carried out under relatively constant environmental conditions are needed to determine whether early effects of siblings persist or whether they fade out in time. Contemporary ecological studies, using both observation and interview methods, could relate sibling interactions to older people's behaviors. Regression analyses might be used to determine whether contemporary or childhood sibling variables explain the greater amount of variance in behavior in old age.

Future Trends in Sibling Research

Broadening the Concept of the Sibling Relationship

In addressing the issue of deterioration of sibling relationships in old age, a variety of constructs have been used, from interaction frequency (visiting, telephoning, or writing), to interaction content (sharing family occasions and holidays, participating in recreational activities), to emotional attributes (feelings of closeness and affection, sympathy, empathy, and so on). Other attributes of the sibling relationship become relevant, however, in adulthood and old age, particularly helping and supporting behaviors (serving as a confidante, giving advice, aiding in decision making, boosting morale, nursing care, homemaking, home repairs, shopping, lending money). Siblings can improve morale among older people (Cumming & Henry, 1961). A few interview studies have reported that siblings are generally ready to give aid in time of trouble, although their help is usually called for only when adult children are absent (Allan, 1977; Cicirelli, 1979; Cumming & Schneider, 1961). In the Cicirelli study 7% of all older people reported turning to a sibling as a primary source of psychological support; fewer used siblings as the main source of help in other areas. However, when asked who they would desire as a primary source of help, should an occasion arise where such help was needed, from 5% to 7% of these older persons named siblings in 8 of the 16 areas of service studied. It is likely that the percentage of siblings regarded as a supplementary or occasional source of help would be much higher. These studies suggest that the very existence of siblings as a possible source of support may be important, though such help is rarely used.

Socialization may be an important attribute of the sibling relationship in later life, as it is in childhood. One sibling might act as a role model or standard of comparison for the other, serve as critic, exert pressures for desired behaviors, present norms and values, perpetuate the strengths and traditions of the family, and serve as a formal or informal teacher. Bank and Kahn (1975) have noted the pioneering function of siblings in youth, where a sibling who ventures into a new area of behavior is quickly followed by others; something similar may occur in later life as well. Siblings may serve as role models for successful aging, widowhood, bereavement, retirement, and so on, or they may serve as challengers and stimulators to encourage new activities. This may be a fruitful area for investigation of the elderly.

Finally, negative or dysfunctional attributes of the relationship for example, sibling rivalry, should be considered. Other examples are conflict, domination, overdependency, and communication problems.

The entire range of attributes of a sibling relationship should be explored more thoroughly to determine its full extent and depth in old age.

Formulating Sibling Developmental Tasks

In the style of Havighurst (1972), one can hypothesize certain developmental tasks to be accomplished by most, if not all, siblings in Western culture through the course of adulthood and old age. (Weisner, 1979, has pointed out great differences in sibling roles and influence in various non-Western cultures.) In early adulthood siblings offer mutual support in establishing themselves socially and psychologically as independent persons in the community. They assist, if only through interest and psychological support, in the rearing of nieces and nephews. Parallel to establishing independence of parents as individuals and later achieving filial maturity (Blenkner, 1965), siblings establish independence of each other and come to accept each other as mature individuals.

Evidence of sibling maturity is observed when siblings resolve early jealousies and conflicts and are able to cooperate in common family interests. A major task of middle-aged siblings is the care and support of their parents during the periods of their decline and death and the achievement of the division of parental property (or the settlement of parental obligations) without rancor and bitterness. Siblings may offer support to each other as they face the problems of aging. Finally, siblings must come to accept the inevitable decline and death of members of their own generation and to face thoughts of their own mortality in the process. Thus far, evidence for these developmental tasks has not been gathered, other than anecdotal and clinical evidence regarding sibling conflicts over parental care. Further study is needed to determine the usefulness and validity of these conceptions of sibling developmental tasks.

Sibling Process, Structure, and Dynamics

As yet, very little is known about how adult siblings behave when they come together under various circumstances. Observational studies of siblings' interactions are needed to determine what kinds of topics are discussed, who initiates what, who dominates the conversation, what emotional responses are present, what verbal reinforcements are given, what problems are brought up, and so on. We need to know what happens when one sibling faces a crisis situation—how the others learn of the crisis, how they respond, and what their feelings are.

Ways in which sibling interactions, feelings, and attitudes change with age or major life events need to be explored. How do interpersonal relationships between siblings change from middle-age to "young-old" to "old-old" age? What are the psychological effects of the death of a sibling at various stages of life? What are the effects of the "empty nest"—with its termination of child rearing—on interpersonal relationships between siblings? What about such events as divorce, death of spouse, death of parents, retirement, and chronic illness? Would siblings aid in any life review process, since they have so many common memories?

Research is also needed into the relation between

position in the sibling structure (birth order, family size, sex, age spacing) and older persons' psychological characteristics and behavior (e.g., memory, longevity, successful aging). Most existing studies have examined only sex; several variables should be considered simultaneously in controlled studies, as in Sutton-Smith and Rosenberg's (1970) work with children and adolescents.

A third line of inquiry concerns the dynamics of sibling influence. If siblings do indeed influence each other in later life, how does it come about? Such topics as the means of sibling socialization (modeling, perception of shared values, direct persuasion); sources of influence when contact is limited (existence, proximity, psychological closeness); and effects of feelings, attitudes, and quality of interactions between siblings need to be investigated.

As yet, there are no clear theories of sibling influence in adulthood to guide the inquiry into dynamics. Toman's (1976) duplication theorem is essentially a theory of early influence, holding that traits and roles determined by sex and birth order are acted out in relationships in later life. This would mean that sibling effects could appear without any contact with siblings in later life. Cumming and Schneider's (1961) substitution concept implies that where an individual remains unmarried or loses a spouse, the sibling relationship substitutes for the missing relationship. This would imply that sibling influence should be greater for such individuals than for those who remain happily married and are the head of their own families.

A theory of sibling rivalry (Adler, 1959/1929) might be used to explain sibling influence in later life, with the rivalry a motivational basis for later actions. This would imply that sibling influence should be greatest where rivalry is greatest, usually between pairs of brothers. Competition between sisters may be greater than heretofore realized, however, and there may be direct rivalry between sisters as they move to occupy leadership roles in the family after the mother's death, for example, looking after brothers and maintaining family relationships (Troll, 1971).

Some theoretical explanation is needed if sibling influence in old age appears at a time when there may be relatively infrequent interaction between the siblings. One can hypothesize that the closeness (at least early in life) and long duration of the uniquely intimate and egalitarian sibling relationship gives sibling interactions particular salience; this salience may be intensified as other relationships and life roles are lost. If siblings maintain strong images of each other and their attitudes and values, then such images can serve as models to guide behavior when the sibling is not physically present. The more a new situation is perceived as something to which the sibling image or model could be applied, the stronger the influence. Clearly much more research is required before this or any other theoretical explanation of sibling influence in old age is established.

Changing Family Patterns

Studies of sibling relationships and sibling influence in the future need to take account of the changes in family patterns that will have an effect on the family relationships of middle-aged adults and on older cohorts within a few decades.

The number and proportion of older people in American society has been increasing steadily, with the greatest increases found for women and for those over 75. If more couples remain childless or have only one or two children, children will become less available for companionship, psychological support, and other forms of help in old age. Since greater longevity and vigor among current elderly and those now middle-aged also implies greater availability of siblings, the strength of sibling relationships could be expected to become greater. There may be a greater exchange of help between siblings as fewer children are available. In later decades there will be fewer siblings as well.

Another trend that needs to be considered for its implications for sibling relationships is the steadily increasing rate of divorce and remarriage in American society. Rather than a single marriage that lasts a lifetime, there is now a state that has been termed "serial monogamy" (Tiger, 1978). The implication for sibling relationships is that there will be more half-siblings and stepsiblings than ever before. Traditional sex and birth-order roles in the family may be blurred. A second possibility is that a pattern of serial monogamy will lead to a decreased commitment to the spouse and an increased commitment to more enduring sibling relationships. We could use studies on younger adults now, with extensions to old age later.

This chapter has indicated what is known about sibling relationships and influence at the present time and has suggested directions for the future. Until recently, the complex dimensions of relationships between siblings in adulthood and old age have barely been investigated. It is hoped that by the time the 1980s come to an end, sibling influence throughout the life span will be much better understood.

REFERENCES

Adams, B. N. *Kinship in an urban setting.* Chicago: Markham, 1968.

Adler, A. *Understanding human nature.* New York: Premier Books (Fawcett), 1959. (Originally published, 1929.)

Allan, G. Sibling solidarity. *Journal of Marriage and the Family,* 1977, *39,* 177–184.

Atchley, R. C. *The social forces in later life* (2nd ed.). Belmont, Calif.: Wadsworth, 1977.

Bank, S., & Kahn, M. D. Sisterhood-brotherhood is powerful: Sibling sub-systems and family therapy. *Family Process*, 1975, *14*, 311–337.

Berezin, M. A. Partial grief for the aged and their families. In E. Pattison (Ed.), *The experience of dying*. Englewood Cliffs, N.J.: Prentice-Hall, 1977.

Bild, B. R., & Havighurst, R. J. Senior citizens in great cities: The case of Chicago. *Gerontologist*, 1976, *16*, 1–88.

Blenkner, M. Social work and family relationships in later life with some thoughts on filial maturity. In E. Shanas & G. F. Streib (Eds.), *Social structure and the family: Generational relations*. Englewood Cliffs, N.J.: Prentice-Hall, 1965.

Cicirelli, V. G. Sibling constellation, creativity, IQ, and academic achievement. *Child Development*, 1967, *38*, 481–490.

Cicirelli, V. G. The effect of sibling relationships on concept learning of young children taught by child teachers. *Child Development*, 1972, *43*, 282–287.

Cicirelli, V. G. Sibling influence on the development of the individual. In K. F. Riegel & J. A. Mechan (Eds.), *The developing individual in a changing world. Vol. 3. Social and environmental issues*. The Hague, The Netherlands: Mouton, 1976.

Cicirelli, V. G. Relationship of siblings to the elderly person's feelings and concerns. *Journal of Gerontology*, 1977, *131*, 309–317.

Cicirelli, V. G. *Social services for elderly in relation to the kin network*. Report to the NRTA-AARP Andrus Foundation, Washington, D.C., 1979.

Cicirelli, V. G. A comparison of college women's feelings toward their siblings and parents. *Journal of Marriage and the Family*, 1980, *42*, 95–102. (a)

Cicirelli, V. G. Relationship of family background variables to locus of control in the elderly. *Journal of Gerontology*, 1980, *35*, 108–114. (b)

Clark, M., & Anderson, B. *Culture and aging*. Springfield, Ill.: Charles C Thomas, 1967.

Cumming, E., & Henry, W. *Growing old*. New York: Basic Books, 1961.

Cumming, E., & Schneider, D. Sibling solidarity: A property of American kinship. *American Anthropologist*, 1961, *63*, 498–507.

Farber, B. *Kinship and family organization*. New York: Wiley, 1966.

Harris, I. D. *The promised seed: A comparative study of eminent first and later sons*. New York: Free Press of Glencoe, 1964.

Havighurst, R. J. *Developmental tasks and education* (3rd ed.). New York: David McKay, 1972.

Laverty, R. Reactivation of sibling rivalry in older people. *Social Work*, 1962, *7*, 23–30.

Manney, J. D. *Aging*. Washington, D.C.: Office of Human Development, DHEW, 1975.

Riley, M. W., & Foner, A. *Aging and society*. Vol. 1. *An inventory of research findings*. New York: Russell Sage Foundation, 1968.

Rosenberg, G. S., & Anspach, D. F. Sibling solidarity in the working class. *Journal of Marriage and the Family*, 1973, *35*, 108–113.

Rothbart, M. K. Birth order and mother–child interaction in an achievement situation. *Journal of Personality and Social Psychology*, 1971, *17*, 113–120.

Schachter, S. *The psychology of affiliation*. Stanford, Calif.: Stanford University Press, 1959.

Schooler, C. Birth order effects: Not here, not now! *Psychological Bulletin*, 1972, *78*, 161–175.

Shanas, E., Townsend, P., Wedderburn, D., Friis, H., Milhoj, P., & Stehouwer, J. *Older people in three industrial societies*. New York: Atherton, 1968.

Sutton-Smith, B., & Rosenberg, B. G. *The sibling*. New York: Holt, Rinehart & Winston, 1970.

Tiger, L. Omigamy: The new kinship system. *Psychology Today*, July 1978, pp. 14–17.

Toman, W. *Family constellation: Its effects on personality and social behavior* (3rd ed.). New York: Springer, 1976.

Townsend, P. *The family life of old people: An inquiry in East London*. New York: Free Press of Glencoe, 1957.

Troll, L. E. The family of later life: A decade review. *Journal of Marriage and the Family*, 1971, *33*, 263–290.

Troll, L. E. *Early and middle adulthood*. Monterey, Calif.: Brooks/Cole, 1975.

Troll, L. E., Miller, S., & Atchley, R. *Families of later life*. Belmont, Calif.: Wadsworth, 1978.

Weisner, T. S. Comments and some comparative perspectives. In B. Sutton-Smith (Chair), *Life span perspectives on sibling socialization*. Symposium presented at the meeting of the American Psychological Association, New York, 1979.

Zajonc, R. B., & Markus, G. B. Birth order and intellectual development. *Psychological Review*, 1975, *82*, 74–88.

Zajonc, R. B., Markus, H., & Markus, G. B. The birth order puzzle. *Journal of Personality and Social Psychology*, 1979, *37*, 1325–1341.

Solomon Cytrynbaum, Lenore Blum, Robert Patrick, Jan Stein, David Wadner, and Carole Wilk

CHAPTER

34

Midlife Development: A Personality and Social Systems Perspective

Recent research and theory on midlife development and the midlife transition is reviewed and integrated into a personality and social systems perspective. This point of view focuses on the analysis of individual midlife personality in social context, the definition of midlife precipitators, developmental tasks, sequential phaselike developments during the midlife transition, and implications for psychopathology. An agenda for the 1980s is proposed that emphasizes a series of research, methodological, and theoretical questions and implications.

The concept of "midlife transition" and even more so the term *midlife crisis* have achieved widespread, perhaps even cultish, popularity in some sectors of our culture. They have been repeatedly described in poetry, novels, plays, and films (e.g., Bellow, 1963; Friedman, 1962, 1970; Kavanaugh, 1970; Kazan, 1967; Miller, 1957; Roth, 1969; Vonnegut, 1969) and in psychological literature stemming in large part from C. G. Jung (1969). Many life span psychologists have remained skeptical, however, about the constructs as described as well as about their explanations.

Some believe that preoccupation with midlife experience is largely a white, middle-class phenomenon associated with increased leisure, more efficient technology, and legitimation of self-involvement (Lasch, 1978; Sobo, 1977). The shift from a survival-oriented to what Lasch calls a narcissistic culture has made it possible for larger segments of the population to engage in introspection and self-expression. The term *midlife crisis* itself, by offering an explanation for trou-

bling aspects of adult development, can reduce anxiety (Cytrynbaum & Patrick, 1979).

Scholarly interest in midlife transition is reflected in a variety of recent publications (Barnett & Baruch, 1978; Brim, 1976; Cahn, 1978; Cohler, 1978; Cytrynbaum & Patrick, 1979; Cytrynbaum, Patrick, Stein, & Wilk, 1978; Gutmann, 1976, 1979a, 1979b; Levinson, Darrow, Klein, Levinson, & McKee, 1976, 1978; Livson, 1976, 1977, 1978; Neugarten & Datan, 1974; Neugarten & Brown-Ruzanka, 1978; Perun & Bielby, 1979; Robertson, 1978; Rosenberg & Farrell, 1976; Rubin, 1979; Troll, 1975).

The existence of a distinct transition involving stress or growth in middle life has been questioned, however. Moreover, studies of personal, marital, or other dissatisfactions provide contradictory results. While some investigators describe stress and crises, others find the same years a relatively stable and even "golden" period of security. It is possible that surface or conscious calm may mask less conscious inner turmoil and that individual differences in defensive and coping strategies may shape the conscious experience (Livson, 1976, 1977, 1978; Kernberg, 1976, 1978; Neugarten, 1968; Rosenberg & Farrell, 1976).

The authors wish to express their appreciation to Springer Publishing Company for permission to present in this chapter the theoretical material and preliminary data that will be forthcoming in greater detail in a book entitled, *Midlife Development: Gender Personality, and Social Systems Influences,* scheduled for publication in 1980.

Questions have also been raised about the data base. With a few exceptions (e.g., Livson, 1976, 1977, 1978; Lowenthal, Thurnher, & Chiriboga, 1975; Neugarten & Associates, 1964; Rubin, 1979; Vaillant, 1977), much of the work has been clinical and/or descriptive in nature. Only a few investigators describe their procedures and identify their samples (Gould, 1972, 1978; Gutmann, 1976, 1979a; Levinson et al., 1978; Lowenthal et al., 1975; Rubin, 1979; Neugarten & Associates, 1964; Vaillant, 1977, 1978; Stein et al., 1978). Even those studies that used relatively systematic procedures fail to report reliability, validity, or sampling.

Despite these limitations, several studies of white, middle-class men suggest that they may experience a stressful period in midlife (Gutmann, 1979a, 1979b; Levinson et al., 1978; Levinson, 1977, 1978; Perun & Bielby, 1979; Vaillant, 1974, 1977, 1978). A similar transition has been identified for women (Livson, 1976, 1977, 1978; Neugarten, 1968; Neumann, 1959; Rubin, 1979). There is more agreement about the existence of a midlife transition, however, than there is about its timing. Our purpose of this chapter is to examine available research findings from the perspective of the personality and social systems variables that could influence midlife development.

Personality and Social Systems

We see midlife as one of several important and inevitable transitions during the life cycle. The term *transition* implies a process of change moving an individual from one relatively stable stage or period of personality development to another (Brim, 1976; Levinson et al., 1978; Lowenthal et al., 1975). Although transitions tend to be experienced as stressful, disruptive, or psychologically painful, they offer opportunity for growth and development. Adults who manage the midlife transition well are thus prepared for later life tasks. Those who do not may be vulnerable to distress and despair in old age.

A *midlife crisis* is here defined as a perceived state of physical and psychological distress that results when internal resources and external social support systems threaten to be overwhelmed by developmental tasks that require new adaptive resources. Our analysis of midlife developmental processes integrates a dynamic view of personality with social systems thinking.

Our primary focus is on personality defined as a set of interrelated structures, including conscious and unconscious cognitive, affective, adaptive, and defensive components. In this context, unconscious processes are seen as operating largely below the level of awareness and thus not under rational control.

Individual personality is seen as embedded in a complex of interpersonal networks and social systems such as couple relationships, families, and work contexts. We use the term *social systems* to refer to a set of relationships in dynamic equilibrium between individuals and activities organized around the pursuit of a task (Miller, 1976; Miller & Rice, 1967; Rice, 1970; Singer, Astrachan, Gould, & Klein, 1975). The concept of task refers to the end toward which effort is directed, an end that must be achieved if the social system is to survive in an adaptive manner (Newton & Levinson, 1973). A family system is composed of intimately interrelated individuals who have close emotional and behavioral ties to each other. The tasks of such systems change over the course of the life cycle of the family (Fleck, 1980; Haley, 1967; Vogel & Bell, 1968).

Certain system properties are particularly relevant to our analysis of midlife. We assume that any major change in one member of a system has dramatic implications for the couple, family, organizational, or work system in which that member is embedded. In any system, a major change in one part reverberates throughout the entire system with immediate as well as longer term implications. Thus, in addition to understanding the individuals' experience of the midlife transition, our analysis focuses on relations to partners or spouses, to children, and to job settings. Relevant systems can exacerbate individual stress, chaos, and conflict or serve as important support structures. Moreover, most systems attempt to maintain some form of dynamic stability or equilibrium. Major changes in a person's life—either intrapsychic or behavioral—will meet with resistance from the family system.

These personality and social systems properties serve to organize much of this chapter. They are shown in schematic form in Table 34-1. The midlife transition incorporates the following components: (a) precipitators or triggers; (b) tasks of midlife; (c) changes in personality; (d) phase-like developments; and (e) outcomes. Each component is introduced in the text that follows by a working assumption, beginning with the contribution of personality predisposition.

Individual Differences in Personality

Assumption 1: Personality differences affect the capacity to cope with the adaptive requirements of midlife.

The contribution of defensive and coping strategies to the outcome of the midlife transition requires examination. We agree with theorists like Erikson (1959, 1963), Neumann (1959), Jung (1970), and Levinson et al. (1978) that developments during midlife are influ-

Table 34-1 A Schematic Overview of Major Personality and Social Systems Parameters and Processes During the Midlife Transition

Predispositions	Developmental processes			Outcomes
Personality	**Precipitators or Triggers**	**Developmental Tasks**	**Developmental Processes**	**Adaptive**
Differences in personality (ego strength, narcissism, coping strategies, defenses, etc.) which predispose individuals to respond differentially to the midlife transition.	**Individual:** Encounter death anxiety; shift in time orientation.	Accept death and mortality.	Destructuring →	Acceptance of mortality; achieve a sense of individuation and coherent identity; integration of creative and destructive forces; attain a sense of community; integrate masculine, feminine, and related emergent components of personality; reinvest narcissism in self.
Interacts with ↕	**Stressful or Unanticipated Life Events:** Biological changes; illness or death of parents, spouse, friends; life-threatening illness.	Accept biological limitations and risks. Restructure self-concept and sexual identity.	Reassessment → Reintegration and restructuring →	Able to cope with developmental tasks of the second half of life.
Systems		Reorientation to work, creativity, and achievement.		**Maladaptive**
Extent to which primary systems (couples, family, work organization) can adapt and support individual member's engagement with midlife tasks as assessed by system's flexibility, communication, boundary management, leadership, role differentiation, culture and myths; vary by social class, racial, ethnic background, etc.	**Social System:** Reduction in parental imperative; work organization or professional culture signals limitations on mobility and rewards or pressures to retire.	Reassess primary relationships.	Behavioral and role change ↑	Failure to establish sexual bimodality which integrates male and female components of personality; failure to transfer narcissism; inability to accept mortality and associated losses. Casualties of one's own developmental potential expressed in midlife-related symptoms (depression, anxiety, decreased appetite for food and sex, poor concentration, fear of homosexuality, alcoholism, psychosomatic disorders) or in vulnerabilities and predispositions to distress and maladaptive symptoms as older adults

enced by the manner in which previous developmental stages and/or tasks have been mastered.

Rosenberg and Farrell (1976) identified four personality patterns in midlife: overtly satisfied, overtly dissatisfied, punitive-disenchanted, and repressed-depressive. These patterns are organized around two dimensions—level of overt experienced satisfaction and level of openness to experiencing stress—and are summarized to Table 34-2.

Speculative typologies of this type have a certain appeal. However, Rosenberg and Farrell fail to demonstrate clearly how such personality differences affect the process of development. Their most important contribution is the identification of the denial-openness dimension. Blum (1979) suggests a parallel between the experience of life-threatening illness and the midlife transition, in that people react to both in a primarily conscious, open, active, adaptive, and masterful manner, or even in a primarily unconscious, passive, defensive, and less masterful manner, or combinations of or oscillations between these polarities.

Livson (1976, 1977, 1978; Livson & Peskin, 1967) studied personality of women from adolescence through midlife (ages 40–50). Two patterns of development were identified: Independents, whose health improved from 40 to 50, were ambitious and intellectual; traditionals, who were healthy at both ages, were gregarious and nurturant. Both traditionals and independents showed key personality traits in early adolescence that persisted to age 50. However, while the presumed stress of the 40s described by many investigators did not affect the traditionals, the independents did have some difficulty (depression and irritability).

Vaillant's work (1974, 1977, 1978) is also longitudinal and focuses on the processes of adaptation in men followed from adolescence through their mid-40s. He suggested that individual differences in adaptive styles are relatively stable and influence coping with stress during the midlife transition.

Precipitators or Triggers of Midlife

Assumption 2: Biological aging, loss, and decline per se are not the necessary or exclusive triggers of a midlife transition. The onset of midlife is a complex, multidetermined process that may involve biological, internalized psychological, and/or sociologically determined events, whose meaning and timing are crucial.

Theorists such as Levinson et al. (1978) adopt a chronological age grading of the life cycle in which, for example, the midlife transition is seen as occurring from age 40 to 50. Others suggest that midlife is a more psychologically and socially delimited period. For some, it may be experienced as a mere "blip" in the life cycle. For others, it may last from 5 to 20 years. Engagement with some midlife tasks may begin in the early 30s or in the mid-50s, and may extend into the late 50s (Brim, 1976).

The onset of midlife is a complex, multidetermined process involving powerful unconscious forces buttressed by a host of contemporary biological, life-stress, and systems (family, work organization, and larger cultural) determinants. However, biological changes, losses of hopes, dreams, parents, close relatives, or friends, and life-threatening illness must be understood in the context of their relation to death and mortality concerns as well as whether they are anticipated (Neugarten, 1970).

Several theorists argue that personal confrontation with death and a shift in time orientation are central triggers of the midlife transition for both men and women (Jacques, 1955; Neugarten & Associates, 1964; Levinson et al., 1978). For example, Jacques (1955) focuses on the preoccupation with death and its accompanying unconscious ontological anxiety as the major trigger of the midlife crisis:

The entry upon the psychological scene of the reality and inevitability of one's own eventual personal death is

Table 34-2 Patterns of Midlife Experience

Degree of overt satisfaction	Degree of openess	
	Open	Denying
Satisfied	Assesses past and present with conscious sense of satisfaction. Few symptoms of distress. Open to own feelings. Acceptance of others. Feels in control of fate.	Overtly satisfied. Attitudinally rigid. Denies feelings. High authoritariansim. High in covert depressions and anxiety. High in symptom formation. Ritualistic conformer.
Dissatisfied	High alienation. Active identity struggle. Ego-oriented, uninvolved interpersonally, low authoritarianism.	Highest in authoritarianism. Conflict with children. Dissatisfaction associated with environmental factors.

the central and crucial feature of the midlife phase—the feature which precipitates the critical nature of this period. (p. 506)

How one tackles the reality of eventual death—whether one faces this reality or denies it—will depend on the working through of prior depressive positions.

Jacques seeks to account for the compulsive attempts to remain young—the hypochondriachal concern with health and appearance, the emergence of sexual promiscuity, and the frequency of increased religious concern—as defensive attempts to race against time. The thought of death could also be worked through internally and not predominantly in projective identification. The most reliable conscious indicator of entry into midlife is death anxiety and the related shift in time orientation to "time left to live."

Blum (1979) argues that life-threatening illness can contribute to the onset of midlife as well as to the intensification of the experience. She maintains that such illness, with its parallel tasks, demands, and concerns about loss, is experienced by the middle-aged adult as a compressed, condensed, "larger-than-life" version of the total midlife experience, and that responses to that illness parallel responses to issues of midlife. Based on in-depth studies of mastectomy patients and comparisons of cohorts of male and female myocardial infarction patients (early, middle, and late adulthood), Blum concludes that life-threatening illness in midlife, *as opposed to in early or late adulthood*, exacerbates and accelerates midlife developmental activity by (a) facilitating the resolution of premorbid stage-related conflicts, or (b) intensifying the premorbid regressive orientation. Specifically, she reports that unlike younger and older adults, midlife subjects conceptualized the illness explicitly in terms of the prevailing developmental and life-space struggles at the time of onset, projecting previously unconscious wishes into the "message" of the illness with unanticipated consistency and clarity. Thus the transitional (chaotic, vulnerable, ambiguous) nature of midlife, in contrast to the more stable character of earlier and later adulthood, reflected the constructive "use" of the illness to resolve or deny conflict by many of the midlife subjects.

The contribution of social system and status changes to the onset of the transition must also be noted. Examples are Gutmann's analysis of the parental imperative and Rosenbaum's (1979) study of organizational career expectations, mobility, and limitations at midlife. Under certain circumstances, biological and social status changes can be so powerful as to precipitate early engagement with midlife tasks. For example, consider the professional dancer who is forced to retire at age 30. There is some evidence to suggest that such a transition is accompanied by a painful process of reassessment and mourning for this loss of identity that parallels midlife processes (Lee-Nelson, 1979).

The question has been raised of whether the anticipation of the "empty nest" as a developmental milestone in the life cycle can serve as an inevitable precipitator of midlife crisis for women. Recent work by Barnett and Baruch (1978), Cohler (1978), Livson (1976, 1977, 1978), Neugarten (1979), and Rubin (1979) indicates that the experience of "empty-nesting" ranges from distress to relief and varies in meaning and timing. Investment in parenthood, individual differences in personality, simultaneous changes in the couple's relationships, and the woman's sense of security in what lies ahead all shape the experience.

Similarly, menopause has been seriously questioned as a major biological determining event of midlife. Notman (1979), in a recent critical review, appropriately suggests that the meaning and impact of menopause should be understood in the context of broader and more complex midlife changes.

The Developmental Tasks of Midlife

Assumption 3: The analysis of the midlife transition can be conceptualized in terms of a series of interrelated tasks to be mastered.

According to Levinson et al. (1978), the central task of a transition is "to terminate a time in one's life: to accept the losses that termination entails; to review and evaluate the past; to decide which aspects of the past to keep and which to reject; and to consider one's wishes and possibilities for the future" (p. 51). A constellation of specific psychosocial, interpersonal, biological, and social systems tasks to be mastered in midlife include (a) acceptance of death and mortality; (b) recognition of biological limitations and health risks; (c) restructuring of sexual identity and self-concept; (d) reorientation to work, career, creativity, and achievement; and (e) reassessment of primary relationships.

The commitment to address these tasks signals one's entry into and participation in midlife. The work of midlife involves a continual and deep examination of inner experiences, feelings, fantasies, conflicts, values, and attitudes. It culminates in an integration of old and new components in personality and interpersonal relationships.

It should be emphasized that the quality of work carried on during midlife in mastering these developmental tasks can set the stage for considerable growth and adaptation. As is argued below, failure to do so may predispose postmidlife people to distress.

The extent to which these tasks are inevitable and universal is unknown. There is some evidence to suggest that they apply not only to white middle-class populations (e.g., Brim, 1976; Cytrynbaum et al., 1978; Havighurst, 1952, 1953; Levinson et al., 1978; McCoy, Ryan & Lichtenberg, 1978) but also to blue-collar workers (Danielson & Cytrynbaum, 1979; Levinson et al., 1978). For example, a recent survey and interview study in the Chicago area of over 200 midlife blue-collar workers ranging in age from 30 to 55 (Danielson & Cytrynbaum, 1979) identified the following themes and preoccupations: (a) concern with job security and boredom, monetary preparedness, and retirement; (b) commitment to the future development and launching of children; (c) awareness of a shortening life span; (d) preoccupation with losses of varying magnitudes, including lost opportunities to relate to "empty-nesting" children; (e) self-assessment and reassessment of primary relationships; (f) the significance of the "dream" (Levinson, 1978); and (g) the importance of past military service in shaping occupational goals and opportunity. Although these data are generally consistent with previous findings on middle-class subjects, further systematic studies across racial, ethnic, gender, and cultural lines are required.

Changes in Personality during the Midlife Transition

Assumption 4: For some people, the midlife transition is a time of significant personality change.

Two major personality changes reported for midlife are increasing interiority and the emergence of previously suppressed or repressed characteristics. The latter shift is of particular interest because of its potential for stressing the family system.

Neugarten and Gutmann (1968) note that youth (up to the 50s) is more outer directed than is middle or old age. During the later years there is a turning inward of ego functions accompanied by a move from active to passive modes of environmental mastery. With age, therefore, there is increased emphasis on introspection.

Levinson et al. (1978), C. G. Jung (1970), and Neumann (1959) describe a reversal in the pattern of inward/outward focus around midlife. This development parallels a presumed change in sexual identity and self-concept, involving the integration of previously suppressed contrasexual components of personality (characteristics that are traditionally, and often stereotypically, associated with the opposite sex).

C. G. Jung (1970), Wolff (1956), Neugarten and Gutmann (1968), Gutmann (1975, 1976, 1979a, 1979b), Levinson et al. (1978), and Gutmann, Grunes, and Griffin (1979), among others, provide empirical or clinical evidence that women tend to move toward greater instrumentality, integrating more autonomous, independent, competitive, and aggressive qualities into their personalities, while men are more able to experience expressive, passive, sensuous, and dependent components. For Jungians (C. G. Jung, 1970; E. Jung, 1969; Neumann, 1959;. Wolff, 1956) this integration of the contrasexual opposite—the animus and anima—results in a sense of sexual bimodality that is a prerequisite for further individuation.

Gutmann (1975, 1976, 1979a, 1979b) has repeatedly argued that the emergence of the contrasexual opposite, the resulting sexual bimodality, and the refocusing of energy away from children to self occur as the sense of parental imperative recedes. By parental imperative he refers to the culturally imposed requirement that certain potentialities be blunted in the service of procreation and parenting tasks. According to Gutmann, it is the requirements of parenthood that establish traditional sex role distinctions in early adulthood; masculine and feminine qualities are distributed not only by sex but by life period and the requirements of parenthood. He further argues that each sex lives out, through the other, those "closeted" aspects of their nature. Middle and later life are periods during which men and women move toward the "normal unisex of later life." These developments can be stressful, especially for couples and families.

The universal nature of the parental imperative and the gender hypothesis have been challenged. Self (1975), for instance, argues that Gutmann's analysis may be less relevant for contemporary couples, especially dual-career couples, and that Gutmann's data may reflect generational changes rather than shifts within individuals. On the basis of a series of in-depth interviews and projective testing of a small sample of male and female midlifers, Stein (1979) has questioned the contrasexual-opposite hypothesis on other grounds. Her preliminary data suggest that what is activated and reintegrated into the personality at midlife are all previously lost, rejected, or not yet realized components, not only contrasexual ones.

Developmental Phases Within the Midlife Transition

Assumption 5: Developmental processes during the midlife transition can be ordered in a series of stages.

Brim (1976) argues against the notion of developmental stages, while Levinson et al. (1978) describe a two-stage process of destructuring and restructuring. Regardless of the age of onset of midlife transitions or of their durations, we believe there is order to the progressive changes that occur. Recent in-depth interview data suggest a process of progressive and regressive cycles (Stein, 1979).

Building upon Levinson et al.'s (1978) and our own findings, we propose that there are at least three phases within the midlife period: destructuring, reassessment, and reintegration and restructuring. The final phase involves integrated behavioral and/or role change. These phases are outlined in Table 34-3.

We believe that early midlife work is not under the conscious control of the individual and is triggered by personal confrontation with death anxiety and the challenge of previously denied, neglected, or repressed components of personality to the existing structure. The first phase is destructuring.

In nonpathological individuals, preexisting personality organization is oriented to the demands of family and society. The process of destructuring is often accompanied by oscillations between euphoria and depression. The psychological task of this phase is to tolerate the emergent changes in self-perception and the loss of old identities while maintaining sufficient functioning capacity to cope with everyday matters.

The transition from destructuring to reassessment occurs at the moment when the individual realizes that the process of change that is under way cannot be reversed. The ambiguous and indeterminate qualities associated with the reassessment are expressed in certain images. For example, our research interviews elicit images of being lost, alienated, alone in the desert, and wandering aimlessly.

The restructuring phase is characterized by (a) the appearance in consciousness of other, emerging aspects of the personality, (b) inclusion of these formerly suppressed aspects in conscious identity, and (c) modification of defense and adaptive structures toward allowing new, more differentiated patterns of behavior and experiencing. The individual's sense of these new structures tends to be that they are authentic, based on personal experience, and rooted in self rather than in social and cultural expectations. A person who has successfully negotiated the transition emerges not only with more individuality and complexity but also with greater self-confidence and self-knowledge.

Like Levinson and Gutmann, we view the ultimate task of this period to be the integration of intrapsychic components and the achievement of a sense of indi-

Table 34-3 Developmental Phases in Midlife

	Precipitators of the Destructuring Process ⟶			Reassessment ⟶	Reintegration and Restructuring ⟶	Behavioral and Role Change
Conscious ↑	Biological change and decline.	Death and illness of significant others.	"Time left to live."	Reassessment of primary relationships and current identity and life structure.	Testing in reality, and/or rehearsing in fantasy different visions of primary relations to men, women and children.	Recommit, modify, or dramatically change behavior and/or relationships to primary family and/or work systems
	Life-threatening illness.	Cultural and social structural transitions such as "empty nesting," parental imperative, early retirement, status loss.		Denial and externalization leads to defensively premature role change (in family or work).	Integration of the more creative forces in personality in the form of a revised dream or legacy and of existing and emergent masculine and feminine components of personality.	Act on creating legacy, sense of community, mentoring, or other expressions of generativity.
				Emergence of real or fantasized transitional partners.		
	Confrontation with death, mortality, death anxiety.			Mourning and grieving losses: dream, mentors, idealism, legacy. Oscillate between depression and elation.	Realignment of defenses and consolidation of primary polarities, such as male-female and destructiveness-creativeness.	
Unconscious ↓				Internal distress, re-emergent contrasexual and other suppressed components of personality.		
				Reactivation of mother-son, mother-daughter separation/individuation struggle.		

viduation and coherent identity that involves (a) an acceptance of mortality, (b) an acceptance of the more destructive and creative forces of the self, (c) a sense of commitment to community, (d) the integration of masculine and feminine and other previously blunted components of the personality, and (e) a successful transfer of narcissism from children to self.

Dramatic or premature changes in primary relationships or careers before first undertaking the necessary intrapsychic work could result in temporary relief but could also increase the chances of ultimate inappropriate or maladaptive solutions. Transitional partners (significant others outside of marriage) can facilitate movement through developmental phases by offering support, reality testing, exploration of ambivalent feelings, or validation of the emergence of frightening aspects of the self (Wadner, 1979). Transitional relationships thus can serve unique and important functions during midlife.

Midlife and Psychopathology

Assumption 6: A developmental perspective should be incorporated into the analysis of psychopathology in adulthood.

Little attention has been paid to the relation between the adult life cycle and psychopathological states. With a few notable exceptions (e.g., Gutmann, 1979a, 1979b; Gutmann et al., 1979; Stein et al., 1978; Vaillant, 1977), most studies of psychopathology in midlife individuals tend to ignore current theoretical notions about adult development. It is appropriate to ask how midlife developmental processes (intrapsychic, social, and biological) affect psychological well-being. For most men and women, this period of change and concomitant stress is met with mastery, adaptive resolution, and expansion of life's goals. For others, such adaptation is not so easily achieved. The transition to older adulthood may be laden with debilitating anxiety and an increased sense of vulnerability that may ultimately set the stage for later psychological and emotional distress (Gutmann, 1979a, 1979b). Psychopathology may occur for the first time in some people during midlife. Other midlifers may encounter a resurgence of previous disturbances or the exacerbation of latent conflicts. If these difficulties are unattended, they could require treatment during the second half of life (Gutmann, 1979a, 1979b).

Although there is some disagreement (e.g., Brim, 1976), there is also evidence that midlife is indeed a period of increased vulnerability to psychopathology. There is evidence of increased frequency of paranoid ideation and psychosis (Cath, 1963; Gutmann, 1979a,

1979b; Steiner, 1973); psychosomatic disorders and hypochondriasis (Blumenthal, 1959; Cath, 1963; Gutmann, 1976, 1979b; Hargreaves, 1975; Lowenthal & Chiriboga, 1972; Steiner, 1973); alcoholism (Curlee, 1969; Fillmore, 1975; Gutmann, 1975, 1976, 1979a, 1979b; Moon & Palton, 1963; Steiner, 1973); sexual difficulties (Horn, 1970; Kernberg, 1976; Pfeiffer & Davis, 1972; Pfeiffer, Verwoerdt, & Davis, 1972); depression in association with weight loss, gastrointestinal, and sleep disturbances (Braceland, 1972; Cath, 1963; Gutmann, 1976, 1979a, 1979b; Hargreaves, 1975; Livson, 1976, 1977, 1978; Steiner, 1973); and disturbances in marital, family, and work relationships (Gutmann, 1976, 1979a, 1979b; Gutmann et al., 1979; Hargreaves, 1975; Kernberg, 1978; Livson, 1976, 1977, 1978; Lowenthal & Chiriboga, 1972; Pineo, 1968; Steiner, 1973; Thurnher, 1976).

The contribution of personality predispositions to severe distress or disturbance during midlife has been largely ignored according to Gutmann, (1976, 1979a, 1979b), Hargreaves, (1975), Horn, (1970), Kernberg, (1976, 1978), and Steiner, (1973).

Kernberg's (1976, 1978) work on midlife patients suggests that narcissistic people are particularly vulnerable to midlife distress because they cannot sustain their self-regard without constant input from others. They are therefore dependent, envious, and unempathetic. In youth they believe that admiration will solve all their problems, and they are therefore poor candidates for therapy. Only when they perceive the emptiness of their existence are they interested in trying to change.

Some efforts have been made to explain why certain people become particularly susceptible to clinical disturbance during midlife. The most interesting of these approaches are Cath's (1976) theory of changing human anchorages, Gutmann's (1979b) ideas of emergent sexual bimodal components of personality, and Jacques's (1955) theory of reworking early infantile depression, which is revived by awareness of death.

The most systematic work in this area is being carried on by Gutmann and his associates. As indicated earlier, the cornerstone of Gutmann's analysis is the return of the repressed opposite-sex components of personality and the refocusing of narcissism as the parental imperative recedes. "Healthy" development involves the successful reintegration of these formerly suppressed aspects of personality.

Threats from emerging opposite-sex components can precipitate pathological symptoms for both men and women. Gutmann speculates that the man's emerging passivity-dependence needs may no longer be gratified by their new, more autonomous, independent, and assertive wives or other female partners. Men can then develop alcoholic or psychosomatic symptoms as a means of gratifying oral needs. The midlife husband who leaves his wife for a younger, more seductive woman may be doing so not as a means of reaffirming his sexual potency but to externalize the more passive components of his personality. A more dependent, adoring younger woman may help him deny his emerging passivity. Accordingly, those who fail to resolve, or who successfully deny, these and related conflicts in midlife may become vulnerable to distress and despair or predisposed to selective symptoms in later years.

Other interpersonal implications of the contrasexual shift can be seen in dual-career families (Hall & Hall, 1979; Lowenthal et al., 1975; Wilk, 1979). The emergence of passive-dependent needs in husbands can, as noted above, lead to powerful wishes to be cared for, to be loved, and to love. Their needs for more intimate, caring relationships may come at a time when their wives are moving toward autonomy, independence, and assertiveness. Circumstances can become further complicated in couples who have maintained a stable system by projecting their unexpressed opposite-sex stereotyped characteristics onto the other—the husband his more passive, dependent, demanding feelings onto his wife, and the wife her more aggressive and autonomous feelings onto her husband. Disruption of the system can occur when these shifts are on different developmental time frames.

An Agenda for the 1980s

Studies on midlife to date have identified several important research, methodological, and theoretical questions.

Research Needs for the Future

1. To extend existing work with predominantly white middle- and upper-class males to women, blue-collar and cross-cultural samples.
2. To look further into the effects of individual differences in personality on the experience of midlife transition.
3. To investigate the impact of social structure and such major cultural and political forces as the women's movement on developmental variations.
4. To look at neglected populations like never-married career women, as well as career women who had children later than average.
5. To study the contribution of external support systems like the extended family, the larger community, and work settings.

6. To explore the contribution of intrapsychic and interpersonal variables to predisposition to pathology in the latter half of life.

Methodology

Some methodological implications for the study of midlife processes should be noted. Careful reviews of current research designs, techniques, and methods in the study of midlife suggest that systematic experimental designs and large-scale surveys may still be premature, especially in the investigation of complex personality processes that require in-depth consideration (Cytrynbaum et al., 1978; Neugarten, 1973). Our most pressing need is for an extensive descriptive data base encompassing diverse racial, ethnic, and social class samples. Such a knowledge base requires the use of case-study methods tailored to specific populations. In-depth and carefully focused interview schedules and midlife theme-oriented TAT cards for studying dual career families, black and white middle-class females, and blue-collar workers are being developed (Cohler, 1978; Danielson & Cytrynbaum, 1979; Gutmann, 1979a; Gutmann et al., 1979; Stein, 1979; Wilk, 1979). We particularly need information about the consequences of midlife transition on later life.

REFERENCES

Barnett, R. C., & Baruch, G. Women in the middle years: A critique of research and theory. *Psychology of Women Quarterly*, Winter 1978, *3* (2).

Bellow, S. *Herzog.* New York: Viking, 1963.

Blum, L. S. Implications of life-threatening illness for midlife development. In S. Cytrynbaum (Chair), *Midlife development: Influences of gender, personality and social system.* Symposium presented at the meeting of the American Psychological Association, New York, September 1979.

Blumenthal, I. S. *Research and the ulcer problem.* Los Angeles: Rand Corporation, 1959.

Braceland, F. J. Stresses that cause depression in middle life. *Geriatrics*, 1972, *27*, 45–56.

Brim, O. G. Theories of male midlife crisis. *Counseling Psychologist*, 1976, *1*, 21–25.

Cahn, A. F. Highlights of eighteen papers on problems of midlife women. In *Women in midlife—security and fulfillment* (A compendium of papers submitted to the House Select Committee on Aging). Washington, D.C.: U.S. Government Printing Office, 1978.

Cath, S. J. Some dynamics of middle and later years. *Smith College Studies in Social Work*, 1963, *33*, 97–126.

Cath, S. J. Individual adaptation in the middle years: A testing of faith in self and object constancy. *Journal of Geriatric Psychiatry*, 1976, *9*, 19–40.

Cohler, B. J. Developmental research on the second half of life. *Career Directions*, 1978, *5*, 19–35.

Curlee, J. Alcoholism and the empty nest. *Bulletin of the Menninger Clinic*, 1969, *33*, 165–171.

Cytrynbaum, S., & Patrick R. Midlife developments from a systems perspective. In S. Cytrynbaum (Chair), *Midlife development: Influence of gender, personality, and social systems.* Symposium presented at the meeting of the American Psychological Association, New York, September 1979.

Cytrynbaum, S., Patrick, R., Stein, J., & Wilk, C. *Gender and adult midlife development: Critical appraisal.* Paper presented at the meeting of the American Psychological Association, Toronto, May 1978.

Danielson, K., & Cytrynbaum, S. *Midlife development for blue-collar working men: Preliminary findings.* Unpublished manuscript, Northwestern University, 1979.

Erikson, E. H. *Identity and the life cycle: Psychological issues* (Monograph 1). New York: International Universities Press, 1959.

Erikson, E. H. *Childhood and Society* (2nd ed.). New York: Norton, 1963.

Fillmore, K. M. Relationships between specific drinking problems in adulthood and middle age: An exploratory 20-year follow-up study. *Journal of Studies on Alcohol*, 1975, *36*, 882–907.

Fleck, S. Family functioning and family pathology. *Psychiatric Annals*, 1980, *10*(2), 17–35.

Friedman, B. J. *Stern.* New York: Simon and Schuster, 1962.

Friedman, B. J. *The dick.* New York: Knopf, 1970.

Gould, R. The phases of adult life: A study in developmental psychology. *American Journal of Psychiatry*, 1972, *129*, 521–531.

Gould, R. *Transformations.* New York: Simon & Schuster, 1978.

Gutmann, D. Parenthood: A key to the comparative psychology of the life cycle. In N. Datan & L. Ginsberg (Eds.), *Life-span developmental psychology.* New York: Academic Press, 1975.

Gutmann, D. Individual adaptation in the middle years: Developmental issues in the masculine mid-life crisis. *Journal of Geriatric Psychiatry*, 1976, *9*, 41–59.

Gutmann, D. *The clinical psychology of later life: Developmental paradigm.* Paper presented at the meeting of the West Virginia Gerontology Conference: Transitions of Aging, Morgantown, West Virginia, 1979. (a)

Gutmann, D. *The post parental years: Clinical problems and developmental possibilities.* Unpublished manuscript, Northwestern University, 1979. (b)

Gutmann, D., Grunes, L., & Griffin, B. *The clinical psychology of later life: Developmental paradigms.* Paper presented at the meeting of the Gerontological Society, Washington, D.C., December 1979.

Haley, J. Toward a theory of pathological systems. In G. Zuk & E. Boszornenyi-Nagy (Eds.), *Family therapy and disturbed families.* New York: Science & Behavior Books, 1967.

Hall, D. T., & Hall, F. S. *Two career couples.* Reading, Mass.: Addison-Wesley, 1979.

Hargreaves, A. G. Making the most of the middle years. *American Journal of Nursing*, 1975, *75*, 1772–1776.

Havighurst, R. J. *Developmental tasks and education.* New York: David McKay, 1952.

Havighurst, R. J. *Human development and education.* New York: Longman, 1953.

Horn, R. E. Psychosexual problems of the middle years. *Clinical Obstetrics and Gynecology*, 1970, *13*, 746–755.

Jacques, E. Death and the mid-life crisis. *International Journal of Psychoanalysis*, 1955, *46*, 502–514.

Jung, C. G. The stages of life. In G. Adler et al. (Eds.) *Collected Works of Carl G. Jung: Vol. 8. Structure and dynamics of the psyche* (R. F. C. Hull, trans.) (2nd ed.) Princeton, N.J.: Princeton University Press, 1970.

Jung, E. *Animus and anima.* New York: Spring Publication, 1969.

Kavanaugh, J. *There are men too gentle to live among wolves.* New York: Dutton, 1970.

Kazan, E. *The arrangement.* New York: Stein & Day, 1967.

Kernberg, O. *Borderline conditions and pathological narcissism.* New York: Aronson, 1976.

Kernberg, O. Why some people can't love. *Psychology Today*, June 1978, pp. 55–59.

Lasch, C. *The culture of narcissism.* New York: Norton, 1978.

Lee-Nelson, S. *The Dance Factory: A collegiate dance company as an artistic enterprise.* Unpublished doctoral dissertation, Northwestern University, 1979.

Levinson, D. Middle adulthood in modern society: A sociopsychological view. In G. DiRenzo (Ed.), *We the people: Social change and social character.* Westport, Conn.: Greenwood Press, 1977.

Levinson, D. Growing up with the dream. *Psychology Today*, January 1978, p. 20.

Levinson, D., Darrow, C. N., Klein, E. B., Levinson, M. H., & McKee, B. Periods in the adult development of men: Ages 10 to 45. *Counseling Psychologist*, 1976, *76*(6), 21–25.

Levinson, D. J., Darrow, C. N., Klein, E. B., Levinson, M. H., & McKee, B. *Season's of a man's life.* New York: Knopf, 1978.

Livson, F. B. Patterns of personality development in middle-aged women: A longitudinal study. *International Journal of Aging and Human Development*, 1976, *7*, 107–115.

Livson, F. B. Coming out of the closet: Marriage and other crises of middle age. In L. E. Troll, J. Israel, & K. Israel (Eds.), *Looking ahead.* Englewood Cliffs, N.J.: Prentice-Hall, 1977.

Livson, F. B. Personality development in men and women in the middle years. Paper presented at the annual meeting of the American Association for the Advancement of Science, Washington, D.C., February 1978.

Livson, F. B., & Peskin, H. Prediction of psychological health in longitudinal study. *Journal of Abnormal Psychology*, 1967, *72*, 509–518.

Lowenthal, M., & Chiriboga, D. Transition to the empty nest. *Archives of General Psychiatry*, 1972, *26*, 8–14.

Lowenthal, M. F., Thurnher, M., & Chiriboga, D. *Four stages of life: A comparative study of women and men facing transition.* San Francisco: Jossey-Bass, 1975.

McCoy, V. R., Ryan, C., & Lichtenberg, J. *The adult life-cycle training manual and reader.* Lawrence, Kansas: Adult Life Resource Center, University of Kansas, 1978.

Miller, A. *Collected plays.* New York: Viking, 1957.

Miller, E. *Task and organization.* New York: Wiley, 1976.

Miller, E. J., & Rice, A. K. *Systems of organization.* London: Tavistock, 1967.

Moon, L. E., & Palton, R. F. The alcoholic psychotic in New York State Mental Hospitals, 1951–1960. *Quarterly Journal of Studies in Alcohol,* 1963, *24,* 664–681.

Neugarten, B. L. Adult personality: Toward a psychology of the life-cycle. In B. L. Neugarten (Ed.), *Middle age and aging.* Chicago: University of Chicago Press, 1968.

Neugarten, B. L. Dynamics of transition to old age. *Journal of Geriatric Psychiatry,* 1970, *4,* 71–87.

Neugarten, B. L. Personality change in late life: A developmental perspective. In C. Eisdorfer and M. P. Lawton (Eds.), *Psychology of adult development and aging.* Washington, D.C.: American Psychological Association, 1973.

Neugarten, B. Time, age and the life cycle. *American Journal of Psychiatry,* 1979, *136,* 887–894.

Neugarten, B. L., & Associates (Eds.). *Personality in middle and later life.* New York: Atherton, 1964.

Neugarten, B. L., & Brown-Ruzanka, L. Midlife women in the 1980's. In *Women in midlife—security and fulfillment* (A compendium of papers submitted to the House Select Committee on Aging). Washington, D.C.: U.S. Government Printing Office, 1978.

Neugarten, B. L., & Datan, N. The midlife years. In S. Arioti (Ed.), *American handbook of psychiatry* (2nd ed.). New York: Basic Books, 1974.

Neugarten, B. L., & Gutmann, D. Age-sex roles and personality in middle age: A TAT study. In B. L. Neugarten (Ed.), *Middle Age and Aging.* Chicago: University of Chicago Press, 1968.

Neumann, E. *Psychological stages of feminine development.* New York: Spring Publications, 1959.

Newton, P., and Levinson, D. The work group within the organization: A sociopsychological approach. *Psychiatry,* 1973, *36,* 115–142.

Notman, M. Midlife concerns of women: Implications of the menopause. *American Journal of Psychiatry,* 1979, *136,* 1270–1274.

Perun, P. J., & Bielby, D. D. Midlife. *Research on Aging,* 1979, *1*(3), 275–300.

Pfeiffer, E., & Davis, G. Determinants of sexual behavior in middle and old age. *Journal of the American Geriatric Society,* 1972, *20,* 151–158.

Pfeiffer, E., Verwoerdt, A., & Davis, C. Sexual behavior in middle life. *American Journal of Psychiatry,* 1972, *129,* 1262–1267.

Pineo, P. C. Disenchantment in later years of marriage. In B. Neugarten (Ed.), *Middle age and aging.* Chicago: University of Chicago Press, 1968.

Rice, A. K. Individual, group and intergroup processes. *Human Relations,* 1970, *22*(6), 565–584.

Robertson, J. F. Woman in midlife: Crisis, reverberations, and support networks. *Family Coordinator,* October 1978, pp. 375–382.

Rosenbaum, J. Organizational career mobility: Promotion chances in a corporation during periods of growth and contraction. *American Journal of Sociology,* 1979, *85*(1), 21–48.

Rosenberg, S. D., & Farrell, M. P. Identity and crisis in middle-aged men. *International Journal of Aging and Human Development,* 1976, *7,* 153–170.

Roth, P. *Portnoy's complaint.* New York: Random House, 1969.

Rubin, L. *Women of a certain age: The midlife search for self.* New York: Harper & Row, 1979.

Self, P. A. The further evolution of the parental imperative. In N. Datan and L. H. Ginsberg (Eds.), *Life-span developmental psychology.* New York: Academic Press, 1975.

Singer, D., Astrachan, B. M., Gould, L. J., & Klein, E. B. Boundary management in psychological work with groups. *Journal of Applied Behavioral Sciences,* 1975, *2,* 137–176.

Sobo, S. Narcissism as a function of culture. In R. S. Eissler et al. (Eds.), *Psychoanalytic study of the child* (Vol. 32). New Haven, Conn.: Yale University Press, 1977.

Stein, J. Gender and midlife developmental processes: Commonalities and differences. In S. Cytrynbaum (Chair), *Midlife development: Influences of gender, personality and social systems.* Symposium presented at the meeting of the American Psychological Association, New York, September 1979.

Stein, S. P., Holzman, S., Karasu, T. B., & Charles, E. S. Mid-adult development and psychopathology. *American Journal of Psychiatry,* 1978, *135,* 676–681.

Steiner, B. W. The crisis of middle age. *Canadian Medical Journal,* 1973, *109,* 1017–1018.

Thurnher, M. Midlife marriage: Sex difference in evaluation and perspectives. *International Journal of Aging and Human Development,* 1976, *7,* 129–135.

Troll, L. *Early and middle adulthood.* Monterey, Calif.: Brooks/Cole, 1975.

Vaillant, G. Natural history of male psychological health. II: Some antecedents of healthy adult adjustments. *Archives of General Psychiatry,* 1974, *31,* 15–22.

Vaillant, G. *Adaptation to life.* Boston: Little, Brown, 1977.

Vaillant, G. Natural history of male psychological health. VI: Correlates of successful marriage and fatherhood. *American Journal of Psychiatry,* 1978, *135*(6), 653–659.

Vogel, E. & Bell, N. The emotionally disturbed child as the family scapegoat. In N. Bell & E. Vogel (Eds.), *The family.* New York: Free Press, 1968.

Vonnegut, K. *Slaughterhouse five.* New York: Delta, 1969.

Wadner, D. Object relations theory as a function for the dream and transitional partners in midlife. In S. Cytrynbaum (Chair), *Midlife development: Recent work on gender, personality and social systems influences.* Symposium presented at the annual meeting of the Illinois Psychological Association, Decatur, Illinois, 1979.

Wilk, C. Coping and adaptation in midlife dual career families. In S. Cytrynbaum (Chair), *Midlife development: Influences of gender, personality and social systems*. Symposium presented at the meeting of the American Psy-

chological Association, New York, September 1979.

Wolff, T. *Structural forms of the feminine psyche*. Zurich: C. G. Jung Institute, 1956.

Lillian E. Troll

CHAPTER
35

Grandparenting

Although population profile changes have shown an increase in both the numbers of families that include grandparents and the number of grandparents, there is a remarkably small nonspeculative literature on the subject. Conclusions to date are that grandparent–grandchild interchanges are usually peripheral in the lives of both and that these relationships are personal and idiosyncratic rather than normative. Ages of both grandparent and grandchild appear to have an effect, as do sex and social group. Furthermore, this relationship may provide a clue to family integration and may also reflect coming shifts in family dynamics, such as those that result from divorce and remarriage.

Grandparents have rarely been considered in either individual or family developmental research. There are fewer than a dozen studies in this area at the present time, although this number does not include speculative excursions, didactic exercises, or sweeping conclusions derived from clinical practice. What is more, findings are notably inconsistent. When our scraps of information are integrated, we are left with two general conclusions: that grandparent–grandchild interchanges are usually peripheral in the lives of both, and that these relationships are idiosyncratic rather than normative. Variation is so large that it is better to talk about diversity of patterns of relating than to try to derive any central tendency. And certainly, trying to generalize from present studies would be premature and presumptuous. In this spirit, then, I will summarize several lines of inquiry and some issues that they address.

Demography

In spite of the present marginal nature of grandparenting, population shifts over the past century have had three significant effects that point to a possibility for greater significance of grandparenting. First, the numbers of and the proportion of older people in the population have increased, making both the potential number of families that include living grandparents and the number of people who are grandparents larger than they used to be. Second, becoming a grandparent is now more a middle-age than an old-age event. Third, grandparents can be more distinctly identified as grandparents within their families—they are not simultaneously parents of their own young children.

The picture is not simple, however, since demographic shifts and population profiles vary by sex and social class, religion, race, and geographic location. To make matters more complicated, new demographic changes are over the horizon. Generalizations based on the last few cohorts of grandparents have to be tentative and time-bound. It is safe to say that so far, more and more people are living out their full life span, while at the same time, the number of children per parenting couple has been steadily decreasing. There was also a trend during the first two thirds of this century for couples to marry earlier and to have their first child sooner after their marriage. Not only did they have fewer children altogether, but these children were closely spaced. Many present-day older people, therefore, are likely to have become grandparents as

475

early as their 40s and are thus still vigorous when their grandchildren reach adulthood and make them great-grandparents. At the same time, many middle-aged people have living parents of their own, and occasionally even grandparents, to divide their attention.

Changes in employment patterns also have their effect. More grandfathers are likely to be retired than in previous eras, and more grandmothers are likely to be employed outside the home. These grandfathers are more likely to be married or remarried and living in their own homes with wives. Grandmothers, on the other hand, are more likely to be widowed or divorced but also living in their own homes, though near at least one of their children. The rocking-chair grandparent is no longer an appropriate image; neither is the child carer, cookie baker, or fishing companion.

About three fourths of people over 65 in the United States have living grandchildren, and three fourths of these see their grandchildren at least once every week or two (Harris & Associates, 1975) and nearly half of them, every day or so. On the other hand, only about 5% of *households* headed by older people contain grandchildren (Atchley, 1977). Thus, contacts involve an outing on somebody's part—unless they are by telephone or letter; they are not routine within-household encounters. One of them has to *want* to visit the other.

Much of the general literature on grandparenting uses the term *grandparent* as a synonym for "old person." In fact, one of the earliest studies on grandparenting (Apple, 1956) focused on the effect that the modern old people's loss of traditional societal power has had on their relationships with their grandchildren. Such a loss could be associated with rapid cultural change following industrialization, which makes the lore of earlier generations obsolete and thus its transmission to descendants unnecessary. This loss of power could also follow shifts in population profiles, or in supply and demand. The explosion in the proportion of living grandparents may have something to do with their value; seeing many of them around may make them less likely to be treasured.

One sign of such a shifting scene may be the predominating theme in the family literature of surprise on the part of family therapists at the intrusion and disruption grandparents are perceived as bringing to "normal" family interaction. Most of our ideas of "normal" family interaction must derive from an era of rare, preoccupied, or feeble grandparents. Family counselors and therapists thus tend to assume—on the basis of their experience with troubled families who come for help—that the cause of the trouble is the alien element—the grandparent. The possibility that grandparents might also be on the scene in less troubled families has not seemed to be considered, nor has the possibility that grandparents are more likely to be around when there *is* trouble than when there is not.

Arguments over nuclear versus extended family structures held center stage during the 1960s. The isolated nuclear family was assumed to be the prevalent pattern of modern times. Therefore, many concluded, in a teleological fashion, that it must also be the *right* pattern for modern times. By the time I reviewed the decade's literature on the family of later life (Troll, 1971), however, it seemed clear that at least a modified form of the extended family is most characteristic of modern life. Findings and conclusions derived from large-scale surveys of older people (e.g., Shanas, Townsend, Wedderburn, Friis, Milhhoj, & Stehouwer, 1968) and from more intensive investigations of intergenerational family relations (e.g., Hill, Foote, Aldous, Carlson, & McDonald, 1970) continue to be replicated. Both nuclear and extended families are neither dead nor, apparently, dying. This is true for child-rearing family units and also for postchild-rearing family units. When Hill and his colleagues interviewed three generations of couples (young adults, their middle-aged parents, and their older grandparents), they found that practically all grandparents had visited with or been visited by their grandchildren within the year and that one third had experienced such a visit within the week. While this is less frequent than Harris reports, part of the difference may be due to more involved lives on the part of young adults. Some of the grandchildren in the Harris survey could have been very young and visiting along with their parents. The Minneapolis young adults whom Hill and his colleagues interviewed saw their parents as often as did those in the Harris sample. Their visits with their grandparents, however, were not necessarily in conjunction with parental visits and thus perhaps represent more truly an intentional and thus meaningful decision of their own.

Age

When we consider that the ages of grandparents may be anywhere between 40 and 120 years, and of grandchildren anywhere up to 80 years old, we have to wonder about the effect of age on grandparent–grandchild relations. This is not to deny that chronological age is a treacherous index, particularly in later life, or that for many behaviors family position is much more useful for predictions. Nonetheless, ignoring age altogether makes an opposite kind of error. Thus, when Neugarten and Weinstein (1965) examined variations in styles of grandparenting, they found age difference. Young grandparents had more diverse styles than older. Some younger grandparents were fun seekers and some were distant figures, but older grandparents were almost always formal and distant. In an ongoing study, I have found that responses about grandchildren are more likely to show positive affect if the respondents are in their 50s, 60s, or 70s than if they are in their 40s or 80s. Respondents in their 40s or 80s were comparatively neutral in their statements. These findings are consistent with Neugarten's theory of age-appropriateness, at least so far as the youngest grandparents are concerned, who may have been made grandparents earlier than they considered "proper" (Neugarten, Moore & Lowe, 1965). Kahana and Kahana (1970) and Clark (1969) report that younger grandchildren are more appealing to older grandparents, but there may be a limit here. Grandparents in their 80s may find very young grandchildren physically trying and older grandchildren disappointing—another generation of betrayed promise. Clearly we have many questions about the effect of age on the grandparent–grandchild relationship. In my ongoing three-generation study mentioned above, there were generational differences in unsolicited mention of the relationship. While 27% of the grandparents brought up the subject of their grandchildren—usually when talking about high points in their life, the kinds of things they like to do, or their ideal living arrangements—only 10% of the other two generations (their children and young-adult grandchildren) referred to grandparents.

The effect of grandparents' life conditions on their relations with their grandchildren is another unknown. Do more feeble grandparents prefer older grandchildren, for example, and relatively immobile infants? Do more idea-oriented grandparents like older, presumably more idea-capable grandchildren? What is the effect of employment and retirement? Does lineage position—being first or second or third surviving generation—contribute? That is, what is the effect of having living parents or grandparents of their own on grandparent's attitudes and feelings toward their grandchildren? It is easy to generate dozens of questions in this area.

As for age of grandchildren, almost all studies have focused on the years of childhood and adolescence. When adult grandchildren have been studied, age-related dimensions are almost always ignored. Kahana and Kahana (1970) report that children feel closer to their grandparents up to about age 10 than later and that this feeling is reciprocal; further, four- and five-year-olds value indulgence in grandparents whereas eight- and nine-year-olds remove themselves altogether. These preliminary data, based on a small sample, certainly need replicating. There seem to be two opposing conclusions about adolescents: Either they are permanently alienated from grandparents or they turn to grandparents as important family resources when they are in conflict with their parents. So far, several studies have shown the importance of grandparents to young adults (Gilford & Black, 1972; Hagestad, 1978; Robertson, 1977), so if there is alienation during adolescence, it must be only temporary or limited. A note of caution in interpreting self-reports of the relationships between different generations is related to what Bengtson and Kuypers (1971) have so aptly called the "generational stake." Youth, in the process of differentiating their own unique identity, tend to underestimate the importance of parents and family in their lives; older generations, in the process or recognizing the finiteness of their *direct* influence on society, overestimate their contribution to and identity with their children and grandchildren and thus their *indirect* influence on the future.

A final note of caution to conclude the discussion of age and population structure concerns the possible uniqueness of the cohort upon which most of these data are based. Just as this cohort of grandparents differs from past cohorts in the numbers of older people and the number of family generations, so may it differ from future cohorts in the same ways. To cite only one relevant predictor: Age of marriage and of birth of first child have recently been shifting upward again. The generation born to mothers in their 30s will again have older grandparents. The future may also hold fewer grandchildren than grandparents and, considering divorce statistics, more step-grandparents and step-grandchildren. We know very little about "reconstituted families." We know nothing so far about grandparenting relationships in such families.

Sex Differences

Throughout the family literature, sex of parent and sex of child create important differences in interaction. Families in our society tend to be female-linked, for example. Hagestad (1978) found that grandmothers are more likely to have warm relationships with their grandchildren than are grandfathers, and most of these warm relationships are along the maternal line. This prominence of maternal grandmothers, however, is not true for intergenerational *influence*, especially since grandfathers tend to underreport their attempts to influence their grandchildren. Grandmothers seem to differentiate more than do grandfathers in their influencing of grandsons and granddaughters and to concentrate on a smaller number of areas in which to influence. They state that their advice to grandsons should be different from their advice to grand-daughters: They may guide grandsons about money, for example, but this would not be appropriate, they feel, for granddaughters.

Sex differences in the grandchildren studied did not seem to affect their perceptions of their grandparents' influence. Granddaughters did not differ significantly from grandsons in how much they felt their grandparents influenced them. How much shifting sex role norms affect these differences in generational perceptions we cannot say. While grandparents, brought up in a more sex-differentiated era, would seek to influence their grandsons one way and their grand-daughters another, these young-adult grandchildren might not be receptive to such messages. Finally, explanations for female family linkage are altogether absent. Why is it that women take over kin-keeping functions even before they are kin? Barbara Turner found, for example, that her undergraduate women students were writing to their boyfriends' parents instead of the sons' doing so themselves. This occurred long before they were married (Troll & Turner, 1976). Sex differences in socialization for affiliation, or even innate sex differences in affiliative tendencies, have been hypothesized but not substantiated.

Social Group Differences

The cross-cultural study of Apple (1956), cited earlier, found that grandparents in societies where the old have diminished power tend to have more egalitarian, indulgent, and warm relationships with their grandchildren than do grandparents in those societies where the old have economic power and prestige. The parallel in our society would be those grandparents with money and power, compared to those without. Such a comparison has not, to my knowledge, been attempted. Studies of ethnic groups within our country (e.g., Cantor, 1977; Parron, 1979) show that where family relationships are concerned, and particularly where social class is controlled, there is little significant difference between blacks and whites. Hispanic grandparents who have been socialized to expect respect from their grandchildren, may be upset because they are instead experiencing irrelevance to the concerns of their Americanized children and grandchildren. Aside from the younger ages at which blacks become grandparents, relations with grandchildren between blacks and whites are more alike than they are different (Parron, 1979). We might postulate that middle-class grandparents, who would have more status and power in the larger society than lower-class

grandparents, could also have more influence on their grandchildren. One problem facing such research is the within-family cohesiveness in all social groups.

Styles of Interaction

Even though the term *grandparent* could imply ascriptive, normative, or ritualized behavior, the actual interactions between modern American grandparents and their grandchildren seem to be characterized more by idiosyncratic or personality-determined behaviors. This point has been made repeatedly by investigators from Neugarten and Weinstein (1964) to Robertson (1977). While parents are responsible for and expected to perform an array of functions, grandparents are usually free to pick the style they wish. The same grandparents can be one thing with one grandchild and another with a different grandchild, and they can alter these styles as the grandchildren develop, or as they themselves age.

The now classic study of Neugarten and Weinstein (1964) found five general styles that varied with subculture, life stage, and personality. All 70 sets of grandparents they studied—half maternal and half paternal—lived in separate households from their children, although nearby (a modal pattern). They were also all middle class and relatively young—in their 50s and 60s—as well as reportedly comfortable with their role of grandparent. They listed one or more of the following kinds of gratification: (a) biological renewal, true more for grandmothers than for grandfathers (29% grandmothers, 16% grandfathers); (b) emotional self-fulfillment (13% grandmothers, 19% grandfathers); (c) being regarded as a teacher or resource person (3% grandmothers, 8% grandfathers); and (d) a feeling of extension of the self, or vicarious achievement (3% grandmothers and grandfathers).

On the other hand, roughly one fifth of them said that being a grandparent had little effect on them. The old people in the Kansas City studies on aging (Cumming & Henry, 1961) also felt relatively removed from their grandchildren. They said they were "glad to see them come and glad to see them go."

The five styles of grandparental interaction demonstrated by the respondents in the Neugarten and Weinstein study are as follows:

1. Formal—maintaining clearly demarcated lines between parent and grandparent, with an occasional gift or minor service (22% grandmothers, 23% grandfathers).

2. Fun-seeker—a leisure orientation characterized by grandparental self-indulgence and mutuality of pleasure (20% grandmothers, 17% grandfathers).

3. Surrogate parent—almost always the grandmother (10% grandmothers, 0% grandfathers), who substitutes for the children's mother if she is employed or otherwise unable to care for her children.

4. Reservoir of family wisdom—more the grandfather (1% grandmothers, 4% grandfathers) and reminiscent of the traditional power role described by Apple (1956).

5. Distant figure—emerging "from the shadows" ritually and fleetingly (13% grandmothers, 20% grandfathers).

Contingent Relationship

The importance to the grandparenting relationship of the intervening generation—the parents of the grandchildren and children of the grandparents—is evident. Hill et al. (1970) spoke of the *lineage bridge* provided by the middle generation in mediating interactions between first and third generations. Robertson (1977) similarly reports that the middle generation, by either facilitating or hindering such interactions, influences the closeness of ties between grandparents and grandchildren. Gilford and Black (1972) paid particular attention to this mediation and noted the importance of residential distance or other factors that might determine opportunities for direct interaction between grandparents and their grandchildren when the latter are young. Where opportunities for such early direct personal bonds tended to develop between the first and third generations, feelings engendered could be either positive or negative in affect, presumably, but in either case the relationship was important to both participants. In the absence of opportunity or encouragement for direct interaction, grandparents still tended to be important figures to their grandchildren but perhaps more in symbolic or ritualistic ways. In any case, these nondirect relationships were even more contingent upon intervening parent–child dyadic bonds than were direct relationships. If parents and children feel close and like each other, their attitudes and feelings are likely to be transferred to the next generation or generations. In most cases, parent–child ties tend to be strong and positive throughout life (Troll, Miller, & Atchley, 1978). Further, in most cases these ties and feelings need not depend on continuous direct interaction. This can also be true in a way for grandparental bonds. Few grandparents seem to want to resume parenting activities with their grandchildren, as noted by Cumming and Henry (1961) and also by Lopata (1973). As Neugarten and Weinstein (1964) noted, the "surrogate parent" style of grandparenting is determined more by necessity than by choice.

While some investigators find greater grandparental contact in black families than in white (e.g., Hays & Mindel, 1973), this finding is not always replicated, particularly when social class is controlled. Parron (1979) found no significant differences in either frequency of interaction or importance of relationships between black and white golden wedding couples matched for education.

Family as a System

Viewing the family as a system has been suggested by a few theorists over the years, notably Hess and Handel (1959). This view has mostly focused on child-rearing family units. Yet the examination of common family themes and strength of family boundaries becomes even more interesting when expanded over several generations. Commonality of values among members of three-generation lineages is related to frequency of interactions and perception of influence (Hill et al., 1970; Troll & Bengtson, 1979). What has not been done is an examination of the effect of differences among families in shared family themes and strength of family boundaries on differences in grandparent–grandchild relationships. Gilford and Black (1972) and Robertson (1977) both suggest that there are family systemic as well as personal components to the grandparent–grandchild relationship. When family units are located close to each other geographically, there is some possibility that the units will be close to each other psychologically as well. Adams (1968) found this to be more typical for working-class than middle-class adults, but other data suggest that geographical separation of middle-class generations in the service of career success may be a temporary rather than a permanent condition (Troll, 1971). Thus when grandparents form more personal, tightly knit relationships with grandchildren, if they have been in immediate contact with each other (Gilford & Black, 1972) they may have stayed in close contact because of their tight family organization. Clausen (1974) found greater value similarity between youths and their parents when the youths reported "closeness" of feeling than when they did not.

Since grandparenting is more commonly a contingent, peripheral relationship to both generations (grandparent and grandchild), its significance may lie more in the clue it provides to the strength of general family unity than in its interpersonal aspects. The interpersonal importance of grandparenting may instead lie more in parent–child and other adult–adult relationships than in the adult–child ties themselves. It is hoped that future research will address these issues.

Reciprocal Influencing

In Apple's (1956) historically focused study, cited earlier, modern grandparents were seen as losing influence and turning to more egalitarian modes of interaction with their grandchildren. That this may be a premature conclusion is suggested by recent data. Early findings from a three-generation Chicago study (Hagestad, 1978) show that both grandparents and adult grandchildren acknowledge reciprocal attempts to influence each other. They not only acknowledge influence, they respect it as a legitimate activity and admit that they *are* influenced. One of the most interesting aspects of these interchanges is the distinction made—covertly—between areas in which influence can be legitimately exerted and those that should be avoided for the sake of maintaining family ties. Hagestad uses the term *demilitarized zones* to apply to such sensitive areas. Her concept is similar to that of Troll and Bengtson (1979), who refer to *generational themes* that are to be distinguished from intergenerational similarities. Against a backdrop of intergenerationally shared values and personality traits within the family are the identity-providing themes of each new generation as it comes of age.

In a review of family generational similarities in five general areas—politics, religion, sex, work, and life-style—Troll and Bengtson found that across family generations of the last few decades, there was greater "transmission" of general political orientation and general religious orientation than of specific political policies or specific religious practices. The orientation was similar, but the way of carrying it out was different. In general, transmission is enhanced where social forces or, to use Mannheim's term, *zeitgeist* are consistent with particular values or behavior. Transmission is reduced in areas where particular characteristics emerge as "keynotes" of a new rising generational unit. Older generations—both parents and grandparents—can exchange views with their young adult descendants and strengthen each other's attitudes, but this can occur only where there is perceived similarity. If the area is sensitized because it has come to represent youth's maturation or individuation needs, it will tend to be avoided. During the 1960s a study of college student radicals (Troll, Neugarten, & Kraines, 1969) found that the parents of the leftist students (and maybe thus their grandparents) approved of most of their ideas and actions and the parents of a matched group of nonleftist students approved of *their* ideas and actions: They were equally disinterested in the ferment on campus. It was curious that the parents of the leftist students were less troubled by their children's dropping out of school, living with a lover or

getting in trouble with the police, than they were with their long hair, irregular hours, and slovenly clothes (see Troll, 1972). Hair and clothes were important parts of the 1960s' generational theme and were best avoided in intergenerational discussions for the sake of the more important family unity.

In the 80 grandparent–grandchild dyads studied by the Chicago team of Hagestad, Cohler, and Neugarten (Hagestad, 1978), less than 20% of the grandparents and even fewer grandchildren reported no attempt to influence the other. Grandmothers' influence covered many areas: style of life, including basic principles for dealing with life's challenges, important values, and basic outlooks; work and education; and interpersonal issues. Grandfathers were more likely to confine their influence to work and education. They were also likely to limit their influencing to their grandsons, at least in their own reports. On the other hand, two thirds of their granddaughters said their grandfather had exerted an influence on their style of life and on interpersonal issues. Hagestad states that "people in families go to great lengths to protect their relationship. One such protective measure is to avoid conflict." The grandparents often said, "We never have disagreements," and one way this is accomplished is through silent pacts on what *not* to discuss. Among the 80 pairs, 34 had topics they recognized as "trouble" and as necessary to avoid. These usually represented sociocultural changes that produced marked generational contrasts in life-style, for example, sexual and religious practices.

Conclusions

While studies that focus on grandparenting as a relationship to young children show it as a contingent, relatively peripheral role, more recent focus on the adult grandchild–grandparent relationship suggests that it has more importance than was originally thought. The fact that more people now become grandparents in middle rather than old age and that they are thus not interested in a "surrogate parent" style and are more interested in "doing their own thing" may point to an emphasis on adult interactions as a preferred style for older people, within the family as well as outside of it. On the other hand, the "generational stake" of grandparents may be even stronger than that of parents, since they are one degree more removed from direct influence on the outcome of society and thus more concerned with their grandchildren's continuing "family themes." Certainly, affectional ties between adult grandchildren and their grandparents are reported. Obviously, we need to extend survey data beyond visting frequencies so that we can assess the incidence of different kinds of relationships between grandparents and grandchildren, not only by race, class, and proximity but also by age and health. We also need to pursue more studies like those of Hagestad and her colleagues to look at the interpersonal dynamics. Finally, we need new kinds of studies that look at grandparenting, a secondary family relationship, as an index of extended family systems.

Projections from current family demography include some interesting questions about possible future grandparental importance. For example, the high incidence of divorce suggests that we may see even more tilting toward the significance of maternal grandparents—or grandmothers (since grandparents are also divorcing)—over other grandparents. Will divorce lead to an increase in surrogate parenting? Will the importance of such grandparenting by mother's mother increase as reconstituted families will seek ties that are safe from disruption? What about the role of stepgrandparents? What about great-grandparents?

If we are going to be witnessing less mobility, even among the middle classes, will this lead to greater personal ties with grandparents than exist now? On the other hand, if there are more options for older people, will they prefer to sever their bonds with their children and grandchildren, at least for a while, during a period of transiton like that of early youth? Finally, if the father's role continues to be emphasized more in the future than it has in the recent past, will more involved fathers become more central grandfathers—to both their granddaughters and their grandsons? There is no dearth of questions for research in this arena.

REFERENCES

Adams, B. *Kinship in an urban setting*. Chicago: Markham, 1968.

Apple, D. The social structure of grandparenthood. *American Anthropologist*, 1956, *58*, 656–663.

Atchley, R. *Social forces of later life* (2nd ed.). Belmont, Calif.: Wadsworth, 1977.

Bengtson, V., & Kuypers, J. Generational difference and the generational stake. *Aging and Human Development*, 1971, *2*, 249–260.

Cantor, M. *The extent and intensity of the informal support system among New York's inner-city elderly—Is ethnicity a factor?* Paper presented at Hunter College School of Social Work, 1977.

Clark, M. Cultural values and dependency in later life. In R. Kalish, (Ed.),*The dependencies of old people*. Ann Arbor: University of Michigan Institute of Gerontology, 1969.

Clausen, J. *Value transmissions and personality resemblance in two generations*. Paper presented at meeting of American Sociological Association, 1974.

Cumming, E., & Henry, W. *Growing old, the process of disenagement*. New York: Basic Books, 1961.

Gilford, R., & Black, D. *The grandchild-grandparent dyad: Ritual or relationship*. Paper presented at meeting of the Gerontological Society, 1972.

Hagestad, G. *Patterns of communication and influence between grandparents and grandchildren in a changing society*. Paper presented at the World Congress of Sociology, Sweden, 1978.

Harris, L., & Associates. *The myth and reality of aging in America*. New York: National Council on Aging, 1975.

Hayes, W. C., & Mindel, C. H. Extended kinship relations in black and white families. *Journal of Marriage and the Family*, 1973, *35*, 51–57.

Hess, R., & Handel, G. *Family worlds*. Chicago: University of Chicago Press, 1959.

Hill, R., Foote, N., Aldous, J., Carlson, R., & McDonald, R. *Family development in three generations*. Cambridge, Mass.: Schenkman, 1970.

Kahana, B., & Kahana, E. Grandparenthood from the perspective of the developing grandchild. *Developmental Psychology*, 1970, *3*, 98–105.

Lopata, H. Z. *Widowhood in an American city*. Cambridge, Mass.: Schenkman, 1973.

Neugarten, B., Moore, J. W., & Lowe, J. C. Age norms, age constraints, and adult socialization. *American Journal of Sociology*, 1965, *70*, 710–717.

Neugarten, B., & Weinstein, K. The changing American grandparent. *Journal of Marriage and the Family*, 1964, *26*, 199–204.

Parron, E. *A study of intimacy in black and white golden wedding samples*. Unpublished doctoral dissertation, Rutgers University, 1979.

Robertson, J. F. Grandmotherhood: A study of role conceptions. *Journal of Marriage and the Family*, 1977, *39*, 165–174.

Shanas, E., Townsend, P., Wedderburn, D., Friis, H., Milhoj, P., & Stehouwer, J. *Older people in three industrial societies*. New York: Atherton, 1968.

Troll, L. The family of later life: A decade review. *Journal of Marriage and the Family*, 1971, *33*, 263–290.

Troll, L. Is parent-child conflict what we mean by the generation gap? *Family Coordinator*, July 1972, pp. 347–349.

Troll, L., & Bengtson, V. Generations in the family. In W. Burr, R. Hill, F. I. Nye, & I. Reiss, (Eds.), *Contemporary theories about the family*. New York: Free Press, 1979.

Troll, L., Miller, S., & Atchley, R. *Families of later life*. Belmont, Calif.: Wadsworth, 1978.

Troll, L., Neugarten, B., & Kraines, R. Similarities in values and other personality characteristics in college students and their parents. *Merrill-Palmer Quarterly*, 1969, *15*, 323–337.

Troll, L., & Turner, B. *The effect of changing sex roles on the family of later life*. Paper Presented at the Ford Foundation Conference on Changing Sex Roles in the Family, Merrill-Palmer Institute, Detroit, 1976.

Methodological Issues

John R. Nesselroade and Stephen W. Harkins, *Section Editors*

Introduction

A topic as broad as the one covered in this section requires a great deal of selectivity in the choice of material and therefore a series of compromises among authors and editors. Our principal objective in this section is to emphasize techniques and methods that, at this time in history, appear to be particularly salient and promising for the study of behavioral aging. There are, of course, many other sources that should be consulted by the researcher interested in designing and conducting psychological research in aging. These include various handbooks (e.g., Birren & Schaie, 1977; Nesselroade & Baltes, 1979), textbooks on developmental research design (Achenbach, 1978; Baltes, Reese, & Nesselroade, 1977; Wohlwill, 1973), and numerous individual articles that present a broad array of appropriate tools for studying aging-related changes in behavior.

The chapters included can be divided into three parts that were prepared for three separate symposia presented at the 87th annual meeting of the American Psychological Association in New York City, September 1979. The first part contains chapters by Labouvie, Horn and McArdle, and Krauss, which, broadly speaking, are concerned with design, measurement, and analysis of intellectual abilities and personality in relation to normal aging. The four chapters comprising the second part, by Danziger, Williams, Hertzog, and Marks and Stevens, reflect the recent increase in interest in sensoriperceptual studies in psychological gerontology. These chapters focus specifically on the use of signal detection theory (SDT) and the value of this methodology in specifying whether age-related changes in the performance of psychophysical, recognition, and memory tasks are due to changes in ability or to changes in response strategies. The third part concerns the complex impact of physical health on studies in psychological gerontology. The reader should be forewarned of the diversity of methodological issues, dependent measures, and theoretical constructs reflected in this collection of chapters and, therefore, should approach the material selectively.

General Issues of Design, Measurement, and Analysis

Life Span Orientation

It is our expectation that in the 1980s, the perspectives on aging offered by life span development orientations will exert a considerable influence on research activity. Research on aging deriving from a life span approach has generated several important concepts that seem advantageous for researchers to consider. We identify a few of these ideas below in relation to the chapters that follow.

The life span perspective of developmental research has led researchers to confront aspects of design, measurement, and analysis in ways not previously required. Baltes and Baltes (1980; see also Baltes, Reese, & Lipsitt, 1980), for example, identified and described three essential concomitants of a life span orientation to the study of aging. These are that (a) changes occur in different patterns defined over many attributes (multidimensionality); (b) behavioral changes of interest to the developmentalist occur along different trajectories for different people and behaviors (multidirectionality); and (c) for many behavioral dimensions, there is a tendency toward increasing variability among people with age.

These three characteristics require explicit attention in the design and conduct of research aimed at understanding the nature of aging. First, consider the concept of *multidimensionality*. Individuals are complex multidimensional organisms that possess both physical and psychological characteristics, each of which can be divided into a very large number of attributes. Given the great variety of dimensions along which individuals differ and exhibit change, the potential exists for changes to begin at different times, to occur at different rates, and/or to manifest different forms, depending on the attributes. For example, within the domains of fluid (Gf) and crystallized (Gc) intelligence, while there is much disagreement as to the actual shapes and forms of Gf and Gc curves, most researchers generally agree that fluid and crystallized intelligence do show different patterns of change. Thus it is far less informative to speak of intellectual decline per se than to isolate and characterize appropriate subsets of attributes that relate to intelligence.

The second parameter identified by Baltes and Baltes (1980) is *multidirectionality*. Developmental trajectories on some dimensions may show first an increase and then a decrease, or vice versa. Also, individuals may simultaneously display increases on some attributes and decreases on others. Therefore, one must allow for the possibility of a complicated pattern of change when studying aging processes. Some normative patterns, for example, as represented by generalized growth curves, may be useful in charting selected features of development, but to fit data well one may also have to recognize differences and to use appropriately sensitive modeling procedures.

The third characteristic described by Baltes and Baltes (1980) is the *increasing interindividual variability* associated with age that is observed for many attributes. People do not become more homogeneous as they age. On the contrary, for many dimensions, the nature of interindividual differences in intraindividual change tends to promote increasing variability, effectively negating a tidy, universal, growth-oriented approach to behavioral aging.

These substantive foci reflect a critical need for more specialization of research design, measurement, and analysis if behavioral research on aging is to be productive. Consider, for example, the difference in measurement requirements when trying to measure the same processes across two or more segments of the life span, versus conceptualizing various ages or stages as qualitatively different and perhaps incapable of being directly linked except as stagelike progressions. From theoretical discussions of measurement equivalence issues to practical attempts to develop "age-appropriate" measures of psychological constructs, there is a need to move beyond traditional measurement principles and evaluation criteria to more specialized considerations. These and related problems are explored by Labouvie (Chapter 36). Similar emphases in the areas of analysis and design are identifed by Horn and McArdle (Chapter 37) and by Krauss (Chapter 38).

If aging is conceptualized as a series of changes, both monotonic and multidirectional, and as a time of increasing interindividual variability with different patterns of changes across different subsets of attributes, and if one's focus includes not only describing these changes but also uncovering their antecedents, the challenge to researchers does indeed appear to be great. Resolving some of the pertinent design, measurement, and analysis issues is the major concern of the first three chapters in this section.

Research Design

Research design is an area in which many important, widely accepted principles have been firmly established and validated (Campbell & Stanley, 1963; Cook & Campbell, 1975; Underwood, 1957). Given the objectives of aging research mentioned above, designing schemes with which to study the nature of intraindividual change and interindividual differences in intraindividual change is a primary concern. In addition to long-standing concerns stemming from the experimental and differential traditions in behavioral research, the developmental literature over the past few years has focused on cross-sectional, longitudinal, and time-lag designs and on their particular strengths and weaknesses within the framework of age, period or time of measurement, and cohort effects (Baltes, 1968; Schaie, 1965). The confounds inherent in the basic designs are well-known, and the apparent merits and utility of alternatives (e.g., sequential strategies) have been amply demonstrated.

Aside from the need to study aging in multiple cohorts and to approximate solid causal inferences whenever possible, we believe that those designs that provide for repeated measurements of subjects are most advantageous in answering many developmental research questions. Development and aging index processes, and the study of processes is intrinsically linked to repeated-measurement design. McCall (1977), in the child development literature, persuasively reiterated that long-standing argument. However, repeated-measurement designs cannot be of the simple longitudinal kind. Simple longitudinal designs are preexperimental and are beset with many confounds, such as selective sampling, dropout, and effects of repeated testing, that jeopardize their internal and external design validity. Rather, longitudinal designs that allow for control of confounds while permitting an examination of intraindividual change and interindividual differences can contribute most successfully to developmental research (Baltes & Nesselroade, 1979).

Baltes and Nesselroade offered several rationales for the application of longitudinal research designs to the study of development. The advantages of using longitudinal designs include (a) the *direct* representation of both intraindividual change and interindividual differences in intraindividual change, and (b) the assessment of *interrelations* among behavioral variables as they change, which thus permits examination of multivariate structures. Longitudinal designs also allow for the *direct* analysis of determinants of change, including the causes of intraindividual change, which may include patterns of multiple or delayed causation, and the analysis of causes of interindividual differences in intraindividual change. Longitudinal research, then, needs to transcend description by incorporating features of control and experimentation.

Krauss (Chapter 38), writing on design of between- and within-group comparisions in the study of aging, gives special attention to the study of variability exhibited by older adults. She pleads for researchers to give careful thought to the framing of research questions, so that, when appropriate, variables such as education, health, and sex will be studied and used to help understand the differential patterns of aging rather than incorporated as mere design controls to reduce otherwise unaccounted-for variance.

Measurement

The research questions raised above, including the identification of interindividual differences in change, the detection of increasing variability with age, and the multidirectionality and multidimensionality of developmental trajectories, place a large burden on the measurement devices used. One important theme in this context is that of measurement equivalence (Eck-

ensberger, 1973; Gulliksen, 1968). For example, in a longitudinal study the researcher must be concerned with whether the same construct is being measured on all occasions. The same general concern applies in comparing young and old subjects on the same measure. Do apparent increases of variability with age represent the same measurement units at different points in time and thus provide a basis for characterizing differences in variability? In the case of multivariate representations, are comparisons of structure meaningfully performed?

Chapter 36 is a direct reflection of concern with measurement issues. Labouvie identifies four general questions concerning the nature of measures: (1) Do instruments measure the same concept? (2) If the same concept is indeed being measured, are metrics, or units of measurement, identical? (3) Do differences in observed means reflect differences in the means of the underlying construct? and (4) Do the measures have comparable reliabilities in all age groups? Labouvie's concern with equivalence of measurement complements a great deal of research in the last half century, much of which has stemmed from concerns with "factor invariance" (see Nesselroade, 1977, for a summary). Many of the resolutions to these questions are currently centered around the model-fitting procedures developed by Jöreskog (1979) and others which fall within the approach discussed in Horn and McArdle's chapter.

Model Fitting and Confirmatory Data Analysis

It is in the nature of development and aging that not all relevant mechanisms and factors are subject to manipulation. Moreover, the phenomenon is complex and multivariate. Such a situation invites the formulation and use of designs providing alternative approaches to the establishment of causal relations within multivariate frameworks. In the 1970s a potentially powerful set of such techniques gained visibility in behavioral research. For example, Kenny (1979) identified exploratory and confirmatory data analyses as two promising areas for future research in social psychology, but their value clearly extends to the study of behavioral aging. Horn and McArdle, in their chapter on statistical modeling procedures and methods, discuss such applications of confirmatory, or hypothesis-testing, analyses.

The use of structural models for representing behavioral change phenomena (Bentler, 1980; Jöreskog, 1979; Rogosa, 1979) is one of the most promising examples of confirmatory analysis from the standpoint of the study of aging. Perhaps one of the greatest contributions that structural analysis approaches have made has been the formal recognition of the distinction between measurement models and structural models. This distinction allows for the integration of long-standing traditions of psychometric, factor-analytic work on test construction, the study of multivariate structures, and the systematic testing of hypothesized causal relations among variables.

Horn and McArdle (Chapter 37) provide both a good introduction and a very thorough discussion of the use of mathematical and statistical modeling in aging research. They not only examine the benefits that modeling offers to scientific theorizing and data evaluation but also provide a valuable perspective on some of the weaknesses of the approach.

Sensation and Perception Issues in Studying Performance Differentials

There are also methodological developments germane to the study of aging that have emerged from research in substantive areas rather than from general considerations of design. Methods should be evaluated not only from a design point of view, but also on the basis of theory and the unique set of instruments that evolve in a specific substantive domain. In the second part of this section, the area of sensation and perception provides an illustrative example.

The chapters by Danziger, Williams, Hertzog, and Marks and Stevens (Chapters 39–42) are concerned with measurements that utilize modern psychophysical techniques, particularly those from the methodology provided by signal detection theory (SDT). The dichotomy between performance and ability has been recognized as a major issue in aging research. The relatively new approach to quantification of sensory, perceptual, and cognitive processes provided by signal detection theory is consistent with the need, in the assessment of age changes in these processes, to separate people's ability to sense, perceive, or remember some aspect of an event from their willingness to report items as different. SDT provides separate estimates of individual subjects' ability (often symbolized as d', a specific parametric estimate of sensitivity) and their response criterion or response bias.

SDT in its classical form is applied to data collected in a task in which an observer judges the presence or absence of a signal in background noise. Neutral (noise alone) and positive (signal plus noise) stimuli are presented in random order over many trials, and the observer reports whether the signal occurred. A response is correct if the signal is accurately identified when present, but wrong if the neutral stimulus (noise)

is reported as involving a signal. Over many trials the rate of correct responses (hits), specified as the proportion of hits to opportunities, is termed the *hit rate* (HR). The rate of erroneous positive responses, termed the *false affirmative rate* (FAR) is similarly specified.

When HR and FAR are examined over several experimental conditions, such as three types of instructions (e.g., "be conservative when guessing," "be moderate," or "be liberal; don't worry about mistakes"), it becomes evident that HR and FAR are related. Swets (1973) and Williams and Hertzog in this volume (Chapters 40 and 41) explain in detail how a plot of several sets of HR and FAR values from the same observer yields a function containing information about the observer's ability to perform, as well as the observer's response bias. The contour that can be constructed from such sets of HR and FAR is an isosensitivity contour, or a receiver operating characteristic (ROC).

The chapter by Danziger (Chapter 39) briefly reviews the sensory-perceptual studies that have investigated age differences in response to bias. Danziger raises issues concerning measurement of bias and also discusses the relation of bias estimation to the concept of "cautiousness." However, as Marks and Stevens (Chapter 42) note, a conservative approach in drawing a strong parallel between the psychological concept of "cautiousness" and SDT estimates of criterion is advisable, particularly where group differences are of concern.

Williams (Chapter 40) calls attention to the limiting assumptions upon which many parametric signal detection measures are based. He discusses parametric SDT measures and illustrates distributional effects for the normal, exponential, and gamma distributions, assuming equal variances in each case. (The normal but unequal variance situation is discussed in Chapter 41 by Hertzog.) Williams notes that the assumption of normality of the subject's internal, associated probabilities that an observed event was caused by the presence of noise alone or noise plus signal is a strong one. He suggests that, in many circumstances, it is likely that young and elderly observers have different associated distributions, and he illustrates this problem with data from a four-alternative, forced-choice task. Of particular importance is Williams's observation that much of the SDT research evaluating age differences in behavior has involved use of only one set of HR and FAR rather than specification of the position of the ROC curve (Swets, 1973).

The extension of the basic SDT procedure to include the use of rating scales for the observer's responses, while of importance to aging research, has often been ignored. The advantages of this procedure are that (a)

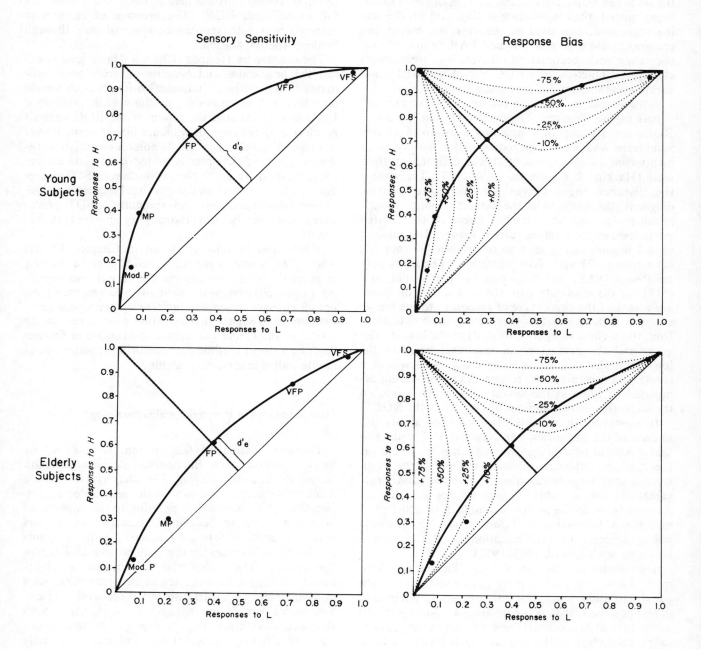

Receiver operating characteristic depicting the effect of age on discrimination ability (d'_e, sensory sensitivity, left side) and response criteria, (percentage of bias, right side). These functions are a plot of the percentage of responses to the higher stimulus (H), on the ordinate, cumulated over the rating-scale categories from the more painful to the less painful rating categories, and the percentage of responses to the lower stimulus (L), plotted on the abscissa, cumulated in a similar manner. Mod. P = moderate pain; MP = mild pain; FP = faint pain; VFP = very faint pain; VFS = very faint sensation. (From "Detection and Decision Factors in Pain Perception in Young and Elderly Man" by S. W. Harkins and C. R. Chapman, *Pain*, 1976, *2*, 253–264. Copyright 1976 by the International Association for the Study of Pain. Reprinted by permission.).

the scale can help clarify characteristics of the material being judged, thus facilitating testing; and (b) the rating scale categories used by the observer, except one category, yield a pair of HR and FAR values, so that the rating scale becomes an efficient way to establish clearly the function (the ROC curve) needed for accurate estimation of sensitivity and response bias.

An example of ROCs is presented in the two left panels of the diagram. These data present the mean ROCs for a group of young and a group of elderly volunteers who were required to make sensory judgments concerning a series of shocks delivered to their teeth (Harkins & Chapman, 1976, 1977). The greater the distance these curves are from the positive diagonal, the better was the subject's ability to discriminate among the shocks. Each of the plotted points represents a rating scale category. The subjects used a 6-point rating scale to report whether they felt (1) nothing; (2) very faint sensation (VFS); (3) very faint pain (VFP); (4) faint pain (FP); (5) mild pain (MP); or (6) moderate pain (Mod. P). The functions are a plot of the percentage of responses to the higher stimulus (H), cumulated over rating-scale categories from the highest category (Mod. P) to the lowest category, and the percentage of responses given to the lower stimulus (L), cumulated across categories in a similar manner. Since the responses to both stimuli cumulated to 100% at the lowest category (nothing) on the scale, this point could not be plotted on the ROCs.

It is possible to measure discrimination ability (d') at each of the categories, and classical SDT maintains that d' should be identical at each category, except for the random influences of measurement error. Substantial unsystematic variation in d' across rating-scale categories for a subject indicates poor quality of measurement. In the present example, it is sufficient to note that elderly subjects performed less well than the young subjects in discrimination of dental shocks (Harkins & Chapman, 1976, 1977).

The results of this experiment (Harkins & Chapman, 1976) are also plotted in the diagram (right panels) to allow visual inspection of group differences in response bias. Bias was computed as Hodos's (1970) percentage of bias estimate and a series of isobias contours. Inspection of the pair of panels on the right of the diagram reveals that the older subjects exhibited a higher percentage of bias than the younger subjects at the VFP category. This may reflect that the elderly are more willing to report low-level stimuli as pain, than are young subjects. This age effect for low-level stimuli appears to be a robust phenomenon (Harkins & Chapman, 1976, 1977; Rees & Botwinick, 1971). An important issue raised by Danziger, however, is whether this effect is due to a true age effect on criterion or results only because young and old observers fall on different ROCs. The problem of changes in response bias with age can be resolved only through further experimentation.

The chapter by Hertzog (Chapter 41) reviews in detail the limitations and benefits of single-point estimates in the study of individual differences in simple detection and recognition paradigms. Like Williams, Hertzog suggests that the power of the ROC analysis in addressing the issue of response bias in aging makes it more desirable than single-point estimation paradigms. Hertzog's chapter is of particular interest because he treats in depth the application of SDT procedures to between-groups designs that block on age. Detection, discrimination, and recognition SDT procedures are clearly and thoroughly covered in his chapter.

Marks and Stevens point out in Chapter 42 that while SDT is one of the most well-supported theories in psychology and has contributed to our understanding of age differences in sensitivity and response bias, not all changes in sensory functioning are amenable to evaluation through signal detection procedures. In the course of discussing this problem, Marks and Stevens describe a direct method for measuring sensation magnitude, called magnitude matching.

Health Factors in Psychological Gerontology

The last chapter of this section, Chapter 43 by Siegler, Nowlin, and Blumenthal, deals with health factors in the study of aging. This chapter has a strong focus on substance, although with methodological implications. For example, in pointing to the importance of health status in behavioral research, the authors note that psychologists are frequently guilty of ignoring health differences in the populations of different age groups. The differential distribution of illness across the life span constitutes an important dimension of design validity. Clearly, since the probability of disease increases with age, changes in the elderly in both simple and complex cognitive processes may result from subclinical disease states and not necessarily from age per se.

The authors point to the practical difficulty in the measurement of health status in psychological gerontology. There is a growing need for increased collaboration between the medical and psychological sciences in this regard. Most important, the authors draw attention to the reciprocal relation of health and behavior. They note that most of the research in psychological gerontology has focused on the effect of disease processes on behavior. Equally important is the relation between behavior and health status.

Concluding Remarks

This overview and the chapters to follow range widely. The methodological issues and procedures identified, and the array of data that they imply, are quite diverse, yet they cannot be considered comprehensive, as pointed out above.

Early in the past decade, Riegel (1973) stressed that advances in knowledge in psychological gerontology will depend not on the accumulation of additional data but on the success in organizing those already available. Despite the diversity of the materials presented, one may view with some optimism the fact that many of the discussions in this section are focused on novel approaches to the organization of data rather than on a refinement of existing methods. Perhaps this decade will see us move significantly nearer to the success that Riegel envisioned. Such advances are most likely when neither theory nor methodology is allowed to define singlehandedly what is being studied.

REFERENCES

Achenbach, T. M. *Research in developmental psychology: Concepts, strategies, methods.* New York: Free Press, 1978.

Baltes, P. B. Longitudinal and cross-sectional sequences in the study of age and generation effects. *Human Development*, 1968, *11*, 145–171.

Baltes, P. B., & Baltes, M. M. Plasticity and variability in psychological aging: Methodological and theoretical issues. In G. Guerski (Ed.), *Aging and the CNS.* Berlin: Schering, 1980.

Baltes, P. B., & Nesselroade, J. R. History and rationale of longitudinal research. In J. R. Nesselroade & P. B. Baltes (Eds.), *Longitudinal research in the study of behavior and development.* New York: Academic Press, 1979.

Baltes, P. B., Reese, H. W., & Lipsitt, L. P. Life-span developmental psychology. In M. R. Rosenzweig & L. W. Porter (Eds.), *Annual review of psychology.* Palo Alto, Calif.: Annual Reviews, 1980.

Baltes, P. B., Reese, H. W., & Nesselroade, J. R. *Life-span developmental psychology: Introduction to research methods.* Monterey, Calif.: Brooks/Cole, 1977.

Bentler, P. M. Multivariate analysis with latent variables: Causal modeling. In M. R. Rosenzweig & L. W. Porter (Eds.), *Annual review of psychology.* Palo Alto, Calif.: Annual Reviews, Inc. 1980.

Birren, J. E., & Schaie, K. W. (Eds.). *Handbook of the psychology of aging.* New York: Van Nostrand Reinhold, 1977.

Campbell, D. T., & Stanley, J. C. Experimental and quasi-experimental designs for research on teaching. In N. L. Gage (Ed.), *Handbook of research on teaching.* Chicago: Rand McNally, 1963.

Cook, T. D., & Campbell, D. T. The design and conduct of quasi-experiments and true experiments in field settings. In M. D. Dunnette (Ed.), *Handbook of industrial and organizational research.* Chicago: Rand McNally, 1975.

Eckensberger, L. H. Methodological issues of cross-cultural research in developmental psychology. In J. R. Nesselroade & H. W. Reese (Eds.), *Life-span developmental psychology: Methodological issues.* New York: Academic Press, 1973.

Gulliksen, H. Methods for determining equivalence of measures. *Psychological Bulletin*, 1968, *70*, 534–544.

Harkins, S. W., & Chapman, C. R. Detection and decision factors in pain perception in young and elderly man. *Pain*, 1976, *2*, 253–264.

Harkins, S. W., & Chapman, C. R. The perception of induced dental pain in young and elderly woman. *Journal of Gerontology*, 1977, *32*, 428–435.

Hodos, W. Nonparametric index of response bias for use in detection and recognition experiments. *Psychological Bulletin*, 1970, *74*, 351–354.

Jöreskog, K. G. Statistical estimation of structural models in longitudinal-development investigations. In J. R. Nesselroade & P. B. Baltes (Eds.), *Longitudinal research in the study of behaviors and development.* New York: Academic Press, 1979.

Kenny, D. A. New directions in methods for social psychology. *SASP (The Society for the Advancement of Social Psychology) Newsletter*, 1979, *5*, 14–15, 22.

McCall, R. B. Challenges to a science of developmental psychology. *Child Development*, 1977, *48*, 333–344.

Nesselroade, J. R. Issues in studying developmental change in adults from a multivariate perspective. In J. E. Birren & K. W. Schaie (Eds.), *Handbook of the psychology of aging.* New York: Van Nostrand Reinhold, 1977.

Nesselroade, J. R., & Baltes, P. B. (Eds), *Longitudinal research in the study of behavior and development.* New York: Academic Press, 1979.

Rees, J. N., & Botwinick, J. Detection and decision factors in auditory behavior of the elderly. *Journal of Gerontology*, 1971, *26*, 133–136.

Riegel, K. F. An epitaph for a paradigm: Introduction for a symposium. *Human Development*, 1973, *16*, 1–7.

Rogosa, D. Causal models in longitudinal research: Rationale, formulation, and interpretation. In J. R. Nesselroade & P. B. Baltes (Eds.), *Longitudinal research in the study of behavior and development.* New York: Academic Press, 1979.

Schaie, K. W. A general model for the study of development problems. *Psychological Bulletin*, 1965, *64*, 92–107.

Swets, J. A. The relative operating characteristic in psychology. *Science*, 1973, *182*, 990–1000.

Underwood, B. J. *Psychological research.* New York: Appleton-Century-Crofts, 1957.

Wohlwill, J. F. *The study of behavioral development.* New York: Academic Press, 1973.

Erich W. Labouvie

36

Identity Versus Equivalence of Psychological Measures and Constructs

Studies of human development and aging need to consider the possibility that a given measure may apply to different concepts in different age/cohort populations and/or that formally different measures may be required to tap the same concept across various groups. The question of functional equivalence can be raised for both independent and dependent variables, antecedents, and consequents. Equivalence of measures for underlying concepts involves several components: (a) conceptual equivalence, (b) metric equivalence, (c) equality of error variances, and (d) equality of systematic errors, or consistency between true and observed group means. Since empirical information can only take the form of sets of observed relations among measures, investigations of measurement equivalence require that the notions of convergent and discriminant validity be systematically made operational.

According to Campbell and Stanley (1963, p. 6), "Securing scientific evidence involves making at least one comparison," or as Gulliksen (1968, p. 534) stated, it requires "an investigation of the relationship between two attributes." While these statements may reflect some long-standing differences between experimental and correlational research traditions in psychology (Cronbach, 1957, 1975), proponents of either one would probably agree that, whenever scientific comparisons are made and relations investigated, the basic interest, with few exceptions, is not in specific arbitrary and unique measures but in more general concepts.

The distinction between specific measures on the one

hand and concepts that can be made operational in many different ways on the other has also been important to developmentalists (e.g., Baltes, 1973; Wohlwill, 1973), including students of adult development and aging. As pointed out by Schaie (1978), developmentalists like to suggest not only that the variability of human behavior increases with age but, what is more important, that many psychological genotypes or concepts that have been studied in younger populations take on different phenotypic expressions in adulthood and old age. Conversely, formally identical phenotypes or measures may be related to different genotypes in populations of different age. Recognition of these two situations and their implications for research in adult development and aging are important foci of the following discussion.

At a methodological level, the distinction between measures and concepts leads to a corresponding distinction between theoretical models and measurement models (e.g., Bentler, 1978). Theoretical models specify structural or causal relations hypothesized to be present in a set of latent constructs. In contrast, measurement models denote the relation of these latent concepts to a set of observed variables. As illustrated in Figure 36-1, inferences about structural or causal relations cannot be made without either implicit or explicit assumptions about the relations between one's measures and the concepts of interest. In the past the ensuing methodological questions have usually been referred to as measurement problems and have been dealt with under measurement equivalence, dif-

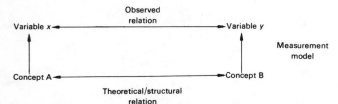

Figure 36-1. Representation of the distinction between concepts and measures. The observed relation between two measures is assumed to involve a measurement model (specifying relations between measures and concepts) and a theoretical/structural relation.

ferential validity, and differential reliability (e.g., Baltes, Reese, & Nesselroade, 1977; Wohlwill, 1973).

As far as previous discussions of the issue are concerned, two points are noteworthy. First, whether or not the equivalence issue is raised in the context of a specific empirical investigation will depend on a variety of different factors. These factors may range, for example, from theoretical model considerations that specify limits of external validity and corresponding population boundaries, to selected properties of the empirical data such as the presence of floor or ceiling effects in various subpopulations, to subjects simply telling the experimenter that the administered tests and tasks are meaningless. According to the position taken here, the issue can and should be considered in all empirical studies that include both longitudinal and cross-sectional comparisons of different age groups. Second, as an indication of unnecessary and misleading biases in past approaches to the concept of equivalence, it is interesting to realize that the issue has been raised primarily with regard to measures of dependent variables and in the context of so-called quasi-experimental designs (Campbell & Stanley, 1963). However, once it is recognized that the issue applies equally well when considering measures of independent variables in true experimental designs, it becomes clear that it is as much a design problem as it is a measurement problem.

The Concept of Equivalence

Since the equivalence issue can, in principle, be considered in any kind of empirical investigation, and since the issue has been raised chiefly in comparative, quasi-experimental designs, it seems appropriate to introduce and illustrate it with an example in which its salience and relevance will be generally recognized.

An Example: The Age × Treatment Interaction Design

Quite popular among students of human development and aging is the so-called age-by-treatment interaction design (e.g., Baltes & Goulet, 1971; Labouvie, 1978). Representative of a wide variety of empirical studies, this design combines features of both true and quasi-experimental designs. That is, the independent variables include chronological age, an assigned variable, and one or more experimental variables that permit a random assignment of subjects within each of several age groups. As the name suggests and as Baltes and Goulet pointed out, the primary objective is a demonstration not of main age and treatment effects but of age-by-treatment interactions. In other words, the emphasis is on relations within different age groups and their comparability across age levels.

To illustrate the psychometric assumptions that underlie the use of this design, or any other design for that matter, consider the following example. Previous studies of problem solving have reported that elderly persons perform less well than younger adults (e.g., Botwinick, 1978). It has also been suggested (e.g., Layton, 1975; Schonfield, 1974) that with increasing age there is an increasing inability to disregard irrelevant information. Suppose we are interested in investigating the relation between problem-solving performance and different amounts of irrelevant information and the comparability of this relation across different age populations. We present a series of tasks like those reported by Hoyer, Rebok, and Sved (1979) to subjects of different ages and ask them to indicate which of two stimulus arrays is more similar to a given standard array. The stimulus arrays are characterized by four dimensions—color, form, position, and number—only one of which is relevant for correct matching. The other dimensions are irrelevant because the three arrays that are presented simultaneously are either all identical or all different on those dimensions. Using reaction time and number of matching errors as dependent variables, we find not only main effects for age and number of irrelevant dimensions but also significant interactions of age with number of irrelevant dimensions. We conclude that age-related decrements in problem-solving performance are due in part to an inability to efficiently discard irrelevant information and that the size of this decrement is related to the amount of irrelevant information presented.

The degree of validity that can be attributed to the conclusions stated above depends largely on what kind of answers are given to the following questions.

1. How reasonable is it to assume, or what empir-

ical evidence is available to suggest, that the measures employed are in fact measuring the same concepts in all age groups? Given a particular type of task, how do we know that reaction time and number of errors are measuring problem-solving performance in both young and old? The possibility that a formally identical measure may be related to different concepts in different age groups is, of course, not limited to the class of dependent variables but applies equally to all the independent variables and corresponding experimental manipulations. For instance, how do we know that a series of tasks with a particular variation in stimulus array represents a variation in the amount of irrelevant information to all age groups?

2. Even if we are reasonably sure that the dependent and independent variables are measuring the same concepts in all age groups, it does not automatically follow that their metrics, or units of measurement, are also equal or invariant across all age populations. Of course, the assumption of equal metrics becomes crucial whenever the magnitude of differences and the strength of a relation are compared across different groups, that is, whenever the emphasis is on interactions. When and how can we assume that a 1-second difference in reaction time or a 1-point difference in number of errors represents similar differences in problem-solving performance in both young and old subjects? And how do we know whether a given variation in the stimulus material represents a comparable increase or decrease in the amount of irrelevant information for all age groups?

3. Even if all variables measure the same concepts with equivalent metrics within all of the age groups, it is still possible that the mean differences observed between age groups do not reflect differences between true means. In other words, conceptual and metric equivalence as discussed in the two previous questions are not generally sufficient to ensure consistency between true and observed means. For instance, can we assume that the age differences observed in reaction time or in the number of errors represent true differences in problem-solving performance between the various age groups? And conversely, even though we presented the same variation of stimulus arrays to all groups, can we assume that, on the average, comparable amounts of irrelevant information were presented to all age levels?

4. Finally, we may ask whether the dependent and independent variables possess comparable reliabilities across all age groups. Although reliability and validity are generally dealt with as two separate properties of empirical measures, it is also recognized that a high degree of reliability is required before it becomes

meaningful to discuss the validity of measures (Nunnally, 1967). In fact, it might be asserted that those forms of reliability that are based on homogeneity and equivalence (e.g., internal consistency, split-half reliability) represent nothing less than specific operational definitions of the notion of convergent validity (Campbell & Fiske, 1959). While the reliabilities of dependent variables are commonly checked, experimental control over the independent variables is generally assumed to ensure a high degree of reliability and standardization across all groups. This assumption may be questionable whenever the various age groups are tested and observed in somewhat different surroundings.

The problem of differential reliability across age groups needs to be considered for at least two reasons, both of which have a bearing on the issue of equivalence. First, dependent and/or independent measures, although conceptually and metrically equivalent across several age groups, may be more or less useful in various age groups, depending on the amount of true

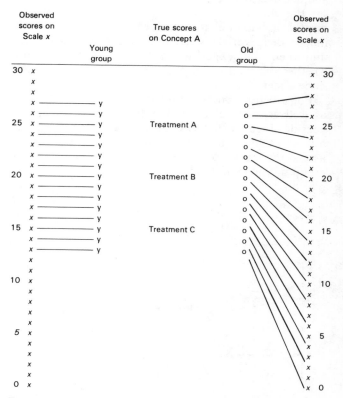

Figure 36-2 Example of a scale *x* that is assumed to be conceptually equivalent across two age groups but exhibits metric nonequivalence and inconsistency between observed and true means.

variance explicated in each group. Second, differential reliability may lead to a differential attenuation of within-age relations. This attenuation needs to be considered when the invariance of a relation across different age groups is investigated.

In considering measures of dependent variables, the problems of conceptual equivalence, metric equivalence, consistency between true and observed means, and equal reliabilities can, in principle, be raised in any empirical investigation, including true experiments. That is, even if the groups to be compared represent random samples from the same population *before* the onset of different treatment conditions, it is possible that subsequent measures of the dependent variables will no longer be equivalent. For instance, empirical evidence from Labouvie, Frohring, Baltes, and Goulet (1973) suggests that performance on a given learning task is likely to tap different underlying concepts as a function of varying amounts of practice on the task.

With measures of independent variables, the same problems are likely to be most critical in comparative and quasi-experimental studies. However, this is not to say that all of these issues do not arise in true experimental designs. For instance, whenever two (or more) independent variables x_1 and x_2 are considered simultaneously, experimenters will want to know whether the levels of x_1 represent variations along the same underlying concept for all levels of x_2.

For a better understanding of the problems at hand, as well as some of the points to be discussed below, consider Figures 36-2 through 36-4. In Figure 36-2 it is assumed that the same test scale or measure is used to assess the effect of three different treatments in a group of young and old subjects. Although true differ-

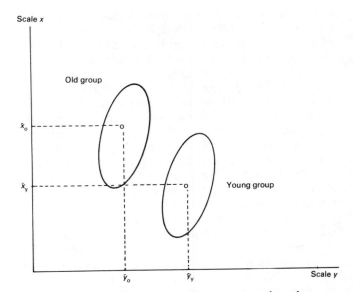

Figure 36-4 Example of two measures x and y that are assumed to be conceptually and metrically equivalent across two age groups. Inconsistencies between observed means suggest inconsistencies between true and observed means.

ences between treatments are assumed to be equal across ages together with an absence of true age differences, postulated differences in metric and inconsistency between true and observed means lead to the typical result of age-by-treatment interaction designs, namely, main effects of age and Age × Treatment interactions. Figure 36-3 merely replicates the assumptions of Figure 36-2 for the case of an independent variable. Finally, inconsistency between true and observed means is shown in Figure 36-4 as inconsistency between the observed means of conceptually equivalent measures. That is, although both measures are highly positively correlated in a group of young and old subjects, the observed mean differences between age groups are not consistent with each other. In other words, the observed means of either one or both variables are not consistent with true mean differences between age groups.

Measurement and Assignment of Numbers

Because a considerable body of literature deals with the theory and practice of empirical measurement (e.g., Harris, 1963; Krantz, Luce, Suppes, & Tversky, 1971; Lord & Novick, 1968; Nunnally, 1967), no attempt is made here to provide a detailed account of measurement models, scales, or procedures. It is more appropriate to point out here that the process of

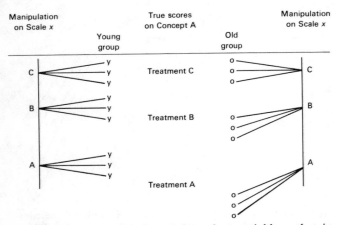

Figure 36-3 Example of an independent variable x that is assumed to be conceptually equivalent across two age groups but exhibits metric nonequivalence and inconsistency between true and observed means.

measurement and the activities involved in that process can and should be viewed from two perspectives.

According to the more traditional view of measurement espoused in most textbooks, measurement begins with the construction or invention of attributes for a specified set of individuals, objects, or events, together with a relational structure assumed to hold among the members of that set (Baltes & Goulet, 1970; Krantz et al., 1971). Measurement involves essentially the subsequent translation of that attribute and its relational structure into a corresponding *numerical* relational structure, as represented by the scores of a scale. Since relational structures can be conceptualized in different ways, the resulting numerical scales are represented as different levels of measurement (e.g., Baltes et al., 1977). In other words, although scale scores are typically represented in the form of real numbers, it is not always implied that all properties of the system of real numbers are valid and applicable.

At the simplest level, relational structures can be based solely on the notion of pair-wise identity. That is, members of a given set are either pair-wise identical or not and may be assigned to a usually smaller set of mutually exclusive categories. While such a structure and corresponding *nominal* scales are unordered in a quantitative sense, it is nevertheless possible to impose an order externally by relating nominal concepts and scales to other variables that are already intrinsically ordered themselves. For instance, a set of developmental stages (e.g., Kohlberg, 1969; Piaget, 1960) can always be ordered in relation to variables such as time or age.

Intrinsically ordered relational structures are, of course, those that rank order the members of a given set in terms of the quantity of an attribute possessed by each member. The corresponding numerical structures may result in ordinal, log-interval, interval, or ratio scales (Krantz et al., 1971). The concept of metric, or unit of measurement, is relatively unimportant for ordinal structures and scales in contrast to the other three types of structures and scales.

Clearly, the traditional view of measurement gives an accurate description of those activities that are generally associated with the construction of psychological tests and measures. However, it does not take full account of the fact that measurement instruments, once they are constructed, can be applied to new and independent sets of individuals, objects, or events. In fact, with the rapid proliferation of measurement instruments in the behavioral sciences, it has become easy to apply any number of test scales to any population or subpopulation and to assign numbers to all members without necessarily knowing whether the sets of scores obtained correspond to any theoretically meaningful attribute and associated relational structure. In other words, the assignment of numbers to individuals according to some well-defined and replicable procedure may sometimes precede the invention of underlying concepts and attributes.

The latter view of measurement activities is as important as the more traditional view, and it is certainly a legitimate one whenever the question of measurement equivalence is raised. In fact, it highlights a crucial issue that can be mentioned here only briefly: Namely, it is one thing merely to state that concepts and measures may or may not be equivalent across different sets of individuals; it is quite another to specify limiting criteria for the external validity of one's concepts and measures and to determine the boundaries between nonequivalent populations of individuals (e.g., Gulliksen, 1968). It is also quite a different matter to design widely acceptable strategies that allow an empirical assessment of the degree and kind of equivalence that may exist across two or more populations. Of course, these questions are closely intertwined with the problem, raised earlier, of explicating factors that determine the pertinence of the equivalence issue in a particular research context. The following discussion is based on the premise that the issue having been raised for whatever reason, the primary objective is to specify both general and specific conditions that permit an empirical investigation of various aspects of equivalence.

Data Comparability and Equivalence

Formal Identity Versus Conceptual Equivalence of Measures

Once the distinction between measures and concepts is acknowledged, it becomes possible to compare measures at two different levels. Considering only the concrete formal and physical characteristics, it should be possible to categorize pairs of measures as either formally identical or not, or at least as formally similar or not. The most obvious physical properties that one may select for such comparisons are likely to include the wording, format, and timing of instructions, tasks, test items, and response choices. However this should not suggest that different researchers will always agree on whether two measures are formally identical (e.g., Guttman, 1953, 1955). Nevertheless, the notion of formal identity or formal similarity—regardless of the particular criteria chosen for its definition—is important and is maintained in the following discussion.

In contrast to the formal characteristics of measures, there stands what might be called their functional properties. Whether these properties are referred to as face validity or construct validity, a concern for them implies that measures are considered in reference to underlying concepts, latent variables, unmeasured variables, true scores, and so forth. In other words, the functional equivalence or nonequivalence of formally identical or formally dissimilar measures is defined only in terms of their relations to such underlying concepts (Eckensberger, 1973).

Types of Measurement Equivalence

Before considering possible ways to determine the functional equivalence of formally similar or dissimilar measures, it is important to recognize that different types and levels of functional equivalence can be distinguished. Strictly speaking, any notion of equivalence needs to acknowledge that concepts and their associated relational structures are always construed in reference to certain sets of objects. For instance, Cattell's (1946) data-relational matrix specifies sets of individuals, sets of variables, and sets of occasions leading to a variety of covariation techniques and possible approaches to the notion of equivalence. The following discussion, however, considers only sets of individuals and interindividual differences as the relevant relational structures.

The most basic form of functional equivalence is what might be called *conceptual equivalence*. In test-theoretical terms (e.g., Lord & Novick, 1968) conceptually equivalent tests are referred to as *congeneric* tests. Although they measure the same concept, they have unequal metrics and reliabilities. Measures that are not only conceptually equivalent but also have the same metric are called *tau-equivalent*. Finally, measures that are tau-equivalent and have the same reliabilities are called *fully equivalent*. As Table 36-1 indicates, these definitions may be applied to both formally identical and formally dissimilar measures.

Regardless of the kind of functional equivalence that is desired in a particular study, empirical investigations of the equivalence issue need to be based on the following two considerations:

1. Although establishing equivalence is ultimately a problem of determining the relation between measures and underlying concepts, relevant empirical evidence is obtainable only in the form of observed relations among the measures themselves. Moreover, for such information to be systematic and sufficient, the sampling of observed relations among sets of measures should be based on the notions of convergent and discriminant validity (Campbell & Fiske, 1959).

Table 36-1 Types of Functional Equivalence Among Psychological Measures

Measurement equivalence	Measures	
	Formally different	Formally identical
Congeneric	Measuring the same concept in one or more populations	Measuring the same concept in different populations
Tau-equivalent	Measuring the same concept with the same metric in one or more populations	Measuring the same concept with the same metric in different populations
Fully equivalent	Measuring the same concept with the same metric and reliability in one or more populations	Measuring the same concept with the same metric and reliability in different populations

2. Since equivalence involves three components—sets of individuals, sets of measures, and sets of underlying concepts—it can be approached from three somewhat different directions, depending on which set is chosen to provide a stable or invariant frame of reference.

Invariant Frames of Reference

Using formally different tests to measure potentially different concepts in different populations results in comparisons so indeterminate as to be undesirable and even meaningless. Instead, researchers prefer to hold constant either the set of concepts to be measured, the set of measures to be used, or the set of individuals to be observed. Once a stable frame of reference is chosen, it is possible to consider more systematically the relation between the two remaining sets, by varying one and exploring changes in the other.

Universal Concepts. Whether or not concepts are introduced as a stable frame of reference in an a priori sense does not depend on the kind of world view one is committed to. Thus, mechanistic theories may posit universal quantitative dimensions, and organismic models are likely to postulate a set of qualitatively different categories or stages as universal across a variety of populations (Reese & Overton, 1970). In either case, the assumed universality or invariance of the concepts of interest makes it possible to express comparisons between populations in a quantitative form, either as differences along a quantitative dimension or as differences in a set of frequencies. But more important in this context, for a comparison of different populations to be scientifically meaningful does not require *all* the concepts of interest be universal or invariant (see also Baltes, 1973; Eckensberger, 1973).

An a priori and exclusive focus on universal concepts represents more of a theoretical than an empirical strategy for dealing with the issue of equivalence. Therefore, it is less relevant to this discussion. Nevertheless, how the issue may be approached by such a position should be pointed out. As illustrated by studies of intellectual development within the context of psychometric models of intelligence (e.g., Schaie, 1978), the primary objective is to determine whether formally similar or formally different measures are needed to tap the same concepts in different populations. However, actual empirical attempts to obtain sets of equivalent measures must utilize a combination of the following two frames of reference.

Stable individuals. Perhaps the most basic test of the presence or absence of functional equivalence among formally dissimilar measures occurs when a multiple set of measures is obtained from the same group of individuals. More specifically, the covariation pattern that exists among the sampled variables is analyzed in an exploratory or confirmatory sense through any of several procedures (e.g., internal consistency, factor analysis, multitrait–multimethod matrix), with the assumption that the resulting concepts reflect relational structures among individuals that were stable at least over the time interval in which the measures were obtained. Of course the validity of this assumption becomes less convincing, the longer the time interval being considered.

Besides requiring the assumption of intraindividual stability over limited periods of time, this approach and the results obtained by it are further limited in that functional equivalence is considered only within a single population at one time. This limitation leads to the possibility that concepts and associated relational structures will become population specific and that formally different measures will be misclassified as functionally equivalent when, in fact, the measures tap different concepts that happen themselves to be correlated in the particular population studied.

Formally identical or similar measures. Instead of asking (a) whether the same or different sets of measures are needed to measure the same set of concepts in different populations, or (b) whether formally different measures tap the same or different concepts in a specified single population, it is also possible to approach the issue of equivalence by considering whether the same set of variables measures the same

or different concepts in different populations. In other words, by holding constant the set of measures, this approach focuses on similarities and differences in the covariation patterns of the variables across several populations. Besides being limited to sets of variables whose formal identity or similarity can be maintained across different populations, this strategy can also lead to erroneous conclusions by misclassifying sets of variables as functionally equivalent across populations when in fact they are not. That is, a high degree of similarity in covariation patterns is necessary but not sufficient to establish equivalence.

The previous discussion presented the three frames of reference as separate and independent of each other. However, the empirical explication of measurement equivalence, when seen in the long-term context of scientific inquiry, will most likely use all three in varying combinations, each one contributing in different ways to the overall task. The notion of invariant or universal concepts may be more important in guiding the systematic sampling of measures within and across populations. In comparison, the notion of stable individuals provides a vehicle for establishing equivalence of measures within populations and is, in that sense, a logical prerequisite for considerations of equivalence across populations. Finally, the notion of formally identical or similar measures seems to bear most directly on the formulation of strategies aimed at the systematic empirical investigation of equivalence across populations. Consequently, the following section deals more explicitly with that matter.

Determination of Equivalence

No attempt is made here to review all of the procedures that have been proposed to deal with the problem of equivalence (e.g., Eckensberger, 1973; Gulliksen, 1968). Instead, the focus is on some general guidelines and one specific methodological strategy that has been developed in the context of multivariate covariance structure analysis (Jöreskog, 1971a, 1971b).

General Guidelines

Whenever measurement equivalence is not merely assumed to be given but is made the subject of a systematic empirical investigation, the overall approach, as stated before, is likely to be formulated around the choice of one or more stable frames of reference. Such frames of reference are obtained in the form of universal or invariant concepts, stable individuals, and formally identical or similar measures. Strictly speaking, the invariance of concepts is not amenable to the same kind of experimental control and manipulation as are the stability of individuals and the formal identity of measures. It is manipulable only in the sense that the assumption may or may not be introduced, especially in situations where formally identical or similar measures are used across different populations.

The primary objective of whatever empirical strategy is eventually chosen is to render operational the notions of convergent and discriminant validity of differences both within and between the populations that are studied. Since any such procedure involves a relevant context defined in terms of certain sets of measures, concepts, and individuals or events, the empirical explication of equivalence is not an all-or-none phenomenon but has to be seen in that particular context. Furthermore, since empirical frames of reference can be obtained only via a set of stable individuals or a set of formally identical or similar measures, relevant empirical strategies cannot be formulated when both sets are empty at the same time. For instance, if two age groups are compared on two formally different sets of measures without any variables common to the two sets, alignment of concepts across groups is purely a matter of theoretical conjecture.

Whenever two or more populations are compared, the set of stable individuals *across* groups is empty by definition. Consequently, the set of formally identical or similar measures that is given to all groups cannot be completely empty. Of course, it would seem desirable in those circumstances to obtain a set of measures that maintains not only its formal identity or similarity across populations but also its functional equivalence (Eckensberger, 1973; Frijda & Jahoda, 1966; Hudson, Barakat, & LaForge, 1959). Although it is likely that formally identical and functionally equivalent sets of measures can always be found in relation to the populations of interest, the corresponding set of underlying concepts may not be of primary interest. On the other hand, if such a system of variables can be identified as representing a meaningful set of concepts, it can be employed as a frame of reference to investigate the functional equivalence of additional sets of measures within and across different populations. The use of such a system of invariant measures and concepts was demonstrated by Labouvie et al. (1973), who studied the equivalence of learning-performance measures across trials for a set of intellectual abilities of different age groups. Finally, in considering the issue of equivalence in a empirical context, it is not sufficient merely to state that the functional equivalence of measures depends on their relations to a set of underlying concepts. The identity of those underlying concepts is ultimately defined in terms of both those variables that are and those that are not related to them.

Actual empirical strategies suited to an investigation of the equivalence issue will vary in both kind and amount of information that may be indicative of patterns of convergence and divergence among multiple measures. For instance, internal consistency estimates (Nunnally, 1967) reflect only the overall convergence among a set of items or measures. In contrast, multivariate methods such as factor analysis and covariance structure analysis yield considerably more detailed information regarding patterns of convergence and divergence (Bock & Bargmann, 1966; Harman, 1960; Jöreskog, 1978). Generally, these procedures can be applied only when both dependent and "independent" variables are observed rather than manipulated. A major reason for this limitation is that the notion of multiple indicators for a given concept is difficult to translate into a research design when subjects are randomly assigned to the levels of each specific independent variable.

Analysis of Covariance Structures Across Populations

Studies of human development and aging that are concerned with the explication of antecedent-consequent relations rely either on the cross-sectional and longitudinal observation of predictor-criterion relations or on the comparison of the effects of experimental treatment across age levels via age-by-treatment interaction designs (Baltes & Goulet, 1971; Labouvie, 1974; Wohlwill, 1973). In the first case it is possible and desirable to obtain multiple measures for all concepts of interest. In the second case it is possible at least to sample the dependent variables as multiple measures of the corresponding concepts.

As stated before, the empirical representation of hypothesized concepts by multiple measures or indicators is a prerequisite for the explication of patterns of convergence and divergence among variables and thus is necessary for an empirical assessment of the equivalence of criterion variables, or predictor variables, or both. Consequently, studies with multiple measures allow a more systematic test of the psychometric properties of those measures and their equivalence across age groups. In particular, it becomes possible to employ a procedure proposed by Rock, Werts, and Flaugher (1978) and based on previous work by Jöreskog and associates (Jöreskog, 1978; Sörbom & Jöreskog, 1976).

Suppose a set of measures x_k ($k = 1,2,..,K$) and a corresponding set of similar measures y_k ($k = 1,2,..,K$)

are each obtained from one of two different age groups. The requirement of strict formal identity of corresponding measures across groups is not necessary as long as a one-to-one correspondence between the x_k and y_k can be specified and as long as the response scales of corresponding measures are formally identical. Also assume that multiple indicators are sampled to provide sets of congeneric tests for each concept of interest (Jöreskog, 1971b). According to Rock et al. (1978), application of the COFAMM program for confirmatory factor analysis across populations (Sörbom & Jöreskog, 1976) considers the following sequence of tests: (a) homogeneity or equality of variance–covariance matrices across populations, and (b) equality of number of factorial dimensions and of subsets of congeneric measures. If the data are consistent with the assumption that factor spaces are equal across populations in terms of both their dimensionality and sets of congeneric measures, the notion of conceptual equivalence is supported, and it is meaningful to proceed to test for (c) equality of metrics, or units of measurement, (d) equality of true variances and reliabilities of factor scores, and (e) equality of true means and equality of intercepts of the regression of observed onto true scores. Sets of variables that are found to satisfy conditions (a) through (d) will be of particular interest, since they can be used to provide a conceptual and empirical reference system that is invariant across the populations of interest.

Conclusions

The need to establish equivalence of measures and concepts across different populations has gained increased recognition in the area of human development and aging for two reasons. First, increased interest in adulthood and aging has led to the realization that most psychological measures were developed for young populations and are therefore of questionable reliability and validity when applied to older individuals. Second, mounting popularity of life span approaches to the study of development and aging has led to greater concern about the differential reliability and validity of measures that are potentially age- and cohort-specific (Baltes, 1973; Baltes et al., 1977).

A systematic empirical investigation of equivalence needs to be based on the following considerations. Theoretical concepts and their associated relational structures are invented or construed for specified sets of individuals, objects, or events. Each concept with its relational structure, regardless of whether it is used to refer to antecedents or consequents, or to causes or effects, can be empirically represented by a multiple set of indicators in the form of arbitrary, unique, and specific measures and scales. Independent of the formal identity or similarity of measures, their functional equivalence can only be determined in relation to underlying concepts and, in turn, the identity of concepts is ultimately defined only in terms of their empirical referents. However, empirical evidence is provided and obtained only through covariation patterns among the various arbitrary and specific measures. Depending on the sampling of measures, the information contained in such covariation patterns may or may not be sufficient to indicate patterns of convergence and divergence among measures according to the notions of convergent and discriminant validity (Campbell & Fiske, 1959). Finally, when comparing different populations, it is also necessary to recognize that a complete analysis of the equivalence issue requires a distinction between units of analysis and associated covariation patterns. In other words, similarity of several *within-group* covariation patterns is not sufficient to ensure that the covariation patterns of *between-group* differences will be consistent with them.

REFERENCES

Baltes, P. B. Prototypical paradigms and questions in life-span research on development and aging. *Gerontologist*, 1973, *13*, 458–467.

Baltes, P. B., & Goulet, L. R. Status and issues of a life-span developmental psychology. In L. R. Goulet & P. B. Baltes (Eds.), *Life-span developmental psychology: Research and theory*. New York: Academic Press, 1970.

Baltes, P. B. & Goulet, L. R. Explorations of developmental variables by simulation and manipulation of age differences in behavior. *Human Development*, 1971, *14*, 149–170.

Baltes, P. B., Reese, H. W., & Nesselroade, J. R. *Life-span developmental psychology. Introduction to research methods*. Monterey, Calif.: Brooks/Cole, 1977.

Bentler, P. M. The interdependence of theory, methodology, and empirical data: Causal modeling as an approach to contruct validation. In D. B. Kandel (Ed.), *Longitudinal research on drug use: Empirical findings and methodological issues*. New York: Wiley, 1978.

Bock, R. D., & Bargmann, R. E. Analysis of covariance structures. *Psychometrika*, 1966, *31*, 507–534.

Botwinick, J. *Aging and behavior* (2nd ed.). New York: Springer, 1978.

Campbell, D. T. & Fiske, D. W. Convergent and discriminant validation by the multitrait-multimethod matrix. *Psychological Bulletin*, 1959, *56*, 81–105.

Campbell, D. T. & Stanley, J. C. *Experimental and quasi-experimental designs for research*. Chicago: Rand McNally, 1963.

Cattell, R. B. *The description and measurement of personality*. New York: World Book, 1946.

Cronbach, L. J. The two disciplines of scientific psychology. *American Psychologist*, 1957, *12*, 671–684.

Cronbach, L. J. Beyond the two disciplines of scientific psychology. *American Psychologist*, 1975, *30*, 116–127.

Eckensberger, L. H. Methodological issues of cross-cultural research in developmental psychology. In J. R. Nesselroade & H. W. Reese (Eds.), *Life-span developmental psychology: Methodological issues*. New York: Academic Press, 1973.

Frijda, N., & Jahoda, G. On the scope and methods of cross-cultural research. *International Journal of Psychology*, 1966, *1*, 109–127.

Gulliksen, H. Methods for determining equivalence of measures. *Psychological Bulletin*, 1968, *70*, 534–544.

Guttman, L. Reliability formulas that do not assume experimental independence. *Psychometrika*, 1953, *18*, 225–239.

Guttman, L. Reliability formulas for noncompleted or speeded tests. *Psychometrika*, 1955, *20*, 113–124.

Harman, H. H. *Modern factor analysis*. Chicago: University of Chicago Press, 1960.

Harris, C. W. (Ed.). *Problems in measuring change*. Madison: University of Wisconsin Press, 1963.

Hoyer, W. J., Rebok, G. W., & Sved, S. M. Effects of varying irrelevant information on adult age differences in problem solving. *Journal of Gerontology*, 1979, *34*, 553–560.

Hudson, B. B., Barakat, M. K., & LaForge, R. Problems and methods of cross-cultural research. *Journal of Social Issues*, 1959, *15*, 5–19.

Jöreskog, K. G. Simultaneous factor analysis in several populations. *Psychometrika*, 1971, *36*, 409–426. (a)

Jöreskog, K. G. Statistical analysis of sets of congeneric tests. *Psychometrika*, 1971, *36*, 109–133. (b)

Jöreskog, K. G. Structural analysis of covariance and correlation matrices. *Psychometrika*, 1978, *43*, 443–477.

Kohlberg, L. Stage and sequence: The cognitive-developmental approach to socialization. In D. A. Goslin (Ed.), *Handbook of socialization theory and research*. Chicago: Rand McNally, 1969.

Krantz, D. H., Luce, R. D., Suppes, P., & Tversky, A. *Foundations of measurement* (Vol. 1). New York: Academic Press, 1971.

Labouvie, E. W. Developmental causal structures of organism-environment interactions. *Human Development*, 1974, *17*, 444–452.

Labouvie, E. W. Experimental sequential strategies for the exploration of ontogenetic and socio-historical changes. *Human Development*, 1978, *21*, 161–169.

Labouvie, G. V., Frohring, W., Baltes, P. B., & Goulet, L. R. Changing relationship between recall performance and abilities as a function of stage of learning and timing of recall. *Journal of Educational Psychology*, 1973, *64*, 191–198.

Layton, B. Perceptual noise and aging. *Psychological Bulletin*, 1975, *82*, 875–883.

Lord, F. M., & Novick, M. R. *Statistical theories of mental test scores*. Reading, Mass.: Addison-Wesley, 1968.

Nunnally, J. C. *Psychometric theory*. New York: McGraw-Hill, 1967.

Piaget, J. *The moral judgment of the child*. Translated by M. Gabain. New York: Free Press, 1960.

Reese, H. W., & Overton, W. F. Models of development and theories of development. In L. R. Goulet & P. B. Baltes (Eds.), *Life-span developmental psychology: Research and theory*. New York: Academic Press, 1970.

Rock, D. A., Werts, C. E. & Flaugher, R. L. The use of covariance structures for comparing the psychometric properties of multiple variables across populations. *Multivariate Behavioral Research*, 1978, *13*, 403–418.

Schaie, K. W. External validity in the assessment of intellectual development in adulthood. *Journal of Gerontology*, 1978, *33*, 695–701.

Schonfield, D. Translations in gerontology—from lab to life: Utilizing information. *American Psychologist*, 1974, *29*, 796–801.

Sörbom, D., & Jöreskog, K. G. COFAMM: Confirmatory factor analysis with model modification. User's guide. Chicago: National Educational Resources, 1976.

Wohlwill, J. F. *The study of behavioral development*. New York: Academic Press, 1973.

John L. Horn and J. Jack McArdle

CHAPTER
37

Perspectives on Mathematical/Statistical Model Building (MASMOB) in Research on Aging

Issues in developmental psychology are considered in terms of reticular analysis modeling (RAM) procedures and linear structural relations (LISREL) programs, as these unfold through the specification, estimation, evaluation, and re-adjustment stages of mathematical/statistical model building. Analyses indicate that many problems that might otherwise be analyzed with analysis of variance, multivariate analysis of variance, regression (path) analysis, factor analysis, canonical correlation, and discriminant function analysis can be addressed effectively with modeling procedures. Advantages and disadvantages of modeling approaches are noted. On balance, it seems that modeling presents exciting possibilities for those who would do serious research on aging, but it also presents awesome challenges for those who intend to use the methods properly and insightfully.

Of the many recent advances in procedures for analyzing data, those that have been discussed under headings such as structural equation model building (e.g., Bentler, 1978; Bock, 1960; Bock & Bargmann, 1966; Goldberger, 1973; Jöreskog, 1966, 1973; Jöreskog & Sörbom, 1977; Kenny, 1979) have most often been heralded as the glad tidings that will usher in a new era in the behavioral sciences and usher out a sad, primitive period of researching and theorizing in these fields. While it seems clear that on occasion these mathematical statistical model building (MASMOB) procedures have been oversold, or at least overbought (as discussed by Kaiser, 1976, for example; see also Horn, 1979), it is clear that the ideas of the methods

have much to commend them. They represent worthy efforts to integrate many of the major concepts of univariate and multivariate analysis of variance, factor analysis, multiple regression analysis, and path analysis (Van de Geer, 1971). The ideas and the methods can help researchers to think in better ways about data and substantive theory and to bring together in constructive ways generic concepts of measurement, mathematics, and statistics. The ideas have stemmed from a number of disciplines, and the overall effort has tended to promote a unity among the disciplines. It may not be an exaggeration to characterize the intellectual activity associated with these ideas as "revolutionary" (see Bentler, 1978).

Yet we must be on guard. There is a faddish quality about some of the heralding of MASMOB methods, and some people who only dimly understand the methods seem particularly keen to force them onto all analyses. We have seen journal reviewers and grant

---

The authors are particularly indebted to John Nesselroade for his help and encouragement in the preparation of this chapter. We also thank Walter Cunningham, Gary Donaldson, Harry Gollob, Chris Hertzog, William Meredith, and Dag Sörbom, with whom we discussed many of the basic ideas. Financial support for the research of this chapter was provided by Grant R01 AG0058302 from the National Institute on Aging and Grant SER77-06935 from the National Science Foundation (Research Initiation and Support Program, RIAS).

evaluators demand the use of such methods when, clearly, other procedures were equally or even more appropriate. We should regard these new ideas and methods rather in the way that a promising new antibiotic is regarded in pharmacology: MASMOB will cure some ills, but we must carefully note the side effects, identify where and when the methods can and cannot work effectively, and seek to accompany our prescriptions with proper warnings. The main purpose of this chapter is to help with this kind of pure-food-and-drug analysis of MASMOB.

The field of research on aging has been particularly open to new ideas about methods of research (Nesselroade, 1977). No doubt this receptivity reflects, in part, the fact that the field requires more complicated procedures than can suffice in some other areas of study. Although developmental psychologists have often acted as if this were not the case—for example, by using analysis of variance (ANOVA) designs that can work effectively only when development is not at issue—they have done so at a cost of saying practically nothing of value about development. Increasingly, in recent years, it has been recognized that use of simple designs will not permit notable advance in the field of developmental psychology, that designs must include a clear provision for development. It is inevitable that some early efforts to deal with this requirement (e.g., Schaie, 1965) were not entirely satisfactory (Baltes, 1968). That such efforts have been made and have been readily accepted into aging research (often too readily, we will argue) is an indication that in this field there is clear need for methods that are appropriate to the phenomena of interest. It is therefore particularly fitting to evaluate MASMOB within the context of developmental psychology and, specifically, within the area of research on aging in adulthood.

Our concrete examples center around analyses of the Wechsler Adult Intelligence Scale (WAIS). For those who have studied the psychology of adulthood we need not emphasize that the Wechsler tests have played an important role in current formulations about the aging of intellectual functions (Botwinick, 1978; Horn, 1977). Because the tests are so important for both theory and practice in the field of adult development, we are undertaking a major study in which we propose to use MASMOB methods to provide an integrative framework for the many WAIS studies now in the literature. We have used the occasion of preparing this chapter to lay down some parts of a foundation for our study proposal. This foundation should help to provide an improved indication of what can and cannot be learned about adult development from use of the Wechsler scales.

In the section that follows we describe a set of WAIS data that are analyzed in a variety of ways in subsequent sections of the chapter. In a second section we describe methods of analysis, develop some language for talking about methods, and indicate the logic and procedures for evaluating models. Then follows a section in which analysis-of-variance procedures are criticized within a context of analysis of the WAIS data. Here, too, we will introduce some ideas about better ways of doing analyses for group means to provide information of relevance for developmental theory. In the next section we consider the idea that for some forms of developmental theory it is most sensible to suppose that several different manifest variables are indicative of a latent variable; that is, we look at models of a kind that have stemmed from use of factor analysis. We then attempt to integrate some of the major ideas of previous sections within the context of an expanded version of path analysis. A further section is devoted to the use of this expanded model to develop in testable form, and to test, a broad substantive theory about intellectual behavior of the kind that is exemplified in WAIS performances. After indicating some results and problems arising from model tests for this theory, we close with a section in which major ideas are summarized.

Throughout this chapter, we have tried to speak in two ways: (a) to technical issues, as such, and (b) to implications for efforts to produce a substantively based theory about adult development of intellectual capacities. These two forms of speaking involve rather different languages. Moreover, it seems that some of those who speak one of the languages do not always think very well in the other language. As much as possible, while still dealing with essential concepts that can be understood in only one or the other of these languages, we have endeavored to communicate in a manner that will enable all who understand English to comprehend the major ideas. We suspect that the chapter will not prove to be easy reading, however. We suggest that a quick reading will suffice to indicate the major ideas and to indicate where, if at all, one might want to read with more care in order to follow the threads that hold up the major arguments.

Description of the WAIS Data to be Analyzed

Subsequent empirical analyses are based on measurements obtained from the 11 subscales of the WAIS. A summary description of the samples for these analyses is provided in Table 37-1.

As can be seen in the table, cohorts of three different historical periods were tested in each of three years, 1954, 1964, and 1974. In the first year of testing, 1954, the averages of the ages within the cohort groupings were 30 (range 25 to 34), 40 (range 35 to

Table 37-1 Basic Data Layout for a Sample of Wechsler Adult Intelligence Scale (WAIS) Scores

| | Repeated testing date | | | | | |
| | 1954 | | 1964 | | 1974 | |
Cohort (and birth date)	Age	Sample size	Age	Sample size	Age	Sample size
Not used (post-1924)	<25	≈1000	<35	≈600	<45	≈250
2 (1924)	25–34	300	35–44	247	45–54	160
1 (1914)	35–44	300	45–54	198	55–64	128
0 (1904)	45–54	300	55–64	124	65–74	80
Not used (pre-1904)	>54	≈300	>64	≈60	>74	≈20

Note. These data represent (but are not in fact—see Technical Appendix at the end of this chapter) a collection (previously uncollated) of WAIS data. The scores represent a partial standardization sample. They can be obtained from the American Documentation Institute or from the authors.

44), and 50 (range 45 to 54) years of age. From extant samples of 300 in each cohort, actual data were obtained for samples of 160, 128, and 80 at all three times of testing over the 20-year follow-up period. These 1954 data are representative of the standardization sample for the WAIS (Wechsler, 1955); the 1964 and 1974 data represent only those parts of the original data that were available in the repeated-measures follow-up.

Subsamples of the data represented in Table 37-1 have been analyzed by other investigators, including Birren and Morrison (1961), Cohen (1957), Doppelt and Wallace (1955), Kangas and Bradway (1971), Radcliffe (1966), and, of course, Matarazzo (1972) in his tour-de-force summary and analysis of over 33 years of previous research and application of the Wechsler scales.

The subgroup means and standard deviations for the full-scale IQ (F) and the Verbal (V) and Performance (P) subscale scores are shown in Table 37-2. These means are pictured in Figure 37-1. One can obtain a fairly good idea about the nature of the data from a careful examination of Table 37-2 and Figure 37-1. We shall refer to these results at several points in this presentation.

Modeling Procedures

The procedures used in the analyses in this chapter derive from several fairly recent attempts to formulate general approaches, and computer programs, for modeling. The approach that most influenced our thinking is represented in the linear structural relations (LISREL) theory and algorithms of Jöreskog and Sörbom (1978; see also Long, 1976). We have reformulated these procedures, and brought together a number of programs for doing analyses, under the heading of reticular analysis modeling (RAM) (McArdle, 1979). Basic path-graphic concepts of this approach are indicated in Figure 37-2 and in the following brief descriptions:

I. **RAM Variables.** These are of two basic types:
  A. *Manifest* (*M*) variables are defined either by operations of measurement or by assignment; these are drawn as *squares* in Figure 37-2 (and in all subsequent figures).
  B. *Latent* (*L*) variables are postulated in a theory; these are drawn as *circles*. (Italics notation is used in place of the ususal Greek letters to designate postulated model variables or parameters.)

Table 37-2 Observed Means (and Standard Deviations) for WAIS Scales on Repeated-Samples Data

Sample size	Cohort	Testing time	Average age	Full IQ	Verbal	Performance
80	Cohort 0 (1904)	1954	50	90.4 (8.1)	52.0 (6.0)	38.4 (7.8)
		1964	60	97.9 (19.4)	62.7 (11.8)	35.2 (11.1)
		1974	70	63.1 (25.2)	42.0 (15.6)	21.1 (11.6)
128	Cohort 1 (1914)	1954	40	109.0 (9.0)	60.3 (7.3)	48.6 (7.2)
		1964	50	115.7 (22.4)	73.1 (13.6)	42.6 (11.8)
		1974	60	84.9 (24.0)	54.2 (14.4)	30.7 (12.3)
160	Cohort 2 (1924)	1954	30	109.0 (11.2)	58.4 (8.0)	50.6 (7.4)
		1964	40	126.4 (21.2)	75.8 (13.0)	50.6 (11.6)
		1974	50	109.6 (22.7)	65.0 (13.3)	44.5 (12.2)

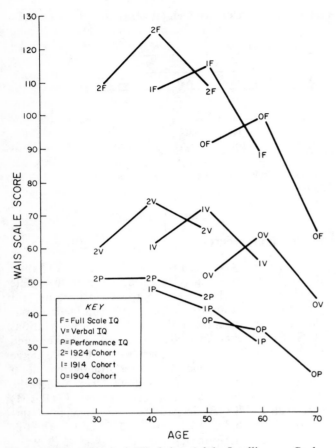

Figure 37-1. Observed Wechsler Adult Intelligence Scale mean levels by age, time, and cohort (also see Table 37-1).

II. **RAM Relations.** The basic forms of relationship among variables are also of two types:
   A. *Directed* (*D*) relations are conditional in the input/output sense of regression; these are drawn as *one-headed arrows* pointing *to* an ouput variable from an input variable.
   B. *Undirected* (*U*) relations are unconditional in the nonspecific regression sense of covariance; these are depicted simply as lines (paths) connecting both of two related variables.

Figure 37-2 is intended to indicate that each kind of RAM relation can, in theory, be specified for every possible combination of M and L variables. See McArdle (1979) or the Technical Appendix at the end of this chapter for further algebraic details.

The SEER Steps of Modeling

Essential features of application of RAM modeling can be described under four main headings: specification, estimation, evaluation, readjustment (SEER). Let us consider these SEER features one by one.

Specification. To specify a model one must describe a theory, or at least an organized set of hypotheses, in terms of manifest (M) and latent (L) variables and the relations, directed (D) or undirected (U), among variables. There are many reasonable ways to do this and thus many different kinds of models. The models we will consider here are mathematical, with added structural and possibly statistical features (Bock & Bargmann, 1966). A key feature of specification for these models is that parameters are set on *D* and *U* relations in ways that prescribe limits on the kinds of data that can be consistent with the model. A mechanism in a population that can generate particular samples of data is described by the parameter settings.

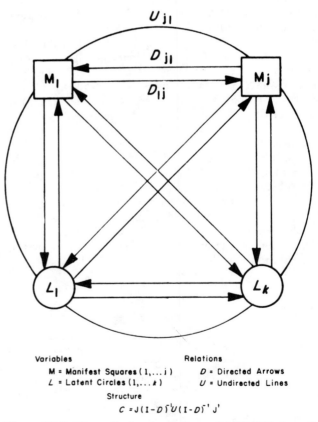

Figure 37-2. The reticular analysis model (RAM) in path nomography. (Note: Here all *D* and *U* labels and other possible *U* relations are assumed.).

This kind of mechanism can be represented by a mathematical (matrix) equation, as in Figure 37-2 and Equation A-1 in the Technical Appendix. The algebra of this kind of equation is isomorphic with extended path-analytic nomography (McArdle, 1980), which is used to present many of the basic ideas of the present chapter.

Equation A-1 well represents the idea that structural models are mathematical. Such models can involve statistical features as well. The variables might be required (in specification) to have particular distribution characteristics (normal, Poisson), for example, and the population mechanism that is said to generate samples of data might involve particular theories about how chance operates. The statistical features of model specification, as well as the mathematical features, might or might not be well represented in the procedures of estimation.

Estimation. To estimate the parameters of a model, appropriate observations must be made and proper operations must be carried out with these observations. In the mathematical models considered here, parameter estimates are derived from application of multiple variable algorithms (Lee & Jennrich, 1979) that have been designed to meet the criteria of particular functions such as those of maximum likelihood based on a Wishart distribution or those for determining the latent roots and latent vectors for a matrix that is assumed to have (but might not have) gramian properties. In theory, but not necessarily in practice, such procedures will converge on parameter estimates that are, in accordance with the particular criteria being served, the best possible for the structural model. There are many reasons, however, why computer programs may not in practice achieve the objectives they are designed to achieve in theory. The equations they serve can be highly complex, and there can be a large number of such equations. Some computer programs require cyclic approximation and reapproximation of many, many partial derivatives of different orders. The gradients of change in recalculations may be very gradual and hampered by what seem to be local maxima and minima. Much is not known about convergence under different conditions that data might present. Moreover, the mathematical criteria that computer programs serve need not be consistent with statistical criteria that could be specified for a particular model. In short, there can be many problems with the procedures that have thus far been developed to provide estimates for models that a scientist might reasonably specify.

There are also problems of ensuring internal consistency within the model. These problems are difficult for the scientist to see and therefore difficult indeed to solve. It is possible to specify a seemingly reasonable model (when considered substantively, for example) that at the same time contains internal contradictions that make it impossible mathematically to obtain accurate estimates of parameters. These are the problems of identification (Anderson & Rubin, 1956; McDonald & Krane, 1977). Such problems can be very subtle and yet disastrous for parameter estimation. They can produce quite misleading results. We will not try to indicate pitfalls of this kind in the present chapter because, frankly, we do not yet understand them well enough to advise on how to avoid them. However, we caution those entering the terrain of model fitting to be wary: Theoretically interesting specifications can yield unidentified models in which particular parameters can, in estimation, take on a wide variety of values that all yield nearly the same outcome for the objective function on which the estimation program is based.

Evaluation. Crucial questions about the goodness of fit of data to model are not answered by obtaining the best possible parameter estimates. Parameter estimates must be reasonably and fairly compared with results from plausible alternative mechanisms for generating samples of data. One class of such alternatives derives from theories about chance, or statistical theories. Evaluation in accordance with such theories should include consideration of various features of the theories that are not the focus of particular tests. These considerations point to the assumptions one must make in using a statistical theory. In the model fitting considered here, the assumptions are those of (a) multivariate normality, on which the Wishart distribution is based, and (b) the large sample chi-square tests that derive from maximum-likelihood estimation theory (Jöreskog & Sörbom, 1977; Krane & McDonald, 1978). Psychometric as well as statistical features of the test also need to be considered (Horn & Engstrom, 1979).

Readjustment. In the practice of model fitting, the three basic steps outlined above are usually followed by a fourth step that is not always mentioned but that can be more important for understanding results than any other part of the analysis. This step, which we have designated readjustment, might be less dryly referred to as tinkering with the model—and tinkering in which one uses results indicating that the original model does not fit. For example, the sampling errors and derivatives for parameters and other program diagnostics can be used to suggest changes in what is estimated and what is fixed in a model. Such changes permit a better model fit (Saris, dePijper, & Zewaart, 1978; Sörbom, 1978). The changes may be made in ways that only slightly alter the basic model without changing its essential scientific implications. But such changes can also lead an investigator to a model that is entirely different from the one originally postulated in substantive theory. Such models can represent only fanciful capitalization on chance. This can occur with models that appear to be sensible (see, for example, Horn & Knapp, 1973, 1974). Thus, readjustment of models, while usually necessary, should be carried out gingerly.

Problems at the Outset

In general, then, structural modeling can be characterized as using RAM with SEER; that is, a theory is RAMmed into data, so to speak, and further analyses are carried out to determine how well data and theory conform, from which readjustments in theory are made, and the new theory is then RAMmed into the data. At this point we have, at best, only alluded to some of the many problems of building a science with research based on these kinds of procedures.

The logical problems alone are considerable. In specification, for example, Hempel (1952), Margenau (1950), and other philosophers of science have shown in logical detail that a model must have a requisite number of operationally defined (M) variables and proper rules of correspondence (D relations) if variables that are defined constitutively (L variables) are to have empirical meaning. Such meaning is required if a model is to be taken seriously in science. It is required, also, that statements of theory be sufficiently removed from tests (of hypotheses) of the theory to ensure objectivity. But what are the necessary and sufficient conditions for meeting such requirements? A full explication of these conditions would require more space than is available here. Even a summary of such considerations would take us far afield. Hence, we mention only that such logical analyses are important for modeling, and we move on to consider simpler concrete lessons derived from our experience in using MASMOB procedures.

Some of the logical requirements for adequate use of the SEER steps seem to be embodied, in part, in such mundane requirements for good data analysis as those stipulating that factors (L variables) should be overdetermined, that one should guard against capitalization on chance, and that analyses should be consistent with theory and hypotheses. But model fitting is more complicated than most other forms of data analysis. The requirements for good use are more difficult to identify. A model fitter should be aware of this fact,

but beyond that we can say little. For example, suppressor influence and the fact that all variables and relations operate simultaneously are extremely important in MASMOB. Our experience suggests that MASMOB results are highly sensitive to suppressor influences. But how should a model fitter deal with this condition? There is no fully satisfying answer to this question. It is not possible to specify all the ways in which suppressor influences operate to make the results from model fitting delicate and difficult to interpret. The sections that follow, however, provide examples that should point to some of the general influences of this kind that have important implications for data analysis.

Modeling of Means: Some Anova Concepts

A large proportion of research in developmental psychology has been based on analysis of variance (ANOVA). Unfortunately, much of this work has been done with little consideration of what ANOVA can and cannot do, and many an investigator who has learned a bit about ANOVA has learned precious little about its limitations or about alternative methods of data analysis. Not uncommonly such analyses can be characterized, as Humphreys (1978) characterized them recently, as "doing research the hard way."

The problems in general of using ANOVA in developmental research are exacerbated in those applications where the objective is to sort out separate effects that might be associated with age (A), cohort (C) and the time of measurement (T). It has been recognized for several years that interpretations of ANOVA results based on these classifications are ambiguous because of logical confounding of the three pseudo-independent variables of age, cohort, and time. This kind of confounding has been recognized in the literature at least since Schaie's (1965) seminal work and Baltes (1968) critical appraisal of that work (see also Adam, 1977; Botwinick & Arenberg, 1976; Buss, 1973; Cattell, 1970; Donaldson, 1979; Donaldson & Horn, 1978; Horn & Donaldson, 1976; Jackson, 1976). Despite these rather ancient recognitions that ANOVA results for age, cohort, and time are confounded and ambiguous, a number of extravagant claims have been made about the importance of the effects of one confounded variable relative to another and about how essential it is to do the very analyses that are known to lead to ambiguous results. It seems, indeed, that investigators have been cowed into doing these analyses, or into giving obeisance to the carrying out of such analyses even when good judgment dictates otherwise and the data at hand do not permit such analysis in any case.

For these reasons alone, therefore, it is worthwhile to begin a consideration of models for developmental data with explication of some ANOVA models. However, our major purpose in discussing these models is to use ANOVA designs as a kind of ground of contrast against which to regard the field of other (seemingly more complex) models. Our purpose is to show that the problems that arise with ANOVA are, in a sense, generic and thus should be considered when thinking about other kinds of models.

Problems With ANOVA Designs for A, C and T

Donaldson (1979) has recently provided a thorough explication of the conditions under which statistical associations reasonably can and cannot be separately estimated for age, cohort, and time classifications. Our analysis begins with a summary of Donaldson's work. In this we note that one basic problem is that most A, C, T models are not identified when initially specified. That is, there is not enough information in the data to provide a basis for estimating all of the parameters of the usual ANOVA model. The parameters can be estimated only if certain assumptions are made. These assumptions can be, and in typical applications have been, quite arbitrary. For example, Mason, Mason, Winsborough, and Poole (1973) have shown that a sufficient condition for estimation and statistical evaluation for a simple A, C, T ANOVA model is to constrain either two age parameters, two cohort parameters, or two time parameters to be equal. But which two parameters should be so constrained? The answer to this question is critical, for results and interpretations can be drastically different for two or more rather reasonable ways of dealing with the question (as illustrated by Adam, 1977; Botwinick & Arenberg, 1976; Donaldson, 1979; Jackson, 1976).

This basic problem can be demonstrated in concrete form with the simplest possible linear statistical model. This is depicted schematically in Table 37-3 and in the following summary equation:

$$Y_{ijkm} = g + a_i + c_j + t_k + e_{ijkm} \qquad (1)$$

This equation states that an observed score—say, an ability measurement—is (assumed in the model to be) a linear function of

g = a location parameter (possibly arbitrary);
a_i = an effect associated with the ith age;
c_j = an effect associated with the jth cohort;
t_k = an effect associated with the kth time of measurement;
e_{ijkm} = an effect due to error associated with observation of the mth subject.

Under an assumption that error has a random distribution with mean equal to zero, a least-squares model for estimating the means of Table 37-2 can be written as

$$\bar{Y}_{ijk} = E(Y_{ijkm}) = g + a_i + c_i + t_k. \qquad (2)$$

Here we have represented the cell mean for a variable (say $\bar{Y}$ = mean full-scale IQ) in terms of the parameters of a specific A, C, and T design.

The problems of estimation with this simple model can be seen in terms of the following matrix-equation representation of data like those depicted in Table 37-3.

$$
\begin{bmatrix}
Y_{1211} \\
Y_{1212} \\
Y_{1321} \\
Y_{1322} \\
Y_{2111} \\
Y_{2112} \\
Y_{2221} \\
Y_{2222}
\end{bmatrix}
=
\begin{bmatrix}
1 & 1 & 0 & 0 & 1 & 0 & 1 & 0 \\
1 & 1 & 0 & 0 & 1 & 0 & 1 & 0 \\
1 & 1 & 0 & 0 & 0 & 1 & 0 & 1 \\
1 & 1 & 0 & 0 & 0 & 1 & 0 & 1 \\
1 & 0 & 1 & 1 & 0 & 0 & 1 & 0 \\
1 & 0 & 1 & 1 & 0 & 0 & 1 & 0 \\
1 & 0 & 1 & 0 & 1 & 0 & 0 & 1 \\
1 & 0 & 1 & 0 & 1 & 0 & 0 & 1
\end{bmatrix}
\begin{bmatrix}
g \\
a_1 \\
a_2 \\
c_1 \\
c_2 \\
c_3 \\
t_1 \\
t_2
\end{bmatrix}
+
\begin{bmatrix}
e_{1211} \\
e_{1212} \\
e_{1321} \\
e_{1322} \\
e_{2111} \\
e_{2112} \\
e_{2221} \\
e_{2222}
\end{bmatrix}
\qquad (3)
$$

$$Y \qquad = \qquad X \qquad\qquad \hat{P} \qquad + \qquad E$$

Notice that all of the elements of the cells of Table 37-3 are represented in this equation.

Table 37-3 A Very Simple ANOVA Model For Age, Cohort, And Time (After Donaldson, 1979)

	Time 1 (1954)	Time 2 (1964)
	Cohort 1 (1914)	**Cohort 2 (1924)**
Age 1 (40)	$Y_{1211} = g + a_1 + c_1 + t_1 + e_{1211}$	$Y_{1321} = g + a_1 + c_2 + t_2 + e_{1321}$
	$Y_{1212} = g + a_1 + c_1 + t_1 + e_{1212}$	$Y_{1322} = g + a_1 + c_2 + t_2 + e_{1322}$
	$Y_{121} = g + a_1 + c_1 + t_1$	$Y_{132} = g + a_1 + c_2 + t_2$
	Cohort 0 (1904)	**Cohort 1 (1914)**
Age 2 (50)	$Y_{2111} = g + a_2 + c_0 + t_1 + e_{2111}$	$Y_{2221} = g + a_2 + c_1 + t_2 + e_{2221}$
	$Y_{2112} = g + a_2 + c_0 + t_1 + e_{2112}$	$Y_{2222} = g + a_2 + c_1 + t_2 + e_{2222}$
	$Y_{211} = g + a_2 + c_0 + t_1$	$Y_{222} = g + a_2 + c_1 + t_2$

In accordance with the usual procedures for estimating the parameters of $\hat{P}$, one minimizes $E'E$, thereby obtaining the normal equation

$$(X^tX)\hat{P} = X'Y, \tag{4}$$

which requires that

$$\hat{P} = (X^tX)^{-1} X^tY. \tag{5}$$

Thus, in order to solve for P one needs to multiply by $(X^tX)^{-1}$, which requires that the rows and columns of X be *linearly independent*. The columns of X are not linearly independent, however (nor can they be, no matter how many subjects are sampled to define the rows of X). The X^tX matrix is singular and thus cannot be inverted. The linear equations of (3) do not have a unique solution. Many possible combinations of parameter values estimate the data with equal fit, so there is no clear way to choose a best fit. The equations can be solved uniquely only by imposing constraints. An infinity of such constraints can be imposed. Most important for present considerations, however, is the fact that the reasonable constraints characteristically imposed in applications of ANOVA reasoning do not enable one to solve the present problem because age, cohort, and time are confounded.

There are several ways to become convinced of this conclusion. Perhaps the simplest is to recognize that even if one eliminates the first column in X, which is obviously a linear combination of Columns 2 and 3, the other columns remain linearly dependent. For example, Column 2 is the following linear combination of Columns 4, 6, and 7;

$$\begin{bmatrix} 1 \\ 1 \\ 1 \\ 1 \\ 0 \\ 0 \\ 0 \\ 0 \end{bmatrix} = (-1) \begin{bmatrix} 0 \\ 0 \\ 0 \\ 0 \\ 1 \\ 1 \\ 0 \\ 0 \end{bmatrix} + \begin{bmatrix} 0 \\ 0 \\ 1 \\ 1 \\ 0 \\ 0 \\ 0 \\ 0 \end{bmatrix} + \begin{bmatrix} 1 \\ 1 \\ 0 \\ 0 \\ 1 \\ 1 \\ 0 \\ 0 \end{bmatrix}$$

This is merely one way of recognizing that when the usual reasonable constraints of ANOVA models are imposed, the equations of (3) are still linearly dependent in the case of age, cohort, and time analyses, and thus an additional constraint must be imposed in order to obtain a unique solution.

The usual constraints are most often represented by the idea of setting the sum of all effects within each factor equal to zero, that is,

$$\Sigma a_i = \Sigma c_j = \Sigma t_k = 0. \tag{6}$$

These constraints can be seen to be reasonable in many applications of analysis of variance, because all that is needed, or that can be reasonably inferred from the data, are constrast effects within particular factors (as the contrasts for the a_i effects, for example). No basis is sought within the model for comparing the effects of one factor with the effects of another (as the a_i effects with the c_j effects, for example). Stated another way, the usual constraints are reasonable when the contrast effects for one factor are not arbitrarily influenced by the particular levels and contrasts of another factor.

These conditions do not hold for the analysis of age, cohort, and time. As Donaldson (1979) has emphasized, the usual constraints

> are not reasonable because the parameters are thought to have intrinsic, rather than relative, meaning. That is, the effect of being age 30 (for example) is not thought to depend on which other ages are sampled, as is the case when the centering constraint $\Sigma a_i = 0$ is imposed. (p. 5)

Also, investigators who have done age, cohort, and time analyses have sought to compare the effects for one design factor with those for another (e.g., Baltes & Schaie, 1976), and the results for such analyses are conditional on the choice of contrasts within each factor (Adam, 1977; Botwinick & Arenberg, 1976).

Particular instances of the problem of arbitrariness in age, cohort, and time analyses can be seen in the recommendations that Schaie (1965, 1973, 1977) has offered in discussions of his "general developmental model." Schaie regards data of the form shown in Table 37-3 as representing a "time-sequential design." He does not specify an explicit mathematical/statistical model for this design, but Jackson (1976) and Donaldson (1979) have shown that such a model can reasonably be inferred from the hypothesis tests that are recommended by Schaie. Such an implicit model for data of the kind shown in Table 37-3 is depicted in Table 37-4. Here, it should be noted, the c_j terms, representing cohort effects in Equations 1 through 3, have been replaced with q_{ik} terms representing interaction parameters.

What we have referred to as the usual constraints of ANOVA models have been imposed in Schaie's work with models of the kind shown in Table 37-4. As Donaldson (1979) has pointed out in detail, this set of

Table 37-4 Implicit Model For Schaie's Time-Sequential Model (After Donaldson, 1979)

	Time 1	Time 2
Age 1	$\overline{Y}_{11} = g + a_1 + t_1 + q_{11}$	$\overline{Y}_{12} = g + a_1 + t_2 + q_{12}$
Age 2	$\overline{Y}_{21} = g + a_2 + t_1 + q_{21}$	$\overline{Y}_{22} = g + a_2 + t_2 + q_{22}$

arbitrary restrictions requires, in the simple 2×2 example, that all interaction parameters be equal in absolute magnitude, even though no logical or theoretical arguments are advanced to support the idea that such relations exist for the cohort effects that the interaction parameters represent.

In larger designs, the number of unlikely implications proliferates. It is thus only under a very unlikely set of circumstances (e.g., when all cohort effects are zero) that the parameters of Schaie's implicit model and their associated hypothesis tests can yield coherent, substantively interpretable results. (Donaldson, 1979, p. 13)

The restrictions imposed implicitly by making the usual ANOVA constraints for "cross-sequential designs" are no more defensible. In short, imposing the usual assumptions for analyses of variance of age, cohort, and time leads to model equations (Equations 2, 3, and 4) that contain a formal ambiguity which renders results arbitrary, not interpretable within the ANOVA framework that is assumed, and therefore potentially misleading (for other examples of these kinds of problems, see Donaldson & Horn, 1978; Horn & Donaldson, 1976, 1977).

Dealing With the Problems by Modeling

We see then that the principal problem with application of ANOVA to A, C, T models is one of being clear and not arbitrary in imposing those constraints that must be imposed in order to estimate the parameters of the models and evaluate goodness of fit. This is the kind of problem that modeling forces one to consider. There is a plethora of assumptions one might make, and it is by no means a cut-and-dried matter to choose one set of assumptions over another. We shall look at this kind of dilemma in terms of several kinds of models one might specify for time-sequential data like shown in Tables 37-1 and 37-2.

To ease into an understanding of the symbols and language used in some of our more involved models, consider first the simple models of Figure 37-3. The diagram on the left (a) represents the idea of two manifest variables Y_1 and Y_2 that may be unconditionally related to each other (the line for the c_{12} covariance) and to themselves (the lines for the s_{11}^2 and s_{22}^2 variances). The K in this diagram represents a constant which itself adds no variance or correlation to the variable set. It is used to represent directed (D) relations for the means ($\overline{Y}_1$ and $\overline{Y}_2$) which can now be regarded as parameters of the model. When the means are thus specified as parameters of a model that also includes parameters for variances and covariances, significance tests pertaining to the saliency (e.g., $\overline{Y}_j = 0$)

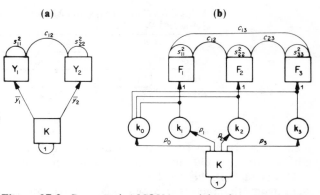

Figure 37-3. Structural ANOVA models of means: (a) moment structure parameters (K = constant); (b) elementary structured means model for a single group.

or equality (e.g., $\overline{Y}_j = \overline{Y}_k$) of means can be considered within a context of explicit statements of assumptions, such as those of homogeneity of variance or, more to the point of the present essay, those concerning whether particular age or cohort effects are to be regarded as equal. This significance testing is accomplished by analysis of the constant-augmented moment structure matrix W (see Technical Appendix).

When this kind of thinking is applied to consideration of A, C, T models in a repeated-measures context (McArdle, 1978), new complications arise. Some of these complications are indicated in Table 37-5 and in Figure 37-3 (b). The figure shows a specification for F, the full-scale WAIS IQ, measured at three times in one cohort group. In this model the variances and covariances have not been restricted in any way, but the directed relations for the K (that represents mean effects) are modeled to be mediated by a set of extended variables, k_i, which represent latent contrasts in the following fixed design matrix:

$$\begin{array}{c} \text{X} \\ (3 \times 4) \end{array} = \begin{array}{c} \\ F_1 \\ F_2 \\ F_3 \end{array} \begin{array}{cccc} k_0 & k_1 & k_2 & k_3 \\ \hline 1 & 1 & 0 & 0 \\ 1 & 0 & 1 & 0 \\ 1 & 0 & 0 & 1 \end{array} \qquad (8)$$

(as in the usual matrix algebra developments of ANOVA models). In analyses with modeling algorithms, there is a solution for a set of free parameters

$$\begin{array}{c} P' \\ (1 \times 4) \end{array} = [p_0, p_1, p_2, p_3] \qquad (9)$$

that represent the relations between the K constants and the contrast variables. The contrast variables

Table 37-5 Cell Means and Model Parameters for an Age-Only Model of the Full-Scale (F_i) WAIS Means

Cohort	Age				
	30	40	50	60	70
1924	$\overline{F}_1 = g + a_{30}$	$\overline{F}_2 = g + a_{40}$	$\overline{F}_3 = g + a_{50}$		
1914		$\overline{F}_1 = g + a_{40}$	$\overline{F}_2 = g + a_{50}$	$\overline{F}_3 = g + a_{60}$	
1904			$\overline{F}_1 = g + a_{50}$	$\overline{F}_2 = g + a_{60}$	$\overline{F}_3 = g + a_{70}$

themselves are allowed no interrelations and thus are not used to represent any of the covariance in the data.

The virtues of this kind of modeling of the means stem from the fact that when one conceptualizes a design in this way, one achieves flexibility in considering just what, according to substantive theory, should vary or remain constant. Also, one can gain some insights into logical difficulties in a theory and/or a model.

For example, suppose a theory stipulates that a general factor is modified in a somewhat different way over each of several aging periods, as suggested in Table 37-5. This table shows where the model parameters are assumed to operate in a layout of actual scores and cell means. Each cell mean $\overline{F}_j$ is a simple additive function of the overall mean g and a single age-effect parameter a_i. Notice that the cohort groups contain rather different sets of parameters, although a given parameter has the same value no matter where it appears in the cohort classifications.

Since there are 9 means and 6 mean parameters to estimate in Table 37-5, it seems reasonable to suppose that the model can be identified and a solution can be obtained. Applying the LISREL-IV program to arrive at parameter estimates, however, reveals a diagnostic that suggests that the a_{70} parameter is not identified. This message reflects a condition of singularity for a particular matrix that must be inverted in a LISREL solution (namely, the information matrix). We discover, in this way, that although we seem to be attacking a rather tractable problem in a sensible way, in fact we have encountered the condition we described earlier as lack of independence. This is by no means obvious in the design layout of Table 37-5. However, if one notices that the two extreme means at age 30 and

age 70 are required by this design to provide a basis for estimating three parameters (g, a_{30}, and a_{70}), then one can see the source of the singularity. Without further specification of the model, no unique solution can be obtained for our parameters.

How does one achieve this further specification? Therein lies a rub that Donaldson (1979) has analyzed in its logical, mathematical, statistical, and substantive complexity. A major conclusion from Donaldson's analyses is that strong substantive theory *or* a reasonable metatheory convention must be brought to bear to set a particular parameter in situations of the kind that is created in Table 37-5. Otherwise any solution can only be regarded as arbitrary. To illustrate this point we have fixed a_{30} to zero in order to obtain parameter estimates. The estimates obtained with this further specification, together with their standard errors, are shown in Table 37-6.

The results of Table 37-6 suggest that 107.2 is a good probability estimate of the grand mean and the "starting" mean of age 30, that this mean increases 3.9 units from age 30 to 40, then decreases to −8.6 units by age 50, −21.8 units by age 60, and −49 units by age 70. Since the standard errors are small relative to magnitude of the contrast effects, there is evidence that the shifts are statistically significant. Our model-fitting approach permits us to be cautious about making this kind of interpretation, however, for in examining the overall fit of the model we obtain $\chi^2(4) = 222$ ($df = 9$ means minus 5 parameters estimated), which we convert to a normal deviate of $Z = 12$ (see Technical Appendix). This result indicates that our model does not fit. We conclude that we have not specified a good model for the cell means.

Our modeling approach has presented us with two

Table 37-6 Maximum-Likelihood Parameters for a Particular Specification of the Age Model

Parameter (P)	Group 1 (1924 cohort)	Group 2 (1914 cohort)	Group 3 (1904 cohort)
p_0	$g = 107.2 \,(.9)$	$g = 107.2 \,(*)$	$g = 107.2 \,(*)$
p_1	$a_{30} = 0$	$a_{40} = 3.9 \,(*)$	$a_{50} = -8.6 \,(*)$
p_2	$a_{40} = 3.9 \,(1.1)$	$a_{50} = -8.6 \,(*)$	$a_{60} = -21.8 \,(*)$
p_3	$a_{50} = -8.6 \,(1.2)$	$a_{60} = -21.8 \,(1.8)$	$a_{70} = -49 \,(2.8)$

Note. X given in Equation 8 is used in all groups. Standard errors are in parentheses, but * indicates parameter is required to be equal to one shown elsewhere.

rather interesting awarenesses in this simple example: (1) that we need a rationale for further specifying our "reasonable" way of regarding an aging change, and (2) that the "reasonable" rationale we brought in to deal with this problem (namely, that we can set an arbitrary origin for an age-change curve at age 30) does not lead to a model that represents the data well. Thus we are driven back to the drawing board (and we have considered only a very simple situation indeed, relative to the kind of theory that developmental psychologists seek to consider). The modeling approach has also made it evident that had we wanted to do so—that is, had theory so dictated—we could have specified a no-change condition for any of the age periods here at hand. The a_{50} parameter, for example, could be constrained to equal the a_{30} parameter. Of course, this same utility of modeling could be realized by use of planned comparisons in ANOVA (although this form of ANOVA seems often to be neglected in developmental research). In contrast to the usual applications of ANOVA, however, the significance tests derived from our modeling need not be based on pooled standard-error estimates and assumptions of equality of covariances. Also, although an overall test of goodness of fit is usually available in outputs from applications of ANOVA (by evaluation of the residual sums of squares), it is hardly ever considered. Again one wonders whether investigators really realize they can, and perhaps should, do restricted modeling.

In Table 37-7 we present some results accrued from our return to the drawing board. The principal conclusion we seek to drive home with these results is that there are many ad hoc but "reasonable" ways to conduct analyses on A, C, and T classifications. The first row of the table contains the parameter estimates and standard errors for the simple aging model we have just considered.

The second row of Table 37-7 provides results for an analysis of time differences (the first time period being regarded as the "starting point," analogous to treating age 30 as the "starting point" in the simple aging model). Implicit in an analysis of this kind is an assumption that there are no age or cohort effects. The chi square ($\chi^2(6) = 231$) and normal deviate ($Z = 13$) for overall fit indicate that this model does not account for the means. One might to tempted to compare this fit with that achieved with Model 1. To make this comparison in the present case is an exercise in futility, however, because neither model even approaches a good fit, and one is not nested in the other.

Table 37-7 Summary of Mean Models for Age, Time, and Cohort

Model	$\chi^2(df)/Z$	g	a_{30}	a_{40}	a_{50}	a_{60}	a_{70}	t_1	t_2	t_3	c_2	c_1	c_0
1. Age (A) only	222(4)/12	107.2 (.9)	0	3.9 (1.1)	−8.6 (1.2)	−21.8 (1.8)	−49 (2.8)	—	—	—	—	—	—
2. Time (T) only	231(6)/13	107.7 (1.2)	—	—	—	—	—	0	12.6 (1.4)	−9.4 (.6)			
3. Cohort (C) only	316(6)/14	110.4 (.8)	—	—	—	—	—	—	—	—	0	−3.3 (1.1)	−18.2 (1.2)
4. A + T	20(2)/3.8	109.4 (.9)	0	−1.6 (1.1)	−17.6 (1.3)	−38.4 (2.2)	−65.9 (3.7)	0	22.1 (1.3)	16.8 (1.9)	—	—	—
5. A + C	131(2)/9.4	108.7 (.9)	0	15.5 (1.6)	3.6 (1.8)	−2.6 (2.3)	−33.2 (3.1)	—	—	—	0	−15.1 (1.7)	−19.9 (1.8)
6. T + C	89(4)/7.9	111.6 (.9)	—	—	—	—	—	0	11.4 (1.2)	−14.7 (1.5)	0	−3.6 (1.1)	−21.6 (1.2)
7. A + T + C	15(1)/3.6	109.2 (.9)	0	−10.3 (2.6)	−30.7 (3.4)	−58.4 (4.8)	−91.3 (5.5)	0	29.1 (2.3)	29.1 (*)	0	9.6 (2.5)	12.8 (3.3)
8. A Linear + T + C	89(4)/7.9	111.6 (.9)	0	−26.1 (1.3)	−52.2 (*)	−78.3 (*)	−114.4 (*)	0	37.5 (2.0)	37.5 (*)	0	22.5 (1.7)	30.7 (2.7)
9. A + C + T, for Verbal (V) + Performance (P)	V 17(2)/3.46	58.5	0	−7.9	−20.2	−37.7	−58.0	0	25.9	25.9	0	9.8	13.8
	P	50.7	0	−2.6	−10.7	−20.9	−33.7	0	3.3	3.3	0	−.1	−.7
10. A + C + T, with V + P proportional	V 21(5)/3.12	58.2	0	−7.0	−19.6	−36.9	−57.1	0	25.5	25.5	0	0.5	13.6
	P	51.1	0	$b = -.63\ (.04)$				0	4.3	4.3	0	1.0	.4
11. Equal covariances	69(44)/2.35	(Same as Model 9)											

Note. Full-scale WAIS scores used unless otherwise noted. 0 = specially fixed parameter. Standard errors are in parentheses; (*) indicates parameter equality.

The third row of Table 37-7 provides parameter estimates for a model of cohort groupings that is analogous to the Model 1 contrasts of age groupings. Again the model does not fit, and there is no known statistical procedure for comparing this lack of fit with the lack of fit for Model 1.

Row 4 contains parameter estimates for a model in which the conditions represented in Rows 1 and 2 are combined. The chi square and normal deviate for overall goodness of fit are much lower than the values for previously considered models, thus suggesting that we are getting closer to an accurate representation of the cell means. Because the models of Rows 1 and 2 are nested within the model of Row 4, there is a basis for a claim that the A + T model provides a better fit to the data than either the first or the second model alone. The chi squares and degrees of freedom are additive (subtractive) under these conditions. Thus, the chi-square difference for Models 1 and 4 is 202 ($df = 2$), which is clearly significant and indicates that Model 4 is an improvement in fit. Similarly, the chi-square difference for Models 2 and 4 is 211 ($df = 4$), which provides a basis for asserting that an adequate model for the data should include parameters for both age and time. In making such claims one should be careful not to imply that Model 4 provides an adequate representation of the data. All that can be fairly said is that Model 4 provides a better fit than either Model 1 or Model 2. Similar conclusions can be drawn for the models of Rows 5 and 6, although neither of these models appears to fit very well.

Notice that in the fit of Model 4, the t_3 is positive (seemingly significantly so when the standard error is considered), whereas in the earlier fit of Model 2, t_3 is negative (and again seemingly significantly so if one chooses to believe the information about the standard errors and to ignore the information indicating that the model does not fit). Such changes in parameter values have not been unusual in results we have obtained with applications of model-fitting technology to a variety of kinds of data and for several kinds of models. We have come to regard such changes much as we regard changes in the weights estimated in regression and canonical analysis when variables are added or subtracted. That is, reasonable changes in what one wishes to consider in a model, and changes that might seem to make little difference in how one would regard a particular influence, may in fact generate powerful suppressor and enhancer effects. These dramatic shifts in parameter values need not be confusing—just as a change in a beta-weight need not be puzzling—provided one understands the phenomena under investigation well enough to explain why the shift comes about. We know in multiple regression analysis, for example,

that if we introduce a predictor that is highly correlated with another predictor, we can reduce the beta weight for the second predictor from a high positive value to zero or even to a negative value. The same kinds of effects can be produced in modeling of the kind we are considering here. Also, in principle at least, an investigator can have as much control over a suppressor effect in complex modeling as some (e.g., Humphreys, 1978) obtain in multiple regression analysis (although we have yet to achieve this control in practice, but see Horn, in press).

The model of Row 7 is of particular interest. Here we have estimated parameters for age, cohort, and time under restrictions that might, if derived from adequate theory, provide a sound basis for analysis. A special path diagram could be drawn to represent this model, but it seemed to us that the information presented in Table 37-8 provides a better "picture." Here one can see clearly where the "starting point" assumptions are made. Also, it is evident in this table that a particular a_i, c_j, or t_k parameter is the same no matter where it appears. Finally, too, the table makes evident the assumption that any time effect occurring between the first and second testing would be the same (on the average) as an effect occurring between the second and third testing (i.e., $t_2 = t_3$). This assumption was derived from logical and psychological analysis of the meaning of a time effect (Donaldson, 1979).

Model 7 provides an overall fit that in our experience is about as good as one can hope to get without activating the readjustment phase of SEER. The chi square of 15 converts to a normal deviate (Z) of 3.6, still significant at better than the .01 level, but the significance in this case might well represent influences (systematic, to be sure) that one could never account for in a scientific theory (see Horn & Engstrom, 1979, for a discussion of some of such influences). However, perhaps the most interesting outcome of estimation in accordance with Model 7 is the difference between the parameter estimates obtained with it and the comparable estimates obtained with other models. For example, in this more nearly complete model, the c_1 and c_0 cohort effects are notably positive, whereas in the models of Rows 3, 5 and 6 these estimates are negative. The general conclusion we derive from consideration of such changes is worth repeating: An estimate of an effect is, in part, a function of the company it keeps.

Some aspects of the generality of the A, C, and T model (given the same set of parameter restrictions) are considered in the models of Rows 8 through 12 of Table 37-7. In Row 8 age changes are modeled to be linear; only one parameter is estimated—the shift from the starting point (age 30) to the next age (40)—and all

Table 37-8 Parameter Specification for an Age, Time, and Cohort Model

		k_0	k_1	k_2	k_3	k_4	k_5	k_6	k_7	k_8	k_9
X (3 × 10) =	F_1	1	1	0	0	1	0	0	1	0	0
	F_2	1	0	1	0	0	1	0	0	1	0
	F_3	1	0	0	1	0	0	1	0	0	1

		Cohort 1 (1924)	Cohort 2 (1914)	Cohort 3 (1904)
P [(10 × 1) × 3] =	k_0	g = 109.2 (.9)	g = 109.2 (*)	g = 109.2 (*)
	k_1	a_{30} = 0	a_{40} = −10.3 (*)	a_{50} = −30.7 (*)
	k_2	a_{40} = −10.3 (2.6)	a_{50} = −30.7 (*)	a_{60} = −58.4 (*)
	k_3	a_{50} = −30.7 (3.4)	a_{60} = −58.4 (4.8)	a_{70} = −91.3 (5.5)
	k_4	t_1 = 0	t_1 = 0	t_1 = 0
	k_5	t_2 = 29.1 (2.3)	t_2 = 29.1 (*)	t_2 = 29.1 (*)
	k_6	t_3 = 29.1 (*)	t_3 = 29.1 (*)	t_2 = 29.1 (*)
	k_7	c_2 = 0	c_1 = 9.6 (2.5)	c_0 = 12.8 (3.3)
	k_8	c_2 = 0	c_1 = 9.6 (*)	c_7 = 12.8 (*)
	k_9	c_2 = 0	c_1 = 9.6 (*)	c_0 = 12.8 (*)

Note. X is the same in all groups. $\chi^2(1)$ = 15, Z = 3.6. 0 indicates specially fixed parameters. Standard errors are in parentheses; (*) indicates equality with other parameters.

other a_j values are simple additive functions of this. To thus restrict the conception of aging moves the chi square from 15 to 89 with a saving of only 3 degrees of freedom. This difference in chi square and degrees of freedom suggests that a linear model (at least the particular linear model considered here) is too simple to account for the data.

In Model 9 (of Table 37-7), the model of Row 7 is applied jointly to the Verbal (V) and Performance (P) subscales of the WAIS. The results indicate that the model fits as well for the separate subscores as for the full-scale IQ. Here one might note also that the parameter estimates for a model in which V and P are considered simultaneously are the same as if V and P had simply been added together. This is true because no joint restrictions were placed.

These results suggest the rather surprising conclusion that there is more aging decline for verbal abilities than for performance abilities. This result is not consistent with much previous work (as reviewed by Botwinick, 1978, p. 213, for example). However, in the present case the outcome is mediated by the fact that there is virtually no cohort or time effect for the performance variable—that is, these parameter estimates are virtually zero—whereas there are cohort and time effects for the verbal scale. These latter effects can reflect an age-related repeated-measures influence in the verbal measures conditional upon time and cohort. For example, a person who does not know the meaning of a word when it is presented in a first testing could well be encouraged to look up the meaning so that it would be available on a second testing (+25.9 units). When effects of this kind are filtered out

through a cohort (+9.8 and 13.8) effect, the aging decline for the verbal scale seems to be notable, even though it does not appear in the original obtained means (see Figure 37-1 and Table 37-2).

In Model 10 three restrictions have been placed on the relation between V and P. These restrictions derive from a theory that the declines in V and P are the same except for a constant of proportionality b that represents a difference in the scaling (i.e., measurement units are not the same for the two scales). This model is not notably different from the model of Rows 9 and 10, in which the aging decline was not required to be the same for V and P (the chi-square difference of 4, Z = .64, is not significant for 3 degrees of freedom).

Finally the bottom row of Table 37-7 illustrates that the covariances can also be considered simultaneously. In this row, Model 9 has been refitted with the additional assumption of equality of group covariances across cohorts, an assumption that is analogous to the one usually imposed in multivariate analysis of variance (MANOVA). The test for equality of covariances can be obtained under the principle of additivity of chi squares by subtracting the chi square of Model 9 from the chi square of Model 11. This test is equivalent to using the test developed by Box (1954) when the chi square and degrees of freedom for the means are removed. It can be seen that the hypothesis of equal covariance is plausible [$\chi^2(42)$ = 52].

These examples are probably sufficient to illustrate our main point: A researcher has many options to consider when age, cohort, and time can be assumed to represent important influences in data for which a developmental interpretation is sought. Analyses of variance with such data should be based on clear thinking about these options. If the assumptions of analysis are not clearly understood and stated, results are as likely to confuse and mislead as they are to clarify and enlighten. Specification of an explicit model is not the only way to be clear about assumptions, but it is an easy and easily communicated way to do this. MASMOB tends to force one to gain increased awareness not only about assumptions but also about alternative hypotheses and theories—in general, about alternative ways to think about phenomena.

Modeling of Structures: Some Factor-Analysis Concepts

The ANOVA models we have just considered can be defective for reasons that pertain to the nature of the dependent variable, rather than because interdependence among the independent variables is not properly taken into account (as in the examples of the previous section). Often in psychological research it is reasonable to suppose that the dependent variable, or several such variables, represent rather different processes, or components, or factors. Such possibilities can be considered in model fitting. Equational details are given in the Technical Appendix. Table 37-9 sum-

marizes results from some analyses designed to explore this aspect of modeling with the WAIS subscale measurements obtained in different age groups.

Each row of the table contains an identification of the latent structure (factor) model that is fitted, together with the degrees of freedom for evaluation of the goodness of fit, and in the other columns, the chi squares and corresponding normal deviate Z values. The model fits are for each of the nine separate subject samples described in Table 37-1.

The first model represents a model fit under an assumption that the 11 WAIS subscales do not measure anything, an assumption equivalent to the hypothesis that the matrix of intercorrelations (intercovariances) among the 11 subscales is well regarded as a diagonal matrix (for further explication of such hypotheses, see Horn & Engstrom, 1979). The 318/13 in the first column for this model indicates that when a model was fitted under this assumption to the data for subjects of Cohort 2 (1924) at 30 years of age (on the average) on the first testing in 1954, the chi square was 318 and the corresponding Z score was 13. This indicates that the "zero common factor" model does not fit at all well. By looking across the columns, one can see that a zero-factor model does not fit in any of the subsamples of subjects. Therefore the WAIS scales must measure something in common.

The fit for a model for one general common factor is indicated next. Again, the chi squares and Z values

Table 37-9 Restricted Factor-Analysis Models by Age, Time, and Cohort

Model (and df)	χ^2/Z				
	Age 30	Age 40	Age 50	Age 60	Age 70
Zero factors baseline (55)					
Cohort 0			158/6.7	369/14	469/16
Cohort 1		257/11	648/20	728/22	
Cohort 2	318/13	675/21	785/22		
One general factor (44)					
Cohort 0			88/3.7	186/8.8	101/4.6
Cohort 1		146/7.0	276/12	?	
Cohort 2	181/8.5	275/12	228/10		
Verbal and Performance (43)					
Cohort 0			78/3.1	107/5.0	66/2.2
Cohort 1		122/5.9	144/7.0	166/8.0	
Cohort 2	128/6.2	149/7.2	149/7.2		
Verbal, Performance, and Number (38)					
Cohort 0			69/2.95	93/4.6	52/1.5
Cohort 1		95/4.7	101/5.1	116/6.0 ?	
Cohort 2	110/5.6	105/5.4	113/5.8		
Derivative fit (7 out of 55 possible) (31)					
Cohort 0			46/1.7 ?	65/3.4 ?	29/−.2
Cohort 1		52/2.3 ?	57/2.7	89/5.1	
Cohort 2	82/4.6	82/4.6	79/4.4		

Note. ? represents a numerical anomaly that prevents clear interpretation.

Table 37-10 Hypothesized Factor Pattern Loadings for a Verbal and Performance WAIS Measurement Model

Variable	Factor loadings[a]			Factor correlations		
	Verbal (V)	Performance (P)	Unique (U)		V	P
Information	b_1	0*	u_{13}		1.0*	sym
Comprehension	b_2	0*	u_{14}	V		
Arithmetic Reasoning	b_3	0*	u_{15}	P	q_{12}	1.0*
Similarities	b_4	0*	u_{16}			
Memory Span for Digits	b_5	0*	u_{17}			
Vocabulary	b_6	0*	u_{18}			
Digit Symbol	0*	b_7	u_{19}			
Picture Completion	0*	b_8	u_{20}			
Block Design	0*	b_9	u_{21}			
Picture Assembly	0*	b_{10}	u_{22}			
Object Assembly	0*	b_{11}	u_{23}			

Note. Factor model is given as $C = BQB^t + U^2$ (see Technical Appendix).

[a] 0* indicates a "fixed at zero" value, and 1.0* indicates a "fixed at one" parameter; other entries are free parameters.

indicate a poor fit. Thus more than one common factor is apparently measured by the subscales of the WAIS. Also, while the model for one common factor cannot be said to fit when the hypothesis is evaluated statistically, it can be said to provide a better fit than the model for no common factors. This conclusion follows from the fact that the one-factor model is nested within the zero-factor model. The difference in the two chi squares is evaluated using the difference in the two degrees of freedom, and because the chi-square difference is significantly large by this comparison, the one-factor model can be said to provide a fit that is significantly better than that provided by the zero-factor model.

This same kind of logic can be applied in evaluating the fit obtained under a hypothesis that the Verbal and Performance measures of the WAIS represent two common factors, V and P, as indicated in Table 37-10. While the chi squares and Z values are too large to provide clear support for this hypothesis (see Table 37-9), evaluation of the difference in the chi squares for this fit and for the fit of the one-factor model support a hypothesis that the two-factor model provides a better fit than the one-factor model. This can be a particularly straightforward conclusion because the difference in degrees of freedom for the two models is unity, so the one model is simply nested in the other, and evaluation of the chi-square difference is a simple one-degree-of-freedom test (that the factor correlation is 1.0).

One among several possible three-factor models is the next model represented in Table 37-9. In forming this model, the hypotheses of Osborne and Lindsey (1967) were used to suggest that performances on the WAIS subscales indicate not only individual differences in verbal and performance abilities, but

also individual differences in numerical/mathematical (N) abilities. In particular, numerical/mathematical abilities seem called for in the WAIS subscales labeled Arithmetic, Memory Span, and Digit Span. It can be seen that the fit obtained with this addition to the V and P factors is better but is still not good. Most of the chi squares and Z values indicate a significant departure from good model fit. Also, while the two-factor model is nested in a simple way in the three-factor model and most of the chi-square differences are significant, we should not be confident that this particular three-factor solution represents a good conception of the structure or is notably better than the V and P two factor solution. The results tell us mainly that some form of three-factor solution is better than this particular two-factor solution, not that we know the three-factor structure of the WAIS.

What we referred to earlier as the readjustment step in model fittings is represented in the last model of Table 37-9 and in the diagram of Figure 37-4. Here, for one set of subjects we took Sörbom's (1975) suggestions for using derivatives to modify a model. In the vicinity where a derivative for a fixed parameter was particularly large, parameters were estimated that had not previously been estimated. Such procedures are often referred to as "freeing-up parameter estimation." This usually ensures a better fit, even though it typically can support only ad hoc explanations. This is true partly because questions about the stability of readjustment fits in cross-validation have not been answered definitively. There is some capitalizing on chance in the procedure, and so it is reasonable to suppose that stability will vary inversely with size of sample on which the statistics for estimation are based.

The readjustments for the models at hand were based on examinations of the derivatives in the fit for

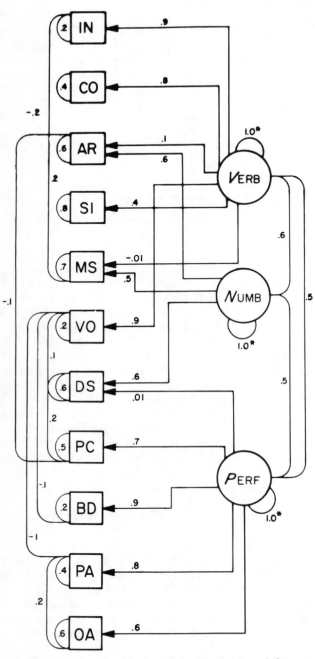

Figure 37-4. Derivative fit model for WAIS data [$\chi^2(31) = 57$; $Z = 2.7$]. Data are for $N = 128$, 1914 cohort, second testing (1964), and average age of 50. Note that 1.0* indicates a specially fixed parameter. (Abbreviations: IN = Information; CO = Comprehension; AR = Arithmetic Reasoning; SI = Similarities; MS = Memory Span; VO = Vocabulary; DS = Digit Symbol; PC = Picture Completion; BD = Block Design; PA = Picture Arrangement; OA = Object Assembly.)

the target group for which age = 50, cohort = 1914, and time = 2. Freeing up seven parameters for these data yielded a model for which the fit was good. These same seven parameters were then relaxed in the models for all of the other data sets. This led to improvement in fit in every case.

Figure 37-4 shows the parameter estimates for the fit to the target group. Here it can be seen that the readjustments that were made to achieve improved fit were relaxations of the usual factor-model assumption that specific factors are uncorrelated. The readjustments left these correlations negative, a condition that is at variance with the common findings and with prevalent theory that intellectual abilities are positively correlated. Other oddities were introduced by the readjustments. For example, the Digit Span loading on the Performance factor dropped to near zero ($-.01$). The changes brought about by the readjustment thus lead one to wonder whether the modified model is genuinely stable and does indeed provide an improved basis for understanding the data.

Modeling Moment Structures: Extending Path-Analysis Concepts

Figure 37-5 illustrates an elementary combination of several features of the modeling for both covariance and means over age, cohort, and time of testing. To simplify things a bit, we have considered only the subscales of the Verbal scale of the WAIS—Information (IN), Comprehension (CO), Arithmetic Reasoning (AR), Similarities (SI), Memory Span (MS), and Vocabulary (VO). All of these subscales are represented with a simple symbol, WV, with a subscript to indicate age. The WV scores are related to verbal ability through a structure (factor pattern) that is symbolized as L_v. As a model hypothesis, we required that this structure remain *invariant* across both repeated-measures and cross-sectional age variations of testing. This means that the verbal factor was required to be measured as the same weighted linear combination of subscales at every age and time of testing. The B_v symbol represents regression relations between the common factor estimates over time. The D_w symbolizes a diagonal matrix of covariances for the specific factors over time. The S^2 represents variances and the U^2 represents disturbances (unique variances).

The parameters for mean effects are symbolized with letters drawn on top of arrows extending from the constant K to a latent variable V or a manifest variable WV. In order to estimate the mean effects for the latent attribute, the relations for the manifest variable means were all set at G, a vector of grand means (i.e.,

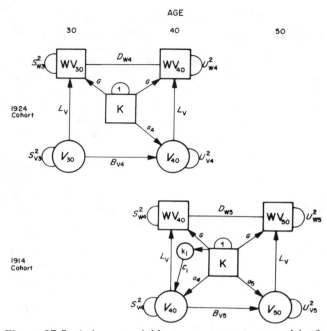

Figure 37-5. A latent-variable moment-structure model of verbal ability. (See text for full explanation.)

The chi square for model fit is 267 ($df = 126$); the corresponding normal deviate is 6.82. Thus the latent model does not fit very well.

Interestingly, with verbal ability defined here as a weighted linear combination of the manifest variables that work best over four groups, the latent attribute increases to age 50, whereas with verbal ability defined in accordance with the WAIS scoring, a decrease with aging was suggested (see Table 37-9). These results reflect the difference in the weighting of the subscales used here in obtaining the latent attribute and the weighting used in obtaining the V of previous analyses. For example, in the L_v vector, Memory Span has a loading of only .16, whereas the loading for Similarities is .45. In obtaining the WAIS V score, on the other hand, these two subscales are assigned the same nominal weights (Horn, 1963) as the other subscales. This illustrates an important difference between path-analysis modeling, as it is usually done, and extended path modeling in which structure and mean effects, as well as relations, are considered simultaneously.

Some piece-by-piece elaborations of the models of Figure 37-5 are illustrated in Figure 37-6. The purpose of these models is to examine the verbal and performance distinction when these abilities are regarded as latent attributes within the context of repeated-measures and cross-sectional change with aging. To simplify illustration of possibilities in this regard, we will consider only the groupings for subjects of 30 and 40 years of age. Even with this highly simplified selection of data there are quite a number of possibilities to consider in specifying a model for analysis.

over the four groups). The mean for the latent variable at age 30 ($\bar{V}_{30}$) was fixed at zero in order to achieve identification.

Some features of this model are particularly worth examining. For example, in the 1924 cohort the latent attribute mean at age 40 is specified exclusively in terms of the a_4 age parameter—that is, indirect regression effects on $\bar{V}_{40}$ are nonexistent because $\bar{V}_{30} = 0$. In the 1914 cohort, however, $\bar{V}_{40}$ is specified in terms of two components a_4 and c_1, representing the difference between the 1914 and 1924 cohorts. In this group the $\bar{V}_{50}$ is directly determined by the a_5 parameter in a somewhat different manner from the a_4 parameter, because $\bar{V}_{50}$ is also determined in part by the additive indirect effects of a_4 acting through B_{v4} and c_1 acting through B_{v5}. That is, the $\bar{V}_{50}$ mean reflects the effects of having been (in this sampling) age 40 and having started aging in the 1914 cohort. These indirect effects are mediated through the stability of measure of the latent attribute.

The parameters actually estimated under these conditions, with an added requirement that $B_{v4} = B_{v5}$, are

$$
\begin{array}{ccccccc}
& \text{IN} & \text{CO} & \text{AR} & \text{SI} & \text{MS} & \text{VO} \\
L_v = & [.99 & .69 & .62 & .45 & .16 & 1.0^*] \quad (10) \\
\end{array}
$$
$$
B_v = .43(.13), \quad a_4 = 1.8(.25), \quad a_5 = 1.2(.31),
$$
$$
c_1 = -1.2(.28)
$$

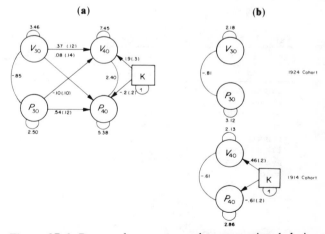

Figure 37-6. Repeated-measures and cross-sectional designs as latent-variable moment structures: (a) repeated-measures model for 1924 cohort at 1954 and 1964 testings [$\chi^2(195) = 390$; $Z = 7.73$]; (b) cross-sectional model for 1914 and 1924 cohorts at 1954 testing [$\chi^2(95) = 235$; $Z = 7.3$].

Figure 37-6 (a) depicts a repeated-measures model for V and P for the 1924 cohort as these individuals move from 30 to 40 years of age. In this model, structure over time is examined in a manner that has been exhaustively considered by Nesselroade (1970, 1972), Schmidt and Crano (1974), and Jordan (1978). Estimates of various possible cross-lag relations are of particular interest. The numbers on the arrows for these relations represent, first, the regression coefficient for predicting one measure from another and, second, in parentheses, the standard error for this coefficient. The numbers suggest that P ability at age 30 is significantly and notably predictive of P at age 40 (.54) and that the same is true for the V abilities at the two ages (.37). However, early-age V is not very predictive of later-age P, and similarly, early-age P is not very predictive of later-age V.

With conclusions such as those just stated, it is important to realize that they are conditional on the proviso that all relations are considered simultaneously. Thus a conclusion that performance ability at age 30 does not predict verbal ability at age 40 should be tempered by awareness that the interrelations between V and P at each particular age, and the autocorrelations over age of V and P, are also simultaneously taken into account, along with several other possible relations (such as invariant L_v and L_p). All manner of suppressor influences can operate, and unless one has insight into how these are in fact, operating, one can be grievously deceived by results (McFatter, 1979). This is exemplified by comparing the L_v loadings in the present solution with those obtained and assumed (in standard calculations of V and P) in models considered earlier. Memory Span in the present model has a loading of -1.47 on V, and Arithmetic Reasoning has a loading of .06 (relative to a fixed 1.0* loading for Vocabulary). Also, the forced invariance of L_v itself may place strain on estimating the other model parameters. The major lesson in such observations is one we stated earlier: An effect in modeling is largely conditional on the other effects that are allowed to operate, and subtle suppressor/enhancer influences can operate throughout a model.

The variances for latent variables can be mediated and determined in rather complex ways. The variances at V_{40} and V_{50}, for example, are a function of the V_{30} and P_{30} variances as these are mediated through the crossed and lagged regressions and the unique variances (of 7.45 and 5.38). Note that the V and P variances are considerably larger at age 40 than at age 30. This may result because the age 40 variables can covary through a number of paths and can be affected by unique components.

The latent attribute means at age 40, $\bar{V}_{40}$ and $\bar{P}_{40}$, are specified relative to $\bar{V}_{30}$ and $\bar{P}_{30}$ when these latter are set equal to zero. Again there is a suggestion of aging increase in verbal ability expressed as a latent variable ($\bar{V}_{40} = 1.9$, with standard error SE of .3), whereas the aging change for the latent performance ability is not different from zero ($\bar{P} = -.2$, SE = .2).

Figure 37-6 (b) presents a model that is similar to that of Figure 37-6 (a) except for cross-sectional groupings at age 30 (1924 cohort) and age 40 (1914 cohort). Only group difference parameters are considered here; no cross-lag or specific regressions are evaluated. Forcing invariance on L_v and L_p permits

Table 37-11 Summary of Two Group Latent-Variable Models: Repeated Measures and Cross-Sectional

Model	$\chi^2(df)/Z$	Latent means						Latent variances					
		$\bar{V}_2$	(SE)	$\bar{P}_2$	(SE)	$\bar{N}_2$	(SE)	V_1	V_2	P_1	P_2	N_1	N_2
Repeated samples (1954 and 1964)													
From age 30 to age 40 (1924 cohort)	390(195)/7.73?	1.9	(.3)	$-.2$	(.2)	1.10	(.9)	3.46	8.00	2.5	6.00	.91	3.50
From age 40 to age 50 (1914 cohort)	359(195)/6.72	.86	(.3)	-1.86	(.3)	1.20	(.9)	2.24	9.87	2.59	7.37	4.54	21.81
From age 50 to age 60 (1904 cohort)	367(195)/6.99	1.0	(.4)	-1.20	(.4)	.58	(.4)	1.07	7.31	3.35	6.91	.83	2.31
Cross-sectional (1954)													
Age 30 vs. age 40	234(95)/7.30	.46	(.2)	$-.69$	(.2)	.09	(.5)	2.18	2.13	3.12	2.86	6.82	3.57
Age 40 vs. age 50	274(95)/8.80	-1.39	(.3)	-2.36	(.3)	-1.60	(.7)	1.79	.85	2.23	2.98	1.51	2.62
Age 30 vs. age 50	212(95)/6.39	-1.04	(.3)	-2.97	(.3)	-1.40	(.46)	2.61	.94	2.65	3.10	.91	.48

Note. V, P, and N, = Verbal, Performance, and Numerical factors, respectively, and subscripts indicate first or second occasion.

evaluation of latent-factor covariances and mean-level differences. The model fits suggest that common-factor covariances are nearly equal for V and P. The mean levels differ, however. The shifts (relative to $\bar{V}_{30} = \bar{P}_{30} = 0$) are $\bar{V}_{40} = .46$ and $\bar{P}_{40} = -.61$, which suggest that V increases from age 30 to 40 while P declines.

Thus the repeated measures suggest no decrease in P, but the cross-sectional results suggest a decrease (and a smaller increase in V). Which conclusion is correct? Perhaps both are, for different hypotheses can be at issue, even as repeated-measures and cross-sectional data have often been assumed to represent the same processes. As noted elsewhere in some detail (Horn & Donaldson, 1980), repeated-measures data should contain a number of systematic influences that are not contained in cross-sectional data, and vice versa. The modeling in Figure 37-6 is intended merely to adumbrate this fact.

The reader might well have reasoned at this point that analyses such as those of Figure 37-6 are inadequate for considering issues raised by repeated-measures and cross-sectional data because the two kinds of data are not analyzed simultaneously. The summary given in Table 37-11 represents an attempt to respond to such reasoning.

All of the models of Table 37-11 were required to have invariant L_i ($i = V, P, N$). When the repeated-measures data are evaluated under these conditions, performance ability declines with age (although the change from age 30 to 40 is not significant) and verbal ability increases with age: A variance increase is systematic throughout. The cross-sectional differences present a different picture. Here V decreases with age and the variances become smaller. Again, however, note that no model fits the data very well, and less than all of the WAIS data have been analyzed simultaneously.

Figure 37-7 represents an extension of the modeling we have just considered to a case in which all of the available WAIS data are analyzed simultaneously. The numbers in the figure do not represent the outcome of this modeling, however. In fact we have never obtained estimates of the parameters for the full model—that is, when structure as well as moment parameters were estimated (and for the rather simple case in which all L_i are the same). LISREL ran 250 iterations and used a huge amount of computer processing time but did not reach a solution. Even when the model was cut in half by considering only verbal ability, the result was the same: no convergence under reasonable limits of patience and funding.

This outcome is the same as we have obtained in other problems in which what seemed to be a reason-

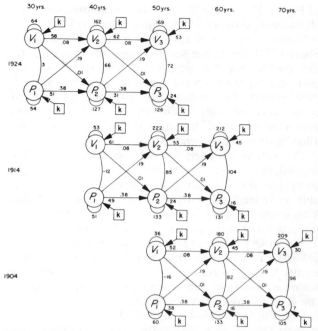

Figure 37-7. A developmental systems model for the WAIS data [$\chi^2(39) = 151$; $Z = 7.6$].

able model was identified and, indeed, was close to a correct model but was large and complex. Under such conditions, maximum-likelihood algorithms such as those of LISREL may fail to yield a solution in a reasonable amount of computer time. As will become evident later in this chapter, in the present case there is a model that fits the total WAIS data—a model somewhat similar to the verbal/performance and developmental model represented by Figure 37-7. Yet the verbal performance model could not be fitted with 250 iterations of the LISREL algorithms. This condition presents a serious practical deterrent to using modeling in some of the very situations for which it is most needed, namely, situations with complex patterns of phenomena for which investigators do not have, at the time, very good ideas about correct models.

The results of Figure 37-7 were obtained by deciding not to estimate the measurement structure parameters of the model (L_i). Instead, verbal and performance abilities were specified as manifest variables, defined in accordance with WAIS scoring for V and P. Prior to fitting under these conditions, models were tried in which the parameters for time effects within cohorts were all set to be equal. A finding of very poor model fit under these conditions suggested that time-of-testing influences should not be assumed to operate in the same way for all age groupings. In applying the model of Figure 37-7 to the V and P variables, therefore, time effects were estimated (i.e., allowed to vary).

Some of the restrictions imposed in the model of Figure 37-7 are rather severe. Note, for example, that the coefficients for across-age auto-regression and cross-lag regression were required to be the same in each cohort. This means that although these coefficients were estimated (allowed to vary) in the total group represented by all cohorts, they were not allowed to vary *between* cohorts.

The values obtained for the model of Figure 37-7 suggest that there is a strong effect in the cross-lag structure for the early measures of performance ability. Indeed, the early P is more predictive of later V than are the early V scores. Such results must be interpreted within the context of simultaneous relations.

The model permits variations between the means for cohorts. This means that the earliest-age "starting points" for assessing repeated-measures changes within each cohort can be different. As can be seen in the K relations of the figure, these starting points are indeed different (58, 61, and 52 for $\overline{V}$). Such results suggest that there is systematic cross-sectional decline in $\overline{P}$ (51, 49, and 38). The model restricted these changes to be equal for all means beyond the initial one. It is perhaps noteworthy that under the conditions of this model the cross-sectional age differences are similar to the repeated-measures age differences.

The model does not fit χ^2 (39) = 151, and Z = 7.6. Thus, though the interpretations provided above do illustrate possibilities, one should be wary about using them.

A *Gf/Gc* Model of the WAIS

In the previous discussion, what seemed to be a reasonable structure/mean model could not be fitted within liberal computer time limits, and eliminating structure features of the model still did not result in a good fit. What is wrong here? Probably several things are wrong, but one problem seems to be that the "reasonable" verbal/performance measurement model is not sufficiently close to a really good structural conception of the data and that many intricacies operate in the model. Under such conditions the algorithms of LISREL can run for an inordinate amount of time before yielding parameter estimates and, indeed, they may never arrive at a solution. Our experience in working with several kinds of data has suggested that when reasonable and only slightly incorrect structures are posited for models in which there are several before-to-after relations, LISREL may run for as many as 1,000 iterations without deciding whether pa-

Table 37-12 Measurement Model Coefficients (Factor Pattern Loadings) for Alternative WAIS Theory (See Figure 37-8)

WAIS subtest	Factor						
	Gc	Gf	Gs	SAR	TSR	U^2	t
Information	.8	—	—	—	1.0	4.0	—
Comprehension	.4	.4	—	—	.4	4.0	.2
Arithmetic Reasoning	.2	—	.2	1.0	.4	6.0	.2
Similarities	.4	.4	—	—	—	6.0	.2
Memory Span	—	.4	.2	.4	—	4.0	.2
Vocabulary	1.0	—	—	—	.8	2.0	.2
Digit Symbol	—	—	1.0	.6	.6	6.0	.2
Picture Completion	.2	.8	.2	—	—	4.0	.2
Block Design	—	1.0	.2	.2	—	2.0	.2
Picture Arrangement	.2	.8	.2	.2	—	4.0	.2
Object Assembly	—	.8	.2	—	—	6.0	.2

Note. Factors: *Gc* = Crystallized Intelligence; *Gf* = Fluid Intelligence; *Gs* = Broad Speediness; *SAR* = Short-Term Acquisition and Retrieval; *TSR* = Tertiary Storage and Retrieval; U^2 = Uniqueness; *t* = Simplex Weights—Inputs From Previous Variable.

rameters can or cannot be estimated. Perhaps in some problems of this kind solutions can never be obtained. At this point in our studies, we simply do not know whether this is true or not.

Compared to a general factor theory, a theory that specifies the performance scoring for the WAIS provides an improved clue to the intellectual processes at work in the subscale performances. This was revealed by the comparisons of structures in the previous section. But the WAIS scoring model for V and P did not fit and thus apparently does not give a truly adequate characterization of the subscale structure. There are indications that a three-factor model is needed. Such a model can be derived from the theory of fluid (*Gf*) and crystallized (*Gc*) intelligence (Cattell, 1971; Cattell & Horn, 1978; Horn, 1970, 1978a; in press). A general statement of a measurement model based on this theory is provided numerically in Table 37-12 and graphically in Figure 37-8.

For present purposes, we used only a subset of the attribute concepts of *Gf/Gc* theory. These may be described briefly as follows:

Gc: Crystallized Intelligence. A broad collection of abilities representing the extent to which an individual has appropriated the intelligence of the dominant culture for his or her own use.

Gf: Fluid intelligence. Also a broad collection of abilities that are quite generally regarded as indicating intelligence, but these abilities are developed largely independently of the systematic influences that characterize acculturation.

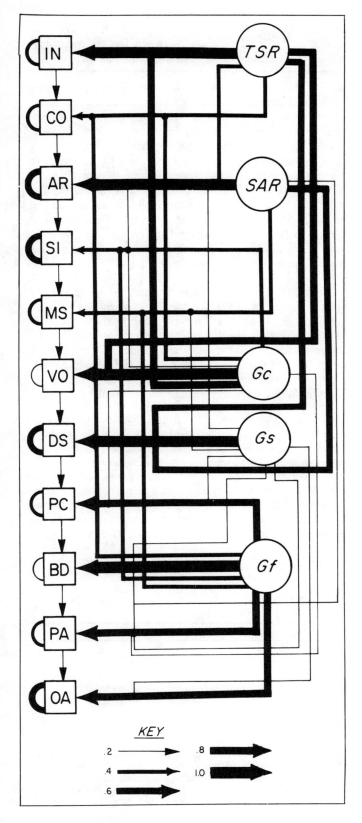

KEY

.2 ⟶   .8 ⟶

.4 ⟶   1.0 ⟶

.6 ⟶

SAR: Short-Term Acquisition and Retrieval. A broad collection of the abilities of becoming aware, maintaining attention, recording information, and retaining it for short periods of time (roughly from 3 to 30 seconds).

TSR: Long-Term Storage and Retrieval. Abilities of storing information in such a way that it is retained for long periods of time—minutes, months, years.

Gs: Broad Speediness. Abilities of rapidly doing clerical and perceptual problems of a kind that all people solve if given enough time.

These concepts have been indicated as common factors in several studies of the structure in broad samples of ability test performances (for summaries see Horn, 1977, 1978b, 1980).

As can be seen in Table 37-12, *Gc* is in several respects similar to the Verbal subscales of the WAIS and *Gf* is similar to the Performance subscales, as has been noted before (e.g., Horn, 1970, in press; Matarazzo, 1972). However, the performances in Memory Span and Arithmetic (which is greatly dependent on Memory Span) are not thought to be highly characteristic of *Gc*. Also, *Gf* is thought to be implicated in the verbal test abilities of Comprehension, Similarities, and Memory Span, as well as in the Performance subscales, excluding, however, Digit Symbol.

The theory also uses the concept of unique factors, the idea that most tasks involve reliably measured processes that are not involved in other tasks.

Developmental concepts are also an important feature of *Gf/Gc* theory. Some aspects of this part of the theory were mentioned in the descriptions of *Gf* and *Gc*. One such feature of importance for present ventures into model fitting can be designated *simplex alteration*. One idea represented by this concept is the notion that the major skills of intelligence build up systematically from simple to elaborated (although the build-up occurs in many ways, and in different ways for different abilities). This is termed *simplex accretion*. Simplex alteration also represents the idea that as skills are lost (and the prior assumption is that some are lost), they build down, as it were, systematically. This is termed *simplex depreciation*.

One result of the operation of these simplex influences is that correlations among repeated measures of abilities show patterns of a kind that Guttman (1954) described under the heading of radex theory. One of the simplest of these patterns is a regular simplex ac-

Figure 37-8. System diagram of measurement structure (factor pattern loadings) for our alternative WAIS theory (see Table 37-12).

cretion. A hypothesis of simplex accretion specifies that the w_i processes of a skill at time t_i are involved also in the w_{i+j} performances at time t_{i+j} in which, however, accretions (refinements, elaborations, etc.) to the skill have been made. Although this pattern is certainly too simple to well represent much of the systematic variation of development, it is about as complex as is realistic in any current theory that purports to rest on empirical knowledge.

The simplex feature of *Gf/Gc* theory implies that it is impossible to attain perfect validity in the prediction of an ability at time t_{i+j} from knowledge of the ability at time t_i because influences that systematically alter the ability occur between the two times. The correlation between manifestations of an ability at two different times can be high, however, if little systematic influence intervenes between the two times of measurement.

A particular application of the simplex concept was employed in our modeling of the latent structure for the WAIS subscales. This application may be designated *simplex warmup*. It represents a hypothesis that when people take the WAIS subtests, which are always given in the same order, systematic individual differences in learning, relaxing, becoming comfortable with the tests, etc., operate to produce more or less enhancement in performance w_{i+j} (on subtest s_{i+j}) as a consequence of prior experience w_i with subtest s_i.

The modeling of this simplex warmup effect is indicated in the column headed t in Table 37-12. The coefficients in this column represent the idea that performance on each subtest is influenced by performance on the just-previous subtest, the extent of this influence being the same .2 for every step from one subtest to the next.

Figure 37-8 illustrates these same ideas graphically. The width of each arrow represents parameter size. The principal purpose of Figure 37-8 is to indicate that the measurement model derived from *Gf/Gc* theory, although considerably simplified compared to the model implied by more general statements of the theory (e.g., Horn, in press), is quite a bit more complex than the verbal/performance model implied by the scoring of the WAIS or even the verbal/performance/number model that we fitted earlier (see Figure 37-4).

It is assumed that the structural model of Table 37-12 and Figure 37-8 is *invariant* for all cohorts, for each of the ages at which cohorts are observed, and (as is now implicit) at each time of measurement (cf. Meredith, 1964). However, the relations between factors at different times of measurement, and the means and standard deviations, can vary from age to age, cohort to cohort, or time to time. Indeed, the hypoth-

esis of simplex alteration that is part of the theory requires that the correlations between factors measured at different stages of development be less than unity, even when the factors are measured with perfect reliability. This does not mean that one could not, in principle, and perhaps in analysis of data, account for the extent to which predictions from one occasion of testing to another deviate from being perfect. Indeed, modeling can help one to clarify thinking, and even to develop testable hypotheses, about such possibilities. If the events between Time 1 and Time 2 that produced a simplex pattern could be identified and measured, for example, then the pattern itself could be accounted for in a model in which the intervening influences were added to the initial individual differences to give perfect predictability. An example of how this might be accomplished is displayed in Figure 37-9 and Table 37-13.

Figure 37-9 represents the notion that while the attribute concepts of *Gf/Gc* are latent variables in relation to the "manifest" subtest scores of the WAIS, they might be regarded as "manifest" in relation to other factors. In particular, the model of Figure 37-9 helps to systematize parts of *Gf/Gc* theory which stipulate that the ability organizations represented by *Gf*, *Gc*, *SAR*, *TSR*, etc., are brought about by

NE: Organization of *Neurological* processes (subscript N)
AC: Systematic *Acculturational* influences (subscript A)
SM: *Situational* influences, such as particular-occasion individual differences in motivation (subscript S)

The widths of the arrows are again intended to be roughly proportional to the strengths of relation between these underlying determinants and the more nearly manifest (but still latent) *Gf*, *Gc*, *SAR*, etc., factors.

Table 37-13 Latent Structure Path Loadings for a *Gf/Gc* Theory of the WAIS (See Figure 37-9)

	Gc	Gf	Gs	SAR	TSR	SM	AC	NE	K
Gc	$\sqrt{.2}$	—	.2	—	.2	—	.6	—	—
Gf	—	$\sqrt{.2}$	.2	.2	—	—	—	.6	—
Gs	—	—	$\sqrt{.2}$	—	—	.2	—	—	—
SAR	—	—	—	$\sqrt{.2}$	—	.2	—	—	—
TSR	—	—	—	—	$\sqrt{.2}$	.2	—	—	—
SM	—	—	—	—	—	u_S	.2	.2	$\bar{g}_S$
AC	—	—	—	—	—	—	u_A	.4	$\bar{g}_A$
NE	—	—	—	—	—	—	—	u_N	$\bar{g}_N$
K	—	—	—	—	—	—	—	—	1

Note. Gc = Crystallized Intelligence; *Gf* = Fluid Intelligence; *Gs* = Broad Speediness; *SAR* = Short-Term Acquisition and Retrieval; *TSR* = Tertiary Storage and Retrieval; *SM* = Situational Motivation; *AC* = Acculturation; *NE* = Neurological Organization.

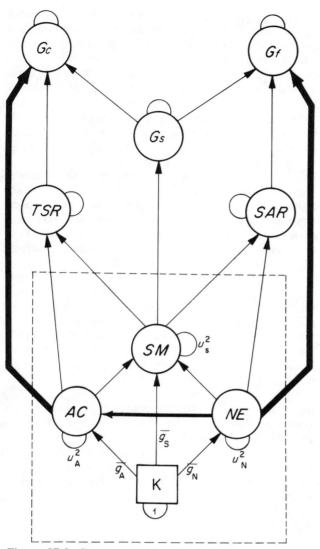

Figure 37-9. System nomograph of latent structure (path coefficients) for a *Gf/Gc* theory of the WAIS. (Controlling parameters are in dashed box; see Table 37-13.)

Figure 37-9 has been designed to illustrate several generic kinds of concepts that one can represent in a strong-theory model for data. For example, the $\bar{g}_A$, $\bar{g}_S$, and $\bar{g}_N$ symbols represent a concept of unique means. That is, just as unique variance (symbolized by u_A^2, u_S^2 and u_N^2 in the figure) represents the idea that there can be reliable variation (in *SM* and *AC*) that is not accounted for by other variation (in *AC* and *NE*), so does unique mean represent the idea that level on one variable is not accounted for by level on other variables.

The diagram also illustrates how indirect influences could produce manifest relations and might be

modeled. The *NE* (Neurological) influence, for example, does not affect *Gc* directly. It operates on *AC* (acculturation), the path influence being .4 (see Table 37-13), which in turn has a major influence (.6) on *Gc*. Multiplication of these two influences (.4 × .6 = .24) gives a measure of the extent to which *Gc* is produced by *NE* through the particular *NE-AC-Gc* pathway. *NE* also affects *Gc* through several other pathways (e.g., *NE/SM/Gs-Gc*), so the overall effect could be considerable.

The model of Figure 37-9 represents a theory that fully accounts for the *Gf, Gc, Gs, TSR* and *SAR* latent variables (and their interrelations) and consequently also fully accounts for the phenotypic characteristics of the 11 WAIS subscore variables that were measured directly. That is, the relations depicted in the model of Figure 37-8, which was regarded as indicating latent variables, are controlled in fact (according to theory) by the six parameters of the model of Figure 37-9, namely, the unique variances and the means of *NE*, *AC*, and *SM*. These high-level theoretical controls are isolated inside the dashed box of Figure 37-9.

Now, then, consider how the truly basic influences represented by *NE*, *AC*, and *SM* might operate over time and circumstances (dynamically) to produce age, cohort, and time effects that would be manifested in *Gf, Gc, Gs, TSR*, and *SAR* and also in the directly measured WAIS subscores. Such dynamic control at the high level is portrayed in Figure 37-10. Here the size of the arrows from one circle to another represents the strength of a control or influence. The smallest arrow path represents a .20 influence. Thus *NE* at age 30

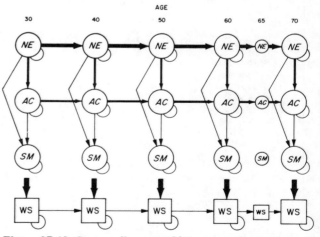

Figure 37-10. System diagram of latent covariance processes (dynamic path coefficients) for the *Gf/Gc* theory of the WAIS. (WS = Weschler Scale variables; see Table 37-14.)

strongly (b = .80) controls *NE* at age 40 but only moderately (b = .40) influences *AC* at age 30 and even more weakly (b = .20) affects *SM* at age 30. The single arrow from one *WS* (Weschler Scale variable) to another represents a model assumption that the unique component of a WAIS variable at one age controls (b = .20) the unique component of that variable at the later age. It can be seen in the figure that for all of the variables, the influences are assumed to be the same for all of the 10-year aging intervals except the one between 60 and 70 years of age. For this period it is assumed that aging over a 5-year span is equivalent to the aging that occurs over a 10-year span elsewhere (in the portion of adulthood considered in this study). The dynamic influences modeled for age 60 to age 70 are smaller [e.g., NE_{60} to $NE_{70} = (.8)(.8) = .64$] under an assumption that there are mediating variables at 65 (represented by small circles).

Figure 37-11 extends the dynamics of Figure 37-10 by depicting the mean changes for the basic controlling variables (of the theory) as these changes are dictated by the relations shown in Figures 37-9 and 37-10. It indicates that in accounting for changes in the means of *NE*, *AC*, *SM*, and *WS*, one must consider the possibility of a unique mean influence, as well as influences expressed through other variables of the model. For example, the shift in the mean of *AC* is affected (a) by the regression influence of *NE* (as depicted in Figure 37-9), which tends to produce aging decline (represented by AO in Figure 37-11), and (b) by a component that is not affected by *NE* or any other variable in the model (and thus is unique), which influence is modeled to increase with age (as represented by Au in the figure). In contrast to the model for *AC*, the model for *NE* specifies that it is not affected by any other modeled variable, and thus the unique mean shift for this variable is all that is specified.

Table 37-14 provides numerical values to indicate the relative magnitude of controlling variable parameters that yield the model relations shown in Figures 37-9 through 37-11. For example, the numbers 10, 11, 12, 13, 15 immediately under *NE* in the table represent variances assumed (in the model) for *NE* at the age periods represented by 30, 40, 50, 60, and 70. Immediately below the numbers representing variances are other numbers representing means for the five age groupings.

The major point to derive from the preceding discussion of Table 37-14 and Figures 37-9 through 37-11 is that we have specified a model in which all the observables associated with the WAIS subscores and with the *Gf*, *Gc*, *Gs*, *TSR*, and *SAR* latent attributes are produced by the neurological, acculturational, and situational influences symbolized as *NE*, *AC*, and *SM*. Thus, *Gf/Gc* theory is pushed up, as it were, to where the influences that yield the structural and developmental outcomes of research are themselves modeled. The suggestion is that if *NE*, *AC*, and *SM* were measured and their relations were determined, this information could be used to reproduce results such as are modeled to depict the structure of the WAIS subscales or describe the aging changes of *Gf* and *Gc*. This is a top-down view of the matter. When we reverse this view and move from the bottom up, supportive results from low-level modeling can serve as a

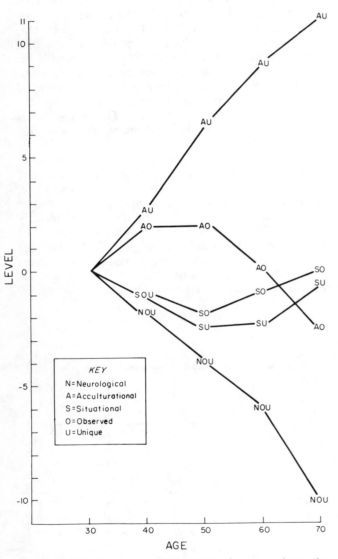

Figure 37-11. Latent-variable means for our alternative WAIS theory. (Note: Only the 1924 cohort group starts at 0; 1914 starts at −1, and 1904 starts at −2. See Table 37-14.)

foundation for building high-level models to represent the "true state of nature" influences of *NE*, *AC*, and *SM*.

The effort to build a model in accordance with this plan encountered huge practical problems stemming from our lack of a computer with infinite storage or budget director who would give us infinite time on the computer that was at our disposal. To work around these problems, we proceeded in the following fashion. First, the data of the 1924 cohort measured in 1954 (ages 25 to 34, $N = 30$) were used to fit the structural (measurement) model alone. The parameter estimates obtained from these analyses were then used as the starting values for estimating corresponding parameters for all of the other groups considered simultaneously, and all other parameters were also estimated. Need we say that the program ran for the maximum number of iterations (250) allowed for a single estimation run? It did. The diagnostics indicated that several more runs through a maximum number of iterations would be needed before a convergent solution could be obtained. Nevertheless, after the first run, $\chi^2(4) = 10.0$, with $Z = 1.8$. The results thus suggest that the departure from good fit is not significant. It seems that a model derived from the developmental and structural stipulations of *Gf/Gc* theory could indeed account for age, cohort, and time changes in WAIS subscale performances—given enough model simplification and computer time!

At this point the reader might suspect that the results are a bit too pat. Surely nature is not that simple. Indeed, a reader familiar with the literature on the WAIS may have been skeptical when the data of this chapter were first described (Table 37-1). In fact, *there are no such data for real people.* The data were generated in a computer. Thus, to the question "How could anyone fit the complex model described in this section, particularly when the indicants of such all-powerful latent variables as *NE*, *AC* and *SM* appear to be so vague?" we can answer quite simply: We can fit the model because *we generated the data from the model.* That is, the data set we have been referring to as "representing WAIS scores" was produced by first specifying the model summarized in Table 37-14 and Figures 37-8 through 37-11 and then applying this model to a set of computer-generated variables to produce 33 variables having the distribution characteristics (means, sigmas, intercorrelations) of genuine data reported in standardizations of the WAIS (Wechsler, 1955). Some of the details of this procedure are described in the Technical Appendix. Here we need only add that the simulation procedure produced data having properties similar to the properties of the genuine data and that subject selection emulated what

Table 37-14 Latent Process Coefficients (Dynamic Path Loadings) for All Controlling Parameters in Our *Gf/Gc* WAIS Theory (See Figures 37-10 and 37-11)

Parameter	Variables			
	NE	*AC*	*SM*	WS
Dynamic Age Regression	.8	.4	0	.2
Observed variances (s^2)				
30	10	10	3	
40	11	10	3	
50	12	10	3	≈ 10.0
60	13	10	3	
70	15	10	3	
Observed means ($\bar{X}$)				
30	0	0*	0	9.25
40	−2	2	−1	9.25
50	−4	2	−2	9.25 $\Big\} = G$
60	−6	0	−1	9.25
70	−10	−2	0	9.25
Unique variances (U^2)				
30	10	8.4	2.2	
40	4.6	6.64	2.16	≈ 4.0
50	4.96	6.48	2.12	(see
60	5.32	6.32	2.08	Table
70	9.675	6	2	37-12
Unique means ($\bar{g}$)				
30	0	0*	0	—
40	−2	2.8	−1	—
50	−2.4	3.6	−1.6	—
60	−4.08	2.4	.2	—
70	−6.16	2	2	—

* Means for *AC* at starting point depend on cohort: 0 = 1924, −1 = 1914, −2 = 1904.

has often been observed in studies of aging (Horn & Donaldson, 1976; Siegler & Botwinick, 1979). As to the first point, the means, variances, and intercorrelations for the WAIS standardization sample of 25- to 34-year-olds ($N = 300$) were well represented by the comparable statistics for the simulated data, $\chi^2(4) = 14$, $Z = 2.14$. Concerning the second point, selection usually eliminated proportionately more of the subjects with low full-scale IQ scores.

Perhaps the most interesting outcome of this effort to model a "true state of nature" is not that we got the model to fit but that after 250 iterations of LISREL we were still some distance away from the near-perfect fit that could be expected. This denouement emphasizes a point made earlier, namely that even with a model that is almost correct, when many intricacies are involved, present-day computing technology may not be adequate to guarantee convergence to a maximum-likelihood solution within a reasonable amount of computer time.

Summary, Conclusions, and Extrapolations

Although this review of issues in the use of MASMOB has been brief in view of the many issues that might be considered, it has left us with a rather complex account of how to view modeling procedures and what to do and not to do to obtain dependable and interesting results with these procedures. What general conclusions are indicated? In this section we attempt to locate such conclusions and at the same time to summarize major points and qualifications. The section is organized in terms of the SEER steps in modeling, although it sometimes seemed rather arbitrary to put an idea under one rather than another of the SEER headings.

Specification

All of the models considered here were specified within the general RAM nomographical system (McArdle, 1980). The RAM provides a framework for specifying a wide range of models that a behavioral scientist might want to consider (Underwood, 1975). While there are, of course, many ways to organize the logic and mathematics of model fitting, in most cases the path-nomographic system representation of RAM proved to be comprehensive, simple, concise, and easy to use.

Our analysis of the application of ANOVA to an A, C, T conception of developmental issues illustrates some of the values of RAM. The flexibility of the RAM modeling approach is one major value, because it helps one to become clear about assumptions, particularly arbitrary assumptions, and to think about the assumptions that reasonably might or might not be imposed. When MASMOB thinking is applied to the use of ANOVA with A, C, T data, it becomes clear that substantive theory is needed to provide a sensible rationale for data analysis. This is a well established principle of good data analysis (cf. Horn, 1979), which has been dictated by much thoughtful consideration of how scientific investigation should be conducted. It is by no means a discovery derived from modeling. But the principle is too often neglected in behavioral science research. Modeling virtually forces an investigator not to neglect it. How modeling can help to improve scientific thinking is illustrated simply and straightforwardly by considering ANOVA models for A, C, T variables.

Our modeling of structure (factors) illustrated opportunities for comparing hypotheses. We know that no model can provide a completely adequate representation of reality and that a principle of good scientific investigation dictates that research should lead to a basis for comparing competing theories. But this principle has been more often ignored than attended to in the behavioral sciences. Factor analytic research in psychology—while probably no worse than other research—has been flawed because although different studies produce different results and lead to different conclusions, the differences are not analyzed in a manner that allows one to conclude with reasonable certainty that the theory of one study is better than the competing theory. Comparison of models, as illustrated in this article, does not, of course, provide a complete solution for this kind of problem, but it does indicate the kinds of halting steps that can be taken along a path toward solution.

Modeling of factor-analytic problems has also helped to uncover an important limitation of MASMOB methods. Present-day procedures require that coefficients that are assumed to represent only hyperplanar relations must be restricted to exactly zero. Most factor theories stipulate, however, that hyperplanar relations are zero only on an average and have a distribution around zero that varies with size of sample. It may be sensible for metric and statistical reasons to constrain coefficients to lie within a boundary—that is, not be precisely zero or (if a free parameter) be allowed to be virtually any real number. Present-day model-fitting programs do not permit this kind of flexibility, however. (Sörbom has indicated in a personal communication that he is working on a version of LISREL that does permit it).

We did not consider metatheories of factor differentiation and integration over development, nor did we consider issues pertaining to the emergence and loss of factors (Cattell, 1957, 1978; Nesselroade, 1970, 1979; Rozeboom, 1978). Modeling may be useful in dealing with some of the problems in these areas, but we need to look at the matter more carefully before we conclude that this is true.

The basic ideas of path analysis are extended by a system in which there is simultaneous specification of structure (factors) for independent variables as well as dependent variables, and for the means, variances, directed relations, and undirected relations of latent variables. Application of such systems logic to developmental problems has been suggested by others (e.g., Bentler, 1978; Royce & Buss, 1976; Urban, 1978; although the mathematics needed to implement the logic were not indicated in the last two papers). To our knowledge, however, no one had tried to apply this logic to the kind of complex developmental problem for which the logic was advocated. The examples we have considered thus provide a first concrete illustration of the potential of this approach to data analysis.

It seems likely that many problems that were formerly attacked with regression analysis, factor analysis, MANOVA, canonical correlation, and discriminant factor analysis can be addressed effectively with MASMOB procedures. Specification for such problems can be quite intricate, however, and problems can be created that are well beyond our present understanding of modeling procedures.

The simulation of *Gf/Gc* theory in a hierarchical model attests to the power and flexibility of RAM nomographical specification. Good indications of what can be done were illustrated in this modeling by the specification of higher order factors in the form of controlling mechanisms, interrelations among means, variances, and covariances, and simplexes within simplexes for invariant measurement structures. It should be recognized, however, that several kinds of conceptions that could be important for simulation or for understanding phenomena are not easily expressed in terms of RAM. For example, the developmental modeling of Figures 37-10 and 37-11 contains no provisions for dependency in subject sampling (Meredith, 1979) or nonrandom attrition—both central problems of inference in research on aging.

In general, then, RAM specification provides a general and flexible way to merge theory with data through data analysis. Use of RAM should help to enforce principles of good scientific investigation. On the other hand, the power of the methods—their ability to make almost any thought look like a hypothesis or even a theory—can lead down primrose paths. The elegance of the methods may also tend to hide important assumptions that are made when models are actuated in estimation and evaluation.

Estimation

The program LISREL-IV (Jöreskog & Sörbom, 1978), as actualized in a Burroughs 6700 computer, was used for all the parameter estimation considered in this chapter. This program provides maximum-likelihood (ML) parameter estimates under the assumptions of a Wishart distribution (which in turn is based on assumption of multivariate normal distribution for variables). The algorithms of the program depend heavily on the Davidon-Fletcher-Powell routine for constrained nonlinear optimization (Lee & Jennrich, 1979). Identification failures are evaluated within the program by indicants of singularity of what is known as the information matrix.

The analyses reported in this chapter indicate that LISREL provides a means for doing many kinds of data analysis that might otherwise be done with a be-wildering array of different programs. LISREL performed well in many applications. However, if computer costs are a genuine concern, one should consider alternatives. In some cases, parameters can be estimated with least-squares or direct calculation procedures that cost far less than the ML and iterative procedures that are embodied in LISREL-IV (e.g., McArdle, 1979; McDonald, 1978, Meredith, 1979; Rozeboom, 1978; Wold, 1975). Also, our use of LISREL-IV has indicated problems of convergence for adequately specified models that are intricate.

But the major problems of estimation are not algorithmic or even mathematical: They are logical problems of design. Some of the most important of these problems deal with suppressor influences. The difficulty is that every parameter estimate is, in part, a function of every other parameter that is or is not estimated in a model. Parameter estimate X is one value if Parameter Y is estimated; X is quite another value if Y is not estimated, or if U, V, and W are not estimated. Some of the examples in this chapter (e.g., in the modeling of A, C, and T variables) illustrated that there can be quite large fluctuations in parameter estimates, with rather minor changes of conditions for inclusion or exclusion of other parameters in the estimation scheme. The problem appears to be the same in principle as the problem of taking proper cognizance of suppressor influences in multiple regression analysis, but the matter is considerably more complex for many applications of modeling.

The work with factor models raised some questions about separate estimation within segments of a system, particularly segments that might reasonably be considered in isolation from the total system. If modeling is done only with structure, and other implications (e.g., developmental) of a theory are ignored, a reasonably good fit can be obtained for models that do not, strictly speaking, represent reality. We found, for example, that the fit of the model for Verbal, Performance, and Numerical factors was reasonably good (see Figure 37-4), even though the example did not represent a sample version of the population model that generated the data. This is not an entirely undesirable outcome, of course. We know that we can never obtain a perfect model of reality, and we want our data-analytic procedures to provide a basis for retaining models that are at least reasonable approximations. The *V*, *P*, and *N* model is not an unreasonable approximation to the structure we know to exist, and it is certainly better than some other models that might have been considered. In this sense, therefore, the results indicating a fit for this model are not misleading. But the question raised by these findings is, "Do modeling results warn a researcher sufficiently that while a given model is not bad, and is better than some other models, it is not really the best model for the data?"

Our results on joint structure-and-development modeling may provide a few clues about how to deal with this question even though they fail to provide an answer to the question. These results suggest that as one moves away from consideration of structure alone to consideration of both structural and the developmental (or other) implications of a theory, then a correction for the error of accepting a wrong (but approximate) model may emerge. We have found that under these conditions, in other sets of data as well as here, it is difficult indeed to fit a model when the submodel for structure is wrong (at either the independent-variable or dependent-variable side of an equation or, as here, when there are several conditions, or occasions, for which a structure is posited). The goodness of fit is poorer than one would expect on the assumption that a structure that provides a reasonably good approximation to the best structure should provide a reasonably good basis for defining the model overall. It seems, therefore, that if the model for structure is wrong, an even poorer fit will result when this structure is included in a modeling of dynamic relations than if the structure mistake were not made.

In sum, then, major problems of estimation in model fitting are indicated by the considerable fluctuation found in the estimates. One might be inclined to attribute this fluctuation to smallness of the sample of subjects or to the unusualness of such sampling. But while subject sampling is no doubt one important factor, the results presented here make it clear that fluctuations in parameter estimates result in large part because of suppressor influences associated with sampling of variables. As a model becomes more and more similar to the "true" model, fluctuations in parameter estimates become smaller. Maximum-likelihood estimates of parameters are good estimates only if the correct model is posed and the genuine minimum for the criterion function is obtained. There is a Catch-22 quality about all of this. One needs to know the correct model in order to get the parameter estimates that provide the basis for deciding whether or not one has the correct model. The way out of this dilemma is along a trial-and-error road that has few trustworthy signposts and several subtly deceptive turns.

Important practical problems of estimation also revolve around computer capabilities and features of algorithms. Model-fitting programs can devour huge amounts of computer time, and even a model that is scientifically plausible though intricate, can eradicate a computer budget. Moreover, it can be very difficult to defend this outcome to a funding agency or depart-

ment chairperson, because even after the budget is gone there may be no solution for the model-fit problem, and the results at hand may indicate very little about what needs to be done to obtain a solution.

This practical difficulty can motivate researchers to specify simpler models, and indeed, some researchers experiencing the practical difficulties of fitting intricate models have reacted by simplifying their models. This may be the wrong reaction, however. Perhaps the practical difficulties of using maximum-likelihood (ML) algorithms for estimation should lead investigators to ask for, and use, simpler least-squares (LS) procedures (see Appendix, p. 536). One problem with this recommendation is that LS programs that will do the estimation that is done by ML programs (such as LISREL) need to be more fully developed. Also, it seems (to us at least) that for intricate latent-structure models we do not know how to identify the conditions under which ML and LS estimates can, or will, be the same and can, or must, differ. If mathematicians already have answers to questions of this kind, then we need better communication to get the answers to programmers and behavioral scientists; if such answers have not been developed, then we need to induce good mathematicians to provide the answers. If we could be sure that LS parameter estimates are the same as ML estimates (as they are with multiple regression coefficients, for example), then the statistical theory associated with ML estimation could be applied as well to estimates obtained with LS procedures, and several of the practical problems of intricate modeling (e.g., nonconvergence) could be solved.

Evaluation

What constitutes an adequate statistical test of a hypothesis? Not an easy question to answer even when only single-occasion univariate hypotheses are considered, it is particularly difficult to deal with in multivariate, latent-structure modeling. The chi square that emerges at the end of such modeling results from a large number of influences. What is meant when this single statistic is said to indicate that a model does not fit, or that it does? We have seen that with some data, if only minor specifications of a model are wrong, the model will not fit but that, on the other hand, one can free up parameters to obtain a fit for a model that is known to be wrong. Where between these two bogs of misinformation is the solid ground on which one can build sound interpretations?

One feature of this ground requires that statistical tests be appropriate for hypotheses that really represent a theory. The examples provided earlier of models for problems that have been treated with ANOVA illustrate that the modeling approach tends to force one to be explicit about hypotheses to be tested. This helps to ensure that the statistical tests of evaluation correspond rather closely to hypotheses that really are, or at least can be, derived from a theory. Also, hypotheses need not be evaluated only in terms of a main effect for means. Individual parameter salience can be evaluated within the context of an overall model. When a model does not fit, questions can be raised about where specifically the fault resides. Such questions frequently are not considered in hypothesis testing with ANOVA.

The modeling approach to data analysis encourages the researcher to compare one plausible hypothesis, or theory, with another. Such an approach is much recommended by espistemological analyses. The statistical features of this approach to modeling rest on the logic, when it can be invoked, of adding and subtracting chi squares and degrees of freedom for different models. This may be the most important feature of MASMOB methods. There is much we have yet to learn, however, before the power of this feature can be effectively used and not abused.

When one model is neatly nested within another, the additivity feature of chi-square analysis can be most unambiguously employed. Application of this logic to the modeling of factor structures in our examples made it evident, however, that in one application (at least) a comparison of chi squares for different models is nothing more than still another test for the number of factors in factor analysis (Horn & Engstrom, 1979). Cogent analyses of this almost ancient problem make it evident that the chi-square comparison test will not prove to be the final best solution (cf. Kaiser, 1976). This nuclear example of an inadequacy of the chi-square comparison features of modeling cautions against acceptance of sanguine pronouncements (sometimes made) that modeling will provide the panacea for all the ills of drawing inferences in the behavioral sciences.

The orderliness of additive chi-square analysis of models that are successively nested within each other is also an attractive feature of evaluation ML model fitting. But what, really, is the universe of inference after several such steps have been taken through a given set of data? The successive tests involve the same sampling and measurement errors. Although the results at each step may be mathematically independent, they are not statistically independent. A chi square representing conditional probability is needed, but such a chi square is not made available in any model-fitting routine of which we are aware (cf. Harris, 1976; Horn, 1965).

We noted in our application of model fitting to factoring problems that in testing successive fits for nested models, the model was sure to get better at each step. Quite simply, the more factors extracted, the better the model fitted. This illustrates another problem that probably exists for all model fitting, not simply that of factoring. It is generally acknowledged that merely by extracting more factors in factor analysis, one does not necessarily arrive at a better conception of data. Similarly, improvement in fit of a model need not imply that one is moving in the right direction to arrive at the "true model" for data. Perhaps the best corrective for inference errors of this kind is to compare models but avoid straw-man comparisons—as when any of an infinity of models for X factors is compared with models (another infinity) for $(X + 1)$ factors. The corrective is to ensure that models to be compared represent truly competing (in substantive theory) explanations of phenomena.

Our piecemeal analyses illustrated that it can be very difficult to find a best model for data by analyzing subsections of a total. The "total model" that was created for our analyses is no doubt much simpler than a model for a true state of nature. Even so, attempts to fit models representing pieces of the whole often led in a wrong direction or provided no information about direction. Indeed, if chi-square tests indicating a poor fit for a piecemeal model are accepted at face value, they can stop further efforts at fitting with that piece of the data. In this sense the statistical evidence from piecemeal model fitting may help the researcher avoid wrong turns even though it does not signal correct turns.

The conclusions of previous sections need to be carefully tempered with awareness of how size of sample (N) affects statistical tests in model fitting. The chi square provides a test that a model does not fit: The larger the chi square, the more unlikely it is that the model fits. The chi square is also a function of the size of sample: The larger the N, the larger the chi square. This presents the interesting possibility that if an investigator is careful to choose a small enough sample, he can demonstrate that his model fits. There is a corrective for this, of course, in that the standard errors for the statistics on which such a model fit would be based increase with decrease of N. Nevertheless, one should be on guard. Our practical experience has left an awareness that small N can indeed lead to the conclusion that a model fits when it does not. One should beware also of inference error that can be associated with large N. If a sample is large, chi square may be so large as to suggest the rejection of a hypothesis of fit for even a good model.

The question of model evaluation is broad indeed.

We have only scratched the surface of major issues in this chapter. Adequate evaluation must take into account many factors in addition to a simple goodness-of-fit statistic. The effort required to put this statistic in proper perspective is formidable indeed (cf. Burt, 1973; Finifter, 1972; Jöreskog, 1966; Specht, 1975).

Readjustments

The major problem with readjustment is that, in effect, it involves discarding the initial theory on which statistical inference is based and adopting a conditional (Bayesian) theory for which the distribution properties are not known. The question becomes, "What is the likelihood of such-and-such, given that, after examining the data, so-and-so has been set at (readjusted to be) a particular value?" What is seen in examining the data may be—in general is—a feature of a particular sample of observations, not a population condition. Thus the conditional that is implicitly assumed in readjustment is difficult to represent in a general theory about chance events.

A generally accepted solution to this kind of problem does not exist for even rather simple univariate statistics. It is not surprising, therefore, that no solution is at hand for the multivariate modeling versions of the problem. A procedure that is widely used, if not widely accepted, for dealing with the problem is simply to ignore it and use statistical tests as if no conditional were imposed. About all we can add to this implicit advice is caution, and cautions probably do little more than generate anxieties. Perhaps such anxiety can be mildly adaptive, however.

Our results with readjustments of factor models taught a lesson with ML modeling that we had learned before with what were referred to as procrustean, or subjective, procedures of rotation (Horn, 1967; Horn & Knapp, 1973, 1974): With enough tinkering one can often get data to conform to one's cherished ideas about the nature of reality. In the examples of the present study we were able to make readjustments that led to a "good" fit for a model that we knew was not an exemplar of the model that generated the data. Our reasoning to justify this step reflected similar reasoning often found in the literature of model fitting, namely, that because our initial model did not fit, we should look for a model that "does fit" (Saris et al., 1978). The trouble with this reasoning is not that it is itself wrong but that the inferences that are drawn from it are wrong. The model that is found to fit by readjustments is a model for the data at hand. It is an example of how one can describe these data. As such, it is not a demonstration of support for an inference about a model or a theory that was developed independently of the data; it is not support for a hypothesis of a theory. The statistics of inference associated with the model fit should be thrown away, and investigators should clearly recognize that all they are doing is describing the data at hand.

Ptolemy's descriptions of the paths of planets provide an example that illustrates this point. Recall that long before Copernicus or Galileo, Ptolemy was able, by detailed study of information on the movements of planets, to work out elliptical pathways for planets that described the data very well—indeed, as well as they were described by later scientists—but for a model in which the earth was the center of the planetary–sun system! Ptolemy's efforts exemplify the same kind of painstaking adjustments to fit existing data to a conception of reality as are exemplified by modern-day readjustments to make a model fit (e.g., Guilford, 1967) or to find the model that does fit (as here). Ptolemy's making the model fit provided only weak support for his theory, however, because theory development and procrustean model fitting were not kept sufficiently independent. His work netted some (weak) support because this model represented a possible way that reality might be explained, and this possibility was based on observations. This is Guilford's (1974) defense of criticisms that his model-fitting studies provide support for his structure-of-intellect theory.

As in our earlier work, there were some signs in the results obtained here to indicate when we were being led astray by our procrustean procedures—signs that might have cautioned us against incorrect inference if we were disposed to read them and take them seriously. Our readjustments allowed correlations between specific factors to be nonzero, certainly not an unreasonable relaxation of a model. The tell-tale sign that this did not lead to a correct model in the present instance appeared when the specific correlations turned out to be negative. Even this finding could be rationalized to seem reasonable, particularly after the fact. The lesson to be learned here is that such rationalization should be done with clear awareness that it is descriptive, not inferential.

We have stressed the negative aspects of the readjustment phase of model fitting, but they should not lead one to ignore the positive. Readjustment affords an opportunity to use observations to improve thinking about phenomena. The thoughts that direct the gathering of data in genuine research are always wrong in important respects. The failure of a model to fit data is one bit of information that can be used to improve these thoughts. A searching of the data to find what really does describe the sample at hand can provide valuable information for improving these thoughts—provided one does not read too much into this description. Such description provides a basis for forming hypotheses, not a basis for confirming them. If this distinction is kept clearly in mind, the readjustment phase of modeling can be the most valuable part of the process.

Denouement Cautions

There is a fifth phase of modeling that in many applications is more important than any of the SEER phases. This is a phase of replication under conditions of no readjustment. It is particularly important to follow with this phase when there has been extensive readjustment to achieve a model fit. When a model of one study can be found to provide an adequate description in another study with no readjustments, one can indeed gain confidence that there is understanding of the modeled phenomena. Often this seems to be what is meant when there is reference to a causal model for data.

The reader may have noticed that we have avoided using terms such as *causal modeling* in discussing the methods outlined in this chapter. This avoidance was quite intentional. The connotations of the word "cause" can be very misleading, particularly if more explanatory power is suggested than can be realized from the statements that contain the word *cause*. To model cause adequately requires one to satisfy a number of requirements that are difficult indeed to satisfy—even only in theory—and that are virtually impossible to realize in an actual experiment for which a model might be specified (Suppes, 1970). For example, there is a requirement (dating from J. S. Mill's analyses of the 19th century) that if we are to say that A causes B, then all conditions other than A that might cause B must somehow be neutralized or held constant. How does one model this requirement of comprehensiveness? A reasonable answer is that one cannot model this requirement, because one cannot be explicit about the infinity of "possible conditions other than A" that must be controlled.

One can deal with this problem in a theory of causal modeling, however, by imposing "what if" conditions that put boundaries on what is considered in a model. For example, to deal with the requirement of compre-

hensiveness, one can specify that *if* all conditions are somehow held constant, then a directed arrow from A to B can represent the idea that A causes B. In a similar manner one can specify requirements of temporal order and conditional probability. In this way an internally consistent model for cause can be described (in formal terms). The term *causal modeling* is appropriately used under these "what if" conditions, for it is made clear that only if the assumptions of specification are met, can one unambiguously infer cause, and it becomes clear in such full description that in all likelihood the assumptions cannot be met with any data a model might be said to represent. In this way the conditions needed to assert cause can be stated rather explicitly in a model and thereby kept separate from the procedures for actually inferring cause by, for example, using a model description to account for actual data. Thus it can be argued that when causal modeling is separated from causal inferences, one can decrease misleading connotations of the term *cause*.

Unfortunately, much of the discussion of causal modeling that has appeared in recent years has not been qualified in the manner just discussed. As a result, it has too often been suggested that evaluation of a model is a test of assumptions that are not even considered in specifying the model. For example, an implicit assumption in specifying that the latent variable L causes manifest variables C, D, E, and F would be that L precedes the manifest variables. Yet in many situations where such a model is specified and evaluated, there is no possibility of considering the assumption of temporal order, because all variables (manifest and latent) are based on observations made at one instant. It is not misleading to say that a causal model assumes that L precedes C, D, E, and F, but it is misleading to suggest that this assumption has been tested by a finding that a model "fits" the data. It is this kind of misleading connotation that we have sought to avoid by not using the term *causal modeling* in the present chapter. We recommend such caution in other discussions of MASMOB methods.

Given these cautions, however, the current and widespread interest in causal modeling can be salubrious. As long as one remains aware that modeling is only an adjunct to good scientific thinking, and not a substitute for such thinking, then the potentially misleading connotations of terms such as *causal modeling* need not lead one astray.

TECHNICAL APPENDIX

Some Fundamental Features of RAM

RAM Moment Structure

The mathematical and statistical aspects of RAM are fully discussed elsewhere (McArdle, 1980). Only a brief description of the approach is offered here.

The RAM system is a combination of a psychometric organization developed by Cattell (1966) and a mathematical/statistical formulation of Jöreskog (1973). Also important in the development of RAM are the early work of Wright (1934) on path analysis (cf. Kenny, 1979) and the recent mathematical formulations of McDonald (1978, 1979), Sörbom (1978), and Bentler and Weeks (1979).

The sample data are assumed to be describable in terms of two sets of moments: first (mean vector $\bar{m}_g$) and second (covariance matrix C_g) moments for a distribution of a specified number (j_g) of manifest variables, obtained for N_g subjects deployed in G groups ($g = 1, \ldots, G$). Thus the sample data for the gth group can be described in terms of the following matrix equation:

$$W = E\{M^t M\} = J (I - D)^{-1} U (I - D)^{-t} J^t \quad \text{(A-1)}$$

where

j = number of manifest variables M;
k = number of latent variables L;
t = the total number of variables ($j + k$);
E = expected value operator over N subjects (N without subscript represents number of subjects in any single group);
W = general moment matrix (size j by j);
M = data matrix (N by j) of j manifest scores for N subjects;
J = Index matrix (j by t) of zeros except where a unit value is used to designate a manifest variable;
I = Identity matrix (t by t);
D = Directed matrix (t by t) of conditional relations;
U = Undirected matrix (t by t) of unconditional relations.

A full development of rationale for this equation is presented elsewhere (McArdle & McDonald, 1980). At first it might appear to be somewhat complex. However, there is simplicity in the algebra because it is isomorphic with an extended system/path geometry. In such geometric representations the J matrix is used to differentiate *squares* from *circles*, the D matrix represents all *one-headed arrows*, and the U represents all no-headed lines. Thus the equation can be used to specify the proposed population covariance for any diagram that one might draw with path-analysis conventions. This simple translation for specification is described in the next section.

RAM Specification

As noted, a major feature of RAM is isomorphism between path diagram and algebraic equation. Any system model that can be geometrically diagrammed using latent-variable path-analytic conventions (Jöreskog & Sörbom, 1977), in which variables are represented as circles (for latent) or squares (for manifest) and relations are drawn as one-headed or no-headed arrows, can also be presented algebraically in the analogous form of Equation A-1. This is not to say that estimates can be obtained for every set of lines one can draw in a path diagram merely because the diagram can be specified algebraically. The steps for translation from diagram to equation and back again can be summarized as follows:

1. Draw (for your substantive theory) a system of (a) variables, namely, j manifest and k latent, connected by arrows representing (b) relations, for the particular free and fixed (and other) *settings* desired, directed D and undirected U.

2. To obtain the Index J write a rectangular matrix with the j manifest variables M as rows and all t variables (manifest and latent) V as columns; then fill the main diagonal of the first part of this matrix (the j by j part) with unities.

3. To obtain the directed matrix D, align all k of the variables V (as in J) along the rows and columns of a large square zero matrix. In the cells of this matrix replace zeros with numbers or other symbols to represent the one-way path parameters. Let column variables be input to row variables—that is, column-to-row represents the direction of a path-diagram arrow.

4. To obtain the undirected matrix U, align all variables along both the rows and columns of a large (square and symmetric) null matrix, and replace zeros with numbers or other symbols to represent two-way path parameters in the lower (or upper) triangle sector.

A useful example to illustrate diagram-to-equation specification is a model for factor analysis, represented in covariance form for f factors as

$$C = BQB^t + UU^t \quad \text{(A-2)}$$

where

C = sample covariance matrix (j by j);

B = factor loading matrix (j by f) of regression coefficients for estimating manifest variables (as output) from common factors (as input);

Q = interfactor covariance matrix (f by f) of allowed relations among common factors;

U = unique factor loading matrix (j by j) of regression coefficients for estimating manifest variables (output) from unique factors (input). In many treatments this part of the model would be represented as U^2, a diagonal matrix of unique factor variances. For reasons that will become evident as we go along, it is desirable to regard unique factor loadings (common factor loadings) as regression coefficients.

When this model is given parameters in RAM, the B is always considered a submatrix of RAM-D and Q is a submatrix of RAM-U. However, the U, filled with parameters, can serve as a diagonal submatrix of either RAM-D or RAM-U, or both.

To illustrate this flexibility in specifying U, we will describe a model for three variables and one common factor. The three manifest variables x_i are decomposed into one common factor h, with pattern loadings b_i and variance q. Following Jöreskog (1966), three unique factors e_i, with fixed unit regression and variance u_{ii}^2, are also postulated. A model for all variables (V) can now be translated into RAM equations of the following form (where "ed" stands for element diagonal form):

$$V = \begin{bmatrix} x_1 & x_2 & x_3 & h & e_1 & e_2 & e_3 \end{bmatrix} \quad \text{(A-3)}$$

$$J = \begin{bmatrix} 1 & 0 & 0 & 0 & 0 & 0 & 0 \\ 0 & 1 & 0 & 0 & 0 & 0 & 0 \\ 0 & 0 & 1 & 0 & 0 & 0 & 0 \end{bmatrix}$$

$$D = \begin{bmatrix} 0 & 0 & 0 & b_1 & 1 & 0 & 0 \\ 0 & 0 & 0 & b_2 & 0 & 1 & 0 \\ 0 & 0 & 0 & b_3 & 0 & 0 & 1 \\ 0 & 0 & 0 & 0 & 0 & 0 & 0 \\ 0 & 0 & 0 & 0 & 0 & 0 & 0 \\ 0 & 0 & 0 & 0 & 0 & 0 & 0 \\ 0 & 0 & 0 & 0 & 0 & 0 & 0 \end{bmatrix}$$

$$U = \text{ed} \begin{bmatrix} 0 & 0 & 0 & q & u_{11}^2 & u_{22}^2 & u_{33}^2 \end{bmatrix}.$$

We may also create parameters for this same model without the e_i elements, which are unnecessary for many calculation purposes, and therefore without the parts of the matrices that pertain to e_i. The resulting smaller, but equivalent, set of *crucial path* RAM matrices are

$$V = \begin{bmatrix} x_1 & x_2 & x_3 & h \end{bmatrix} \quad \text{(A-4)}$$

$$J = \begin{bmatrix} 1 & 0 & 0 & 0 \\ 0 & 1 & 0 & 0 \\ 0 & 0 & 1 & 0 \end{bmatrix}$$

$$D = \begin{bmatrix} 0 & 0 & 0 & b_1 \\ 0 & 0 & 0 & b_2 \\ 0 & 0 & 0 & b_3 \\ 0 & 0 & 0 & 0 \end{bmatrix}$$

$$U = \text{ed} \begin{bmatrix} u_{11}^2 & u_{22}^2 & u_{33}^2 & q \end{bmatrix}.$$

Another version of this model is useful to consider, particularly if Heywood cases are possible. This *unique path* specification effectively restricts unique variance estimates to non-negative values because their square roots u_{ii} are the estimated parameters. Thus the possibility of a Heywood case for variances is eliminated (although other problems may arise). In this specification, V and J are as in Equation A-3, but D and U are as follows:

$$D = \begin{bmatrix} 0 & 0 & 0 & b_1 & u_{11} & 0 & 0 \\ 0 & 0 & 0 & b_2 & 0 & u_{22} & 0 \\ 0 & 0 & 0 & b_3 & 0 & 0 & u_{33} \\ 0 & 0 & 0 & 0 & 0 & 0 & 0 \\ 0 & 0 & 0 & 0 & 0 & 0 & 0 \\ 0 & 0 & 0 & 0 & 0 & 0 & 0 \\ 0 & 0 & 0 & 0 & 0 & 0 & 0 \end{bmatrix} \quad \text{(A-5)}$$

$$U = \text{ed} \begin{bmatrix} 0 & 0 & 0 & q & 1 & 1 & 1 \end{bmatrix}$$

The crucial-path and unique-path ideas may be combined into a *compact path* parameterization.

The means can be introduced into models as covariances for dummy contrast variables, as in regression analysis (Cohen & Cohen, 1975). Also, Sörbom (1978) has introduced the idea of using differential group intercept parameters. Scheifley and Schmidt (1978) and Rock, Werts, and Flaugher (1978) have used this idea to consider, simultaneously, hypotheses about both mean and covariances. Recently Sörbom has modified his earlier formulations to allow the entire moment structure to be evaluated with covariance equations based on the independence of means and co-variances (Sörbom, personal communication, May 1979). These ideas are incorporated into RAM logic.

In order to represent the means in path diagrams, a square is used to denote a *constant* k. That is, k is considered to be a special variety of manifest variable, namely, a "variable" on which all subjects have exactly the same score. Thus, the variance for this "variable" is zero, and its correlation with all other variables is also zero.

Input data consist of means ($\overline{M}$) and covariances C, with the addition of the k as a manifest variable. In the simple case of two manifest variables, k-augmented equations (denoted by asterisks) are

$$M^* = [x_1 : x_2 : k] \qquad (A\text{-}6)$$

$$\overline{M}^* = [\bar{x}_1 : \bar{x}_2 : k]$$

$$C^* = \begin{bmatrix} s_1^2 & & \text{sym} \\ c_{12} & s_2^2 & \\ 0 & 0 & 0 \end{bmatrix} ;$$

therefore,

$$W^* = C + \overline{M}^t\,\overline{M} = \begin{bmatrix} (s_1^2 + \bar{x}_1^2) & & \text{sym} \\ (c_{12} + \bar{x}_1\bar{x}_2) & (s_2^2 + \bar{x}_2^2) & \\ \bar{x}_1 & \bar{x}_2 & 1 \end{bmatrix}$$

This moment structure W^* is analyzed in the same way that a covariance matrix is typically analyzed in multivariate programs (e.g., in maximum-likelihood programs). In the results, the directed relation of k, as input to the other variables, represents the *mean* parameters. For example, this could be described in RAM with $t^* = 3$, $J^* = I$, and

$$V = [x_1 : x_2 : k] \qquad (A\text{-}7)$$

$$D = \begin{bmatrix} 0 & 0 & 0 \\ 0 & 0 & \bar{x}_1 \\ 0 & 0 & \bar{x}_2 \end{bmatrix}$$

$$U = \begin{bmatrix} s_1^2 & & \text{sym} \\ c_{12} & s_2^2 & \\ 0 & 0 & 1 \end{bmatrix}$$

Now that the means are RAM parameters, inferences about their saliency (i.e., $\bar{x}_1 = 0$), equality (i.e., $\bar{x}_1 = \bar{x}_2$), or more complex patterns (McArdle, 1978) can be evaluated by further restrictions on D. The mathematical proof that hypothesis testing can be based on this full moment structure lies in showing that the objective function for W^* is the same as the comparable function for the matrix usually evaluated in multivariate analysis. Meredith demonstrated this equality in a personal communication to us in June 1979.

RAM Estimation

The computational problems of estimation for complex models can be quite severe. The procedures proposed here are not new. They represent a combination of existing algorithms.

RAM requires estimation under conditions in which both "free" parameters (to be estimated from the data) and "fixed" parameters (usually set at zero or one) are considered simultaneously (Jöreskog, 1973; McDonald, 1978). The nonlinearity of these equations can be seen when the inverse of I-D is written equivalently as the Neumann-series sum of increasing powers of D. The condition of nonlinearity does not permit general solutions of closed form, and so numerical methods of "constrained nonlinear optimization" must be used (Chambers, 1977; Lee & Jennrich, 1979). Assuming that identification is adequate, these methods require a complete model specification and starting values for an iterative Newton-based solution, as well as a set of first- and (sometimes) second-order partial derivatives associated with an objective function (F) to be minimized. Bock and Bargmann (1966) provide the necessary matrix calculus rules. However, Jöreskog (1973) and Sörbom (1978) (as well as McDonald, 1978) have derived general equations that become simpler when particular unnecessary model matrices can be eliminated. The required solutions are based on first-order partial derivatives (δ) that can be written as follows:

$$\delta F/\delta D_g = 2Ng(A_g J_g^t B_g J A_g U_g A_g) \qquad (A\text{-}8)$$

$$\delta F/\delta U_g = N_g(A_g J_g^t B_g J_g A_g)$$

where

$$A_g = (I_g - D_g)^{-1}$$

$$B_g = Q_g\,(W_g - W_g)\,Q_g.$$

In this last equation the Q_g is particularly important. This weight matrix Q_g derives from the formulation of Krane and McDonald (1978) and Lee and Jennrich (1979). The utility of the Q_g weight-matrix is realized when one considers the kind of minimization that can be used in obtaining parameter estimates. For example, when $Q_g = I$, an unweighted-least-squares (ULS) solution is obtained; when $Q_g = W_g^{-1}$ (i.e., the inverse of the *observed* W), then the minimization is in accordance with generalized least squares (GLS); when $Q^* = W_g^{-1}$ (i.e., the inverse for the *population* W), a Wishart-based maximum-likelihood (MLW) function is minimized. This illustrates that modeling in general, and thus RAM, need not be tied to any particular estimation method. It also illustrates that the ULS, GLS, and MLW procedures are interrelated. The ULS might be said to be data oriented, while the MLW is population oriented, and GLS is in between. Also, the GLS is asymptotically equivalent to MLW (i.e., the W is a best unbiased sample estimate of population W). A practical value of this relation is that computation is often much cheaper by GLS than by MLW (e.g., because W^{-1} can be calculated once and stored).

Computer algorithms are generally available for most of the kinds of models one can specify with RAM. One of the most popular sets of such algorithms is LISREL-IV (Jöreskog & Sörbom, 1978). Unfortunately, this program permits only MLW estimation by means of the Davidon-Fletcher-Powell methods (also see McDonald, 1978).

Long (1976) presents a model description of LISREL as an expanded algebraic sequence. More typically, this model is presented as a supermatrix containing eight separate parameter matrices that can be written (using LISREL-IV notation) as

$$\sum = E\{[yvar:xvar]^t \, [yvar:xvar]\} = \qquad \text{(A-9)}$$

$$(NI \times NI)$$

$$\begin{bmatrix} (LY)(BE)^{-1}[(GA)(PH)(GA)^t + (PS)](BE)^{-t}(LY)^t & \text{sym} \\ \qquad\qquad\qquad\qquad\qquad\qquad\qquad + (TE) & \\ (LY)(BE)^{-1}(GA)(PH)(LX)^t & (LX)(PH)(LX)^t + (TD) \end{bmatrix}$$

All eight matrices can be given parameters for any number of groups (NG > 0), each possibly involving a different number of observations (NO > 0).

The elements in any of these parameter matrices can be allowed to be (1) fixed—at some specified value, (2) free—to be estimated from the data, or (3) equal—constrained to be the same as one or more other parameters. Any RAM model can be specified for estimation within the LISREL program by setting up a model for only three parameter matrices: fixed LY, free BE, and free PS. To accomplish this, five matrices must be zeroed (ZE) out. This specific RAM to LISREL translation is indicated in the following equalities:

LX = ZE, GA = ZE, TD = ZE, TE = ZE,
    PH = ZE;
LY = J and fixed;
BE = (I − D); and
PS = U; thus leaving only
$\sum$ = $(LY)(BE)^{-1}(PS)(BE)^{-t}(LY)^t$.   (A-10)

Of importance in this translation of LISREL to RAM is the equivalence of RAM and LISREL matrices: Index J is fixed in LY, directed D, is a transformation to BE, and undirected U, is equivalent to PS. The translation of D to BE needs to be done carefully but is straightforward: All off-diagonal d_{ij} parameter signs must be reversed and the main-diagonal d_{ii} parameters must be increased in value by one. This transformation must be done if path values are to be obtained from LISREL calculations.

A RAM formulation need not represent the most economical (of computer time) way to assign parameters to a given problem. A major feature of LISREL-IV is that it breaks up the D matrix (which needs to be inverted) into small and meaningful subsections for which no inversion is necessary. For any given computation problem, the various possibilities for such breakdown should be studied before solution is attempted, in order to achieve good computing efficiency (cf. Jöreskog & Sörbom, 1978). In the analyses presented here, every effort has been made to maximize program efficiency.

RAM Evaluation

As mentioned in the text, there are several ways to evaluate goodness of fit of model to data. One popular statistical procedure is based on the relation between a likelihood ratio and a chi-square (χ^2) distribution. The chi square for the MLW estimation indicated in Equation A-8 can be calculated in terms of the objective function that is minimized; thus

$$\chi^2 = \sum_{g=1}^{G} (N_g - 1)\, F_g. \qquad \text{(A-11)}$$

The evaluation of fit is based on a comparison of gain in information (i.e., lower F values) relative to the number of independent free parameters estimated. Some aspects of this basis for evaluation can be seen in terms of degrees of freedom (df_P) for a specific set of parameters (P):

$$df_P = p_w - [(p_D + p_U) - p_B], \qquad \text{(A-12)}$$

where

$p_w = j(j+1)/2 =$ number of independent parameters in W;
$p_D =$ number of free parameters in D;
$p_U =$ number of free parameters in U;
$p_B =$ number of dependent parameters in both D and U

Thus, df for any model is based on the difference between information available in the data and information required by the model. Asymptotic statistical tests of hypothese are available when the more global alternative P^* is strictly defined as P without specific restrictions. This canonically nested form permits a test of χ^2 difference where

$$\chi_D{}^2 = \chi_P{}^2 - \chi_{P^*}{}^2,$$

and

$$df_D = df_{P*} - df_P, \qquad \text{(A-13)}$$

which is evaluated as a chi-square variate with df_D to test the hypothesis that the $P*$ alternative is significantly better than the P model. One important test here is when the $P*$ equals the most general alternative that $W = $ W. In this case the $df_{P*} = p_w$ and the test is one of overall fit of model to data.

It can be seen that the χ^2 itself (Equation A-11) is partially determined by the sample size, whereas the df (Equation A-12) are not. Therefore, one must take care in setting overall alpha levels (see Horn & Engstrom, 1979, for some guidelines). One indicator that is useful in this regard is the Wilson-Hilferty normal deviate Z-score (see Bishop, Fienberg, & Holland, 1975). Given any χ^2 and df, this statistic is

$$Z = \{(\chi^2/df)^{1/3} - [1 - (2/9\ df)]\} / \{(2/9\ df)^{1/2}\}. \qquad \text{(A-14)}$$

Other procedures for evaluation of fit, such as the metrical variable-sampling, are discussed by Burt (1973), Horn and Engstrom (1979), and Specht (1975). Further research is required to provide guidelines indicating the strengths and weaknesses of these different approaches.

RAM Simulation

As mentioned in the text, RAM provides a convenient set of procedures for simulation of samples of data that correspond to specified parameter sets (as, for example, genuine WAIS data). One way to approach such simulation is to set up a complete RAM model in terms of the M, L, D, and U indicated in Equation A-1. Such a model, whether all parameters are identified or not, yields a specific moment matrix W that can be regarded as the "population." Of course, if all parameters are not identified, the entire structure cannot be recovered in reverse (i.e., from W to D and U). If means and covariances are to be simu-

lated, the k model is used, although the means are removed in obtaining sample data sets for different groups. These are created by applying a triangular factorization procedure (such as that available in the International Mathematical and Statistical Library [1977] GGNRM routine) to the population covariances. When the population means are included, the data should have the sample distributional properties of the population moment structure (McArdle, 1980).

By applying these general procedures to a specific problem, the WAIS data of the present study were generated as follows:

1. A complete RAM model was created for each cohort group using a higher order conception of G_f/G_c theory (see pp. 522–527).

2. The covariance and means from this model were calculated for 33 variables for each cohort, and scores having desired distribution properties were simulated for 500 subjects in each cohort.

3. Variables were made comparable to WAIS standard scores by forcing raw scores within appropriate bounds, rounding to the nearest integer, and then using the overall raw-to-standard-score translation tables (Wechsler, 1955).

4. Full-scale IQ scores (F) were calculated, and a selection mechanism was put into effect to simulate attrition: The lowest 20% of F scores were eliminated for all ages, and the top 10% were also eliminated from the early ages (20, 30, and 40).

5. The final data used in analyses were for three groups ($N = 160$, $N = 128$, and $N = 80$) and 33 measures. These data are available on request.

6. This simulation has not been verified in entirety owing to the horrendous CPU problems of evaluating the full model in LISREL-IV. However, some tests of interest were performed. For example, the scores for the initial $N = 500$ (before boundary, rounding, and selection conditions were imposed) were fitted to the true measurement model with a nonidentifiable, nonconvergent outcome of $\chi^2 = 5.6$ ($Z = .7$). Other similarity checks to real WAIS data are described in the text.

REFERENCES

Adam, J. Statistical bias in cross-sequential studies of aging. *Experimental Aging Research*, 1977, *3*, 325–333.

Anderson, T. W., & Rubin, H. Statistical inference in factor analysis. In J. Neyman (Ed.), *Proceedings of the Third Berkeley Symposium on Mathematical Statistics and*

Probability. Berkeley: University of California Press, 1956.

Baltes, P. B. Longitudinal and cross-sectional sequences in the study of age and generation effects. *Human Development*, 1968, *11*, 145–171.

Baltes, P. B., & Schaie, K. W. On the plasticity of intelligence in adulthood and old age: Where Horn and Donaldson fail. *American Psychologist*, 1976, *31*, 720–725.

Bentler, P. M. The interdependence of theory, methodology, and empirical data: Causal modeling as an approach to construct validation. In D. B. Kandel (Ed.), *Longitudinal research on drug abuse: Empirical findings and methodological issues.* New York: Wiley, 1978.

Bentler, P. M. & Weeks, D. G. Interrelations among models for the analysis of moment structures. *Multivariate Behavioral Research*, 1979, *14*, 169–186.

Birren, J. E., & Morrison, D. F. Analysis of WAIS subtests in relation to age and education. *Journal of Gerontology*, 1961, *16*, 363–369.

Bishop, Y. M. M., Fienberg, S. E., & Holland, P. W. *Discrete multivariate analysis: Theory and Practice.* Cambridge, Mass.: MIT Press, 1975.

Bock, R. D. Components of variance analysis as a structural and discriminal analysis for psychological tests. *British Journal of Statistical Psychology*, 1960, *13* (Pt. 2), 151–163.

Bock, R. D., & Bargmann, R. E. Analysis of covariance structures. *Psychometrika*, 1966, *31*, 507–533.

Botwinick, J. *Aging and behavior.* New York: Springer, 1978.

Botwinick, J., & Arenberg, D. Disparate time-spans in sequential studies of aging. *Experimental Aging Research*, 1976, *2*, 55–61.

Box, G. E. P. Some theorems on quadratic forms applied to the study of analysis of variance problems. II. Effects on inequality of variance and of correlation between errors in the two-way classification. *Annals of Mathematical Statistics*, 1954, *25*, 484–498.

Burt, R. S. Confirmatory factor-analytic structures and the theory construction process. *Sociological Methods and Research*, 1973, *2*, 131–190.

Buss, A. R. An extension of developmental models that separate ontogenetic and cohort differences. *Psychological Bulletin*, 1973, *80*, 466–479.

Cattell, R. B. *Personality and motivation structure and measurement.* New York: World Books, 1957.

Cattell, R. B. Higher order factor structures and reticular vs. hierarchical formulae for their interpretation. In C. Banks and P. L. Broadhurst (Eds.), *STEPANOS: Studies in psychology.* New York: Barnes & Noble, 1966.

Cattell, R. B. Separating endogenous, exogenous, ecogenic, and epogenic component curves in developmental data. *Developmental Psychology*, 1970, *3*, 151–162.

Cattell, R. B. *Abilities: Their structure, growth and action.* Boston: Houghton Miffin, 1971.

Cattell, R. B. *The scientific use of factor analysis in behavioral and life sciences.* New York: Plenum Press, 1978.

Cattell, R. B., & Horn, J. L. A cross-social check on the theory of fluid and crystallized intelligence with discovery of new valid subtest designs. *Journal of Educational Measurement*, 1978, *15*, 139–164.

Chambers, J. M. *Computational methods for data analysis.* New York: Wiley, 1977.

Cohen, J. A factor analytically based rationale for the Wechsler Adult Intelligence Scale. *Journal of Consulting Psychology*, 1957, *21*, 451–457.

Cohen, J., & Cohen, P. *Applied multiple regression/correlation analysis for the behavioral sciences.* New York: Wiley, 1975.

Donaldson, G. *On the formulation, estimation, and testing of a developmental model of human abilities specifying age, cohort, and time parameters.* Unpublished doctoral dissertation, University of Denver, Dept. of Psychology, May 1979.

Donaldson, G., & Horn, J. L. *Logical and inferential problems in the analysis of developmental change.* Unpublished manuscript, University of Denver, Department of Psychology, 1978.

Doppelt, J. E., & Wallace, W. L. Standardization of the Wechsler Adult Intelligence Scale for older persons. *Journal of Abnormal and Social Psychology*, 1955, *51*, 312–330.

Finifter, B. M. The generation of confidence: Evaluating research findings by random subsample replication. In H. L. Costner (Ed.), *Sociological methodology, 1972,* San Francisco: Jossey-Bass, 1972.

Goldberger, A. S. Structural equation models: An overview. In A. S. Goldberger and O. D. Duncan (Eds.), *Structural equation models in the social sciences.* New York: Seminar Press, 1973.

Guilford, J. P. *The nature of human intelligence.* New York: McGraw-Hill, 1967.

Guilford, J. P. Rotation problems in factor analysis. *Psychological Bulletin*, 1974, *81*, 495–501.

Guttman, L. The radex: A new approach to factor analysis. In P. Lazersfeld (Ed.), *Mathematical thinking in the social sciences.* New York: Columbia University Press, 1954.

Harris, R. J. The invalidity of partitioned-U tests in canonical correlation and multivariate analysis of variance. *Multivariate Behavioral Research*, 1976, *11*, 353–356.

Hempel, C. G. Fundamentals of concept formation in empirical science. In *International encyclopedia of united science* (Vol. 2). Chicago: University of Chicago Press, 1952.

Horn, J. L. Equations representing combinations of components in scoring psychological variables. *Acta Psychologica*, 1963, *21*, 184–217.

Horn, J. L. A rationale and test for the number of factors in factor analysis. *Psychometrika*, 1965, *30*, 179–185.

Horn, J. L. On subjectivity in factor analysis. *Educational and Psychological Measurement*, 1967, *27*, 811–820.

Horn, J. L. Organization of data on life-span development of human abilities. In L. R. Goulet and P. B. Baltes (Eds.), *Life-span developmental psychology.* New York: Academic Press, 1970.

Horn, J. L. Personality and ability theory. In R. B. Cattell and R. M. Dreger (Eds.), *Handbook of modern personality theory.* Washington D.C.: Hemisphere, 1977.

Horn, J. L. Human ability systems. In P. B. Baltes (Ed.), *Life-span development and behavior.* New York: Academic Press, 1978. (a)

Horn, J. L. The nature and development of intellectual

abilities. In R. T. Osborne, C. E. Noble, & N. Weyl (Eds.), *Human variation: The biopsychology of age, race, and sex*. New York: Academic Press, 1978. (b)

Horn, J. L. Some correctable defects in research on intelligence. *Intelligence*, 1979, *3*, 307–322.

Horn, J. L. Concepts of intelligence in relation to learning and adult development. *Intelligence*, in press.

Horn, J. L., & Donaldson, G. On the myth of intellectual decline in adulthood. *American Psychologist*, 1976, *31*, 701–709.

Horn, J. L., & Donaldson, G. Faith is not enough: A response to the Baltes-Schaie claim that intelligence does not wane. *American Psychologist*, 1977, *32*, 369–373.

Horn, J. L., & Donaldson, G. Cognitive development. II: Adulthood development of human abilities. In O. G. Brim & J. Kagan (Eds.), *Constancy and change in human development: A volume of review essays*. Cambridge, Mass.: Harvard University Press, 1980.

Horn, J. L., & Engstrom, R. Cattell's scree test in relation to Bartlett's chi-square test and other observations on the number of factors problem. *Multivariate Behavioral Research*, 1979, *14*, 283–300.

Horn, J. L., & Knapp, J. R. On the subjective character of the empirical base of Guilford's structure-of-intellect model. *Psychological Bulletin*, 1973, *80*, 33–43.

Horn, J. L., & Knapp, J. R. Thirty wrongs do not make a right: A reply to Guilford. *Psychological Bulletin*, 1974, *81*, 502–504.

Humphreys, L. G. Doing research the hard way: Substituting analysis of variance for a problem in correlational analysis. *Journal of Educational Psychology*, 1978, *70*, 873–876.

International Mathematical and Statistical Library. *International mathematical and statistical library* (Vol. 6). Houston, Texas: Author, 1977.

Jackson, D. *A reformation of Schaie's model of developmental change*. Unpublished manuscript, 1976.

Jordan, L. A. Linear structural relations, longitudinal data, and the cross-lag idea. In *Proceedings of the Business and Economics Section, American Statistical Association*. Washington, D.C.: American Statistical Association, August 1978.

Jöreskog, K. G. Testing a simple structure hypothesis in factor analysis. *Psychometrika*, 1966, *31*, 165–178.

Jöreskog, K. G. A general method for estimating a linear structural equation system. In A. S. Goldberger and O. D. Duncan (Eds.), *Structural equation models in the social sciences*. New York: Seminar Press, 1973.

Jöreskog, K. G., & Sörbom, D. Statistical models and methods for analysis of longitudinal data. In D. J. Aigner and A. S. Goldberger (Eds.), *Latent variables in socio-economic models*. Amsterdam: North-Holland, 1977.

Jöreskog, K. G., & Sörbom, D. *LISREL-IV: Analysis of linear structural relationships by the method of maximum likelihood*. Chicago: National Educational Resources, 1978.

Kaiser, H. F. Review of Lawley and Maxwell's "Factor analysis as a statistical method." *Educational and Psychological Measurement*, 1976, *36*, 586–588.

Kangas, J., & Bradway, K. Intelligence at middle age: A thirty-eight year follow-up. *Developmental Psychology*, 1971, *5*, 333–337.

Kenny, D. A. *Correlation and causality*. New York: Wiley, 1979.

Krane, W. R., & McDonald, R. P. Scale invariance and the factor analysis of correlation matrices. *British Journal of Mathematical Statistical Psychology*, 1978, *31*, 218–228.

Lee, S. Y., & Jennrich, R. I. A study of algorithms for covariance structure analysis with specific comparisons using factor analysis. *Psychometrika*, 1979, *44*, 99–113.

Long, J. S. Estimation and hypothesis testing in linear models containing measurement error. *Sociological Methods and Research*, 1976, *5*, 157–206.

Margenau, H. *The nature of physical reality*. New York: McGraw-Hill, 1950.

Mason, K., Masson, M., Winsborough, H., & Poole, K. Some methodological issues in cohort analysis of archival data. *American Sociological Review*, 1973, *38*, 242–258.

Matarazzo, J. D. *Wechsler's measurement and appraisal of adult intelligence* (5th ed.). Baltimore: Williams & Wilkins, 1972.

McArdle, J. J. A structural view of longitudinal repeated measures. In *Proceedings of the Social Sciences Section, American Statistical Association*. Washington, D.C.: American Statistical Association, 1978.

McArdle, J. J. The development of general multivariate software. In *Proceedings of the Association for the Development of Computer-Based Instructional Systems*. Akron, Ohio: University of Akron Press, 1979.

McArdle, J. J. Causal modeling applied to psychonomic systems simulation. *Behavioral Research Methods and Instrumentation*, 1980, *12*, 193–209.

McArdle, J. J. & McDonald, R. P. *A simple algebraic representation for moment structures*. Manuscript submitted for publication, 1980.

McDonald, R. P. A simple comprehensive model for the analysis of covariance structures. *British Journal of Mathematical Statistical Psychology*, 1978, *31*, 59–72.

McDonald, R. P. The structural analysis of multivariate data: A sketch of a general theory. *Multivariate Behavioral Research*, 1979, *14*, 21–28.

McFatter, R. The use of structural equation models in interpreting regression equations including suppressor and enhancer variables. *Applied Psychological Measurement*, 1979, *3*, 123–135.

Meredith, W. Notes on factorial invariance. *Psychometrika*, 1964, *29*, 177–185.

Meredith, W. *Factor analytic and principal components approaches to longitudinal/repeated measures data*. Paper presented at a University of Denver Colloquium, June 1979.

Nesselroade, J. R. Application of multivariate strategies to problems of measuring and structuring long-term change. In L. R. Goulet & P. B. Baltes (Eds.), *Life-span developmental psychology: Research and theory*. New York: Academic Press, 1970.

Nesselroade, J. R. Notes on the "longitudinal factor analysis" model. *Psychometrika*, 1972, *37*, 187–191.

Nesselroade, J. R. Issues in studying developmental change in adults from a multivariate perspective. In J. E. Birren & K. W. Schaie (Eds.), *Handbook of the psychology of aging*. New York: Van Nostrand Reinhold, 1977.

Osborne, R. T., & Lindsey, J. M. A longitudinal investigation of changes in the factorial compositions of intelligence with age in young school children. *Journal of Genetic Psychology*, 1967, *110*, 49–58.

Radcliffe, J. A. WAIS factorial structure and factor scores for ages 18 to 54. *Australian Journal of Psychology*, 1966, *18*, 229–238.

Rock, D. A., Werts, C. E., & Flaugher, R. L. The use of analysis of covariance structures for comparing the psychometric properties of multiple variables across populations. *Multivariate Behavioral Research*, 1978, *13*, 403–418.

Royce, J. R., & Buss, A. R. The role of general systems and information theory in multi-factor individuality theory. *Canadian Psychological Review*, 1976, *17*, 1–21.

Rozeboom, W. W. *General Linear Dynamic Analysis (GLDA)*. Paper presented at a University of Denver Colloquium, December 1978.

Saris, W. E., dePijper, M., & Zewaart, P. Detection of specification errors in linear structural equation models. In K. F. Schuessler (Ed.), *Sociological methodology*. San Francisco: Jossey Bass, 1978.

Schaie, K. W. A general model for the study of developmental problems. Psychological Bulletin, 1965, *64*, 92–107.

Schaie, K. W. Methodological problems in descriptive developmental research on adulthood and aging. In J. R. Nesselroade, & H. W. Reese (Eds.), *Life-span developmental psychology: Methodological issues*. New York: Academic Press, 1973.

Schaie, K. W. Quasi-experimental research designs in the psychology of aging. In J. E. Birren, & K. W. Schaie (Eds.), *Handbook of the psychology of aging*. New York: Van Nostrand Reinhold, 1977.

Scheifley, V. M., & Schmidt, W. H. Analysis of repeated measures data: A simulation study. *Multivariate Behavioral Research*, 1978, *13*, 347–362.

Schmidt, F. L., & Crano, W. D. A test of the theory of fluid and crystallized intelligence in middle and low-socioeconomic-status children: A cross-lagged panel analysis. *Journal of Educational Psychology*, 1974, *66*, 255–261.

Siegler, I. C., & Botwinick, J. A long-term longitudinal study of intellectual ability of older adults: The matter of selective subject attrition. *Journal of Gerontology*, 1979, *34*, 242–245.

Sörbom, D. Detection of correlated errors in longitudinal data. *British Journal of Mathematical and Statistical Psychology*, 1975, *28*, 138–151.

Sörbom, D. An alternative to the methodology for analysis of covariance. *Psychometrika*, 1978, *43*, 381–396.

Specht, D. A. On the evaluation of causal models. *Social Science Research*, 1975, *4*, 113–133.

Suppes, P. *A probabilistic theory of causality*. Amsterdam: North-Holland, 1970.

Underwood, B. J. Individual differences as a crucible in theory construction. *American Psychologist*, 1975, *30*, 128–134.

Urban, H. B. The concept of development from a systems perspective. In P. B. Baltes (Ed.), *Life-span development and behavior*. New York: Academic Press, 1978.

Van de Geer, J. P. *Introduction to multivariate analysis for the social sciences*. San Francisco: W. H. Freeman, 1971.

Wechsler, D. *Manual for the Wechsler Adult Intelligence Scale*. New York: Psychological Corporation, 1955.

Wold, H. O. A. Path models with latent variables: The NIPALS approach. In H. M. Blalock, A. Aganbegian, F. M. Borodkin, R. Boudon, & V. Capecchi (Eds.), *Quantitative sociology*. New York: Academic Press, 1975.

Wright, S. The method of path coefficients. *Annals of Mathematical Statistics*, 1934, *5*, 161–215.

Iseli K. Krauss

CHAPTER
38

Between- and Within-Group Comparisons in Aging Research

Many of the factors used in controlling unexplained variances in aging research are of interest in themselves. Education, sex, and health variables, for example, may account for other differences obtained among the elderly. Equating young and old groups on these factors is not always appropriate, since women, ill health, and lower levels of education are disproportionately represented in the elderly population. The use of such variables differs according to the research question involved. Past research demonstrated large individual differences within the older adult and elderly populations. These differences, frequently disregarded in aging research, must become a central focus of investigation if we are to understand the aging process.

The necessity for experimental control of extraneous or confounding variables is, of course, critical in all areas of research. Control factors that are routinely incorporated into much psychological research take on special significance in developmental research—significance that is less than perfectly understood and is frequently ignored. The primary purposes of this chapter are to explore several issues relating to the use of control factors in aging research and to suggest ways that may improve the use of these factors. The first part of the chapter contains a discussion of the control factors of sex, education, and health. The second part focuses on age as a control factor and, finally, on the necessity for research directed to the detection of differences within the elderly population and to antecedents and consequences of those differences.

Confounds in Age-Group Comparisons

Investigators who are aware that factors not relevant to their research questions may confound their data take steps to minimize those problems for age-group comparisons. For example, if both sexes are to be included in a study an attempt is made to test equal numbers of men and women. When health factors are pertinent, subjects are screened for the presence of health problems that might obscure findings of central interest. Education is often "controlled for" by equating education levels of young and old groups. But although demographic, health, and other factors are routinely incorporated into studies of aging, their use may present unacknowledged risks of experimental error. Once we understand the implications of the use of each of these factors, we may consider how to use them most effectively.

Common to these specific control factors is an intriguing notion concerning research questions. It is important to distinguish between research questions for which the central concern involves comparisons between the sexes, between groups of people with a particular, specified level of education, or between groups

This work was supported in part by NIMH Grant 1 RO1 MH29277 and was completed while the author was Visiting Research Fellow at Princeton University. The author would like to thank Joachim F. Wohlwill for his insightful comments on an earlier draft.

of people with specified health histories and research questions for which these variables, though largely irrelevant, may influence the findings. Current use does not usually distinguish between these types of research questions. The importance of using these control factors appropriately, depending on the nature of the research question asked, is discussed separately for each of the three control factors under consideration.

Differential Representation of Sexes

A common complaint among graduate students is the difficulty of finding elderly male research subjects. Small wonder, since there is a higher proportion of women than men at all adult ages, and this differential is still greater in the elderly population (Botwinick, 1978; Hendricks & Hendricks, 1977). An experimental design incorporating equal numbers of old and young men and women does not reflect accurately the proportions of men and women in the respective age groups. Furthermore, the older women may be healthier than the men of the same age, and thus more willing to participate in the research and perhaps able to perform at a higher level than those men who do volunteer. That is, a smaller proportion of available men may volunteer because of health problems and those who do participate may be in poorer health than the women. If sex differences in particular abilities or attributes are the primary concerns of the research, then equal numbers of males and females may quite reasonably be tested. The issue in that case is whether in the existing population of older men and women, there are sex differences in the incidence of particular attributes. If, however, the question concerns only an age difference in attributes and the sex differences are incidental, proportions of males and females representing the respective proportions in the population might better be included. Statistical analyses would, unfortunately, become more complex, but the results would be more representative of true age differences, or lack of differences, in the general population on the issue in question.

Health Status Differences

Health factors are even more complex to consider. Even the simplest screening procedures are likely to eliminate more older than younger potential subjects. For instance, fewer young people would have difficulty demonstrating 20/20 or 20/40 vision with or without glasses. Of course the research participants have to be able to see the stimuli, but the more screening procedures employed and the more stringent the criteria, the

less likely is the successful group to represent the general elderly population. Admittedly, most studies with rigorous health screening procedures are clearly directed toward the unrepresentative group of exceptionally healthy elderly, and no assertions are made that the results of such studies can be generalized to the larger population (Botwinick & Birren, 1963). This is also true for studies involving individuals selected precisely because they have a particular health problem, although in such studies it is the younger group that is less likely to be representative of the larger population. Obviously researchers must screen out potential research participants who cannot see the stimuli, who are not able to perform motor components of the research task, or who are unable to concentrate because of illness or pain. But if the same researchers could also modify their procedures so that a larger proportion of the elderly population could participate in the research, the findings would apply for larger numbers of elderly adults.

Education Differences

Equating age groups for education presents somewhat different, but no less serious, problems. No standard exists for assigning levels of education for individuals with irregular educational histories. Courses taken during adult years, technical training, professional training, and training during military service all present problems for reliable assignment of individuals to educational categories or levels. It is also unclear whether years of education or highest level of education attained is the more appropriate educational index. Fifty years ago, a physician was out on his—and occasionally her—own after 12 years of primary and secondary school plus as few as 2 years of undergraduate work and 3 to 4 years of medical school and internship. Current training procedures require considerably greater expenditure of time, perhaps as long as 23 or 25 years. Even comparing contemporary college graduates may present problems, since diplomas from different institutions or programs within a single institution may not represent equivalent educational attainment.

An even more complex predicament is presented by educational comparisons between the young and the elderly simply because a lower proportion of the elderly than of the young were highly educated. These educational differences do not necessarily reflect differences in aptitude for academic achievement but, rather, social class and economic differences and changes in accessibility or attitude toward education over the past half century. Comparing college graduates of 1979 to college graduates of 1929 may be extremely misleading if social class and economic conditions are not taken into account. Selecting subjects on the basis of equal years of education will result in a highly select group of elderly, if the criterion is high, or in narrowly selected group of young subjects, if the criterion is low. In order for research findings relating education and subsequent measures of performance to have meaning, the educational attainment variable should be much more carefully defined.

As a first step in reducing the error in the use of the education variable in aging research, I would suggest a regularization in the assignment of educational levels. Quite arbitrarily we may make the decision to increase the possibility of either overestimating or underestimating educational attainment. Once we have made that decision, we should be as consistent as possible in estimating how much education the subjects have completed. My own preference is to risk overestimating, since older people may have accumulated a great deal of experience outside educational institutions that younger people may have absorbed in an educational setting. Many skills that were previously learned through apprentice programs are now taught through academic institutions of one sort of another. For example, training for woodworking, for auto mechanics, for artistic expression, and for several professions is provided through degree-granting institutions. Since the training represented by educational degrees and certificates is constantly changing and is increasingly accessible to a higher proportion of the population, I propose that the elderly be given maximum credit for any education they have obtained. A person with a sixth-grade education and 2 full years of community college courses should be considered to have an educational level equivalent to 14 rather than 8 years. Years of technical training should be considered equivalent to years of academic training for research purposes, unless academic or technical training per se is of particular interest. Kindergarten and nursery school attendance should not be included in the calculations for years of education, since in the past children attended such classes only if their parents could afford the tuition fees or if because of child care needs, they had to afford them. Since preschool education is a relatively new phenomonon in this country, including those years would maximize the chances of confounding social class, generation, and education. If these suggested basic guidelines are followed by a significant number of researchers, at least arbitrary uniformity will be achieved and results from study to study will be more comparable.

Again, as with the health factor, if the research question is directed toward comparisons of young and old individuals having particular educational attainments, such as high-school graduates, university faculty, and so on, there should be no problems in interpreting the data. However if it is desirable to generalize the results to the population at large and the years-of-education variable is not of immediate concern, matching groups for educational level may not be appropriate. In that case, the optimal research design might include people in two or more age groups who have reached the median level of education for their own age groups. This procedure would vastly increase the problems in obtaining large samples, and I doubt that most researchers will give it serous consideration. But serious consideration should certainly be given to the implications of generalizing from results based on two or more age groups "controlled for education" on the basis of equivalent educational levels.

Sex, health, and education are not the only factors that should be considered in equating groups in aging research, but they illustrate the complexity involved in making comparisons among age groups. Researchers would be well advised to avoid the casual use of such factors in their understandable desire to appear to be meeting rigorous experimental standards.

Individual Differences

Between-Age Comparisons

There is a strong view in the field of aging that the best research design is one in which the performance of an elderly group on a measure of interest is compared with the performance of a young group on the same measure. The primary question in the field is "How do the old differ from the young?" The young group is seen as a standard against which the older group is to be compared. With few exceptions, the older group is expected to perform less well than the younger group. Even in training studies, the aim is to increase the performance of the elderly as nearly as possible to the level of the young. In studies in which old and young subjects are compared, obtained performance differences have been attributed to the difference in ages of the two groups. Such studies have usually demonstrated that old people are less intelligent than young people (Wechsler, 1958); that their reaction times are slower (Welford, 1977); that they are poorer problem solvers (Storck, Looft, & Hooper, 1972), have worse memories (Arenberg, 1973), and so on. By relying on comparisons between age groups, investigators reinforce any existing impressions that old people form a homogeneous population whose members differ consistently from members of younger populations. Differences within the elderly groups are treated as noise, as error variance, as random, and as unimportant (Shen, 1942). Factors other than age, however, have been found to contribute to the performance differences between the young and the elderly. For instance, there is a large and growing literature indicating that generational differences (Schaie, 1974, 1979) may explain in part why old and young people differ so widely on measures of intellectual abilities. The factors discussed above—sex, health, and education—have also been shown to be related to age differences in ability (Hertzog, Schaie, & Gribbin, 1978; Tesch, Whitbourne, & Nehrke, 1978; Young, 1971).

Within-Age Comparisons

A small but determined group of investigators asserts that differences among the elderly present research questions of great interest and importance. In many cases the differences found within the elderly population exceed the differences found between the young and the elderly (Sheppard, 1977). These researchers argue that it is extremely valuable to the growth of our knowledge of aging to understand how large numbers of people have maintained or increased their abilities while many others have shown decremental changes in one or several areas. Comparisons between the successful and the less successful aged on factors associated with maintenance of abilities should provide insight into the etiology of many of the detrimental effects of aging.

Titchener (1910), in a lecture delivered in 1909 on the occasion of the 20th anniversary of the opeining of Clark University, stated that "individual psychology . . . furnishes the key to many otherwise inexplicable differences of result, and it promises to allay many of the standing controversies of the textbooks; there can be no doubt that it will play a part of steadily increasing importance in the immediate future" (pp. 418–419). Perhaps individual differences provided a primary focus for research interest in Titchener's immediate future, but the same cannot be said for our immediate past.

Not even the strong tradition in psychological testing adequately considers within-age group comparisons. Leaders in the testing field have made general statements stressing the importance of investigating individual differences, and unless one were to read beyond the general statements, one might be led to believe that such investigations had become commonplace immediately after the appearance of that particular publication. In 1942 Shen pointed out that psychologists are generally interested in the effects of a

particular treatment on subsequent behavior and treat individual differences as "an unfortunate source of error to be eliminated as far as possible" (p. 261). Anastasi (1958) pleaded the cause of "differential psychology" by stating that an understanding of individual differences in behavior would lead to a clarification of the "basic mechanisms of behavior." But as is common in the testing field, she considered age as a grouping factor, so the old are compared to the young just as males are compared to females and rural dwellers are compared to urban dwellers. Anastasi did mention that individuals should be thought of as belonging to several groups that intersect, but her overall emphasis was not consistent with that approach.

Horrocks (1964) reminded us that if it were not for individual differences, we would need to measure only one individual. Although Willerman's book (1979) discusses both individual and group differences, a major section concerns group comparisons for sex, age, and racial differences on a number of variables. An exception to the psychometric tradition of using age as a grouping variable appeared in the recent volume on assessment instruments for the elderly. Ernst and Ernst (1978) contend that chronological age obscures individual differences. By making such a statement they imply that age is not a valid predictor of individual variations in behavior.

Another tradition with a more theoretical emphasis has evolved within the area of individual differences. Cronbach (1957), Emmerich (1968), and Wohlwill (1970, 1973) have written extensively on the topic. According to Cronbach, experimental methodology is primarily useful in controlling or at least accounting for individual differences so that causation may be determined. Correlational techniques, according to Cronbach, were devised for the study of what "man has never learned to control or can never control." (p. 672). Cronbach believed that correlational methods were most useful in studying differences among individuals and "experimental psychology" was useful in investigations of differences among treatments. His main point was that *only* with intervention is it possible to demonstrate causation. In another context Kempthorne made the same point, just as emphatically, in 1978. Baltes and Nesselroade (1973) stated in contradiction that with the advent of multivariate techniques, the choice of experimental or correlational designs is less mandated by the distinction between individual differences and treatment than by subject matter and preference of the investigator.

Emmerich (1968) provided a somewhat different analysis, equally relevant to the study of aging. After identifying classical development analysis as being based on an invariant sequence of stages appearing at different rates for individuals, he distinguished between differential and ipsative analyses. Using the differential approach, an investigator may chart changes in differences among individuals along several attributes. The ipsative approach permits the investigator to follow intraindividual changes in organization of attributes over time. Hoyer (1974) presented several convincing arguments for the use of the ipsative approach.

Wohlwill (1973), in a thorough analysis of behavioral-developmental methodology, distinguished between two conceptual approaches to the study of individual differences. Individual differences may be seen either as deviations or variations around a common pattern of development or as the central focus, tracing the development of the differences themselves. In a further distinction within the latter approach, individuals can be compared according to group characteristics such as sex, intellectual level, or socioeconomic level, or alternatively, interrelations among the variables themselves may be scrutinized and followed over time (Wohlwill, 1970, 1973).

If we consider age as a group characteristic and compare the elderly to the young, the research based on that premise falls squarely within one of Wohlwill's definitions of individual-difference research, for in some respects a chronological age variable is not different from years-of-education or health variables. We cannot assign an individual to an age group younger than the number of years lived, nor can we assign a highly educated person to a sixth-grade level or a person in poor health to a healthy category. It is true that we may be able to raise some of the less highly educated people to higher levels and some of the sick people to healthier levels (I will omit the possibility of making well people ill). But we do not have the freedom of assigning individuals to education or health categories at our whim or for experimental convenience. Age is not precisely commensurate with education and health as a variable, however. So far, we are not able to modify age in either direction. Nevertheless, following Wohlwill's reasoning if not his predisposition, assignment to groups by age is not entirely inappropriate in the study of individual differences. And so we are back to the distinction with which we began—Research in aging may focus on group comparisons or on individual comparisons, and what one person calls a grouping characteristic, others may call an individual characteristic.

More technical questions of design and analysis for investigation of individual differences have been presented by Nesselroade (1970), Wohlwill (1973), Baltes and Nesselroade (1973), Nunnally (1973), and Hoyer (1974), among others, and Tyler (1974) has compared several methodologies.

Variability Within and Between Age Groups

In a discussion of variability and age, Wohlwill (1973) stated that increasing differentiation accompanies increasing age, but differentiation is greater for some people than for others. That is, specific skills develop at different rates within each individual, and the discrepancy in the rates of development of several skills may be compared among individuals. From that perspective intraindividual differences contribute to increasing interindividual differences. The expected increase in standard deviations is not always found, however, as Wohlwill demonstrated with longitudinal data originally published by Kagan and his colleagues (Kagan, Rosman, Day, Albert, & Phillips, 1964), in which standard deviations decreased with age for children and adolescents.

Wohlwill contended that intersubject variability is largely ignored, even as a methodological topic. Certainly its implications for data analysis are underplayed if not ignored. On the other hand, more significance may be accorded to an apparent increase in variance than is warranted by closer inspection of the data. Since variability is frequently correlated positively with test scores, it is difficult to be certain that an increase in variability accompanying age is not due to an artifact of the scale. For instance, a particular test may fail to distinguish among individuals at the lower end of the distribution, resulting in an artificial limit to the variability among scores. But since ability levels increase more rapidly in some individuals than in others, the group mean score will increase and so will the variance. Had the scale provided for a wider range of scores at the lower end, the original variance would have been greater and the subsequent increase in apparent group variance would have been less pronounced. This particular possibility should not present an insurmountable difficulty in aging research, since there is considerable evidence that although mean levels of performance may drop for the elderly as a group, variance remains high. This point is demonstrated below with data from the current literature.

In discussing performance variance in aging research, we may consider overlapping variability between young and old groups or variability among the elderly themselves. Although neither has been a prominent topic, both are occasionally brought to our attention. Anastasi (1958) compared three early cross-sectional studies in which ages varied from 10 to 60 and 10 to 80 (Jones & Conrad, 1933; Miles & Miles, 1932; Wechsler, 1944) and found that in all three, variance within each age group was large and individual differences tended to increase with age. She noted that there was a great deal of performance overlap among widely spread age groups.

In a study published by Sward (1945), performance on several indexes of intellectual abilities was compared for young and old men. For all subtests, except word meanings, performance of the two groups was significantly different. Sward made several interesting comparisons showing that although a high percentage of the older subjects performed at a level comparable to the lowest quartile of younger men, many older men performed at high levels. Nearly 80% of the older group scored at or above the median of the young on a synonyms and antonyms test. The remaining figures range from a low of 4.6% for the symbol-digit subtest to 39.8% for the word-meanings subtest. Sward pointed out that large individual differences were evident on every test. Using an index of relative variability of $(100\ SD)/M$, he demonstrated 30%–50% higher variability in the scores of the older men. He concluded, after considering several other explanations, that old age does lower the ability to perform well on some tests of mental ability for some men, and that variability increases with age.

Demonstrating variability among the elderly or young–old performance overlap from the current literature is not as easy as it could be. Few articles include standard deviation or variance figures. Furthermore, each experimental design permits its own variance comparisons. Though no single study can explain any aspect of the aging process completely, some studies come closer to that goal than others. Cross-sectional studies, the most prevalent, provide the least definitive answers to our questions directed toward the detection of age-related changes, and variance information in cross-sectional investigations is generally ignored or less than fully explored. Studies of elderly populations offer a second approach toward investigating behaviors associated with aging. Specific cognitive, health, personality, or other factors are used to predict successful or less successful performance on other measures of behavior. While cross-sectional studies are confounded by cohort differences, within-age studies are confounded by lifelong differences. Differences in performance at age 70 may be less at age 20. Longitudinal studies of the elderly, the next step, demonstrate change or stability over time, the relation between the current state and earlier predictor variables, and the change among variables over time. Sequential designs involving longitudinal studies of several age groups over time (Schaie, 1977) provide all of the information of the less complex investigations plus the extremely important dimension of long-term differential change among age groups. Of course adding new groups at each age at each time of testing (Schaie, 1977) allows for all of the analyses of the designs lower in the hierarchy and for the added benefit of cohort analyses.

To illustrate the infrequency with which variance among the elderly and performance overlap between the young and the elderly are considered, all of the articles in the Psychological Sciences Section of the first four issues of Volume 39 of the *Journal of Gerontology* were examined. The animal studies were excluded, and the remaining articles were then grouped by the design of the study and were examined for evidence of performance variance among the elderly or between the young and the elderly, of large overlap in scores of the young and the old, or of relatively larger variance among the elderly than among the young. Few of the articles examined included variance information, even for purely methodological reasons.

Cross-sectional studies. Of the 15 articles using a cross-sectional design, one reported that intergroup variance assumptions were met (Ford, Hink, Hopkins, Roth, Pfefferbaum, & Kopell, 1979), and one discussed homogeneity-of-variance assumptions for the particular analysis employed (Watson, Turpenoff, Kelly, & Botwinick, 1979). Five other articles using cross-sectional design indicated neither performance overlap nor variance for the two or more age groups. Weiner's (1962) often-quoted and reassuring opinion of the robustness of analysis of variance and the small risk attendant on violating homogeneity-of-variance assumptions may provide justification for omitting variance data. Without those data, however, rich source of information is lost.

Nine studies included wider age ranges for older groups than for younger groups; the widest differential was a 4-year span for the youngest group and a 24-year span for the oldest group, though several others approached it. Only three studies had equal age ranges in all groups, and one study had no information on age ranges. Unfortunately none of the three articles reporting studies with equal age ranges included variance data, although one study (described later) had nearly equal age ranges and did present variance data (Jacewicz & Hartley, 1979). Given this information, generalizations about age differences in variability may result more from unequal age ranges than from true age differences in intragroup variability.

As Shen (1942) pointed out, "Any two sources of variation may be, of course, legitimately compared and the ratio of their variances tested for significance, provided one knows exactly what is being done" (p. 262). It should follow that we may compare the variances of performance on relevant measures for young and older groups to determine whether the older individuals differ more among themselves than do the younger ones. The variance ratios may then be tested for one-tailed significance with the appropriate degrees of freedom. Four of the articles question were based on cross-sectional designs and reported variance data. These four studies provide fascinating evidence on variability.

Jacewicz and Hartley (1979) accounted for the lack of a significant difference in reaction time for reversed, rather than regular, spatial stimuli by the presence of a wide range of individual differences. This observation is especially noteworthy, since the age ranges of the older and younger groups were nearly equal. A subsequent variance-ratio analysis did not show age differences in variability, however.

In a study of problem solving and intelligence, Hayslip and Sterns (1979) found no differences between the oldest and youngest of their three age groups on crystallized intelligence, but they found a significant difference on fluid intelligence. Comparing the variances of the two age groups confirms that although they do not differ for crystallized intelligence, there is a significant difference between the group variances on the fluid-intelligence measures. Means and variances on all the problem-solving tasks were significantly higher for the older group. In this study, however the age ranges for the three groups were different, that is, the age range of the oldest group was three time that of the youngest group. Nevertheless it was evident from the performance ranges that there was a great deal of overlap among the groups. On many of the measures at least one individual in the older group performed at the level of the highest performing individuals in the younger group. It would not be entirely correct to conclude from this study that older people performed less well than younger people, even if the group means were significantly different, only that some older people performed less well.

In a study on visual masking, Walsh, Williams, and Hertzog (1979) found reliable age differences in the length of interstimulus interval needed for the subject to escape visual masking, which varied with target duration. But the variances within young and old performance at each target duration form an interesting picture. The ratio between the variances of the two age groups increases with target duration such that while the variances of the two groups are approximately equal at the shortest duration, they differ significantly at the longest duration. The variance of the young group remains fairly stable, with changes in target duration after an initial decrease, but that of the older group increases dramatically. While the reported findings tell us a great deal about differences between the young and the elderly groups, further analyses of the wide differences in performance among the elderly at long target durations could be equally informative about the aging of perceptual processes.

Although not so striking or consistent, Rankin and

Kausler's (1979) study on false recognition showed the same pattern of results with significant differences in variances between the young, middle-aged, and elderly groups at some target durations under some conditions. Investigating the source of the variance among the elderly subjects would be the next logical step in understanding the relation between age and false recognition.

Variance comparisons for these four studies tell us little more than that the elderly differ widely among themselves on several cognitive measures and may differ among themselves more or less than do the young. Studies are obviously called for to investigate the origin of the within-group differences and the rate of change of variance differences.

One cross-sectional study did include an analysis of individual differences. In a study on the discrimination of food odors, Shiffman and Pasternak (1979) used scaling procedures designed to allow for individual comparisons. According to their evidence, the young may be more widely dispersed than the elderly on measures of discrimination of food odors.

Within-group studies of the elderly. Two studies concerned elderly subjects with whom measurements were taken only once. Markides and Martin (1979) found that among the elderly, health and activity were strong predictors of satisfaction with life. Linn and Hunter (1979) found that among the elderly there was a relation between personality variables and perception of age. Using a similar approach Krauss, Quayhagen, and Schaie (1980) tested elderly men and women for differences in performance on several spatial tasks. Far from finding uniformity of performance, we found that elderly persons who had performed at high levels when comparison and test stimuli were presented simultaneously showed a greater performance decrement when the stimuli were presented sequentially than did those who had performed at much lower levels on simultaneous tasks. Although this study is far from a model, it does point the way for useful studies of differences within the elderly population.

Longitudinal studies. Studies designed to document changes in individual differences across time are enormously rich data sources. Longitudinal studies demonstrate age changes in behaviors, whereas cross-sectional studies demonstrate differences between age groups, which may reflect systematic influences of generational differences in education, diet, health, or other factors. Longitudinal studies may also demonstrate changes in interindividual differences across time. Three longitudinal studies, reported in the journal from which the previous examples were drawn, were directed toward the detection of individual differences and examined changes in two or more related variables.

Siegler and Botwinick (1979) found that the more intellectually able returned for testing twice over a 30-year period. Witt and Cunningham (1979) found a relation between cognitive speed and intellectual development. On the basis of their own data, Pierce and Chiriboga (1979) suggested that the relations among variables may change over time because of changes in social conditions or other factors.

In the particular issues of the *Journal of Gerontology* surveyed, there were no articles based on a sequential model, but such articles are well represented in other volumes of that journal and other journals. This level of investigation may be the ideal, but each of the other types of studies has the potential to provide important, relevant, and reliable information on the aging process. Choice of approach depends on pragmatic concerns such as time, available subjects, and funds and personnel. The critical points here are that whatever the design, possible conclusions are limited by the design of choice and no comparisons permitted by the design should be overlooked. Individual-difference information is available in any of the designs discussed above, but change in intraindividual differences, interindividual differences, and intergroup differences may be investigated in longitudinal or sequential rather than cross-sectional or single age-group studies. How the process of aging affects different individuals in different ways over time cannot be determined in a single-testing-session study, yet one that is well-designed can provide information on performance differences related to age differences and individual differences.

Conclusions

If we are to understand the process of aging at anything more than the most general level, we must begin to give closer attention to individual variation in aging and its origins. Promising signs are evident to those who are concerned with individual-difference research. An issue of *Experimental Aging Research* was devoted to an exploration of memory in the elderly, specifically, individual differences and their implications for the development of intervention strategies (Costa & Fozard, 1978; Kahn & Miller, 1978; Poon, Fozard, & Treat, 1978; Treat, Poon, Fozard, & Popkin, 1978). A symposium held at the 1978 meeting of the Gerontological Society was devoted to discussion of a longitudinal study involving cognitive training of older adults, in which individual differences

were of critical importance (chaired by Baltes and Willis). Neimark (1979), in a discussion of formal operations research, presents a convincing argument that not only are individual differences central to an understanding of the development of formal operations, but they interact with tasks and instructions in less than perfectly understood complex ways. Hayslip and Sterns (1979) examined individual differences in the relation between crystallized and fluid intelligence. Several papers presented at the 1979 meetings of the American Psychological Association were devoted to the exploration of individual differences among the elderly and their origins.

Old people are different from each other. Old people may be more different from each other than are young people. Old people may even be more different from each other than they are, as a group, from young people. If these statements are true, they offer several good reasons for investigating differences within the elderly population in our attempts to understand the aging process. Determining the contributing causes of the large individual differences among the elderly will provide valuable information on both the origins of decrements associated with aging and the factors contributing to successful aging. Rather than using variables such as education, health, and sex as control variables, we should be using those and others to determine the causes of differential aging within and among elderly individuals, as well as between the young and the elderly.

REFERENCES

Anastasi, A. *Differential psychology* (3rd ed.). New York: Macmillan, 1958.

Arenberg, D. Cognition and aging: Verbal learning, memory, and problem solving. In C. Eisdorfer & M. P. Lawton (Eds.), *The psychology of adult development and aging.* Washington, D.C.: American Psychological Association, 1973.

Baltes, P. B., & Nesselroade, J. The developmental analysis of individual differences on multiple measures. In J. R. Nesselroade & H. W. Reese (Eds.), *Life-span developmental psychology: Methodological issues.* New York: Academic Press, 1973.

Botwinick, J. *Aging and behavior* (2nd ed.). New York: Springer, 1978.

Botwinick, J., & Birren, J. E. Cognitive processes: Mental abilities and psychomotor responses in healthy aged men. In J. E. Birren, R. N. Butler, S. W. Greenhouse, L. Sokoloff, & M. R. Yarrow (Eds.), *Human aging: A biological and behavioral study.* Washington, D.C.: U.S. Government Printing Office, 1963.

Costa, P. T., Jr., & Fozard, J. L. Remembering the person:

Relations of individual difference variables to memory. *Experimental Aging Research*, 1978, *4*, 291–304.

Cronbach, L. J. The two scientific disciplines of scientific psychology. *American Psychologist*, 1957, *12*, 671–684.

Emmerich, W. Personality development and concepts of structure. *Child Development*, 1968, *39*, 671–690.

Ernst, M., & Ernst, N. S. *Measures of functional capacity. The development of an instrument bank: Assessment of available instruments and measurement scales for the study of aging and the elderly* (Report to the Administration on Aging, Office of Human Development, Department of Health, Education, and Welfare). Kansas City: University of Missouri, Midwest Council for Social Research in Aging, May 1978.

Ford, J. M., Hink, R. F., Hopkins, W. F., Roth, W. T., Pfefferbaum, A., & Kopell, B. S. Age effects on event-related potentials in a selective attention task. *Journal of Gerontology*, 1979, *34*, 388–395.

Hayslip, B., Jr., & Sterns, H. L. Age differences in relationships between crystallized and fluid intelligences and problem solving. *Journal of Gerontology*, 1979, *34*, 404–414.

Hendricks, J., & Hendricks, C. D. *Aging in mass society: Myths and realities*. Cambridge, Mass.: Winthrop, 1977.

Hertzog, C., Schaie, K. W., & Gribbin, K. Cardiovascular disease and changes in intellectual functioning from middle to old age. *Journal of Gerontology*, 1978, *33*, 872–883.

Horrocks, J. E. *Assessment of behavior*. Columbus, Ohio: Charles E. Merrill, 1964.

Hoyer, W. J. Aging as intraindividual change. *Developmental Psychology*, 1974, *10*, 821–826.

Jacewicz, M. M., & Hartley, A. A. Rotation of mental images by young and old college students: The effects of familiarity. *Journal of Gerontology*, 1979, *34*, 396–403.

Jones, H. E., & Conrad, H. S. The growth and decline of intelligence: A study of a homogeneous group between the ages of ten and sixty. *Genetic Psychology Monographs*, 1933, *13*, 223–298.

Kagan, J., Rosman, B. L., Day, D., Albert, J., & Phillips, W. Information processing in the child: Significance of reflective attitudes. *Psychological Monographs*, 1964, *78* (1, Whole No. 578).

Kahn, R. L., & Miller, N. E. Adaptational factors in memory function in the aged. *Experimental Aging Research*, 1978, *4*, 273–289.

Kempthorne, O. Logical, epistemological and statistical aspects of nature-nurture data interpretation. *Biometrics*, 1978, *34*, 1–23.

Krauss, I. K., Quayhagen, M., & Schaie, K. W. Spatial rotation in the elderly: Performance factors. *Journal of Gerontology*, 1980, *35*, 199–206.

Linn, M. W., & Hunter, K. Perception of age in the elderly. *Journal of Gerontology*, 1979, *34*, 46–52.

Markides, K. S., & Martin, H. W. A causal model of life satisfaction among the elderly. *Journal of Gerontology*, 1979, *34*, 86–93.

Miles, C. C., & Miles, W. R. The correlation of intelligence scores and chronological age from early to late maturity. *American Journal of Psychology*, 1932, *44*, 44–78.

Neimark. E. Current status of formal operations research. *Human Development*, 1979, *22*, 60–67.

Nesselroade, J. R. Application of multivariate strategies to problems of measuring and structuring long-term change. In L. R. Goulet & P. B. Baltes (Eds.), *Life-span developmental psychology: Research and theory*. New York: Academic Press, 1970.

Nunnally, J. Research strategies and measurement methods for investigating human development. In J. R. Nesselroade & H. W. Reese (Eds.), *Life-span developmental psychology: Methodological issues*. New York: Academic Press, 1973.

Pierce, R. C., & Chiriboga, D. A. Dimensions of adult self-concept. *Journal of Gerontology*, 1979, *34*, 80–85.

Poon, L. W., Fozard, J. L., & Treat, N. J. From clinical and research findings on memory to intervention programs. *Experimental Aging Research*, 1978, *4*, 235–253.

Rankin, J. L., & Kausler, D. H. Adult age differences in false recognitions. *Journal of Gerontology*, 1979, *34*, 58–65.

Schaie, K. W. Translations in gerontology— From lab to life: Intellectual functioning. *American Psychologist*, 1974, *29*, 802–807.

Schaie, K. W. Quasi-experimental research designs in the psychology of aging. In J. E. Birren & K. W. Schaie (Eds.), *Handbook of the psychology of aging*. New York: Van Nostrand Reinhold, 1977.

Schaie, K. W. The primary abilities in adulthood: An explanation of psychometric intelligence. In P. B. Baltes & O. G. Brim, Jr. (Eds.), *Life-span development and behavior* (Vol. 2). New York: Academic Press, 1979.

Shen, E. The place of individual differences in experimentation. In Q. McNemar & M. A. Merrill (Eds.), *Studies in personality*. New York: McGraw-Hill, 1942.

Sheppard, H. L. (with the assistance of L. Passarell & T. Romashko). *Research and development strategy on employment-related problems of older workers*. Washington, D.C.: American Institutes for Research, Center on Work and Aging, 1977.

Shiffman, S., & Pasternak, M. Decreased discrimination of food odors in the elderly. *Journal of Gerontology*, 1979, *34*, 73–79.

Siegler, I. C., & Botwinick, J. A long-term longitudinal study of intellectual ability of older adults: The matter of selective subject attrition. *Journal of Gerontology*, 1979, *34*, 243–245.

Storck, P. A., Looft, W. R., & Hooper, F. H. Interrelationships among Piagetian tasks and traditional measures of cognitive abilities in the mature and aged adult. *Journal of Gerontology*, 1972, *27*, 461–465.

Sward, K. Age and mental ability in superior men. *American Journal of Psychology*, 1945, *58*, 443–479.

Tesch, S., Whitbourne, S. K., & Nehrke, M. F. Cognitive egocentrism in institutionalized adult males. *Journal of Gerontology*, 1978, *33*, 546–552.

Titchener, E. B. The past decade in experimental psychology. *American Journal of Psychology*, 1910, *21*, 404–421.

Treat, N. J., Poon, L. W., Fozard, J. L., & Popkin, S. J. Toward applying cognitive skill training to memory problems. *Experimental Aging Research*, 1978, *4*, 305–319.

Tyler, L. E. *Individual differences: Abilities and motiva-*

tional directions. New York: Appleton-Century-Crofts, 1974.

Walsh, D. A., Williams, M. V., & Hertzog, C. K. Age-related differences in two stages of central perceptual processes: The effects of short duration targets and criterion differences. *Journal of Gerontology*, 1979, *34*, 234–241.

Watson, C. S., Turpenoff, C. M., Kelly, W. J., & Botwinick, J. Age differences in resolving power and decision strategies in a weight discrimination task. *Journal of Gerontology*, 1979, *34*, 547–552.

Wechsler, D. *The measurement of adult intelligence* (3rd ed.). Baltimore, Md.: Williams & Wilkins, 1944.

Wechsler, D. *The measurement and appraisal of adult intelligence* (4th ed.). Baltimore, Md.: Williams & Wilkins, 1958.

Weiner, B. J. *Statistical principles in experimental design*. New York: McGraw-Hill, 1962.

Welford, A. T. Motor performance. In J. E. Birren & K. W. Schaie (Eds.), *The handbook of the psychology of aging*. New York: Van Nostrand Reinhold, 1977.

Willerman, L. *The psychology of individual and group differences*. San Francisco: Freeman, 1979.

Witt, S. J., & Cunningham, W. R. Cognitive speed and subsequent intellectual development: A longitudinal investigation. *Journal of Gerontology*, 1979, *34*, 540–546.

Wohlwill, J. F. The age variable in psychological research. *Psychological Review*, 1970, *77*, 49–64.

Wohlwill, J. F. *The study of behavioral development*. New York: Academic Press, 1973.

Young, M. L. Age and sex differences in problem solving. *Journal of Gerontology*, 1971, *26*, 330–336.

Warren L. Danziger

CHAPTER
39

Measurement of Response Bias in Aging Research

Analysis of response bias tendencies by signal detection theory is a valid method for inferring cautiousness. Whereas several studies have reported that older adults set stricter criteria and had lower sensitivity than young adults, two studies found no age differences in either response bias or sensitivity. These findings and their implications are discussed, and present measures of bias are described.

In recent years many researchers have become interested in applying signal detection methodology to investigations of age differences in response bias. The purposes of this chapter are (a) to review at an introductory level the sensory-perceptual studies that have investigated age differences in response bias, and (b) to explore some issues concerning the measurement of bias. The chapters by Williams (Chapter 40), Hertzog (Chapter 41), and Marks and Stevens (Chapter 42) examine other associated issues concerning the use of signal detection methodology in aging research.

Sensory thresholds obtained by traditional psychophysical methods can be influenced by nonsensory variables. These include past learning experiences, attitudes, pathological conditions, mental sets the subject brings into the testing situation, and mental sets induced by the experimenter's instructions. By failing to consider the psychological factors involved in making a decision, experimenters may overestimate the extent of learning deficit or sensory loss present in elderly people. Signal detection theory (SDT) provides a method for distinguishing between subjects' sensitivity for detecting a stimulus and their response bias or criterion for reporting the presence of a stimulus (Green & Swets, 1966).

Theoretically, subjects' criteria are independent of their sensitivity. For a given level of sensitivity, a criterion can be set anywhere along the decision axis (see Figure 39-1). A criterion (C_2) that is set where the signal plus noise (SN) and noise (N) curves intersect represents unbiased decision making, since the subject is equally likely to respond either "Yes, I detect something" or "No, I don't." Criterion C_1 indicates a stricter criterion, since the subject has low hit and false-alarm rates. And criterion C_3 is a lax criterion, with the subject making more correct detections and more false alarms. Thus, SDT, which concerns the ways in which choices are made, is useful for investigating how people of different ages make decisions.

Background

The performance of older subjects is often characterized as cautious or conservative in comparison to the performance of younger subjects on a variety of tasks. Older adults have been labeled cautious when it was inferred (a) that they took more time than necessary in responding to difficult visual discriminations (Botwinick, Brinley, & Robbin, 1958); (b) that they chose to make no response rather than an incorrect one (Korchin & Basowitz, 1957); (c) that from a list of risky alternatives, they chose one that involved little risk (Wallach & Kogan, 1961); and (d) that they set stricter criteria for making decisions than did younger adults (e.g., Clark & Mehl, 1971, Rees & Botwinick, 1971). In SDT research one subject is said to be more cautious than another when he or she has set a stricter criterion than the other.

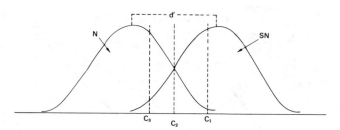

Figure 39-1. Hypothetical distributions of signal plus noise (SN) and noise (N). d' is the distance between the means of the two distributions, and C_1, C_2, and C_3 represent possible criteria.

Sensory-Perceptual Tasks

Several aging studies have employed statistical decision procedures in an effort to investigate response bias independently of sensitivity. Craik (1969) tested young and old men for auditory detection in two response conditions: a yes/no procedure and a 5-point rating-scale procedure. In the yes/no series, old subjects adopted a stricter criterion than did young subjects. In the confidence-rating-scale procedure, age differences in criterion placement where not significant, but there was a slight tendency for old subjects to restrict the range of their criteria.

Rees and Botwinick (1971) found no age differences for d' but reported that elderly men set stricter criteria than did young men in reporting the presence of faint auditory signals. Older subjects tended to avoid reporting the presence of low-intensity inputs, even though their performance in a threshold task affirmed their sensitivity to these stimuli. Potash and Jones (1977) reported that "old" adults (55–64 years) had lower sensitivity and greater response bias than young adults. When the sensitivity of the young group at 30 dB was compared with that of the older group of 50 dB, no age difference in sensitivity was found, though a significant age difference in response bias remained.

The effect of age on pain perception has been investigated in three studies using SDT procedures. Clark and Mehl (1971) observed that middle-aged subjects seemed to report pain only when they were certain that pain was present, whereas younger subjects were more liberal in their use of the pain criterion. And Harkins and Chapman (1976, 1977) found that elderly men and women were less likely than young subjects to report a low level of perceived stimulus intensity as painful, although they were more likely to report high levels as painful.

In a study of weight discrimination, Watson, Turpenoff, Kelly, and Botwinick (1979) found no significant age differences in either sensitivity or response

bias. However, Danziger and Botwinick (1980) reported that young adults had significantly higher d' values than older adults and suggested that the older adults had set stricter criteria than the young adults. Results from yes/no data indicated that older adults set stricter criteria than young adults; however, when the data from a rating-scale procedure were analyzed in an analysis of variance design, no significant age difference was found. There was, however, a significant interaction between age and measurement of bias across the 5-point rating scale. Older adults had more relaxed bias values than younger adults at the first rating category, but stricter values at the last (fifth) category. Also, when the old and young subjects in the study were matched for sensitivity, there was no age difference in their response bias (Danziger & Botwinick, 1980).

In a recent study in which Danziger (1979) tested young, middle-aged, and older men and women in a visual discrimination task, no significant age differences were found in either sensitivity or response bias measures.

Recognition Memory

Correct recognition of previously presented words can also be influenced by decision-making strategies. Several researchers have used signal detection methodology to test Schonfield and Robertson's (1966) finding of no age difference in recognition memory.

In a pilot experiment Craik (1969) reported that young and middle-aged adults were similar in recognition memory and that there was some indication that the middle-aged group adopted higher criteria than did the young adults. Gordon and Clark (1974a) tested young and older adults for differences in sensitivity and response bias on a prose recognition task. The elderly were poorer at recognizing the old words, but no significant differences in response bias were found between the two age groups. (The young subjects actually set stricter criteria than the elderly. For a possible explanation of this occurrence, refer to the discussion of Figure 39-2.)

Gordon and Clark (1974b) also tested the same young and old adults on recognition memory for words and nonsense syllables. The elderly had lower recognition scores than young adults for both types of stimuli. The elderly set stricter criteria than the young for the first word trial and similar criteria to theirs on the second trial. For nonsense syllables the elderly's criteria were lower than the young adults' on the first trial and approached the same level as theirs on the second trial. The authors suggested that the elderly were more cautious than the young on the first word trial but more anxious on the first trial with unfamiliar material.

More recently, Harkins, Chapman, and Eisdorfer (1979) studied recognition memory in young and elderly women. The young women discriminated between the old and new words significantly better than the older women. A rating-scale procedure was employed, and differences in response bias were tested at each category. No age differences in bias were reported at the three middle categories; however, the elderly women were found to restrict the range of their criteria such that they initially set a more lax criterion than the young women but at the fifth category, a much stricter criterion.

Bias Differences

In most of these studies, age differences were found in both sensitivity and response bias, but when there were no age differences in sensitivity, there were also none in response bias. Given equal sensitivity, subjects with strict criteria and subjects with lax criteria appear to undergo similar sensory experiences. That is, comparing subjects not likely to label the stimuli as different with subjects more likely to do so is meaningful only if the two groups of subjects have similar sensory abilities. Therefore it may not be useful to compare subjects for differences in response bias if they differ in sensory ability.

Two receiver operating characteristic (ROC) curves have been generated, based on hypothetical group rating-scale data (see Figure 39-2). The data may be interpreted as follows: At the lower curve (A) $d' = .5$, and at the upper curve (B) $d' = 1.5$. Assume the difference in sensitivity to be statistically significant. Each curve has five criterion points (reading from left to right), with the third point falling on the negative diagonal. In a yes/no task the third point is the only data point that would be obtained from both groups of subjects, and a statistical test would indicate no difference in bias. At Point 2, Group A ($\beta = 1.5$) set a stricter criterion than Group B ($\beta = 1.3$), but the difference is probably not significant. At Point 4, A set a stricter criterion than B, and the difference might be statistically significant.

In examining Points 1 and 5, which are approximately mirror images of one another, it is apparent that the differences between Groups A and B are probably statistically significant. However, at Point 1, Group B has set a stricter criterion than Group A, while at Point 5, Group A has set a stricter criterion than Group B. At Point 1 it is not clear whether the difference in bias is due to the stricter criterion of Group B compared to Group A or whether the differ-

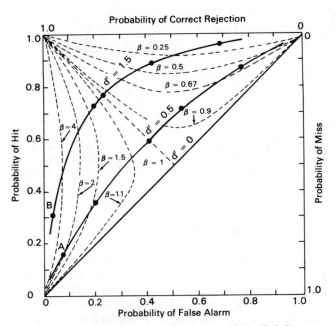

Figure 39-2. A receiver operating characteristic (ROC) curve with β isobias contours (dashed lines) and three isosensitivity curves (solid lines).

ence is a function of sensitivity. Because A has low sensitivity there is a high probability that its criteria will have a range between $\beta = 1.5$ and $\beta = .67$. However, it is not likely that B's criteria will fall into that range, particularly Criteria 1 and 5. Intuitively, it appears to be improper to compare A and B for differences in bias when they differ in sensitivity.

Further support for this position comes from Danziger and Botwinick (1980), who studied age groups differing in both sensitivity and response bias. Correlational analyses indicated that the relations between d' and β were significant for each subject group. In general, the correlations between measures of sensitivity and response bias were moderately positive for young men, highly negative for young women, somewhat negative for older men, and slightly negative for older women. In an effort to test for differences in response bias independent of differences in sensitivity, young and older subjects were matched for sensitivity and then tested for differences in response bias. No significant age differences were found.

Whenever possible, therefore, experimenters should compare differences in bias only among subjects who are similar in sensitivity. This does not mean that subjects who differ in sensitivity cannot be compared for differences in response bias. It does suggest, however, that interpretation and generalization of the results should be made with care. Only with subjects who are similar in sensitivity can the experimenter be certain that elicited bias differences are independent of sensitivity differences.

Measures of Response Bias

The purpose of this section is (a) to discuss those measures of criterion or response bias reported in the aging literature, and (b) to determine whether the different measures of criterion yield similar results. For a discussion of the experimental and statistical foundations for current treatments of bias, the reader is referred to Dusoir (1975) and Hertzog (Chapter 41, this volume).

Four measures of response bias have been reported in the aging literature: β, log β, percentage bias, and B. β is the traditional measure of bias and is theoretically independent of d'. It is defined as the ratio of the heights of the probability density functions at the criterion, and it is equal to the slope at which a given ROC curve passes through a particular point. When the subject is unbiased, β equals 1.0. If a subject has a lax criterion, β has a range between 0 and 1.0; if a subject has a strict criterion, however, β has a range from 1.0 to infinity. Therefore, a distribution of β values may be skewed (McNicol, 1972, p. 123), although the transformation of β to log β equalizes the intervals between degrees of response bias.

Although percentage bias (Hodos, 1970) has been considered a nonparametric index of response bias, this label has been disputed by Dusoir (1975), who calls it "a new (arbitrary) bias parameter." The measurements of percentage bias correlate highly with the measures β and log β (Danziger, 1979; Danziger & Botwinick, 1980), and the percentage bias isobias contours are visually similar to those of β.

The last measure of response bias discussed here is B (McNicol, 1972)—the interpolated rating-scale category in which the subject is unbiased. B provides a crude assessment of whether a subject is biased toward reporting the presence or absence of a signal. The measure B is only moderately correlated with the other three measures of bias (Danziger, 1979; Danziger & Botwinick, 1980), and its role in the measurement of bias is not clear, since it has been reported in only one other study (Potash & Jones, 1977). Of the four available measures, the measure of choice would seem to be log β because it equalizes the intervals between degrees of response bias.

A measure of bias such as β is simply a unit of measurement that reflects deviations from equal heights of the probability density functions. The heights of the probability density functions are equal, and $\beta = 1.0$ at the intersection of the SN and N curves

or anywhere along the decision axis that the SN and N curves overlap exactly. The negative diagonal of the ROC curve represents criteria placed at the intersection of the SN and N curves, and the positive diagonal represents chance performance. Although criteria placed along either diagonal are interpreted similarly—that is, that a subject is equally likely to respond, "Yes, a signal was presented" as "No, only noise was presented"— intuitively they appear to reflect different decision-making processes. Future research must determine whether criterion at chance performance along the positive diagonal is equivalent to unbiased performance along the negative diagonal, where d' is greater than zero.

Inspection of Figure 39-2 reveals a simplistic, but perhaps novel, interpretation of bias measurement. The β isobias contours of the ROC curve measure bias as deviation from the positive and negative diagonals. At a very low d'—slightly above chance performance—the SN and N curves of Figure 39-1 would overlap almost completely. Although criteria could be located at some distance from the intersection of the two curves, that is, where the subject is unbiased, the ratio of the heights of the two probability density functions would still approach 1.0. This can be seen more clearly in Figure 39-2 by imagining a curve approximately halfway between the $d' = 0$ and $d' = .5$ curves. A criterion could be located at some distance from the negative diagonal, but never far from the positive diagonal.

Conversely, for widely separated SN and N curves, the subject is operating well above chance performance, and criteria can be set at some distance from the point of unbiased performance. In Figure 39-2 a criterion placed along the curve where $d' = 1.5$ at some distance from the negative diagonal would only approach the positive diagonal at the endpoints of the curve. This suggests that it is inappropriate to compare individuals or groups for differences in response bias when they differ in sensitivity. A subject with low sensitivity has a restricted range of bias values, in contrast to the subject with high sensitivity who is likely to have a wider range of bias values and more extreme values. This may account for the restricted ranges of criteria in elderly subjects observed by Harkins and colleagues in their studies (Harkins and Chapman, 1976, 1977; Harkins et al., 1979).

A proposed bias measure meriting further investigation is c (Ingham, 1970). According to Ingham, if the variances of the SN and N distributions are equal, then d' and c are orthogonal. While d' is the difference between the means of the two distributions (i.e., Zn − Zsn), c is twice the distance from the intersection of the two distributions to the criterion and is the sum of the two deviates from unbiased decision making (see

Figure 39-3). Further research is needed to determine whether *c* is indeed independent of *d'* when subjects differ in sensitivity.

Interpretation and Implication

Several studies (Danziger & Botwinick, 1980; Harkins et al., 1979) have reported that on a rating-scale task, young subjects had higher bias values than older subjects at the first ROC point and lower bias values at the fifth ROC point. A similar occurrence in the hypothetical data discussed earlier suggests two possible interpretations. One is that young subjects may be less willing to respond "I'm very certain a signal was presented" than are older subjects but more willing to respond "I'm moderately certain that only noise was presented." The importance of this disparity is unclear, nor can it be told whether one group is more cautious than the other. According to a second interpretation, older subjects are more cautious than young subjects because they have a restricted range of criteria, implying that older subjects are avoiding extreme responses.

This situation might arise and require interpretation even when the two groups are similar in sensitivity. At the fifth ROC point, older subjects set a stricter criterion which is less extreme than the young subjects'

criterion, but at the first ROC point, older subjects set a criterion that is less extreme and also more lax than the response criterion of young subjects. The best interpretation for these data is still uncertain.

Finally, what are the implications of the research findings? Do older adults set stricter criteria, that is, are they more cautious than young adults? Certainly this is implied by the auditory detection and pain perception literature, but in those studies young adults had higher sensitivity than older adults. In the two studies in which young and older adults were similar in sensory ability, they did not differ in response bias. Therefore, the strict criteria of older adults may be a natural concomitant of decreased ability, because when young and older adults were similar in ability, they were similar in response bias. The increase in cautiousness noted in older adults—at least in these studies—appears to reflect declining performance in their old age rather than a change in their criteria.

REFERENCES

Botwinick, J., Brinley, J. F., & Robbin, J. S. The interaction effects of perceptual difficulty and stimulus exposure time on age differences in speed and accuracy of response. *Gerontologia*, 1958, *2*, 1–10.

Clark, W. C., & Mehl, L. Thermal pain: A sensory decision theory analysis of the effect of age and sex on *d'*, various response criteria, and 50% pain threshold. *Journal of Abnormal Psychology*, 1971, *78*, 202–212.

Craik, F. I. M. Applications of signal detection theory to studies of aging. In A. T. Welford & J. E. Birren (Eds.), *Decision making and aging*. Basel, Switzerland: Karger, 1969.

Danziger, W. L. *Adult age differences in sensitivity and response bias in a visual discrimination task*. Unpublished doctoral dissertation, Washington University, 1979.

Danziger, W. L., & Botwinick, J. Age and sex differences in sensitivity and response bias in a weight discrimination task. *Journal of Gerontology*, 1980, *35*, 388–394.

Dusoir, A. E. Treatments of bias in detection and recognition models: A review. *Perception & Psychophysics*, 1975, *17*, 167–178.

Gordon, S. K., & Clark, W. C. Application of signal detection theory to prose recall and recognition in elderly and young adults. *Journal of Gerontology*, 1974, *29*, 64–72. (a)

Gordon, S. K., & Clark, W. C. Adult age differences in word and nonsense syllable recognition memory and response criterion. *Journal of Gerontology*, 1974, *29*, 659–665. (b)

Green, D. M., & Swets, J. A. *Signal detection theory and psychophysics*. New York: Wiley, 1966.

Harkins, S. W., & Chapman, C. R. Detection and decision factors in pain perception in young and elderly men. *Pain*, 1976, *2*, 253–264.

Harkins, S. W., & Chapman, C. R. The perception of in-

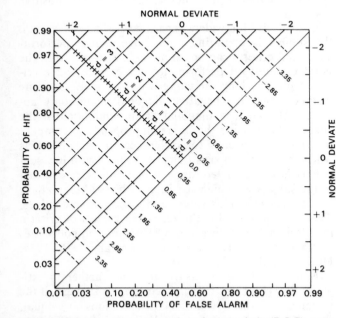

Figure 39-3. A receiver operating characteristic (ROC) curve plotted in normal deviate coordinates. The solid lines are isosensitivity curves, and the dashed lines are bias curves, as measured by *c*.

duced dental pain in young and elderly women. *Journal of Gerontology*, 1977, *32*, 428–435.

Harkins, S. W., Chapman, C. R., & Eisdorfer, C. Memory loss and response bias in senescence. *Journal of Gerontology*, 1979, *34*, 66–72.

Hodos, W. Nonparametric index of response bias for use in detection and recognition experiments. *Psychological Bulletin*, 1970, *74*, 351–354.

Ingham, J. G. Individual differences in signal detection. *Acta Psychologia*, 1970, *34*, 39–50.

Korchin, S. J., & Basowitz, H. Age differences in verbal learning. *Journal of Abnormal and Social Psychology*, 1957, *54*, 64–69.

McNicol, D. *A primer of signal detection theory.* Winchester, Mass.: Allen & Unwin, 1972.

Potash, M., & Jones, B. Aging and decision criteria for the detection of tones in noise. *Journal of Gerontology*, 1977, *32*, 436–440.

Rees, J. N., & Botwinick, J. Detection and decision factors in auditory behavior of the elderly. *Journal of Gerontology*, 1971, *26*, 133–136.

Schonfield, D., & Robertson, B. Memory storage and aging. *Canadian Journal of Psychology*, 1966, *20*, 228–336.

Wallach, M. A., & Kogan, N. Aspects of judgment and decision making: Interrelationships and changes with age. *Behavioral Science*, 1961, *6*, 23–36.

Watson, C. S., Turpenoff, C. M., Kelly, W. J., & Botwinick, J. Age differences in resolving power and decision strategies in a weight discrimination task. *Journal of Gerontology*, 1979, *34*, 547–552.

M. Virtrue Williams

40

Receiver Operating Characteristics: The Effect of Distribution on Between-Group Comparisons

Recent research into age differences in the processing of information has emphasized the importance of separating sensitivity differences (d') from response criterion (beta). It is equally important to determine the nature of the receiver operating characteristic (ROC) to assure the appropriateness of parametric (d' and beta) comparisons. Both d' and beta assume normal distributions as the basis of subjects' ROCs. If the distribution is non-normal and the researcher uses d' and beta for comparison, incorrect conclusions are likely. Examples of non-normal distributions are discussed, and effects on data comparisons are demonstrated.

As this chapter emphasizes, the study of adult and late-life behavioral changes is complicated by what is termed a *performance–ability dichotomy*. It is possible that older people do not choose to demonstrate the same proportion of their ability as do young people. Botwinick (1973), in a well-articulated hypothesis on the performance–ability dichotomy, as has suggested that the problem stems from a pervasive cautiousness of behavior. Botwinick has argued that older subjects are generally more inclined to withhold an uncertain response, thereby reducing their percentage of correct responses compared with the young subjects. Reciprocally, the young subjects' percentage of correct responses may be inflated by their increased tendency to make educated guesses. Until recently, with the exception of simple corrections for guessing or analyses of errors of omission versus commission, little could be

done to investigate scientifically the impact of such systematic trends in between-group comparisons of performance. The theory of signal detection has ameliorated this situation by allowing investigators to separate subjects' response strategies from their sensitivity in a detection task.

Clearly, any approach that permits the separation of sensitivity from response strategy will be the method of choice, especially when an investigator expects systematic between-group differences. Understandably, there has been a rather enthusiastic application of signal detection theory to age-difference research (see Chapter 42 in this volume). Unfortunately, however, few researchers have noted the more recent publications that have emphasized the limiting assumptions on which many of the parametric signal detection measures are based. Investigation of groups that may have systematically different response strategies has led to widespread application of signal detection analysis (see Chapter 39 in this volume). However, it is important to judge the conformance of the data to the assumptions of parametric signal detection measures before they are applied.

While the investigator who is not concerned with between-age group comparisons can be satisfied with the weaker assumption of random variation among individuals, the developmentalist interested in possible group differences is not afforded such an assumption.

Thus it becomes important to investigate the degree to which the data conform to the assumptions that underlie the parameters, and to be cognizant of the impact that violations of assumptions have on the parameters.

This chapter deals explicitly with the assumption of normality of the subject's internal, associated probabilities that an observed event was caused by the presence of noise alone or by noise plus signal. (See Chapter 41 in this volume for a discussion of the normal but unequal variance case.) First, the most common approaches in the literature on age differences to signal detection parameters are described, followed by an explanation of the limits of these approaches. The concept of internal probability distributions and the impact of non-normality on this concept are discussed next, followed by a more detailed description of the three types of distributions (normal–normal, exponential, and gamma) that are used at length in this chapter. A data-based example of variability in conclusions, given differing assumptions of distributions, is then presented. Finally, a possible approach is offered for dealing with tasks for which the investigator does not have prior knowledge of the subjects' probability distributions.

Parametric Signal Detection Measures

The study of the performance–ability distinction has been greatly enhanced by the application of signal detection analysis. Investigators of adult–life behavioral changes, concerned that older adults' performance on given tasks does not reflect their true ability, but rather betrays a hesitancy to respond in uncertainty, can treat this hesitancy as a conservative response bias. For example, Rees and Botwinick (1971) used this approach in reporting age differences in an auditory detection task. They found that the older group adopted a more stringent criterion for response, as measured by the parameter beta (β) (old = 2.41; young = 1.21), while showing equal discriminability of the target, as measured by the detectability index d' (old = 1.44; young = 1.36). The ability to allow parametric comparison of subjects' response strategy and their sensitivity has led to the rapid application of this theory to the study of adult development. In Rees and Botwinick's study, without such a measure performance differentials between groups would have been ascribed to sensitivity differences rather than to differences in response strategy. However, while such an approach indicates the nature of the between-group differences, it is far from definitive. In order to generate beta and d' estimates, as this and succeeding chapters em-

phasize, the experimenter must make powerful assumptions concerning the signal and noise distributions used by the observer.

Assumption of Normality

The data gathered in most adult-development experiments allow estimation of one point in the receiver operating characteristics space (ROC space). To allow comparison, the assumption is made that the signal and noise distributions perceived by the subject are normal and have equal variance. As demonstrated in Rees and Botwinick's data, and shown in Figure 40-1A, two points are identified in ROC space, one for each age group. To compare these points it must be assumed that each observer has an internal ordering of observational evidence and, associated with the evidence, a probability that it is produced by signal or noise. These probability distributions (shown in Figure 40-1B) are assumed to be normal and of equal variance. As they are separated (i.e., as discriminability increases), such distributions will generate a family of ROC curves, only one of which will pass

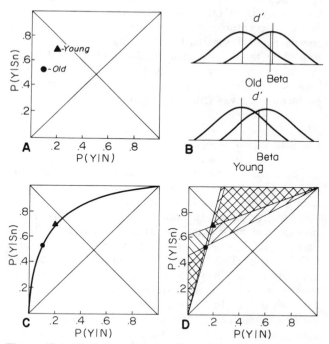

Figure 40-1. Various representations of the data reported by Rees and Botwinick (1971). A: the performance means in receiver operating characteristic (ROC) space. B: underlying signal-plus-noise and noise curves, assuming normal distributions. C: normal–normal ROC giving rise to the d' of the Rees and Botwinick report. D: area traversed by possible proper ROC curves that could intercept the data points.

through each of the points in ROC space. Thus, the ROC defines each point uniquely and allows experimental comparison. In the Rees and Botwinick experiment, both young and old subjects fall on the same curve (Figure 40-1C). When two points fall on the same curve, the subjects are said to have equal discriminability of signal, since the normal–normal ROC is determined by the distance between the signal and noise distributions. However, beta, a measure of bias, is different for the two groups, as is indicated by the different locations on which each group falls on the ROCs. As Figure 40-1B illustrates, the old subjects make fewer correct responses but they also have fewer incorrect identifications of noise as signal.

The Use of Forced Choice

A second approach, which involves removing the potential problem of between-group differences in bias by employing a forced-choice procedure, has been used frequently in visual discrimination tasks (Hertzog, Williams, & Walsh, 1976; Walsh, 1976). By generating a symmetrical ROC, the percentage of correct responses is shown to be an unbiased estimate of the area under the ROC (Green & Swets, 1966). This approach, acceptable if the only point of interest is a comparison of sensitivity levels, can be viewed as a procedure that normalizes the distributions and forces the subject to use an unbiased response strategy (i.e., beta = 1). However, it offers no information about performance away from the negative diagonal.

Limiting Assumptions

The most commonly used measures of detectability are based on the assumption that the probability distributions that observers associate with their ordered evidence for signal and noise (as in Figure 40-1B) are normal and have equal variance. If this is true, each point in ROC space is defined by one, and only one, ROC curve. The set of these curves is created by generating ROCs from low-detectability conditions (nearly overlapping signal-plus-noise and noise curves) to high-detectability conditions (widely separated curves). Such a set of ROCs is designated an ordered family of ROCs. As no two ROCs so generated will overlap, each point in ROC space is traversed by one and only one ROC. This has been labeled the N–N (normal–normal) ROC family by Egan (1975).

The popular signal-detection-theory parameter d' is defined as the distance between the means of the signal-plus-noise and the noise-associated probability distributions. It is, as stated above, precisely this variable that gives rise to the N–N ordered family. Therefore, if the normality assumption holds, each point in ROC space is associated with one and only one d'. As discussed by Green and Swets (1966), the ROC of a given d' is generated by systematically varying cut-off—the point on the observation axis of beta (see Figure 40-1B—from very high to very low. Thus, if two points in ROC space are defined as falling on the same N–N ROC, they must differ in beta.

Clearly, both parameters d' and beta rely for their derivation on the assumptions of normality and equal variance for the observers' likelihood functions (probability distributions). If these distributions are not normal (or are not of equal variance, see Chapter 41, this volume), the experimenter may be greatly misled if these parameters are generated from one observation per group. If the assumption is made that the ROC is proper—constantly decreasing (see Egan, 1975)—there are still an infinite number of ROCs that can pass through any given point in ROC space. In Figure 40-1D, the double crosshatched area illustrates where proper ROCs will cross the ROC data points gathered by Rees and Botwinick (1971) in their study.

Distributional Effects

It is the premise of this chapter that the impact of changes in the assumed underlying distributions for signal and noise are often completely disregarded. This may be due to the familiarity and appeal of normal distributions and, hence, the understandable reluctance of researchers to reject them. Alternatively, it may be that some researchers believe mistakenly that the assumption of normality for these distributions is intuitively satisfying and not overly restrictive. At all events, this assumption is taken rather cavalierly, and often without even prima facie appeal when the data are considered. There is little reason to assume normal distribution in detection experiments. A number of other distributions are more frequently used for neural models of detection systems; indeed, Green and Swets (1966) noted that in visual experiments non-normal-appearing ROCs were frequently found. Also, while many researchers believe that such assumptions are not overly restrictive, relaxing this assumption may reverse the behavioral predictions. Three distributions—normal, exponential, and gamma—are compared in this chapter; however, it should be noted that these three do not constitute all the possible forms of underlying distributions. (The reader is referred to Egan, 1975, for an excellent treatment of a large number of distribution types.)

Normal Distributions

The effect of a normal distribution on ROCs is discussed at some length in Chapter 41 of this volume. It was employed by Green and Swets (1966) to permit estimation of d' and beta as signal detection parameters. The impact of violation of the Gaussian assumption on the detectability parameter d' is severe (Pollack & Hsieh, 1969). While the evidence for N–N distributions in psychophysical experiments is limited, there is some evidence that when MOC functions are generated in memory experiments N–N curves may be found (e.g., Wickelgren & Norman, 1966).

Exponential Distributions

Negative exponential distributions occur in the form ke^{-kx} with a family (as defined above) generated by manipulations of the single parameter k. Such distributions have been recommended under circumstances in which vigilance due to uncertainty of signal onset is part of the detection task (Egan, Greenberg, & Schulman, 1961; Green & Swets, 1966). Also, when the subject is detecting visual signals, data can be fitted by assuming exponential distributions (S. Kline, personal communication, 1979).

It is very difficult to determine empirically whether data are the result of underlying negative exponential distributions or of unequal-variance Gaussian distributions. Green and Swets (1966, p. 79) discuss this problem and state, "The justification for the Gaussian model with unequal variance is, we believe, not to be made on theoretical but rather on practical grounds." They go on to argue that there are also practical grounds for preferring the exponential distribution as underlying, primarily because this allows the use of a single-parameter specification.

Arguments for parsimony aside, there are reasonable theoretical grounds for expecting exponential distributions in certain detection paradigms, particularly in cases where power-law models of neuronal response might be anticipated (e.g., early visual processing), and in fixed-interval, speeded detection tasks. In the latter, a Rayleigh function has been used to describe random walk models for choice response (see Green & Swets, 1966, p. 301; Ratcliff, 1978). In any case, researchers should not be misled into believing that selection between Gaussian and exponential distributions is an atheoretical choice made simply on the basis of convenience of data reduction. The problem arises because of limitations in empirical discrimination between the unequal-variance Gaussian and exponential distributions.

Gamma Distributions

In experiments in which the observer is asked to respond quickly within an interval or to an externally timed interval, a gamma-type distribution might be expected. This distribution has been discussed extensively n regard to reaction-time tasks (McGill, 1967; Waugh, Fozard, Talland, & Erwin, 1973). The gamma distribution is not a single-parameter density function, and is described as:

$$g(t|mr) = \frac{m^r t^{r-1} \exp(-mt)}{(r-1)!}$$

with $t \geq 0, r = 1, 2, \ldots$. If r is fixed, then a family of ROCs based on $\mu_{sn}|\mu_s$ is described.

As with the exponential function, it is difficult in practice to discriminate between the unequal-variance Gaussian case and the case of a gamma-distribution-based ROC. Indeed in cases in which the observer lacks information concerning the signal, distributions based on unequal variance may be much like that derived from the gamma case. However, in timed detection tasks and decision-speed tasks, a number of neuronal models predict gamma- and Poisson-type distributions (see Pike, 1973; Restle & Davis, 1962).

Age and Distributions

Each of these distributions has theoretical and practical advantages. The equal-variance Gaussian, negative exponential, and gamma functions may each be appropriate under certain conditions and may each have theoretical backing. If it were possible to assume that regardless of what the distributional characteristics of signal and noise probability functions were, all subjects would use similar distributions, then the particular one chosen might be of minor import. However, the development assumption implies precisely the opposite, and indeed contends that in many circumstances young and old subjects would very likely have quite different distributions.

For example, the most disparate distributions in terms of their ROCs are the exponential and gamma-type probability distributions. It might be the case that following a warning stimulus in a visual discrimination task, the young subjects would have one distribution type and the old another. Young persons might be affected by the phase and intensity characteristics of the signal, while the old might be affected by the time estimation introduced by the warning stimulus. This would be most plausible if equal intensity signals were used. When attempting to identify the signal, the young subjects would be expected to show detection characteristics that conformed to neuronal models based on exponential response characteristics. Conversely, the old, attempting to compensate for both decreased sensitivity and decreased accuracy in time estimation, might show a gamma distribution. This ROC would reflect a greater sensitivity to the need for estimating the interval between the warning stimulus and signal. Thus, the old subjects' ROC would reflect models of neuronal timing (i.e., a gamma-type distribution).

The argument is not that one of these distributions is necessarily correct for young observers and another for old observers but rather that, in the absence of data, it is difficult to ascertain which distribution is correct. Further, researchers should be aware that the choice of a particular distribution (usually N–N) will affect the way in which the data are interpreted.

Detection Data

In order to demonstrate the impact of different assumed signal and noise probability distributions, data were gathered on a group of young and a group of old subjects in a backward-masking experiment. Backward masking is particularly useful for this type of problem because, by varying the stimulus-onset asynchrony, it is possible to vary systematically the detectability of the target. In order to generate estimates of detectability alone, a four-alternative forced-choice procedure was employed first. Second, to describe the ROC, subjects were asked to rate the certitude of their judgment. These ROCs were then fitted by eye as each of the three underlying distributions discussed above (Gaussian, exponential, gamma) was assumed in turn. The effect of the alternative distributions on the interpretation of the data was marked.

Four-Alternative Forced Choice

A four-choice detection task was performed under conditions of backward masking on 10 subjects, five in each of two age groups (18–28 years, and 60–70 years). In the first forced-choice procedure, five asynchronies between mask and target were employed: 0, 20, 40, 60, and 80 msec. At each of these asynchronies 20 target–mask pairs were presented, and the subject was required to choose among the target alternatives (Block letters T, V, X, or Y) for each pairing. With this method, the percentage of correct responses is an unbiased estimate of the area under the ROC, which is generally considered to be the best estimate of detectability (e.g., Egan, 1975; Green & Swets, 1966).

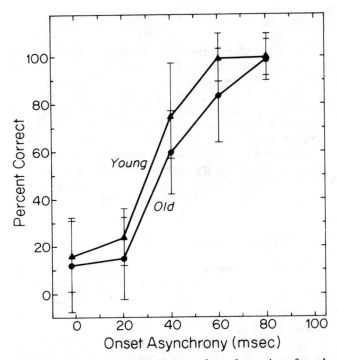

Figure 40-2. Data gathered in a four-alternative, forced-choice, masking experiment.

The results of this analysis are presented in Figure 40-2. The finding of lower detectability at each stimulus onset asynchrony is in accord with several reports (e.g. Walsh, Williams, & Hertzog, 1979). The lower percentage of correct responses for older subjects is generally interpreted as reflecting slower visual information processing by this group (Walsh, 1976). Such slowness of information processing is thought to be pervasive (see Chapter 21 of this volume) and is found at various levels of the information-processing sequence. The result of this slowness in information processing by older subjects is that at any given onset asynchrony, the target is subject to more interference by the masking stimulus.

Rating Curves

In order to generate ROCs, subjects were given 100 trials at each of two onset asynchronies (20 and 60 msec). They were asked to rate the certitude of their response on a five-level scale, and the resulting data were averaged to generate group ROCs. The rating data were then fitted with three ROCs, with Gaussian, exponential, and gamma distributions assumed, in turn, as the underlying distribution.

Since fitting these curves is somewhat arbitrary, they were equated at the negative diagonal. The point

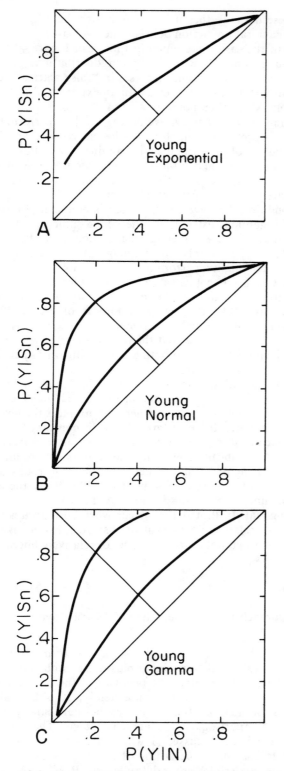

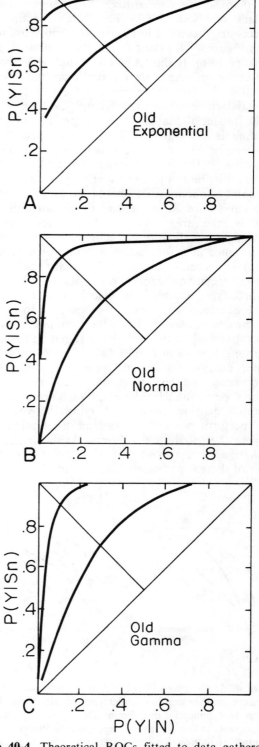

Figure 40-3. Theoretical ROCs fitted to data gathered at stimulus onset asychronies of 40 and 60 msec under conditions of backward masking for five young subjects.

Figure 40-4. Theoretical ROCs fitted to data gathered at stimulus onset asychronies of 40 and 60 msec under conditions of backward masking for five old subjects.

at which such curves cross the negative diagonal has proved to be fairly insensitive to sampling variability (Pollack & Hsieh, 1969). The ROCs for the young subjects are presented in Figure 40-3 and those for the old in Figure 40-4. (The data points are presented later in Figure 40-6). It should be noted that while the standard-deviation ranges are omitted from the figure for the sake of clarity, all three distributions fall within one standard deviation of each empirical point.

The impact of changing the assumed underlying distribution is illustrated in Figures 40-3 and 40-4. In both figures, Plot A features the exponential distribution, Plot B the N–N distribution, and Plot C the gamma distribution as the underlying signal and noise probability functions. It should be emphasized that these curves are all equated at the negative diagonal. That is, the area under each of these curves is equivalent, and all three are equivalent in terms of the performance in a forced-choice task (for a given age group). However, it is equally clear that at points other than the negative diagonal, performance will vary for the three types of underlying distributions.

The distributional effects are best seen in the most extreme comparison, which is the gamma compared to the exponential as the underlying signal and noise distributions, (shown in Figure 40-5). Plot A presents the gamma distribution as underlying the young subjects' performance and the exponential as underlying the old subjects' performance, whereas, Plot B presents the exponential distribution as underlying the young subjects' performance and the gamma distribution as underlying that of the old subjects. Again, it should be emphasized that the intent here is not to argue that either of these is necessarily the correct distribution for these data. Rather it is to emphasize the difference in behavioral prediction between the two cases.

In the case represented in Plot A of Figure 40-5 the young subjects, with a gamma distribution, gain in "hits" for very small increases in "false alarms" compared to the old subjects, with an exponential distribution. Also, when both young and old subjects are operating as very conservative observers, their performance is theoretically equal (i.e., the curves cross). This equality of performance is obtained even though in both the 20- and 60-msec stimulus onset asynchrony conditions, the old subjects are operating at approximately 10% less perceptual accuracy in a forced-choice condition. However, notice what is predicted if instead of a gamma distribution, the young subjects' data are fitted with an exponential distribution, as in Plot B of Figure 40-5. In this plot, although the young start with a much higher performance level, any improvement they achieve comes at a much higher cost in false alarms. The old, in this case fitted by a gamma distribution (like the young in Plot A of Figure 40-5), gain in hits for small increments in false alarms. The result of reversal is that the performance of young and old equilibrates when both are using liberal rather than conservative criteria.

It should be emphasized that in Figure 40-5 the group rise in performance in the forced-choice condition has not changed. Further, in both plots the level of detectability for each group is held constant, as it is determined by the area under the curve (Green & Swets, 1966). However, the points of predicted equivalent performance between the two groups have essentially reversed. The points in Plot B are the mirror image of those in Plot A across the negative diagonal. In Plot A they occur when both groups consist of relatively conservative observers; in Plot B they occur when both groups consist of relatively liberal observers.

Approaches to Determination of Distributions

The thrust of this chapter is that the form of the underlying signal and signal-plus-noise probability distributions determines the behavior of the observer in a detection experiment. Consequently, it is crucial to understand what this form may be, particularly when age comparisons are being considered. These points having been discussed, I will address briefly how the researcher might determine the nature of the distributions underlying the data-derived ROCs. One approach to this problem is recommended: normal trans-

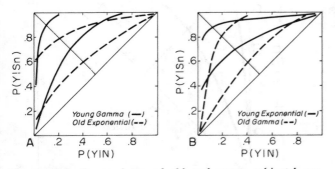

Figure 40-5. Comparisons of old and young subjects' performance with alternative underlying distributions. Plot A utilizes an exponential distribution for the old subjects and a gamma distribution for the young, whereas Plot B utilizes a gamma distribution for the old subjects and an exponential for the young.

formation of the data and fitting of the straight-line approximation by a maximum-likelihood solution.

Normalizing the ROC

It is both the strength and the major limitation of ROC analysis that transformation of data to normal–normal coordinate space generally produces straight or nearly straight curves. For instance, all three functions discussed in this chapter are either straight lines, or so close to straight that the empirically derived functions are in practice, indistinguishable from straight in normal transformation.

N–N ROCs in Normal Coordinates

A ROC based on normal underlying distributions will be a straight line in normal–normal coordinates. For various reasons, researchers interested in age differences have been slow to use this fact in testing the conformity of the data to the normal-normal ROC. Hertzog (in Chapter 41 of this volume) discusses the use of maximum-likelihood statistics for determining the agreement between the data and the normal–normal equal-variance model. However, beyond a test for unity of slope, this approach is susceptible to overinterpretation.

It has been widely reported that the slope of the ROC in normal–normal space for N–N ROC is equal to the ratio of noise variance to signal-plus-noise variance (e.g., Egan, 1975, p. 87). While this fact is not contested, it should be recognized that such a solution does not sufficiently demonstrate that the underlying distributions are indeed N–N based. (For a discussion of the unequal variant case see Chapter 41 of this volume.)

Exponential Distributions

Exponential distributions are very nearly linear when plotted in normal–normal coordinates. In general, they show slopes less than unity, although as detectability approaches zero their slope approaches one. This tendency of the slope to flatten illustrates once again the potentially misleading nature of single-point ROC comparisons in which the N–N equal-variant form is assumed but not demonstrated. Note that the exponential function of the old subjects crosses the gamma distribution of the young subjects. If the normal–normal assumption is made, and only the common point is generated, the researcher will assume that both groups fall on the same N–N ROC

with detectability halfway between the two non-normal distributions. Egan (1975, p. 99) states, "If d' be defined as $z_n - z_{sn}$, then, for each of the power law ROCs, d' continually decreases as the false-alarm rate increases." He then goes on to warn against the use of single-point signal detection comparisons.

The slope of a normal–normal ROC plotted in normal–normal coordinate space will be equal to s_n/s_{sn}. Similarly, if an exponential-distribution-based ROC is plotted in log-log coordinates, its slope will yield the parameter k. It has been suggested that such an approach can be used like the z-transform if an exponential is believed to be the underlying function. In this circumstance the parameter k is the ratio of the log $P(Y|sn)$ to the log $P(Y|n)$ (Egan, 1975, p. 98).

Gamma Distributions

The gamma distribution, like the exponential distribution, is approximately a straight line in normal–normal coordinates. The distributions in Figures 40-5 and 40-6 are the mirror image across the negative diagonal of the exponential distribution. It should be recognized that the gamma distribution has two parameters, so that this relationship with the negative exponential is not inevitable. In this presentation, r was set equal to 1, making the contrast between the exponential and gamma distributions clearer for purposes of exposition (a discussion of the gamma distribution as the basis of a ROC is given in Egan, 1975).

Family ROCs Transformed

The data, with the best-fitting of the three theoretical curves, are presented in normal transform in

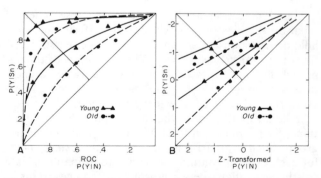

Figure 40-6. The data points for old and young groups presented (A) in untransformed ROC space, and (B) in normal transformed ROC space. The best-fitting theoretical curves are presented (fitted by eye).

Figure 40-6. This figure makes it clear that the gamma distribution is not the distribution of choice in any of the four ROCs, as none show a slope greater than unity. The data all appear to be best fitted by slopes less than one or, in one case with the smallest detectability, equal to one. It would be interesting to be able to choose between the two remaining alternative distributions. This could in fact be done, though the simplifying assumption would have to be made that within an age group, the form of the distributions does not change between levels of detectability. Stated more explicitly, it is assumed that within a task, observers' underlying probability functions do not change their shapes, even when their levels of detectability shift. If this assumption holds, then the normal–normal equal-variance distributions may also be rejected, since the only case fitted by such a function is the low-detectability condition for the old subjects.

Of the distributions presented, the best fit to these data is offered by the exponential family of ROCs, a finding frequently found for visual detection tasks (see above). However, researchers should also be aware that normal–normal unequal-variance distributions will also fit these data, and the choice between these alternatives is difficult. One possible approach would be to assume one or the other distribution to be viridical and to compare goodness-of-fit statistics. However, as these distributions remain underdetermined, it is enough at this time to know the general shape of the distribution and the specification of an equation with parameters that will reproduce the data. Between exponential and unequal-variance Gaussian distributions, the exponential, by being single-parameter, has some advantage.

Summary

Signal detection analysis allows the researcher to separate the bias of a subject toward offering or withholding a response (e.g., cautiousness in older subjects) from the subject's sensitivity. The usefulness of the approach has led to its rapid acceptance by researchers interested in age-related differences in behavior. However, there has been a widespread tendency for researchers to gather data that allows only the specification of one point on a ROC for each experimental group. Such comparisons, based on only a single point for each experimental group, can lead to inappropriate conclusions about between-group differences. This is because these conclusions are based on restrictive assumptions about the form of the distributions that observers have associated with the presence of signal or noise in a trial.

A large number of well-defined distributions can be used to generate theoretical ROCs. Many such distributions have sufficient a priori theoretical justification for consideration as possible underlying distributions in ROC analysis. Choosing among these distributions can lead to radically different conclusions on the nature of between-group differences in perception—or even on whether between-group differences exist. It is crucial, therefore, to determine the shape of the ROC if anything other than the most rudimentary behavior (e.g., behavior in a forced-choice condition) is to be described.

Specification of the underlying distributions is best achieved by transforming the data to normal–normal coordinates and determining the slope of the best-fitting linear-regression line. If the data conform to the usual normal–normal equal-variance assumptions, this slope will be unitary. If the slope is not one, the distributions are either non-normal or unequal variance. Distinguishing between these two cases may be impractical; however, the form of the data can be described numerically with one or the other of the alternatives chosen, allowing self-consistent between-group comparisons. The most promising approach for distinguishing among underlying distributions is through the generation of a family of ROCs and a comparison of goodness of fit of alternative theoretical ROC families.

REFERENCES

Botwinick, J. *Aging and behavior.* New York: Springer, 1973.

Egan, J. P. *Signal detection theory and ROC analysis.* New York: Academic Press, 1975.

Egan, J. P., Greenberg, G. Z., & Schulman, A. I. Operating characteristics, signal detectability, and the method of free response. *Journal of the Acoustical Society of America,* 1961, *33,* 993–1007.

Green, D. M., & Swets, J. A. *Signal detection theory and psychophysics.* New York: Wiley, 1966.

Hertzog, C. K., Williams, M. V., & Walsh, D. A. The effect of practice on age differences in central perceptual processing. *Journal of Gerontology,* 1976, *31,* 428–433.

McGill, W. J. Neural counting mechanisms and energy detection in audition. *Journal of Mathematical Psychology,* 1967, *4,* 351–375.

Pike, R. Response latency models for signal detection. *Psychological Review,* 1973, *80,* 53–80.

Pollack. I., & Hsieh, R. Sampling variability of the area, under the ROC-curve and of *d'. Psychological Bulletin,* 1969, *71,* 161–173.

Ratcliff, R. A theory of memory retrieval. *Psychological Review,* 1978, *85,* 59–108.

Rees, J. N., & Botwinick, J. Detection and decision factors in auditory behavior of the elderly. *Journal of Gerontology*, 1971, *26*, 133–136.

Restle, F., & Davis, J. H. Success and speed of problem solving by individuals and groups. *Psychological Review*, 1962, *69*, 520–536.

Walsh, D. A. Age differences in central perceptual processing: A dichoptic backward masking investigation. *Journal of Gerontology*, 1976, *31*, 181–188.

Walsh, D. A., Williams, M. V., & Hertzog, C. K. Age-related differences in two stages of central perceptual processes: The effects of short target durations and criterion differences. *Journal of Gerontology*, 1979, *34*, 234–241.

Waugh, N. C., Fozard, J. L., Talland, G. A., & Erwin, D. W. Effects of age and stimulus repetition on two-choice reaction time. *Journal of Gerontology*, 1973, *28*, 466–470.

Wickelgren, W. A., & Norman, D. A. Strength models and serial position in short-term recognition memory. *Journal of Mathematical Psychology*, 1966, *3*, 316–347.

Christopher Hertzog

CHAPTER

41

Applications of Signal Detection Theory to the Study of Psychological Aging: A Theoretical Review

It has been suggested that signal detection theory (SDT) provides a useful methodology for comparing age groups in detection and recognition performance because it explicitly separates sensitivity from response criterion. This chapter provides an introductory review of the principles of SDT and its methods. The advantages and limitations of single-point estimation techniques, common in gerontological application, are discussed extensively. The alternative SDT method, receiver operating characteristic (ROC) analysis, is recommended both as a means of testing assumptions enabling single-point estimation and as a more fully informative approach in assessing observers' sensitivity and response criteria.

Psychologists interested in studying age differences in psychological constructs such as perception or memory have been justifiably concerned that age differences in performance on an experimental task may reflect age differences in task-specific performance skills rather than age differences in the construct of interest per se, (see Botwinick, 1967, 1978). A potentially important performance-related confound is an age difference in the decision processes involved in the selection of a response from the set of possible response alternatives; it has been suggested that old subjects tend to be more cautious or conservative in their decision making and more likely to show inappropriate response biases that would impair performance (Botwinick, 1978; Okun, 1976).

Signal detection theory (SDT) has been advocated as an ideal method to approach the problem of age differences in decision processes (e.g., Craik, 1969), since it explicitly separates a subject's level of discrimination among stimulus alternatives from his or her decision processes in response selection. Several studies have employed SDT methods to study age differences in a variety of tasks (see Danziger, Chapter 39, this volume) including auditory perception (Rees & Botwinick, 1971) and recognition memory (Craik, 1969; Gordon & Clark, 1974; Harkins, Chapman, & Eisdorfer, 1979). Such studies are to be commended for their attempt to use a strong, theory-based methodology to disentangle age differences in "sensitivity" from age differences in decision criteria. However, a critical review of this literature indicates an un-

Most of the concepts, equations, and so forth, presented in this chapter come directly from other sources, most notably Egan (1975) and Green and Swets (1974), and no claim of originality is made. Of the few original ideas presented here, most were tested and sharpened in extended conversations with Michael Williams, whom I thank for his effort and interest. Thanks also to John A. Swets, Marcy Lansman, and Stephen Harkins for their comments and suggestions.

Work on this paper was supported by a U.S. Public Health Service Postdoctoral Fellowship from the National Institute on Aging (AG05150-01).

fortunate tendency toward a somewhat superficial application of SDT methods. Most studies have generated SDT-based parameters in the quickest and most economical way, without sufficient consideration of whether the strict assumptions required for the "quick and dirty" approach have been violated. This is indeed unfortunate, since violation of certain basic assumptions will produce contaminated SDT parameters, which may not be much better than the traditionally used indices of performance. In fact, they may be worse, since they are believed to be "pure" measures of sensitivity and response bias. Moreover, the prevalent usage of the simplest SDT method seems to have obscured the potential utility of the more complex SDT methods, which, though more costly and time-consuming, provide a fuller, richer description of subjects' sensitivity and decision processes.

The aim of this chapter is to provide an introductory overview of SDT and its methods and their application to between-groups designs that block on the age factor. The discussion covers a wide range of SDT paradigms potentially useful in the study of age differences in detection and recognition tasks. Special attention is given to the problem of individual differences in SDT parameters and to how these differences should be analyzed. This treatment of SDT is relatively untechnical and may therefore seem unsatisfactory to the mathematically sophisticated; those readers are referred to more advanced treatments of the topic.

Recognition and Detection Tasks

SDT applies concepts derived from statistical decision theory to the analysis of data obtained from a decision or recognition task (Green & Swets, 1974). Following Bush, Galanter, and Luce (1963) and Luce (1963), we can characterize these detection and recognition tasks as incorporating the following principles:

1. These tasks are usually complete identification experiments, because there is a one-to-one correspondence between the elements of the response set R and the stimulus presentation set S. Thus, each response is uniquely identified with one and only one stimulus alternative.

2. The detection experiment asks the question, "Is there a stimulus present?" There is a set of stimuli $S = (0, S_1, S_2 \ldots S_m)$, in which 0 is a null or noise stimulus, and $S_1, S_2 \ldots S_m$ represent m alternative non-null stimuli. The subject's task on each trial is to determine whether a stimulus has been presented.

3. The recognition experiment asks the question, "Which of several possible stimuli are present?" The

subject is asked to distinguish among the m stimulus alternatives $S = (S_1, S_2, \ldots S_m)$ by giving the corresponding response from set $R = (R_1, R_2, \ldots R_m)$.

Variations in detection and recognition tasks are possible and are best illustrated by inspection of the stimulus-response matrix shown in Figure 41-1. In the general case, this matrix has $m + 1$ rows and $m + 1$ columns, where the rows are identified with the stimulus set $S = (0, S_1, S_2, \ldots S_m)$ and the columns are identified with the response set $R = (0, R_1, R_2, \ldots R_m)$. The different detection and recognition tasks involve combination of subsets of S and R (see Green & Birdsall, 1978).

Simple Detection

The simple detection task consists of two stimulus alternatives, $S = (0, S_1)$. Either a signal is added to background noise (S_1) or it is not (0). There are two response alternatives: $R = (0, R_1)$. These responses are generally "No, a signal was not present" (0), or "Yes, a signal was present" (R_1). Simple detection is therefore often called a yes–no (Y, N) task. It is the task most often employed in applications of SDT.

1-of-m Detection

The 1-of-m detection task uses all cells in the matrix shown in Figure 41-1, except that all non-null stimuli are treated the same; the stimulus set is still $S = (0, S_1, S_2, \ldots S_m)$, but the subject is required only to determine whether any of the m potential signals were presented. Hence the response set is still $R = (0, R_1)$ or $R = $ (no, yes). This is the only task considered here in which there is not a complete one-to-one mapping of R on S; R_1 is appropriate for all non-null elements of S.

Pure Recognition

The pure recognition task omits the null stimulus and its corresponding response; the stimulus set is restricted to one of the m stimuli, $S = (S_1, S_2, \ldots S_m)$, and the response set is $R = (R_1, R_2, \ldots R_m)$.

Detection and Recognition

The detection and recognition task uses the complete stimulus–response matrix shown in Figure 41-1. There are $m + 1$ stimulus alternatives (0 plus the m signals) such that on a given trial one of the signals

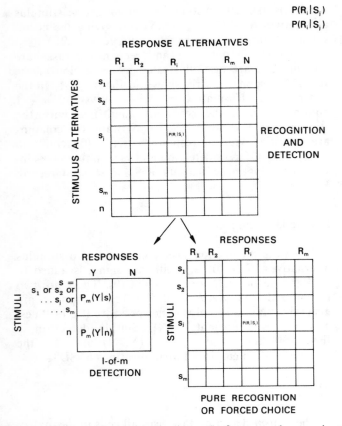

Figure 41-1. Stimulus–response matrix for general recognition and detection task. Two subtypes, the 1-of-*m* detection and the pure recognition task, are also shown. Rows correspond to the stimulus set, columns to the response set; cell entries are conditional probabilities of response R_i, given stimulus S_j. (From "Detection and Recognition" by D. M. Green and T. G. Birdsall, *Psychological Review*, 1978, *85*, 192–206. Copyright 1978 by the American Psychological Association. Reprinted by permission.)

$(S_1, S_2, \ldots S_m)$ or none (0) is presented. There are corresponding $m + 1$ response alternatives, $R = (0, R_1, R_2, \ldots R_m)$. The subject must answer two questions: (1) Was a stimulus presented? and (2) If so, which stimulus was it?

Additional compexities are added by allowing for the possibility of multiple observation intervals. In the four tasks considered above, only one observation, or stimulus event, occurred in each trial. If we allow more than one observation interval, a new class of detection experiments can be developed.

Two-Interval, Forced Choice

In this experiment, a simple detection experiment is expanded into two observation intervals, one for each stimulus alternative (0 and S_1). The signal (S_1) is randomly presented in one of the two intervals, and the subject must indicate which interval contained the non-null stimulus S_1. This response set can be denoted as $R = (I_1, I_2)$.

m-Interval, Forced Choice

The *m*-interval forced-choice task is a generalization of the 2-interval forced-choice task, except that the number of intervals is greater than two. S_1 is presented in only one of the *m* intervals; all other intervals contain 0 alone. Again, the subject is asked to select the interval containing S_1 where $R = (I_1, I_2, \ldots I_m)$.

Several other complex recognition and detection paradigms exist (see Green & Swets, 1974), but the ones defined above are sufficient for the purposes of this chapter. There is one important additional design feature worth mention: Forced-choice experiments may be run as a single-interval, *m*-alternative forced choice if the alternative observations can be presented simultaneously (e.g., visual stimuli presented simultaneously in multiple spatial locations). The characteristics of *m*-interval forced-choice experiments hold for *m*-alternative forced-choice experiments as well.

One source of confusion regarding the forced-choice paradigm should be made explicit: All of the tasks considered above are "forced choice" in the sense that the subject is always required to respond by giving one of the response alternatives. Subjects are not allowed to respond "I don't know" or "Maybe any of them!" (Models allowing for a noncommittal response category are feasible but much more complex.) This feature might be called *forced response* to avoid confusion. The forced-choice experiment, however, requires the subject to choose among different observation intervals, only one of which contains the non-null stimulus. Thus *forced choice* has a special interpretation above and beyond *forced response*.

Classifications of Response Data

The basic datum of the detection and recognition tasks listed above is the relative frequency, or probability (P), of any stimulus–response pairing. Each cell of the stimulus–response matrix of Figure 41-1 consists of a union of elements in S and R. The diagonal elements of the matrix are the correct responses, that is, where S_j is paired with R_i ($i = j$). The off-diagonal elements of the matrix are incorrect responses, that is, where S_j is paired with R_i ($i \neq j$).

Although the basic datum is the frequency of joint

occurrence of R_i and S_j, it is common practice to use estimates of conditional probabilities, denoted $P(R_i|S_j)$, or "the probability of R_i, given S_j." The conditional probabilities give the probability of R_i on trials when S_j is presented, and they are generally preferable because they do not depend on variation in the frequency of $P(S_j)$ across levels of j. In other words, the conditional probabilities are independent of differences in the probability of occurrence of each of the stimulus alternatives. These conditional probabilities are estimated from the experimental data by the relative frequencies of the response set and the stimulus set; one estimates $P(R_1|S_1)$ by obtaining the frequency of R_1 when S_1 is presented, and by then dividing by the frequency of S_1 presentations, ignoring which R_j was given. Formally, the empirically obtained relative frequency is denoted as $\hat{P}(R_i|S_j)$ and then

$$\hat{P}(R_i|S_j) = \frac{f(R_i, S_j)}{\sum_{s=1}^{m} f(R_i, S_j)} \quad (1)$$

where $f(R_i, S_j)$ stands for the frequency of the joint occurrence of R_i and S_j.

Signal Detection Theory: Basic Principles

SDT derives from the application of fundamentals from statistical decision theory (Green & Swets, 1974). This section provides a rudimentary sketch of the logic of SDT. The concepts are developed more formally in the following section covering the simple detection task.

SDT assumes that a fallible observer is asked to perform in a detection or recognition task under experimental conditions in which the alternatives in the stimulus presentation set are not perfectly discriminable. SDT assumes further that the observer uses internally processed information about the stimulus event as the evidence with which to decide among the response alternatives. The nature of this evidence depends on the characteristics of the observer's perceptual processing of the stimulus event. SDT assumes that, regardless of the number of dimensions present in the evidence, the evidence can be mapped on a unidimensional axis. The central problem is that since the evidence distribution of one stimulus event on this unidimensional axis overlaps the evidence distributions of the remaining stimulus events, (a) the observer confuses stimuli with one another, and (b) the observer requires a decision rule using the available evidence to select the best response alternative. The optimal decision strategy is to compute and estimate the condi-

tional probability for each stimulus alternative, given the evidence, to form a likelihood ratio of these conditional probabilities and then to adopt a cutoff rule to assign the response alternatives to regions of the likelihood-ratio axis. It can be shown that decisions based on the use of the likelihood ratio (or its functional equivalent) are optimal for several different classes of decision goals (Egan, 1975; Green & Swets, 1974).

The detectability of a given stimulus alternative is a function of the physical parameters of the stimulus and the observer's evidence process, but the performance of the observer within a given level of stimulus detectability is a function of the observer's likelihood ratio. This is the basis for SDT's ability to provide a measure of the relative detectability of the stimulus, independent of the observer's use of the likelihood ratio in making a decision. These concepts are given more formal attention in the following explication of the simple detection task.

The Simple Detection Task

Recall that the simple detection, or Yes–No, task consists of two stimulus alternatives and two response alternatives; the stimulus–response matrix is given in Figure 41-2. To assist the reader's understanding, an

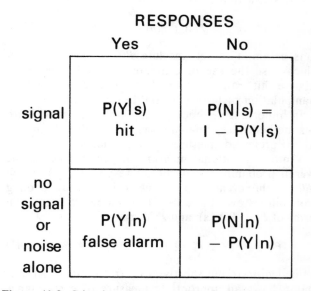

RESPONSES

	Yes	No
signal	P(Y|s) hit	P(N|s) = 1 − P(Y|s)
no signal or noise alone	P(Y|n) false alarm	P(N|n) 1 − P(Y|n)

Figure 41-2. Stimulus–response matrix for simple detection (Yes–No) task. Rows correspond to the stimulus set, columns to the response set; cell entries are conditional probabilities of the response, given the stimulus. (From "Detection and Recognition" by D. M. Green and T. G. Birdsall, *Psychological Review*, 1978, *85*, 192–206. Copyright 1978 by the American Psychological Association. Reprinted by permission.)

explicit Yes–No notation is used: Let (n,s) be substituted for $(0, S_1)$ in S and let (N, Y) be substituted for $(0, R_1)$ in R. The four cells in the stimulus–response matrix, (Y,s), (N,s), (Y,n), (N,n), are commonly termed *hits*, *misses*, *false alarms*, and *correct rejections*, respectively. The conditional probabilities $P(Y|s)$, $P(N|s)$, $P(Y|n)$, and $P(N|n)$ are termed *hit rate*, and *miss rate*, etc. This matrix has only two independent parameters because of the conditional probabilities. That is,

$$P(Y|s) + P(N|s) = 1$$
$$P(Y|n) + P(N|n) = 1 \qquad (2)$$

so that if $P(Y|s)$ and $P(Y|n)$ are given, the two remaining conditional probabilities are determined by

$$P(N|s) = 1 - P(Y|s)$$
$$P(N|n) = 1 - P(Y|n). \qquad (3)$$

By convention, the hit rate and false-alarm rate are the two conditional probabilities used to measure performance in the simple detection paradigm; as stated above, these conditional probabilities are independent of the prior probabilities, that is, the probabilities of presentation of the two stimulus events, $P(s)$ and $P(n)$. Obviously, with the two stimulus alternatives,

$$P(s) + P(n) = 1. \qquad (4)$$

It is common to set absolute $P(s) = P(n) = .5$, in which case the use of estimates of hit frequency or relative hit rate is equivalent. The experimenter's manipulation of prior probabilities where $P(s) \neq P(n)$ is an important method that is discussed below. With this method the estimated hit rate and false alarm rate are the preferred measures of performance.

A more traditional measure of performance is the overall probability of a correct response $P(C)$, which ignores the event/response classification by pooling probabilities over the cells. $P(C)$ can be represented in terms of $P(s)$, $P(Y|s)$, and $P(Y|n)$:

$$P(C) = P(Y|s) P(s) + [1 - P(Y|n)] [1 - P(s)]. \qquad (5)$$

As is demonstrated shortly, a central thesis of SDT is that $P(C)$ is an appropriate measure of performance levels only under certain conditions.

We are now in a position to develop a more formal understanding of the SDT theory and the simple detection task. SDT assumes that the observer's rational decision about responding yes or no in a given trial is based a value x of a random variable X, which represents a unidimensional evidence domain. Each event, s

or n, is assumed to be mapped onto this variable X (by a functional rule unknown to the experimenter and perhaps even to the subject); however, this mapping varies across trials for s and n, producing two separate probability distributions for each stimulus alternative. While these probability distributions may be continuous or discrete, X is treated here as continuous for simplicity of presentation. Then $f(x|n)$ and $f(x|s)$ are the probability density functions and $f(x|sn)dx$ and $f(x|n)dx$ are the heights of the evidence distributions at a given value of X.

An example of two probability density functions is shown in Figure 41-3. The distributions overlap because s and n are not perfectly discriminable; that is, there is a range of values for X where there is a nonzero probability for both event s and event n.

How is the evidence variable used by the observer to respond Y or N? Statistical decision theory assumes that the observer's decision is based on a probabilistic decision rule. The observer is assumed to calculate two conditional probabilities, one for the presentation of s and one for the presentation of n, given the evidence x. These probabilities, $P(s|x)$ and $P(n|x)$, are termed the posterior probabilities because they are calculated from the evidence after a stimulus presentation. The observers compute $P(s|x)$ and $P(n|x)$ by using their

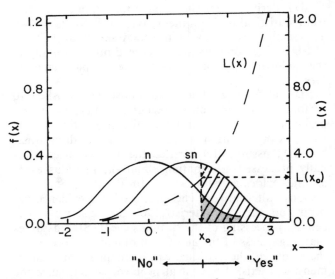

Figure 41-3. Evidence distributions for Events s and n mapped on unidimensional evidence axis X. Superimposed curve is for the likelihood ratio of s presentation, $L(x)$. Criterion cutoff at $L(x_c)$ divides X axis into two disjoint acceptance regions. (From *Signal Detection Theory and ROC Analysis* by J. P. Egan [New York: Academic Press, 1975]. Copyright 1975 by Academic Press. Reprinted by permission.)

knowledge about prior probabilities of stimulus presentation, $P(s)$ and $P(n)$, and their knowledge of the evidence value x generated by s and n events. Statistical decision theory assumes that the observer has learned enough about the probability distributions of X for s and n to be able to estimate $P(x|s)$ and $P(x|n)$ for any given value x. Then, by application of Bayes's theorem,

$$P(s|x) = \frac{P(x|s)\,P(s)}{P(x)} = \frac{f(x|s)\,P(s)}{f(x|s)\,P(s) + f(x|n)\,P(n)} \cdot \quad (6)$$

An analogous application of Bayes's theorem yields $P(n|x)$; it is then possible to calculate the posterior odds in favor of Stimulus s being presented as a ratio of the posterior probabilities:

$$\frac{P(s|x)}{P(n|x)} = \frac{P(s)}{P(n)} \frac{f(x|s)}{f(x|n)} \cdot \quad (7)$$

The first element of Equation 7 is the ratio of the prior probabilities indicating the relative likelihood that Stimulus s is presented. The second element on the right side of Equation 7, $f(x|s)/f(x|n)$ is called the likelihood ratio, denoted $L(x)$, and it indicates the relative likelihood of obtaining the value x when s has been presented.

SDT assumes that the observer uses the posterior odds to form a decision rule for responding Y or N. This decision rule establishes a cutoff point c for $L(x)$, such that

$$\text{if } L(x)\,\frac{P(s)}{P(n)} < c, \text{ respond N};$$
$$\text{if } L(x)\,\frac{P(s)}{P(n)} > c, \text{ respond Y}. \quad (8)$$

Obviously, when $P(s) = P(n)$, the decision rule can be expressed solely in terms of $L(x)$. The likelihood ratio at the cutoff c is denoted $L(x_c)$.

In theory, the decision goal of the observer determines placement of the likelihood-ratio cutoff criterion. Different values of $L(x)$ are optimal for different decision goals. A traditional decision goal in psychological experiments is to maximize the probability of correct responses, denoted $P(C)$. This goal is accomplished if one responds Y if $P(s|x) > P(n|x)$. In terms of the likelihood ratio, this goal implies that the observer responds Y if $L(x) > P(n)/P(s)$, and N otherwise. Other decision goals are possible (see Egan, 1975; Green & Swets, 1974); it can be shown formally that a likelihood-ratio criterion rule is optimal for a variety of such decision goals.

The Receiver Operating Characteristic

The observer's placement of the likelihood-ratio cutoff criterion determines the hit rate and false alarm rate. If the criterion is varied for a fixed pair of evidence distributions for s and n, the hit rate and false alarm rate will vary, even though the overlap of the distributions (and hence, the relative detectability of s from n) remains the same. $P(C)$ will also covary with the response criterion. Thus, any comparison of hit rates or $P(C)$ values between subjects or across experimental conditions will reflect both the discriminability of s from n and the criterion location. If, as is usually the case, the experiment is designed to test the hypothesis that detectability levels differ between conditions, a statistical test of differences in $P(C)$ or $P(Y|s)$ will be inappropriately biased when $L(x_c)$ varies between conditions as well. Fortunately, SDT provides a method for estimating an unbiased measure of detectability—namely, by using a statistic that reflects the overlap in the distributions of $f(x|s)$ and $f(x|n)$. Before discussing methods for measuring detectability, it is useful to discuss the concept of a receiver operating characteristic.

The conditional probabilities $P(Y|s)$ and $P(Y|n)$ may be plotted against each other on a two-dimensional graph with coordinates $P(Y|n)$, $P(Y|s)$. This graph is called the unit square, since the probability coordinates range from 0 to 1 (see Figure 41-4). The diagonals in the unit square have important properties: The positive diagonal—the line from (0,0) to (1,1)—is the line of chance performance, where $P(Y|s) = P(Y|n)$; the negative diagonal—the line from (1,0) to (0,1)—represents the line where responses Y and N are equally probable, that is, where $P(Y|s) = 1 - P(Y|n)$.

The results of a simple detection experiment with unchanging signal strength are graphed as a single point on the unit square (Figure 41-4A). If the relative overlap of the evidence distributions is held constant (e.g., by holding the physical characteristics of the stimuli constant) while the observer's likelihood-ratio cutoff is varied, a set of points is generated that lies along a smoothed curve (see Figure 41-4B). This curve is an isosensitivity curve (Luce, 1963), since the overlap of the evidence distributions has not changed. Theoretically, an observer can operate anywhere along this isosensitivity curve by adjusting the likelihood-ratio criterion; conversely, an observer operating with a given criterion is located on a single point on the curve. Hence the curve is named the receiver operating characteristic, or ROC.

The theoretical ROC has several important features (Egan, 1975):

1. If the observer's decision rule is a consistent func-

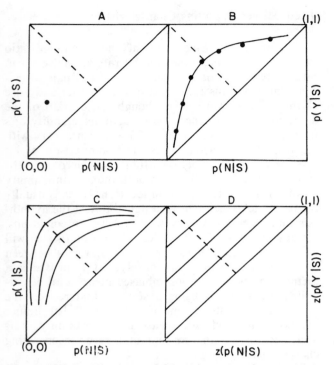

Figure 41-4. A: Hit rate and false alarm rate from a single experimental condition is graphed as a single point in the unit square. **B:** Iso-sensitivity curve (ROC) generated by holding stimulus detectability constant and varying the likelihood-ratio cutoff, $L(x_c)$. **C:** Family of proper ROCs generated for three levels of stimulus detectability. **D:** Family of normal, equal-variance ROCs graphed in normal deviate coordinates. (For all four plots, $R_1 = Y$, $R_2 = N$, $S_1 = S$, $S_2 = N$.)

the physical parameters of the stimuli) change the discriminability of s from n. If, for a discrete set of detectability levels, $L(x)$ is varied as before, a family of ROC curves is traced across the unit square, with one ROC for each level of detectability (see Figure 41-4C). A family of ROCs is termed an *ordered family* if the individual ROCs do not intersect (note that the ROC family in Figure 41-4C is ordered). If the evidence distributions are completely overlapping, such that Event s cannot be distinguished from Event n, then the ROC is the positive diagonal, $P(Y|s) = P(Y|n)$. As the degree of overlap of the evidence distributions decreases (detectability increases), the ROC moves upward in the unit square, being bounded by (0,1), where the s event is always correctly detected. Since the area under the ROC is a monotonic function of detectability, it can be used as an index of detectability.

5. It is possible to locate a point on each member of an ROC family where an observer using a consistent decision rule should be performing. For the likelihood-ratio observer, this point is often $L(x) = c$, where the likelihood-ratio cutoff is constant. This curve is an isocriterion (or isobias) contour with an exact form dependent on the decision goal of the observer. There are a wide variety of isocriterion contours, since there are many possible decision goals and decision rules. An important isocriterion contour for some observers is the negative diagonal of the unit square, where $P(Y|s) = P(N|n)$. The optimal operating point for an observer seeking to maximize $P(C)$ lies on the negative diagonal (Egan, 1975).

Normal Evidence Distributions

As stated above, the shape of an ideal ROC depends largely on the form of the underlying probability distributions for the evidence variable X. Classic SDT assumes that the evidence distributions for all stimuli, including the null or noise stimulus, are normally distributed. There are several reasonable justifications for this assumption, including the pragmatic rationale that normality assumptions greatly simplify the mathematical relations described in an ROC function (Egan, 1975, pp. 57–59; Green & Swets, 1974, pp. 57–58).

This normal (Gaussian) distribution assumption is useful because the normal density function is specified by only two parameters, the mean (μ) and variance (σ^2):

$$f(x) = (\sigma^2\pi)^{-1/2} \exp[-(x - \mu)^2/2\sigma^2], \quad (9)$$

where $\exp(a) = e^a$.

Under the assumption of normal distributions,

$$f(x|n) = (2\pi_n^2)^{-1/2} \exp[-(x - \mu_n)/2\sigma_n^2], \quad (10)$$

tion of $L(x)$, holding across the domain of $L(x)$ such that only the cutoff value $L(x_c)$ is changing, then a proper ROC is generated. A proper ROC is bounded by coordinates (0,0) and (1,1) and is monotonically increasing from (0,0) to (1,1) along the interior points of the unit square.

2. The slope of the ROC at any interior point is equal to the likelihood ratio $L(x)$. The slope of a proper ROC is monotonically decreasing from (0,0) to (1,1). The slope is infinite at (0,0), 0 at (1,1), and equal to 1 at the negative diagonal.

3. The shape of the ROC along the interior points of the unit square is dependent on the nature of the evidence distributions $f(x|s)$ and $f(x|n)$. Different ROC shapes are produced by different probability density functions for X. For example, normally distributed evidence distributions produce a qualitatively different ROC from that produced by exponential distribution functions.

4. Shifts in the overlap of the evidence distributions on the X dimension (generally produced by changes in

where μ_n is the mean of the evidence distribution for n and σ_n^2 is its variance. The same substitution gives $f(x|s)$ in terms of the evidence distribution parameters for s, where μ_s is its mean and σ_s^2 is its variance. For a given cutoff $x = c$, the hit rate $P(Y|s)$ and the false alarm rate $P(Y|n)$ are equal to the area under the normal density function from the tails of the s and n distributions to cutoff c.

SDT, in its classic form, assumes that the normal evidence distributions for s and n have equal variance, $\sigma^2 = \sigma_s^2 = \sigma_n^2$. Under this assumption the degree of overlap between the two evidence distributions is completely specified by $(\mu_s - \mu_n)/\sigma$, the difference between the means of the distributions, scaled by the common standard deviation. The scaled difference is defined as d'. The parameter d' is independent of the likelihood-ratio criterion of the observer; it remains constant for a given pair of X distributions when the criterion cutoff is varied. Given the normal equal-variance assumption, the standard scores (z scores) for the s and n evidence distributions at cutoff c are

$$z_s = \frac{c - \mu_s}{\sigma}$$

and $\hspace{10em}$ (11)

$$z_n = \frac{c - \mu_n}{\sigma} .$$

The difference between the two standard scores is

$$z_n - z_s = \frac{\mu_s - \mu_n}{\sigma} = d' \qquad (12)$$

and is independent of the actual criterion c, which cancels out of the equation. The hit rate and false alarm rate at c are

$$P(Y|s)_c = 1 - \Phi(z_s)$$
$$P(Y|n)_c = 1 - \Phi(z_n), \qquad (13)$$

where Φ is the normal distribution function associated with the normal density function of Equation 9. Equation 13 shows formally that while d' is invariant with changing criterion, the hit rate and false alarm rate covary with changes in that criterion.

The ROC curve under the normal, equal-variance assumption is symmetrical about the negative diagonal of the unit square and is completely determined by the parameter d'. Thus the normal equal-variance ROC is a "single-parameter" isosensitivity curve (Luce, 1963). If the normal equal-variance ROC is plotted on a normal-deviate coordinate system, using the z-score transforms of $P(Y|n)$ and $P(Y|s)$, then the ROC is a

straight line with unit slope and intercept $-d'$, since from Equation 12

$$z_s = z_n - d'. \qquad (14)$$

The utility of the assumption of normal evidence distributions with equal variance should be apparent in Equations 12 and 14, since d' is simply the difference between the z-scores corresponding to the false alarm rate and hit rate. (By convention, the signs of z-scores are reversed in SDT analysis so that d' is always positive.) Equation 12 implies that d' can be estimated from any interior point in ROC space, since one and only one normal equal-variance ROC passes through a single interior point. Figure 41-4D shows a family of normal equal-variance ROCs graphed in normal-deviate coordinates.

Although d' is the vertical intercept in Equation 14, the fact that the negative diagonal in normalized coordinates is defined as $z_s = z_n$ means that any point on the negative diagonal has an abcissa (x coordinate) of $z_n = d'/2$. Therefore, the distance up the negative diagonal from the midpoint of the unit square is a linear function of d', and the negative diagonal may thus be scaled in terms of d' values (Egan, 1975, pp. 68–69).

Although the normal equal-variance ROC is completely specified by parameter d', the operating point of an observer on any such ROC is determined by the likelihood-ratio cutoff, or $L(x_c)$, the slope of the ROC at criterion cutoff. In the case of normal distributions, the likelihood-ratio cutoff is defined as β. Since $L(x) = f(x|n)/f(x|s)$, β is equal to the ratio of the ordinates corresponding to z_s and z_n at cutoff c (see McNicol, 1972, Chap. 3).

If $\sigma_s^2 \neq \sigma_n^2$ (the general Gaussian case), then the ROC curve for the simple detection experiment is not a single-parameter isosensitivity function. In the general case for normal evidence distributions, the values of z_s and z_n at a particular criterion c are

$$z_n = \frac{c - \mu_n}{\sigma_n}$$

and $\hspace{10em}$ (15)

$$z_s = \frac{c - \mu_s}{\sigma_s} ,$$

the difference being that each probability is scaled by the standard deviation of its own distribution, σ_n or σ_s, rather than by a common σ. The degree of overlap between the distributions is still independent of Criterion c, since c can be eliminated by expressing z_n and z_s in Equations 15 in terms of the common element c:

$$c = \sigma_n z_n - \mu_n = \sigma_s z_s - \mu_s . \qquad (16)$$

Thus the equation becomes

$$z_s = \left(\frac{\sigma_n}{\sigma_s}\right)z_n - \left(\frac{\mu_n - \mu_s}{\sigma_s}\right), \qquad (17)$$

which shows that the normalized ROC in the unequal-variance case is still a straight line with two parameters, slope σ_n/σ_s and intercept $-(\mu_n - \mu_s)/\sigma_s$. Green and Swets (1974) define these parameters as (Δ_m, s), where Δ_m is the intercept of the ROC (at $z_s = 0$) and s is the slope. Although both parameters are needed to specify the normal unequal-variance ROC, the parsimony of a single index of detectability has led several authors to suggest a detectability parameter analogous to d' (see Simpson & Fitter, 1973). The most prevalent index is Egan's d_e' (or d_s), which corresponds to the intercept at the point where the ROC intersects the negative diagonal. Its advantage as a single detectability index is that it gives equal weight to the units of the n and s evidence distributions (Egan & Clarke, 1966; Treisman, 1977). The abundance of other single-parameter estimates of detectability need not be discussed in the present context.

An additional complexity in the general Gaussian case is that a proper ROC is generated only if $L(x)$ is used to partition the evidence axis into discrete response regions. A single cutoff in terms of the untransformed evidence variable X will result in an improper ROC (Egan, 1975, Chapters 1–3). Actually this was not the case when equal variances were assumed; then a single cutoff on the untransformed evidence was functionally equivalent to a likelihood-ratio cutoff. In other words, X is a proper decision variable in the Gaussian case when $\sigma_s = \sigma_n$, but not otherwise. Nevertheless, the operating point of an observer on a normal unequal-variance ROC is still determined by the likelihood-ratio cutoff β; its computation is more difficult in the unequal-variance case (McNicol, 1972, Chapter 4).

Although the assumption of normal evidence distributions is common in applications of SDT to studies of simple detection, there are other evidence distributions that can be specified formally and whose properties are important in certain types of SDT models (Egan, 1975). For example, the exponential distribution is often used in SDT-oriented models of response latency. Williams (Chapter 40, this volume) discusses some of the properties of different types of evidence distributions and their importance in psychological studies of aging.

Empirical Applications of SDT

The basic principles of signal detection theory, as just outlined for the simple detection task, can be used to study psychological phenomena in several ways.

Empirical applications of SDT may be divided roughly into two categories: (1) primarily psychophysical studies, which study with care empirically generated ROCs in a small number of trained observers, and (2) studies of individual differences in sensitivity and criterion measures, which usually compare experimentally or "naturally" defined groups of subjects.

In the first category, the examination of individual differences in ROC curves is of secondary importance; the primary purpose is to understand the mechanics of perceptual phenomena by using empirical ROCs to differentiate among different theories of perceptual sensitivity. Basic studies validating SDT models of perceptual task performance have examined the invariance of d' across different methods of generating empirical ROCs or have tested the tenability of normal equal-variance assumptions for different kinds of psychophysical tasks. ROC analysis has been used primarily in auditory and visual psychophysical studies to test different theories of psychophysical thresholds; SDT studies have challenged traditional psychophysical theories of perceptual threshholds by demonstrating the importance of decision processes in psychophysical tasks (e.g., Green & Swets, 1974, Chapter 5; other complex threshold theories compatible with decision-theory application are discussed by Luce, 1963, and Krantz, 1969). In all of these studies, emphasis was placed on obtaining stable estimates of ROC functions in observers whose high level of training virtually guaranteed asymptotic performance levels and who were most likely to be able to adjust their criterion according to experimenter instructions. ROC curves were generally plotted separately for each observer, but the individual differences in ROCs were rarely emphasized.

In contrast, a considerable number of studies have studied individual differences in SDT-derived measures of sensitivity and criterion in widely varied psychological tasks (Grossberg & Grant, 1978). Studies of age differences in SDT parameters obviously fall into this second category. When emphasis has been placed on studies of individual differences, the time-consuming task of training observers and generating empirical ROCs from hundreds, or even thousands, of experimental trials has been generally avoided. Individual-differences studies have generally sought to obtain more "economical" SDT parameters on a large number of subjects. Such studies have often turned to the analysis of individual differences in single point estimates of d' and β.

Single-Point Estimates

The term *single-point estimate* refers to the fact that d' and β are calculated from a single pair of hit-rate and false-alarm-rate probabilities, and thus from a single point in the unit square. The underlying ROC is not empirically estimated. Single-point estimates of d' and β are possible under the normal equal-variance distribution assumptions, since, as discussed above, there is only one ideal ROC derived from such distributions that passes through a given interior point in the unit square.

Single-point estimates of d' and β are economical since estimation of an empirical ROC over several values of $L(x_c)$ requires many more experimental trials. If the normal equal-variance assumptions hold true, then the single-point estimates of d' and β are unconfounded (orthogonal) estimates of sensitivity and criterion. The experimenter is then able to examine individual or group differences in subjects' sensitivity to the signal (d'), "corrected" for differences in operating point on the normal equal-variance ROCs. The experimenter is also able to analyze individual or group differences in operating points (β).

The method of obtaining single-point estimates of d' and β is relatively straightforward. Consider an experiment employing a simple detection (yes–no) task with $P(s) = P(n)$ and with subjects instructed to maximize $P(C)$. There is one experimental condition for each level of signal strength (defined by variation in physical attributes of s, e.g., increasing luminance in a luminance-detection task). For each condition the experimenter obtains a single pair of relative response frequencies $\hat{P}(Y|s)$ and $\hat{P}(Y|n)$ (see Equation 1), which is taken to be an unbiased estimate of the true hit and false alarm rates $P(Y|s)$ and $P(Y|n)$. Since $P(Y|s)$ and $P(Y|n)$ are the areas under the normal evidence distributions for s and n at Criterion c, the tables of the standard normal curve can be used to find the z-score values of areas under the standard normal density function corresponding to the two empirical probabilities, $\hat{P}(Y|s)$ and $\hat{P}(Y|n)$. An estimate of d' is the difference between the two z-scores, and an estimate of β is the ratio of the ordinates corresponding to the two z-scores (McNicol, 1972). For convenience, Elliott (1964) has provided a table of d' values corresponding to different pairs of empirical hit rates and false alarm rates.

It is necessary to calculate separate estimates of d' and β for each subject, because pooling relative response frequencies within groups can distort averaged estimates of d'. Once estimates of d' have been obtained, they may be treated as $P(C)$ is usually treated. If, for example, the signal strengths are chosen as part of the method of constant stimuli, then a psychometric function plotting d' against a measure of signal strength can be obtained for each subject. It has been more common in practice to employ a single experimental condition and to use the estimates of d' and β as dependent measures in a statistical analysis of the significance of between-groups differences; analysis of variance is often used for this. The logarithm of β is often used instead of β, since the log transform has a symmetric interval for degree of bias to responses Y and N (Danzinger, Chapter 39, this volume; McNicol, 1972).

On the surface, the analysis of single-point estimates of d' and β represents an excellent method for comparing age groups for differences in sensitivity and bias. There are, however, several major limitations to this approach that may well vitiate the utility of these indices in many research applications. There are three major areas of concern:

1. What are the consequences of violating the basic assumptions enabling the single-point estimation?

2. How reliable are interindividual differences in the single-point estimates?

3. What are the appropriate statistical tests of between-group and within-individual differences in the estimates?

Assumption violations. The first area of concern, the violation of assumptions enabling the single-point estimation procedure, is most important. The major assumptions are summarized in Table 41-1. The most general assumption is that the subjects behave as rational observers, using the likelihood-ratio decision rule (or its functional equivalent) to select among response alternatives (Y and N in the simple detection case), the likelihood ratio being a function of the posterior probabilities computed by the subjects. The assumption of asymptotic performance implies that the subjects have learned the task requirements and the stimulus set elements and have developed a stable, consistent method of computing posterior probabilities. This implies that the subjects have built up sufficient information about the task to be performing at their own optimal level (with maximum possible sensitivity). This assumption, plus the assumptions of independence of trials and of a constant likelihood-ratio

Table 41-1 Assumptions for Single-Point Estimates of d' and β

General Assumptions
1. Rational observer used likelihood-ratio decision rule on posterior probabilities to select response.
2. Asymptotic performance levels have been achieved prior to experimental trials.
3. Relative response frequencies are statistically independent across trials.
4. The likelihood-ratio cutoff criterion is held constant over all trials.

Distributional Assumptions
1. Conditional evidence distributions for events s and n, $f(x|s)$ and $f(x|n)$, are normally distributed.
2. Normal distributions $f(x|s)$ and $f(x|n)$ have equal variances ($\sigma_s^2 = \sigma_n^2$).

criterion, simplifies the critical SDT equations and enables the experimenter to pool relative response frequencies over trials (ignoring sequential effects) in computing estimates of d' and β. The assumption of a constant likelihood-ratio criterion is also important because any estimate of d' under variable cutoff criteria can be shown to be biased downward (Green & Swets, 1974; Wickelgren, 1968)—that is, true sensitivity is underestimated.

Taken together, the assumptions listed above, if true, guarantee that subjects will produce a proper ROC that represents their own optimal performance in the task. Any type of "irrational" or mixed decision rule (not using likelihood ratio or its equivalent) will produce an improper ROC (see Egan, 1975, Chapter 2) that cannot be accurately summarized by classic SDT parameters, however estimated. The other assumptions ensure stable asymptotic performance by the subject over all trials.

The form of the proper ROC is determined by the evidence distribution assumptions. Assumptions of normal equal-variance evidence distributions yield the single-parameter isosensitivity ROC discussed above.

In practice, none of the assumptions listed in Table 41-1 will be strictly met; for example, sequential dependencies in detection task data have frequently been found (Dusoir, 1975). The critical issues are what the degree of bias in single point estimates of d' and β is when assumptions are violated, and what can be done to minimize the biasing influences. The usual psychophysical procedure of providing the subject with extensive practice represents an effort to minimize bias by producing an asymptotic performance level for the subject.

A formal treatment of the biases introduced by violating different assumptions is beyond the scope of the present article. If the decision rules are mixed, the rule must be explicitly stated, and there is a large if finite, number of such rules.

An informal illustration of the possible danger of assumption violations will suffice in the present context. Suppose that of the assumptions listed in Table 41-1, all hold except the equal variance assumption; that is, the evidence distributions are normal, but $\sigma_s \neq \sigma_n$. Typically, ideal ROCs for such cases have slopes less than unity, but the slopes increase with decreasing detectability (Green & Swets, 1974, pp. 62–64, pp. 94–99). The solid lines in Figure 41-5 show two such ROCs. These ROCs belong to the same family under the general Gaussian assumption. Now assume that two subjects are constrained by this unequal-variance Gaussian ROC family but that Observer 1, who is more sensitive than Observer 2, performs along the upper ROC and Observer 2 along the lower ROC, for equivalent signal strengths. These ROCs illustrate why $P(C)$ is often an inappropriately biased measure of de-

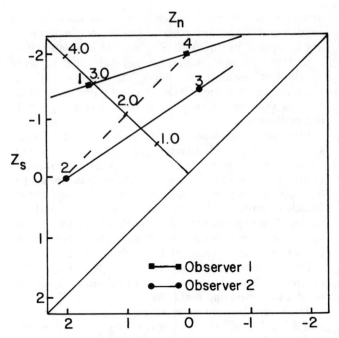

Figure 41-5. Hypothetical data from Table 2 for two observers constrained by normal evidence distributions of unequal variance. Single-point estimates of d' will be misleading since equal variance assumption is violated (see text).

tectability in subjects with differing operating points. The two points plotted on the ROC of Observer 1 have different criteria, different hit and false alarm rates, and different percentages of correct values, even though the points lie on the same isosensitivity curve (see Table 41-2). Therefore, two observers constrained by the same ROC will have differing $P(C)$ values unless they are operating at the same point. If the observers have different sensitivities for a given stimulus "strength," then comparisons of $P(C)$ will be biased indices of the differences in sensitivity unless the operating points are the same. In other words, the observers' operating points lie on an isocriterion contour.

Parenthetically, if the observers were ideal and seeking to maximize $P(C)$, their performance would lie along the negative diagonal [if $P(s) = P(n)$; see above], and $P(C)$ would be an unbiased measure of detectability. In practice, however, human observers often show less than optimal response biases—particu-

Table 41-2 Hypothetical Data for Single-Point Estimates [a]

Observer	$P(Y\|n)$	$P(Y\|s)$	$P(C)$	Z_n	Z_s	d'	β
Observer 1	.055	.933	.939	1.60	−1.50	3.10	.82
Observer 1	.500	.977	.739	0.00	−2.00	2.00	7.39
Observer 2	.123	.500	.689	2.00	0.00	2.00	.14
Observer 2	.421	.919	.749	0.20	−1.40	1.60	.18

[a] Data are depicted in Figure 41-5. See text for explanation.

Figure 41-6. Empirical ROCs for three observers in an expected value experiment. Note the individual differences in ROC slope and in spread of data points in unit square. (From "Decision Processes in Perception" by J. A. Swets, W. P. Tanner, Jr., and T. G. Birdsall, *Psychological Review*, 1961, *68*, 301–340. Copyright 1961 by the American Psychological Association. Reprinted by permission.) →

larly if they are not given feedback to avoid bias—and their operating points rarely lie on a common isocriterion contour; thus derives the inappropriate bias in $P(C)$ as a comparison measure of individual differences in sensitivity.

The question is, would single-point estimates of d' be better indices of sensitivity in this case? Recall that single-point estimates of d' from the points provided may be represented as scaled units along the negative diagonal. In Figure 41-5 these single-point d' estimates can be taken as the intersection of the unit-slope line projection from the data point to the negative diagonal (the dashed line). For Observer 1, operating at Point 1, estimated d' is 3.1, whereas for Observer 2, operating at Point 2, estimated d' is 2.0. For these points, d' reflects the sensitivity difference (although this difference is greater than that which would be obtained from d'_e, as taken from the negative diagonal). Note, however, that if Observer 1 operates at Point 4, the dashed line projection of d' passes through both Points 2 and 4; the estimated d' value is 1.0, which is the same as that estimated for Observer 2 (at Point 2). In other words, with radically different operating points and unequal variances, point estimates of d' can indicate no differences in sensitivity for observers when in fact there are true differences in sensitivity (as shown by the areas under the ROCs). In the present example, the data would probably be misinterpreted as showing no sensitivity differences between Observers 1 and 2 and only large criterion differences. This result is not surprising, since, given $\sigma_s \neq \sigma_n$, the relative superiority of Observer 1 over Observer 2 decreases with increasing false-alarm rate, due to the slope differences. Given freely varying operating points on their ROCs, single-point estimates of d' may underestimate or overestimate "true" detectability differences between individuals. Given an unfavorable configuration of individual differences in β, use of single-point estimates of d' [rather than $P(C)$] may merely be replacing one biased discriminability estimate with another.

The problem may be even more severe than is illustrated in Figure 41-5, since studies of empirical ROCs have often found qualitative individual differences in the shape of ROC curves (e.g., Markowitz & Swets, 1967). Empirical ROCs for three different trained observers, taken from Swets, Tanner, & Birdsall (1961), are shown in Figure 41-6. These ROCs were generated in a visual detection task by using a payoff matrix manipulation (see below).[1] The data contained a great

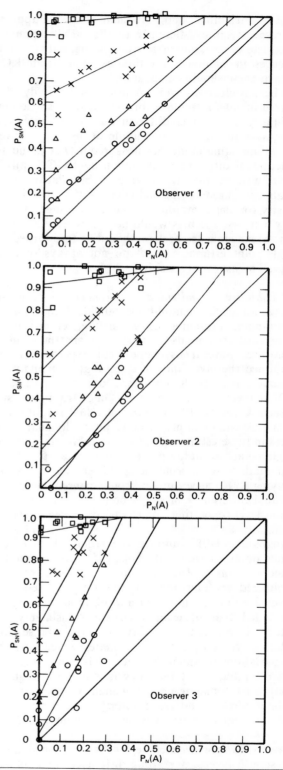

[1] The data in Figure 41-6 are plotted on standard arithmetic coordinates, that is, the probabilities have *not* been normalized. The reader should not be misled; the poor fit of the straight lines in Figure 41-6 is therefore not necessarily indicative of non-normal evidence distributions.

deal of variability, and individual observers appeared to respond quite differently to the payoff manipulation. The danger inherent in comparing individual differences in single-point estimates of d' from ROCs such as these should be apparent.

There is clearly a great need for formal study of the degree of bias introduced in $P(C)$ and of single point estimates of d' under different assumption violations, both as a function of magnitude of disparity between actual operating points, as measured by $L(x_c)$, and as a function of different locations on an ROC family. It could well be that the degree of bias introduced is small compared to the individual differences in sensitivity for the commonly encountered range of $L(x_c)$, in which case the bias would not be as serious a problem. Meanwhile researchers should be forewarned that single-point estimates of d' do not always represent "pure" measures of sensitivity.

Reliability of individual differences. Little is now known about the reliability of individual differences in single-point estimates of d'; neither empirical nor theoretical treatments of this topic are found in the literature. Several psychophysical experiments have examined the invariance of d' estimates for individual observers over trials, days, and different methods of ROC-curve generation, with encouraging results (Green & Swets, 1974). Intraindividual stability in d' estimates would imply reliable interindividual differences in these estimates, but studies have not examined single-point estimates per se. The major problem is that qualitative interindividual differences in the underlying ROC curves might produce unreliable interindividual differences in single point d' estimates if criterion level (operating point) varied between measurement points.

Ingham (1970) examined the reliability of d' estimates obtained from rating-scale data in an auditory detection task. Interindividual differences were minimized by adjusting stimulus intensity separately for each subject, aiming for a d' of about 1.5. Ingham concluded that d' estimates were "reasonably consistent" within and between two experimental sessions, but that was only after d' estimates were "corrected for variations in signal intensity." Moreover, the "corrected" reliability estimate was only .62. Ingham's study provides some encouragement on the reliability of interindividual differences in d', but more definitive work is needed, particularly on single-point estimates.

Statistical significance tests. As mentioned above, the significance of age group differences in d' is commonly tested with an analysis of variance (ANOVA). Thus the ratio of between-group variance in estimated d' to the pooled within-group variance in estimated d'

is compared with a critical value from the F distribution to test the null hypothesis of no group differences. The application of ANOVA methods seems straightforward, but there is a potential problem: The variance in the point estimate of d' is not equivalent across the unit square; the sampling variance of the empirical relative response frequencies about the true conditional probabilities varies in magnitude with the magnitude of the conditional probabilities themselves (see Green & Swets, 1974, Appendix III). In other words, the variance of the conditional probabilities is larger for extreme probability values, and the variance of the single-point d' estimate increases as the point moves toward the borders of the unit square.

Gourevitch and Galanter (1967) showed that an appropriate test of the null hypothesis that two independent estimates of d' are not different requires an estimate of the variance of d' at the two data points, and they developed formulae for the estimated variance of d' and a test statistic for evaluating the null hypothesis. Specifically, Gourevitch and Galanter (1967) showed that for a given d' estimate $\hat{d}'_1$, the variance estimate is

$$\hat{V}(\hat{d}'_1) = \frac{P_1(1 - P_1)}{n_1(\text{ord } z_1)^2} + \frac{P_2(1 - P_2)}{n_2(\text{ord } z_2)^2} \quad (18)$$

where $P_1 = P(Y \mid n)$, $P_2 = P(Y \mid s)$, $n_1 = P(n)$, $n_2 = P(s)$, and ord (z) is the ordinate for z_n or z_s. A test statistic for evaluating the significance of the difference between two estimates of d', $\hat{d}'_1$ and $\hat{d}'_2$, is then

$$G = \frac{\hat{d}'_1 - \hat{d}'_2}{[\hat{V}(\hat{d}'_1) + \hat{V}(\hat{d}'_2)]^{1/2}}. \quad (19)$$

Marascuilo (1970) extended Gourevitch and Galanter's (1967) method to the comparison of K d' estimates. He stated that the test statistic

$$U'_0 = \sum_{k=1}^{K} W_k(\hat{d}'_k - \hat{d}'_0)^2 \quad (20)$$

is approximated by a chi-square distribution with $K - 1$ degrees of freedom, where $W_k = 1/\hat{V}(\hat{d}'_k)$, and

$$\hat{d}'_o = \frac{\sum_{k=1}^{K} W_k \hat{d}'_k}{\sum_{k=1}^{K} W_k}. \quad (21)$$

The basic principle is that the sum of squared deviations of the $\hat{d}'_k$ about the pooled estimate $\hat{d}'_0$ is weighted by the different variances of estimate. This is clearly not the case for a traditional ANOVA analysis of $\hat{d}'$, where the test statistic is merely a function of the squared deviations about the marginal means or the grand mean, irrespective of the standard errors of estimate for each $\hat{d}'_k$.

It would appear therefore, that the more appropriate test of significant group differences in d' should be based on an F ratio formed from Marascuilo's test statistic U'_0, rather than on the traditional ANOVA F ratio, particularly if the single-point estimates of d' are widely scattered across the unit square.

One could define a group structure with subscript g, and then compute U'_0 for the variation of the marginal means, $\hat{d}'_g$, about $\hat{d}'_0$ as

$$U'_B \sum_{g=1}^{G} W_g(\hat{d}'_g - \hat{d}'_0)^2 \qquad (22)$$

where

$$W_g = \sum_{K=1}^{K_g} 1/\hat{V}(\hat{d}'_{k_g}) \qquad (23)$$

in the gth group. Then the pooled within-group variance is estimated from a modification of Equation 20 to reflect the group structure:

$$U'_w = \sum_{g=1}^{G} \sum_{k=1}^{K_g} W_{K_g}(\hat{d}'_k - \hat{d}'_g)^2. \qquad (24)$$

As in the usual ANOVA procedure, under the null hypothesis, H_0: all $\hat{d}'_g$ equal. The ratio of $[U'_B (K - G)]/[U'_w (G - 1)]$ should be asymptotically distributed as F with $(G - 1, K - G)$ degrees of freedom.

Again, no information is currently available on the degree of statistical bias introduced when the traditional ANOVA F test is used to analyze differences in d' estimates. Thus the practical importance of failing to use a more appropriate test statistic is unknown. For example, could one merely set a higher α level for the traditional F test?

Incidentally, Marascuilo's test statistic is well suited for the statistical analysis of individual differences in $\hat{d}'$. Not only does one obtain a χ^2 test of the overall significance of individual differences in $\hat{d}'_k$ (an omnibus significance test) but Marascuilo's post-hoc analysis techniques can be used to determine which individuals differ significantly.

Single point estimates: Concluding comments. Under favorable conditions, the conversion of routinely collected experimental data into single-point estimates of d' and β provides an economical method for indexing sensitivity and bias and for comparing age differences in sensitivity in individuals who differ in decision criteria. However, as has been noted, there are major pitfalls in the conversion to single-point SDT in-

dices if the assumptions enabling the conversion are violated, and there are problems in the use of these single-point estimates in between-group comparisons. Gerontologists who are interested in using indices of sensitivity unconfounded with response bias to measure age differences in behavior may thus be ill-advised in routinely using and interpreting single-point estimates of d' as an appropriate sensitivity index. Use of a single-point β estimate as a measure of bias is also problematic (see below; also see Danziger, Chapter 39, this volume).

One alternative to single point estimates of d' is to use a single-point estimate of the area under the ROC curve, since (as discussed earlier) this area is nonparametric—that is, it is an appropriate measure of sensitivity regardless of the form of the underlying evidence distributions. Norman (1964; Pollack & Norman, 1964) developed a formula for estimating the area under the ROC curve using only a single-point in ROC space; this method is based on the fact that a proper ROC passing through a given interior point in the unit square is constrained to lie inside a subspace of the unit square defined by that interior point (see also McNicol, 1972, Chapter 2). This measure, denoted A', averages the upper- and lower-bound areas possible for a given interior point. While this measure seems to be an attractive alternative to the single-point d', the difference between the upper and lower bounds of the proper ROC is rather large. Thus the measurement error is nontrivially large and may exceed the magnitude of individual differences in A' found in an experiment. The imprecision of its estimation severely limits the utility of A' for studies of individual differences in sensitivity.

Given the potential problems with single-point estimates, behavioral scientists should consider using alternative SDT methods to develop measures of sensitivity and bias, or at least to test the normal equal-variance assumptions in pilot data before proceeding with single-point d' estimates. There are two important and useful alternatives to the single-point estimation procedure: (1) use of the forced-choice paradigm (to estimate sensitivity only), and (2) generation of empirical ROCs from the simple detection paradigm. The following section outlines methods of generating ROC curves empirically and using these empirical ROCs to test important assumptions and to calculate appropriate measures of sensitivity.

Empirical ROC Curves

Empirical ROC curves are generated by holding the physical parameters of the stimulus set constant while experimentally manipulating the subject's placement of the criterion cutoff. A separate data point is generated for each manipulation condition, and this point should lie on an isosensitivity curve (assuming asymptotic performance levels). The experimental manipulation is necessarily indirect, since the criterion placement is under the subject's control; hence the manipulation generally involves informing the subject of changes in the task conditions, or simply changing instructions, in order to induce the subject to alter the criterion setting.

The criterion levels can be manipulated indirectly by (1) varying the a priori stimulus presentation probabilities $P(s)$ and $P(n)$, (2) varying the costs and values in a payoff matrix, (3) giving explicit instructions to vary the criterion, and (4) requiring a confidence rating with each response.

Manipulation of the stimulus presentation probabilities should affect the criterion by increasing the evidence value necessary to respond yes as $P(s)$ decreases. For example, a trained observer should require more definitive evidence to respond yes if $P(s) = .1$ than if $P(s) = .5$. This principle is explicit in Equation 8 above, where $L(x)$ is weighted by the ratio $P(s)/P(n)$. Thus, a subject who is fully informed of variations in the stimulus presentation probabilities should adjust the criterion accordingly.

The payoff-matrix approach assigns a positive or negative value to each of the event-response conjunctions, that is, the joint occurrence of (Y,N) and (s,n). Generally, the positive values are assigned to the correct responses (Y,s) and (N,n), while the negative values are assigned to incorrect responses (Y,n) and (N,s). When costs and values are introduced into the likelihood-ratio decision function, the likelihood-ratio observer must consider the expected value of the event-response conjunctions (Egan, 1975, pp. 16–19). The decision rule for the expected value observing is an extrapolation of Equation 8:

$$\text{If } L(x) > \frac{P(n)}{P(s)} \frac{V_{n,N} - V_{n,Y}}{V_{s,Y} - V_{s,N}} \qquad (25)$$

say yes; otherwise, say no (where V denotes the value of the subscript event-response conjunction). The term incorporating the V elements in Equation 25 can be interpreted as follows: The numerator, $V_{n,N} - V_{n,Y}$, is the relative value of a correct rejection against a false alarm, whereas the denominator, $V_{s,Y} - V_{s,N}$, is the relative value of a hit against a miss. Both terms should affect the decision of whether to choose Response Y or N, as shown in Equation 25; for example, a symmetrical payoff matrix with $V_{n,N} = V_{s,Y}$ and $V_{n,Y} = V_{s,N}$ weights equally both types of correct and incorrect response, and there is no differential

value for choosing Y over N. Hence, performance should lie on the negative diagonal, where both types of response are equally probable. Asymmetrical payoff matrices should produce a degree of bias toward Y or N, depending on the weights.

The use of explicit instructions is the simplest method of manipulating criterion; the subject is instructed to adopt a "strict" criterion on some trial blocks and a "lax" criterion on others. While this method may seem simplistic, it has been used with good results and is recommended by Wickelgren (1968) over the previous two methods in some cases.

In contrast, the confidence rating procedure is the most complex, in that its data require special treatment. The procedure itself is straightforward: The subject is required to give a confidence rating, taken from a predefined rating scale, with each response. For example, the subject may be instructed to use a 5-point rating scale, with 1 representing the highest degree of confidence and 5 representing the lowest degree of confidence. Each point on the rating scale is assumed to correspond to a different criterion setting, with high confidence that the event was a signal corresponding to a strict criterion, and low confidence that the event was a signal corresponding to a lax criterion. The experimenter then provides as large a number of trials as is required for the subject to use all of the rating categories and to generate reliable data.

The ROC data points are found by assuming that the subject is using several criterion settings simultaneously, with the j rating scale points corresponding to $j - 1$ different criterion settings. Then a hit rate and a false-alarm rate are calculated for, say, Rating Category 1. A second ROC point is found for Rating Category 2 by pooling probabilities for Categories 1 and 2. This procedure is repeated for all but the last rating category, and $j - 1$ ROC points are generated. These data points are clearly not independent of one another. McNicol (1972) provides an excellent introductory treatment of the rating-scale task and the method of calculating data points for a rating-scale ROC.

The confidence-rating procedure is probably the most frequently used method of generating empirical ROCs, because it usually requires fewer experimental trials to estimate the same number of points on the ROC. The confidence-rating procedure is not without drawbacks, however; it may be difficult to train subjects to use the confidence ratings reliably, and subjects may underutilize some of the confidence ratings, especially at the extreme ends of the scale. Indeed, there is some evidence that older subjects avoid the extreme confidence ratings (Craik, 1969; Danziger, Chapter 39 this volume). Also the lack of independence among the data points may place hidden constraints on the shape of the ROC. Nevertheless, the economy of the rating scale procedure makes it use advantageous (see Green & Swets, 1974).

The selection of a method for generating an empirical ROC is determined largely by the objectives of the experiment. As suggested above, if economy is the overriding consideration, then a rating-scale procedure is the method of choice. The use of payoff matrices or manipulation of the a priori probabilities potentially provides a fuller description of the subject's decision behavior, since an optimal criterion placement can be defined to maximize payoff or percentage correct for each manipulation condition (Swets, Tanner, & Birdsall, 1961). The subject's decision "efficiency" may then be characterized by the deviation of the empirically obtained criteria from the optimal criteria. Since human observers tend to avoid extreme criterion settings, even when they are optimal for a given experimental condition, the deviation from obtained and optimal criteria may be substantiated in some conditions (see Green & Swets, 1974, Chapter 4). There is some evidence that manipulation of a priori stimulus probabilities produces distortions in empirical ROC slopes because the slope varies with $P(s)$ (e.g., Markowitz & Swets, 1967; Schulman & Greenberg, 1970). This evidence may contraindicate general use of a priori stimulus probabilities to generate empirical ROCs without attention to this problem.

In general, it is most useful to estimate an empirical ROC for at least two different levels of stimulus strength (sensitivity), that is for two or more members of an ROC family. As the number of sensitivity levels assessed grows, the economy of the confidence-rating-scale procedure becomes increasingly attractive.

Assume for the moment that a family of empirical ROCs has been obtained for two or more age groups, by whatever method. The experimenter's interest will usually be focused on testing the hypothesis of age differences in "true" sensitivity (detectability) as defined by SDT (comparisons of criterion are considered below). How should the data analysis proceed?

The first step is to fit the ROC function for each member of the ROC family. Then, once the ROC function has been estimated, appropriate sensitivity parameters can be calculated. Since nonlinear curve fitting may present formidable problems, it is common practice to assume normal evidence distributions and to use the z-scores z_s and z_n corresponding to $P(Y|S)$ and $P(Y|n)$. As shown in Equation 17 the normalized ROC is a straight line under the assumption of normal distribution; thus a linear function may be fitted for each ROC of the family.

The fitting is often done by eye—that is, by simply drawing the "best looking" line through the data (Green & Swets, 1974). Curve fitting by eye is subject to bias, however, particularly if the data points deviate from the visualized line. Fortunately, exact maximum-likelihood methods for fitting linear ROC functions are now available for ROCs with independent and interdependent data points (e.g., Dorfman & Alf, 1968, 1969; Grey & Morgan, 1972; Ogilvie & Creelman, 1968). In addition to estimating the slope and intercept parameters of the normalized ROC, these programs provide a goodness-of-fit statistic that is useful for deciding whether the data lie along a straight line. If the linear function fits poorly, the assumption of normal evidence distributions may be untenable (see also Williams, Chapter 40, this volume).

Because individual differences in ROC slopes and deviation about the linear function might be obscured in pooled data, the curve fitting must be done separately for each subject. There may be substantial individual differences in the goodness of linear fit and in the estimated slopes. In the empirical ROCs shown in Figure 41-6, note the individual differences in both of the ROC slopes and the deviations about the visually fitted linear functions. These differences may be even larger when relatively untrained observers are used.

Once the slope and intercept parameters have been estimated for each normalized ROC, the problem is to select appropriate measures of sensitivity. The use of d' is justified under the equal-variance assumption; hence it is critical to test the hypothesis that the normalized ROCs have unit slope (Pastore & Scheirer, 1974). Some of the available maximum-likelihood programs (e.g., Grey & Morgan, 1972) provide variances of the estimators, which may be used to construct confidence intervals around the slope parameters. If the confidence intervals do not contain the value 1, then the hypothesis of unit slopes may be rejected. Unfortunately, since no available program uses restricted-information, maximum-likelihood methods, the hypothesis of unit slopes cannot be tested directly by comparing the fit of models with and without ROCs of fixed unit slope.

Actually, testing the hypothesis of unit slopes provides only a weak test of the equal-variance assumption, since the slope of the ROC may reflect more than just the ratio of the variances of the signal and noise distributions. The major additional factor is criterion variance, and it can be shown that the slope of the ROC with confounded criterion variance is

$$S = \frac{(\sigma_c{}^2 + \sigma_n{}^2)^{1/2}}{(\sigma_c{}^2 + \sigma_s{}^2)^{1/2}}, \tag{26}$$

where $\sigma_c{}^2$ is the criterion variance (Wickelgren, 1968).

If σ_c^2 is larger than σ_n^2 and σ_s^2, then σ_s will be biased toward 1 and the difference in σ_n^2 and σ_s^2 will be underestimated. Since other factors may also affect the slopes of empirical ROCs (Markowitz & Swets, 1967), interpretation of the ROC slope in terms of signal and noise variance is therefore somewhat hazardous.

Nevertheless, if the slopes depart significantly from unity (by whatever standard), an alternative detectability measure other than d' may be used. Work with empirical ROCs suggests that d_e' (twice the ordinate at the intersection of the ROC with the negative diagonal, also denoted d_s) is a useful sensitivity parameter because, in addition to the advantages noted above, it remains stable over trials and methods of ROC generation in empirical data (Egan & Clarke, 1966; Markowitz & Swets, 1967; Treisman, 1977). However, as Treisman notes, d_e' was originally conceived as an alternative detectability measure when the ideal ROCs were constrained by normal equal-variance evidence distributions, but the empirical ROC slopes differed from unity owing to experimental error. Treisman argues that when other than unit slopes are suspected on theoretical grounds to be a consistent feature of an ROC, no single sensitivity parameter suffices, because both the slope and intercept are needed to characterize the ROC fully (see also Green & Swets, 1974). While Treisman's point is well taken, the attractiveness of using a single sensitivity parameter, along with the useful properties of d_e', will probably continue to make d_e' a widely used measure of detectability.

Another generally applicable sensitivity index is the area under the empirical ROC, which is independent of the form of the underlying evidence distributions. The area under the empirical ROC, denoted here as $P(A)$ (for proportional area) may be estimated by applying the trapezoidal rule to the data (Green & Swets, 1974, Appendix III). The accuracy of estimation for $P(A)$ obviously increases as the number of empirically generated points upon the ROC increases, although the accuracy is also a function of the spread of the empirical data points. With unfavorable data, the measurement precision of the trapezoidal rule's $P(A)$ may be only slightly better than the single-point area estimated A'.

Pollack and Hsieh (1969) studied the sampling variability of $P(A)$ using computer simulation techniques and found the sampling variability of $P(A)$ to be acceptably small, dependent upon the mean value of $P(A)$, and realtively free of the form of the underlying evidence distributions. The sampling variability was slightly less than the value predicted from binomial sampling variability, with the sampling variability of $P(A)$ growing differentially smaller as the upper bound of 1.0 was approached. Their results suggest that the binomial estimate of the standard error of $P(A)$

$$\sigma_A = [P(A)(1 - P(A))/n]^{1/2} \qquad (27)$$

may be used in statistical significance testing with $P(A)$, in a manner analogous to the significance tests for d' advanced by Gourevitch & Galanter (1967) and Marascuilo (1970).

To date, few researchers into psychological aging have employed ROC analysis techniques in SDT-based studies (but see, e.g., Harkins, Chapman, & Eisdorfer, 1979), even though ROC analysis represents a more valid application of SDT than the traditional single-point procedures. Perhaps researchers investigating aging have been unaware of the power of ROC analysis techniques. It may be useful, therefore, to refer interested readers to the excellent recent paper by Swets, Pickett, Whitehead, Getty, Schnur, Swets, & Freeman (1979) describing applications of ROC analysis to the problem of neuropsychological assessment. Swets et al. had trained medical observers use confidence ratings while employing two different methods to detect brain lesions, and empirical ROCs were then generated.

Data were analyzed for each subject with a modification of Dorfman and Alf's (1969) maximum-likelihood estimation program, which not only produced estimates for ROC slopes and intercepts but also yielded maximum-likelihood estimates of the area under the normalized ROC. Pooled ROC curves were also analyzed, but only after individual differences among the observers were found to be surprisingly small. Review of the substance of Swets et al.'s (1979) findings is beyond the scope of this chapter, but their work constitutes an impressive example of ROC application that certainly merits emulation.

Assessment of Criterion

Much of the current interest in using SDT methods to study adult psychological development grew out of the apparent usefulness of SDT for the study of age differences in decision-making criteria. Some studies have discussed age differences in β within the context of evaluating the hypothesis that older subjects are more conservative or cautious in their willingness to respond affirmatively in psychological experiments (e.g., Rees & Botwinick, 1971). This approach is discussed by Danziger (Chapter 39, this volume), and the present discussion is not intended to duplicate his chapter. Instead, an outline of some preliminary concepts regarding the assessment of criterion differences should complement Danziger's dicussion of bias.

The concept of decision criteria, and of bias in these criteria, can be understood only by realizing that the criterion that subjects use for response selection is a function of their own decision goals. There are many different decision goals, and the field of decision theory has devoted much attention to categorizing them and to evaluating human decision makers' efficiency in attaining explicit and implicit goals (e.g., Lee, 1971). As stated above, the decision goal used most commonly by experimental psychologists is to maximize the percentage of correct responses, although this goal may be implicit—i.e., not explicitly emphasized in the instructions given the subjects. Other types of decision goals are also important in detection and recognition experiments. For example, the Neyman-Pearson decision goal—to maximize $P(Y|s)$ for fixed $P(Y|n)$—is the basis for most statistical tests of the null hypothesis, where α corresponds to the fixed value of $P(Y|n)$. Another important decision goal is to maximize expected value; this decision goal is used in association with a payoff matrix, as described in the previous section. Each event–response conjunction has an assigned value (cost), and the subject attempts to maximize expected value (payoff), often in terms of monetary reward.

For each of these decision goals, the subject who uses a likelihood-ratio criterion is most likely to achieve optimal performance levels, where the desired maximization defined by the decision goal is attained. An optimal likelihood-ratio criterion may then be defined for any explicit decision goal; for instance, the subject maximizing the percentage of correct responses should use a likelihood-ratio cutoff of $P(s)/P(n)$ (the optimal criterion in an expected value experiment was given in Equation 25. A biased criterion may then be defined as any one other than the optimal criterion. A biased criterion, by definition, depresses performance levels [indexed by $P(C)$, payoff, etc.] below those achievable at the optimal criterion.

In the usual psychological experiment, with a decision goal of $P(C)$ maximization and $P(s) = P(n) = .5$, the optimal criterion is at $L(x_c) = 1$, the negative diagonal of the unit square. One should therefore expect all subjects' performance to fall on the negative diagonal. Of course, that does not happen, which is one of the justifications for using SDT to estimate "true" sensitivity, eliminating the influence of bias. The question is, "Why doesn't a subject (particularly an older subject) perform at optimal criterion points?" Out of several possible answers, the one that seems to be implicitly assumed in a cautiousness-oriented interpretation is that the subject is really maximizing an intrinsic expected value function, while assigning a greater cost to $P(Y|n)$ than to $P(N|s)$. Such a subject

is intrinsically biased toward Response N. The cautiousness hypothesis is often tested by evaluating age group differences in β, the empirical estimates of the likelihood-ratio criterion.

The internal validity of inferences on significant age differences in β as indicating criterion differences is intimately related to whether β is the appropriate bias parameter to use in characterizing the decision behavior of the subjects. Dusoir (1975) suggests that a bias parameter is appropriate for a given subject if it remains constant when the objective discriminability of the stimuli is varied (assuming a fixed decision function). The bias parameter is therefore directly analogous to a sensitivity parameter such as d', which remains constant under fixed stimulus parameters as the subject's criterion is varied. The equivalent to the isosensitivity curve (ROC) with parameter d' is an isocriterion (isobias) curve or contour, for which a bias parameter is sought. Parsimony suggests that a single bias parameter should be used, if possible, to define the isocriterion contours generated by a given subject. For β to be an appropriate single-parameter characterization of bias, it is necessary to demonstrate that it does indeed specify the subject's isocriterion contour obtained by varying the discriminability of s from n.

There are actually many possibilities other than β for bias parameters, as has been ably reviewed by Dusoir (1975). To characterize these possibilities more formally, Dusoir defined $P(Y|n) = F_1(z)$, $P(Y|s) = F_2(z)$, where F_1 and F_2 are continuous functions of a real variable z (criterion). He then identified three ways to classify measures of degree of bias ($z = z_c$): (1) in terms of $F_1(z_c)$, $F_2(z_c)$, or some combination of the two; (2) in terms of the local behavior of F_1 and F_2 around $z = z_c$; or (3) in terms of the distance ($z_c - r$) between some arbitrarily scaled reference point (pp. 169–170). Different isocriterion contours are defined by different bias parameters (Figure 41-7).

The parameter β is of the second type listed above, namely,

$$\beta = \frac{dP(Y|s)/dz}{dP(Y|n)/dz}\bigg|_{z=z_c} \qquad (28)$$

the slope of the ROC at Point z_c. The problem is that β, as a single parameter, does not characterize the isobias contours of all decision goals, as can be seen in Figure 41-7. It is a suitable single-parameter bias measure if the subject acts as specified in SDT and seeks to maximize $P(C)$. If some other response operator is functioning (say, probability matching; Thomas & Legge, 1970), or if the decision function is a mixed decision rule with complex partitions of acceptance regions, then the use of β to describe criterion will be

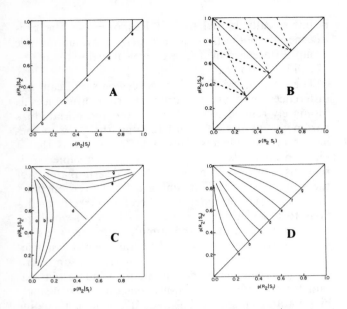

Figure 41-7. Illustrative isobias contours. **A:** $P(\text{Y} \mid \text{n})$, given as $p(\text{R}_2 \mid \text{S}_2)$: (a) .1, (b) .3, (c) .5, (d) .7, (e) .9. **B:** Isocriterion contours for bias parameter $P(\text{Y})$, given as $p(\text{R}_2)$; solid lines with $P(\text{s}) = .5$, dashed lines with $P(\text{s}) = .3$, dotted and dashed lines with $P(\text{s}) = .7$: (a) .3, (b) .5, (c) .7. **C:** Isocriterion contours for β under normal equal-variance assumptions: (a) 2.3, (b) 1.7, (c) 1.3, (d) 1.0, (e) .9, (f) .7, (g) .5. **D:** Isocriterion contours for Luce's b: (a) 3.9, (b) 2.3, (c) 1.5, (d) 1.0, (e) .9, (f) .5, (g) .3. (From "Treatments of Bias in Recognition and Detection Experiments" by A. E. Dusoir, *Perception & Psychophysics*, 1975, *17*, 167–178. Copyright 1975 by the Psychonomic Society. Reprinted by permission.)

inadequate. The Neyman-Pearson observer, for example, uses a complex likelihood-ratio decision function to enable maximum $P(C)$ for fixed-alarm rate, and $P(\text{Y} \mid \text{n})$, not β, is the single parameter characterizing the subject's isocriterion contours.

The problem, then, is that individuals may differ in intrinsic decision functions (and thus, in intrinsic isocriterion contours), even though they are presumed to be using a simple likelihood-ratio cutoff $L(x_c)$ to maximize $P(C)$. Use of β to assess criterion differences is therefore valid only if β reflects the criterion operator used by all subjects. At worst, different β values could obtain if observers not only have identical criteria in some decision other than the one specified by SDT but also have inherently different levels of sensitivity. For example, two Neyman-Pearson observers with different sensitivity levels and identical criteria—identical $P(\text{Y} \mid \text{n})$—would differ in empirical estimates of β in spite of the fact that they did not differ in criterion. Unless β can be shown to be a sufficient parameter to characterize the subject's isocriterion contours, then it

is at best an arbitrary bias parameter useful only for describing variation in the operating points of different subjects on an ROC family. The descriptive utility of such an arbitrary bias parameter should not be denigrated, for the experimental data cannot be summarized completely without some information on the spread of observed data points along the ROC. One could, of course, argue for a different bias parameter on other grounds, as Hodos (1970) did in developing a nonparametric bias measure that does not require the normal distribution assumption for its calculation. But as Dusoir (1975) notes, this remains an arbitrary bias parameter (albeit with descriptive utility) without additional theoretical import vis-à-vis the actual decision criteria employed by the subjects. Note that the interpretation of such an arbitrary bias parameter becomes highly problematic when the observers differ in sensitivity, since one cannot assume in general that distances along isosensitivity curves of differing slope are reflected equivalently by all bias parameters. This conclusion is softened for ROCs with coincident slope over the range of sensitivity. Thus the distance measure defined by Ingham (1970; also see Chapter 39, this volume) is a useful bias parameter in describing equivalently the spread of ROC points along any member of the normalized unit-slope ROC family, even if these ROCs are not determined in the way assumed by SDT. In the general case, however, one can well wonder (as does Danziger in Chapter 39, this volume) about the meaning of differences in an arbitrary bias parameter when sensitivity also differs.

The problems inherent in analyzing individual differences in β underscore the need for ROC analysis in aging studies. It is critical to examine the sufficiency of bias parameters such as β in describing the isocriterion contours of subjects of different ages. This can only be accomplished by examining the isocriterion contours obtained by generating a family of empirical ROCs. If the subjects are given explicit instructions on the desired decision goals (and their practical implications), the form of the empirical isocriterion contours will be helpful in evaluating whether they are indeed acting as likelihood-ratio observers using bias parameter β, as is usually assumed in SDT. The empirically obtained β values corresponding to the isocriterion contours may be contrasted with optimal β values if payoff matrices or a priori probabilities are manipulated, thus providing a richer characterization of the individual and age-related differences in maximizing certain decision goals. In short, the position taken here is that SDT applications in gerontological research should move away from comparisons of single-point β estimates as general indicators of cautiousness, and toward more complex studies of age differences in ability to formulate and maximize basic decision goals.

The Forced-Choice Paradigm

The forced-choice paradigm represents the best alternative to ROC analysis for estimating a criterion-independent measure of sensitivity, although usually at the price of explicitly ignoring the measurement of criterion differences. Thus, when a study focuses solely on the issue of sensitivity differences, the economy of the forced-choice procedure makes it an attractive and viable alternative to full-blown ROC analysis. The following discussion is limited to the multiple-interval, forced-choice paradigm, as opposed to a multiple-alternative, single-interval, forced-choice paradigm, although the principles discussed apply equally well to both.

Two-Interval, Forced Choice

In the two-interval forced-choice paradigm (2IFC), the signal s may be presented with equal probability in either the first or second interval. Let [s,n] be defined as the occurrence of s in the first observation interval, and [n,s] be defined as the occurrence of s in the second interval. Each observation interval is a simple detection observation, where the usual SDT treatment applies; that is, the subject is assumed to compute posterior probabilities as the likelihood that s was presented by using the evidence x. The decision of the subject is assumed to be a function of the likelihood ratio that s was presented instead of n.

There are two likelihood ratios involved in the 2IFC, one for the likelihood of an s presentation in each interval. The optimal decision rule (the one that maximizes the percentage of correct responses) is simply

$$\text{Choose response } I_1 \text{ iff } L(x)_{[s,n]} > L(x)_{[n,s]}. \qquad (29)$$

That is, one simply computes a likelihood ratio for each event and chooses the larger of the two. This decision rule is optimal regardless of the form of the evidence distributions for x, $f(x|s)$ and $f(x|n)$, for each interval. The advantage of the forced-choice procedure is that the subject's criterion cutoff $L(x_c)$ in the simple detection task is immaterial; the decision can be made simply on the relative size of the two likelihood ratios. Thus the forced-choice procedure removes the influence of the subject's intrinsic bias to response set (Y,N). Of course, response bias to set (I_1, I_2) has become a factor, but psychophysicists have generally assumed that there is less intrinsic bias involved with this response set and have used feedback, with some success, to minimize this bias (Green & Swets, 1974). Thus the 2IFC paradigm is well suited to studying de-

tection in situations where response bias is not the focus of the study.

Additional importance was added to the 2IFC paradigm by Green's (1964) theorem, which showed that, under the assumptions of independent events and response symmetry, the percentage correct in the 2IFC paradigm, denoted $P_2(C)$, is equal to the area under the simple detection ROC (see Green, 1964; or Green & Swets, 1974, pp. 46–47, for the entire proof).

Green's proof treats each interval as a sample from the signal and the noise distribution. The observer will be correct if the likelihood-ratio value from the signal distribution is some real number k, and the likelihood-ratio value for the noise sample is less than k; that is,

$$P_2(C) = [P(L(x)_s = K)] \cdot [P(L(x)_n < k)] \qquad (30)$$

Green's (1964) theorem uses Equation 29 to show that

$$P_2(C) = \int_0^1 [1 - P(Y|n)] \, dP_k(Y|s), \qquad (31)$$

which is the area under the yes–no ROC.

The fact that $P_2(C) = P(A)$ in the yes–no task further legitimates $P_2(C)$ as a valid nonparametric measure of sensitivity that is independent of the subject's yes–no criterion. It is, in a sense, the best single-point detectability estimate available, since an equivalent measure to $P(A)$ can be estimated with a relatively small number of trials. Thus the 2IFC paradigm can be highly recommended for gerontological studies, although it has not to this author's knowledge, been employed previously. Again, it is important for the experimenter to make sure that subjects indeed show no bias to respond I_1 or I_2. If interval bias persists, however, a correction formula for $P_2(C)$ can be found in Green and Swets (1974, Appendix III).

The assumption of symmetry can be relaxed by introducing a bias parameter c into Equation 29:

$$\text{Choose } I_1 \text{ iff } L(x)_{[s,n]} > cL(x)_{[n,s]}. \qquad (32)$$

In this case, the analysis of detectability requires the 2IFC ROC curve, using the conditional probabilities $P(I_1|[s,n])$ and $P(I_1|[n,s])$, which completely specify performance on the task. The treatment of the 2IFC ROC is highly similar to the simple detection ROC; indeed, the values of the 2IFC ROC coordinates may be determined from the simple detection ROC (Green & Swets, 1974). Hence, ROC analysis for the 2IFC will not be treated in any detail here. An interesting property of the 2IFC ROC is that it is symmetrical about the negative diagonal, even when the parent yes–no ROC is not. The reader may consult Atkinson and Kinchla (1965), Markowitz and Swets (1967), or

Schulman and Mitchell (1966) on the use of confidence ratings to generate empirical 2IFC ROCs.

The preceding comments about the 2IFC paradigm hold irrespective of the form of the evidence distributions. Under the assumption of normal equal-variance evidence distributions, a d' value may be calculated for the 2IFC experiment, denoted d'_{2IFC}. Under the assumption that $\sigma_s^2 = \sigma_n^2 = 1$, and $\mu_n = 0$, the distance between the means is d' (see above). The relation of d' to d'_{2IFC} is found by the following argument (Green & Swets, 1974; Luce, 1963). Define the evidence variable for 2IFC as the difference in evidence variables for the two intervals, $D = X_{I_1} - X_{I_2}$. Then, when the signal occurs in the first interval, the evidence difference distribution ($D\,|\,[s,n]$) is normally distributed with mean d' and variance 2 (because the mean of the difference distribution is $\mu_s - \mu_n$ and the variance of the difference distribution is $\sigma_n^2 + \sigma_s^2$). Conversely, the evidence difference distribution ($D\,|\,[n,s]$) is normally distributed with mean $-d'$ and variance 2. Then the difference in the evidence distribution means is $2d'$ with standard deviation $\sqrt{2}$, and

$$d'_{2IFC} = \sqrt{2d'}. \qquad (33)$$

(See Green & Swets, 1974, Chapter 3, for additional details.) Elliott (1964) provides a table for estimating d_{2IFC} from the conditional probabilities of a single data point in 2IFC ROC space.

Analysis of this single-point estimate is subject to the same concerns expressed for single-point estimates of d'.

M-Interval, Forced Choice

The arguments for the 2IFC paradigm may be extended to the general case of m observation intervals. In the MIFC paradigm, the subject is again assumed to choose a response from set ($I_1, I_2, \ldots I_m$) by selecting the interval with the largest likelihood ratio. Then, by extension of Equation 30, the probability of a correct response (again assuming independent events) is

$$P_m(C) = [P(L(x)_s = k)] \cdot [P(L(x)_n < k)^{m-1}]. \qquad (34)$$

The likelihood ratio for the noise distribution is raised to the $m-1$ power because there are $m-1$ intervals containing noise along. Since Green's (1964) theorem showed that

$$P_m(C) = \int_0^1 [1 - P_k(Y\,|\,n)^{m-1}] dP_k(Y\,|\,s) \qquad (35)$$

the percentage correct in an MIFC paradigm is still a function of the area under the yes–no ROC. As before,

the assumption of symmetry (no interval bias) must be invoked.

The MIFC task may well be more prone to interval bias than the 2IFC, particularly when the number of intervals is relatively large (e.g., greater than 3; Green & Swets, 1974). Unfortunately, no reasonably simple correction formula for $P_m(C)$ corresponding to the correction formula for $P_2(C)$ exists. This means that the experimenter using MIFC paradigms runs the risk that $P_m(C)$ will underestimate $P(A)$, given interval bias, and that nothing can be done about it. This problem would seem to reduce the value of adding more noise intervals to the 2IFC task.

The problem in allowing interval bias and computing an MIFC ROC is the large number of parameters required to describe the m-dimensional observation space. The m-dimensional space may be analyzed by invoking the homogeneity of noise assumption—that is, by assuming that all noise observations are identical (Green & Swets, 1974). The problem then essentially reduces to studying the 2IFC ROC above. (The interested reader is referred to Green and Swets, 1974, pp. 64–69; see also Luce, 1963.) From a cost-benefit perspective, the complexities introduced by adding m-2 additional noise intervals in the MIFC paradigm make it a less attractive alternative than the 2IFC paradigm for application by gerontologists unsophisticated in SDT. However, the MIFC paradigm may be particularly useful for evaluating complex threshold theories and for estimating age differences in the resulting parameters.

Complex Detection and Recognition

A comprehensive treatment of the decision theory techniques available to analyze results from the complex detection and recognition tasks listed above would be impossible to present in the available space. Instead, some basic concepts and associated references are cited.

Pure Recognition

The standard SDT methods used in the simple detection paradigm are equally applicable to a recognition task with two stimuli: $S = (S_1, S_2)$. One simply substitutes S_1 for 0 in S, and R_1 for 0 in R. The mathematics are then formally identical. However, when the number of stimuli to be recognized is greater than two, alternative methods for analyzing the confusion matrix data from Equation 1 are necessary.

The usual procedure is to treat the pure recognition task as formally equivalent to an m-interval forced-choice paradigm. If there are no response biases among the elements of R, then the average correct response from the main diagonal (see Figure 41-1) can be taken as a measure of performance, since it estimates the expected value of $P(C)$ (Green & Birdsall, 1978). If the assumption of orthogonal or independent signals can be invoked, then Green's (1964) area theorem for $P(C)$ in a forced-choice task can be applied to pure recognition as well (Green & Birdsall, 1978).

However, if response bias is expected, $P(C)$ is not generally an appropriate measure of discriminability among the S_j. Unfortunately, there is no generally accepted method of computing a more appropriate index of discriminability. Some provisional models have applied Luce's (1959) choice theorem and multidimensional scaling techniques to the problem, and more advances in this area may be hoped for in the future. Getty, Swets, Swets, and Green (1979) recently discussed predicting recognition confusion matrices from the results of a multidimensional scaling of similarity judgments among the stimulus alternatives. However, although their model for predicting the confusion matrices allows for nonorthogonal stimuli, it assumes no response bias. Thus asymmetry in the confusion matrix is attributed solely to correlated positions of stimuli in the multidimensional perceptual space and is assumed to be unrelated to response bias. A problem with Getty et al. (1979) is the low frequency of off-diagonal elements (i.e., confusions) in the confusion matrix, which may have forced a spurious fit of their model to the data. Nevertheless, both their model and their analysis are impressive, particularly the validation of the multidimensional scaling results by prediction of an independent recognition task. One hopes that their later work will provide parameters for response bias.

An interesting set of models reported by Townsend (1971) did use response bias parameters to predict alphabetic confusion matrices. Townsend listed three models of interest: (1) an all-or-none activation model, in which the subjects either receive information enabling a perfect identification or are thrown into an uncertain state of guessing according to their response bias; (2) an overlap-activation model that adds some partial information to (1) so that the subject has partial information consistent with two possible stimuli and must choose among these alternatives (again with some response bias); and (3) a choice model in which the choice of a response is determined by the strength of that response, given the information, relative to the total strength relating the presented stimulus to other stimuli in the stimulus set. The relative strengths are estimated by ratio scale similarity and bias parameters from Luce's (1959, 1963) model. Townsend (1971) used both maximum-likelihood techniques to predict the empirical confusion matrix from an alphabetic

recognition task and multidimensional scaling techniques to analyze the empirical confusion matrix. He achieved good fits for the choice model and the multidimensional scaling solution to the empirical confusion matrix.

Nakatani (1972) introduced a complex confusion-choice model that also used Luce's (1959) choice theorem and multidimensional scaling techniques to analyze confusion-matrix data. Nakatani's (1972) model is notable in that it combines SDT-based conceptualizations about the nature of perceptual evidence with the choice-theorem analysis of response selection. Nakatani's model subsumes Townsend's (1971) choice model as a special case, but the number of freely estimated parameters in Nakatani's (1972) model is considerable. References for other (mostly earlier) models using the choice theorem and/or multidimensional scaling to analyze recognition confusion matrices may be found in Luce (1977) and Luce and Green (1974).

Recognition and Detection

The formal treatment of the 1-of-m detection and the generalized recognition and detection tasks has been recently advanced in papers by Starr, Metz, Luted, and Goodenough (1975), Green, Weber, and Duncan (1977), and Green and Birdsall (1978). The starting point for much of this work was the "One of M Orthogonal Signals Model" described by Green and Swets (1974). The work of Starr et al. (1975) and Green et al. (1977) has led to theorems relating the probability of correct recognition *and* detection to the probability of a false alarm in the 1-of-m detection and simple-detection paradigms. Green and Birdsall (1978) review this work and include a discussion of the ROC for the 1-of-m, orthogonal-signals paradigm under the assumption of Gaussian noise. They also derive some interesting ROC functions for a binary detection-state model. Some of these theoretical developments have been applied with considerable success to the problem of detection, localization, and recognition in medical diagnosis by Starr et al. (1975) and Swets et al. (1979) and may well be applicable in psychogerontological research.

Concluding Statement

This review has considered the potential utility of several SDT paradigms for the study of detection and recognition performance in adults of different ages. Other potentially important approaches, such as the theory of ideal observers, may be particularly useful for studies in which the physical dimensions of the stimuli can be specified exactly (Green & Swets, 1974). Related developments, such as Thurstonian scaling techniques, are covered in references cited by Green and Swets (1974) in an additional topical bibliography. Swets (1973) reviews a wide range of ROC analysis applications.

This chapter has covered in considerable detail the rationale and limitations of the application of single-point estimates to the study of individual differences in simple detection and recognition paradigms and has emphasized the potential utility of ROC analysis. The purpose of this treatment is not to imply that single-point estimation is invalid and should invariably be replaced by ROC analysis, but rather to suggest that for some applications, the economy of this method may be outweighed by its inherent problems. Still, single-point estimation should not be performed to the exclusion of ROC analysis; indeed, one could argue that it should follow a careful ROC study, justifying its use for a particular paradigm and population. After all, the time, effort, and expense of ROC analysis prohibit its use as a general research strategy for experimental aging research on detection and recognition problems. Consequently, a forced-choice approach may be the best general method for generating economical, yet valid, detectability estimates. Nevertheless, the power of ROC analysis to address the response criterion problem—which led to gerontological applications of SDT in the first place—makes it a prime candidate for advancing experimental research on psychological aging in the 1980s.

REFERENCES

Atkinson R. C., & Kinchla, R. A. A learning model for forced choice detection experiments. *British Journal of Mathematical and Statistical Psychology*, 1965, *18*, 183–206.

Botwinick, J. *Cognitive processes in maturity and old age*. New York: Springer, 1967.

Botwinick, J. *Aging and behavior* (2nd ed.). New York: Springer, 1978.

Bush, R. R., Galanter, E., & Luce, R. D. Characterization and classification of choice experiments. In R. D. Luce, R. R. Bush, & E. Galanter (Eds.), *Handbook of mathematical psychology*, (Vol. 1). New York: Wiley, 1963.

Craik, F. I. M. Applications of signal detection theory to studies of aging. *Interdisciplinary Topics in Gerontology*, 1969, *4*, 147–157.

Dorfman, D. D. & Alf, E., Jr. Maximum likelihood estimation of parameters of signal detection theory—a direct solution. *Psychometrika*, 1968, *33*, 117–124.

Dorfman, D. D. & Alf, E., Jr. Maximum likelihood estimation of parameters of signal detection theory and determi-

nation of confidence intervals—rating method data. *Journal of Mathematical Psychology*, 1969, *6*, 487–496.

Dusoir, A. E. Treatment of bias in detection and recognition models: A review. *Perception & Psychophysics*, 1975, *17*, 167–178.

Egan, J. P. *Signal detection theory and ROC analysis*. New York: Academic Press, 1975.

Egan, J. P., & Clarke, F. R. Psychophysics and signal detection. In J. B. Sidowsky (Ed.), *Experimental methods and instrumentation in psychology*. New York: McGraw-Hill, 1966.

Elliott, P. B. Appendix 1—Tables of d'. In J. A. Swets (Ed.), *Signal detection and recognition by human observers*. New York: Wiley, 1964.

Getty, D. J., Swets, J. A., Swets, J. B., & Green, D. M. On the prediction of confusion matrices from similarity judgments. *Perception & Psychophysics*, 1979, *26*, 1–19.

Gordon, S. K., & Clark, W. C. Adult age differences in word and nonsense syllable recognition memory and response criterion. *Journal of Gerontology*, 1974, *29*, 659–665.

Gourevitch, V., & Galanter, E. A significance test for one-parameter isosensitivity functions. *Psychometrika*, 1967, *32*, 25–34.

Green, D. M. General prediction relating yes–no and forced choice results. *Journal of the Acoustical Society of America*, 1964, *36*, 1042(A).

Green, D. M., & Birdsall, T. G. Detection and recognition. *Psychological Review*, 1978, *85*, 192–206.

Green, D. M., & Swets, J. A. *Signal detection theory and psychophysics*, (2nd ed.). New York: Krieger, 1974.

Green, D. M., Weber, D. L., and Duncan, J. E. Detection and recognition of pure tones in noise. *Journal of the Acoustical Society of America*, 1977, *62*, 948–954.

Grey, D. R., & Morgan, B. J. T. Some aspects of ROC curve fitting: Normal and logistic models. *Journal of Mathematical Psychology*, 1972, *9*, 128–139.

Grossberg, J. M., & Grant, B. F. Clinical psychophysics: Applications of ratio scaling detection methods to research on pain, fear, drugs, and medical decision making. *Psychological Bulletin*, 1978, *85*, 1154–1176.

Harkins, S. W., Chapman, C. R., & Eisdorfer, C. Memory loss and response bias in senescence. *Journal of Gerontology*, 1979, *34*, 66–72.

Hodos, W. Nonparametric index of response bias for use in detection and recognition experiments. *Psychological Bulletin*, 1970, *74*, 351–354.

Ingham, J. G. Individual differences in signal detection. *Acta Psychologica*, 1970, *34*, 39–50.

Krantz, D. H. Threshold theories of signal detection. *Psychological Review*, 1969, *76*, 308–324.

Lee, W. *Decision theory and human behavior*. New York: Wiley, 1971.

Luce, R. D. *Individual choice behavior*. New York: Wiley, 1959.

Luce, R. D. Detection and recognition. In R. D. Luce, R. R. Bush, & E. Galanter (Eds.), *Handbook of mathematical psychology* (Vol. 1). New York: Wiley, 1963.

Luce, R. D. The choice axiom after twenty years. *Journal of mathematical psychology*, 1977, *15*, 215–233.

Luce, R. D., & Green, D. M. Detection, discrimination, and recognition. In E. C. Carterette and M. P. Friedman (Eds.), *Handbook of perception* (Vol. 2). New York: Academic Press, 1974.

Marascuilo, L. A. Extensions of the significance test for one-parameter signal detection hypotheses. *Psychometrika*, 1970, *35*, 237–243.

Markowitz, J., & Swets, J. A. Factors affecting the slope of empirical ROC curves: Comparison of binary and rating response. *Perception & Psychophysics*, 1967, *2*, 91–100.

McNicol, D. *A primer of signal detection theory*. London: Allen and Unwin, 1972.

Nakatani, L. H. Confusion-choice model for multidimensional psychophysics. *Journal of Mathematical Psychology*, 1972, *9*, 104–127.

Norman, D. A. A comparison of data obtained with different false alarm rates. *Psychological Review*, 1964, *71*, 243–246.

Ogilvie, J. C., & Creelman, C. D. Maximum likelihood estimation of receiver operating characteristic curve parameters. *Journal of Mathematical Psychology*, 1968, *5*, 377–391.

Okun, M. Adult age and cautiousness in decision: A review of the literature. *Human Development*, 1976, *19*, 220–233.

Pastore, R. E., & Scheirer, C. J. Signal detection theory: Considerations for general application. *Psychological Bulletin*, 1974, *81*, 945–958.

Pollack, I., and Hsieh, R. Sampling variability of the area under the ROC and of d'_e. *Psychological Bulletin*, 1969, *71*, 161–173.

Pollack, I., & Norman, D. A. A non-parametric analysis of recognition experiments. *Psychonomic Science*, 1964, *1*, 125–126.

Rees, J. N., & Botwinick, J. Detection and decision factors in auditory behavior of the elderly. *Journal of Gerontology*, 1971, *26*, 133–136.

Schulman, A. I., & Greenberg, G. Z. Operating characteristics and a priori probability of the signal. *Perception & Psychophysics*, 1970, *8*, 317–320.

Schulman, A. I., & Mitchell, R. R. Operating characteristics from yes–no and forced choice procedures. *Journal of the Acoustical Society of America*, 1966, *40*, 473–477.

Simpson, A. J., & Fitter, M. J. What is the best index of detectability? *Psychological Bulletin*, 1973, *80*, 481–488.

Starr, S. J., Metz, C. E., Lusted, L. B., & Goodenough, D. J. Visual detection and localization of radiographic images. *Radiology*, 1975, *116*, 533–538.

Swets, J. A. The relative operating characteristic in psychology. *Science*, 1973, *182*, 990–1000.

Swets, J. A., Pickett, R. M., Whitehead, S. F., Getty, D. J., Schnur, J. A., Swets, J. B., & Freeman, B. A. Assessment of diagnostic technologies. *Science*, 1979, *205*, 753–759.

Swets, J. A., Tanner, W. P., Jr., & Birdsall, T. G. Decision processes in perception. *Psychological Review*, 1961, *68*, 301–340.

Thomas, E. A. C., & Legge, D. Probability matching as a basis for detection and recognition decision. *Psychological Review*, 1970, *77*, 65–72.

Townsend, J. T. Theoretical analysis of an alphabetic confusion matrix. *Perception & Psychophysics*, 1971, *9*, 40–50.

Treisman, M. On the stability of d_s. *Psychological Bulletin*, 1977, *84*, 235–243.

Wickelgren, W. A. Unidimensional strength theory and component analysis of noise in absolute and comparative judgments. *Journal of Mathematical Psychology*, 1968, *5*, 102–122.

Lawrence E. Marks and Joseph C. Stevens

CHAPTER

42

Measuring Sensation in the Aged

The signal detection approach and the direct scaling approach to sensory-perceptual behavior hold great promise for evaluating sensory and associated cognitive changes that may take place with age. Signal detection theory has already contributed and will continue to contribute importantly to understanding differences in sensitivity (discriminability) and response bias, especially when applied to individual performance. A new scaling method—magnitude matching—can give information about sensation magnitude. In this method people give magnitude estimations of sensation intensities aroused by stimuli from two or more continua; the data yield cross-modality matching functions, which can show individual differences in sensation magnitude besides differences in numerical judgment.

Decision Making and Sensory Discrimination

The theory of signal detectability—discussed so ably in the preceding three chapters—is undoubtedly one of the best supported theories in psychology. It is based on what is essentially a simple statistical model for the way people make decisions in the face of uncertainty, and this statistical decision model has a broad range of applications—not only to sensory and perceptual functions but also to reaction time (Green & Swets, 1966), memory (Parks, 1966), attention (Sperling, 1978), categorization (Kubovy, 1977), and other forms of behavior that can be cast in a decision-making mold. For instance, the processes of recognizing previously encountered stimuli resemble processes of signal detection, notably in the parallels between correct recognitions of old items and hits and between false recognitions of new items as old and false alarms. One can construct a *memory operating characteristic*, by

analogy to the *receiver operating characteristic* (ROC), to separate, in principle, "bias" from "sensitivity." Recently Sperling (1978) showed how one can construct an *attention operating characteristic* (Kinchla, cited by Sperling, 1978) to describe the trade-off between attention to two different channels or sets of conditions.

We mention these topics not just because they provide interesting ways to apply the same kind of theoretical model to a variety of behaviors, but because those of us concerned with people's performance as they grow older may find it instructive and valuable to look at a wide variety of behaviors. And to the extent that sensation, perception, reaction time, memory attention, and classification or categorization fall under the rubric of decision making, signal detection paradigms can be useful to assess possible patterns in the way performance changes with age. (For brief view, see Craik, 1969.)

Signal detection methods are especially powerful because they permit one to parcel out the effects of a person's criterion or changes in criterion from measures of the person's sensitivity to a stimulus or the pure discriminability of two stimuli (whether sensory, mnemonic, or whatever). The chapters in this book by Williams, Hertzog, and Danziger all treat important issues in evaluating data collected with signal detection paradigms, and they point out some of the potential difficulties that one may encounter—for example, in

This research was supported in part by National Institutes of Health Grant AG 01331-01.

deciding when individuals or groups do show a difference in response bias or criterion. This is especially important in aging research, where, as has been indicated, it is often reported that older people tend to be conservative in making judgments and setting criteria.

The fact that people differ in how they set their criteria raises several issues. Danziger (Chapter 39, this volume) noted that the degree of bias may be related to the discriminability of the stimuli, which is to say that the location of the criterion in some ways depends jointly on the hit rate and the false-alarm rate. Note that the theory of signal detectability can yield normative rules. From knowledge of the a priori probabilities of the two stimuli and of the payoff structure for hits and false alarms, the theory can specify, for instance, a cutoff or a criterion that will maximize the expected value. But there are other optimizing strategies that people might employ: They could maximize the overall probability of making a correct response (correct detections of signals plus rejection of nonsignals), or they could minimize false alarms (Neyman-Pearson rule). (See Green & Swets, 1966, for a review.) It is possible to ask not only how well people adhere to a given normative rule, but what rule they try to follow, whether they try to follow a single rule under all conditions or for all tasks, and whether the rule or rules they try to follow change with age. Perhaps we should be cautious in using terms like conservatism.

It is noteworthy that so-called conservatism has been evaluated in the other tasks alluded to, notably in probabilistic categorization: Kubovy (1977) presented to his (young) subjects four-digit numbers randomly selected from two overlapping distributions and asked them to identify the source of each number or to judge the probability that it came from one of the distributions. Results suggested that conservatism may arise from subjects' nonveridical judgments of the probabilities. It might be worthwhile to investigate possible tendencies toward conservatism in nonperceptual tasks like Kubovy's, where individual differences in sensitivity to the input are better controlled and can perhaps be eliminated. In any case, it is certainly worth testing the same subjects on a variety of tasks, especially in the light of a recent suggestion (Harkins, Chapman, & Eisdorfer, 1979; Watson, Turpenoff, Kelly, & Botwinick, 1979) that conservatism in the aged may depend on the task.

One of the main themes that come across from the previous three chapters is that understanding the behavior of the aged, and in particular assessing how behavior may change with age, requires thorough, parametric experimental analyses. For example, as Hertzog (Chapter 41, this volume) showed, it does not suffice to measure a single point on an ROC. The entire curve, or at least a large portion of it, needs to be determined to ensure that the form of the ROC is comparable in different groups or in different individuals. This leads to another point of Hertzog's that needs to be reinforced: Because people do differ, great attention must be given to the ROCs of individuals. Averaging or pooling data across individuals can bias the average result. But even if it does not, averaging can at the very least obscure the range of interindividual variation.

Measuring Sensation Magnitude

It is with the goal of assessing individual differences in sensory functioning—and especially of measuring differences that may occur in the aged—that we have developed a new method to measure magnitudes of sensation, one that promises to uncover absolute differences in sensation magnitude across groups or individuals. This method arises from a methodological approach distinct from that used in signal detection analyses, for the present approach seeks to provide ways to answer rather different types of questions—questions about magnitude rather than about discrimination.

Sensory functioning often changes notably with age, but not all changes are amenable to measurement and interpretation through signal detection paradigms. These paradigms, after all, are geared toward measuring the discriminability of pairs of stimuli or stimulus conditions. Measures of discriminability may not in some instances tell us very much about, say, the magnitude of sensation—about the degree of brightness or loudness; the warmth or coldness; the taste, smell, or pain intensity. A given individual may have an elevated absolute threshold—or reduced absolute sensitivity as measured by a detection paradigm—and yet have perfectly normal sensation above threshold (where most of the action is in day-to-day living). Or one person's ability to discriminate between a pair of easily detected stimuli could be poor in comparison to another person's, and yet the average perceived magnitudes aroused by the same two stimuli could be exactly the same in the two people. Remember that discriminability is ultimately limited by variability or noise. Increasing the variances of two sensory response distributions, keeping their means (e.g., the average sensation magnitudes) constant, will diminish the discriminability.

Still other possibilities exist. It is conceivable that individuals with identical absolute sensitivity could have sensory systems that function quite differently at levels above threshold. This possibility is strengthened by a recent report by Bartoshuk (1978), who studied the taste functioning of a woman who had undergone radiation therapy for cancer of the neck. Absolute taste sensitivity decreased at first but recovered subsequently. Even after absolute sensitivity returned to preradiation levels, however, the woman still experienced "weakness" in taste sensation, and scaling by the method of magnitude estimation suggested that taste substances no longer aroused the magnitudes they had before. We find this report of interest because old people often say food tastes less palatable than it used to. Might the magnitudes of flavor sensations (taste, smell, and pungency) decline with age? It is not prima facie clear that the methodology of signal detection theory provides a means to evaluate such a change. What is needed is a way to measure absolute sensation levels.

The potentially most fruitful procedure to measure magnitude of sensation is S. Stevens's (1956) method of magnitude estimation, in which a subject tries to assign numbers in proportion to the strength of sensations. But just as in measurements of sensitivity or discriminability, there is the need here to distinguish real sensory changes or differences among people from differences in judgment, cognition, or criterion. Just as a given measure of a traditional threshold represents a combination of the sensitivity of the sensory system and response bias or criterion, so a given set of judgments of sensation intensity, as obtained by the method of magnitude estimation, represents the concatenation of sensory processing plus a host of biases that can stem from contextual effects or from differences in people's conceptions of what makes a sensory ratio.

Under many conditions of stimulation, and for a wide variety of sensory and perceptual continua, magnitude estimates of sensory intensity adhere closely to S. Stevens's (1957) power law, which in its simplest form reads

$$\psi = k\phi^\beta \tag{1}$$

where ψ is the quantitatively judged sensation magnitude, ϕ is stimulus intensity, k is a proportionality constant, and β is the power-function exponent. The sizes of k and of β characterize the sensory or perceptual continuum under investigation and the parameters of stimulation. The example of loudness may be useful. Given stimulus intensity reckoned as sound pressure, the exponent β governing the loudness function is about .6 when sound frequency is greater than about 300 Hz (Marks, 1979; S. Stevens, 1956); as frequency declines below 300 Hz, β increases steadily (S. Stevens, 1966). Even when the exponent β is constant, the relative size of k can vary. For instance, when the duration of a sound is reduced below one or two tenths

of a second, loudness decreases: The way loudness depends on duration (temporal summation of loudness) expresses itself quantitatively in a change in the value of the proportionality constant k, even while β remains unchanged (J. Stevens & Hall, 1966).

Even if all the stimulus parameters are the same, the actual values of the parameters of the power function for loudness that one obtains from a given experiment will fluctuate from individual to individual. Indeed, the form of the psychophysical function itself will vary—sometimes obeying a power law better than other times (e.g., Luce & Mo, 1965)—although the power function generally provides a good fit to individual loudness data (J. Stevens & Guirao, 1964). Even when subjects give good power functions, the size of the exponent β can vary notably, with about a twofold range from smallest to largest for a typical group of 10–12 subjects.

Might such a range of variation represent real differences in sensory functioning? Perhaps in part, but is seems likely that most of this variation represents differences in the ways people assign numbers to sensation magnitudes in the direct scaling tasks. Number behavior can be a characteristic of an individual. Some people assign big numbers to sensations, whereas other people assign small numbers. Some people give a big range of numbers to a set of stimuli, whereas others give a small one. The range that a subject gives to stimuli from one modality tends to correlate positively with the range given to stimuli from another modality (Jones & Marcus, 1961; see Marks, in press, for review), implying that number behavior may be a pervasive characteristic of an individual. Such differences in numerical response bias can camouflage, or at least make it difficult to assess, any real differences in sensory functioning. For this reason, one must view with caution results like those of Rovee, Cohen, and Shlapack (1975), who reported that power-function exponents for odor intensity of n-propanol were greatest in subjects 45 years old, smaller in younger and older subjects. Does this variation in exponent represent complex sensory changes or cognitive (response bias) differences? Methods like magnitude estimation need both theoretical frameworks and empirical paradigms akin to those of signal detection if the methods are to be capable of providing convincing evidence for sensory, as distinct from judgmental, differences among people.

This is not the place to describe the sort of theoretical framework that one of us thinks might emerge (some hints may be gleaned from Marks, 1979), but we would like to describe some steps we have taken to develop an empirical tool for evaluating and comparing sensory magnitudes across individuals

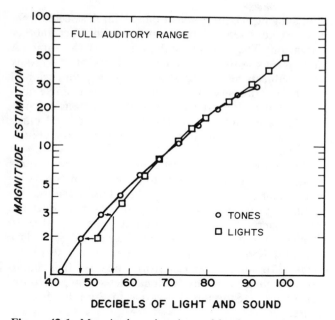

Figure 42-1. Magnitude estimations of loudness and brightness as functions of decibels of sound (re 2×10^{-5} N/m²) and decibels of light (re 10^{-10} lambert). The spacing on the ordinate is logarithmic, as is the decibel scale itself on the abscissa. The arrows show how two matching points may be determined by finding decibel levels of light and sound that produce the same magnitude estimation. In the experiment the full auditory range of 40–95 dB was employed.

(J. Stevens & Marks, 1980). The method—which we call magnitude matching—involves using the method of magnitude estimation to obtain cross-modality matching functions. In short, the method requires subjects to judge the sensation magnitudes of stimuli that are selected from two or more continua and that are interspersed within a single test session. The crux of the procedure involves instructing the subject to judge all of the sensations aroused by these stimuli on a single, common scale of sensation magnitude without regard to the modality; it is important to instruct the subject not to assume that the ranges of sensations or absolute levels of sensations are necessarily the same in different modalities. A cross-modality matching function can then be determined by finding the pairs of stimulus intensities on the two continua that yield the same average magnitude estimate.

In essence, the method of magnitude matching uses magnitude estimation as a matching device; the fundamental assumption is that the subject will, on the average, assign the same number to a stimulus when the sensation magnitude is the same.

Magnitude matching provides what is actually a second major extension in this direction of magnitude

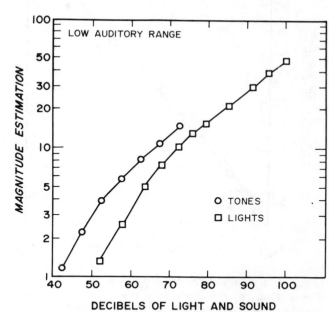

Figure 42-2. Magnitude estimations for lights of the same luminance but under a small (low) range (40–75 dB) of sound.

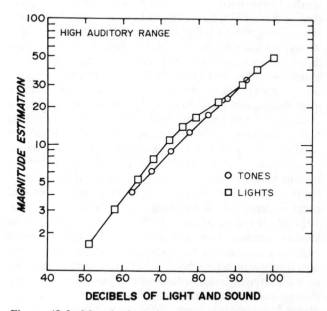

Figure 42-3. Magnitude estimations for lights of the same luminance but under a small (high) range (60–95) dB) of sound.

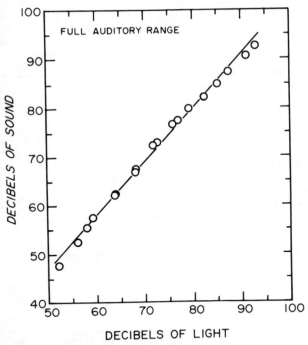

Figure 42-4. A cross-modality matching function relating sound and light, derived from the data in Figure 42-1.

estimation. The first major extension came when the method was used as an *intramodal* matching device (see Marks, 1974, for review). In that method, subjects are called upon to judge the perceived magnitudes of a variety of stimuli, all of which belong to a single modality, but which vary along two or more stimulus dimensions. This first extension—from simple scaling of an intensity series to mapping sensation onto a multidimensional stimulus array—made it possible to evaluate complex psychophysical relations in ways that had previously been time consuming and often not feasible. To take but one example, studies of spatial summation in the warmth sense were conducted by having subjects judge the warmth of each of a set of stimuli defined by a matrix of radiant intensities and areal extents of stimulation (J. Stevens & Marks, 1971; J. Stevens, Marks, & Simonson, 1974). These studies showed how summation changes in degree; from full reciprocity between intensity and area at the absolute warmth threshold, summation decreases to nil at high intensity, near the absolute pain threshold. Although such information could in principle have been gleaned by direct warmth-matching procedures, so long and tedious an approach is hardly practical if the goal is to study warmth summation over the entire dynamic range of the system.

The use of magnitude estimation as a *cross-modal*

matching device (its application to stimuli selected from two or more sense departments) provides yet another extension. The fundamental principle is the same. A stronger assumption is required, however. Not only must subjects be able to abstract a single dimension of perceived intensity from sensations in a single modality, but they must abstract a single dimension common to sensations from several modalities and make judgments using a unitary scale common to the unitary dimension.

The magnitude matching procedure circumvents biases or contextual effects by using one modality or continuum as a control for another. Traditional scaling methods provide no certain way to answer the question of whether, say, all taste stimuli appear weaker to Subject A than to Subject B. The present procedure provides a possible means to make such an assessment, relative to some other (control) modality. It is analogous to measuring, by a signal detection procedure, sensitivity to Stimulus A relative to Stimulus B or to noise.

Given two continua that conform to power functions like the one in Equation 1, $\psi_1 = k_1\psi_1^{\beta_1}$ and $\psi_2 = k_2\phi_2^{\beta_2}$. The cross-modality matching function expresses equality between ψ_1 and ψ_2, so it too will be a power function, having the form

$$k_1\phi_1^{\beta_1} = k_2\phi_2^{\beta_2}$$

or

$$\phi_1 = c\phi_2^{\beta_2/\beta_1}, \tag{2}$$

where $c = (k_2/k_1)^{1/\beta_1}$. In other words, the exponent of the matching function will be the ratio of the exponents governing the two modalities.

Two main advantages accrue to this procedure over traditional direct cross-modality matching. First, magnitude matching avoids "regression" bias (the direct cross-modality matching functions vary somewhat in exponent, depending on which continuum the subject adjusts; see S. Stevens, 1959; S. Stevens & Greenbaum, 1966); hence the present procedure avoids the need to match both Continuum 1 to Continuum 2, and 2 to 1. Second, in the present procedure the stimuli need not be continuously adjustable. Moreover, the method is fast, efficient, and sensitive and can be used to assess individual as well as group differences.

As we have said, the validity of the method rests on the assumption that subjects can judge sensations of different continua on a common scale of magnitude. We tested this prediction in a study of brightness and loudness (J. Stevens & Marks, 1980). Each of a dozen college-aged subjects served in three test sessions in which they made magnitude estimations of the perceived intensities of various levels of a 1000-Hz tone and a white light alternated within a session. The range and luminance levels of the light were the same in all sessions, but the range and levels of the tone were intentionally varied to induce some contextual effects on the numerical judgments. If subjects can judge magnitudes on a common scale, the contextual effects should express themselves in judgments of both sounds and lights but should leave the cross-modality matching relation unaltered. As Figures 42-1 through 42-3 show, context exerted some small effect on the magnitude estimates, but by and large the derived cross-modality functions (Figures 42-4 through 42-6) are similar across conditions.

Perhaps the single most important finding of the experiment was that the cross-modality matching functions varied much less across individuals than did the magnitude-estimation functions from which the matches were derived. As a whole, the cross-modality matches (a) were more uniform, providing better fits to power functions (Equation 2); (b) varied less in exponent (β_2/β_1); and (c) varied less in position (proportionality constant c).

The method of magnitude matching holds great promise for evaluating sensory losses (and individual differences in general), including sensory losses in the aged. It should be sensitive enough, for instance, to pick out easily a constant hearing loss equivalent to 15

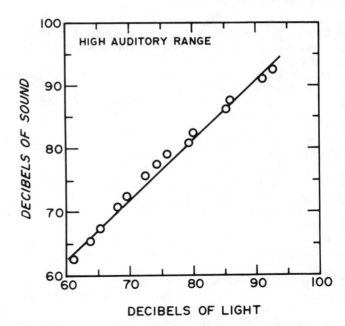

Figure 42-6. A cross-modality matching function relating sound and light, derived from the data in Figure 42-3.

dB, with a false-alarm rate of only .1%. Of course the method has its limitations. It requires some standard continuum to serve as a yardstick, a continuum that is the same for the different subjects. In practice this may mean that an experimenter will have to test several different continua; note, though, that stimuli from more than two perceptual continua can be interspersed in the same test session. To be sure, if a given subject's sensations in all modalities were proportionately weaker, in some absolute ontological way, than all the sensations of another subject, the method could not uncover the discrepancy. But it is doubtful whether any possible method could.

REFERENCES

Bartoshuk, L. M. The psychophysics of taste. *American Journal of Clinical Nutrition*, 1978, *31*, 1068–1077.

Craik, F. I. M. Applications of signal detection theory to studies of aging. In A. T. Welford & J. E. Birren (Eds.), *Decision making and age*. Basel, Switzerland: Karger, 1969.

Green, D. M., & Swets, J. A. *Signal detection theory and psychophysics*. New York: Wiley, 1966.

Harkins, S. W., Chapman, C. R., & Eisdorfer, C. Memory loss and response bias in senescence. *Journal of Gerontology*, 1979, *34*, 66–72.

Jones, F. N. & Marcus, M. J. The subject effect in judgments of subjective magnitude. *Journal of Experimental Psychology*, 1961, *61*, 40–44.

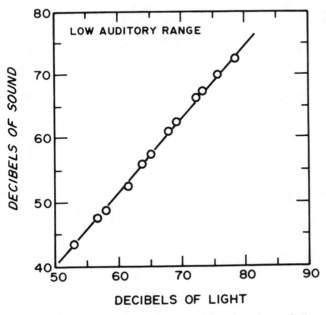

Figure 42-5. A cross-modality matching function relating sound and light, derived from the data in Figure 42-2.

Kubovy, M. A possible basis for conservatism in signal detection and probabilistic categorization tasks. *Perception & Psychophysics*, 1977, *22*, 277–281.

Luce, R. D., & Mo, S. S. Magnitude estimation of heaviness and loudness by individual subjects: A test of a probabilistic response theory. *British Journal of Psychology*, 1965, *18*, 159–174.

Marks, L. E. *Sensory processes: The new psychophysics.* New York: Academic Press, 1974.

Marks, L. E. A theory of loudness and loudness judgments. *Psychological Review*, 1979, *86*, 256–285.

Marks, L. E. Psychophysical measurement: Procedures, tasks, scales. In B. Wegener (Ed.), *Social attitudes and psychophysical measurement.* Hillsdale, N. J.: Erlbaum, in press.

Parks, T. E. Signal-detectability theory of recognition-memory performance. *Psychological Review*, 1966, *73*, 44–58.

Rovee, C. K., Cohen, R. Y., & Shlapack, W. Life-span stability in olfactory sensitivity. *Developmental Psychology*, 1975, *11*, 311–318.

Sperling, G. The attention operating characteristic: Examples from visual search. *Science*, 1978, *202*, 315–318.

Stevens, J. C., & Guirao, M. Individual loudness functions. *Journal of the Acoustical Society of America*, 1964, *36*, 2210–2213.

Stevens, J. C., & Hall, J. W. Brightness and loudness as functions of stimulus duration. *Perception & Psychophysics*, 1966, *1*, 319–327.

Stevens, J. C., & Marks, L. E. Spatial summation and the dynamics of warmth sensation. *Perception & Psychophysics*, 1971, *9*, 291–298.

Stevens, J. C. & Marks, L. E. Cross-modality matching function generated by magnitude estimation. *Perception & Psychophysics*, 1980, *27*, 379–389.

Stevens, J. C., Marks, L. E., & Simonson, D. C. Regional sensitivity and spatial summation in the warmth sense. *Physiology and Behavior*, 1974, *13*, 825–826.

Stevens, S. S. The direct estimation of sensory magnitudes—Loudness. *American Journal of Psychology*, 1956, *69*, 1–25.

Stevens, S. S. On the psychophysical law. *Psychological Review*, 1957, *64*, 153–181.

Stevens, S. S. Tactile vibration: Dynamics of sensory intensity *Journal of Experimental Psychology*, 1959, *59*, 210–218.

Stevens, S. S. Power-group transformations under glare, masking, and recruitment. *Journal of the Acoustical Society of America*, 1966, *39*, 725–735.

Stevens, S. S., & Greenbaum, H. B. Regression effect in psychophysical judgment. *Perception & Psychophysics*, 1966, *1*, 439–446.

Watson, C. S., Turpenoff, C. M., Kelly, W. J., & Botwinick, J. Age differences in resolving power and decision strategies. *Journal of Gerontology*, 1979, *34*, 547–552.

Ilene C. Siegler, John B. Nowlin, and James A. Blumenthal

CHAPTER
43

Health and Behavior: Methodological Considerations for Adult Development and Aging

This chapter reviews a set of issues related to the assessment of health and behavior and their interaction with the psychology of adult development and aging. Methodological problems are discussed and illustrated, along with contributions from other disciplines of relevance to the study of health and behavior. Particular attention is paid to questions of design and measurement. The methodological and assessment problems are well understood, but the solutions have not yet been found. Recent developments in the area of behavioral medicine are reviewed.

The set of issues dealing with the complex multiple interactions of health, behavior, and aging constitutes an area in which it is easier to raise than to answer questions. This chapter focuses on an exploration of the issues involved in the study of health, behavior, and aging and considers the special methodological problems inherent in this research area.

The larger context of this chapter concerns the societal questions about health as a component of the quality of life (Campbell, Converse, & Rodgers, 1976), the costs of providing appropriate care for increasing numbers of older persons (Brehm, 1978), and the policy implications of the health care system (Maddox, 1980; Shanas & Maddox, 1976). These important social policy issues are beyond the scope of this chapter.

The first section of this chapter focuses on some of the questions of research design in studies that include health and considers briefly some of the contributions from epidemiology and medical sociology. Often, psychological studies pay little attention to the population from which samples are drawn and assume that the external validity of the research will be sufficient if carefully described. Understanding the distribution of health/illness parameters may be useful in the design of psychological studies, since many of the health conditions, though more frequent among older persons, are still relatively rare events. Serious design problems in both cross-sectional and longitudinal or sequential studies result from the differential distribution of health/illness that is found across the life cycle.

The second section focuses on conceptual and measurement problems in the assessment of health status. Studies in this area often depend on the collaboration of a physician or the use of medical data, and thus a better understanding of the types of data and the characteristics of medical health information is required.

The third section concerns the relations between health and behavior. In the psychology of aging, most of the research has considered the impact of certain disease conditions (e.g., cardiovascular diseases) on psychological functioning (e.g., intelligence, reaction

Writing of this chapter was supported in part by Grant AG00364 from the National Institute on Aging. Our special thanks are due to Gerda G. Fillenbaum, Gail R. Marsh, Cecilia Teasley, and Elizabeth Auld.

time). The other side of the relation, the impact of be-havior on health, has been less well studied in the psy-chology of aging. The implications of this area in treatment and research suggest a major new direction.

Social and Epidemiological Considerations: Implications for Design and Theory

Epidemiology is the study of the incidence and dis-tribution of disease in which age is a particularly im-portant variable because (a) the distribution of disease by age is as great or greater for age than for most other variables; (b) the age distribution of a disease may pro-vide important information on its etiology; and (c) age may also prove an important confounding variable that must be controlled for when comparing different populations or subpopulations. In addition, diagnosis of disease and of cause of death at the extremes of the life cycle becomes less accurate, leading to a differ-ential reliability of assessment across the life cycle (MacMahon & Pugh, 1970). As in many areas of re-search on humans, where the phenomena of interest are not amenable to randomization, opportunities for controlled experimentation are rare, and the "natural" experiment must be capitalized on or modeled with more complex designs, including long-term studies (Friedman, 1974; Lilienfeld, 1976).

Two types of epidemiological studies are cross-sec-tional. Prevalence studies describe the relation between a disease and other variables of interest in a defined population at one point in time. Case control studies are prevalence studies to which, after the essential case has been identified, a specific control group is added for comparison. Incidence or cohort studies investigate the development of disease and are similar to longi-tudinal studies. Prospective studies are defined as studies that measure characteristics and wait for dis-ease to develop, whereas retrospective studies measure characteristics of persons already diseased. Thus, pre-valence is a static concept and incidence a dynamic concept within a specified time interval (Friedman, 1974). In addition, concern with single cohort studies (traditional longitudinal studies) that do not replicate across different times of measurement, which have led to the development of sequential strategies in adult de-velopment and aging (see e.g., Riley, 1979; Schaie, 1977), has had a long history in epidemiology as seen in the classic study of Frost (1939) on TB mortality.

Because of the focus on disease, the causal agents in epidemiology (e.g., exposure to a specific agent occur-ring at a particular time or the lagged effect of an ex-posure, as in cancer) give a more concrete nature to the variables, and thus models in epidemiology are less abstruse than models in developmental psychology.

But the logic of the forms of analysis is identical. Most of the epidemiological work in aging to date has con-cerned dementia (Ostfeld & Gibson, 1975).

One important source of public health data often underused by psychologists is information collected and made available by the National Center for Health Statistics (NCHS). The National Health Survey was authorized by Congress in 1956, and data from four surveys are now available from NCHS. The most recent study in the Health and Nutrition Examination Survey (HANES) was conducted from April 1971 to June 1974 and used a national probability sample of individuals from ages 1 to 74. A subsample of adults aged 25–74 years old was included in the HANES Augmentation Study, which included a household survey, physical examination, and laboratory tests. Of the sample of 4,288, 94% had medical histories and household information and 71% had physical exami-nations. The data from this survey are now becoming available and should provide an excellent set of figures for normative data comparisons when smaller psycho-logical samples are drawn. NCHS also publishes a series of methodological studies that deal with the measurement of health variables (see NCHS, 1978).

Recent findings are summarized in *Health—United States 1978* (U.S. Department of Health, Education, and Welfare, 1978): For example, data from the Health Interview Survey about self-assessment of health give figures broken down by age for self-ratings of health as excellent, good, fair, or poor (see Table 55, pps. 234–235). Percentages are given for four age groups (under 17, 17–44, 45–64, 65 and over) and range from 58.8% excellent, 36.4% good, 22.3% fair, and .4% poor for those under 17 years of age to 29.0% excellent, 39.0% good, 22.3% fair, and 9.0% poor for those aged 65 years or older. Other types of studies deal with reporting errors and variations in interviewer behavior (see e.g., Cannell, Oksenberg, & Converse, 1977). These studies and the sets of studies published in the Vital and Health Statistics Series can provide useful comparative data. While focused primarily on issues found in survey research, data about design and administration of questionnaires, reliability and validity of self-report data, and descriptions of the health status of the population of the United States at specified time intervals can supplement the types of findings typically reported in psychological studies. Such data can also help to increase the methodological sophistication of questionnaires and screening instru-ments designed for smaller samples.

Data on breakdowns within the elderly are less com-mon. Thus smaller local surveys may be useful. For example, in 1972–1973, a 10% probability sampling of the elderly was conducted in Durham County, North Carolina, by the Older Americans Resources and

Services (OARS) Survey (Blazer, 1978). The data from the OARS Community Survey presented below indicate the prevalence of disease observed. The survey was conducted with a home-interview format (Service & Heron, 1978) that included an assessment of physical functioning, and respondents were asked to list diseases they had. While reliabilities are not available for individual questions, the reliability for the area of the questionnaire dealing with physical health functioning was determined by a 5-week retest in which 91% of the responses were identical to the original responses (see Fillenbaum, 1978).

Validity studies on the OARS instrument were limited to checking the assessments derived from ratings scales (the physical function scale was one of five). Scale ratings were found to be highly correlated with assessments made by clinicians (Fillenbaum, 1978). The total sample included 997 individuals, of whom 983 had data on diseases. The data are presented in Table 43-1. These data include disease combinations, though approximately 25% of the sample reported no disease. The modal number of diseases was one (40% of the sample). No one reported more than six diseases. The resulting distribution of the sample was two diseases, 22%; three diseases 10%; four diseases, 3%; five diseases, .5%; and six diseases, .1%.

As can be seen from Table 43-1, arthritis was the most commonly mentioned disease. However, the cardiovascular disorders, as a group, were the most common. None of the frequencies of reported diseases were significantly related to age within the elderly age range. As a cross-sectional study, this survey reflects the profiles of only surviving members of the later cohorts. In addition, as the data were self-report and unconfirmed by medical examination, they may reflect an underestimate of diseases that tend to be asymptomatic (e.g., hypertension, early cancers, and diabetes).

The differential distribution of health across the life cycle is a serious problem for the design of research in this area. Whether the task in a particular study is to separate aging from disease or to develop a sample

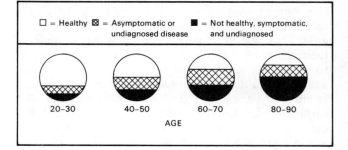

Figure 43-1. Schematic representation of four hypothetical populations.

across the life cycle that contains individuals at the same level of health, the researcher is sampling, depending on the ages of the individuals sampled, from different populations. A synthetic example is presented in Figure 43-1. As can be seen from the figure, in addition to the changes in distribution of subjects within each of the circles, the circles themselves become progressively smaller owing to mortality of the original cohort.

Each circle in Figure 43-1 represents the population available for study at each of four age groups. The unshaded area in each circle represents the proportion of that group of subjects in excellent health, confirmed by a physical examination with associated laboratory tests. The cross-hatched area represents the proportion of that age group with asymptomatic or subclinical disease, where self-report data would indicate no health problems but a physical examination would indicate some minor or potentially serious health problems. The fully shaded portion of the circle represents individuals with significant clinical disease that is known to the individuals and is thus accessible by self-report.

In a typical cross-sectional study, where the subjects are limited to those who are "healthy," defined by the ability to come to the laboratory without assistance

Table 43-1 Prevalence of Common Diseases by Age Group

Disease						
	Age group (N)					
	65–70 (436)	71–75 (270)	76–80 (121)	81–85 (118)	86–93 (38)	65–93 (983)
Arthritis	54.59	57.78	61.16	61.86	55.26	57.17
Hypertension	26.38	25.00	25.62	27.12	13.46	25.48
Heart disease	20.00	24.07	21.49	31.36	29.85	23.01
Diabetes	9.17	10.47	6.61	8.47	10.53	9.16
Stroke	8.15	4.44	4.13	4.24	8.11	6.32
Emphysema	3.67	1.49	4.13	6.78	2.63	3.46
Peptic ulcer	2.08	2.96	3.31	5.13	5.26	2.96
Cancers	.69	.74	.00	2.54	2.63	.92
No disease	25.58	24.63	20.86	20.20	31.58	24.34

Note. All data are percentages of age group that have the disease.

(see Abrahams, Hoyer, Elias, & Bradigan, 1975), the subjects would come from the top 75% of each age group but would represent different subsections of their age groups. In designing studies that include persons who are matched for health status across broad age ranges, a different problem arises. For example, a group of young (e.g., 20–30-year-old) subjects with cardiovascular disease would represent a much different selection from a population of age peers than would a group aged 60–70 with equally serious cardiovascular disease. A similar distribution of subjects by age and disease is given by Speith (1965, p. 271, Figure 1), who points out the unequal distribution by age within various healthy and diseased subjects. One can also remove from the sample all subjects with pathologies known to influence the variables under study (see e.g., Rowe, Andres, Tobin, Norris, & Shock, 1976). However, these procedures result in the exclusion of significantly more older than younger subjects from the study group (Rowe et al., 1976, p. 157, Table 1) and would require a large parent sample, an understanding of potentially confounding conditions, and a simultaneous measurement of appropriate health indices.

The representativeness of samples at different ages of the life cycle is not a problem peculiar to the study of health and behavior with age, but the issues assume a sharper focus in this area of research (see Baltes, Reese, & Nesselroade, 1977; Kuhlen, 1959). Two underlying assumptions in cross-sectional research are (1) that the younger group will, over time, become like the older group, and (2) that the older group was like the younger group some number of years ago. This set of assumptions is often hard to fulfill in health-related studies, because it is known that younger people with equivalent disease are unlikely to survive to the age of the older groups. When various controls are employed in analysis of data from longitudinal data banks, restricting both cross-sectional and longitudinal analyses to subjects who have been screened for health (Rowe et al., 1976) and/or for participation and survival (Botwinick & Siegler, 1980), findings from longitudinal and cross-sectional analyses have been shown to converge when the variable indexed by the method variance is controlled.

The requirements for well-designed research in this area are considerable. Large samples must be developed and maintained, and the variables of interest, along with potential confounding variables, must be measured. Measurement of indices of health also presents many complex problems.

Measurement Issues in Health

Aging processes have been studied extensively and are well characterized for most biological systems. Re-

views of the biology of aging and age-related changes in the various organ systems are available in Comfort (1979) and in Finch and Hayflick (1977). A briefer summary of age-related changes in human organ systems is contained in Rossman (1980) as well as in other general textbooks of geriatric medicine (Brockelhurst, 1978; Steinberg, 1976). In general, the age-related changes are in the direction of functional decline. In fact, no organ system fails to present that pattern as people age. However, in considering these age-associated decrements in human physiological function, one should keep the following qualifications in mind: (1) Research establishing functional decrements has been almost exclusively cross-sectional. Longitudinal and sequential studies may or may not replicate these findings. (2) The cross-sectional decrements typically reported may be partly a function of a design error in studies that do not have sufficient information to exclude subjects with potentially causal disease from the analysis. (3) Individual differences are large, indicating that group means may not accurately reflect the average functioning of the individual. (4) Since physiological systems are markedly redundant in structure, the proportion of function loss at which the system is compromised to the point of breakdown is rarely approached until homeostasis is threatened.

Timiras (1972) provides an excellent conceptual discussion of homeostasis as a biological phenomenon. Elderly individuals do not die of old age per se; instead, they die of diseases that occur when they are older. Even so, the separation of pathological processes from changes associated with normal aging constitutes a major theoretical concern. Busse (1978) has suggested the use of the following terms to make this distinction: Primary aging is defined as time-related changes intrinsic to the organism and hence as "true" aging; secondary aging derives from changes that are a result of disease-related pathology. A clear definition of the boundaries between primary and secondary aging awaits a fuller understanding of aging and of developmental mechanisms. For even if all of the major diseases known to cause death were eliminated, it is not logical to assume that the life span of the human organism would be lengthened, though the average life expectancy would be increased. Thus even the conceptual and empirical separation of aging from disease, if and when it is achieved, will not necessarily have answered the intriguing questions about the relations between aging and survival.

Concerns with mortality (see Upton, 1977) and survival (see Palmore & Jeffers, 1971) also raise issues in interpretation of findings. For example, in a follow-up of the Navy's study of 1000 aviators, MacIntyre, Mitchell, Oberman, Harlan, Graybill, and Johnson (1978) ask the question, Is aging "slower" in the military pilot? They compared the mortality experience of the pilots (aged 23 when first tested in 1940 and followed up most recently in 1977) at age 60 with U.S. Census data. The aviators had significnatly lower mortality than the Census population, and this difference increased as the cohort aged. MacIntyre et al. concluded that the pilots did indeed "age slower." While it is true that as a group the pilots lived longer, the data did not speak to the question of the rate of aging.

Developments in the field of geriatric medicine have focused attention on the special medical problems of older persons. Although geriatrics is primarily a clinical speciality, there is an increasing development of clinical research findings as well. In this chapter, the measurement of health and its relation to behavior has been limited to physical health. This is not because issues in mental health are not important but rather because they are covered elsewhere in this volume.

The dementing disorders, primarily Alzheimer's disease, are of major concern when dealing with the health of the elderly. A major symptom of Alzheimer's disease is cognitive dysfunction (see Eisdorfer & Cohen, 1978), and thus screening for dementia is critical in studies of cognitive functioning across the life cycle. Recent developments in the area of dementia and other aspects of geriatric psychiatry are reviewed in Busse and Blazer (1980). The roles that issues in mental health assessment play in relation to physical health are discussed more fully in Chapter 2 of of this volume. Even if one assumes the mental status of the individual to be intact, assessment of physical health status is still complex.

Health can be assessed by a variety of techniques: a physical examination by a physician or other health care provider, laboratory and diagnostic procedures, ratings scales filled out by the examiner, various types of archival data, and interview and self-report instruments.

Chen and Bryant (1975) and Balinsky and Berger (1975) review the complexities involved in global health assessments. Health ratings of necessity combine two distinct components: degree of pathology and degree of functional impairment. In many cases, these two aspects of health ratings are not well correlated. For example, in many types of cancer, an individual may have a serious malignancy with little or no functional compromise; alternatively, an individual may be functionally impaired without any diagnosable disease process. As well, there are individual differences in response to specific health problems.

Health ratings devised for large population studies may not be useful for individual assessment (Chiang & Cohen, 1973; Fanshel & Bush, 1970). Functional rating scales—such as Williamson's (1969) 6-point scale of impairment related to the ability to work—and activities-of-daily-living scales—such as the one of Katz, Down, Cash, and Grotz (1970) that evaluates independence of functioning in simple daily activities—may be useful to profile populations and in studies of disabled adults or impaired and home-bound or institutionalized elderly persons. But these scales would be expected to show little variance in studies of older persons tested in the laboratory and to be inappropriate at younger ages of the life cycle. Starfield (1974) has suggested the use of a profile indicative of environmental coping. However, such an approach is not differentially sensitive to types of disease.

Another common way to assess health is the self-report symptom questionnaire. One of the most common is the Cornell Medical Index (CMI) (Brodman, Erdmann, Lorge, & Wolff, 1949). The CMI is composed of 195 questions answered yes or no and is divided into (a) 12 scales that are summed to get a physical-symptoms score and (b) 6 scales that are summed to get a psychological-symptoms score. Scores on the CMI appear to be better validated against emotional well-being than against physical illness (Abramson, 1966), and older persons' scores have been studied by McCrae, Bartone, and Costa (1976) and by Wood, Elias, Schultz, and Pentz (1978). McCrae et al. reported that the CMI psychological-symptoms score was related to anxiety across the adult age range (25–82) in men, while the CMI physical-symptoms score was related to anxiety only through age 54. Correlation between physician-rated illness and the CMI physical-symptoms score was low but significant. Wood et al., who compared hypertensives and normals on the CMI, found that hypertensives of all ages had both more psychological and physical symptoms. Differences between hypertensives and normals were found on a large variety of scales. These two studies suggest that the CMI cannot be used in place of more detailed medical screening. In addition, knowledge that one has a disease may be a better predictor of anxiety than the disease itself (Costa, McCrae, Andres & Tobin, in press).

Self-ratings of health (generally of the form "Would you rate your health as excellent, good, fair, or poor?") are among the easiest health ratings to collect. Such ratings by the elderly have been found to be generally valid when compared to physicians' ratings (Maddox & Douglass, 1973), to physicians' ratings and survival (LaRue, Bank, Jarvik, & Hetland, 1979), and to objective reports of symptoms, drug usage, and rated degree of impairment from health concerns (Fillenbaum, 1979). For example, in comparing self-health ratings with a concurrent physician's examination, Maddox and Douglass (1973) summarized the experience of the first six examinations from the Duke First Longitudinal Study. Overall, 64% of the responses were congruent, and 36% were noncongruent. When the two indices were noncongruent, the self-rating tended to be higher than the physician rating. Examining the data longitudinally with cross-lagged panel correlations, Maddox and Douglass found that the self-ratings were more predictive of future physician ratings than physician ratings were of future self-ratings.

Fillenbaum (1979), using data from the OARS Survey, compared elderly individuals residing in the community with institutionalized elderly people. Three self-assessments were used: overall assessment of health (from excellent to poor), concern about health (from not concerned to very much concerned), and degree of impairment of daily activities due to health (from none to a lot). These self-assessments were validated against self-reports of more objective data: number of health problems checked on a 23-item list, number of medications taken from a list of 18 drugs, and number of disabilities checked on a list of 16 disabilities. The results indicated that the subjective self-assessments were related to the objective indices for the community residents but not for the institutional residents. Also, while self-assessments were equivalent for both men and women, women reported more objective health problems.

LaRue et al. (1979) looked at self- versus physician ratings of health along a scale of excellent to poor, and at the relation of those ratings to a 5-year survival criterion in survivors from a study of aged twins (Blum, Clark, & Jarvik, 1973). The survivors had a median age of 84.25 years. The results indicated that for the younger subjects (those under 84), both self- and physician ratings were predictive of survival. Self-ratings tended to be somewhat higher than physician ratings, and sex differences were not important.

Thus, the three studies mentioned above suggest that in older persons (aged 60–84), self-assessments of health, though they may slightly overestimate health when compared with physician ratings, are probably useful indicators for community-dwelling populations. However, the reports may be tapping somewhat different constructs for men and women.

In the Duke Longitudinal Studies (see Palmore, 1971, 1974), two functional health ratings were developed. These ratings, which were filled out by the physician after examination of the subject, combined both pathological and functional information. The physical function rating (PFR; Dovenmuehle, Busse, & Newman, 1961) was used in the first longitudinal study and had a 6-point range. A similar scale with a 10-point range (Karnofsky & Burchenal, 1948) was used in the second longitudinal study. These scales proved predictive of health outcomes in both studies and show appropriate relations with behavioral measures (Nowlin, 1979, 1980; Siegler, 1979). A recent study concerning the Karnofsky scale (Hutchinson,

Boyd, & Feinstein, 1979) reported poor reliability when two physician raters were compared after examining a group of hospital emergency-room drop-in patients. However, the study format posed many difficulties (for example, no standard schema for evaluating patients) that might in themselves have produced the rater discrepancy.

A second type of health information is derived from the use of disease-diagnostic categories. Comparisons of groups of diseased and disease-free groups have the potential for clarifying many large-scale issues in gerontology. Specifically, to what extent are many so-called "normative" aging changes merely the impact of coincident disease states (perhaps not obvious and only distinguished by a discerning eye). Caution should be an integral part of any utilization of diagnostic categories: Categories of disease may not always be what they seem. A prominent example is found in testing the widely held assumption that many "normative aging changes" in intellectual and psychomotor function might, in reality, derive from subtle changes in the central nervous system produced by atherosclerosis.

Patently, all vascular or circulatory diseases are not a result of atherosclerotic pathology. Hence a person with rheumatic heart disease should not be categorized with a group of people who demonstrate the classic clinical manifestations of atherosclerosis (i.e., angina, heart attack, etc.). Unfortunately, differences in diagnostic categories are not all as clear-cut as the example just offered.

The availability of a vast array of accessory clinical testing has pertinence for the psychologist interested in aging. These procedures can establish diagnosis and can often provide some clue to the extent or severity of illness. The number of test procedures accessible is legion, far beyond the scope of this chapter to summarize. One relatively understandable source of information is Volume 2 in the Harper and Row *Practice of Medicine* series (Spittell, 1979), which is largely devoted to discussion of laboratory measures. Moreover, there is frequent updating with supplements, an unusual and attractive feature.

Some procedures merit special emphasis, either because they are easily accessible or because they provide particularly useful information in evaluation of psychological functioning. Blood pressure recordings are one such measure. Despite its value as a health correlate, blood pressure is quite variable, and this characteristic should be kept in mind as the investigator makes use of it. Harbin and Cunningham (1978) have recently reported on a study of blood pressure in the elderly, with focus on assessing multiple measures and variability. Systolic pressure proved to be more variable than diastolic pressure. Thus indices that combine the two may provide a somewhat distorted picture of blood pressure responsivity, even though a single index is tidier for purposes of statistical analysis.

For definition of hypertension, diastolic blood pressure provides the better index. Criteria demarcating high from normal blood pressure levels are almost as inconsistent as the variable itself. For the older person, lower limits of normal are generally considered higher than for the younger individual. For example, persistent diastolic readings of 90 mm Hg or greater for people up to age 60 are usually considered within the hypertensive pressure range. Higher values, 95–100 mm Hg diastolic, are acceptable for the older person. Systolic pressure is a less reliable indicator of hypertension. There is a more striking (and variable) increase in this value with age than with diastolic pressure; presumably the systolic-pressure increase reflects the stiffening of the arterial walls that accompanies aging.

Finally, the investigator should be aware that the traditional method of recording blood pressure (blood pressure cuff and stethoscope) generally underestimates systolic values and overestimates diastolic values. Newer blood pressure recording apparatuses—such as the semiautomatic pressure-detection devices—provide a reasonable estimate of this cardiovascular measure.

Visualization of the retinal arteries provides a useful index of hypertension and atherosclerotic disease. Vessels are rated on a scale from 1 to 4, with higher values indicative of increasingly severe disease. Changes in retinal arteries have been demonstrated to correlate with extent of atherosclerotic disease found with coronary artery cineangiography (an invasive x-ray technique that permits visualization of the coronary arterial network).

The clinical electrocardiogram offers substantial evidence of presence or absence of heart disease. While a "negative" electrocardiogram does not exclude the likelihood of heart disease, the presence of changes on the electrocardiogram provide incontrovertible evidence. In the older age group, any "significant change" is most probably secondary to atherosclerotic vascular disease.

Kidney function and its assessment offer some highly pertinent health information with potential behavioral correlates. By virtue of its two primary interrelated functions (ridding the body of waste chemicals built up by cell work and maintaining appropriate concentrations of various body chemicals), the kidney affects the efficiency of all body system workings, including the central nervous system. Hence slight changes in kidney function, even those that seem insignificant to the medical clinician, could be associated with subtle alteration in state of the sensorium. Two blood tests offer a reasonable gauge of kidney func-

tion: serum creatinine and blood urea nitrogen (BUN) levels. The former test is more frequently employed for this assessment. Since age, sex, and body surface all influence blood level of creatinine, a formula has been derived to account for these factors, along with a nomogram (see Kampmann, Giersback-Wieler, Kristense, & Hansen, 1974; Rowe et al., 1976).

Also, drug usage among older persons is high. Failure of the kidney to clear the blood of active medications or their immediate breakdown products permits the accumulation of relatively high concentrations of drug with a resulting enhanced effect. A good summary of drug effects on older persons on a drug-by-drug basis can be found in Lawson and Chaptron (1978).

Relation Between Health and Behavior: Methodological Problems, Illustrative Findings, and Therapeutic Implications

The literature in the psychology of adult development and aging concerning health and behavior has been reviewed by Abrahams (1976), Eisdorfer and Wilkie (1977), and Elias, Elias, and Elias (1977, see Chapter 12). Two studies that have become classic studies in this area illustrate problems that have yet to be adequately solved. The two studies are the NIMH Human Aging Study (Birren, Butler, Greenhouse, Sokoloff, & Yarrow, 1963; Granick & Patterson, 1971) and Speith's study of speeded performance tasks in relation to various forms of cardiovascular disease (Speith, 1964, 1965). In the Human Aging Study, 47 healthy men were divided into two groups: Group 1—those in optimal health—and Group 2—those with asymptomatic disease. These 47 men were followed up 5 and 11 years later. At the 11-year follow-up, 63% of Group 1 had survived versus 30% Group 2. At the 11-year follow-up it was no longer reasonable to distinguish between the two groups on basis of health, since all of the survivors would then have been classified in the second group. Analyses at the first measurement point turned up many significant differences in psychological functioning between the two health groups. Speith reported changes in a variety of speeded psychological tasks that declined with both age and increasing severity of disease.

In general, current research has supported the basic findings of these studies, and each study illustrates problems that have yet to be adequately solved. The Human Aging Study started with a relatively small number of subjects (47). At the 5-year follow-up, 29 of 39 survivors were tested. Survival was related to initial health status. In Group 2 there had been a subgroup with arteriosclerosis, and none of that group survived for later evaluation. Aside from the problem of limited *N*, which often accompanies studies in which many detailed measurements are made, the differential survival of the various health groups did not permit the evaluation of the patterns of change within various health/disease groups. The study was successful, however, in describing the relations between health and various behaviors at the initial measurement point, and in using the data to develop predictors of survival (see Granick & Patterson, 1971).

In Speith's study, the subject population included men representative of a wide adult age range (23–59) as well as a range of known cardiovascular status. However, an examination of Speith's Figure 1 (1965, p. 371) indicates that the severity of disease increased with age. Thus the potential interaction of age with disease in that study could not be separated. Similarly, in a study by Light (1978), where subjects were recruited from a hypertensive clinic, although a broad age range (18–77) was sampled, the distributions of diseases within the age groups precluded direct tests of the separation of age from disease. Covariance procedures were used for age and a relationship was found between reaction time and disease.

Similar problems can be found in other studies. Often, in the analysis of large-scale aging studies that are designed for multiple purposes, special attention is paid to health/behavior relationships. Whenever the variables of interest in a particular analysis are not the focus of the design of the study, problems can be anticipated. For example, a recent paper (Hertzog, Schaie, & Gribbin, 1978), from Schaie's sequential study of cognitive behavior across the life cycle, looked at the relation between various forms of cardiovascular disease (CVD) and intellectual functioning and behavioral rigidity. All of the health data were based on abstracted records of health histories and thus were not under the experimenters' control. Because of changes in the subjects' health during the 14 years of the study, the grouping of subjects into disease categories varied as a function of the records evaluated. Sufficient information was available to provide for an analysis of the relations among participation, drop-out, and disease, but the resulting number of cases with various forms of cardiovascular disease required that the analysis with the most interest (CVD × Cohort × Sex × Time) be done with a dichotomous CVD variable. While this was required by the number of subjects for the design, the combinations of disease in the disease groups, fully described by the authors, suggest that differential findings would have resulted if the various groups had been evaluated separately. In addition, the classification of the sample into CVD groups was problematical.

Another approach to similar problems is illustrated in recent findings from our second longitudinal study (Siegler & Nowlin, 1979). In this longitudinal study, in order to evaluate the relation between cardiovascular status, intellectual functioning as assessed by the Weschler Adult Intelligence Scale, and anxiety as assessed by Cattell's Sixteen Personality Factor Questionnaire (16PF) (Form C, factor QII), subjects were classified according to their health status across the full six years of the study. That is, the normal group had no evidence of cardiovascular disease at any of the four measurement times; the groups with hypertension, coronary artery disease, and both disease categories were assessed as having had the disease throughout the study, based on evidence from at least three out of four examinations. These classification procedures resulted in the loss of 102 of the 345 participating surviving subjects from the original panel of 502 subjects. When the original panel, then aged 46 to 69, was evaluated between 1968 and 1976, 63 had died, and 114 had dropped out or missed at least one examination. As mentioned above, 102 subjects had ambiguous health histories, with 24 subjects remaining in the hypertensive group, 32 in the coronary-artery disease group, and only 8 with both hypertension and coronary artery disease (CAD). The results indicated a main effect for anxiety that separated people with no disease from those with disease. The anxiety remained consistently higher at all times of measurement for those in whom the disease was present.

Intelligence tended to increase slightly over the course of the study for all groups. The hypertensive group, which was receiving medication for the hypertension, had the highest scores and the increase reached a plateau after the third examination. The normal group showed the same pattern but had slightly lower scores. Those with CAD and with both CAD and hypertension had lower scores and increased only through the second examination, indicating a different pattern of change over time as a function of the degree and type of disease present. Even with an original population of approximately 500 people, we were hampered by the insufficient number of subjects available on which to compare the behavioral data with the development of the disease observed over the course of the study. Similar problems in the study of personality and hypertension are reviewed by Costa et al. (in press). Costa et al. report data from the Baltimore Longitudinal Study and discuss the requirements for research in this area.

The other side of the health/behavior relationship is the impact of behavior on health. This can be illustrated by considering the well-documented relation of behavior patterns and coronary heart disease (CHD).

Epidemiological studies have identified a number of risk factors associated with increased risk for coronary heart disease, including advancing age, sex (being male), elevated blood pressure, high serum-cholesterol levels, obesity, and cigarette smoking (Dawber & Kannel, 1961; Epstein, 1965; Kannel, McGee, & Gordon, 1976). However, the failure of these indices to predict the incidence of new cases of CHD prompted investigators to look for additional variables, including psychological and behavioral factors.

The notion that a particular behavioral predisposition may place persons at risk for CHD has received growing attention in the past 20 years (Jenkins, 1971). While clinical observations by Osler (1897), Dunbar (1943), Arlow (1945), and the Menningers (Menninger & Menninger, 1936) described coronary patients as hostile, competitive, chronically tense, and frequently overcommitted to work without deriving lasting satisfaction, those reports were generally ignored in the medical community. Studies were criticized for their retrospective designs, small and select patient samples, and lack of scientific rigor. However, in the late 1950s, two cardiologists, Meyer Friedman and Ray Rosenman, integrated these psychological characteristics and added overt behavioral features in their formulation of the coronary-prone, or "Type A," behavior pattern. They described the Type A person as characterized by excessive competitive drive, a persistent desire for recognition, enhanced aggressiveness, and a habitual propensity to accelerate the pace of living (Rosenman, Friedman, Straus, Wurm, Kostichek, Hahn, & Werthessen, 1964). The converse, Type B, behavior pattern was defined by a relative absence of these characteristics.

The methods for assessing the Type A behavior pattern have undergone a subtle transformation over the past 10 years. Typically, Type A is assessed by a structured interview (Rosenman et al., 1964), a variety of psychometric instruments including the Jenkins Activity Survey for Health Prediction (Jenkins, Rosenman, & Friedman, 1967), the Framingham Type A Scale (Haynes, Levine, Scotch, Feinlab, & Kannel, 1978) and the Bortner Type A Scale (Bortner, 1969), or a performance battery (Bortner & Rosenman, 1967). Currently, the two most widely accepted techniques are the structured interview and the Jenkins Activity Survey (JAS). The structured interview is generally considered the most valid measure of Type A. Initially it was developed to assess the more enduring psychological characteristics of the individual as well as the overt behavioral stylistics displayed during the interview procedure. Recently the structured interview has been shown to rely more on the speech style and psychomotor behaviors than on the content of the interviewee's response. For example, evidence suggests that speech speed and volume account for almost 50% of the variance in behavior pattern classification (Scherwitz, Berton, & Leventhal, 1977; Schucker & Jacobs, 1977). The JAS has also undergone changes in the original instrument. Today there are a number of different forms for various specific populations including women, unemployed or retired persons, and college students (see Dembroski, Weiss, Shields, Haynes, & Feinlab, 1978).

The Western Collaborative Group Study (WCGS) is the landmark study in the Type A literature. Retrospective studies of men and women had previously shown that the relation of behavior pattern to CHD was from four to seven times stronger for Type A than for Type B behavior (Friedman & Rosenman, 1959; Rosenman & Friedman, 1961). The WCGS project was initiated in 1960–1961 as a longitudinal study of the incidence of CHD in over 3,500 employed males in several California communities. At the beginning of the study subjects underwent extensive medical evaluation in which a complete medical history was obtained, blood studies and other laboratory tests were performed, and the behavioral structured interview was administered. Initially, 113 men were found to have manifest CHD; 80 men, or 71%, were concurrently assessed as being Type A (Rosenman et al., 1964). The remaining subjects in the sample, who were diagnosed as free from CHD, were subsequently followed annually for a mean period of 8½ years. The final report from the study indicated that Type A subjects exhibited 2.37 times the rate of new CHD compared to their Type B counterparts (Rosenman, Brand, Jenkins, Friedman, Straus, & Wurm, 1975). A statistical adjustment procedure, provided by the multiple logistic model, was used to control for differences in age, serum cholesterol, blood pressure, and smoking, reducing the relative risk to approximately 1.97 (Brand, 1978).

In 1965 subjects participating in the WCGS also completed the 1965 version of the JAS (Jenkins, Rosenman, & Zyzanski, 1974). Results indicated that those men who developed CHD after testing scored significantly higher on the Type A scale than a random sample of controls. Thus, while the JAS Type A scale does not classify subjects in the same way as the structured interview does, the Type A scale of the JAS has also been shown to be a significant predictor of CHD, though not as good a one as the interview method (Brand, Rosenman, Jenkins, Sholtz, & Zyzanski, in press). Numerous retrospective studies have confirmed the association of the JAS Type A scale and CHD. (For a review, see Dembroski et al., 1978; Glass, 1977; Jenkins, 1976.)

Several studies have reported an association between the Type A behavior pattern and coronary atherosclerosis. In 1968 Friedman, Rosenman, Straus, Wurm, and Kositchek found evidence that Type A men have twice the extent of coronary atherosclerosis as Type B men when studied at autopsy. In fact, 26 subjects considered to have the most severe coronary occlusions were classified Type A, while only four classified Type B had severe disease. In an effort to extend these findings to an actual patient population, several investigative teams attempted to relate the Type A behavior pattern to coronary atherosclerosis determined by coronary angiography. In the Duke study, Blumenthal, Williams, Kong, Schanberg, and Thompson (1978) reported that the Type A behavior pattern was associated with significantly greater severity of coronary artery disease than the contrasting Type B behavior pattern. This study was important, since it suggested that behavioral patterns might be related to the development of disease as well as to the clinical manifestation of disease.

Several cross-sectional studies have reported a relation between age and the Type A behavior pattern. Zyzanski (1978) noted that linear correlations approach zero among populations with restricted age ranges. For example, no relation was found between Type A behavior and age in the 39–59-year age group in the WCGS. In studies including a wider age range, however, small inverse relations are found between age and men classified as Type A (Mettlin, 1976; Shekelle, Schoenberger, & Stamler, 1976). In contrast, the Type A scores of employed women rise with age, while men's scores show a slight decline with age (Waldron, Zyzanski, Shekelle, Jenkins, & Tannenbaum, 1977). In the study documenting the greatest correlation of age with Type A—the Boston study of 390 air traffic controllers reported by Zyzanski (1978)—age does not account for more than 4% of the variance in Type A scores. Most studies have focused on middle-aged employed males. In one of the few studies of Type A in the elderly, Haynes et al. (1978) administered a self-report measure of Type A behavior (Framingham Type A scale) to 176 men and 232 women aged 65–77, as well as to a middle-aged group, 45–64. For both sexes, age and the Type A score were inversely related. Unpublished data from our own laboratory (Blumenthal & Herman, in preparation) indicate that adjectives descriptive of Type A men remain constant throughout adulthood, whereas, applied to women, the Type A adjectives are found more often in the younger decades. However, these data were interpreted as reflecting a cohort effect rather than a true age effect.

There have been few studies of the psychology of Type A in middle age, although there is evidence that

the Type A behavior pattern may exert its greatest influence on the development of CHD in the middle decades of life. For example, Jenkins (1975) noted that younger Type A men generated higher relative risk ratios than older Type A men.

Aside from CHD, recent statistics have implicated overt behavioral factors in the manifestation of five of the six leading causes of death in the United States. Diseases of the cardiovascular system, cancer, diabetes mellitus, cirrhosis of the liver, and accidents all have been shown to be associated with such life-style factors as cigarette smoking, improper diet and eating habits resulting in obesity, "coping styles," lack of physical exercise, alcohol and drug misuse, cultural patterns, and the failure to follow prescribed medical regimens (see Houpt, Orleans, George, & Brodie, 1979; Pomerleau, 1979).

The potential of intervention for the modification of deleterious behaviors and how this will affect aging in populations with and without such intervention present intriguing questions for the future.

One could speculate that if children and young adults are trained in the proper habits, they might well enter adult life with a lowered probability of disease, as evidenced by a lowered incidence of disease during the later years. Sequential studies plus a careful monitoring of sex differences and times of these shifts will be required to interpret future data correctly.

Not only is there interest in modifying behaviors for preventive reasons, but in the last few years there has been an increasing interest in the use of psychological and behavioral principles for treating the physically ill. A new term, *behavioral medicine*, has recently been adopted and has received widespread attention. The term is distinguished from its predecessor, psychosomatic medicine, in several important ways. The conceptual origins of psychosomatic medicine were imbedded in Freudian psychoanalytic theory. The emphasis was on understanding the unconscious determinants in the etiology and pathogenesis of physical disease. Consequently therapeutic interventions emphasized treatment of underlying conflicts, drives, and motives.

The recent development of behavioral medicine, on the other hand, is derived from interest in behavior modification and behavior therapy. Behavior modification uses principles derived from the experimental analysis of behavior, social learning theory, and classical conditioning theory (see Pomerleau, 1979; Pomerleau & Brady, 1979; Schwartz & Weiss, 1977, 1978).

A number of behavioral intervention techniques have been successfully developed. Biofeedback, a treatment involving psychological and technological intervention, has been employed in treatment of a variety of psychophysiological disorders. The selectivity of the physiological control achieved by biofeedback is thought to give biofeedback an advantage in treating disorders in which the symptom is quite specific, such as sinus tachycardia, Raynaud's disease, seizure disorders, and various neuromuscular disorders. In applications where specificity is not important, such as in hypertension, muscle-contraction headaches, and asthma, the operant conditioning aspect of biofeedback is regarded as less important, and more general relaxation procedures are emphasized.

To date, most research in the area of behavioral medicine has not considered age a significant variable (Gentry, 1978). Behavioral techniques have been largely ignored in the treatment of medical disorders that are particularly prevalent in the elderly. An informal survey of patients undergoing behavioral treatment in the Biofeedback Laboratory at Duke University Medical Center indicated that less than 5% of the patients seen are over 65 years of age. The reasons for this are unclear. Older persons appear to be able to benefit from behavioral treatments in a wide variety of contexts (Lopez, Hoyer, Goldstein, Gershaw, & Sprafkin, 1980; Richards & Thorpe, 1978). Roberts 1980 reported on the treatment of chronic pain patients with behavioral techniques and found that age was not related to treatment outcome. Basic research on the relation of classical and instrumental conditioning to age (for reviews, see Botwinick, 1967, 1973; Jerome, 1959) suggests that older persons may learn more slowly than younger persons. However, most current work on conditioning and age appears in the animal literature (Arenberg & Robertson-Tchabo, 1977). The 1980s will see an increase (a) in the use of behavioral interventions for modifying risk factors that have been associated with various diseases, and (b) in studies designed to assess the efficacy of attempts to modify health-related behavior in older persons.

The problems encountered in studying health and behavior in the psychology of aging are considerable. We have tried to point out some of the more obvious ones. As current problems are solved, the future will probably bring us more sophisticated, but hopefully different, methodological problems.

REFERENCES

Abrahams, J. P. Psychological correlates of cardiovascular disease. In M. F. Elias, B. E. Eleftheriou, & P. K. Elias (Eds.), *Special review of experimental aging research: Progress in biology*. Bar Harbor, Maine: Experimental Aging Research Inc., 1976.

Abrahams, J. P., Hoyer, W. J., Elias, M. F., & Bradigan, B. Gerontological research in psychology published in the *Journal of Gerontology*, 1963–1974: Perspectives and progress. *Journal of Gerontology*, 1975, *30*, 668–673.

Abramson, J. H. The Cornell Medical Index (CMI) as an epidemiological tool. *American Journal of Public Health*, 1966, *56*, 287–298.

Arenberg, D., & Robertson-Tchabo, E. A. Learning and aging. In J. E. Birren & K. W. Schaie (Eds.), *Handbook of the psychology of aging*. New York: Van Nostrand Reinhold, 1977.

Arlow, J. A. Identification mechanisms in coronary occlusions. *Psychosomatic Medicine*, 1945, *7*, 195–209.

Balinsky, W., & Berger, R. A review of the research on general health status indexes. *Medical Care*, 1975, *13*, 283–293.

Baltes, P. B., Reese, H. W., & Nesselroade, J. R. *Life-span developmental psychology: Introduction to research methods*. Monterey, Calif: Brooks/Cole, 1977.

Birren, J. E., Butler, R. N., Greenhouse, S. W., Sokoloff, L., & Yarrow, M. *Human aging* (PHS No. 986). Washington, D.C.: U.S. Government Printing Office, 1963.

Blazer, D. G. The OARS Durham surveys: Description and application. In, *Multidimensional functional assessment: The OARS methodology*. Durham, N.C.: Duke University, Center for the Study of Aging and Human Development, 1978.

Blum, J., Clark, E. T., & Jarvik, L. F. *The New York State Psychiatric Institute study of aging twins*. New York: Springer, 1973.

Blumenthal, J. A., & Herman, S. *Type A behavior and adult development*. Manuscript in preparation.

Blumenthal, J. A., Williams, R. B., Kong, Y., Schanberg, S. M., & Thompson, L. W. Type A behavior pattern and coronary atherosclerosis. *Circulation*, 1978, *58*, 634–639.

Bortner, R. W. A short rating scale as a potential measure of Pattern A behavior. *Journal of Chronic Diseases*, 1969, *22*, 87–91.

Bortner, R. W., & Rosenman, R. H. The measurement of Pattern A behavior. *Journal of Chronic Diseases*, 1967, *20*, 525–533.

Botwinick, J. *Cognitive processes in maturity and old age*. New York: Springer, 1967.

Botwinick, J. *Aging and behavior*. New York: Springer, 1973.

Botwinick, J., & Siegler, I. C. Intellectual ability among the elderly: Simultaneous cross-sectional and longitudinal comparisons. *Developmental Psychology*, 1980, *16*, 49–53.

Brand, R. J. Coronary prone behavior as an independent risk factor for coronary heart disease. In T. M. Dembroski, S. M. Weiss, S. G. Haynes, & M. Feinlab (Eds.), *Coronary prone behavior*. New York: Springer-Verlag, 1978.

Brand, R. J., Rosenman, R. H., Jenkins, C. D., Sholtz, R. I., & Zyzanski, S. J. Comparison of coronary heart disease prediction in the Western Collaborative Group Study using the structured interview and the Jenkins Activity Survey assessments of the coronary-prone Type A behavior pattern. *Journal of Chronic Diseases*, in press.

Brehm, H. P. The future of U.S. health care delivery for the elderly. In B. R. Herzog (Ed.), *Aging and income*. New York: Human Science Press, 1978.

Brockelhurst, J. C. (Ed.) *Textbook of geriatric medicine and gerontology* (2nd ed.). Edinburgh, Scotland: Churchill Livingstone, 1978.

Brodman, K., Erdmann A. J., Lorge, I., & Wolff, H. G. The Cornell Medical Index: An adjunct to medical interview. *Journal of the American Medical Association*, 1949, *140*, 530–534.

Busse, E. W. Duke Longitudinal Study I: Senescence and senility. In R. Katzman, R. D. Terry, & K. L. Beck (Eds.), *Alzheimer's Disease: Senile dementia and related disorders* (Aging Vol. 7). New York: Raven Press, 1978.

Busse, E. W., & Blazer, D. G. (Eds.). *Handbook of geriatric psychiatry*. New York: Van Nostrand Reinhold, 1980.

Campbell, A., Converse, P. E., & Rodgers, W. L. *The quality of American life: Perceptions, evaluations & satisfactions*. New York: Russell Sage Foundation, 1976.

Cannell, C. F., Oksenberg, L., & Converse, J. M. *Experiments in interviewing techniques: Field experiments in health reporting, 1971–1977* [DHEW Publication No. (HRA) 78-3204]. Hyattsville, Md.: National Center for Health Services Research, 1977.

Chen, M. K., & Bryant, B. E. The measurement of health—A critical and selective overview. *International Journal of Epidemiology*, 1975, *4*, 257–264.

Chiang, C. L., & Cohen, R. D. A stochastic model for an index of health. *International Journal of Epidemiology*, 1973, *2*, 7–13.

Comfort, A. *Aging: The biology of senescence* (3rd ed.). New York: Elsevier, 1979.

Costa, P. T., McCrae, R. R., Andres, R., & Tobin, J. D. Hypertension, somatic complaints, and personality. In D. Streeten & M. F. Elias (Eds.), *Hypertension and behavior*. Mt. Desert, Maine: Beech Hill Enterprises, in press.

Dawber, T. R., & Kannel, W. B. Susceptibility to coronary heart disease. *Modern Concepts in Cardiovascular Disease*, 1961, *30*, 617–676.

Dembroski, T. M., Weiss, S. M., Shields, J. L., Haynes, S. G., & Feinlab, M. *Coronary prone behavior*. New York: Springer-Verlag, 1978.

Dovenmuehle, R. H., Busse, E. W., & Newman, G. Physical problems of older people. *Journal of American Geriatric Society*, 1961, *9*, 208–217.

Dunbar, F. *Psychosomatic diagnosis*. New York: Hoeber & Harper, 1943.

Eisdorfer, C., & Cohen, D. Differential diagnosis. In M. Storandt, I. C. Siegler, & M. F. Elias (Eds.), *The clinical psychology of aging*. New York: Plenum Press, 1978.

Eisdorfer, C., & Wilkie, F. Stress, disease, aging and behavior. In J. E. Birren & K. W. Schaie (Eds.), *Handbook of the psychology of aging*. New York: Van Nostrand Reinhold, 1977.

Elias, M. F., Elias, P. K., & Elias, J. W. *Basic processes in adult developmental psychology*. St. Louis, Mo.: Mosby, 1977.

Epstein, F. The epidemiology of coronary heart disease: A review. *Journal of Chronic Diseases*, 1965, *18*, 735–774.

Fanshel, S., & Bush, J. W. A health index and its application to health research outcomes. *Operations Research*, 1970, *18*, 1021–1029.

Fillenbaum, G. G. Validity and reliability of the MFAQ. In, *Multidimensional functional assessment: The OARS methodology*. Durham, N.C. Duke University, Center for the Study of Aging and Human Development, 1978.

Fillenbaum, G. G. Social context and self-assessment of health among the elderly. *Journal of Health and Social Behavior*, 1979, *20*, 45–51.

Finch, C. E., & Hayflick, L. (Eds.) *Handbook of the biology of aging*. New York: Van Nostrand Reinhold, 1977.

Friedman, G. *Primer of epidemiology*. New York: McGraw-Hill, 1974.

Friedman, M., & Rosenman, R. H. Association of specific overt behavior pattern with blood and cardiovascular findings. *Journal of the American Medical Association*, 1959, *169*, 1286–1296.

Friedman, M., Rosenman, R. H., Straus, R., Wurm, M., & Kositchek, R. The relationship of behavior Pattern A to the state of the coronary vasculature: A study of fifty-one autopsy subjects. *American Journal of Medicine*, 1968, *44*, 525–537.

Frost, W. H. The age selection of mortality from tuberculosis in successive decades. *American Journal of Hygiene*, 1939, *30*, 91–96.

Gentry, W. D. Psychosomatic issues in assessment. In M. Storandt, I. C. Siegler, & M. F. Elias (Eds.), *The clincial psychology of aging*. New York: Plenum Press, 1978.

Glass, D. C. *Behavior Patterns, stress and coronary disease*. New York: Wiley, 1977.

Granick, S., & Patterson, R. D. (Eds.) *Human aging II* [DHEW Publication No. (HSM) 71-9037]. Washington, D.C.: U.S. Government Printing Office, 1971.

Harbin, T. J., & Cunningham, W. R. Influence of contextual variables on blood pressure in the elderly. *Experimental Aging Research*, 1978, *4*, 521–534.

Haynes, S. B., Levine, S., Scotch, N. A., Feinlab, M., & Kannel, W. B. The relationship of psychosocial factors to coronary heart disease in the Framingham study: Methods and risk factors. *American Journal of Epidemiology*, 1978, *107*, 362–383.

Hertzog, C., Schaie, K. W., & Gribbin, K. Cardiovascular disease and changes in intellectual functioning from middle to old age. *Journal of Gerontology*, 1978, *33*, 872–883.

Houpt, J. L., Orleans, C. S., George, L. K., & Brodie, H. K. H. *The importance of mental health services to general health care*. Cambridge, Mass.: Ballinger, 1979.

Hutchinson, T. A., Boyd, N. F., & Feinstein, A. R. Scientific problems in clinical scales as demonstrated in the Karnofsky index of performance status. *Journal of Chronic Diseases*, 1979, *32*, 661–666.

Jenkins, C. D. Psychological and social precursors of coronary disease. *New England Journal of Medicine*, 1971, *284*, 244–255; 307–317.

Jenkins, C. D. The coronary prone personality. In W. D. Gentry (Ed.), *Psychological aspects of myocardial infarction*. Cambridge Mass.: Ballinger, 1975.

Jenkins, C. D. Recent evidence supporting psychological and social risk factors for coronary disease. *New England Journal of Medicine*, 1976, *294*, 987–994; 1033–1038.

Jenkins, C. D., Rosenman, R. H., & Friedman, M. Development of an objective psychological test for the determination of the coronary prone behavior pattern in employed men. *Journal of Chronic Diseases*, 1967, *20*, 371–379.

Jenkins, C. D., Rosenman, R. H., & Zyzanski, S. J. Prediction of clinicial coronary heart disease by a test for the coronary prone behavior pattern. *New England Journal of Medicine*, 1974, *290*, 1271–1275.

Jerome, E. A. Age and learning: Experimental studies. In J. E. Birren (Ed.), *Handbook of aging and the individual*. Chicago: Univeristy of Chicago Press, 1959.

Kampmann, J., Giersback-Wieler, K., Kristense, M., & Hansen, M. J. Rapid evaluation of renal clearance. *Acta Medica Scandinavia*, 1974, *196*, 517–520.

Kannel, W. B., McGee, D., & Gordon, T. A general cardiovascular risk profile: The Framingham study. *American Journal of Cardiology*, 1976, *38*, 46–51.

Karnofsky, D. A., & Burchenal, J. H. The clinical evaluation of chemotherapeutic agents in cancer. In C. M. Macleod (Ed.), *Evaluation of chemotherapeutic agents*. New York: Columbia University Press, 1948.

Katz, S., Down, T. D., Cash, H. R., & Grotz, R. C. Progress in development of ADL. *Gerontologist*, 1970, *21*, 20–30.

Kuhlen, R. G. Aging and life-adjustment. In J. E. Birren (Ed.), *Handbook of aging and the individual*. Chicago: University of Chicago Press, 1959.

LaRue, A., Bank, L., Jarvik, L., & Hetland, M. Health in old age: How do physicians' ratings and self-ratings compare? *Journal of Gerontology*, 1979, *34*, 687–691.

Lawson, I., & Chaptron, D. A basic pharmacopoeia for geriatric practice. In W. Riechel (Ed.), *Clinical aspects of aging*. Baltimore, Md.: Williams & Wilkins, 1978.

Light, K. C. Effects of mild cardiovascular and cerebrovascular disorders in serial reaction time performance. *Experimental Aging Research*, 1978, *4*, 3–22.

Lilienfeld, A. M. *Foundations of epidemiology*. New York: Oxford University Press, 1976.

Lopez, M. A., Hoyer, W. J., Goldstein, A. C., Gershaw, N. J., & Sprafkin, R. P. Effects of overlearning and incentive on the acquisition and transfer of interpersonal skills with institutionalized elderly. *Journal of Gerontology*, 1980, *35*, 403–408.

MacIntyre, N. R., Mitchell, R. E., Oberman, A., Harlan, W. R., Graybill, A., & Johnson, E. Longevity in military pilots: 37-year followup of the Navy's "1000 aviators." *Aviation Space & Environmental Medicine*, 1978, *49*, 1120–1122.

MacMahon, B., & Pugh, T. C. *Epidemiology: Principles and methods*. Boston: Little, Brown 1970.

Maddox, G. L. The continuum of care: Movement toward the community. In E. W. Busse & D. G. Blazer (Eds.), *Handbook of geriatric psychiatry*. New York: Van Nostrand Reinhold, 1980.

Maddox, G. L., & Douglass, E. B. Self-assessment of health. *Journal of Health and Social Behavior*, 1973, *14*, 87–93.

McCrae, R. R., Bartone, P. T., & Costa, P. T. Age, anxiety and self reported health. *Journal of Aging and Human Development*, 1976, *7*, 49–58.

Menninger, K. A., & Menninger, W. C. Psychoanalytic observations in cardiac disorders. *American Heart Journal*, 1936, *11*, 10–21.

Mettlin, C. Occupational careers and the prevention of coronary prone behavior. *Social Science Medicine*, 1976, *10*, 367–372.

National Center for Health Statistics. *Current listing and topical index to the vital and health statistics, Series 1962–1977* [DHEW Publication No. (PHS) 78-1301]. Hyattsville, Md., May 1978.

Nowlin, J. B. *Health status, age, and intellectual functioning*. Paper presented at the Conference on Longitudinal Studies, University of Missouri—St. Louis, May 1979.

Nowlin, J. B. *Health in the Duke Longitudinal Studies* (Unpublished tech. rep.). Duke University, Durham, N.C., 1980.

Osler, W. *Lectures on angina pectoris and allied states*. New York: D. Appleton, 1897.

Ostfeld, A., & Gibson, D. C. *Epidemiology of aging* [DHEW Publication No. (NIH) 75-711]. Washington, D.C.: U.S. Government Printing Office, 1975.

Palmore, E. (Ed.) *Normal aging I*. Durham, N.C.: Duke University Press, 1971.

Palmore, E. (Ed.) *Normal aging II*. Durham, N.C.: Duke University Press, 1974.

Palmore, E., & Jeffers, F. C. (Eds.) *Prediction of lifespan: Recent findings*. Lexington, Mass: Heath, 1971.

Pomerleau, O. F. Behavioral medicine: The contribution of the experimental analysis of behavior to medical care. *American Psychologist*, 1979, *34*, 654–663.

Pomerleau, O. F., & Brady, J. P. (Eds.) *Behavioral medicine: Theory and practice*. Baltimore Md.: Williams & Wilkins. 1979.

Richards, W. S., & Thorpe, G. L. Behavioral approaches to the problem of later life. In M. Storandt, I. C. Siegler, & M. F. Elias (Eds.), *The clinical psychology of aging*. New York: Plenum Press, 1978.

Riley, M. W. (Ed.) *Aging from birth to death*. Boulder. Colo.: Westview Press, 1979.

Roberts, A. *Behavioral management of chronic pain*. Paper presented at the Nova Behavioral Conference on Aging, Ft. Lauderdale, Fla., January 1980.

Rosenman, R. H., Brand, R. J., Jenkins, C. D., Friedman, M., Straus, R., & Wurm, M. Coronary heart disease in the Western Collaborative Group study: Final follow-up experience of 8½ years. *Journal of the American Medical Association*, 1975, *233*, 872–877.

Rosenman, R. H., & Friedman, M. Association of specific behavior pattern in women with blood and cardiovascular findings. *Circulation*, 1961, *24*, 1173–1184.

Rosenman, R. H., Friedman, M., Straus. R., Wurm, M., Kositchek R., Hahn, W., & Werthessen, N. T. A predictive study of coronary heart disease. *Journal of the American Medical Association*, 1964, *20*, 371–379.

Rossman, I. Bodily changes with aging. In E. W. Busse & D. G. Blazer (Eds.), *Handbook of geriatric psychiatry*. New York: Van Nostrand Reinhold, 1980.

Rowe, J. W., Andres, R., Tobin, J. D., Norris, A. H., & Shock, N. W. The effect of age on creatinine clearance in men: A cross-sectional and longitudinal study. *Journal of Gerontology*, 1976, *31*, 155–163.

Schaie, K. W. Quasi-experimental research designs in the psychology of aging. In J. E. Birren & K. W. Schaie

(Eds.), *Handbook of the psychology of aging*. New York: Van Nostrand Reinhold, 1977.

Scherwitz, L., Berton, K., & Leventhal, H. Type A assessment and interaction in the behavior pattern interview. *Psychosomatic Medicine*, 1977, *39*, 229–240.

Schucker, G., & Jacobs, D. R. Assessment of behavioral risk for coronary disease by voice characteristics. *Psychosomatic Medicine*, 1977, *39*, 229–240.

Schwartz, G., & Weiss, S. What is behavioral medicine? *Psychosomatic Medicine*, 1977, *36*, 377–381.

Schwartz, G., & Weiss, S. Behavioral Medicine revisited: An amended definition. *Journal of Behavioral Medicine*, 1978, *1*, 249–251.

Service, C., & Heron, B. Administration of the OARS MFAQ. In *Multidimensional functional assessment: The OARS methodology*. Durham, N.C.: Duke University Press. Center for the Study of Aging and Human Development, 1978.

Shanas, E., & Maddox, G. L. Aging, health and the organization of health resources. In R. Binstock & E. Shanas (Eds.), *Handbook of aging and the social sciences*. New York: Van Nostrand Reinhold, 1976.

Shekelle, R. B., Schoenberger, J. A., & Stamler, J. Corelates of the JAS Type A behavior pattern score. *Journal of Chronic Diseases*, 1976, *29*, 381–394.

Siegler, I. C. *Relationships between health status and terminal drop*. Paper presented at the conference on Longitudinal Studies, University of Missouri—St. Louis, May 1979.

Siegler, I. C., & Nowlin, J. B. *Health and behavior in the Duke Longitudinal Studies*. Paper presented at the meeting of the American Psychological Association, New York, September 1979.

Speith, W. Cardiovascular health status, age and psychological performance. *Journal of Gerontology*, 1964, *19*, 277–284.

Speith, W. Slowness of task performance and cardiovascular disease. In A. T. Welford & J. E. Birren (Eds.), *Behavior, aging, and the nervous system*. Springfield, Ill.: Charles C Thomas, 1965.

Spittell, J. A. (Ed.) *The practice of medicine: Laboratory diagnosis* (Vol. 2). New York: Harper & Row, 1979.

Starfield. B. Measurement of outcome: A proposed scheme. *Milbank Memorial Fund Quarterly: Health and Society*, 1974, *52*, 39–50.

Steinberg, F. U. (Ed.) *Cowdry's The care of the geriatric patient* (5th ed.). St. Louis Mo.: Mosby, 1976.

Timiras, P. *Developmental physiology and aging*. New York: Macmillan, 1972.

Upton, A. C. Pathobiology. In C. E. Finch & L. Hayflick (Eds.), *Handbook of the biology of aging*. New York: Van Nostrand Reinhold, 1977.

U.S. Department of Health, Education, and Welfare. *Health–United States 1978* [DHEW Publication No. (PHS) 78-1232]. Washington, D.C.: Author, 1978.

Waldron, I., Zyzanski, S., Shekelle, R. B., Jenkins, C. D., & Tannenbaum, S. The coronary prone behavior pattern in employed men and women. *Journal of Human Stress*, 1977, *3*, 2–18.

Williamson, J. W. Outcomes of health care: Key to health improvement. In *Methodology of identifying, measuring and evaluating outcomes of health service programs, systems, and subsystems* (HSMHA Conference Series, Outcome Conference I–II). Washington, D.C.: U.S. Government Printing Office, 1969.

Wood, W. G., Elias, M. F., Schultz, N. R., & Pentz, C. A. Symptoms reported in the Cornell Medical Index. *Experimental Aging Research*, 1978, *4*, 421–431.

Zyzanski, S. J. Coronary prone behavior patterns and coronary heart disease: Epidemiological evidence. In T. M. Dembroski, S. M. Weiss, J. L. Shields, S. G. Haynes, & M. Feinlab (Eds.), *Coronary prone behavior*. New York: Springer-Verlag, 1978.

Epilogue

A. T. Welford

Where Do We Go From Here?

The chapters in this book have shown that psychological research on aging has come a long way from the 1930s and 1940s and has produced a substantial body of knowledge, much of it at a high level of sophistication. What is to be done next? If one looks at the history of psychological research, one can see progression along four largely independent dimensions: first, from observation through the induction of unifying concepts to the formulation of models of process; second, from studies of experience and behavior alone to their integration with data from other biological sciences such as physiology and biochemistry; third, from qualitative classification to quantitative measures; and fourth, a to-and-fro progression between pure theory and application. A quick answer about the future, therefore, can be found by looking at the stage any line of research has reached and estimating its potential for development in any or all of these directions. Whether development actually occurs or not depends on many circumstances, such as opportunity for exchange of ideas within and across disciplines, progress in related lines of work, breakthroughs in technique, and the quality of mind of those carrying out particular studies.

Observation, Concepts, and Models

Those of us who pioneered the modern psychological study of aging in the 1940s found ourselves faced with deeply entrenched popular stereotypes about the nature of age changes, based on commonsense observation and the somewhat wishful-thinking postulate that all could be explained in terms of well-known deficits in sense organs, muscles, and joints. It was one of our tasks to show that this view neglected a number of important changes in the cognitive and decisional processes mediating sensory input and motor output. We were greatly helped by the fact that our research took place against the background of a ferment of theoretical ideas, derived from the collaboration of psychologists with engineers in the design and use of equipment for the armed services during and after the Second World War. This theorizing, which came to be known as the *skills* approach and was one of the main contributors to what is now termed the *information-processing* approach, had already advanced in several areas to the stage of model building, in which attempts were made to spell out the chains of events in various performances. Much of our effort, therefore, was directed to identifying the key points at which age changes were important in different types of tasks. Essentially we found that any or all of the links between input and output and back again might be affected. The extent to which each link showed changes with age appeared to differ according to the extent to

I am grateful to James Birren, Bernice Neugarten, Anderson Smith, and Martha Storandt for their comments on earlier drafts of this epilogue.

615

which it was loaded by the demands of the particular task concerned. For instance, a simple reaction leading to a powerful responding movement showed greater age effects in the time taken by the response than by the reaction (Pierson & Montoye, 1958), whereas a choice reaction coupled with a relatively light movement showed the reverse (e.g., Singleton, 1955).

Broadly speaking, human performance can be conceived in terms of three types of elements. First are *demands* made by the external, including social, environment and by the individual's internal desires and standards. Second are *capacities*, both physical and mental, possessed by the individual. Third are various techniques, methods or, as they have come to be termed, *strategies* by which these capacities are deployed to meet the demands. Strategies used for any task differ between individuals, and within the same individual on different occasions, according to fatigue, stress, and other states affecting the organism. Some strategies are more efficient than others, in the sense that they enable a given demand to be met with the expenditure of less capacity, or a given capacity to meet a greater demand. It is the use of such efficient strategies that seems to mark what we call *skill* (Welford, 1978).

The skills approach enabled the main lines of change in sensory-motor performance from young adulthood onward to be mapped out by the 1960s in a way that has survived well since (see Welford, 1977), although further development may be hoped for with the interest currently being taken by experimental psychologists in studying sports and athletics. The approach is being rapidly extended to social performance, personality, and coping, and I discuss these later as examples of what may be expected along the model-building line. Let me emphasize that they are given as illustrations only and that I do not intend to imply that they are the most important that can be envisaged.

The explicit study of social skill began at Oxford in 1966 when a leading social psychologist, Michael Argyle, joined with an expert on industrial skill, E. R. F. W. Crossman. In studies of automation, Crossman (1960) had been impressed by the extent to which the effectiveness of operators of process plants depended on their ability to maintain good social relations with others in the organizational hierarchy. There had, of course, been many studies of social relations and human interaction before, but the work by Argyle and Crossman marked the beginning of attempts to link these interactions to the ideas worked out in the field of sensorimotor skill. The essential concept is that just as skill can be displayed in efficient interaction between, say, an operator and a machine tool in industry, so can it be displayed in the interaction

between one person and another—in conveying messages efficiently, preventing fatigue due to overloading or boredom due to underloading, and keeping friendly to-and-fro communication going in a system of mutual feedback (see Argyle, 1967; Welford, 1966a; 1979). Work in this area expanded rapidly until in 1979 a conference held at Leuven in Belgium revealed a wide range of high-grade research and the beginnings of practical applications in several countries of Europe and the United States (Singleton, Spurgeon, & Stammers, 1979). Such research and application seem almost certain to expand further during the next two decades and to be of importance to social and clinical gerontology. Explicit training in social skill and similar clinical procedures for helping people with communication problems have already produced highly beneficial effects among young and middle-aged people in several walks of life. Such training can also be expected to become a powerful means of reducing the interpersonal problems of old people who become self-centered, disagreeable, lonely in the midst of relatives, or otherwise "difficult," especially under conditions of dependency when help from others must be obtained to meet the demands of daily life.

The foundations of the strategies that form the basis of skill seem to be laid down in childhood and young adulthood, when they are conditioned not only by the person's capacities but also by the person's circumstances at the time, so that they are based partly on innate characteristics and partly on experience. They tend to be applied subsequently in broad terms to many tasks: In other words, they become *characteristic types* of strategy, which pervade large areas of performance. Examples that come readily to mind are tendencies to caution versus speed, to anxious activity versus easygoing idleness, to selfishness versus altruism, and to optimistic preparation for the best versus pessimistic anticipation of the worst. It is these characteristic strategies that seem to constitute what is commonly termed *personality*.

Capacities obviously change with age, and so also do demands, as children grow up and leave home and, later, when the time comes to retire. Optimum strategies will thus change also. However, because strategies are built up and anchored in the past, they may not reach optimum levels spontaneously in old age. This will lead to some degree of maladjustment that may be compounded by anxiety if the individual becomes aware of the possibility of failure. The reaction of many of the people responsible for the care of the elderly is to treat such anxiety with tranquilizing drugs, but this may be the worst possible treatment, since it diminishes capacity still further and thus exacerbates the condition that has caused the anxiety.

Instead, the need is to pinpoint the source of difficulty and to treat it, either by changing the demands, including any excessively high standards the elderly are setting for themselves, or by teaching more appropriate strategies. In severe organic cases the scope for these measures will, of course, be limited, but in a wide band of milder cases such measures could well prevent drug treatment, hospitalization, and reduction of the patient to a state of dependency, while enhancing quality of life and improving relationships with others. Older people can obviously adjust to lowered capacities by reducing the demands they attempt to meet—shedding responsibilities and restricting interests—although this needs to be done with caution if life is not to become narrow and lacking in the variety needed to prevent boredom. The more positive alternative is a deliberate attempt to acquire efficient means of coping, partly by learning new or revised strategies at later ages, and partly by acquiring sound habits early that can be carried into old age.

The model of skill in terms of which the foregoing discussion has been couched is a powerful aid to understanding human performance and its changes with age. It is, of course, not the only useful model and, like all theories and models, it must be used with caution. Any theorizing has a constraining effect on the way data are regarded. If the theorizing fits the facts well, it can bring simplicity and clarity to what would otherwise be a mass of seemingly conflicting observations. If, however, the fit is not good, strong attachment to a particular theory can lead to neglect or distortion of discrepant facts, or alternatively, attempts to accommodate them may make the theory overelaborate and lead to its becoming trivial. The protection against going too far up a theoretical blind alley is, perhaps, to follow the precept, current in many psychological laboratories during the 1920s and 1930s, of observing subjects closely while they are performing in experiments and questioning them afterwards. The evidence obtained in this way was regarded as secondary but as a useful supplement to the objective measurements made. Especially in the field of gerontology, observations made of old people and the opinions and observations of those in close touch with them need to be taken seriously. At the very least, they may provide some valuable null hypotheses to be tested by objective measurement. Often they can help to prevent premature, oversimple theorizing.

Interdisciplinary Research

Chapters in this book have shown that there has been considerable progress in gerontological research that combines the study of behavior with the study of other biological disciplines such as physiology and biochemistry. The reason is probably twofold: First, the enormous strides made during recent years in neurological research have had far-reaching implications for the understanding of behavior, and second, modern gerontological research has been pursued simultaneously in several biological disciplines and in clinical medicine. Research workers in all of these disciplines have regularly come together at conferences and worked together in some research laboratories. Such collaboration has, of course, been a feature of some branches of psychology since the 19th century, and the traffic has been two-way. Not only have psychologists turned to other biological disciplines and medicine for help in explaining their findings, but other disciplines have used measures of performance as an aid to sensory research and diagnostic procedures, for instance, in the location of brain tumors. Cooperation seems likely to increase as the theoretical models in both psychology and other disciplines become more precise and descriptive of actual functional mechanisms rather than notional ones.

One area that seems especially ripe for such development is that of *personality*. It has been many years since physiologists noted behavioral correlates of endocrine disorders and suggested the possibility of a physical basis for some personality traits (e.g., Mottram, 1944). More recently, the dimension of extraversion–introversion has been related to variations in functions such as physiological reactivity, sedation threshold, and diurnal temperature rhythm (see Broadbent, 1971; Welford, 1966a). With the rapid expansion of knowledge of endocrine and other physiological changes that accompany aging, the opportunity is favorable to look again at these factors and to see how far they can account not only for gross disturbances such as depression but also for more subtle changes of personality that come with age.

Other areas, discussed in this book, where cooperative research has already produced important results are *cognitive performance* and *memory*; in these fields it has been possible to relate some failures during old age to physiological conditions that are reversible. Success of this kind, combined with the study of brain and behavior in mental deficiencies of various types, seems to offer the possibility of supplying what has always been lacking, namely, understanding of the nature of *intelligence*. Despite the widespread use of intelligence tests, clear definition is still lacking, and discussion of how far intelligence declines with age is consequently inconclusive.

Psychology stands between physiology, on the one hand, and the social sciences such as sociology, on the other, and a further area of interdisciplinary research clearly lies in this latter direction. An example can be seen in the organization and staffing of homes for old people. It is important that the people who are inevitably thrown closely together in communal living should be reasonably compatible. Many social and political idealists, believing that people from different backgrounds should be mixed together, have used old people's communities to further their aims. Yet living is likely to be easier, less stressful, and more efficient among those of like mind who share common interests, temperaments, and values (Welford, 1979). This means that people of different occupational and social backgrounds should be housed in different communities if they are to enjoy as high a quality of life as possible. Just what facets of similarity make for compatibility among older people appears to be a worthwhile topic for cooperative research between sociologists and those concerned with social skills.

From Qualities to Quantities

A great deal of psychological research—much more than is often recognized—is essentially concerned with whether or not an event occurs, whether a particular quality of performance is or is not shown. For example, many studies of child development are concerned with the ages at which particular qualities of behavior appear, with little or no regard for their extent, effectiveness, or efficiency. Gerontological psychology has been more fortunate, having grown up during a period of rapidly increasing interest in quantitative measurement of the demands of tasks and performance at them. The development first of information theory and later of signal detection theory also enabled many theoretical models that would otherwise have been catalogs of stages in a process to be cast in quantitative, mathematical forms.

Interest in quantification coincided with the use of statistical tests for assessment of both qualitative and quantitative data. In retrospect, however, these may appear as only a temporary stage. The late G. Udny Yule, who was one of the fathers of statistical methods and very sympathetic to psychology, once remarked during a conversation in the late 1930s that the use of statistical tests was a confession of failure—if one had controlled one's experiments properly, results should be expressible not in terms of significant differences but of functional relations. He recognized that this was seldom possible at the stage psychology had then reached, but he urged it as a goal at which to aim. There are now examples—particularly of times taken to react (e.g., Hick, 1952), to make movements (e.g.,

Fitts & Peterson, 1964), or to recover items from memory (e.g., Sternberg, 1975)—where rationally defined functions fit the data so well that statistical tests are unimportant. The attainment of such precision should enable age changes to be assessed with more confidence than has been possible hitherto and, it is to be hoped, will in due course provide defined functional relations between changes of performance and various physiological and physical changes associated with age. Many investigators have looked forward to the time when a combination of such relationships would provide an index of overall *functional age*, but this is a false hope. Within any one individual, different functional capacities change at different rates with age, and the rate for any one functional capacity differs between one individual and another. Moreover, changes of capacity that limit performance of a task making one set of demands may not do so for another task making different demands. Functional age of individuals can, therefore, be assessed only for particular tasks: One individual may be functionally older than another for one task but functionally younger for a different task. No meaningful overall index of functional age is possible.

Again, it is hazardous to point to areas where progress in quantification is likely, but two areas in which a need exists can be indicated briefly. One is *intelligence*. Despite the many attempts that have been made to express intelligence quantitatively in test scores, measurement has so far consisted essentially of ranking items and testees—no effective attempts have been made to quantify the demands of the items. Recently a possible approach to at least some types of "fluid" intelligence has opened up with the concept of *working memory*. For many tasks, substantial amounts of data, such as rules of procedure or tallies of developing events, have to be held in mind until the task is completed, whereupon they are completely dismissed. The memory involved seems to be more robust than that used for, say, a digit span repeated back immediately, but it is nevertheless ephemeral and therefore different from long-term memory, although it may include a selection of material held there. Talland (1968) suggested that such medium-term retention in a fairly protracted activity might be a possible mechanism within the limbic system required for permanent registration to occur: Working memory might be represented by such activity that does not continue through to long-term registration.

The concept of working memory in turn provides a way into one of the problems that has baffled psychologists ever since the subject began, namely, *thinking*. Introspectively, thinking seems to consist of a series of "stages" in which a "leap" is made from one idea or partial solution of a problem to another.

Between these stages, verbal, visual, and other images seem to store the data already gathered and the partial solutions already attained while the next leap is being made. It is a fair guess that a major limitation in thinking is the amount of data that can be stored in this way, and there is evidence that this is so in older people (Rabbitt, 1977; Welford, 1958, Chapter 8). It seems fair to argue that many, if not all, items that test "fluid" intelligence involve some form of thinking of this kind and that their demands might be quantified in terms of the amount of data to be carried and the attentional demands of other operations over which they have to be retained. Studies of working memory are as yet little developed, but the subject appears to be of great importance in several areas of work and everyday life. Its study in relation to age could not only throw light on some types of intellectual strength and weakness and improve understanding of orientation in older people but could also contribute to general understanding of the processes involved. It is likely that the capacity of working memory declines with age but that the decline may be at least partly, or sometimes even more than, offset by the better coding of data that comes with experience. Similarly with thinking, better coding may enable older people to compensate for reduced storage capacity. On the other hand, if the leaps in thinking take longer, as they may in older people, the load imposed on storage may be increased. The relation between storage, coding, speed, and age is important, because if storage is a source of limitation, it should be possible to reduce its effects by developing aids, such as note taking, and training people in their use. Both working memory and thinking have been discussed further from these standpoints elsewhere (Welford, 1980).

A second area in which quantification seems to be needed is *human motivation*. In the past, most studies of human motives have been concerned with defining certain instincts, drives, interests, attitudes, and incentives and with studying their separate effects. Yet it is clear that human motivation cannot be described adequately in such terms. For instance, the motives leading to one act or activity may be many, and any one motive may lead to a variety of actions. This is true in two ways. First, motives can be regarded as demands that are related to capacities by different strategies, according to the extent to which circumstances make one strategy more appropriate than another. Second, performance seems typically to be organized hierarchically, with larger "units" formed of several smaller ones. The larger units can be said to motivate the smaller in the sense that the results of the smaller have their main significance as means to a larger end (Welford, 1966a, 1972).

Readiness to undertake action seems to depend on some kind of ratio between the benefit hoped for and the effort or other cost involved in obtaining it. In other words, it can be conceived in terms of an anticipated *cost-benefit ratio*, with readiness to act diminishing as the ratio becomes larger. Costs and benefits are not, of course, to be thought of merely in monetary terms but rather in terms of satisfaction and dissatisfaction, pleasure and unpleasantness attaching to any and every level in the hierarchy (Welford, 1976a). One complicating factor must be noted. While a high cost-benefit ratio may tend to deter action, it seems to enhance the *value* subsequently placed on achievement (Lewis, 1965), so that the worthwhileness of any action may appear very different at the time it is taken and later in retrospect.

In considering older people, three points deserve emphasis. First, we need to think quantitatively in terms of cost-benefit ratios because (a) failing capacities mean rising costs, in that actions once performed easily may become laborious, and (b) changing circumstances may mean altered benefits. For example, the benefits of a large income decrease when a family has grown up and left home. Statements to the effect that old people desire to be "wanted" or "valued" may be true in an absolute sense but can be misleading unless the further question is asked of what cost in effort and cooperation with others they would accept in order to have this desire realized.

Second, the complex nature of motivation means that the true reasons for an action may not be at all obvious to an observer who is not in possession of a wide context of knowledge about the previous experience and future aims of the person concerned. Indeed, the individuals themselves may not know or may have a distorted idea of why they do what they do. This is especially likely with older people because their longer previous experience will tend to mean that more long-term aims are either fulfilled or frustrated, more past achievements, vividly remembered, may distort present values, and more habits and customs are carried forward from a time when they were very different from today. In consequence, behavior of the elderly that appears strange, inappropriate, stilted, or even bizarre to younger observers may be understandable if its background is known.

Third, if undesirable behavior is to be changed, we need to know not only what costs and benefits are involved but how much of each the individual derives from particular actions, so that calculations can be made of the balance between them and of how this balance would be affected by any change of circumstance or behavior we desire to bring about. In making such calculations, the time scale of changes needs to be estimated, and the problem that a long-term benefit may involve a short-term cost in effort while the old-established habits and routines are being replaced by the new must also be dealt with.

Theory and Application

Much of the spur to the development of psychology in the 19th and early 20th centuries came from people interested in education, astronomy, clinical medicine, and industry who sought understanding of human performance in their fields, and there has always been some concern to apply the results of pure psychological research to practical problems. Both pure and applied research workers need to keep in touch with one another. Attempts to solve practical field problems without a theoretical background tend to become isolated ad hoc studies that are inefficient because it is not possible to generalize from one situation to another. At the same time, theory without application is apt to become trivial, caught up with minutiae, and liable to build conceptual structures that prove to be houses of cards, even if they sometimes take years to collapse.

Once again, psychological research in aging has been fortunate. The pioneering work of Miles and his co-workers in the United States (Miles, 1965) and of the units sponsored by the Nuffield Foundation and the Medical Research Council in Britain (see Welford, 1966b, 1976b) was oriented toward determining the potential of older people for industrial work, and most research done since has had the idea, even if only in the far background, that findings might be relevant to clinical problems of mental health or to the social and material needs of the elderly. While, as in other areas, it is hazardous to predict future developments, there are two fields where past achievements point clearly to application. First, enough is now known about sensorimotor performance and the types of work that are and are not done satisfactorily by older people (Griew, 1964; Powell, 1973; Smith, 1973; Welford, 1966b) to undertake field trials to test the validity of job modifications and personnel placements that previous research findings have suggested would help older people use their abilities to best advantage.

Second, the last decade or so has witnessed a great increase in research on learning by older people, and this could have important implications for methods of training. In fact, some highly significant work has already been done in Britain on the industrial training of middle-aged and older people (e.g., E. Belbin, 1964; R. M. Belbin, 1965, 1969; Belbin & Belbin, 1972; see also Shooter, Schonfield, King, & Welford, 1956; Entwisle, 1959). This work has shown that young people learn well from a variety of training methods but that only some of these are effective in middle age and beyond. Training at later ages was especially more efficient when procedures were based on the "discovery" method in which trainees did not merely follow instructions but had to make active decisions under conditions arranged so that errors were unlikely to be made or were quickly corrected. These studies have not been followed up to the extent they appear to deserve, seemingly because unemployment has made the training of older people for industrial work appear less important and because the training of old people for leisure activities has had a low priority during a decade of financial stringency for research. Yet even if the need to train older people no longer ranks as high as it once did, there is an urgent special need to train personnel to look after the elderly in sheltered accommodation and long-stay geriatric nursing homes and, indeed, to provide relatives and members of the general public who have to deal with the old with insight into their needs and problems. Many such people are themselves in later middle or "young" old age—a time of life when special training methods are important if understanding and competence are to be gained efficiently.

It seems fair to suggest that there are many other areas in which a wealth of knowledge exists ready to be applied and that in these areas, as well as in the two discussed here, the experience gained in application would be a valuable means of refining present theoretical understanding and pinpointing future research needs.

A Concluding Thought

Development in gerontological psychology must depend to a large extent on development in general psychology and to some extent on development in the gerontological aspects of other disciplines, both biological and social. Yet, as has been indicated here, gerontological psychology has, over the years, remained well to the fore in its ideas and techniques, and those research workers involved have often led their colleagues concerned with other areas of psychology. The reasons are, perhaps, two. First, old age holds, as it were, a magnifying glass to many aspects of human performance, whether sensory, cognitive, intellectual, motor, or social, so that problems and limitations that would have gone unnoticed in young subjects become clearly visible in middle and old age. Had psychological research down the years been conducted on older people instead of on students, the picture we now have would probably have been fuller and clearer. Second, almost certainly the contacts maintained with other disciplines and with practitioners have given gerontological psychologists a broader perspective and sympathy across the biological and social sciences. Gerontological psychologists are thus well poised to lead the way to a more thorough integration of the study of the human species, one in which there will not only be cooperative interdisciplinary research but, at least for some key personnel, training that spans existing disciplinary boundaries to join parts of the vast field that is now psychology to parts of other cognate sciences.

REFERENCES

Argyle, M. *The psychology of interpersonal behaviour.* Harmondsworth, England: Penguin, 1967.

Belbin, E. *Training the adult worker* (D.S.I.R. Problems of Progress in Industry, No. 15). London: Her Majesty's Stationery Office, 1964.

Belbin, E., & Belbin, R. M. *Problems in adult retraining.* London: Heinemann, 1972.

Belbin, R. M. *Training methods for older workers.* Paris: O.E.C.D., 1965.

Belbin, R. M. *The discovery method: An international experiment in retraining.* Paris: O.E.C.D., 1969.

Broadbent, D. E. *Decision and stress.* London: Academic Press, 1971.

Crossman, E. R. F. W. *Automation and skill.* London: Her Majesty's Stationery Office, 1960.

Entwisle, D. G. Ageing: The effects of previous skill on training. *Occupational Psychology,* 1959, *33,* 238–243.

Fitts, P. M., & Peterson, J. R. Information capacity of discrete motor responses. *Journal of Experimental Psychology,* 1964, *67,* 103–112.

Griew, S. *Job re-design: The application of biological data on ageing to the design of equipment and the organization of work.* Paris: O.E.C.D., 1964.

Hick, W. E. On the rate of gain of information. *Quarterly Journal of Experimental Psychology,* 1952, *4,* 11–26.

Lewis, M. Psychological effect of effort. *Psychological Bulletin,* 1965, *64,* 183–190.

Miles, W. R. The Stanford University studies of later maturity. In A. T. Welford & J. E. Birren (Eds.), *Behavior, aging and the nervous system.* Springfield, Ill.: Charles C Thomas, 1965.

Mottram, V. H. *The physical basis of personality.* Harmondsworth, England: Penguin, 1944.

Pierson, W. R., & Montoye, H. J. Movement time, reaction time and age. *Journal of Gerontology,* 1958, *13,* 418–421.

Powell, M. Age and occupational change among coalminers. *Occupational Psychology,* 1973, *47,* 37–49.

Rabbitt, P. Changes in problem solving ability in old age. In J. E. Birren & K. W. Schaie (Eds.), *Handbook of the psychology of aging.* New York: Van Nostrand Reinhold, 1977.

Shooter, A. M. N., Schonfield, A. E. D., King, H. F., & Welford, A. T. Some field data on the training of older people. *Occupational Psychology,* 1956, *30,* 204–215.

Singleton, W. T. Age and performance timing on simple skills. In *Old age in the modern world. Report of the 3rd Congress of the International Association of Gerontology.* Edinburgh, Scotland: Livingstone, 1955.

Singleton, W. T., Spurgeon, P., & Stammers, R. B. (Eds.). *The analysis of social skill.* New York: Plenum, 1979.

Smith, J. M. Age and occupation: The determinants of male occupational age structures—hypothesis H and hypothesis A. *Journal of Gerontology,* 1973, *28,* 484–490.

Sternberg, S. Memory scanning: New findings and current controversies. *Quarterly Journal of Experimental Psychology,* 1975, *27,* 1–32.

Talland, G. A. *Disorders of memory and learning.* Harmondsworth, England: Penguin, 1968.

Welford, A. T. *Ageing and human skill.* London: Oxford University Press for the Nuffield Foundation, 1958. (Reprinted in 1973 by Greenwood Press, Westport, Conn.)

Welford, A. T. The ergonomic approach to social behaviour. *Ergonomics,* 1966, *9,* 357–369. (a)

Welford, A. T. Industrial work suitable for older people: Some British studies. *Gerontologist,* 1966, *6,* 4–9. (b)

Welford, A. T. The future motivation of man. *Search,* 1972, *3,* 113–120.

Welford, A. T. Motivation, capacity, learning and age. *International Journal of Aging and Human Development,* 1976, *7,* 189–199. (a)

Welford, A. T. Thirty years of psychological research on age and work. *Journal of Occupational Psychology,* 1976, *49,* 129–138. (b)

Welford, A. T. Motor performance. In J. E. Birren & K. W. Schaie (Eds.), *Handbook of the psychology of aging.* New York: Van Nostrand Reinhold, 1977.

Welford, A. T. Mental work load as a function of demand, capacity, strategy and skill. *Ergonomics,* 1978, *21,* 151–167.

Welford, A. T. The concept of skill and its application to social performance. In W. T. Singleton, P. Spurgeon, & R. B. Stammers (Eds.), *The analysis of social skill.* New York: Plenum, 1979.

Welford, A. T. Memory and age: A perspective view. In L. W. Poon, J. L. Fozard, L. S. Cermak, D. Arenberg, & L. W. Thompson (Eds.), *New directions in memory and aging: Proceedings of the George A. Talland Memorial Conference.* Hillsdale, N.J.: Lawrence Erlbaum, 1980.

Leonard W. Poon

A Last Word

Research is, after all, an intensely personal matter. Professional fame may not be the goal of every investigator, but each of us cherishes his own ideas as if they were his children and is as little likely to be willing to forego recognition of his parentage. Our allegiance to our discipline is stronger than we are prepared to believe. It is painful to see how a cherished principle which may constitute an essential component of one's scientific or professional identity may be utterly ignored or treated as quite inconsequential by a colleague from another field. It is thus that many efforts at collaboration prove abortive, or, if carried through, are poorly productive, since each participant feels he has sacrificed an important tenet in the interests of a common goal which is depreciated thereby. (Cohen, 1963, p. ix)

If these well-worded thoughts reflect the experience of most researchers, we must marvel at the strength of the trend toward collaborative efforts that we see among investigators in and across fields, and among researchers, clinicians, and service providers. This volume has aimed to support and continue the trend by presenting collaborative efforts within and between disciplines, by illuminating a broad variety of points of view, and by putting psychological aging into perspective for the new decade of the 1980s.

Although every aspect of psychological aging could not be covered in any one volume, a great deal of recent research is reviewed here, and directions have been proposed for future studies—from the perspectives of health, environment, behavior, and the combined effects of all three on the aging person. I believe the information is representative of what we now know in the nine areas covered by the sections of this book.

As we evaluate the state of the art in the psychology of aging, we are faced with the gaping holes in our knowledge base and the numbers of important issues that need to be explored. At the same time, we can take pleasure in what has been accomplished in the last 30 years and in what may be achieved in the next decade. This final note will not rehash the ideas and concepts presented in the preceding pages, for they can stand up and be examined in their own right. Rather, I hope to establish some continuity between what has been accomplished and what lies ahead.

The preceding chapters provide ample evidence that the seeds planted just a decade ago in the recommendations of the APA Task Force on Aging to the White House Conference on Aging (Eisdorfer & Lawton, 1973) have germinated and show promise of bearing flower and fruit. To begin with, the recommendation for a National Institute of Gerontology became a reality when the National Institute on Aging (NIA) was established in 1975. An office of Associate Director for Behavioral and Social Sciences Programs in NIA has the responsibility for initiating research and training programs, forming policies, and allocating funds for research on the behavioral aspects of aging. The recommendation for a Center for the Mental Health of the Aged within the National Institute of Mental Health—with authority and funds for research, training, and services for the aged in the community and in hospitals—has been realized with the establishment of the Center for Studies of the Mental Health of the Aging in 1976. During the last decade, programs and directions have become consolidated in other federal agencies concerned with aging and the aged.

Although the last decade has seen a steady increase in financial support for investigations into psychological aging, the increase has not kept pace proportionally with funding in the biological sciences (see the Prologue to this book). This lag should provide the impetus for gerontological psychologists in the 1980s to examine the present systems of research, training, applications, and methods of disseminating information and utilizing knowledge and to work to upgrade their quality.

The findings and theories presented in this book reflect an active pursuit of knowledge and understanding of (1) the normative changes that accompany advancing age, (2) the facts and artifacts that appear to tie advancing age to a loss of intellectual and cognitive functioning and to psychological and adjustment difficulties, and (3) the changing social, personality, and environmental influences on elderly behavior. All of these issues were identified by the 1971 APA Task Force on Aging as priority research areas for the decade of the 1970s. Through these research priorities new vistas opened in the study and treatment of problems associated with aging.

These priorities should be extended into the 1980s, with perhaps a renewed emphasis on demonstrating the *application* of new knowledge to the elderly, both those who need long-term care and those who still function productively in the community. Exploratory research has shown that practical benefits can be achieved in the following areas: human-factors design for improvement of physical environments; prostheses to compensate for weakened senses and limited mobility; early recognition, clinical diagnosis, and treatment of mental health and cognitive problems; use of family, peer, and social support systems to supplement available services; and application of management techniques to control for everyday stress, to expand potentialities for leisure, work, and retirement, and to prepare for bereavement.

One area that has received limited attention is the study of the exceptionally gifted elderly and of ways to profit from their cumulated wisdom, knowledge, and experience. The 1980s seem to provide a promising decade in which to tap the tremendous productive and creative resources of our elderly population. As evidenced by the number of multidisciplinary chapters in this book, the 1980s should show a rich interdisciplinary collaboration among psychologists and other social and biomedical scientists to improve the lives of the elderly.

Finally, what breakthroughs might we achieve in the 1980s? The answer to that question will take more than the collective effort of the 95 contributors to this volume. Riegel (1973) put it succinctly when he wrote,

> Progress in knowledge and science is always codetermined by the nonscientific conditions and demands of the society in which they develop. Society, in turn, will be modified by the scientific progress made. . . . Little do we recognize that both our observations as well as the theoretical models proposed are selectively dependent upon social, economic, and political conditions of the society in which we happen to live. (p. 56)

I hope, then, that it is not a futile exercise to define what we now know, to question our clinical, fund-allocating, and information-disseminating practices, and to propose ways to make them better, even though controversy may result if our conclusions run counter to our current teachings and our current systems of research, training, and practice. Such an exercise could form the basis for a new and exciting perspective on aging in the 1980s.

REFERENCES

Cohen, R. A. Preface, In J. E. Birren, R. N. Butler, S. W. Greenhouse, L. Sokoloff, and M. R. Yarrow (Eds.), *Human aging.* Baltimore, Md.: U.S. Department of Health, Education and Welfare, 1963.

Eisdorfer, C., & Lawton, M. P. (Eds.). *The psychology of adult development and aging.* Washington, D.C.: American Psychological Association, 1973.

Riegel, K. On the history of psychological gerontology. In C. Eisdorfer and M. P. Lawton (Eds.), *The psychology of adult development and aging.* Washington, D.C.: American Psychological Association, 1973.

Author Index

Subject Index